Microsoft® Access 2016 Comprehensive

Amy Kinser

MORIARITY | KINSER | KOSHAREK

PEARSON

Boston Columbus Indianapolis New York San Francisco
Amsterdam Cape Town Dubai London Madrid Milan Munich Paris Montréal Toronto
Delhi Mexico City São Paulo Sydney Hong Kong Seoul Singapore Taipei Tokyo

Editorial Director: Andrew Gilfillan
Senior Editor: Samantha McAfee Lewis
Team Lead, Project Management: Laura Burgess
Project Manager: Anne Garcia
Program Manager: Emily Biberger
Development Editor: Lori Damanti
Editorial Assistant: Michael Campbell
Director of Product Marketing: Maggie Waples
Director of Field Marketing: Leigh Ann Sims
Product Marketing Manager: Kaylee Carlson
Field Marketing Managers: Joanna Sabella & Molly Schmidt
Marketing Assistant: Kelli Fisher
Senior Operations Specialist: Maura Zaldivar-Garcia
Senior Art Director: Diane Ernsberger
Manager, Permissions: Karen Sanatar
Interior and Cover Design: Studio Montage
Cover Photo: Courtesy of Shutterstock® Images
Associate Director of Design: Blair Brown
Product Strategy Manager: Eric Hakanson
Vice President, Product Strategy: Jason Fournier
Digital Product Manager: Zachary Alexander
Media Project Manager, Production: John Cassar
Full-Service Project Management: Cenveo Publisher Services
Composition: Cenveo Publisher Services

Credits and acknowledgments borrowed from other sources and reproduced, with permission, in this textbook appear on appropriate page within text.

Pearson Education Ltd., London
Pearson Education Singapore, Pte. Ltd
Pearson Education, Canada, Inc.
Pearson Education–Japan
Pearson Education Australia PTY, Limited
Pearson Education North Asia Ltd., Hong Kong
Pearson Educación de Mexico, S.A. de C.V.
Pearson Education Malaysia, Pte. Ltd.

Library of Congress Cataloging-in-Publication Data available upon request

2 16
ISBN-10: 0-13-447955-6
ISBN-13: 978-0-13-447955-2

Dedications

I dedicate this series to my Kinser Boyz for their unwavering love, support, and patience; to my parents and sister for their love; to my students for inspiring me; to Sam for believing in me; and to the instructors I hope this series will inspire!

Amy S. Kinser

I dedicate this book to my beautiful and amazing wife, April. Without her support and understanding, this would not have been possible. Also, to my wonderful son, Patton, whose strength to overcome so many obstacles in his life inspires me to continue to do my best work.

Brant Moriarity

For my wife, Amy, and our two boys, Matt and Aidan. I cannot thank them enough for their support, love, and endless inspiration.

J. Eric Kinser

To my husband John, for his love, patience, and encouragement to follow through with my desire to write; to my sons Alex and Justin for their love and support; to my parents, who pushed me to "do" and told me I could; to a special colleague, Ann, for her help and support; and to the memory of my best friend Betty who lives on in my heart.

Diane L. Kosharek

About the Authors

Amy S. Kinser, Esq., Series Editor

Amy holds a B.A. degree in Chemistry with a Business minor from Indiana University, and a J.D. from the Maurer School of Law, also at Indiana University. After working as an environmental chemist, starting her own technology consulting company, and practicing intellectual property law, she has spent the past 15 years teaching technology at the Kelley School of Business in Bloomington, Indiana. Currently, she serves as the Director of Computer Skills and Senior Lecturer at the Kelley School of Business at Indiana University. She also loves spending time with her two sons, Aidan and J. Matthew, and her husband J. Eric.

Brant Moriarity

Brant P. Moriarity earned a B.A. in Religious Studies/Philosophy and a M.S. in Information Systems at Indiana University. He is a Senior Lecturer at the Indiana University's Kelley School of Business, where he teaches topics such as data management and analysis, as well as the strategic use of Information Systems in business. He is also the founder of Beats Per Minute Technologies, LLC, bringing the benefits of business analytics to small businesses and non-profit organizations.

J. Eric Kinser

Eric Kinser received his B.S. degree in Biology from Indiana University and his M.S. in Counseling and Education from the Indiana School of Education. He has worked in the medical field and in higher education as a technology and decision support specialist. He is currently a senior lecturer in the Operations and Decision Technology Department at the Kelley School of Business at Indiana University. When not teaching he enjoys experimenting with new technologies, traveling, and hiking with his family.

Diane L. Kosharek

Diane is a full-time Business Technology faculty member at Madison College in Madison, WI. In addition to her faculty role, she works closely with business and industry specialists, developing and delivering tailored training solutions to employees in areas such as customer service, software applications, and business writing skills. Prior to joining Madison College, she worked as a Technology Training Consultant, providing consultation and production assistance to teaching faculty and staff to incorporate appropriate technology in their courses to enhance learning. Diane holds a Bachelor's Degree in Education from the University of Wisconsin-Madison and a Master's Degree in Educational Computing from Cardinal Stritch University.

Brief Contents

COMMON FEATURES

ACCESS

Contents

Acknowledgments

The ***Your Office*** team would like to thank the following reviewers who have invested time and energy to help shape this series from the very beginning, providing us with invaluable feedback through their comments, suggestions, and constructive criticism.

We'd like to thank all of our conscientious reviewers, including those who contributed to our previous editions:

Sven Aelterman
Troy University

Nitin Aggarwal
San Jose State University

Heather Albinger
Waukesha County Technical College

Angel Alexander
Piedmont Technical College

Melody Alexander
Ball State University

Karen Allen
Community College of Rhode Island

Maureen Allen
Elon University

Wilma Andrews
Virginia Commonwealth University

Mazhar Anik
Owens Community College

David Antol
Harford Community College

Kirk Atkinson
Western Kentucky University

Barbara Baker
Indiana Wesleyan University

Kristi Berg
Minot State University

Kavuri Bharath
Old Dominion University

Ann Blackman
Parkland College

Jeanann Boyce
Montgomery College

Lynn Brooks
Tyler Junior College

Cheryl Brown
Delgado Community College West Bank Campus

Bonnie Buchanan
Central Ohio Technical College

Peggy Burrus
Red Rocks Community College

Richard Cacace
Pensacola State College

Margo Chaney
Carroll Community College

Shanan Chappell
College of the Albemarle, North Carolina

Kuan-Chou Chen
Purdue University, Calumet

David Childress
Ashland Community and Technical College

Keh-Wen Chuang
Purdue University North Central

Suzanne Clayton
Drake University

Amy Clubb
Portland Community College

Bruce Collins
Davenport University

Linda Collins
Mesa Community College

Margaret Cooksey
Tallahassee Community College

Charmayne Cullom
University of Northern Colorado

Christy Culver
Marion Technical College

Juliana Cypert
Tarrant County College

Harold Davis
Southeastern Louisiana University

Jeff Davis
Jamestown Community College

Jennifer Day
Sinclair Community College

Anna Degtyareva
Mt. San Antonio College

Beth Deinert
Southeast Community College

Kathleen DeNisco
Erie Community College

Donald Dershem
Mountain View College

Sallie Dodson
Radford University

Joseph F. Domagala
Duquesne University

Bambi Edwards
Craven Community College

Elaine Emanuel
Mt. San Antonio College

Diane Endres
Ancilla College

Nancy Evans
Indiana University, Purdue University, Indianapolis

Christa Fairman
Arizona Western College

Marni Ferner
University of North Carolina, Wilmington

Paula Fisher
Central New Mexico Community College

Linda Fried
University of Colorado, Denver

Diana Friedman
Riverside Community College

Susan Fry
Boise State University

Virginia Fullwood
Texas A&M University, Commerce

Janos Fustos
Metropolitan State College of Denver

John Fyfe
University of Illinois at Chicago

Saiid Ganjalizadeh
The Catholic University of America

Randolph Garvin
Tyler Junior College

Diane Glowacki
Tarrant County College

Jerome Gonnella
Northern Kentucky University

Lorie Goodgine
Tennessee Technology Center in Paris

Connie Grimes
Morehead State University

Debbie Gross
Ohio State University

Babita Gupta
California State University, Monterey Bay

Lewis Hall
Riverside City College

Jane Hammer
Valley City State University

Marie Hartlein
Montgomery County Community College

Darren Hayes
Pace University

Paul Hayes
Eastern New Mexico University

Mary Hedberg
Johnson County Community College

Lynda Henrie
LDS Business College

Deedee Herrera
Dodge City Community College

Marilyn Hibbert
Salt Lake Community College

Jan Hime
University of Nebraska, Lincoln

Cheryl Hinds
Norfolk State University

Mary Kay Hinkson
Fox Valley Technical College

Margaret Hohly
Cerritos College

Brian Holbert
Spring Hill College

Susan Holland
Southeast Community College

Anita Hollander
University of Tennessee, Knoxville

Emily Holliday
Campbell University

Stacy Hollins
St. Louis Community College Florissant Valley

Mike Horn
State University of New York, Geneseo

Christie Hovey
Lincoln Land Community College

Margaret Hvatum
St. Louis Community College Meramec

Jean Insinga
Middlesex Community College

Kristyn Jacobson
Madison College

Jon (Sean) Jasperson
Texas A&M University

Glen Jenewein
Kaplan University

Gina Jerry
Santa Monica College

Dana Johnson
North Dakota State University

Mary Johnson
Mt. San Antonio College

Linda Johnsonius
Murray State University

Carla Jones
Middle Tennessee State University

Susan Jones
Utah State University

Nenad Jukic
Loyola University, Chicago

Sali Kaceli
Philadelphia Biblical University

Sue Kanda
Baker College of Auburn Hills

Robert Kansa
Macomb Community College

Susumu Kasai
Salt Lake Community College

Linda Kavanaugh
Robert Morris University

Debby Keen
University of Kentucky

Mike Kelly
Community College of Rhode Island

Melody Kiang
California State University, Long Beach

Lori Kielty
College of Central Florida

Richard Kirk
Pensacola State College

Dawn Konicek
Blackhawk Tech

John Kucharczuk
Centennial College

David Largent
Ball State University

Frank Lee
Fairmont State University

Luis Leon
The University of Tennessee at Chattanooga

Freda Leonard
Delgado Community College

Julie Lewis
Baker College, Allen Park

Suhong Li
Bryant Unversity

Renee Lightner
Florida State College

John Lombardi
South University

Rhonda Lucas
Spring Hill College

Adriana Lumpkin
Midland College

Lynne Lyon
Durham College

Nicole Lytle
California State University, San Bernardino

Donna Madsen
Kirkwood Community College

Susan Maggio
Community College of Baltimore County

Michelle Mallon
Ohio State University

Kim Manning
Tallahassee Community College

Paul Martin
Harrisburg Area Community College

Cheryl Martucci
Diablo Valley College

Sebena Masline
Florida State College of Jacksonville

Sherry Massoni
Harford Community College

Lee McClain
Western Washington University

Sandra McCormack
Monroe Community College

Sue McCrory
Missouri State University

Barbara Miller
University of Notre Dame

Johnette Moody
Arkansas Tech University

Michael O. Moorman
Saint Leo University

Kathleen Morris
University of Alabama

Alysse Morton
Westminster College

Elobaid Muna
University of Maryland Eastern Shore

Jackie Myers
Sinclair Community College

Russell Myers
El Paso Community College

Bernie Negrete
Cerritos College

Melissa Nemeth
Indiana University, Purdue University, Indianapolis

Jennifer Nightingale
Duquesne University

Kathie O'Brien
North Idaho College

Michael Ogawa
University of Hawaii

Janet Olfert
North Dakota State University

Rene Pack
Arizona Western College

Patsy Parker
Southwest Oklahoma State Unversity

Laurie Patterson
University of North Carolina, Wilmington

Alicia Pearlman
Baker College

Diane Perreault
Sierra College and California State University, Sacramento

Theresa Phinney
Texas A&M University

Vickie Pickett
Midland College

Marcia Polanis
Forsyth Technical Community College

Rose Pollard
Southeast Community College

Stephen Pomeroy
Norwich University

Leonard Presby
William Paterson University

Donna Reavis
Delta Career Education

Eris Reddoch
Pensacola State College

James Reddoch
Pensacola State College

Michael Redmond
La Salle University

Terri Rentfro
John A. Logan College

Vicki Robertson
Southwest Tennessee Community College

Jennifer Robinson
Trident Technical College

Dianne Ross
University of Louisiana at Lafayette

Ann Rowlette
Liberty University

Amy Rutledge
Oakland University

Candace Ryder
Colorado State University

Joann Segovia
Winona State University

Eileen Shifflett
James Madison University

Sandeep Shiva
Old Dominion University

Robert Sindt
Johnson County Community College

Cindi Smatt
Texas A&M University

Edward Souza
Hawaii Pacific University

Nora Spencer
Fullerton College

Alicia Stonesifer
La Salle University

Jenny Lee Svelund
University of Utah

Cheryl Sypniewski
Macomb Community College

Arta Szathmary
Bucks County Community College

Nasser Tadayon
Southern Utah University

Asela Thomason
California State University Long Beach

Nicole Thompson
Carteret Community College

Terri Tiedeman
Southeast Community College, Nebraska

Lewis Todd
Belhaven University

Barb Tollinger
Sinclair Community College

Allen Truell
Ball State University

Erhan Uskup
Houston Community College

Lucia Vanderpool
Baptist College of Health Sciences

Michelle Vlaich-Lee
Greenville Technical College

Barry Walker
Monroe Community College

Rosalyn Warren
Enterprise State Community College

Sonia Washington
Prince George's Community College

Eric Weinstein
Suffolk County Community College

Jill Weiss
Florida International University

Lorna Wells
Salt Lake Community College

Rosalie Westerberg
Clover Park Technical College

Clemetee Whaley
Southwest Tennessee Community College

Kenneth Whitten
Florida State College of Jacksonville

MaryLou Wilson
Piedmont Technical College

John Windsor
University of North Texas

Kathy Winters
University of Tennessee, Chattanooga

Nancy Woolridge
Fullerton College

Jensen Zhao
Ball State University

Martha Zimmer
University of Evansville

Molly Zimmer
University of Evansville

Mary Anne Zlotow
College of DuPage

Matthew Zullo
Wake Technical Community College

Additionally, we'd like to thank our MyITLab team for their review and collaboration with our text authors:

LeeAnn Bates
MyITLab content author

Jennifer Hurley
MyITLab content author

Becca Lowe
Media Producer

Ralph Moore
MyITLab content author

Jerri Williams
MyITLab content author

Preface

Real World Problem Solving for Business and Beyond

The *Your Office* series provides the foundation for students to learn real world problem solving for use in business and beyond. Students are exposed to hands-on technical content that is woven into realistic business scenarios and focuses on using Microsoft Office as a decision-making tool.

Real world business exposure is a competitive advantage.

The series features a unique running business scenario—the Painted Paradise Resort & Spa—that connects all of the cases together and exposes students to using Microsoft Office to solve problems relating to business areas such as finance and accounting, production and operations, sales and marketing, and more. Look for the icons identifying the business application of each case.

Active learning occurs in context.

Each chapter introduces a realistic business case for students to complete via hands-on steps that are easily identified in blue-shaded boxes. Each blue box teaches a skill and comes complete with video, interactive, and live auto-graded support with automatic feedback.

Coursework that is relevant to students and their future careers.

Real World Advice, Real World Interview Videos, and Real World Success Stories are woven throughout the text and in the student resources. These share how former students use the Microsoft Office concepts they learned in this class and had success in a variety of careers.

Outcomes matter.

Whether it's getting a good grade in this course, learning how to use Access to be successful in other courses, or learning business skills that will support success in a future job, every student has an outcome in mind. And outcomes matter. That is why we added a Business Unit opener to focus on the outcomes students will achieve by working through the cases and content of each chapter as well as the Capstone at the end of each unit.

No matter what career students may choose to pursue in life, this series will give them the foundation to succeed. And as they learn these valuable problem-solving and decision-making skills while becoming proficient in using Microsoft Office as a tool, they will achieve their intended outcomes, making a positive impact on their lives.

Key Features

The **Outcomes focus** allows students and instructors to focus on higher-level learning goals and how those can be achieved through particular objectives and skills.

- **Outcomes** are written at the course level and the business unit level.
- **Chapter Objectives list** identifies the learning objectives to be achieved as students work through the chapter. Page numbers are included for easy reference. These are revisited in the Concepts Check at the end of the chapter.
- **MOS Certification Guide** for instructors and students directs anyone interested in prepping for the MOS exam to the specific series resources to find all content required for the test.

Business Application Icons

Customer Service

Finance & Accounting

General Business

Human Resources

Information Technology

Production & Operations

Sales & Marketing

Research & Development

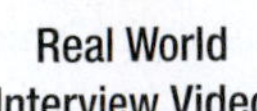

Real World Interview Video

Blue Box Videos

Soft Skills

The **real world focus** reminds students that what they are learning is practical and useful the minute they leave the classroom.

- **Real World Success** features in the chapter opener share anecdotes from real former students, describing how knowledge of Office has helped them be successful in their lives.
- **Real World Advice boxes** offer notes on best practices for general use of important Office skills. The goal is to advise students as a manager might in a future job.
- **Business Application icons** appear with every case in the text and clearly identify which business application students are being exposed to (finance, marketing, operations, etc.).
- **Real World Interview Video icons** appear with the Real World Success story in the business unit. Each interview features a real businessperson discussing how he or she actually uses the skills in the chapter on a day-to-day basis.

Features for active learning help students learn by doing and immerse them in the business world using Microsoft Office.

- **Blue boxes** represent the hands-on portion of the chapter and help students quickly identify what steps they need to take to complete the chapter Prepare Case. This material is easily distinguishable from explanatory text by the blue-shaded background.
- **Starting and ending files** appear before every case in the text. Starting files identify exactly which student data files are needed to complete each case. Ending files are provided to show students the naming conventions they should use when saving their files. Each file icon is color coded by application.
- **Side Note** conveys a brief tip or piece of information aligned visually with a step in the chapter, quickly providing key information to students completing that particular step.
- **Consider This** offers critical thinking questions and topics for discussion, set apart as a boxed feature, allowing students to step back from the project and think about the application of what they are learning and how these concepts might be used in the future.
- **Soft Skills icons** appear with other boxed features and identify specific places where students are being exposed to lessons on soft skills.

Study aids help students review and retain the material so they can recall it at a moment's notice.

- **Quick Reference boxes** summarize generic or alternative instructions on how to accomplish a task. This feature enables students to quickly find important skills.
- **Concept Check** review questions, which appear at the end of the chapter, require students to demonstrate their understanding of the objectives.
- **Visual Summary** offers a review of the objectives learned in the chapter using images from the completed solution file, mapped to the chapter objectives with callouts and page references, so students can easily find the section of text to refer to for a refresher.

- **MyITLab™ icons** identify which cases from the book match those in MyITLab™.
- **Blue Box Video icons** appear with each Active Text box and identify the brief video, demonstrating how students should complete that portion of the Prepare Case.

Extensive cases allow students to progress from a basic understanding of Office through to proficiency.

- **Chapters all conclude with Practice, Problem Solve, and Perform Cases** to allow full mastery at the chapter level. Alternative versions of these cases are available in Instructor Resources.
- **Business Unit Capstones all include More Practice, Problem Solve, and Perform Cases** that require students to synthesize objectives from the two previous chapters to extend their mastery of the content. Alternative versions of these cases are available in Instructor Resources.
- **More Grader Projects** are offered with this edition, including Prepare cases as well as Problem Solve cases at both the chapter and business unit capstone levels.

Resources

Instructor Resources

The Instructor's Resource Center, available at www.pearsonhighered.com/irc, includes the following:

- AACSB mapping that identifies which cases and exercises in the text prepare for AACSB certification
- Business application mapping, which provides an easy-to-filter way of finding the cases and examples to help highlight whichever business application is of most interest
- Annotated Solution Files with Scorecards, which assist with grading the Prepare, Practice, Problem Solve, and Perform cases
- Data and solution files
- Rubrics for Perform cases in Microsoft Word format, which enable instructors to easily grade open-ended assignments with no definite solution
- PowerPoint presentations with notes for each chapter
- Lesson plans that provide a detailed blueprint to achieve chapter learning objectives and outcomes and best use the unique structure of the business units
- Complete test bank, also available in TestGen format
- Syllabus templates for 8-week, 12-week, and 16-week courses
- Additional Practice, Problem Solve, and Perform cases to provide variety and choice in exercises at both the chapter and business unit levels
- Scripted Lectures, which provide instructors with a lecture outline that mirrors the chapter Prepare case

Student Resources

Student Data Files

Access the student data files needed to complete the cases in this textbook at www.pearsonhighered.com/youroffice.

MyITLab®

Available in MyITLab

- **Blue Box Videos** walk students through the activity in each blue box, illustrating how to perform a task while explaining the business context of the case.
- **Real World Interview Videos** introduce students to real professionals discussing how they use Microsoft Office in their daily work. These videos provide real world relevance to answer the question "Why is this content important to me?" There are videos in each Business Unit.
- **Audio PowerPoints** provide a lecture review of the chapter content and include narration.
- **Grader Projects** provide live-in-the-application training and assessment with immediate feedback and detailed reports for students to practice, learn, and remediate.
- **eText** is available in some MyITLab courses.

MyITLab for Office 2016 is a solution designed by professors for professors that allows easy delivery of Office courses with defensible assessment and outcomes-based training. The new **Your Office 2016** system will seamlessly integrate online assessment, training, and projects with MyITLab for Microsoft Office 2016!

Dear Students,

If you want an edge over the competition, make it personal. Whether you love sports, travel, the stock market, or ballet, your passion is personal to you. Capitalizing on your passion leads to success. You live in a global marketplace, and your competition is global. The honors students in China exceed the total number of students in North America. Skills can help set you apart, but passion will make you stand above. ***Your Office*** is the tool to harness your passion's true potential.

In prior generations, personalization in a professional setting was discouraged. You had a "work" life and a "home" life. As the Series Editor, I write to you about the vision for ***Your Office*** from my laptop, on my couch, in the middle of the night when inspiration struck me. My classroom and living room are my office. Life has changed from generations before us.

So, let's get personal. My degrees are not in technology, but chemistry and law. I helped put myself through school by working full time in various jobs, including a successful technology consulting business that continues today. My generation did not grow up with computers, but I did. My father was a network administrator for the military. So, I was learning to program in Basic before anyone had played Nintendo's Duck Hunt or Tetris. Technology has always been one of my passions from a young age. In fact, I now tell my husband: don't buy me jewelry for my birthday, buy me the latest gadget on the market!

In my first law position, I was known as the Office guru to the extent that no one gave me a law assignment for the first two months. Once I submitted the assignment, my supervisor remarked, "Wow, you don't just know how to leverage technology, but you really know the law too." I can tell you novel-sized stories from countless prior students in countless industries who gained an edge from using Office as a tool. Bringing technology to your passion makes you well rounded and a cut above the rest, no matter the industry or position.

I am most passionate about teaching, in particular teaching technology. I come from many generations of teachers, including my mother who is a kindergarten teacher. For over 12 years, I have found my dream job passing on my passion for teaching, technology, law, science, music, and life in general at the Kelley School of Business at Indiana University. I have tried to pass on the key to engaging passion to my students. I have helped them see what differentiates them from all the other bright students vying for the same jobs.

Microsoft Office is a tool. All of your competition will have learned Microsoft Office to some degree or another. Some will have learned it to an advanced level. Knowing Microsoft Office is important, but it is also fundamental. Without it, you will not be considered for a position.

Today, you step into your first of many future roles bringing Microsoft Office to your dream job working for Painted Paradise Resort & Spa. You will delve into the business side of the resort and learn how to use ***Your Office*** to maximum benefit.

Don't let the context of a business fool you. If you don't think of yourself as a business person, you have no need to worry. Whether you realize it or not, everything is business. If you want to be a nurse, you are entering the health care industry. If you want to be a football player in the NFL, you are entering the business of sports as entertainment. In fact, if you want to be a stay-at-home parent, you are entering the business of a family household where ***Your Office*** still gives you an advantage. For example, you will be able to prepare a budget in Excel and analyze what you need to do to afford a trip to Disney World!

At Painted Paradise Resort & Spa, you will learn how to make Office yours through four learning levels designed to maximize your understanding. You will Prepare, Practice, and Problem Solve your tasks. Then, you will astound when you Perform your new talents. You will be challenged through Consider This questions and gain insight through Real World Advice.

There is something more. You want success in what you are passionate about in your life. It is personal for you. In this position at Painted Paradise Resort & Spa, you will gain your personal competitive advantage that will stay with you for the rest of your life—***Your Office***.

Sincerely,

Amy Kinser

Series Editor

Painted Paradise

RESORT & SPA

Welcome to the Team!

Welcome to your new office at Painted Paradise Resort & Spa, where we specialize in painting perfect getaways. As the Chief Technology Officer, I am excited to have staff dedicated to the Microsoft Office integration between all the areas of the resort. Our team is passionate about our paradise, and I hope you find this to be your dream position here!

Painted Paradise is a resort and spa in New Mexico catering to business people, romantics, families, and anyone who just needs to get away. Inside our resort are many distinct areas. Many of these areas operate as businesses in their own right but must integrate with the other areas of the resort. The main areas of the resort are as follows.

- The **Hotel** is overseen by our Chief Executive Officer, William Mattingly, and is at the core of our business. The hotel offers a variety of accommodations, ranging from individual rooms to a grand villa suite. Further, the hotel offers packages including spa, golf, and special events.

  Room rates vary according to size, season, demand, and discount. The hotel has discounts for typical groups, such as AARP. The hotel also has a loyalty program where guests can earn free nights based on frequency of visits. Guests may charge anything from the resort to the room.

- **Red Bluff Golf Course** is a private world-class golf course and pro shop. The golf course has services such as golf lessons from the famous golf pro John Schilling and playing packages. Also, the golf course attracts local residents. This requires variety in pricing schemes to accommodate both local and hotel guests. The pro shop sells many retail items online.

  The golf course can also be reserved for special events and tournaments. These special events can be in conjunction with a wedding, conference, meetings, or other events covered by the event planning and catering area of the resort.

- **Turquoise Oasis Spa** is a full-service spa. Spa services include haircuts, pedicures, massages, facials, body wraps, waxing, and various other spa services—typical to exotic. Further, the spa offers private consultation, weight training (in the fitness center), a water bar, meditation areas, and steam rooms. Spa services are offered both in the spa and in the resort guest's room.

  Turquoise Oasis Spa uses top-of-the-line products and some house-brand products. The retail side offers products ranging from candles to age-defying home treatments. These products can also be purchased online. Many of the hotel guests who fall in love with the house-brand soaps, lotions, candles, and other items appreciate being able to buy more at any time.

  The spa offers a multitude of packages including special hotel room packages that include spa treatments. Local residents also use the spa. So, the spa guests

3355 Hemmingway Circle • Santa Fe, New Mexico 89566

are not limited to hotel guests. Thus, the packages also include pricing attractive to the local community.

- **Painted Treasures Gift Shop** has an array of items available for purchase, from toiletries to clothes to presents for loved ones back home including a healthy section of kids' toys for traveling business people. The gift shop sells a small sampling from the spa, golf course pro shop, and local New Mexico culture. The gift shop also has a small section of snacks and drinks. The gift shop has numerous part-time employees including students from the local college.
- The **Event Planning & Catering** area is central to attracting customers to the resort. From weddings to conferences, the resort is a popular destination. The resort has a substantial number of staff dedicated to planning, coordinating, setting up, catering, and maintaining these events. The resort has several facilities that can accommodate large groups. Packages and prices vary by size, room, and other services such as catering. Further, the Event Planning & Catering team works closely with local vendors for floral decorations, photography, and other event or wedding typical needs. However, all catering must go through the resort (no outside catering permitted). Lastly, the resort stocks several choices of decorations, table arrangements, and centerpieces. These range from professional, simple, themed, and luxurious.
- **Indigo5** and the **Silver Moon Lounge**, a world-class restaurant and lounge that is overseen by the well-known Chef Robin Sanchez. The cuisine is balanced and modern. From steaks to pasta to local southwestern meals, Indigo5 attracts local patrons in addition to resort guests. While the catering function is separate from the restaurant—though menu items may be shared—the restaurant does support all room service for the resort. The resort also has smaller food venues onsite such as the Terra Cotta Brew coffee shop in the lobby.

Currently, these areas are using Office to various degrees. In some areas, paper and pencil are still used for most business functions. Others have been lucky enough to have some technology savvy team members start Microsoft Office Solutions.

Using your skills, I am confident that you can help us integrate and use Microsoft Office on a whole new level! I hope you are excited to call Painted Paradise Resort & Spa ***Your Office***.

Looking forward to working with you more closely!

Aidan Matthews
Aidan Matthews
Chief Technology Officer

Common Features of Microsoft Office 2016

Chapter 1 | UNDERSTANDING THE COMMON FEATURES OF MICROSOFT OFFICE

OBJECTIVES

1. Understand the Office suite and applications p. 4
2. Start, save, and manipulate Office applications and use the Office ribbon p. 5
3. Manipulate, correct, and format content using tools such as the Font group and Tell me what you want to do p. 21
4. Formatting using the ribbon, contextual tools, and other menus p. 32
5. Use the Help window and ScreenTips p. 39
6. Printing and sharing files p. 41
7. Insert Office add-ins p. 44

Prepare Case

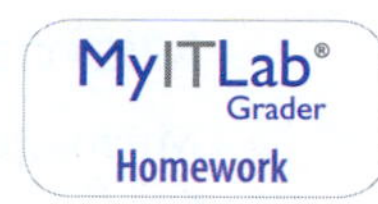

Sales & Marketing

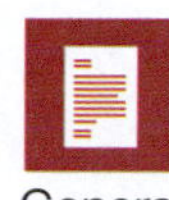
General Business

Painted Paradise Resort & Spa Employee Training Preparation

The gift shop at the Painted Paradise Resort & Spa has an array of items available for purchase, from toiletries to clothes to souvenirs for loved ones back home. There are numerous part-time employees, including students from the local college. The gift shop frequently holds training luncheons for new employees. Your first assignment will be to prepare three documents for a meeting with your manager, Susan Brock: a starting file for meeting minutes, the agenda for the meeting, and an Excel budget. To complete this task, you need to understand and work with the common features in the Microsoft Office Suite.

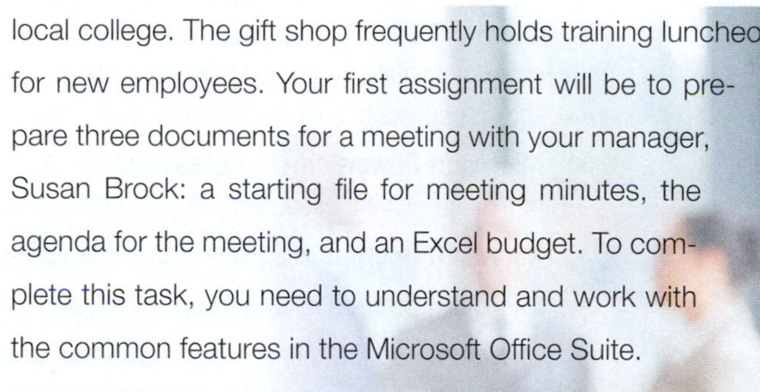

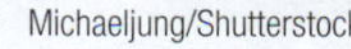
Michaeljung/Shutterstock

Student data files needed for this chapter:

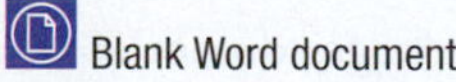
Blank Word document

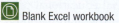

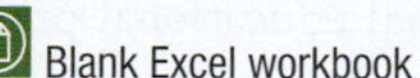
Blank Excel workbook

cf01ch01Agenda.docx

cf01ch01Logo.jpg

You will save your files as:

cf01ch01Minutes_LastFirst.docx

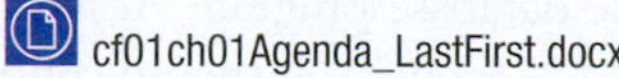
cf01ch01Agenda_LastFirst.docx

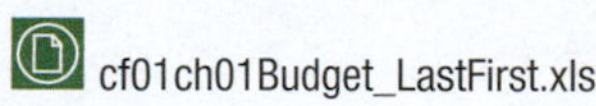
cf01ch01Budget_LastFirst.xlsx

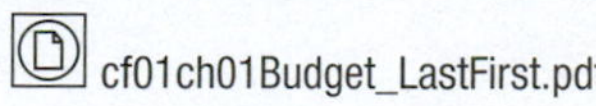
cf01ch01Budget_LastFirst.pdf

Working with the Office Interface

When you walk into a grocery store, you usually know what you are going to find and that items are likely to be in approximately the same location, regardless of which store you are visiting. The first items you usually see are the fresh fruits and vegetables, while the frozen foods are typically near the end of the store. This similarity among stores creates a comfortable and welcoming experience for the shopper, even if the shopper has never been in that particular store. The brands may be different, but the food types are the same. Canned corn is canned corn.

Microsoft Office was designed to create that same level of familiarity and comfort with its ribbons, features, and functions. Each application has an appearance or user interface that is similar to the appearance or interface of the other applications. The interface for Microsoft Office 2016 has introduced new color schemes, the default being a colorful appearance. The new look is minimalist; even the ribbon is hidden by default — unless a setting from a prior version of Office carries into your Office 2016 installation. In this section, you will learn to navigate and use the Microsoft Office interface.

Microsoft Office Suite and Different Versions

Microsoft Office 2016 is a suite of productivity applications or programs that are available for purchase separately or as a package. The exact applications available depend on the package installed. Office 2016 is available in greater variety and flexibility than ever before.

QUICK REFERENCE | **Programs in Office 2016**

- **Microsoft Word** is a word-processing program. This application can be used to create, edit, and format **documents** such as letters, memos, reports, brochures, resumes, and flyers.
- **Microsoft Excel** is a **spreadsheet** program — a two-dimensional grid that can be used to model quantitative data and perform accurate and rapid calculations with results ranging from simple budgets to financial and statistical analyses.
- **Microsoft PowerPoint** is a **presentation** program — an oral performance aid that uses slides or a stand-alone presentation such as those at kiosks.
- **Microsoft OneNote** is a planner and note-taking program.
- **Microsoft Outlook** is an e-mail, contact, and information management program.
- **Microsoft Access** is known as a **relational database** — or three-dimensional database software — because it is able to connect data in separate tables, allowing you to make the most efficient storage of your data.
- **Microsoft Publisher** is a desktop publishing program that offers professional tools and templates to help communicate a message easily in a variety of publication types, saving time and money while creating a polished and finished look.
- **Microsoft Skype for Business** — formerly known as Lync — is a unified communication platform.

With Office 2016 and Windows 10, Microsoft has embraced the concept of flexible versions for multiple platforms such as Windows Phone, iPads, Android devices, and even a web browser. Different versions of Office have different levels of functionality, but Microsoft has tried to keep the universal user interface as similar as possible.

Microsoft Office 2016 is available in several different suite packages from home to enterprise. This book is written with Microsoft Office 365 ProPlus — other packages do not contain the database program Access. Furthermore, most schools have special educational pricing and versions. You should consult your instructor or institution for further information.

For non-educational consumers, Office 2016 is available in two main pricing schemes. You can purchase Office 2016 the traditional way from a retailer for a one-time fee. You can then install the software on exactly one computer. Alternatively, Office 2016 can be purchased by subscription for a yearly or monthly fee. This version is called Office 365. It is the same product as Office 2016, but it comes with more frequent updates, the ability to be installed on more than one computer, more OneDrive storage space, free minutes in Skype, and several other additional perks. At the time of this writing, the Office 365 version is competitively priced to be less expensive for most people despite the monthly or yearly fee. For the latest in pricing and options, you can visit http://office.microsoft.com.

REAL WORLD ADVICE **Help, I Have a Mac!**

Traditionally, Office has been available in different versions for Windows and Macs with different functionality, such as the absence of the Access program in the Mac versions. Instead of using the Mac version of Office, two other popular options exist for using Office on a Mac: virtualization and dual boot.

Virtualization of Office on a Mac uses software that mimics Windows in order to run Office. In any major search engine, search for "PC virtualization on Mac" and you will find many software options for emulating a PC on a Mac. While many virtualization programs promise to mimic entirely, there can be some — usually minor — differences.

Dual boot is the ability to choose the operating system on startup. **Bootcamp** is the Mac software that allows the user to decide which operating system — Mac operating system or Windows — to run. When the computer is turned on, the user is given the choice of operating system. Thus, the user can run the Windows version of Office under the Windows operating system.

You should consult your instructor about the policy in your course. Policies on the usage of the Mac operating system vary greatly from course to course and from school to school.

Typically, using Office requires you to have a free Microsoft account. If you are working in a computer lab or enterprise version of Windows 10, you may not need to sign into a Microsoft account to run Office or Windows 10. If you are running Office on a personal computer, you will need to have a Microsoft account. You can create the account when you install Windows 10. If you do not have an account, you need to sign up for one at https://signup.live.com and follow the on-screen instructions. Your first name, last name, and profile image for your Microsoft account will appear in various screens of Windows and Microsoft Office.

Start, Save, and Navigate Office Applications

Each Office application has its own specific application Start screen. From the **application Start screen**, you can select a blank document, workbook, presentation, database, or one of many application-specific templates. Files that have already been created can also be opened from this screen. When existing files are double-clicked from a File Explorer window, the Start screen is not needed and does not open.

Opening Microsoft Word and the Start Screen

Once you start working with these applications, you can have more than one application or more than one instance of the same application open at a time. This means that you can open one file in Word in one window and also open another file in Word in a different window. In this exercise, you will start Microsoft Word so you can create a beginning file for meeting minutes.

CF01.01

To Open Microsoft Word and Use the Start Screen

SIDE NOTE

Windows 10

This book is written for Windows 10. If you are using Windows 8, open your charms, click Search, and then type Word. If using Windows 7, search the Start menu for Word.

a. On the taskbar, click into the **Ask me anything** or **Search the web and Windows** box. Type Word. The search results display. Verify the first result is Word 2016, and then press Enter. Pressing Enter automatically selects the first search result. Microsoft Word opens to the Word Start screen.

Troubleshooting

If Word 2016 is not the first option, you will need to use your mouse to select Word 2016 from the search results.

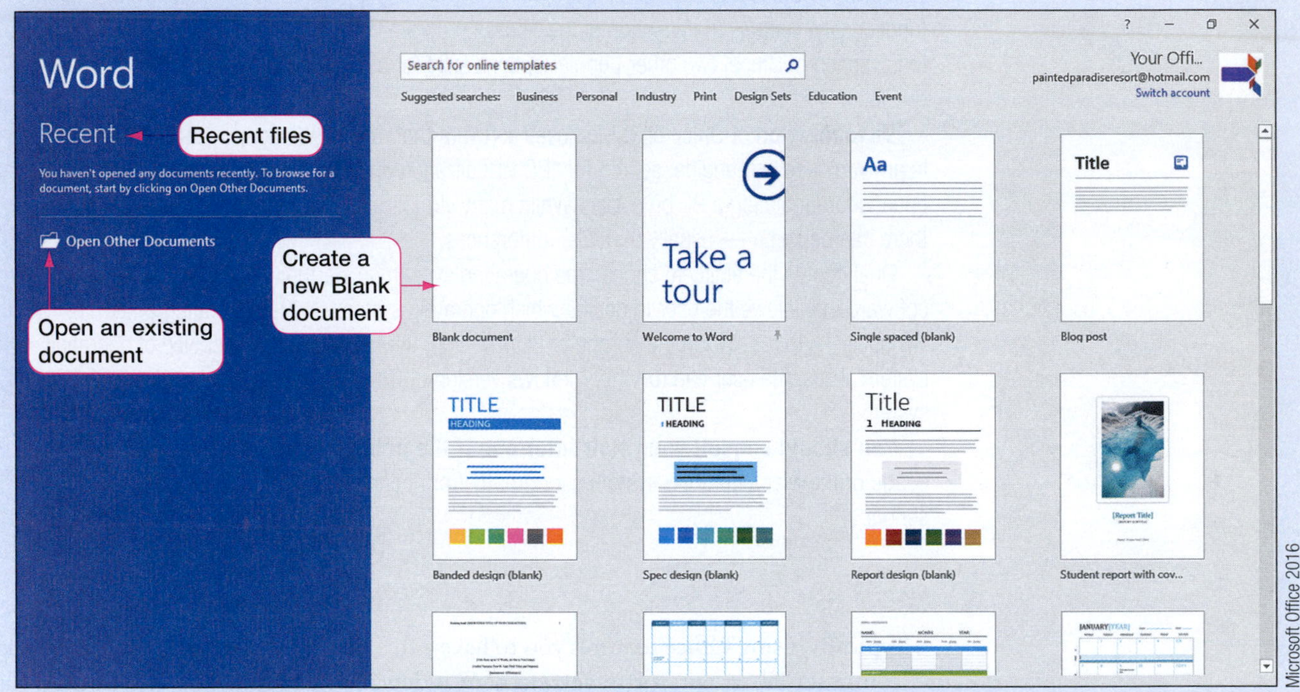

Figure 1 Word Start screen

b. Click **Blank document**. A new Word document opens.

Notice the words Document1 – Word appear on the title bar. This means that the document has not been saved yet. The insertion point is at the beginning of the document.

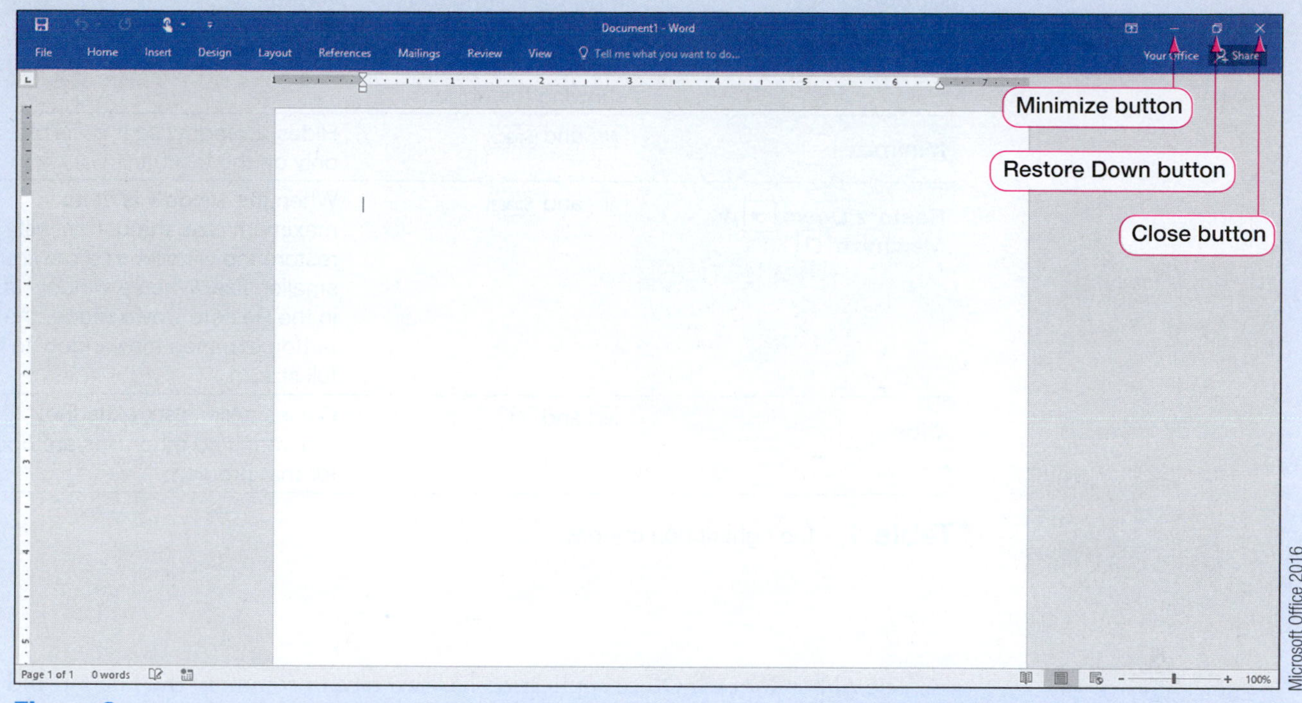

Figure 2 New Word document

Using the Ribbon and Ribbon Display Options

Office has a consistent design and layout that help to make its programs familiar and comfortable to the user. Once you learn to use one Office 2016 program, you can use many of those skills when working with other Office programs. The **ribbon** is the row of tabs across the top of the application. The ribbon display changes according to the screen resolution of your monitor. The figures in this text are set to a screen resolution of 1366 × 768. When open, the ribbons look like Figure 3.

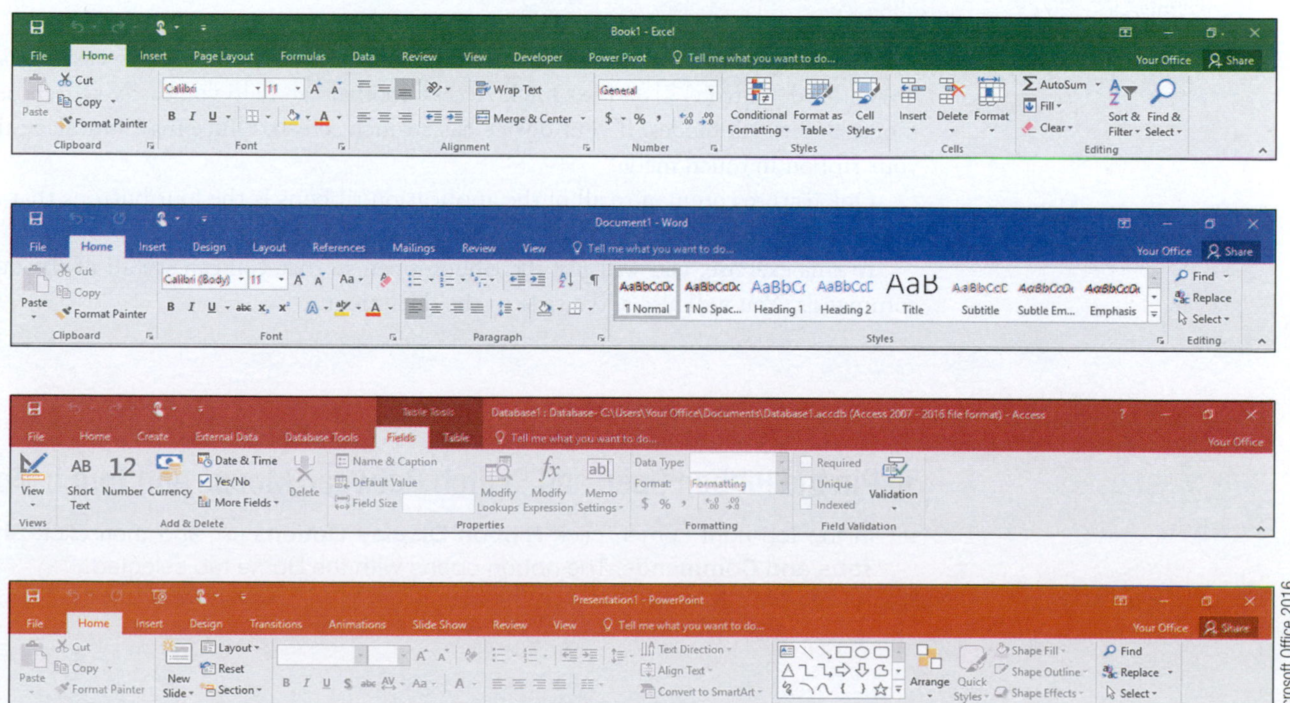

Figure 3 Ribbons of Excel, Word, Access, and PowerPoint

Button	Keyboard Shortcut	Action
Ribbon Display Options	Ctrl and F1 (toggles between collapsing and showing the ribbon)	Auto-Hide Ribbon, Show Tabs, and Show Tabs and Commands
Minimize	Alt and Space	Hides a window so it is visible only on the taskbar
Restore Down or **Maximize**	Alt and Space	When the window is at its maximum size, the button will restore the window to a previous, smaller size. When a window is in the Restore Down mode, the button expands the window to its full size.
Close	Alt and F4	Closes a file; also, exits the program if no other files are open for that program

Table 1 Top right ribbon buttons

The ribbon for each Office application has two tabs in common: the File tab and the Home tab. The File tab is the first tab on the ribbon and is used for file management needs such as saving and printing. The Home tab is the second tab and contains the commands for the most frequently performed activities, such as copying, cutting, and pasting. The commands on these tabs may differ from program to program. Other tabs are program specific, such as the Formulas tab in Excel, the Design tab in Word and PowerPoint, and the Database Tools tab in Access. The ribbon is further subdivided into **groups** — logical groupings of related commands.

By default, the ribbon is hidden. This allows you more room to work with your document rather than having the ribbon take up screen space with buttons and tools. However, hiding the ribbon makes it harder to perform tasks while learning Office. To open the ribbon, you need to pin it open. All directions and figures in this book will assume that the ribbon is pinned open.

Touch mode switches Office into a version that makes a touch screen easy to use. The Touch Mode button on the Quick Access Toolbar can help you easily switch between mouse and touch modes. If your device has a touch screen, Office may automatically put your ribbon in touch mode.

One feature common to all of the application ribbons is the four buttons that appear in the top right corner of an application title bar as shown in Table 1.

In this exercise, you will pin the ribbon open so that you can see all of the tabs and commands. You will also add a title to the document.

To Pin the Ribbon Open and Switch Between Mouse and Touch Mode

a. In the top right corner, click **Ribbon Display Options** and then click **Show Tabs and Commands**. The ribbon opens with the Home tab selected.

CHAPTER 1

Troubleshooting

Does your ribbon looks different? Your ribbon may seem to have condensed or expanded buttons and groups. The most common causes are different screen resolution, auto-detecting touch mode, or a smaller program window. Since the ribbon changes to accommodate the size of the window or screen, buttons can appear as icons without labels, and a group can be condensed into a button that must be clicked to display the group options. So do not worry! All of the same features are on the ribbon and in the same general area.

All of the figures in this book use a screen resolution of **1366 × 768**. Setting your computer to that resolution, if it is available, will minimize this issue. In Windows 10, you can find the screen resolution by right-clicking the desktop, clicking Display settings, and clicking Advanced display settings.

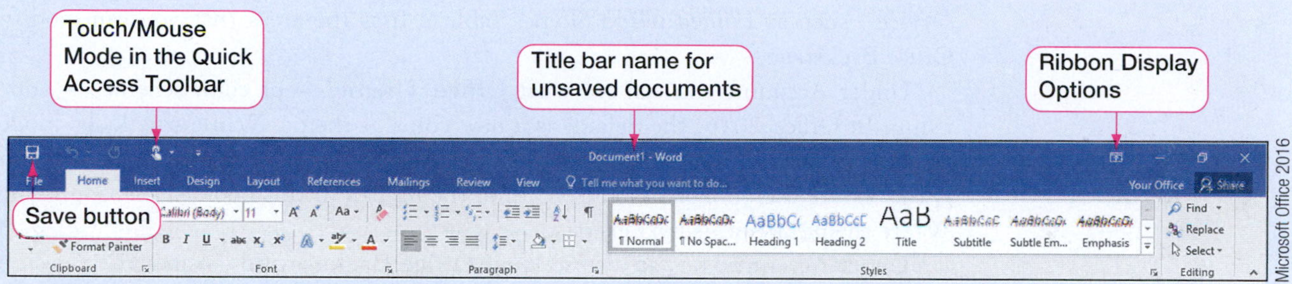

Figure 4 Word with ribbon pinned open

b. In the Quick Access Toolbar in the top left corner, click **Touch/Mouse Mode**. Then click **Touch**. If your ribbon does not change, you were already in Touch mode — and you most likely have a device with a touch screen.

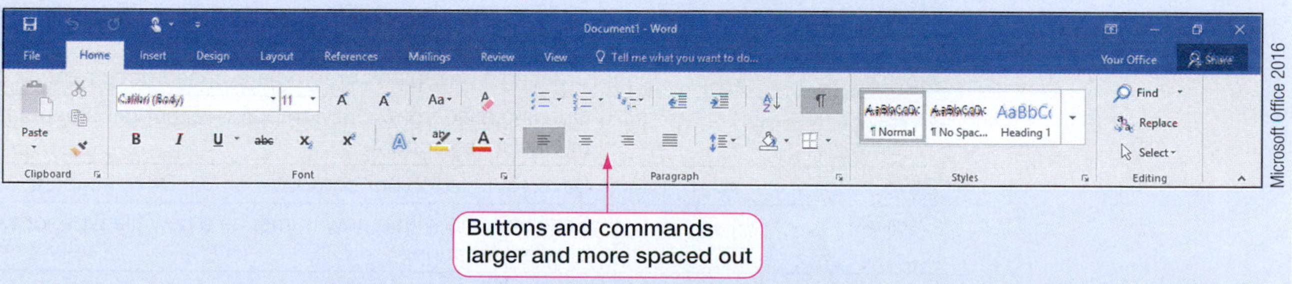

Figure 5 Word ribbon in Touch mode

SIDE NOTE

Customize the Quick Access Toolbar

You can customize the Quick Access Toolbar for favorite or frequently used commands such as Quick Print, Spelling & Grammar, or New.

c. All the figures in this text were made in mouse mode. In the Quick Access Toolbar in the upper left, click **Touch/Mouse Mode**. Then click **Mouse** to ensure that you are in mouse mode.

d. With your insertion point still at the beginning of the document, type Meeting Minutes – Budget Meeting.

CONSIDER THIS | Advantages of a Common Interface

The ribbon provides a common user interface. This common interface can help you learn additional applications quickly. What elements have you noticed that are common? What elements have you noticed that are different? Of the elements that are different, how are they still presented in a common way?

Using Office Backstage, Your Account, and Document Properties

Office Backstage provides access to the file-level commands, such as saving a file, creating a new file, opening an existing file, printing a file, and closing a file, as well as program options and account settings. Backstage is accessed via the File tab. Office Backstage includes an area called Account. This enables you to log into your Microsoft account or switch accounts. You can also see a list of connected services and add services, such as LinkedIn and Skype. Table 2 lists the areas that you can modify in Office Backstage.

Under Account, you can see what **Office Theme** — or color scheme — you are using. In Office 2016, the default is a new colorful theme. While this looks modern, the best theme for accessibility for people with vision impairments or color blindness is the White theme. For this reason, all of the figures in this book were made with the White theme after this next exercise.

Under Account, you can also see your **Office Background** — an artistic design in the upper right area of the title bar. Again for accessibility reasons, all the figures in this text were made with No Background. In this exercise, you will look at Backstage for your meeting minutes starting document.

Area	Description
Info	Adding properties, protecting, inspecting, and managing a document.
New	Creating a new blank or template-based document.
Open	Opening a file from your computer, recent documents list, or OneDrive account.
Save	Save your file to your computer or OneDrive account.
Save As	Save your file with a new name, as a new file type, or to a different location.
Print	Preview and print your document.
Share	Share your file by invitation, e-mail, online presentation, or blog post.
Export	Change the file type or create a PDF/XPS document.
Close	Close the file without closing the application.
Account	User and product information, including connected services.
Options	Launches the Application Options dialog box with many options, including advanced options.

Table 2 Office Backstage

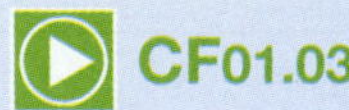

CF01.03

To Use Backstage to Set Account Settings and View Document Properties

a. Click the **File** tab and then, in the left pane, click **Info**.

Notice the file properties on the right side of the window. Since you have not saved yet, most of the properties are blank. The properties will appear once the file has been saved.

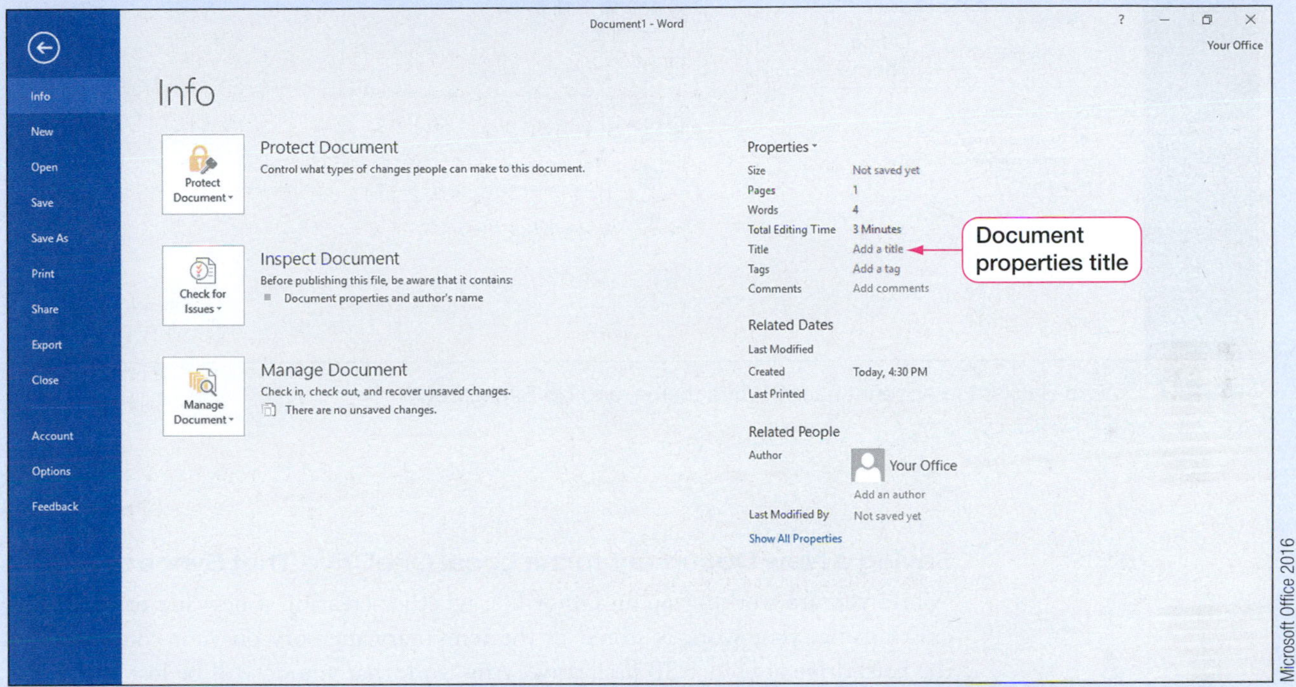

Figure 6 Word Backstage, info page

b. In the properties, click **Add a title**, and then type Budget Meeting Minutes LastFirst, using your last and first name.

c. In the left pane, click **Account**.

If your Microsoft account is already connected, you will see your information and links to access and modify your account. If it is not connected, you will see an option to sign in. In a computer lab, you may see something entirely different, depending on your administrator's setup. If desired and needed, you can sign in to your account now.

Notice that you can also check for updates and see your version of Office. As Microsoft updates in between new versions of Office, your version may change the way the interface works slightly from these instructions. This book is written for version 16.0.6001.1033.

d. If you would like your screen to match the figures in this text, ensure that the **Office Background** is set to **No Background** and the **Office Theme** is set to **White**. Leave Backstage open for the next exercise.

The best theme for accessibility for people with vision impairments or color blindness is the White theme and No Background. For this reason, from this point forward all figures in this book were made with the White theme.

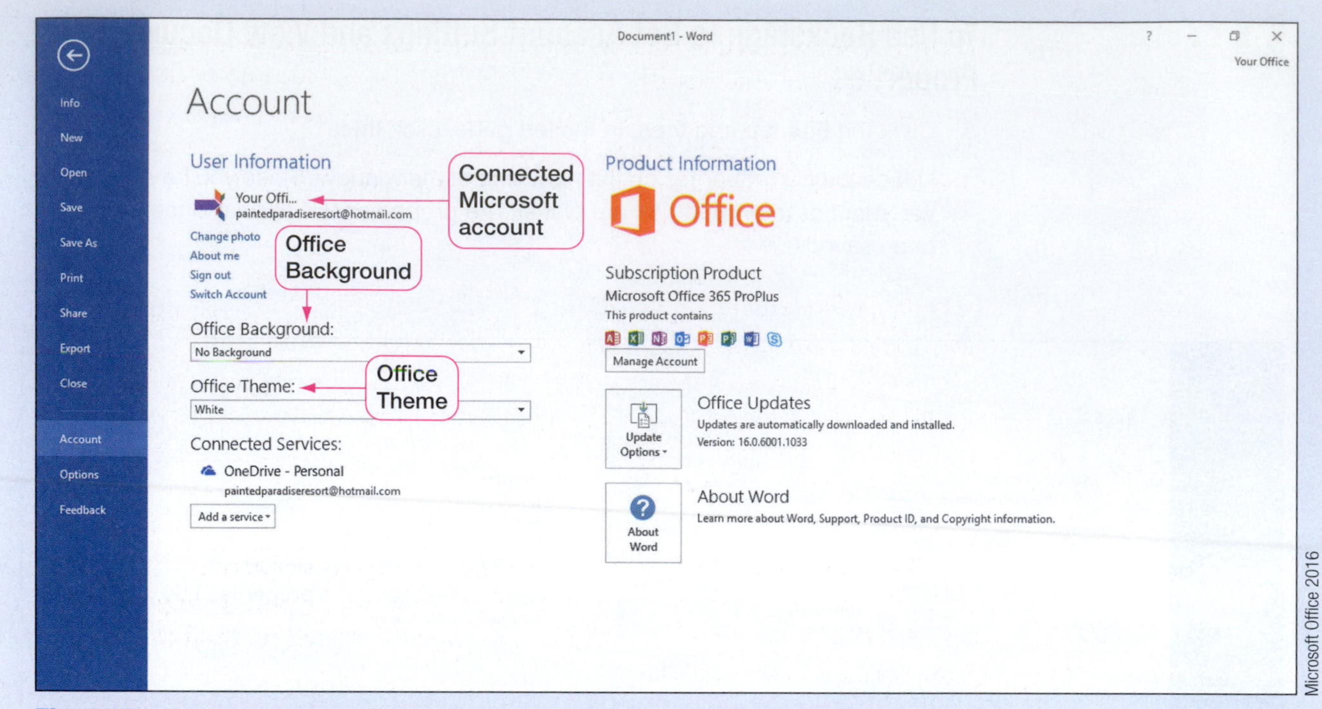

Figure 7 Word Backstage Account name, White theme, and No Background

Saving a New Document to the Local OneDrive That Syncs to the Cloud

While you are working on an Office file, whether creating a new file or modifying an existing file, your work is stored in the temporary memory on your computer, not on the hard drive or your USB flash drive. Any work that you do will be lost if you exit the program, turn off the computer, or experience a power failure or computer crash without you or the program's automatic save function saving your work. To prevent losing your work, you need to save your work and remember to do so frequently — at least every 10 minutes or after adding several changes. That saves you from having to re-create any work you did before the last save.

You can save files to the hard drive, which is located inside the computer; to an external drive, such as a USB flash drive; to a network storage device; or to OneDrive or another cloud storage service. Office has an **AutoRecovery** feature — previously called AutoSave — that will attempt to recover any changes made to a document since your last save if something goes wrong, but this should never be relied upon as a substitute for saving your work manually.

Traditionally, for file storage, files are saved locally on a hard drive or an external storage device such as a USB drive. A **USB drive** is a small, portable storage device — popular for moving files back and forth between a lab, office, and/or home computer. However, USB drives are easily lost, and file versions and backups are usually maintained manually, potentially causing versioning problems.

With Windows 10 and Office 2016, cloud file storage technologies are easier to use than ever. **OneDrive** — Microsoft's cloud storage solution — is fully integrated into File Explorer and Backstage. **Cloud computing** is computing resources, either hardware or software, on remote servers being used by a local computer over the Internet. Apps exist for all of your devices, even Apple and Android devices, that connect to your files on the cloud. Other cloud storage systems also exist, such as Dropbox, Google Drive, and Box.

When you edit a file, your computer or device automatically updates the file in the online storage location. All of the other computers and devices check the online storage for changes and update as needed. Thus, when saving your file, you automatically place a copy online and in all of your synced computers. This creates an online backup if your computer crashes. Additionally, there is no USB drive to lose. File versioning problems are also minimized — in fact, OneDrive by default keeps all versions of your file for you, just in case. Once all applications have been properly set up, you have your files everywhere you want them and shared with exactly who needs them without having multiple copies of files around or e-mailing attachments.

REAL WORLD ADVICE **Not All Terms of Service Are the Same**

Terms of service for online cloud storage services vary. Some services require you to waive your rights to file content. You really should read the terms of service before signing up for any online service. If you do not, you may not "own" your own files.

Your school's computer lab may or may not be integrated with cloud storage. In this case, you can always log into the cloud storage via a web browser and upload your files. For OneDrive, the URL is http://onedrive.live.com. If you are unsure about your school's computers, ask your instructor.

REAL WORLD ADVICE **Backing Up to the Cloud**

Best practice still dictates bringing files to important meetings on a physical drive such as a USB drive as backup. Cloud technologies are dependent on an Internet connection. Suppose you show up for a presentation and cannot get to your files because of a poor Internet connection. Your presentation is likely to be a disaster.

The Save As option in Office Backstage gives you direct access to OneDrive, which you can access with your Microsoft account — except Access, which requires you to save locally. With Windows 10, you have a local folder that is directly accessible from the File Explorer and automatically syncs with OneDrive. Thus, you can sync Access files in the local syncing OneDrive folder.

When you save a file, you must provide a name. A file name includes the name you specify and a **file extension** — a few letters that come after the period in the name — assigned by the Office program to indicate the file type. The file extension may or may not be visible, depending on your computer settings. You can check your computer's setting in the File Explorer window under the View tab in the Show/Hide group. The check box for File name extensions should be checked to see file extensions, as shown in Figure 8. Each Office program adds a period and a file extension after the file name to identify the program in which that file was created. Table 3 shows the common default file extensions for Office.

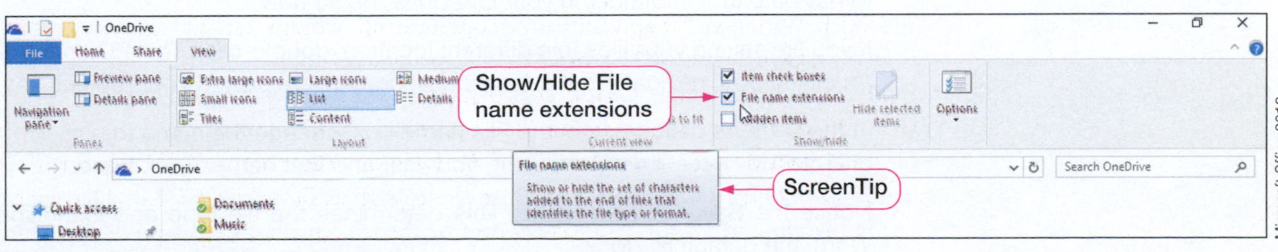

Figure 8 File Explorer extension setting

Application	Extension
Microsoft Word 2016	.docx
Microsoft Excel 2016	.xlsx
Microsoft PowerPoint 2016	.pptx
Microsoft Access 2016	.accdb

Table 3 Office 2016 default file extensions

Name your file with a descriptive name that accurately reflects the content of the document, workbook, presentation, or database, such as "January 2017 Budget" or "012017 Minutes". The descriptive name can include uppercase and lowercase letters, numbers, hyphens, spaces, and some special characters — excluding ? "/ | < > * : — in any combination.

A file exists on your local machine at a **file path** — the physical location of the file starting with a letter that represents the drive and separating folders with a "\". This could be to your hard drive, usually the C:\ drive. Or it could be a USB drive that could be any letter of the alphabet, such as G:\. Assuming your main hard drive is C:\, the OneDrive location on your local computer is C:\Users\username\OneDrive — where username is the username you logged in with. Thus, if you put a file called Meeting.docx in your local OneDrive — and not in a subfolder — the file path combined with the file name would be C:\Users\username\OneDrive\Meeting.docx.

The file path and name combined can include a maximum of 255 characters including the extension. Even though Windows 10 can handle a long file name, some systems cannot. Thus, shorter names can prevent complications in transferring files between different systems.

In this exercise, you will save the meeting minutes document to OneDrive or the location where you are saving your files.

To Save a Workbook to the Local OneDrive Folder That Syncs to the Cloud

SIDE NOTE
Saving a File
To save in OneDrive, you must be signed in. You can also save to This PC or Add a Place.

a. If necessary, return to Backstage by clicking the **File** tab. Then, on the left pane, click **Save As**.

   Notice there is an option for Save and Save As. Save saves a file to the location in which it already exists with the same name. Since this is a new, never saved file, Save and Save As work the same. You will work with an existing file to understand the difference later in this chapter.

b. Click on **This PC**. You may see a folder icon that links to Documents. You will also see recent locations, potentially your OneDrive. If you see OneDrive here, you can click on it. You can also click on Browse to open the Save As dialog box.

c. If you are logged into your Microsoft account, double-click **OneDrive**. If you want to navigate to a subfolder in your OneDrive, do so now.

   If you are saving your files to a different location, double-click This PC. In the Save As dialog box, navigate to the location where you are saving your project files.

d. In the Save As dialog box in the File name box, change the name to cf01ch01Minutes_LastFirst, using your last and first name. Click **Save**.

   Notice the Save as type menu. This determines the file type and extension. In Word, the default is .docx.

Troubleshooting

You are not connected to OneDrive! If this is your PC, log into your Microsoft account as directed in the previous exercise. If you cannot do that, such as in a computer lab, double-click **This PC** or **Browse** and navigate to a location where you would like to store your files.

You can store the files on the desktop and then upload them at http://onedrive.live.com when you are finished. If you do this, make sure all files are closed before you upload them.

Alternatively, you can save the files to a USB drive or other location of your choosing.

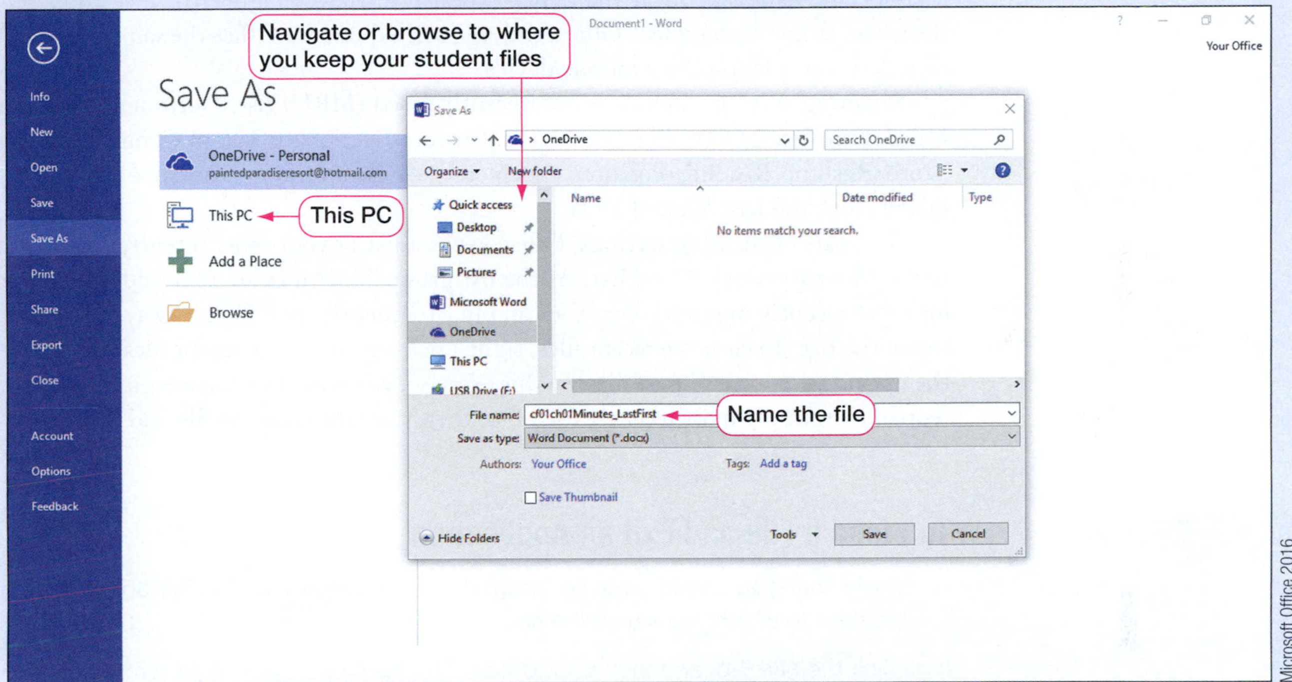

Figure 9 Word Save As

e. Click **Minimize** [–]. Then on the taskbar, click **File Explorer**.

f. In the left Navigation pane, Click **OneDrive** or otherwise navigate to where you saved your file. In the file list, verify that your file is there.

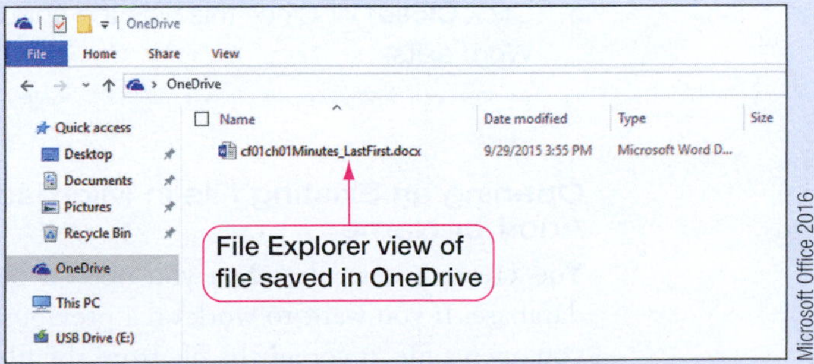

Figure 10 Word file in File Explorer

g. In the top right corner of File Explorer, click **Close** [×].

h. On the taskbar, point to the **Word icon** until you see the Live Preview of your file. Click the **Live Preview** to maximize your file again.

Closing a File, Reopening from the Recent Documents List, and Exiting an Application

When you are ready to close a file, you can click the Close command in Office Backstage. If the file you close is the only file that's open for that particular program, the program window remains open with no file in the window. You can also close a file by using the Close button [×] in the top right corner of the window to exit the window. If you exit the window, it will close both the file and the program. Exiting programs when you are finished with them helps to save system resources and keeps your Windows desktop and taskbar uncluttered. It also prevents data from being accidentally lost. Importantly, files must be closed before being uploaded to the web, copied to a new location, or attached to an e-mail; otherwise you risk corrupting the file.

Office's **roaming settings** are a group of settings that offer easy remotely synced user-specific data that affect the Office experience. Across logins, these settings remain the same. When signing into Office, the user will experience Office the same way, whether on a desktop, a laptop, or a mobile device.

Roaming settings include Most Recently Used (MRU) list, Documents and Places, MRU Templates, Office Personalization, Custom Dictionary, List of Connected Services, Word Resume Reading Position, OneNote — custom name a notebook view, and in PowerPoint the Last Viewed Slide.

As a part of roaming settings, Office keeps a list of your most recently modified files in the **Most Recently Used list**. As the list grows, older files are removed to make room for more recently modified files. You can pin a frequently used file to always remain at the top of the list. To clear the recent files, right-click any file in the recent files list, and select the option to clear unpinned files. In this exercise, you will close the meeting minutes and reopen it from the most recently used list; then you will close the file and Word.

To Close a File and Exit an Application

a. Verify that you saved your file properly in the previous exercise and know the location to which you saved the file.

b. Click the **File** tab, and then click **Close**. The file closes, but Word remains open.

c. Click the **File** tab, and then click **Open**. On the right, you should see your file in the Most Recently Used list organized by last saved date — labeled Today, Yesterday, Last Week, or Older.

d. Click **cf01ch01Minutes_LastFirst**. Your file opens from the originally saved location.

e. Click **Close** [×]. Since this was the only open document, the document closes and Word exits.

Opening an Existing File in Microsoft Word and Then Saving as Another Name

You create a new file when you open a blank document, workbook, presentation, or database. If you want to work on a previously created file, you must first open it. When you open a file, it copies the file from the file's storage location to the computer's temporary memory and displays it on the screen. When you save a file, it updates the storage location with the changes. Until then, the file exists only in your computer's memory. If you want to open a second file while one is open, the keyboard shortcut of pressing [Ctrl] and then pressing [O] will display the Open tab of Office Backstage. Using the keyboard shortcut of [Ctrl] + [F12] will launch the Open dialog box without taking you to Office Backstage.

Many times, you will open a file that already exists rather than starting a new file. You can open the program and then open the file. You also can double-click a file in File Explorer, and the file will open in the associated program. When you have an existing file open, the Save command saves the file to the current location with the same name. If you want to change the name of a file or save it to a different location, you will need to use the Save As command. This allows you to specify the save options. When you use Save As, it allows you to select any location and give the file a new name.

When you open files that you downloaded from the Internet, accessed from a shared network, or received as an attachment in e-mail, the file usually opens in a read-only format called **Protected View** in Reading Mode. In Protected View, the file contents can be seen and read, but you cannot edit, save, or print the contents until you enable editing. If you see the information bar right under the ribbon and you trust the source of the file, simply click the Enable Editing button on the information bar.

REAL WORLD ADVICE **Sharing Files Between Office Versions**

Different Office versions are not always compatible with one another. The general rule is that files created in an older version can always be opened in a newer version but not the other way around — an Office 2016 file is not easily opened in earlier versions of Office. Sharing files with Office 2003 users is a concern because different file extensions were used. For example, .doc was used for Word files instead of docx, .xls instead of .xlsx for Excel, and so on.

It is possible to save the Office 2016 files in a previous file format. To save in one of these formats, use the Save As command, and click the 97-2003 file format. If the file is already in the format of a previous version of Office, it will open in Office 2016 and be saved with the same format in which it was created. However, if a file is saved with the extension of a previous version, it may lose anything created with newer features.

If you have not already done so, you need to download the files for this text at http://www.pearsonhighered.com/youroffice. In this exercise, you will open an existing file and save it with another name. Susan Brock has already started an agenda for your meeting with her but has asked you to finish it.

To Open an Existing File

a. On the taskbar, click in **Ask me anything** or **Search the web and Windows** and type Word. Click the **Word 2016** search result. The Word Start screen opens.

b. Click **Open Other Documents** in the left pane, and then click **Browse**. Navigate through the folder structure to the location of your student data files, and then double-click **cf01ch01Agenda**.

The agenda previously started by Susan Brock opens in Word.

c. If necessary, click Enable Editing. If you needed to click Enable Editing, your file opened in Protected View.

d. Click the **File** tab, click **Save As**, and then double-click **This PC**. In the Save As dialog box, navigate to the location where you are saving your project files, and then change the file name to cf01ch01Agenda_LastFirst, using your last and first name. Click **Save**.

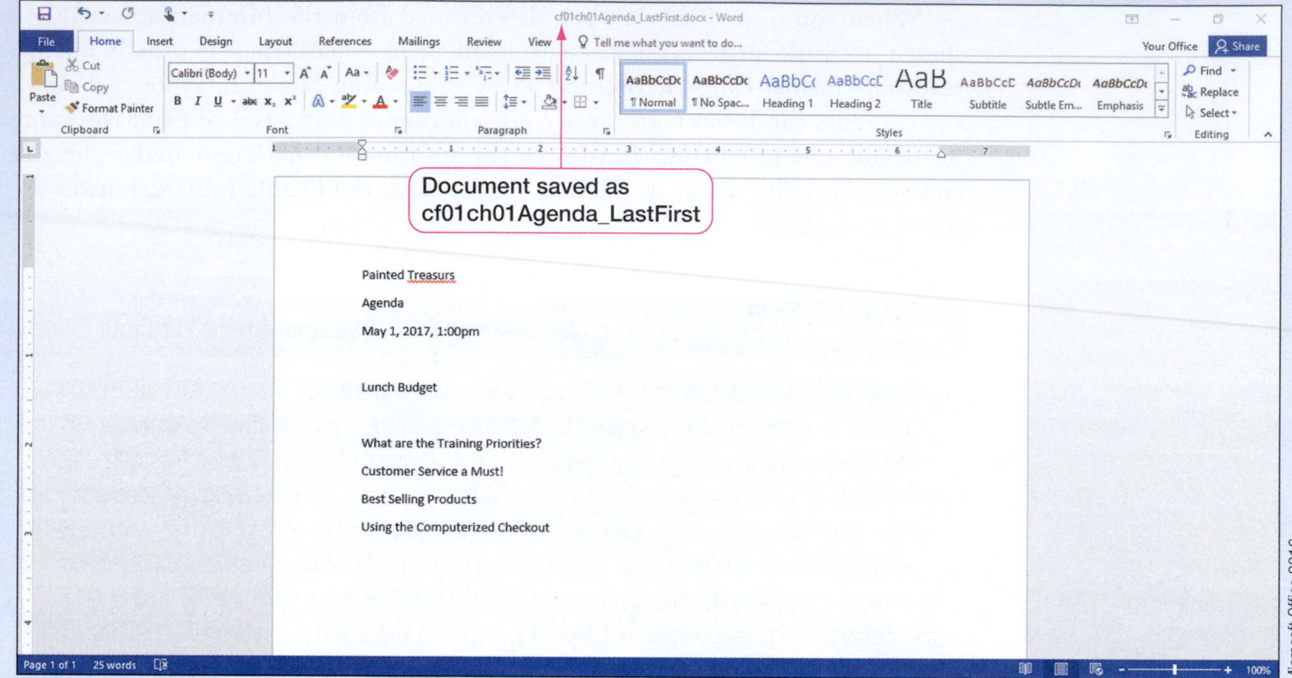

Figure 11 Beginning the Agenda document

Zooming, Scrolling, and Navigating with Keyboard Shortcuts

To get a closer look at the content within the program, you can zoom in. Alternatively, if you would like to see more of the contents, you can zoom out. Keep in mind that the zoom level affects only your view of the document on the screen and does not affect the printed output of the document. It is similar to using a magnifying glass on a page of a book to make the words look bigger — the print on the page is still the same size. Therefore, do not confuse the zoom level with how big the text will print — it affects only your view of the document on the screen.

On the right side of the status bar in the lower right corner is a slide control that permits zooming in Word from 10% to 500%. The minus and plus buttons provide an easy method to change the view size, or you can drag the Zoom Slider. In Excel and PowerPoint, the zoom range is from 10% to 400%. When zoom is used, text is sometimes shifted off the viewing screen. Depending on the program and the zoom level, you might see the vertical or horizontal scroll bars or both scroll bars, which can be used to adjust what is displayed in the window. The scroll bars have arrows that can be clicked to shift the workspace in small increments in a specific direction and a scroll box that can be dragged to move a work space in larger increments. Touch screens allow you to zoom in and out by using pinch and stretch gestures. In addition to zooming and scrolling, you can navigate the file using keyboard shortcuts.

REAL WORLD ADVICE | **Using Keyboard Shortcuts and KeyTips**

Keyboard shortcuts — keyboard equivalents of software commands — are extremely useful, and some are universal to all Windows programs. They allow you to keep your hands on the keyboard instead of reaching for the mouse — increasing efficiency and saving time. Some companies have even take the mouse away from their interns to force them to use keyboard shortcuts. Keyboard shortcuts are also very useful for accessibility and people with vision impairments.

Pressing Alt will toggle the display of **KeyTips** — or keyboard shortcuts — for items on the ribbon and Quick Access Toolbar. After displaying the KeyTips, you can press the corresponding letter or number to request the action from the keyboard.

For multiple-key shortcuts, you hold down the first key listed and press the second key once. Some common keyboard shortcuts are listed below.

Ctrl + C	Copy the selected item
Ctrl + X	Cut the selected item
Ctrl + V	Paste a copied or cut item
Ctrl + A	Select all the items in a document or window
Ctrl + B	Bold selected text
Ctrl + Z	Undo an action
Ctrl + Home	Move to the top of the document
Ctrl + End	Move to the end of the document

In this exercise, you will zoom in and out on the agenda document and navigate it with keyboard shortcuts.

CF01.07

SIDE NOTE
Methods for Zooming
Several ways exist to zoom Office applications: Zoom Slider, View tab in the Zoom group, Ctrl and a mouse wheel, and touch gestures.

SIDE NOTE
End of the Document
When this text requests that the insertion point be at the end of the document, use this keyboard shortcut to avoid mistakes.

To Zoom, Scroll, and Navigate with Keyboard Shortcuts

a. The insertion point should be at the beginning of the document right before the word "Painted," and the insertion point should be blinking.

b. On the Word status bar, drag the **Zoom Slider** to the right until it reaches **500%**. The document is enlarged to its largest size. This makes the text appear larger.

c. Press Ctrl + End. This takes you to the end of the document.

Troubleshooting

As discussed in the Windows 10 chapter, if the End key is shared with a function key as on many laptops, you may have had a different result. Ensure that your button is behaving as the End key and not as a function key. This is device specific, and you may need to do a web search to figure it out. If necessary, use the scroll bar instead.

d. On the Word status bar, click **500%**.

Notice that this percentage is the Zoom level button that opens the Zoom dialog box. This dialog box provides options for custom and preset settings.

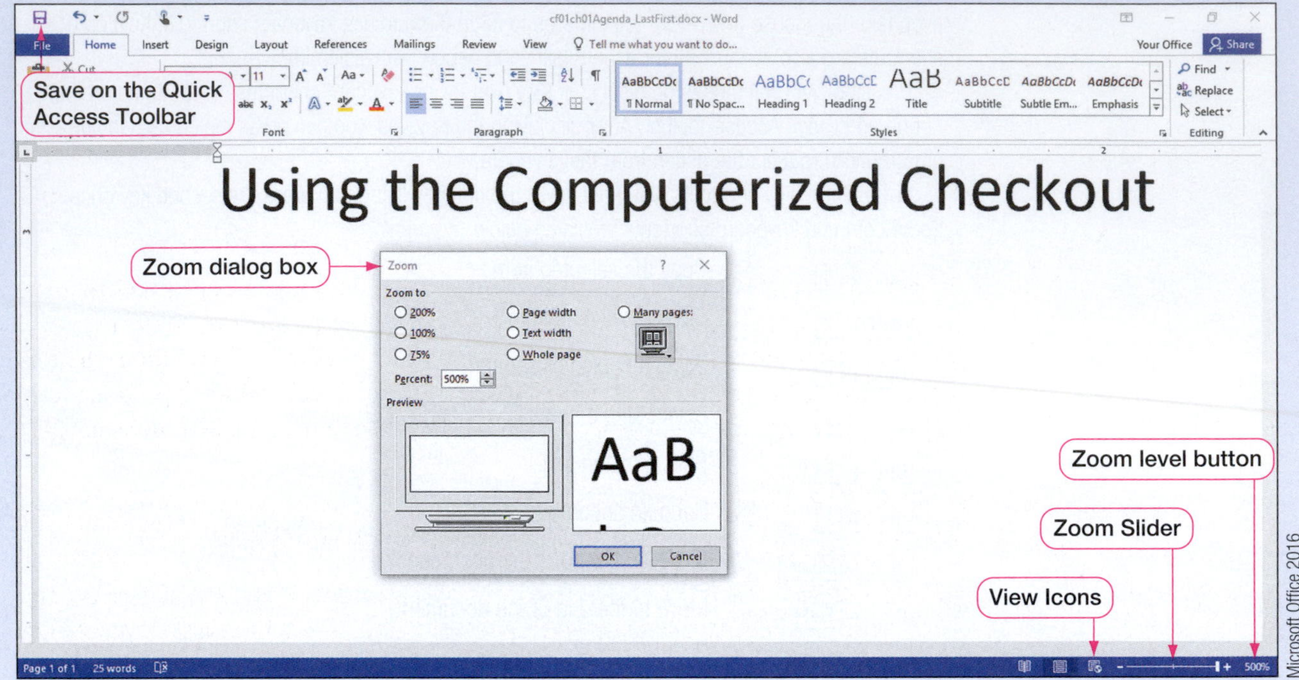

Figure 12 Zoom controls and dialog box

SIDE NOTE

Long Documents

When you are scrolling in long documents, it is fastest to right-click the scroll box in the scroll bar and select your desired option.

e. Click **Page width**, and then click **OK**.

The Word document zooms to its page width. Notice that this zoom level will give you the maximum size without creating a horizontal scroll bar.

f. Right-click the **scroll box** in the scroll bar. Then select **Top** to return to the beginning of the document.

Notice that the document scrolled to the top but did not move the insertion point. The keyboard shortcut of Ctrl + Home takes you to the top and moves the insertion point.

g. Press Ctrl + Home and notice that the insertion point moves to the top as well.

h. **Save** the document.

Using the Quick Access Toolbar to Save a Currently Open File

In addition to Office Backstage, Office provides several ways to save a file. To quickly save a file, simply click Save on the Quick Access Toolbar or use the keyboard shortcut of pressing Ctrl + S. The **Quick Access Toolbar** is the series of small icons in the top left corner of the title bar that can be customized to display commonly used buttons.

When this method is used, the program simply saves the file to its current location with the same name. Once you save a file the first time, the simple shortcut methods to save any changes to the file work fine to update the existing file — as long as you do not need to change the file name or location with the Save As command. In this exercise, you will save your file to its current location with the same name as previously given.

SIDE NOTE

Save Keyboard Shortcut

You can also save with the keyboard shortcut of Ctrl + S.

To Save an Existing File with the Quick Access Toolbar

a. In the top left corner in the Quick Access Toolbar, click **Save**.

The file is now saved to the same location and with the same name you designated earlier in this chapter. Although you have not made changes since the document was last saved, best practice is to save your files frequently.

Manipulate, Correct, and Format Content in Word

A personal brand is important in business. If a person dresses poorly, colleagues may assume that this person's work is poor as well. In the business world, everything a person does influences the way colleagues and superiors view that person, including the content and formatting of the files he or she produces. Thus, understanding appropriate content and formatting is very important — it is a direct reflection of you as a professional.

REAL WORLD ADVICE | **It Is Not the Place for Jokes!**

Business documents and files are rarely if ever appropriate for jokes. Consider a job applicant who lists, as the last thing in his or her resume, "Will work for food" — this has actually happened. The job applicant may have wanted to convey that he or she had a good sense of humor. But in reality, the message shows that the job applicant did not understand that humor was inappropriate in this situation or he or she did not take getting the job seriously.

CONSIDER THIS | **Consider Your Personal Brand**

Have you thought about your personal brand? Are you the creative person? Are you the efficient person? Describe your brand. Give an example of how you were influenced positively or negatively by the way another person presented themselves or their work.

Checking Spelling

Checking spelling is a must — and it is easy in Office. There are no excuses for spelling mistakes. Everyone makes typos, but that is no excuse for poor spelling. Further, you need to understand your audience and purpose before using jargon, acronyms, text abbreviations, or other informal language. Using informal language in a business chat in Skype is appropriate. However, in a business meeting agenda, formal language is expected.

In this exercise, you will correct a spelling mistake.

To Correct Spelling

SIDE NOTE
Spelling Pane
The spelling pane can also be an effective way to check an entire document. Subsequent chapters will cover more on spell check.

a. Notice the second word on the first line is misspelled as "Treasurs" instead of "Treasures." Since it is misspelled, Word put a wavy red line under the word to indicate the mistake. A green wavy line indicates a grammar mistake. A blue wavy line indicates that there could be a mistake but it is not grammar or spelling — such as using "from" instead of "form".

b. Right-click the misspelled word **Treasurs**. Click the first option for **Treasures**.

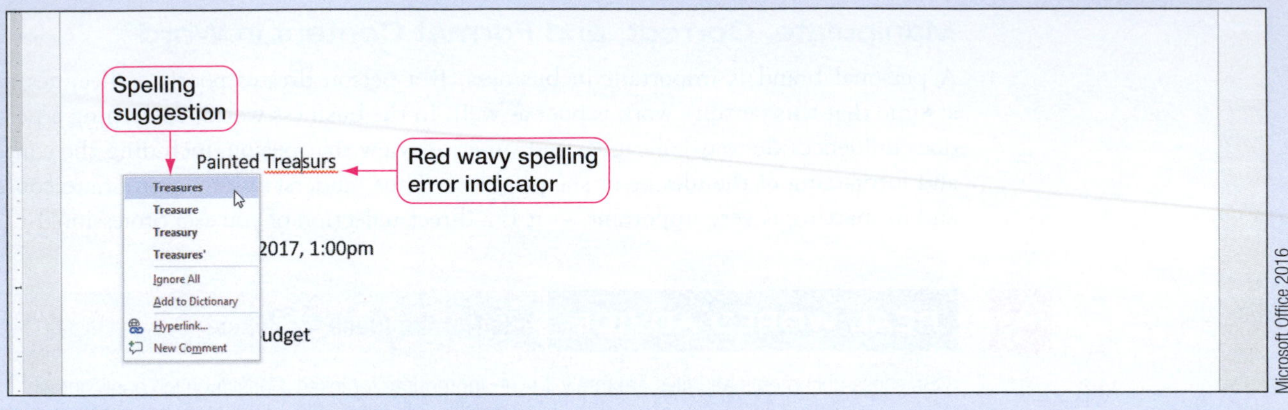

Figure 13 Correcting spelling in a document

c. **Save** the document.

Showing Formatting Symbols, Entering, Copying, and Pasting Text

Many keys, such as Spacebar, Enter, and Tab, insert nonprinting characters in a document. For example, when you press Tab, text is indented and a tab "character" is inserted. Sometimes called formatting marks, nonprinting characters are by default not displayed on the screen. These formatting marks are not shown when the document is printed, even when they are displayed on the screen. When content is entered, these marks can change the way the text is shown, is located, and is formatted. Thus, displaying formatting symbols can help you see everything in your document.

As you add content, you will inevitably find an occasion when copying and pasting the text will save you time. Of course, someone looking at the end product will have no way of knowing what you typed by hand and what you copied and pasted. In many instances, copy and paste not only will save you time but also will increase accuracy — assuming that you do not copy a mistake! In this exercise, you will enter the top three products at the gift store. Along the way, you will copy and paste to enter text as efficiently as possible.

CF01.10

To Show Formatting Symbols, Enter, Copy, and Paste Text

a. On the Home tab, in the Paragraph group, click **Show/Hide** ¶. The hidden formatting symbols now show. Notice the only hidden symbols in this document are a paragraph mark indicating the end of a paragraph and a dot representing spaces.

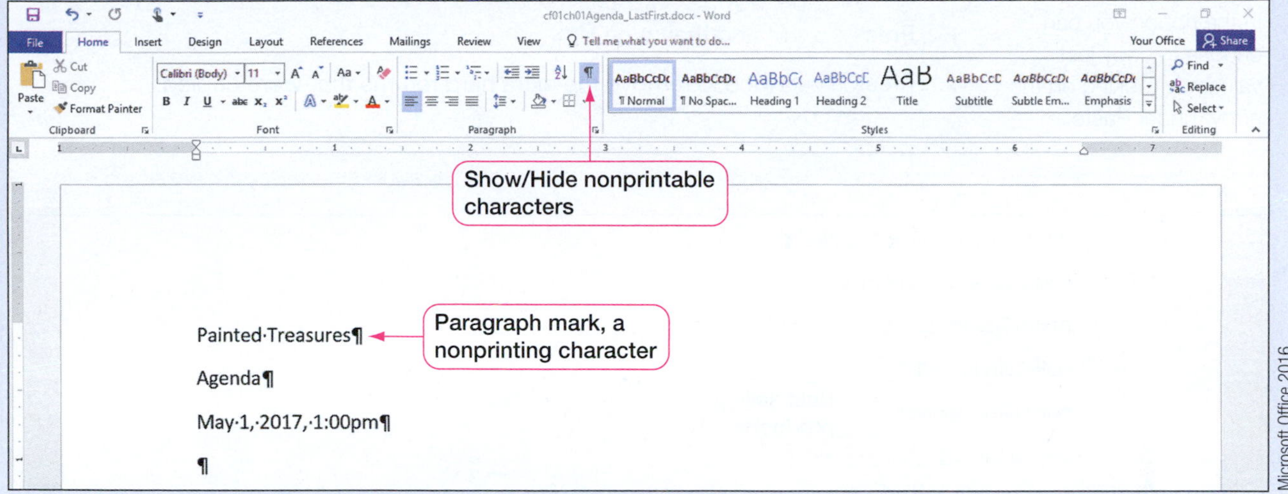

Figure 14 Hidden formatting characters

> **SIDE NOTE**
> **Mouse Versus Keyboard**
> If you have trouble using the keyboard to select text, use the mouse instead. In the end, it does not change your document. Knowing both methods is about speed.

b. If necessary, scroll until you see the words **Best Selling Products** and then click after the **s** in Products to place your insertion point at the end of that line. Press Enter.

Pressing Enter creates a hard return that creates a new paragraph. Word will automatically wrap text in a paragraph down to the next line.

c. Type Golf Clubs. The top three products are three different kinds of golf clubs. To save time, you will use copy and paste.

d. Hold down the Shift key, and press the ← **ten** times to select the words Golf Clubs.

You can use Shift and arrow keys to select, rather than the mouse. Depending on the situation, the mouse could be faster or the keyboard could be faster. Therefore, it is useful to know how to use both. Notice when you pressed the arrow for the tenth time, it automatically selected the paragraph mark.

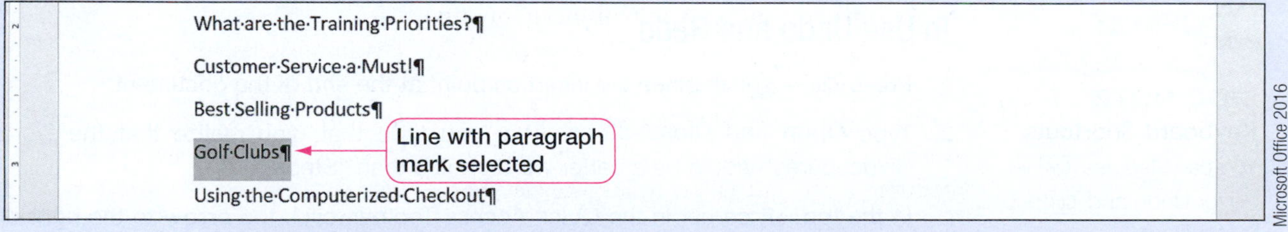

Figure 15 Paragraph mark selected

e. Press Ctrl + C. This copies the text to the Office Clipboard to use anytime you want, even multiple times, until the clipboard is replaced with something else.

f. Click after the **s** in Golf Clubs to place the insertion point at the end of the line. Then press Spacebar and type Junior.

SIDE NOTE
Copy without Formatting
The keyboard shortcut copies everything, including formatting. In the ribbon you can choose to copy just values by clicking on the arrow under Paste.

g. Press Enter and then press Ctrl + V. This pastes the contents of the Clipboard onto that line. Then press ← to return to the second line that says "Golf Clubs."

h. Press Spacebar and then type **Beginner**.

i. Press Enter and then press Ctrl + V. This pastes the contents of the Clipboard onto that line. Then press ← to return to the third line that says "Golf Clubs."

j. Press Spacebar and then type **Pro**.

k. Press Delete twice to remove the extra hard returns that were copied.

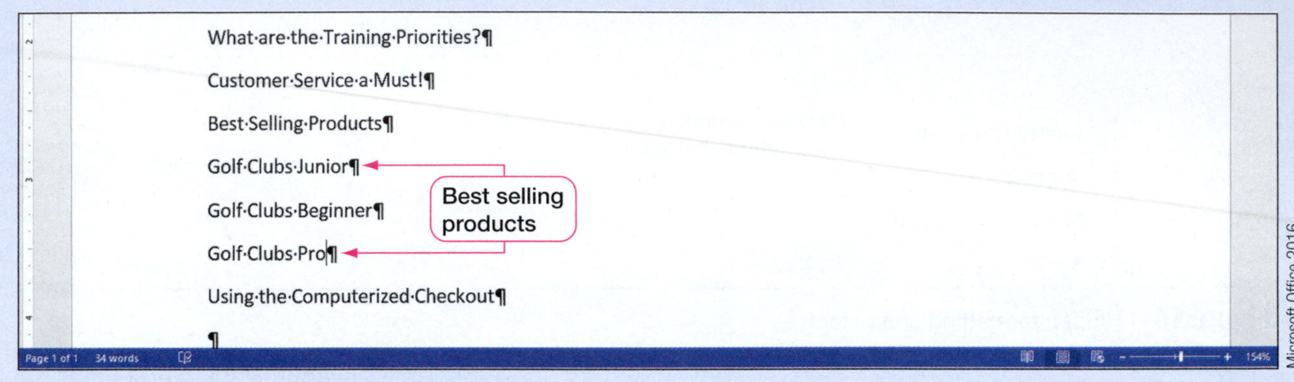

Figure 16 Top products entered

l. **Save** the document.

Using Undo and Redo

Everyone makes a typo from time to time, and you are going to make mistakes that you need to undo. The easiest way to do that is through the Undo and Redo buttons in the Quick Access Toolbar. In this exercise, you will add some text to your agenda, undo it, and then add better text.

CF01.11

SIDE NOTE
Keyboard Shortcuts
You can also use Ctrl + Z for Undo and Ctrl + Y for Redo.

To Use Undo and Redo

a. Press Ctrl + End to place the insertion point at the end of the document.

b. Type **Open and Close Steps**. After you type that, you realize that the word "Procedures" would be a better word choice than "Steps."

c. In the top left corner in the Quick Access Toolbar, click the **arrow** to the right of Undo Typing.

SIDE NOTE

Redo

Redo works similar to Undo. If you undo something and then change your mind, you can reverse the Undo by clicking Redo.

d. Verify that the list is letting you undo by the letter. If not, see the troubleshooting below. Click the item on the list that says **Typing "S"** that was the first letter to the word Steps.

Troubleshooting

If your version of Office does not undo by the letter, you may see an option for only the phrase Typing "Steps." If you do, click that option. You may also see an option for the whole phrase Typing "Open and Close Steps." If you do, click that option and then, in the next step, you will have to redo the entire line by typing Open and Close Procedures.

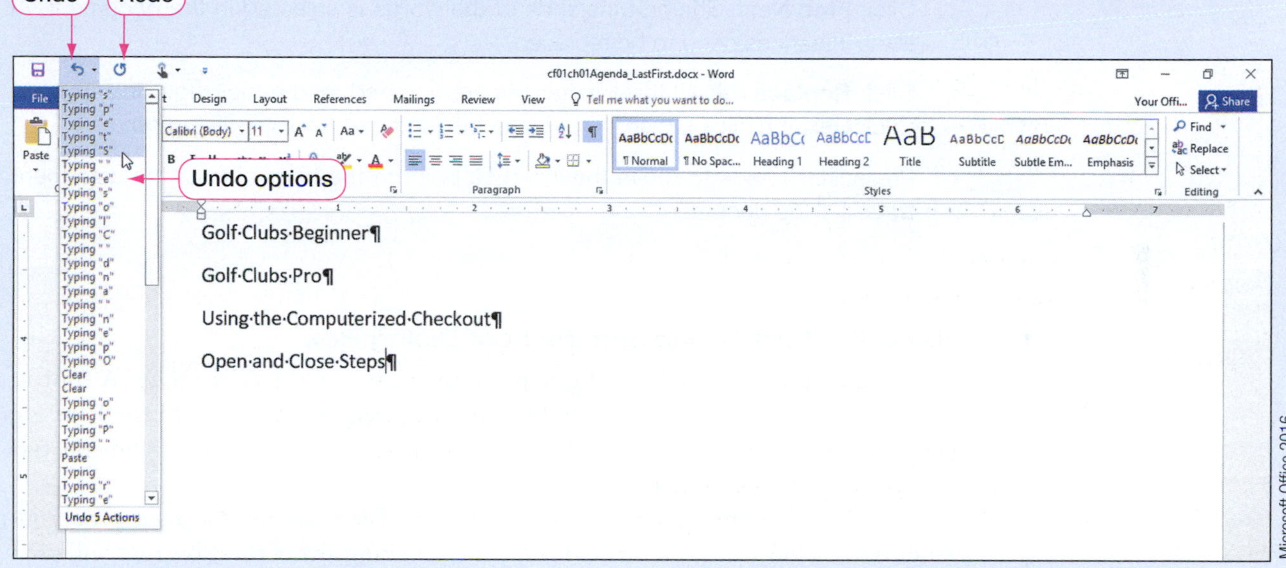

Figure 17 Undo typing steps

e. Type Procedures. The word "Steps" is undone, and you have entered a better word choice. Undo and Redo can be used for almost anything you do, not just typing.

f. **Save** the document.

Using the Navigation Pane, Finding Text, and Replacing Text

Sometimes, you may not know where certain text is in a document. Or you may need to replace text with something different. You can use Find and Replace on the ribbon rather than manually looking for text and changing it. If you click Find on the Home tab, it opens the Navigation pane on the left side of the window with a search box. A **pane** is a smaller window that often appears to the side of the program window and offers options or helps you to navigate through completing a task or feature. If you click Replace, it opens the Find and Replace **dialog box**, which is a window that provides more options or settings beyond those provided on the Navigation pane. All three of the top-selling products are actually Wilson Golf clubs. In this exercise, you will find the words "Golf Clubs" and replace them with the more precise brand of Wilson Golf Clubs.

REAL WORLD ADVICE | **What to "Find" in a Find and Replace?**

Be careful what you look for in a find and replace. If you are not careful, you can end up replacing items that should not have been. If this ever happens, remember the Undo command!

SIDE NOTE

Be Careful with Replace All

When using Replace All, be very careful. It is easy to unintentionally change text that should not have been changed.

To Use Find and Replace

a. On the Home tab, in the Editing group, click **Find**. The Navigation pane appears on the left. You could find all of the instances of Golf Clubs from this pane. However, you cannot do a find and replace operation from here. In the top right corner of the Navigation pane, click **Close** ☒ to close that pane.

b. On the Home tab, in the Editing group, click **Replace**. The Find and Replace dialog box opens.

c. Click in the **Find what** box, and type Golf Clubs.

d. Click in the **Replace with** box, and type Wilson Golf Clubs.

e. Click **Find Next**. The first instance of the words is selected in the document. All three instances need to be replaced.

f. Click **Replace All**. All three instances are updated, and a message box appears. Click **OK**, and click **Close** ☒ to close the Find and Replace dialog box.

g. Press Ctrl + Home to move the insertion point to the beginning of the document. **Save** the document.

Using the Font Group and the Font Dialog Box

One of the most commonly used groups on the ribbon is the Font group. A **font** is the way the letters in words look, including the size, weight, and style. In the Font group, you can change many attributes of the words, including color, size, alignment, type of font, and common emphasis.

Clicking a command will produce an action. For example, the Font group on the Home tab includes buttons for bold and italic. Clicking any of these buttons will produce an intended action. So if you have selected text to which you want to apply bold formatting, simply click the Bold button, and bold formatting is applied to the selected text.

Some buttons are **toggle buttons** — one click turns the feature on and a second click turns the feature off. When a feature is toggled on, the button remains highlighted. Clicking toggles the setting on and off. Bold is an example of a toggle button.

Some buttons have two parts: a button that accesses the most commonly used setting or command and an arrow that opens additional options. A **gallery** is a set of menu options that appears when you click the arrow next to a button. A normal arrow will bring up the options or enable you to scroll through the options. If there is a More arrow, it brings up all of the options.

For example, on the Home tab, in the Font group, the Font Color button includes a gallery of the different colors that are available for fonts. If you click the button, the default is to apply the last color used, which is displayed on the icon. To access the gallery for other color options, click the arrow next to the Font Color button.

Some commands open other menus. These commands expand to a list of options when the arrow next to the list is selected. Whenever you see an arrow next to a button, this is an indicator that more options are available. Then you can click on the option from the list that you want.

Some ribbon groups include a diagonal arrow in the bottom right corner of the group, called a **Dialog Box Launcher**, which opens a corresponding dialog box. Click the Dialog Box Launcher to open a dialog box. It often provides access to more precise or less frequently used commands along with the commands that are offered on the ribbon; thus, using a dialog box offers the ability to apply many related options at the same time and from one location.

In this exercise, you will change the formatting of the font to be more appropriate.

CF01.13

To Use the Font Group and Font Dialog Box

SIDE NOTE

Text Selection

You can double-click to select a single word or triple-click to select the entire paragraph. You can also use Shift and arrow keys to select text.

a. If necessary, press Ctrl + Home to place your insertion point at the beginning of the document.

b. On the Home tab in the Paragraph group, click **Center**. The title is centered across the top.

c. On the first line, click before the **P** in Painted Treasures, and then drag to right after the **s** to select the words "Painted Treasures."

d. On the Home tab, in the Font group, click **Increase Font Size** three times. The title is now larger.

e. On the Home tab, in the Font group, click the **arrow** next to the Font gallery. Scroll down the list, and click **Verdana**. The font changes.

f. On the Home tab, in the font group, click the **arrow** next to Font color. Under Standard Colors, select **Dark Red**.

g. On the Home tab, in the font group, click **Bold** B.

h. Click before the **L** in Lunch Budget, and drag to the **t** to select Lunch Budget.

i. On the Home tab, in the Font group, click the **arrow** next to Font Size 11. Click **14**. The font increases in size to 14 points.

j. On the Home tab, in the Font group, click the **Dialog Box Launcher**. The Font dialog box opens. Under Font style, click **Italic**.

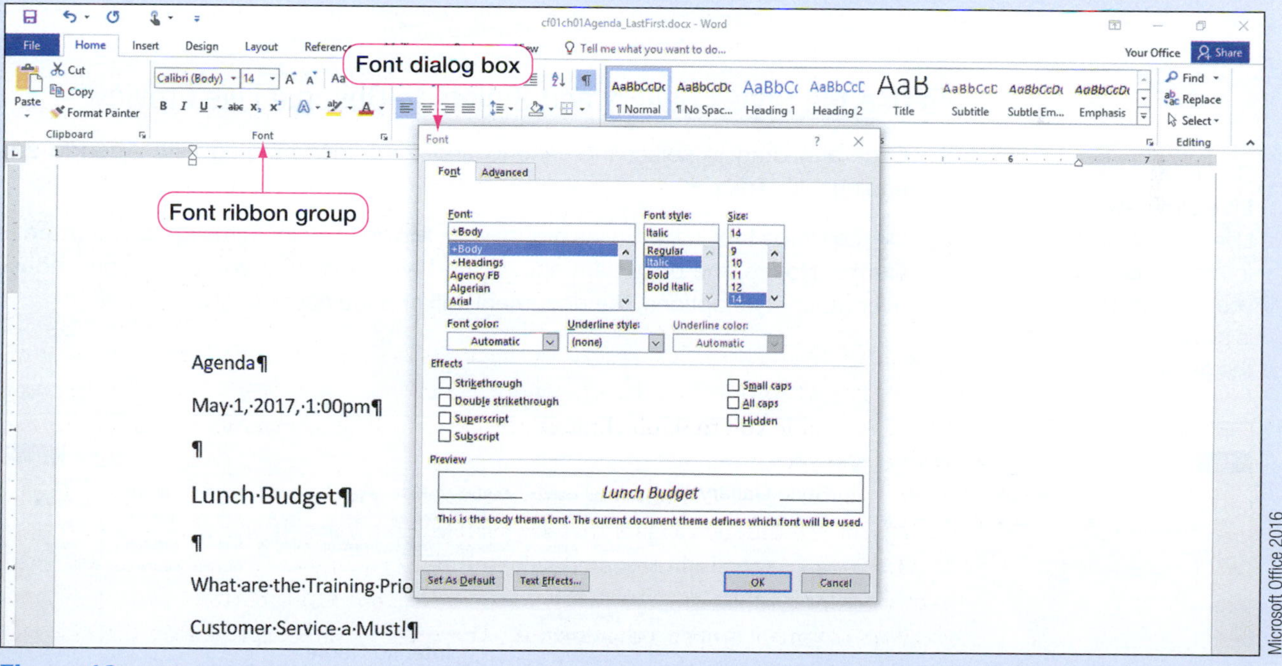

Figure 18 Font dialog box

k. Click **OK**. The dialog box closes.

l. **Save** the document.

Using the Style Gallery and Bullets with Live Preview

Live Preview lets you see the effects of menu selections on your document file or selected item before making a commitment to a particular menu choice. The menu or grid shows samples of the available options. Not all additional options under arrows have Live Preview. Using Live Preview, you can experiment with settings before making a final choice.

Predefined Styles are a type of preset formatting. You will learn more about styles later. However, styles allow for more advanced features, such as a Table of Contents. They can also be customized. So if you later decide that Heading 2 should be in a larger font size, you change the style, and it changes every instance of Heading 2 in your document. Finally, and for the purpose of this chapter, styles help you apply aesthetically pleasing formatting very quickly — and can also be helpful for users with vision color impairments.

When you click on the More arrow for styles, you will see the Styles gallery. Point to a text style in the Styles gallery, and the selected text or the paragraph in which the insertion point is located appears with that text style. Moving the pointer from option to option results in quickly seeing what your text will look like before you make a final selection. To finalize a change to the selected option, click the style.

Bullets are symbols that appear before each item to create a list of items. Typically, bullets also have different spacing than a normal paragraph and have the Live Preview option. When you click on the Bullets arrow, a library menu appears that allows you to pick the symbol you wish to use.

In this exercise, you will add a style to the gift shop agenda using styles and some simple bulleting. In business, agendas usually do not need a lot of formatting. However, a little bit of formatting can actually change what the content conveys to others and provide clarity to your content.

To Use the Styles Gallery and Bullets to Observe Live Preview

SIDE NOTE

Live Preview

Live Preview shows how formatting looks before you apply it. This feature is available for many of the galleries.

a. Click and drag to select the second and third lines starting with **Agenda** and ending with **1:00pm**.

b. On the Home tab, in the Styles group, click **More**. Point to the option for **Intense Quote**. Notice, the document shows the Live Preview. If you move your mouse over other style options, the document will change accordingly.

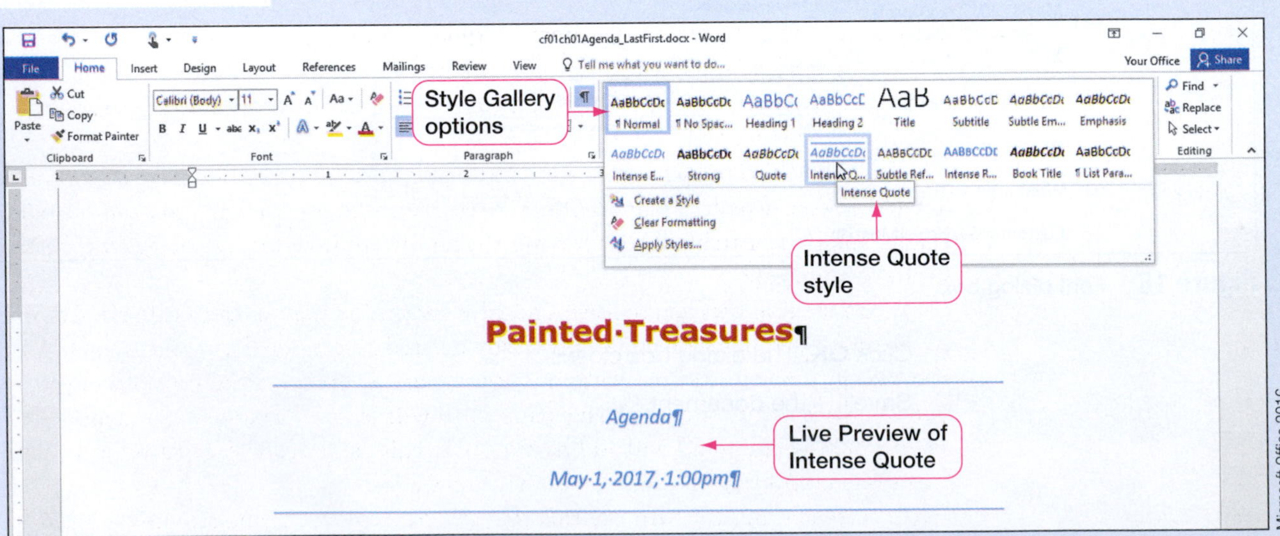

Figure 19 Styles Live Preview

SIDE NOTE

Closing a Gallery

Press Esc to close a gallery without making a selection. Alternatively, you can click outside the gallery menu.

c. Click **Intense Quote**. The Intense Quote style is now applied to those two lines.

d. If necessary, scroll down until you see the golf clubs you entered. Click and drag starting with **Wilson Golf Clubs Junior** down to the last of the three types of golf clubs, **Wilson Golf Clubs Pro**.

e. On the Home tab, in the Paragraph group, click **Bullets**. The lines now display as a bulleted list. Notice that after the bullet symbol, the formatting symbol for a tab appears, indicating space between the symbol and the words.

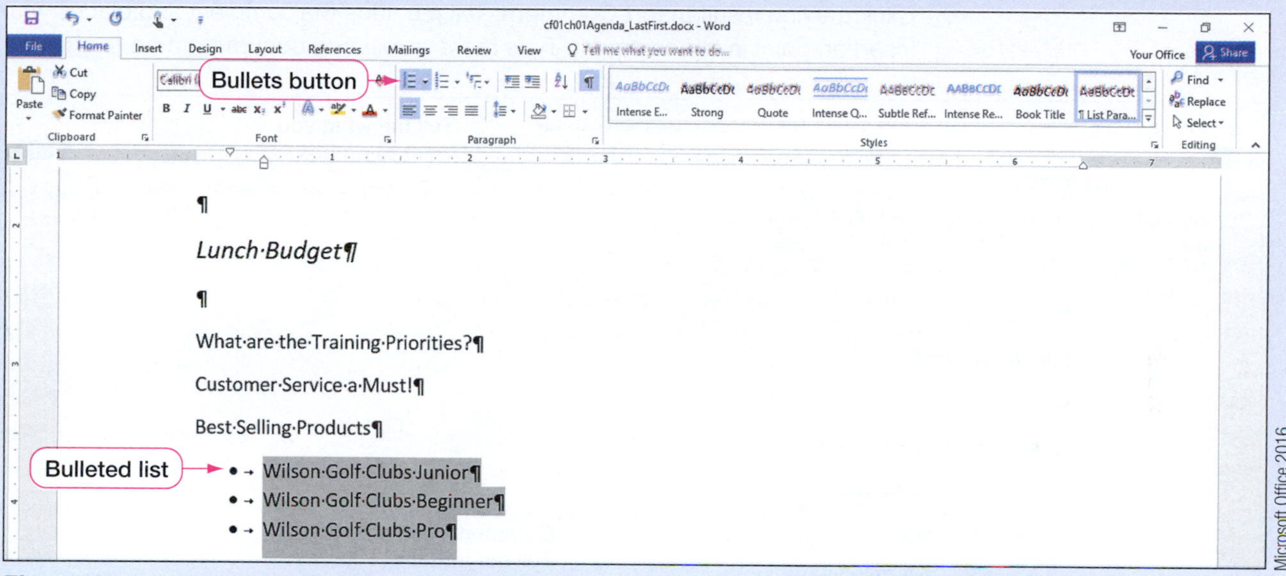

Figure 20 Bulleted list

f. **Save** the document.

Inserting a Comment and Footer Using the Tell me what you want to do Box

New in Office 2016, all of the programs have a **Tell me what you want to do** box in the title bar — "Tell me" for short. This tool is particularly useful when you want to do something but do not know where a command is located in the ribbon. This tool will not just take you to help on that item — though it does provide options for that as well. It actually performs the action for you. Although the Tell me feature is not currently connected to Cortana or speech recognition, it is easy to see that as a potential feature upgrade in the future.

Under the Tell me what you want to do search results, you also have an option for a Smart Lookup, which is new to Office 2016. With Smart Lookup, you can open search results and do research without leaving the application. Instead, it brings up the results in the Inights pane.

A comment allows you to leave a note for another person to read and reply. Comments are great for collaboration and can be easily deleted before the document is final. A footer allows you to put text at the bottom of every page. Footers are great for placing the page number, your name, or even the file name. You will learn more about comments and footers in a later chapter and will add basic ones in this exercise. The Tell me feature is great for using and finding features you do not know a lot about.

In this exercise, you will use this tool to add a comment and a footer to the agenda. Susan, the gift shop manager, has asked you to send back to her the updated agenda. You need to add a comment to ask her a question.

CF01.15

To Use Tell Me to Insert a Comment and Footer

a. Place your insertion point at the end of the line Using the Computerized Checkout so that the insertion point is after the **t** and before the **paragraph** mark.

b. In the title bar, click in the **Tell me what you want to do . . .** box and type Add Comment. Notice that command options are listed first. Next, you have the option to open the Help window on the topic you entered. Finally, you can select Smart Lookup, which opens the Insights pane on the right with Bing web search results.

c. Click the first result **Insert Comment**. Tell me adds the comment and places your insertion point in the comment. Type Is there existing documentation to use?

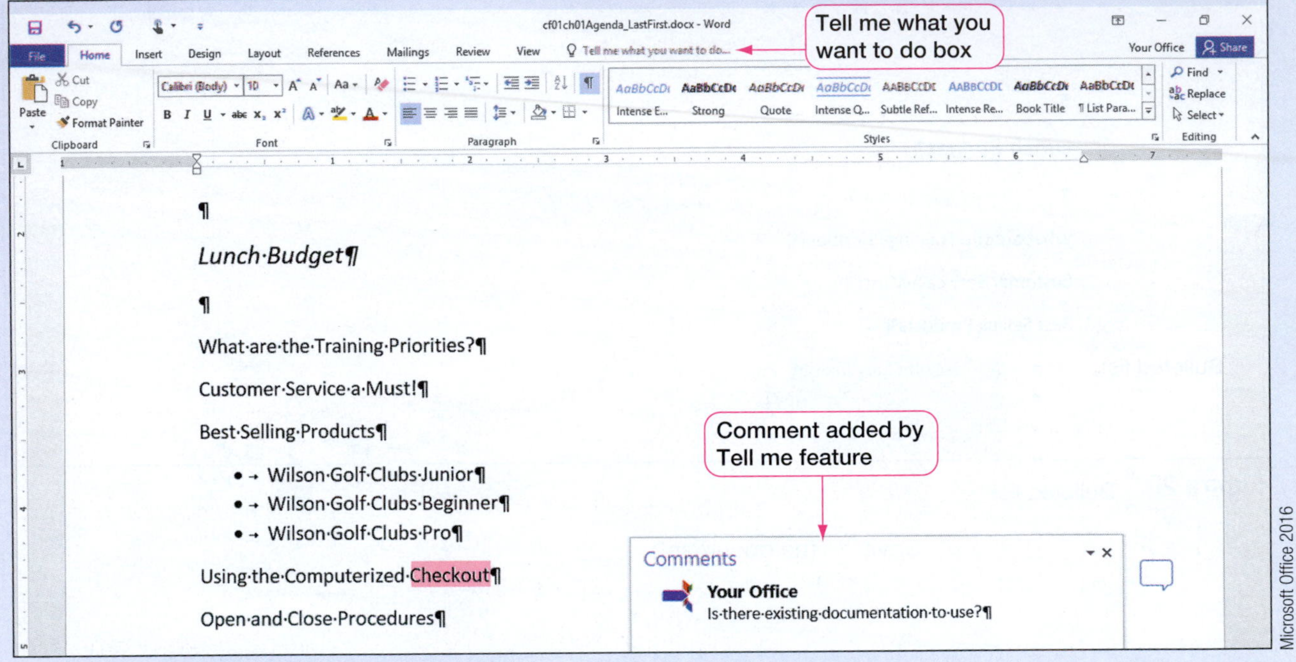

Figure 21 Inserted comment

d. If necessary, scroll to the left and press Ctrl + End to place your insertion point at the end of the document.

e. In the title bar, click in the **Tell me what you want to do . . .** box and type Add a footer, and then click the first result **Add a Footer**. In the submenu, select the second option **Blank (Three Columns)**. Tell me adds the footer and places your insertion point in the footer.

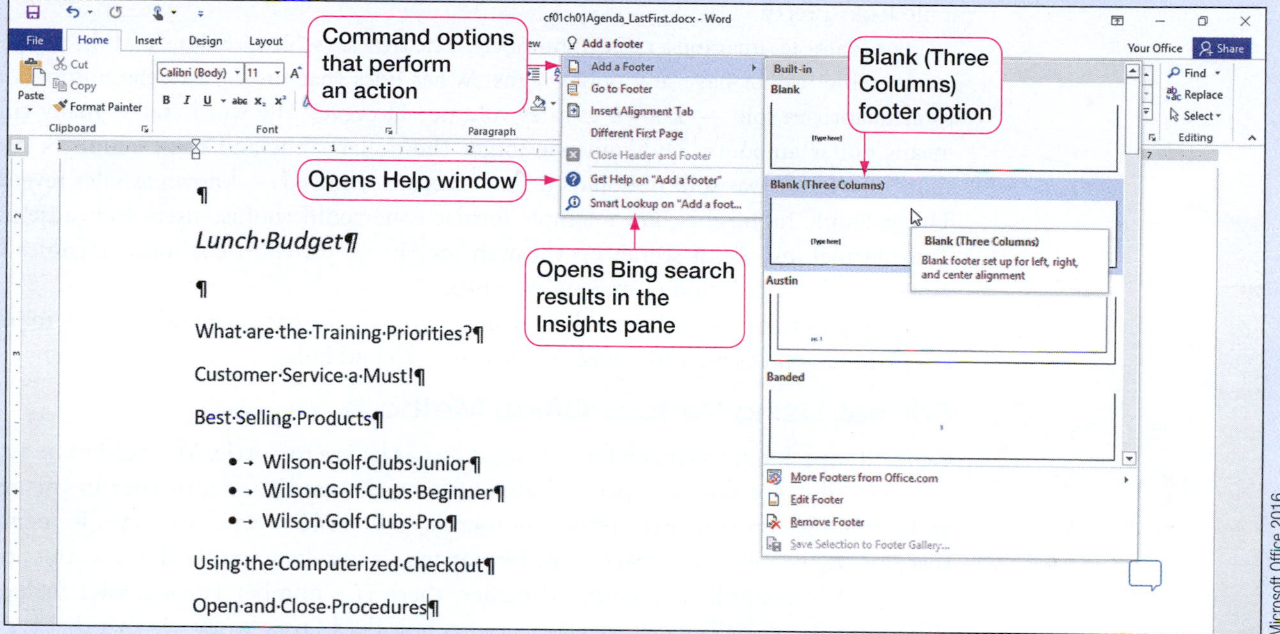

Figure 22 Adding a footer with Tell me

f. On the left side, click **[Type here]** and type First Last, using your first and last name.

g. In the middle, click **[Type here]** and type Course Name, using your class's name.

h. On the right side, click **[Type here]** and type InstructorLast, using your instructor's last name.

i. Press Esc to exit the footer, and then press Ctrl + Home to return to the beginning of the document.

j. **Save** the document, and then click **Close** to close Word. Submit your file as directed by your instructor. If you need to take a break before finishing this chapter, now is a good time.

REAL WORLD ADVICE Saving Files

Most programs have an added safeguard or warning dialog box to remind you to save if you attempt to close a file without saving your changes first. Despite that warning, best practice dictates that you save files before closing them or exiting a program. If you select the wrong option on the warning by accident, you will lose work. Remembering to save before you close prevents this kind of accident.

Best practice also dictates saving often. The more often you save, the less work you can lose in the event of an unexpected closing of the application. Pressing Ctrl + S takes only a few seconds. Train yourself now to use this keyboard shortcut regularly and often. If you do, it will become second nature and save you from losing work in the future!

Formatting, Finding Help, and Printing in Office

The accuracy and quality of your content are the most important aspect of your files. However, even the most high-quality, accurate file is much harder to use if it is formatted poorly causing confusion for anyone who looks at it. After accuracy, clarity of your file to others — and even yourself — is extremely important. It is much more than just making a file look "pretty."

For example, imagine a table of numbers. The title says "2016 Sales," and the numbers in the table do not have any dollar signs. What does that mean? Are the numbers the total quantities sold — known as sales volume? However, the word "sales" many times means dollar amounts. Did someone forget the dollar signs and these numbers really show how much was sold in dollars before costs are removed — known as sales revenue? This example highlights how a simple format issue could confuse users and cause poor decision making. Do a search on the web for "Excel mistakes costing companies big money" and you will find numerous examples.

In this section, you will learn how to appropriately format your budget, how to print a copy to take notes on at the meeting, and how to find help.

Format Using Various Office Methods

Generally speaking, too much formatting is just as bad as too little. You need to be aware of accessibility for vision-impaired individuals — discussed in depth later in this text. Styles in Office provide nice options for users who don't have an artistic eye. Remember that less can be more. However, some formatting, if not done, can lead to incorrect conclusions. For example as mentioned earlier, there is a number labeled Sales in Excel. Without a clearer title or currency formatting, how does a user know whether that is sales in dollars or in quantity sold?

Earlier in the chapter, you added a small amount of formatting that helped the clarity of your agenda. Now you are ready to create your budget in Excel.

Creating a New Excel Workbook

An Excel file is referred to as a **workbook**. Each Excel workbook can contain many different worksheets. Each sheet has rows represented by numbers and columns represented by letters of the alphabet. The intersection of any row and column is a **cell**. For example, cell B2 refers to the cell where column B and row 2 intersect. The **active cell** is the currently selected cell. In a new worksheet, the active cell is the first cell of the first row, cell A1.

On a personal computer, you may prefer to use the Windows Start menu to open the program, but in a computer lab or on an unfamiliar computer, the search method may be preferable. In this exercise, you will search for and open Microsoft Excel to create a new workbook to start a budget for the training budget that you will finish in your meeting with Susan Brock, the gift shop manager.

To Create a New Excel Workbook

a. On the taskbar, click **Ask Me Anything** or **Search the web and Windows**. Type **Excel**.

b. Click on **Excel 2016** in the search results. The Excel Start screen is displayed.

c. Click **Blank workbook**. A new Excel spreadsheet opens.

   Notice, the words Book1 - Excel appear on the title bar. This means that the workbook has not been saved yet. This opens a blank workbook with one worksheet named Sheet1. The active cell is A1.

d. Press Ctrl + F1. The ribbon is pinned open so that you can see all of the commands. on the Home tab.

CHAPTER 1

Troubleshooting

You pressed the keyboard shortcut, but nothing happened or something else happened. Are you working on a laptop? If so, then you may need to hold down the Fn key as well. The function keys on a laptop are generally assigned to other things, such as volume. You can change these key assignments, but they are specific to the device — you may need to search the web to find out how to change them on yours.

On a Microsoft Surface, you can press Fn and CapsLock to make the function keys work without pressing the Fn keys. If you have a laptop, it is worth the time to figure out how to do this on your machine. Keyboard shortcuts greatly increase your speed and efficiency. Finally, you can always use the Ribbon Display Options button instead.

e. Click the **File** tab, click **Save As**, and then double-click **This PC**. In the Save As dialog box, navigate to the location where you are saving your project files, and then change the file name to cf01ch01Budget_LastFirst, using your last and first name. Click **Save**.

Using Excel to Enter Content, Apply Italics, and Apply a Fill Color

As was discussed earlier in the chapter, Office uses a common interface between all of the applications. This does not mean an identical interface. While some things are the same, how they are applied or how they work may be slightly different. For example, in Excel, if you select the cell, the formatting options apply to the entire cell — not just part of the text inside of a cell. By contrast, in Word, you select precisely the words for which to change the font color. To make only a single word a different color in Excel, you must select the specific text you want inside the cell first. Some formatting must be applied to the entire cell, such as number type — Currency, Text, and Date, among others. When exploring features that are common to the Office applications, you need to experience how a feature can be slightly different or very different in an application-specific way.

In this exercise, you will add content to the budget, apply italic to some cells, and apply different background color to others.

CF01.17

To Use the Italic Button and the Fill Color Button

a. Click cell **A6** to make it the active cell. Then type Budget and press Enter. The text is inserted into the cell, and the cell below becomes the active cell.

b. Click cell **A8**. Type Expenses and press Enter.

c. In cell A9, type Food and press Enter.

d. In cell A10, type Drinks and press Enter.

e. Click cell **A8** to make it the active cell. Then, on the Home tab, in the Font group, click **Italic** I. The toggle button applies italic to cell A8, and the button is highlighted.

f. Click cell **B6**. Type 500 and press Ctrl + Enter. The value is entered in the cell, and the active cell remains B6.

g. With B6 active, on the Home tab, in the Font group, click the **Fill Color arrow** . The color options appear. Point to the colors to find **Green, Accent 6, Lighter 60%**. At the writing of this text, that is the third color down in the far right column. Click **Green, Accent 6, Lighter 60%**.

Troubleshooting

What if that color is not there? Microsoft has taken to updating Office more often than just every new version. Thus, things can change over time — and color placement in the galleries is one of those things. The best way to find the color is to point to the name. If the color you need is not there, pick the standard color — which does not change — of light green.

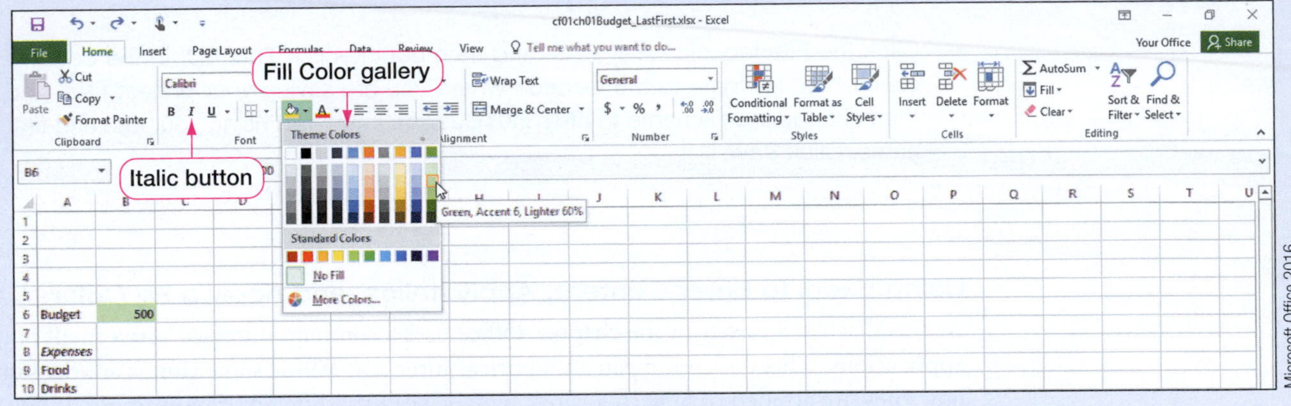

Figure 23 Fill color

h. **Save** the spreadsheet.

Opening an Excel Dialog Box

Excel has dialog boxes, just like Word. The Format Cells dialog box is probably the most used dialog box in Excel, as it allows you to specify many things. Most important, it allows you to specify the type of data in the cell, such as Currency or Text. Since spreadsheets use many calculations, specifying the type of data is very important.

In this exercise, you will use a dialog box to format some of the cells in the budget you are beginning for your manager, Susan Brock.

To Use the Dialog Box Launcher to Format a Number

a. If necessary, click cell **B6** to make it the active cell. Then, on Home tab, in the Number group, click on **Number Format Dialog Box Launcher** . The Format Cells dialog box opens to the Number tab.

b. On the left side, under Category, click **Currency**.

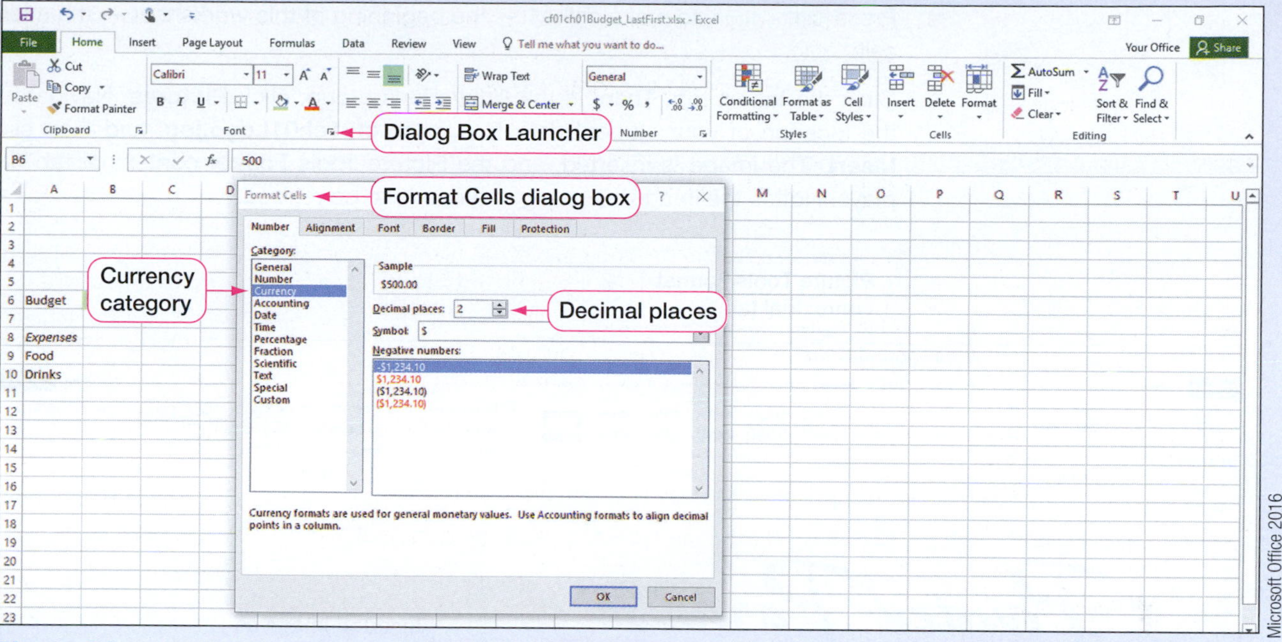

Figure 24 Format Cells dialog box, Number tab

c. Click **OK**. The cell now shows a dollar sign before the number. Notice that the default of two decimals is applied.

d. **Save** the spreadsheet.

Inserting Images and Using Contextual Tools to Resize

In Word, Excel, PowerPoint, and Publisher, you can insert pictures from a file, a screen shot, or various online sources. The online options include inserting images within the Office Online Pictures collection, via a Bing search, or from your own OneDrive. Be careful when you insert Online Pictures — you must ensure that you have the right to use the image you selected for the purpose you want.

The term "contextual tools" refers to tools that appear only when needed for specific tasks. Some tabs, toolbars, and menus are displayed as you work and appear only if a particular object is selected. Because these tools become available only as you need them, the workspace remains less cluttered.

A **contextual tab** contains commands related to selected objects so that you can manipulate, edit, and format the objects. Examples of objects that can be selected to display contextual tabs include a table, a picture, a shape, or a chart. A contextual tab appears to the right of the standard ribbon tabs. The contextual tab disappears when you click outside the selected object — in the file — to deselect the object. In some instances, contextual tabs can also appear as you switch views.

In this exercise, you will insert a Painted Treasures Gift Shop logo into the budget you are beginning for your manager, Susan Brock. This budget will become a part of Susan's larger budget that she must present to the CEO of Painted Paradise in an internal memo once a year. Logos are an excellent way to brand both internal and external communications.

To Insert an Image and Use the Contextual Tab to Resize

a. Press Ctrl + Home to make cell A1 — the beginning of this worksheet — the active cell.

b. Click the **Insert** tab. Then, in the Illustrations group, click **Pictures**. Navigate to the location of your student data files, click **cf01ch01Logo.jpg**, and then click **Insert**. The image is inserted, and the Picture Tools Format contextual tab displays. Notice the image is too big and needs to be resized.

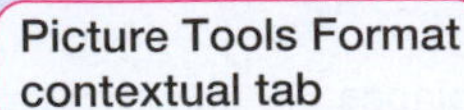

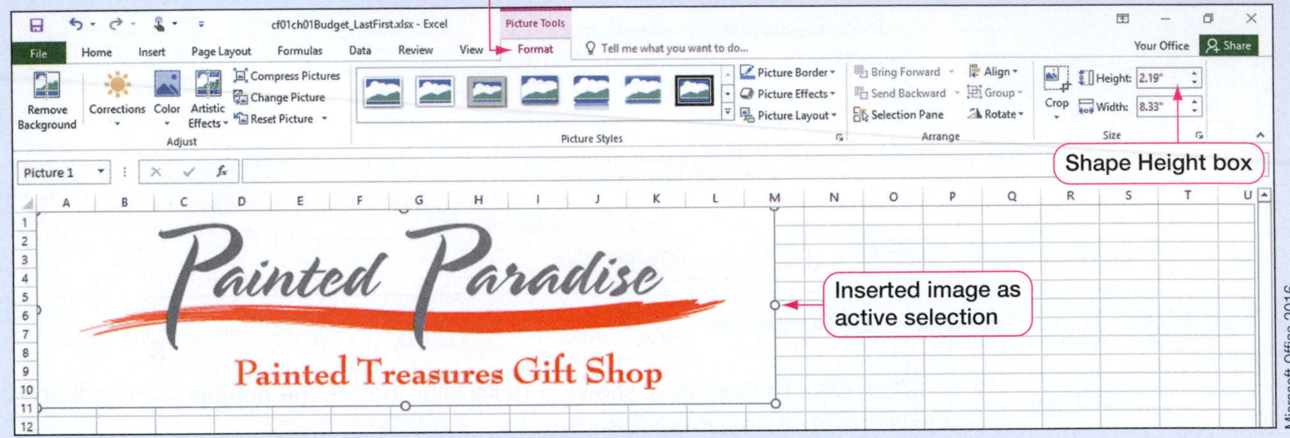

Figure 25 Picture Tools Format contextual tab

c. In Picture Tools, on the Format contextual tab, in the Size group, click in the **Shape Height** box. Then type 1 and press Enter. The image now fits the spreadsheet more appropriately.

d. Click cell **A6**. The contextual tab disappears because the image is no longer selected.

e. **Save** the spreadsheet.

REAL WORLD ADVICE — What Is Creative Commons and Why Should You Care?

Office used to provide clip art pictures that were free to use. Office 2016 instead searches web sources for images. By default, it will find images that have Creative Commons licenses. These are images for which the copyright owner has chosen to allow anyone to use the image without commercial compensation. However, it is up to YOU to make sure that image really is free to use. You must read the specific license for that image to be sure your use is acceptable — otherwise, you could be sued for copyright infringement — which is why you should care. When you insert the image, the source URL will be listed on the bottom. Click the link to open the source URL. From there, it may or may not be easier to find the license that is specific to that URL. When in doubt, do not use the file, or contact the owner before using.

Formatting Using the Mini Toolbar

The **Mini toolbar** appears after text has been selected and contains buttons for the most commonly used formatting commands, such as font, font size, font color, center alignment, bold, and italic. The Mini toolbar button commands vary for each Office program. The toolbar disappears if you move the pointer away from the toolbar, press a key, or click the workspace. All the commands on the Mini toolbar are available on the ribbon; however, the Mini toolbar offers quicker access to common commands, since you do not have to move the mouse pointer far away from the selected text for these commands.

In this exercise, you will edit some of the cells in your budget with the Mini toolbar.

To Use the Mini Toolbar to Make a Cell Bold

a. Double-click cell **A6** to place the insertion point in the cell. Double-clicking a cell enables you to enter edit mode for the cell text.

b. Double-click cell **A6** again to select the text. The Mini toolbar appears, coming into view directly above the selected text. If you move the pointer off the cell, the Mini toolbar becomes transparent or disappears entirely. If you don't move it too far away, you can move the pointer back over the Mini toolbar, and it becomes completely visible again. If it doesn't reappear, double-click on the text again.

Troubleshooting

If you are having a problem with the Mini toolbar disappearing, you may have inadvertently moved the mouse pointer to another part of the document. If you need to redisplay the Mini toolbar, right-click the selected text, and the Mini toolbar will appear along with a shortcut menu. Once you have selected an option on the Mini toolbar, the shortcut menu will disappear and the Mini toolbar will remain while in use — or repeat the prior two steps, then make sure the pointer stays over the toolbar.

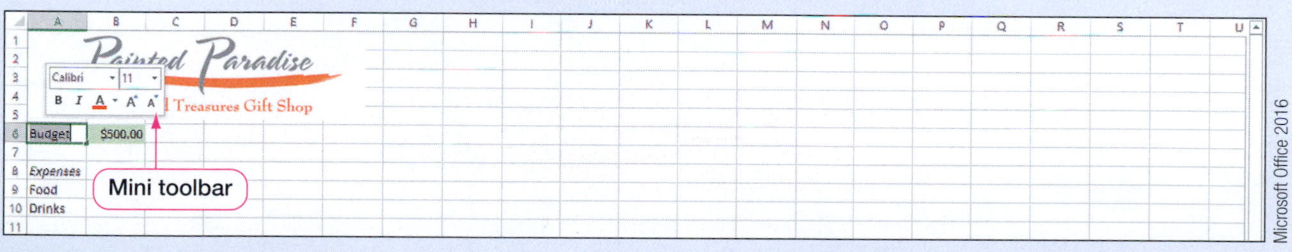

Figure 26 The Mini toolbar

c. In the Mini toolbar, click **Bold** [B] and press [Enter].

d. **Save** [Save icon] the spreadsheet.

The Mini toolbar is particularly helpful with the touch interface. When Office recognizes that you are using touch instead of a mouse or digitizer pen, it displays Mini toolbars that are larger and designed to work with fingers more easily. An example of a touch Mini toolbar in Excel Touch mode is shown in Figure 27.

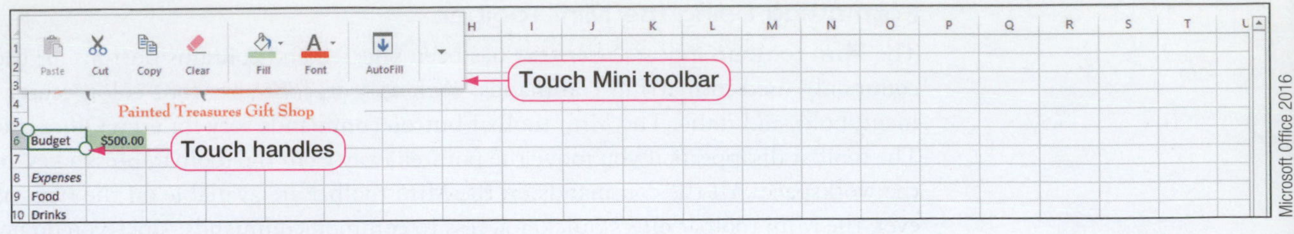

Figure 27 The Mini toolbar in Touch mode

Opening Shortcut Menus and Format Painter

A **shortcut menu** is a list of commands related to a selection that appears when you right-click — click the right mouse button. Shortcut menus are also context sensitive and enable you to quickly access commands that are most likely to be needed in the context of the task being performed. This means that you can access popular commands without using the ribbon. Included are commands that perform actions, commands that open dialog boxes, and galleries of options that provide a Live Preview. The Mini toolbar also opens with the shortcut menu when you click the right mouse button. If you click a button on the Mini toolbar, the shortcut menu closes, and the Mini toolbar remains open, allowing you to continue formatting your selection.

The **Format Painter** allows you to copy a format and apply it to other selections. This allows you to format in one place and quickly apply all of the same formatting elsewhere. If you click the Format Painter button once, Format Painter will turn off after you use it just once. If you double-click the Format Painter, it leaves Format Painter active until you click the Format Painter button again or press Esc; leaving Format Painter active allows you to apply the formatting to multiple locations.

In this exercise, you will add some additional information to the budget you are beginning for your manager. You will also edit some of the cells using a shortcut menu and copy the format using Format Painter.

To Use a Shortcut Menu and Format Painter

a. Click cell B9. Type 450 and press Enter. Cell B10 should now be the active cell.

b. With cell B10 active, type 50 and press Enter.

c. Right-click cell **B9** to display the shortcut menu.

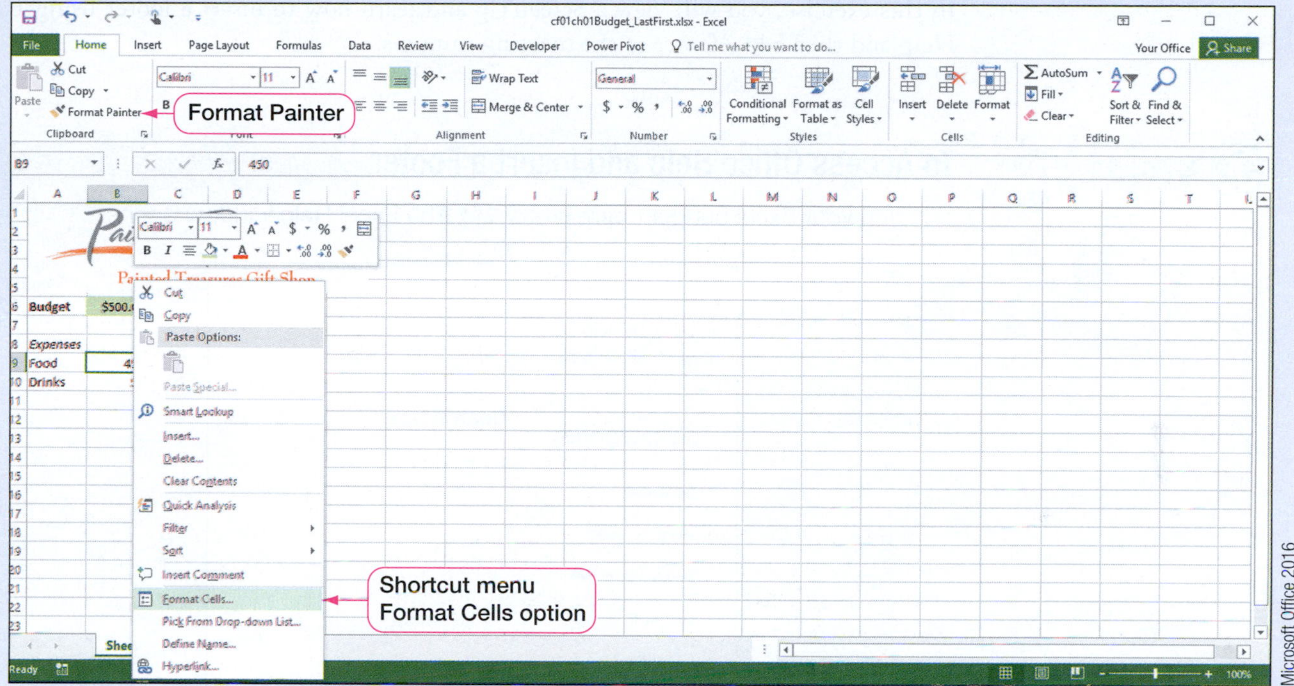

Figure 28 The shortcut menu

> **SIDE NOTE**
> **Double-click the Format Painter**
> If you double-click the Format Painter, it will stay on until you click the Format Painter again, allowing you to apply the formatting to more than one cell.

d. Click **Format Cells**.

e. In the Format Cells dialog box, under Category, click **Currency** and then click **OK**.

f. With B9 as the active cell, on the Home tab, in the Clipboard group, single-click **Format Painter**. Your insertion point now appears with a paintbrush next to it.

g. Click cell **B10**. Notice that B10 changes to currency format and the Format Painter is turned off.

h. **Save** the spreadsheet.

Find Help, Print, and Share in Office

Office **Help** can give you additional information about a feature or steps for how to perform a new task. Your ability to find and use Help can greatly increase your Office proficiency and save you time from seeking outside assistance. Office has several levels of help, from a searchable search window to more directed help such as ScreenTips.

The Help window provides detailed information on a multitude of topics, as well as access to templates, training videos installed on your computer, and content available on Office.com — the website maintained by Microsoft that provides access to the latest information and additional Help resources. To access the contents at Office.com, you must have access to the Internet from the computer. If there is no Internet access, only the files installed on the computer will be displayed in the Help window. The easiest way to access Help is through pressing F1 — in some of the programs. If available, this will take you directly to an article about what is actively selected.

Pointing to any command on the ribbon will display a **ScreenTip** with screen text to indicate more information. You may have seen these while working earlier in the chapter. They are very useful to learn what the command on the button will do.

Using the Help Window and ScreenTips

In this exercise, you will view a ScreenTip and learn how to insert a footer using Excel Help and then add a footer to the meeting minutes.

CF01.22

To Access Office Help and Insert a Footer

a. With your Excel budget open, press F1. The Excel Help window opens.

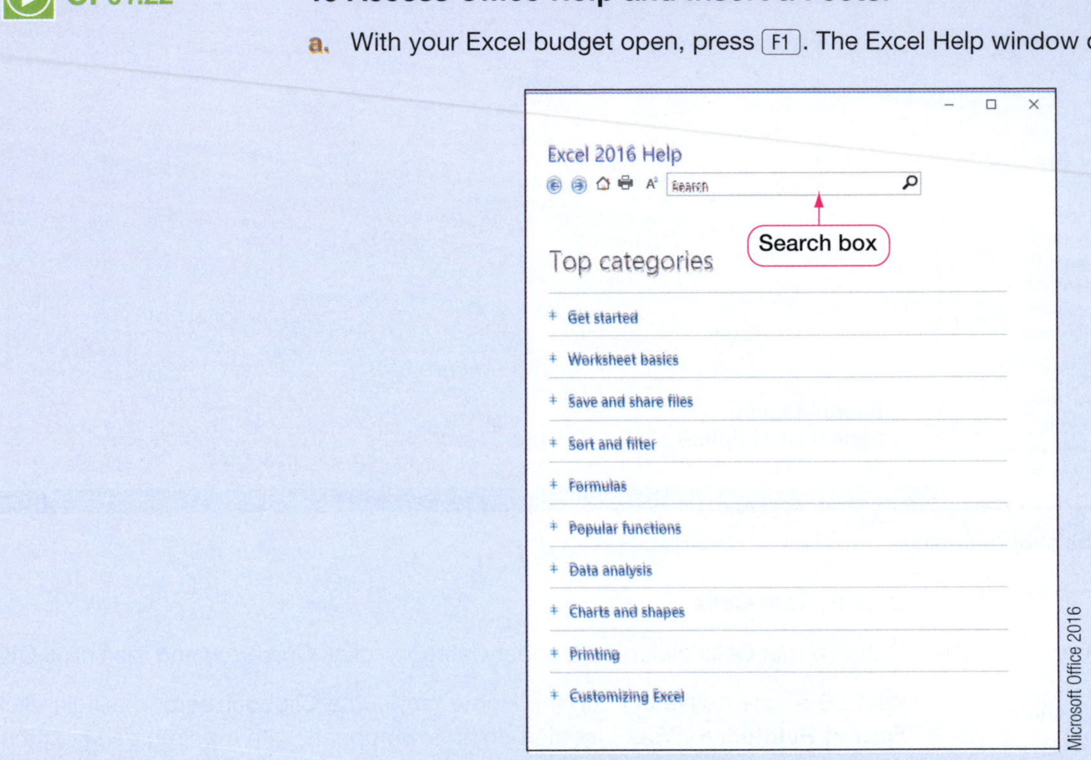

Figure 29 The Excel Help window

b. In the search box, type add a footer and press Enter. Then click the first link, and read about how to add a footer. When you are done, click **Close** ✕ to close the Help window.

c. Click the **Page Layout** tab, and then, in the Page Setup group, point your mouse to **Print Titles**. Notice the ScreenTip with a link for Tell me more. If you clicked on Tell me more, it would take you to the Help window specifically for Print Titles.

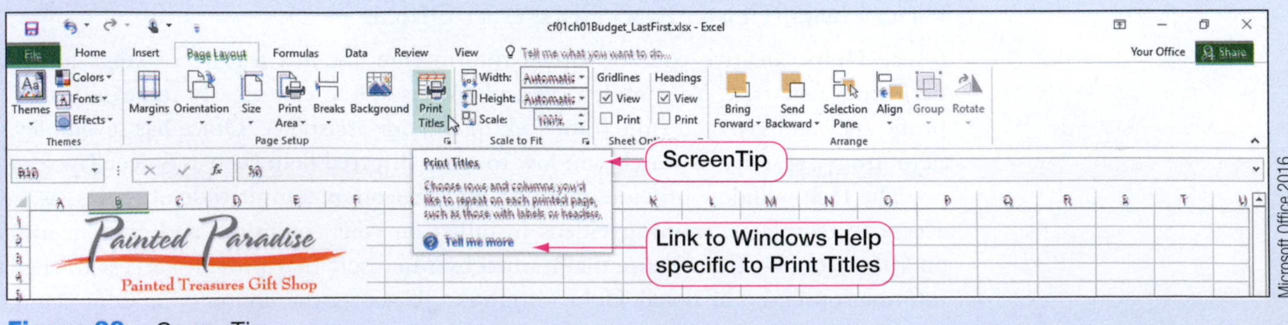

Figure 30 ScreenTip

d. On the **Page Layout** tab, in the Page Setup group, point your mouse to the **Page Setup Dialog Box Launcher**. Notice the ScreenTip, this time without the Tell me more option. Click the **Page Setup Dialog Box Launcher**.

e. Click the **Header/Footer** tab, and then click **Custom Footer** to display the Footer dialog box.

f. Click in the **Left section** and type First Last, using your first and last name.

g. Click in the **Center section** and click **Insert File Name**.

h. Click in the **Right section** and type InstructorLast, using your instructor's last name.

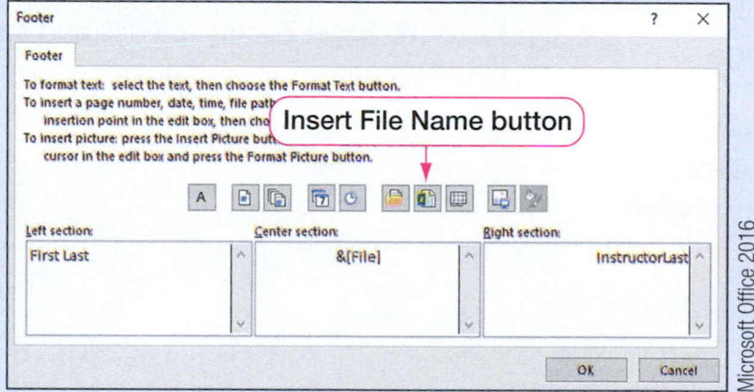

Figure 31 The Footer dialog box

> **SIDE NOTE**
> **ScreenTip and F1**
> If a topic for a ScreenTip does not exist in Help, the window will open to the starting search page.

i. Click **OK**, and then click **OK** again. The footer is inserted. In Normal view, you will not see the footer. You will see the footer in the next exercise.

j. **Save** the spreadsheet.

Accessing the Share Pane

In Office, many ways exist for sharing files. There are times when you will need a paper copy — also known as a hard copy — of an Office document, spreadsheet, or presentation. When a printed version is not needed, a digital copy will save paper and costs. Office provides many ways to share your document. You can use traditional ways of sharing by printing or exporting a PDF. From the Share link in Office, you can invite other people to share the document, and you can specify whether others are allowed to edit the document if the file is saved to OneDrive. From Office Backstage, the document can be e-mailed to others, transformed into an online, browser-not-required presentation, or posted to a blog.

New in Office 2016, you can share your file without leaving your file. In the top right corner, next to your account image, click Share. This will open the Share task pane. From there, you can add a person, choose whether he or she can edit or just view the file, and even give a personal message. In addition, new with Office 2016, you and those you share with can all be editing the document in real time. You will be able to see the changes being made to the document while you are also making changes. To do this, you must have the file saved in your OneDrive and be logged into your Microsoft account.

Changing Views

In each of the Office applications, there are different ways to view the file. For example, in Word, you can view in Read Mode, as a Web Layout, Outline, or Draft. In Excel, it is particularly important to change your view to Page Break Preview before attempting to print a file. This view shows you where the page breaks will happen and, if needed, allows you to modify them. Also, Page Layout view will allow you to view any headers and footers before printing. In this exercise, you will change to Page Break Preview and the Page Layout view to ensure that everything will fit on one page.

CF01.23

SIDE NOTE

Adjusting Page Breaks

From Page Break Preview you can click and drag to adjust page break lines.

To Change Views to Preview How a File Will Print

a. Click the **View** tab, and then, in the Workbook Views group, click **Page Break Preview**. Excel Zooms to 60% and shows each page with blue lines. The budget will fit on one page, and no adjustments are needed.

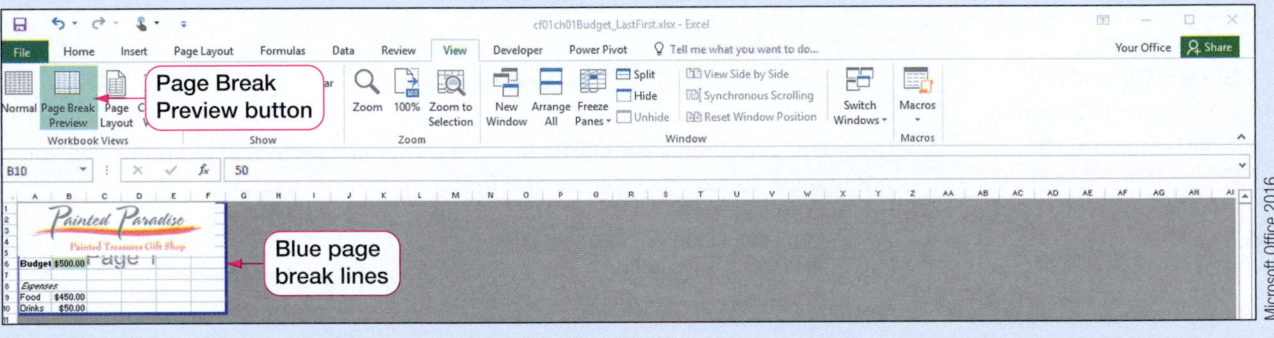

Figure 32 Page Break Preview

b. On the View tab, in the Workbook Views group, click **Page Layout**. Scroll down and verify that the footer you created in a prior exercise looks correct.

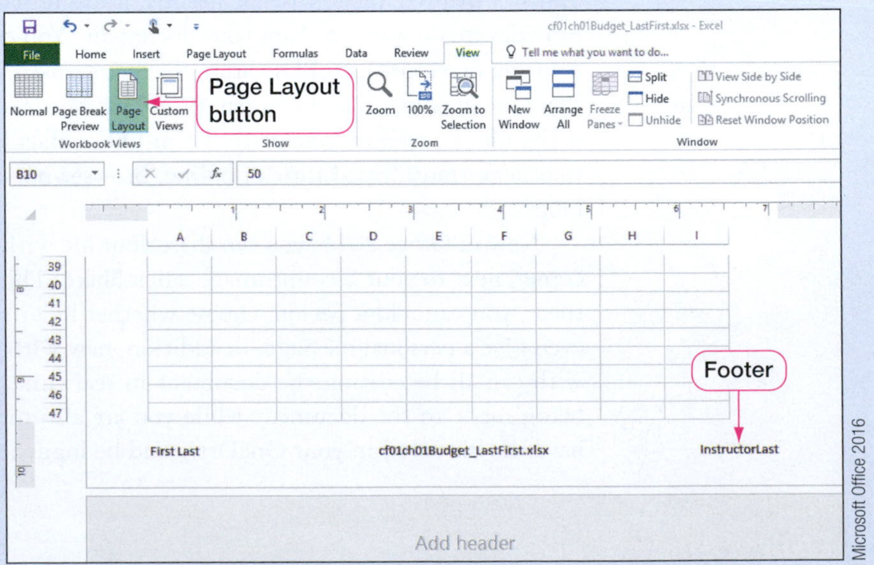

Figure 33 Page Layout view

c. On the View tab, in the Workbook Views group, click **Normal** to return to the normal Excel view. Press Ctrl + Home to make cell A1 the active cell.

d. **Save** the spreadsheet.

Printing a File

Before printing, carefully consider whether a paper copy is necessary. Even in the digital world, paper copies of documents make more sense in many situations. Always review and preview the file and adjust the print settings before sending the document to the printer as you did in the prior exercise. Many options are available to fit various printing needs, such as the number of copies to print, the printing device to use, and the portion of the file to print. The print settings vary slightly from program to program. Printers also have varied capabilities; thus, the same file may look different from one computer to the next, depending on the printer that is connected to it. Doing a simple print preview will help to avoid having to reprint your document, workbook, or presentation, which requires additional paper, ink, and energy resources.

In this exercise, you will print the budget on which notes can be handwritten during the meeting so that you can update the spreadsheet with more detail later.

CF01.24

To Print a File

a. In Excel, click the **File** tab to open Office Backstage.

b. Click **Print**. The Print settings and Print Preview appear. Verify that the Copies box displays **1**.

c. Verify that the correct printer — as directed by your instructor — appears in the Printer box. Choices may vary depending on the computer you are using. If the correct printer is not displayed, click the Printer arrow, and then click to choose the correct or preferred printer from the list of available printers.

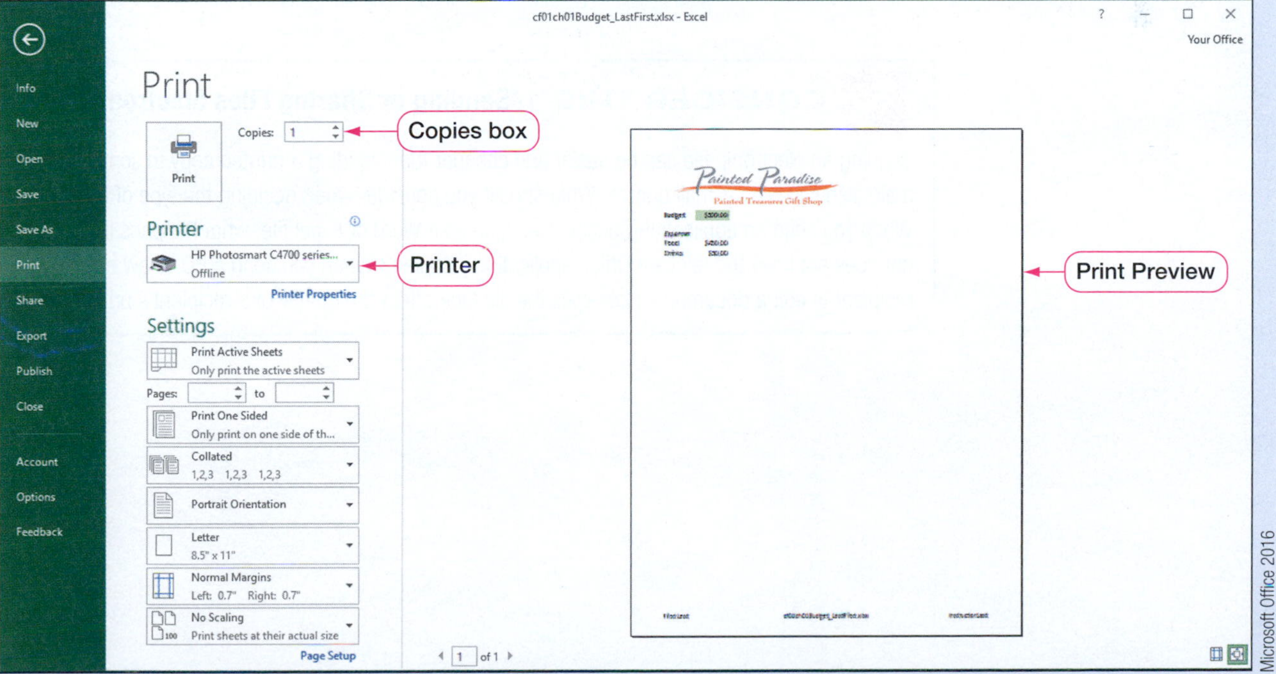

Figure 34 Backstage Print

d. If your instructor asks you to print the document, click **Print**.

Exporting a PDF

When you want to give someone else a document, consider whether an electronic version of the file is better than a printed copy. A **portable document format (PDF)** file is a type of file that ensures that the document will look the same on someone else's computer. For example, different computers may have different fonts installed. A PDF maintains the fonts used in the original document. Even if the computer on which the file is being viewed does not have the same fonts as the computer that was used to create the file, the viewer will see the correct font. PDFs are a common file format used in business to share documents because of the readily available free readers. In Word, you can edit a PDF. Also, in Windows 10, the default PDF reader is now the new Edge browser. You can still install the Adobe reader program and set it as the default if you prefer.

In this exercise, you will export a PDF of the budget file so you can e-mail a copy to your colleagues who are also attending the meeting.

To Create a PDF File

a. If you are not already in Office Backstage, click the **File** tab. Click **Export**, and then click **Create PDF/XPS**.

b. Navigate to the location where your student files are stored. Verify that the file name selected is **cf01ch01Budget_LastFirst.pdf**. Notice settings in the Publish as PDF or XPS dialog box for optimizing for publishing online versus printing. Since your colleague will print this document, the default setting of Standard is appropriate.

c. Click **Publish**. Close the **PDF** file. If the PDF opens in the default reader — in the Windows 10 Edge browser — then close the reader.

d. **Save**  the spreadsheet and click **Close** ✕ to close this file and exit Excel. Submit your files as directed by your instructor.

CONSIDER THIS | Sending or Sharing Files Electronically

Sending an electronic file can be easier and cheaper than sending a printed copy to someone. Sharing a file also saves on e-mail quotas. What should you consider when deciding the type of file to send? When you send an application-specific file, such as a Word or Excel file, what happens if the recipient does not have the relevant Office application installed? When you send a PDF, how easy is it for a recipient to edit a document? How does the file type affect the quality of a recipient's printout?

Insert Office Add-ins

To enhance the features of Office, you can install **Add-ins for Office** from Microsoft's Office Store. These Add-ins run in the side pane to provide extra features such as web search, dictionary, and maps. There are different Add-ins for the different Office programs. You must be signed into Office with your Microsoft account to take advantage of them.

QUICK REFERENCE	Installing Add-ins for Office

1. Open up any Office application in which you want to use apps.
2. Go to the Insert tab, and then select My Add-ins arrow. Select See All from the menu.
3. The Office Add-ins window appears, showing all the apps you have installed to your Microsoft account under My Apps. If you see the app you want, select the app, and then click Insert.
4. If you do not see the app you want, click Store link or Office Store button.
5. Search for the Add-in you want, and then follow the steps online to install the Add-in to your account. You may have to sign into your Microsoft account.
6. Once the Add-in has been installed, return to the Office application and repeat steps 2 and 3.

Concept Check

1. What kind of Microsoft program do you need to create a budget? p. 4
2. What are the advantages of using OneDrive instead of a USB flash drive? p. 12
3. What is the difference between Save and Save As? p. 10
4. How do you pin open the ribbon? Explain what can be done in Office Backstage. p. 8–10
5. Explain a way to copy and paste. What advantages are there to knowing keyboard shortcuts? p. 18
6. What is the Tell me what you want to do feature and how is it different from Help? p. 29
7. Describe three different ways of making text bold. p. 37
8. What is a contextual tab? p. 35
9. Describe ways to obtain help in Office 2016. p. 39
10. How could you share a newsletter with all the members of your business fraternity without printing the document? p. 41, 44
11. What are the Add-ins for Office? p. 45

Key Terms

Visual Summary

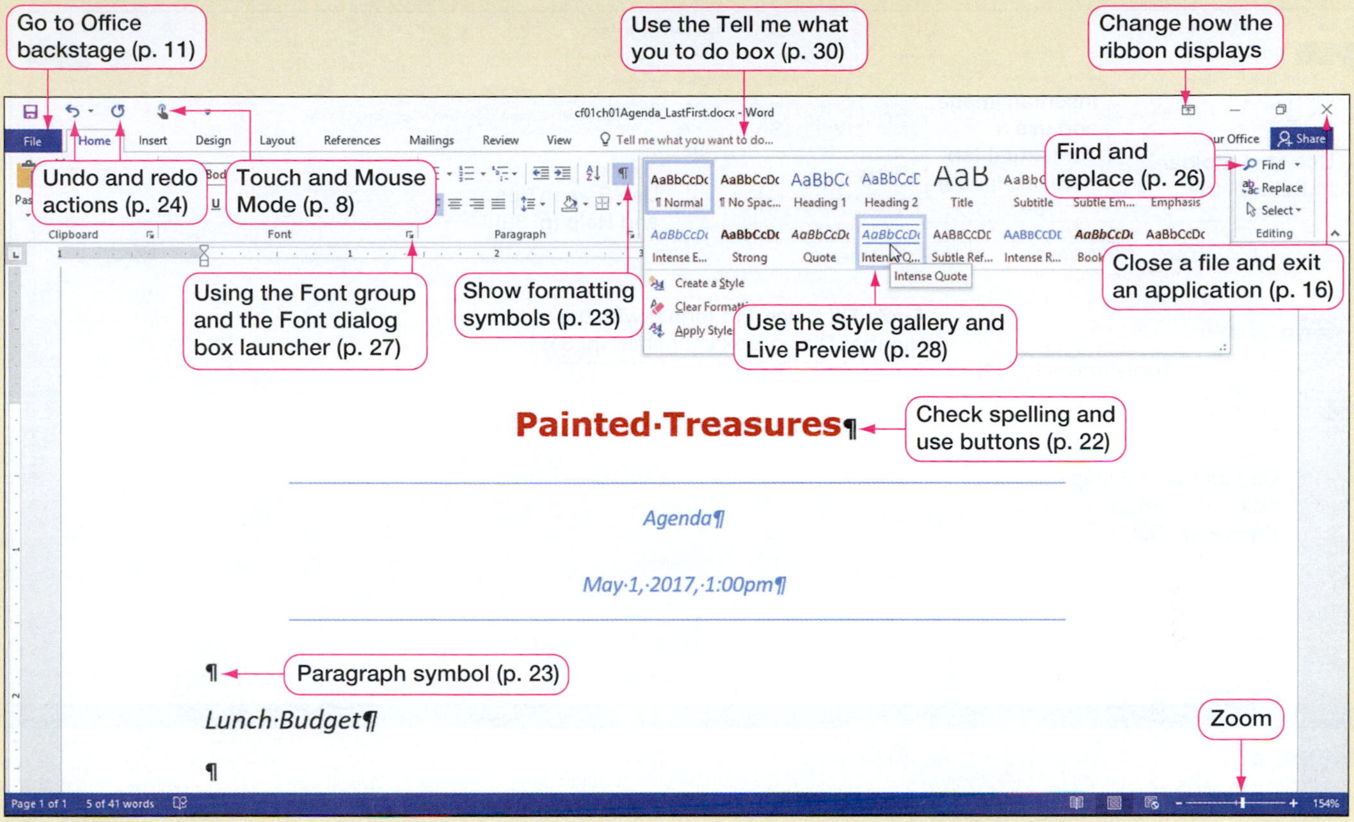

Go to Office backstage (p. 11)
Use the Tell me what you to do box (p. 30)
Change how the ribbon displays
Undo and redo actions (p. 24)
Touch and Mouse Mode (p. 8)
Find and replace (p. 26)
Close a file and exit an application (p. 16)
Using the Font group and the Font dialog box launcher (p. 27)
Show formatting symbols (p. 23)
Use the Style gallery and Live Preview (p. 28)
Check spelling and use buttons (p. 22)
Paragraph symbol (p. 23)
Zoom
cf01ch01Agenda_LastFirst.docx - Word
Painted·Treasures¶
Agenda¶
May·1,·2017,·1:00pm¶
Lunch·Budget¶

Microsoft Office 2016

Figure 35

Document properties (p. 11)
Open an existing file and the Recent Documents list (p. 17)
Save an existing file
Save an existing file as a different name, location, or to OneDrive
Print a file (p. 43)
Office Theme and Background (p. 11)
Export a PDF (p. 44)
Manage account settings (p. 11)
Document1 - Word
Product Information
Office
Subscription Product
Microsoft Office 365 ProPlus
Office Updates
About Word

Microsoft Office 2016

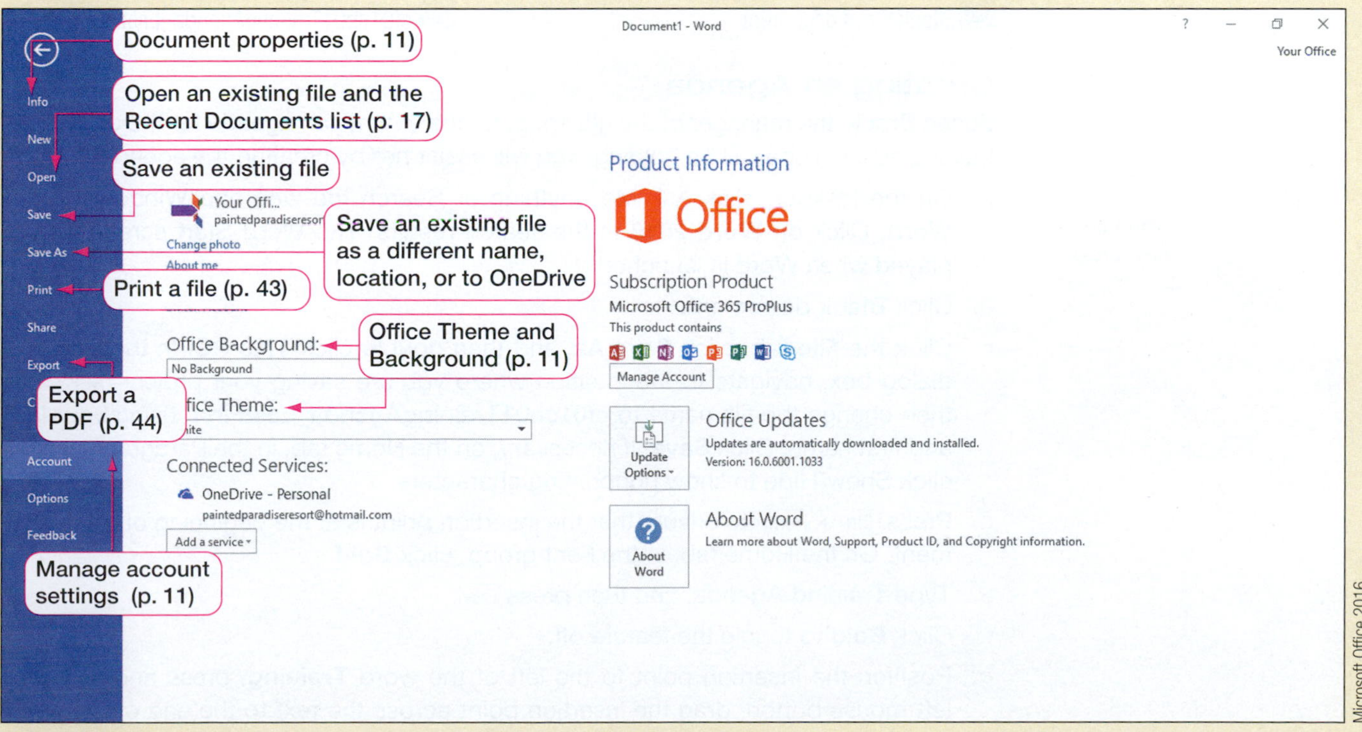

Figure 36

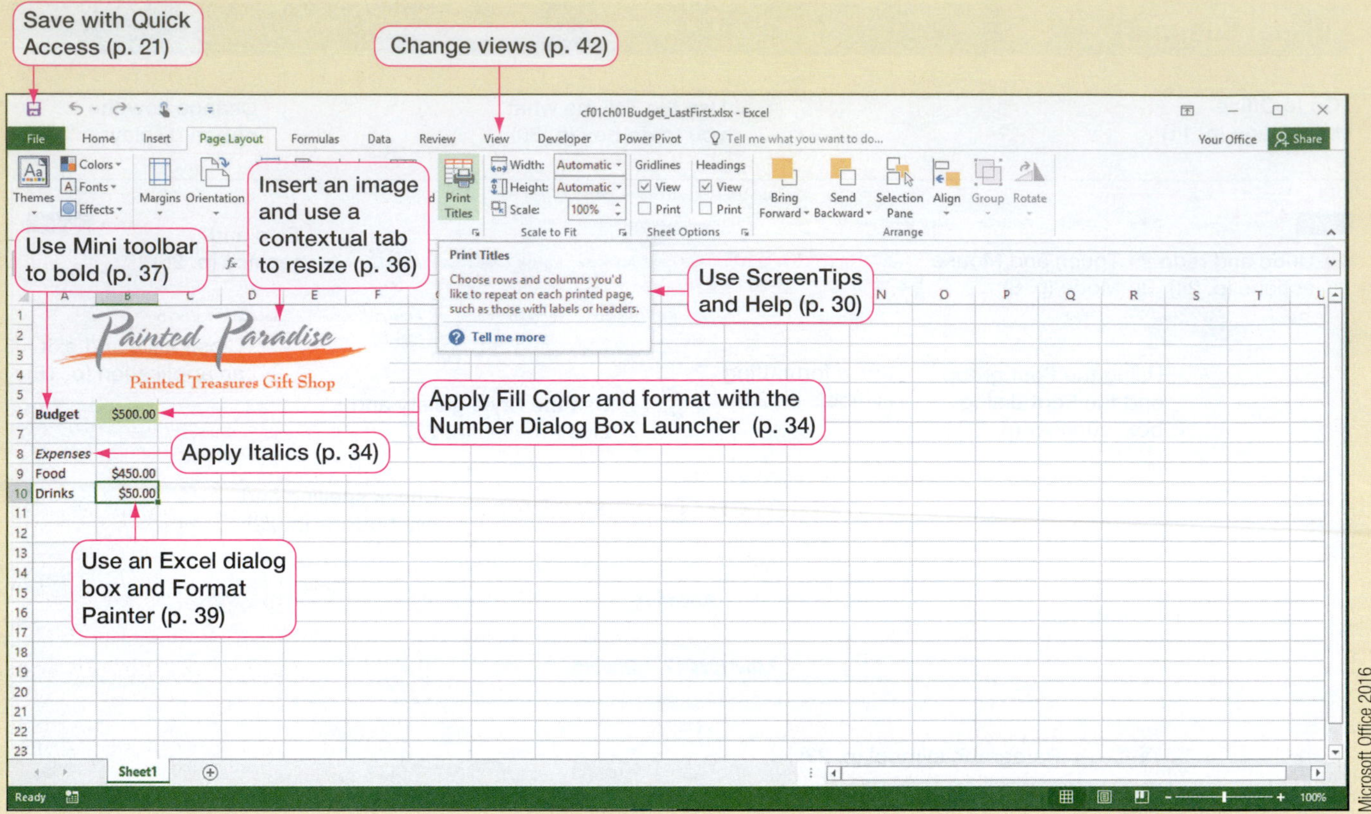

Figure 37

Practice 1

Student data file needed:

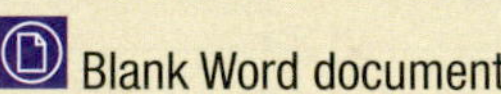

Blank Word document

You will save your file as:

cf01ch01TrainingAgenda_LastFirst.docx

Creating an Agenda

Human Resources

Susan Brock, the manager of the gift shop, needs to write an agenda for the upcoming training session she will be holding. You will assist her by creating the agenda.

a. On the taskbar, click Ask Me Anything or Search the web and Windows. Type Word. Click on **Word 2016** in the search results. The Word Start screen is displayed when Word is launched.

b. Click **Blank document**.

c. Click the **File** tab, click **Save As**, and then double-click **This PC**. In the Save As dialog box, navigate to the location where you are saving your project files, and then change the file name to cf01ch01TrainingAgenda_LastFirst, using your last and first name. Click **Save**. If necessary, on the Home tab, in the Paragraph group, click Show/Hide to show nonprinting characters.

d. Press Ctrl + Home to ensure that the insertion point is at the beginning of the document. On the Home tab, in the Font group, click **Bold**.

e. Type Training Agenda, and then press Enter.

f. Click **Bold** to toggle the feature off.

g. Position the insertion point to the left of the word **Training**, press and hold the left mouse button, drag the insertion point across the text to the end of the word **Agenda**, and then release the mouse button. All the text in the line should be highlighted.

h. On the Home tab, in the Font group, click the **Font Size** arrow. Select **20** to make the font size larger.
i. In the Paragraph group, click **Center**. In the Font group, click the **arrow** next to Font Color and select **Blue**.
j. Click the second line, type **today's date**, and then press Enter twice.
k. In the Paragraph group, click the **Bullets** arrow. Under the Bullet Library, click the **circle** bullet.
l. Type Welcome trainees 2:00 pm, and then press Enter.
m. Type Using the Register, and then press Enter.
n. Type Customer Service Policies, and then press Enter.
o. Type Wrap-Up, and then press Enter twice to turn off bullets.
p. Type Questions?. On the Home tab, in the Styles group, click **Heading 2**.
q. **Save** the document.
r. Click the **Insert** tab, and then, in the Header & Footer group, click the **Footer** arrow, and then select the first option **Blank**.
s. On the Header & Footer Tools Design tab, in the Insert group, click **Document Info**, and then click **File Name**.
t. On the Header & Footer Tools Design tab, in the Close group, click **Close Header and Footer** to exit the footer.
u. **Save** the document, exit Word, and then submit your file as directed by your instructor.

Problem Solve 1

Student data files needed:

cf01ch01Letter.docx

cf01ch01Cookies.jpg

You will save your file as:

cf01ch01Letter_LastFirst.docx

Midnight Sweetness Loan Letter

Finance & Accounting

Recently, you opened a business with a few partners called Midnight Sweetness. With the slogan "No more starving late-night studies," the business specializes in delivering freshly baked cookies, brownies, and other sweet treats to local college students. Midnight Sweetness has been a huge success. Currently, you rent a small building that includes major kitchen appliances. Now you and your partners are looking for a bank loan to expand your business. As part of your presentation to the bank, you must write a cover letter highlighting some parts of your business. The letter is written, but now you will add formatting to make it easier to read.

a. Open the cf01ch1Letter document. Save your file as **cf01ch01Letter_LastFirst**, using your last and first name. Click Enable Editing if necessary. If necessary, show nonprinting characters.
b. Place the insertion point before the **M** in Midnight Sweetness. Insert the **cf01ch01Cookies** image.
c. Resize the image to be **1"** in height.
d. Format the company name, Midnight Sweetness, to **bold**, **Dark Red** font color, font size **36**, and font of **Georgia**.
e. Find the two spelling errors with a red wavy line, and correct the **mistakes** in the text.
f. Midnight Sweetness has three offerings: Freshly baked cookies, Homemade brownies, and Other sweet treats. Change the three paragraphs listing the offerings to a **bulleted** list using regular bullets.

g. Midnight Sweetness is trying to achieve four things: a larger kitchen, more office space, additional baking equipment, and additional baking supplies. Change the four paragraphs of what the company is trying to achieve to a **numbered** list with **Number alignment: Left** style that uses the number without the parenthesis.
h. Select the second and third lines of the document containing the address. Cut the address to the clipboard.
i. Insert a **blank** footer. Paste the **two address lines** to the footer. Verify that the footer does not have any blank paragraphs — only the two address lines. Verify that there is only one blank paragraph between the company name and the line that reads "Dear Mr. Garth."
j. In the footer, change the font color of both lines of the address to **Dark Red**, and **Center** the text.
k. In the blank line between the company name and "Dear Mr. Garth," type the **current date**.
l. After the letter closing, on the paragraph below "Sincerely," type First Last, using your first and last name. Erase any blank paragraphs below your name.
m. Apply the style **Emphasis** to your name, change the font size to **14**, and change the font color to **Dark Red**. Press Ctrl + Home to place the insertion point at the beginning.
n. Save the document, exit Word, and then submit your file as directed by your instructor.

Critical Thinking

These directions told you how to format the letter. Do you have any suggestions for improvements or anything that might be problematic? Do you think the letter looks professional? Is the content of the language in the letter professional and appropriate? You may suggest changes that you have not learned how to make yet. Answer as directed by your instructor.

Perform 1: Perform in Your Career

Student data files needed:

cf01ch01Herb.xlsx

cf01ch01Herb.docx

You will save your files as:

cf01ch01Herb_LastFirst.xlsx

cf01ch01Herb_LastFirst.docx

Harry's Herbs

General Business

You are interning for a local nursery. One of the employees, Harry, specializes in herbs. Every year, he does an herb sale as a fundraiser for the local homeless shelter. Another intern began to create these files — but is unexpectedly unavailable to finish them. Your supervisor has asked you to help get ready for the event by preparing documents associated with the schedule.

a. Open the Excel file **cf01ch01Herb**. Save your file as **cf01ch01Herb_LastFirst**, using your last and first name.
b. Change the **font, fill color**, and **font color** of the merged cell A1:D1, and make the font size **16 or larger**. Choose professional colors.
c. Format the merged cell from A2:D2 to be **bold**.
d. Format cells A3:A5 as **italic**.
e. Format cell **A6** so that it matches or complements the coloring you applied to the merged cell A1:D1, and make the font size **larger**.
f. Paint the format from cell A6 to **A13**, **A19**, **A24**, and **A28**.
g. Change the text in cell **D7** to **Details**, and make D7 **bold**. Then copy and paste to put the same label in cells **D14**, **D20**, **D25**, and **D29**.

h. Apply bold to all of the cells with one of these three labels **Master Gardener Advice and Classes**, **Daily** and **Hourly**.

i. Add any other formatting that will make this spreadsheet look more professional or have more clarity. Do not change any more of the content or move cells.

j. Add a custom footer that contains **First Last**, using your first and last name, in the Left section and the **File Name** in the Right section. Do not worry if the file will not print on a single page.

k. **Save** the spreadsheet, exit Excel, and then submit your file as directed by your instructor.

l. Open the Word file **cf01ch01Herb.docx**. Save your file as **cf01ch01Herb_LastFirst.docx**, using your last and first name.

m. Correct all spelling mistakes.

n. Before the word Schedule in the title, add the word **Tuesday**.

o. Add **am** and **pm** to the times appropriately — Tuesdays overall hours are 10:00 am to 8:00 pm.

p. Change the **font colors**, **background colors**, **font sizes**, and **styles** to make the schedule easier to read and understand. Match the colors you used in cf01ch1Herb_LastFirst.xlsx.

q. Add a custom footer with **First Last**, using your first and last name.

r. **Save** the document, and close Word. Submit your work to your instructor as directed.

Perform 2: Perform in Your Life

Student data files needed:

 Blank Word document

 cf01ch01Vintage.docx

cf01ch01Dinner.xlsx

You will save your file as:

 cf01ch01Critique_LastFirst.docx

Human Resources

Finance & Accounting

Improving the Appearance of Files

Your boss at a local vintage clothing store has asked you to review a spreadsheet and a document — made by a prior employee — and make suggestions on what to do to improve the appearance of the document and spreadsheet. Examine the two files cf01ch01Vintage and cf01ch01Dinner. Then do the following.

a. Open a new blank document in Word, and then save the file as **cf01ch01Critique_LastFirst**, using your last and first name.

b. List five items that you would change in the document and why.

c. List five items that you would change in the spreadsheet and why.

d. Add a footer with First Last, using your first and last name, and the file name.

e. Exit Word, and then submit your file as directed by your instructor.

Additional Cases

Additional Chapter Cases are available at www.pearsonhighered.com/youroffice

Access Business Unit 1

Understanding and Using a Relational Database

Today's businesses rely heavily on having access to accurate, reliable, and consistent data to make decisions. Database management systems (DBMS) such as Microsoft Access provide organizations with the ability to develop relational databases for collecting, storing, and accessing valuable data via tables, queries, forms, and reports.

Learning Outcome 1

Understand the purpose for main database objects in Access: tables, queries, forms, and reports.

Real World Success 

"I used Access to create ad hoc reports for managers. My ability to quickly provide data has made me their 'go to' person."

– Art, alumnus, materials analyst

Learning Outcome 2

Based on the needs of an organization, understand and create various types of relationships using different types of keys: primary, foreign, and composite.

Real World Success 

"Reports on open issues were very important to my project manager. I set up a database with a main table of open issues. I used foreign keys to link it to employee tables and to a table of priorities. That way, I could generate a report that included the details of any open issues, including who reported it and the priority level of the issue."

– Joseph P., IT intern

Microsoft Access 2016

Chapter 1 | THE FOUR MAIN DATABASE OBJECTS

OBJECTIVES

Prepare Case

Production & Operations

Red Bluff Golf Course Putts for Paws Charity Tournament

The Red Bluff Golf Course & Pro Shop is sponsoring a charity tournament, Putts for Paws, to raise money for the Santa Fe Animal Center. An intern created a database to help run the tournament but did not finish it before leaving. You have been asked to finish the database to track the participants who enter the tournament, the orders they have placed, and the items they have purchased.

Kati Molin / Shutterstock

Student data files needed for this chapter:

 a01ch01Putts.accdb

 a01ch01Participant.accdb

You will save your file as:

 a01ch01Putts_LastFirst.accdb

Understanding the Basics of Databases and Tables

Businesses keep records about everything they do. If a business sells products, it keeps records about its products. It keeps records of its customers, the products it sells to each customer, and each sale. It keeps records about its employees, the hours they work, and their benefits. These records are collected and used for decision making, for sales and marketing, and for reporting purposes. A **database** is a collection of these records. The purpose of a database is to store, manage, and provide access to these business records.

In the past, many databases were paper based. Paper records were stored in files in file cabinets. Each file would be labeled and put in a drawer in a file cabinet. Elaborate filing schemes were developed so that any record could be located quickly. This was highly labor intensive and prone to error. Today, while most businesses use automated databases to store their records, you still see the occasional paper-based system. For example, a realtor's office may still use paper files for client records.

Data can be defined as facts about people, events, things, or ideas. Data is an important asset to any organization as it allows companies to make better business decisions after the data is converted into useful information. **Information** is data that has been manipulated and processed to make it meaningful. For example, if you see the number 2,000 out of context, it has no meaning. If you are told that 2,000 represents the amount of an order in dollars, that piece of data becomes meaningful information. Businesses can use meaningful information to gain a competitive advantage, such as by providing discounts to customers who order more expensive items. An automated database management system, such as Microsoft Access 2016, makes that possible.

Databases are used for two major purposes: for operational processing and for analytical purposes. In operational or transaction-based databases, each sale or transaction that a business makes is tracked. The information is used to keep the business running. Analytical databases are used for extracting data for decision making. The data in these databases is summarized and classified to make information available to the decision makers in the business.

Automated databases provide many advantages over paper databases. The information in the databases is much easier to find in automated form. The information can be manipulated and processed more rapidly. Automated databases can be used to enforce accuracy and other quality standards. In today's fast-paced world, a business needs to manipulate information quickly and accurately to make decisions. Without today's automated databases, a business cannot compete. In this section, you will learn what Access is and learn about the four main object types in an Access database.

Understand the Purpose of Access

Access is a relational **database management system (DBMS)** program created by Microsoft. It is a tool to organize, store, and manipulate data and to select and report on data. Access stores data in tables. Similar data is stored in the same table. For example, if one is storing data about participants in an event, he or she would include all the participants' names, addresses, and telephone numbers in one table.

The power of a database management system comes from the ability to link tables together. A separate table of purchases for the tournament can be linked with the participant table. This allows users to easily combine the two tables; for example, the tournament manager would be able to print out the participants with a record of their tournament purchases.

REAL WORLD ADVICE | **What Advantage Does Access Afford to Its Users?**

- Access is an easily available DBMS. It is included with many Microsoft Office suites, which makes Access very attractive to businesses.
- Access is a relational DBMS. What you learn about Access is transferable to other relational DBMSs.
- Access allows for easy interaction with other products in the Office suite. You can export data and reports into Word, PowerPoint, or Excel. You can also import from Excel and Word into Access.
- Access is often used as a stand-alone DBMS, meaning a DBMS used by a single user. Even if a company uses another DBMS for many users, you can easily link to that database with Access. You can use Access queries to output the data you need to interact with other Office applications to perform tasks such as mail merges.
- Access allows you to create an app database and either give it to others or put it on the Windows App Store.

Understanding the Four Main Objects in a Database

Access has four main database **objects**: tables, queries, forms, and reports. A **table** is the database object that stores data organized in an arrangement of columns and rows. A **query** object retrieves specific data from other database objects and then displays only the data that you specify. Queries allow you to ask questions about the data in your tables. You can use a **form** object to enter new records into a table, edit or delete existing records in a table, or display existing records. The **report** object summarizes the fields and records from a table or query in an easy-to-read format suitable for printing.

QUICK REFERENCE | **Access Object Types**

There are four main database object types:

1. Table objects store data. Each row is a person, place, or thing. Each column is a field.
2. Query objects allow you to ask questions about your data. You can select, summarize, and sort data in a query.
3. Form objects give you a formatted way to add, modify, or delete data in your tables. They can also be used to display data.
4. Report objects provide an easy-to-read view of your data that is suitable for business purposes. Data in reports can be grouped, sorted, and totaled.

Access objects have several views. Each **view** gives you a different perspective on the objects and different capabilities. For example, **Datasheet view** of a table shows the data contents within a table. Figure 1 shows Datasheet view of a participant table. **Design view** shows how fields are defined. Depending on the object, other views may exist. Figure 1 shows a toggle button you can use to switch between Datasheet view and Design view. Figure 2 shows how a participant table would appear in Design view. In Datasheet view, you see the actual participants and their related information. In Design view, you see how the information is defined and structured. Figure 1 shows the charity event participant table. Each row contains corresponding pieces of data about the participant listed in that row. Each row in Access is called a **record**. A record is all of the data pertaining to one person, place, thing, or event. There are 17 participant records in the table. The second participant is John Trujillo.

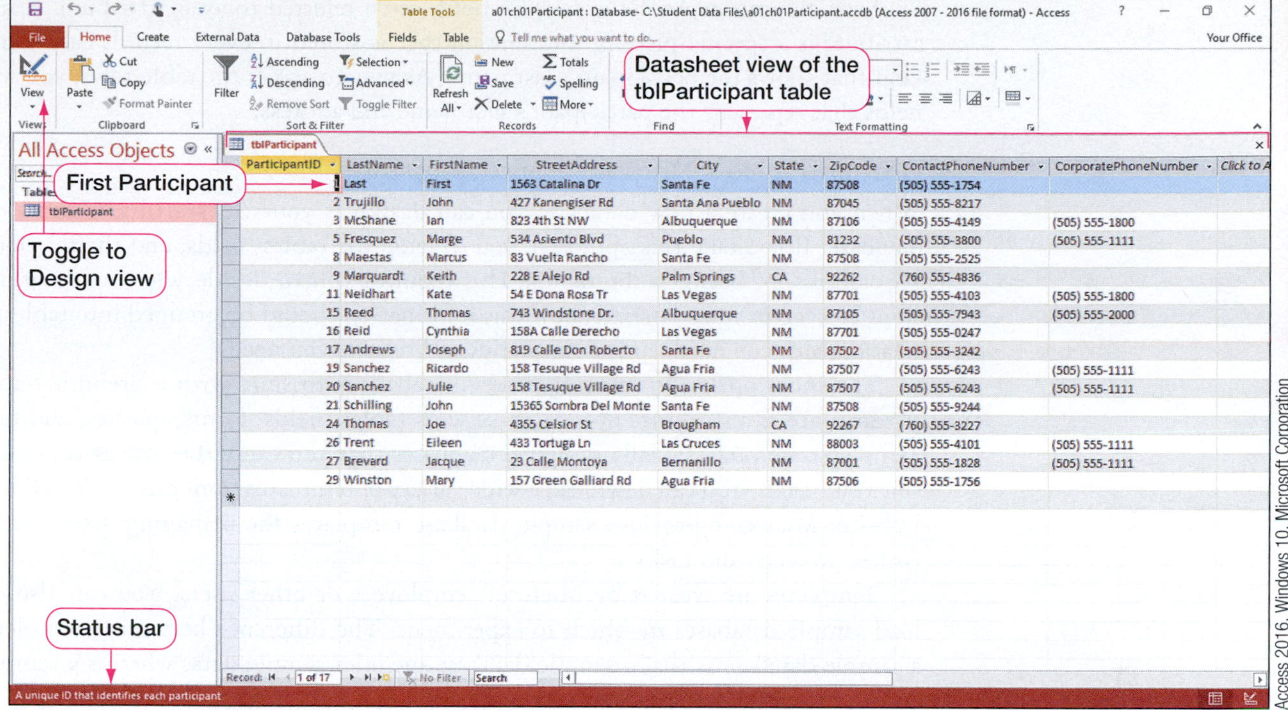

Access 2016, Windows 10, Microsoft Corporation

Figure 1 Datasheet view of the tblParticipant table

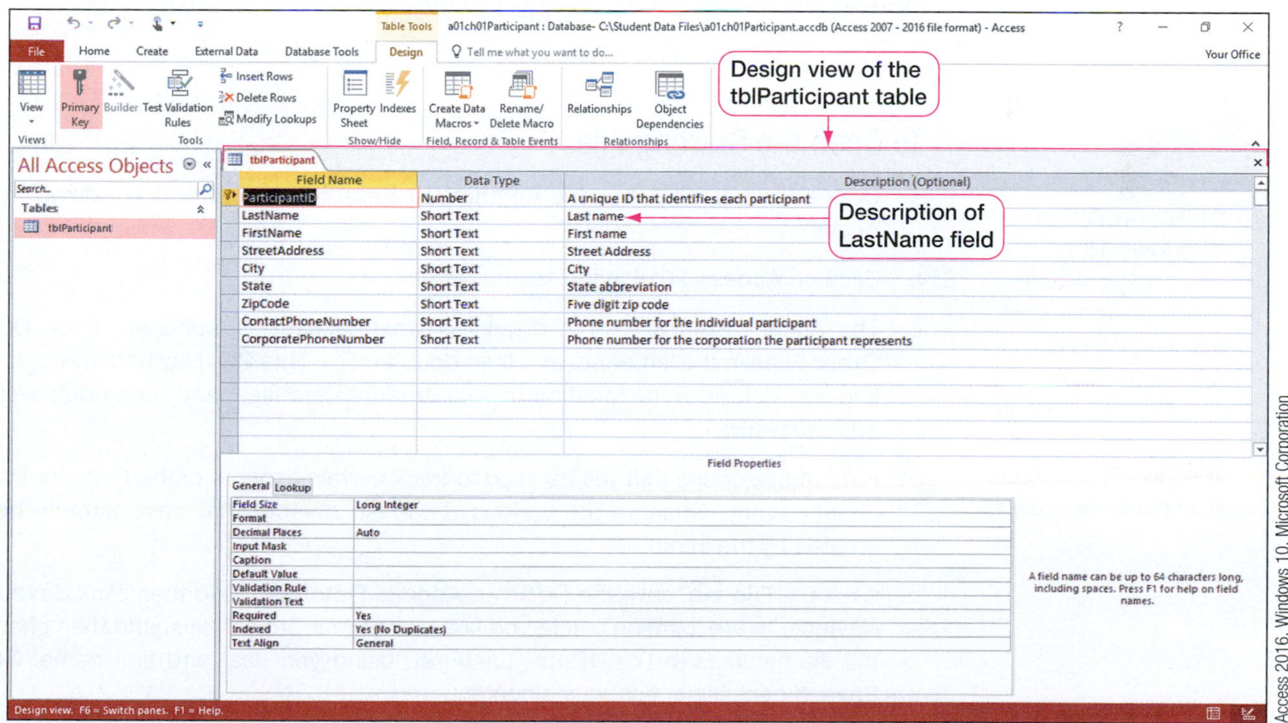

Access 2016, Windows 10, Microsoft Corporation

Figure 2 Design view of the tblParticipant table

Each column in Access is called a **field**, often referred to as an attribute. A field or attribute is a specific piece of information that is stored in every record. LastName is a field that shows the participant's last name. As you go across the table rows, you will see fields that represent the participant's first name and address.

Creating a New Database and Templates

When you create a new database, you can design it yourself, starting with an empty database. If you take this approach, you develop the tables, fields, and the relationships — or links — between the tables. This requires you to decide what information you want to keep in your database, how this information should be grouped into tables, what relationships you need, and what queries and reports you need.

The other option in creating a new database is to start with a prebuilt template. A **template** is a structure of a database with tables, fields, forms, queries, and reports. Templates are professionally designed databases that you can either use as is or adapt to suit your needs. You can download a wide variety of templates from Microsoft's Office.com website. Microsoft provides sample database templates for managing assets, contacts, issues, projects, and tasks.

Templates are created by Microsoft employees or other users. You can also download sample databases in which to experiment. The difference between a template and a sample database is that a sample database includes sample data, whereas a template is empty except for the structure and definitions.

Opening the Starting File

For the tournament, the intern created a new database and defined tables specifically for Putts for Paws. You will work with the database that has already been created. In this exercise, you will launch Access and open the database to get started.

A01.00

> **SIDE NOTE**
> **Windows 10**
> This book is written for Windows 10. If you are using Windows 8, open your charms, click Search, and then type Access. If using Windows 7, search the Start menu for Access.

To Open the Starting File

a. On the taskbar, click **Ask Me Anything** or **Search the web and Windows**. Type Access.

b. Click on **Access 2016** in the search results.

c. The Access Start screen is displayed when Access is launched. Click **Open Other Files** in the left pane, and then double-click **This PC**. Navigate through the folder structure to the location of your student data files, and then double-click **a01ch01Putts**.

d. A database opens that will be used to track certain aspects of the Putts for Paws charity event. Observe the various database objects that have already been created by the intern.

e. Click the **File** tab, save the file as an **Access Database**, and then click **Save As**. Navigate to the location where you are saving your project files, and then change the file name to a01ch01Putts_LastFirst, using your last and first name. Click **Save**. If necessary, enable the content.

REAL WORLD ADVICE **Why a Security Warning?**

Access databases can contain dangerous code that can infect your computer with a virus. Therefore, Access displays a security warning asking you whether you trust the content of the database. Until you tell Access that you trust this content, Access disables features that might allow the virus to infect your computer.

- Make sure you run a virus scan on any file before you say that it should be trusted. You should not trust content that you are unsure about.
- You have the option to trust the content for a single use. Click Enable Content to say that you trust the file.
- To trust a database permanently, you can store it in a trusted location. Depending on your computer and operating system, certain locations are predefined as trusted. Click the File tab, click Options, and then select Trust Center for the Access Trust Center, where you can add other locations to the trusted locations.

Maneuver in the Navigation Pane

When a database is opened, Access displays the **Navigation Pane** on the left side as shown in Figure 3. This pane allows you to view the objects in the database. The standard view in the Navigation Pane shows all objects in the database organized by object type. You can see that the database has three tables: tblItem, tblOrder, and tblOrderLine. There is one query, one form, and one report.

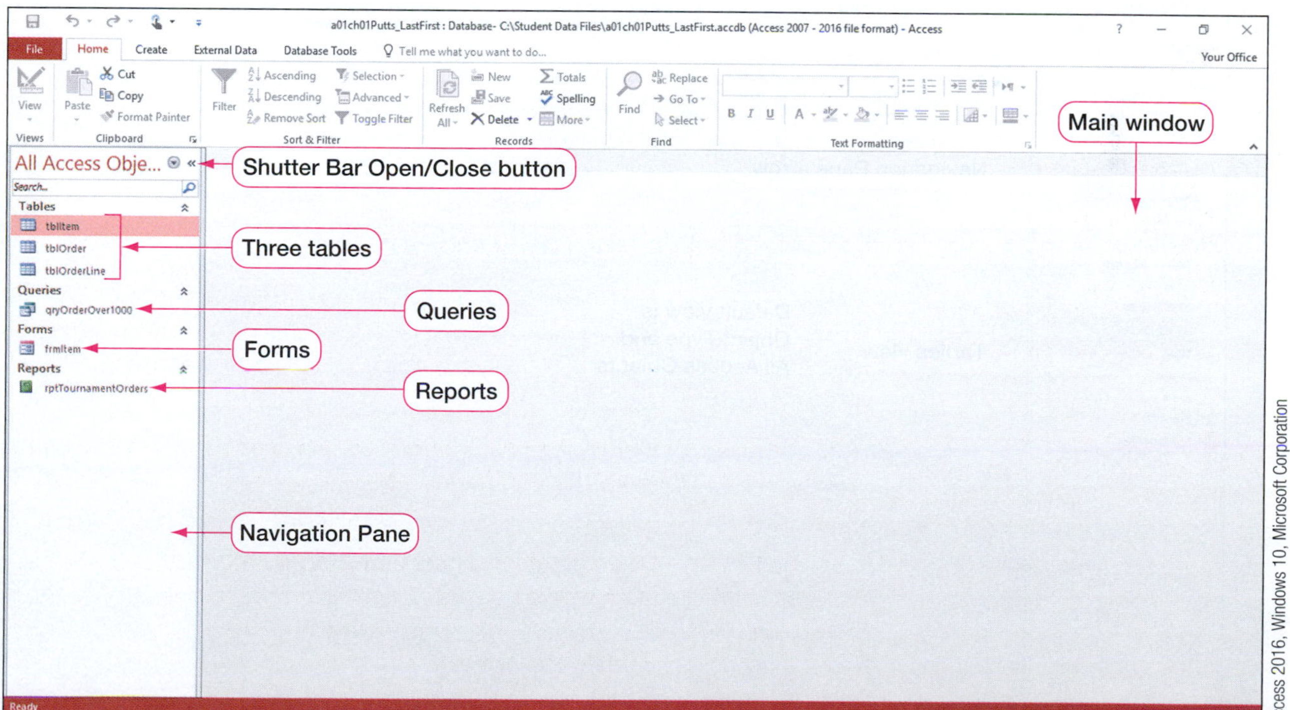

Figure 3 Navigation Pane

Opening and Closing the Shutter Bar

You can work in Access with the Navigation Pane open or closed. In this exercise, you will use the Shutter Bar Open/Close button at the top of the pane to open and close the pane.

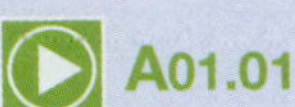

A01.01

SIDE NOTE

Pin the Ribbon

If your ribbon is collapsed, pin your ribbon open. Click the Home tab. In the lower right-hand corner of the ribbon, click Pin the Ribbon [pin icon].

To Open and Close the Shutter Bar

a. Click the **Shutter Bar Close** button « to close the Navigation Pane. Access closes the pane, allowing for a larger workspace in the database, but it leaves the Navigation Pane on the side of the window for when you need it.

b. Click the **Shutter Bar Open** button » to open the pane again.

Customize the Navigation Pane

While the default view of the Navigation Pane shows all objects such as tables, queries, forms, and reports, organized by object type, you have several choices of views. In this exercise, you will explore the various views.

A01.02

To Customize the Navigation Pane

a. Click the **Navigation Pane arrow** [arrow icon] to display the Navigation Pane view options. The default view is displayed, which is Object Type and All Access Objects.

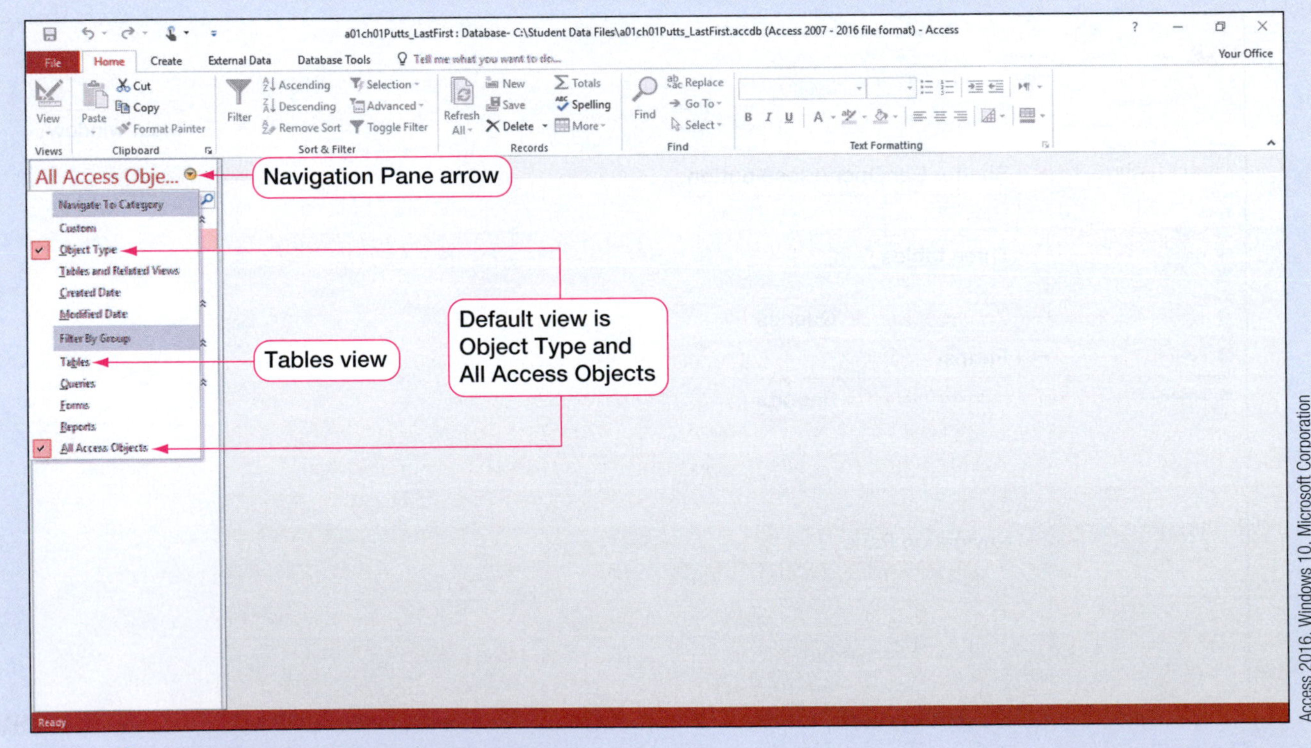

Figure 4 Navigation Pane options: default view

b. Click **Tables**.

Only the three tables are displayed in the Navigation Pane. When you have many objects in a database, it helps to restrict objects that are shown in the Navigation Pane.

c. Click the **Navigation Pane arrow** [icon] again, and then click **Tables and Related Views**.

The objects are organized by tables. Any query, report, or form related to a table is listed with that table.

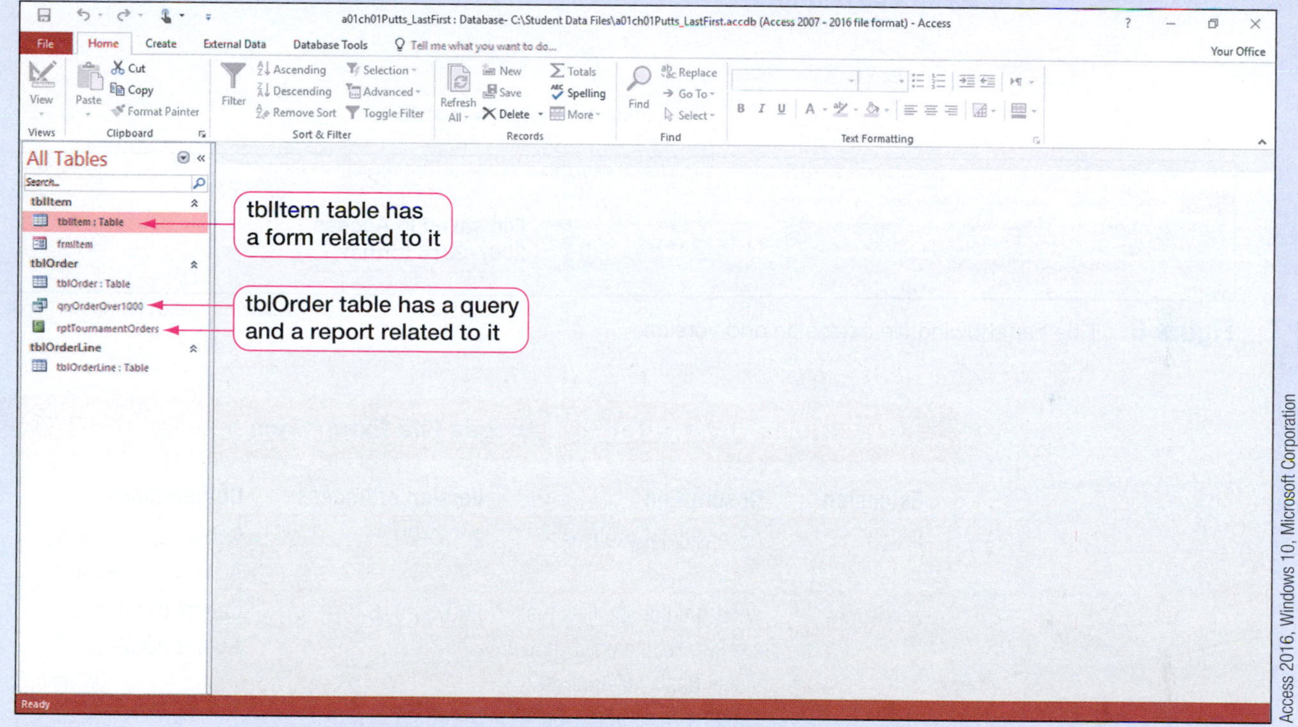

Figure 5 Tables and Related Views in Navigation Pane

Using the Search Box

Currently, there are only a few objects in your database. However, as you work with a database, more objects may be added as you develop reports and queries. As a result, to help you find objects, Access provides a Search box. In this exercise, you will use the search box to locate specific objects within the database.

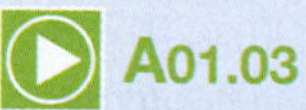
A01.03

To Use the Search Box

a. Click in the **Search** box at the top of the Navigation Pane, and then type Order. Access searches for and displays all objects with the word Order in their name.

b. Click the **Clear Search String** button [icon] to see all objects again.

c. Click the **Navigation Pane arrow** [icon], click **Object Type**, click the **Navigation Pane** arrow [icon] again, and then select **All Access Objects**. This returns you to the default view, which is what will be used throughout this text.

Understanding File Extensions in Access

A **file extension** is the suffix on all file names that helps Windows determine what information is in a file and what program should open the file. However, Windows automatically hides these extensions, so they often go unnoticed. The file name in Figure 6 shows the file name and location followed by its extension ".accdb". Access 2016 uses the same file extension that was used in Access 2007, Access 2010, and Access 2013. This ".accdb" extension indicates that databases created in the four versions are compatible with one another. The file name at the top of the window in Figure 6 also shows that the file version is Access 2007-2016. Be careful not to confuse the DBMS with the database. The DBMS software you are using is Access 2016, but the database is in Access 2007-2016 format.

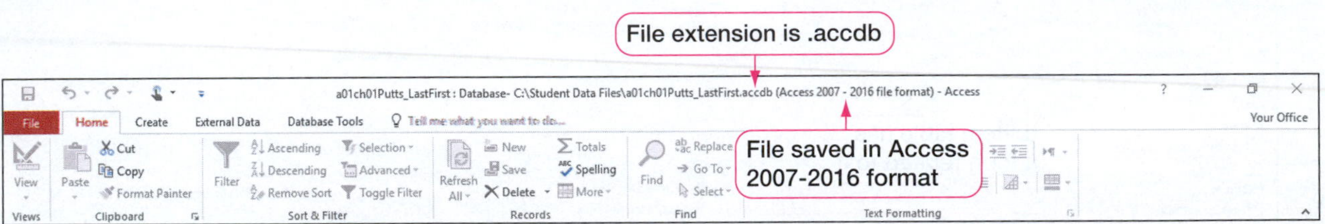

Access 2016, Windows 10, Microsoft Corporation

Figure 6 Title bar showing file extension and version

QUICK REFERENCE | **Access File Extensions**

Extension	Description	Version of Access	Compatibility
accdb	Access database files	2007–2016	Cannot be opened in Access 2002–2003
accde	Access database files that are in "execute only" mode; Visual Basic for Applications (VBA) source code is hidden	2007–2016	Cannot be opened in Access 2002–2003
accdt	Access database templates	2007–2016	Cannot be opened in Access 2002–2003
mdb	Access 2002–2003 database files	2002–2003	Can be opened in Access 2007–2016. Access 2007–2016 can save files in this format
mde	Access database files that are in "execute only" mode; Visual Basic for Applications (VBA) source code is hidden	2002–2003	Can be opened in Access 2007–2016. Access 2007–2016 can save files in this format

Understand the Purpose of Tables

Tables store data organized in an arrangement of columns and rows. For illustration, think about the charity event, Putts for Paws. There are many ways participants and companies can participate in the event and help the charity. For example, a participant can play in the event, a company can pay for a foursome to play in the event, or the company can sponsor various items such as a cart, hole, or flag. Painted Paradise needs to keep a record of the available options and what corporations or participants have purchased, as shown in Table 1.

Item ID	Item Description	Quantity Available	Amount To Be Charged	Notes
G1	Golfer — one	100	$200.00	
TEAM	Golfers — team of four	10	$550.00	
CTEAM	Golfers — corporate team of four	10	$850.00	Includes hole sponsorship
CART	Cart sponsor	40	$2,000.00	Logo or brand displayed on cart
HOLE	Hole sponsor	18	$500.00	Logo or brand displayed on hole
FLAG	Flag sponsor	18	$500.00	Logo or brand displayed on flagstick

Table 1 Data in the tblItem table

As was mentioned previously, the power of a **relational database** comes in when you link tables. A relational database is a database in which data is stored in tables with relationships between the tables. The tblItem table shown in Table 1 contains information about items that a participant or corporation can buy to support the charity, including the items available, a description, the quantity available to be sold, the amount that will be charged for the item, and notes about the item. However, you cannot see who has ordered these items. That additional information becomes available when you use relationships to look at other tables.

Importing a Table

Recently, a colleague compiled a list of participants in the charity event in an Access table in another database. In this exercise, you will begin your work for Putts for Paws by importing this participant table from the Participant database into your database. **Importing** is the process of copying data from another file, such as a Word file or Excel workbook, into a separate file, such as an Access database.

To Import a Table

a. Click the **External Data** tab, and then, in the Import & Link group, click **Access**. The Get External Data - Access Database dialog box is displayed.

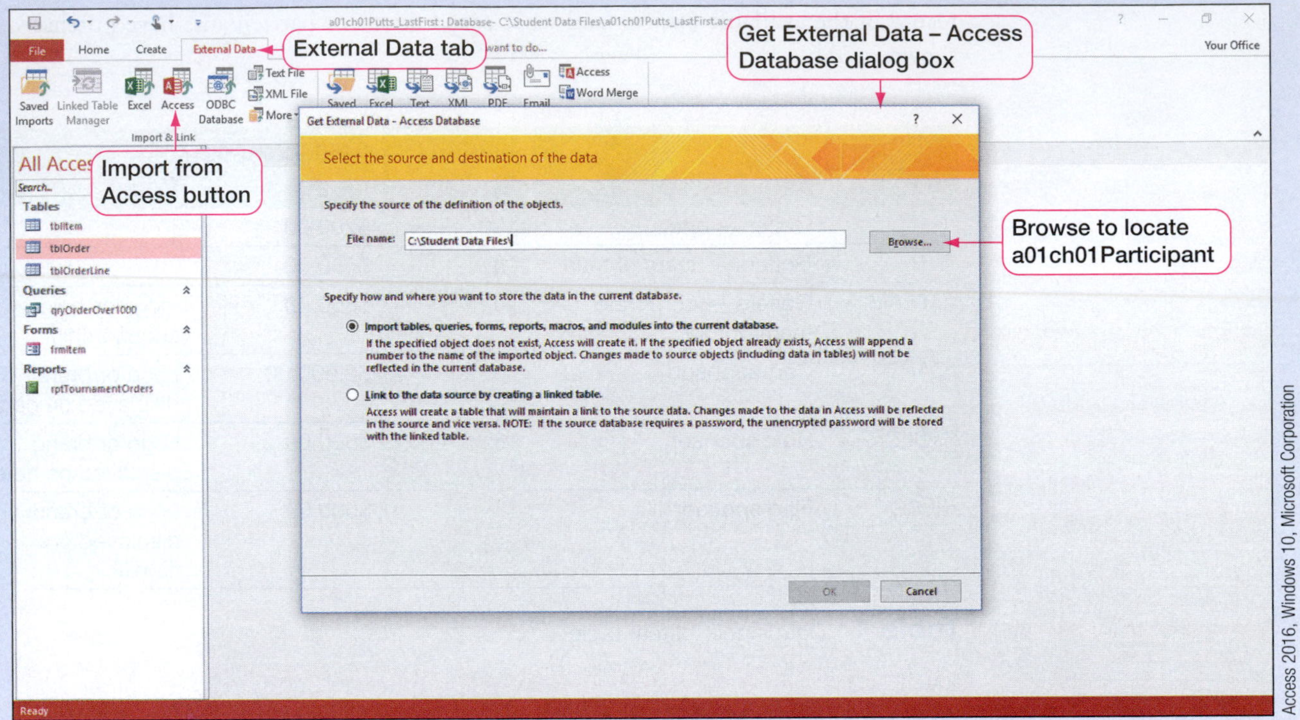

Figure 7 Get External Data - Access Database dialog box

b. Click **Browse**, navigate through the folder structure to the location of your student data files, double-click **a01ch01Participant**, and then click **OK**. Access opens the Import Objects dialog box.

> **Troubleshooting**
>
> If you do not see the Import Objects dialog box, you may have chosen Access from the Export group on the ribbon rather than from the Import & Link group.

c. If necessary, click the **Tables** tab. Click **tblParticipant**, and then click **OK**. Access displays the message "All objects were imported successfully."

d. Click **Close** at the bottom of the dialog box.

e. Double-click **tblParticipant** in the Navigation Pane.

Access opens the table. You may not see exactly the same number of columns and rows in your table, because how much of the table is visible depends on how large your Access window is. You can change the size of the Access window by using your mouse to resize it or by clicking the Maximize button □ to maximize the Access window.

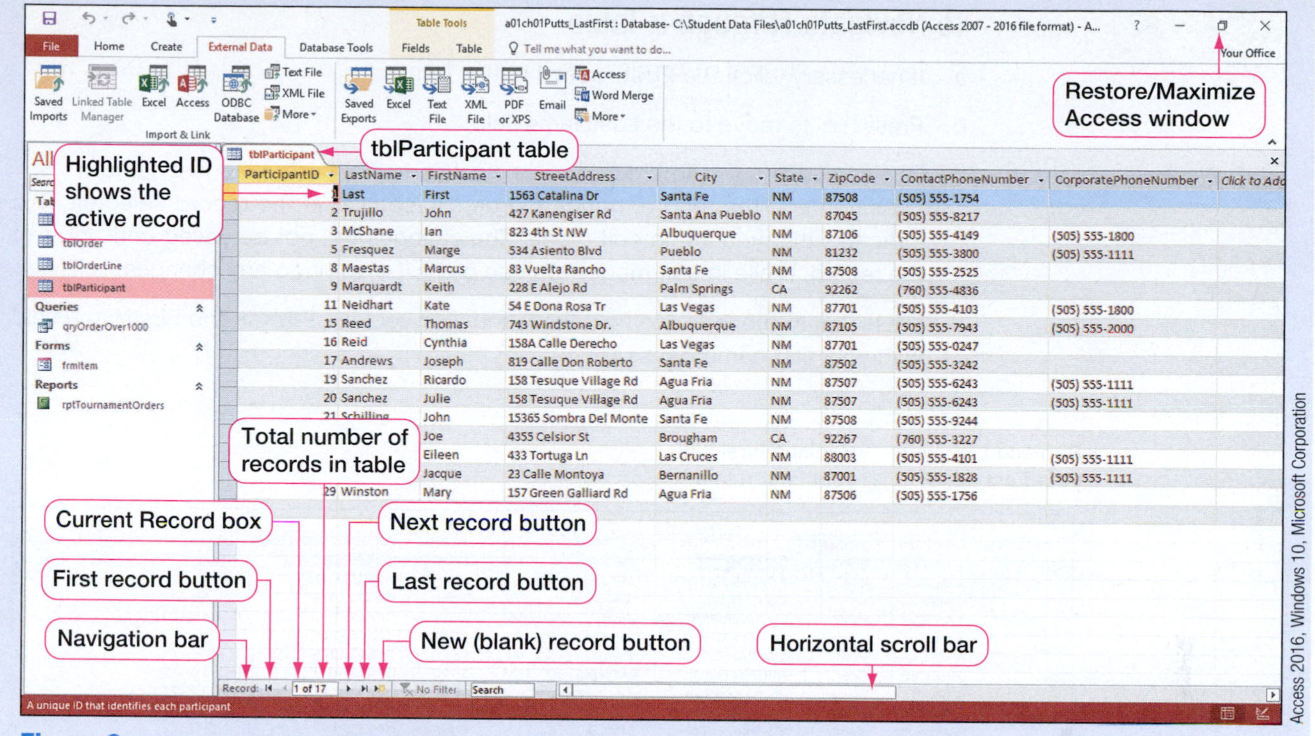

Figure 8 Imported tblParticipant table

REAL WORLD ADVICE **What Should You Name Your Tables?**

If other people use the database and cannot find the right table, how useful is your database? Therefore, you want to use names that are easy to understand. While Access allows you to give any name you want to a table, the name "tblParticipant" follows a standard naming convention:

- Use a name that starts with "tbl". That allows you to distinguish tables from queries at a glance.
- Follow with a name that is descriptive. You want it to be easy to remember what is in the table.
- Make the name short enough that it is easy to see in the Navigation Pane.
- You can use spaces in table names (e.g., tbl Participant), but avid Access users avoid them because using spaces in table names makes advanced tasks more difficult.
- You can use special characters in names. Some people use underscores where a space would otherwise be, such as tbl_Participant.

Navigating Through a Table

Carefully examine the tblParticipant table. Each row of data contains information about the participant listed in the LastName field. There are 17 participant records in the table, the second record being John Trujillo. In this exercise, you will change the name in the record for the first participant to your name.

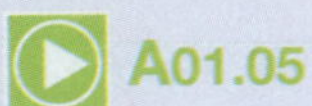

To Navigate Through a Table

a. If necessary, click the **First record** button.

b. Press Tab to move to the LastName field.

c. Replace **Last** in the first record of the LastName field with your last name.

As you edit the record, notice the pencil icon in the record selector. This indicates that you are in edit mode. The changes will not be saved until you exit the record. While in edit mode, you can press Esc to undo any changes.

d. Press Tab to move to the next field, and then replace **First** in the FirstName field with your first name. Press Enter.

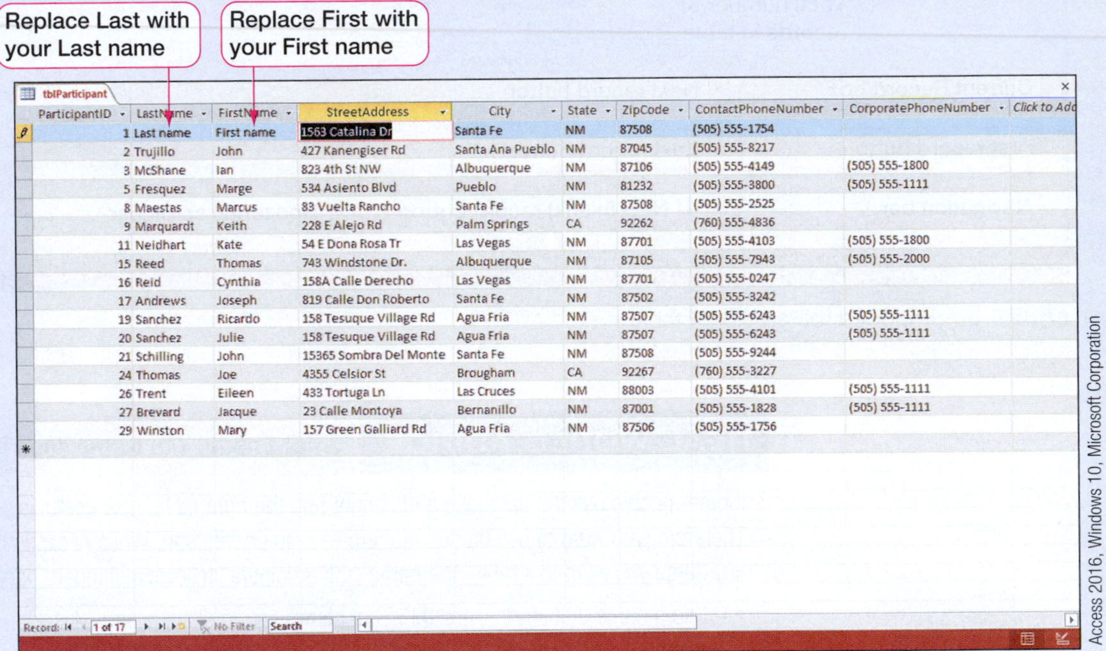

ParticipantID	LastName	FirstName	StreetAddress	City	State	ZipCode	ContactPhoneNumber	CorporatePhoneNumber	Click to Add
1	Last name	First name	1563 Catalina Dr	Santa Fe	NM	87508	(505) 555-1754		
2	Trujillo	John	427 Kanengiser Rd	Santa Ana Pueblo	NM	87045	(505) 555-8217		
3	McShane	Ian	823 4th St NW	Albuquerque	NM	87106	(505) 555-4149	(505) 555-1800	
5	Fresquez	Marge	534 Asiento Blvd	Pueblo	NM	81232	(505) 555-3800	(505) 555-1111	
8	Maestas	Marcus	83 Vuelta Rancho	Santa Fe	NM	87508	(505) 555-2525		
9	Marquardt	Keith	228 E Alejo Rd	Palm Springs	CA	92262	(760) 555-4836		
11	Neidhart	Kate	54 E Dona Rosa Tr	Las Vegas	NM	87701	(505) 555-4103	(505) 555-1800	
15	Reed	Thomas	743 Windstone Dr.	Albuquerque	NM	87105	(505) 555-7943	(505) 555-2000	
16	Reid	Cynthia	158A Calle Derecho	Las Vegas	NM	87701	(505) 555-0247		
17	Andrews	Joseph	819 Calle Don Roberto	Santa Fe	NM	87502	(505) 555-3242		
19	Sanchez	Ricardo	158 Tesuque Village Rd	Agua Fria	NM	87507	(505) 555-6243	(505) 555-1111	
20	Sanchez	Julie	158 Tesuque Village Rd	Agua Fria	NM	87507	(505) 555-6243	(505) 555-1111	
21	Schilling	John	15365 Sombra Del Monte	Santa Fe	NM	87508	(505) 555-9244		
24	Thomas	Joe	4355 Celsior St	Brougham	CA	92267	(760) 555-3227		
26	Trent	Eileen	433 Tortuga Ln	Las Cruces	NM	88003	(505) 555-4101	(505) 555-1111	
27	Brevard	Jacque	23 Calle Montoya	Bernanillo	NM	87001	(505) 555-1828	(505) 555-1111	
29	Winston	Mary	157 Green Galliard Rd	Agua Fria	NM	87506	(505) 555-1756		

Figure 9 Record edited with your name

Navigating Through a Table with the Navigation Bar

At the bottom of the table, Access provides a **Navigation bar** that allows you to move through the table. You can move record by record, or skip to the end, or if you know a specific record number, you can jump to that record. The highlighted ID shows the active record. When you open the table, the first record is active. In this exercise, you will navigate through the table using the Navigation bar.

To Navigate Through a Table with the Navigation Bar

a. Click the **Next record** button [▶] to move to the second record. The Current Record box changes to show 2 of 17. Access highlights the street address of participant John Trujillo.

b. Click the **Next record** button [▶] again to move to the third participant. The Current Record box changes to show 3 of 17.

c. Click the **First record** button [|◀] to return to the first participant.

d. Click the **New (blank) record button** [▶*] to go to the first blank row. Alternatively, you could click in the ParticipantID field of the first blank row.

The first blank row at the end of the table is the **append row**. This row allows you to enter new records to the table. Notice that Access displays an asterisk in the **record selector** box — the small box at the left of the record — to indicate that it is the append row. When you type data here, you create a new participant record. Whenever you add a participant, make sure you are in the append row so you are not changing the information for an existing participant. You will add a participant to this empty row.

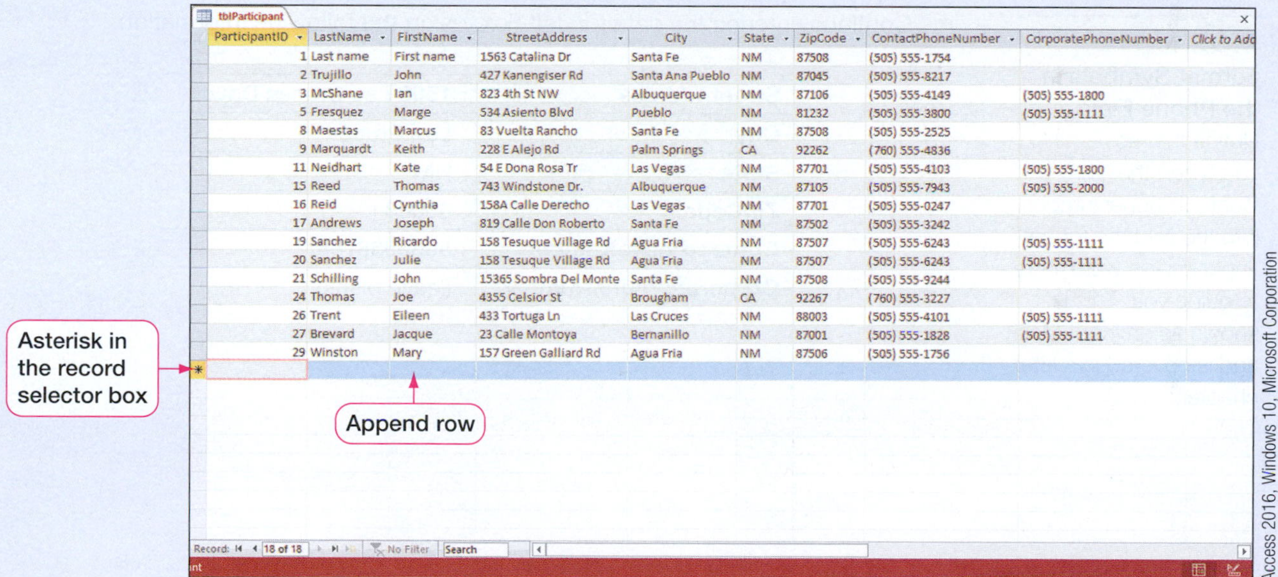
tblParticipant

ParticipantID	LastName	FirstName	StreetAddress	City	State	ZipCode	ContactPhoneNumber	CorporatePhoneNumber	Click to Add
1	Last name	First name	1563 Catalina Dr	Santa Fe	NM	87508	(505) 555-1754		
2	Trujillo	John	427 Kanengiser Rd	Santa Ana Pueblo	NM	87045	(505) 555-8217		
3	McShane	Ian	823 4th St NW	Albuquerque	NM	87106	(505) 555-4149	(505) 555-1800	
5	Fresquez	Marge	534 Asiento Blvd	Pueblo	NM	81232	(505) 555-3800	(505) 555-1111	
8	Maestas	Marcus	83 Vuelta Rancho	Santa Fe	NM	87508	(505) 555-2525		
9	Marquardt	Keith	228 E Alejo Rd	Palm Springs	CA	92262	(760) 555-4836		
11	Neidhart	Kate	54 E Dona Rosa Tr	Las Vegas	NM	87701	(505) 555-4103	(505) 555-1800	
15	Reed	Thomas	743 Windstone Dr.	Albuquerque	NM	87105	(505) 555-7943	(505) 555-2000	
16	Reid	Cynthia	158A Calle Derecho	Las Vegas	NM	87701	(505) 555-0247		
17	Andrews	Joseph	819 Calle Don Roberto	Santa Fe	NM	87502	(505) 555-3242		
19	Sanchez	Ricardo	158 Tesuque Village Rd	Agua Fria	NM	87507	(505) 555-6243	(505) 555-1111	
20	Sanchez	Julie	158 Tesuque Village Rd	Agua Fria	NM	87507	(505) 555-6243	(505) 555-1111	
21	Schilling	John	15365 Sombra Del Monte	Santa Fe	NM	87508	(505) 555-9244		
24	Thomas	Joe	4355 Celsior St	Brougham	CA	92267	(760) 555-3227		
26	Trent	Eileen	433 Tortuga Ln	Las Cruces	NM	88003	(505) 555-4101	(505) 555-1111	
27	Brevard	Jacque	23 Calle Montoya	Bernanillo	NM	87001	(505) 555-1828	(505) 555-1111	
29	Winston	Mary	157 Green Galliard Rd	Agua Fria	NM	87506	(505) 555-1756		

Record: 18 of 18 No Filter Search

Figure 10 Append a new record

e. Make sure that the append row (blank row) is selected and that the record selector box contains an asterisk. In the ParticipantID field, type 30. Press [Tab] to move to the next field, and then, in the LastName field, type Fox.

Alternatively, you can press [Enter] after typing text in a field to move to the next field. Also, notice that when you start typing, the record indicator changed from an asterisk to a pencil [✎]. The pencil means that you are in edit mode. The record after Fox now becomes the new append row.

f. Press [Enter], and then, in the FirstName column, type Jeff.

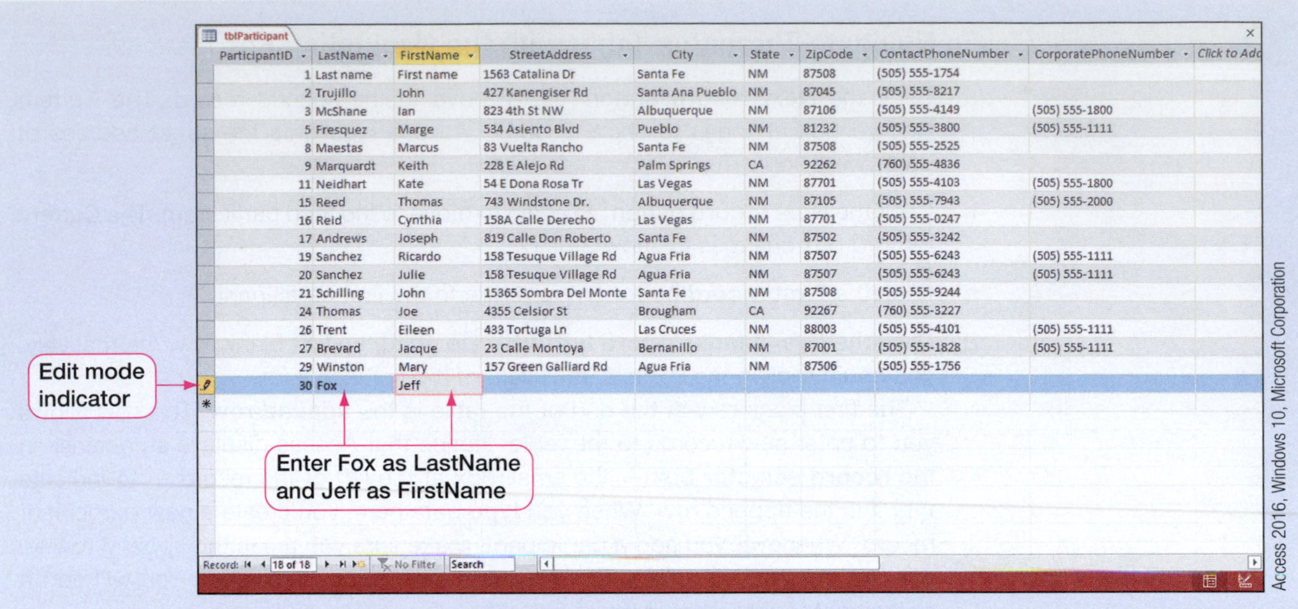

tblParticipant

ParticipantID	LastName	FirstName	StreetAddress	City	State	ZipCode	ContactPhoneNumber	CorporatePhoneNumber	Click to Add
1	Last name	First name	1563 Catalina Dr	Santa Fe	NM	87508	(505) 555-1754		
2	Trujillo	John	427 Kanengiser Rd	Santa Ana Pueblo	NM	87045	(505) 555-8217		
3	McShane	Ian	823 4th St NW	Albuquerque	NM	87106	(505) 555-4149	(505) 555-1800	
5	Fresquez	Marge	534 Asiento Blvd	Pueblo	NM	81232	(505) 555-3800	(505) 555-1111	
8	Maestas	Marcus	83 Vuelta Rancho	Santa Fe	NM	87508	(505) 555-2525		
9	Marquardt	Keith	228 E Alejo Rd	Palm Springs	CA	92262	(760) 555-4836		
11	Neidhart	Kate	54 E Dona Rosa Tr	Las Vegas	NM	87701	(505) 555-4103	(505) 555-1800	
15	Reed	Thomas	743 Windstone Dr.	Albuquerque	NM	87105	(505) 555-7943	(505) 555-2000	
16	Reid	Cynthia	158A Calle Derecho	Las Vegas	NM	87701	(505) 555-0247		
17	Andrews	Joseph	819 Calle Don Roberto	Santa Fe	NM	87502	(505) 555-3242		
19	Sanchez	Ricardo	158 Tesuque Village Rd	Agua Fria	NM	87507	(505) 555-6243	(505) 555-1111	
20	Sanchez	Julie	158 Tesuque Village Rd	Agua Fria	NM	87507	(505) 555-6243	(505) 555-1111	
21	Schilling	John	15365 Sombra Del Monte	Santa Fe	NM	87508	(505) 555-9244		
24	Thomas	Joe	4355 Celsior St	Brougham	CA	92267	(760) 555-3227		
26	Trent	Eileen	433 Tortuga Ln	Las Cruces	NM	88003	(505) 555-4101	(505) 555-1111	
27	Brevard	Jacque	23 Calle Montoya	Bernanillo	NM	87001	(505) 555-1828	(505) 555-1111	
29	Winston	Mary	157 Green Galliard Rd	Agua Fria	NM	87506	(505) 555-1756		
30	Fox	Jeff							

Record: 18 of 18 No Filter Search

Figure 11 Enter participant Jeff Fox into the append row

> **SIDE NOTE**
> **Format Symbols in the Phone Field**
> Notice that as you typed the ContactPhoneNumber into the field the formatting symbols were there to guide you. This is known as an Input Mask and is covered in a later chapter.

g. Continue entering the data for Jeff Fox, using the following information.

StreetAddress	1509 Las Cruces Drive
City	Las Cruces
State	NM
ZipCode	88003
ContactPhoneNumber	5055558786
CorporatePhoneNumber	(leave blank)

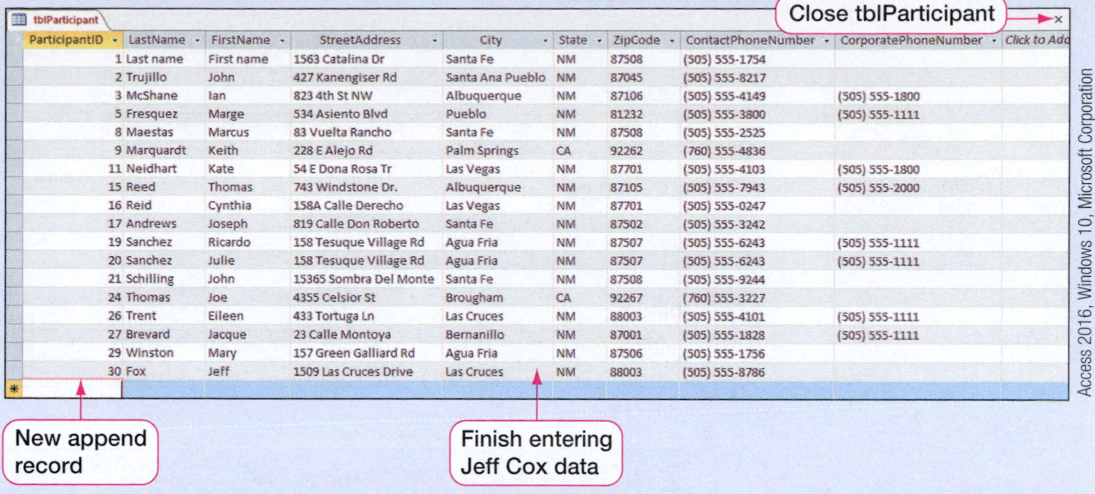

ParticipantID	LastName	FirstName	StreetAddress	City	State	ZipCode	ContactPhoneNumber	CorporatePhoneNumber	Click to Add
1	Last name	First name	1563 Catalina Dr	Santa Fe	NM	87508	(505) 555-1754		
2	Trujillo	John	427 Kanengiser Rd	Santa Ana Pueblo	NM	87045	(505) 555-8217		
3	McShane	Ian	823 4th St NW	Albuquerque	NM	87106	(505) 555-4149	(505) 555-1800	
5	Fresquez	Marge	534 Asiento Blvd	Pueblo	NM	81232	(505) 555-3800	(505) 555-1111	
8	Maestas	Marcus	83 Vuelta Rancho	Santa Fe	NM	87508	(505) 555-2525		
9	Marquardt	Keith	228 E Alejo Rd	Palm Springs	CA	92262	(760) 555-4836		
11	Neidhart	Kate	54 E Dona Rosa Tr	Las Vegas	NM	87701	(505) 555-4103	(505) 555-1800	
15	Reed	Thomas	743 Windstone Dr.	Albuquerque	NM	87105	(505) 555-7943	(505) 555-2000	
16	Reid	Cynthia	158A Calle Derecho	Las Vegas	NM	87701	(505) 555-0247		
17	Andrews	Joseph	819 Calle Don Roberto	Santa Fe	NM	87502	(505) 555-3242		
19	Sanchez	Ricardo	158 Tesuque Village Rd	Agua Fria	NM	87507	(505) 555-6243	(505) 555-1111	
20	Sanchez	Julie	158 Tesuque Village Rd	Agua Fria	NM	87507	(505) 555-6243	(505) 555-1111	
21	Schilling	John	15365 Sombra Del Monte	Santa Fe	NM	87508	(505) 555-9244		
24	Thomas	Joe	4355 Celsior St	Brougham	CA	92267	(760) 555-3227		
26	Trent	Eileen	433 Tortuga Ln	Las Cruces	NM	88003	(505) 555-4101	(505) 555-1111	
27	Brevard	Jacque	23 Calle Montoya	Bernanillo	NM	87001	(505) 555-1828	(505) 555-1111	
29	Winston	Mary	157 Green Galliard Rd	Agua Fria	NM	87506	(505) 555-1756		
30	Fox	Jeff	1509 Las Cruces Drive	Las Cruces	NM	88003	(505) 555-8786		

Figure 12 Finish entering the record for Jeff Fox

h. Click **Close** [X] to close the tblParticipant table. Keep Access and the database open.

Notice that Access did not ask you whether you want to save the table. Access is not like Word or the other Office applications in which you must choose an option to save the file. Access automatically saves the data you enter as you type it.

Understanding Differences Between Access and Excel

An Access table looks similar to an Excel worksheet. Both have numbered rows of data and columns with labels. In addition, both applications allow you to manage data, perform calculations, and report on the data. The major difference between them is that Access allows multiple tables with relationships between the tables, thus the term "relational database." For example, if you are keeping track of participants and the items they order, you create a table of participants and another table of orders. Excel 2016 has some of these features, so it now blurs the distinction between spreadsheets and relational databases.

When you look at Access, you notice that several tables are used for an order. Why use multiple tables for a single order? Figure 13 shows how an order would look in Access and in Excel. The Excel version has to repeat the participant's information on multiple lines. This leads to the following problems.

- **Data redundancy** — With repetition, you create redundant information. John Trujillo bought a cart and a team, so in Excel, you have two rows. You would have to repeat the address information on both records. It is not efficient to enter the address information twice.
- **Errors** — Redundant information leads to errors. If the address needs to be changed, you have to look for all records with that information to make sure it is fixed everywhere.
- **Loss of data** — Suppose that John Trujillo orders just one item. If you deleted the ordered item, it would mean deleting all the information about him as well as the order.

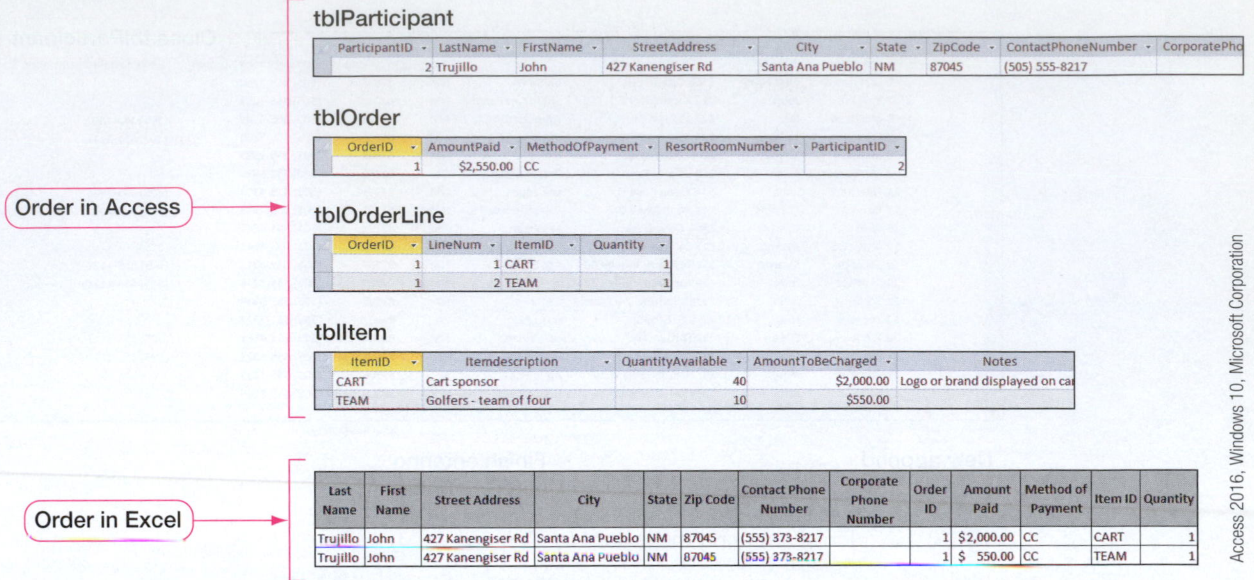

tblParticipant

ParticipantID	LastName	FirstName	StreetAddress	City	State	ZipCode	ContactPhoneNumber	CorporatePho
2	Trujillo	John	427 Kanengiser Rd	Santa Ana Pueblo	NM	87045	(505) 555-8217	

tblOrder

OrderID	AmountPaid	MethodOfPayment	ResortRoomNumber	ParticipantID
1	$2,550.00	CC		2

tblOrderLine

OrderID	LineNum	ItemID	Quantity
1	1	CART	1
1	2	TEAM	1

tblItem

ItemID	Itemdescription	QuantityAvailable	AmountToBeCharged	Notes
CART	Cart sponsor	40	$2,000.00	Logo or brand displayed on ca
TEAM	Golfers - team of four	10	$550.00	

Last Name	First Name	Street Address	City	State	Zip Code	Contact Phone Number	Corporate Phone Number	Order ID	Amount Paid	Method of Payment	Item ID	Quantity
Trujillo	John	427 Kanengiser Rd	Santa Ana Pueblo	NM	87045	(555) 373-8217		1	$2,000.00	CC	CART	1
Trujillo	John	427 Kanengiser Rd	Santa Ana Pueblo	NM	87045	(555) 373-8217		1	$ 550.00	CC	TEAM	1

Figure 13 John Trujillos's order in Access and in Excel

Because Access and Excel have so many common functionalities, many people use the tool that they are more confident using. If you prefer to use both, however, you can easily switch by exporting your data from Access to Excel or from Excel into Access. You can also use one tool for most uses and import your data into the other when you need to.

REAL WORLD ADVICE | **When Do You Use Access Instead of Excel?**

Generally, Access is designed to store data, and Excel is designed to analyze data and model situations. Fortunately, you can easily store data in Access and export a query to Excel for analysis.

Use Access for the following:

- You need to store data in multiple tables.
- You have a very large amount of data, perhaps thousands of records.
- You have large amounts of nonnumeric data.
- You want to run many different queries and reports from your data.

Use Excel for the following:

- Your data fits well into one table.
- You primarily want to do calculations, summaries, or comparisons of your data.

Manually Navigate a Database

Before exploring a database using Access queries, it will prove useful to explore the database manually. This will provide an understanding of what Access can do. Additionally, before developing queries and reports, one should examine the tables and fields so that he or she understands the database.

Using a Manual Query to Explore a Database

Patti Rochelle, the events coordinator at Painted Paradise, wants to send follow-up letters to the participants who have booked a corporate team for the Putts for Paws charity event. She asks you which participants have booked a team. In this exercise, you will first need to discover how a team is indicated in the database. Teams are items that participants can order, so you will start in the tblItem table.

A01.07

To Use a Manual Query to Discover a Database

a. In the Navigation Pane, double-click **tblItem**.
Access opens tblItem in Datasheet view. Explore the data, and you will notice that a corporate team is indicated as CTEAM.

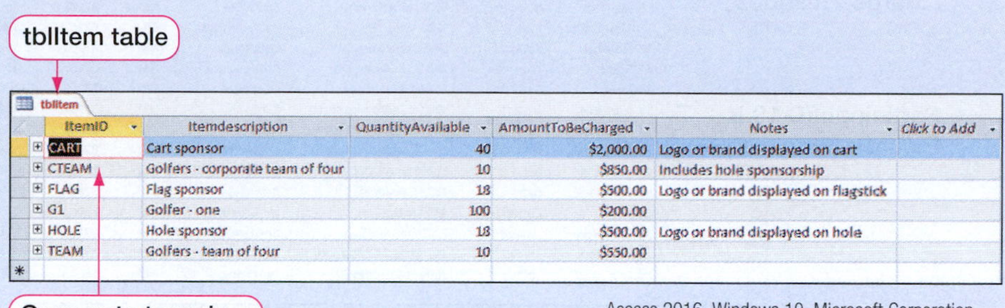

ItemID	ItemDescription	QuantityAvailable	AmountToBeCharged	Notes	Click to Add
CART	Cart sponsor	40	$2,000.00	Logo or brand displayed on cart	
CTEAM	Golfers - corporate team of four	10	$850.00	Includes hole sponsorship	
FLAG	Flag sponsor	18	$500.00	Logo or brand displayed on flagstick	
G1	Golfer - one	100	$200.00		
HOLE	Hole sponsor	18	$500.00	Logo or brand displayed on hole	
TEAM	Golfers - team of four	10	$550.00		

Access 2016, Windows 10, Microsoft Corporation

Figure 14 tblItem table

b. **Close** ☒ the tblItem table.
Next you need to determine which orders include CTEAM. Orders are composed of data from tblOrderLine and tblOrder.

c. Double-click **tblOrderLine** to open the table.
Scan for orders that include CTEAM. There are two: OrderID 4 and OrderID 11.

d. **Close** ☒ the tblOrderLine table.

e. Double-click **tblOrder** to open the table, and then find OrderID 4 and 11.
You need to find which participants placed these orders. Access uses common fields to relate tables. tblParticipant and tblOrder have ParticipantID in common. You find that the ParticipantID for OrderID 4 is 5 and the ParticipantID for OrderID 11 is 19.

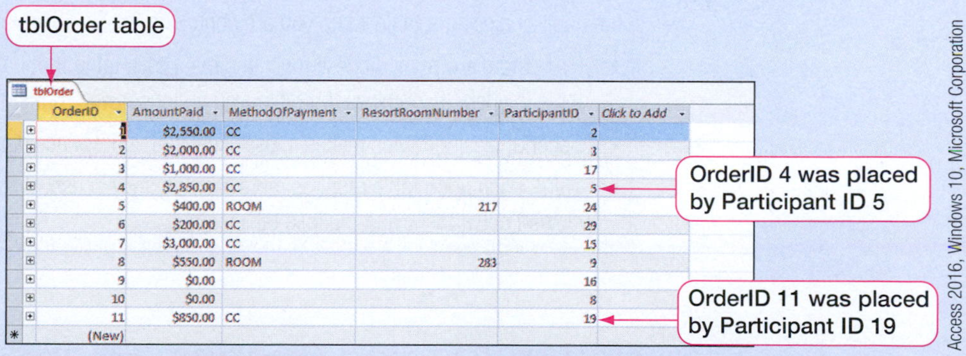

OrderID	AmountPaid	MethodOfPayment	ResortRoomNumber	ParticipantID	Click to Add
1	$2,550.00	CC		2	
2	$2,000.00	CC		3	
3	$1,000.00	CC		17	
4	$2,850.00	CC		5	
5	$400.00	ROOM	217	24	
6	$200.00	CC		29	
7	$3,000.00	CC		15	
8	$550.00	ROOM	283	9	
9	$0.00			16	
10	$0.00			8	
11	$850.00	CC		19	
(New)					

Access 2016, Windows 10, Microsoft Corporation

Figure 15 tblOrder table

f. **Close** ☒ the tblOrder table.

g. Double-click **tblParticipant** to open the table.
Scan for the participants that match the two ParticipantIDs you identified earlier, 5 and 19. You find that OrderID 4 was placed by ParticipantID 5, Marge Fresquez. OrderID 11 was placed by ParticipantID 19, Ricardo Sanchez.

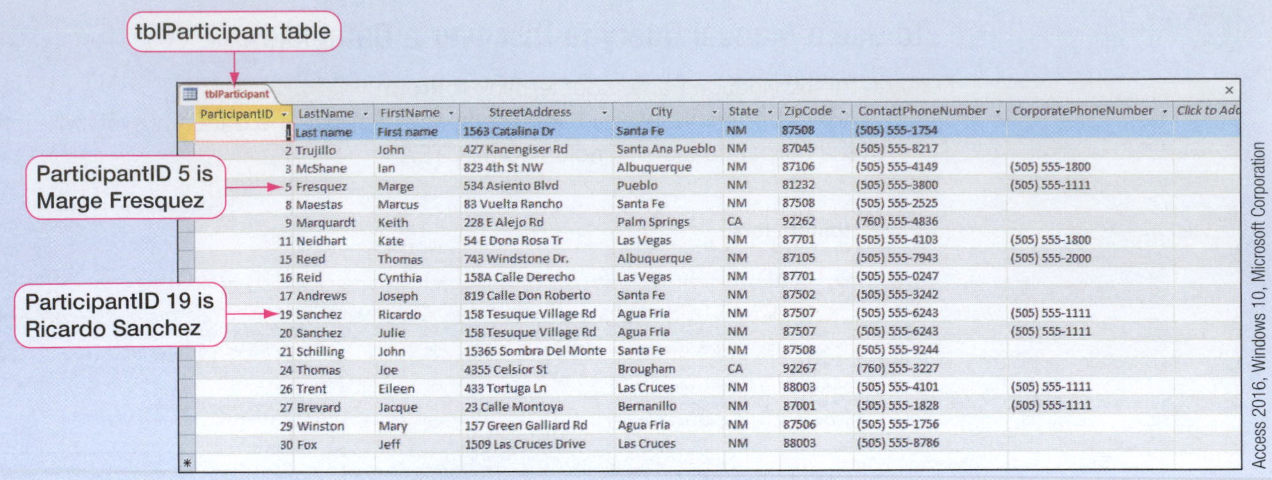

tblParticipant

ParticipantID	LastName	FirstName	StreetAddress	City	State	ZipCode	ContactPhoneNumber	CorporatePhoneNumber	Click to Add
1	Last name	First name	1563 Catalina Dr	Santa Fe	NM	87508	(505) 555-1754		
2	Trujillo	John	427 Kanengiser Rd	Santa Ana Pueblo	NM	87045	(505) 555-8217		
3	McShane	Ian	823 4th St NW	Albuquerque	NM	87106	(505) 555-4149	(505) 555-1800	
5	Fresquez	Marge	534 Asiento Blvd	Pueblo	NM	81232	(505) 555-3800	(505) 555-1111	
8	Maestas	Marcus	83 Vuelta Rancho	Santa Fe	NM	87508	(505) 555-2525		
9	Marquardt	Keith	228 E Alejo Rd	Palm Springs	CA	92262	(760) 555-4836		
11	Neidhart	Kate	54 E Dona Rosa Tr	Las Vegas	NM	87701	(505) 555-4103	(505) 555-1800	
15	Reed	Thomas	743 Windstone Dr.	Albuquerque	NM	87105	(505) 555-7943	(505) 555-2000	
16	Reid	Cynthia	158A Calle Derecho	Las Vegas	NM	87701	(505) 555-0247		
17	Andrews	Joseph	819 Calle Don Roberto	Santa Fe	NM	87502	(505) 555-3242		
19	Sanchez	Ricardo	158 Tesuque Village Rd	Agua Fria	NM	87507	(505) 555-6243	(505) 555-1111	
20	Sanchez	Julie	158 Tesuque Village Rd	Agua Fria	NM	87507	(505) 555-6243	(505) 555-1111	
21	Schilling	John	15365 Sombra Del Monte	Santa Fe	NM	87508	(505) 555-9244		
24	Thomas	Joe	4355 Celsior St	Brougham	CA	92267	(760) 555-3227		
26	Trent	Eileen	433 Tortuga Ln	Las Cruces	NM	88003	(505) 555-4101	(505) 555-1111	
27	Brevard	Jacque	23 Calle Montoya	Bernanillo	NM	87001	(505) 555-1828	(505) 555-1111	
29	Winston	Mary	157 Green Galliard Rd	Agua Fria	NM	87506	(505) 555-1756		
30	Fox	Jeff	1509 Las Cruces Drive	Las Cruces	NM	88003	(505) 555-8786		

Figure 16 tblParticipant table

h. **Close** [X] the tblParticipant table. If you need to take a break before finishing this chapter, now is a good time to take a break.

You now can tell Patti which participants have booked corporate teams and the addresses to which the follow-up letters should be sent. However, it may seem like that was a lot of work to find out who booked the corporate teams. Access queries make this task easier. It is important to know what data is in your database. While Access will do the hard part of matching tables on common fields and finding the results, you still need to tell it what fields you want and where the fields are located.

REAL WORLD ADVICE | **Closing Tables**

While Access allows you to leave several tables open at the same time, it is a good idea to get into the habit of closing a table when you are done with it.

- First, there are many Access functions that use a table that cannot be completed while the table is open. If you close the table, you no longer risk running into this problem.
- Second, closing tables makes it less likely that you will accidentally change the wrong table.
- Third, each open table requires more memory for Access. With larger tables, Access could be slowed down by having multiple tables open.

Understanding Queries, Forms, and Reports

You have explored tables, the first of the four main object types in Access. As was mentioned previously, the other three object types are queries, forms, and reports. Each object provides a different way to work with data stored in tables. A query is used to ask questions about your data. A form is primarily used to enter data into your database or display data in your database. Reports are used to provide professional-looking displays of your tables that are suitable for printing. In this section, you will work with queries, forms, and reports within your database.

Understand the Purpose of Queries

A query is a way to ask questions about the data. For example, with the Putts for Paws Charity database, queries can be used to get answers to questions like the one asked in the manual query exercise or other questions, such as "What has John Trujillo ordered?", "What orders are over $1,000?", and "Which charity participants are from Santa Fe?" More complex queries can also be created, such as calculating a score given a player's strokes and handicap.

One of the strengths of Access is the ability to ask such questions and get answers quickly. In the previous exercise, you traced who ordered corporate teams. That was difficult because you had to keep track of fields such as ParticipantID in one table and then look them up in another table. If you use queries, Access can match common fields in the tables and trace the order for you.

You will look at two different views of queries in this chapter.

- Datasheet view shows the results of your query.
- Design view shows how the query is constructed. It shows the tables, fields, and selection criterion for the query.

Using the Query Wizard

Access provides wizards to help you with tasks. A **wizard** is a step-by-step guide that walks you through tasks by asking you questions to help you decide what you want to do. Once you have some experience, you can also do the task yourself without a guide.

You would like to know which participants are from Santa Fe, New Mexico. In this exercise, you will use the Query Wizard to create the query getting all participants, and then you will modify the query design to select those from Santa Fe.

REAL WORLD ADVICE | **Using Wizards in Access**

Wizards can sometimes save you time. Access wizards are shortcuts to building objects such as queries, reports, and forms. They select fields, format the data, and perform calculations. After the wizard does the initial formatting, you can always modify the resulting query, report, or form to get exactly what you want.

However, anything that can be done with a wizard could also be done without a wizard. A wizard may limit your choices. On the other hand, starting in Design view requires you to make choices without guidance. Whether you start with a wizard or with Design view is usually personal choice. As you become more comfortable with Access, pick the method you prefer. The results will be the same.

A01.08

To Use the Query Wizard

a. If you took a break, open the **a01ch01Putts** database. Click the **Create** tab, and then, in the Queries group, click **Query Wizard**.

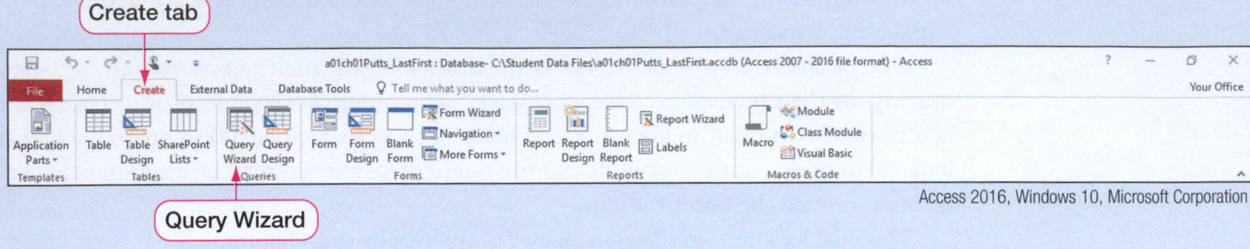

Access 2016, Windows 10, Microsoft Corporation

Figure 17 Create tab on the ribbon

Access displays the New Query dialog box and asks you what kind of query you want to create.

Troubleshooting

If this is the first time that you have used an Access wizard, Access will need to set up the wizards. You will get the message "Setting up wizard" and will need to wait while the wizards are installed.

b. If necessary, click **Simple Query Wizard**, and then click **OK**.

Access asks you which fields you want to include in the query. You have choices of tables or queries as the source for your fields. Your database has four tables to select as a source. You will choose only one table. You could choose fields from multiple tables, but that is not necessary in this query.

c. Click the **Tables/Queries** arrow to see available field sources, and then select **Table: tblParticipant** as the source of your fields.

The dialog box has two lists. The box on the left shows you all available fields from the selected table or query. The box on the right shows you all the fields that you have selected for this query. You use the buttons between the two lists to move fields from one box to the other. By selecting a field and clicking the One Field button [>], you move that field from the Available Fields box to the Selected Fields box. Clicking the All Fields button [>>] moves all fields.

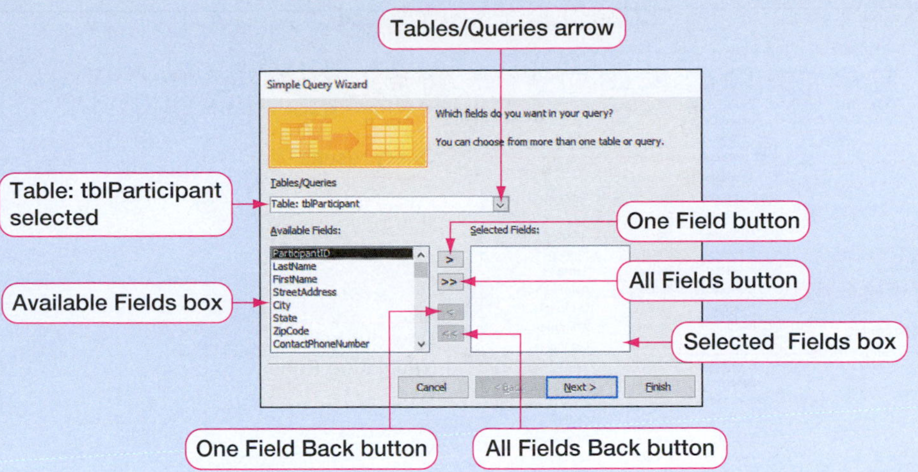

Figure 18 Select tblParticipant

CHAPTER 1

> **SIDE NOTE**
> **Selecting Fields**
> Alternatively, you can double-click the field name to move it from the Available Fields box to the Selected Fields box.

d. Under Available Fields, click **LastName**, and then click the **One Field** button [>]. Access moves the LastName field to the Selected Fields box.

e. If necessary, click **FirstName**, and then click the **One Field** button [>].

f. Click **City**, and then click the **One Field** button [>].
Your field list in the Selected Fields box should display fields in the following order: LastName, FirstName, and City.

Troubleshooting

If you accidentally add the wrong field to the Selected Fields box, select the field and use the One Field Back button [<] to place it back in the Available Fields box.

If you select the fields in the wrong order, Access does not have a way to reorder the fields. It is best to place them all back in the Available Fields box using the All Fields Back button [<<] and then select them again in the correct order.

g. Click **Next** to continue to the next page of the wizard. In the **What title do you want for your query?** box, type qryParticipantSantaFe.

h. Click **Finish**.
Access shows you the results of your query. Once you have created this query, the query name is displayed under All Access objects in the Navigation Pane.

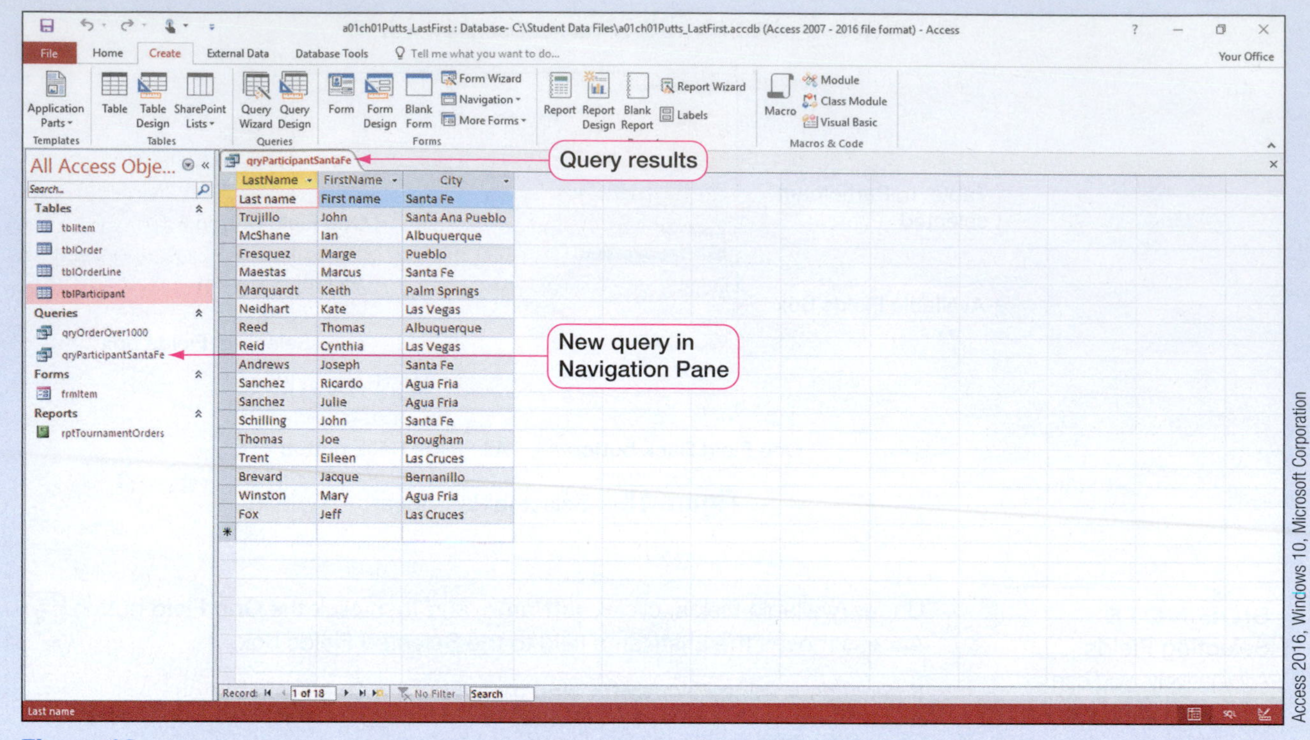

Figure 19 Results of query

i. **Close** [X] the query.

REAL WORLD ADVICE | **Naming Queries**

Similar to tables, Access will allow you to give your query any name you want. There are two important considerations.

- You want to remember what a query does, so make the name as descriptive as possible. A query named "tblParticipant Query" will probably have no meaning for you in a few days. It will be easier to remember that "qryParticipantSantaFe" shows participants from Santa Fe.
- When you are looking at field sources, you often have a choice between tables and queries. Starting all your tables with "tbl" and all your queries with "qry" makes it easy to distinguish what you are choosing.

Switching to the Design View of a Query

The Query Wizard uses a question-and-answer dialog box to create a query. The other method of creating a query is to use Design view. Design view goes behind the scenes of the data and shows you the detailed structure of an Access object. In this exercise, you will switch to Design view of a query.

A01.09

To Switch to Design View to Modify a Query

a. Right-click **qryParticipantSantaFe** in the Navigation Pane.

b. Select **Design View** from the shortcut menu.

Access opens the Design view of your query. The Design tab is open on the ribbon. The left side of the screen shows the Navigation Pane. The top half of the screen shows the **query workspace**, which is the source for data in the query. In this case, the source is the table tblParticipant. The bottom half is called the **query design grid**. It shows which fields are selected in this query: LastName, FirstName, and City.

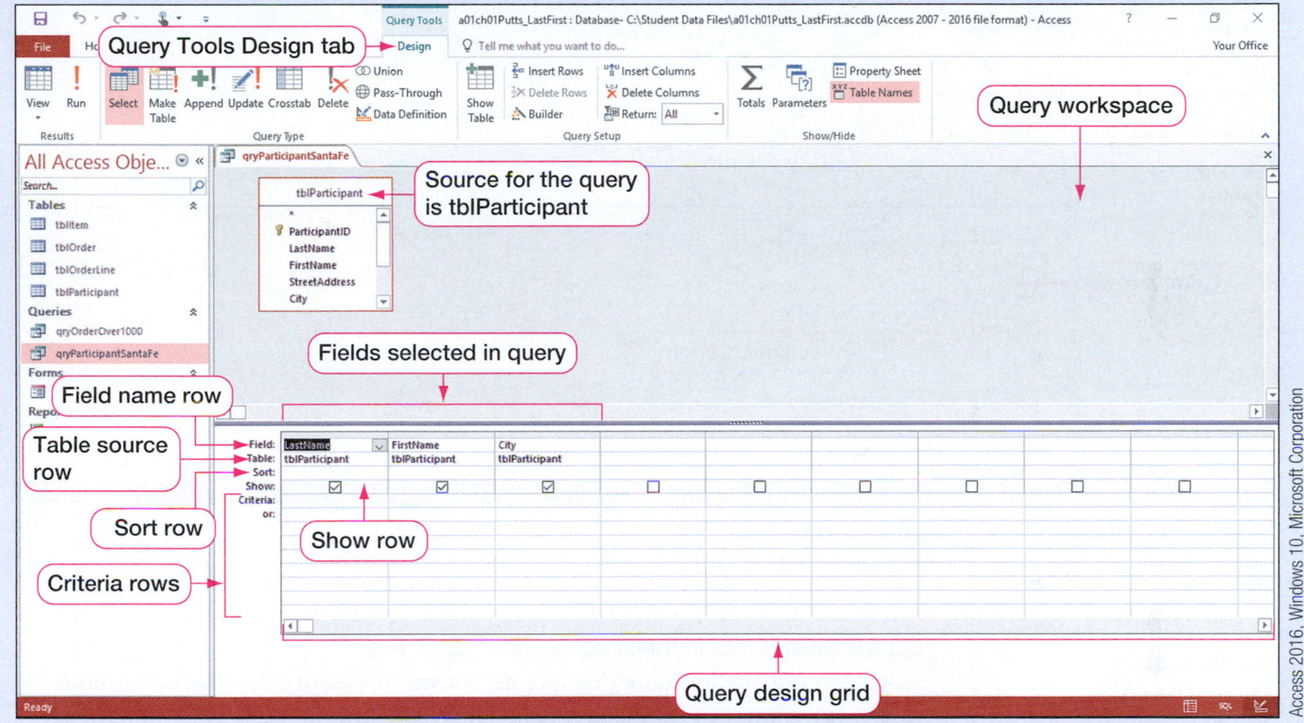

Figure 20 Design view of qryParticipantSantaFe

Specifying Selection Criteria

Each row in the design grid shows information about the field. The top row is Field name. The next row shows the table or source for this field. The Sort row allows you to specify the order of records shown in your query results by setting one or more sort fields. The Show row is a check box that specifies whether the field is shown in the table of query results. The Criteria rows allow you to select certain records by setting conditions for the field contents. In this exercise, you are going to change the query to see which participants are from Santa Fe. You will do that by adding a selection criterion.

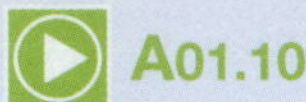
A01.10

To Specify Selection Criteria

a. In the Query Design Grid, click the **Criteria** cell in the City column.

b. Type Santa Fe, and then press Enter.

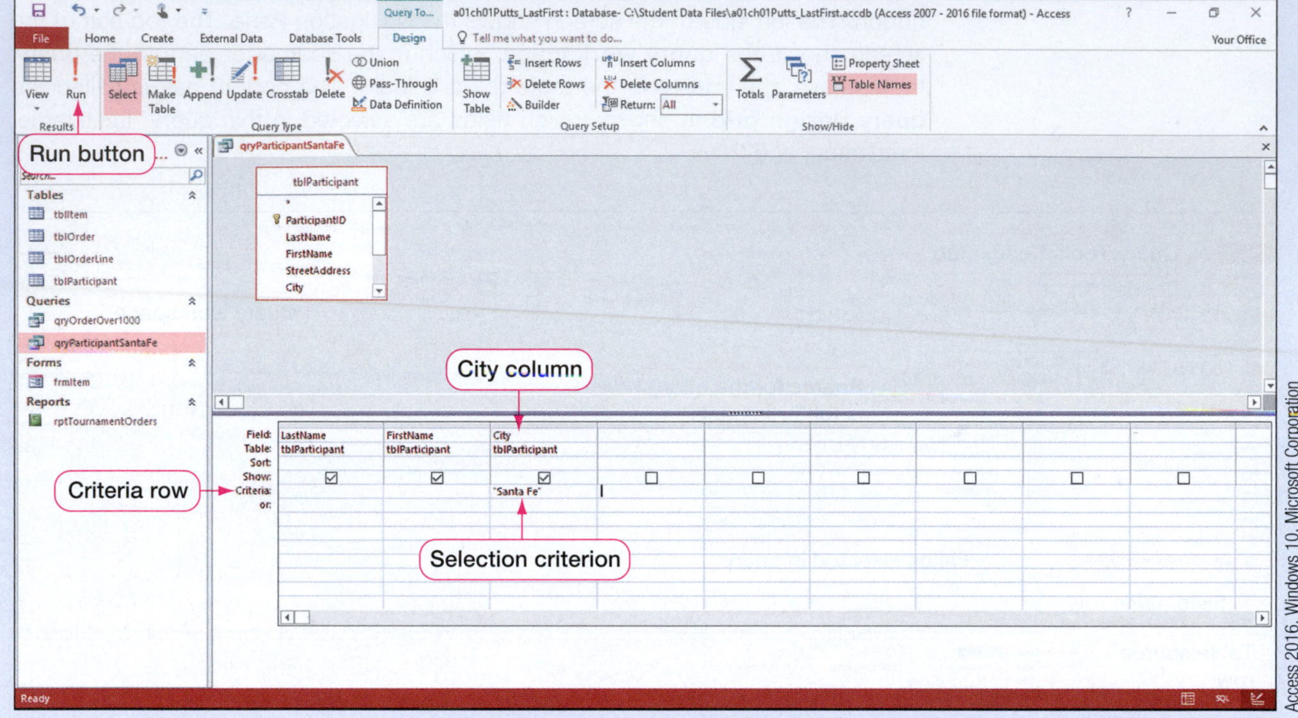

Access 2016, Windows 10, Microsoft Corporation

Figure 21 Selection criterion added to City field

> **SIDE NOTE**
> **Query Criteria**
> Because "City" is a text field, the criterion is treated as text, and Access adds quotation marks. You can also type the quotation marks.

c. On the Design tab, in the Results group, click **Run**.

Access returns the query results as shown in Figure 22. When you run a query, you should check the results to make sure they make sense. You wanted the participants with a city of Santa Fe, and the participants shown are only from Santa Fe.

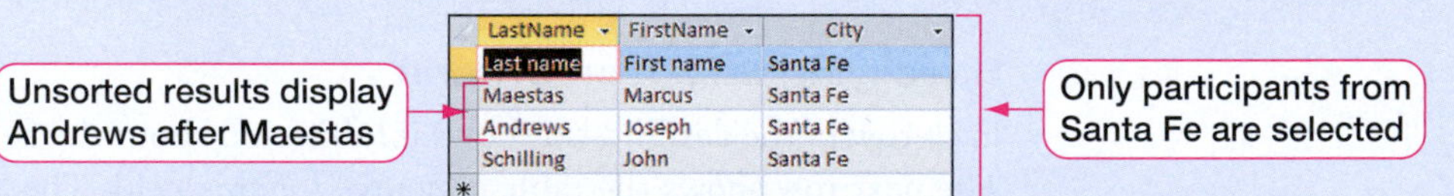

LastName	FirstName	City
Last name	First name	Santa Fe
Maestas	Marcus	Santa Fe
Andrews	Joseph	Santa Fe
Schilling	John	Santa Fe

Access 2016, Windows 10, Microsoft Corporation

Figure 22 Query results showing participants from Santa Fe

Troubleshooting

If your query results are not what you expect (compare to Figure 22), you made an error in entering your selection criterion. Click the View button on the Home tab to switch back to Design view. Compare your criterion with Figure 21. Make sure that you spelled "Santa Fe" correctly and that it is in the City column.

QUICK REFERENCE	Selection Criteria

When you typed Santa Fe as the criterion, you asked Access to select the participants who had a city equal to "Santa Fe". The equals sign is implied, though you can enter it if you wish. Other operators that can be entered in the selection criteria are as follows.

Operator	Meaning	Description
=	Equal to	Selects the records in which the field value is equal to the value provided. If no operator is used, equal to is assumed.
<	Less than	Selects the records in which the field value is less than the value provided.
>	Greater than	Selects the records in which the field value is greater than the value provided.
< =	Less than or equal to	Selects the records in which the field value is less than or equal to the value provided.
> =	Greater than or equal to	Selects the records in which the field value is greater than or equal to the value provided.
< >	Not equal	Selects the records in which the field value is not equal to the value provided.
Between	Between	Selects the records in which the field values listed are within the two values. For example, between 1 and 7 is true for any value between 1 and 7; this includes the value of 1 and the value of 7.

Sorting Query Results

When Access runs a query, it puts the results in a default order based on how the table is defined. As Figure 22 illustrates, having the participants sorted by ID does not make much sense. If no sorting sequence is specified, Access will sort the results of the query by the primary key. In addition, if the query result shows many records, it will be difficult to find a specific record with the default sorting. Usually, you will want to change the sort order so that the order of the results makes sense. In this exercise, you will sort the participants in alphabetical order.

To Sort Query Results

a. On the Home tab, in the Views group, click the **View** arrow, and then select **Design View**.

b. Click the **Sort cell** in the LastName column, click the **Selection** arrow, and then select **Ascending**.

c. Click the **Sort cell** in the FirstName column, click the **Selection** arrow, and then select **Ascending**.

   Although sorting in Datasheet view is possible, it is best practice always to sort a query in Design view. This allows for sorting by multiple rows with ease, and the sorting sequence becomes part of the underlying query code, which means it can be exported into other applications.

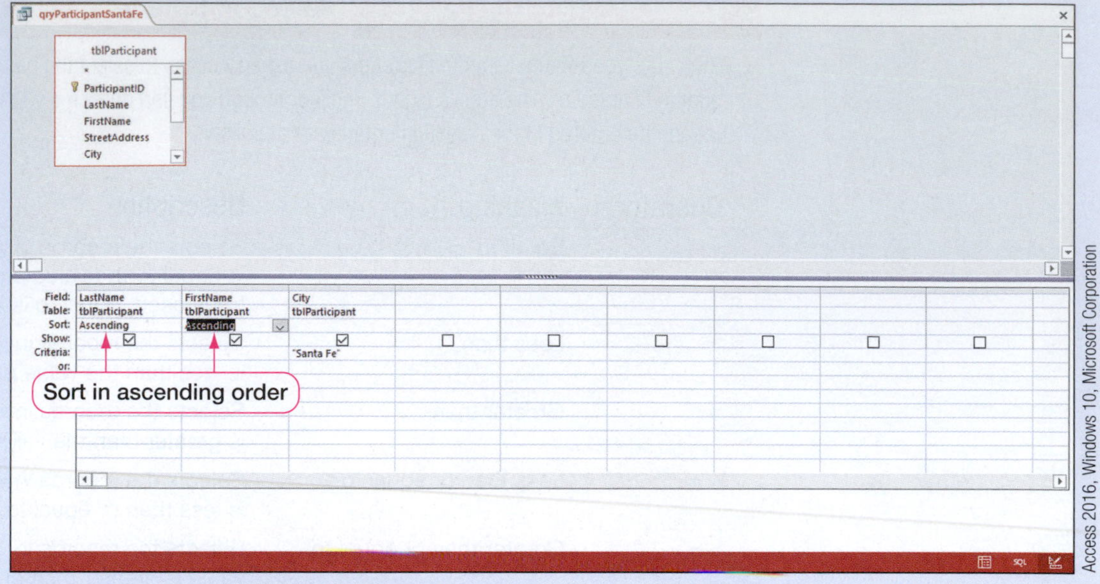

Figure 23 Sorting results of a query

d. On the Design tab, in the Results group, click **Run**.
Access puts the participants in alphabetical order by last name. If there were two participants with the same last name, they would be sorted alphabetically by first name.

Printing Query Results

If you want to print your query results, you can do this on the File tab. Printing tables is done the same way. In this exercise, you will print the results of the qryParticipantSantaFe query.

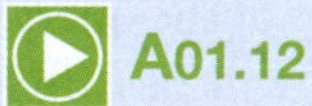

To Print Query Results

a. Click the **File** tab to display Backstage view.
b. Click **Print**, and then click **Print Preview** to see what the results would look like if printed.
c. If your instructor asks you to print your results, on the Print Preview tab, click **Print**. In the Print dialog box, select the correct printer, and then click **OK**.
d. On the Print Preview tab, click **Close Print Preview**.
e. Click **Save** .
f. **Close** the qryParticipantSantaFe query.

Troubleshooting

If you accidentally closed Access instead of just the query, open Access the same way you did at the beginning of the chapter. In the Recent databases, click the name a01ch01Putts_LastFirst to open the database again.

REAL WORLD ADVICE | **Do You Need to Print?**

Before you decide to print the results of a query, you may want to consider whether you really need a printed version. If you want to share the results with someone else, often you can share them via e-mail. Access provides an export-to-PDF feature for a query or table that allows you to save the results in PDF format. Right-click the object in the Navigation Pane, point to Export, and then select PDF or XPS. You can then publish your object as a PDF file, which you can e-mail to someone. Alternatively, you can use the External Data tab to export to a PDF format

CHAPTER 1

Understand the Purpose of Forms

A form provides another interface to a table or query beyond the table in Datasheet view. In corporate databases, end users of a database computer system often use forms to enter and change data. You can also use forms to limit the amount of data you see from a table. In a personal database, you can create forms for entering data if you wish.

Forms have three views.

- **Form view** shows the data in the form. This is the view you use to enter or change data. You cannot change the form design in this view.
- **Layout view** shows the form and the data. Some of the form design, such as field lengths and fonts, can be changed in this view. The data cannot be changed.
- Design view shows the form design but not the data. Any aspect of the form design can be changed. The data cannot be changed.

REAL WORLD ADVICE | **Layout View Versus Design View**

Both Layout view and Design view allow you to change the design of forms. Which view is best for changing design? Part of this is personal preference, but some features can be changed only in Design view. Following are some considerations.

- Layout view shows both the form and the data. When you are changing column widths or field lengths, it is often easier if you see both. You can adjust the sizes while seeing the data and make sure you pick a size that is appropriate.
- Many features can be changed only in Design view. How do you remember which ones? If you prefer Layout view, try it in that view first, and switch to Design view whenever you have trouble changing something.

Creating a Form

There are different types of forms that can be created. The default form shows one record at a time and has each field clearly labeled. In this exercise, you will create a form to make it easier to enter new participants and edit the records of existing participants.

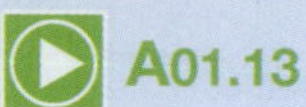

To Create a Form

a. Click **tblParticipant** in the Navigation Pane. Click the **Create** tab, and then, in the Forms group, click **Form**.

b. Click **Save** to save the form. In the Save As dialog box, type frmParticipant, and then click **OK**.

Access creates a form. Notice that the form displays the same Navigation bar that you had in the table. That is because a form is a data entry or display tool for the table. You can use it to navigate through your table. The form is created in Layout view, which allows you make minor changes to the design. You cannot enter data when the form is in Layout view.

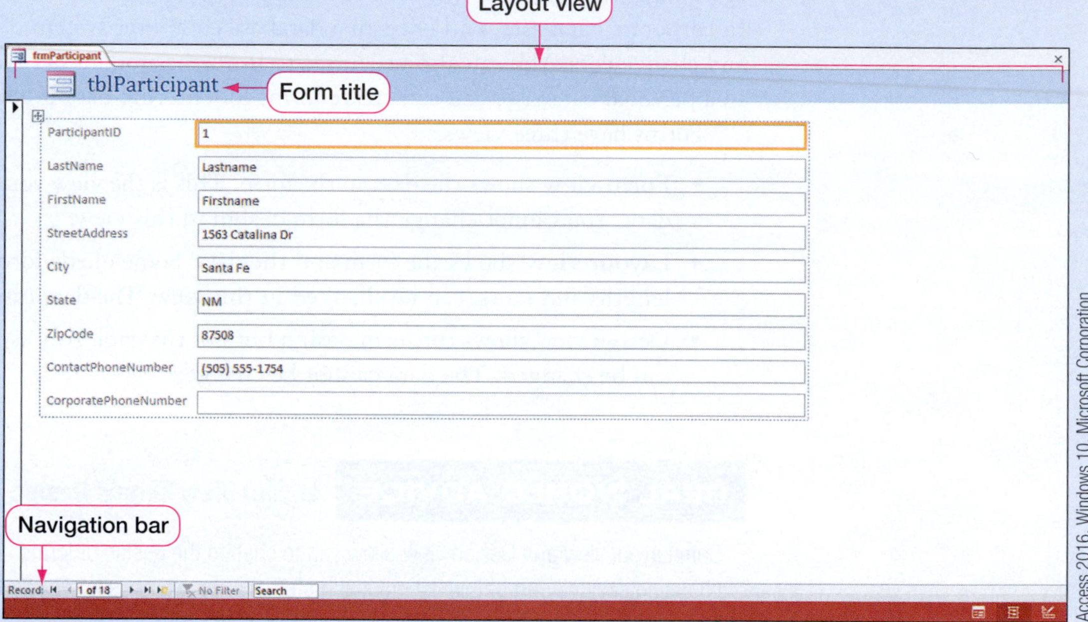

Figure 24 frmParticipant form in Layout View

c. Click the **title** of the form, and then click again to select the **text**. Replace the current title with Participant Form, and then press Enter.

d. **Save** the form.

Entering Data Using a Form

Jackie Silva has asked to register for the tournament. When you are adding a new record, it is very important that you navigate to the append row so you enter the information into a blank record instead of overriding an existing record. In this exercise, you will use your newly created form to add a new record to the participant table.

A01.14

To Enter Data Using a Form

a. On the Design tab, in the Views group, click the **View** arrow, and then click **Form View**. This view allows you to use the form to enter data into the table. Form view opens to existing records, so you must be careful that you do not override any existing data.

b. Click the **New (blank) record button** on the Navigation bar. If you see a participant's name in the form, try again. This will be record 19 of 19 in the Navigation bar.

Figure 25 Blank append record

c. Type the following information into the form. Press Enter or Tab to move to each field.

ParticipantID	31
LastName	Silva
FirstName	Jackie
StreetAddress	1509 Main Street
City	Santa Ana Pueblo
State	NM
ZipCode	87044
ContactPhoneNumber	5055553355
CorporatePhoneNumber	(leave blank)

d. **Close** the form. The participant data you entered in the form is saved to the table.

e. On the Navigation Pane, under Tables, double-click **tblParticipant**.

f. Click the **Last Record button** on the Navigation bar. Verify that Jackie Silva has been added to your table.

g. **Close** the table.

CONSIDER THIS | **Adding Data Directly into a Table Versus Adding Data into a Form**

You have added two participants to your table. Earlier, you added a row to the table and added Jeff Fox. Now you have added Jackie Silva via a form. Which was easier for you? Why would most companies use forms to enter data?

Understand the Purpose of Reports

A report provides an easy-to-read format suitable for printing. A sample report is shown in Figure 26. You can easily provide column totals as needed. When printing data for management presentations, you usually use a report rather than a query. The source of the data for a report can be a table or a query.

Reports have four views.

- **Report view** shows how the report would look in a continuous page layout.
- **Print Preview** shows how the report would look on the printed page. This view allows you to change the page layout.
- Layout view shows the report and the data. Some parts of the report design, such as field lengths and fonts, can be changed in this view.
- Design view shows the report design but not the data. Any aspect of the report design can be changed.

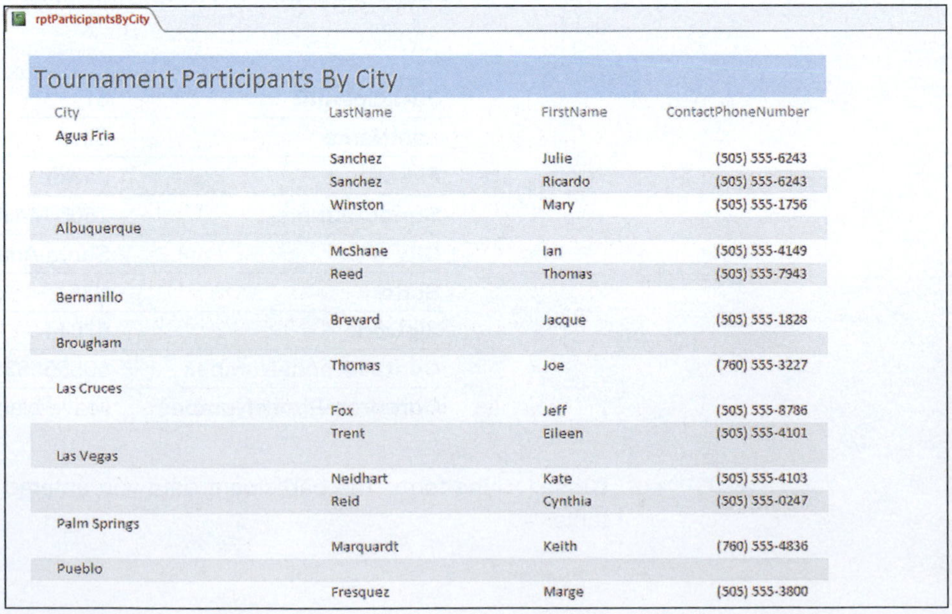

rptParticipantsByCity

Tournament Participants By City

City	LastName	FirstName	ContactPhoneNumber
Agua Fria			
	Sanchez	Julie	(505) 555-6243
	Sanchez	Ricardo	(505) 555-6243
	Winston	Mary	(505) 555-1756
Albuquerque			
	McShane	Ian	(505) 555-4149
	Reed	Thomas	(505) 555-7943
Bernanillo			
	Brevard	Jacque	(505) 555-1828
Brougham			
	Thomas	Joe	(760) 555-3227
Las Cruces			
	Fox	Jeff	(505) 555-8786
	Trent	Eileen	(505) 555-4101
Las Vegas			
	Neidhart	Kate	(505) 555-4103
	Reid	Cynthia	(505) 555-0247
Palm Springs			
	Marquardt	Keith	(760) 555-4836
Pueblo			
	Fresquez	Marge	(505) 555-3800

Access 2016, Windows 10, Microsoft Corporation

Figure 26 An Access report

Creating a Report Using a Wizard

The report feature in Access allows you to easily design reports that can serve management purposes and look professional. The Report Wizard starts similarly to the Query Wizard in selecting fields for the report. After that, the wizard asks questions about report formatting that were not part of the Query Wizard.

In this exercise, you will create a report listing the participants entered in the tournament with their contact phone numbers. You will group all participants in a city into a single group, alphabetized in ascending order by their names.

A01.15

To Create a Report Using a Wizard

a. Click the **Create** tab, and then, in the Reports group, click **Report Wizard**. Click the **Tables/Queries** arrow, and then click **Table: tblParticipant**.

b. Using the One Field button [>], move these fields to the Selected Fields box: **LastName**, **FirstName**, **City**, and **ContactPhoneNumber**.

> **SIDE NOTE**
> **Adding Fields**
> Alternatively, you can double-click each field name that you want to add to the query.

c. Click **Next**. The wizard asks whether you want to add grouping levels.

d. Click **City**, and then click the **One Field button** [>] to group by city. When you make this selection, the box on the right of the dialog box shows a preview of what the report grouping will look like.

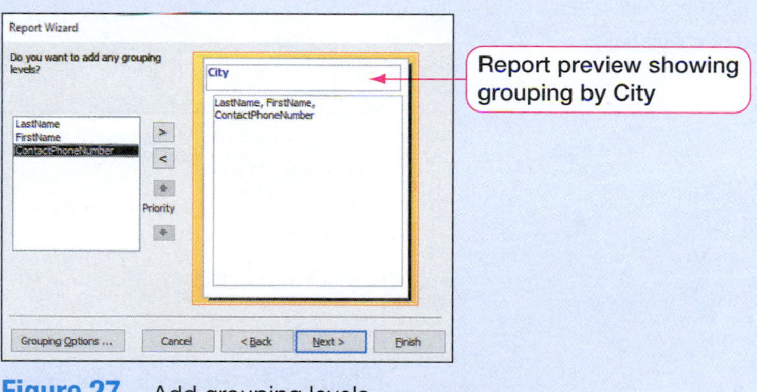

Access 2016, Windows 10, Microsoft Corporation

Figure 27 Add grouping levels

e. Click **Next**.
The wizard asks what sort order you want. You always want to put your report in some order that makes it easy to read and understand. Otherwise, a report with a lot of information is difficult to understand. In this report, you will list participants alphabetically.

f. In the 1 box, click the **Selection arrow** [v], and then select **LastName**. If necessary, make sure that the sort order is **Ascending**, meaning in alphabetical order from A to Z.

g. In the 2 box, click the **Selection arrow** [v], and then select **FirstName**.

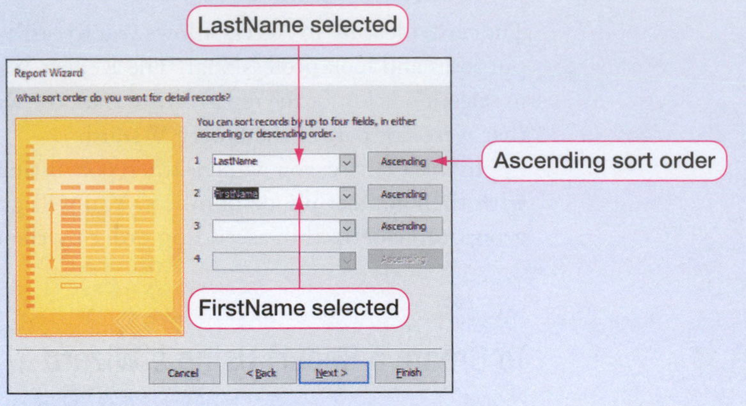

Figure 28 Add sorting

SIDE NOTE

Previewing Reports

Print Preview is the only view that allows you to see page headers and footers and is therefore the best place to check how your report will look when printed or converted to a PDF.

h. Click **Next**. Make sure the default **Stepped** layout and **Portrait** orientation are selected.

i. Click **Next**. In the **What title do you want for your report?** box, type rptParticipantsByCity.

j. Click **Finish**.

Access displays the report in Print Preview. You notice that the ContactPhoneNumber heading is not fully shown. You can fix that easily in Layout view.

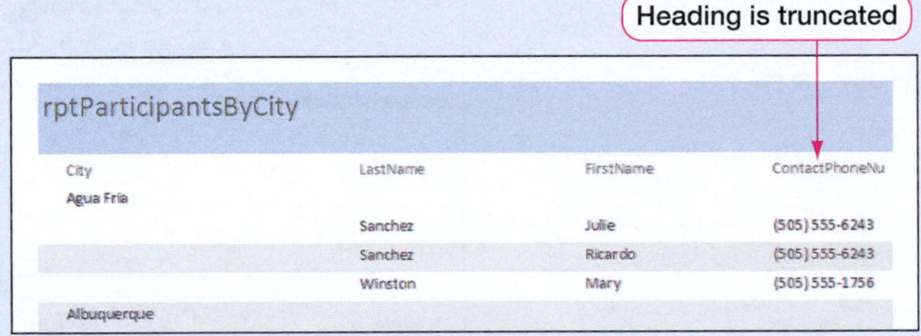

Figure 29 Report in Print Preview

k. Right-click anywhere on the report, and then click **Layout View** from the shortcut menu. Click the heading of the **ContactPhoneNumber** column.

Troubleshooting

If either the Field List Pane or the Property Sheet shows on the right side of the field, click ☒ to close it.

l. Point to the **left border** of the selected heading (ContactPhoneNumber) until the Horizontal Resize pointer is displayed ↔.

m. Drag to the left until you can see the entire column heading.

n. Double-click the **title** of the report, and then change the report title to Tournament Participants By City. Your report should look like Figure 26.

o. **Save** the report.

Notice that the City data is a line above the data in the other columns. That is because the participants are grouped by city. Within a city, participants are sorted alphabetically.

S_S CONSIDER THIS | Grouping Versus Sorting

Grouping arranges records together by the value of a single field. Sorting puts the records within a group in a specific order based on field values. When would you choose to sort your records, and when would you group before sorting?

Printing a Report

Reports can be printed in the same way as queries, using the File tab. You can also take advantage of Print Preview to print a report. In this exercise, you will switch from Layout View to Print Preview to see how the report will be printed.

A01.16

To Print a Report

a. Click **Print Preview** on the Status Bar to change to Print Preview. Alternatively, you could change to Print Preview using the View button on the ribbon, as you have done before. If necessary, widen the Report Title so that the entire title is visible.

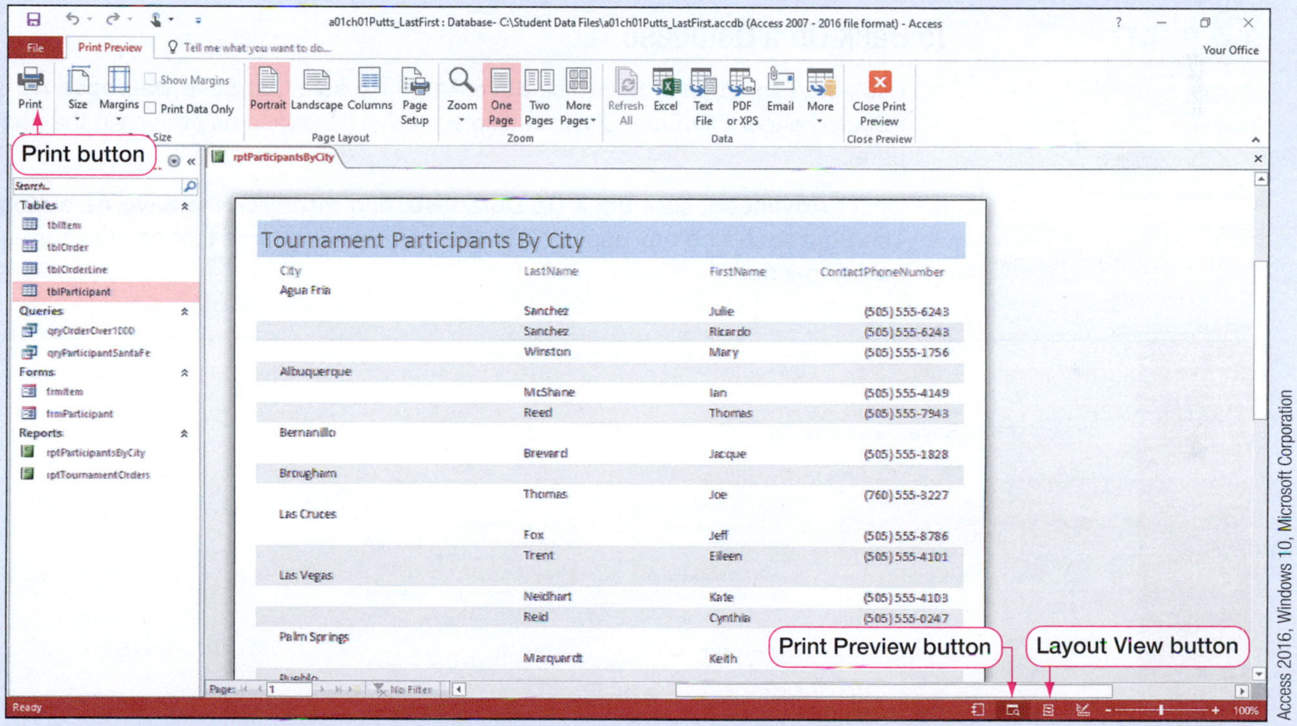

Figure 30 Switch views using the status bar

b. If your instructor directs you to print the report, in the Print group, click **Print**, and then click **OK**.

c. In the Close Preview group, click **Close Print Preview**, and then **close** ☒ the report.

REAL WORLD ADVICE | When Do You Use a Report Versus a Query?

Both reports and queries can be used to view data. A report provides a more formal presentation of data and is designed for printing. A query has more selection capabilities, but the formatting is not as attractive. You can combine the two capabilities by first creating the query object and then creating a report using the query as your source.

Back Up a Database

A **backup database** is an extra copy of your database that you can use to protect yourself from the accidental loss of data. You can return to the backup copy if you accidentally delete the real database. The backup copy may not be as current, but it may save you from having to recreate the whole database. If you store the backup on another storage medium, it can also help in cases of hardware failure such as a hard drive crash.

Backing Up a Database

In Access, you make backups by using the Back Up Database command, which is available on **Backstage view** under Save As. If you make multiple backup copies, you will want to give them different names. The backup feature appends the current date to the suggested file name. That allows you to easily distinguish between various versions of the backups, and you can be sure that you are getting the most recent one.

If you ever need a backup, simply return to the most recent copy that you have, and start working with that file. In this exercise, you will back up the a01ch01Putts database.

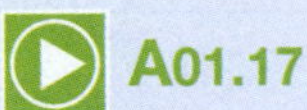

A01.17

To Back Up a Database

a. Click the **File** tab, and then click **Save As**. Make sure that **Save Database As** is selected under File Types. Access displays Save Database As options in the right pane.

b. Under **Advanced**, click **Back Up Database**, and then click the **Save As** button. The Save As dialog box appears with a suggested file name that has the current date appended.

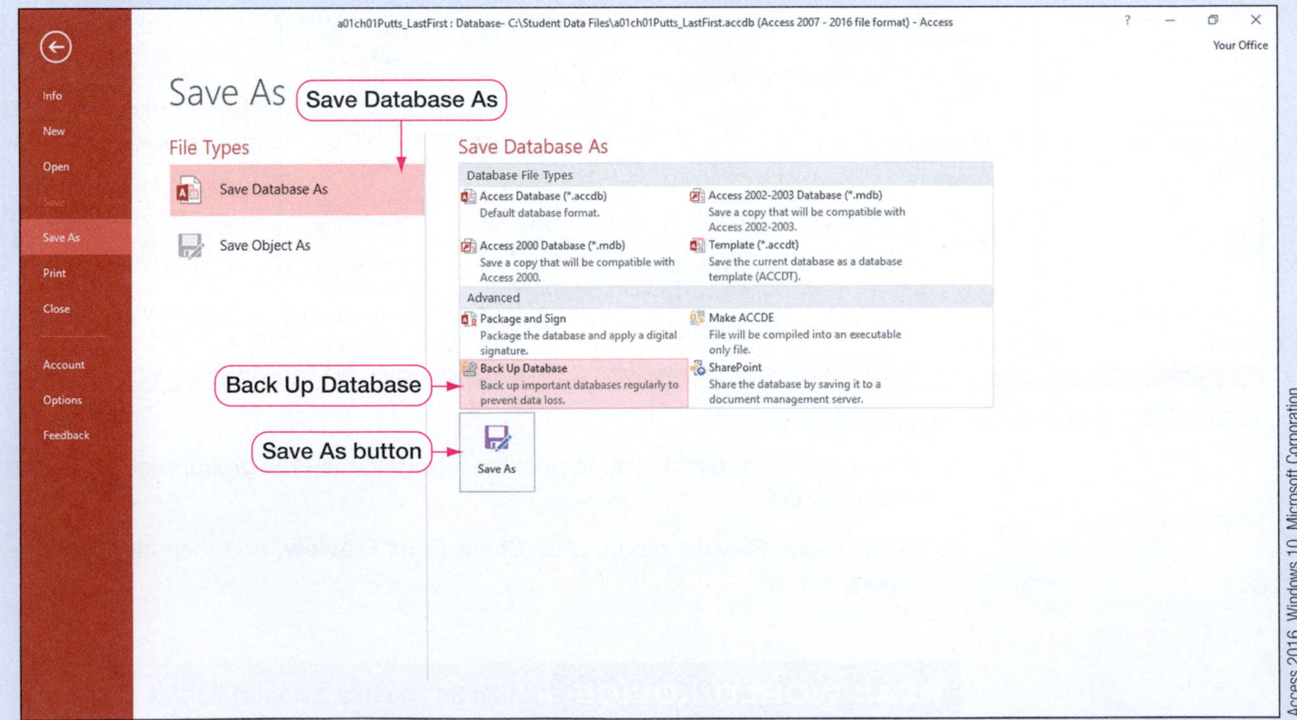

Figure 31 Making a backup copy of a database

c. Navigate to the drive and folder where you want to store your backup, and then click **Save**.

CHAPTER 1

CONSIDER THIS | Backups

What would you lose if your PC's hard drive crashed? Do you have copies of school work, photographs, or music? You may never need to retrieve the backup, but which would be worse: making unnecessary backups or losing all your files?

Compact and Repair a Database

As you work on an Access database, the size of the database file increases. When you delete a record or object or if you make changes to an object, Access does not reuse the original space. Access provides a compacting feature that makes more efficient use of disk space. **Compacting** rearranges objects to use disk space more efficiently, thus releasing the now unused space to be used again. If you do not compact your database, its size can get very large quickly. The compact option also looks for damaged data and tries to repair it.

Compacting Your Database

You have two options for compacting.

1. You can perform a single Compact and Repair Database action at any time.
2. You can select Compact on Close.

If you select Compact on Close, Access automatically compacts your database anytime you close it. Both options are available on Backstage view. In this exercise, you will compact and repair the a01ch01Putts database.

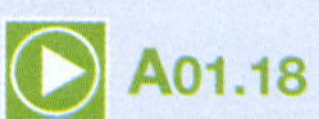

A01.18

To Compact Your Database

a. Click the **File** tab.

b. Click **Compact & Repair Database**.

Access compacts your database, fixes it if necessary, and returns you to the Home tab. On a small database such as Putts for Paws, this action is very fast. On a larger database with many changes made, there may be a noticeable delay.

c. Click the **File** tab, and then click **Options**.

d. Click **Current Database** in the left pane, and then, under Application Options, click the **Compact on Close** check box.

By default, Compact on Close is turned off. Many professionals like to turn on Compact on Close so they do not need to remember to compact the database themselves.

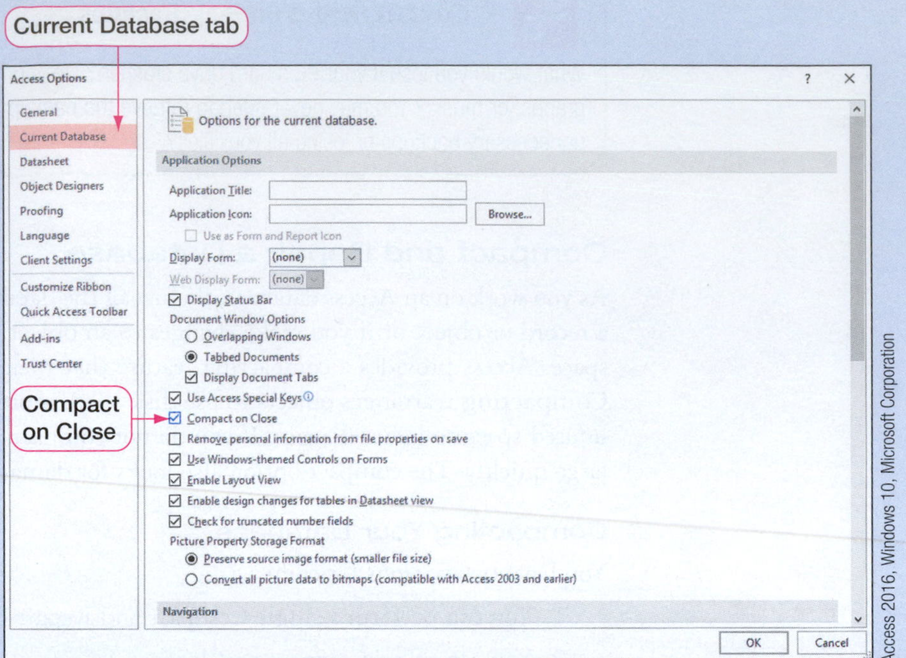

Figure 32 Select Compact on Close

e. Click **OK** to turn this option on. Access warns you that the option will not take effect until you close and reopen the database.

f. Click **OK** again.

g. Exit Access, and then submit your file as directed by your instructor.

Concept Check

1. What is Access? When would you use Access instead of Excel? p. 55, 69
2. What is the Navigation Pane? Where do you find it? p. 59
3. What is a record? What is a field? How are they represented in Access? p. 56, 57
4. How do you manually navigate a database? p. 70
5. How is a query used? What is the difference between Datasheet view and Design view of a query? p. 73
6. How is a form used? p. 81
7. How is a report used? What is Report Layout view? p. 84
8. What is a database backup, and how is it used? p. 88
9. What does it mean to compact and repair your database? What is the difference between a single compact and a compact on close? p. 89

Key Terms

Visual Summary

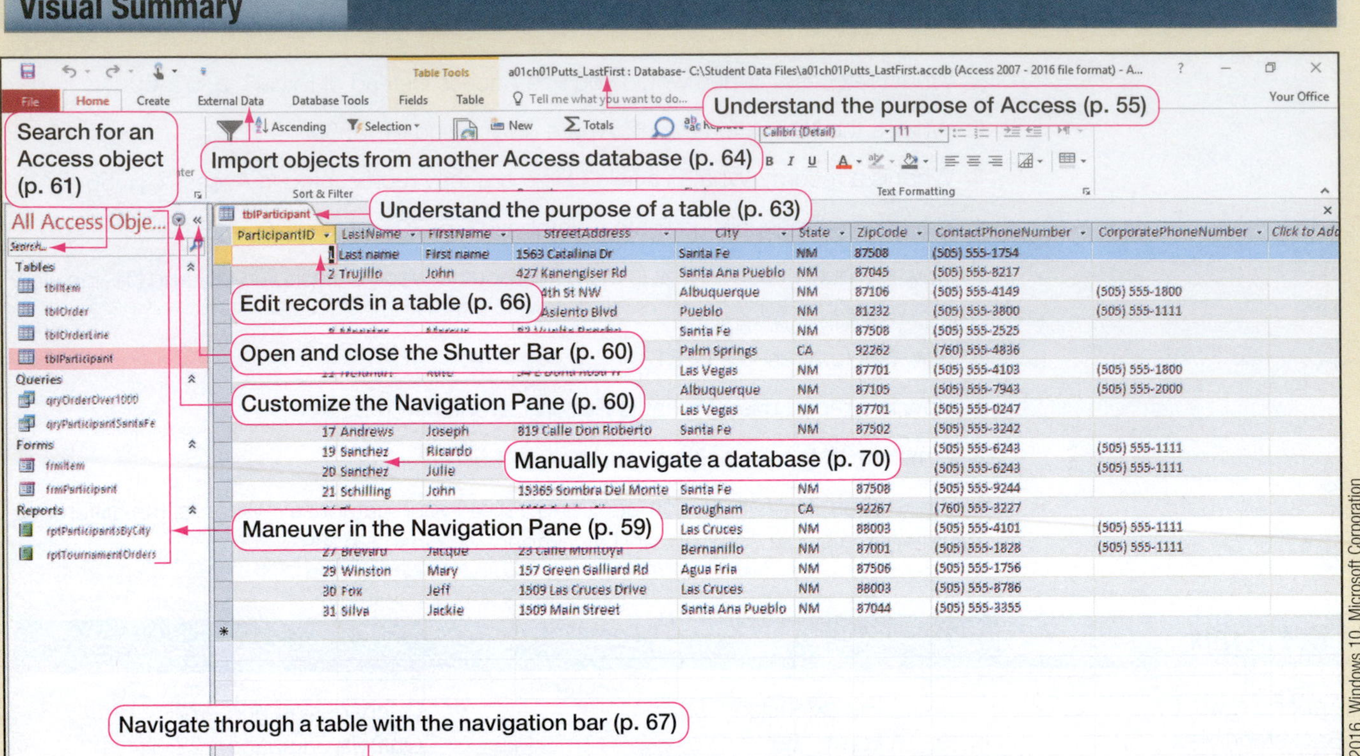

Access 2016, Windows 10, Microsoft Corporation

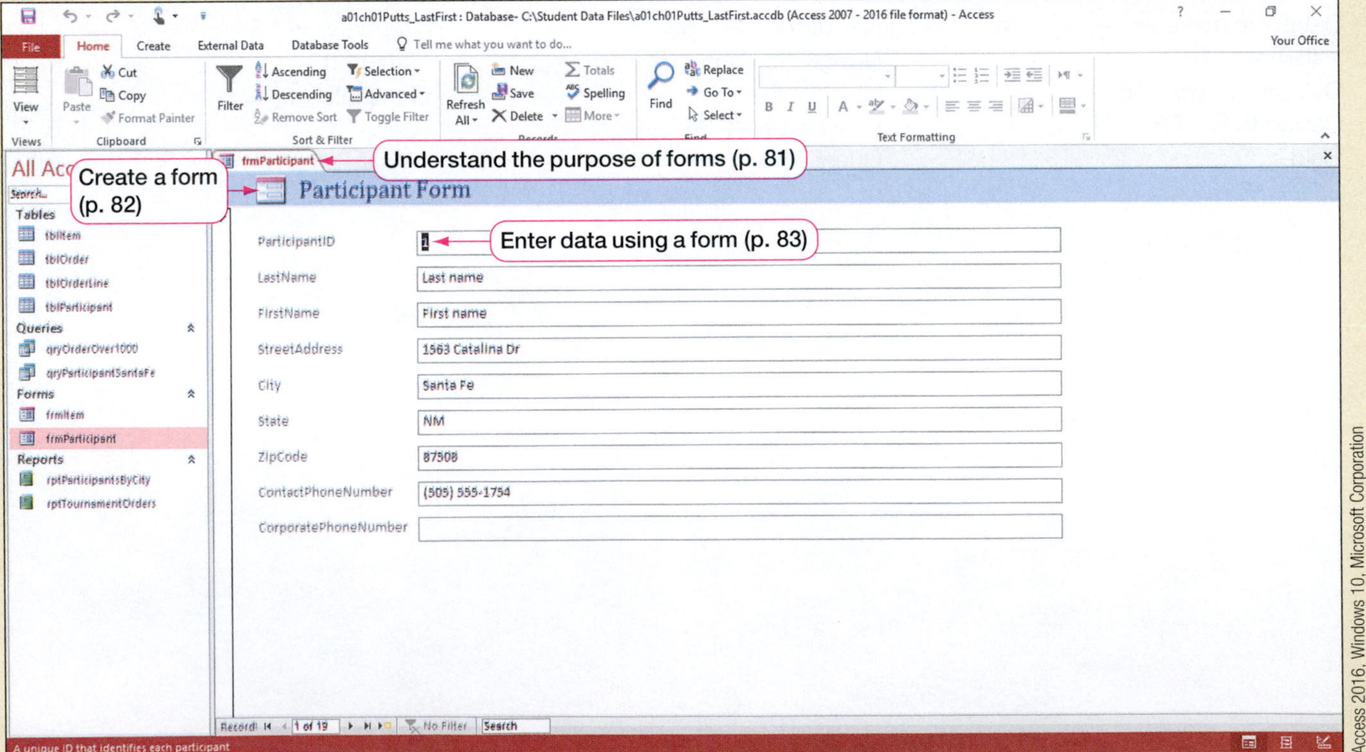

Access 2016, Windows 10, Microsoft Corporation

Figure 33

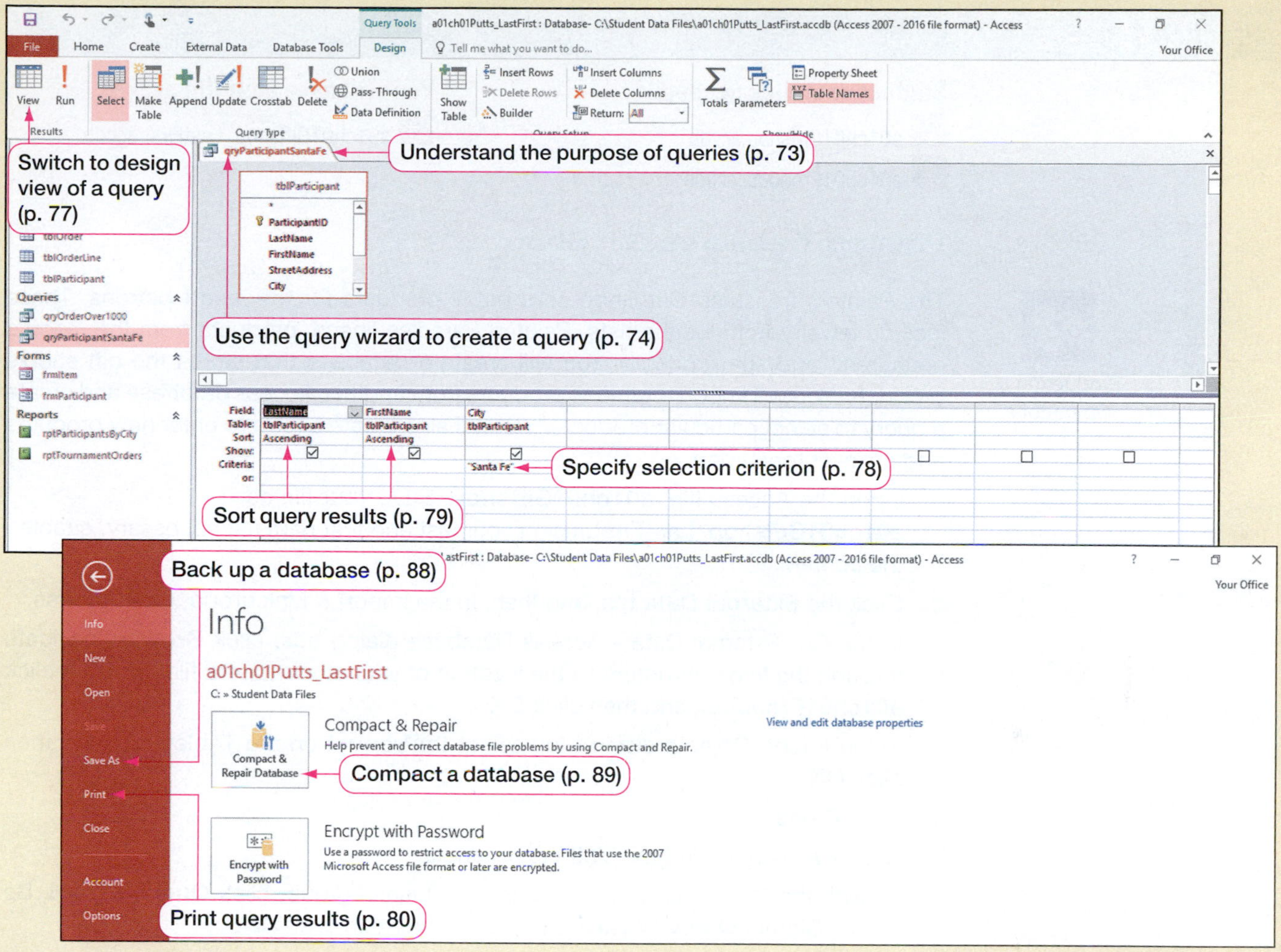

Switch to design view of a query (p. 77)
Understand the purpose of queries (p. 73)
Use the query wizard to create a query (p. 74)
Specify selection criterion (p. 78)
Sort query results (p. 79)
Back up a database (p. 88)
Compact a database (p. 89)
Print query results (p. 80)

Access 2016, Windows 10, Microsoft Corporation

Figure 34

Understand the purpose of reports (p. 84)
Create a report using a wizard (p. 85)
Print a report (p. 87)

Access 2016, Windows 10, Microsoft Corporation

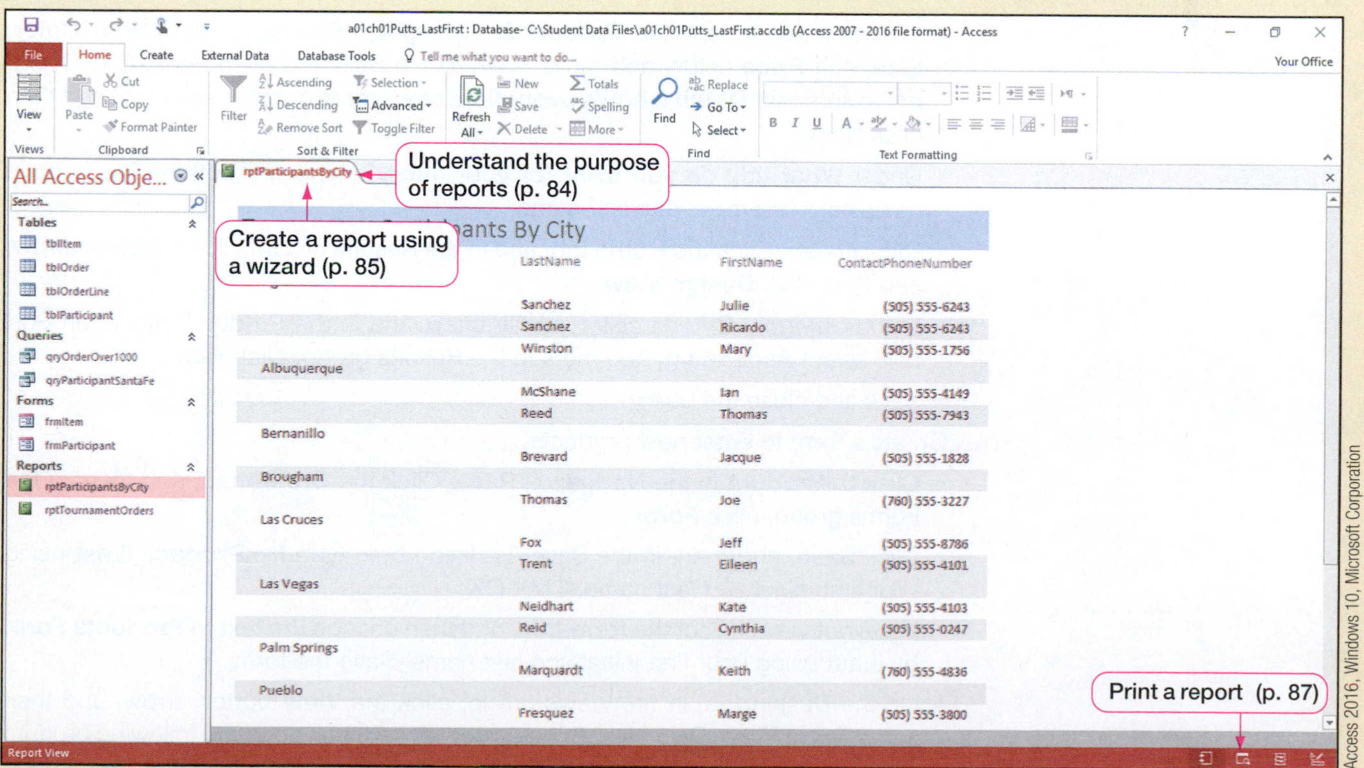

Figure 35

Practice 1

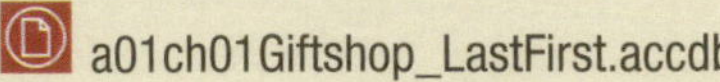

Student data files needed:

a01ch01Giftshop.accdb

a01ch01Products.accdb

You will save your file as:

a01ch01Giftshop_LastFirst.accdb

Painted Treasures Gift Shop

Production & Operations

The Painted Treasures Gift Shop sells many products for the resort patrons. These include jewelry from local artists, Painted Paradise linens, products from the resort's restaurant, and spa products. You will create a database that stores the gift shop's products. You will import a table of products from another Access database and create a query to select particular products. You will also create a form to enter new products and an inventory report.

a. Open the Access file, **a01ch01Giftshop**. Save your file as **a01ch01Giftshop_LastFirst**, using your last and first name. If necessary, enable the content.

b. Click the **External Data** tab, and then, in the Import & Link group, click **Access**.

c. In the Get External Data - Access Database dialog box, click **Browse**, navigate through the folder structure to the location of your student data files, double-click **a01ch01Products**, and then click **OK**.

d. In the Import Objects dialog box, select **tblProduct** on the Tables tab, and then click **OK**.

e. Click **Close**.

f. Create a query to find the clothing products.
   - Click the **Create** tab, and then, in the Queries group, click **Query Wizard**. Be sure **Simple Query Wizard** is selected, and then click **OK**.
   - Click the **Tables/Queries** arrow, and then click **Table: tblProduct** as the source of your fields.
   - In this order, select the **ProductID**, **Category**, **ProductDescription**, **Color**, **Size**, and **Price** fields, and move them to the Selected Fields box. Click **Next**, make sure that **Detail (shows every field of every record)** is selected, and then click **Next**.
   - Under **What title do you want for your query?**, type qryClothingTypes_iLast using your first initial and last name.
   - Click **Finish**. Click the **Home** tab, and in the Results group, click the **View** arrow, and then click **Design View**.
   - In the Category Criteria cell, type Clothing, and in the ProductDescription Sort cell, select **Ascending**, and then, in the Results group, click **Run**.
   - Save and close the query.

g. Create a form to enter new products.
   - Click **tblProduct** in the Navigation Pane. Click the **Create** tab, and then, in the Forms group, click **Form**.
   - Click **Save**, and then, in the Save As dialog box, type **frmProduct_iLast** using your first initial and last name. Click **OK**.
   - In Layout view, select the **form title**, and then change the text to **Products Form by iLast** using your first initial and last name. Save the form.
   - On the Design tab, in the Views group, click the **View** button arrow, and then select **Form View**. Click **New (blank) record**, and then enter the following product in the blank append record.

ProductID	42
ProductDescription	Polo Shirt
Category	Clothing
QuantityInStock	35
Price	30.00
Size	L
Color	Blue

- Close the form.

h. Create an inventory report.
- Click the **Create** tab, and then, in the Reports group, click **Report Wizard**.
- Click the **Tables/Queries** arrow, and then click **Table: tblProduct**.
- Select the fields in the following order: **Category**, **ProductDescription**, **Color**, **Size**, and **QuantityInStock**, and then click **Next**.
- Under **Do you want to add any grouping levels?**, double-click **Category** and **ProductDescription**, and then click **Next**.
- In the 1 box, click the **arrow**, and then select **Color**. In the 2 box, click the **arrow**, select **Size**, and then click **Next**.
- Make sure the layout is set to **Stepped**, change the Orientation to **Landscape**, and then click **Next**.
- Type rptInventory_iLast, using your first initial and last name, as the title for your report, and then click **Finish**.
- Click **Close Print Preview.** On the Design tab, in the Views group, click the **View** arrow, and then click **Layout View**. Change the report title to Inventory Report by iLast using your first initial and last name.

i. Save the database, exit Access, and then submit your file as directed by your instructor.

Problem Solve 1

Student data files needed:

a01ch01Planner.accdb

a01ch01PlanItems.accdb

You will save your file as:

a01ch01Planner_LastFirst.accdb

Rakes Event Management

Production & Operations

Beth Rakes runs an event-planning service. She is moving toward using Access to manage her business more effectively. In one database, she tracks clients, events, and menus that each client has booked. In another database, she has many decorations reserved for events. She has hired you to consolidate the databases and make some additional changes, which will improve the database's functionality.

a. Open the Access file, **a01ch01Planner**. Save your file as a01ch01Planner_LastFirst using your last and first name. If necessary, enable the content.

b. Import the **tblEventItems** table from the **a01ch01PlanItems** Access database, located with your student data files.

c. Import the **tblDecorations** table from the **a01ch01PlanItems** Access database, located with your student data files.

d. Open **tblClients**. In record **8**, change client **Colorado Rojas'** street address to 725 Second Avenue.

e. Create a form to enter decorations into the **tblDecorations** table, naming the form **frmDecorations**. Change the title of the form to Decorations.

f. Enter the following products as new records. Notice that you do not have to enter the DecorID or the Extended Price because Access automatically fills them in.

DecorID	DecorItem	Color	Category	Quantity	Price	Extended Price
Access automatically fills	Balloons	Red	Miscellaneous	12	1.99	Automatically calculated
Access automatically fills	Balloons	White	Miscellaneous	12	1.99	Automatically calculated

g. **Save** and **close** the form.

h. Create a query for Beth to use to retrieve information on all the different balloon decorations available for events. Use the Query Wizard to create a query listing **DecorID**, **DecorItem**, **Color**, **Quantity**, and **Price** from tblDecorations. Save your query as qryBalloonDecorations.

i. Switch to Design view, and type Balloons in the Criteria row for the DecorItem field. Run the query to observe the results. Save and close the query.

j. Create a query that will return the various types of buffet meals offered for events. Using the Query Wizard, create a query that selects **MenuType**, **CostPerPerson**, and **ServiceType** from tblMenuChoice. Save your query as qryBuffetMeals.

k. Switch to Design view, and type Buffet in the Criteria row for the ServiceType field. Sort the results by **CostPerPerson** in ascending order. Run the query to observe the results. Save and close the query.

l. Create a report showing **EventDate**, **EventName**, **StartTime**, **EndTime**, **Location,** and **TotalAttendees** from tblEvents. Do not add any grouping levels. Sort by **EventDate** and then **EventName** in ascending order. Change to **Landscape** orientation. Name your report rptEvents. In Layout view, change the report title to read Event Report.

m. Save the database, exit Access, and then submit your file as directed by your instructor.

Perform 1: Perform in Your Career

Student data file needed:

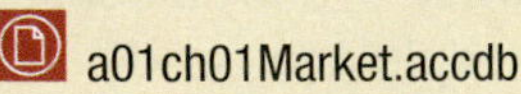

a01ch01Market.accdb

You will save your file as:

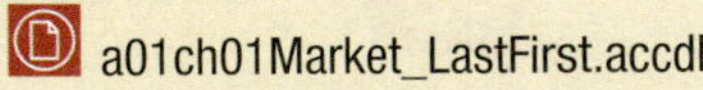

a01ch01Market_LastFirst.accdb

Farmer's Market

Production & Operations

You are the owner of a small herb business that cultivates various herbs to sell at the local farmer's market. All of the data from the sale of the herbs are stored in an Access database. You will create a form, a query, and a report to be able to make decisions from the data stored in the database.

a. Open the Access file, **a01ch01Market.accdb**. Save your file as a01ch01Market_LastFirst using your last and first name.

b. Create a form based on **tblHerb**, and name the form frmHerb_iLast using your first initial and last name. Note that since the tblHerb table has a relationship to another table, the form you create includes a subform that shows data related to orders in which the particular herb was sold.

c. Add a new record using **frmHerb_iLast**. Use the following information.

Field Name	Data
HerbID	130
HerbName	Sweet Basil
PotSize	8
Cost	6
Price	18
Light	Full Sun
Height	14"
Spacing	18"
Type	Annual
Uses	Makes Pesto
Other	Pinch flowers to keep the leaves from turning bitter.

d. Create a query based on the **tblHerb** table. Include the fields for **HerbID**, **HerbName**, **PotSize**, **Cost,** and **Price**. Name the query qryHerb_iLast using your first initial and last name. Select only the herbs that come in **8**-inch pots. Sort the results by the **Cost** field in ascending order.

e. Save and close the query.

f. Create a report based on **tblHerb**. Include the fields for **HerbID**, **HerbName**, **PotSize**, **Cost**, and **Price**.

g. Group the report by **PotSize**, and sort it in alphabetical order by **HerbName**. Save the report. Name the report rptHerb_iLast using your first initial and last name.

h. Save the database, exit Access, and then submit your file as directed by your instructor.

Additional Cases

Additional Chapter Cases are available at www.pearsonhighered.com/youroffice

Microsoft Access 2016

Chapter 2 | TABLES, KEYS, AND RELATIONSHIPS

Production & Operations

OBJECTIVES

Prepare Case

Red Bluff Golf Course Putts for Paws Charity Tournament Database

The Red Bluff Golf Course & Pro Shop is sponsoring a charity tournament, Putts for Paws, to raise money for the local pet shelter. You are modifying a database for the tournament that tracks money being raised from the event. The scope of this database is limited to tracking monies. Thus, in this instance, you are not tracking whether a participant is a golfer, volunteer, or other role. Anyone can donate money in the form of hole sponsorship or another donation item. You will want to track monies derived from corporate sponsorship. You will bring in data for the event from various sources, including Excel worksheets and text files.

Rayjunk/Shutterstock

Student data files needed for this chapter:

 a01ch02Putts.accdb

 a01ch02PuttsGolf.xlsx

 a01ch02PuttsCont.xlsx

 a01ch02PuttsVol.xlsx

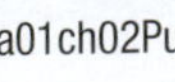 a01ch02PuttsDon.txt

You will save your file as:

 a01ch02Putts_LastFirst.accdb

Inserting Data into a Database

To manage the golf tournament, the participants, the corporations that participate, the tee times, and the items each participant purchases have to be tracked. Each of these sets of data will be entered into a separate table in the database. In this chapter, you will load tables from already existing databases and from Excel worksheets in addition to creating two new tables.

Understand Database Design

Database design can be thought of as a three-step process:

1. Identify the entities — they become the tables.
2. Identify the attributes — they become the fields.
3. Specify the relationships between the tables.

An **entity** is a person, place, item, or event for which data is to be tracked. For the Putts for Paws tournament database, data on participants, including golfers, donors, and corporate representatives, need to be tracked. The participant data will be stored in a participant table. A single participant is an instance of the participant entity and will become a record in the participant table.

An **attribute** is information about an entity. For example, for each participant, the person's name and address would be considered attributes that will need to be tracked. Each of the attributes will become a field in the table.

A **relationship** is an association between tables based on common fields. The power of Access is easily seen when relationships are created between tables. For example, a relationship can be created between the participant table and the table that contains the orders that participants place.

Later in the chapter, you will look more closely at designing a database. While you explore the database tables and data, think about these general principles or steps to follow.

1. Brainstorm a list of all the types of data you will need.
2. Rearrange data items into groups that represent a single entity. These groups will become your tables.
3. If one item can have several attributes, such as a credit card number, expiration date, name on the card, and security code, then put it into one group that will later become a table of its own. In this example, it would be a group named "credit card".
4. Break each attribute into the smallest attributes; they will become the fields. Give each attribute a descriptive name. For example, split addresses into street, city, state, and ZIP Code.
5. Do not include totals, but do include all of the data needed so the calculation can be done in a query. For example, include the price of an item and the quantity ordered so the total cost can be calculated.
6. Remove any redundant data that exists in multiple groupings. For example, do not put customer names in both the customer grouping and the sales grouping.
7. Ensure that common fields connect the groupings. For example, make sure that there is a common field between the customer grouping and the sales grouping so they can be connected. Later in this chapter, you will learn more about common fields.

Table 1 contains the attributes being tracked for the participant entity in the Putts for Paws tournament database. Next to each attribute is the data type, description, and field size for that attribute. These will be discussed later in the chapter.

Field Name	Data Type	Description	Field Size
ParticipantID	Number	A unique ID that identifies each participant	Long Integer
LastName	Short Text	Last name	25
FirstName	Short Text	First name	20
StreetAddress	Short Text	Street address	35
City	Short Text	City	25
State	Short Text	State abbreviation	2
ZipCode	Short Text	Five-digit ZIP Code	5
ContactPhoneNumber	Short Text	Phone number for the individual participant	14
CorporatePhoneNumber	Short Text	Phone number for the corporation the participant represents	14

Table 1 Fields for tblParticipant

REAL WORLD ADVICE **Break Compound Fields into Their Parts**

You might wonder why the name and address fields are divided into multiple fields. Would it not be easier to have a single field for Name and a single field for Address? It might be easier for data entry, but it is much more difficult for reporting.

- Break names into first name and last name fields. That means you can sort on people alphabetically by last name and, if two people have the same last name, by first name.
- Break addresses into fields such as StreetAddress, City, State, and ZipCode. This allows reporting by state, city, or other fields.
- For other fields, consider whether you might want to report on smaller parts of the field. For example, for PhoneNumber in some applications, you might want to report on AreaCode. However, that would be rare, so you usually use just one field.

Opening the Starting File

For the golf tournament, you will need to keep track of participants, the corporations that participate, and the items each participant purchases. There are several files that tournament organizers have been keeping about the tournament. In this exercise, you will open the main database file.

A02.00

To Open the Starting File

a. Start **Access**, click **Open Other Files** in the left pane, and then double-click **This PC**. Navigate through the folder structure to the location of your student data files, and then double-click **a01ch02Putts**. A database opens, displaying tables related to the Putts for Paws tournament.

b. Click the **File** tab, save the file as an Access database, and then click **Save As**. Navigate to the location where you are saving your project files, and then change the file name to a01ch02Putts_LastFirst using your last and first name. Click **Save**. If necessary, enable the content.

Viewing the Design View of a Table

Tables have two views: Datasheet view and Design view. Datasheet view shows the values of the data within the table. Design view shows the structure of the table with the fields and their definitions. In this exercise, you will open a table and switch to Design view to examine the table structure and field properties.

A02.01

SIDE NOTE

Pin the Ribbon

If your ribbon is collapsed, pin your ribbon open. Click the Home tab. In the lower right-hand corner of the ribbon, click Pin the Ribbon.

To View the Design View of a Table

a. In the Navigation Pane, double-click **tblParticipant** to open it.

When you open the tblParticipant table, it opens in Datasheet view. In Datasheet view, you can see the information about the participants.

b. On the Home tab, in the Views group, click the **View** arrow, and then select **Design View**. When you switch to Design view, you see the structure of the fields and the field properties.

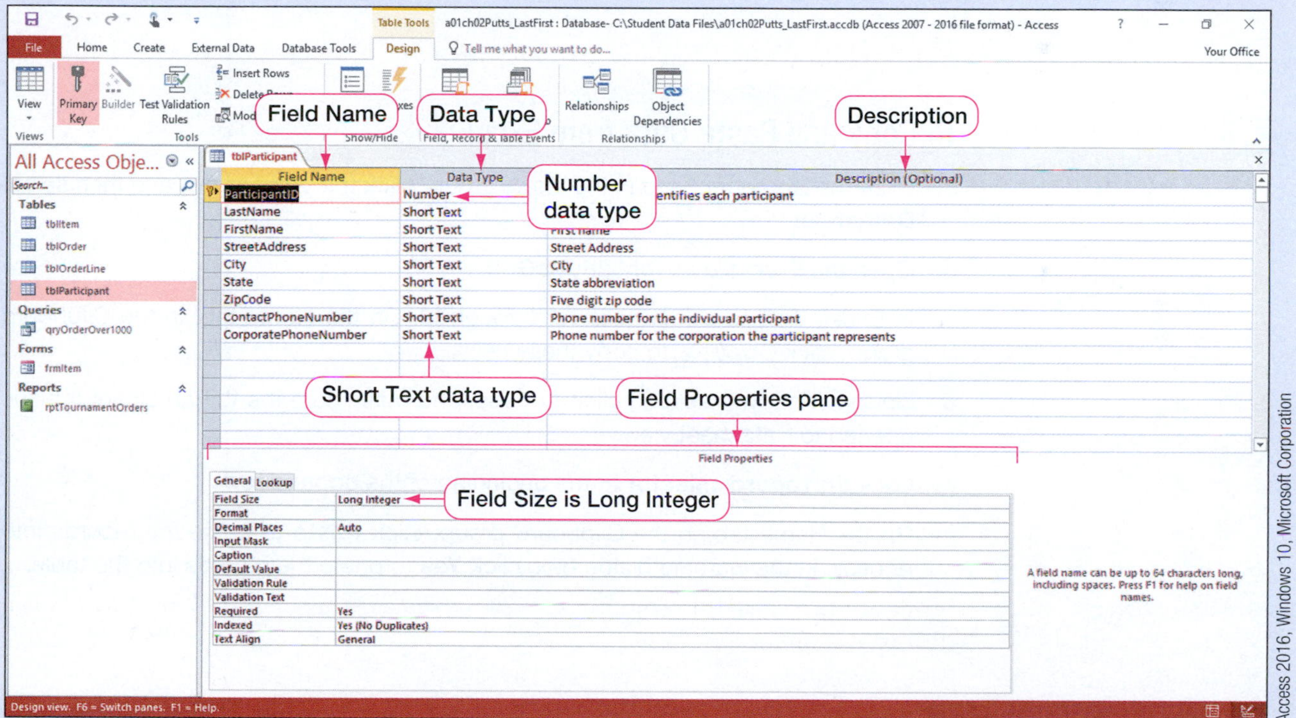

Figure 1 Design view of tblParticipant

The upper pane of Design view has three columns: Field Name, Data Type, and Description. The Field Name is the column label in Datasheet view. **Data types** define the kind of data that can be entered into a field, such as numbers, text, or dates. The data type tells Access how to store and display the field. Number and Short Text are the two most common data types. In this table, you can see that one field is stored as a **Number data type**. That means the data can contain only numeric characters. The **Short Text data type** allows any text and numeric characters to be stored. StreetAddress is the Short

Text data type, so a street address in this database can contain numbers, letters, and special characters. The third column, Description, helps the user to discern the meaning of the field.

The Field Properties pane in Design view gives more information on how the data is stored, entered, and processed. If the ParticipantID field is selected, you can see that its Field Size is Long Integer.

Import Data from Other Sources

The Red Bluff Golf Course & Pro Shop has had different employees collecting data in different ways. Luckily, the applications in the Microsoft Office suite work together. This allows you to import and export — transfer data — easily between Excel and Access. You will import the files from Excel, Access, and Notepad. After importing the data, you will be able to further analyze and refine the table structure for the database. Even though other employees have kept track of the roles that each participant plays, remember that the scope of this database does not include tracking the participants' roles in the event. You are tracking only corporate involvement.

Copying and Pasting Data from Excel

Only a few golfers were entered into the tblParticipant table. Some others were put in an Excel worksheet. In this exercise, you will copy and paste them from Excel into your Access table.

To Copy and Paste Data from Excel

a. Click the **Home** tab, and in the Views group, click the **View** arrow, and then select **Datasheet View**.

b. Open the Excel file **a01ch02PuttsGolf**.

c. In Excel, drag to select **cells A1** through **I9**. On the Home tab, in the Clipboard group, click **Copy** to copy these cells.

d. On the Windows taskbar, click **Access**, and make sure the tblParticipant table is opened to Datasheet view.

e. Click the **record selector** at the beginning of the append row.

f. On the Home tab, in the Clipboard group, click **Paste** to paste the records into Access. In the warning dialog box, click **Yes** to paste the records into the table.

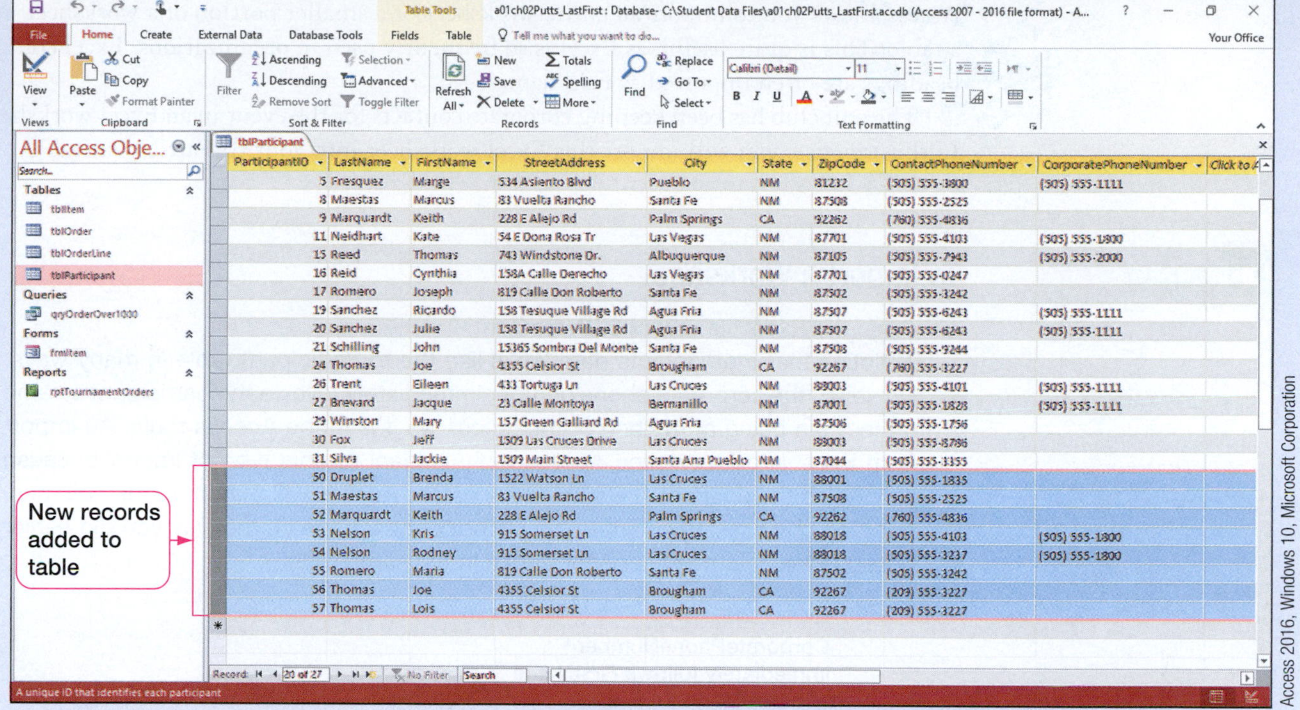

Figure 2 New records added to the tblParticipant table

Troubleshooting

If you accidentally click in a single cell of the append row and try to paste there, you get the error message "The text is too long to be edited." It appears that you are trying to paste all the data into one cell, and Access will not let you continue. If this happens, click OK, indicating that you do not want to put all the text into the one cell.

After that, it may be difficult to exit that row and click in the record selector column. It appears you are trying to paste an invalid row, and Access will not let you continue. You will get an error message saying, "Index or primary key cannot contain a Null value." When you click OK and try to recover, the message will reappear. If this happens, press Esc, indicating that you do not want to keep that record.

g. On the Windows taskbar, click **Excel**, and then **close** ☒ Excel.

h. If necessary, on the Windows taskbar, click Access and then **Close** ☒ tblParticipant.

REAL WORLD ADVICE — Copying and Pasting from Excel into Access

If you want to copy and paste from Excel into Access, the columns must be exactly the same in the two applications. There cannot be missing columns or columns in different orders. You cannot paste fields that are nonnumeric into numeric fields. If you have any doubt about the data being compatible, use the Import feature to append the data to the table.

Use Copy and Paste in these situations.

- You started in Access and exported the data to Excel, made additions, and now want to import the data into Access. That way, you know the columns are the same.
- You are copying and pasting the contents of a single field from Excel into Access, such as a street address.

Importing a Worksheet

Access allows you to import an entire worksheet or a smaller portion of a worksheet into a table. This is quite useful, as Excel is so frequently used in organizations. Excel column headings are often imported as field names.

The golf club has been keeping corporate contacts for the event in an Excel worksheet. In this exercise, you will import this Excel worksheet into your tblParticipant table.

To Import a Worksheet

a. Open the Excel file, **a01ch02PuttsCont**.

Notice that the contacts data looks like the tblParticipant table in many ways. However, the corporate phone number immediately follows the participant's name rather than being at the end of the record, as it is in the Access table. An import from Excel into an existing Access table is ideal for this type of import because as long as the columns have the same name, Access will match up the columns, skipping any missing column. You cannot copy and paste the way you did earlier because the columns are not arranged in the same order.

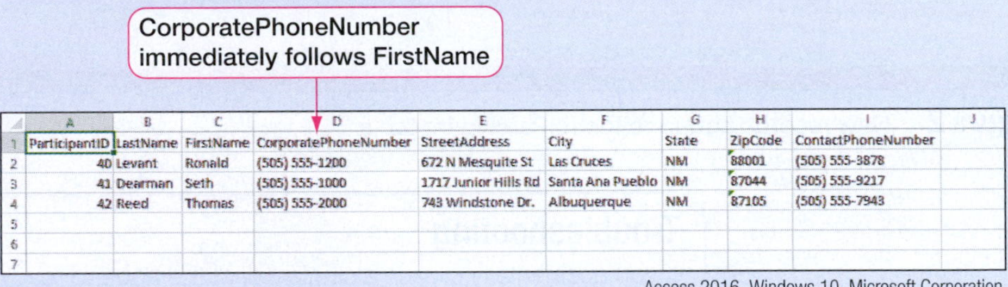

ParticipantID	LastName	FirstName	CorporatePhoneNumber	StreetAddress	City	State	ZipCode	ContactPhoneNumber
40	Levant	Ronald	(505) 555-1200	672 N Mesquite St	Las Cruces	NM	88001	(505) 555-3878
41	Dearman	Seth	(505) 555-1000	1717 Junior Hills Rd	Santa Ana Pueblo	NM	87044	(505) 555-9217
42	Reed	Thomas	(505) 555-2000	743 Windstone Dr.	Albuquerque	NM	87105	(505) 555-7943

Access 2016, Windows 10, Microsoft Corporation

Figure 3 Contact data in Excel

b. **Close** ☒ Excel.

c. In Access, click the **External Data** tab, and then, in the Import & Link group, click **Excel**.

The Get External Data - Excel Spreadsheet dialog box appears.

d. Click **Browse**, navigate through the folder structure to the location of your student data files, and then double-click **a01ch02PuttsCont**.

e. Select **Append a copy of the records to the table**, click the **arrow**, select **tblParticipant**, and then click **OK**.

The Import Spreadsheet Wizard opens, which displays worksheets and named ranges in the Excel workbook.

f. Make sure **Show Worksheets** is selected and the **Corporate contacts** worksheet is highlighted, and then click **Next**.

Access displays the next page of the wizard. This shows that Access found the column headings in Excel and matched them to the field names in Access.

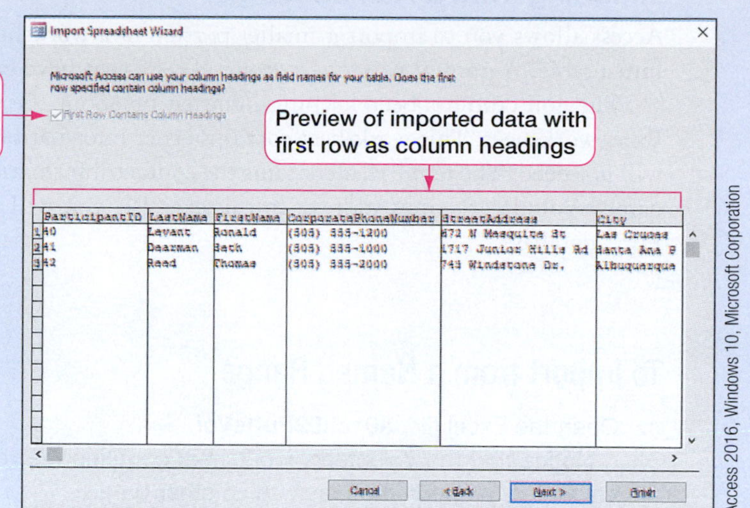

Figure 4 Worksheet to be imported

> **SIDE NOTE**
> **Records Are Sorted by the Primary Key**
> When you added the contacts, they were added in the middle of the table because Access orders records in tables by the primary key field.

g. Click **Next**, click **Finish**, and then click **Close**.

h. In the Navigation Pane, double-click **tblParticipant** to open the table.

Your table has the three corporate contacts added. The contacts were imported, and because the field names in Access matched the Excel column headings, the fields were rearranged to match the Access table order.

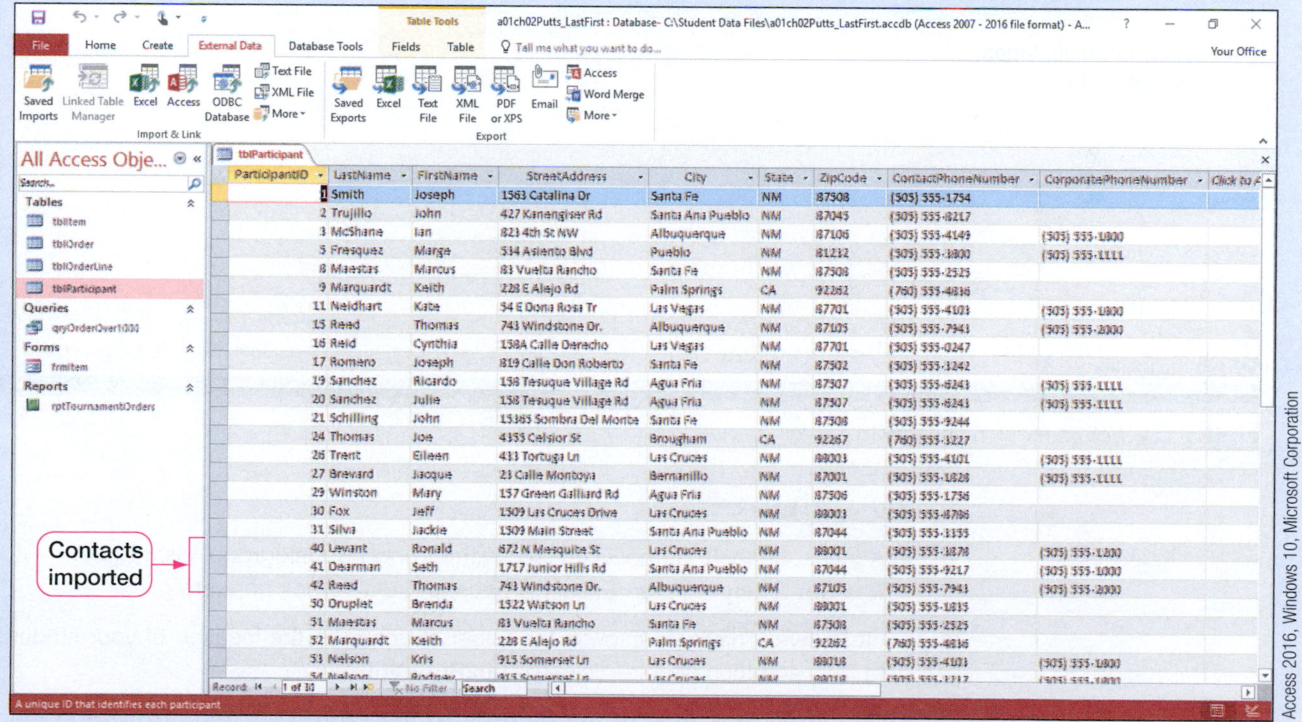

Figure 5 Corporate contacts imported into the tblParticipant table

i. **Close** [X] tblParticipant.

Importing from a Named Range

Access allows you to import a smaller portion of a worksheet, known as a named range, into a table. A **named range** is a group of cells that have been given a name.

The golf club has been keeping information about the volunteers for the event in an Excel worksheet. This worksheet contains other information about volunteering that you will not need. The range that contains the contact information for the volunteers has been named VolunteerNamesAddress. In this exercise, you will import those records into the Putts database.

A02.04

To Import from a Named Range

a. Open the Excel file, **a01ch02PuttsVol**.

Notice that the Volunteers worksheet contains the volunteer information, in the Volunteers named range, as well as other data.

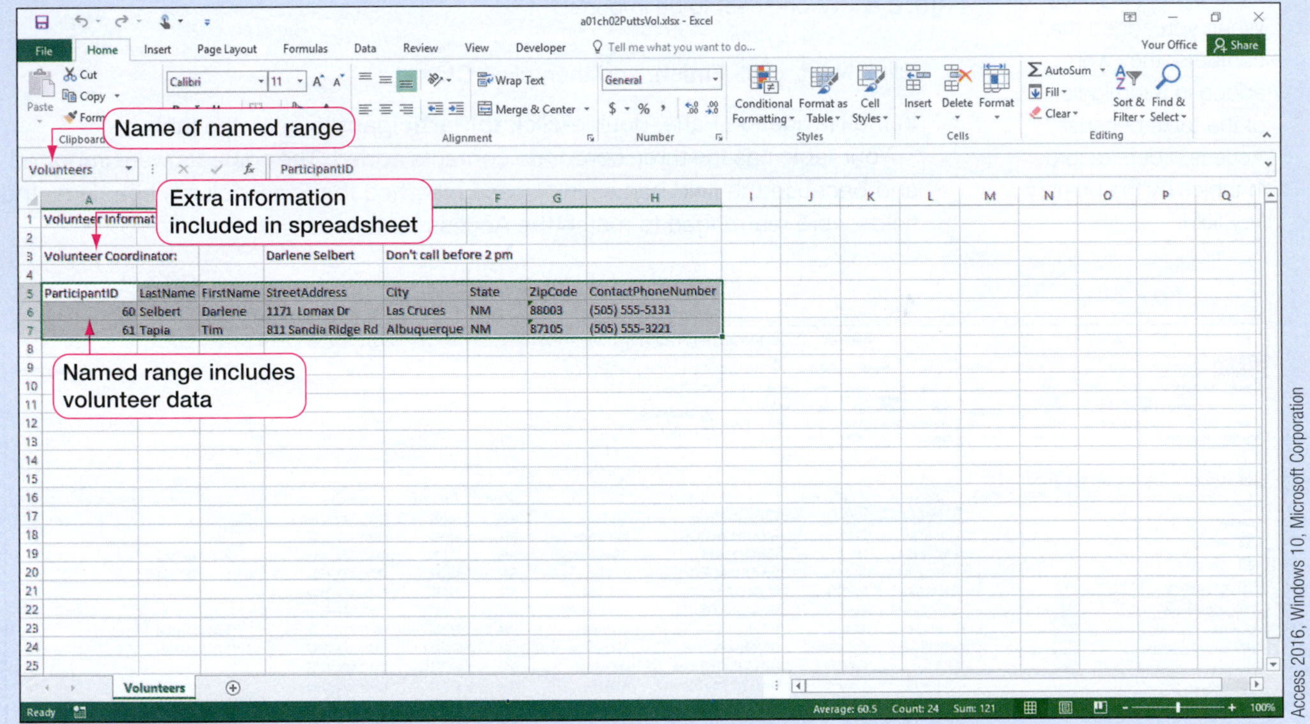

Figure 6 Volunteer worksheet with extra information

b. **Close** [X] Excel.

c. In Access, on the External Data tab, in the Import & Link group, click **Excel**.

The Get External Data - Excel Spreadsheet dialog box appears.

d. Click **Browse**, navigate through the folder structure to the location of your student data files, and then double-click **a01ch02PuttsVol**.

e. Select **Append a copy of the records to the table**, click the **arrow**, and then select **tblParticipant**.

f. Click **OK**, and then click **Show Named Ranges**.

One named range, VolunteerNamesAddress, is displayed and highlighted in the list box.

g. Click **Next**. Access tells you that it found your column headings in Excel and matched them to the field names in Access. Click **Next**.

h. Click **Finish**, and then click **Close**.

i. In the Navigation Pane, double-click **tblParticipant** to open the table. Your table has the two volunteers added for a total of 32 volunteers.

j. **Close** [X] the tblParticipant table.

Importing from a Text File

Access enables you to import data from text and Word files. Typically, these files would have data organized in tables. In Word, these tables will have actual rows and columns. In text files, the tables are implied by the separation of the columns. This separation is done by delimiter characters. A **delimiter** is a character such as a tab or comma that separates the fields. The rows in the text tables will be imported as records into your Access table.

The golf course has been keeping information about the donors for the event in a text file. In this exercise, you will import those records into the Putts database.

To Import from a Text File

a. Open the text file **a01ch02PuttsDon**.

Notice that there are three donors in this file. The fields are separated by unseen tabs.

> **Troubleshooting**
>
> Your columns may not line up the way Figure 7 shows them lining up. This happens because Notepad does not save font formatting. Notepad does save tabs, so you do not need to worry about any display differences.

Three donors in text file

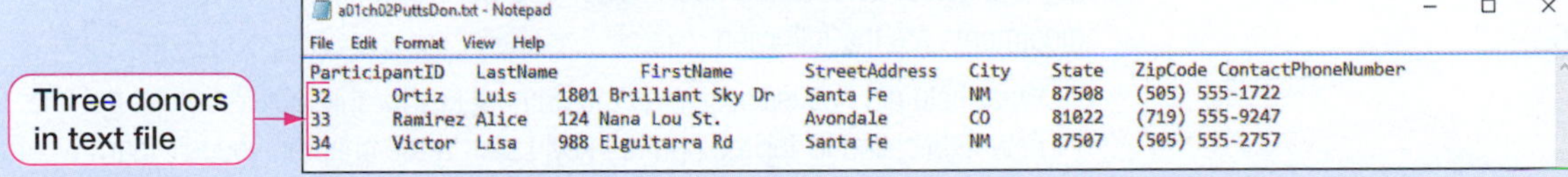

a01ch02PuttsDon.txt - Notepad

File Edit Format View Help

ParticipantID	LastName	FirstName	StreetAddress	City	State	ZipCode	ContactPhoneNumber
32	Ortiz	Luis	1801 Brilliant Sky Dr	Santa Fe	NM	87508	(505) 555-1722
33	Ramirez	Alice	124 Nana Lou St.	Avondale	CO	81022	(719) 555-9247
34	Victor	Lisa	988 Elguitarra Rd	Santa Fe	NM	87507	(505) 555-2757

Access 2016, Windows 10, Microsoft Corporation

Figure 7 Donor text file in Notepad

b. **Close** [X] Notepad.

c. In Access, on the External Data tab, in the Import & Link group, click **Text File**.

The Get External Data - Text File dialog box appears.

d. Click **Browse**, navigate through the folder structure to the location of your student data files, and then double-click **a01ch02PuttsDon**.

e. Click **Append a copy of the records to the table**, click the **arrow** to select **tblParticipant**, and then click **OK**.

f. Click **Next**, make sure that the **Tab** delimiter is selected, and then click to select the **First Row Contains Field Names** check box.

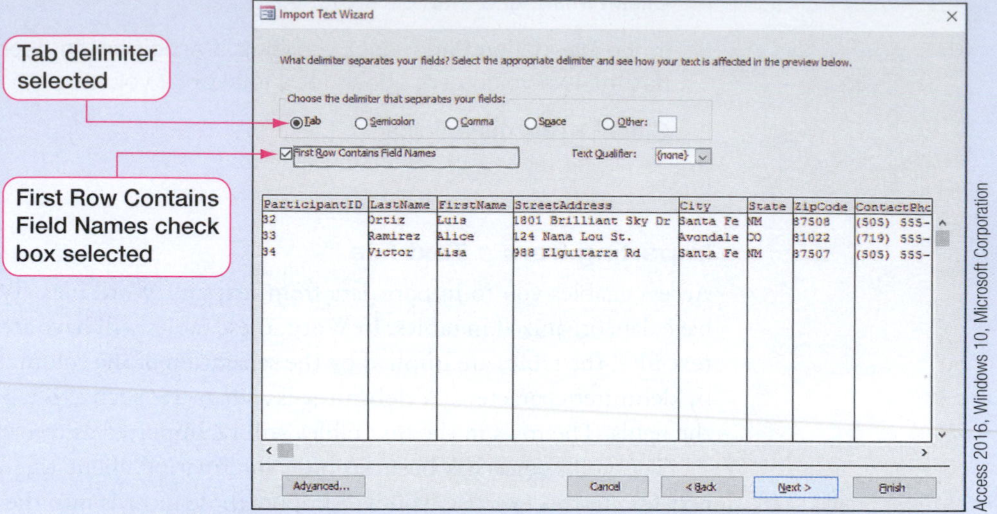

Figure 8 Tab delimiter Delimited with First Row Contains Field Names

g. Click **Next**, and then click **Finish**.

h. Click **Close**. Double-click **tblParticipant** to open the table, and verify that the records for Luis Ortiz, Alice Ramirez, and Lisa Victor were imported.

REAL WORLD ADVICE **Importing an Excel Worksheet into a New Table**

In all the previous examples of importing, you imported into an already existing table. You can also import into a new table. Access creates a table using the column headings for field names. Access defines fields with default definitions. After performing the import, open the table in Design view and adjust fields and properties as necessary. Some things that you should consider in these adjustments are the following.

- What field did Access assign as the primary key for the table? Access defaults to creating a new field called ID for the primary key. Later in the chapter, you will learn what field might work better as a primary key.
- The default length for all short text fields is 255 characters. Adjust the field size properties to sizes that are appropriate for your fields. Check all field definitions for errors.
- Are the field names descriptive? The column headings from Excel might not be appropriate as field names in Access.

Enter Data Manually

If the data does not already exist in another form, you can type the data directly into Access. There are two methods: entering data directly into the table or entering the data in a form.

Entering Data Using Datasheet View

When you open a table in Datasheet view, you can type data directly into the table. In this exercise, you will add a new participant to the tournament by creating a new record in the tblParticipant table.

A02.06

To Enter Data Using Datasheet View

a. In the tblParticipant table, click in the **ParticipantID** column of the append row, and then type 62.

As you type the "62", a pencil icon appears in the record selector on the left. The pencil icon means that this record is actively being modified.

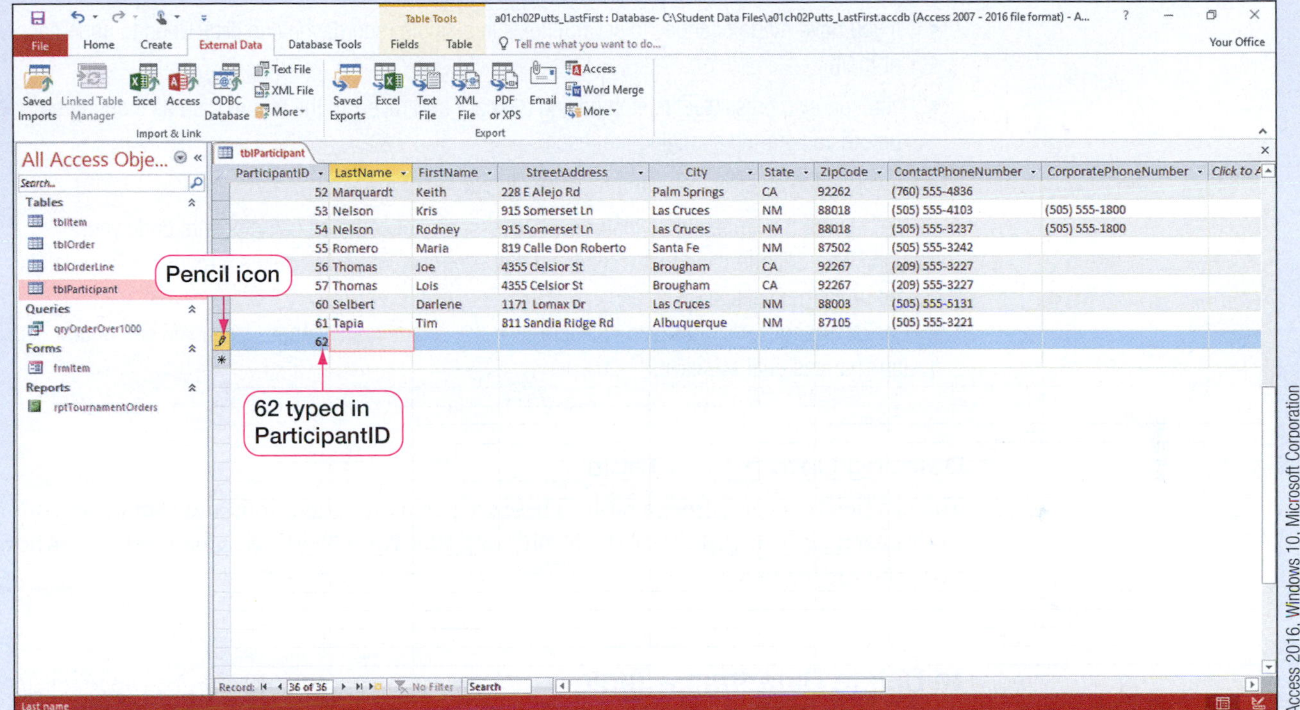

Figure 9 Type 62 in ParticipantID

b. Press Tab to continue filling in the record using the following data.

LastName	FirstName	Street Address	City	State	ZipCode	ContactPhone Number
Gupta	Sanjay	3544 Cornice Blvd	Las Cruces	NM	88001	5055557789

c. Press Tab to go to the next field, and press Tab again to go to the next record. The pencil icon disappears. Unlike Word and Excel, Access immediately saves the data change.

REAL WORLD ADVICE — Undoing in Access

Access immediately saves the changes you make to data. There is very limited undo/redo functionality in Access. If the Undo button [↶] is dimmed, you cannot undo the change you made.

- Typically, you can undo a single typing change even if you have gone on to the next record. However, if you made several changes to different records, you cannot undo more than the changes to the last record.
- If you have made changes to several fields in a single record, you can click Undo to undo each of them.
- You can also press Esc to stop editing a record and revert to the record data as it appeared before you started changing the record.
- If you make an error, you can press Esc to get out of the error.

Because of the limited undo features in Access, do not count on being able to undo your changes. You will often find that you cannot. For example, when you delete a record or records, you cannot undo the deletion.

Design changes are not saved until you save the object you changed. Thus, you can undo design changes until you save.

Deleting Data from a Table

You can delete records from a table. These are permanent deletions and cannot be undone. In this exercise, you will delete the record for golfer Kate Neidhart, who needs to withdraw from the tournament.

To Delete Data from a Table

a. In the tblParticipant table, click the **record selector** for record 7, Kate Neidhart, ParticipantID 11, to select the row.

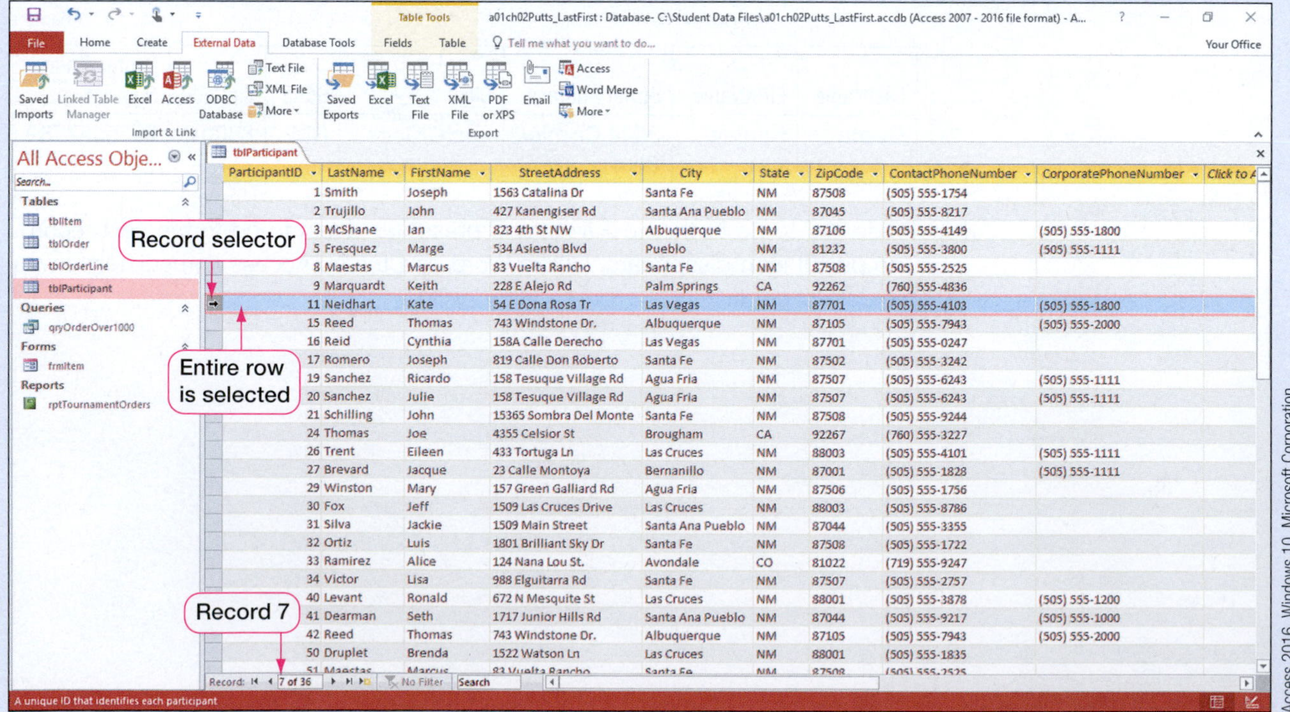

Figure 10 Delete Kate Neidhart's record

b. Right-click the **row**, and then select **Delete Record**.

Because you cannot undo a delete, Access asks whether you are sure you want to delete this record.

c. Click **Yes**. The record is deleted.

> **Troubleshooting**
>
> If you do not get the Access confirmation message asking whether you are sure you want the deletion to occur, the confirmation message setting may be turned off. If you would like to turn it back on, on the File tab, click Options, and then click Client Settings. Scroll down to find the Confirm section under Editing, click the Document deletions check box, and click OK.

Deleting a Field from a Table

You can also delete individual fields from a table. These are also permanent deletions and cannot be undone. The design of the database will be changed to track individual participants separate from corporations. Later in this chapter, you will create a table for the corporations involved with the tournament and include the CorporatePhoneNumber field there. In this exercise, you will delete the CorporatePhoneNumber field from the tblParticipant table. You can delete a field in either Design view or Datasheet view. In Datasheet view, you can see the contents of the field that you are deleting, which gives you an extra check on whether you really want to delete the field.

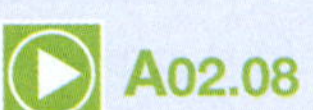

To Delete a Field from a Table

a. In the tblParticipant table, scroll to the right to find the **CorporatePhoneNumber** column. Point to the **column heading** until it changes to a black down arrow, and then click so the entire column is highlighted. Make sure that you selected **CorporatePhoneNumber** and not **ContactPhoneNumber**.

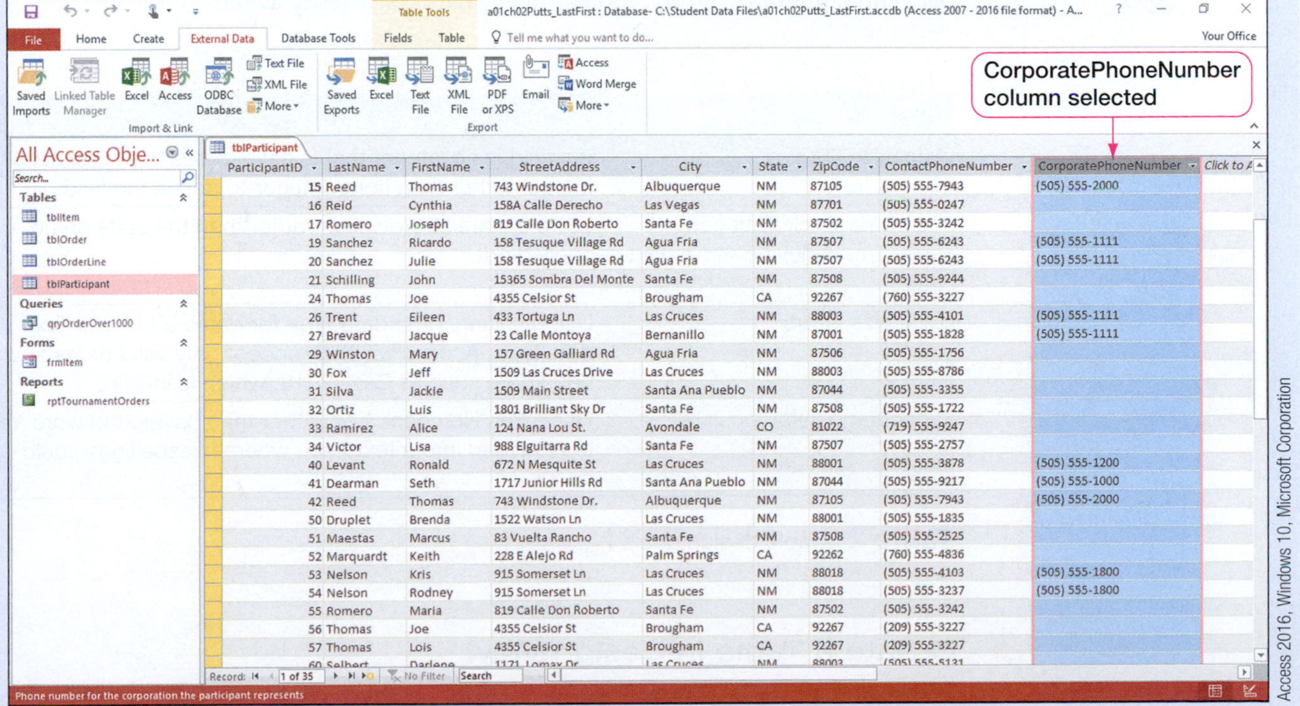

Figure 11 Select the CorporatePhoneNumber column

b. Click the **Home** tab, and then in the Records group, click **Delete**.

Because you cannot undo a deletion, Access asks, "Do you want to permanently delete the selected field(s) and all the data in the field(s)? To permanently delete the field(s), click Yes." Because you are in Datasheet view, you can glance at it and make sure this is the data you want to delete.

c. Click **Yes**. The column is deleted.

d. **Close** [X] tblParticipant.

Troubleshooting

If, when you clicked in the column heading, you accidentally double-clicked and then clicked Delete, Access blanked out the field name rather than deleting the column. This put you in edit mode, ready to rename the field. Press Esc to cancel edit mode and try again.

e. If you need to take a break before finishing this chapter, now is a good time.

Understanding Tables and Keys

The database needs to be further examined and evaluated with regard to how the tables have been set up. Tables represent entities — or people, places, things, or events that you want to track. Each row represents a single person, place, or other entity. To identify that entity, a primary key field is typically used. A **primary key** field is a field that uniquely identifies the record; it can be any data type, but it should be a field that will not change. For example, a person's name is not a good primary key for two reasons. First, it is not unique — several people may have the same name. Second, a person's name could change. If you define a primary key for a table, the field cannot be blank.

In this section, you will create a table from scratch, minimize file size, facilitate quick data entry, minimize errors, and encourage data consistency as shown in Table 2.

Goal	Example
Minimize file size	If a field is an integer that is always less than 32,767, use Integer rather than Long Integer to define the field.
Facilitate quick data entry, including removing redundant data	Store a state abbreviation rather than the state name spelled out.
Minimize errors	Use the Date/Time data type for dates and not a Text data type. Access will then accept only valid dates and not a date such as 2/31/2018, which is invalid.
Encourage data consistency	Use a Yes/No check box rather than having the word Yes or No typed into a text field, where misspellings could occur.

Table 2 Table design goals

Create a Table in Design View

You want to keep track of corporations that are involved with the tournament. You do not have a source that you can import, so you will need to design and create the table. You will use Design view to enter fields, data types, and descriptions.

Defining Data Types

Data types define the kind of data that can be entered into a field, such as numbers, text, or dates. The data type tells Access how to store and display the field.

QUICK REFERENCE | **Data Types**

Data Type	Description	Examples
Short Text	Used to store textual or character information. Any character or number can be entered into this type of field. You should store any data that will never be used in calculations, such as a Social Security number, as text, not a number. There is an upper limit of 255 characters that can be stored in a Short Text field.	Names, addresses
Long Text	Used to capture large amounts of text. Can store up to 1 gigabyte of characters, of which you can display 65,535 characters in a control on a form or report. This is a good data type to use if you need more than 255 characters in one field.	Comments
Number	Used for numeric data.	Quantity
Date/Time	Used to store a date and/or time.	Start time
Currency	A numeric value that is used for units of currency. It follows the regional settings preset in Windows to determine what the default currency should be. In the United States, the data is displayed with a dollar sign and two decimal places.	Salary
AutoNumber	Used for keys. Access generates the value by automatically incrementing the value for each new record to produce unique keys. For example, it would set the value as 1 for the first record, 2 for the next, and 3 for the third.	ProductID
Yes/No	A checked box in which an empty box is no and a checked box is yes.	EntryPaid
OLE Object	Use to attach an OLE object, such as a Microsoft Office Excel worksheet, to a record. An OLE object means that when you open the object, you open it in its original application, such as Excel. This allows cross-application editing.	SalarySpreadsheet
Hyperlink	Text or combinations of text and numbers stored as text and used as a hyperlink address.	CompanyWebsite
Attachment	Images, worksheet files, documents, charts, and other types of supported files that are attached to the records in your database, similar to attaching files to e-mail messages.	EmployeePhoto
Calculated	A field calculated from other fields in the table. A calculated field may not be edited, as it performs a calculation on other data that is entered.	GrossPay, which is calculated on the basis of HoursWorked and HourlySalary
Lookup Wizard	Lists either values retrieved from a table or query or a set of values that you specified when you created the field.	ProductType, which gives a list of valid types

REAL WORLD ADVICE | **Number or Text?**

Any character can be used in a text field. However, if you expect a field to contain only numbers, you should store the data in a text field only if the numbers will never be used in a calculation. If you store numbers as text, you cannot use them in calculations. Conversely, if you improperly store numeric text as a number, Access will remove any leading zeros. For example, you would not use ZIP Codes in calculations, so a ZIP Code should be stored as text. A person living in Boston might have a ZIP Code of 02108. If you stored the ZIP Code as a number, Access would store this as 2108.

Determining Field Size

Field size indicates the maximum length of a data field. Whenever you use a Short Text data type, you should determine the maximum number of text characters that can exist in the data to be stored. That number would then be the field size. For example, a state abbreviation can be only two characters long, so the size for this field should be 2. If you allow more than two characters, you are likely to get a mix of abbreviations and spelled-out state names. Limiting the size will limit errors in the data. There is an upper limit of 255 characters for a Short Text field. If you need more than 255 characters, use a Long Text data type.

For numeric fields, the type defines the maximum length or range of values. You should use the number size that best suits your needs. For example, if a value in a field is always going to be a whole number and is never going to be above 32,768, then Integer is the best field size. If the number is currency, you should use the Currency data type instead of Number.

QUICK REFERENCE | **Number Field Sizes**

Field Size	Description
Byte	For integers that range from 0 to 255. These numbers can be stored in a single byte.
Integer	For integers that range from –32,768 to +32,767. Must be whole numbers. Integers cannot have decimal places.
Long Integer	For integers that range from –2,147,483,648 to +2,147,483,647. Long Integers cannot have decimal places. (AutoNumber is a long integer.)
Single	For large numbers with up to seven significant digits. Can contain decimal places. Numbers can be negative or positive. For numeric floating point values that range from -3.4×10^{38} to $+3.4 \times 10^{38}$.
Double	For very large numbers with up to 15 significant digits. Can contain decimal places. Numbers can be negative or positive. For numeric floating point values that range from -1.797×10^{308} to $+1.797 \times 10^{308}$.
Decimal	For numeric values that contain decimal places. Numbers can be negative or positive. For numeric values that range from $-9.999\ldots \times 10^{27}$ to $+9.999\ldots \times 10^{27}$.

Creating a Table in Design View

In this exercise, you will create a new table to track data on the corporations participating in the tournament. You will name the table tblCorporate, add the necessary fields, define data types, add descriptions, and specify field sizes.

A02.09

To Create a Table in Design View

a. If you took a break, open the **a01ch02Putts** database.

b. Click the **Create** tab, and then, in the Tables group, click **Table Design**.
Access opens a blank table in Design view. You will enter each field in the appropriate row.

c. Type **CompanyName** for the Field Name, and then press Tab to move to the Data Type column.
Notice that Short Text is the default data type, so you do not need to make a selection to keep Short Text for this field. For other data types, click the arrow and select the data type.

d. Press Tab to move to the Description column, and then type Name of the company.

e. In the Field Properties pane, type 50 in the Field Size box.

SIDE NOTE
Select Data Type
Alternatively, you can type the first letter of the data type, and it will appear, such as "N" for Number.

SIDE NOTE
Switch Panes
You can press the F6 key to quickly switch to the Field Properties pane.

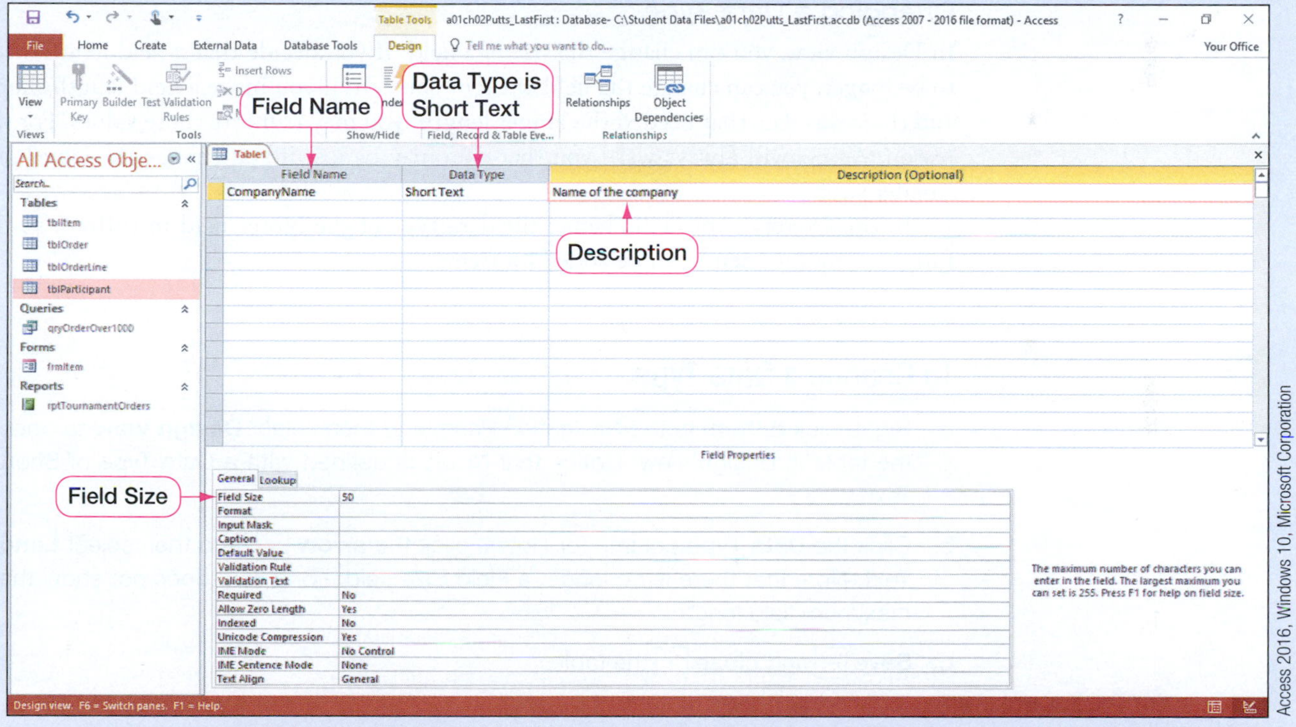

Figure 12 First field in the tblCorporate table

f. Continue defining the table with the following information.

CHAPTER 2

Field Name	Data Type	Description	Field Size
StreetAddress	Short Text	Company's street address	40
City	Short Text	Company's city	40
State	Short Text	State abbreviation	2
ZipCode	Short Text	ZIP Code either 5 or 9 character format	10
PhoneNumber	Short Text	Phone number with area code	14

g. **Save** the table, name it tblCorporate, and then click **OK**. In the warning message that asks whether you want to create a primary key, click **No**. You will define a key later.

h. **Close** tblCorporate.

Changing a Data Type

In Design view, you can change the size of a field. If you decide that a field length needs to be longer, you can change the field without concern. If you make a field length shorter and there was data that needed the longer length, you may truncate those values. For that reason, Access will always warn you that data may be lost if you change the length to a smaller size.

In this exercise, you will change the data type of the Notes field in tblItem so that full, lengthy comments can be added for items.

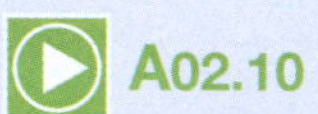

A02.10

To Change a Data Type

a. Right-click **tblItem** in the Navigation Pane, and then select **Design View** to open the table in Design view. Notice that Notes is defined with a Data Type of Short Text.

b. Click the **Data Type** column for Notes, click the **arrow**, and then select **Long Text**. Note that there is no longer a Field Size field. Long Text does not show the maximum field length.

c. **Save** and **close** the table.

Understand Masks and Formatting

One of the values of using a DBMS is that it can make sure that information is entered, stored, and displayed consistently. Masks and formatting are two of the methods that assist in that process.

Defining Input Masks

Access provides a way to consistently enter data, called input masks. For example, phone numbers can be typed (555) 555-5555, 555-5555, or 555-555-5555. An **input mask** defines a consistent template and provides the punctuation, so it does not have to be typed manually. Access also has a wizard that creates automatic masks for Social Security numbers, ZIP Codes, passwords, extensions, dates, and times. You can also create your own custom masks. Input masks can affect how data is stored. In this exercise, you will create an input mask for the PhoneNumber field in tblCorporate.

To Define an Input Mask

a. Right-click **tblCorporate** in the Navigation Pane, and then select **Design View** to open the table in Design view.

b. Click the **PhoneNumber** Field Name to select the PhoneNumber field. In the Field Properties pane, click in the **Input Mask** box.

c. Click the **Build** button [...] to start the Input Mask Wizard. If necessary, select **Phone Number**.

d. Click **Next** to start the phone number Input Mask Wizard.

Access suggests the format !(999) 000–0000. This means that the area code is optional and will be enclosed in parentheses. The rest of the phone number is required and will have a dash between the two parts. The exclamation mark specifies that characters should be typed from left to right.

e. Click **Next** to accept the format.

f. Access asks whether you want to store the symbols with the data. Select **With the symbols in the mask, like this**.

To save space, Access recommends that an input mask be saved without the symbols. However, the mask characters in this instance will not utilize much space. Keeping the symbols will add clarity for users looking at the data.

g. Click **Next**, and then click **Finish**.

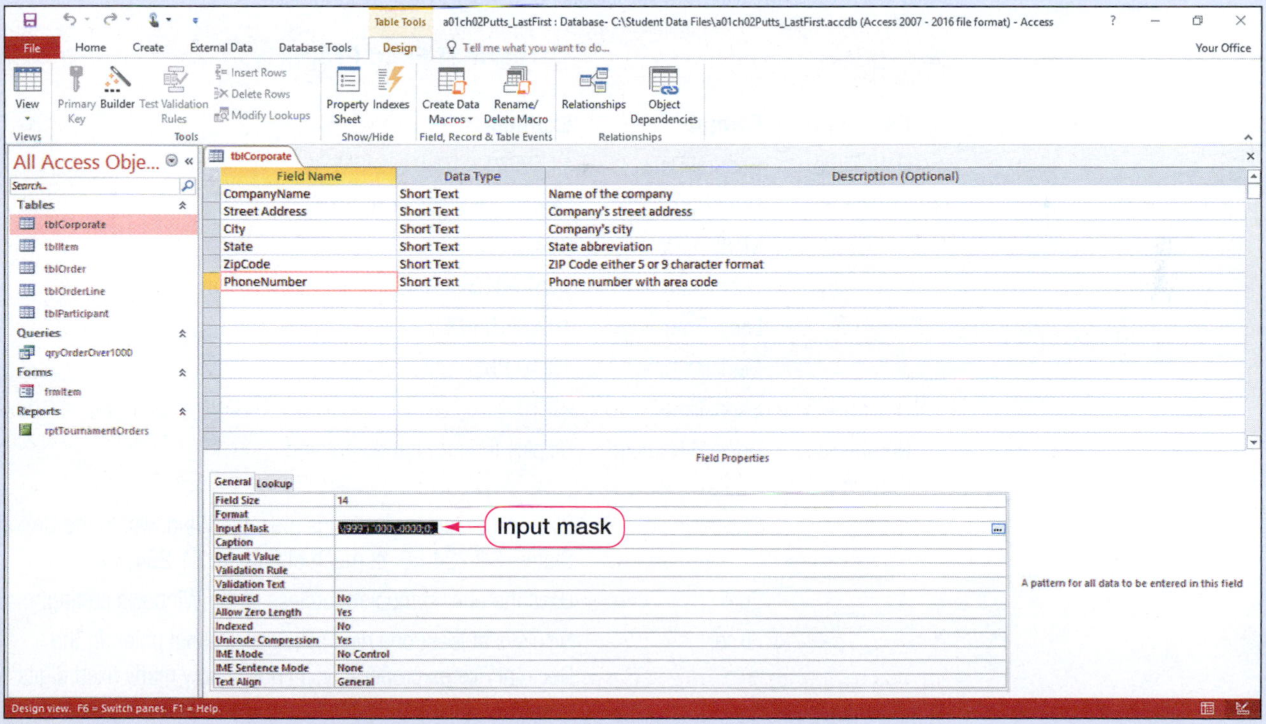

> **SIDE NOTE**
> **Semicolons in Input Mask**
> The semicolons indicate that there are three sections of the mask. The dash in the last section shows the placeholder.

Figure 13 Finished input mask

h. **Save** [save icon] the table design. On the Design tab, in the Views group, click the **View** arrow, and then select **Datasheet View**.

i. Notice that the columns are not wide enough for the entire heading text to show. Move your mouse pointer to the border between **CompanyName** and **StreetAddress** until it becomes the Horizontal resize pointer [+], and then double-click the **border** to widen the column.

j. Double-click the **border** after the **StreetAddress** and **PhoneNumber** headings to widen the columns.

k. In the append row, type Tesuque Mirage Market in the CompanyName field. Press Tab to move to StreetAddress.

l. Continue entering the records as follows.

StreetAddress	City	State	ZipCode	PhoneNumber
8 Tesuque Mirage Rd	Santa Fe	NM	87506	5055551111

Notice the input mask in the PhoneNumber makes it easier to type in phone numbers.

m. Double-click the borders in between all fields so that all data are visible. **Close** ☒ tblCorporate, and then, in the Microsoft Access dialog box, click **Yes** to save the layout.

Formatting a Field

In a table design, you can define a Format field property that customizes how data is displayed and printed in tables, queries, reports, and forms. The **Format** property tells Access how data is to be displayed. It does not affect the way the data is stored. For example, you can specify that currency fields are displayed in dollars, such as $1,234.56, in American databases or in euros, such as €1.234,56, in European databases. Formats are available for Date/Time, Number, Currency, and Yes/No data types. You can also define your own custom formats for Short Text and Long Text fields.

QUICK REFERENCE | **Format Field Property**

Data Type	Format	Example
Date/Time	General Date	11/9/2015 10:10:10 PM
	Long Date	Monday, November 9, 2015
	Medium Date	9-Nov-15
	Short Date	11/9/2015
	Long Time	10:10:10 PM
	Medium Time	10:10 PM
	Short Time	22:10
Number and Currency	General Number	Display the number as entered
	Currency	Follows the regional settings preset in Windows. In the United States, $1,234.56. In much of Europe, €1.234,56.
	Euro	Uses the euro symbol regardless of the Windows setting.
	Fixed	Displays at least one digit after the decimal point. In the Decimal Places property, you choose how many fixed digits to show after the decimal point.
	Standard	Use the regional settings preset in Windows for the thousands divider. In the United States, 1,234; in much of Europe, 1.234.
	Percent	Multiply the value by 100 and follow with %.
	Scientific	Use standard scientific notation, for example, 4.5E + 13.
Yes/No	Yes/No	Yes or No display options.
	True/False	True or False display options.
	On/Off	On or Off display options.

To Format a Field

a. In the Navigation Pane, right-click **tblOrder**, and then select **Design View**.

b. In the first **blank row**, in the Field Name column, type OrderDate. Select a Data Type of **Date/Time**, and then enter a Description of Date order was placed.

c. Click in the **Input Mask** box.

d. Click **Build** [...] to start the Input Mask Wizard. When prompted to save, click **Yes**. Select **Short Date**, and then click **Next**.
   Access suggests the format 99/99/0000. This means that the month and day are optional and that a four-character year is required. The backslashes are used to separate the month, day, and year.

e. Click **Next** to accept the format, and then click **Finish**.

f. Click in the **Format** property, click the **Format** arrow, and then select **Medium Date**.
   Notice that the Property Update Options button appears. Clicking it would display an option to change the format of OrderDate wherever else it appears. Because it does not appear anywhere else yet, you do not need to click the button.

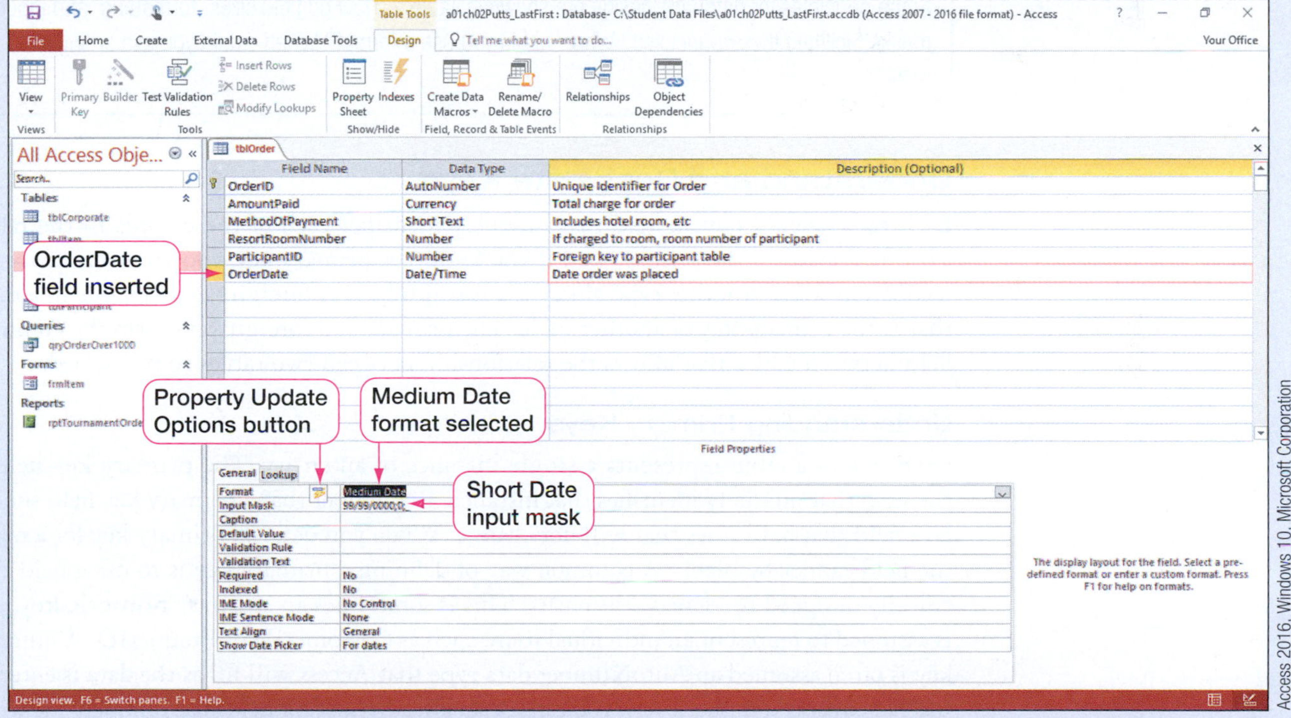

Figure 14 Input mask and formatting

g. **Save** the table design, and then, in the Views group, click the **View** button to switch to Datasheet view.
   The orders were placed on May 4, 2018, but no date was entered.

h. For the first order, in the OrderDate field, type 05042018. Press the down arrow [↓] to move to the next record.
   Notice that the input mask provides the placeholders and the backslashes, and the display changes to **04-May-18**, the medium date format.

SIDE NOTE

Copy and Paste Values

To save time and to avoid making errors, after typing the date and before moving to the next record, select 05042018, press Ctrl+C to copy, and then press Ctrl+V to paste the order date into the other orders.

Troubleshooting

When clicking inside the OrderDate field, be sure to click in the left side of the field to avoid starting in the middle of the input mask.

i. For the second order, type 05042018, and then press the down arrow ↓ to move to the next record. Again, the display changes to medium date format.

j. Continue typing 05042018 for all the orders.

Input masks are generally useful for increasing the efficiency and ensuring consistency of data entry. Formatting is useful for changing the way data appears to the end users. As you can see from the above example, having a Short Date input mask makes entering dates easier, and applying a Medium Date format makes viewing the dates easier.

k. **Close** ✕ the table.

CONSIDER THIS | Database Design Principles

Some principles for database design are shown in Table 2. How do field sizes, formatting, and input masks facilitate these principles? When would you use a format? When would you use an input mask?

Understand and Designate Keys

Each table should have a field that uniquely identifies each of the records in the table. This field is called the primary key. If you know the primary key, you know exactly what record you want. Another type of key is a **foreign key**. A foreign key is a value in a table that is the primary key of another table. The primary and foreign keys form the common field between tables that allows the relationship between two tables to be formed.

Understanding Primary Keys

Each row of a table represents a single instance of an entity. The primary key field is the field that uniquely identifies that instance. Remember that a primary key field should be a field that has values that will not change. When you define a primary key for a table, the field cannot be blank. A common way of defining a primary key is to use a field specifically designed to identify the entity. This is sometimes an arbitrary **numeric key** that is assigned to represent an individual item, such as CustomerID or ProductID. A numeric key is often assigned an AutoNumber data type that Access will fill as the data is entered. Instead of using a numeric key, you can use an already existing field that uniquely identifies the person or item, such as the person's employee ID.

REAL WORLD ADVICE | Do You Need a Primary Key?

While Access does not require a primary key for every table, you almost always want to give the table a primary key. What are the advantages of having a primary key?

- It helps to organize your data. Each record is uniquely identified.
- Primary keys speed up access to your data. Primary keys provide an index to a record. In a large table, that makes it much faster to find a record.
- Primary keys are used to form relationships between tables.

Understanding Foreign Keys

A foreign key is a field in a table that stores a value that is the primary key in another table. It is called foreign because it does not identify a record in this table; it identifies a record in another — foreign — table. For example, you have two tables, tblParticipant and tblOrder, in your database. You want to know which participants have placed certain orders. The primary key for your Participant table is ParticipantID. You can add a field called ParticipantID to the Order table that indicates which participant placed the order. ParticipantID is the foreign key in the tblOrder table; it identifies the participant in the tblParticipant table. Figure 15 illustrates this relationship. Foreign keys do not need to be unique in the table. Participants can place several orders.

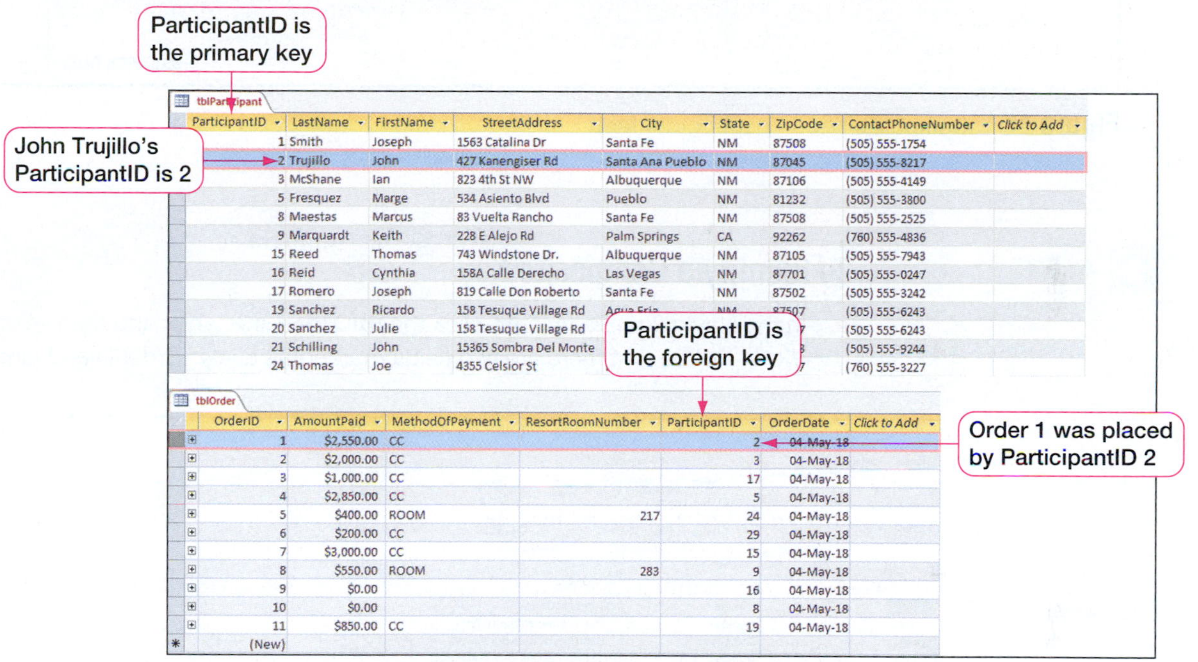

tblParticipant

ParticipantID	LastName	FirstName	StreetAddress	City	State	ZipCode	ContactPhoneNumber	Click to Add
1	Smith	Joseph	1563 Catalina Dr	Santa Fe	NM	87508	(505) 555-1754	
2	Trujillo	John	427 Kanengiser Rd	Santa Ana Pueblo	NM	87045	(505) 555-8217	
3	McShane	Ian	823 4th St NW	Albuquerque	NM	87106	(505) 555-4149	
5	Fresquez	Marge	534 Asiento Blvd	Pueblo	NM	81232	(505) 555-3800	
8	Maestas	Marcus	83 Vuelta Rancho	Santa Fe	NM	87508	(505) 555-2525	
9	Marquardt	Keith	228 E Alejo Rd	Palm Springs	CA	92262	(760) 555-4836	
15	Reed	Thomas	743 Windstone Dr.	Albuquerque	NM	87105	(505) 555-7943	
16	Reid	Cynthia	158A Calle Derecho	Las Vegas	NM	87701	(505) 555-0247	
17	Romero	Joseph	819 Calle Don Roberto	Santa Fe	NM	87502	(505) 555-3242	
19	Sanchez	Ricardo	158 Tesuque Village Rd	[illegible]	[illegible]	87507	(505) 555-6243	
20	Sanchez	Julie	158 Tesuque Village Rd	[illegible]	[illegible]	[illegible]	(505) 555-6243	
21	Schilling	John	15365 Sombra Del Monte	[illegible]	[illegible]	[illegible]	(505) 555-9244	
24	Thomas	Joe	4355 Celsior St	[illegible]	[illegible]	[illegible]	(760) 555-3227	

tblOrder

OrderID	AmountPaid	MethodOfPayment	ResortRoomNumber	ParticipantID	OrderDate	Click to Add
1	$2,550.00	CC		2	04-May-18	
2	$2,000.00	CC		3	04-May-18	
3	$1,000.00	CC		17	04-May-18	
4	$2,850.00	CC		5	04-May-18	
5	$400.00	ROOM	217	24	04-May-18	
6	$200.00	CC		29	04-May-18	
7	$3,000.00	CC		15	04-May-18	
8	$550.00	ROOM	283	9	04-May-18	
9	$0.00			16	04-May-18	
10	$0.00			8	04-May-18	
11	$850.00	CC		19	04-May-18	
(New)						

Figure 15 Relationship between the tblParticipant and tblOrder tables

Identifying a Composite Key

Sometimes, two fields are needed to uniquely identify a record. In that case, both fields are used to create the key and are called a **composite key**. For example, a university might identify a class by subject area and course number. The university could have classes Math 101, Math 102, and MIS 101. It takes both subject and course number to identify a single course.

A typical use of a composite key is on an order form. Figure 16 shows a paper form that the golf tournament organizers used before they used Access. To uniquely identify the items that have been ordered, a composite key can be made that combines the order number with the line number of the order form. In this exercise, you will identify a composite key used in the Putts for Paws tournament database.

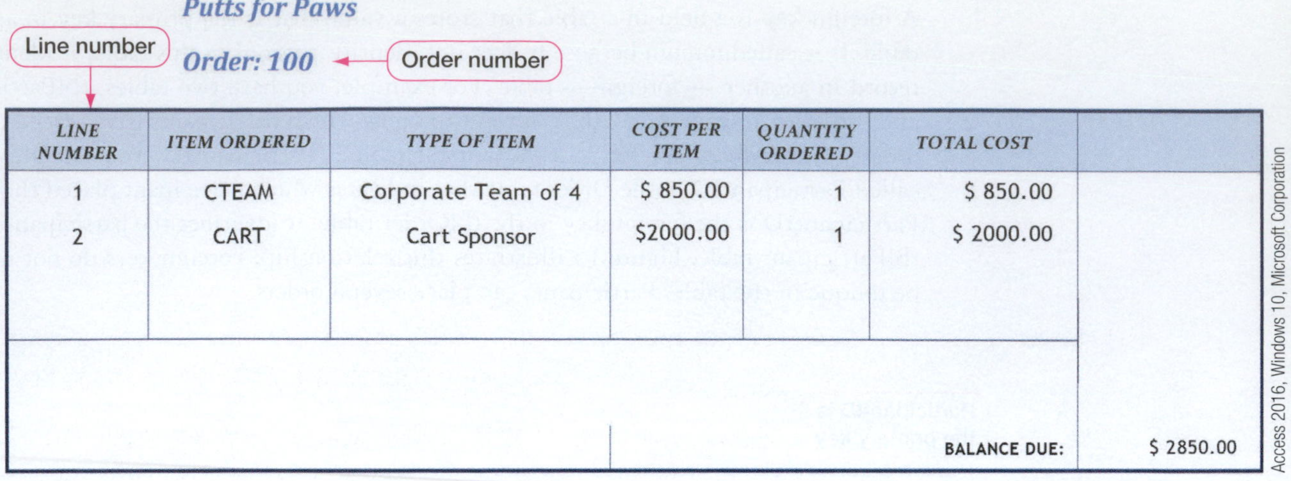

Putts for Paws

Order: 100

LINE NUMBER	ITEM ORDERED	TYPE OF ITEM	COST PER ITEM	QUANTITY ORDERED	TOTAL COST
1	CTEAM	Corporate Team of 4	$ 850.00	1	$ 850.00
2	CART	Cart Sponsor	$2000.00	1	$ 2000.00
				BALANCE DUE:	$ 2850.00

Figure 16 Composite key on paper order form

A02.13 To Identify a Composite Key

a. In the Navigation Pane, right-click the **tblOrderLine** table, and then select **Design View**. Notice that there are two fields marked as a key: OrderID and LineNum.

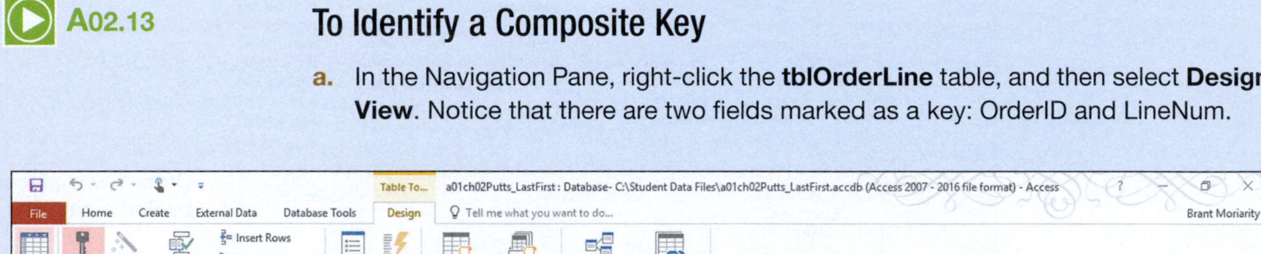

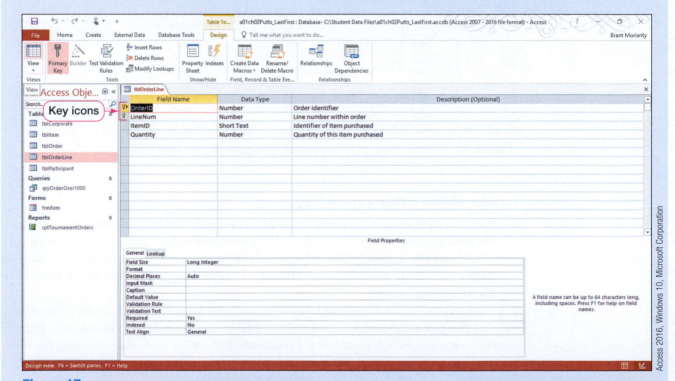

Figure 17 Composite key in the tblOrderLine table

b. **Close** [X] the tblOrderLine table.

CHAPTER 2

Defining a Primary Key

Sometimes your data will have a unique identifier that is a natural part of your data. When that is true, you can use the field as a **natural primary key**. If you already identify orders by order number, that would make a good primary key.

The important point is that the natural primary key is a value that will not change. You might start by thinking that telephone number is a natural way to identify a customer. But people change their telephone numbers. When the natural key might change, it is better to use an arbitrary unique number to identify the customer. When natural keys do exist, they are favored over numeric keys.

CONSIDER THIS | Social Security Number as a Primary Key

While a Social Security number seems like the perfect primary key, it is seldom used. What privacy concerns might arise in using Social Security numbers? Are there other issues that might arise with using Social Security numbers?

You can use the data type AutoNumber for the primary key. In that case, Access will automatically assign a unique value for every record. You can also define a key as numeric and fill the key values yourself. In this exercise, you will create a numeric primary key for the tblCorporate table.

To Define a Primary Key

a. In the Navigation Pane, right-click **tblCorporate**, and then select **Design View**.

b. On the Design tab, in the Tools group, click **Insert Rows**. Because CompanyName was the active field, a blank row is added above CompanyName.

c. Type CorporateID in the Field Name column.

d. Select **AutoNumber** as the Data Type. The field size is set to Long Integer.

e. Type Unique corporate identifier in the Description column.

f. With the CorporateID row still selected, on the Design tab, in the Tools group, click **Primary Key** to make CorporateID the primary key. A key icon is displayed in the record selector bar.

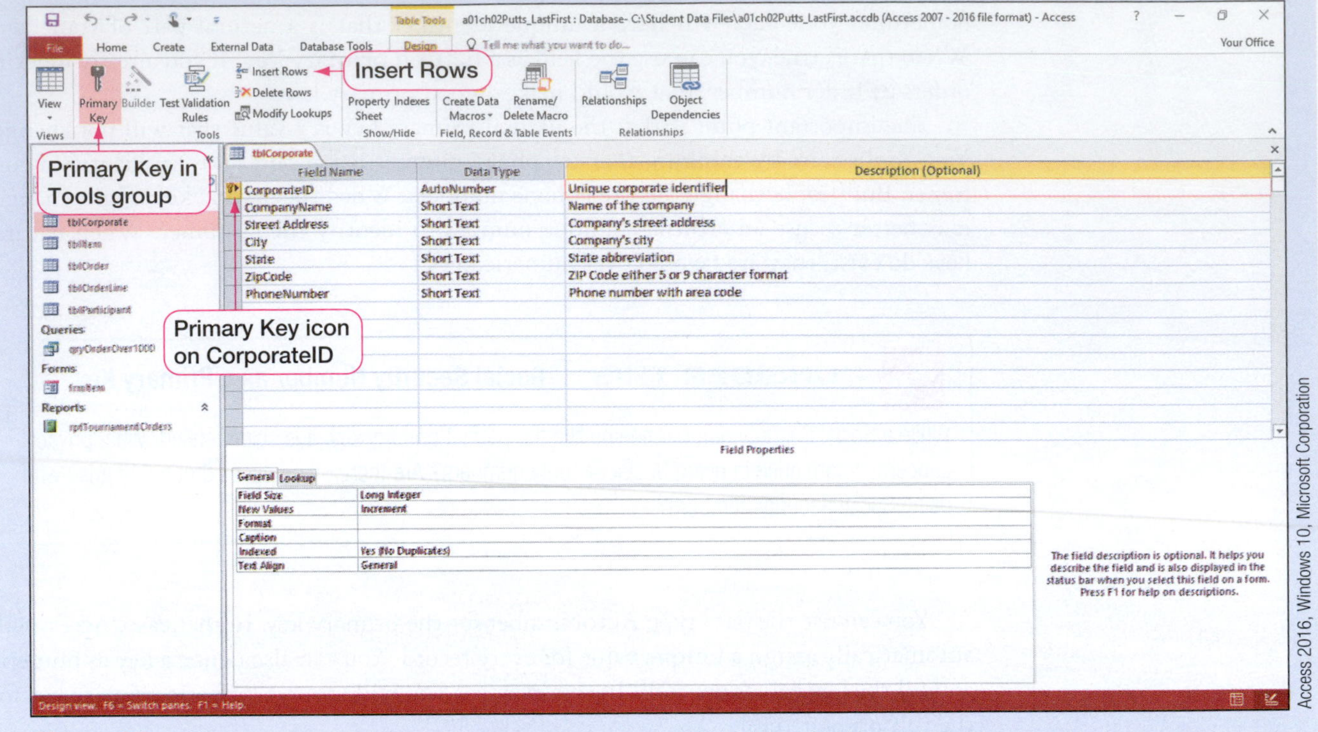

Access 2016, Windows 10, Microsoft Corporation

Figure 18 Defining a primary key

g. **Save** your table design. On the Design tab, in the Views group, click **View** to switch to Datasheet view. Notice that Access has populated the CorporateID field with an automatic number of 1. When new records are added the CorporateID field will automatically increment the value by 1.

h. **Close** the tblCorporate table. If you need to take a break before finishing this chapter, now is a good time.

REAL WORLD ADVICE **Read Error Messages**

The error message "Index or primary key cannot contain a Null value" is one example of an error message that Access displays when you make changes to an Access database that would break the rules you set up in your table design. You should read the error message carefully to understand what it is telling you.

If you get the error message "Index or primary key cannot contain a Null value," that means that one of your records has no entry in the primary key field. Enter the primary key. Often, the issue is that you accidentally entered data in the append record. If you do not want that record to be created, press Esc to cancel the addition of the record.

Understanding Relational Databases

One of the benefits of using Access is the ability to add relationships to the tables. This allows you to work with two or more tables in the same query, report, or form. For the tournament database, when you relate tables together, you can ask such questions as "Which golfers are playing for the Tesuque Mirage Market?", "Did the market agree to purchase any other items?", and "Have they paid for those items yet?"

Relationships in a relational database are created by joining the tables together. A **join** is created by establishing a relationship between two tables based on a common field in the two tables, as shown in Figure 19. The tblParticipant table has a field named ParticipantID. The tblOrder table also has a field named ParticipantID. When you create the relationship, Access will match the ParticipantID fields between the two tables to find which participants placed an order. Looking at the table, you can mentally join the two tables to see that John Trujillo has placed an order for $2,550. In this section, you will create relationships between tables, create a report, and check to make sure the relationships you are creating between the tables make sense.

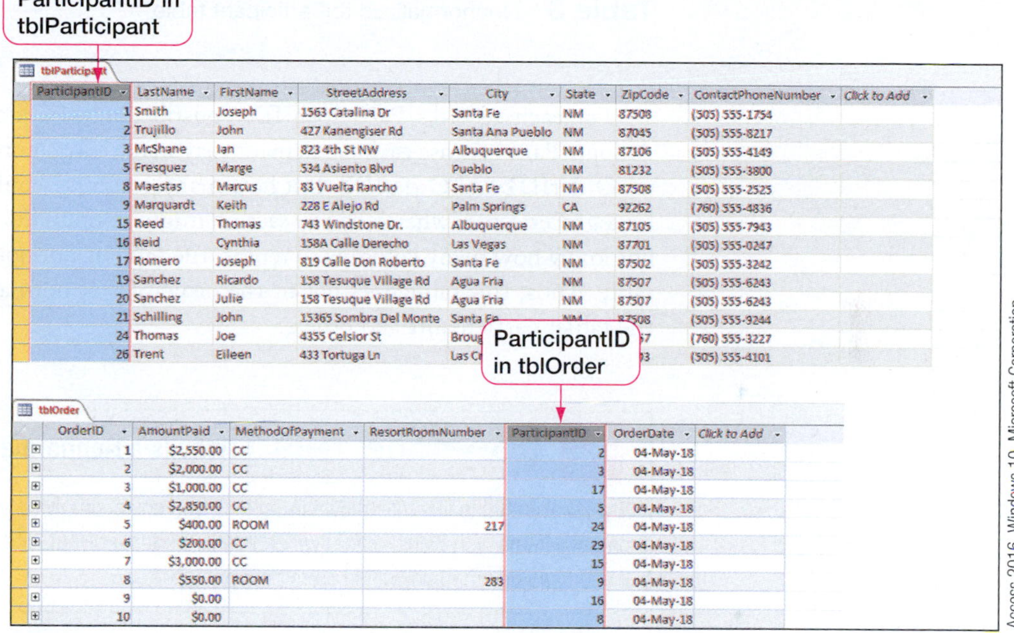

tblParticipant

ParticipantID	LastName	FirstName	StreetAddress	City	State	ZipCode	ContactPhoneNumber	Click to Add
1	Smith	Joseph	1563 Catalina Dr	Santa Fe	NM	87508	(505) 555-1754	
2	Trujillo	John	427 Kanengiser Rd	Santa Ana Pueblo	NM	87045	(505) 555-8217	
3	McShane	Ian	823 4th St NW	Albuquerque	NM	87106	(505) 555-4149	
5	Fresquez	Marge	534 Asiento Blvd	Pueblo	NM	81232	(505) 555-3800	
8	Maestas	Marcus	83 Vuelta Rancho	Santa Fe	NM	87508	(505) 555-2525	
9	Marquardt	Keith	228 E Alejo Rd	Palm Springs	CA	92262	(760) 555-4836	
15	Reed	Thomas	743 Windstone Dr.	Albuquerque	NM	87105	(505) 555-7943	
16	Reid	Cynthia	158A Calle Derecho	Las Vegas	NM	87701	(505) 555-0247	
17	Romero	Joseph	819 Calle Don Roberto	Santa Fe	NM	87502	(505) 555-3242	
19	Sanchez	Ricardo	158 Tesuque Village Rd	Agua Fria	NM	87507	(505) 555-6243	
20	Sanchez	Julie	158 Tesuque Village Rd	Agua Fria	NM	87507	(505) 555-6243	
21	Schilling	John	15365 Sombra Del Monte	Santa Fe	NM	87508	(505) 555-9244	
24	Thomas	Joe	4355 Celsior St	Broug[illegible]	[illegible]	[illegible]7	(760) 555-3227	
26	Trent	Eileen	433 Tortuga Ln	Las C[illegible]	[illegible]	[illegible]3	(505) 555-4101	

tblOrder

OrderID	AmountPaid	MethodOfPayment	ResortRoomNumber	ParticipantID	OrderDate	Click to Add
1	$2,550.00	CC		2	04-May-18	
2	$2,000.00	CC		3	04-May-18	
3	$1,000.00	CC		17	04-May-18	
4	$2,850.00	CC		5	04-May-18	
5	$400.00	ROOM	217	24	04-May-18	
6	$200.00	CC		29	04-May-18	
7	$3,000.00	CC		15	04-May-18	
8	$550.00	ROOM	283	9	04-May-18	
9	$0.00			16	04-May-18	
10	$0.00			8	04-May-18	

Figure 19 Tables joined between primary and foreign keys

Understand Basic Principles of Normalization

When you work with tables in Access, you want each table to represent a single entity and have data about only that entity. For example, you want tblParticipant to have data about participants and nothing else. You do not want to have data about the corporation they represent or the order they placed. This is why you deleted the CorporatePhoneNumber field earlier in the chapter.

Representing Entities and Attributes

Recall that an entity is a person, place, or item that you want to keep data about. The data you keep about an entity are called attributes. An entity is generally stored in a single table in a relational database. The attributes form the fields or columns of the table. **Normalization** is the process of minimizing the duplication of information in a relational database through effective database design. If you know the primary key of an entity in a normalized database, each of the attributes will have just one value. When you normalize a database, you will have multiple smaller tables, each representing a different thing. There will be no redundant data in the tables. A complete discussion of normalization is beyond the scope of this chapter, but the following sections will give you an idea of why tables should be normalized.

Table 3 shows a nonnormalized view of tblParticipant. Suppose John Trujillo places two orders: Order 1 for $2,550 and Order 2 for $500. You can easily fill in his name and address. However, when you get to the order fields, you cannot fill in the attributes with just one value. You want to enter Order 1 for Order ID and Order 2 for Order ID. You want to enter $2,550 for AmountPaid and $500 for AmountPaid. But you have only one field for each.

Participant ID	Last Name	First Name	Street Address	Other Address Fields	Order ID	Amount Paid
2	Trujillo	John	427 Kanen-giser Rd		??????	????

Table 3 Nonnormalized tblParticipant table

For each record's ParticipantID, you do not have a single value for OrderID and AmountPaid because each participant may make several orders. You could have a column for OrderID1 and OrderID2. But how many columns would you make? What if this was for a grocery store where one transaction might contain dozens of items? Any time you do not know how many columns to repeat, the table is not normalized and you need another table. Thus, this table does not fit the principles of normalization. It has two entities in the table: participants and orders.

CONSIDER THIS | **Why Is a Nonnormalized Table Undesirable?**

If you have a table like that shown in Table 3, you could simply enter a record for each item. If you had five items, you would enter five records in the table. What kind of redundancy does that create? If you used this method, would there be a primary key?

Minimizing Redundancy

Table 4 shows a nonnormalized view of the tblOrder table. In this case, when you know the OrderID, you are able to know the amount paid, the method of payment, and the name and address of the customer who purchased the order.

OrderID	Amount Paid	Method of Payment	Last Name	First Name	Address
1	$2,550.00	CC	Trujillo	John	427 Kanengiser Rd
12	$500.00	CC	Trujillo	John	427 Kanengiser Rd

Table 4 Nonnormalized tblOrder table

However, the table has redundant data. **Redundancy** occurs when data is repeated several times in a database. All of the data about John Trujillo is repeated for each order he makes. That means that the data will need to be entered multiple times. Beyond that, if the data changes, it has to be changed in multiple places. If his address or phone number changes, it will need to be changed in all his order records. Forgetting to change it in one place will lead to inconsistent data and confusion. Again, this table is not normalized because it contains data about two different entities: participant and orders.

In a normalized database, redundancy is minimized. The foreign keys are redundant, but no other data about the entity is repeated.

Understand Relationships Between Tables

To normalize the database, you need to have two tables: one for participants and one for orders. How then do you form a relationship between them? A table represents an entity — or the nouns — in the database. The relationship represents the verb that connects the two nouns. In the example, the two nouns are "participant" and "order." Is there a relationship between these two nouns? Yes. You can say that a participant places an order.

Once you have determined that there is a relationship between the entities, you need to describe the relationship. You do that by asking yourself two questions starting with each entity in the relationship.

- Question 1, starting with the Participant entity: If you have one participant, what is the maximum number of orders that one participant can place? The only two answers to consider are one or many. In this case, the participant can place many orders.
- Question 2, starting with the Order entity: If you have one order, what is the maximum number of participants that can place that order? Again, the only answers to consider are one or many. An order is placed by just one participant.

The type of relationship in which one question is answered "one" and the other is answered "many" is called a one-to-many relationship. A **one-to-many-relationship** is a relationship between two tables in which one record in the first table corresponds to many records in the second table. One-to-many is called the cardinality of the relationship. **Cardinality** indicates the number of instances of one entity that relates to one instance of another entity.

Viewing the Relationships Window

Access stores relationship information in the Relationships window as shown in Figure 20.

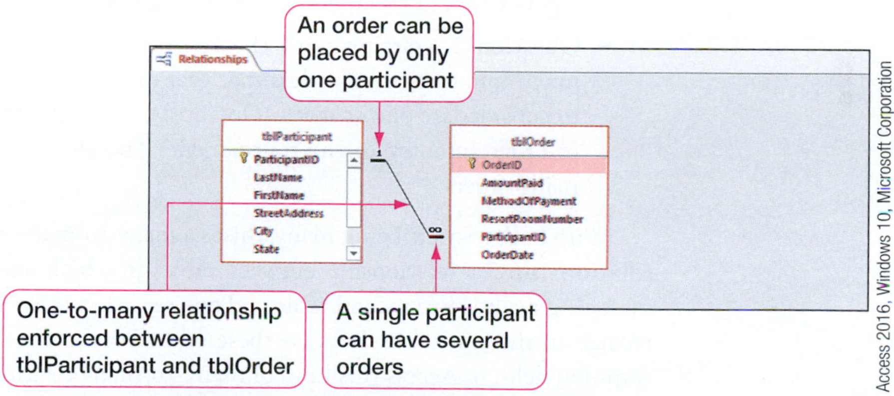

Figure 20 Relationships window

The Relationships window shows tables and the relationships between those tables. Notice the join line between tblParticipant and tblOrder. There is an infinity symbol on the line next to tblOrder. The infinity symbol indicates that a single participant can have several orders. There is a "1" on the line next to tblParticipant. The "1" indicates that an order can be placed by just one participant. Access indicates that a one-to-many relationship is being enforced by displaying a "1" on the one side of the join line and an infinity symbol on the many side.

REAL WORLD ADVICE	Other Uses for the Relationships Window

The Relationships window gives you an overview of all your tables and the relationships between them. It also shows all the fields in all the tables. It is often helpful to return to the Relationships window in developing queries and reports.

In this exercise, you will view the Relationships window in the database.

To View the Relationships Window

a. If you took a break, open the **a01ch02Putts** database.

b. Click the **Database Tools** tab, and then, in the Relationships group, click **Relationships**.

The Relationships window opens. The window shows tables and the relationships between those tables.

Determining Relationship Types

The relationship between tblParticipant and tblOrder is a one-to-many relationship. There are other types of relationships. Consider the relationship between tblOrder and tblItem: An item can be on an order. What is the cardinality? You need to ask yourself the two questions to determine the cardinality.

- Question 1, starting with the Order entity: If you have one order, what is the maximum number of items that can be part of that order? You care about only two answers: one or many. In this case, the order can contain many items. For example, a golfer could buy an entry into the tournament and a T-shirt.
- Question 2, starting with the Item entity: If you have one item, what is the maximum number of orders that that item can be part of? Again, the only answers to consider are one or many. Obviously, you want more than one person to be able to order an entry to the tournament. Therefore, you say that an item can be on many orders.

With both answers being many, this is a many-to-many relationship. A **many-to-many relationship** is a relationship between tables in which one record in one table has many matching records in a second table and one record in the related table has many matching records in the first table. Because these two tables in the charity database do not have a common field, in Access this kind of many-to-many relationship must have an additional table in between these two. This intermediate table is referred to by several synonymous terms: "intersection," "junction," or "link table." You will look at this later in the chapter.

A one-to-one relationship occurs when each question is answered with a maximum of one. A **one-to-one relationship** is a relationship between tables in which a record in one table has only one matching record in the second table. In a small business, a department might be managed by no more than one manager, and each manager manages no more than one department. That relationship in that business is a one-to-one relationship.

There are three types of relationships: one-to-many, many-to-many, and one-to-one. The relationship type is based on the rules of the business. In the charity golf tournament, the relationship between the order and the item is many-to-many, but in another business, it might not be. For example, consider a business that sells custom-made jewelry in which each item is one of a kind. In this case, an item can appear on just one order. Thus, the relationship between order and item in that business would be one-to-many.

CHAPTER 2

REAL WORLD ADVICE | **Use of One-to-One Relationships**

When you have a one-to-one relationship, you could combine the two tables into a single table. A single table is simpler than two tables with a one-to-one relationship between them.

- You could keep the two tables separate when the two tables are obviously two different things, such as manager and department. You might want to keep private information about the manager in the manager table. Additionally, this would be easier to change if business rules were to change and multiple managers might manage the same department.
- You should combine the two tables when there are just a few attributes on one of the tables. For example, suppose you wanted to keep only the manager's name in the manager table with no other information about the manager. Then you might consider the manager's name to be an attribute of the department.

Create a One-to-Many Relationship

Consider the relationship between tblParticipant and tblOrder. This is a one-to-many relationship. To form a relationship between two tables, you need the tables to have a field in common. The easiest way to accomplish this is to put the primary key from the table on the one side in the table on the many side. In this case, you would use the ParticipantID from the one side table and add it as a field to tblOrder. The field that you add to the many side is called a foreign key because it is a key to another, or foreign, table. ParticipantID is already a field on the many side table, so you can use it to form the relationship.

QUICK REFERENCE | **Creating a One-to-Many Relationship in Access**

Creating a one-to-many relationship in Access takes three steps.

1. Make sure the two tables have a field in common. Use the primary key from the one side, and add it as a foreign key in the many side table.
2. Form the relationship in the Relationships window. This is done by connecting the primary key of the one side table to the foreign key in the many side table.
3. Populate the foreign key by adding data to the foreign key in the many side table.

Forming a Relationship

Because tblParticipant and tblOrder already have a field in common, you can form the relationship. In this exercise, you will connect the primary key of the one side table to the foreign key in the many side table.

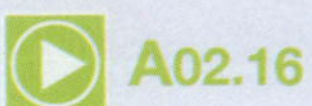

A02.16

To Form a Relationship

SIDE NOTE

Adding Tables to the Relationship Window

You can also add tables to the Relationships window by dragging a table from the Navigation Pane to the window.

a. On the Database Tools tab, in the Relationships group, click **Show Table**, click **tblParticipant**, and then click **Add**.

b. Click **Close** to close the Show Table dialog box, and then drag the **tblParticipant** table to appear below tblOrder in the Relationships window.

c. Use your pointer to resize **tblParticipant** by dragging the corner of the field list so all fields show. Drag **tblOrder** to the right.

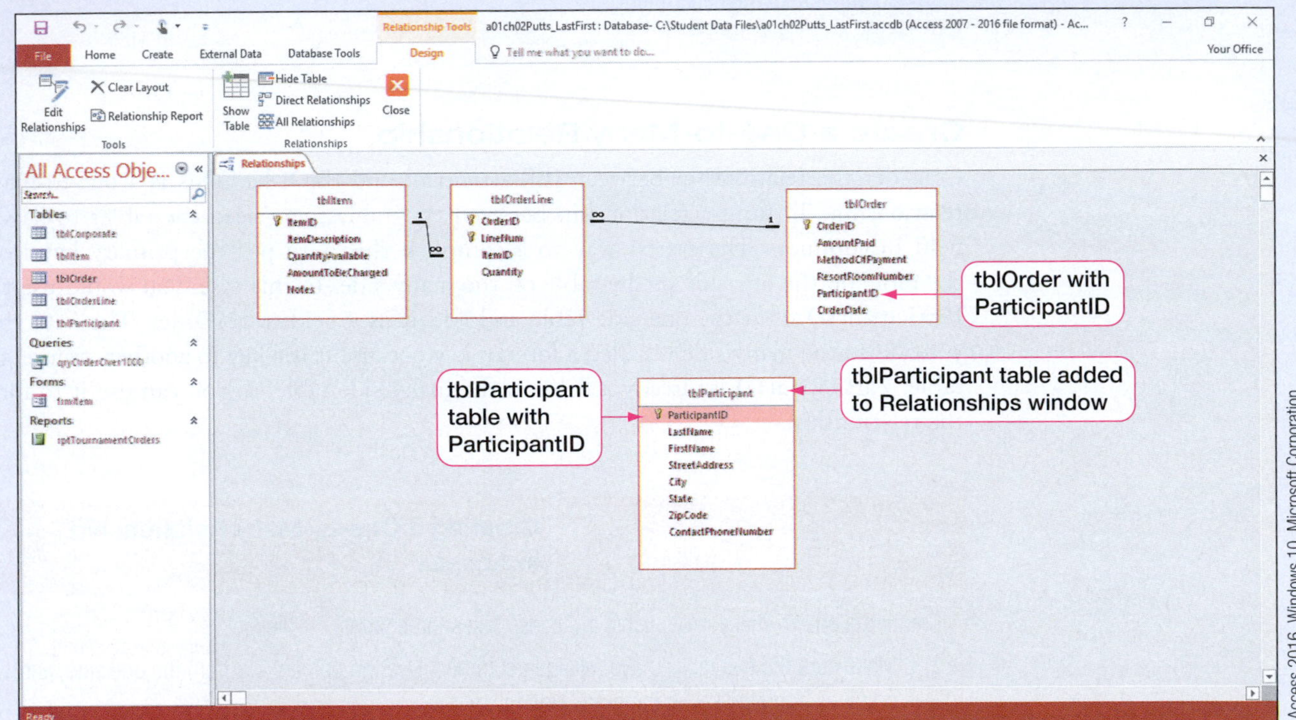

Figure 21 Add tblParticipant table to the Relationships window

SIDE NOTE

Duplicate Tables in the Relationship Window

Be careful not to add a table more than once to the Relationships window. If you do, simply click a field in the table to select it, and press Delete.

d. Drag the primary key, **ParticipantID**, from tblParticipant to **ParticipantID** in tblOrder. Alternatively, you could drag from ParticipantID in tblOrder to ParticipantID in tblParticipant.

e. The Edit Relationships dialog box is displayed. Check that the fields shown in the box are both ParticipantID.

Troubleshooting

If you do not see two fields named ParticipantID in the Edit Relationships dialog box, click Cancel and retry step d.

Notice that Access calls the relationship a one-to-many relationship. This is because the relationship is between a primary key and a foreign key.

f. Click **Enforce Referential Integrity** to select it, and then click **Create**. Later in the chapter, you will look further at what referential integrity accomplishes.

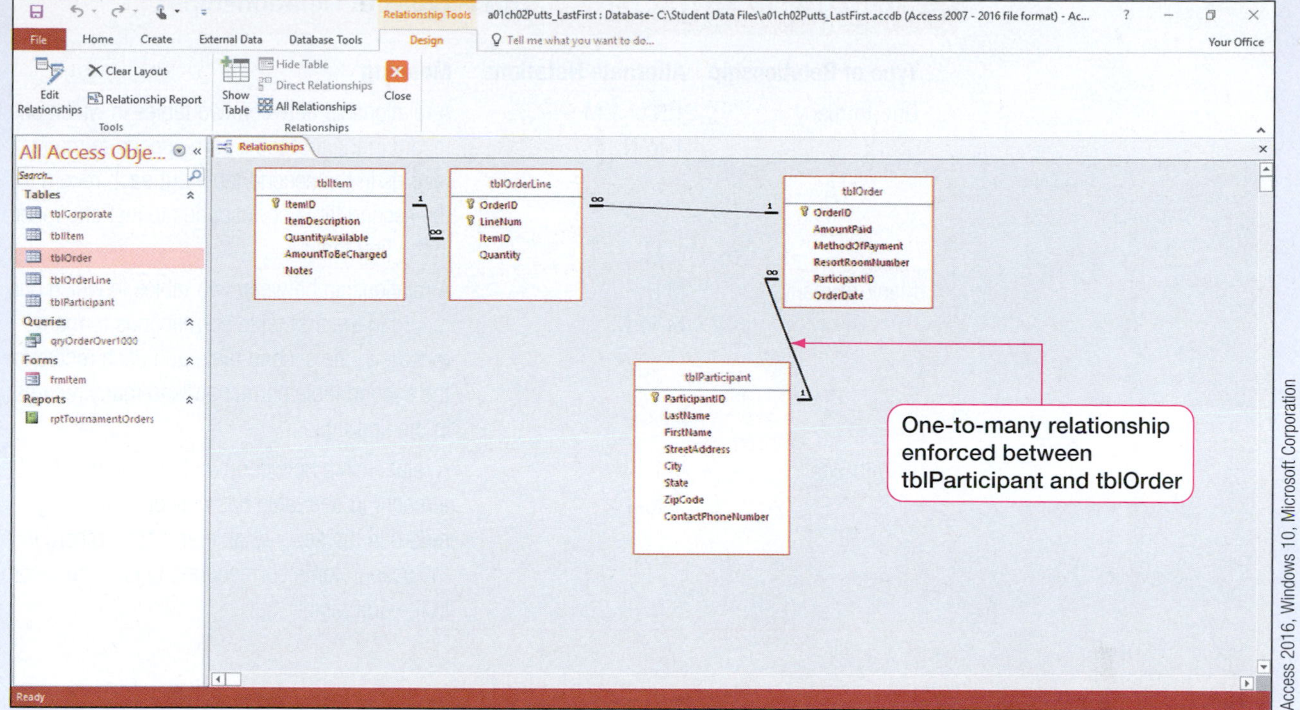

Figure 22 Relationship between tblParticipant and tblOrder

g. On the Relationship Tools Design tab, in the Relationships group, click **Close**. Click **Yes** to save the changes made to the layout.

Troubleshooting

If you get the error message "The database engine could not lock table 'tblParticipant' because it is already in use by another person or process," this means that the tblParticipant table is still open. Close the table, and try again to form the relationship. You should get in the habit of closing tables when you are done with them.

If you get the error message "Relationship must be on the same number of fields with the same data type," this means that the data types for the primary key and the foreign key are different. For example, they must be both Numeric and Long Integer or both Text. Make sure that you are creating the relationship between the correct fields. If you are, check the table designs, and fix the field with the wrong data type.

If you add a relationship that you do not want, right-click the join line, and click Delete. If you want to edit a relationship, right-click the join line, and click Edit Relationship.

QUICK REFERENCE	Three Types of Relationships	
Type of Relationship	**Alternate Notations**	**Meaning**
One-to-many	1:N or 1:M 1-to-N	A relationship between two tables in which one record in the first table corresponds to many records in the second table but each record in the second table corresponds to just one record in the first table.
Many-to-many	M:N M-to-N	A relationship between two tables in which one record in the first table corresponds to many records in the second table and each record in the second table corresponds to many records in the first table.
One-to-one	1:1 1-to-1	A relationship between two tables in which a record in one table has only one matching record in the second table and each record in the second table corresponds to just one record in the first table.

Create a Many-to-Many Relationship

Unless you are connecting a common field such as a foreign key to the same foreign key in a different table, Access cannot form a many-to-many relationship with a single relationship. Instead, you need to make two one-to-many relationships to represent the many-to-many relationship. As was stated before, tblOrder and tblItem have a many-to-many relationship. An order can have many items on it. Each item can be on many orders. To form this relationship, a new table, tblOrderLine, needs to be added. Both tblOrder and tblItem are related to the new table. The third table is called a junction table. A **junction table** breaks down the many-to-many relationship into two one-to-many relationships.

Look at the relationship between tblOrder and tblOrderLine in Figure 23. It is a one-to-many relationship with orders having many order lines but each order line on just one order. There is also a relationship between tblOrderLine and tblItem. It also is a one-to-many relationship with each order line having just one item but an item being able to be on many order lines, as shown in Figure 23.

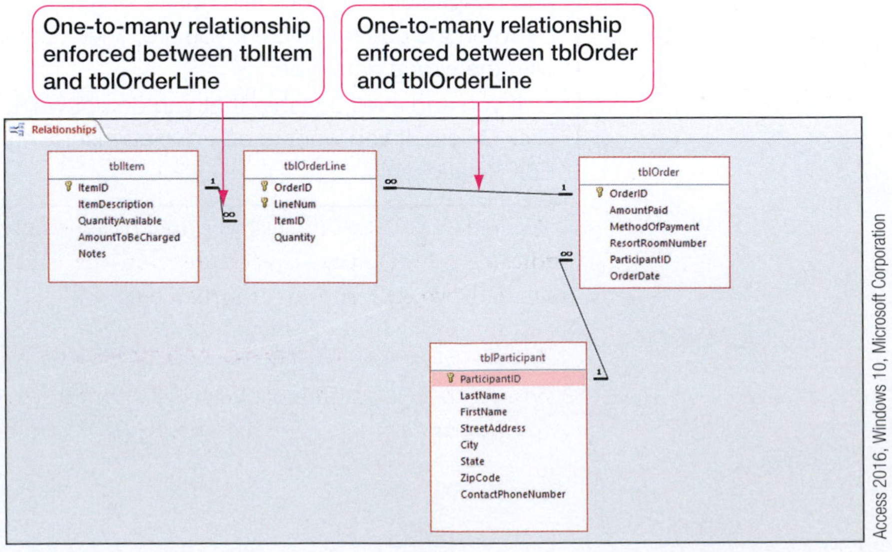

Figure 23 Relationship between tblOrder and tblItem with tblOrderLine

As shown in Figure 24, OrderID 4 has two order lines: one with an item of a corporate team and one with a cart. By traveling from left to right across the three tables, you see that OrderID 4 has many items on it. OrderID 6 has one line: an entry to the tournament. By traveling from right to left across the three tables, you see that an entry to the tournament can be on many orders. Hence, the junction table tblOrderLine forms a many-to-many relationship between tblOrder and tblItem.

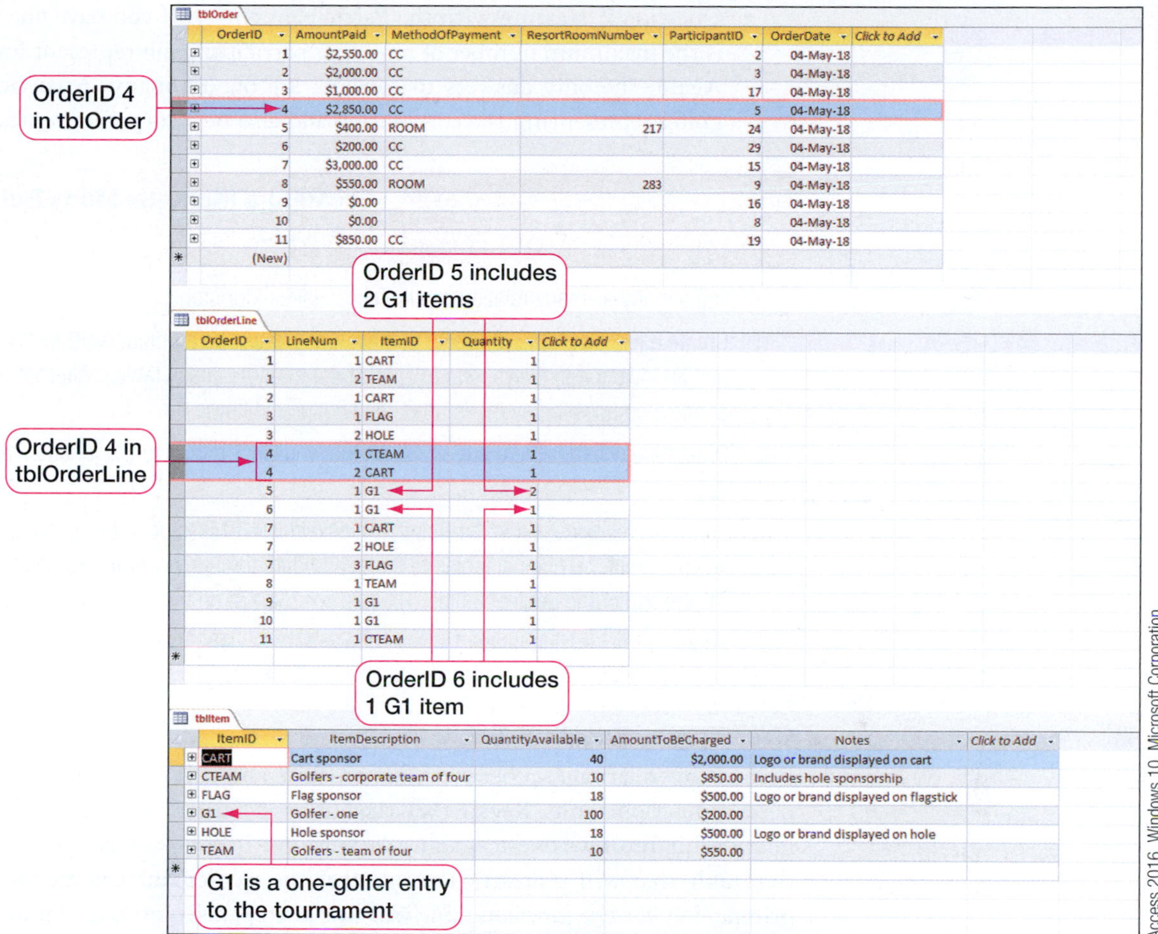

tblOrder

OrderID	AmountPaid	MethodOfPayment	ResortRoomNumber	ParticipantID	OrderDate	Click to Add
1	$2,550.00	CC		2	04-May-18	
2	$2,000.00	CC		3	04-May-18	
3	$1,000.00	CC		17	04-May-18	
4	$2,850.00	CC		5	04-May-18	
5	$400.00	ROOM	217	24	04-May-18	
6	$200.00	CC		29	04-May-18	
7	$3,000.00	CC		15	04-May-18	
8	$550.00	ROOM	283	9	04-May-18	
9	$0.00			16	04-May-18	
10	$0.00			8	04-May-18	
11	$850.00	CC		19	04-May-18	
(New)						

tblOrderLine

OrderID	LineNum	ItemID	Quantity	Click to Add
1	1	CART	1	
1	2	TEAM	1	
2	1	CART	1	
3	1	FLAG	1	
3	2	HOLE	1	
4	1	CTEAM	1	
4	2	CART	1	
5	1	G1	2	
6	1	G1	1	
7	1	CART	1	
7	2	HOLE	1	
7	3	FLAG	1	
8	1	TEAM	1	
9	1	G1	1	
10	1	G1	1	
11	1	CTEAM	1	

tblItem

ItemID	ItemDescription	QuantityAvailable	AmountToBeCharged	Notes	Click to Add
CART	Cart sponsor	40	$2,000.00	Logo or brand displayed on cart	
CTEAM	Golfers - corporate team of four	10	$850.00	Includes hole sponsorship	
FLAG	Flag sponsor	18	$500.00	Logo or brand displayed on flagstick	
G1	Golfer - one	100	$200.00		
HOLE	Hole sponsor	18	$500.00	Logo or brand displayed on hole	
TEAM	Golfers - team of four	10	$550.00		

Figure 24 Data in tblOrder, tblOrderLine, and tblItem

tblOrderLine has foreign keys to tblOrder and tblItem. This allows the relationships to be formed. Notice that the relationship between tblOrder and tblOrderLine is formed with OrderID in tblOrder joined to OrderID in tblOrderLine. Similarly, the relationship between tblItem and tblOrderLine is formed from ItemID in tblItem to ItemID in tblOrderLine.

The junction table, tblOrderLine, has one field beyond the key fields: Quantity. This indicates the quantity of each item on the order. As shown in Figure 24, OrderID 5 included two entries to the tournament.

Forming a New Many-to-Many Relationship

Consider the relationship between tblCorporate and tblParticipant. There is a relationship: A participant can represent a corporation. A participant can be a golfer for a corporation, the corporate representative, or a donor. What is the cardinality? You need to ask yourself the two questions to determine the cardinality.

- Question 1, starting with the Corporate entity: If you have one corporation, what is the maximum number of participants that can represent that corporation? You care about only two answers: one or many. In this case, the corporation could be represented by many participants. A corporate team might have four golfer participants.
- Question 2, starting with the Participant entity: If you have one participant, what is the maximum number of roles that participant can represent for the corporation? Again, the only answers to consider are one or many. A participant could be a golfer representing the corporation and also be a corporate representative.

QUICK REFERENCE	Creating a Many-to-Many Relationship in Access

Creating a many-to-many relationship in Access takes four steps.

1. Create a junction table. Create a primary key that will be a unique field for the junction table, and add two foreign keys, one to each of the many-to-many tables. Alternatively, you can create a composite key made up of the two foreign keys.
2. Determine whether there are any fields that you want to add to the junction table beyond the keys.
3. Form two relationships in the Relationships window. This is done by connecting the primary key of one of the original tables to the appropriate foreign key of the junction table. Repeat for the second of the original tables. The junction table is on the many side of both relationships.
4. Populate the junction table.

Creating a Junction Table

Because the relationship between tblCorporate and tblParticipant is many-to-many, you need a junction table. Recall that the junction table breaks down the many-to-many relationship into two one-to-many relationships. In this exercise, you will create the junction table that will represent the role that the participant has for the corporation. The primary key for the junction table will be ParticipantRoleID, an AutoNumber field. You will have two foreign keys: the CorporateID field and the ParticipantID field. You will also add a field named Role that describes the role of the participant. Because the table represents roles, you will call the table tblParticipantRole.

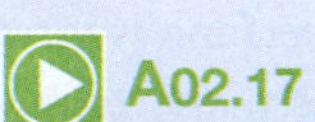

To Create a Junction Table

a. Click the **Create** tab, and then, in the Tables group, click **Table Design**.
   Access opens a blank table in Design view. You will enter each field in the appropriate row.

b. In the Field Name column, type ParticipantRoleID. Press Tab to move to the Data Type column, click the **arrow**, and then select the **AutoNumber** data type.
   Alternatively, you can type the A and "AutoNumber" will appear.

c. Notice that Field Size in the Field Properties pane defaults to Long Integer. Press Tab to move to the Description column, and then type Primary key for tblParticipantRole.

d. On the Design tab, in the Tools group, click **Primary Key** to make the ParticipantRoleID field the primary key.

e. Press Tab to move to the next field. Continue filling in the table with the following information, being sure to enter the field size in the Field Properties pane.

Field Name	Data Type	Description	Field Size
CorporateID	Number	Foreign key to tblCorporate	Long Integer
ParticipantID	Number	Foreign key to tblParticipant	Long Integer
Role	Short Text	Role that participant fills for the corporation	40

f. **Close** ☒ the table, and then, in the Microsoft Access dialog box click **Yes**. Name the table tblParticipantRole, and then click **OK**.

Forming Two Relationships to a Junction Table

The many-to-many relationship will turn into two one-to-many relationships between each of the original tables and the junction table. The rule is that the junction table is on the many side of the two relationships. But you can ask yourself the two questions to determine the cardinality.

- Question 1, starting with the Corporate entity: If you have one corporation, what is the maximum number of participant roles that can represent that corporation? You care about only two answers: one or many. In this case, the corporation could be represented by many participant roles. A corporation could have golfers and corporate contacts.
- Question 2, starting with the ParticipantRole entity: If you have one ParticipantRole, what is the maximum number of corporations that the participant can represent? Again, the only answers to consider are one or many. A ParticipantRole is for a single participant.

Thus, tblCorporate to tblParticipantRole is a one-to-many relationship with Corporate on the one side. You can ask the same questions about the relationship between tblParticipant and tblParticipantRole.

In this exercise, you will create the two one-to-many relationships to the tblParticipantRole table.

A02.18

To Form Two Relationships to a Junction Table

a. Click the **Database Tools** tab, and then, in the Relationships group, click **Relationships**.

b. On the Design tab, in the Relationships group, click **Show Table**. Select **tblCorporate**, click **Add**, select **tblParticipantRole**, and then click **Add**.

c. **Close** the Show Table dialog box, and then drag the **tables** in the Relationships window so there is some space between the tables to form the relationships.

d. Drag the primary key **ParticipantID** from tblParticipant to **ParticipantID** in tblParticipantRole. Alternatively, you could drag from ParticipantID in tblParticipantRole to ParticipantID in tblParticipant.

e. Access displays the Edit Relationships dialog box. Click **Enforce Referential Integrity** to select it, and then click **Create**.

f. Drag the primary key **CorporateID** from tblCorporate to **CorporateID** in tblParticipantRole.

g. Access displays the Edit Relationships dialog box. Click **Enforce Referential Integrity** to select it, and then click **Create**.

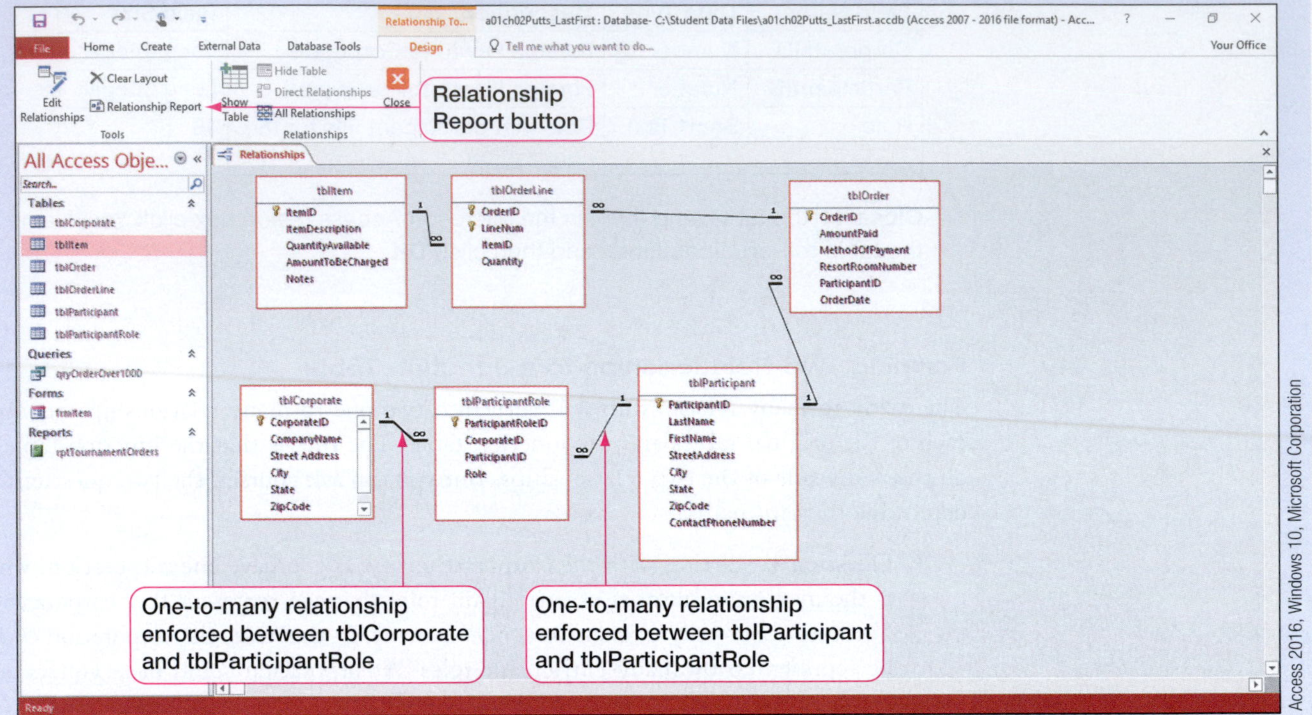

Figure 25 Junction table with two one-to-many relationships

h. On the Design tab, in the Tools group, click **Relationship Report** to create a report for your relationships. **Save** the report, accepting the report name **Relationships for a01ch02Putts_LastFirst**, and then click **OK**.

i. If your instructor asks you to print your report, on the Print Preview tab, in the Print group, click **Print** to print the report.

j. In the Close Preview group, click **Close Print Preview**, and then **close** the Relationships report.

k. **Close** the Relationships window.

Populating the Junction Table

In this exercise, you will populate the junction table with data to complete the many-to-many relationship.

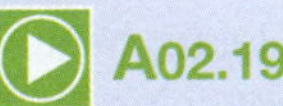
A02.19

To Populate the Junction Table

a. Double-click **tblParticipantRole** to open the table in Datasheet view.

b. Click in the **CorporateID** field in the **append row**. Enter a CorporateID of 1, a ParticipantID of 5, and a Role of Corporate Contact. Access automatically numbers ParticipantRoleID as 1.

c. Because the last field is not totally visible, place your pointer in the **border** on the right of the **Role** column heading. When your pointer is a double-headed arrow [+], double-click the **border** to resize the column. Repeat for each field.

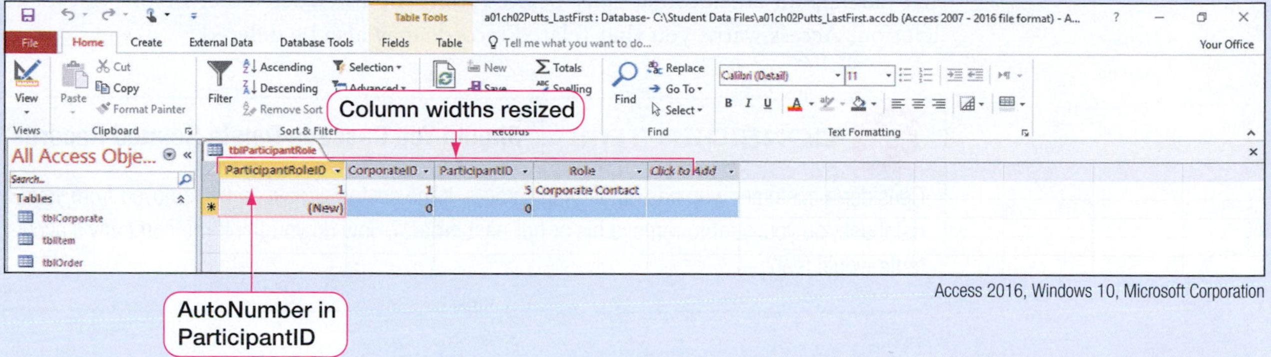

Figure 26 tblParticipantRole columns resized

d. Enter the following data in new records as follows.

CorporateID	ParticipantID	Role
1	1	Golfer
1	26	Golfer

e. **Close** [X] the table, and then, in the Microsoft Access dialog box, click **Yes** to save the changes to the table layout.

Defining One-to-One Relationships

One-to-one relationships in Access are formed very similarly to one-to-many relationships. You can put a foreign key in either table and establish the relationship by dragging with the primary key in one table joined to the foreign key. You can also make both tables have the same primary key.

Understand Referential Integrity

Referential integrity is a database concept that ensures that relationships between tables remain consistent. When one table has a foreign key to another table, the concept of referential integrity states that you may not add a record to the table that contains the foreign key unless there is a corresponding record in the linked table. Recall that when you created the relationship between tblParticipant and tblOrder, you told Access to enforce referential integrity.

Selecting Cascade Update

When you ask Access to enforce referential integrity, you can also select whether you want Access to automatically cascade update related fields or cascade delete related records. These options allow some deletions and updates that would usually be prevented by referential integrity. However, Access makes these changes and replicates or cascades the changes through all related tables so referential integrity is preserved.

If you select Cascade Update Related Fields when you define a relationship, then when the primary key of a record in the one side table changes, Access automatically changes the foreign keys in all related records. For example, if you change the ItemID in the tblItem table, Access automatically changes the ItemID on all order lines that include that item. Access makes these changes without displaying an error message.

If the primary key in the one side table was defined as AutoNumber, selecting Cascade Update Related Fields has no effect, because you cannot change the value in an AutoNumber field.

Selecting Cascade Delete

If you select Cascade Delete Related Records when you define a relationship, any time you delete records from the one side table, the related records in the many side table are also deleted. For example, if you delete a tblParticipant record, all the orders made by that participant are automatically deleted from the tblOrder table. Before you make the deletion, Access warns you that related records may also be deleted.

CONSIDER THIS | Should You Cascade Delete Related Records?

Consider a customer who has made many orders. If the customer asks to be removed from your database, do you want to remove his or her past orders? How do you think the company's accountants would feel?

Testing Referential Integrity

Enforcing referential integrity ensures that the following rules will be applied when you define the fields in Design view.

- The value in the field on the one side of the relationship is unique in the table. You must use either the primary key of the one side in the relationship or a field that you have set as unique in the table.
- You cannot add a foreign key value on the many side that does not have a matching primary key value on the one side.
- The matching fields on both sides of the relationship are defined with the same data types. For example, if the primary key is numeric and Long Integer, the foreign key must be numeric and Long Integer too. (For purposes of relationships, an AutoNumber primary key is considered Long Integer.)

If these rules are violated, when you try to form the relationship, you will get the following error message: "Relationship must be on the same number of fields with the same data type."

CONSIDER THIS | Why Enforce Referential Integrity?

You can decline to enforce referential integrity on a relationship. What are the pros and cons of enforcing referential integrity? What are the pros and cons of not enforcing referential integrity?

You also cannot change the primary key value in the one side table if that record has related records.

QUICK REFERENCE | Referential Integrity

Access enforces the following rules on defining a relationship with referential integrity.

1. The primary key field values on the one side of the relationship must be unique in the table.
2. The foreign key values on the many side of the relationship must exist as the primary key field for a record on the one side of the relationship.
3. The matching fields on both sides of the relationship are defined with the same data types.

(Continued)

QUICK REFERENCE	Referential Integrity *(Continued)*

The following rules are applied to data changes when referential integrity is enforced.

1. You cannot enter a value in the foreign key field on the many side table that is not a primary key on the one side table. However, you can leave the foreign key unfilled, indicating that this record is not in the relationship. However, it is not good practice to do this.
2. You cannot delete a record from the one side table if matching records exist in a many side table, unless Cascade Delete has been selected for the relationship, in which case all the matching records on the many side are deleted.
3. You cannot change a primary key value in the one side table if that record has related records in the many side unless Cascade Update has been selected for the relationship, in which case all the matching records on the many side have their foreign key updated.

CHAPTER 2

In this exercise, you will test referential integrity being enforced between the tblParticipant and tblOrder tables by attempting to enter a new order and assign it to a ParticipantID that does not exist and by attempting to delete a participant that has records in the tblOrder table.

A02.20

To Test Referential Integrity

a. Right-click **tblParticipant**, and then select **Design View**. Notice that ParticipantID is defined as Number and Long Integer.

b. **Close** [X] tblParticipant, right-click **tblOrder**, select **Design View**, and then click the **ParticipantID** field. Notice that ParticipantID is also defined as Number and Long Integer in the tblOrder table.

c. Click the **Home** tab, and then, in the Views group, click the **View** button to switch to Datasheet View for tblOrder.

d. In the ParticipantID for the last record in the table, type 70, and then press Enter twice.
   Access responds with the error message "You cannot add or change a record because a related record is required in table tblParticipant." That is, you cannot add an order to participant 70 because there is no participant 70.

e. Click **OK**, and then change the ParticipantID for the last order to 1. Press Enter twice. ParticipantID 1 is a valid participant, so you can make that change.

f. **Close** [X] the tblOrder table.
   If you enforce referential integrity, you also cannot delete a record from the one side table if matching records exist in the many side table. If you want to delete the record, you must delete the matching records or use Cascade Delete.

g. In the Navigation Pane, double-click **tblParticipant** to open it in Datasheet view.

h. Click the **record selector** of the second row, John Trujillo.

i. On the Home tab, in the Records group, click **Delete**.
   Access responds with the error message "The record cannot be deleted or changed because table 'tblOrder' includes related records." That means John Trujillo has placed an order.

j. Click **OK**.

k. **Close** [X] the tblParticipant table.

Creating a Report Using Two Related Tables

The reason you create a relationship is to join two tables for queries, reports, and forms. In this exercise, you will create a simple report showing participants and their orders by using two related tables.

To Create a Report Using Two Related Tables

a. Click the **Create** tab, and then, in the Reports group, click **Report Wizard**.

b. In the Report Wizard dialog box, click the **Tables/Queries** arrow, and then select **Table: tblParticipant**. Select the **LastName** field, and then click **One Field** [>]. Select the **FirstName** field, and then click **One Field** [>].

c. Click the **Tables/Queries** arrow, and then select **Table: tblOrder**. Select the **OrderID** field, and then click **One Field** [>]. Select the **AmountPaid** field, and then click **One Field** [>].

> **Troubleshooting**
>
> If you clicked Next instead of selecting the tblOrder fields, you can go back a step in the wizard by clicking Back.

d. Click **Next**.

You can see a preview of how your report will look if you group the report by participants, using the data in tblParticipant. Access uses the one side of a one-to-many relationship as the default for the grouping. This is the grouping you want.

e. Click **Next**. The wizard asks whether you want more grouping levels; however, you do not want any other grouping levels.

f. Click **Next**.

g. Use the arrow to select **OrderID**. Ascending sort order is already selected. Click **Next**.

The wizard asks you to choose a layout and orientation for your report. You will accept the default Stepped layout and Portrait orientation.

h. Click **Next**.

i. Title your report rptParticipantOrders. Click **Finish**.

Access connects the participants and orders in a report.

j. Right-click anywhere on the report, and then select **Layout View** from the shortcut menu.

> **Troubleshooting**
>
> If the Field List shows on the right side of the Access window, close it so you can see the entire report layout.

k. Double-click the **title** of the report. Change the report title to Participants and Orders, and press Enter. **Save** your report.

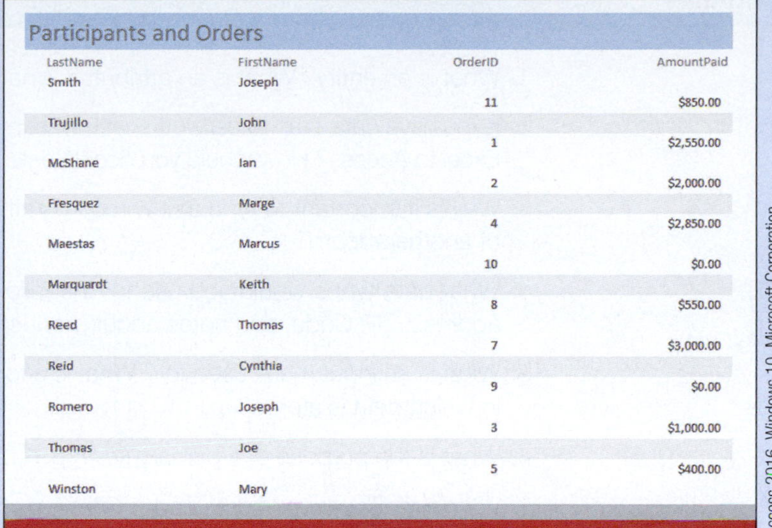

Participants and Orders

LastName	FirstName	OrderID	AmountPaid
Smith	Joseph	11	$850.00
Trujillo	John	1	$2,550.00
McShane	Ian	2	$2,000.00
Fresquez	Marge	4	$2,850.00
Maestas	Marcus	10	$0.00
Marquardt	Keith	8	$550.00
Reed	Thomas	7	$3,000.00
Reid	Cynthia	9	$0.00
Romero	Joseph	3	$1,000.00
Thomas	Joe	5	$400.00
Winston	Mary		

Figure 27 Completed report

l. If your instructor directs you to print the report, right-click anywhere on the report, switch to **Print Preview**, click **Print** in the Print group, and then click **OK**.

m. **Close** [X] the report.

n. Exit Access and then submit your file as directed by your instructor.

Concept Check

1. What is an entity? What is an attribute? What is a relationship? p. 99
2. If you have data in an Excel worksheet, what methods could you use to move the data in Excel to Access? How would you decide between the methods? p. 102, 104, 106, 108
3. Why is it important to type a new record in the blank (append) row rather than on top of another record? p. 108
4. What data types would you use for the following fields: price, phone number, street address, ZIP Code, and notes about product usage? p. 113
5. What is an input mask used for? What is a format used for? Which can affect the way in which data is stored? p. 116, 118
6. What is the purpose of a primary key? p. 112
7. Why is redundancy of data undesirable? p. 126
8. What does it mean to say that there is a relationship between two tables? p. 127
9. How do you create a one-to-many relationship in Access? p. 129
10. How do you create a many-to-many relationship in Access? p. 132–137
11. What does it mean for a relationship to have referential integrity enforced? p. 137

Key Terms

Attribute 99
Cardinality 127
Composite key 121
Data type 101
Delimiter 107
Entity 99
Field size 114
Foreign key 120
Format 118
Input mask 116
Join 125
Junction table 132
Many-to-many relationship 128
Named range 106
Natural primary key 123
Normalization 125
Number data type 101
Numeric key 120
One-to-many relationship 127
One-to-one relationship 128
Primary key 112
Redundancy 126
Relationship 99
Short Text data type 101

Visual Summary

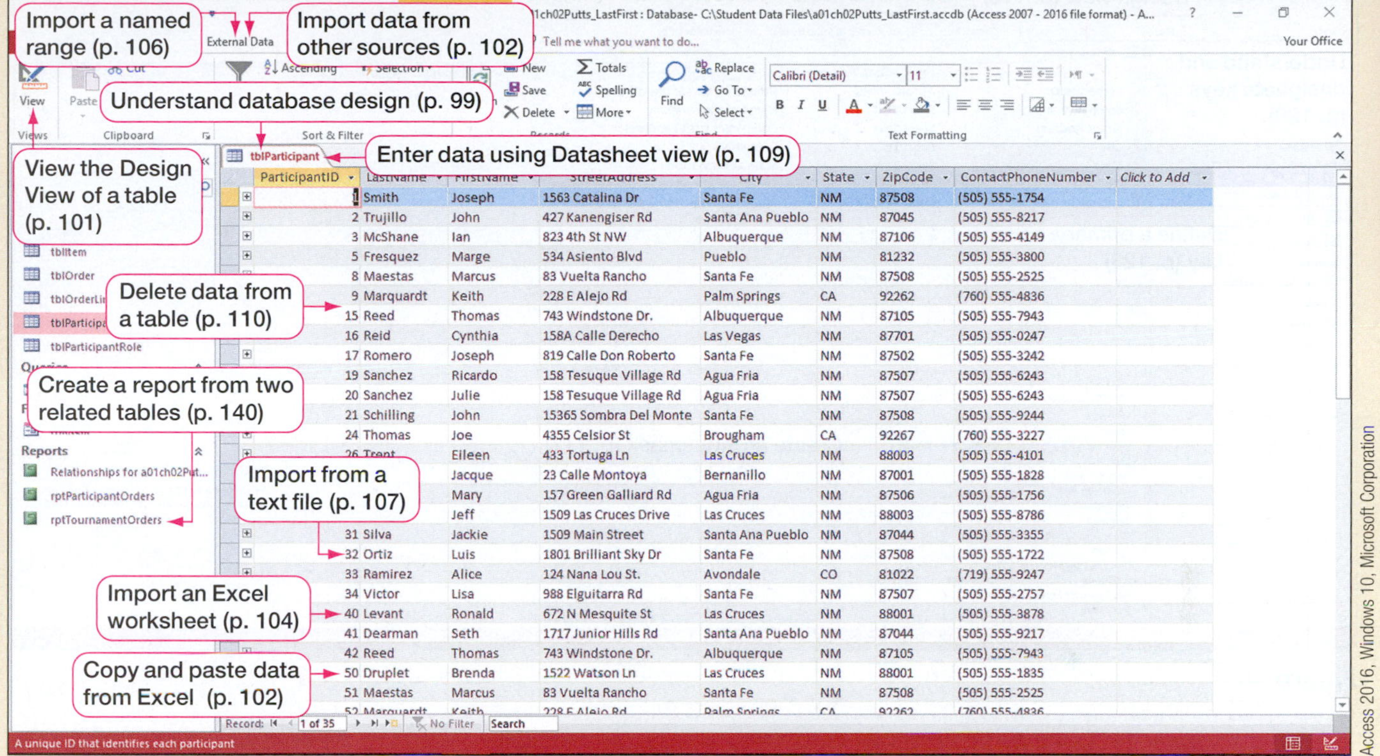

Figure 28

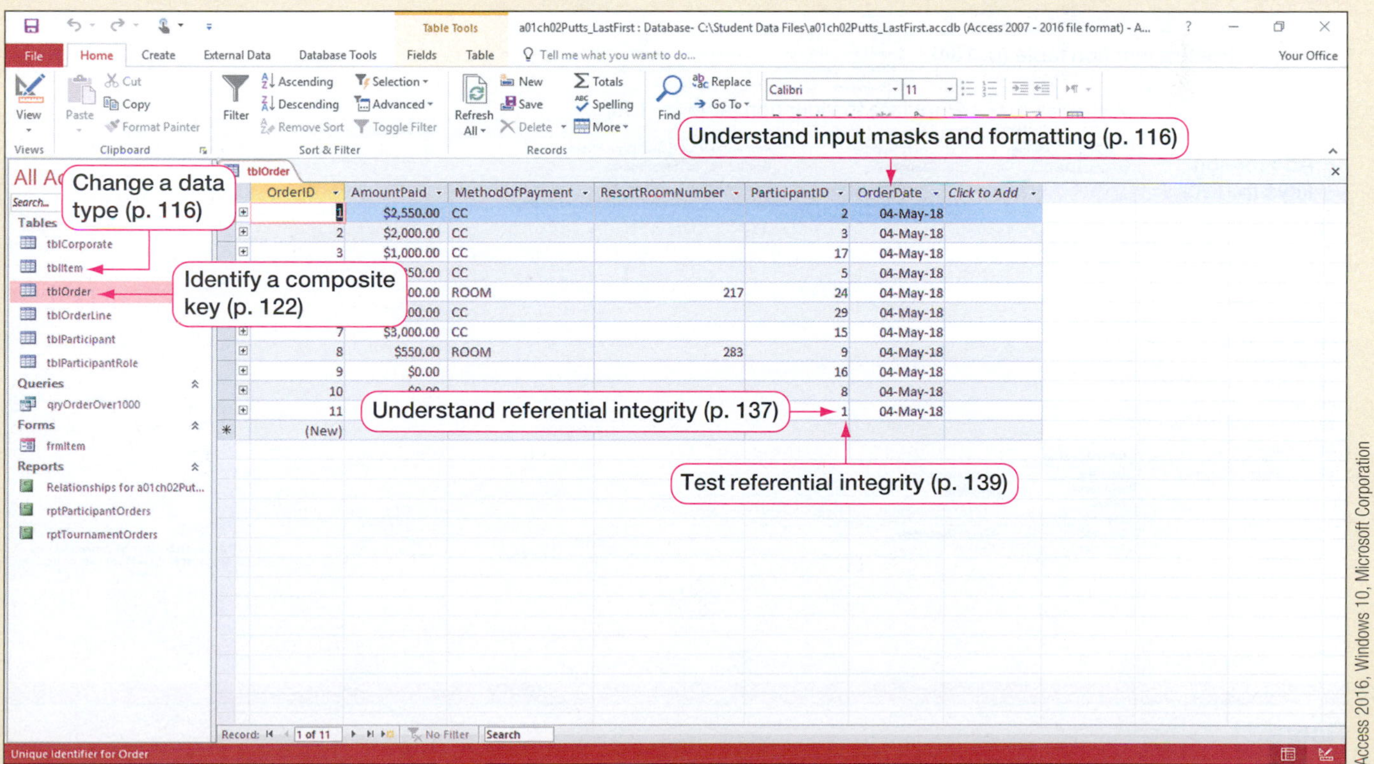

Figure 29

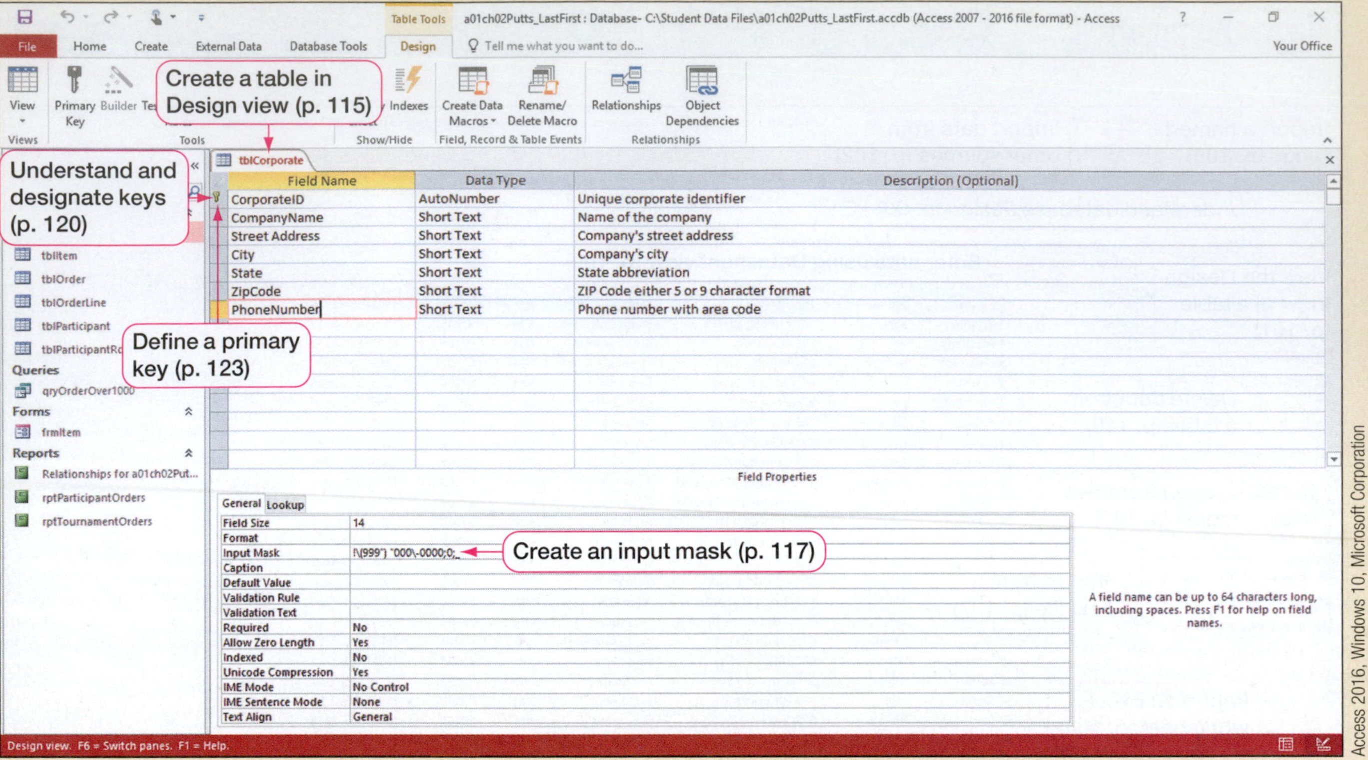

Figure 30

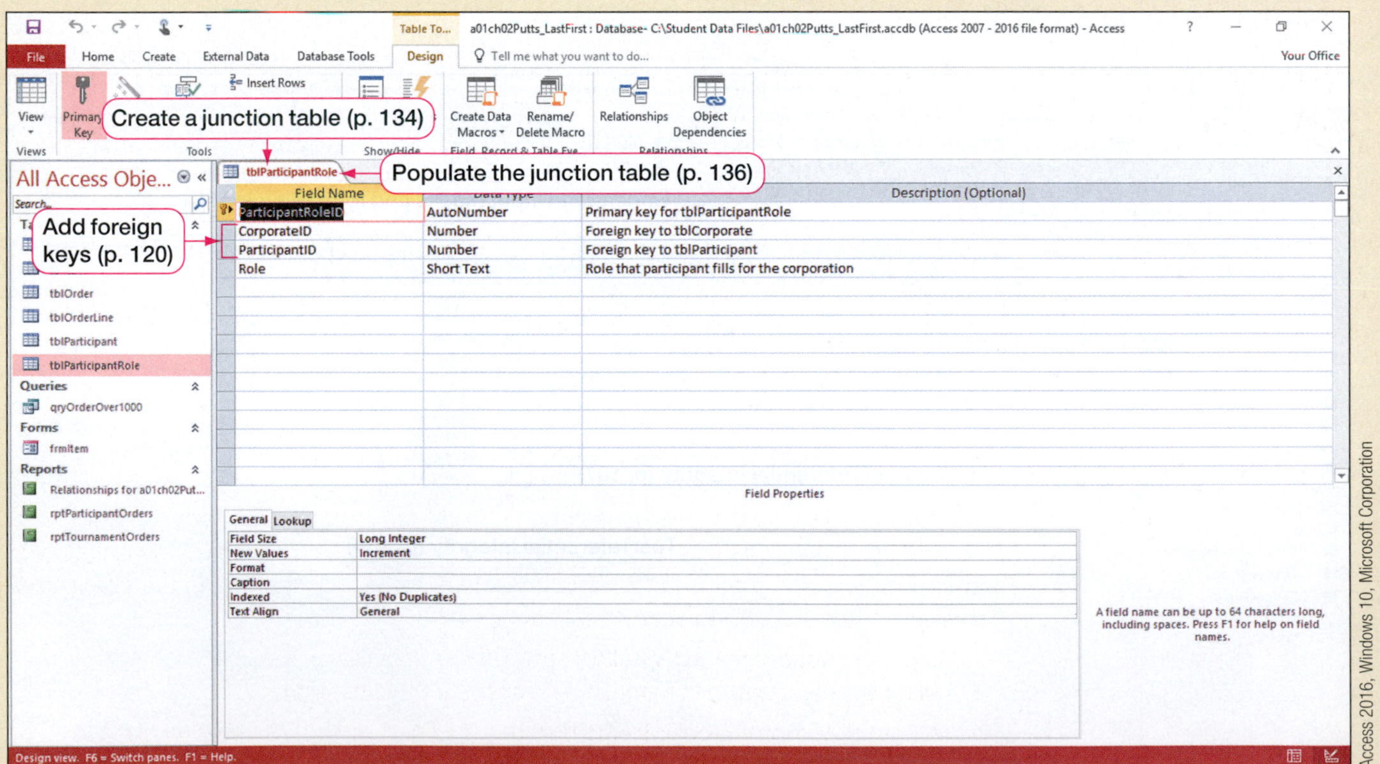

Figure 31

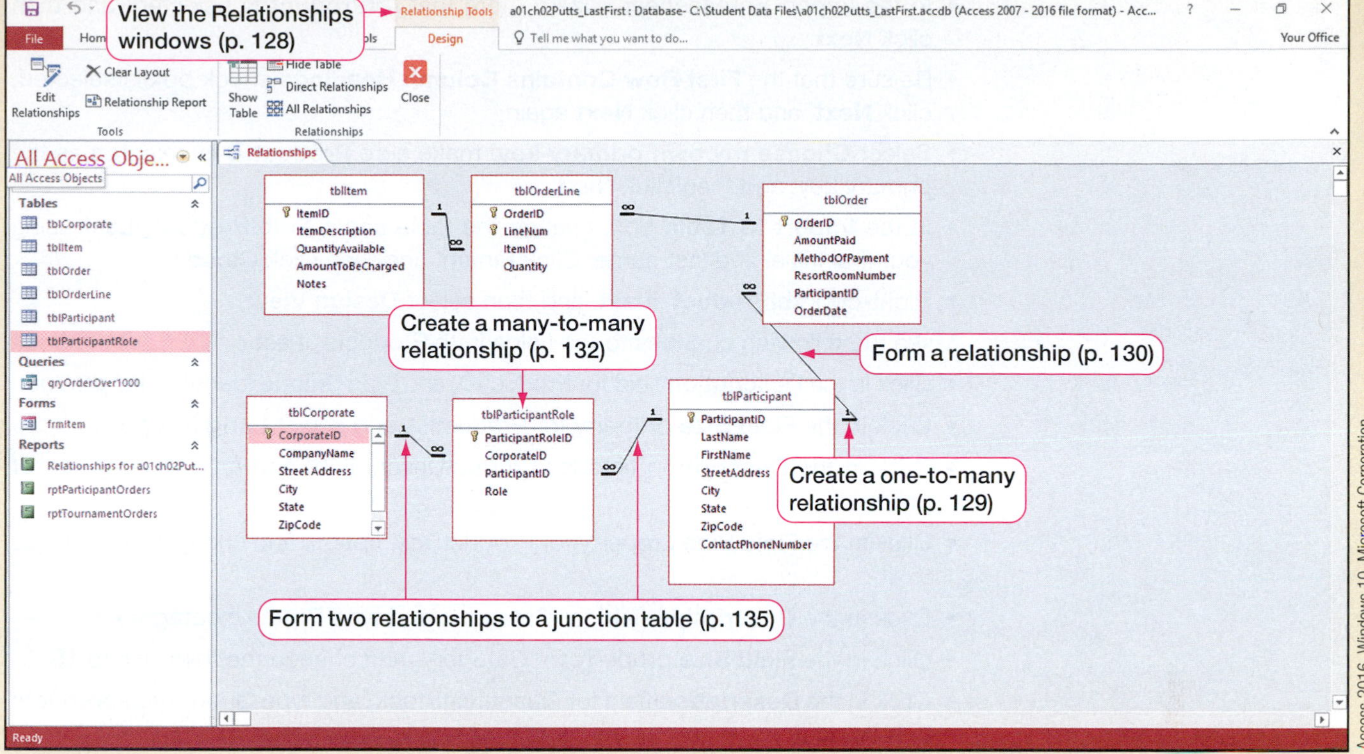

Access 2016, Windows 10, Microsoft Corporation

Figure 32

Practice 1

Student data files needed:

a01ch02Giftshop.accdb

a01ch02Products.xlsx

a01ch02Customers.xlsx

You will save your file as:

a01ch02Giftshop_LastFirst.accdb

Painted Treasures Gift Shop

Sales & Marketing

The Painted Treasures Gift Shop sells many products for the resort patrons, including jewelry, clothing, and spa products. You will create a database of customers and their purchases. The three tables that you need are customers, purchases, and products. What are the relationships between these three tables? You will need to create a new table that will serve as a junction table between the two tables, as is necessary to accommodate a many-to-many relationship.

a. Open the Access file, **a01ch02Giftshop**. Save your file as a01ch02Giftshop_LastFirst using your last and first name. If necessary, enable the content.

b. Import data from Excel into the database by completing the following steps.

- Click the **External Data** tab, and then, in the Import & Link group, click **Excel**.
- Click **Browse.** Navigate through the folder structure to the location of your student data files, and then double-click **a01ch02Products**. Make sure **Import the source data into a new table in the current database** is selected, and then click **OK**.

- In the Import Spreadsheet Wizard, note that **tblProduct** is selected, and then click **Next**.
- Be sure that the **First Row Contains Column Headings** check box is selected, click **Next**, and then click **Next** again.
- Select **Choose my own primary key**, make sure **ProductID** is selected as the primary key, and then click **Next**.
- In the **Import to Table** box, change the table name to tblProduct_iLast using your first initial and last name. Click **Finish**, and then click **Close**.
- Right-click **tblProduct_iLast**, and then select **Design View**.

c. Make the following changes to the fields in tblProducts_iLast.
- Click in the **Description** field for ProductID, and type Unique identifier for product.
- Click in the **Field Size** property for ProductID, and select **Long Integer**.
- Click in the **Description** field for ProductDescription, and type Description of product.
- Click in the **Field Size** property for ProductDescription, and change the field size to 40.
- Click in the **Description** field for Category, and type Product category.
- Click in the **Field Size** property for Category, and change the field size to 15.
- Click in the **Description** field for QuantityInStock, and type Quantity of products in stock.
- Click in the **Field Size** property for QuantityInStock, and select **Integer**.
- Click in the **Data Type** field for Price, and select **Currency**.
- Click in the **Description** field for Price, and type Price to charge customer.
- Click the **Description** field for Size, and type Size of product.
- Click in the **Field Size** property for Size, and set the size to 10.
- Click the **Description** field for Color, and type Color of product.
- Click in the **Field Size** property for Color, and set the size to 15.

d. Save the table. Access tells you that some data might be lost because you are making fields shorter in length. Accept this by clicking **Yes**, and then close the table.

e. Create a table in Design view by completing the following steps.
- Click the **Create** tab, and then click **Table Design**. Access opens a blank table in Design view.
- Fill in the fields and change field sizes as noted.

Field Name	Data Type	Description	Field Size
CustomerID	AutoNumber	A unique ID that identifies each customer	Long Integer
LastName	Short Text	The customer's last name	25
FirstName	Short Text	The customer's first name	20
StreetAddress	Short Text	Street address	40
City	Short Text	City address	25
State	Short Text	State abbreviation	2
ZipCode	Short Text	Five-digit ZIP Code	5
ResortHotelRoom	Short Text	Leave blank if not guest	6

- Highlight the **CustomerID** row by clicking the record selector to the left of the field, and then, on the Design tab, in the Tools group, click **Primary Key** to make CustomerID the primary key.
- Save your table design, naming it tblCustomer_iLast using your first initial and last name, and then close the table.

f. Import data into the table by completing the following steps.
   - Click the **External Data** tab, and then, in the Import & Link group, click **Excel**.
   - Click **Browse**. Navigate through the folder structure to the location of your student data files, and then double-click **a01ch02Customers**.
   - Click **Append a copy of the records to the table** if necessary, click the arrow to select **tblCustomer_iLast**, and then click **OK**.
   - Click **Next** twice, and then, in the Import Spreadsheet Wizard dialog box, in the Import to Table box, accept the name **tblCustomer_iLast**. Click **Finish**, and then click **Close**. Double-click **tblCustomer_iLast** to open it in Datasheet view.
   - In the first record in the table, change the **LastName** and **FirstName** fields to your **last name** and **first name**. Close the table.

g. Create relationships between your tables by completing the following steps.
   - Click the **Database Tools** tab, and then, in the Relationships group, click **Relationships**, and then click **Show Table** if necessary.
   - Add all four tables in the order **tblCustomer_iLast**, **tblPurchase**, **tblPurchase-Line**, and **tblProduct_iLast** to the Relationships window, and then close the Show Table dialog box.
   - Drag the primary key **CustomerID** from tblCustomer_iLast to **CustomerID** in tblPurchase.
   - Click **Enforce Referential Integrity**, and then click **Create**.
   - Drag the primary key **PurchaseID** from tblPurchase to **PurchaseID** in tblPurchaseLine. Click **Enforce Referential Integrity**, and then click **Create**.
   - Drag the primary key **ProductID** from tblProduct_iLast to **ProductID** in tblPurchaseLine. Click **Enforce Referential Integrity**, and then click **Create**.
   - Click **Relationship Report**, and then save the report, accepting the name **Relationships for a01ch02Giftshop_LastFirst**. If your instructor directs you to print your results, print the report.
   - Close the report, and then close the Relationships window.

h. Create a report of the customers, purchases, and products by completing the following steps.
   - Click the **Create** tab, and then, in the Reports group, click **Report Wizard**.
   - In the Report Wizard dialog box, click the **Tables/Queries** arrow, and then select **Table: tblCustomer_iLast**. Select the **LastName** and **FirstName** fields.
   - Click the **Tables/Queries** arrow, click **Table: tblPurchase**, and then select **PurchaseDate**.
   - Click the **Tables/Queries** arrow, click **Table: tblPurchaseLine**, and then select **Quantity**.
   - Click the **Tables/Queries** arrow, click **Table: tblProduct_iLast**, select **ProductDescription**, and then click **Next**.
   - Accept grouping by **tblCustomer_iLast** and then by **PurchaseDate** by clicking **Next**.
   - You do not want any other grouping levels, so click **Next**.

- Click the **arrow** to sort your report by ascending **ProductDescription**, and then click **Next**.
- Change the Orientation to **Landscape**, and then click **Next**.
- Title your report **rptCustomerPurchases_iLast** using your first initial and last name, and then click **Finish**.
- Switch to Layout view.
- Change the title of your report to **Customers and Purchases by iLast** using your first initial and last name.

i. Save the report, exit Access, and then submit your file as directed by your instructor.

Problem Solve 1

Student data files needed:

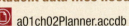

a01ch02Planner.accdb

a01ch02PlannerDec.txt

You will save your file as:

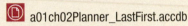

a01ch02Planner_LastFirst.accdb

Sue Morris has a small event-planning business. She recently decided to transfer her company's data to a database. Although she has started on the database, she is too busy to finish it, so she has hired you to complete the implementation.

a. Open the Access file, **a01ch02Planner**. Save your file as a01ch02Planner_LastFirst using your last and first name. If necessary, enable the content.

b. Sue wants to ensure that certain data is entered correctly. Open **tblClients** in Design view.
   - For **Phone**, add an input mask so that fields appear as **(555) 555-5555** with a placeholder of "_", and save with symbols in the mask.
   - Change the field size of **State** to 2.
   - Change the field size of **ZipCode** to 5.

c. Import the decorations data stored in **a01ch02PlannerDec.txt** into a new table.
   - The data is delimited and separated with commas.
   - Choose your own primary key of **Field1**.
   - Name the table tblDecorations.
   - Do not save the import steps.

d. In Design view for **tblDecorations**, make the following changes to the fields.

Current Field Name	New Field Name	Data Type	Description	Field Size
Field1	DecorationID	Number	A unique identifier for the decoration	Long Integer
Field2	Decoration	Short Text	Decoration label	20
Field3	Color	Short Text	Decoration color	10
Field4	Category	Short Text	Type of decoration	20

e. Sue wants to be able to record the decorations that are being reserved for each event. This creates a many-to-many relationship between events and decorations. Create a junction table in Design view.

- Add the following fields (in this order).

Field Name	Data Type	Description	Field Size
EventID	Number	The primary key from tblEvents	Long Integer
DecorationID	Number	The primary key from tblDecorations	Long Integer
NumberReserved	Number	The number of decorations reserved	Long Integer

- Create a composite key using **EventID** and **DecorationID**.
- Save the new table as tblEventDecoration.

f. Open the **Relationships** window, create a one-to-many relationship between **ClientID** in tblClients and **ClientID** in tblEvents. Enforce referential integrity.

g. Create a many-to-many relationship between **tblEvents** and **tblDecorations** using the new junction table.

- Add the **tblEventDecoration** table to the Relationships window.
- Create a one-to-many relationship between **EventID** in tblEvents and **EventID** in tblEventDecoration. Enforce referential integrity.
- Create a one-to-many relationship between **DecorationID** in tblDecorations and **DecorationID** in tblEventDecoration. Enforce referential integrity.
- Create a relationships report accepting the name **Relationships for a01ch02Planner_LastFirst**.
- If your instructor directs you to print the relationships, print your relationship report.

h. Sue has one order to put into **tblEventDecoration**. Type the following new records in the table.

EventID	DecorationID	NumberReserved
3	7	4
3	9	40
3	17	4

i. Use the Report Wizard to create a report showing decorations needed for each event.

- Use the **LastName** and **FirstName** fields from tblClients.
- Use the **EventDate** field from tblEvents.
- Use the **Decoration** and **Color** fields from tblDecorations.
- Use **NumberReserved** from tblEventDecoration.
- View by **tblClients**, and accept the default grouping.
- Sort by **Decoration** in ascending order.
- Change Orientation to **Landscape**.
- Name the report rptEventDecorations, and then modify the report title to be Event Decorations.
- Fix the report columns as necessary so the report fits on one page. If your instructor directs you to print your results, print your report.

j. Save the report, exit Access, and then submit your file as directed by your instructor.

Critical Thinking

Name one other entity that would be useful for Morris Event Management to track in the database and provide an explanation as to why it would be useful.

Perform 1: Perform in Your Career

Student data files needed:

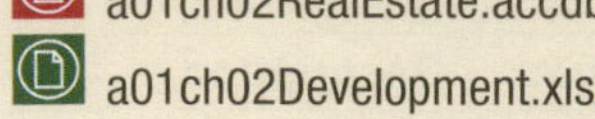

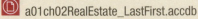

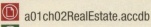

a01ch02RealEstate.accdb

a01ch02Development.xlsx

You will save your file as:

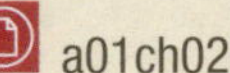

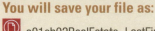

a01ch02RealEstate_LastFirst.accdb

Real Estate Listings Database

Sales & Marketing

You are interning for a local real estate firm. You have been asked to work with a database of your firm's real estate listings. There is data describing each development in the area and listing its amenities in an Excel workbook. Your boss asks that you incorporate the Excel data into the database and report some findings.

a. Open the Access file, **a01ch02RealEstate**. Save your file as a01ch02RealEstate_LastFirst using your last and first name.

b. Open **tblAgent**. Change the first and last name fields for record 1 to your first and your last name.

c. Add a new field named Phone. Create an input mask so that the numbers appear as (336) 555-1234. Store the data without the symbols. Set the field size to 12. Enter ten-digit phone numbers for all the agents.

d. Import the data contained in the Excel file **a01ch02Development** into the database as a table named tblDevelopment_iLast using your first initial and last name. Set **DevelopmentID** as the primary key.

e. Open tblDevelopment _iLast in Design view. Change the field size of DevelopmentID to 15. Change the field size of DevelopmentName to 40. Define the Pool, Playground, BikeTrail, and DogPark fields as **Yes/No** fields. Define HOADues as **Currency**.

f. Create a one-to-many relationship between the **DevelopmentID** field in tblDevelopment_iLast and tblListing. Enforce referential integrity.

g. Create a Relationship Report showing the relationships in the database. Name this report rptRelationships_iLast using your first initial and last name.

h. Use the Report Wizard to create a report showing the sales for each agent.
   - From tblAgent, select the **LastName** and **FirstName** fields.
   - From tblListing, select the **SoldDate** and **SoldPrice** fields.
   - From tblDevelopment_iLast select the **DevelopmentName** field.
   - View the data in the report by tblAgent, and sort in ascending order by SoldDate.
   - Keep the default Stepped layout and Portrait orientation.
   - Name this report rptAgentSales_iLast using your first initial and last name.

i. Edit the report title to read Agent Sales Report.

j. Save the report, exit Access, and then submit your file as directed by your instructor.

Additional Cases

Additional Chapter Cases are available at www.pearsonhighered.com/youroffice

Understanding and Using a Relational Database

This business unit had two outcomes:

Learning Outcome 1:

Understand the purpose for main database objects in Access: tables, queries, forms, and reports.

Learning Outcome 2:

Based on the needs of an organization, understand and create various types of relationships using different types of keys: primary, foreign, and composite.

In Business Unit 1 Capstone, students will demonstrate competence in these outcomes through a series of business problems at various levels from guided practice, problem solving an existing database, and performing to create new databases.

More Practice 1

Student data files needed:

a01Recipe.accdb

a01RecipePrep.xlsx

a01RecipeIng.xlsx

a01RecipeJunc.csv

You will save your file as:

a01Recipe_LastFirst.accdb

Indigo5 Restaurant

Production & Operations

Robin Sanchez, the chef of the Painted Paradise Resort's restaurant, Indigo5, wants to keep track of recipes and the ingredients they include in an Access database. This will allow her to plan menus and run reports and queries on the ingredients that are needed. Ingredients have already been stored in Excel worksheets and can be imported from Excel into Access. The dish preparation instructions can be copied from Excel and pasted into Access. Other data will need to be entered. Complete the following tasks.

a. Open the Access file **a01Recipe**. Save your file as a01Recipe_LastFirst using your last and first name. If necessary, enable the content.

b. Create a new table in **Design** view. This table will store specific recipe items.

- Add the following fields, data types, and descriptions. Change field sizes as noted.

Field Name	Data Type	Description	Field Size
RecipeID	Short Text	The recipe ID assigned to each menu item (primary key)	6
RecipeName	Short Text	The recipe name	30
FoodCategory	Short Text	The food category	15
TimeToPrepare	Number	Preparation time in minutes	Integer
Servings	Number	The number of servings this recipe makes	Integer
Instructions	Long Text	Cooking instructions	

- Designate **RecipeID** as the primary key. Save the new table as tblRecipes_iLast using your first initial and last name, and then close the table.

c. Create a form to enter recipes. Select **tblRecipes_iLast**, click the **Create** tab, and then, in the Forms group, click **Form**. Save the form as frmRecipes_iLast using your first initial and last name.

- Enter the following data into frmRecipes_iLast in Form view.

RecipeID	RecipeName	FoodCategory	TimeToPrepare	Servings
REC001	Chicken Soup	Soup	45	8
REC002	Black Beans	Beans	90	6

d. Open the Excel file, **a01RecipePrep**. For each recipe, copy the **Cooking Instructions** from the Excel worksheet, and paste these instructions into the Access field **Instructions**. Close the form, and then close Excel.

e. Import the Excel file **a01RecipeIng**, appending it to **tblIngredients**. Use the **Ingredients** worksheet. There are headers in the first row of this worksheet. Do not save the import steps.

f. Create a new table in **Design** view. This table will serve as the junction table between the tblIngredients and tblRecipes_iLast tables.

- Add the following fields, data types, and descriptions in this order. Change field sizes as noted.

Field Name	Data Type	Description	Field Size
RecipeIngredientID	AutoNumber	The recipe ingredient ID automatically assigned to each recipe ingredient (primary key)	Long Integer
RecipeID	Short Text	The recipe ID from tblRecipes (foreign key)	6
IngredientID	Number	The ingredient ID from tblIngredients (foreign key)	Long Integer
Quantity	Number	The quantity of the ingredient required in the recipe	Double

- Assign **RecipeIngredientID** as the primary key.
- Save the new table as tblRecipeIngredients_iLast using your first initial and last name.
- Close the table.

g. Open the **Relationships** window, and add all three tables to the window.

- Create a one-to-many relationship between **RecipeID** in tblRecipes_iLast and **RecipeID** in tblRecipeIngredients_iLast. Enforce referential integrity. Do not cascade update or cascade delete.
- Create a one-to-many relationship between **IngredientID** in tblIngredients and **IngredientID** in tblRecipeIngredients_iLast. Enforce referential integrity. Do not cascade update or cascade delete.
- Create a relationship report accepting the default name.
- Save the relationships, and then close the Relationships window.

h. The Recipe Ingredients junction data were stored in a comma-separated values file, also known as a csv file. This is a comma-delimited format that can be read by Excel. Access treats a csv file as a text file. Import **a01RecipeJunc** as **Text**, appending it to **tblRecipe-Ingredients_iLast**. Select **Delimited**, **Comma**, and **First Row Contains Field Names**. Do not save the import steps.

i. Use the Simple Query Wizard and the data in tblRecipes_iLast, tblRecipeIngredients_iLast, and tblIngredients to create a query that displays the ingredients for each dish. The query results should list **RecipeName**, **Quantity**, **Ingredient**, and **Units**. This will be a **Detail** query. Run your query. Adjust the width of the query columns as necessary. Save your query as qryRecipeIngredients_iLast using your first initial and last name.

j. Create a report with the source **qryRecipeIngredients_iLast** using the Report Wizard. Select all fields, group by **RecipeName**, and then sort by **Ingredient**. Accept all other defaults. Name your report rptRecipeIngredients_iLast using your first initial and last name.

k. Modify the report title to be Recipe Ingredients Report by iLast using your first initial and last name. Adjust the report columns as necessary.

l. Save the report, exit Access, and then submit your file as directed by your instructor.

Problem Solve 1

Student data file needed:

 a01HotelEvent.accdb

You will save your file as:

 a01HotelEvent_LastFirst.accdb

Group Reservations Database

Production & Operations

Patti Rochelle, corporate event planner, wants to be able to track group reservations with the conference rooms that are booked for the event. This will involve tracking conference rooms, groups, and events.

A group can book several events. Each event is booked by just one group. Each event could require multiple conference rooms. Conference rooms can be booked for several events (on different days). You will need a junction table for this relationship. Complete the following tasks.

a. Open the Access file **a01HotelEvent**. Save your file as a01HotelEvent_LastFirst using your last and first name. If necessary, enable the content.

b. Create a new table in Design view. This table will store conference rooms.

- Add the following fields (in the following order). Where necessary, decide upon data types.

Field Name	Data Type	Description	Field Size
ConfRoomID	AutoNumber	A unique identifier for the conference room	Long Integer
RoomName	Pick an appropriate data type.	The name of the conference room	40
Capacity	Pick an appropriate data type.	The capacity of the conference room	Integer

- Assign **ConfRoomID** as the primary key.
- Save the new table as **tblConfRooms**.

c. In this order, enter the following rooms into the table.

RoomName	Capacity
Musica	500
Eldorado	100
Pueblo	25

d. Create a new table in Design view. This table will store groups.

- Add the following fields, data types, and descriptions (in the following order). Where necessary, decide upon data types.

Field Name	Data Type	Description	Field Size
GroupID	AutoNumber	A unique identifier for the group (primary key)	Long Integer
GroupName	Pick an appropriate data type.	Group name	40
ContactFirstName	Pick an appropriate data type.	Contact person first name	30
ContactLastName	Pick an appropriate data type.	Contact person last name	40
ContactPhone	Pick an appropriate data type.	Contact phone number	14

- Define an input mask for contact phone number. Use a mask that will show phone numbers as **(555) 555-5555** with a placeholder of "_", and save with the symbols in the mask.
- Assign **GroupID** as the primary key. Save the new table as tblGroup.

e. Create a new table in Design view. This table will store events.

- Add the following fields, data types, and descriptions (in the following order). Where necessary, decide upon data types.

Field Name	Data Type	Description	Field Size
EventID	AutoNumber	A unique identifier for the event (primary key)	Long Integer
EventName	Pick an appropriate data type.	The name of the event	40
EventStart	Pick an appropriate data type.	Starting date for the event	Short Date
EventLength	Pick an appropriate data type.	Length of the event (in days)	Integer
GroupID	Number	The Group ID from tblGroup (foreign key)	Long Integer

- Make sure that you have assigned EventID as a primary key. Save the new table as tblEvent.

f. Create a new table in Design view. This table will serve as the junction table between tblConfRooms and tblEvent.

- Add the following fields, data types, and descriptions (in the following order). Where necessary, decide upon the field names and data types.

Field Name	Data Type	Description	Field Size
ReservationID	AutoNumber	A unique identifier for the conference reservation (primary key)	Long Integer
EventID	Number	The Event ID from tblEvent (foreign key)	Long Integer
ConfRoomID	Number	The Conference Room ID from tblConfRooms (foreign key)	Long Integer
ReservationDate	Pick an appropriate data type.	Reservation date	Short Date
DaysReserved	Number	Number of days reserved	Integer

- Make sure that you have assigned ReservationID as a primary key. Save the new table as tblConfRes.

g. Open the **Relationships** window.

- Create a one-to-many relationship between the correct field in tblGroup and the correct field in tblEvent. Enforce referential integrity. Do not cascade update or cascade delete.
- Create a one-to-many relationship between the correct field in tblEvent and the correct field in tblConfRes. Enforce referential integrity. Do not cascade update or cascade delete.
- Create a one-to-many relationship between the correct field in tblConfRooms and tblConfRes. Enforce referential integrity. Do not cascade update or cascade delete.
- Create a relationship report, keeping the default name.

h. Enter the following data into the appropriate tables (in the following order). You may need to determine keys along the way.

Group:	Benson & Diaz Law Group
	Contact: Mary Williams (505) 555-1207
Benson & Diaz's Event:	Company Retreat
	Start Date: 2/17/2018
	Length of Event: 2 days
Benson & Diaz's Reservation of the Pueblo Room:	
	Date: 2/17/2018
	Number of Days: 2 days

Group:	Dental Association of Nova Scotia
	Contact: Firstname Lastname (replacing Firstname Lastname with your own name) (902) 555–8765
Dental Association's Event:	Annual Meeting
	Start Date: 2/17/2018
	Length of Event: 5 days
Dental Association's Reservation of the Eldorado Room:	
	Date: 2/17/2018
	Number of Days: 2 days
Dental Association's Reservation of the Pueblo Room:	
	Date: 2/20/2018
	Number of Days: 2 days

Group:	Orchard Growers of the United States
	Contact: Will Goodwin (212) 555-7889
Orchard Growers' Event:	Annual Meeting
	Start Date: 2/17/2018
	Length of Event: 2 days
Orchard Growers' Reservation of the Musica Room:	
	Date: 2/17/2018
	Number of Days: 5 days

i. Create a query using **RoomName** from tblConfRooms and **ReservationDate** and **DaysReserved** from tblConfRes. Save your query as qryEldoradoRoom. Modify the query to select the room named **Eldorado**, sort by **ReservationDate**, and then run the query. Adjust the width of the query columns as necessary. If your instructor directs you to print your results, print your query.

j. Use data from four tables to create a query about the Dental Association of Nova Scotia. The query results should list **GroupName**, **EventName**, **EventStart**, **EventLength**, **RoomName**, **ReservationDate**, and **DaysReserved**. Save your query as qryDentalAssociation. Modify the query to select the group named **Dental Association of Nova Scotia**, sort by **ReservationDate**, and then run the query. Adjust the width of the columns as necessary. If your instructor directs you to print your results, print your query.

k. Create a report from **qryDentalAssociation**. Select all fields. Accept the default view by tblGroup. Sort by **RoomName** and **ReservationDate**. Select **Landscape orientation**. Name your report rptDentalAssociationBooking. Adjust the width of the report columns as necessary. Modify the report title to be Dental Association Booking. If your instructor directs you to print your results, print your report.

l. Save the report, exit Access, and then submit your file as directed by your instructor.

Critical Thinking

In this project, you were asked to pick an appropriate data type for several of the fields. Explain how you determined which data types were most appropriate. Do you think there was more than one appropriate data type for any of the fields? Explain your thinking for one of the choices you made.

Problem Solve 2

Student data files needed:

 a01HotelRoom.accdb

 a01HotelType.txt

 a01HotelItems.xlsx

You will save your file as:

a01HotelRoom_LastFirst.accdb

Room Inventory Database

Production & Operations

For each room at the hotel, the resort wants to track room types and all inventory items such as furniture, artwork, and appliances. You will build an Access database to do this tracking. The database will have four new tables: tblRoomType, tblRoom, tblItem, and a junction table between tblRoom and tblItem, named tblRoomItem.

a. Open the Access file, **a01HotelRoom**. Save your file as a01HotelRoom_LastFirst using your last and first name. If necessary, enable the content.

b. Create a new table in Design view. This table will store the room types.

- Add the following fields (in the following order).

Field Name	Data Type	Description	Field Size
RoomType	Short Text	The name of the room type	20
RoomAmenities	Long Text	The amenities that this type of room has	

- Do not assign a primary key yet.
- Save the new table as tblRoomType.

c. The data for this table has been stored in a text file delimited with tabs, **a01HotelType**. Import the data, and append it to **tblRoomType**.

- Add a new field to be the primary key. The field should be the first field in the table and should have the following characteristics.

Field Name	Data Type	Description	Field Size
RoomTypeID	AutoNumber	A unique identifier for the room type	Long Integer

d. Create a new table in Design view. This table will store individual rooms.

- Add the following fields, data types, fields sizes, and descriptions (in the following order).

Field Name	Data Type	Description	Field Size
RoomNumber	Short Text	A unique identifier for the room	30
ResortFloor	Number	Floor that the room is on	Integer
SquareFeet	Number	Square feet of this room	Long Integer
RoomTypeID	Number	Foreign key to tblRoomType	Long Integer

- Assign a primary key using the most appropriate field.
- Name the table tblRoom.

e. Enter the following data into the tblRoom table.

RoomNumber	ResortFloor	SquareFeet	RoomTypeID
101	1	500	1
102	1	520	1
106	1	600	2
206	2	600	2
112	1	700	3
120	1	1000	4
231	2	1400	5

f. The resort has been tracking inventory items in Excel. Import the spreadsheet **a01HotelItems** into a new table named tblItem. The first row contains column headings. Do not assign a primary key yet.

g. Make the following design changes to **tblItem**, adding descriptions for all fields.

Action	Field Name	Data Type	Description	Field Size
Add as primary key.	ItemID	AutoNumber	A unique identifier for inventory items	Long Integer
Modify field.	ItemName		Name of item	20
Modify field.	ItemDescription		Description of item	40
Modify field.	Color		Color of item	20
Modify field.	ItemCount		Number of items in hotel	Long Integer
Remove field.	Which rooms			

h. Create a new table in Design view. This table will serve as the junction table between tblRoom and tblItem.

- Add the following fields, data types, field sizes, and descriptions (in the following order).

Field Name	Data Type	Description	Field Size
RoomItemID	AutoNumber	A unique identifier for the room item (primary key)	Long Integer
RoomNumber	Short Text	The room number from tblRoom (foreign key)	30
ItemID	Number	The item ID from tblItem (foreign key)	Long Integer
InventoryCount	Number	Number of items of this type in this room	Long Integer

- Make sure that you have assigned RoomItemID as a primary key. Save the new table as tblRoomItem.

i. Create the following relationships using existing fields and enforcing referential integrity. Do not cascade update or cascade delete.

- Each room is of a single room type. There are many rooms of each type.
- A room may have many items in it. Each type of inventory item may be in many rooms. You will need to use the junction table tblRoomItem to create this relationship.
- Create a relationship report accepting the default report name. If your instructor directs you to print your results, print your report.

j. Enter the following data into **tblRoomItem**.

RoomItemID	RoomNumber	ItemID	InventoryCount
Let Access autonumber as 1.	101	1	1
Let Access autonumber as 2.	102	1	1
Let Access autonumber as 3.	120	1	1
Let Access autonumber as 4.	120	3	1
Let Access autonumber as 5.	120	4	1
Let Access autonumber as 6.	120	8	4
Let Access autonumber as 7.	120	9	3
Let Access autonumber as 8.	101	8	2
Let Access autonumber as 9.	102	8	2
Let Access autonumber as 10.	101	3	1

k. Create a report showing **RoomType** and **RoomAmenities** from **tblRoomType** and **ResortFloor** and **RoomNumber** from **tblRoom**. View by **tblRoomType**, and add a grouping by **ResortFloor**. Sort by **RoomNumber**. Select **Landscape** orientation. Name your report rptRoomType. Change the title of your report to Rooms Listed by Room Type. Adjust the column widths as needed so that all four columns are displayed on each page. If your instructor directs you to print your results, print your report.

l. Create a query listing **RoomNumber** from **tblRoom**, **InventoryCount** from **tblRoomItem**, and **ItemName** from **tblItem**. Save your query as qryTelephone. Modify the query to select the items named **Telephone**, sort by **RoomNumber**, and then run the query. Fix column widths. If your instructor directs you to print your results, print your query.

m. Create a query listing **RoomNumber** and **ResortFloor** from **tblRoom**, **InventoryCount** from **tblRoomItem**, and **ItemName** from **tblItem**. Save your query as **qryRoom120Contents**. Modify the query to select the room numbered **120**, sort by **ItemName**, and then run the query. Fix column widths. If your instructor directs you to print your results, print your query.

n. Save the query, exit Access, and then submit your file as directed by your instructor.

Perform 1: Perform in Your Life

Student data file needed:

 Blank Access database

You will save your file as:

 a01Contacts_LastFirst.accdb

Personal Contact Database

Research & Development

You have decided to keep better track of the contact information of your family, friends, and acquaintances. You will begin with a blank database file, building tables, forms, queries, and reports for typical ways you would use contact information in your personal life. You will track data to include names, mailing addresses, e-mail addresses, cell phone numbers, and birthdates.

a. Start **Access**, and then create a new blank database. Save the database as **a01Contacts_LastFirst** using your last and first name.

b. When saving any objects in this project, add **_iLast** using your first initial and last name, to the end of the name.

c. Design a table to store contact information for your family, friends, and acquaintances. Use the following fields: **LastName**, **FirstName**, **Street**, **City**, **State**, **ZIP**, **Cell#**, **Email**, and **BirthMonth**.

- Insert an AutoNumber field as the first field with the name, **ContactID**.
- Add an Input Mask to Cell# with symbols for phone numbers as appropriate.
- Add an Input Mask with symbols for **ZIP**.
- For all other fields, determine and enter appropriate data types, descriptions, and field sizes.
- Save your table as **tblContacts_iLast**.

d. Enter a minimum of ten records in **tblContacts_iLast**. Widen fields as appropriate to ensure that all information is visible.

e. Using **tblContacts_iLast**, design a columnar form with all fields, and name the form **frmContacts_iLast**.

f. Using **tblContacts_iLast** and the Report Wizard, design a tabular report named **rptPhoneBook_iLast** that displays the fields **LastName**, **FirstName**, and **Cell#**. Sort in ascending order by **LastName**. Display report in portrait orientation. Modify the title to be **Last Name's Phone Book** using your last name. Adjust column widths as appropriate to ensure that all information is visible.

g. Create another report that would be useful, using the Report Wizard. Apply any appropriate groupings and sorting. Adjust column widths as appropriate to ensure that all information is visible. Give the report an appropriate title, and save the report with an appropriate name.

h. Create a query that would be useful. Use a specific criterion to select only a subset of your contacts, and be sure to apply appropriate sorting. Save the query with an appropriate name.

i. Using **tblContacts_iLast**, create a query named **qryCity_iLast** to find out which contacts reside in a city of your choice. Show the fields **LastName**, **FirstName**, and **City**. Modify the query design to show only the contacts who reside in the city of your choice. Sort in ascending order by **FirstName** or **LastName**. Run the query.

j. Save the query, exit Access, and then submit your file as directed by your instructor.

Student data file needed:

 Blank Access database

You will save your file as:

 a01HorseStable_LastFirst.accdb

Bluff Creek Stables Inventory Database

Production & Operations

You live in the Midwest and work as a stable hand for Bluff Creek Stables, a regionally well-known horse barn. This stable provides guided trail rides, horse-drawn wagon and sleigh rides, horse camps, and horseback riding lessons for people of all ages. The stable manager has asked you to complete an inventory database of the horses, farrier care (equine hoof care), and saddle time.

a. Start **Access**, and then create a new blank database. Save the database as **a01HorseStable_LastFirst** using your last and first name.

b. When saving any objects in this project, add _iLast, using your first initial and last name, to the end of the name.

c. Design a table to store an inventory of the stable's horses. Use the following fields: **HorseID**, **HorseName**, **Breed**, **TrailHorse**, **LessonHorse**, and **GuideHorse**.

- Assign **HorseID** to be the primary key with the AutoNumber data type.
- For all fields, enter appropriate data types and descriptions, and apply field sizes. Save your table as **tblHorses_iLast**.
- Enter the following data into the table, in this order.

HorseID	HorseName	Breed	TrailHorse	LessonHorse	GuideHorse
1	Pecos	Draft Cross	Yes	Yes	No
2	Joey	Thoroughbred	Yes	No	Yes
3	Tahnee	Paint	Yes	No	Yes
4	Buck	QuarterHorse	Yes	Yes	No
5	Moose	Draft Cross	Yes	Yes	Yes
6	Chip	Paint	Yes	Yes	No
7	Doc	QuarterHorse	Yes	Yes	Yes
8	Buzzard	Draft Cross	Yes	No	No
9	Patches	Warmblood	No	Yes	Yes
10	Champ	Warmblood	No	Yes	No

d. Design a table to store farrier data. Use the following fields: **HorseID** and **DateTrimmed**.

- For all fields, enter appropriate data types and descriptions, and apply field sizes.
- Save your table as **tblFarrier_iLast**.

e. Enter the following data into tblFarrier_iLast, in this order.

HorseID	DateTrimmed
1	9/29/2018
2	7/26/2018
3	9/29/2018
4	9/27/2018
5	9/27/2018
6	7/21/2018
7	9/27/2018
8	9/27/2018
9	9/29/2018
10	7/26/2018

f. Design a table to store saddle time. Use the following fields: HorseID, 2016Hours, 2017Hours, and 2018Hours.
   - Assign **HorseID** to be the primary key.
   - For all fields, enter appropriate data types and descriptions, and apply field sizes.
   - Save your table as tblSaddleTime_iLast.

g. Enter the following data into **tblSaddleTime_iLast**, in this order.

HorseID	2016Hours	2017Hours	2018Hours
1	154	115	138
2	37	56	42
3	76	64	106
4	45	55	98
5	90	83	75
6	50	30	30
7	102	80	115
8	45	58	75
9	50	52	120
10	85	67	15

h. Open the Relationships window. Create a one-to-many relationship between HorseID in tblHorses_iLast and HorseID in tblFarrier_iLast. Enforce referential integrity. Do not cascade update or cascade delete.

i. Create a one-to-one relationship between HorseID in tblHorses_iLast and HorseID in tblSaddleTime_iLast. Enforce referential integrity. Do not cascade update or cascade delete.

j. Create a relationship report named rptRelationships_iLast.

k. Create a form based on tblHorses_iLast named frmHorses_iLast.

l. Create a report showing the most current information for each horse. Display the fields **HorseID**, **HorseName**, **Breed**, **DateTrimmed**, and **2018Hours**. Group by **Breed**, and sort in ascending order by **HorseID**. Display report in landscape orientation. Save the report as rptCurrentInfo_iLast.

m. Create a query to find out which horses are both guide and lesson horses. Show the **HorseID**, **HorseName**, **GuideHorse**, and **LessonHorse** fields. Save the query as qryGuideLessonHorses_iLast.

n. Create a query to find out which horses logged more than 100 hours of saddle time in 2018. Show the **HorseID**, **HorseName**, and **2018Hours** fields. Save the query as qry100+Hours_iLast.

o. Exit Access, and then submit your file as directed by your instructor.

Perform 3: Perform in Your Team

Student data files needed:

 Blank Access database

Blank Word document

You will save your files as:

 a01Music_TeamName.accdb

 a01MusicPlan_TeamName.docx

Production & Operations

Independent Music Label

The owner of an independent music label needs to keep track of the label's groups, the musicians in the groups, and the groups' music, both albums and songs. You have been asked to create a database for the label.

The label owner would like to be able to get a list of groups with all musicians, get a list of groups with albums, select an album and see all songs in the album, and select a group and see their albums with all songs in the album. You will need to design tables, fields, relationships, queries, and reports for the label.

Because databases can be opened and edited by only one person at a time, it is a good idea to plan ahead by designing your tables in advance. You will use a Word document to plan your database and to plan which team member will complete each task.

a. Select one team member to set up the Word document and Access database by completing steps b through e.

b. Open your browser and navigate to either https://www.onedrive.com, https://www.drive.google.com, or any other instructor assigned location. Be sure all members of the team have an account on the chosen system. Create a new folder, and name it **a01MusicFolder_TeamName**. Replace TeamName with the name assigned to your team by your instructor.

c. Start **Access**, and then create a new blank database. Save the database as **a01Music_TeamName**. Replace TeamName with the name assigned to your team by your instructor.

d. Upload the **a01Music_TeamName** database to the **a01MusicFolder_TeamName** folder, and then share the folder with the other members of your team. Verify that the other team members have permission to edit the contents of the shared folder and that they are required to log in to access it.

e. Create a new Word document in the assignment folder and then name it **a01MusicPlan_TeamName**. Replace TeamName with the name assigned to your team by your instructor.

f. In the Word document, each team member must list his or her first and last name as well as a summary of his or her planned contributions. As work is completed on the database, this document should be updated with the specifics of each team member's contributions.

g. Use the Word document to list the fields you need in each table, the primary keys for each table, and the foreign keys.

h. In Access, your team members will need to complete the following steps.

- Design your tables.
- Enter data for three music groups into your tables.

Groups	Group Members	Albums	Songs
Clean Green, an Enviro-Punk band	Jon Smith (vocalist and guitar) Lee Smith (percussion and keyboard)	Clean Green	Esperando Verde Precious Drops Recycle Mania Don't Tread on Me
		Be Kind to Animals	It's Our Planet Too Animal Rag Where Will We Live?
Spanish Moss, a Spanish Jazz band	Hector Caurendo (guitar) Pasquale Rodriguez (percussion) Perry Trent (vocalist) Meredith Selmer (bass)	Latin Latitude	Attitude Latitude Flying South Latin Guitarra Cancion Cancion
Your band	Your team members (and their instruments)	You decide	You decide

- Create your relationships. Create a relationship report.
- Create a report showing all groups with all musicians.
- Create a report showing all groups, each group's type, and each group's albums.
- Create a query to select an album from your band and see all songs in the album.
- Create a query to select your band and see all your albums with all songs in the albums.

i. Save the database and the document, exit Access and Word, and then submit your files as directed by your instructor.

Perform 4: How Others Perform

Student data file needed:

 a01Textbook.accdb

You will save your file as:

 a01Textbook_LastFirst.docx

College Bookstore

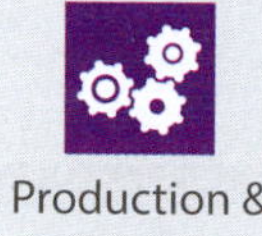

Production & Operations

A colleague has created a database for your college bookstore. He is having problems creating the relationships in the database and has come to you for your help. What problems do you see in his database design? He has three tables in his database: one for sections of courses, one for instructors, and one for textbooks, as shown in Figures 1, 2, and 3.

a. Open the Access file, **a01Textbook**. Save your file as a01Textbook_LastFirst using your last and first name. You do not need to make changes to this database, but you will want to look at the database in more detail than is shown in the figures.

b. Create a Word document named a01Textbook_LastFirst using your last and first name, where you will answer the remaining questions.

c. Are there any errors in the way fields are defined or named in the tables? In your a01Textbook_LastFirst Word document, list these errors by table.

d. Are there any errors in the way tables are named or defined? In your a01Textbook_LastFirst Word document, list these errors by table.

e. How would you want to define the relationships?
   - An instructor can teach many sections; a section is taught by just one instructor.
   - A section can have many textbooks; a textbook can be used in many sections.

f. Save the database and the document, exit Access and Word, and then submit your files as directed by your instructor.

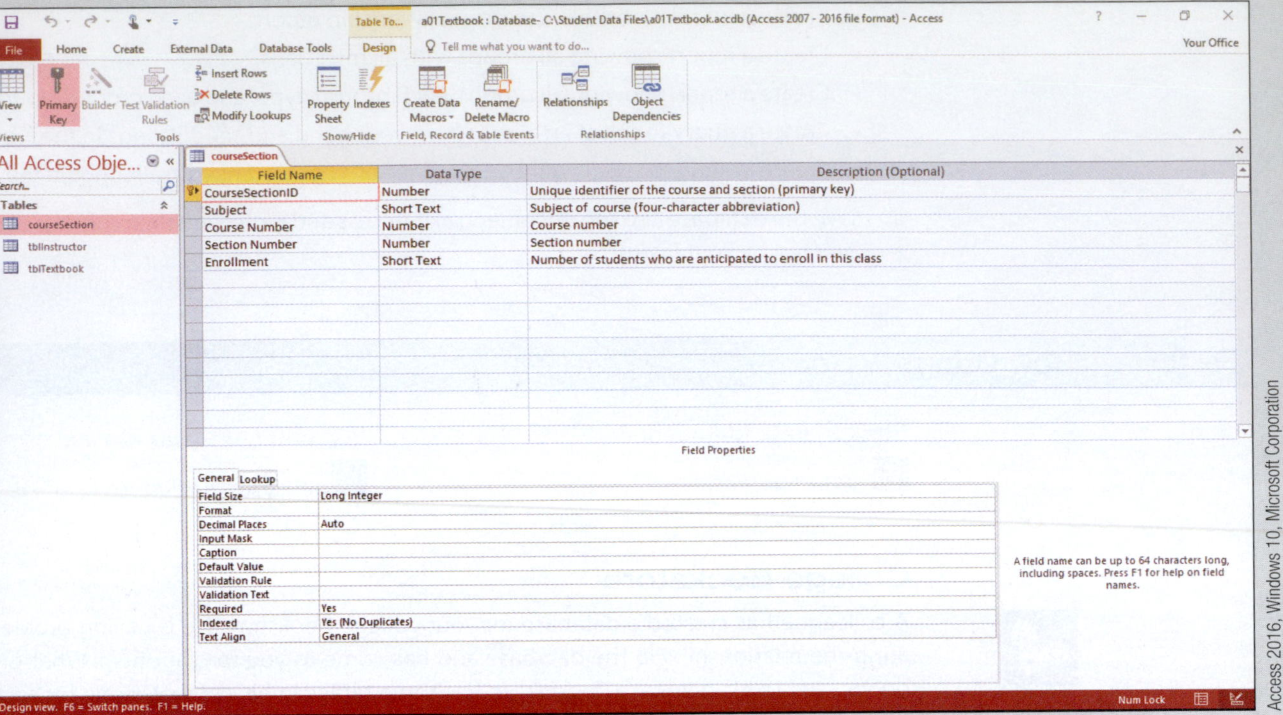

Access 2016, Windows 10, Microsoft Corporation

Figure 1 Table design for courseSection

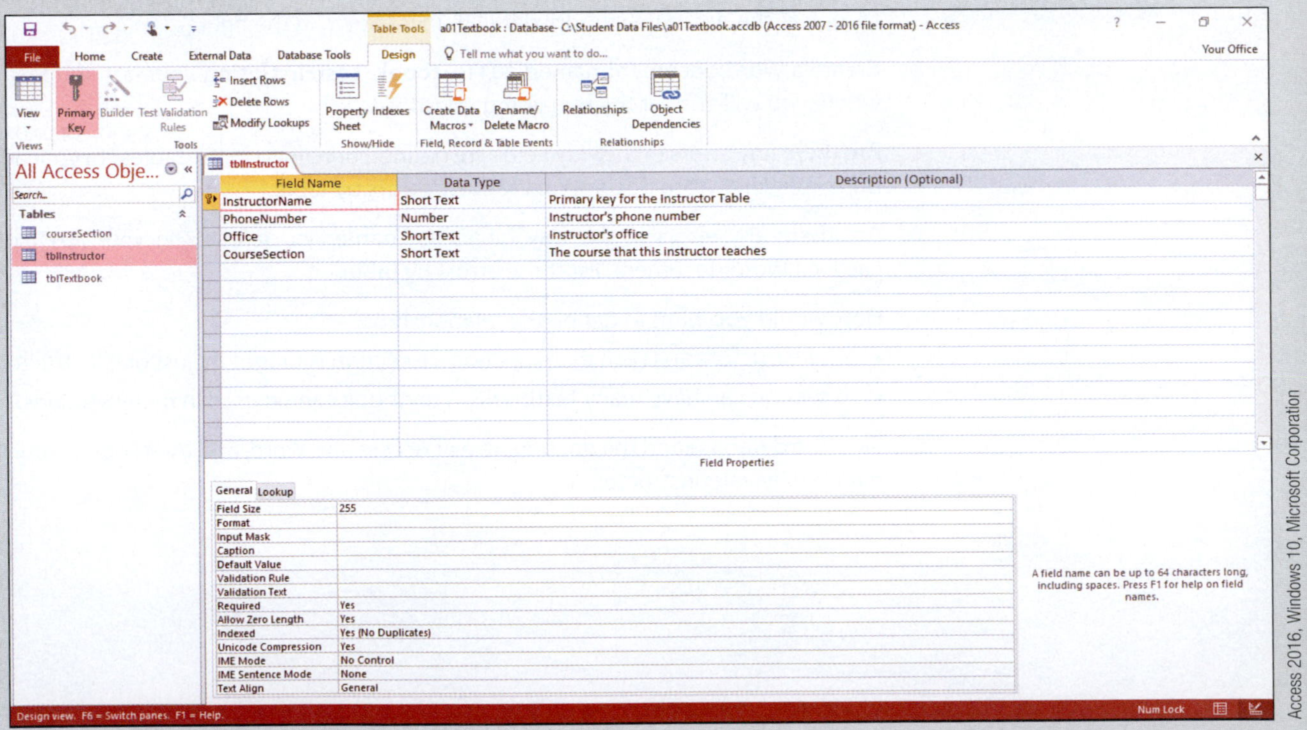

Access 2016, Windows 10, Microsoft Corporation

Figure 2 Table design for tblInstructor

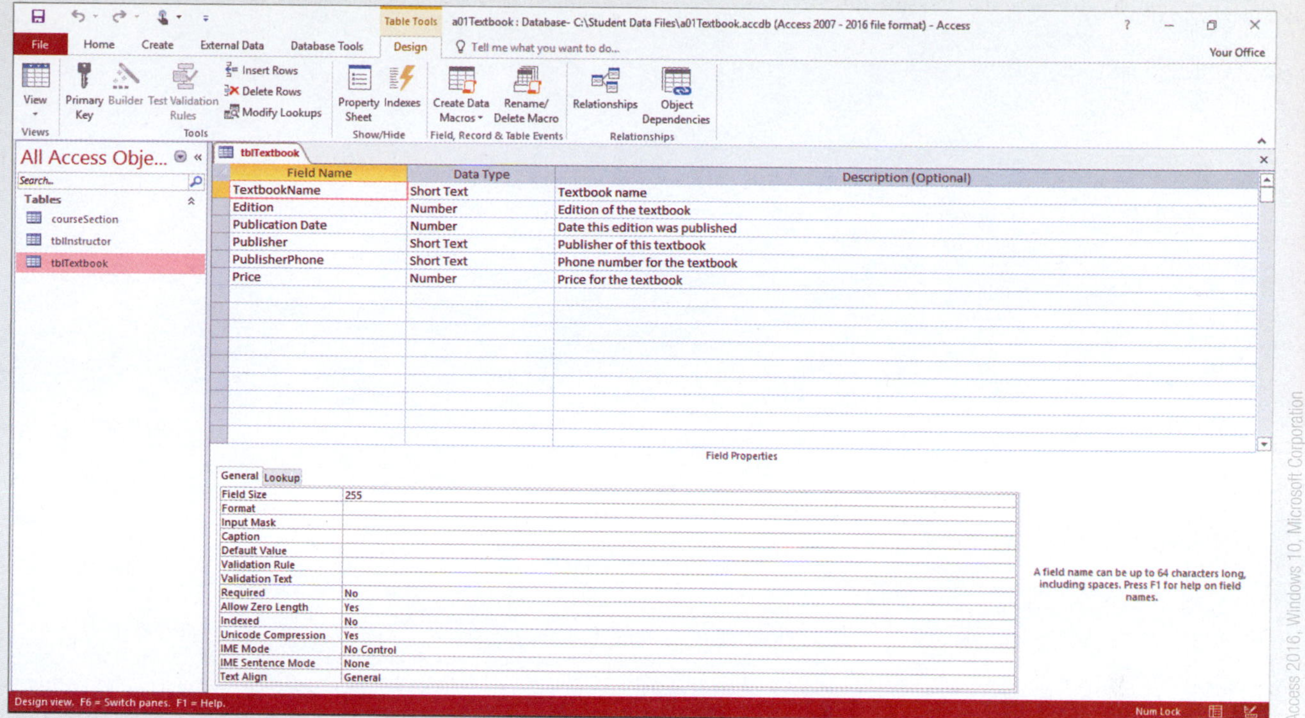

Figure 3 Table design for tblTextbook

Access Business Unit 2

Accessing, Maintaining, and Presenting Information

Databases are an essential part of operating a business. The ability to navigate and search for data as well as present data is a crucial business function of a database. While simply searching a database table for a specific record is helpful, searching data across multiple tables using sophisticated criteria can reveal important business information. Using forms in Access allows the database user to navigate and enter new information into a database simply and quickly. Queries allow for searching single or multiple tables using complex criteria to return data or reveal new insights from the database. Reports provide a method of presenting data from tables or queries for viewing, printing, or exporting to formats such as PDF documents.

Learning Outcome 1:

Find data in a database by searching tables and designing queries that sort, aggregate, and calculate complex search results.

Real World Success 

"My company sells luxury appliances. Sometimes we run out of products and don't have time to wait for the supplier. In the past, I'd have to get on the phone and call all our other locations in the region to see if they had extra that they could spare. Now I run a query, and in less than a minute, I know which location has it and how fast they can ship it. The queries are so popular that I've shared them with all of the managers."

- David, alumnus and procurement specialist

Learning Outcome 2:

Navigate and update information in a database using forms and present information in a database by creating customized reports.

Real World Success 

"After I started using Access for entering my data and running reports, my supervisor asked whether I could set up a database for my coworker to use for her job. She didn't know Access, so I created forms for her data entry. She just enters today's data and runs her daily reports."

- Elaine, marketing analyst and alumnus

Microsoft Access 2016

Chapter 3 | QUERIES AND DATA ACCESS

OBJECTIVES

1. Find and replace records in the datasheet p. 169
2. Modify datasheet appearance p. 174
3. Run query wizards p. 175
4. Create queries in Design view p. 178
5. Sort table and query results p. 185
6. Define selection criteria for queries p. 187
7. Create aggregate functions p. 202
8. Create calculated fields p. 209

Prepare Case

Production & Operations

Turquoise Oasis Spa Data Management

The Turquoise Oasis Spa has been popular with resort clients. The owners have spent several months putting spa data into an Access database so they can better manage the data. You have been asked to help show the staff how best to use the database to find information about products, services, and customers. For training purposes, not all the spa records have been added yet. Once the staff has been trained, the remaining records will be entered into the database.

Subbotina Anna/Fotolia

Student data file needed for this chapter:

 a02ch03Spa.accdb

You will save your file as:

 a02ch03Spa_LastFirst.accdb

CHAPTER 3

Working with Datasheets

Datasheets are used to view all records in a table at one time. Each record is viewed as a row in the table. Records can be entered, edited, and deleted directly in a datasheet. When a table becomes so large that all the records and fields are no longer visible in the datasheet window without scrolling, the Find command can be used to quickly find specific values in a record. In this section, you will find records in a datasheet and modify the appearance of a datasheet.

Find and Replace Records in the Datasheet

The Navigation bar allows you to move to the top and bottom of a table or scroll to a specific record; however, this can be inefficient if your table is large. To manage larger tables, Access provides ways for you to quickly locate information within the datasheet. Once that information has been found, it can then be easily replaced with another value by using the **Replace command**.

If you do not know the exact value you are looking for because you do not know how it is spelled or how someone entered it, you can use a **wildcard character**. A wildcard character is used as a placeholder for an unknown part of a value or to match a certain pattern in a value. For example, if you know that the value you are looking for contains the word "market", you can use a wildcard character at the beginning and end such as *market*.

Opening the Starting File

The owners of the spa have spent several months entering spa data into an Access database so they can better manage the data. You have been asked to help show the staff how best to use the database to find information about products, services, and customers. For training purposes, not all the spa records have been added yet. In this exercise you will open the database and save it with a new file name.

A03.00

To Open the a02ch03Spa Database

a. Start **Access**, click **Open Other Files** in the left pane, and then double-click **This PC**. Navigate through the folder structure to the location of your student data files, and then double-click **a02ch03Spa**. A database opens displaying tables and queries related to the spa.

b. On the File tab, click **Save As**, save the file as an **Access Database**, and click **Save As**. Navigate to the location where you are saving your project files and then change the file name to a02ch03Spa_LastFirst using your last and first name. Click **Save**. If necessary, enable the content.

Finding Records in a Table

In Datasheet view, you can use the **Find command** to quickly locate specific records using all or part of a field value. In this exercise, a staff member found a book left by one of the guests. A first name was printed on the inside of the book cover. The staff member remembers helping a man named Guy who said he was from North Carolina, but the staff member is not certain of his last name. In this exercise, you will show the staff how to use the Find command to quickly navigate through the table to search for this guest.

A03.01

To Find Records in the Datasheet

SIDE NOTE
Pin the Ribbon
If your ribbon is collapsed, pin your ribbon open. Click the Home tab. In the lower right-hand corner of the ribbon, click Pin the Ribbon [pin].

a. In the Navigation Pane, double-click **tblCustomer** to open the table.

b. Add a record at the end of the table with your first name, last name, address, city, state, phone, and e-mail address. Press Tab until the record selector is on the next row and your record has been added to the table.

c. On the Navigation bar, click **First Record** [First Record] to go to the first record in the table. On the Home tab, in the Find group, click **Find** to open the Find and Replace dialog box.

d. Replace the text in the Find What box with Guy. Click the **Look In** arrow, and then select **Current document**.

SIDE NOTE
Find Shortcut
Ctrl+F is the keyboard shortcut for Find.

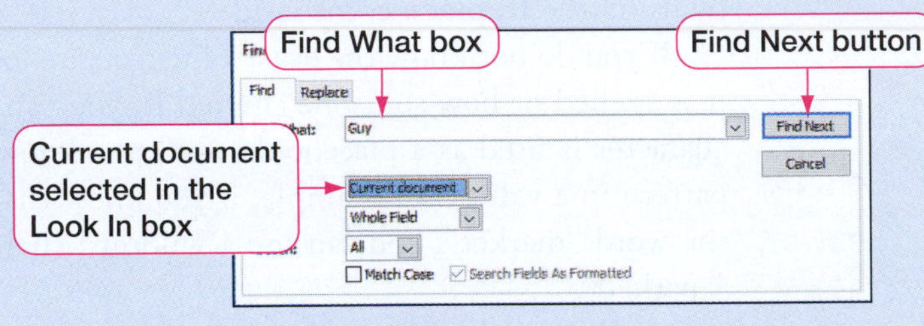

Figure 1 Find and Replace dialog box to find all records for "Guy"

Access 2016, Windows 10, Microsoft Corporation

SIDE NOTE
Spelling Counts
Spelling counts in Access, so if you enter a search item and Access cannot find it, the search value or table value may be spelled wrong.

e. Click **Find Next**. Access highlights the first record found for Guy Bowers from Derby, North Carolina (NC). This is a possibility, but there might be a second Guy.

f. Click **Find Next** again to check for more records with Guy. Guy Blake from Suffolk, Wisconsin, is found.

g. Click **Find Next** again to check for more records with Guy. When Access is done searching and cannot find any more matches, you will see the message "Microsoft Access finished searching the records. The search item was not found."

h. Click **OK**, and then click **Cancel** to close the Find and Replace dialog box.

Troubleshooting

If you did not get the results shown above, go back and carefully check the settings in the Find and Replace dialog box. Make sure Match Case is not checked. When Match Case is checked, the search will be case sensitive. Also check to make sure the Look In box shows Current document. If the Look In box shows Current field, Access will look only in the field selected.

Finding and Replacing Records in a Datasheet

Not only can you find records using the Find command, but you can also replace records once you have found them with the Replace command. In a large table, it is helpful to locate a record using the Find command and then replace the data using the Replace command.

The spa receptionist has received an e-mail from Erica Rocha about her upcoming marriage, which will result in a new last name. The receptionist wants to go through the database and find any records related to Erica and change her last name to her married name, Muer. In this exercise, you will show the receptionist how to find Erica in the database and replace her last name of Rocha with Muer.

To Find and Replace Records

a. Click the **Home** tab, and in the Find group, click **Find** to open the Find and Replace dialog box.

b. In the Find and Replace dialog box, click the **Replace** tab. In the Find What box, type Rocha, and then, in the Replace With box, type Muer.

c. Verify that Look in: Current document is selected. Leave all other options as they are.

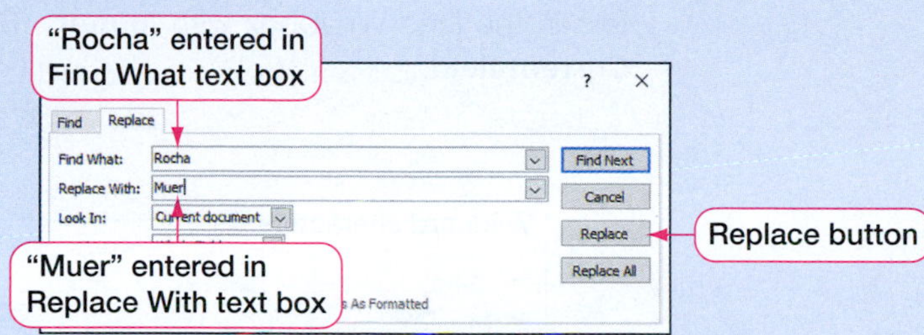

Figure 2 Find and Replace dialog box options

> **SIDE NOTE**
> **Data Is Automatically Saved**
> Access automatically saves data changes when you close the table, without prompting you to save it.

d. Click **Find Next**. Notice that the first record found has the last name Rocha, but the first name is Emily. Click **Find Next** again. Notice that this is the record for Erica Rocha. Click **Replace**. Click **OK** when you get the message that Microsoft Access has finished searching the records. The Last Name should now be Muer instead of Rocha. Click **Cancel** to close the Find and Replace dialog box.

e. **Close** [X] the table.

Using a Wildcard Character

A wildcard character, as shown in Table 1, is used as a placeholder for an unknown part of a value or to match a certain pattern in a value. A wildcard character can replace a single character or multiple characters, which can be both text and numbers.

Wildcard Character	Example
*	Used to match any number of characters; to search for a word that starts with "ar", you would enter ar*.
#	Used to match any single numeric character; to search for a three-digit number that starts with "75", you would enter 75#.
?	Used to match any single character; to search for a three-letter word that starts with "t" and ends with "p", you would enter t?p.
[ ]	Used to match any single character within the brackets; to search for a word that starts with "e", contains any of the letters "a" or "r", and ends with "r", you would enter e[ar]r and get "ear" or "err" as a result.
!	Used to match any single character NOT within the brackets; to search for a word that starts with "e", contains any letter other than "a" or "r", and ends with "r," you would enter e[!ar]r to get anything except "err" or "ear".
-	Used to match any range of characters in ascending order: "a" to "z"; to search for a word beginning with "a" and ending in "e" with any letter between "b" and "t" in between, you would enter a[b-t]e.

Table 1 Wildcard characters

The staff is looking for products with the word "butter" in the name so they can put together a weekly promotion for all these products. In this exercise, you will show them how to use a wildcard character to find the products.

To Use a Wildcard Character to Find a Record

a. In the Navigation Pane, double-click **tblProduct** to open the table.

b. In the first record, click the **ProductDescription** field. Click the **Home** tab, and in the Find group, click **Find** to open the Find and Replace dialog box. Replace the text in the Find What box with *butter*. Click the **Look In** arrow, and then click **Current field**.

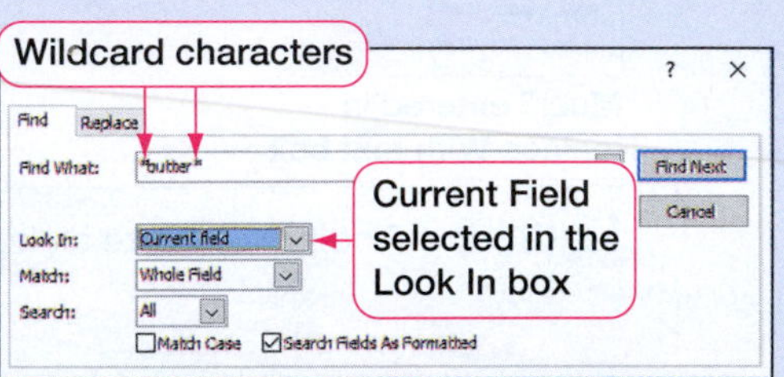

Access 2016, Windows 10, Microsoft Corporation

Figure 3 Find records with "butter" in the ProductDescription field

c. Click **Find Next**. The first record found is for ProductID P018 Cocoa Body Butter. Click **Find Next** again to find the record for ProductID P021 Lemon Body Butter.

d. Click **Find Next** again until Access has finished searching the records. When Access is done searching and cannot find any more matches, you will see the message "Microsoft Access finished searching the records. The search item was not found." Click **OK**, and then click **Cancel** to close the Find and Replace dialog box.

Troubleshooting

If Access highlights a record in the table and you cannot see it, drag the Find and Replace dialog box to another area of the screen.

e. **Close** [X] the table.

Applying a Filter to a Datasheet

A **filter** is a condition you apply temporarily to a table or query. All records that do not match the filter criteria are hidden until the filter is removed or until the table is closed and reopened. A filter is a simple technique to quickly reduce a large amount of data to a much smaller subset of data. You can choose to save a table with the filter applied so when you open the table later, the filter is still available.

You can filter a datasheet by selecting a value in a record and telling Access to filter records that contain some variation of the record you choose, or you can create a custom filter to select all or part of a field value.

When you **filter by selection**, you select a value in a record, and Access filters the records that contain only the values that match what you have selected. A customer came into the spa and stated that she was from Minnesota and had previously been a spa customer but was just browsing today. She left her glasses on the counter, and the staff wants to return them to her. In this exercise, you will help the staff members find all customers from Minnesota to see whether they recognize the customer's name.

A03.04

To Select Specific Records Using a Selection Filter

SIDE NOTE
How to Clear Filters
To delete filters from the table, click Advanced in the Sort & Filter group, and select Clear All Filters.

a. Double-click **tblCustomer** to open the table, locate the first record with an address in the state of Minnesota (MN), and then click the **State** field for that record. Click the **Home** tab, in the Sort & Filter group, click **Selection**, and then click the **Equals "MN"** option.
Access displays three records in which all states are MN for Minnesota.

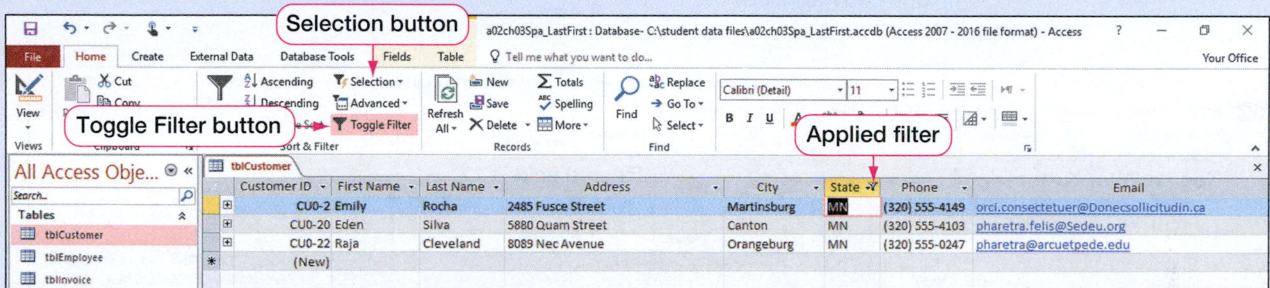

Figure 4 Filtered table for all records containing a state of MN

Access 2016, Windows 10, Microsoft Corporation

b. Click **Save** . This saves the table with the filter.
The filter is temporary unless you choose to save it with the table or query. If you do save it, the next time you open the table or query, you only have to click Toggle Filter to see the records from the state of Minnesota.

c. **Close** the table.

d. Double-click **tblCustomer** to open the table. On the Home tab, in the Sort & Filter group, click **Toggle Filter** to see the filtered records.
The Toggle Filter button in the Sort & Filter group allows you to go back and forth between viewing the filtered records and all the records in the table. To remove the filter, click Toggle Filter in the Sort & Filter group. To show the filter again, click Toggle Filter in the Sort & Filter group.

e. **Close** the table.

CONSIDER THIS | Finding Records

You have now found records using Find and Replace and using a selection filter. What are the advantages of each method? When would you use each?

Using a Text Filter

Text filters allow you to create a custom filter to match all or part of the text in a field that you specify. The staff wants to create a mailing of sample products but cannot send the products to customers with a post office box. In this exercise, you will help the staff find all customers who have "P.O. Box" as part of their address.

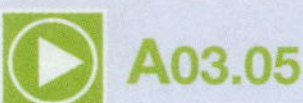

To Select Specific Records Using a Text Filter

a. Double-click **tblCustomer** to open the table. Select the entire **Address** column by clicking the column name. In the column heading, click the **filter** arrow, point to **Text Filters**, and then click **Begins With**.

b. In the Custom Filter dialog box, type P, and then click **OK**.
Access retrieves the nine records in which the addresses contain a P.O. box number. Notice that Toggle Filter in the Sort & Filter group is selected and the Filtered indicator in the Navigation bar is highlighted. You can toggle between the filtered table and the whole table by clicking on either Toggle Filter or the Filtered indicator. The filter indicator in the column heading indicates whether a filter is currently applied.

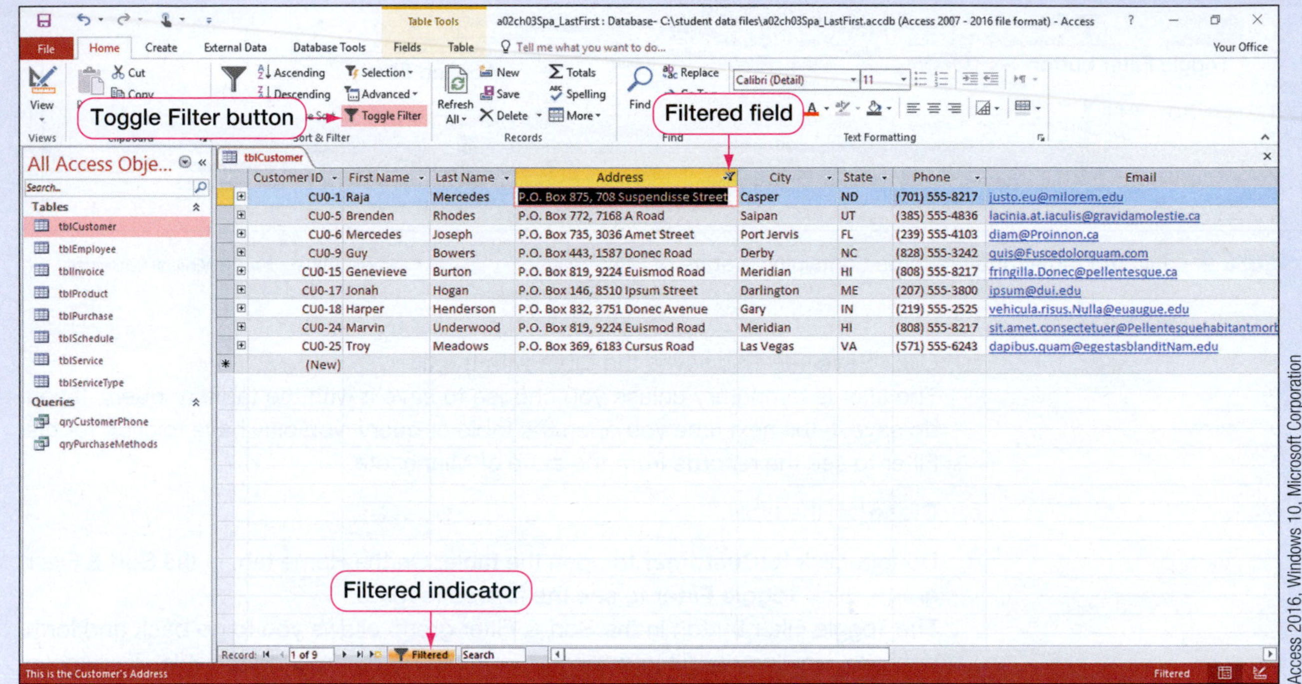

Figure 5 Results of the filter

c. Click **Save** to save the table with the new filter applied. **Close** the table.

Modify Datasheet Appearance

You can change the appearance of your datasheet by changing the font type, font size, column widths, and background colors to make it more readable. **AutoFit** is a feature that can change the column width of the data to match the widest data entered in that field. AutoFit allows you to see all the data in a particular field.

Changing the Look of a Datasheet

The manager is upset because the font is too small and she cannot see all the field headings in the invoice table. In this exercise, you will show her how to make the text larger and the columns wider.

A03.06

To Change Font Size, Column Width, and Alternating Row Colors

SIDE NOTE

Alternative Method for Changing Column Width

You can also drag a column border to make the column wider.

a. Double-click **tblInvoice** to open the table.

b. Click the **Home** tab. In the Text Formatting group, click the **Font Size** arrow [11], and then click **14**.

c. Point to the **right border** of the first field name until the pointer turns into a double-sided arrow [+], and double-click. The AutoFit feature resizes the column to best fit the data. Repeat this action for all the columns.

d. In the Text Formatting group, click the **Alternate Row Color** arrow, and then under Theme Colors, select **Green, Accent 6, Lighter 40%**. This is the tenth column and the fourth row under Theme Colors. The rows will still be alternating colors, but they will be changed to green.

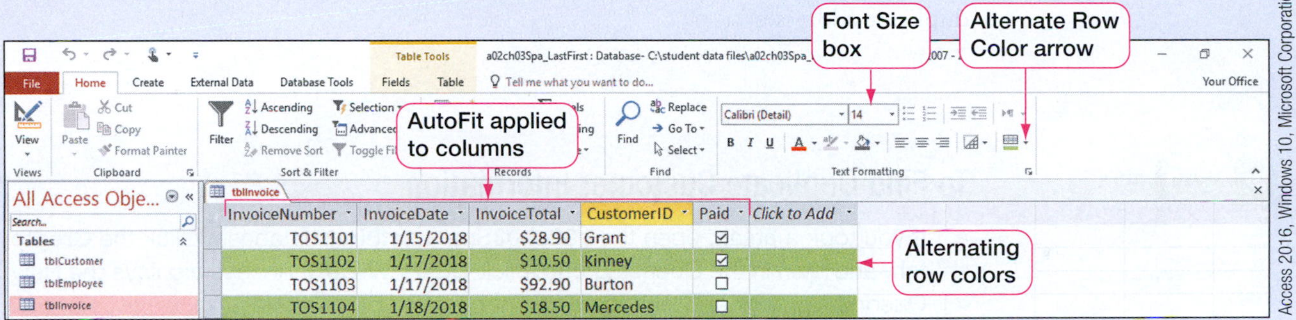

Figure 6 Modified table

e. **Close** [X] the table, and then when prompted to save the changes, click **Yes**. If you need to take a break before finishing this chapter, now is a good time.

Querying the Database

While the Find and Filter features can help you to find data quickly, a query can be created for data that you may need to find again in the future. If you recall, the Simple Query Wizard is used to display fields from one or more tables or queries with the option to choose a detailed or summary query. The Simple Query Wizard does not provide the opportunity to select data criteria. Queries can also be created in Query Design view, which not only allows you to choose the tables and fields to include in the query, but also allows you to select criteria for the field values, create calculated fields, and select sorting options.

In this section, you will create and define selection criteria for queries and create aggregate functions and calculated fields as well as sort query results.

Run Query Wizards

In addition to the Simple Query Wizard, three other query wizards are available to make quick, step-by-step queries.

1. **Crosstab** — Used when you want to describe one field in terms of two or more fields in the table. Example: summarizing information or calculating statistics on the fields in the table.
2. **Find Duplicates** — Used when you want to find records with the same specific value. Example: duplicate e-mail addresses in a customer database.

3. **Find Unmatched** — Used when you want to find the rows in one table that do not have a match in the other table. Example: identifying customers who currently have no open orders.

The Find Duplicates Query Wizard and the Find Unmatched Query Wizard, allow you to find duplicate records or identify orphans by selecting criteria as part of the wizard steps. An **orphan** is a foreign key in one table that does not have a matching value in the primary key field of a related table.

Creating a Find Duplicates Query

The **Find Duplicates Query Wizard** finds duplicate records in a table or a query. You select the fields that you think may include duplicate information, and the wizard creates the query to find records matching your criteria.

The spa receptionist sends out mailings and reminders to spa customers throughout the year. She wants to prevent multiple mailings to the same address to help reduce costs. In this exercise, you will show her how she can use a Find Duplicates query to check for duplicate addresses.

To Find Duplicate Customer Information

a. If you took a break, open the **a02ch03Spa_LastFirst** database. Click the **Create** tab, and then in the Queries group, click **Query Wizard**. Access displays the New Query dialog box and lists the different queries you can select.

b. Select **Find Duplicates Query Wizard**, and then click **OK**.

c. Select **Table: tblCustomer** as the table to search for duplicate field values, and then click **Next**.

Troubleshooting

If you get a Security Notice, click Open.

d. Under Available fields, click **CustAddress**, and then click the **One Field** button [>]. Access moves the CustAddress field to the Duplicate-value fields list. This is the field you think may have duplicate data.

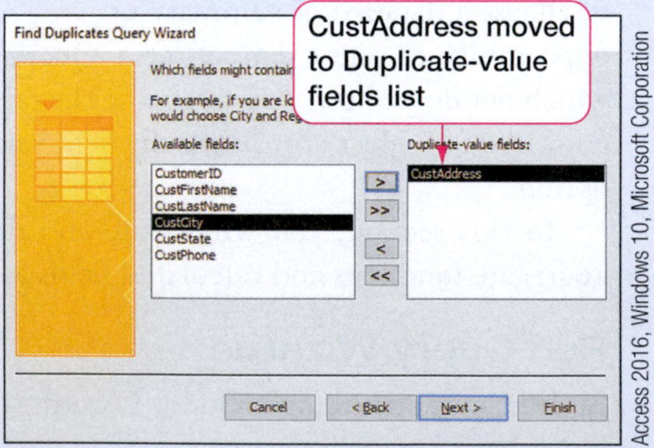

Figure 7 Select the field that may have duplicate data

e. Click **Next**. Click the **All Fields** button [>>] to move all available fields to the Duplicate-value fields list to display all the fields in the query results. Click **Next**.

f. Under "What do you want to name your query?", type qryDuplicateCustomers, and then click **Finish**. The result of the query should have two records with the same address.

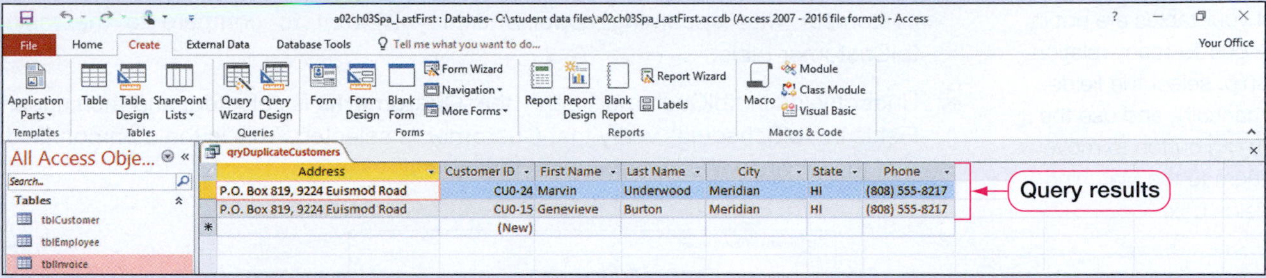

Figure 8 Results from the Find Duplicates query

Access 2016, Windows 10, Microsoft Corporation

g. **Close** [X] the query.

Creating a Find Unmatched Query

The **Find Unmatched Query Wizard** is designed to find records in a table or query that have no related records in a second table or query. This can be very helpful if you want to contact inactive customers or mail a notice to past clients who are still listed in the database. The wizard uses the primary key from the first table and matches it with the foreign key in the second table to determine whether there are unmatched records. If a one-to-many relationship exists between the two tables, the wizard will join the two correct fields automatically.

The wizard will try to match the primary key field and the foreign key field if there is a one-to-many relationship between the two tables. If there is not a one-to-many relationship, you can select the fields to be matched manually.

In this exercise, spa management would like to identify customers who have used the spa's services in the past but do not have a current appointment. This means that a record for the customer would be listed in the customer table but not in the schedule table, as shown in Figure 9.

Customer Table

First Name	Last Name	Address
Suzie	James	124 Marlow Dr
Allison	Williams	617 Burton Ln
Matt	Grofton	1258 8th St

Schedule Table

First Name	Last Name	Appointment
Suzie	James	3/6/15
Matt	Grofton	4/12/15

Figure 9 Tables in a Find Unmatched query

Notice that Allison Williams is a past customer, so she is listed in the customer table, but she does not have an appointment scheduled in the schedule table. Her record would be found in a Find Unmatched query comparing the customer and schedule tables. In this exercise, you will show the staff how to find unmatched records.

 A03.08

To Find Unmatched Records

a. Click the **Create** tab, and then in the Queries group, click **Query Wizard**.

b. Select **Find Unmatched Query Wizard**, and then click **OK**.

SIDE NOTE

Manually Select Fields to Match

If your tables are not in a one-to-many relationship, select the fields manually, and use the <=> button to move them to the Matching fields box.

c. Select **Table: tblCustomer**, and then click **Next**. This is the table you think has past customers with no upcoming appointments.

d. Select **Table: tblSchedule**, and then click **Next**. This is the table that has customers with upcoming appointments you want to compare to the main tblCustomer table.

e. Under Fields in 'tblCustomer', verify that **CustomerID** is selected, and then under Fields in 'tblSchedule', verify that **Customer** is selected. This is the common field that the wizard will use to compare the tables.

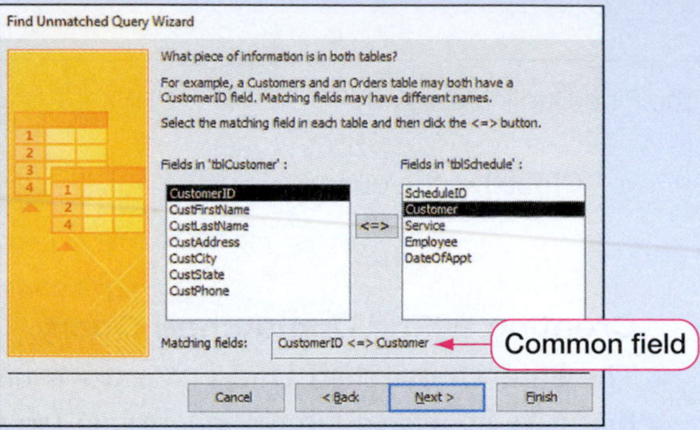

Figure 10 Compare the two tables using their common field

f. Click **Next**, click the **All Fields** button >> to add all the fields to the Selected fields list, and then click **Next**.

g. Under "What would you like to name your query?", type qryCustomersWithoutAppointments, and then click **Finish**. You should see the names, addresses, and e-mail addresses of three customers who do not currently have appointments at the spa, including yourself. **Close** ☒ the query.

Create Queries in Design View

The query wizards work by prompting you to answer a series of questions about the tables and fields to display and then creating the query based on your responses. Alternatively, you can use Design view to manually create queries. The query window in Design view allows you to specify the data you want to see by building a **query by example**. A query by example provides a sample of the data you want to see in the results. Access takes that sample of data and finds records in the tables you specify that match the example. In the query window, you can include specific fields, define criteria, sort records, and perform calculations. When you use the query window, you have more control and more options available to manage the details of the query design than with the Simple Query Wizard.

When you open Design view, by default the Show Table dialog box opens with a list of available tables and queries to add. You can select a table name and click Add, or you can double-click the table name. Either way, the table will be added to the query window. If the Show Table dialog box is closed, you can drag a table or query from the Navigation Pane to the query window to add it to the query.

The next step in building your query is to add the fields you want to include from the various tables selected to the query design grid. There are a number of ways to add fields to the query design grid.

QUICK REFERENCE	Methods to Add Fields to a Query Design Grid
Action	**Description**
Drag	Once you click the field name, drag it to any empty column in the query design grid.
Double-click field name	Double-click the field name to add it to the first empty column in the query design grid.
Select from list	Click in the first row of any empty column, click the selection arrow, and select the field name from the list.
Double-click title bar	Double-click the title bar for the table with the fields you want to add, and all the fields will be selected. Drag the fields to the first empty column.
Click, Shift, click	Click a field name, press and hold down the Shift key, and then click another name to select a range of field names. Drag the selected fields to the query design grid.

If you add a field to the wrong column in the query design grid, you can delete the column and add it to the correct column, or you can drag it to another position in the grid.

All fields that have values you want included in a query — either for the criteria or to show in the results — must be added to the query design grid. For example, you may want to find all customers from New Mexico but not necessarily show the state field in the query results. You can use the Show check box to indicate which fields to show in the results and which fields not to show.

REAL WORLD ADVICE **Increasing Privacy Concerns**

There are many instances in which the person running the query does not have the right to see confidential information in the database. An example of this is Social Security numbers. Although companies are doing away with this practice, many existing databases still use a customer's Social Security number as a unique identifier. You can include a Social Security number in query criteria, but uncheck the Show box so the actual value does not show in the query results.

Creating a Single-Table Query

A single-table query is a query that is based on only one table in your database. The manager of the spa needs your help to print out a price list for all the products. She wants to see the product description, size, and price for each product, and she wants to see all the records. In this exercise, you will show her how to add only the fields she wants to the query.

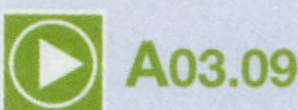

A03.09

To Create a Single-Table Query

a. Click the **Create** tab, and then in the Queries group, click **Query Design** to open the query window with the Show Table dialog box.

b. In the Show Table dialog box, select **tblProduct**, and then click **Add**. Click **Close** to close the Show Table dialog box.

SIDE NOTE
Seeing All Fields in a Table
Alternatively, you can scroll down to see all the fields.

Troubleshooting

If you cannot see the query design grid at the bottom of the query design window, use the pointer [+] to drag the top border of the grid up.

SIDE NOTE
Adding fields to the Query Design Grid
Alternatively, you can click the Field arrow in a column of the query design grid and select a table field.

c. Move the pointer to the lower border of **tblProduct** until it becomes a double-sided arrow [↕]. Click and drag down to see all the fields.

d. Double-click **ProductDescription** to add it to the first column of the query design grid. You can also add fields by dragging a field from the table to a column in the query design grid.

e. Click and drag the **Price** field from tblProduct to the **second column** of the query design grid. Repeat the process for the **Size** field.

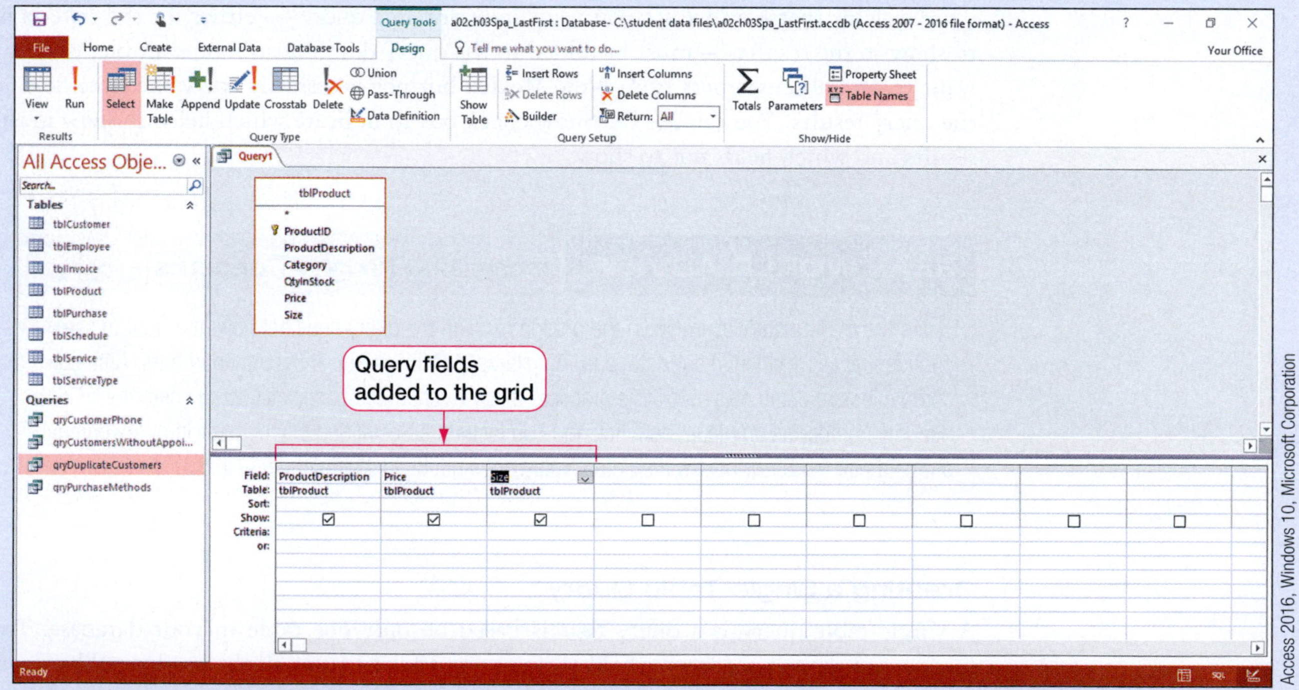

Figure 11 Fields from tblProduct added to the query design grid

f. On the Design tab, in the Results group, click **Run** to run the query. You should have 25 records showing the ProductDescription, Price, and Size (ounces) fields.

g. In the Views group, click the **View** arrow, and then click **Design View**. To move the Size field to the left of the ProductDescription field, point to the **top border** of the **Size** field until the pointer turns into a black arrow [⬇]. Click the **ProductDescription** field while the black arrow is displayed, then drag the **Size field** to the left of the **ProductDescription** field.

h. In the Results group, click **Run** to run the query again. The query will still have 25 records, but the field order will be Size (ounces), ProductDescription, and Price.

i. Click **Save** [Save icon]. In the Save As dialog box, type qryProductPriceList, and then click **OK**. **Close** [X] the query.

QUICK REFERENCE | **Opening or Switching Views**

Access gives you several methods to open objects in different views or to switch views.

1. To open an object in default view, double-click it in the Navigation Pane.
2. To open an object in Design View, right-click it in the Navigation Pane, and select Design View.
3. To switch views for an already open object, on the Home tab, in the Views group, click the View arrow, and then select your preferred view.
4. To switch views for an already open object, right-click the object tab, and then select the preferred view.
5. To switch views for an already open object, the right side of the status bar has small icons for each available view. Hover your mouse pointer over the icon to see the ScreenTip. Click the icon to switch to the preferred view.

REAL WORLD ADVICE | **The Importance of Knowing Your Data**

Many times, databases are shared by many users. Different people may enter data differently causing errors or inconsistency. Inconsistent data entry can affect the validity of query results. If a value is misspelled or is abbreviated when it should be spelled out, a query may not find the record when it searches using criteria. You must know what your data looks like when you create queries. A quick scan of the records or using Find with a wildcard for certain values may help you find misspellings or other data entry errors before you run your query.

Having some idea of what the query results should look like will also help make sure your query has found the right record set. For example, if you query all customers from New Mexico and think there should be about a dozen but your query shows 75, you should check your table records and your query criteria to see why there might be such a big discrepancy from what you expected.

Viewing Table Relationships

A multiple-table query retrieves information from more than one table or query. For Access to perform this type of query, it uses relationships between the tables, or the common field that exists in both tables to "connect" the tables.

If two tables do not have a common field, Access will join the two tables by combining the records, regardless of whether they have a matching field. This is called the **multiplier effect**. For example, if one table has 10,000 records, another table also has 10,000 records, and these two tables do not have a common field, all records in the first table will be matched with all records in the second table for a total of 100,000,000 records! Depending on the computer's processing power and memory, Access could take a long time to run the query or may even become nonresponsive.

You can view how your tables are related in the Relationships window. **Join lines** are the lines connecting the tables that represent relationships. The field to which the line is pointing in each table represents the common field between the tables. It is helpful to understand how tables are related before you try to create a multiple table query. In this exercise, you will view table relationships to determine how the tables are related.

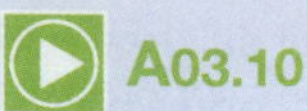

To View Table Relationships

a. Click the **Database Tools** tab, and in the Relationships group, click **Relationships**. Click the **Shutter Bar Open/Close** button « to hide the Navigation Pane and display the whole Relationships window. Take a moment to study the table relationships.

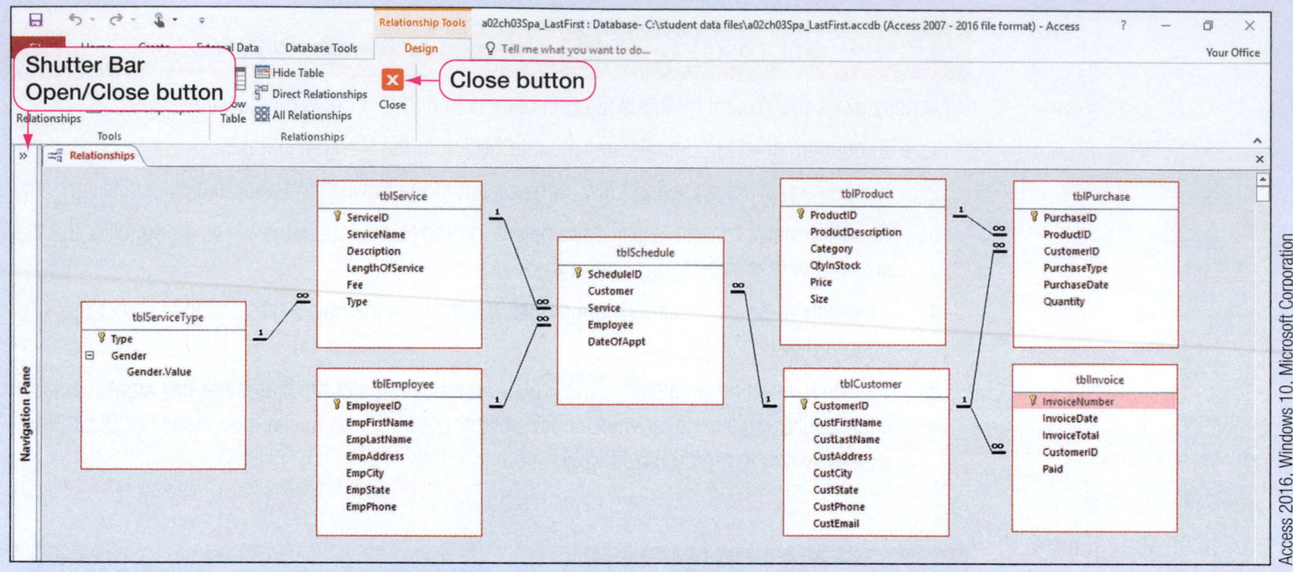

Figure 12 Spa Database table relationships

b. On the Design tab, in the Relationships group, click **Close** to close the Relationships window. Click the **Shutter Bar Open/Close** button » to show the Navigation Pane again.

REAL WORLD ADVICE Which Tables to Choose?

You should select only the tables you need when creating a query in the query window. Access treats all the tables selected as part of the query when it executes the query, which means that unnecessary tables added to the query may cause performance problems or incorrect results. Best practice is to do the following.

- Understand the table structure and relationships before you construct your query — refer to the Relationships window often.
- Choose only the tables from which you need data.
- If no data from a table is needed, do not add the table. The exception to this rule is if a table is required to link the many-to-many relationship together. In other words, no table will be left unconnected, and tables can be added to create that connection.

Creating a Query from Multiple Tables

All tables added to a query should be connected by relationships and have a common field. The staff would like to see all services scheduled for each employee. tblEmployee includes the employee names, and tblSchedule lists the services scheduled for each employee. In this exercise, you will create a query that includes records from two tables into one query.

A03.11

To Create a Query from Multiple Tables

a. Click the **Create** tab, and then in the Queries group, click **Query Design**. Click **tblEmployee**, and then click **Add**. Click **Close** to close the Show Table dialog box.

b. Double-click **EmpFirstName** and **EmpLastName** in that order to add the fields to the query design grid.

c. In the Results group, click **Run**. Notice there are 14 employee records.

d. Switch to **Design** view. From the Navigation Pane, drag **tblSchedule** to the query window. In the Results group, click **Run** to run the query again.
Scroll through the table and notice there are 53 records in the query results now and employees names are repeated. Employee names have been matched up with each scheduled service, of which there are 53, but you cannot see any information about the services because no fields from that table have been added. The relationship between the two tables dictates that each employee be listed for each service he or she has scheduled. The relationship also prevents employees without a scheduled appointment from appearing in the results. For example, Mariah Paul does not appear here because she has no appointments scheduled.

e. Switch to **Design** view. In the tblSchedule table, in the following order, double-click **Service**, **DateOfAppt**, and **Customer** to add the fields to the query design grid.

SIDE NOTE

Adding Tables from the Navigation Pane

Remember that in addition to selecting the tables from the Show Table dialog box, you can drag tables from the Navigation Pane.

SIDE NOTE

Add Only Necessary Tables

Adding a table to a query without adding fields changes the query results, and the results may not make sense.

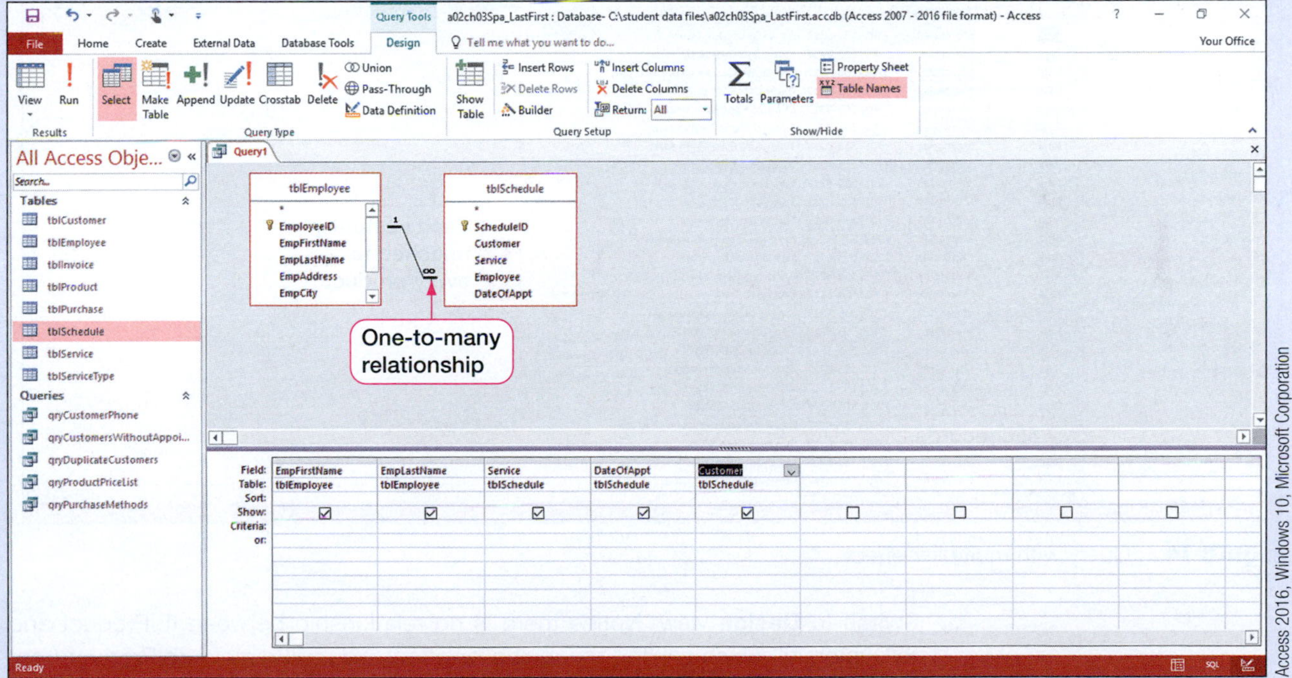

Figure 13 Query window for multiple-table query

f. In the Results group, click **Run** to run the query. Use the **AutoFit** feature on the columns to best fit the data.
Notice there are 53 records again for each service scheduled, but now the details for those services are included in the query because you added the fields to the query design grid.

g. Click **Save**, and under Query Name, type qryEmployeeSchedule, and then click **OK**. **Close** the query.

Removing a Table from a Query to Fix an Undesirable Multiplier Effect

When two tables without a common field are used in a query, you will see the multiplier effect. Recall that the multiplier effect occurs when each record in the first table is matched to each record in the second table.

Someone in the spa wanted to find the phone number for each customer but created a multiple table query using two tables without a common field. One table has 25 records and the other has 26, so the multiplier effect caused the query result to have 650 records! In this exercise, you will run the employee's query and then fix it by removing the second table from the query.

To Remove a Table from a Query

a. In the Navigation pane, double-click **qryCustomerPhone** to run the query. Notice there are 650 records because every customer name is matched with every product. Since there are 25 products, each of the 26 customers is matched with every product for 25 times 26 = 650 records.

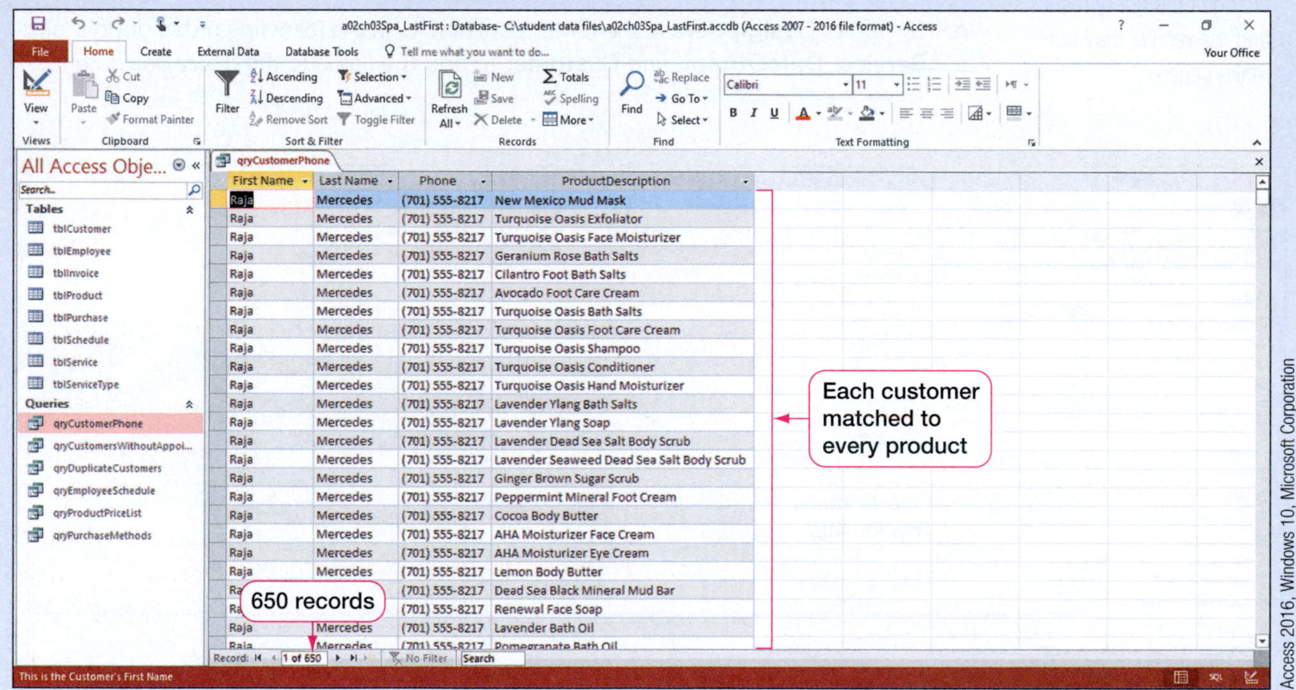

Figure 14 Query with multiplier effect

b. Switch to **Design** view. Notice there is no relationship between tblProduct and tblCustomer, which caused the multiplier effect. You will remove tblProduct from the query.

c. Right-click **tblProduct** in the query window, and then select **Remove Table**. The table is removed from the query window, and the ProductDescription is removed from the query design grid.

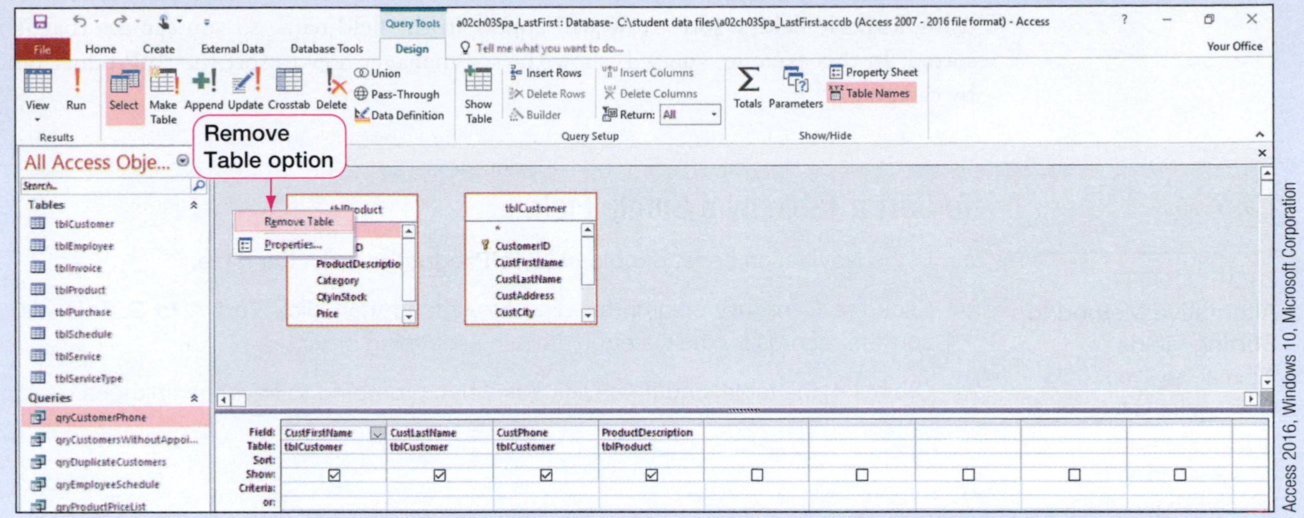

Figure 15 Remove table from query

d. In the Results group, click **Run** to run the query. Notice there are now only 26 records.

e. Click the **File** tab, click **Save As**, and then click **Save Object As**. Click **Save As**, and under Save 'qryCustomerPhone' to, type qryCustomerPhoneFixed, and then click **OK**. **Close** ☒ the query.

Sort Tables and Query Results

Sorting is the process of rearranging records in a specific order. By default, records in a table or query are sorted by the primary key field. You can change the sort order of a table in a query, which will not affect how the data is stored, only how it will appear in the query results.

Sorting by One Field

To sort records, you have to select a **sort field**, or a field used to determine the order of the records. The sort field can be a Short Text, Long Text, Number, Date/Time, Currency, AutoNumber, Yes/No, or Lookup Wizard field as shown in Table 2. A field may be sorted in either ascending (A to Z) order or descending (Z to A) order.

Type of Data	Sorting Options
Short and Long Text	Ascending (A to Z); descending (Z to A)
Numbers (including Currency and AutoNumber)	Ascending (lowest to highest); descending (highest to lowest)
Date/Time	Ascending (oldest to newest); descending (newest to oldest)
Yes/No	Ascending (yes, then no values); descending (no, then yes values)

Table 2 Methods for sorting data

If you have numbers that are stored as text — phone numbers, Social Security numbers, ZIP Codes — then the characters 1 to 9 come before A to Z in the appropriate order sorted as alphanumeric text.

A table may be sorted by a single field in Datasheet view. When a table is sorted by using a single field, a sort arrow will appear in the field name so you can see that it is sorted. In this exercise, you will show the spa manager how to sort the tblProduct table by category.

SIDE NOTE
Alternative Method to Sorting Fields
Alternatively, you can select the field to be sorted and click Ascending or Descending on the Home tab in the Sort & Filter group.

To Sort a Table by a Single Field

a. In the Navigation pane, double-click **tblProduct** to open the table.

b. Click the **Category** column heading arrow, and then click **Sort A to Z**. This will sort the records by the Category field in ascending order.

c. **Close** [X] the table, and then click **Yes** when prompted to save the changes.

Sorting by More Than One Field

You can also sort by multiple fields in Access. The first field you choose to sort by is called the **primary sort field**. The second and subsequent fields are called **secondary sort fields**.

In Datasheet view, you can sort multiple fields by selecting all the fields at one time and using the Sort & Filter group sorts, but there are some restrictions. First, the fields in Datasheet view must be next to each other, and the sort is executed from left to right; that is, the far-left field is the primary sort field, the next field is a secondary sort field, and so on. Second, you can sort only in ascending or descending order for all fields; you cannot have one field sorted in ascending order and another in descending order. These two restrictions do not exist if sorting is set in Design view. Thus, it is more efficient to create a query and sort by multiple fields using Design view.

Using Design view to sort records allows you to sequence the fields from left to right in an order that makes sense for your desired sort results and allows you to combine ascending and descending sorts. You can also sort in an order different from left to right by adding a field multiple times and clearing the Show check box. In this exercise, you will show the staff how to sort the tblSchedule table by Employee, then Date, and then Service by creating a query from the table and setting up the sort options.

SIDE NOTE
How Many Fields Is Too Many?
You may choose up to ten fields to sort by in Design view.

To Sort a Query by More than One Field

a. Click the **Create** tab, and then in the Queries group, click **Query Design**. Double-click **tblEmployee** and **tblSchedule** to add the tables to the query. Click **Close** to close the Show Table dialog box.

b. Double-click **EmpLastName**, **EmpFirstName**, and **EmpPhone** from **tblEmployee** to add those fields to the query design grid. Double-click **DateOfAppt**, **Service**, and **Customer** from tblSchedule to add those fields to the query design grid.

c. Click the **Sort** row for EmpLastName, click the **selection** arrow, and then click **Ascending**. Click **Ascending** for the EmpFirstName, DateOfAppt, and Service fields.
Notice that unlike sorting in Datasheet view, your sorting fields do not need to be next to each other to be sorted in a query.

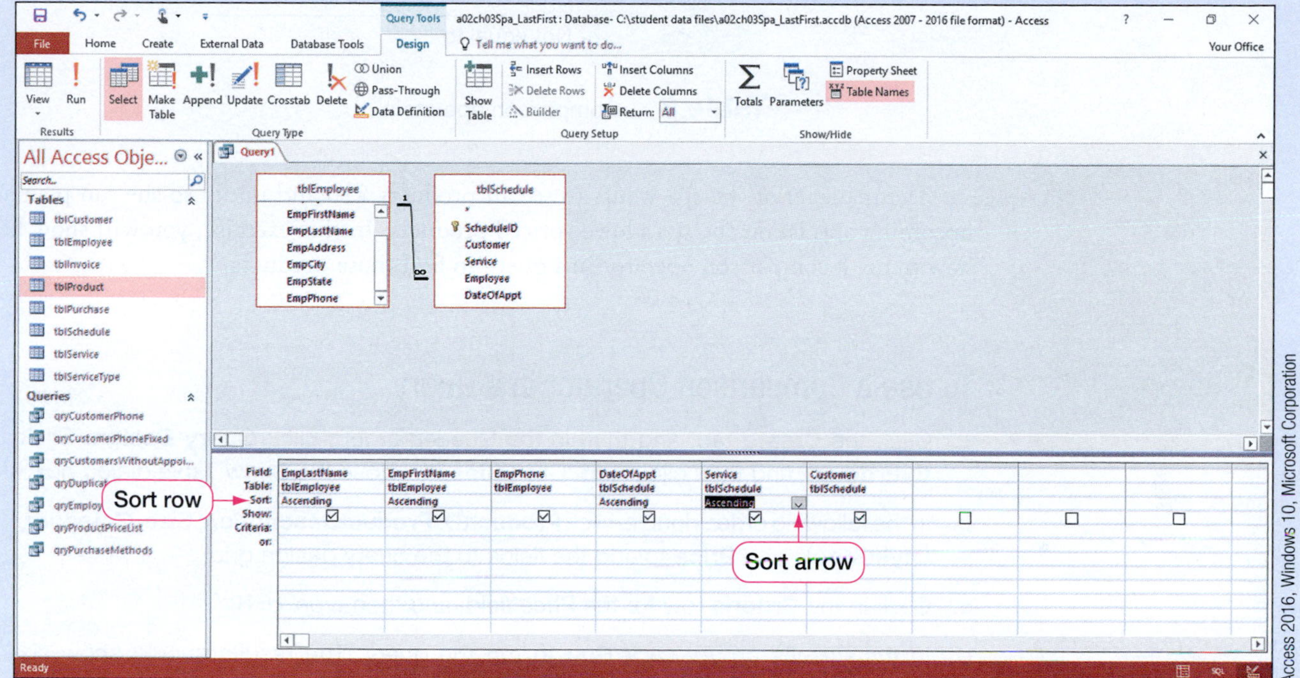

Figure 16 Sort options selected

d. In the Results group, click **Run** to run the query. Use the **AutoFit** feature on the columns to best fit the data.
Notice there are 53 records and the table is sorted by Employee, then Date, then Service.

e. Click **Save** [Save icon], name the query qryEmployeeAppointments, and then click **OK**. **Close** [X] the query.

Define Selection Criteria for Queries

Databases, including Access, provide a robust set of selection criteria that you can use to make your queries well focused. You can use the different kinds of operators described below to choose criteria for one or more fields in one or more tables.

Using a Comparison Operator

Comparison operators compare the values in a table or another query to the criteria value you set up in a query. The different comparison operators, descriptions, and examples are shown in Table 3. Comparison operators are generally used with numbers and dates to find a range or a specific value. Equal to and not equal to can also be used with text to find exact matches to criteria. For example, to find all states that are not NY, you could enter < >"NY" for the state criterion.

In query criteria, text is identified by quotation marks around it and dates with # in front of and at the end of the date. For example, 1/1/18 would appear as #1/1/18#. Access adds the necessary quotation marks and pound signs, but it is a good idea to double-check.

Operator	Description
=	Equal to
< =	Less than or equal to
<	Less than
>	Greater than
> =	Greater than or equal to
< >	Not equal to

Table 3 Comparison operators

The manager of the spa wants to see all products $10 and under so she can plan an upcoming special on the spa's lower-priced products. In this exercise, you will show her how to use a comparison operator in a query to find those products.

To Use a Comparison Operator in a Query

a. Click the **Create** tab, and then in the Queries group, click **Query Design**. Click **tblProduct**, and then click **Add**. Click **Close** to close the Show Table dialog box.

b. In the following order, double-click **ProductID**, **ProductDescription**, **Size**, **Category**, **QtyInStock**, and **Price** to add the fields to the query design grid.

c. Click in the **Criteria** row for the Price field, and then type <=10.

d. In the Results group, click **Run** to run the query. The results should show six records, all with prices $10 or less.

e. Click **Save**, under Query Name type qryLowPriceProducts, and then click **OK**.

Hiding Fields That Are Used in a Query

For a field to be used in a query, it must be added to the query grid. If you just want to use the field to define criteria but do not want to see the results of that field in the query, it cannot be removed from the query grid, but it can be hidden from the results.

The manager is happy with the results of the low-price products query you created above, but she would like to post a list of the products without the prices so she can advertise the list as all $10 and under. In this exercise, you show her how that is possible by using the Show check box in the query design grid.

To Use a Field Value in a Query but Not Show the Field in the Results

a. With the **qryLowPriceProducts** query open, switch to **Design** view.

b. In the Price field, click the **Show** check box to clear the check mark.

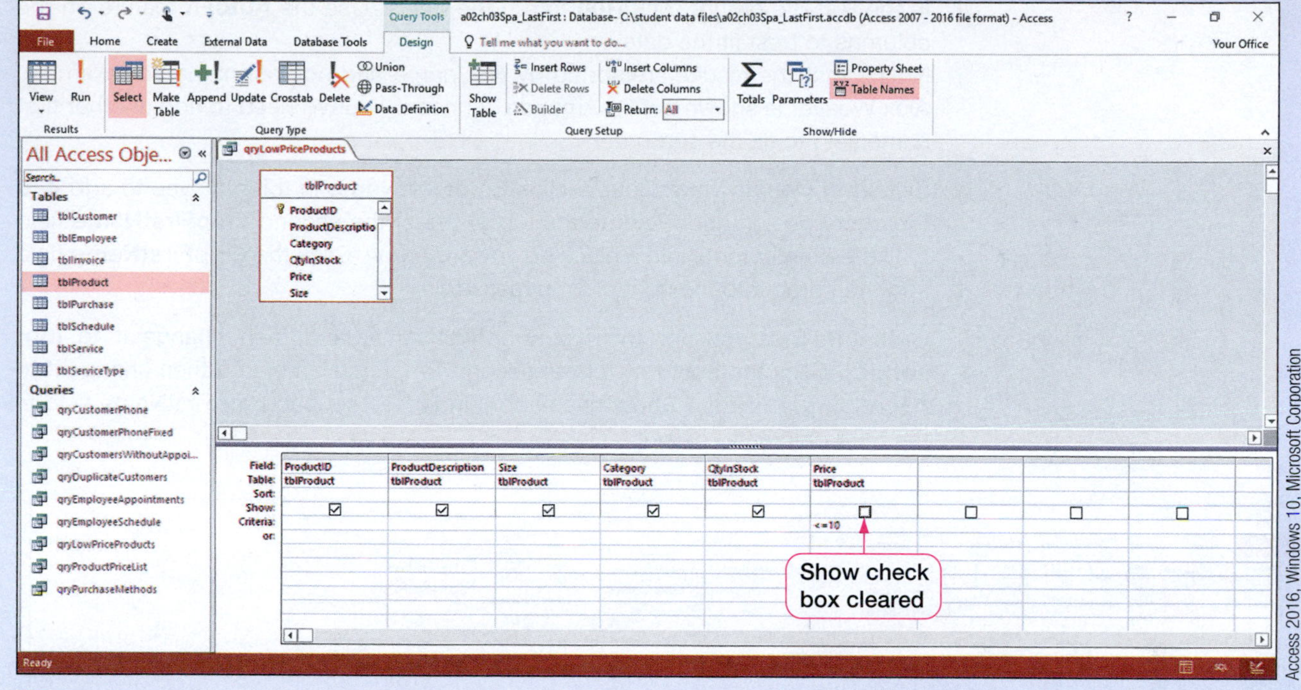

Figure 17 Clearing the Show check box

c. In the Results group, click **Run** to run the query. The results should show the same six records you found in the previous query but without the price field showing.

d. Click the **File** tab, click **Save As**, and then click **Save Object As**. Click **Save As**, and in Save 'qryLowPriceProducts' to:, type qryTenAndUnder, and then click **OK**. **Close** [X] the query.

Sorting on a Field That You Do Not Show

The manager liked the employee schedule query you created, but she would like it to show the employee's first name first in the query results. If you put first name first in the grid and then last name, Access will sort by first name first. In this exercise, you will show her how to add a field multiple times to the query design grid to sort fields one way but display them another way.

 A03.17

To Sort a Query by Multiple Fields in a Different Sort Order

a. Click the **Create** tab, and then in the Queries group, click **Query Design**. Double-click **tblEmployee** and **tblSchedule** to add the tables to the query. Click **Close** to close the Show Table dialog box.

b. Double-click **EmpFirstName** and **EmpLastName** from tblEmployee to add those fields to the query design grid. Double-click **DateOfAppt**, **Service**, and **Customer** from tblSchedule to add those fields to the query design grid.

c. Click the **Sort** row for EmpFirstName, click the **selection** arrow, and then click **Ascending**. Click **Ascending** for the EmpLastName, DateOfAppt, and Service fields.

d. In the Results group, click **Run** to run the query. Use the **AutoFit** feature on the columns to best fit the data.
Notice that the results are sorted by first name and not last name; for example, Alex Weaver is shown before Amanda Johnson. You will need to add another first name field to fix the sort order.

e. Switch to **Design** view. Double-click **EmpFirstName** in tblEmployee to add it to the query design grid. Point to the top of the of the second **EmpFirstName** field until the pointer turns into a black downward arrow. Click the **EmpFirstName** field and then drag it to the right of EmpLastName.

f. Click the **Sort** row for the first EmpFirstName, and then change it to **(not sorted)**. Click the **Sort** row for the second EmpFirstName, and then change it to **Ascending**. Click the **Show** check box under the second EmpFirstName field in the third column to clear it.

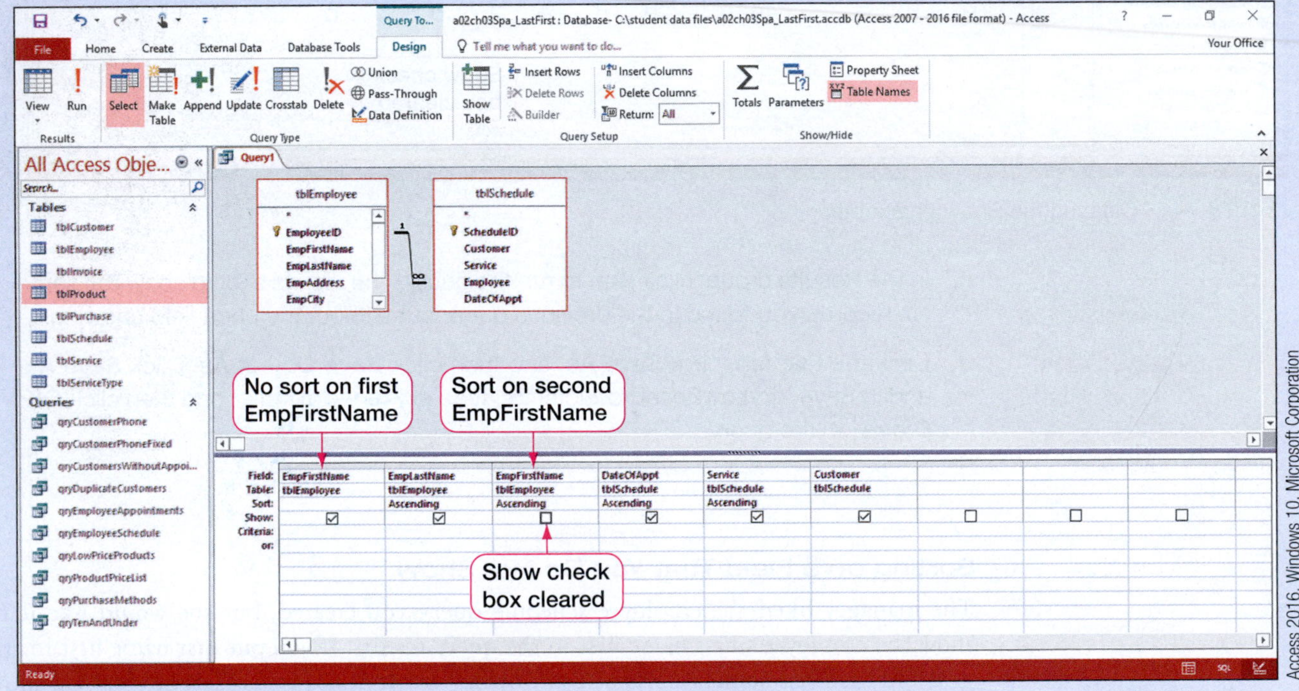

Figure 18 Sort options selected and second EmpFirstName Show check box cleared

g. In the Results group, click **Run** to run the query. The results should show 53 records sorted by employee last name, first name, date, and service. Notice that the main sort is by last name but Alex Weaver comes before Joseph Weaver.

h. Click **Save**, name the query qryEmployeeSort, and then click **OK**. **Close** the query.

Using Is Null Criteria

You practiced entering a criterion value to get all records that meet the criterion. You can also select any records that have no value in a field using the Is Null criterion. Null is the absence of any value and is different from blank or zero.

One of the spa workers has created a purchase record without specifying that the order was placed in person. In this exercise, you will show the manager how to locate a record that is missing a value. You will also show her how to change the value in the query and have it changed in the table.

To Use Is Null Criteria

a. Click the **Create** tab, and then in the Queries group, click **Query Design**. Double-click **tblPurchase**, and **tblCustomer** to add the tables to the query window. Click **Close** to close the Show Table dialog box.

b. In the following order, double-click **PurchaseType** and **PurchaseDate** from tblPurchase, and **CustFirstName** and **CustLastName** from tblCustomer to add them to the query design grid.

c. Click in the **Criteria** row for the PurchaseType field, and then type Is Null.

d. In the Results group, click **Run** to run the query. The results show one record: the purchase by Omar Hinton on 1/18/2018. That is the record that the employee forgot to change to In Person.

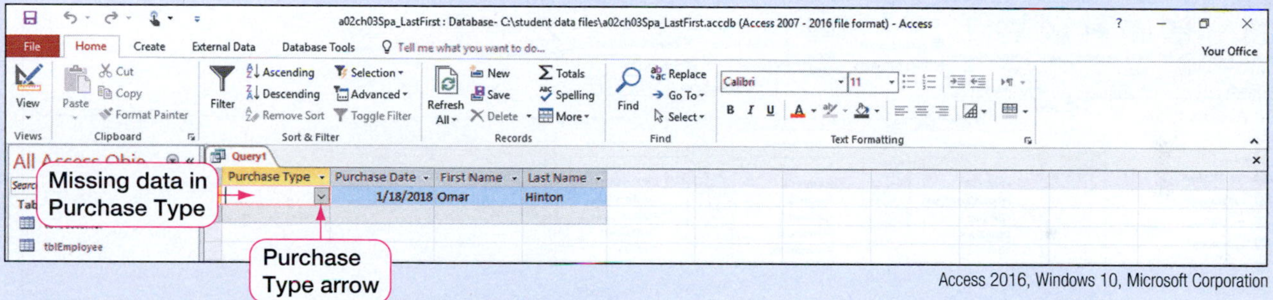

Access 2016, Windows 10, Microsoft Corporation

Figure 19 Change null value in query results

e. Click the arrow under **Purchase Type**, and then change the value to **In Person**. This changes the result in the underlying tblPurchase to be In Person.

f. Click **Save** [Save icon], and under Query Name, type qryNullPurchaseType, and then click **OK**. **Close** [X] the query.

g. Double-click **tblPurchase** to open the table. Notice that Hinton's purchase (PurchaseID = 25) is now indicated as being In Person. **Close** [X] the table.

h. Double-click **qryNullPurchaseType** to run it. Notice that no records are found, since Hinton's record was corrected. **Close** [X] the query.

Using Criteria Row with Multiple Criteria

When you create a query, you can specify criteria for one field or for multiple fields. When selecting criteria for multiple fields, you must show how the query selects the records. When criteria are placed on the same Criteria row, Access logically interprets the criteria as related by an and — all criteria are true. For example, the query may need to return orders placed Online and from customers in New Mexico. The query must contain the criterion in which the PurchaseType is Online and the criterion in which the customer State is New Mexico. This task can be easily completed by using the Criteria row in the query design grid. The Criteria row of the query design grid directs Access to look for the first criterion AND the second criterion and so on for each value typed into the same Criteria row in the query. All criteria on the same line are interpreted by Access as an AND logically. In this exercise, you want to help the manager narrow down a sales strategy. She is trying to determine which customers have placed phone orders for products over $10.

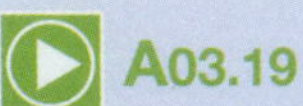

SIDE NOTE
Looks Do Not Matter
How the tables are laid out in the query window does not affect the results. You can move the tables by dragging them to a new location.

To Use the Criteria Row

a. Click the **Create** tab, and then in the Queries group, click **Query Design**. Double-click **tblProduct**, **tblPurchase**, and **tblCustomer** to add the tables to the query window. Click **Close** to close the Show Table dialog box.

b. In the following order, double-click **PurchaseType** from tblPurchase, **ProductDescription** and **Price** from tblProduct, and **CustFirstName** and **CustLastName** from tblCustomer to add them to the query design grid.

c. Click in the **Criteria** row for the PurchaseType field, type Phone, and then for the Price field, type >10.

d. Click in the **Sort** row for the **ProductDescription** field, and then select **Ascending**.

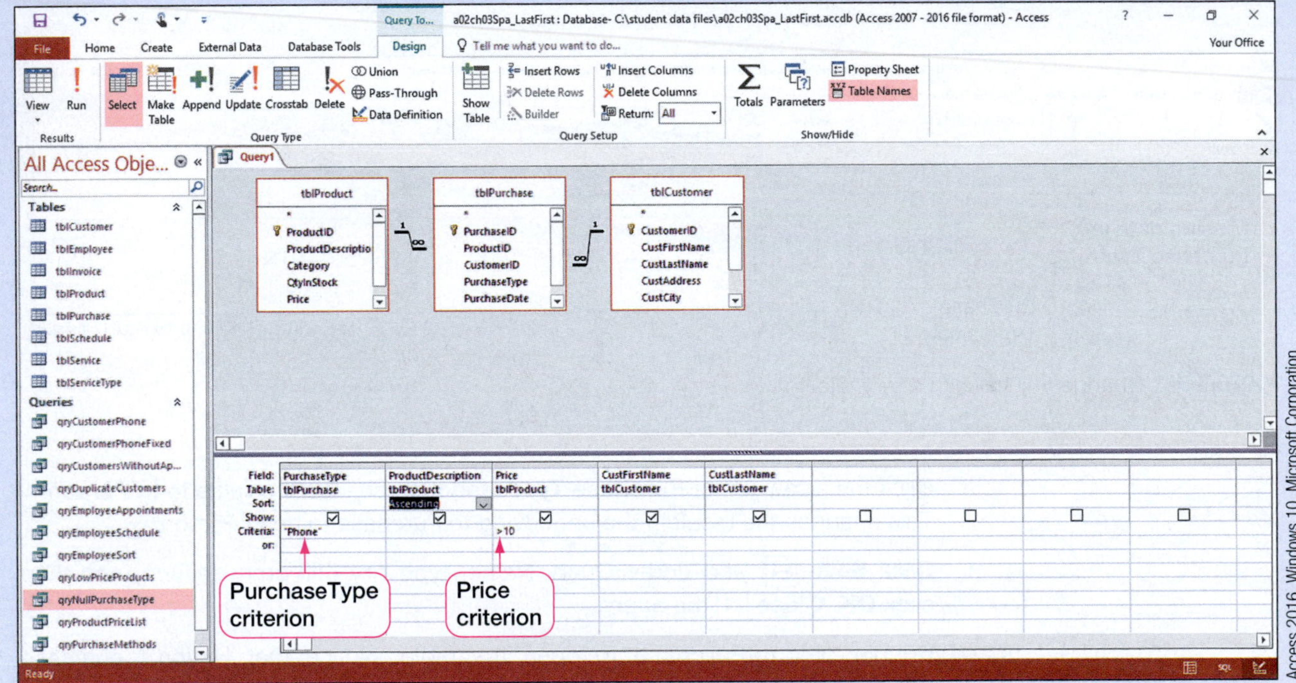

Access 2016, Windows 10, Microsoft Corporation

Figure 20 Criteria added for PurchaseType and Price fields

e. In the Results group, click **Run** to run the query. The results show five records with Phone as the purchase type and a price greater than $10. The results are sorted by ProductDescription.

f. Click **Save** [Save icon], and under Query Name type qryPhoneAndTen, and then click **OK**. **Close** [X] the query.

Using the Or Criteria Row

When specifying two or more different criteria for the same field or different sets of criteria in a query, the or row below the Criteria row can be used. For example, if you wanted to know how many customers live in New Mexico or Nevada, you could enter the criterion for the State field on two different lines for the same field in the query design grid — assuming no other criteria for different fields. The query would then run and return records in which the State field equals New Mexico OR where the state field equals Nevada. In this exercise, you will help the manager find all customers who make purchases either by phone or online.

To Use the Or Criteria Row

a. Click the **Create** tab, and then in the Queries group, click **Query Design**. Double-click **tblProduct**, **tblPurchase**, and **tblCustomer** to add the tables to the query. Click **Close** to close the Show Table dialog box.

b. Double-click **PurchaseType** from tblPurchase, double-click **ProductDescription** from tblProduct, and then double-click **CustFirstName** and **CustLastName** from tblCustomer in that order to add them to the query design grid.

c. Click in the **Criteria** row for the PurchaseType field, type Phone. In the **or criteria** row just below the Criteria row in the PurchaseType field, type Online.

d. Click in the **Sort** row, and then select **Ascending** for the PurchaseType and ProductDescription fields.

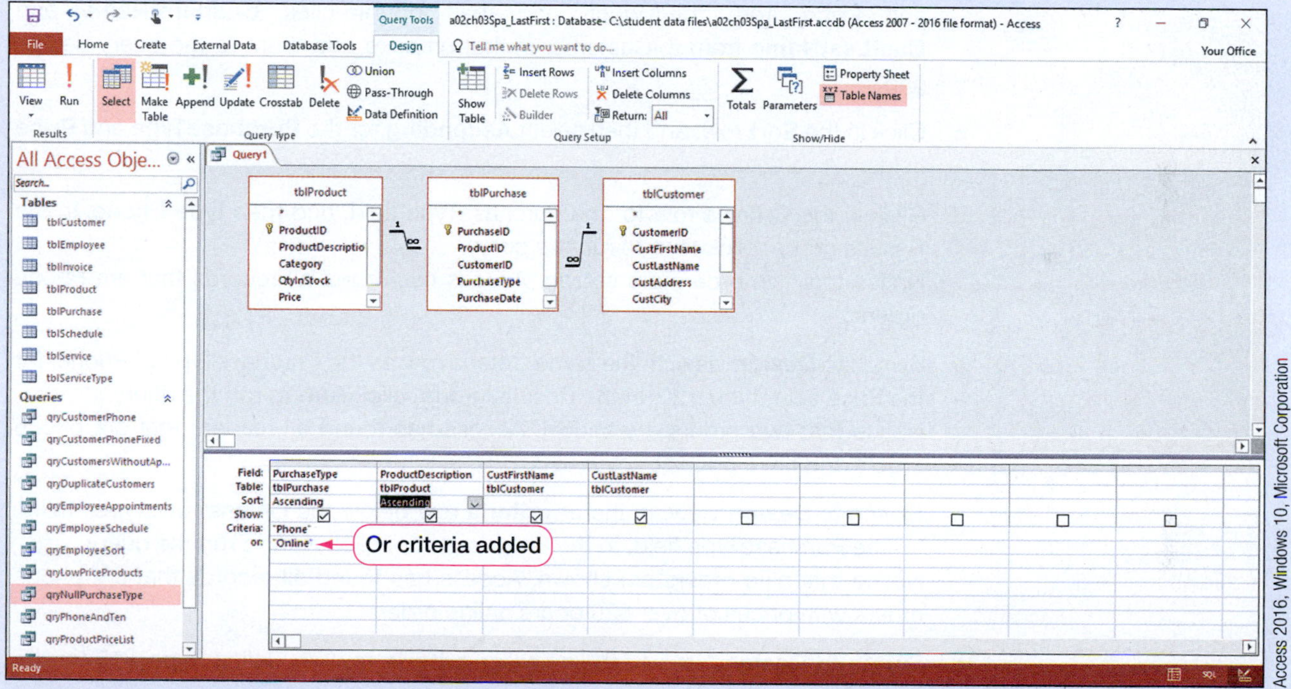

Figure 21 Or Criteria row used for PurchaseType

e. In the Results group, click **Run** to run the query. The results should show 12 records, all with Phone or Online as the purchase type sorted by purchase type and product description.

f. Click **Save**, name the query qryPhoneOrOnline, and then click **OK**. **Close** the query.

Using Both the Criteria Row and the Or Criteria Rows in a Query

More complex queries can be created by combining the use of the Criteria row and the or criteria rows. Each row of criteria in the query design grid is returned as a set of records by the query. In other words, records that meet the values on the first Criteria row are returned by the query as one set of records. Records that meet the values on the or criteria row are also returned by the query, as are records on each successive or criteria row in the query design grid. The result is a query containing records that meet the first set of criteria or the second set of criteria and so on. Each line represents a separate set of connected criteria that is logically compared by an OR.

The manager wants you to find all phone purchase types for products over $20 as well as all online purchase types for products over $15. Phone and greater than $20 are one criterion, while Online and greater than $15 are a separate criterion. By specifying each criterion on a separate or criteria row, the query will combine the records meeting each set of criteria. In this exercise, you will create a query that combines two different sets of criteria using the or criteria row.

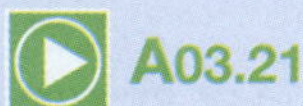

To Use the Criteria and Or Criteria Rows in a Query

a. Click the **Create** tab, and then in the Queries group, click **Query Design**, and then double-click **tblProduct**, **tblPurchase**, and **tblCustomer** to add the tables to the query. Click **Close** to close the Show Table dialog box.

b. Double-click **PurchaseType** from tblPurchase, double-click **ProductDescription** and **Price** from tblProduct, and then double-click **CustFirstName** and **CustLastName** from tblCustomer in that order to add them to the query design grid.

c. Click in the **Sort** row, and then select **Ascending** for the **PurchaseType** and **Price** fields.

d. Click in the **Criteria** row for the PurchaseType field, and then type Phone. In the Results group, click **Run** to run the query.
Notice that five orders are shown. Access has found all records that are Phone orders.

e. Switch to **Design** view. In the same Criteria row as the PurchaseType of Phone, for the Price field, type >20. In the Results group, click **Run** to run the query.
Notice that two orders are shown. Access has found all records that are phone orders and have prices of over $20.

f. Switch to **Design** view. In the **or criteria** row below the Criteria row, type Online for the PurchaseType field. In the Results group, click **Run** to run the query.
Notice that nine orders are shown. Access has found all records that are phone orders with prices of over $20 or are online orders.

g. Switch to **Design** view. In the same **or criteria** row as Online, type >15 for the **Price** field.

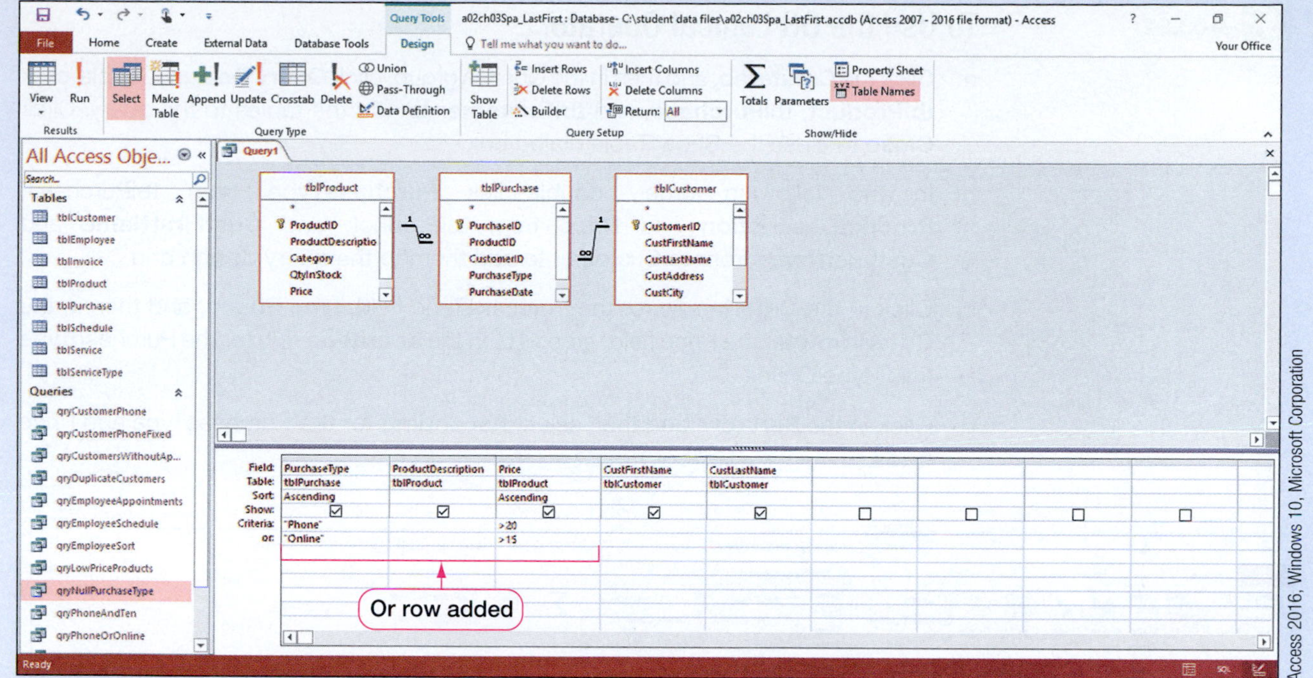

Figure 22 Two criteria rows added for PurchaseType and Price

h. In the Results group, click **Run** to run the query.
Notice that six orders are shown. Access has found all records that are phone orders with prices over $20 or are online orders with prices over $15.

i. Click **Save**, name the query qryPhoneAndOnline, and then click **OK**. **Close** the query.

Using AND and OR Logical Operators

When a query is created, it may be necessary to meet multiple criteria for a single field. This can be easily accomplished in the query design grid with the use of logical operators. **Logical operators** are operators that allow you to combine two or more criteria for the same field. Examples of logical operators are shown in Table 4. For example, if you want a record selected when two or more criteria are met for a field, you would use the AND logical operator typed into the Criteria row of the field. Alternatively, if you want a record selected if only one of the criteria is met, you would use the OR logical operator.

Operator	Description
AND	Returns records that meet both criteria
OR	Returns records that meet one or more criteria
NOT	Returns records that do not meet the criteria

Table 4 Logical operators

The manager of the spa wants you to find all phone and online purchase types for products over $10. If you put the purchase type criteria on two rows and the price of >10 in one row, your results will show all records with phone purchase types over $10 or Online purchase types of any amount. Access will treat "Phone" and >10 as AND criteria and then move to the next row, which it will consider an OR criterion. In this exercise, you will create a query using the OR logical operator to find all phone and online purchases over $10.

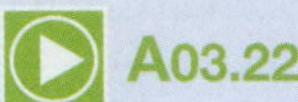

To Use the OR Logical Operator

a. Click the **Create** tab, and then in the Queries group, click **Query Design**. Double-click **tblProduct**, **tblPurchase**, and **tblCustomer** to add the tables to the query. Click **Close** to close the Show Table dialog box.

b. In the following order, double-click **PurchaseType** from tblPurchase, **ProductDescription** and **Price** from tblProduct, and **CustFirstName** and **CustLastName** from tblCustomer to add them to the query design grid.

c. Click in the **Criteria** row for the PurchaseType field, type Phone, and then in the **Criteria** row for the Price field, type >10. In the **or criteria** row for the PurchaseType field, type Online.

d. Click in the **Sort** row, and then select **Ascending** for the PurchaseType and Price fields.

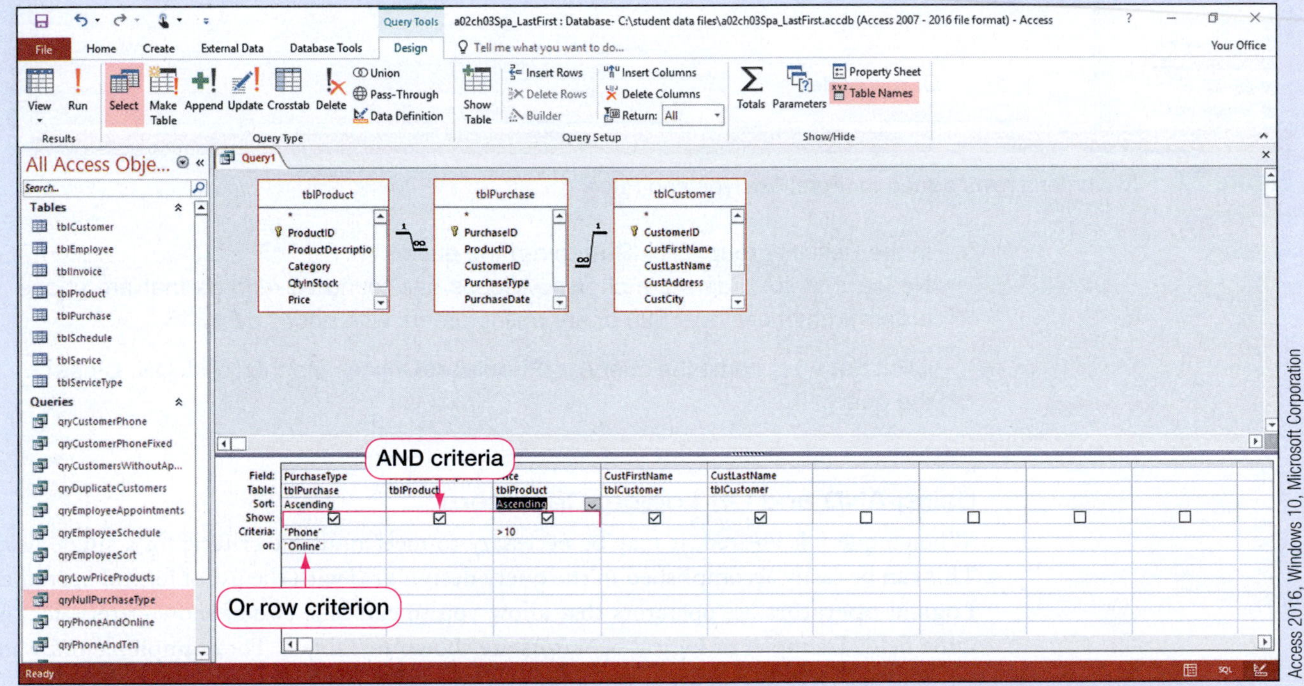

Figure 23 Criteria added to the query design grid

> **SIDE NOTE**
> **Access Puts in Quotes**
> You can leave the quotation marks around "Phone" or remove them. Access will add them for Short Text fields.

e. In the Results group, click **Run** to run the query.
Notice the results are all Phone purchase types with prices over $10 or all Online purchase types, regardless of the price. The manager wants to see Phone or Online purchase types over $10, so this is not correct.

f. Switch to **Design** view. In the **or criteria** row for the PurchaseType field, delete "Online." Click in the **Criteria** row for the PurchaseType field, and then change the criteria to Phone or Online.

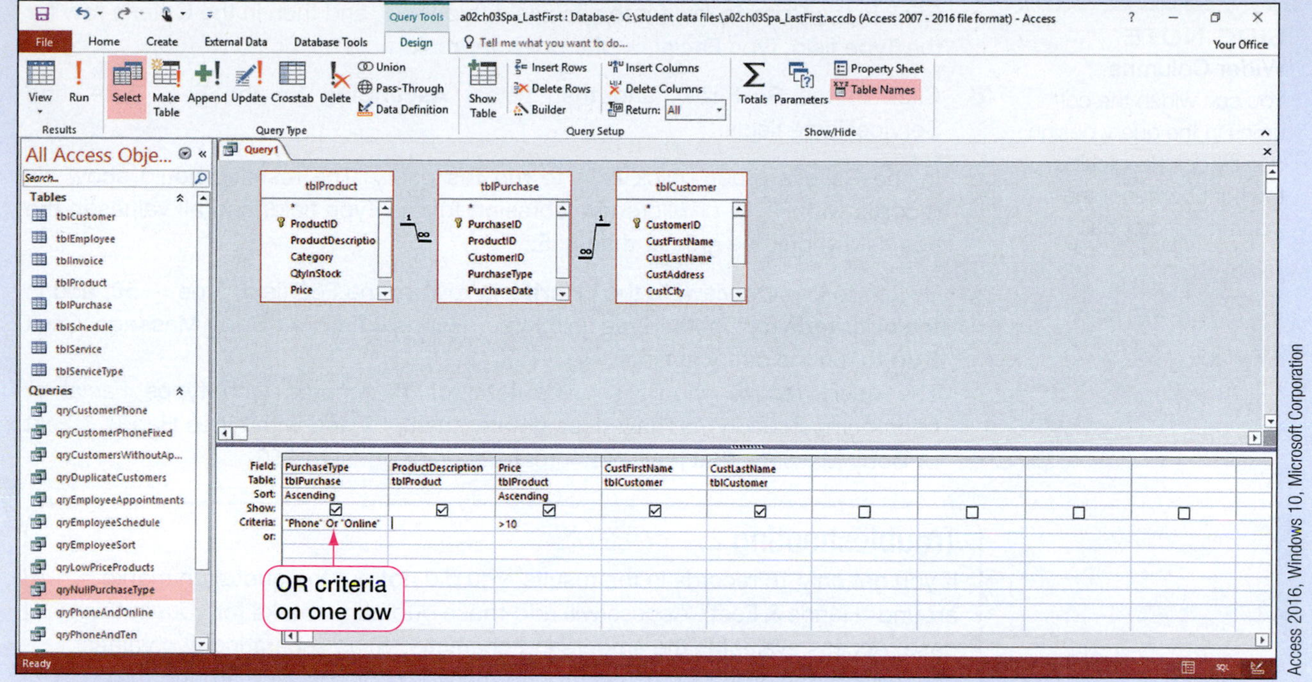

Access 2016, Windows 10, Microsoft Corporation

Figure 24 Or criteria added to the query design grid

g. In the Results group, click **Run** to run the query again. The results should now show the 10 Phone or Online purchase types that are over $10.

h. Click **Save**, and under Query Name, type qryPhoneOrOnlineOverTen, and then click **OK**. **Close** the query.

Combining Operators and Multiple Criteria

The more criteria you add to your query, the more difficult it will be to see whether you have the correct results. With multiple criteria, it is good practice to add one criterion, run the query to make sure you are getting the correct results, and then continue adding criteria one at a time.

The spa manager would like to see all of her high-end services listed by price and then service type, and she would like to break down the criteria as follows: Hands & Feet or Body Massage services $50 or more, Facial or Microdermabrasion services over $55, Beauty or Waxing services over $45, and all Botanical Hair & Scalp Therapy services. In this exercise, you will show her how to do this by combining operators and multiple criteria.

To Combine Operators and Multiple Criteria

a. Click the **Create** tab, and then in the Queries group, click **Query Design**, and double-click **tblService** to add the table to the query window. Click **Close** to close the Show Table dialog box.

b. In the following order, double-click **Fee**, **Type**, and **ServiceName** to add the fields to the query design grid.

SIDE NOTE
Wider Columns
You can widen the columns in the query design grid by double-clicking the right border of the column selector bar.

c. Click in the **Criteria** row for the Fee field, type >55, and then in the Criteria row for the Type field, type Facial or Microdermabrasion.

d. Click in the **Sort** row, and then select **Ascending** for the Fee, Type, and ServiceName fields.

e. In the Results group, click **Run** to run the query. The results should show six records with Facial or Microdermabrasion for the Type field, and all values in the Fee field should be greater than $55.

f. Switch to **Design** view. In the **or criteria** row for the Fee field, type >=50, and in the **or criteria** row for the Type field, type "Hands & Feet" or Body Massage. Click **Run** to run the query again.
The query results should show a total of 19 records with types Facial or Microdermabrasion that have fees greater than $55 and with types Hands & Feet or Body Massage that have fees greater than or equal to $50.

Troubleshooting

If you get only 16 records in the results, you did not put the quotation marks around "Hands & Feet". Access will add those quotation marks for you. In this case, Access evaluates the ampersand character (&) as separating two values, so it will put the quotation marks around the word "Hands" and around the word "Feet" so it will look like "Hands" & "Feet". This is different from having the quotations around the whole phrase, which is what you want it to look like. In this case, you should put the quotation marks around the phrase in order for it to appear as "Hands & Feet".

g. Switch to **Design** view. Click in the first **blank row** under the or criteria row for the Fee field, type >45, and then for the Type field, type Beauty or Waxing. In the Results group, click **Run** to run the query again.
The results should show a total of 23 records with types Facial or Microdermabrasion that have fees greater than $55, with types Hands & Feet or Body Massage that have fees greater than or equal to $50, and with types Beauty or Waxing that have fees greater than $45.

h. Switch to **Design** view. Click in the **next blank row** under the **or criteria** row for the Type field, and then type "Botanical Hair & Scalp Therapy".

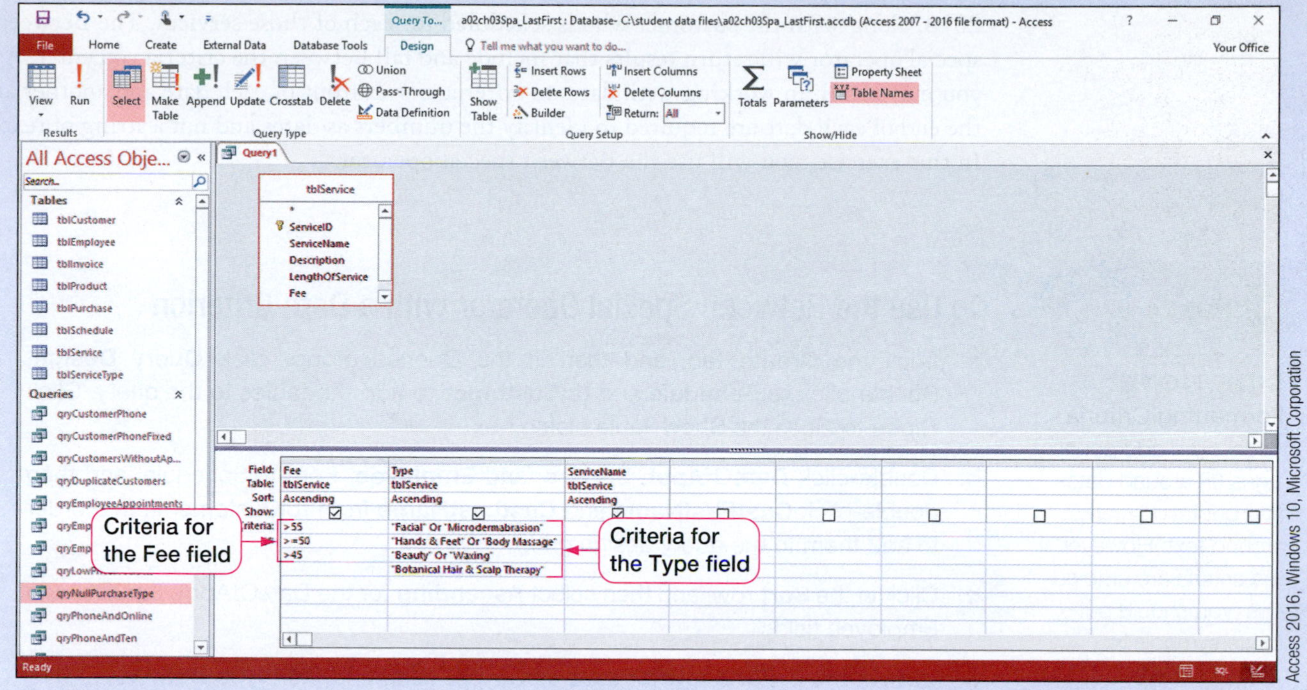

Figure 25 All criteria added to the query design grid

i. In the Results group, click **Run** to run the query again.
The results should show a total of 25 records with types Facial or Microdermabrasion that have fees greater than $55, with types Hands & Feet or Body Massage that have fees greater than or equal to $50, with types Beauty or Waxing that have fees greater than $45, and with all Botanical Hair & Scalp Therapy types.

> **Troubleshooting**
> If you still see 23 records, check to see whether you put the quotation marks around "Botanical Hair & Scalp Therapy" and whether you spelled the type correctly.

j. Click **Save**, name the query qryHighEndServices, and then click **OK**. **Close** the query.

Using Special Operators and Date Criteria

Special operators, as shown in Table 5, are used to compare text values using wildcards (LIKE) to determine whether values are between a range of values (BETWEEN) or in a set of values (IN).

Operator	Description
LIKE	Matches text values by using wildcards. These are the same wildcards that are shown in Table 1.
BETWEEN	Determines whether a number or date is within a range.
IN	Determines whether a value is found within a set of values.

Table 5 Special operators

The manager of the spa would like you to find all services scheduled for February 2018, along with the customer who is scheduled for each of those services. The Between special operator will return results that include and fall between the criteria you enter. As you may recall, in working with dates as criteria, a # in front of each date and another at the end of each date are required to identify the numbers as dates and not a string of text. In this exercise, you will use the Between special operator.

SIDE NOTE

Formatting Criteria

Access will add pound signs (#) around dates and quotation marks around text. However, if the criteria are ambiguous, you should put these symbols in.

To Use the Between Special Operator with a Date Criterion

a. Click the **Create** tab, and then in the Queries group, click **Query Design**. Double-click **tblSchedule** and **tblCustomer** to add the tables to the query. Click **Close** to close the Show Table dialog box.

b. Double-click **DateOfAppt**, **Service**, and **Employee**, from tblSchedule, and then double-click **CustFirstName** and **CustLastName** from tblCustomer in that order to add them to the query design grid.

c. Click in the **Sort** row, and then select **Ascending** for the DateOfAppt, Service, and Employee fields.

d. Click in the **Criteria** row for the DateOfAppt field, and then type Between 2/1/18 and 2/29/18.

e. In the Results group, click **Run** to run the query. Use the **AutoFit** feature on the columns to best fit the data.
Notice that the results do not show services in February. They show services in January. Access is misinterpreting your query criterion.

f. Switch to **Design** view to check the criteria. Move your pointer to the **border** between DateOfAppt and Service until it becomes ⇔. Double-click to see the full criteria.
Notice that since there is no leap day in 2018, Access interpreted the 2/29 as February of 2029 (2/1/2029) and the /18 as a division. This is not what you wanted. This example shows why it is so important to check your results to see whether they make sense.

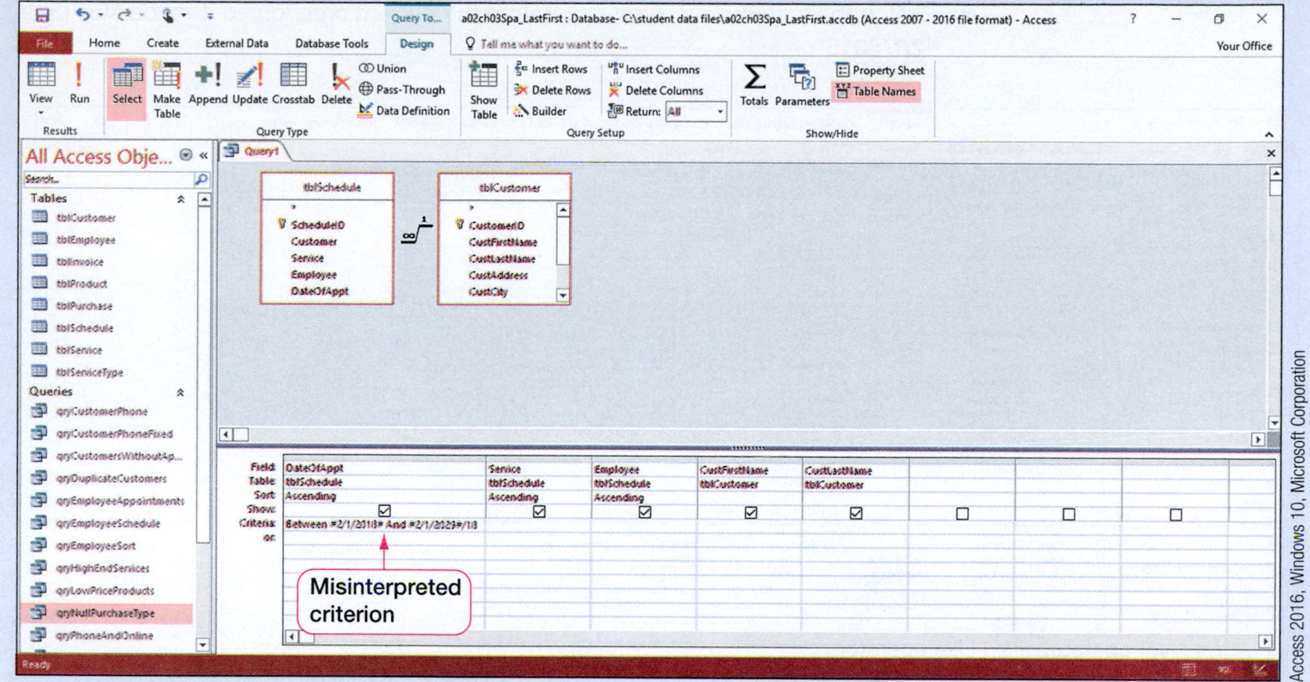

Figure 26 Misinterpreted criterion for DateOfAppt

g. Change the criterion to Between 2/1/18 and 2/28/18. In the Results group, click **Run** to run the query.
This time, the results are as expected and show 47 appointments in February.

h. Click **Save**, and under Query Name, type qryFebruaryServices, and then click **OK**. **Close** the query.

Combining Special Operators and Logical Operators

Special operators can be combined with logical operators. As your criteria get more complex, you need to carefully check how Access interprets your criteria and your results.

The manager of the spa would like you to find all services scheduled for months other than February 2018, along with the customer who is scheduled for each of those services. In this exercise, you will use the LIKE special operator and combine it with the NOT logical operator. This query is very similar to the one you just created, so you will open that query and modify it.

A03.25

To Combine Logical and Special Operators

a. In the Navigation pane, right-click **qryFebruaryServices**, and then select **Copy**. Right-click anywhere in the **Navigation Pane**, and then select **Paste**. In the Query Name box, type qryNotFebruaryServices. Click OK.

b. Double-click **qryNotFebruaryServices** to open it.

c. Switch to **Design** view. Click in the **Criteria** row for the DateOfAppt field, and then replace the current criteria with Like 2/*/2018. Remember that the asterisk (*) is a wildcard that will select all dates that have a month of 2 and a year of 2018.

d. In the Results group, click **Run** to run the query. Notice that the results show 47 February service appointments.

e. Switch to **Design** view. Type Not before the current criterion so it reads **Not Like "2/*/2015"**.

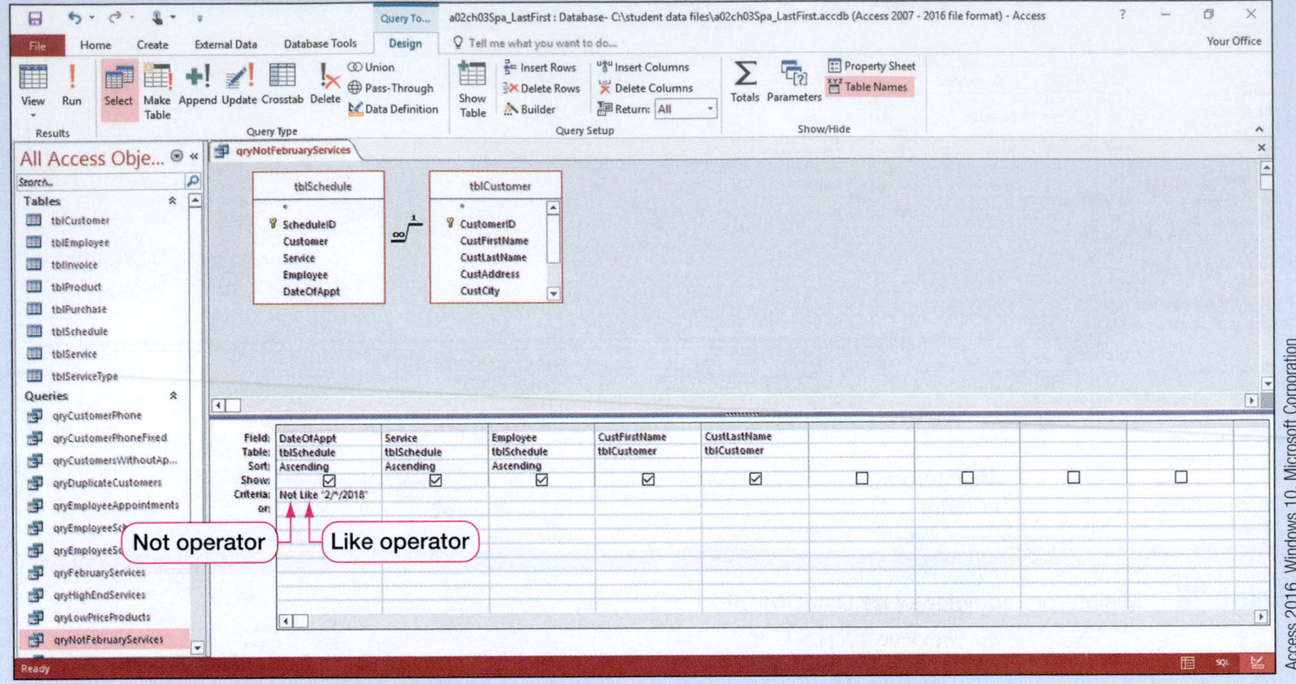

Access 2016, Windows 10, Microsoft Corporation

Figure 27 Combined Not and Like operators

f. In the Results group, click **Run** to run the query. Notice that the results now show the six service appointments not in February.

g. **Save**, and **close** your query.

Create Aggregate Functions

Aggregate functions perform arithmetic operations, such as calculating averages and totals, on records displayed in a table or query. An aggregate function can be used in Datasheet view by adding a total row to a table, or it can be used in a query on records that meet certain criteria.

QUICK REFERENCE | **Commonly Used Aggregate Functions**

There are a number of different aggregate functions that can be used depending on the type of calculation you want to perform.

1. **Sum** — Calculates the total value for selected records
2. **Average** — Calculates the average value for selected records
3. **Count** — Displays the number of records retrieved
4. **Minimum** — Displays the smallest value from the selected records
5. **Maximum** — Displays the largest value from the selected records

Adding a Total Row

If you need to see a quick snapshot of statistics for a table or query, you can use the total row. The **total row** is a special row that appears at the end of a datasheet that enables you to show aggregate functions for one or more fields. In this exercise, you will help the manager quickly find a total for all unpaid invoices listed in the invoices table and a count of the number of invoices in the table. The invoice table has a Yes/No field, so you will show her how to define criteria for Yes/No.

A03.26

To Add a Total Row to a Query

a. In the Navigation pane, double-click **tblInvoice** to open it. Notice that the Paid field is a check box. Switch to **Design** view, and for the Paid field, click the **Data Type** box, and see that the Format is Yes/No. **Close** [X] the table.

b. Click the **Create** tab, and then in the Queries group, click **Query Design**. Double-click **tblInvoice** and **tblCustomer** to add the tables to the query. Click **Close** to close the Show Table dialog box.

c. Double-click **InvoiceDate**, **InvoiceTotal**, and **Paid** from tblInvoice, and then double-click **CustFirstName** and **CustLastName** from tblCustomer in that order to add them to the query design grid.

d. Click in the **Sort** row, and then select **Ascending** for InvoiceDate.

e. Click in the **Criteria** row for the Paid field, and then type No.

f. In the Results group, click **Run** to run the query. The six unpaid invoices are shown.

g. In the Records group, click **Totals** so that the Total row shows.

h. Click in the **Total row** under the InvoiceTotal field, click the **arrow**, and then select **Sum**. Click in the **Total** row under the First Name field, click the **arrow**, and then select **Count**.

SIDE NOTE

Removing Totals

To remove the total row, on the Home tab, click Totals.

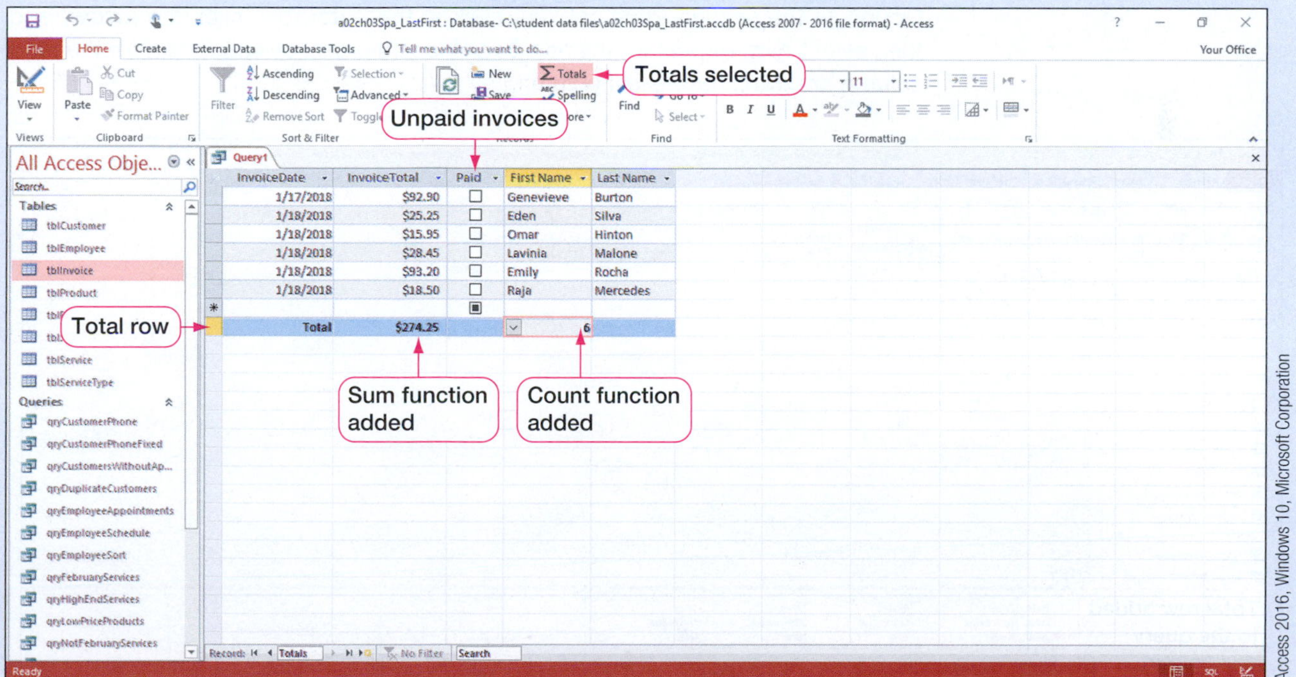

Figure 28 Sum and Count of Unpaid Invoices added to the Total row

i. Click **Save** [save icon], and under Query Name, type qryUnpaidInvoices, and then click **OK**. **Close** [X] the query.

Using Aggregate Functions in a Query

Aggregate functions can be used in queries to perform calculations on selected fields and records. One advantage to using aggregate functions in queries, rather than just a total row, is that you can group criteria and then calculate the aggregate functions for a group of records. By default, the query design grid does not have a place to enter aggregate functions, so the column total row must be added from the Query Tools Design tab. Each column or field can calculate only one aggregate function. So to calculate the sum and average on the same field, the field must be added to the grid multiple times.

You have been asked to provide a statistical summary of the spa's product prices. The manager would like to see how many products are offered, the average product price, and the minimum and maximum product prices. In this exercise, you will use aggregate functions to provide this information.

To Use Aggregate Functions in a Query

a. Click the **Create** tab, and then in the Queries group, click **Query Design**. Double-click **tblProduct** to add the table to the query. Click **Close** to close the Show Table dialog box.

b. Double-click **Price** four times to add the field four times to the query design grid.

> **Troubleshooting**
>
> If you clicked the Price field too many times, click the top of the extra Price fields in the query design grid, and press Delete to remove them.

c. In the Show/Hide group, click **Totals** to add a total row to the query design grid.

d. In the first Price column, click in the **Total** row, click the **arrow**, and then select **Count**. In the second Price column, click in the **Total** row, click the **arrow**, and then select **Avg**. Repeat for the next two Price columns, selecting **Min** for the third column and **Max** for the last column.

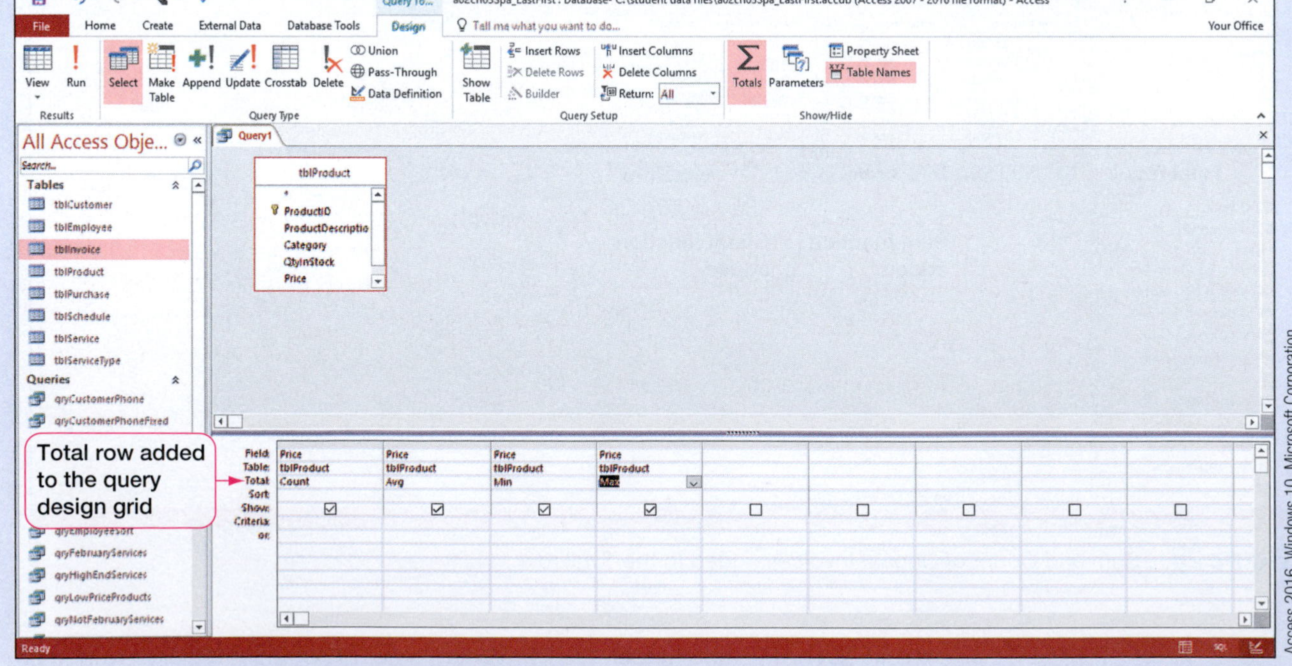

Figure 29 Aggregate functions selected for each column

e. In the Results group, click **Run** to run the query. Because this is an aggregate query and you are calculating one statistic per column, there will be only one record in the results.

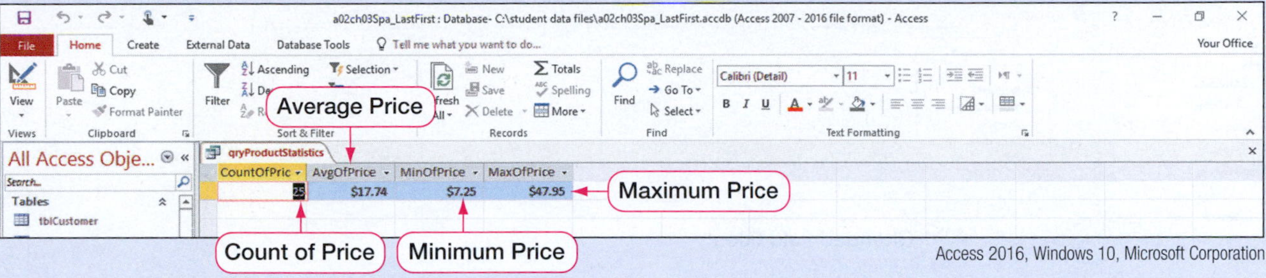

Access 2016, Windows 10, Microsoft Corporation

Figure 30 Aggregate query results

f. Click **Save** [save icon], and under Query name, type qryProductStatistics, and then click **OK**.

Changing Field Names

Field names in aggregate queries are a composite of the selected aggregate function and the table field name. For example, the Count function for Price is named CountOfPrice as shown in Figure 30. This name can be misleading, as the aggregate function actually shows the number of products that have a price. The other functions are more descriptively named but still could have more useful names.

The field names assigned in an aggregate query can easily be changed either before or after the query is run. However, you must keep the original field name in the query design grid so Access knows what field to perform the calculation on. In this exercise, you will change the names of the fields in the aggregate query you just created.

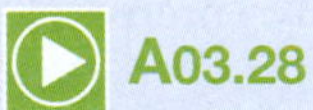
A03.28

To Change the Field Names in an Aggregate Query

a. With qryProductStatistics open, switch to **Design** view.

b. Click in the **Field** row of the first column, and then press Home to move the insertion point to the beginning of the field name. Type Number of Products:. Do not delete the field name Price. The colon identifies the title as separate from the field name. Repeat for the other three fields, and type Average Price:, Minimum Price:, and Maximum Price:. If necessary, use **AutoFit** to resize the columns to see the complete column names.

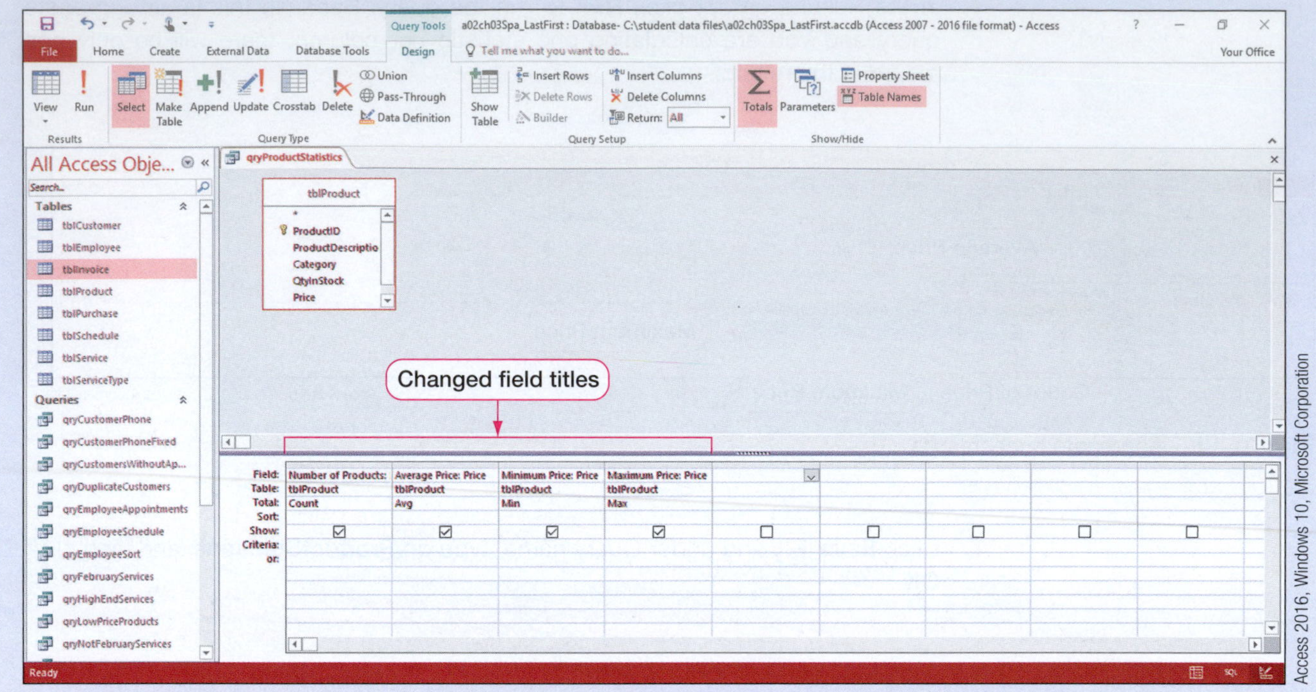

Figure 31 Field titles changed

c. In the Results group, click **Run** to run the query. Use **AutoFit** to resize the columns to see the complete column names.

d. Click **Save** and then **Close** the query.

Creating Calculations for Groups of Records

Not only can you find statistical information for selected records using aggregate functions in a query or for all records using the total row, you can also calculate statistics for groups of records. Creating a group to calculate statistics works the same way as an aggregate query but must include the field to group by. The additional field will not have a statistic selected for the total row, but instead, it will have the default Group By entered in the total row.

In this exercise, you will help the spa manager find the same product price statistics you calculated above but this time grouped by product category.

A03.29

To Create a Group Calculation

a. In the Navigation pane, right-click **qryProductStatistics**, and then select **Copy**. Right-click anywhere in the **Navigation Pane**, and then select **Paste**. In the Query Name box, type qryProductStatisticsByCategory. Click OK.

b. In the Navigation pane, double-click **qryProductStatisticsByCategory** to open it. Switch to **Design** view.

c. Double-click **Category** to add it to the query design grid. Point to the **top border** of the Category field until the pointer turns into a black downward arrow. Click and drag the **Category** field to the left of the Number of Products: Price column. Notice that the Category Total row displays Group By, so the statistics will be grouped by each category type.

d. In the Results group, click **Run** to run the query. Use **AutoFit** on the columns to best fit the data.
Notice that there are five total rows, one for each category of product.

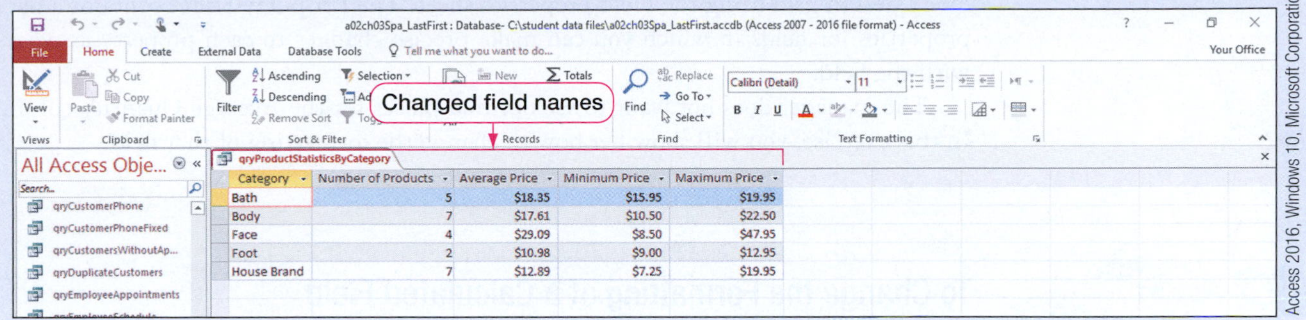

Access 2016, Windows 10, Microsoft Corporation

Figure 32 Query results with calculations

e. Click **Save**, and **Close** the query.

Troubleshooting an Aggregate Query

Caution should be used in using aggregate functions. Forgetting to add a function in the total row can cause a large number of records to be retrieved from the database or can result in a combination of records that do not make any sense. You must carefully select which field should have the Group By operator in the total row; many times, only one field will use Group By. Combining search criteria and aggregate functions in a single query can make the query complex. It also makes troubleshooting more difficult if the query does not work. When in doubt, set all your criteria in one query, and then use the aggregate functions in another query based on the query with the criteria. This way, you can first verify that your criteria worked and then concentrate on the aggregate function results.

The manager tried to create an aggregate query to calculate the total number of items and average number of items purchased by different methods: phone, online, and in person. The results made no sense, and she has asked you to help her figure out why. In this exercise, you will troubleshoot the query to determine the problem and correct it.

To Troubleshoot an Aggregate Query

a. Double-click **qryPurchaseMethods** to open the query. Notice the results in the second and third columns are exactly the same when the intent was to have one column contain a total and the other column contain an average.

b. Switch to **Design** view. Look at the second column, **Quantity**, and notice the Total row shows the Group By operator instead of a function. Change this to **Sum**.

c. Rename the second and third column field titles to **Total Quantity** and **Average Quantity**, remembering to put a colon between the name and the Quantity field name.

d. In the Results group, click **Run** to run the query. Use **AutoFit** on the columns to best fit the data.

e. Click the **File** tab, click **Save As**, click **Save Object As**, and then click **Save As**. Under Save 'qryPurchaseMethods' to:, type qryPurchaseMethodsFixed, and then click **OK**.

Formatting a Calculated Field

An aggregate query may give you the correct results, but the formatting may not be what you expected. The fields used in a query that come from a table use the formatting defined in the table design. However, calculated query fields must be formatted in the query design grid using the Field properties sheet. The **Property Sheet** contains a list of properties for fields in which you can make precise changes to each property associated with the field.

The manager does not want to see decimal places for the Average Quantity column. In this exercise, you will show her how to change the formatting of that field.

To Change the Formatting of a Calculated Field

a. With **qryPurchaseMethodsFixed** open, switch to **Design** view.

b. Click the **Average Quantity: Quantity** column. On the Design tab, in the Show/Hide group, click **Property Sheet**.

c. In the Property Sheet pane, on the General tab, click the **Format** box, click the **arrow**, and then select **Fixed**. Click the **Decimal Places** box, and then type 0.

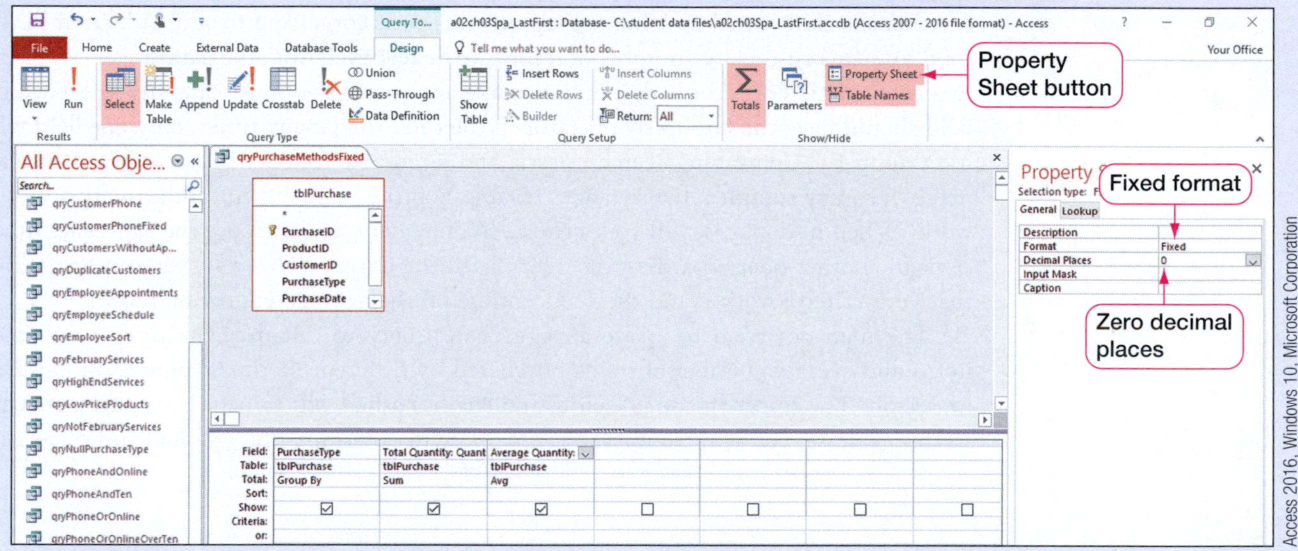

Figure 33 Property sheet open with changes

d. **Close** [X] the Property Sheet pane, and then **run** the query again. The results should be formatted with no decimal places.

e. **Save** [Save] and **close** [X] the query.

CHAPTER 3

SS **CONSIDER THIS** | **How Many Decimal Places?**

Would having many decimal places for an average field give you a more accurate average? Why would you choose to show no decimal places on an average quantity field?

Create Calculated Fields

In addition to statistical calculations using aggregate functions, you can perform an arithmetic calculation within a query to create a new field. The result of the calculated field is displayed each time you run the query. However, this new field is not part of any other table.

A calculated field can be added to a query using the fields in the query or even fields in another table or query in the database. The calculation can use a combination of numbers and field values, allowing you flexibility in how you perform the calculation. For example, you can multiply a product price stored in the table by a sales tax rate that you enter into the calculation.

Building a Calculated Field Using Expression Builder

The **Expression Builder** is a tool in Access that can help you build calculated fields correctly. Expression Builder provides a list of expression elements, operators, and built-in functions. Its capabilities range from simple to complex.

In this exercise, you will help the spa manager create a query to show what the value of her inventory is, using the Quantity in Stock and Price fields for each product.

 A03.32

SIDE NOTE
Expression Box
When you use multiple tables in Expression Builder, the table name is put in front of the field name with an exclamation mark.

To Add a Calculated Field Using Expression Builder

a. Click the **Create** tab, and then in the Queries group, click **Query Design**, and then double-click **tblProduct** to add the table to the query. Click **Close** to close the Show Table dialog box.

b. Double-click **ProductDescription**, **Category**, **QtyInStock**, and **Price** to add the fields to the query design grid.

c. Click in the **Sort** row, and then select **Ascending** for the ProductDescription field.

d. Click **Save**, and under Query Name, type qryProductInventory, and then click **OK**.

e. Click in the **Field** row in the fifth column, and in the Query Setup group, click **Builder**. The Expression Builder dialog box opens, which is where you will build your formula for the calculation.

f. Under Expression Categories, double-click **QtyInStock** to add the field to the expression box, type * for multiplication, and then under Expression Categories, double-click **Price**. Move the insertion point to the beginning of the expression, and then type Total Inventory:.

Troubleshooting

When you click Expression Builder to create a calculated field and you do not see your field names listed in the Expression Categories box in the middle of the dialog box, it may be that the query has not been saved yet. If the query has not been saved, the field names will not appear, and you will have to type them in the Expression Builder manually instead of clicking them to select them. It is good practice to save your query first and then open the Expression Builder to create a calculated field.

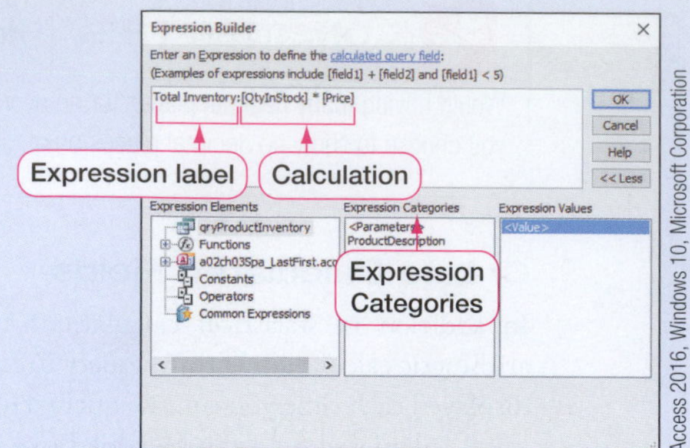

Figure 34 Expression Builder

g. Click **OK** to save the expression and add it to the query design grid. The field name will show Total Inventory: [QtyInStock]*[Price] and will multiply the quantity by the price.

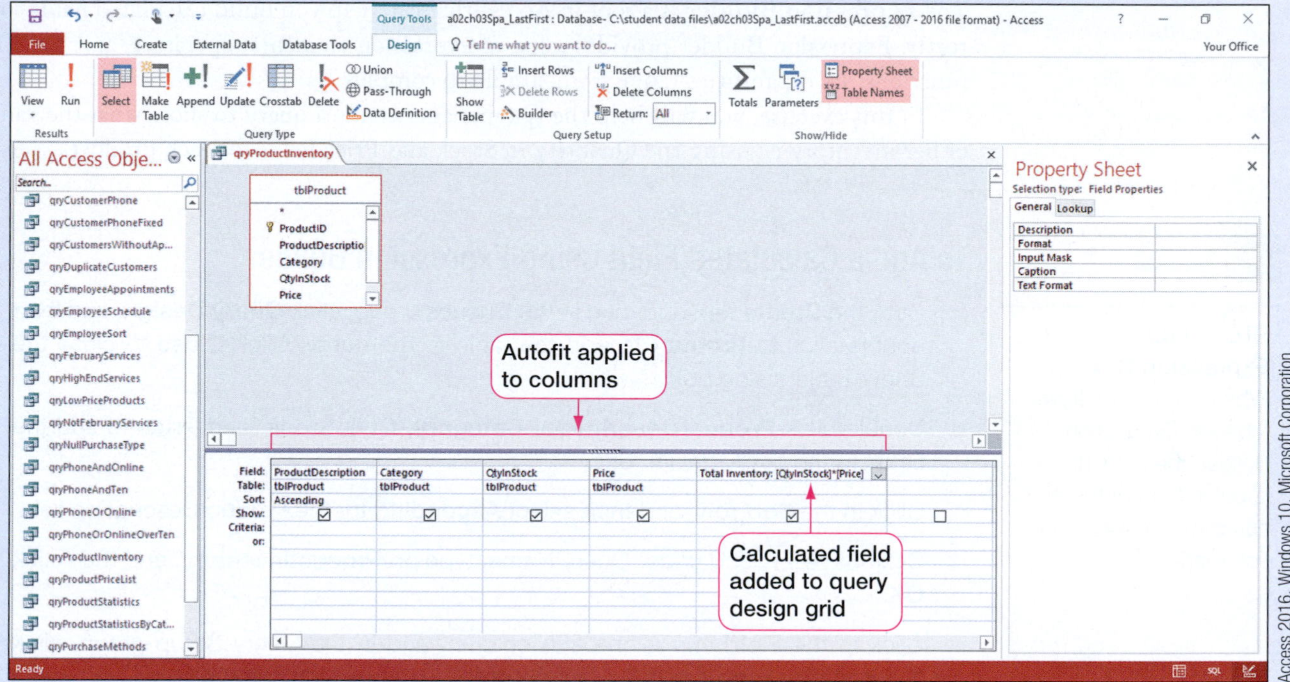

Figure 35 Design grid with calculated expression added

h. In the Results group, click **Run** to run the query. Use **AutoFit** on the Total Inventory column to best fit the data. The results should show 25 records with a new column titled Total Inventory that multiplies the QtyInStock and the Price fields.

i. **Close** [X] the query, and then click **Yes** when prompted to save changes. **Close** Access.

Concept Check

1. What is a wildcard character? How would you use it to find a record? p. 169
2. Does modifying the datasheet appearance change the data in your database? p. 174
3. What is the difference between the Find Duplicates Query Wizard and the Find Unmatched Query Wizard? p. 175–176
4. What is the multiplier effect, and how can you prevent it from happening? p. 181
5. If you sort on two different fields in a query, which sort is done first? p. 186
6. What is the difference between using AND and OR as logical operators in a query? p. 195
7. What is an aggregate query? Why would you add the same field multiple times to an aggregate query? p. 203–204
8. How does a calculated field differ from an aggregate function? p. 208

Key Terms

Aggregate function 202
AutoFit 174
Comparison operator 187
Crosstab query 175
Expression Builder 209
Filter 172
Filter by selection 172
Find command 169
Find Duplicates Query Wizard 175
Find Unmatched Query Wizard 176
Join lines 181
Logical operator 195
Multiplier effect 181
Orphan 176
Primary sort field 186
Property sheet 208
Query by example 178
Replace command 169
Secondary sort field 186
Sort field 185
Sorting 185
Special operator 199
Text filter 173
Total row 202
Wildcard character 169

Visual Summary

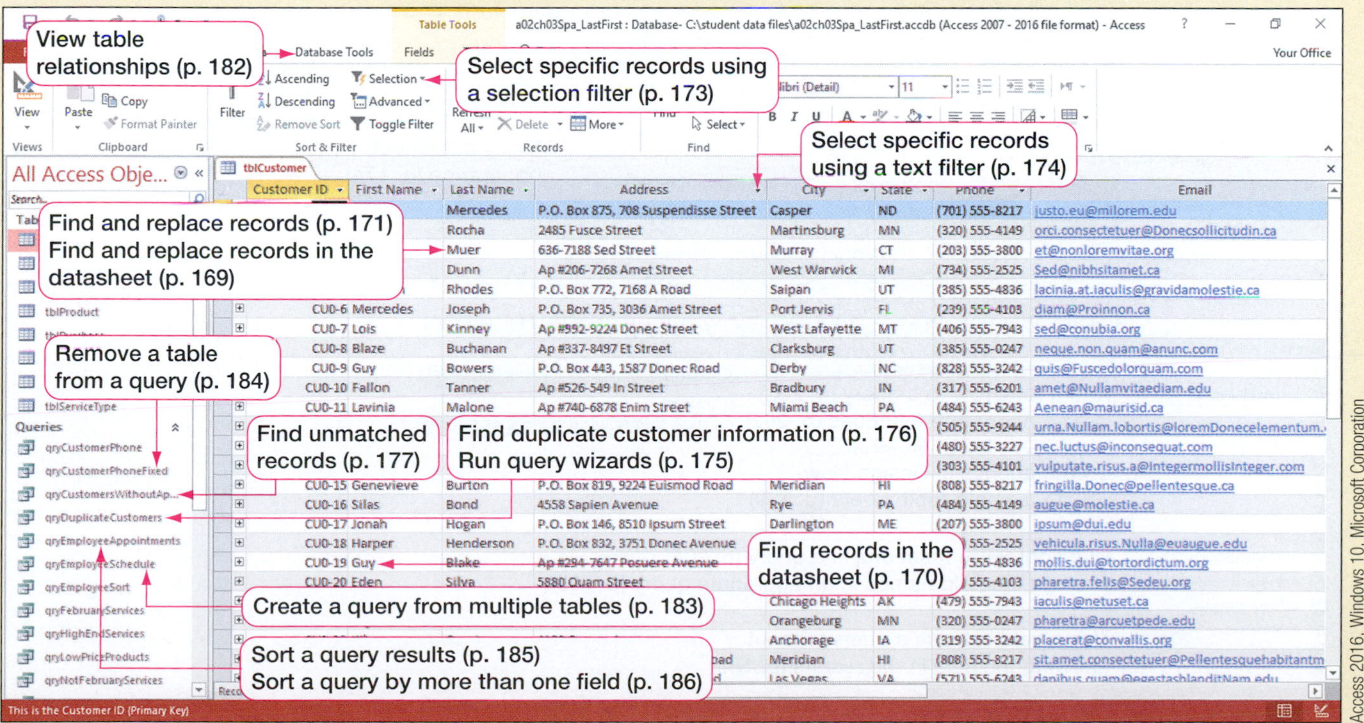

Figure 36

Access 2016, Windows 10, Microsoft Corporation

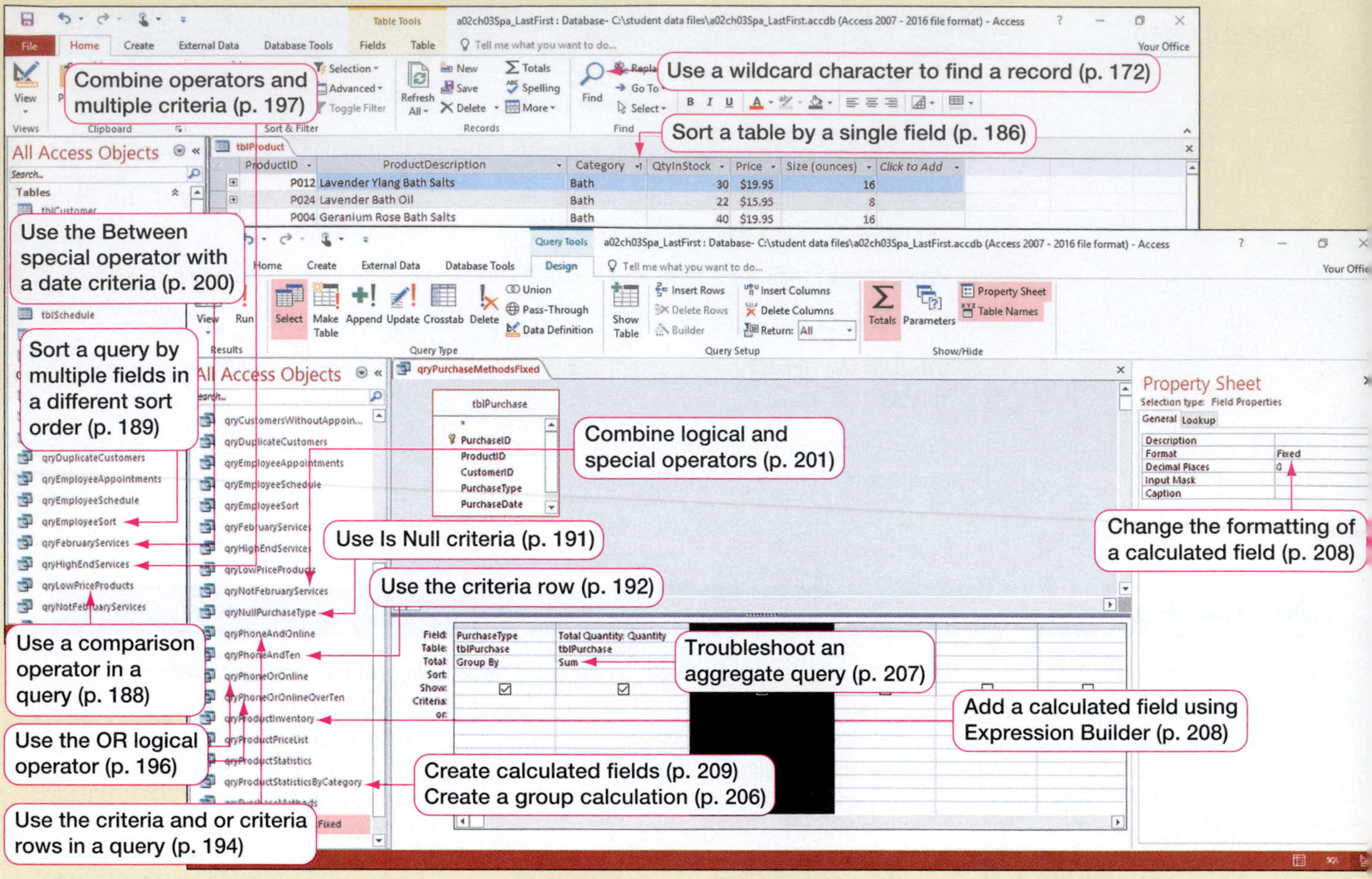

Combine operators and multiple criteria (p. 197)

Use a wildcard character to find a record (p. 172)

Sort a table by a single field (p. 186)

Use the Between special operator with a date criteria (p. 200)

Sort a query by multiple fields in a different sort order (p. 189)

Combine logical and special operators (p. 201)

Use Is Null criteria (p. 191)

Change the formatting of a calculated field (p. 208)

Use the criteria row (p. 192)

Use a comparison operator in a query (p. 188)

Troubleshoot an aggregate query (p. 207)

Add a calculated field using Expression Builder (p. 208)

Use the OR logical operator (p. 196)

Create calculated fields (p. 209)
Create a group calculation (p. 206)

Use the criteria and or criteria rows in a query (p. 194)

Figure 37

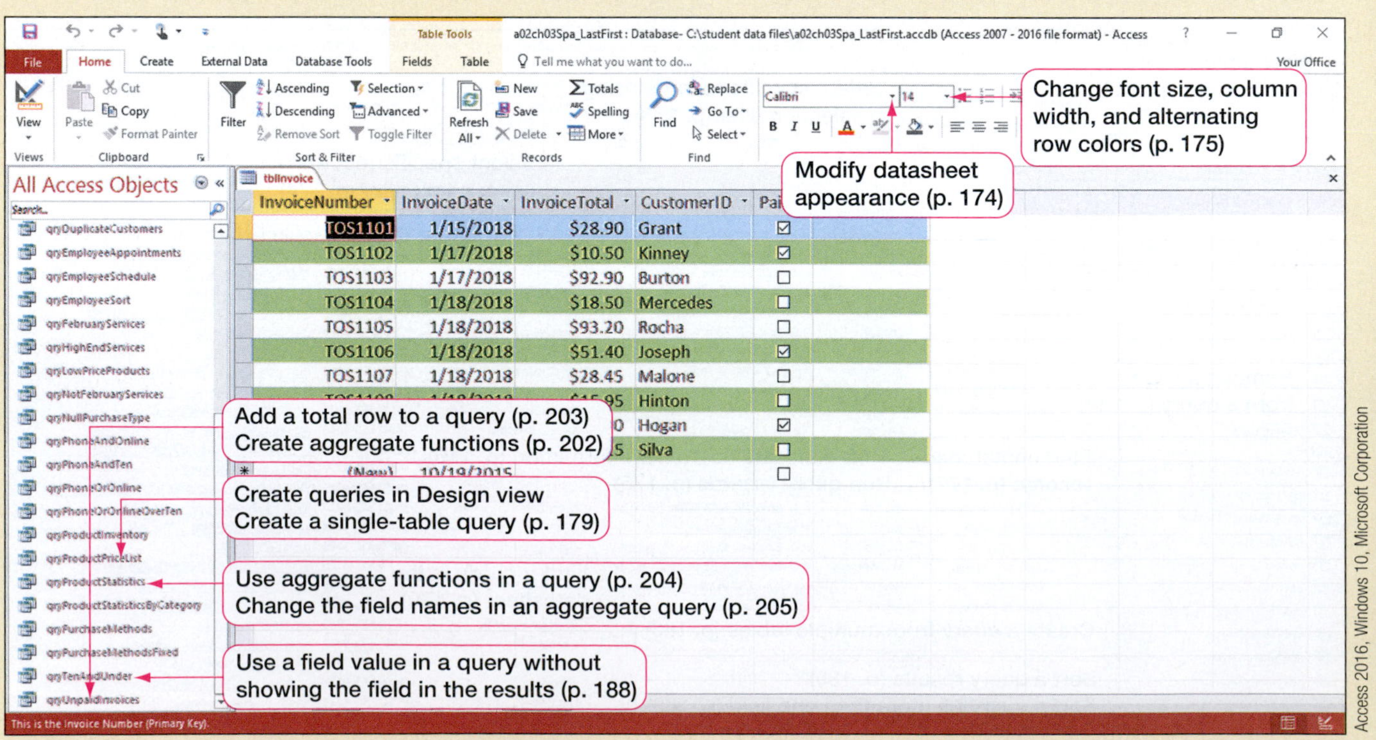

Figure 38

Access 2016, Windows 10, Microsoft Corporation

Practice 1

Student data file needed:

 a02ch03Spa2.accdb

You will save your file as:

 a02ch03Spa2_LastFirst.accdb

Turquoise Oasis Spa

Sales & Marketing

The resort is considering hosting a large convention and is trying to sign a multiple-year contract with an out-of-town group. The spa is being asked to provide information about the services, products, and packages it offers. All the information can be found in the database, but it needs to come together in a coherent fashion. You have been asked to answer a number of questions about the spa and provide information to help answer those questions. You will also look for discrepancies or mistakes in the data and correct them as necessary.

a. Start **Access**, click **Open Other Files** in the left pane, and then double-click **This PC**. Navigate through the folder structure to the location of your student data files, and then double-click **a02ch03Spa2**. A database opens displaying tables related to the spa.

b. Click the **File** tab, click **Save As**, save the file as an **Access Database**, and click **Save As**. Navigate to the location where you are saving your project files, and then change the file name to a02ch03Spa2_LastFirst using your last and first name. Click **Save**. If necessary, enable the content.

c. Double-click **tblCustomer** to open the table. Add a new record with your first name and last name, your address, your city, your state, your phone number, and your e-mail address.

d. Use the **Find** command to find spa customers who come from as far away as Alaska.

- Click in the **State** column for the first record. On the Home tab, in the Find group, click **Find**. Type AK in the Find What box, and then click **Find Next** until Access finishes searching the table. Click **OK**, and then click **Cancel** to close the dialog box. Notice that the Alaska address selected is really a city in Hawaii.

e. Use the Replace command to replace **AK** with HI in the table.

- On the Home tab, in the Find group, click **Find**. Click the **Replace** tab, and type AK in the Find What box. Type HI in the Replace With box, and then click **Find Next**. When Customer ID CU0-21 is selected, click **Replace**. Click **Find Next** to check for any more similar errors. Click **OK**, and then click **Cancel** to close the dialog box.

f. Click the **arrow** on the State field column, point to **Text Filters**, select **Begins With**, type H in the State begins with box, and then click **OK**. Verify that three records are selected. Save and close the table.

g. Create a query to find which products are purchased by more than one customer.

- Click the **Create** tab, and then in the Queries group, click **Query Wizard**. Click **Find Duplicates Query Wizard**, and then click **OK**.
- Click **Table: tblPurchase**, and then click **Next**. Double-click **ProductID**, and then click **Next**. Click the **All Fields** button to add all the fields to the Additional query fields box, and then click **Next**. Under "What do you want to name your query?", type qryDuplicateProducts_iLast using your first initial and last name, and then click **Finish**. Close the query.

h. Create a query to find out which employees currently do not have any customer appointments at the spa.

- On the **Create** tab, in the Queries group, click **Query Wizard**. Click **Find Unmatched Query Wizard**, and then click **OK**.

- Click **Table: tblEmployee**, and then click **Next**. Select **Table: tblSchedule**, and then click **Next**. Verify that Matching fields shows **EmployeeID <=> Employee**, and then click **Next**. Click the **All Fields** button to add all the fields to the Selected fields column, and then click **Next**.
- Name the query qryEmployeesWithoutAppointments_iLast using your first initial and last name, and then click **Finish**.
- In the Results group, switch to **Design** view. Click the **Sort** row for the EmpLastName field, click the **sort** arrow, and then click **Ascending** to sort the query in ascending order by Last Name. On the Design tab, in the Results group, click **Run** to run the query. Close the query, and then click **Yes** when prompted to save the changes.

i. Create a query to list any customers who are not from New Mexico who have purchased bath products.
   - Click the **Create** tab, and then in the Queries group, click **Query Design**. Double-click **tblCustomer**, **tblPurchase**, and **tblProduct** to add the tables to the query window. Click **Close** to close the Show Table dialog box.
   - In the following order, from tblCustomer, double-click **CustLastName**, **CustFirstName**, **CustState**; from tblPurchase, double-click **PurchaseDate**; from tblProduct, double-click **ProductDescription**; and from tblPurchase, double-click **Quantity** to add the fields to the query design grid. Click the **Sort** row for the CustLastName and CustFirstName fields, and then select **Ascending**.
   - In the **Criteria** row for CustState, type Not NM. In the same **Criteria** row for ProductDescription, type *Bath*.
   - Note that the Not in the CustState criteria will be converted to <> by Access and the word Like will be added to the criteria *Bath*.
   - On the Design tab, in the Results group, click **Run** to run the query.
   - Click **Save**, name the query qryBathProductsNotNM_iLast using your first initial and last name, and then close the query.

j. Create a query to list the spa's services by Type, Name, LengthOfService, and Fee.
   - Click the **Create** tab, in the Queries group, click **Query Design**. Double-click **tblService** and **tblServiceType** to add the tables to the query window. Click **Close** to close the Show Table dialog box.
   - In the following order, from tblServiceType, double-click **Type**, and from tblService, double-click **ServiceName**, **LengthOfService**, and **Fee** to add the fields to the query design grid. Click the **Sort** row for the Type field, select **Ascending**, and then for the Fee field, select **Descending**. On the Design tab, in the Results group, click **Run** to run the query.
   - Use **AutoFit** on all columns to better view the data. Click **Save**, name the query qryServicesAndFees_iLast using your first initial and last name, and then close the query.

k. Create a query to find how much each customer spent on his or her product purchase, including 8% sales tax, but only if the purchase was a quantity greater than 1.
   - Click the **Create** tab, and then in the Queries group, click **Query Design**. Add **tblProduct**, **tblPurchase**, and **tblCustomer** to the query window. Click **Close** to close the Show Table dialog box. From tblProduct, double-click **ProductDescription** and **Price**; from tblPurchase, double-click **Quantity**; and from tblCustomer, double-click **CustFirstName** and **CustLastName** in that order to add the fields to the query design grid.
   - Click in the **Criteria** row for Quantity, and then type >1. Click **Save**, name the query qryTotalPurchase_iLast using your first initial and last name, and then click **OK**.

- In the sixth column, click in the **Field** row, and then on the Design tab, in the Query Set-up group, click **Builder**. In the Expression Categories column, double-click **Price** to add it to the expression, type *, double-click **Quantity** to add it to the expression, type *, and then type 1.08. Click at the beginning of the expression, type Total Purchase with tax:, and then click **OK**.
- Click the **Sort** row for the Quantity field, click the **arrow**, and then click **Ascending**. In the Results group, click **Run** to run the query.
- Switch to **Design** view. Click the **Total Purchase with tax** field, on the Design tab, in the Show/Hide group, click **Property Sheet**. On the Property Sheet's General tab, click the **Format** arrow, and then select **Currency**. Click the Decimal Places arrow, and then select **2**. Close the Property Sheet, and then on the Design tab, in the Results group, click **Run** to run the query. The Total Purchase with tax field should be formatted with currency and two decimal places.
- Use **AutoFit** on all the columns.
- Close the query, and then click **Yes** when prompted to save the changes.

l. Create an aggregate query to find the average, minimum, and maximum fee for each type of service the spa offers.
- Click the **Create** tab, and then in the Queries group, click **Query Design**. Add **tblService** to the query window. Click **Close** to close the Show Table dialog box. Double-click **Type** one time, and then double-click **Fee** three times in that order to add the fields to the query design grid. In the Show/Hide group, click **Totals** to add the Total row to the query design grid.
- Click in the **Total** row, for the first Fee column, click the **arrow**, and then click **Avg**. For the second Fee column, select **Min**; and for the third Fee column, select **Max**. Click in the **Sort** row in the Type field, click the **arrow**, and then select **Ascending**. In the Results group, click **Run** to run the query.
- Switch to **Design** view. Change the names of the three Fee columns to Average Fee, Minimum Fee, and Maximum Fee in that order, remembering to put a colon before the Fee field name. In the **Results** group, click **Run** to run the query.
- Use **AutoFit** on all the columns.
- Click **Save**, name the query qryFeeStatistics_iLast using your first initial and last name, and then click **OK**. Close the query.

m. Close Access, and submit your file as directed by your instructor.

Problem Solve 1

Student data file needed:

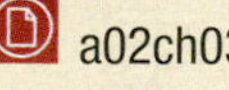

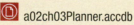

a02ch03Planner.accdb

You will save your file as:

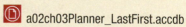

a02ch03Planner_LastFirst.accdb

Rakes Event Management

Production & Operations

Beth Rakes runs an event-planning service. She has a database with clients, events, menus, and decorations. She has hired you to add queries to make the database more useful. You have been given a small database with representative data.

a. Open the Access database **a02ch03Planner**. Save your file as a02ch03Planner_LastFirst using your last and first name. If necessary, enable the content.

b. Open **tblClients**, and change the first and last name in the last record to be your actual name. Create a filter to show only the clients who have a State of **MN**. Save and close the table.

c. Modify tblEvents so the font size is **14**. Adjust the column widths appropriately. Change to an Alternate Row Color of **Gold, Accent 4, Lighter 80%**. Save and close the table.
Create a Find Duplicates query that will show all events on the same date. Show all the fields in the query results. Name the query qryDupDates. Close the query.

d. Create a Find Unmatched query that will return the **last name**, **first name**, **city**, **state**, and **phone** of anyone who is listed as a client in **tblClients** but does not have an event booked. Sort the query in ascending order by last name and then by first name. Name the query qryClientNoEvent. Save and close the query.

Critical Thinking

Of the records returned in this query, which state or states occur most frequently as having clients that do not have booked events?

e. Create a query that will return the client's **last name**, **first name**, **event name**, **event date**, and **rate**. Sort the query in ascending order first by LastName then by FirstName. Name the query qryRates. Add a total row to show total rate. Save and close the query.

f. Create a query that returns all the events with 100 attendees or more. Include event date, event name, location, total attendees, and rate. Sort them by rate (highest to lowest), but do not show the rate in the result. Name the query qryLargeEvents. Save and close the query.

g. Create a query to calculate menu costs. Include from **tblEvents** the **EventDate**, **EventName**, and **TotalAttendees**, and include from **tblMenuChoice** the **MenuType** and the **CostPerPerson**. You will also need to include the **tblMenuItems** table to avoid the multiplier effect. Name the query qryMenuCosts. Calculate MenuCost as TotalAttendees * CostPerPerson. If necessary, format the new field as currency, and sort the results by EventDate (ascending).
Adjust the column widths as necessary. Save and close the query.

h. Create a query that returns the **count**, **sum**, **average**, **minimum**, and **maximum** of all the event rates. Name the fields Event Count, Total Rates, Average Rate, Minimum Rate, and Maximum Rate in that order. Adjust the column widths as necessary. Name the query qryEventRateStats. Save and close the query.

i. Create a query that includes the client **LastName** and **FirstName**, the **EventName**, **EventDate** and **TotalAttendees** for any event in April 2018 that has 200 or more attendees. Sort in ascending order by client LastName and then by FirstName. Name the query qryAprilBigEvents. Save and close the query.

j. Close the database, exit Access, and then submit your file as directed by your instructor.

Perform 1: Perform in Your Career

Student data file needed:

a02ch03HomeSale.accdb

You will save your file as:

 a02ch03HomeSale_LastFirst.accdb

Real Estate Database

Production & Operations

You are interning at a real estate firm. You supervisor was delighted with your Access skills. She asks you to deliver subsets of data from the database so that she can analyze the data and look for trends.

a. Open the Access database, **a02ch03HomeSale**. Save your file as a02ch03HomeSale_LastFirst using your last and first name. If necessary, enable the content.

b. Open the Relationships window to familiarize yourself with the tables, fields, and relationships in the database. Close the Relationships window.

c. Open **tblAgent**, and add your first and last names where indicated. Close the table.

d. Open **tblDevelopment**, and add your name to the **DevelopmentName** field for the sixth record. Close the table.

e. Create a query that displays the **DevelopmentName**, **Address**, **City**, **State**, and **PostalCode**. Add the listing agent's **ID** and **first** and **last** names. Finally, add the **ListPrice** and **SoldPrice**.

f. Limit your query to only the sold properties, and sort it by development name in ascending order. (Hint: Properties that have been sold will have a sold price; all others will be null.) Save the query as qrySoldProperties_iLast.

g. Make the following modifications to the qrySoldProperties_iLast query.

- Calculate the percent of list price for which each property was sold. For example, a property that listed for $100,000 and sold for $98,000 received 98.0% of its listed price, 98,000/100,000. Format the calculation results as a percent with one decimal place. Name the new field PercentList.
- Add a total row to the Datasheet View of the query. Use it to calculate the average percent of list price and the total of the list price and sold prices. If necessary, resize the columns to view the data.

h. Create a new query based on **qrySoldProperties_iLast**. In the Show Table dialog box, use the Queries tab to view a list of queries in the database. Add the **DevelopmentName**, the **ListPrice**, the **SoldPrice**, and the **PercentList** fields. Aggregate by the development name; sum the price fields; and average the PercentList field. Format the PercentList field as **Percent** with **1** decimal place. Save the query as qrySalesByDevelopment_iLast.

i. Create a new query based on qrySoldProperties. Add the agent's first and last names, the ListPrice, the SoldPrice, and the PercentList fields.

j. Group the data by the agent's last name, sum the ListPrice, and SoldPrice, and average the PercentList field. Sort the data in ascending order by the last name.

k. Calculate the listing agent's commission. Multiply the SoldPrice by 3%. In the total row for the expression, select **Sum**. Name the field Commission and format the field as **Currency**. Save the query as qryCommission_iLast.

l. Create a new query. Add the agent's first and last names, the ListingDate, SoldDate, SquareFeet, and SoldPrice fields. Save the query as qrySaleAnalysis_iLast.

m. Limit the query to sales made in 2017 of properties with more than 2000 square feet.

n. Calculate the number of days each property was on the market by finding the difference between the SoldDate and the ListingDate.

o. Run the query. In Datasheet view, calculate the average number of days the 2017 sold homes were on the market.

p. Close the database, exit Access, and then submit your files as directed by your instructor.

Additional Cases

Additional Chapter Cases are available at www.pearsonhighered.com/youroffice

Microsoft Access 2016

Chapter 4 | USING FORMS AND REPORTS IN ACCESS

OBJECTIVES

Prepare Case

Production & Operations

Turquoise Oasis Spa's New Database

The Turquoise Oasis Spa has a database with customer, employee, product, and service information for easier scheduling and access. An intern created the database, and the manager and staff members are struggling to use it to its fullest capacity. You have recently been hired to work in the office of the spa, and you have knowledge of Access, so the manager has asked for your help in maintaining the records and creating forms and reports to help better use the data in the database.

Zadorozhnyi Viktor / Shutterstock

Student data files needed for this chapter:

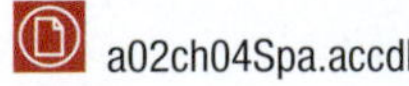

a02ch04Spa.accdb

a02ch04Spa.jpg

a02ch04Spa.thmx

You will save your files as:

a02ch04Spa_LastFirst.accdb

a02ch04SpaEmployeeSchedule_LastFirst.pdf

Creating Customized Forms

Recall that forms are the objects in Access that are used to enter, edit, or view records in a table. Data can be entered, edited, or viewed directly in the table or in a form. Each option offers advantages and disadvantages.

In Datasheet view, data may be updated directly in the table where it is stored. Datasheet view shows all the fields and records at one time, which provides all the information you need to update your data, unlike in a form or query, where some of the fields or records may not be in view. In this section you will navigate datasheets and forms. Then you will edit data in a table and in a form.

Navigate and Edit Records in Datasheets

As you may recall, you can navigate from record to record or from field to field in a table using the Navigation bar or, in Navigation mode, by using Tab, Enter, Home, End, ↑, ↓, ←, and →. **Navigation mode** allows you to move from record to record and from field to field using keystrokes. To update data in a table, you must be in Edit mode. **Edit mode** allows you to edit, or change, the contents of a field. To switch between Navigation mode and Edit mode, press F2.

If you can see the blinking insertion point in a field, you are in Edit mode. When the text of a field is selected and highlighted, you are in Navigation mode.

QUICK REFERENCE — Keystrokes Used in Navigation Mode and Edit Mode

Keystroke	Navigation Mode	Edit Mode
→ and ←	Move from field to field	Move from character to character
↑ and ↓	Move from record to record	Switch to Navigation mode and move from record to record
Home	Moves to the first field in the record	Moves to the first character in the field
End	Moves to the last field in the record	Moves to the last character in the field
Tab and Enter	Move one field at a time	Switch to Navigation mode and move from field to field
Ctrl + Home	Moves to the first field of the first record	Moves to the first character in the field, same as Home
Ctrl + End	Moves to the last field of the last record	Moves to the last character in the field, same as End

Opening the Starting File

The spa collects data about customers, employees, products, and services and uses the data for scheduling. In this exercise, you will open the spa database to get started.

A04.00

To Open the a02ch04Spa Database

a. Start **Access**, click **Open Other Files** in the left pane, and then double-click **This PC**. Navigate through the folder structure to the location of your student data files, and then double-click **a02ch04Spa**. A database opens displaying tables, forms, and a report related to the spa.

b. Click the **File** tab, click **Save As**, and save the file as an **Access Database**, and click **Save As**. Navigate to the location where you are saving your project files, and then change the file name to a02ch04Spa_LastFirst using your last and first name. Click **Save**. If necessary, enable the content.

Editing a Table in Datasheet View

Datasheet view shows all the records and fields at one time, which is one advantage to using it to update your records. Another advantage is the ability to see all the records in the table, which gives you a perspective on the data you are entering. The spa staff has received a note from a customer who has changed his phone number. In this exercise, you will show the staff how to change that customer's record in the Customer table.

 A04.01

SIDE NOTE

Pin the Ribbon

If your ribbon is collapsed, pin your ribbon open. Click the Home tab. In the lower right-hand corner of the ribbon, click Pin the Ribbon [pin icon].

To Edit a Record in a Table in Datasheet View

a. In the Navigation Pane, double-click **tblCustomer** to open the table.

b. Locate the customer with the Customer ID **CU0-12** and the last name **Hinton**.

c. Click in the **CustomerID** field, and then press Tab. You are now in Navigation mode, and the First Name field should be highlighted.

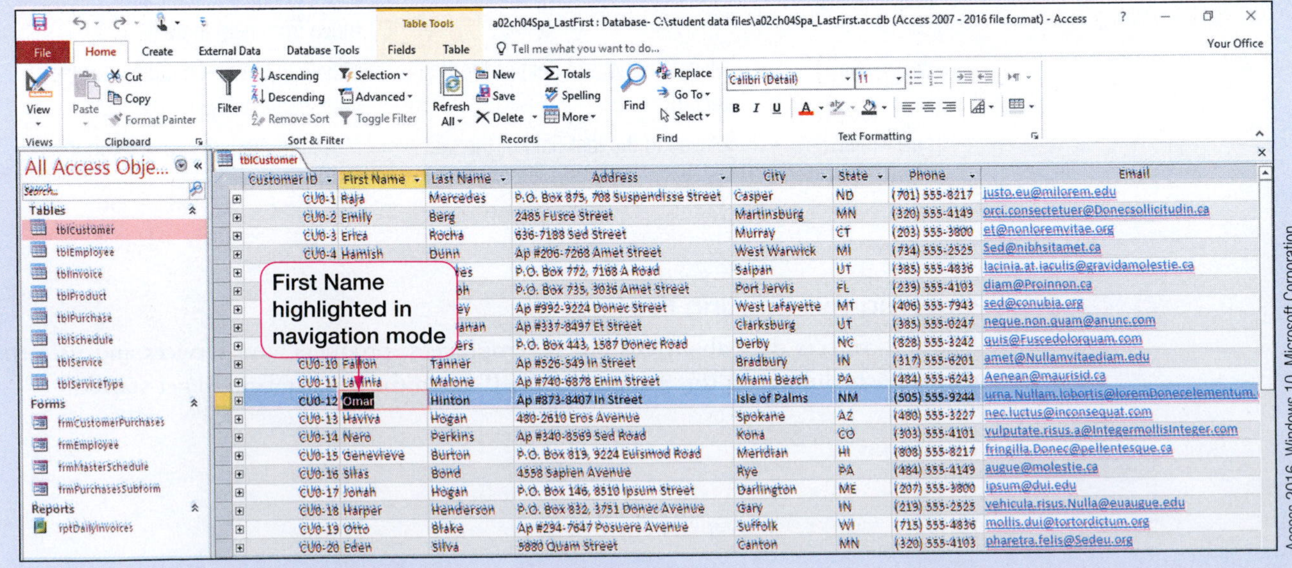

Access 2016, Windows 10, Microsoft Corporation

Figure 1 Table in Navigation mode

SIDE NOTE

Prefix for Key

When you click CustomerID, the "CU0-" disappears. The key is defined as numeric but has a prefix identifying the table to which it is key.

d. Continue pressing Tab until the **Phone** field is highlighted. Press F2 to switch from Navigation mode to Edit mode. Notice the insertion point is at the beginning of the Phone field and the first character is highlighted. Type 5055552923 to enter the new phone number. Because the field is already formatted as a phone number, it is not necessary to enter parentheses or dashes.

e. Press Tab to switch to Navigation mode and move to the next field.

f. **Close**  the table.

CONSIDER THIS | Why Put a Prefix Before a Primary Key?

CustomerID, the primary key for tblCustomer, is defined as AutoNumber but is formatted to have the prefix "CU0-" (0 is a zero) before the number field. Similarly, EmployeeID, the key for tblEmployee, is formatted to have "EMP00" as a prefix before the number field. What is the advantage of putting a prefix before the primary key to a table? Are there disadvantages? Why were these two prefixes chosen?

Navigate Forms and Subforms

A form is an object in Access that you can use to enter, edit, or view records in a table. A simple form allows you to see records one at a time rather than as a group in Datasheet view.

REAL WORLD ADVICE | Data Overload!

You may be asked to create a database for someone else who is not familiar with how a database works or even how the computer works. Your role is to make that person's job as easy as possible so he or she can get work done with as few errors as possible.

Looking at a database table with hundreds or thousands of records in Datasheet view can be very intimidating to some people. Trying to keep track of the record or field you are in can be more difficult as the table grows larger and larger. Often, seeing one record at a time in a form can eliminate data entry errors and allow the user to focus on the information for that particular record.

You navigate records in a form the same way you navigate a table: using buttons on the Navigation bar to move from record to record.

QUICK REFERENCE | Navigation Buttons on the Navigation Bar

Button	Description	What it does
⏮	First record	Moves to the first record in the table
⏭	Last record	Moves to the last record in the table
◀	Previous record	Moves to the record just before the current record
▶	Next record	Moves to the record just after the current record
▶✱	New (blank) record	Moves to a new row to enter a new record

When you create a form from two tables that have a one-to-many relationship, the first table you select becomes the **main form**, and the second table you select becomes the **subform**. A form with a subform allows you to see one record at a time from the main form and multiple records in Datasheet view from the other related table. Because you see only one record at a time or one record and a datasheet, navigation tools become important when you are working with forms, as you cannot see all the records at one time.

Navigating a Main Form

Within each record, you can use a combination of Tab, Home, Enter, and End, as well as ↓, ↑, ←, and →, to move from field to field as shown in the Quick Reference Box.

QUICK REFERENCE | **Navigating Forms**

Navigating a main form

Keystroke	What it does
Tab	Moves from field to field within a record; at the last field in a record, moves you to the first field in the next record
Home	Moves to the first field of the current record
Ctrl + Home	Moves to the first field of the first record of the table
End	Moves to the last field of the current record
Ctrl + End	Moves to the last field of the last record of the table
↓, ↑, ←, →	Move up or down a field of the current record

Navigating a form with a subform

Keystroke	What it does
Tab	Moves from field to field within a main record; at the last field in a record, moves to the first field in the subform; at the last record in the subform, moves to the first field in the next record of the main form
Home	From the main form, moves to the first field of the current record; from the subform, moves to the first field of the current record in the subform
Ctrl + Home	From the main form, moves to the first field of the first record; from the subform, moves to the first field of the first record in the subform
End	From the main form, moves to the last field of the current record in the subform; from the subform, moves to the last field of the current record in the subform
Ctrl + End	From the main form, moves to the last field of the last record of the subform; from the subform, moves to the last field of the last record of the subform
↓, ↑, ←, →	Move up or down a field in the current record in either the form or the subform

In this exercise, you will show the spa staff how to navigate the form frmEmployee, which is a list of all employees, one record at a time.

To Navigate a Single-Table Form

a. In the Navigation Pane, double-click **frmEmployee** to open the form.

b. Click **Last record** [▶|] to go to the last record of the table.

c. Click **First record** [|◀] to return to the first record in the table.

d. Click **Next record** [▶] to go to the next record in the table.

e. Click **Previous record** [◀] to go back to the previous record in the table.

f. **Close** [X] the form.

Navigating a Form with a Subform

When you are navigating forms with a subform, the Navigation bar buttons at the bottom of the main window are used to navigate the records in the main form, and a second Navigation bar at the bottom of the subform datasheet is used to navigate the records in the subform. The same navigation keystrokes are used; however, they work a little differently when a subform is included.

In this exercise, you will show the spa staff members how to navigate the form frmCustomerPurchases, which shows one customer at a time with all the customer's recent product purchases.

To Navigate a Form with a Subform

a. On the Navigation Pane, double-click **frmCustomerPurchases** to open the form.
Notice that the form has two parts. At the top is the main form that shows information about the customer. It contains records from the tblCustomer table. The lower part is the subform that shows all the purchases made by the customer. It contains records from the tblPurchase table. There are also two navigation bars: one for the main form and one for the subform.

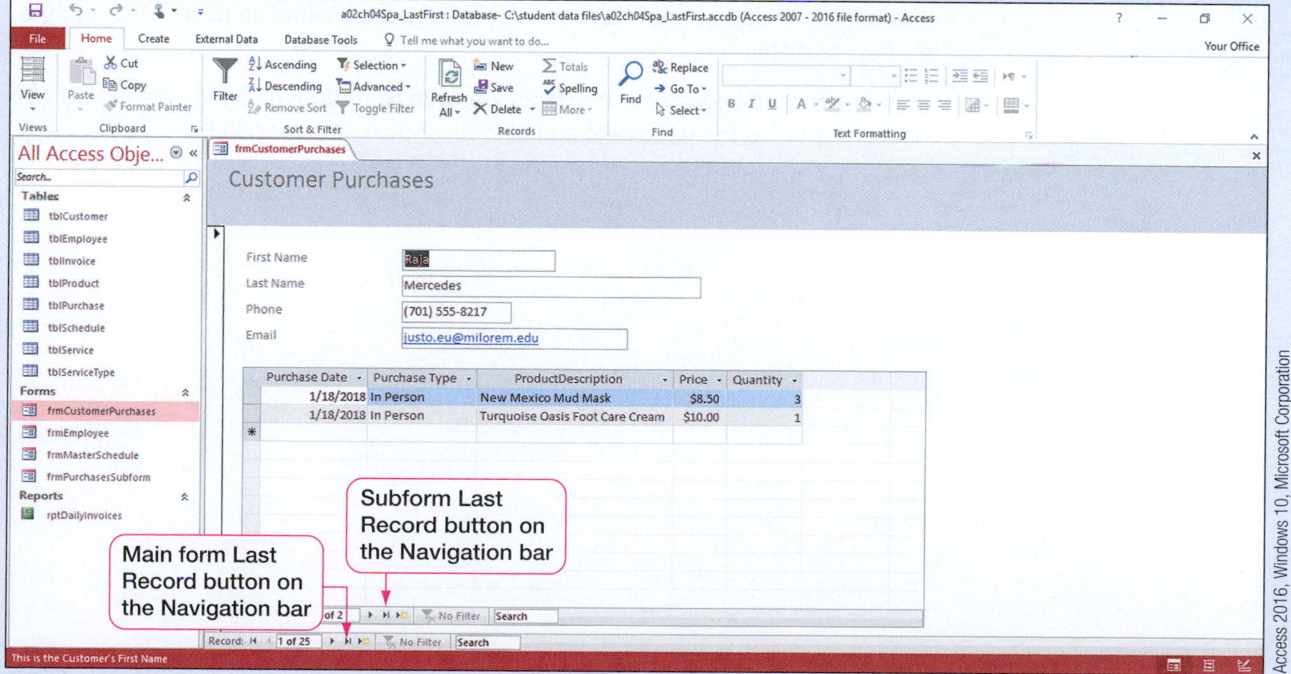

Figure 2 Form with a subform in Datasheet view

b. Click **Last record** [▸|] on the subform Navigation bar to highlight the last record in the subform.

c. Click **Last record** [▸|] on the main form Navigation bar to go to the last record in the table.

d. Click **Previous record** [◂] on the main form repeatedly to go to record 20 with the customer name Eden Silva.

e. Click **Next record** [▸] in the subform to go to the next record in the subform.

f. **Close** [X] the form.

Navigating a Split Form

A **split form** is a form created from one table, but it has a Form view and a Datasheet view in the same window. You can view one record at a time at the top of the window and see the whole table in Datasheet view at the bottom of the window. This kind of form is helpful when you want to work with one record at a time and still see the big picture in the main table. In a split form, there are buttons on the Navigation bar to move only from record to record, and each record shown at the top is the record highlighted in the datasheet at the same time. You cannot highlight a different record in the form part and the datasheet part at the same time.

In this exercise, you will show the spa staff how to navigate the form frmMaster-Schedule, which shows the schedule as a form and a datasheet in the same window.

A04.04

To Navigate a Split Form

a. In the Navigation Pane, double-click **frmMasterSchedule** to open the form.

b. Click **Last record** [▸|] on the Navigation bar to highlight the last record in both the form and the datasheet.
The customer that appears for the last record has a Schedule ID of S053 and the Customer is Raja.

c. Click the **record selector** in the datasheet with **Schedule ID S046**. The record will be highlighted in the datasheet and also be shown at the top in Form view.

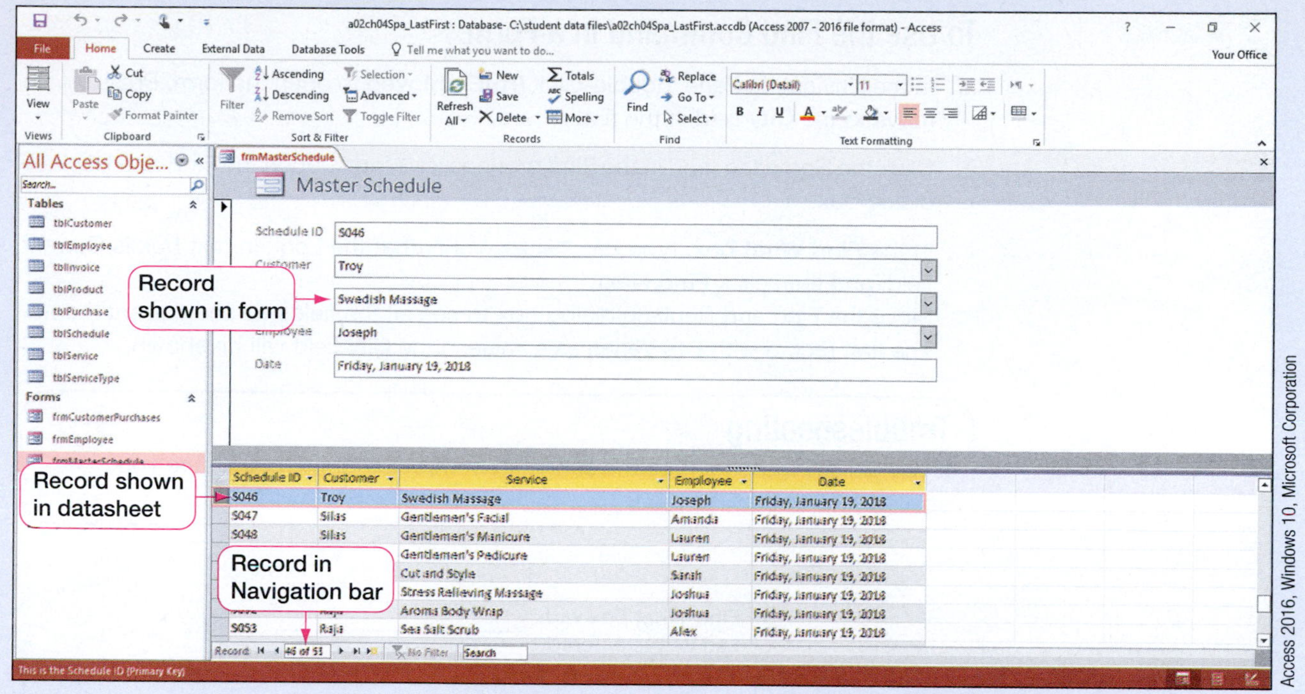

Figure 3 Navigating a split form

d. **Close** [X] the form.

REAL WORLD ADVICE Using Tabs

People have become accustomed to using tabs in browsers, and they tend to have many tabs open at one time. In fact, it makes work more efficient because they do not have to keep opening and closing those windows. Unfortunately, Access does not work the same way. Every time you open an object in Access, it opens in a new tab. However, those tabs do not work the same way as tabs in your browser. While websites can be updated when they are open in a browser tab on your desktop, related Access objects cannot be updated when they are open. For example, design changes cannot be made to a table if a related form is open. It is therefore a good idea to close an object when you are done working with it and then reopen it again later when you need it.

Using the Find Command in a Form

Finding data in a form is similar to finding data in a datasheet — you use the Find command. Because you see only one record at a time with a form, using Find can be a quick way to find a record with a specific value in a field and prevents you from having to scroll through all the records in the table one at a time in Form view.

When you are looking for a specific value in a field, you are looking for an exact match. A staff member has asked you to search the employee table to find any employees who may live in Las Vegas so they can try to set up a carpool. In this exercise, you will show the staff member how to use a form to look for that information.

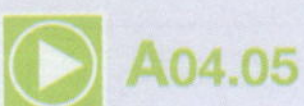

To Use the Find Command in a Form

a. In the Navigation Pane, double-click **frmEmployee** to open the form. Press Tab to move to the **City** field in the first record.

b. Click the Home tab, and in the Find group, click **Find** to open the Find and Replace dialog box.

c. In the **Find What** box, type Las Vegas. Verify that the Look In text box is Current field, and then click **Find Next**.
Move the Find and Replace dialog box to see all the fields for the current record. The first record with Las Vegas as a value in the City field will be shown.

Troubleshooting

If you get the message that the search item was not found, make sure you spelled "Las Vegas" correctly.

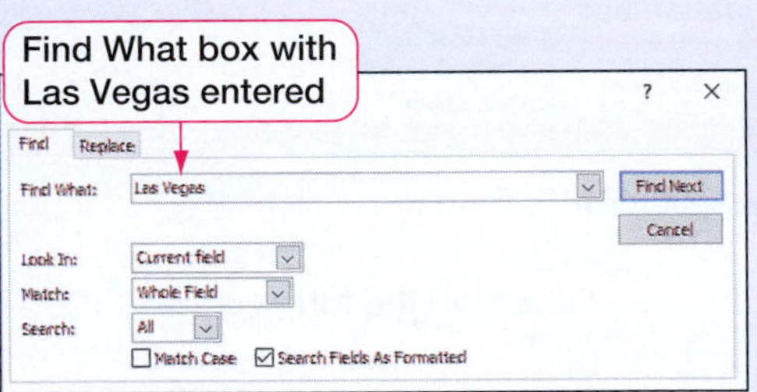

Figure 4 Find and Replace dialog box

Access 2016, Windows 10, Microsoft Corporation

d. Continue to click **Find Next** until Access gives you the message "Microsoft Access finished searching the records. The search item was not found." Click **OK**, and then click **Cancel** to close the Find and Replace dialog box.

Update Table Records Using Forms

Just as you can update data in a datasheet, you can also update data in a form. Remember that a form is just another way to view the data in the table, so when you see a record, you are seeing the record that is actually stored in the table. Nothing is stored in the form.

To make changes to data in a form, you must view the form in Form view. You can also add a record to a table in Form view. Using the Navigation bar, you can go directly to a new record.

QUICK REFERENCE	Updating Tables		

Data can be edited in tables, queries, or forms. There are advantages and disadvantages to each method. The table below will help you decide the most appropriate place to edit data.

Method	Advantages	Disadvantages	Typical Situation to Use
Tables	All the records and fields are visible in the datasheet.	The number of records and/or fields in the datasheet can be overwhelming.	A user familiar with Access needs to add a record quickly to a smaller table.
Queries	There may be fewer records and/or fields in the datasheet, making the data more manageable. A form can be based on a query rather than a table.	Not being able to see all the records and/or fields, you may inadvertently change related data in the fields you can see. Not all queries are editable, such as aggregate queries.	A user familiar with Access needs to see and modify appointments booked for a particular day.
Forms	Being able to view one record at a time can make the data seem more manageable.	Not all fields may be included in a form. If fields are missing, some data may mistakenly be left out of a record. Provides a view of only one record at a time.	A user unfamiliar with Access needs to add data to a large table with many records.

Adding Records

When you add a record to a form, you are actually adding the record to the table in which it will be stored. The form will open in Form view, which is the view that allows you to edit the data. As in a datasheet, new records are added at the end of the table, which means that you must go to a blank record to enter new data. In this exercise, you will use the frmEmployee form to add your name to the list of employees in the tblEmployee table.

To Add a New Record in a Form

a. On the Navigation bar, click **New (blank) record** [icon].

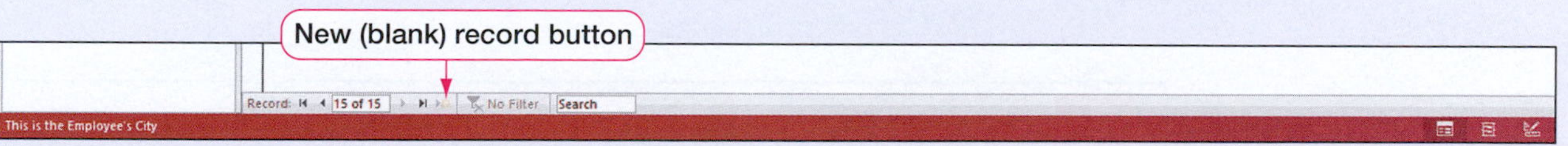

Access 2016, Windows 10, Microsoft Corporation

Figure 5 frmEmployee Navigation bar

b. Type your first name, last name, address, city, state, and phone number in the new record. **Close** [X] the form.

c. In the Navigation Pane, double-click **tblEmployee** to open the table, and then click **Last record** [icon] to see that your record was added. **Close** [X] the table.

Editing Records

When you edit a record in a form, you are actually editing the record in the table in which it is stored. Changes to data are saved automatically but can be undone while the table or form is open by using the Undo button or by pressing Esc just after the change is made while still in Edit mode.

You have been asked to update the tblEmployee table with recent changes. Mary Murphy has recently changed her phone number, but it has not yet been changed in the table. In this exercise, you will show the staff how to find her record using a form and update her phone number.

To Edit Records Using a Form

a. In the Navigation Pane, double-click **frmEmployee** to open the form. Press Tab to move to the **Last Name** field. Click the Home tab, in the Find group, click **Find**, and then in the Find What box, type Murphy. Click **Find Next**.

b. When the record for Mary Murphy is displayed, click **Cancel** to close the Find and Replace dialog box, and then press Tab to move to the **Phone** field. Change Mary's phone number to 5055551289.

c. **Close** the form.

Deleting Records

Records can be deleted from a single table without additional steps if the table is not part of a relationship. If the table is part of a relationship, referential integrity has been enforced, and the cascade delete option has not been chosen, a record cannot be deleted if there are related records in another table until those records have also been deleted. For example, if you want to delete a customer from tblCustomer and that customer has appointments in tblSchedule, then the appointments for the customer have to be deleted from the tblSchedule before the customer can be deleted from the tblCustomer. This prevents leaving a customer scheduled in one table without the corresponding customer information in another table.

The spa manager would like you to remove Peter Klein from tblEmployee because he has taken a new job and is leaving the spa. You explain to her that if Peter has any appointments scheduled in tblSchedule, those will have to be removed first. She tells you that rather than removing those records, she would like to give those appointments to Alex instead. By changing the name to Alex, those appointments will no longer be linked to Peter, and Peter will be able to be deleted from tblEmployee. In this exercise, you will give Peter's appointments to Alex and remove Peter's record from the table of employees.

CONSIDER THIS | Delete with Caution

Deleting records in a table is permanent. Once you confirm a deletion, you cannot use the Undo button. This is very different from programs such as Excel or Word. Can you think of ways in which you could safeguard your data from accidental deletion?

A04.08 To Delete a Record with a Form

a. In the Navigation Pane, double-click **frmEmployee** to open the form. In the Find group, click **Find**, and then in the Find What box, type Peter. Click **Find Next**, and then click **Cancel** to close the Find and Replace dialog box.

b. Click the Home tab, and in the Records group, click the **Delete** arrow, and then click **Delete Record**. Access displays a message saying, "The record cannot be deleted or changed because table 'tblSchedule' included related records." Click **OK**.

Troubleshooting

If Access blanks out the First Name field, you chose Delete rather than Delete Record. Press Esc to undo the deletion, and then choose Delete Record.

c. In the Navigation Pane, double-click **tblSchedule** to open the table. Press Tab to move to the Employee field for the first record. Click the arrow next to **Peter**, and then click **Alex**.

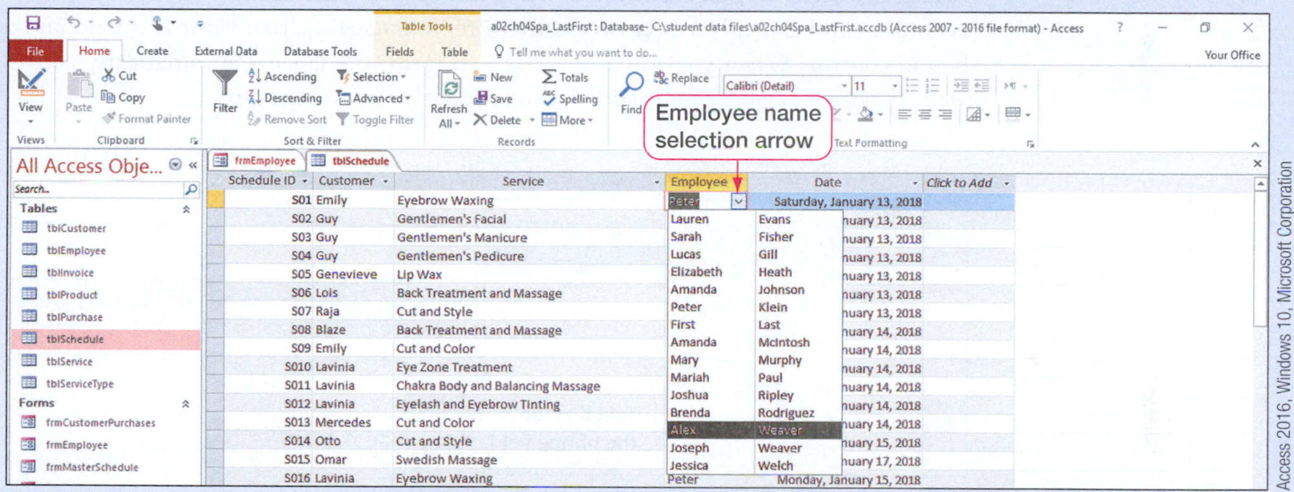

Figure 6 Replacing employee name using the selection arrow

d. On the Home tab, in the Find group, click **Find**, and then in the **Find What** box, type Peter. Click **Find Next**. Click the **arrow** next to the name, and then click **Alex**. Click **Find Next**, and then repeat for the remaining record that has **Peter** listed as the Employee. Click **Cancel** to close the Find and Replace box.

e. **Close** ☒ the table. On the frmEmployee form, make sure the record showing is for **Peter**. On the Home tab, in the Records group, click the **Delete** arrow, and then select **Delete Record**. Click **Yes** to confirm the deletion.

f. **Close** ☒ the form.

Create a Form Using the Form Wizard

Recall that the Query Wizard walks you through the steps to create a query, asking you questions and using your answers to build a query that you can then make changes to if necessary. The Form Wizard works in a similar fashion, walking you through step by step to create a form from one or more tables in your database.

Unlike creating a simple form using the Form button on the Create tab, when you create a form using the wizard, it opens automatically in Form view, ready for you to enter or edit your records. To make changes to the form, you have to switch to either Layout view or Design view.

Creating a Form

Form view is only for viewing and changing data, so to make any changes to the form, you need to switch to either Layout view or Design view. Layout view allows you to make changes to the form while viewing the data at the same time. The effects of your changes can be viewed right away. Design view is a more advanced view that allows you to change the properties or structure of the form. Data is not shown while you are in Design view.

Both Layout view and Design view work with controls, as shown in Figure 7. A **control** is a part of a form or report that you use to enter, edit, or display data. There are three major kinds of controls: bound, unbound, and calculated. A **bound control** is a control whose data source is a field in the table, such as the customer name. An **unbound control** is a control that does not have a source of data, such as the title of the form. A **calculated control** is a control whose data source is a calculated expression that you create. Every field from the table is made up of two controls: a label and a text box. A **label control** may be the name of the field or some other text you manually enter and is an unbound control. A **text box control** represents the actual value of a field and is a bound control. When you add a text box to a form, the label is automatically added as well. However, a label can be added independently from a text box.

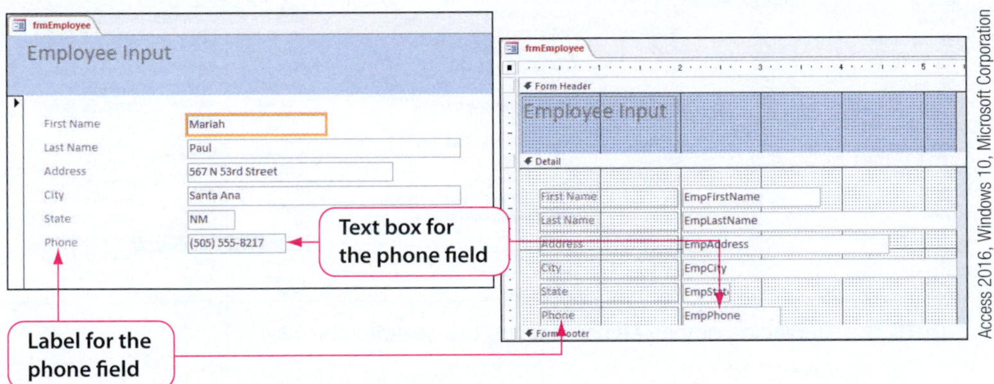

Figure 7 Text box and label controls in Layout view and Design view

The manager of the spa wants the staff to be able to enter and update customer information easily. She thinks it would be much easier to enter data in a form rather than in Datasheet view. In this exercise, you will help her set up the form.

A04.09

To Create a Single-Table Form

a. Click the **Create** tab, and then in the Forms group, click **Form Wizard**. The Form Wizard dialog box opens.

b. Click the **Tables/Queries** arrow, and select **Table: tblCustomer**. Click the **All Fields** button [>>] to add all the available fields to the Selected Fields box, and then click **Next**.

c. Verify that **Columnar** is selected as the form layout, and then click **Next**.

d. Under "What title do you want for your form?", type frmCustomerInput. Verify that the Open the form to view or enter information option is selected, and then click **Finish**.
The form opens in Form view, so you can immediately start adding or editing records. The form name is also displayed in the Navigation Pane under forms.

SIDE NOTE
Alternative Methods to Expand the Footer
You can expand the footer and then add the label, or you can add the label and the footer will automatically expand to fit what you add.

e. On the Home tab, click the **View** arrow and select **Design view**. Notice the Form Footer at the bottom of the form window. On the Design tab, in the Controls group, click **Label** Aa. Point to the Form Footer area, and then when your pointer changes to +A, drag your pointer to draw a label control about 2.5 inches wide in the top left corner of the Form Footer section. In the new label, type Created by initial Lastname using your first initial and last name.

Troubleshooting
If the Field List pane opens, close it.

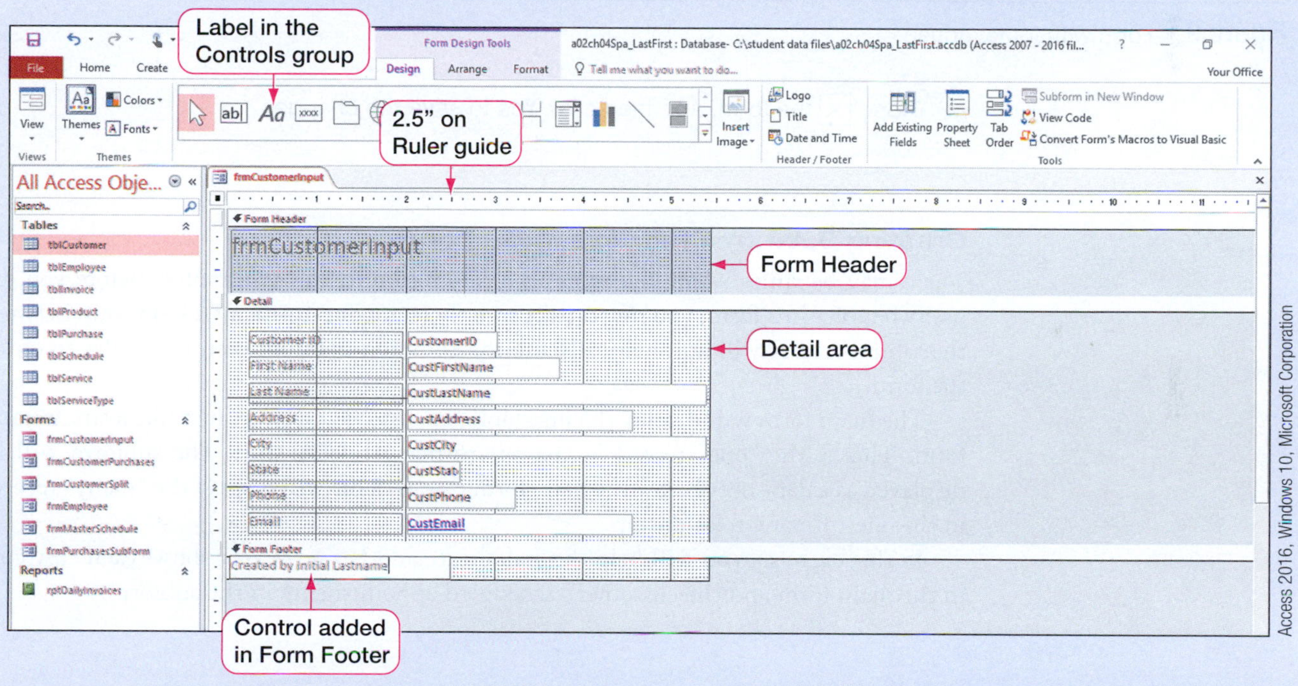

Figure 8 Form in Design view

f. Switch to **Form** view. Verify that your label has been entered in the bottom left corner of the form.

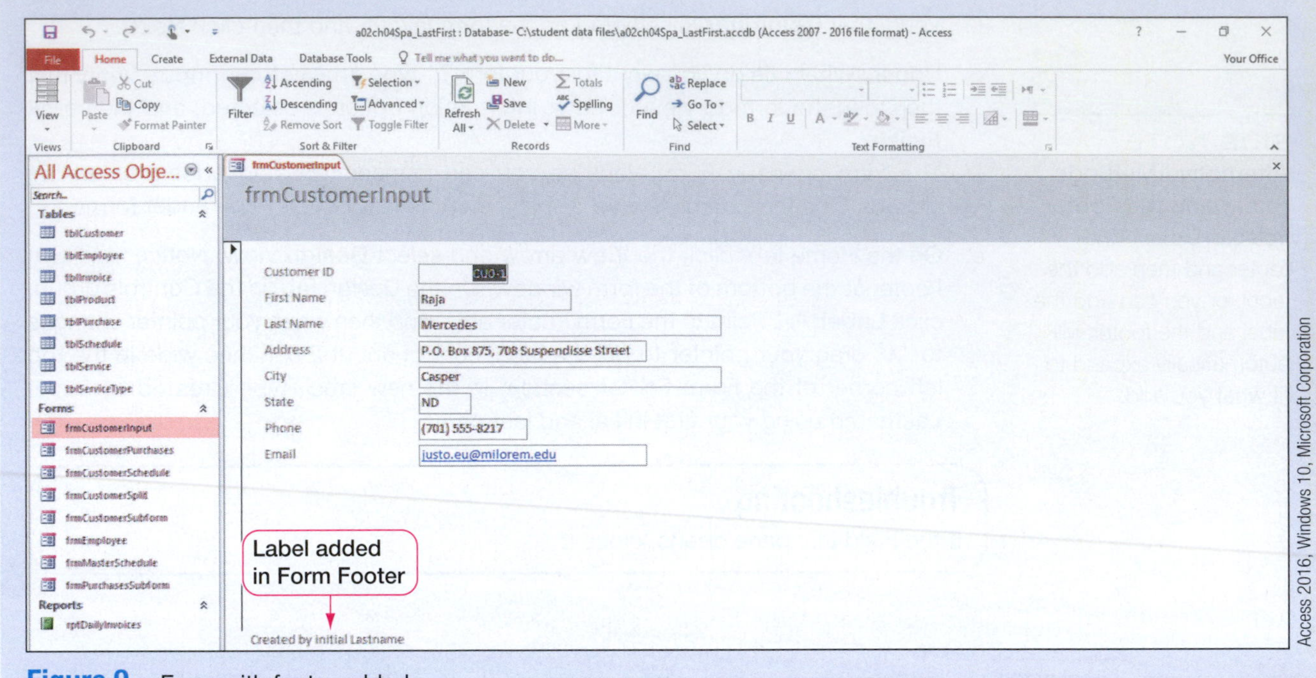

Figure 9 Form with footer added

g. **Close** [X] the form, and then click **Yes** to save the changes.

Creating Subforms (Multiple-Table Forms)

There may be times when you want to create a form using two tables. Before you can use two tables in a form, you must make sure there is a one-to-many relationship between the tables. Access will automatically use the common field between the tables to create the form.

The main form will display the first table one record at a time, just like a single-table form. This is the "one" record in the one-to-many relationship. The subform will be displayed as a datasheet below the main form record. This will display the "many" records in the one-to-many relationship.

In this exercise, you will help the staff create another form that shows each customer in the main form and the customer's scheduled appointments in the subform.

A04.10

To Create a Subform

a. Click the **Create** tab, and then in the Forms group, click **Form Wizard**. The Form Wizard dialog box opens.

b. Click the **Tables/Queries** arrow, and then select **Table: tblCustomer**. Click the **All Fields** button [>>] to add all the available fields to the Selected Fields list.

c. Click the **Tables/Queries** arrow, and then select **Table: tblSchedule**. Click the **All Fields** button [>>] to add all the available fields to the Selected Fields list, and then click **Next**.

d. Verify that by **tblCustomer** is selected and that **Form with subform(s)** is selected, and then click **Next**.

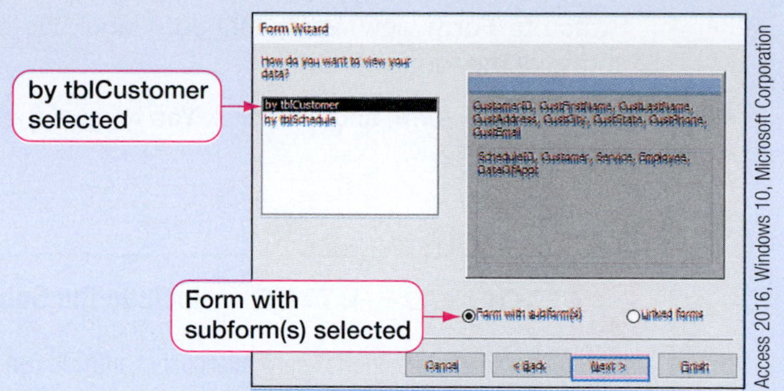

Figure 10 Form options are selected

e. Verify that Datasheet is selected as the subform layout, and then click **Next**.

f. Under What titles do you want for your forms? in the Form field, type frmCustomerSchedule. In the Subform field, type frmCustomerSubform. Verify that the Open the form to view or enter information option is selected, and then click **Finish**.

The form opens in Form view so you can immediately start adding or editing records. The form and subform names are shown in the Navigation Pane.

g. Switch to **Design** view. Scroll to the bottom of the form to see the Form Footer at the base of the main form. On the Design tab, in the Controls group, click **Label** Aa. When your pointer changes to +A, drag your pointer to draw a label control about 2.5 inches wide in the top left corner of the Form Footer section. In the new label, type Created by initial Lastname using your initial and last name.

Troubleshooting

If the Field List pane shows and blocks parts of the form you need to see, close the Field List pane.

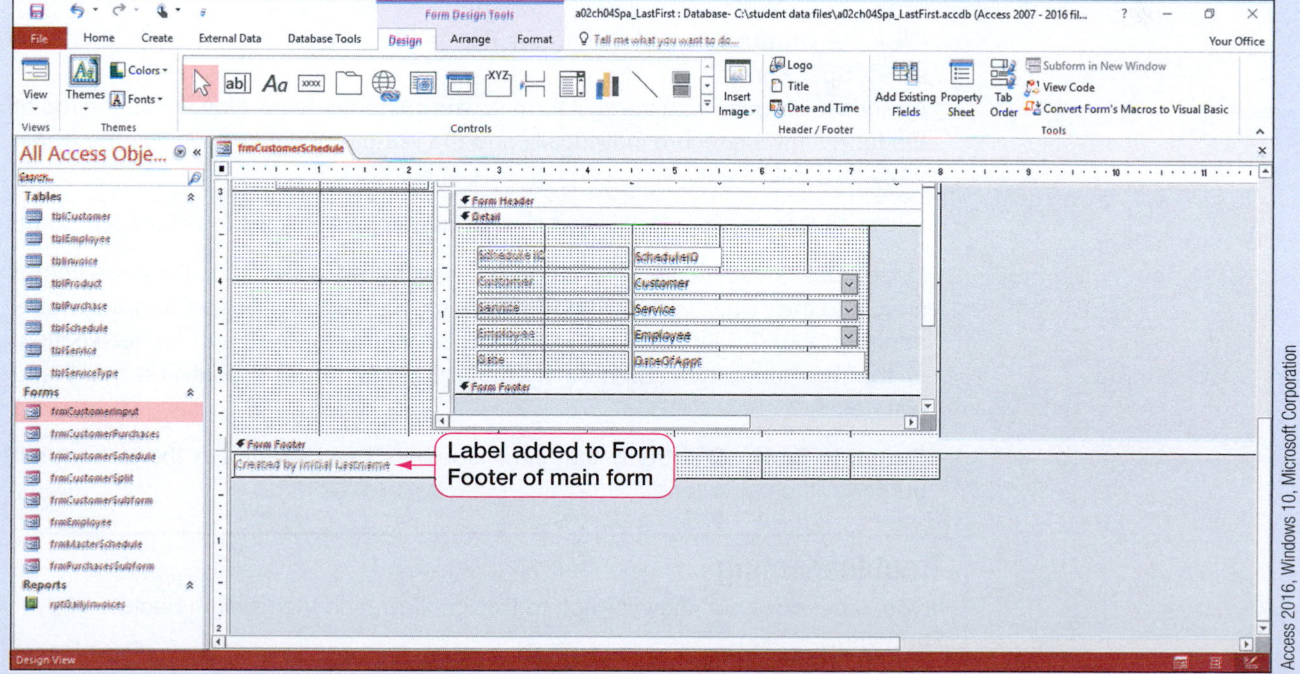

Figure 11 Add footer to main form

h. Switch to **Form** view. Verify that your label has been entered in the bottom left corner of the form.

i. **Close** ☒ the form, and then click **Yes** to save the changes.

SS CONSIDER THIS | Include the Subform?

When two tables are in a one-to-many relationship and you use the Form button to create a form for the table on the one side of the relationship, the wizard automatically adds a subform for the table on the many side. If you create the form using Form Wizard, you can choose whether to include the subform. When would you want to include the subform? When would you not want to include the subform?

Creating a Split Form

A split form is created from one table and displays each record individually at the top of the window and then again as part of the whole table datasheet in the bottom of the window. This type of form gives you the advantage of seeing each record and the whole table in one place.

The manager would like to see each customer's record individually along with all the records from the customer table. In this exercise, you will show her how to create a split form from the customer table.

A04.11

To Create a Split Form

a. In the Navigation Pane, click **tblCustomer** one time to select the table, but do not open it.

b. Click the **Create** tab, and then in the Forms group, click **More Forms**, and then select **Split Form**.
A window will open with the split form for the customer table. Notice that the top of the form shows a record individually and the bottom of the form shows the whole table as a datasheet.

c. Switch to **Design** view. Notice that Design view shows only the top of the split form.

d. On the Design tab, in the Controls group, click **Label** Aa, point to the Form Footer area, and then when your pointer changes to +A, drag your pointer to draw a label control about 2.5 inches wide in the top left corner of the Form Footer section. In the new label, type Created by initial Lastname using your first initial and last name.

e. Switch to **Form** view. Verify that your label has been entered in the bottom left corner of the upper form.

Troubleshooting

If your label does not show, switch to Design view, and then switch back to Form view.

f. Click **Save** 💾, and under **Form Name**, type frmCustomerSplit, and then click **OK**. **Close** ☒ the form.

Modify a Form's Design

While creating a form using the wizard is quick and efficient, there may be times when you will want to change how the form looks or add things to the form after you have created it. Formatting, such as colors and fonts, can easily be changed. Controls can be added to a form to include additional fields or labels with text. Pictures and other objects can also be added to a form to make the form more visually appealing.

Often, forms are customized to match company or group color themes or other forms and reports already created by a user. Customizing forms can make them more personal and sometimes easier to use.

Colors, font types, and font sizes are just a few of the formatting changes you can make to an existing form.

Changing the Form Theme

By default, Access uses the Office theme when you create a form using the Form Wizard. Even though there is not a step in the wizard to select a different theme, you can change it once the form has been created. A **theme** is a built-in combination of colors and fonts. By default, a theme will be applied to all objects in a database: forms, reports, tables, and queries. However, you can choose to apply a theme to only the object you are working with or to all matching objects. You can also select a theme to be the default theme instead of Office.

Because the form is displayed in Form view, once it has been created, the first step is to switch to Layout view to make changes to the form itself. Changing the theme will change not only the colors of the form but also the font type and size and any border colors or object colors added to the form. Once a theme has been applied to the form, the colors and fonts can be changed independently of the theme, so you can combine the colors of one theme and a font of another.

The manager of the spa would like to make the customer input form look more like the colors in the spa. The resort has a set of themes that the manager wants to apply to the selected form. In this exercise, you will show her how to change the theme and the fonts for the form. The theme will be applied to all objects in the database. The font change will be applied to this form only.

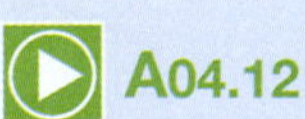

To Change the Theme of a Form

a. In the Navigation Pane, double-click **frmCustomerInput** to open the form. Switch to **Layout** view.

b. Click the Design tab, and in the Themes group, click **Themes** to open the Themes gallery. Click **Browse for Themes**, navigate to where you stored your data files, click **a02ch04Spa**, and then click **Open**. This applies the spa theme to all objects.

c. On the Design tab, in the Themes group, click **Fonts**. Scroll down, and click the Font theme **Corbel**.

d. Double-click the **form title**, select the existing **text**, which by default is the name of the form, and then type Customer Input. Press Enter.

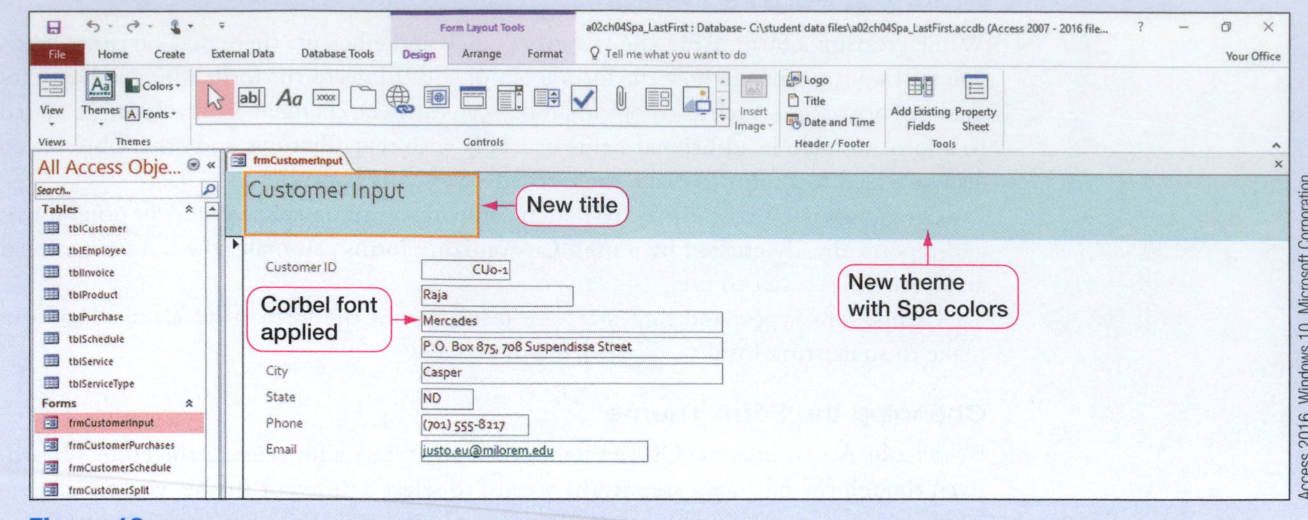

Figure 12 Form with theme, font, and title changed

e. **Save** and **Close** the form.

REAL WORLD ADVICE **Saving Custom Themes**

By default, all themes are saved in the Document Themes folder (C:\Users\username\AppData\Roaming\Microsoft\Templates\Document Themes). If you save a custom theme in the default folder, it will appear as a custom theme in the Themes gallery. If you save the theme in a different folder, you can select Browse for Themes and look for the saved theme in your Documents folder. You can change where you save the theme, but if other people want to use that theme for any of their documents, they may not be able to find it if it has been saved somewhere other than the default folder. One purpose of saving themes is to have them available for a unified look among various documents, and because you may not be the person creating all the documents, you may want to save the theme in a place where everyone can find it.

Resizing and Changing Controls

Controls can be resized to make the form more user friendly. When you create a form using the wizard, the order in which you choose the fields in the wizard step is the order in which the fields are added to the form. Once the form has been created, you may decide the fields should be in a different order. When you click a control in Layout view, an orange border appears around the control. When you select a subform control, an orange border appears around the control, and a layout selector appears in the top-left corner. The **Layout Selector** allows you to move the whole table at one time. Once the control has been selected, you can move it or resize it. You can also change its appearance by adding borders or fill color.

In this exercise, you will work with the spa staff to rearrange the controls on the Customer Schedule form to make data entry easier.

A04.13

To Resize and Change Controls on a Form

a. In the Navigation Pane, double-click **frmCustomerSchedule** to open it. Notice that the spa theme was applied to this form.

b. Switch to **Layout** view. Click the **Last Name** text box control, and an orange border appears around the control. Point to the **right border** of the control, and then drag it to the left so it lines up with the right border of the First Name text box above.

c. Click the **Address** text box control, and then drag the **right border** to the right until it lines up with the right border of the City text box below.

d. Double-click the **form title**, select the existing **text**, which by default is the name of the form, and then type Customer Schedule. Press Enter.

e. Click the **frmCustomer** subform label, and then press Delete to delete it from the form.

f. Use the AutoFit feature on each column of the subform to best fit the data. Use the scroll bar on the Navigation bar of the subform to scroll to the right to see all the fields. Drag the **left border** of the subform to the left so that all fields are visible without scrolling.

g. In the main form, click the **Customer ID** label control, press and hold Shift, and then click the **Customer ID** text box control to select both controls.

SIDE NOTE

Selecting Controls

Each field has two controls — a label and a text box. The field name shows in the label, while the field value shows in the text box.

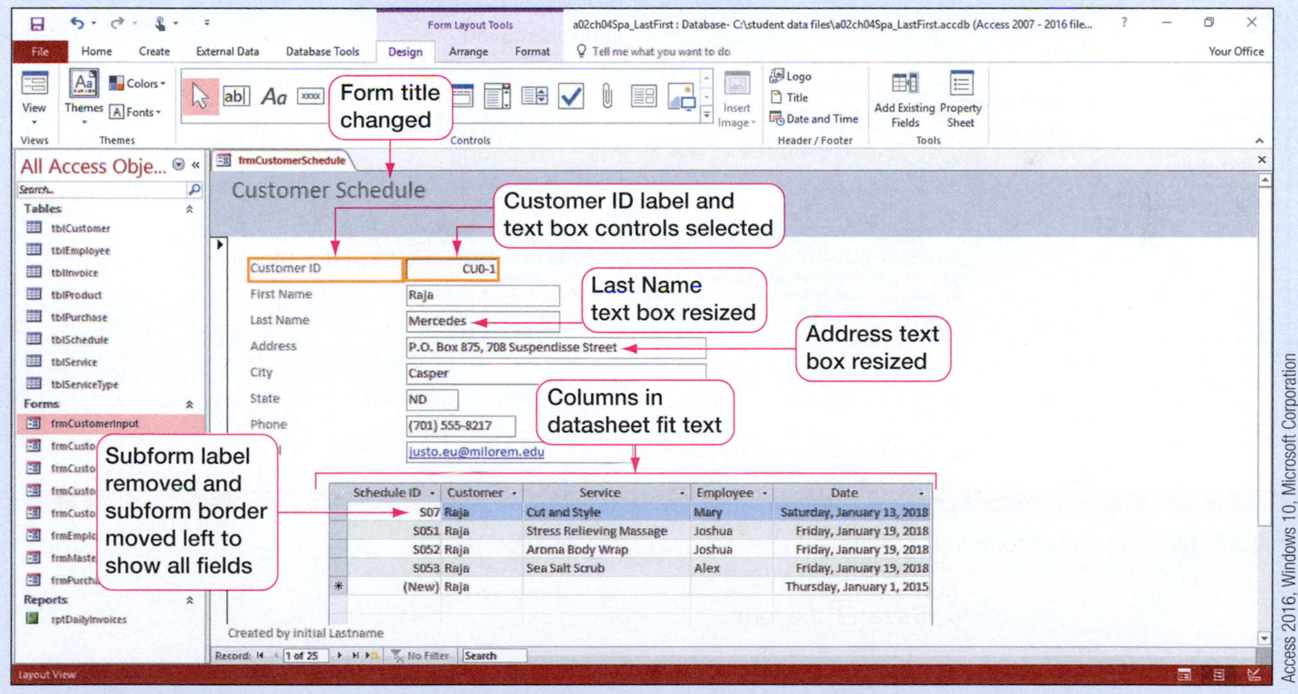

Figure 13 Select both label and name control to delete

h. Press Delete to delete both controls from the form.

i. Click the **Phone** label, hold down Shift, and then click the **Phone** text box, the **Email** label, and the **Email** text box controls.

j. Point to any of the **selected controls**. When the pointer changes to [icon], drag all four controls up and to the right until they are right next to the First Name and Last Name controls.

> **Troubleshooting**
> If, the fields do not line up when you release the pointer, repeat step j, and then adjust the placement.

SIDE NOTE
Limited Visibility
If you cannot see the whole subform, use the scroll arrow on the right side of the window to scroll down the form.

k. Click the **subform** datasheet to select it. Click the **Layout Selector** [icon], and then drag it up and to the left so it is just under the State control.

l. Click the **title** of the form to select it. Click the **Home** tab, and in the Text Formatting group, click **Bold** B, click the **Font size** arrow [11], and then select **28**.

m. Click the **First Name** text box control, hold down Shift, and then click the **Last Name** text box control. On the Home tab, in the Text Formatting group, Click **Bold** B.

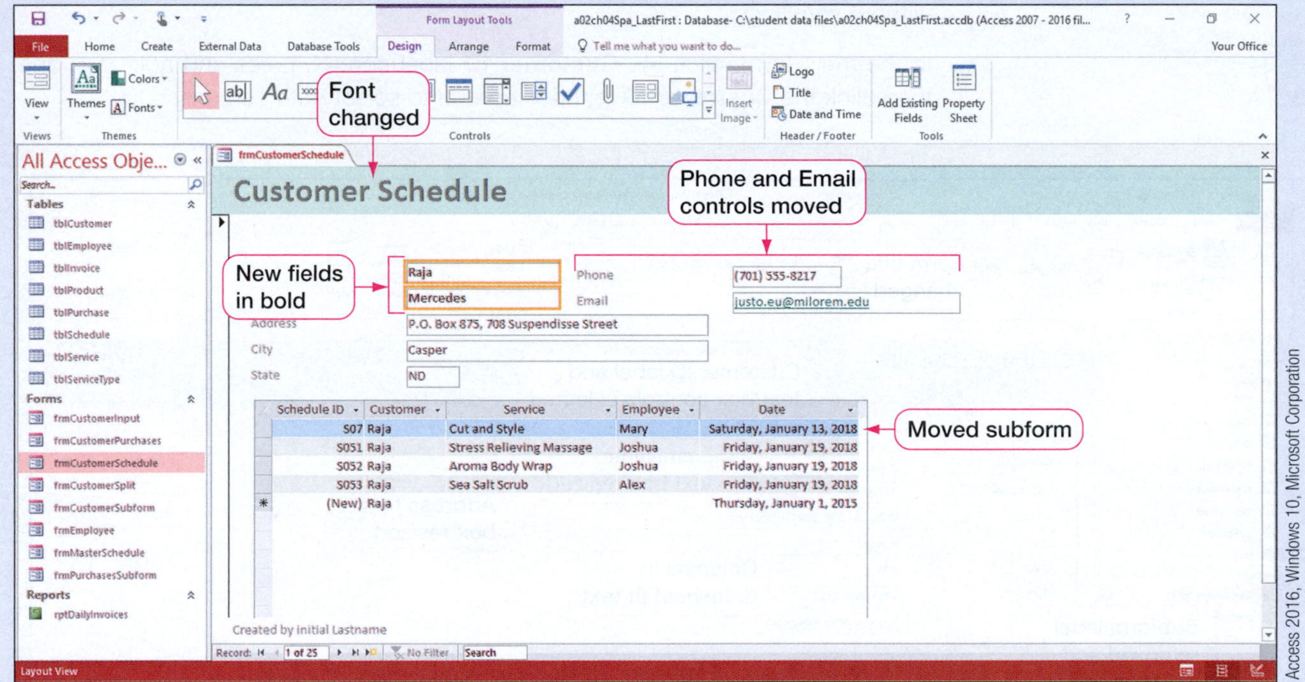

Figure 14 Formatted form and subform

n. **Save** [icon] the form.

Adding a Picture to the Form

Pictures can be added to forms to make them more appealing. When a picture is added to a form, the same picture will appear for every record in the table. A different picture cannot be added for each record. A picture can be inserted in the header, the footer, or the Detail area of the form where the record values are shown. In this exercise, you will insert the spa's logo in the Detail area of the form to make it more personal for the spa.

A04.14

To Add a Picture on the Form

a. With the frmCustomerSchedule open, in Layout view, click in the **Detail area** of the form to select it. If a text box or label is selected, the Insert Image button will not be available to use.

b. Click the **Design** tab, in the Controls group, click **Insert Image**, and then click **Browse**.

c. In the Insert Picture dialog box, navigate to where your student files are located, click **a02ch04Spa**, and then click **OK**. With the image control pointer, click in the **form detail** to insert the picture. Drag the corner until the picture is small enough to fit under Email and above the subform.

d. Click the **Layout Selector** and move the picture under the **Email** text box. Move your pointer to the **bottom right corner** of the picture until it becomes a diagonal resize pointer and drag to make the picture smaller until the picture fits between the Email text box and the subform.

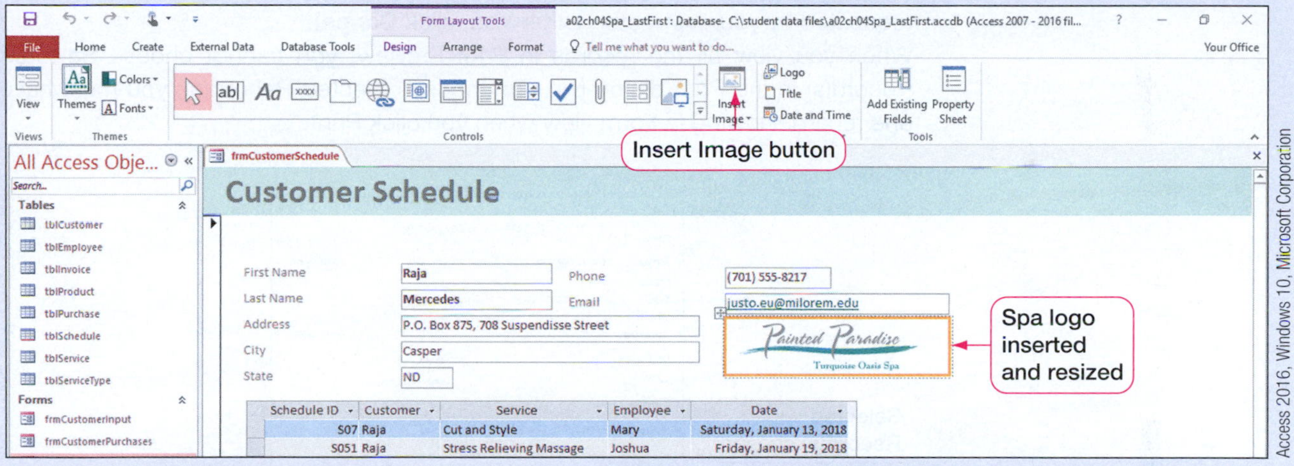

Figure 15 Logo inserted in form

e. **Close** the form, and then click **Yes** to save the changes.

Printing a Record from a Form

Not only can you see one record at a time using a form, but you can also print one record at a time. Printing a form can be useful if you need only one record's information or if you want to use a form for other people to manually fill in the information.

The spa manager would like you to print a record for a particular customer from the customer form. In this exercise, you will show her how to preview the form first, select one record, and then send it to the printer.

A04.15 To Preview and Print a Record from a Form

a. In the Navigation Pane, double-click **frmCustomerInput** to open it, and then switch to **Layout** view.

b. Click the **Address** text box control, and then drag the **right border** to the right until it is lined up with the Last Name and City text box controls.

c. Click the **File** tab, click **Print**, and then click **Print Preview**. Notice all the records will print in Form view.

d. Click **Last Page** [▶|] on the Navigation bar to go to the last record. Notice in the Navigation bar that the number of pages for the printed report will be seven.

e. On the Print Preview tab, in the Close Preview group, click **Close Print Preview**.

f. Using the Navigation bar, advance through the customer records to find the record for **Jonah Hogan**.

g. Click the **File** tab, click **Print**, and then click **Print**. In the Print dialog box, in the Print Range section, click **Selected Record(s)**. Click **OK** to print the record if requested by your instructor. Otherwise, click **Cancel**.
When you view all the records in Print Preview, you cannot choose Selected Record(s) in the Print dialog box. To choose Selected Record(s), you must have one record showing in Form view when you click Print.

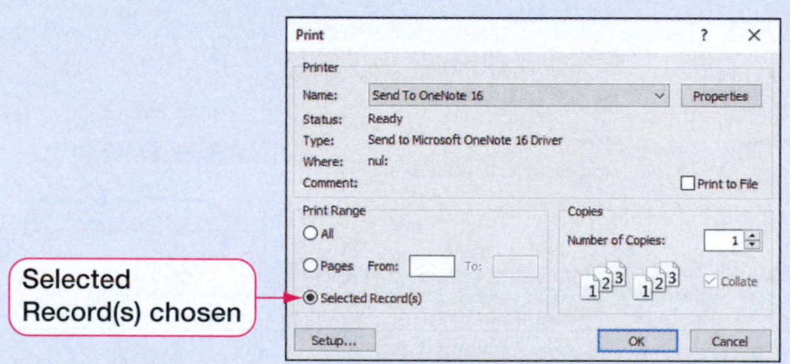

Figure 16 Print one record as a form

Access 2016, Windows 10, Microsoft Corporation

h. **Close** [X] the form, and then click **Yes** to save the changes. If you need to take a break before finishing this chapter, now is a good time.

Creating Customized Reports

While a report and a form may look similar, a form is a method for data entry, and a report is a read-only view of the data that can be formatted for easy printing. A report can be created from either a table or a query. Reports may be based on multiple tables in a one-to-many relationship using a common field to match the records. The "one" record from the first table in the relationship will be shown first — similar to a main form — while the "many" records from the second table will be displayed as detailed records in the **subreport** — similar to a subform. In this section, you will create a report using the Report Wizard and then make changes to the report in Design and Layout views.

Create a Report Using the Report Wizard

The Report Wizard will walk you step by step through the process of building your report. You will choose the table or query to base the report on, and you will choose the fields to include in the report. You will have the option to group the data in your report.

CHAPTER 4

A **group** is a collection of records along with introductory and summary information about the records. Grouping allows you to separate related records for the purpose of creating a visual summary of the data. Groups can be created with data from individual tables or from multiple tables.

For example, a report grouped by the primary table containing customer records would show all the selected fields for a customer and then would list that customer's individual appointments from the secondary table below the customer's record.

Within a report, you can also sort using up to four fields in either ascending or descending order. Once a report has been created using the wizard, it will open in Print Preview. Print Preview provides a view of the report representing how it will look when it is actually printed and provides you with printing options such as orientation, margins, and size. The current date and page numbers are added, and you can navigate the report in this view using the Navigation bar. To make any changes to the report, you can switch to Layout view.

Creating a Single-Table Report

A report can be created by using one table, multiple tables, or a query. A single-table report is a report created from one table. Any or all of the fields can be selected. The spa manager would like to have a report to help the staff with scheduling. In this exercise, you will create a report that will consist of a list of employee names and phone numbers so the staff can contact each other if necessary.

To Create a Single-Table Report Using Report Wizard

a. If you took a break, open the **a02ch04Spa_LastFirst** database. Click the **Create** tab, and then in the Reports group, click **Report Wizard**.

b. Click the **Tables/Queries** arrow, and then select **tblEmployee**.

c. Double-click **EmpFirstName**, **EmpLastName**, and **EmpPhone** from the Available Fields list. Click **Next**.

> **SIDE NOTE**
> **Field Order**
> The order in which you add the fields in the Report Wizard is the order in which the fields will appear on the report.

d. You will not add any grouping levels to this report, so click **Next**.

e. Click the **1 Sort** arrow, select **EmpLastName**, click the **2 Sort** arrow, select **EmpFirstName**, and then click **Next**.

f. Verify that **Tabular** layout and **Portrait** orientation are selected, as well as **Adjust the field width so all fields fit on a page**. Click **Next**.

g. Under What title do you want for your report?, type rptEmployeeList. Click **Modify the report's design**, and then click **Finish**.

h. If necessary, **close** the Field List pane. On the Report Design Tools Design tab, in the Controls group, click **Label**, point to the **Report Footer** area, and then when your pointer changes to +A, drag your pointer to draw a label control about 2.5 inches wide in the top left corner of the Report Footer section. In the new label, type Created by initial Lastname using your first initial and last name.

Troubleshooting

If the Label control is not visible, in the Controls group, click the More button to display the gallery, and then click Label.

i. Switch to **Report** view. Verify that your label is fully shown in the bottom left corner of the report.

j. Switch to **Layout** view. Double-click the **form title**, select the existing text, type Employee List and then press Enter.

In Layout view, you should also check that all the report column headers and data show fully. On this report they do, so no further changes are necessary.

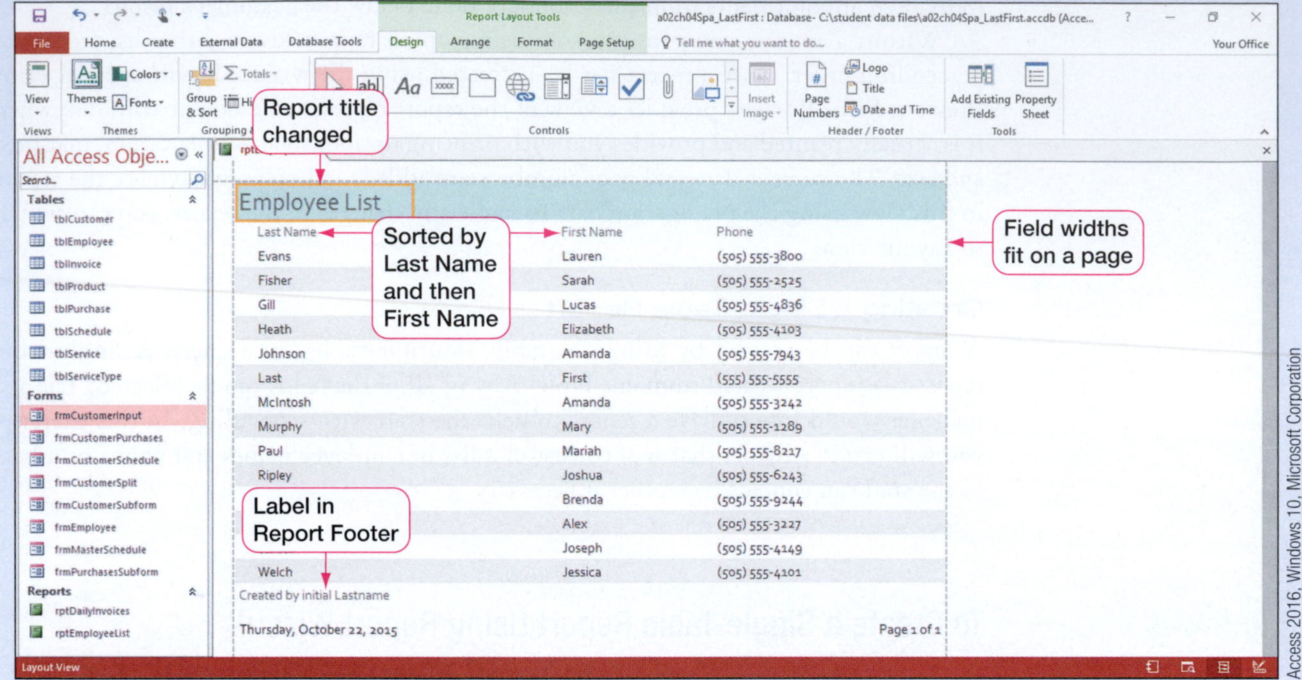

Figure 17 Completed Employee List report

k. **Close** ☒ the report, and then click **Yes** to save the changes.

Creating a Multiple-Table Report

Similar to other objects created by using more than one table or query, a multiple-table report must use tables that have a common field. The first table chosen for the report becomes the primary table, and the next and subsequent tables chosen become the secondary tables.

An employee has a one-to-many relationship with scheduled appointments. Each employee may have more than one appointment, and each appointment is with just one employee. Therefore, tblEmployee will be the primary table, and tblSchedule will be a secondary table.

The manager would like a report that will show all employees' names and their upcoming appointments. This way, the staff members can help coordinate their services for a guest who may be seeing more than one staff member in a day. In this exercise, you will create a multiple-table report that the staff can use for this purpose.

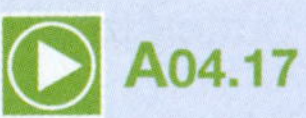

A04.17

To Create a Multiple-Table Report Using the Report Wizard

a. Click the **Create** tab, and then in the Reports group, click **Report Wizard**.

b. Click the **Tables/Queries** arrow, and then select **Table: tblEmployee**. Double-click **EmpFirstName** and **EmpLastName** in the Available Fields list.

c. Click the **Tables/Queries** arrow, and then select **Table: tblSchedule**. Double-click **Service**, **DateOfAppt**, and **Customer** from the Available Fields list, and then click **Next**.

d. Verify that by tblEmployee is highlighted to view the data by Employee, and then click **Next**.
Notice that Access defaults to viewing the data by primary table, tblEmployee.

e. Double-click **DateOfAppt** to group by the date. Click **Grouping Options**, click the **Grouping intervals** arrow, select **Normal**, and then click **OK**.
Access defaults to grouping dates by Month. Normal groups by date value.

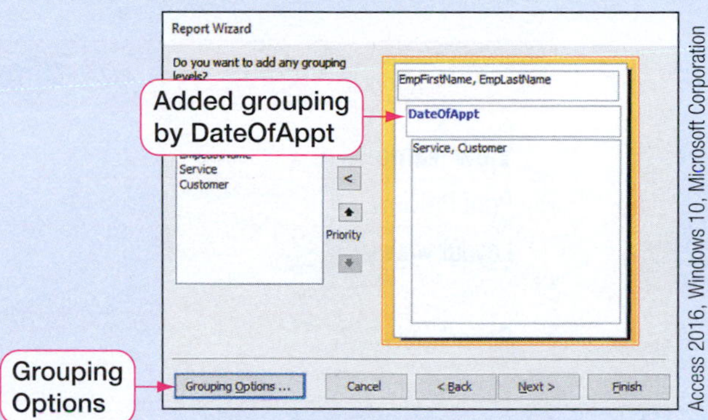

Figure 18 Report Wizard grouping step

f. Click **Next**. Click the **1 Sort** arrow, select **Customer**, and then click **Next**.

g. Verify that Stepped is selected under Layout, and then under Orientation, click **Landscape**. Verify that Adjust the field width so all fields fit on a page is checked. Click **Next**.

h. Under What title do you want for your report?, type rptEmployeeSchedule, and then click **Finish**. The report will open in Print Preview.

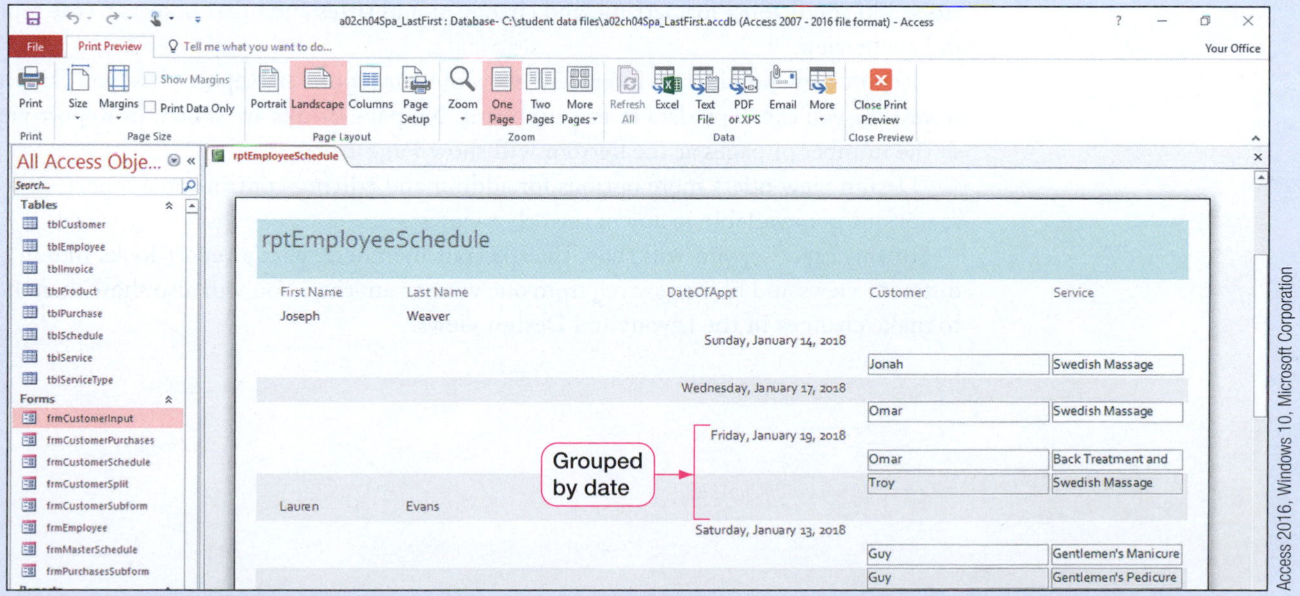

Figure 19 Report in Print Preview

Notice that the appointments are grouped by date. Your date column may not be wide enough to see the dates, but you will fix that in Layout view. Additionally, notice that in Print Preview view, at the bottom of each page of the report is today's date and the page number.

i. Click **Close Print Preview**.

Exploring Report Views

Recall that reports have four different views. Each type of view has its own features.

QUICK REFERENCE — Different View Options for a Report

View Name	What the View Is Used For
Print Preview	Shows what the printed report will look like
Layout view	Allows you to modify the report while seeing the data
Report view	Allows you to filter data or copy parts of the report to the Clipboard
Design view	Allows you to change more details of the report design or add other controls that are available only in Design view

When the Report Wizard has finished creating the report, it shows you the report in Print Preview, which is the view that shows you exactly what the report will look like when it is printed. Print Preview adds the current date and page numbers in the page footer at the bottom of each page.

Layout view allows you to change basic design features of the report while the report is displaying data so the changes you make are immediately visible. You can resize controls, add conditional formatting, and change or add titles and other objects to the report in Layout view.

Report view provides an interactive view of your report. In Report view, you can filter records or you can copy data to the clipboard. No page breaks are shown in Report view, so the number of pages at the bottom will show Page 1 of 1.

Design view offers more options for adding and editing controls on a report, as well as options not available in any of the other views.

In this exercise, you will show the spa staff members what a report looks like in the different views and how to switch from one view to another. You will also show them how to make changes in the Layout and Design views.

To Explore Report Views

a. With the rptEmployeeSchedule open, switch to **Layout** view.

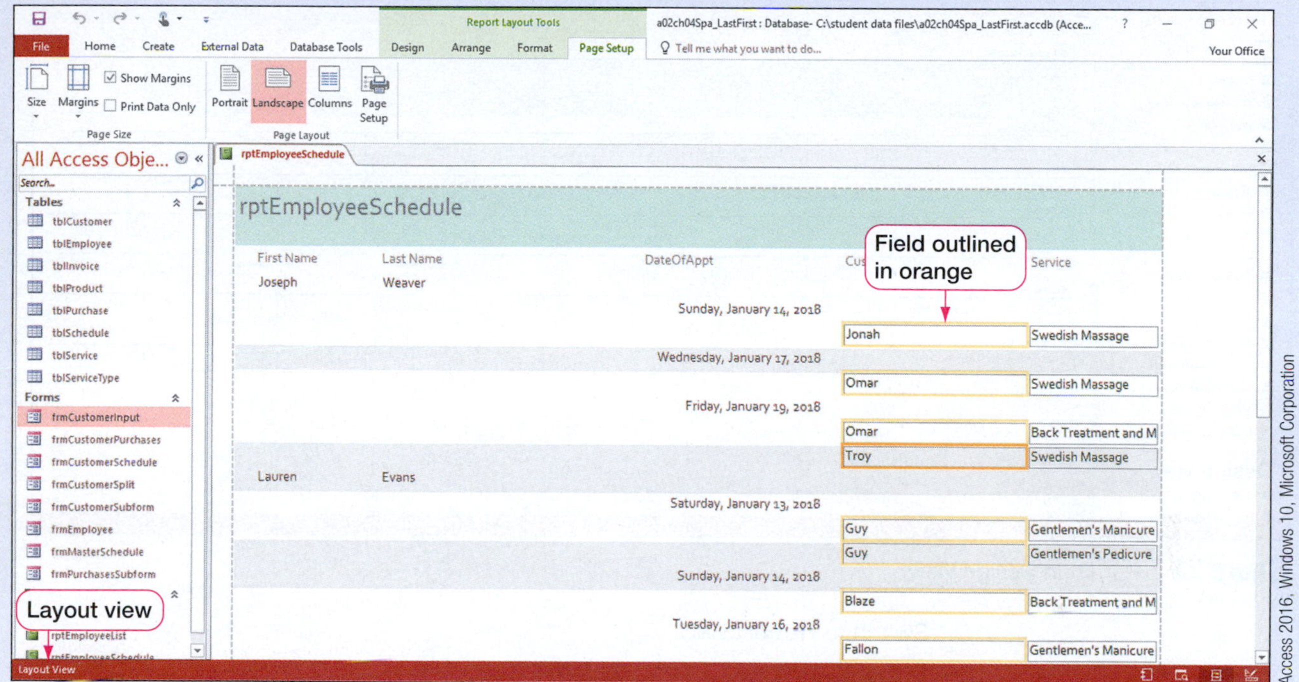

Figure 20 Report in Layout view

Notice the orange border around the first Customer field. Customer is the active field. You can make changes, such as making a column wider, in Layout view.

b. If your dates are not visible, click the **DateOfAppt** column header, press and hold Shift, and then click the **DateOfAppt** text box. Use your pointer to drag the left border of the column to the left so the date is fully shown.

c. Scroll to the **bottom right** of the report.
Notice there is the date and page number in the page footer, but the page number shows page 1 of 1. The actual number of pages will not be calculated until you switch to Print Preview.

d. On the Design tab, switch to **Design** view. Data in Design view is not visible, only the controls in each section of the report are.

e. On the Design tab, in the Controls group, click **Label** Aa, point to the Report Footer area, and then when your pointer changes to +A, drag your pointer to draw a label control about 2.5 inches wide in the top left corner of the Report Footer section. In the new label, type Created by initial Lastname using your first initial and last name.

SIDE NOTE
Two Footers
Be sure to put your label in the Report Footer, not the Page Footer.

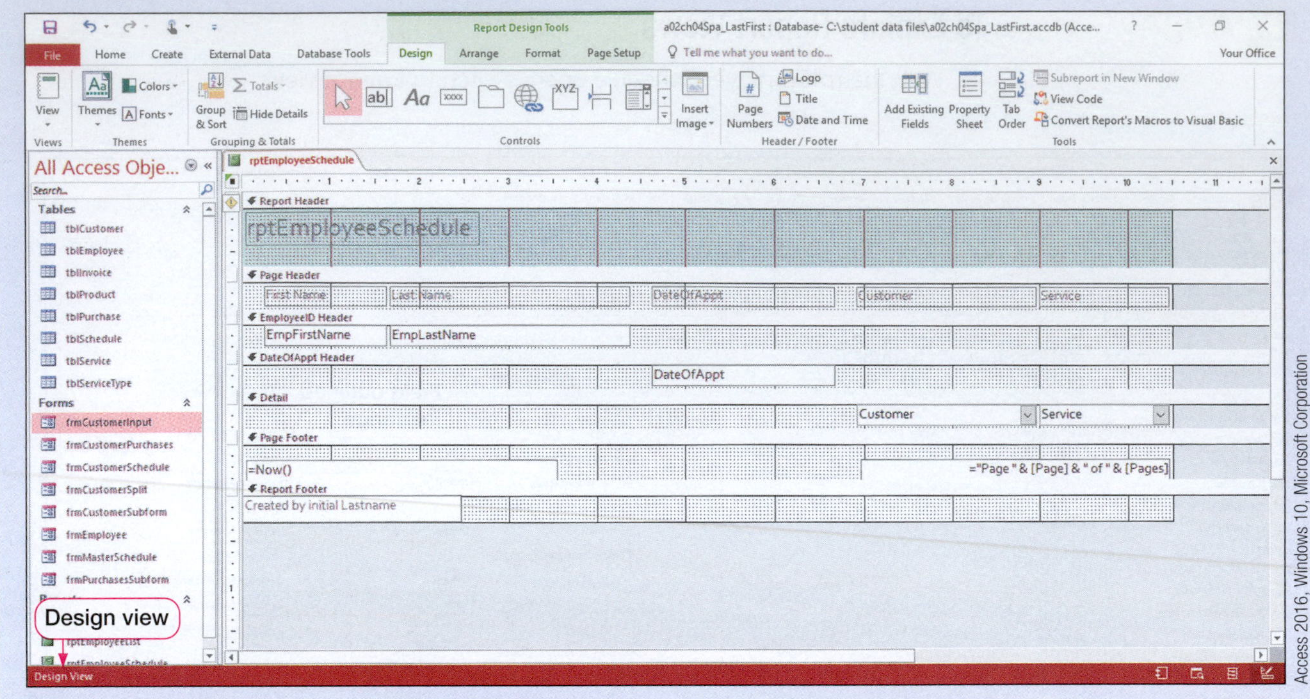

Figure 21 Report in Design view

f. Switch to **Report** view.

g. Scroll to the **bottom** of the report.
Verify that your label has been entered in the bottom left corner of the report. In Report view, there are no page breaks, so the number of pages at the bottom will show Page 1 of 1.

h. **Save** [save icon] and **close** [X] your report.

Creating Totals Using the Report Wizard

When you report on numeric data, Access has the ability to calculate sums, averages, minimums, and maximums of the numeric data. The **grand total** calculates the total for all records. **Subtotals** calculate totals for smaller groups of records. In this exercise, you will use the wizard to request these totals. Later, you will add totals to an already created report.

The spa manager asks you to create a report showing the invoices collected each day. In this exercise, you will show her how to provide a daily total as well as a grand total using the Report Wizard.

To Create Report Totals Using the Report Wizard

a. Click the **Create** tab, and then in the Reports group, click **Report Wizard**.

b. Click the **Tables/Queries** arrow, and then select **Table: tblInvoice**. Double-click **InvoiceDate** and **InvoiceTotal** in the Available Fields list. Click **Next**.

c. Double-click **InvoiceDate** to group by the date. Click **Grouping Options...**, click the **Grouping intervals** arrow, and select **Day**. Click **OK**, and then click **Next**.

d. Click the **1 Sort** arrow, and then select **InvoiceDate**.

e. Click **Summary Options...**, and then click the **Sum** check box.

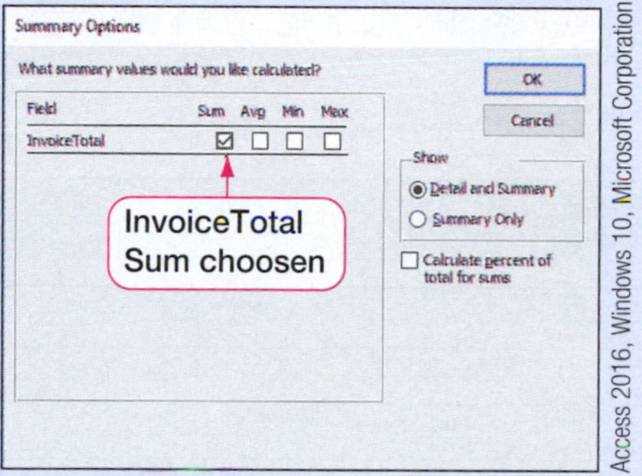

Figure 22 Report Summary Options

f. Click **OK**, and then click **Next**. Verify that Stepped and Portrait are selected, and then click **Next**.

g. Under What title do you want for your report?, type rptInvoiceTotals, and then click **Finish**. The report will open in Print Preview. If necessary, scroll down to see the grand total.

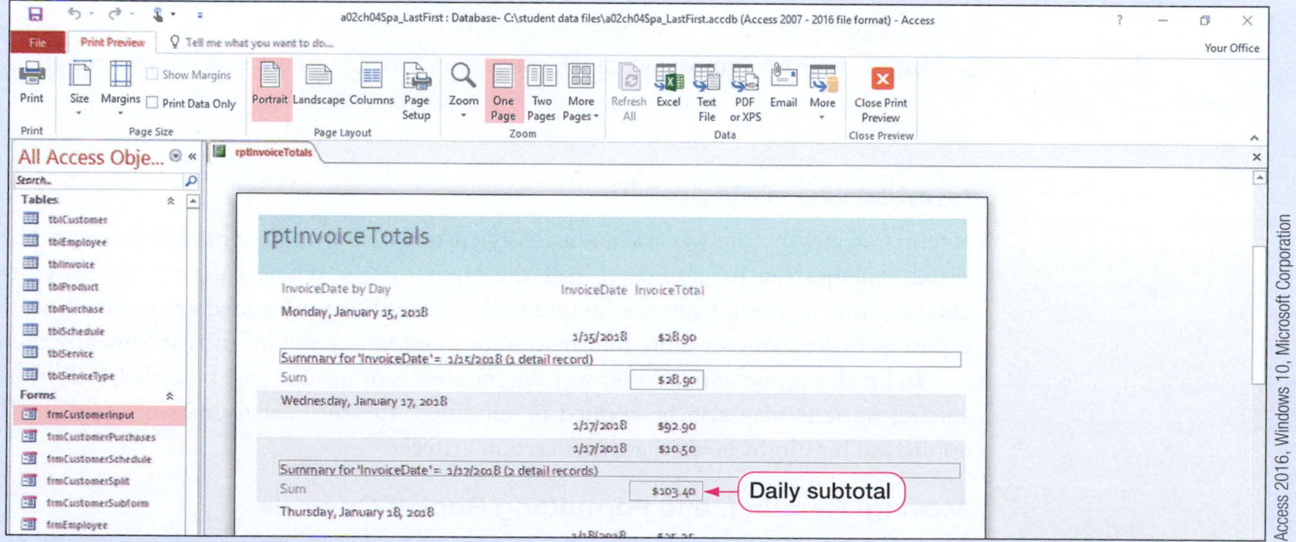

Figure 23 Report with daily subtotals and a grand total

Notice that there is a sum for each day and a grand total of all invoices for all days.

h. **Close Print Preview** and Switch to **Design** view. There is a new footer for InvoiceDate where the sum for each day is shown. There is also a Report Footer where the GrandTotal is shown.

i. On the Design tab, in the Controls group, select **Label**, move your pointer to the **Report Footer** just below the existing Grand Total label, and then when your pointer changes to, drag your pointer to draw a label control about 2.5 inches wide in the Report Footer section. In the new label, type Created by initial Lastname using your first initial and last name.

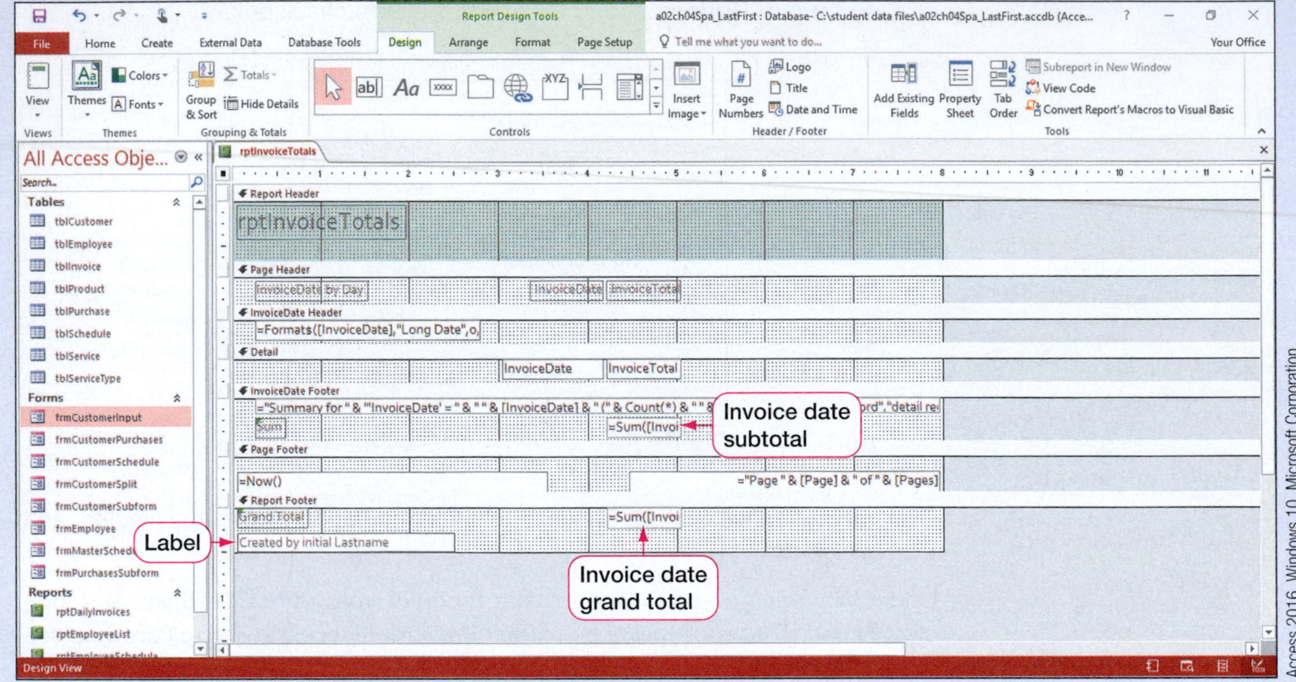

Figure 24 Design view of totals

j. Switch to **Print Preview** to check your label. **Save** and **close** your report.

Customize a Report

Reports created by the wizard can be easily customized after they have been created and saved. Themes can be applied to just the report or the whole database to change the colors, fonts, or both. Controls, bound and unbound, can be added or modified on the report to make room for more information or to rearrange the information already there.

To break a report into smaller sections, subtotals or groups may be added. Additional sorting options may also be applied or modified. Conditional formatting may also be applied to highlight fields that meet certain criteria.

Moving, Resizing, and Formatting Report Controls

Controls, as defined in the section on forms, are also used in reports. A control can be a text box or another object that has been added to the form either by the wizard or manually in Layout or Design view. Controls can be moved or resized to make the report more readable. In this exercise, you will change the rptEmployeeSchedule schedule report to make it look more like what the manager expected. You will move the date, service, and customer name fields below the employee name, change the heading, and change the formatting to match the resort theme.

A04.20

To Move, Resize, and Format a Report Control

a. In the Navigation Pane, right-click **rptEmployeeSchedule**, and then click **Layout View**.

b. Click the **DateOfAppt** text box control to select it, and then drag the field to the left so it is just slightly indented under the employee first name.

c. Click the **First Name** label control — the column header. Press and hold Shift, click the **Last Name** and the **DateofAppt** label controls, and then press Delete.

d. Click the Customer label control, press and hold Shift, and then click the **Customer** text box, the **Service** label, and the **Service** text box controls. Point to and click any field to drag all the controls to the left, just next to the date field.

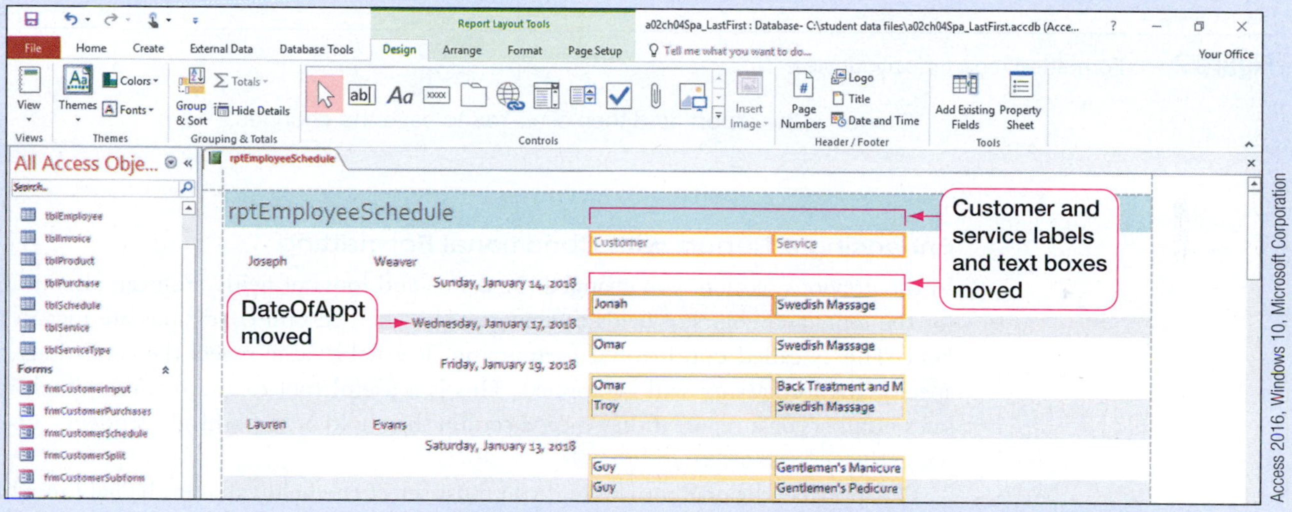

Figure 25 Fields moved

Troubleshooting

If you drag the controls too far to the left, reselect them and then drag them back to the right.

e. Click the **Service** text box control. Drag the **right border** of the box to the right to fit all the service description. Scroll down to check Chakra Body and Balancing Massage to make sure the description is fully shown. If it is not, drag the border to make the field wider.

f. Click the **Service** text box control, press and hold Shift, and then click the **Customer** text box control. Click the **Format** tab, in the Control Formatting group, click **Shape Outline**, and then select **Transparent**.

g. Click the employee's **First Name** text box control, press and hold Shift, and then click the **Last Name** text box control. On the Format tab, in the Control Formatting group, click **Shape Fill**, and then select **Dark Teal Accent 2 Lighter 80%** in the second row of the sixth column under Theme colors. In the Font group, click **Bold** B.

h. Double-click the **title**, select the **text**, type Employee Schedule, and then press Enter.

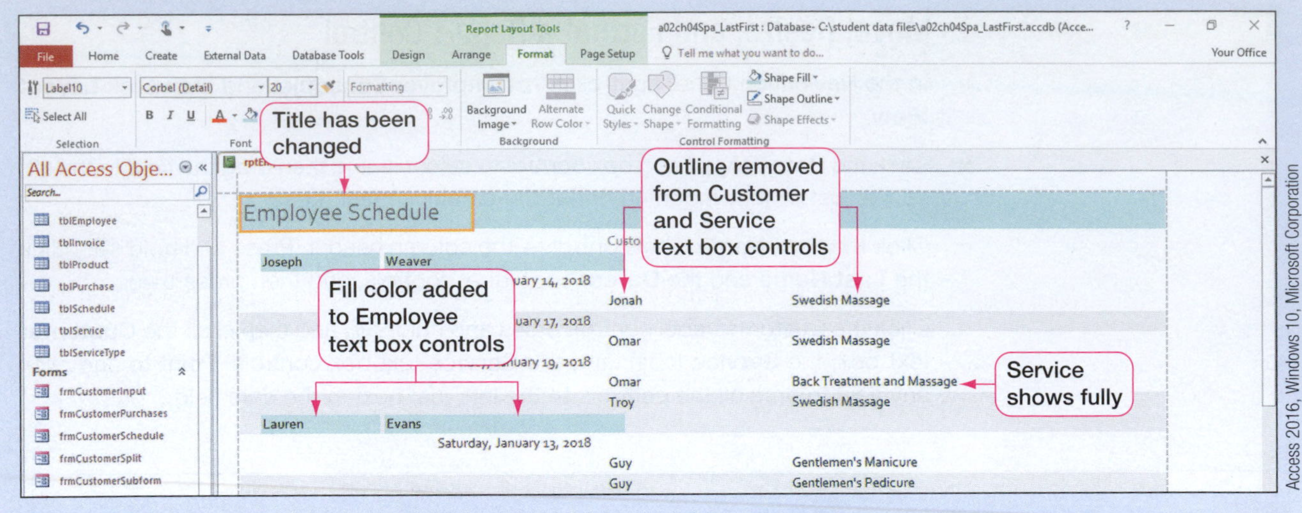

Figure 26 Formatted report in Layout view

i. **Close** [X] the report, and then click **Yes** to save the changes.

Enhancing a Report with Conditional Formatting

In the previous section, you changed the colors and fonts of fields. You can also arrange for the fonts and colors of fields to change only when certain conditions are met in the field. This is called **conditional formatting**. If a field value meets the conditions you specify, the formatting will be applied. This is a useful tool to automatically highlight sales numbers on a report if they meet a certain threshold or to highlight students' grades when they exceed a certain limit.

To apply conditional formatting, you must select the field value in the field to which you want the formatting applied. You can select a different font color and font effects for the formatting.

The spa manager would like a list of services currently scheduled that cost over $100. The customers who buy these services usually get some special treatment, such as complimentary coffee and tea, and the staff would like to be able to easily see which customers are to get special treatment. In this exercise, you will create a report and apply conditional formatting to all services currently scheduled that cost over $100.

 A04.21

To Apply Conditional Formatting to a Report Field

a. Click the **Create** tab, and then in the Reports group, click **Report Wizard**.

b. Click the **Tables/Queries** arrow, and then select **Table: tblSchedule**. Double-click **DateOfAppt**, **Customer**, and **Service** in the Available Fields list. Click the **Tables/Queries** arrow, and then select **Table: tblService**. In the Available Fields list, double-click **Fee**, and then click **Next**.

c. Verify that by tblSchedule is highlighted, and then click **Next**. You will not add any grouping to this report, click **Next**.

d. Click the **1 Sort** arrow, click **DateofAppt**, and then click **Next**. Verify that Tabular is selected under Layout and Portrait is selected under Orientation. Verify that Adjust the field width so all fields fit on a page is checked. Click **Next**.

e. Under What title do you want for your report?, type rptHighFees, and then click **Finish**. The report will open in Print Preview. **Close Print Preview**, and switch to **Layout** view. If necessary, close the Field List pane.

f. Double-click the title, select the text, type High Service Customers, and then press Enter.

g. Click in the **Fee** text box control, and then, click the **Format** tab, and in the Control Formatting group, click **Conditional Formatting**.

h. In the Conditional Formatting Rules Manager dialog box, click **New Rule**. Verify that Check values in the current record or use an expression is highlighted. Find the three condition text boxes. The first should display Field Value Is. Click in the second condition box, and then select **greater than**. In the third condition text box, type 100.

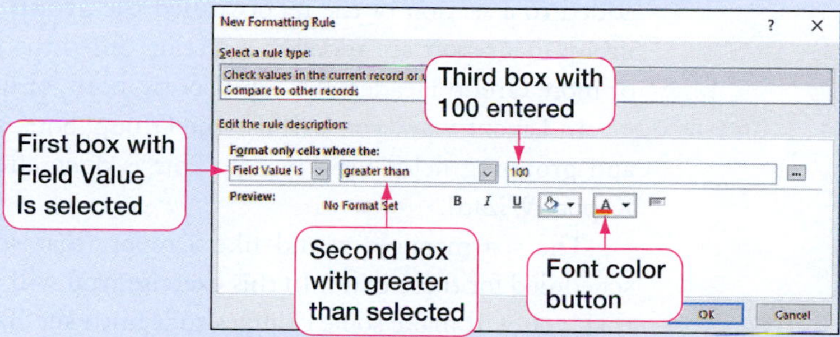

Figure 27 New Formatting Rule dialog box

i. Below the condition text boxes, click **Bold** B, click the **Font color** arrow, and then click **Dark Red**. Click **OK**, verify that your rule states Value >100, and then click **OK**.

All values greater than $100 in the Fee field will now be highlighted in dark red and bold.

j. Click the **Design** tab, and switch to **Design** view. Click the **Design** tab, in the Controls group, select **Label** Aa, move your pointer to the **Report Footer**, and then when your pointer changes to +A, drag your pointer to draw a label control about 2.5 inches wide in the top left corner of the Report Footer section. In the new label, type Created by initial Lastname using your first initial and last name.

k. Switch to **Report** view. Verify that your label has been entered in the bottom left corner of the report.

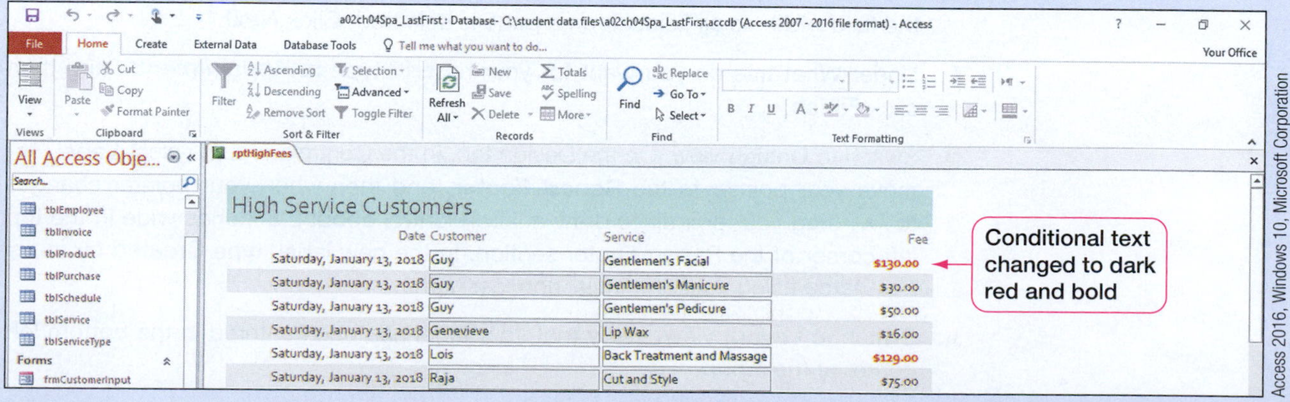

Figure 28 Report with conditional formatting applied

l. **Close** the report, and then click **Yes** to save the changes.

QUICK REFERENCE	To Delete a Conditional Formatting Rule

1. Click the Format tab in Layout view.
2. Click the field that has the conditional formatting applied.
3. In the Control Formatting group, click Conditional Formatting.
4. Click the rule you wish to delete, and then click Delete Rule.

Applying Grouping and Sorting

The Report Wizard gives you the opportunity to sort and group records. Sometimes reviewing the report reveals an alternative way to group and sort the data. You can change the sorting and grouping options from either Layout view or Design view. Groups are added to a section of the report called the **group header**. Calculations performed on a group in a report are added to a section called the **group footer**. A report may have one or more Group Headers, Group Footers, both, or neither.

In Layout view, you will use the Group, Sort, and Total pane to select the sort fields and grouping fields for a report. This is done after the report has been created by the Report Wizard.

The spa manager would like a report that shows appointment dates and services scheduled for those dates. In this exercise, you will show her how to create the report, and then you will make some changes to it until she likes how the information is presented.

To Add Group and Sort Fields to a New Report

a. Click the **Create** tab, and then in the Reports group, click **Report Wizard**.

b. Click the **Tables/Queries** arrow, and then select **Table: tblSchedule**. Double-click **DateOfAppt**, **Service**, **Customer**, and **Employee** from the Available Fields list. Click **Next**.

c. Click the **One Field Back** button [<] to remove the Service grouping level. Click **DateOfAppt**, and then click the **One Field** button [>] to add the date as a grouping level. Click **Grouping Options...**, click the **Grouping intervals** arrow, and then click **Normal**. Click **OK**, and then click **Next**.

d. Click the **1 Sort** arrow, select **Service**, and then click **Next**.

e. Verify that Stepped layout and Portrait orientation are selected. Verify that Adjust the field width so all fields fit on a page is selected. Click **Next**.

f. Under What title do you want for your report? type rptAppointments, and then click **Finish**.

g. Switch to **Design** view. On the Design tab, in the Controls group, select **Label** [Aa], move your pointer to the **Report Footer**, and then when your pointer changes to [+A], drag your pointer to draw a label control about 2.5 inches wide in the top left corner of the Report Footer section. In the new label, type Created by initial Lastname using your first initial and last name.

h. Switch to **Layout** view. Verify that your label has been entered in the bottom left corner of the report.

i. Click the **DateOfAppt** text box control, click the **Format** tab, in the Font group, click **Align Text Left** [≡]. Drag the right border of the DateOfAppt text box to line up with the left border of the Service text box. All the date values should be visible.

j. Click the **Service** text box control, and then drag the left border to the left to make the control wider so all the text can be displayed. Scroll down to the appointments scheduled on January 18, and then confirm that the **Microdermabrasion Treatment (6 sessions)** is showing.

k. Double-click the **title**, select the **text**, and then type Daily Appointments. Press Enter.

l. Click the **Design** tab, in the Grouping & Totals group, click **Group & Sort**, and then notice the Group, Sort, and Total pane that opens at the bottom of the report.

m. Click the line that displays **Sort by Service**, and then click **Delete** ☒ on the far right of the line. This will delete the sort that was added in the Report Wizard.

n. Click **Add a group** in the Group, Sort, and Total pane, and then select **Employee**.

o. Click the **Employee** text box control, and then drag it to the left until it is under the date. Click the **Employee** label control, press and hold Shift, click the **DateOfAppt** label control, and then press Delete.

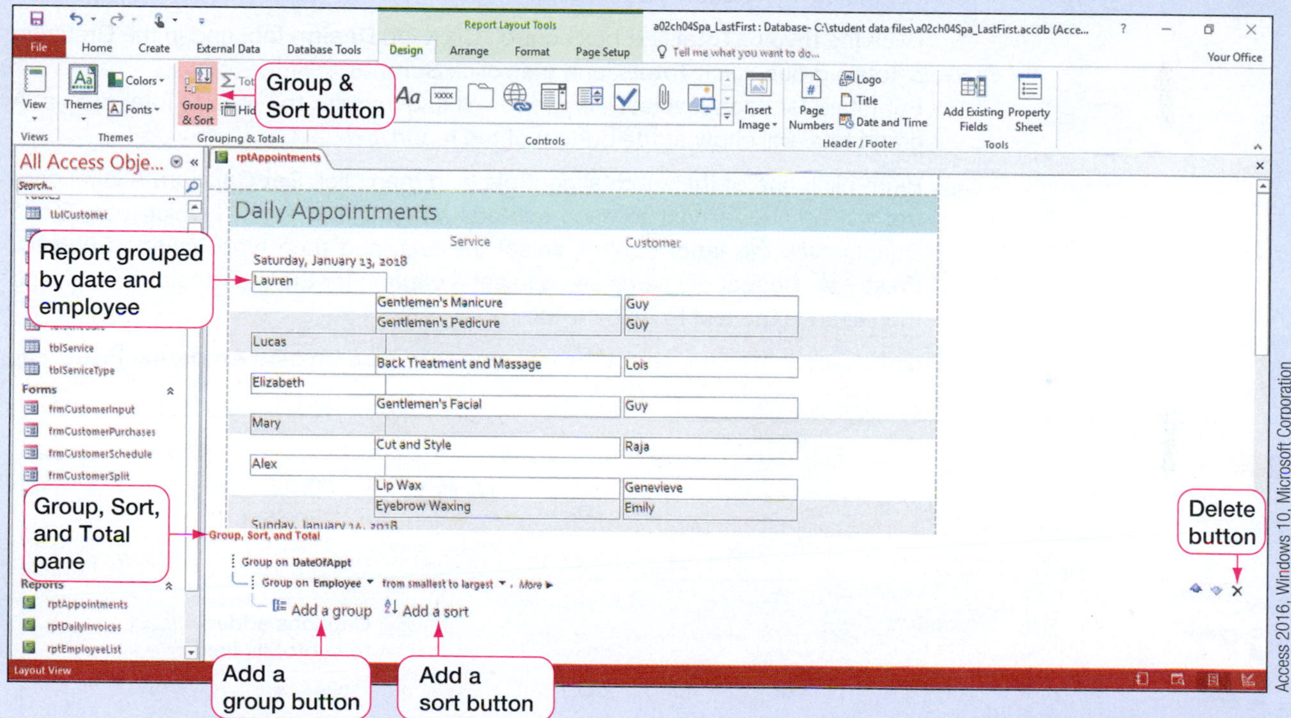

Figure 29 New grouping added to report

p. **Close** ☒ the Group, Sort, and Total pane, being careful that you are clicking Close and not the Delete button. **Close** ☒ the report, and then click **Yes** to save the changes.

Adding Subtotals

Earlier, you added subtotals when you created the report using the wizard. However, sometimes seeing the report makes you realize that subtotals would be useful. You can add them in Layout view, using the Group, Sort, and Total pane when you are selecting or modifying groups and sorts for the reports.

In this exercise, you will show the spa manager how to add subtotals to a report that shows all invoices grouped by date.

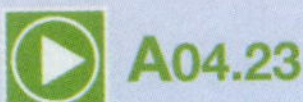

To Add Subtotals to a Report

a. In the Navigation Pane, right-click **rptDailyInvoices**, and then select **Copy**. Right-click in the **Navigation Pane**, and then select **Paste**. In the Paste As dialog box, in the Report Name: box, type rptDailyInvoiceTotals. Click **OK**.

b. In the Navigation Pane, double-click **rptDailyInvoiceTotals** to open the report. Notice the report shows all invoices by day but has no totals.

c. Switch to **Design** view. On the Design tab, in the Controls group, click **Label** Aa. Move your pointer to the **Report Footer**, and then when your pointer changes to +A, drag your pointer to draw a label control about 2.5 inches wide in the top left corner of the Report Footer section. In the new label control, type Created by initial Lastname using your first initial and last name.

d. Switch to **Layout** view. Verify that your label has been entered in the bottom left corner of the report.

e. Click the **Invoice Total** label control, press and hold Shift, click the **Invoice Total** text box control, and then drag the **left border** to the right so the field is narrower but the column heading still shows.

f. Click the **InvoiceTotal** text box control. Click the **Design** tab, and in the Grouping & Totals group, click **Totals**, and then click **Sum**.
Subtotals for each InvoiceDate group will show under the InvoiceTotal details. A grand total will show at the bottom of the report.

g. Right-click one of the subtotal controls, and then click **Set Caption**. A label control will be added next to each subtotal amount that says "InvoiceTotal Total". Double-click the **label** control, select the text, and then type Invoice Subtotal. Press Enter. Repeat the same steps to set a caption for the grand total control, and then change the text to Invoice Total.

h. Double-click the **title**, select the text, and then type **Invoice Amounts**. Press Enter.

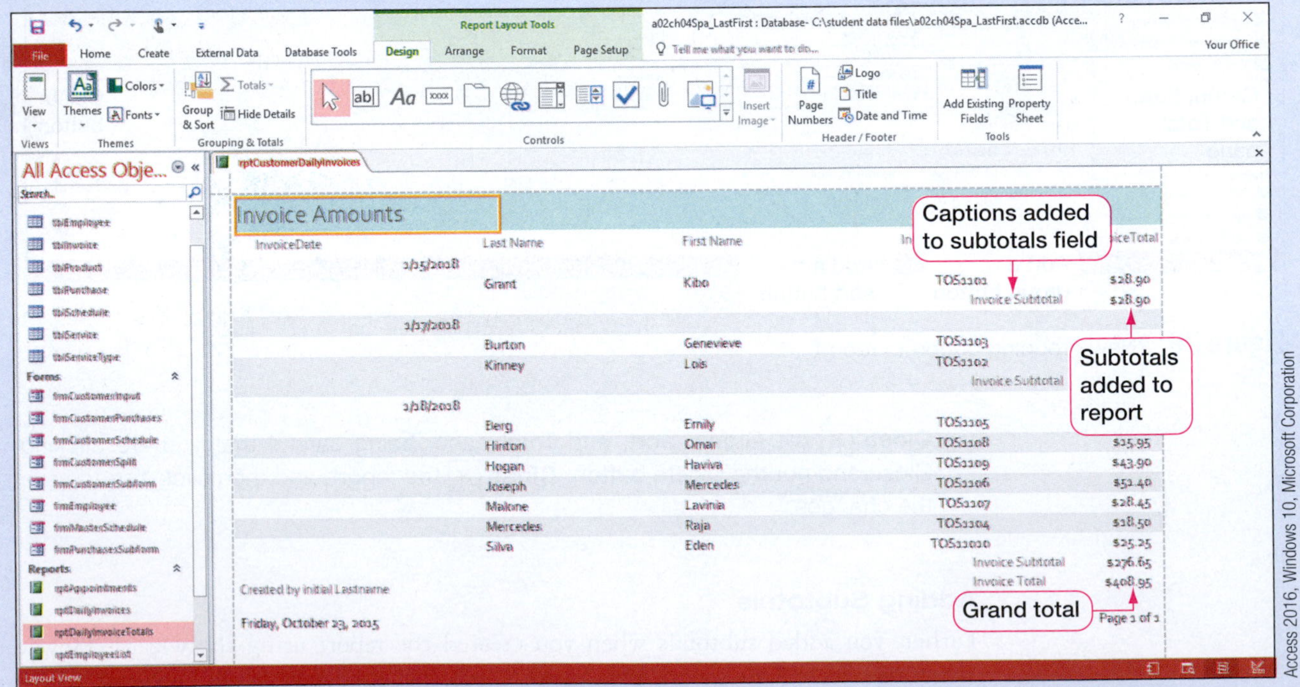

Figure 30 Report with subtotals added

i. **Close** ☒ the report, and then click **Yes** to save the changes.

Save a Report as a PDF File

Reports are formatted printable documents of your data, so the final result of a report will usually be a printout. Alternatively, the report may be shared with other people electronically. When you send a report to someone electronically, they have to have the same program in which the report was created in order to open the report. To avoid this problem, you can save a report as a PDF file, which can be read by Adobe Reader, a free program that can be downloaded from the Internet, or by Word 2016 or several other programs on a computer or mobile device.

To print a report, you use the Print dialog box to select your printing options. Before you print, it is always a good idea to view the report in Print Preview to make sure it looks the way you want. Viewing the report in Layout view and Report view does not show you page breaks and other features of the report as it will look when actually printed. In Print Preview, you have many options to make design changes to your report before you send it to the printer. You can change the margins and orientation, and you can select how many pages, if not all, you want to print.

Creating a PDF File

If you need to distribute the report electronically, you also have the option to save the report as an Adobe PDF file. An **Adobe PDF file** is usually smaller than the original document, is easy to send through e-mail, and preserves the original document look and feel so you know exactly what it will look like when the recipient opens it. The correct terminology for saving a report as a PDF file format is to "publish" the report. When you are saving the report as a PDF, you will see the option to Publish, not to Save or Print.

In this exercise, you will show the staff how to print and publish a PDF file of the employee schedule so it can easily be e-mailed to the staff each week.

To Save a Report as a PDF File

a. In the Navigation Pane, double-click **rptEmployeeSchedule** to open the report. On the Home tab, click the **View** button, and switch to **Print Preview**. Navigate through the pages to make sure the records fit on the pages correctly.

b. On the Print Preview tab, in the Print group, click **Print**.

c. If your instructor instructs you to print, under Print Range, verify All is selected, and then click **OK**. Otherwise, click **Cancel**.

d. On the Print Preview tab, in the Data group, click **PDF or XPS**.

e. In the Publish as PDF or XPS dialog box, navigate to the location where you are saving your files, and then in the File name box, type a02ch04SpaEmployeeSchedule_LastFirst using your last and first name. Click **Publish**. The PDF file automatically opens. **Close** the file and the application in which it opened.

f. **Close** the Export - PDF window. **Close** the report, and then exit Access.

Concept Check

1. What is the difference between Navigation and Edit modes? How can you tell you are in each mode? p. 219
2. When you add, change, or delete a record in a form, how does it affect the underlying table? Why? p. 226–227
3. What are controls? What is a bound control? What is an unbound control? p. 230
4. What is the difference between a label control and a text box control? Which is bound, and which is unbound? p. 230
5. What is a theme? What is the difference between applying a theme to an entire database and to a single object? p. 234
6. What view will you see when the Report Wizard is done creating a report? What is the difference between Report view, Layout view, Design view, and Print Preview when you are creating a report? Which view will show you the most accurate picture of what your printed report will look like? In which views do you see the data? p. 244
7. What is conditional formatting, and when would you use it? p. 250
8. What is a PDF file, and why would you want to save your report as a PDF? p. 255

Key Terms

Adobe PDF file 255
Bound control 230
Calculated control 230
Conditional formatting 250
Control 230
Edit mode 219
Grand total 246
Group 241
Group footer 252
Group header 252
Label control 230
Layout Selector 236
Main form 222
Navigation mode 219
Split form 224
Subform 222
Subreport 240
Subtotals 246
Text box control 230
Theme 235
Unbound control 230

Visual Summary

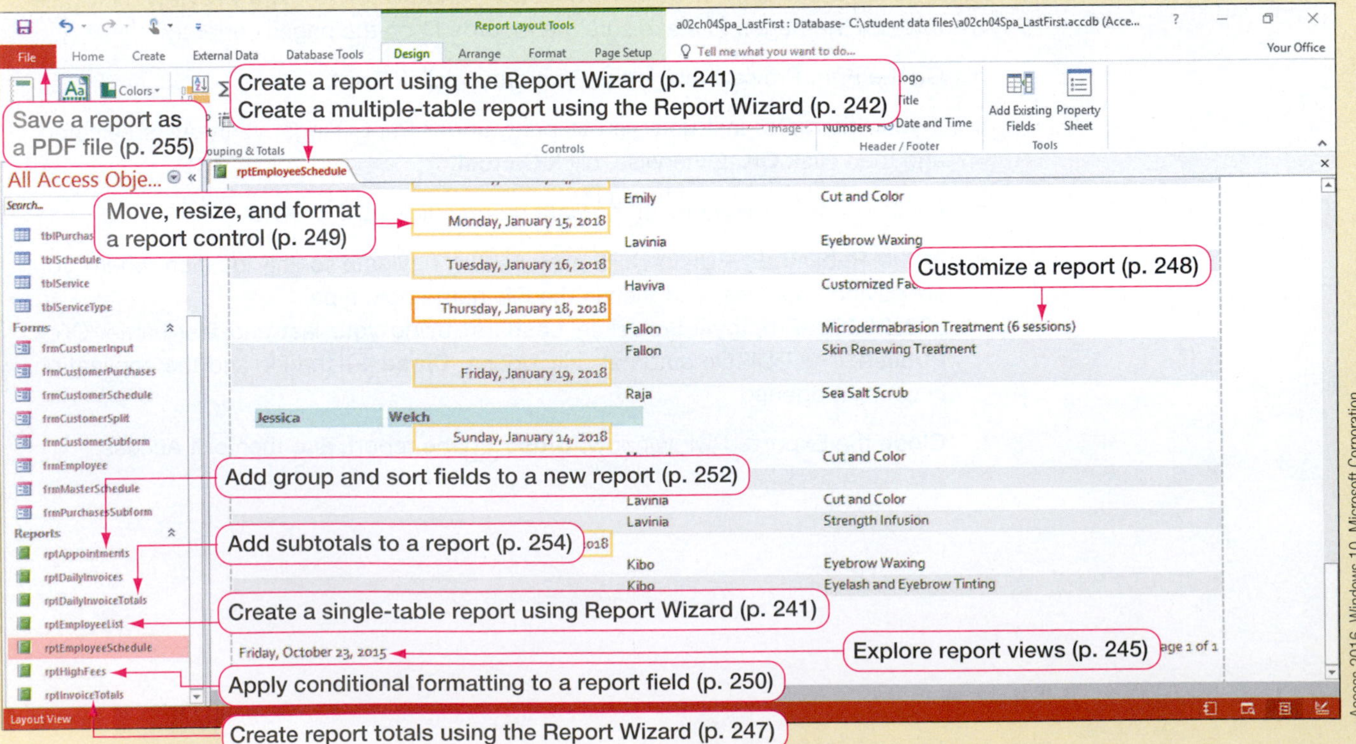

Figure 31

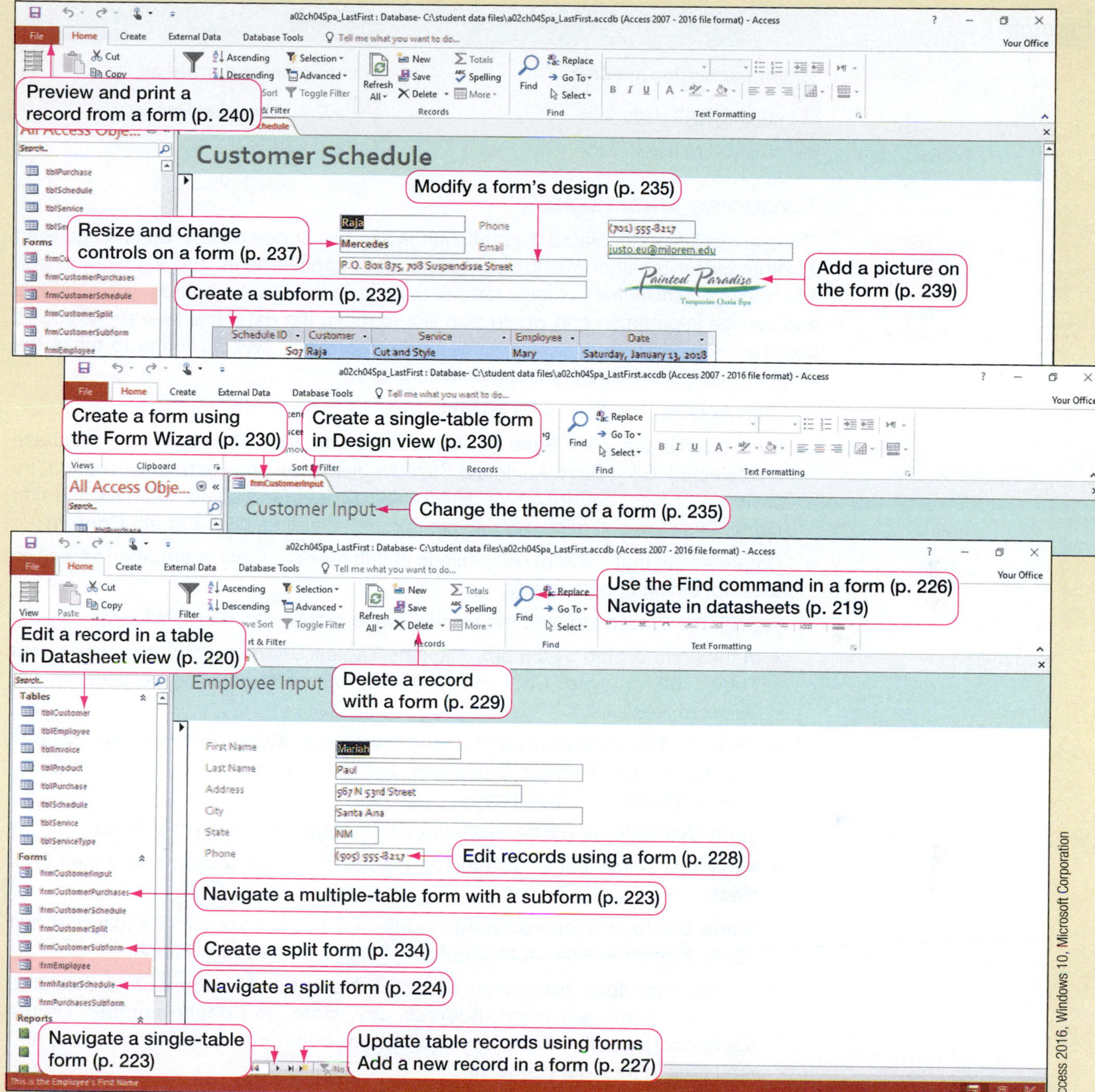
Preview and print a record from a form (p. 240)
Modify a form's design (p. 235)
Resize and change controls on a form (p. 237)
Add a picture on the form (p. 239)
Create a subform (p. 232)
Customer Schedule
Create a form using the Form Wizard (p. 230)
Create a single-table form in Design view (p. 230)
Customer Input
Change the theme of a form (p. 235)
Use the Find command in a form (p. 226)
Navigate in datasheets (p. 219)
Edit a record in a table in Datasheet view (p. 220)
Employee Input
Delete a record with a form (p. 229)
Edit records using a form (p. 228)
Navigate a multiple-table form with a subform (p. 223)
Create a split form (p. 234)
Navigate a split form (p. 224)
Navigate a single-table form (p. 223)
Update table records using forms
Add a new record in a form (p. 227)

Figure 32

Practice 1

Student data files needed:

 a02ch04Spa2.accdb

a02ch04Spa.thmx

You will save your file as:

 a02ch04Spa2_LastFirst.accdb

Turquoise Oasis Spa

Human Resources

The spa has just redecorated the staff lounge and has added bulletin boards and even a computer for the staff members to check their appointments and sign in and out. The manager would like to create reports to post on the bulletin boards with schedule and service information and would also like to make the database as easy to use as possible. You will help to create some of the reports as well as forms to make the database easy for data entry and maintenance.

a. Start **Access**, and then open **a02ch04Spa2**.

b. Click the **File** tab, click **Save As**. Verify Save Database As and Access Database are selected. Click **Save As**. In the Save As dialog box, navigate to where you are saving your files, and then type a02ch04Spa2_LastFirst using your last and first name. Click **Save**. If necessary, in the Security Warning, click **Enable Content**.

c. Create a form that will allow employees to edit their personal information as well as their upcoming appointments.

- Click the **Create** tab, and then in the Forms group, click **Form Wizard**.
- In the Form Wizard dialog box, click the **Tables/Queries** arrow, and then select **Table: tblEmployee**. Click the **All Fields** button to add all the fields to the Selected Fields list.
- Click the **Tables/Queries** arrow, and then select **Table: tblSchedule**. Double-click **Customer**, **Service**, **Employee**, and **DateOfAppt** to add the fields to the Selected Fields list. Click **Next**.
- Verify that the data will be viewed by tblEmployee, and then click **Next**.
- Verify that Datasheet is selected as the layout for the subform, and then click **Next**.
- Name the form frmEmployeeSchedule_iLast using your first initial and last name, name the subform frmSubform_iLast, and then click **Finish**.
- On the main form Navigation bar, click **New (blank) record**, and then add your first name, last name, address, city, state, and phone number. On the Navigation bar, click **First record** to return to the first record in the table, and then click in the **Last Name** field.
- On the Home tab, in the Records group, click the **Delete** arrow, and then click **Delete Record**. Click **Yes** when prompted to delete the record.
- Switch to **Layout** view. Double-click the **title**, select the **text**, and then type Employee Schedule.
- Click the **Last Name** text box control, and then drag the **right border** of the text box to line up with the right border of the First Name text box.
- Click the **subform label**, and then press Delete to delete the control. Click the **Subform**, and then using the layout selector, drag it to the left so it is right below the Phone label. Use AutoFit on all the columns to best fit the data.
- Click the **Employee** field heading in the subform datasheet, and then press Delete to delete the field. Click the **Date** heading in the subform datasheet, and then drag it to the left of the Customer field.

- On the Design tab, in the Themes group, click the **Themes** arrow, click **Browse for Themes**, browse to where you stored data files, click **a02ch04Spa**, and then click **Open**.
- Switch to Design view and, if prompted to save changes, click **Yes**. Click the **Design** tab, and in the Controls group, select **Label**, move your pointer to the **Form Footer**, and then draw a label control about 2.5 inches wide in the top left corner of the Form Footer section. In the new label control, type Created by initial Lastname using your first initial and last name.
- **Close** the form, and then click **Yes** when prompted to save the changes.

d. Create a report to show a list of customers and their purchases.

- Click the **Create** tab, and then in the Reports group, click **Report Wizard**. In the Report Wizard dialog box, click the **Tables/Queries** arrow, and then select **Table: tblCustomer**. Double-click **CustFirstName**, **CustLastName**, **CustState**, and **CustPhone** to add the fields to the Selected Fields list.
- Click the **Tables/Queries** arrow, and then select **Table: tblProduct**. Double-click **ProductDescription** to add the field to the Selected Fields list.
- Click the **Tables/Queries** arrow, and then select **Table: tblPurchase**. Double-click **PurchaseType**, **PurchaseDate**, and **Quantity** to add the fields to the Selected Fields list. Click **Next**.
- Verify that the data will be viewed by tblCustomer, and then click **Next**.
- Double-click **ProductDescription** to add it as a grouping level, and then click **Next**.
- Click the **1 Sort** arrow, click **PurchaseDate**, and then click **Next**. Select a **Stepped** layout and **Portrait** orientation, and then click **Next**.
- Name the report rptCustomerPurchases_iLast using your first initial and last name, and then click **Finish**.

e. Customize the report's appearance.

- Switch to **Layout** view.
- Click the **PurchaseDate** text box control, and then drag the **left border** to the left until the date is visible. Move the **Date** text box control to the left until it lines up under the First Name field.
- Click the **ProductDescription** text box control, and then drag the **right border** to the right until the whole field is visible.
- Click the **ProductDescription** label control, press and hold Shift, click the **PurchaseDate** label control, click the **PurchaseType** label control, and then press Delete to delete the controls.
- Click the **Phone** text box control, and then drag the **right border** so the whole field is visible.
- Double-click the **title**, select the **text**, and then type Customer Purchases.
- **Save** the report.

f. Add totals and subtotals.

- Click the Design tab, and in the Grouping & Totals group, click **Group & Sort** to open the Group, Sort, and Total pane. Click **Group on ProductDescription**, and then click **Delete** to delete the group.
- In the Group, Sort, and Total pane, click **Add a group**, and then select **PurchaseType**. Click the **PurchaseType** text box control — on the far right of report — and then drag it just below the customer's first name and just above the date.
- In the Group, Sort, and Total pane, click **Add a sort**, and then select **ProductDescription**. **Close** the Group, Sort, and Total pane.

- Click the **PurchaseType** text box. Click the **Format** tab, and in the Control Formatting group, click **Conditional Formatting**, and then click **New Rule**. In the second box, select **equal to**, and then in the third text box, type Online. Click the **Font color** arrow, and then under Standard Colors in the first row, select **Purple**. Click **OK** twice.
- With the PurchaseType text box control selected, click the **Design** tab. In the Grouping & Totals group, click **Totals**, and then select **Count Records**. Click the **PurchaseType** text box control, press and hold Shift, and then click the **subtotal** text box control. Click the **Format** tab, and in the Control Formatting group, click **Shape Outline**, and then select **Transparent**.
- Right-click the **Subtotal** text box control for Record Count, and then select **Set Caption**. Replace the text in the caption box with Orders.
- Scroll to the bottom of the report. Click the **Grand Total** text box control, and then move it under the product description. Right-click the **Grand Total** text box control, and then click **Set Caption**. Replace the text in the caption box with Total Orders.
- Switch to **Design** view. Click the **Design** tab, in the Controls group, select **Label**, move your pointer to the **Report Footer**, and then when your pointer changes, drag your pointer to draw a label control about 2.5 inches wide on the left side of the Report Footer. In the new label control, type Created by initial Lastname using your first initial and last name.

g. **Close** the report, and then click **Yes** when prompted to save the changes.

h. Close your database, exit Access, and submit your files as directed by your instructor.

Problem Solve 1

Student data file needed:

 a02ch04Baseball.accdb

You will save your files as:

 a02ch04Baseball_LastFirst.accdb

 a02ch04Baseball_LastFirst.pdf

Baseball Academy

Production & Operations

Matt Davis is a retired baseball player who runs the Baseball Academy, an indoor baseball facility for middle school, high school, and college players. He offers lessons as well as practice times for individuals and teams. Because of his growing clientele and increased record-keeping needs, Matt wants all his records in a database. Although he has already set up a database, he now needs to take the database to the next level of performance by improving his ability to get specific data out of the database. He has hired you to create the forms and reports he needs.

a. Open the Access database, **a02ch04Baseball**. Save the file as a02ch04Baseball_LastFirst using your last and first name. If necessary, enable the content.

b. Create a **split form** to show all the member information from **tblMember**.
   - Save the form as frmMemberInput.
   - Change the title of the form to be **Member Input**.
   - Apply the theme **Organic** to all objects in the database. (Hint: The themes are listed alphabetically.)
   - Add Created by initial Lastname to the Form Footer.
   - Use the form to add your information to the members table.
   - Save and close the form.

c. Use the Form Wizard to create a form that will display in the main form the member's **LastName**, **FirstName**, **Phone**, and **ScheduledDate** and **Fee** in the subform. Keep all other default options. Name the form frmMemberLessons, and name the subform frmSubformLessons.
   - Move the right borders of the Member fields so they are all the same width as FirstName.
   - Remove the subform label. Move the subform to line up with the Phone label.
   - AutoFit the columns in the subform so all the lesson information fits. Resize the subform to fit the columns.
   - Change the title of the form to Member Lessons.
   - Add Created by initial Lastname to the main form footer. Save and close the form.

d. Use the Report Wizard to create a schedule of lessons for an employee. Include employee **LastName**, **FirstName**, **ScheduledDate**, and member **LastName** and **FirstName**. Accept the default view, add a grouping by **ScheduledDate** with **Normal** grouping intervals, sort by member **LastName** and **FirstName**, use a format of **Stepped** and **Landscape**, and save the report as rptEmployeeSchedule.
   - Change the column headers for the member's name to be Member Last Name and Member First Name respectively.
   - **Bold** the employee **LastName** and **FirstName** text boxes.
   - Left align the ScheduledDate text box.
   - Add Created by initial Lastname to the report footer.
   - Change the title of the report to Employee Schedule. Save and close the report.

Critical Thinking

How would this report need to be changed to display the schedule by date instead of by employee? List any changes to the report that would need to be made without removing any existing fields from the report. Be sure to discuss both technical changes to the report and design changes. What business needs would be met with the schedule organized by employee? What business needs would be met with the schedule organized by date?

e. Use the Report Wizard to create a report to summarize lessons taught by each employee. Include employee **LastName**, **FirstName**, **ScheduledDate**, **Fee**, and member **FirstName** and **LastName**. Accept the view, add a grouping by **ScheduledDate** with **Normal** grouping intervals, sort by member **LastName** and **FirstName**, add Summary Options to **Average** the **Fee** field, use a format of **Stepped** and **Landscape**, and save the report as rptEmployeeLessons.
   - Fix the Fee column width so that all fees and averages show fully.
   - Move the **Avg caption** for each date to the right to line up with member's first name. Repeat for the **Avg caption** for employee. Change the captions to read Daily Average and Employee Average.
   - Change the column headers for the member's name to be Member Last Name and Member First Name respectively.
   - In Layout view, click on the field that starts **Summary for 'ScheduledDate'** and delete it.
   - In Layout view, click on the field that starts **Summary for 'EmployeeID'** and delete it.
   - Left-align the ScheduledDate text box, and resize the control to fit under the ScheduledDate label.
   - Select the **First Name** text label and text box controls, and move them to the left so that they are slightly indented under the report title.

- Move the text box controls and labels for the **ScheduledDate**, **Member Last Name**, **Member First Name**, **Fee**, **Daily Average**, and **Employee Average** to the left to minimize the extra space in the report.
- Apply conditional formatting to make any Employee Average greater than **175** display in bold and red.
- Add Created by initial Lastname to the report footer.
- Change the title of the report to Employee Lessons.
- Print the report as a PDF. Save the file as a02ch04Baseball_LastFirst.pdf using your last and first name.
- Save and close the report.

f. Close your database, exit Access, and submit your files as directed by your instructor.

Perform 1: Perform in Your Career

Student data files needed:

a02ch04Rentals.accdb

a02ch04Room.jpg

You will save your file as:

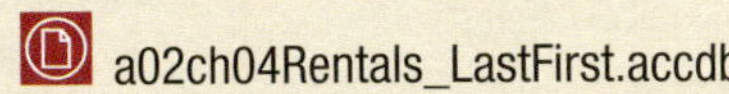

a02ch04Rentals_LastFirst.accdb

Student Housing Rentals

Production & Operations

You are working for a company that specializes in renting apartments and houses to students at your university. The manager is familiar with your Access skills and has asked you to create a series of forms and reports to improve her ability to add and analyze information in the database.

a. Open the Access database, **a02ch04Rentals**. Save the file as a02ch04Rentals_LastFirst using your last and first name. If necessary, enable the content.

b. Open the Relationships window to familiarize yourself with the tables, fields, and relationships in the database. Open **tblEmployees**, and add your name as a new record in the table.

c. Create a columnar form based on **tblProperties**. Use all the fields in the form, and name the form frmProperties_iLast using your first initial and last name.

d. Change the theme of frmProperties_iLast to **Slice**. Make the Slice Theme the default for the database.

e. Change the font color of all labels in the detail area of the form to **Light Turquoise, Background 2** (first row, third column) under Theme Colors.

f. Insert the house picture **a02ch04Room** on the right side of the form. Adjust the image size to fit between the PropertyID field and the PostalCode field. Change the title in the form to Properties. Add Created by initial Lastname, using your first initial and last name, to the form footer.

g. Create a form with a subform from **tblEmployees**. Use **tblProperties** for the subform data. Name the form frmAgents_iLast, and name the subform frmAgentSubform_iLast, using your first initial and last name.

h. Change the title in the form Header to Our Agents.

i. Remove the **frmAgentsSubform** label. Align the left border of the subform to the Phone label. Use AutoFit to adjust the column width of the subform fields. Adjust the right border of the subform so that the PostalCode field can been seen without scrolling to the right. Add Created by initial Lastname, using your first initial and last name, to the form footer.

CHAPTER 4

j. Create a report from **qryNotRented** showing the **City**, **Property Name**, **Address**, **Pool**, **Playground**, **BikeTrail**, **DogPark**, and **MonthlyRental** fields. Name the report rptNotRented_iLast.
k. Change the title of the report to Available Rentals By City. Group the data by the City.
l. Change the text of the MonthlyRental label to Rent.
m. Display the Count of the Property Name field by City for all cities displayed in the report.
n. Change the caption for the property count by city to Available and the caption for all properties in the report to Total Available.
o. Create a conditional format that adds an Aqua Blue fill color (first row, ninth column) to Available values greater than 1.
p. Modify the spaces between column labels and move or resize the columns to fit the report to a single page width. Ensure that no values are cut off. Add Created by initial Lastname, using your first initial and last name, to the report footer.
q. Close your database, exit Access, and submit your file as directed by your instructor.

Additional Cases

Additional Chapter Cases are available at www.pearsonhighered.com/youroffice

Access Business Unit 2 CAPSTONE

Accessing, Maintaining, and Presenting Information

This business unit had two outcomes:

Learning Outcome 1:

Find data in a database by searching tables and designing queries that sort, aggregate, and calculate complex search results.

Learning Outcome 2:

Navigate and update information in a database using forms and present information in a database by creating customized reports.

In Business Unit 2 Capstone, students will demonstrate competence in these outcomes through a series of business problems at various levels from guided practice, problem solving an existing database, and performing to create new databases.

More Practice 1

Student data files needed:

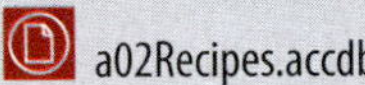

a02Recipes.accdb

a02Indigo5.jpg

You will save your files as:

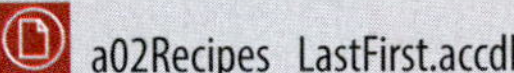

a02Recipes_LastFirst.accdb

a02Recipes_LastFirst.pdf

Indigo5 Restaurant

Production & Operations

Robin Sanchez, the chef of the Painted Paradise Resort's restaurant, Indigo5, has started a database to keep track of the recipes and ingredients that the restaurant includes. Right now, no forms, queries, or reports have been created for this database, so the information available is very limited. You will help to create some queries as well as forms for data entry and reports for the daily management of the food preparation.

a. Start **Access**, click **Open Other Files** in the left pane, and then double-click **This PC**. Navigate through the folder structure to the location of your student data files, and then double-click **a02Recipes**. A database opens displaying tables related to the spa.

b. Click the **File** tab, save the file as an **Access Database**, and click **Save As**. Navigate to the location where you are saving your project files and then change the file name to a02Recipes_LastFirst using your last and first name. Click **Save**. If necessary, in the Security Warning, click **Enable Content**.

c. Click the **Create** tab, and then in the Forms group, click **Form Wizard**. Add all of the fields from **Table: tblRecipes**. From **Table: tblRecipeIngredients**, add **IngredientID**, **Quantity**, and **Measurement**. View the form **by tblRecipes**, and then show the subform as a **Datasheet**. Save the form as frmRecipe_iLast, using your first initial and last name, and save the subform as frmRecipeSubform_iILast using your first initial and last name. Switch to **Design** view. On the Design tab, in the Controls group, click **Label**, and then add a label about 2.5 inches wide in the top left corner of the form footer that says Created by initial Lastname using your first initial and last name.

d. Switch to **Layout** view. Click the **Design** tab, and in the Themes group, click **Themes**. Click the **Ion Boardroom** theme to apply it to all objects in the database.

e. Click the **Design** tab, and in the Themes group, click Fonts, and then click **Office** to apply it to all objects.

f. Double-click the title of the form, and change it to Recipe Details. Click the **Format** tab, and in the Font group, change the title font size to **28**, and then apply **Bold**.

g. Delete the subform label, and then move the subform to the left under the Instructions label. AutoFit the subform fields **Quantity** and **Measurement** to size them appropriately. Move the **right** border of the subform to the left to fit the subform columns.

h. Click in the form body. On the Design tab, in the Controls group, click **Insert Image**. Click **Browse**, navigate to your student data files, and then locate **a02Indigo5**. Insert the image to the right of the Recipe information. Resize the image as necessary to fit above the Instructions text box.

i. Switch to **Form** view. Click the **Recipe Name** text box. Click the **Home** tab, and in the Find group, click **Find**, and then in the Find What box, type Pasta Napolitana, and then click **Find Next**. Click **Cancel**. Change the Quantity for the IngredientID Honey to 1.

j. Click the **New (blank) record** button on the main form Navigation bar, and then enter the following data. Use the field arrows for the Food Category ID and Subcategory fields.

Recipe Name	Food Category ID	Subcategory	Prep Time (minutes)	Servings	Instructions
Avocado Salsa	Appetizer	Vegetarian	10	6	Peel and mash avocados. Add cayenne pepper, salt, chopped onion, and chopped toma-to. Add lime juice and mix well. Refrigerate for at least 4 hours.

Enter the following data into the subform:

IngredientID	Quantity	Measurement
Avocado	2	whole
Tomato	1	cup
Cayenne pepper	.5	teaspoon
Salt	.5	teaspoon
Onions	1	cup
Lime juice	3	tablespoons

Save and close the form.

k. Create a query to show recipes that use the ingredients cumin or paprika. Click the **Create** tab, and in the Queries group, click **Query Design**, and then add **tblRecipes**, **tblRecipe-Ingredients**, and **tblIngredients**. Include **RecipeName**, **Ingredient**, and **Quantity** in the results. In the **Ingredient Criteria**, type cumin or paprika. Sort in **Ascending** order by Quantity. Run the query, and then use AutoFit on the query columns. Save your query as qryCuminOrPaprika_iLast, using your first initial and last name. Close the query.

l. Create a query to show all ingredients not used in any recipe. Click the **Create** tab, and then in the Queries group, click Query Wizard, click **Find Unmatched Query Wizard**, and then click **OK**. Click **Table: tblIngredients**, and then click **Next**. Click **tblRecipe-Ingredients**, and then click **Next**. IngredientID will be the common field between the tables. Click **Next**, and then include all the available fields. Click **Next**. Save the query as qryUnusedIngredients_iLast, using your first initial and last name. Click **Finish**. Switch to **Design** view, and sort IngredientID in **Ascending** order. Save and close the query.

m. Create a query to show all recipes that take less than 30 minutes to prepare and are listed with the category of soup or pizza. Click the **Create** tab, and in the Queries group, click **Query Design**, and then add **tblRecipes** and **tblFoodCategories**. Include **RecipeName**, **TimeToPrepare**, and **FoodCategory** in the results. Add the criterion <30 to the TimeToPrepare field to find all recipes that take less than 30 minutes to prepare. Add the criterion soup or pizza to the FoodCategory field. Sort TimeToPrepare in **Ascending** order. **Run** the query. Use AutoFit on each column. Save the query as qryTimeAndCategory_iLast, using your first initial and last name, and then close the query.

n. Create a query to show all recipes that include tomatoes or garlic in their ingredients. Click the **Create** tab, and in the Queries group, click **Query Design**, and then add **tblRecipes**, **tblRecipeIngredients**, and **tblIngredients**. Include **RecipeName**, **Ingredient**, **Quantity**, **Measurement**, and **RecipeID** from tblRecipeIngredients in the results, in that order. Add the criterion tomato or garlic to the Ingredient field. Sort RecipeID in **Ascending** order. **Run** the query. Use AutoFit on each column. Save the query as qryRecipeIngredients_iLast, using your first initial and last name, and then close the query.

o. Create a report that lists all recipes, their instructions, and a list of ingredients. Click the **Create** tab, and in the Reports group, click **Report Wizard**, and then from Table: tblRecipes, add the fields **RecipeName**, **Instructions**, **TimeToPrepare**, and **Servings**. From Query: qryRecipeIngredients_iLast, add the fields **Ingredient**, **Quantity**, and **Measurement** in that order. View your report **by tblRecipes**. Group by **RecipeName**. Sort in **Ascending** order by Ingredient. Accept all other default settings, and then name the report rptRecipes_iLast using your first initial and last name.

- Switch to **Layout** view, and then move the **Ingredient**, **Quantity**, and **Measurement** text boxes to the left under the Instructions field. Delete the **Ingredient**, **Quantity**, and **Measurement** labels. Move the **Servings text box** and **label** to the right. Make the **Prep Time (minutes)** and **Servings** labels wider so the text is visible. Double-click the report **title**, and then change it to Recipes.
- Click the **RecipeName** text box. Click the **Format** tab, and in the Font group, click **Bold**. Move the right border for the **RecipeName** text box to make it wide enough to fit all the text for every record. Scroll down to **Gambas al Ajillo (Shrimp with Garlic)** to make sure the field is wide enough.
- Click the **Quantity** text box, and then move the **left** border to the right to make the field narrower. Click the **Ingredient** text box, and then move the right border to the right to make the field completely visible. Scroll down to see **Garlic** make sure the field is wide enough.
- Click the **Prep Time** text box, and then in the Control Formatting group, click **Conditional Formatting**. Click **New Rule**, select **greater than** in the second box, and then type 15 in the third box. Click **Bold**, change the font color to **Red**, and then click **OK**. Click **OK** again.
- Switch to **Design** view. Click the **Design** tab, and in the Controls group, click **Label**, and then add a label saying Created by initial Lastname, using your first initial and last name, to the Report Footer.
- Save the report, switch to **Report** view to check your report, and then close the report.
- Right-click **rptRecipes_iLast**. Select **Export**, and then select **PDF or XPS**. Navigate to the folder where you are saving your files, and type a02Recipes_LastFirst using your last and first name. In the Open file after publishing box, **clear** the check box, click **Publish**, and then click **Close**.

p. Create a report that lists all ingredients and which recipes they are used in. Click the **Create** tab, and in the Reports group, click **Report Wizard**, and then from **Table:**

tblRecipeIngredients, add the fields **IngredientID**, **Quantity**, and **Measurement**. From **Table: tblRecipes**, add **RecipeName**. Click **Next**, check to make sure you view your data **by tblRecipeIngredients**, click **Next**, and then double-click **RecipeName** to add grouping. Accept all other default options, and then name your report rptIngredientCount_iLast using your first initial and last name.

- Switch to **Design** view. On the Design tab, in the Controls group, click **Label**, and then add a label saying Created by initial Lastname, using your first initial and last name, to the Report Footer.
- Switch to **Layout** view. Click the **Design** tab, and in the Grouping & Totals group, click **Group & Sort**, and then delete the grouping by RecipeName. Click **Add a group**, and then group by **IngredientID**. Move the **IngredientID** text box to the left margin, under the RecipeName label. Click the **Format** tab, and in the Font group, click **Align Left**. Delete the **RecipeName**, **IngredientID**, **Quantity**, and **Measurement** labels.
- Change the title to Ingredient List. Click the **IngredientID** text box, click **Shape Outline**, and then click **Transparent**. Click **Shape Fill**, and then under Theme Colors, click **Dark Purple, Text 2, Lighter 60%**.
- Click the **Quantity** text box. Click the **Design** tab, and in the Grouping & Totals group, click **Totals**, and then click **Sum** to add subtotals. Right-click the **subtotal** text box, select **Set Caption**, and then change the text to Total. Click the **subtotal** text box, and then click the **Format** tab.
- In the Font group, click **Align Right** to change the alignment. Scroll down to the bottom of the report to find the grand total text box (value 84.5), click the text box, and then press **Delete**. Make the **RecipeName** text box wide enough to fit all the text for every record, and scroll to find **Gambas al Ajillo (Shrimp with Garlic)** to check the width.
- Close the Group, Sort, and Total pane. Close the report, and then save your changes.

q. Close the database, exit Access, and then submit your file as directed by your instructor.

Problem Solve 1

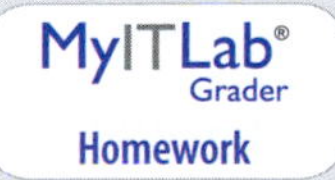

Student data files needed:

 a02Hotel.accdb

 a02Paradise.jpg

 a02PaintedParadise.thmx

You will save your file as:

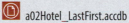

 a02Hotel_LastFirst.accdb

Hotel Reservations

Production & Operations

Painted Paradise Resort & Spa has started a database to keep track of its hotel reservations with guest information, reservation information, and additional room charge information. Because no reports, forms, or queries have been built yet, the hotel staff finds that the database is not easy to use. You will create reports, forms, and queries to help the staff better manage the data in the database. Complete the following tasks.

a. Open the Access file, **a02Hotel**. Save your file as a02Hotel_LastFirst using your last and first name. If necessary, enable the content.

b. Open **tblGuests**, and add a new record with your Last Name, First Name, Address, City, State, ZipCode, and Phone. Close the table.

c. Use the Form Wizard to create a form that will allow the staff to enter Room Charges for each guest during their stay. Include the **GuestLastName**, **GuestFirstName**, **City**, **State**, **ChargeCategory**, and **ChargeAmount**. View the data by **tblGuests**. The subform should be in **Datasheet** layout. Accept all other default options, name the form frmGuestRoomCharges, and name the subform frmGuestSubform.

- Add Created by initial Lastname, using your first initial and last name, to the form footer.
- Delete the subform label. Move the **subform** to the left to line up with State. Resize the subform to fit the columns.
- Apply the theme **a02PaintedParadise** to all objects in your database.
- Insert the image **a02Paradise** to the right of the guest fields, resizing as necessary.
- Resize the **First Name** text field to line up with Last Name.
- Change the **title** to Guest Room Charges, and change the font size of the title to **28** and **bold**. Save and close the form.

d. Create a query to find the number of times (count) a room type has been reserved and the average room rate for the room type. Use **RoomType** and **RoomRate** from tblReservations to perform the aggregate query. Sort the query in **Ascending** order by average **RoomRate**.

- Change the field names to Number of Reservations and Average Room Rate.
- AutoFit the **column widths**.
- Add a total line to the query datasheet results. Show the Total Number of Reservations overall.
- Change the alternating row colors to **Rose, Background 2, Darker 10%**.
- Save the query as qryRoomStatistics.

e. Create a query to find guests who have reservations but do not have any room charges. Include all available fields in the results. Sort the query in ascending order by **CheckInDate**. Save the query as qryGuestsWithoutRoomCharges.

f. Create a query to find guests with multiple room charges. Include **GuestID**, **RoomChargeID**, **ReservationID**, **ChargeCategory**, and **ChargeAmount** from tblRoomCharges. Sort the query in ascending order by **ReservationID**. AutoFit the columns. Save the query as qryMultipleRoomCharges.

Critical Thinking

Consider another version of this query. How could this query be altered to display the total number of room charges and the total amount of these charges for each guest with multiple room charges? Which guest has the most room charges? Which guest has spent the highest total amount on room charges?

g. Create a query to find all guests who have reservations in **2018** and who are staying **two or more nights**. Include **GuestFirstName** and **GuestLastName** from tblGuests, and include **CheckInDate**, **NightsStay**, and **NumberOfGuests** from tblReservations. Sort in ascending order by **CheckInDate**. Save the query as qry2018And2.

h. Create a query to find all guests who have reservations in **2017** with **more than three guests** or all guests who are staying **three or more nights** regardless of their check-in date. Include **GuestFirstName** and **GuestLastName** from tblGuests, and include **CheckInDate**, **NightsStay**, and **NumberOfGuests** from tblReservations. Sort in ascending order by **GuestLastName**. Save the query as qryGuestRelations.

i. Create a query to find all guests who are checking in sometime in **April 2018** and who are staying **between two and four nights**. Include **GuestFirstName** and **GuestLastName** from tblGuests, and include **CheckInDate**, and **NightsStay** from tblReservations. Sort in ascending order by **CheckInDate**, but do not show CheckInDate. Save the query as qryAprilReservations.

j. Use the Report Wizard to create a report for all guests with their reservation information. Include **GuestFirstName**, **GuestLastName**, **CheckInDate**, **NightsStay**, **NumberOfGuests**, **RoomType**, and **RoomRate**. View the data by **tblReservation**. Group the report by **CheckInDate** with normal date grouping options. Sort in ascending order by **GuestLastName** and then by **GuestFirstName**. Add an average of **NightsStay**. Change to **Landscape** orientation, accept all other default options, and name the report rptGuestReservations.
   - Change the report title to Guest Reservations.
   - Add Created by initial Lastname, using your first initial and last name, to the report footer.
   - Delete the line that begins **Summary for 'CheckInDate'**.
   - Move or resize all necessary fields so all the text is visible.
   - Move the caption **Avg** to line up with FirstName. Change the caption to **Average Nights Stay**.
   - Change the border of the RoomType text box control to **Transparent**.
   - Add conditional formatting so that any **NightsStay** that is more than two nights displays in **Dark Red** and **Bold**. Close the form.

k. Close the database, exit Access, and then submit your file as directed by your instructor.

Problem Solve 2

Student data files needed:

 a02Hotel2.accdb

 a02Paradise2.jpg

You will save your files as:

 a02Hotel_LastFirst.accdb

 a02Room_LastFirst.pdf

Additional Hotel Reservations

Production & Operations

The hotel has asked you to further customize their database. The hotel manager is interested in learning more about how often guests stay and how much they spend on reservations. She is also interested in extracting data from the database about the room types in the hotel. You will create reports, forms, and queries to help the staff better manage the data in the database.

a. Open the Access file, **a02Hotel**. Save your file as a02Hotel_LastFirst using your last and first name. If necessary, enable the content.

b. Open **tblGuests**, and add a new record with your Last Name, First Name, Address, City, State, ZipCode, and Phone. Close the table.

c. Create a query to see which guests had reservations between November 1, 2017, and January 31, 2018, that included either a crib or handicapped accommodations. Show **GuestLastName** and **GuestFirstName** from tblGuests, and show **CheckInDate**, **Crib**, and **Handicapped** from tblReservations. Sort by **CheckInDate**. Name the query qryCribReservations.

d. Create a query to calculate the total room charges per guest. Use the **GuestID** from tblGuests and the **ChargeAmount** from tblRoomCharges. Rename the total field **RoomCharges**. Sort in **Descending** order by **RoomCharges**. AutoFit the **RoomCharges** field. Save the query as qryTotalRoomCharges.

e. Create a query to calculate the total amount due for each guest, including room rate and room charges. Include **GuestLastName** and **GuestFirstName** from tblGuests, include **NightsStay** and **RoomRate** from tblReservations, and include **RoomCharges** from qryTotalRoomCharges. Save the query as qryTotalDue.

- Add a new calculated field to the query to calculate each guest's total amount due based on the room rate, the number of nights they stayed, and room charges. Name the new field **TotalDue**. Sort the query by **GuestLastName** and then by **GuestFirstName** in **Ascending** order. Save the changes, and close the query.

f. Use the Report Wizard to create a report showing the **TotalDue** for each guest. Include all the fields from qryTotalDue. Do not add a grouping level. Sort by TotalDue in **Descending** order. Accept all other default options, and name the report rptTotalDue.
   - Add Created by initial Lastname, using your first initial and last name, to the report footer. Change the title to Guest Total Charges. Add conditional formatting in **Dark Red** and **Bold** for all NightsStay between three and five nights. Adjust all the label sizes to see the headings. Save and close the report.

g. Use the Report Wizard to create a report with data from **tblRoomtypes** and **tblReservations** with the **RoomDescription**, **RoomRate**, **DiscountType**, **NightsStay**, and **CheckInDate**. View the data by **tblRoomTypes**, do not add any other grouping, and sort by CheckInDate in **Ascending** order. Accept all other default options, and name the report rptRoomTypes.
   - Add Created by initial Lastname, using your first initial and last name, to the report footer. Change the title to Room Types. Remove the outline around the **DiscountType** text box.
   - Calculate the number of reservations for each RoomRate. Add a caption, and type Number of reservations. Resize the calculated field so the caption is visible. Add the fill color **Blue, Accent 1, Lighter 60%** to the caption.
   - Calculate the average nights' stay for each **RoomDescription**. Add a caption, and type Average Nights Stay. Add the fill color **Blue, Accent 1, Lighter 60%** to the caption.
   - Remove the sort on **CheckInDate**. Add a new sort by **RoomDescription**, and move it above the **Group on RoomID**. Resize the width of all the labels so all text is visible. Save and close the report.

h. Publish the report as a PDF file. Save the file as a02Room_LastFirst using your last and first name.

i. Use the Form Wizard to create a form to enter room charges along with the charge details. Include **RoomChargeID**, **GuestID**, **ChargeCategory**, **ChargeAmount**, and **Purchase**. View the form by **tblRoomCharges**, and view the subform in a tabular layout. Accept all other default options, name the form frmRoomCharges, and name the subform frmRoomSubform.
   - Add Created by initial Lastname, using your first initial and last name, to the form footer. Change the title to Room Charges. Insert the image **a02Paradise2** to the right of the main form detail, with the top border of the image lined up with the top border of the GuestID text box and the bottom border of the image lined up with the bottom border of the Amount text box.
   - Delete the **frmRoom** label, and move the subform to the left so it aligns with the Amount label.
   - Save and close the form.

j. Close the database, exit Access, and then submit your file as directed by your instructor.

Perform 1: Perform in Your Life

Student data file needed:

 Blank Access database

You will save your file as:

 a02Schedule_LastFirst.accdb

Class Schedule

Information Technology

One way to stay organized during the semester is to keep track of your schedule. You will create a database of all your classes and grades. The database should track the class information, your personal schedule, and the location of the class. To be able to use this for more than one semester, you will keep each of the data in separate tables.

Once the tables have been created, you will set up forms to make data entry easier, run queries to get more information, and create reports to help you manage your schedule. For each report, query, or form, make the object attractive and meaningful.

a. Start **Access**, and then click the **Blank desktop database**. Save the database as a02Schedule_LastFirst using your last and first name.

b. To keep track of class information, design a table that includes fields for at least the class number, class description, credits offered, and professor's name. Assign an appropriate primary key, and then save the table as tblClasses.

c. Add the class information for your classes from last semester, or use fictitious classes if necessary. Add at least six classes to the table. AutoFit the columns so all text is visible.

d. To keep track of your class locations, design a table that includes fields for the building number, building name, and campus the building is located on. Assign an appropriate primary key, and then save the table as tblBuilding.

e. Add the location of the classes you entered in step c. Include at least three different locations. Use AutoFit on the columns so all text is visible.

f. To keep track of your schedule, design a table that includes fields for the class number, semester, meeting days, meeting time, location, midterm grade (as a number), and final grade (as a number). Use AutoFit on the columns so all text is visible. Assign an appropriate primary key, and then save the table as tblSchedule.

g. Enter last semester's schedule, or a fictitious one, that includes at least six classes in at least three different locations. The classes and locations should be the ones entered in tblClasses and tblBuildings.

h. Create relationships as appropriate for tblSchedule, tblClasses, and tblBuilding.

i. You would like to be able to enter all your class and schedule information at one time. Create one form that will allow you to enter all the information. Save the form as frmSchedule_iLast, using your first initial and last name.

j. Use the form to enter a new record for this semester. You should enter all the information except grades. Add a new theme to the form, change the title to something more meaningful than the form name, and add Created by initial Lastname, using your first initial and last name, to the form footer. Save and close the form.

k. You would like to see each class individually as well as all the class records at once. Create a form that will show you this view of the data. Change the form title to something meaningful. Save the form as frmClasses_iLast, using your first initial and last name.

l. You want to find out what your average midterm grade and average final grade were each semester. Even though grades are entered for only one semester, create a query to perform this calculation.

- Rename the fields to something more meaningful, and then format the fields to show only two decimal places. Sort the query by Semester in **Descending** order. Save the query as qryAverageGrades_iLast, using your first initial and last name.

m. You want a schedule of last semester's classes only. Create a query that will show you last semester's classes, the instructor for each class, and where and when each class occurred. Save the query as qrySchedule_iLast, using your first initial and last name.

n. Create a report that will show you last semester's schedule organized by each day. Sort it in order of class time.

- Make sure all the fields print on one page of the report and that all the fields are visible. Add Created by initial Lastname, using your first initial and last name, to the report footer. Save the report as rptSchedule_iLast using your initial and last name.

o. You want to know how to schedule your weekends. Create a query to see whether you have classes after 9 A.M. on Friday. When entering your criteria for this query, use the time as formatted in the tblSchedule table. Save the query as qryFridayClasses_iLast using your initial and last name.

p. You also want to know the average of your midterm and final grades for your classes. Create a query to calculate the average grade in each class. Sort the query by an appropriate field. Save the query as qryGrades_iLast using your initial and last name.

q. You want to print a report to show your parents your grades by class for the semester, including the average grade. Create a report that shows the class number, description, credits, midterm grade, final grade, and average grade for each class. Sort by an appropriate field. Resize all labels so all the text is visible. Change the title to something more appropriate. Save the report as rptGrades_iLast using your initial and last name.

- Add Created by initial Lastname, using your initial and last name, to the report footer. Use Conditional Formatting to display all average grades over 90 in red and bold. Save and close the report.

r. Close the database, exit Access, and then submit your file as directed by your instructor.

Perform 2: Perform in Your Career

Student data file needed:

 a02Fitness.accdb

You will save your file as:

 a02Fitness_LastFirst.accdb

Fitness Center

Production & Operations

A new fitness center has opened and is developing a database for keeping track of members. So far the fitness center has two tables, for Membership information and Member information, and another table with Roster Information. No queries, forms, or reports have been created, so the center has asked you to help answer some questions with queries, make data entry easier with forms, and print some reports for reference. For each report, query, or form, make the object attractive and meaningful.

a. Start **Access**, and open the student data file **a02Fitness**. Save the database as a02Fitness_LastFirst using your last and first name.

b. Open each table, and then familiarize yourself with the fields. Open the **Relationships** window, and then note how the tables are related.

c. The staff wants to be able to enter all new member and roster information in the database at one time. Create a form that will allow them to enter the member records and the related membership records for a new member. Give the form a meaningful name. Add Created by initial Lastname, using your initial and last name, to the form footer. Save the form as frmMemberInput_iLast using your initial and last name.

d. Using frmMemberInput, enter yourself as a member. Use your actual name and address; all other information can be fictitious. Join the club today, and have your membership end a year from now.

e. The staff wants to know how old each member is (in whole numbers) as of the date the person joined the club. This will help the staff to plan age-appropriate activities. Create a query to calculate the age of each member as of the date the person joined the club. (Hint: When you subtract one date from the other, you get a total number of days, not years.) Sort the query by an appropriate field. Save the query as **qryMemberAge_iLast** using your initial and last name.

f. The manager wants to know which membership types are creating the most revenue and which types are the most popular. Create a query to calculate the total number of each membership type and the total fees collected for each membership type. Format the query so the manager will understand exactly what each field represents. Save the query as **qryMembershipStatistics_iLast** using your initial and last name.

g. The manager would like to know whether any membership types have not been applied for. Find any membership types that are not assigned to a current member. Include all fields from tblMemberships in the query. Save the query as **qryMembershipTypesUnused_iLast** using your initial and last name.

h. The staff likes to celebrate birthdays at the club. Assume that the current year is 2017. Everyone born in 1977 will turn 40 this year, and the staff would like a list of all those members along with their actual birthdays so the staff can quickly see who is celebrating a birthday each day. Sort the query by an appropriate field. Save the query as **qry1977Birthdays_iLast** using your initial and last name.

i. The staff likes to see each member's data as an individual record while still being able to view the whole table of data. Create a form that will allow the staff to view the data this way. Add **Created by initial Lastname**, using your initial and last name, to the form footer. Give the form a meaningful name. Save the form as **frmMemberRecords_iLast** using your initial and last name.

j. The staff needs a master list of members with their membership information. Create a report that will show member names, date joined, expiration date, and membership type so the staff knows who is a current member and what kind of membership each person has. Save the report as **rptExpirationDates_iLast** using your initial and last name.

- Add **Created by initial Lastname**, using your first initial and last name, to the report footer. Change the report title to something meaningful.
- Modify rptExpirationDates_iLast so the records are grouped by the month of the expiration date. Conditionally format the expiration date field with bold and colored font so it stands out from the other fields.

k. The staff needs a list of members with the facilities their membership type gives them access to. Create a report so the staff can quickly locate a member's name and determine which facilities the member is allowed to access. Save the report as **rptFacilities_iLast** using your initial and last name.

- Add **Created by initial Lastname**, using your initial and last name, to the report footer.
- Change the report theme, change the report title to something other than the name of the report, and save the report.

l. Close the database, exit Access, and then submit your file as directed by your instructor.

Perform 3: Perform in Your Team

Student data file needed:

 a02Cars.accdb

You will save your file as:

 a02Cars_TeamName.accdb

River Bluff Car Dealership

Production & Operations

You work as an office manager for River Bluff Car Dealership, a prosperous car dealership near a metropolitan area on the banks of a river. The car dealership operates from two locations: a main location downtown and a second location on the edge of the city on the sunny side of a river bluff. You work as the office manager at the second location, while another office manager works for the main downtown location. Your supervisor has asked you to work with the other office manager to build a database of the existing used and new vehicles in stock at both locations. This database will make it easier for the sales personnel to suggest vehicles for purchase by customers at either location. Within an existing database file, a table and form of vehicles for each location have already been created with vehicle data entered, including makes, models, year, transmission category, selling price, interior/exterior features, color, and mileage. Your supervisor has asked you to work closely with the other office manager to complete a set of queries and reports for an upcoming meeting for River Bluff's sales staff.

a. Select one office manager to set up the document by completing steps b through d.

b. Open your browser, and navigate to https://www.onedrive.live.com, https://www.drive.google.com or any other instructor-assigned location. Be sure both members of the office manager team have an account on the chosen system, such as a Microsoft or Google account.

c. Open **a02Cars**, and then save the database as a02Cars_TeamName, replacing TeamName with the name assigned to your team by your instructor.

d. Share the database with the other office manager on your team. Make sure each member has the appropriate permission to edit the document.

e. Hold an office manager team meeting to discuss the requirements of the remaining steps. Make an action plan to assign individual and team work, as well as deadlines for each step.

f. Create a query qryBluffside5%DiscountSale_TeamName, using your team name, that calculates the Sales Discount amount and Total Sales Price after discount for each make and model of vehicle in stock at the Bluffside location.
   - Show the fields **Make**, **Model**, and **Price**.
   - Add a new calculated field SaleDiscount that multiplies the **Price** by 5%.
   - Add another new calculated field TotalSalesPrice that subtracts the **SaleDiscount** from the **Price**.
   - Format both calculated fields to display in Currency format in Datasheet view.
   - Run the query results.
   - Add a Total row, and use the SUM aggregate function to find the totals for **Price**, **SaleDiscount**, and **TotalSalesPrice**.
   - Adjust the column width of each field as necessary to display all information.
   - Close and save the query.

g. Create a query qryDowntown6CylinderVehicles_TeamName, using your team name, that finds vehicles in the downtown location that operate on six cylinders.
   - Show the fields **Make**, **Model**, and **Price**.
   - Use the **Cylinder** field for a criterion, but do not show it in the query results.
   - Sort in ascending order by **Make**, then **Model**, then **Price**.
   - Run the query results.

- Adjust the column widths of each field as necessary to display all information.
- Close and save the query.

h. Create a query qryBluffsideUsedCarsunder$15,000_TeamName, using your team name, that finds used vehicles under $15,000 at the Bluffside location only.
- Show the fields **Make**, **Model**, **Used/New**, **Color**, and **Price**.
- Use the appropriate criterion to display used vehicles under $15,000.
- Sort in ascending order by **Price**.
- Run the query results.
- Adjust the column widths of each field as necessary to display all information.
- Close and save the query.

i. Create a query qryDowntownUsedCarsover50,000Miles_TeamName, using your team name, that finds used vehicles with mileage over 50,000 at the downtown location only.
- Show the fields **Make**, **Model**, **Price**, and **Mileage**.
- Use the appropriate criterion to display used vehicles with over 50,000 miles.
- Sort in ascending order by **Mileage**.
- Run the query results.
- Adjust the column widths of each field as necessary to display all information.
- Close and save the query.

j. Create a query qryDowntownPrices_TeamName, using your team name, that finds the overall average, minimum, and maximum prices of vehicles at the downtown location only.
- Use the **Price** field to find the Average Price, Minimum Price, and Maximum Price.
- Run the query results.
- Adjust the column widths of each field as necessary to display all information.
- Close and save the query.

k. Using the Report Wizard, create a report rptBluffside5%DiscountSale_TeamName, using your team name, based on the **qryBluffside5%DiscountSales** query.
- Show all fields **Make**, **Model**, **Price**, **SaleDiscount**, and **TotalSalePrice**.
- Group by **Make**, then by **Model**, then by **TotalSalesPrice**.
- Select an appropriate layout for the report.
- Use the report title Bluffside 5% Discount Sale.
- Adjust the column widths to display on one page in portrait orientation. This will ensure there are no blank pages in the report.
- Close and save the report.

l. Using the Report Wizard, create a report rptDowntownVehicleInventory_TeamName, using your team name, based on the **tblDowntownVehicleInventory** table.
- Show the fields **Make**, **Model**, **Year**, **Price**, and **Used/New**.
- Group by **Used/New**, then by **Year**.
- Sort by **Price**.
- Select an appropriate layout for the report.
- Use the report title Downtown Inventory.
- Adjust the column widths to display on one page in portrait orientation. This will ensure there are no blank pages in the report.
- Adjust alignment of field names as necessary to improve readability and format.
- Close and save the report.

m. Close the database, exit Access, and then submit your file as directed by your instructor.

Perform 4: How Others Perform

Student data file needed:

 a02SummerCamp.accdb

You will save your file as:

 a02Answers_LastFirst.docx

Summer Camp

Production & Operations

You live in the Midwest and volunteer as kitchen help for Kidz Kamp in June, July, and August of each year. At the start of this summer, the head chef had another volunteer complete a database of meal recipes and main ingredients. Specifically, she requested a set of queries and reports that would provide her with information to plan meals for the week-long summer camps. As you began using the database, you noticed that the queries and reports appeared to be either missing data or presenting incorrect results. Answer the following questions about each of the objects as completely as possible.

a. Start **Access**, and then open **a02SummerCamp**.

b. Create a Word document a02Answers_LastFirst, using your last and first name, where you will answer the questions.

c. Open the form **frmRecipes**. This form was created by using the table **tblRecipes**. The form was supposed to display the fields Recipe Card Number, Recipe Name, Total Prep Time, and Total Cook Time and show one recipe (record) at a time in the window. Why is the form showing the first recipe in the top half of the form and then all recipes at the bottom of the form? How was this form created? How should the form have been created to display only a single recipe at a time?

d. The query qryBreakfast was created to find all breakfast food records in which the food category is "Vegetable". Why are records with meal categories other than breakfast listed? Switch to **Design** view, and explain how you would correct the query.

e. The query qryEarlyJune was created to find all recipes that were last used in the first two weeks of June (from June 1 until June 14). Why is the query returning all results from June? Switch to **Design** view, and explain how you would correct the query.

f. The report rptMainIngredients was created from the table tblIngredients. The chef has requested that the report be modified to be grouped by Food Category in alphabetical order. How could this be accomplished? How would the appearance of the report need to be altered to reflect this change?

g. Close the database, exit Access, and then submit your file as directed by your instructor.

Access Business Unit 3

Ensuring Consistent Data and Advanced Querying

One of the most important functions of a database management system is to retrieve useful information for decision making. Using advanced queries, you can find answers to questions related to data stored in your database. To retrieve the data needed, it is important that data be consistent and accurate. The quality of the data that is entered into the database determines the quality of the data displayed in your queries. Placing constraints—rules—on the data helps to prevent errors in data input.

Learning Outcome 1:

Control how data is entered by using input masks, data validation rules, lookup fields, custom formatting, requiring data, and work with field captions and create indexes.

Real World Success

"Last summer, I interned for a major banking firm in Pittsburgh, Pennsylvania. The department database we used to manage clients was built by a former employee who had never used Access before. When I ran queries, all the applicable data never seemed to be displayed, even though I knew the data existed in the tables. I took a look at the tables and noticed that the fields contained inconsistent data. For example, the state field contained three different abbreviations for the same state. I modified the table structure so the fields would only accept data one way. Once the data was cleansed, my queries were completely accurate. The bank asked me to come back the following summer for another internship!"

- Lyndsai, current information systems management student

Learning Outcome 2:

Create useful information for decision making by creating queries to retrieve data, filter data, calculate data totals, update data, append data, and delete data in bulk.

Real World Success

"I am creating an Access database for my internship. This database will track vendor and supplier data my company will be dealing with for its new company acquisition in Canada. Querying data will be the most critical function of this database—wildcard and parameter queries being the highest on the list. When my supervisor asked our department if anyone knew how to use Access, I was the only one who did! Because of this, I was asked to continue my internship once it officially ended."

- Tina, current information systems management student

Microsoft Access 2016

Chapter 5 | ADVANCED TABLES

OBJECTIVES

Prepare Case

Production & Operations

The Red Bluff Golf Course & Pro Shop: Modifying Database Tables

The Red Bluff Golf Course & Pro Shop generates revenue through its golfers, golfer services, and pro shop sales. The current database tracking this data has erroneous data from a lack of good table design. Barry Cheney, the Golf Course manager, has given you a copy of the database and has asked you to modify the tables used to track employees and course members. This will make data entry easier and more consistent. To keep the file small while you work with the database, he removed most of the data and left only some sample data. Once Barry accepts your changes, he will load all of the data and implement the new database.

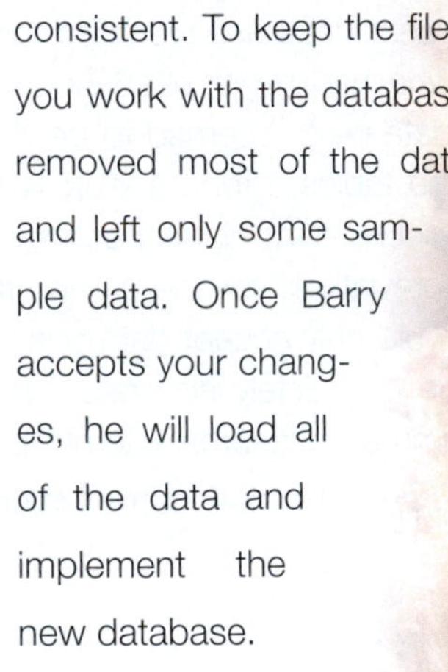

bikeriderlondon/Shutterstock

Student data files needed for this chapter:

 a03ch05Golf.accdb

 a03ch05Liu.jpg

 a03ch05Matrell.jpg

a03ch05Condon.jpg

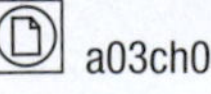 a03ch05Liu.pdf

You will save your file as:

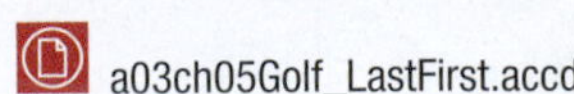 a03ch05Golf_LastFirst.accdb

Controlling the Way Data Is Entered: Advanced Field Options

By ensuring that data is consistent and accurate, you enhance the usability of the data and the database. The quality of data that is entered into a database determines the quality of data that is displayed in query data sets. The **GIGO principle** — Garbage In, Garbage Out — means that inputting inconsistent or inaccurate data leads to inconsistent or inaccurate output. People are not perfect when it comes to data entry. Therefore, database designers have to place constraints — rules — on the data to prevent GIGO errors. In this section, you will learn how to help control the way data is entered through the use of advanced field options such as creating input masks, custom formatting, designing validation rules, and requiring data. Additionally, you will learn how to work with field captions and create indexes.

REAL WORLD ADVICE | **Does It Really Matter How Data Is Entered?**

The quality of the information you produce depends on the quality of data entered into your database. For example, you may want to query all customers who live in Ohio. If you did not restrict the number of characters permitted in a State field or create an input mask to assist in data entry, users could enter the two-character abbreviation or completely spell out the state name. Once you have multiple versions of the state name within the State field, you run the risk of not returning all the customers who reside in Ohio in your query data set. This creates false reporting and ultimately can lead to poor decision making, which is never desirable in the business world.

- Set constraints on as many fields as possible. This will ensure that users are entering data the way you want it to be entered.
- Do not restrict what data can be entered into a field so much that it becomes difficult for users to enter data. You do not want to discourage users from using the database.
- Verify that all restrictions will adequately accept every variant of accurate data. You do not want valid data excluded.
- Remember that garbage in leads to garbage out.

Understand the Purpose and Benefits of Input Masks

Multiple ways exist to standardize data entry into a database. One of the most common methods includes an input mask. An **input mask** controls the way data is entered. Thus, in most cases, an input mask actually controls the way that data is stored. This minimizes the likelihood that users will omit information or enter the wrong data by mistake. The input mask defines a pattern for how all data will be entered in a field. For example, users entering data will know whether or not to include parentheses around a phone number's area code.

Illustratively, you could create an input mask that ensures that all data entered into a Last Name field has an uppercase first letter while the rest remain lowercase, no matter what capitalization the user types. Thus, the data actually is stored as a first capital and the rest in lowercase. You could also format the last name to all uppercase, but the data would still be stored as it was entered and will appear as if it is formatted as all uppercase letters. This technique will ensure that all data on reports and forms will look professional and consistent.

Opening the Starting File

In this exercise, you will open and save a copy of the Golf database. There are multiple tables that list data about employees, members, and other data relevant to running the golf course.

A05.00

To Open the Starting File

a. Start **Access**, click **Open Other Files** in the left pane, and then double-click **This PC**. Navigate through the folder structure to the location of your student data files, and then double-click **a03ch05Golf**. A database opens, displaying the tables related to the Golf Course & Pro Shop.

b. Click the **File** tab, save the file as an **Access Database**, and click **Save As**. Navigate to the location where you are saving your project files and then change the file name to a03ch05Golf_LastFirst, using your last and first name. Click **Save**. If necessary, enable the content.

Using the Input Mask Wizard

Microsoft Access includes several predefined input masks for more common formats such as date, time, Social Security number, password, phone number, and ZIP Code. To apply one of these masks, you can use the **Input Mask Wizard** in the table's Design view. Regardless of the method in which you configure an input mask — manually or via the wizard — you want to select an input mask that is most appropriate for the field. If all the field values contain data with a consistent pattern, you should define an input mask. In this exercise, you will use the Input Mask Wizard to create an input mask for entering phone numbers and hire dates.

A05.01

SIDE NOTE
Pin the Ribbon
If your ribbon is collapsed, pin your ribbon open. Click the Home tab. In the lower right-hand corner of the ribbon, click Pin the Ribbon.

To Use the Input Mask Wizard

a. In the Navigation Pane, right-click **tblMember**, and then click **Design View**.

b. Click the **Phone** field, and under Field Properties, click **Input Mask**, and then click **Build** to open the Input Mask Wizard.

c. If necessary, select **Phone Number**, and then click **Next**.
Notice how the input mask characters are already defined for you. You can enter your phone number in the Try It box to see what your users will see when they enter data into the Phone field.

d. Click **Next**.

e. Under How do you want to store the data?, select **With the symbols in the mask**.

f. Click **Finish**.
Notice that the mask is displayed in the Input Mask field property.

g. Click **Save** to save your changes.

h. Click **Datasheet View** on the Status bar to switch to Datasheet view to see how this input mask works. Enter the following new record.

FirstName	LastName	Address	City	State	ZipCode	Phone
JoAnn	Pollack	124 6th Street	Spring Hill	NM	87588	5055552010

Notice how the phone input mask makes it easier to enter and view data. It also saves time because Access enters the symbols for you.

i. **Close** tblMember.

j. In the Navigation Pane, right-click **tblEmployee**, and then click **Design View**.

SIDE NOTE
Saving Time Equals Accurate Data Entry
Input masks make entering and viewing data easier and save time, but they also help to ensure that data is entered in the same format.

k. Click the **HireDate** field, and then, under Field Properties click the **Input Mask**. Click **Build** [...] to open the Input Mask Wizard.

l. Select **Short Date**. You can enter today's date in the Try It box to see what your users will see when they enter data into the HireDate field.

m. Click **Finish**.

n. **Save** your changes.

o. Click **Datasheet View** on the Status bar. Enter the following new record to see how the input mask works.

FirstName	LastName	Salary	HireDate	Position
Lilly	Baine	21375	07052018	Golf Caddy

p. **Close** [X] tblEmployee.

REAL WORLD ADVICE With or Without the Symbols in the Mask

If you do not store the symbols in the mask, Access will still display them when the field is used on other objects, such as on a form or report. In a Phone Number field, the parentheses and hyphen will not take up storage space. This is a carryover from when storage space was an extreme luxury. Either way, it will look the same to the user. Not storing the symbols saves a little space. If you have hundreds or thousands of customer records in a table and are storing a phone number for each customer, you may decide that you want to save a little space and not store the data with the symbols.

An important item to note is that if you choose not to store the symbols, you will have challenges when working with the data in other programs. For example, if you merge the data into Word or export it into Excel, then symbols will be missing if you did not store them in the mask.

QUICK REFERENCE Three Parts of an Input Mask

Input masks consist of one mandatory part and two optional parts, separated by semicolons as shown in Figure 1.

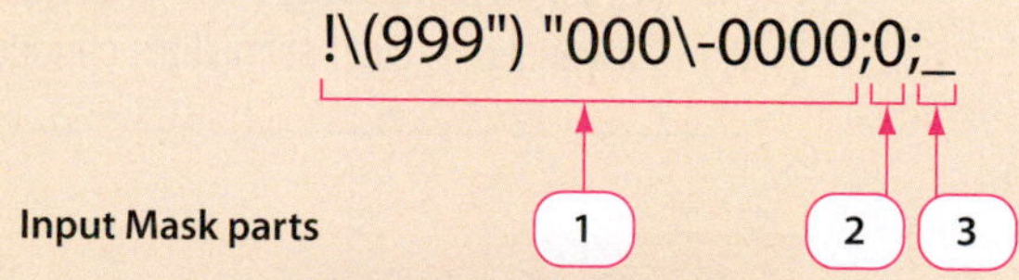

Figure 1 Input Mask parts

1. The first part is mandatory and includes the input mask characters, placeholders, and literal data.
2. The second part is optional. This refers to how the input mask characters are stored within the field. A blank or "1" means that input mask characters will not be stored. A "0" means that input mask characters will be stored. Setting the second part to "1" can save database storage space. In certain cases, setting the second part to "1" can be confusing if the data is ever exported. For example, imagine exporting a list of phone numbers with no parentheses or dashes. A number such as 5555551234 is harder to understand than (555) 555-1234. You should weigh the increase in database size with the potential for confusion.
3. The third part of the input mask is also optional and defines which placeholder symbol appears in the input mask. The default symbol that Access uses is an underscore, but you can choose any character.

Creating a Custom Input Mask

You can manually create an input mask and use special characters to require part of the data to be entered while other parts of the field are optional. For instance, you can require that the area code for a phone number be entered or that other data such as the additional four digits of a ZIP+4 style ZIP Code is optional. These characters specify the type of data — such as a number or character — needed for each character in the input mask.

QUICK REFERENCE | **Common Global Data Variants**

Because business is global, customers can be located all over the world. Different countries format data differently.

- Postal codes: Postal codes outside the United States can contain letters and numbers. For example, the postal code for Niagara Falls in Ontario, Canada, is L2G 2A6.
- Phone numbers: International phone numbers have country codes and a different format. For example, the phone number for a hotel near the Eiffel Tower in Paris, France would be +331 45 55 55 55.
- Dates: In most of the world, a date is formatted with the day first, then the month, and then the year. In the United States, the date 05-07-1967 would be read as May 7, 1967. In many countries, it would be read as July 5, 1967.
- Currency: With businesses competing in a global market, one company could have different locations where the local currency would be used. For example, Alcoa is the world's leading producer of aluminum. In China, Alcoa would use the yuan, and in Europe, they would use the euro, just to name a few.

You can also set the Format property for the same field to define how the data is displayed. For example, your input mask can define that a date is entered in a format such as YYYY/MM/DD but have the date be displayed as DD-MM-YYYY.

CONSIDER THIS | **What Would You Do If You Had International Data?**

Think about what would happen if you had international data along with data from the United States that had to be entered into your table. Consider the common global data variants. How could you change your input masks to allow for these variations? Would you need to create different fields to allow for variations, such as multiple currency fields?

QUICK REFERENCE | **Define Custom Input Masks Using the Following Characters**

The common input mask characters along with their description are as follows.

- 0 — Digit: 0 to 9; data entry is required; plus and minus signs are not permitted.
- 9 — Digit or space; data entry is not required; plus and minus signs are not permitted.
- # — Digit or space; data entry is not required; spaces are displayed as blanks when editing, but blanks are removed when data is saved; plus and minus signs are permitted.
- L — Letter: A to Z; data entry is required.
- ? — Letter: A to Z; data entry is not required.
- A — Letter or digit; data entry is required.
- a — Letter or digit; data entry is not required.

QUICK REFERENCE	Define Custom Input Masks Using the Following Characters (continued)

- & — Any character or a space; entry required.
- \ — Displays the character that follows as the literal character; for example, \A is displayed as just A.
- "" — Characters enclosed in quotation marks are displayed as the literal characters; for example, "Cat" is displayed as Cat.
- C — Any character or a space; entry is optional.
- > — Characters display in uppercase.
- < — Characters display in lowercase.
- ! — Causes the input mask to be displayed from left to right, rather than from right to left.
- ; — Used to separate the three parts of an input mask setting.

In this exercise, you will create a custom input mask that will ensure that when state abbreviations are entered into the tblMember table, they are entered as two capital letters.

A05.02

To Create a Custom Input Mask

a. In the Navigation Pane, right-click **tblMember**, and then click **Design View**. Click the **State** field, and then, in the Format box under Field Properties, type >.

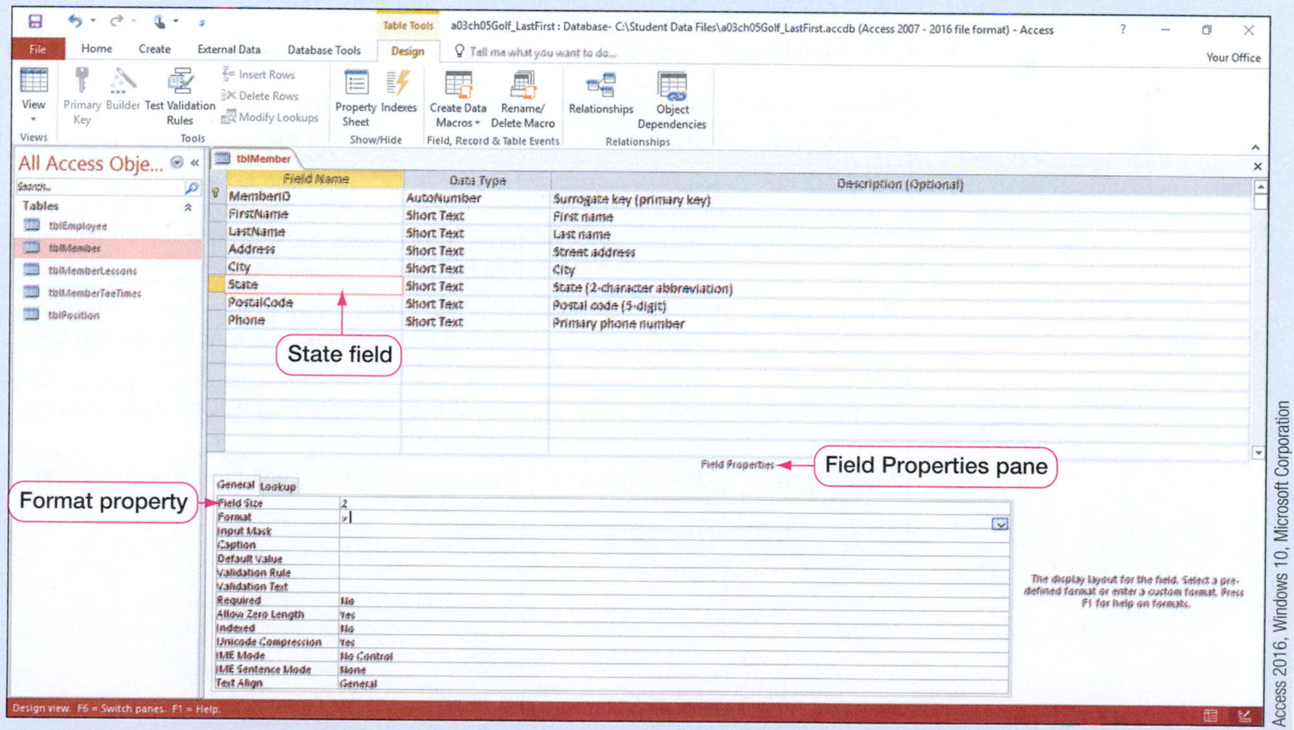

Figure 2 Design view of the tblMember table

b. Click **Save**.

c. Click **Datasheet View** on the Status bar.

d. Enter the following new record, replacing First and Last with your first and last name, to see how the format works.

FirstName	LastName	Address	City	State	ZipCode	Phone
First	Last	323 Bigalow Boulevard	Santa Fe	nm	87594	5055554772

Notice that when you enter data as lowercase in the State field, it is displayed as uppercase. However, if you click back into the State field in the record you just entered, the state abbreviation returns to all lowercase. Now you will reformat this field using a custom input mask.

e. Click **Design View** on the Status bar.

f. Click the **State** field, and under Field Properties click **Input Mask**, and then click **Build** to open the Input Mask Wizard. If Access prompts you to save your table first, click **Yes**.

SIDE NOTE

Changing Input Masks

Input masks can be customized by either changing a predefined mask or manually changing the Input Mask property.

Troubleshooting

If a Microsoft Access Security Notice appears on your screen, it is safe to click Open. To avoid seeing this message in the future, add your database to the Trust Center.

g. Because there is not an input mask already defined for the State field, you need to create a custom input mask. Begin by clicking **Edit List**.

h. Click **New (blank) record**. To create a custom input mask, enter the following.

Where to enter	What to enter	Why you entered this
Description	State	This will be listed in the Input Mask Wizard.
Input Mask	>LL	The ">" is to format the field as uppercase. The "L" indicates that a letter must be entered; thus, users must enter two letters into this field.
Placeholder	_	Using an underscore as the placeholder will make it easy to see how much data can be entered into this field.
Sample Data	NM	This is the example that will be displayed in the wizard.
Mask Type	Text/Unbound	This means that you will type the text in the field.

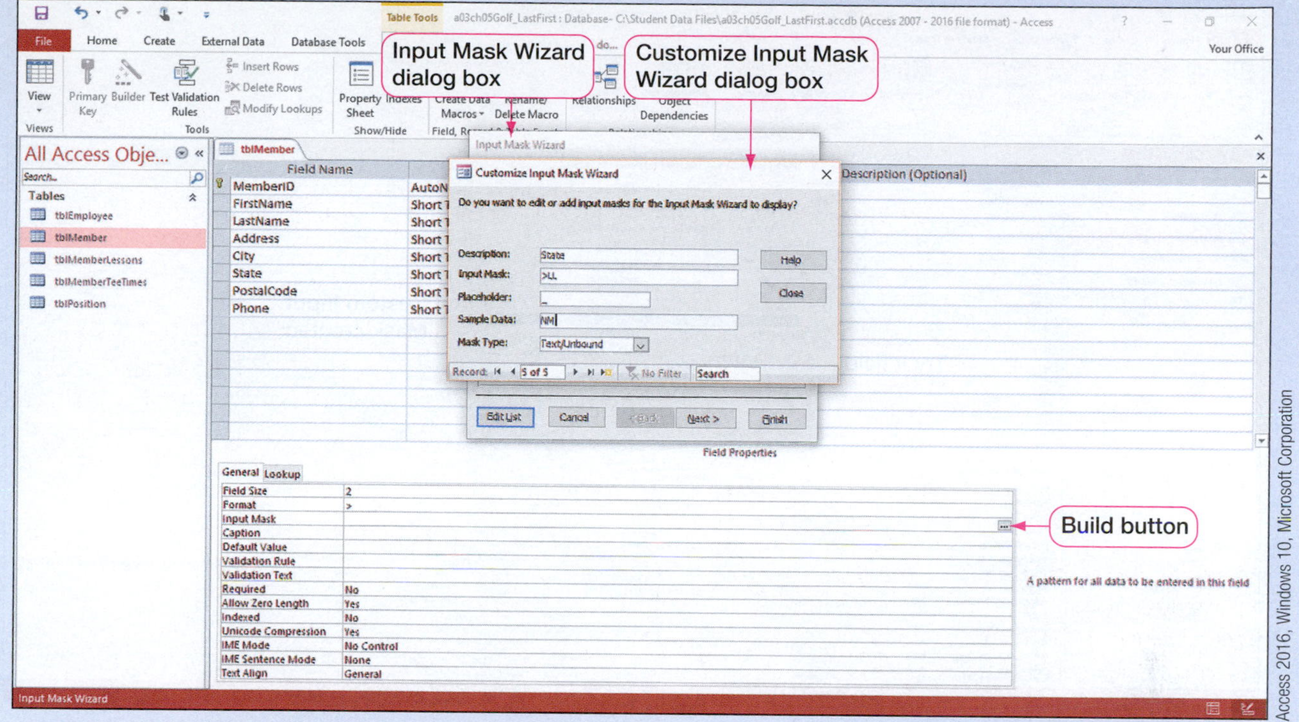

Figure 3 Customize Input Mask Wizard dialog box

SIDE NOTE
Storing Symbols
When disk space was expensive, symbols were not stored, to save space and money. Now you can store them because storage space is so inexpensive.

i. Click **Close**. In the Input Mask Wizard dialog box, scroll down the list if necessary, and then click **State**.

j. Place the insertion point in the **left side** of the Try It box, and then type nm in lowercase.

Notice how Access automatically displays it in uppercase and does not allow you to enter more than two letters.

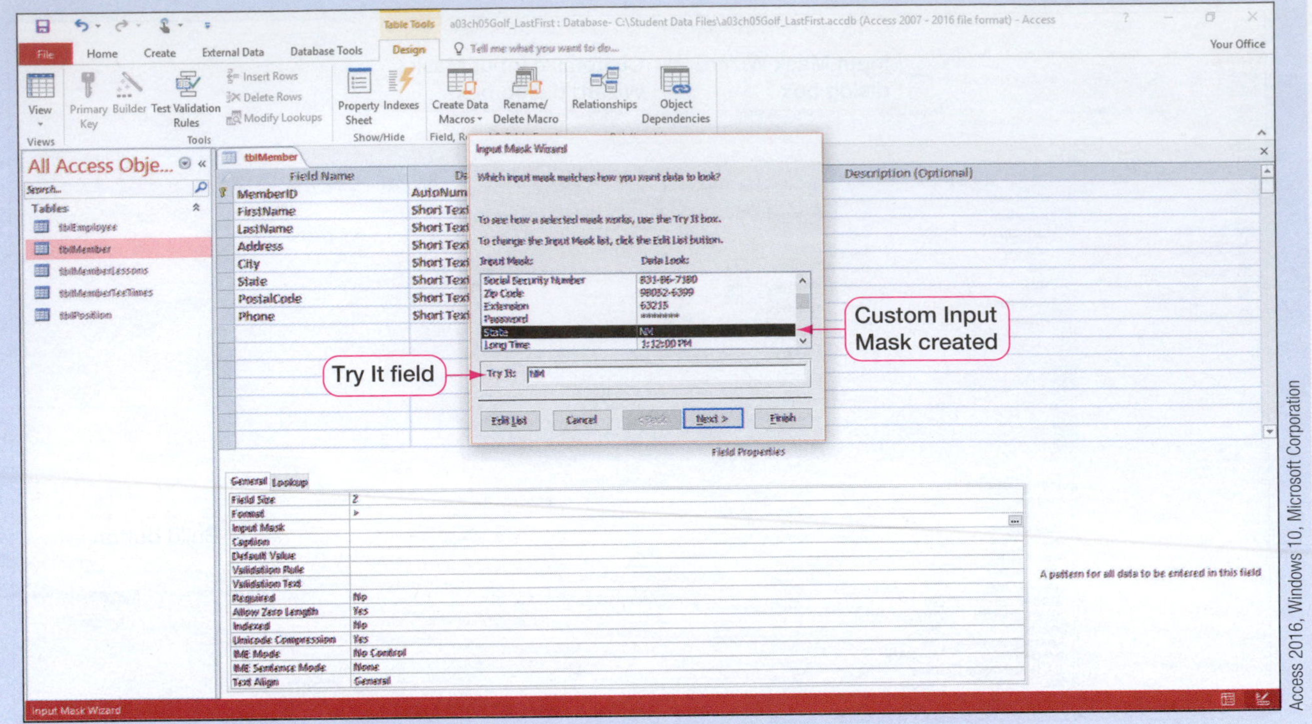

Figure 4 Input Mask Wizard dialog box

k. Click **Next** two times. Because there are no symbols in the custom input mask you created, it does not matter which option you choose on the screen that asks how you want your data to be stored. Keep the default selection, and then click **Next**.

l. Click **Finish**.

Notice that the mask is displayed in the Input Mask field property.

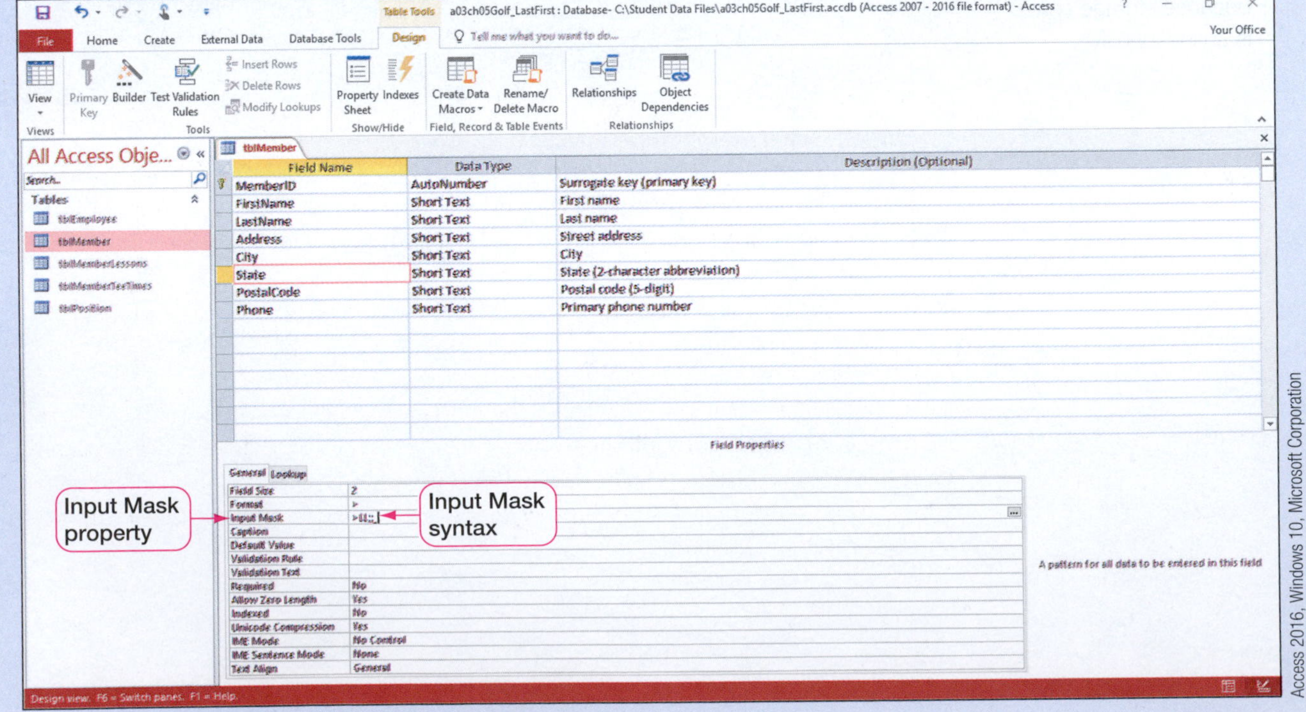

Figure 5 State field custom input mask property

m. Under Field Properties delete > in the Format property.

n. Click **Save** [Save icon]. Click **Datasheet View** [Datasheet View icon] on the Status bar. Enter the following new record to see how the custom input mask works.

FirstName	LastName	Address	City	State	ZipCode	Phone
Charlie	Edwards	191 Drake Court	Santa Fe	nm	87594	5055558676

o. Click the **State** field.

Notice that although you entered the state in lowercase, Access changed the storage of the state you entered into uppercase.

p. **Close** [X] tblMember.

QUICK REFERENCE | **Useful Custom Input Masks**

You can create any number of input masks. Table 1 lists some of the more common input masks.

Type of Data	Input Mask	Data Results
Product number	>L0L 0L0	E8M 8C9
License plate number	>AAA\-AAAA	EZN-0987
Book ISBN-13	000-&-&&-&&&&&&-0	978-0-13-256088-7
Phone number with an extension	\(999") "000\-0000" Ext. "9999	(724) 555-8989 Ext.4484

Apply Custom Formatting

Another common way to control data is through formatting. A **field format** is like makeup. Makeup may change the way a person looks, but it does not change a person's underlying face. The same is true with formatting. Consider an American telephone number. You place parentheses around the area code and a dash between the prefix and last four numbers. The parentheses and dash make the number easier to read, but they do not change the actual number.

You can also create your own type of formatting, called **custom formatting**. You can use the Format property to customize the way numbers, dates, times, and text are displayed and printed by using predefined formats or custom formats. If you set a field's Format property in Design view of a table, Microsoft Access uses that format to display data in datasheets, new form controls, and new report controls.

Creating Custom Formatting

There are times when you may want the convenience of an AutoNumber data type for a primary key but also want the option to change the way that number appears in the table. Custom formatting can be applied in this case, to make the auto number generated appear to be more than just a number. In this exercise, you will create a custom format for the EmployeeID field.

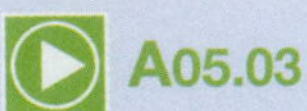

SIDE NOTE

Formatting Data

Formats can be customized by manually changing the Format property where you want the format applied.

To Create Custom Formatting

a. In the Navigation Pane, right-click **tblEmployee**, and then click **Design View**.

b. If necessary, click the **EmployeeID** field, and then, under Field Properties, click the **Format** property.

c. Type **"EMP"0**. The zero will serve as a digit placeholder for the number generated by the AutoNumber data type.

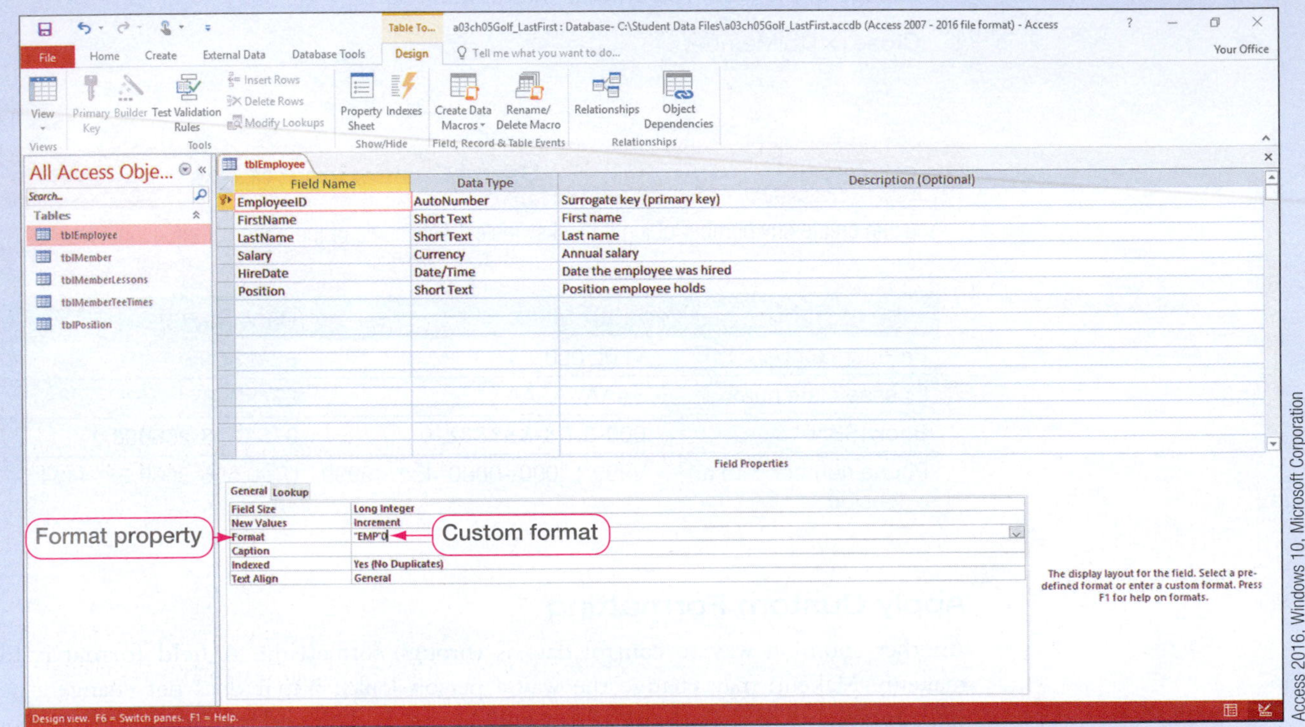

Figure 6 EmployeeID field custom format defined

d. **Save** your changes.

e. Click **Datasheet View** on the Status bar. Enter the following new record to see how the custom format works.

FirstName	LastName	Salary	HireDate	Position
Dennis	Matrell	18200	08122018	Golf Caddy

f. Click the **EmployeeID** field of the record you just entered.

Notice that the format did not change the way the data is stored, just its display.

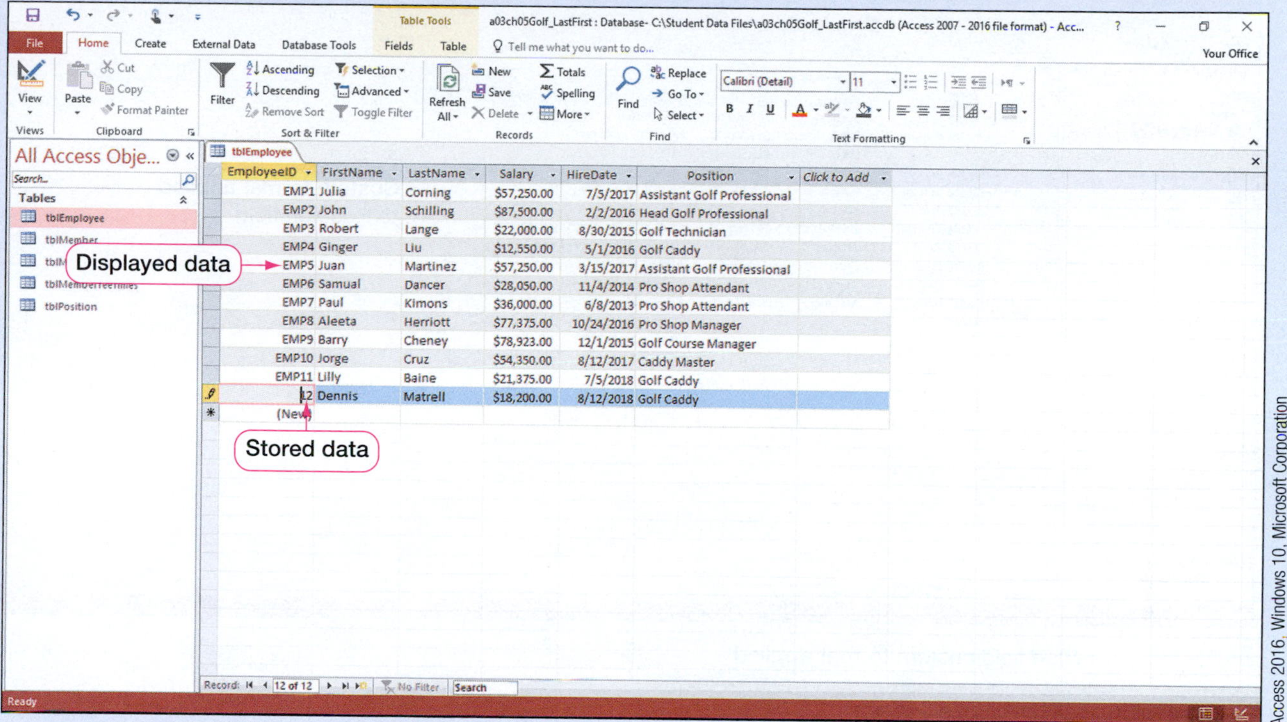

Figure 7 EmployeeID field custom formatting applied

g. Click **Design View** on the Status bar.

h. Click the **Position** field, and then, under Field Properties click the **Format** property. Type &&[Green]. You customized the Format property of the Position field to change the color of the text.

i. **Save** your changes.

j. Click **Datasheet View** on the status bar, and then view the data in the Position field to see how the format works.

Notice that the text is now green.

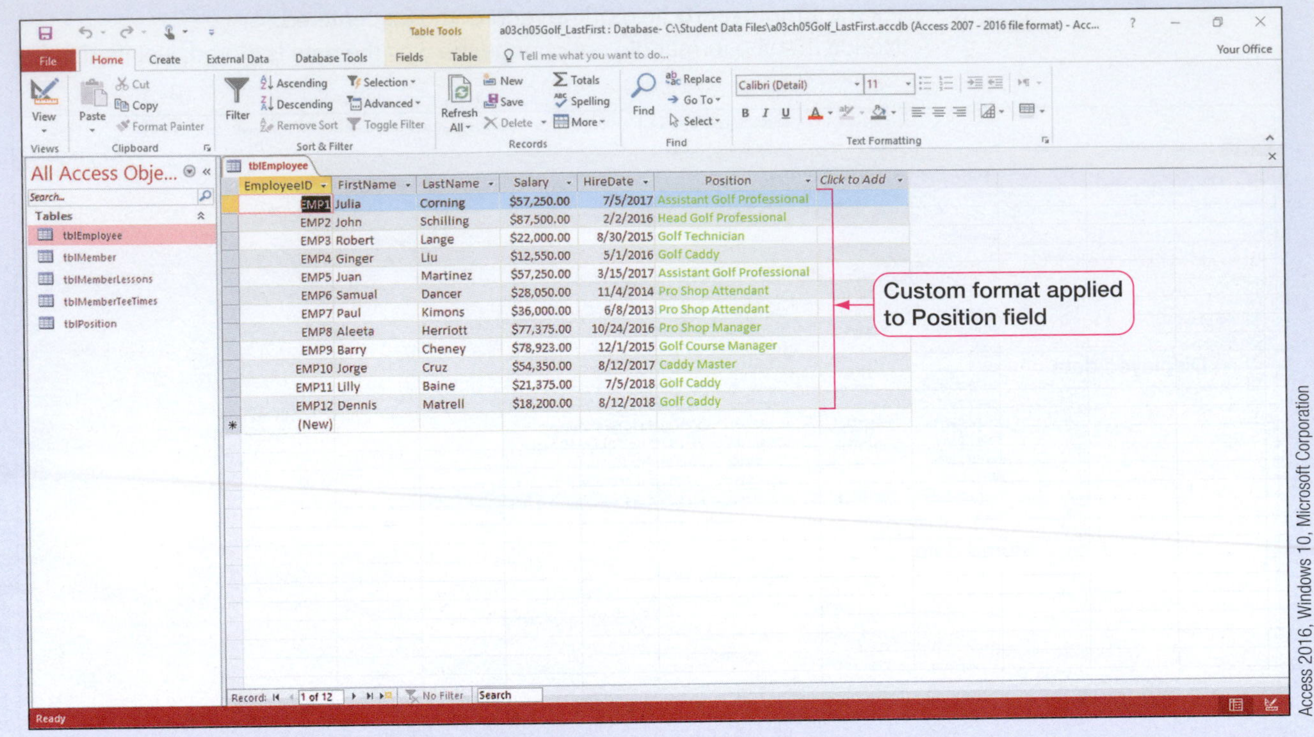

Figure 8 Position field custom format applied

k. Click **Design View** on the Status bar.

l. Click the **HireDate** field, and then, under Field Properties, click the **Format** property, click the **Format Property arrow**, and then select **Medium Date**. The date format for the HireDate field has now been customized with a medium date format.

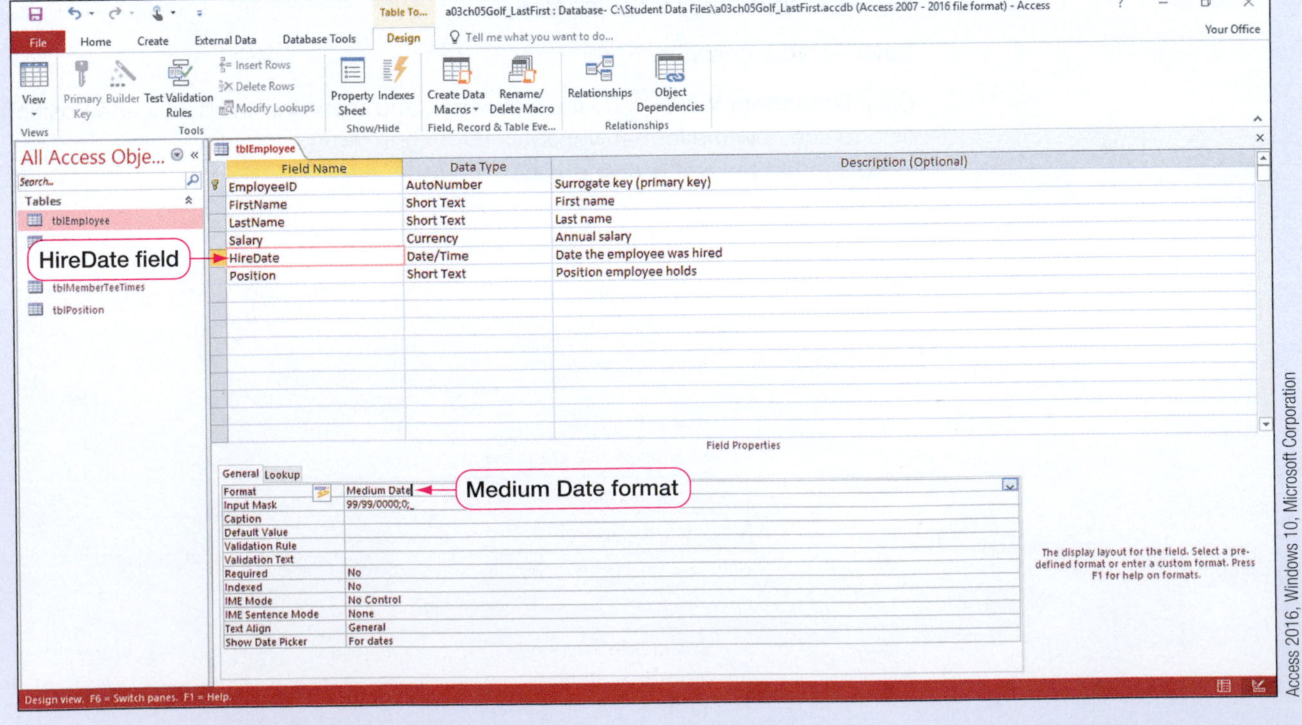

Figure 9 Medium Date format

CHAPTER 5

Troubleshooting

You may have noticed that the Property Update Options button appeared after you changed the HireDate property to Medium Date. If you click the button and choose Update Format everywhere HireDate is used, Access will automatically update all lookup properties everywhere throughout your database where this field is used, including forms, reports, and queries.

SIDE NOTE

The Text Is Still Black

Notice that as you are typing data in the Position field, it remains black. After you leave the field, it will change to green.

m. **Save** your changes.

n. To see how this format works switch to **Datasheet** view, and then enter the following new record.

FirstName	LastName	Salary	HireDate	Position
Antonio	Ruweeze	36900	08242018	Pro Shop Attendant

Notice that because of the input mask, you were able to enter the HireDate as a short date. However, because you formatted the field as a Medium Date, it is displayed in the Medium Date format.

REAL WORLD ADVICE — Can One Property Take Precedence over Another Property?

When you define an input mask that is different from the Format property in the same field, the Format property takes precedence when the data is displayed. Following are some items to note.

1. If you save an input mask, the input mask is ignored when you define a format in the field's Format property.
2. The stored data in the table does not change regardless of how you define the Format property.
3. The Format property affects only how data is displayed, not how it is stored.

QUICK REFERENCE — Define Custom Formats Using the Following Characters

You can enter different formatting syntax — placeholders, separators, literal characters, and colors — in the Format property of a field to create a custom format. By combining these characters, you can make the data easier to read.

Character	Description
Space	Entering a space displays a space.
"ABC"	Characters inside quotes are displayed.
!	Forces left alignment in the field.
*	Fills the available space with the next character.
\	Displays the character that follows.
[color]	A color inside square brackets changes the font color. Available colors are black, blue, green, cyan, red, magenta, yellow, and white.

QUICK REFERENCE — Define Custom Formats Using the Following Characters (continued)

Custom number formats can have one to four sections, with semicolons separating the sections. Each section also holds the format specification for a different type of number.

Section	Description
First	The format for positive numbers
Second	The format for negative numbers
Third	The format for zero values
Fourth	The format for null values

You can also create custom number formats by using the following symbols.

Symbol	Description
.	Decimal separator
,	Thousand separator
0	Display a digit or 0
#	Display a digit or blank
$	Display a dollar sign
%	Value is multiplied by 100, and a percent sign added
E– or e–	Scientific notation with a minus sign next to negative exponents. This symbol must be used with other symbols, as in 0.00E–00 or 0.00E00.
E+ or e+	Scientific notation with a minus sign next to negative exponents and a plus sign next to positive exponents. This symbol must be used with other symbols, as in 0.00E+00.

For example, a custom format for a Date/Time field can contain two sections: one for the date and another for time. The sections are then separated by a semicolon. Thus, you can combine the Short Date format (mm/dd/yyyy) and the Medium Time format (hh:mm followed by AM or PM), as shown in Figure 10.

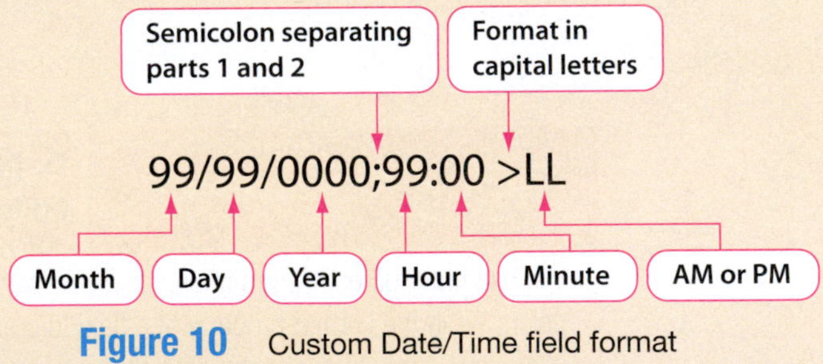

Figure 10 Custom Date/Time field format

Define Data Validation Rules

When data validation rules are used, data can be validated as it is entered; this helps to help improve accuracy and consistency. **Data validation rules** prevent inaccurate data from being entered and consequentially stored in a database. Validation rules can be set for a specific field or an entire record. For example, a validation rule could be created to ensure that a product price is greater than zero.

When data is entered, Access checks to see whether the data meets the validation rule. If the data is not accepted, Access displays a message — known as **validation text** — designed to help users understand why there is a problem. The **Validation Text property** allows you to specify the error message.

There are two basic types of validation rules: field validation rules and record validation rules. **Field validation rules** are used to verify the value that is entered in just one field is accurate. If the validation rule is violated, Access prevents the user from leaving the current field until the problem is fixed. For example, you may want to make sure that a product price entered is greater than 0. In the ProductPrice field, you would enter >0 as the Validation Rule property. If you enter 0 in the field, Access will not permit you to move to another field until the problem has been corrected.

CONSIDER THIS | What Would You Recommend?

What if the resort wants to offer a free item in the inventory? What effect would configuring a validation rule on ProductPrice >0 have? What would you recommend doing in this instance?

A **record validation rule** determines whether a record is valid, or meets all criteria, when a record is saved. In other words, you need to compare and validate the values in one field against the values in another field in the same record. For example, suppose a business requires that products ship within 14 days from when an order was placed. A record validation rule can be defined on the ScheduledShippingDate field, ensuring that someone does not schedule a ship date that breaches the company's 14-day rule.

The only difference between establishing a field validation rule and a record validation rule is its structure. In a record validation rule, you would reference field names rather than simply entering an expression. If your business follows the above 14-day shipping rule, the Validation Rule property compares the date entered in the OrderDate field against the date entered in the ScheduledShippingDate field. You can enter [ScheduledShippingDate]<=[OrderDate]+14.

REAL WORLD ADVICE | Why Bother with Validation Rules?

A fine line exists between rejecting inaccurate data and accepting all data entered. Ultimately, a database is only as good as the data stored within, so it is important to limit bad data from being entered into a field. However, be careful not to overdo validation rules, or you may end up blocking data that is valid yet unanticipated. The goal is to force users entering data to safeguard the validity of the data.

1. Data that does not follow data validation rules can negatively affect business processes. Therefore, data validation should start with a business process definition and a set of business rules within this process.
2. Accuracy is critical in defining data validation rules. Errors in data validation can lead to data corruption or security vulnerability.
3. Periodically evaluate data validation rules. Rather than accepting or rejecting data when it is entered, consider changing the field properties into an acceptable format.

Creating Validation Rules and Validation Text

It is critical for a business that employee records be accurate. Validation rules are another way to prevent errors in your database. In this exercise, you will create and test validation rules that will ensure that an employee's hire date and salary are valid on the basis of the company's policies.

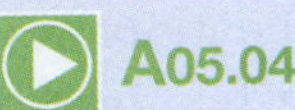

A05.04

To Create Validation Rules and Validation Text

a. Click **Design View** on the Status bar to switch to the Design view of the tblEmployee table.

b. If necessary, click the **HireDate** field, and then, under Field Properties click the **Validation Rule** property.

c. Type >=Date()-14 as the Validation Rule.

You created a field validation rule for the HireDate field so employees cannot be entered into the system after 14 days from the hire date, as it could cause problems with the payroll department.

d. Click inside the Validation Text property, and enter the following validation text, including the punctuation: This employee began working more than 14 days ago. Please call the Corporate Office at (800) 555-4022.

SIDE NOTE

Using an Equal Sign

When entering a validation rule, you do not need to begin the expression with an equal sign (=).

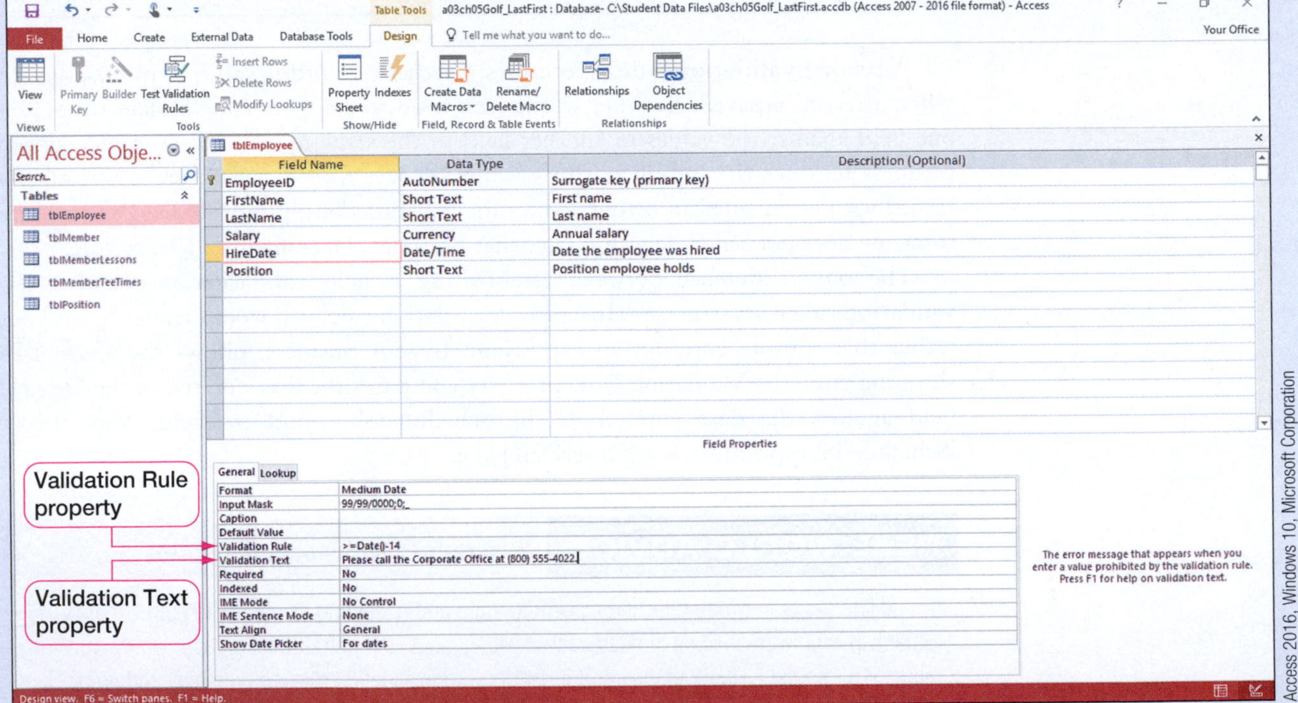

Figure 11 HireDate field validation rule and text

Troubleshooting

At times, data being entered into field properties can become difficult to see. To enlarge your work area and font, right-click the property you are working on, and then click Zoom.

e. **Save** your changes.

f. Click **No** when Access prompts you to confirm whether you want to test the existing data against the new rules.

Troubleshooting

You will notice a warning message stating that you have made changes to the table's data integrity rules and that existing data may not meet the new rules. Access wants to confirm whether you want to test the existing data against the new rules. If you know that the data meets the new rules, you can click No. If you are not sure and you want to make certain that all records meet the requirements, click Yes.

g. To see how the validation rule and validation text work, switch to Datasheet view, and then enter the following new record.

FirstName	LastName	Salary	HireDate
Dolly	Hunt	23600	Enter a date that is at least 15 days before today's date.

Notice that because you entered a date that was more than 14 days ago, Access keeps you from moving to the next field until you correct the mistake.

h. Click **OK**, and then change the date to today's date, and finish entering the record by typing Golf Technician into the Position field.

i. Click **Design View** on the Status bar, click the **Salary** field, and then, under Field Properties, click the **Validation Rule** property.

j. Create a validation rule for **Salary** so that no salary can exceed $200,000. Enter <=200000 as the Validation Rule property.

k. Enter the following validation text with the punctuation: The maximum salary an employee can earn is $200,000. Please re-enter this employee's salary.

l. **Save** your changes, and then click **Yes** to make sure that all existing data meets the new validation rule.

m. Click **Datasheet View** on the Status bar. Enter the following new record to see how the validation rule and validation text work.

FirstName	LastName	Salary
Allie	Madison	800000

Notice that because you entered a salary that was more than $200,000, Access keeps you from entering the rest of the record until you correct the mistake.

SIDE NOTE

Validation Rules and Numbers

When entering numbers or currency into a validation rule, do not enter symbols such as commas or dollar signs.

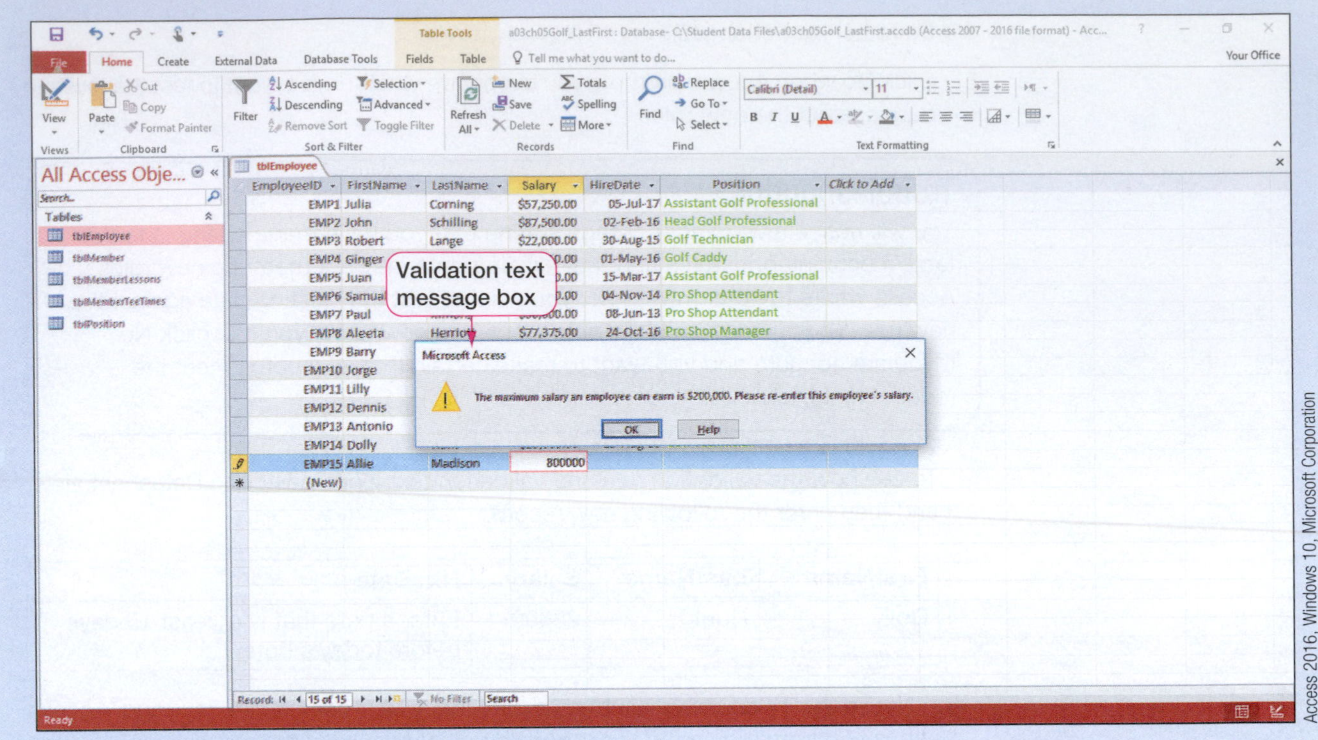

Figure 12 Salary field validation text displayed

n. Click **OK**, change the salary to 80000, and then finish entering the record by typing Today's date in the HireDate field and Golf Professional in the Position field.

Define Caption Names

When naming fields, you should use a name that is easy to understand. Although the field name may be the best choice in designing a database, sometimes those names may not be what you want to display on other database objects such as forms, reports, and queries. Or you may be working with a database that someone else created — someone who did not understand the principles of good design.

Instead of having to modify field names, which could require you to modify other objects or settings in your database (e.g., relationships), it would be easier to simply define the **Caption property**. A caption is like an alias. An alias is another name that someone may use to hide his or her true identity, but the person's legal name is still what is listed on the birth certificate. A caption does not change the actual field name; it just changes the way users see it — like an alias. Once this property has been established, every object you create will display what the caption is instead of the field name. For example, a field named HomePhone would be displayed as "HomePhone" on forms and reports. However, if you enter "Home Phone" in the Caption property, objects such as forms, reports, and queries will look more professional. This will also eliminate the need to change "HomePhone" to "Home Phone" on every object you create. This not only makes it easier for users to understand the data within table fields, but also makes it easier for designers to create other objects within the database.

Creating Captions for Existing Fields

In this exercise, you will modify the Caption property for several fields in the tblEmployee table, making the other objects that reference the fields more user-friendly.

To Create Captions for Existing Fields

a. Click **Design View** on the Status bar to switch to Design view of the tblEmployee table.

b. Click the **FirstName** field, and then, under Field Properties, click the **Caption** property. Type First Name in the Caption property.

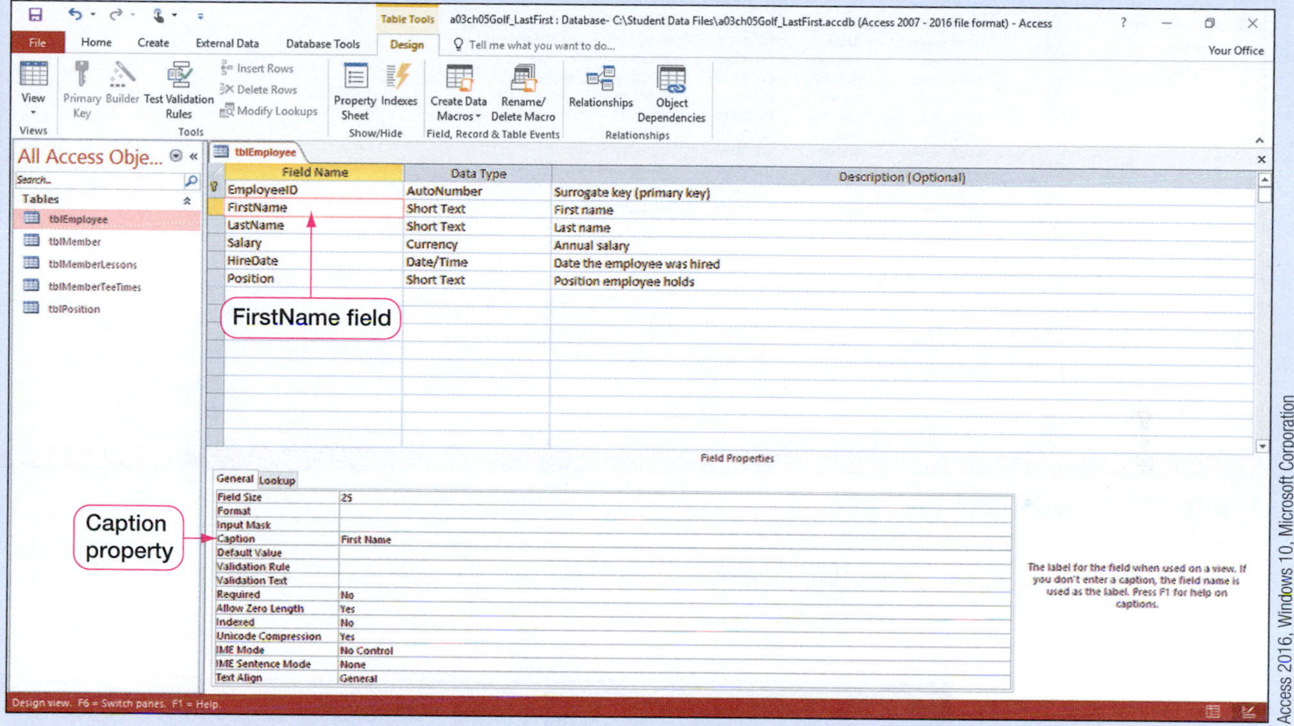

Figure 13 FirstName field caption property

c. **Save** your changes. Click **Datasheet View** on the Status bar, and then look at the field heading to see how the Caption property works.

d. Click **Design View** on the Status bar, and then enter the following captions for each field.
LastName: Last Name
HireDate: Date of Hire
Position: Job Title

e. **Save** your changes. To see how the table looks after creating your captions, switch to **Datasheet** view, and then view the field headings. Resize your fields if you cannot see the entire caption.

SIDE NOTE
Always Resize Fields
Best practices state that when in Datasheet view, you should always resize the fields so all the data is visible.

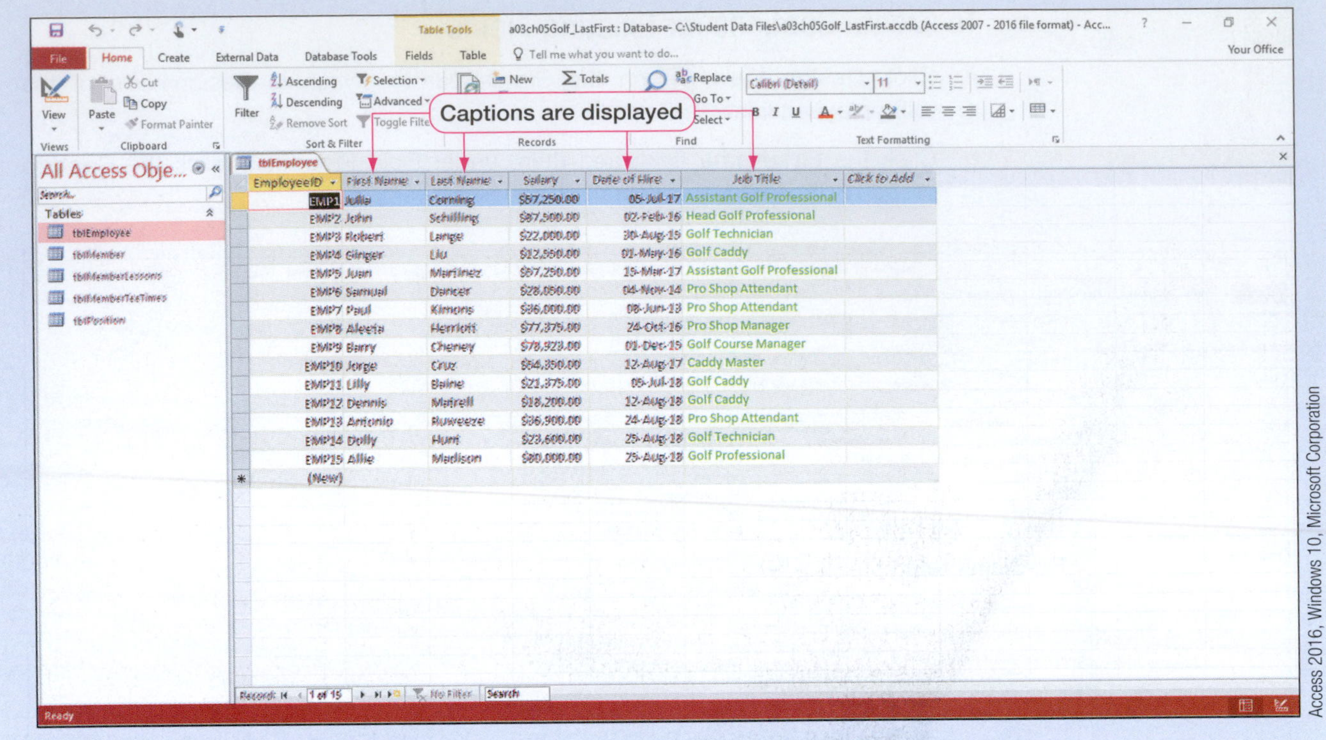

Figure 14 Captions displayed

f. **Save** and **close** tblEmployee.

REAL WORLD ADVICE — Captions Enable You to Use Reserved Words

All relational databases have specific words and symbols that cannot be used as field names because they have a specific meaning within the underlying system files, such as "date" or "time". If you use a reserved word or symbol as a field name, Access will warn you that it is reserved, and you will experience errors when working with the database. The error message you receive will not necessarily communicate that the problem stems from using a reserved word or symbol. Thus, it can be challenging to identify what needs to be revised.

Because there are hundreds if not thousands of reserved words, it is impractical to list them all. Therefore, it is important to read all warning messages thoroughly when you are working in Access. Remember that you can use whatever word or symbol you would like as a caption. When naming a field, create a name that is compliant — Access will let you know if it is not — and then create a caption for the field as you choose.

Create Indexes to Increase Performance

Many databases contain a large amount of data. Indexes are created and used to increase performance. For example, if you repeatedly search or sort your data on a specific field, you could create an index to speed up the procedure. An **index** in Access is similar to an index in a book. It is a lot easier and faster to find a topic in a book's index than to have to search through the book page by page to locate what you need. If you create an index for a field or fields in a table, Access can quickly locate all the records that contain specific values for those fields without having to read through each record in the table.

CONSIDER THIS | **What Will Happen in the Future?**

Right now, the resort database is small enough that you will not recognize a difference in performance after creating an index. If this database is used for three years, how large do you think it will get? What would happen in year 3 if you did not create indexes? Would your database run more slowly?

REAL WORLD ADVICE | **How Do You Decide What Fields to Index?**

- You can index every field if you want to, but it is not a good idea. Indexes can accelerate searches and queries, but they can slow down performance when you add or update data. Performance decreases because the indexes must be updated when data changes.
- You cannot index a field with an OLE Object, Hyperlink, Memo, or Attachment data type.
- Index a field when the data is generally unique and when there are more different entries than duplicate entries.
- Index a field when you plan to search through it or sort it frequently.
- The strategy to indexing efficiently is that an index should improve performance. Do not apply an index for any other reason.

Defining a Single-Field Index

If you create a **single-field index** with the index property Unique set to Yes, Access will not let you enter a new value in the field if that value is already entered in the same field within another record. Access automatically creates an index for primary keys, but you might also want to prevent duplicate values in other fields or simply increase the efficiency when searching or sorting other fields. For example, you may want to create an index on a field that stores a Universal Product Code (UPC) to ensure that all products have a unique UPC. In this exercise, you will create a single-field index on the Position field in the tblPosition table.

To Define a Single-Field Index

SIDE NOTE
Some Indexes Are Automatically Created
For some fields, such as a primary key, Access automatically creates an index for you.

a. In the Navigation Pane, right click **tblPosition**, and then click **Design View**.

b. If necessary, click the **EmployeePosition** field, and then look at the Indexed property under Field Properties.
   Notice that Access automatically created an index for this field when the table was built.

c. On the Table Tools Design tab, in the Show/Hide group, click **Indexes** to create a single-field index. The Indexes dialog box will open.

d. Enter the following index properties starting at the first blank row in the Indexes dialog box.

Index Name	Field Name	Sort Order
Position	PositionType	Ascending

SIDE NOTE
Create Indexes in Field Properties
You can create a single-field index by changing No to Yes in the Indexed property in Field Properties.

Index properties for Position index

Primary	No
Unique	No
Ignore Nulls	No

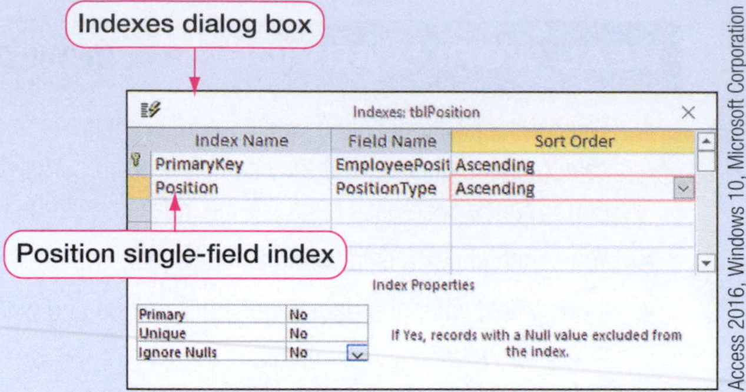

Figure 15 Indexes dialog box with new index property

SIDE NOTE
Using the Indexes Dialog Box
The Indexes dialog box allows you to easily see all the indexes within the table at the same time.

e. **Close** ☒ the Indexes dialog box, and then **Save** your changes.
Creating an Index on the PositionType field will make searching and sorting by this field more efficient.

f. **Close** ☒ tblPosition.

Defining Multiple-Field Indexes

You can also create an index for a combination of fields with a maximum of ten fields. For example, if you frequently specify criteria for the Supplier and UPC fields in the same query, database performance will be improved if you create a multiple-field index on both fields.

When you create a **multiple-field index**, you specify the order of the fields. Once you have sorted a table by defining a multiple-field index, Access sorts the index in the order in which you enter each field into the Indexes dialog box. If there are records with duplicate values in the first field, Access then sorts by the second field defined for the index, and so on. In this exercise, you will create a multiple-field index on the FirstName and LastName fields in the tblMember table.

A05.07

To Define Multiple-Field Indexes

a. In the Navigation Pane, right click **tblMember**, and then click **Design View**.

b. On the Table Tools Design tab, in the Show/Hide group, click **Indexes** to create a multiple-field index. The Indexes dialog box will open.

c. Enter the following index properties, starting at the first blank row in the Indexes dialog box.

Index Name	Field Name	Sort Order
MemberName	LastName	Ascending
	FirstName	Ascending

SIDE NOTE
Reviewing Your Indexes
By clicking Indexes on the Table Tools Design tab, you can easily view and modify all existing indexes.

SIDE NOTE

Is Something Missing?

At first glance, it appears that something is missing. Note that the index name appears only once in a multiple-field index.

Index properties for MemberName index

Primary	No
Unique	No
Ignore Nulls	No

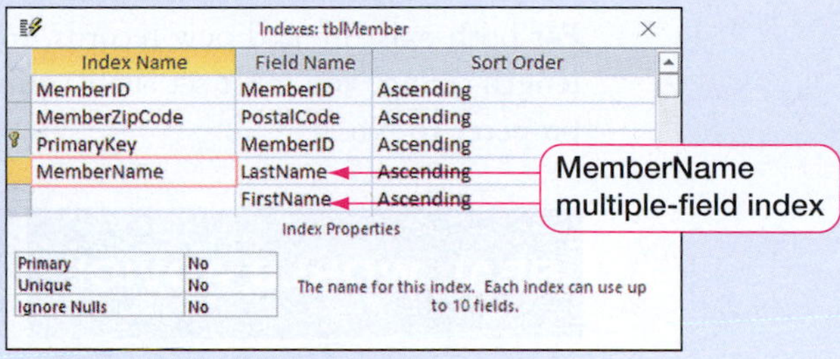

Figure 16 Multiple-field index

Access 2016, Windows 10, Microsoft Corporation

d. **Close** the Indexes dialog box, and then **Save** your changes.
   Creating a multiple-field index on the FirstName and LastName fields will make searching and sorting by these fields more efficient.

QUICK REFERENCE | **Deleting an Index**

If you find that an index becomes unnecessary or has a negative impact on performance, it can be deleted. When you delete an index, you remove only the index and not the field or fields on which it was created.

1. In the Indexes dialog box, select the entire row or rows that contain the index you want to delete, making sure that you select the whole row.
2. Press Delete.
3. Click Save on the Quick Access Toolbar.
4. Close the Indexes dialog box.

Require Data in Fields

Requiring data to be entered into certain fields is a way of ensuring that essential information is not omitted from the database, either accidentally or deliberately. For example, in a sales database, essential data required to place an order may be a credit card number and expiration date. However, other data may prove very useful to the business, such as a customer's name, address, gender, and other data. It is important to distinguish between data that is required for a record to be created and data that is desirable if available.

In Access, you can use the **Required property** to specify whether a value is required in a field, ensuring that the field is not left blank or, in database terms, is not **null**. If the Required property is set to Yes and a user attempts to leave a field blank or removes a value from a required field when trying to save the record, Access will display an error message. The user will need to enter data before moving to the next field. However, the user can still bypass a field with the Required property set to Yes if the user enters what is known as a zero-length string. A **zero-length string** is text that contains no characters and is created by typing two sets of double quotes without a space in between them (""). A zero-length string allows a user to bypass a required field if the data is not available, thus allowing the record to still be created. A real world example of this would be when you buy something at a store and the cashier asks you for your phone number before completing the transaction. The system used by the company may have the phone number field required, but you do not actually have to provide that data to complete the transaction. If you do not give your phone number, the cashier can simply enter a zero-length string into the field and continue with the transaction.

Also, the Required property applies only to new records, not existing ones. Thus, if that is all that is set, you can cause an existing last name to be blank even if it is required. For both existing and new records, to require data in a field that will not allow a zero-length string, you must set the Required property to Yes and set the Allow Zero Length property to No.

REAL WORLD ADVICE | **Changing the Required Setting When a Table Contains Data**

If you change the Required property to Yes for a field that already contains data, Access allows you to verify whether existing records have values entered in that field. You can require that a value be entered in this field for all new records even if there are existing records without values in the field.

Making Fields Required

In this exercise, you will make several fields required in the tblMember table for new and existing records. You will also ensure that none of the fields can be bypassed with a zero-length string.

SIDE NOTE
Changing a Yes/No Property Value
You can double-click inside the property to toggle from Yes to No and vice versa.

To Make Fields Required

a. In Design view of tblMember, click the **FirstName** field, and then, in Field Properties click the **Required** property.

b. Change the **Required** property from No to Yes.

c. Click the **Allow Zero Length** property, and change it from Yes to No.

d. Change the Required property to Yes and the Allow Zero Length property to No for the following fields: **LastName**, **Address**, **City**, **State**, and **PostalCode**.

e. **Save** your changes, and then click **Yes** in the Data Integrity warning dialog box.

CONSIDER THIS | **Customer Data Is Important**

Data about customers gives companies a way to contact the customers for marketing and customer service purposes. Some customers may not want to give out personal information. To allow for customers' personal preferences, do not restrict the database too much. For example, a customer may have an unlisted phone number. Should this be considered in determining whether data in a field is required? Which fields should never have the Required property set to Yes?

Define Default Values

Default values are one of the easiest ways to help with data entry. A **default value** is a value that is automatically entered into a field when a new record is created. For example, perhaps the majority of your customers live in a specific city. In a Customer table, you can set the default value for the City field to that specific city, such as Santa Fe. When users add a record to the table, they can either accept this value by tabbing to the next field or change it by entering the name of a different city.

Setting a Default Value

In this exercise, you will set a default value for the City and State fields in the tblMember table to make entering new records more efficient.

A05.09

SIDE NOTE

Adding Quotation Marks

If you do not enter the quotation marks, Access will enter them for you.

To Set a Default Value

a. Click the **City** field, and then, in Field Properties click the **Default Value** property.

b. Type Santa Fe and then press Enter.

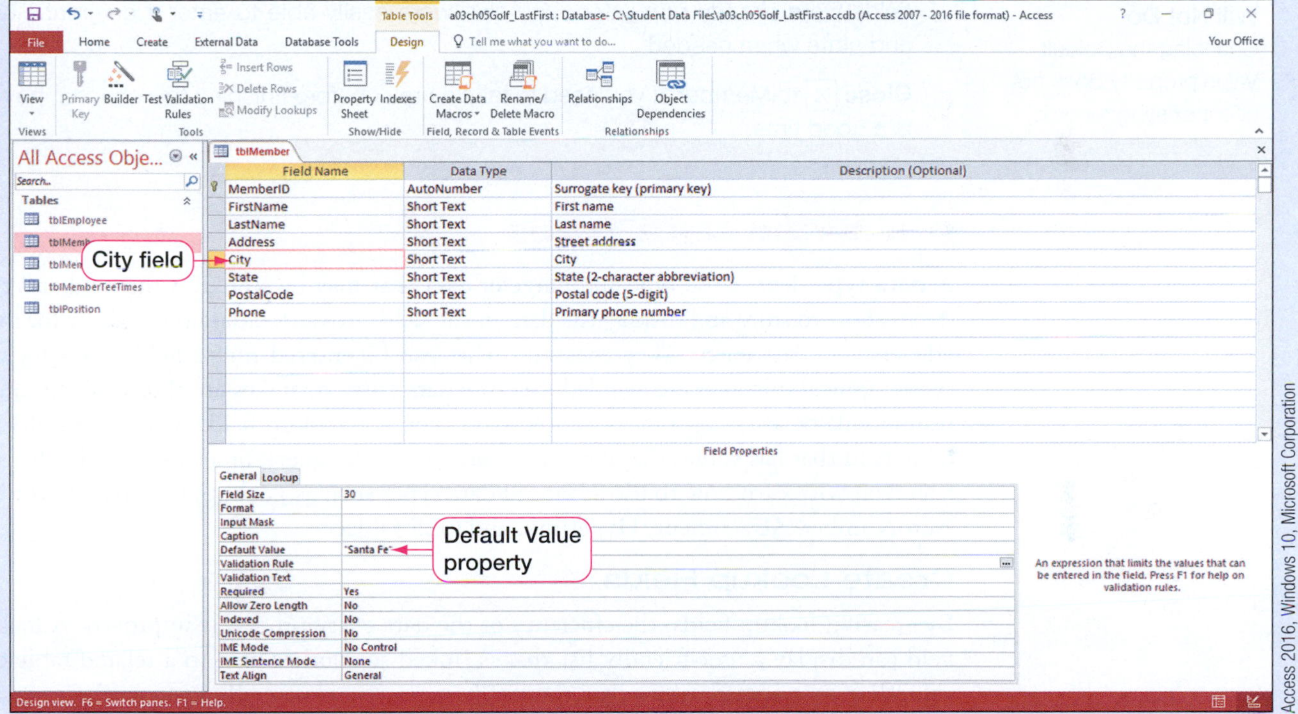

Figure 17 Default Value property

Troubleshooting

Quotation marks are needed around text, also known as string data, to let Access know that it is text. Different data types require specific delimiters or symbols when they become part of an expression: Text needs to be enclosed in quotation marks, and dates need to be enclosed in number signs. Eliminating the quotes would confuse Access because it would think you entered a number or keyword when you really entered text. Notice that Access automatically places quotes around the string if you forget. A **string** is composed of a set of characters that can include spaces, symbols, and numbers. Additionally, if you type in "Santa Fe", Access will automatically recognize it as a string and enter the quotes, unless the word is an operator. For example, if you have a field in which the default value contains the word "like", you have to physically type the quotes because "like" is a reserved word.

SIDE NOTE
When a Default Value Can Be Used
Default values can be used in all fields except AutoNumber or OLE Object data types.

c. Click the **State** field, click the **Default Value** property, and then type NM.

d. **Save** your changes.

e. Click **Datasheet View** on the Status bar, and then click **New (blank) Record** to see how the Default Value property works.

Notice that the City and State fields are already populated.

f. Enter the following records.

FirstName	LastName	Address	City	State	ZipCode	Phone
Karen	Meyer	27 First Avenue	Santa Fe	NM	87594	5055552787
Harry	Shay	60258 Wildwood Road	Snowflake	AZ	85937	9285551638

Notice that you saved time entering the first record because the City and State fields were already populated. You also were easily able to enter a different city and state when needed.

g. **Close** tblMember. If you need to take a break before finishing this chapter, now is a good time.

SIDE NOTE
What a Default Value Will Not Do
Changing the Default Value property does not affect existing records.

Advanced Data Types

A **data type** defines the type and range of data that may be stored in the field and tells Access how to store and display the data in the field. Advanced data types allow for more efficiency in data entry. They constrain what can be entered into a field, ensuring that typographical mistakes are avoided. Because data entry mistakes are thus avoided, query results will be accurate. One advanced data type is a lookup field. A **lookup field** is a table field that has values that come from either a table, query, or a value list. In this section, you will learn how to use advanced data types such as Lookup, Calculated, Yes/No, AutoNumber, Attachment, Hyperlink, and OLE Object.

Create Lookup Fields

By creating lookup fields, the efficiency of the data entry process is improved. A lookup field can display a user-friendly list that is linked to another field in a related table or a value list — a list of values that the database designer manually creates. For example, the lookup field can display a company name that is linked to a corresponding contact identification number in another table, query, or list.

When a lookup field is created that that gets data from a table or query — called a source — Access uses the primary key field from the source to determine which value goes with which record. A lookup field replaces what is displayed, which would be the primary key field by default, with something more meaningful, such as an employee name. The value that is stored is called the **bound value**. The value that is displayed is called the **display value**.

Although a lookup field can be manually defined, the **Lookup Wizard** is the easiest way to create a lookup field. The wizard simplifies the process by automatically populating the appropriate field properties and creating the appropriate table relationships. The Lookup Wizard feature was enhanced in Access 2010 by automatically creating referential integrity settings. At the end of the wizard, you can make a choice to enable referential integrity. The wizard not only creates a relationship, but also makes the correct referential integrity settings.

Another feature in Access is the ability to store multiple values in a **multivalued field**. This helps you to keep track of multiple related facts about a subject. For example, suppose you have a project management database that helps you manage which employees are assigned to what projects. One employee might be working on several projects, and each project might have more than one employee working on it. This kind of data structure is called a many-to-many relationship. Access makes it easy to keep track of this related data by using a multivalued lookup field. After you create the multivalued field, it appears as a check box list in Datasheet view. The selected people are stored in the multivalued field and are separated by commas when displayed.

REAL WORLD ADVICE | **Enforcing Referential Integrity with Multiple Values**

Access will not allow you to store multiple values in one field if you enforce referential integrity. When Access enforces referential integrity, it is checking to see whether related data exists between the primary key and foreign key in two tables. You cannot enter a value in the foreign key field of the related table that does not exist in the primary key field of the primary table. For example, a project cannot be assigned to an employee if that employee does not exist in your database. On the other hand, multiple employees may be assigned to one project. Thus, the foreign key in the Project table — EmployeeID — can have more than one EmployeeID listed, the names being separated by a comma. The combination of the EmployeeIDs will not match any of the EmployeeIDs listed in the Employee table.

When you are building tables, make sure you understand how the data will be used. In many cases, it may be better to create a junction table instead of having a field within a table that allows multiple values to be stored.

CONSIDER THIS | **Multiple Values and Normalization**

Does storing multiple values conform to the principles of normalization? List some examples in which using this feature is useful. What are some examples where storing multiple values would be inappropriate?

The purpose of a lookup field is to replace the display of a number such as an ID — or other foreign key value — with something more meaningful, such as a name. For instance, instead of displaying a product item ID number, Access can display a product name. **Lookup field properties** can be viewed in the bottom pane of the table's Design view under Field Properties. When the first property is initially configured, the list of available properties changes to reflect one's choice. Lookup field properties can be set to change the behavior of a lookup column. When the Lookup Wizard is used, many of the lookup field properties are automatically established by the wizard.

Although the wizard establishes the lookup field properties, there are some properties that may need to be modified on the basis of your own preferences. When the wizard creates the settings of a lookup field, many properties are not established or are configured to the Access default settings. You can set the lookup field properties to change the behavior of the lookup field.

QUICK REFERENCE	Determining Which Setting to Choose

There are three settings that you can select on the last screen in the Lookup Wizard. Choosing the right one depends on how you want to relate your data between the two tables. If you want to create a simple relationship, you would select No Data Integrity. If you want to make sure that the values in the two tables always match, select the Enable Data Integrity check box, and then click one of the following.

1. Restrict Delete: This option activates referential integrity with no Cascades. Thus, if you attempt to delete a record from one table but there is a corresponding record in the other table, the delete operation is not allowed.
2. Cascade Delete: This option activates referential integrity with Cascade Delete. Thus, if you delete a record from one table, corresponding records in the other table are also deleted.

Creating Lookup Fields and Modifying Lookup Properties

In this exercise, you will use the Lookup Wizard to create a lookup field that will increase the efficiency of entering records.

 A05.10

To Create Lookup Fields and Modify Lookup Properties

SIDE NOTE
Lookup Fields Have Limitations
The only data types you can create a lookup field for are Text and Number.

a. If you took a break, open the **a03ch05Golf** database.

b. In the Navigation Pane, double-click **tblMemberLessons** to open the table in Datasheet view.

   Notice that only numbers exist in the MemberID and EmployeeID fields. By creating a lookup field, you will be able to display something other than a number — a key from a different table. This will make it easier to see who is scheduling lessons.

c. Click **Design View** on the Status bar, and then click the **MemberID** field.

d. Select **Lookup Wizard** from the Data Type list. The Lookup Wizard dialog box will open.

> **Troubleshooting**
> If a Microsoft Access Security Notice appears on your screen, it is safe to click Open. To avoid seeing this message in the future, add your database to the Trust Center.

e. If necessary, click **I want the lookup field to get the values from another table or query**, and then click **Next**.

> **Troubleshooting**
> If a relationship already exists on the field in which you want to use the Lookup Wizard, you must open the Relationships window and delete the existing relationship before going through the Lookup Wizard. Access will recreate the relationship automatically upon completion.

SIDE NOTE
Order Is Important
Select the fields in the same order as stated here. This specifies how the data will be displayed in the lookup field.

f. Select **tblMember**, and then click **Next**.

g. Select the **MemberID**, **LastName**, and **FirstName** fields to be included in your lookup field. You can move each one to the right side by either double-clicking the field name or clicking once on **One Field** [>].

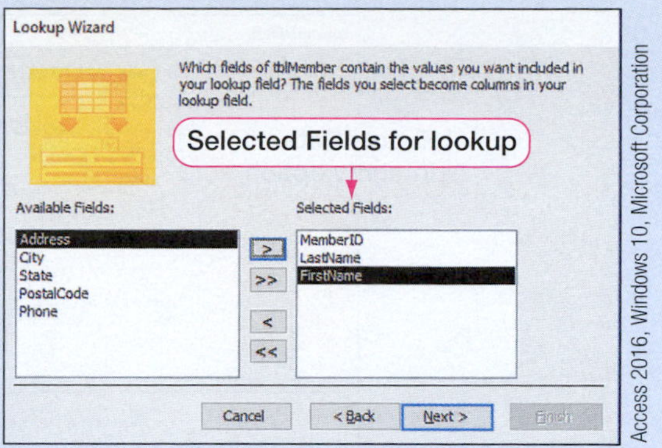

Figure 18 Selecting data in the Lookup Wizard dialog box

> **SIDE NOTE**
> **Using Descending Order**
> Ascending order is the default sort order. If you want to sort a field in descending order, click Ascending to change the sort order.

h. Click **Next**, and then sort the following fields in ascending order: LastName, FirstName.

Figure 19 Sorting data in the Lookup Wizard dialog box

i. Click **Next**, and then clear the **Hide key column** check box.

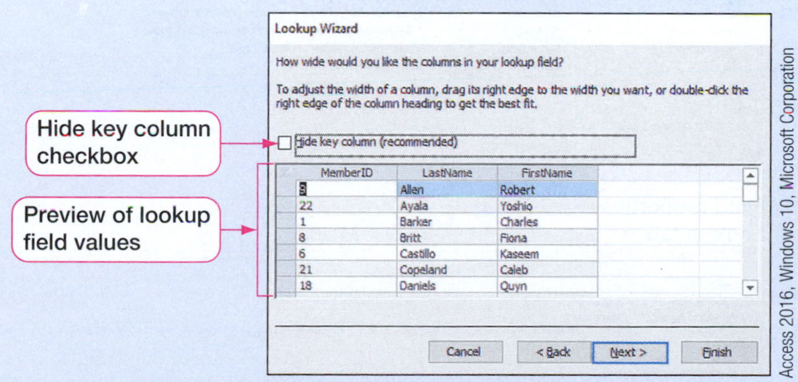

Figure 20 Unhide the Key column

> **SIDE NOTE**
> **Should You Rename the Lookup Field Label?**
> Because your field is already named, you do not need to rename it.

Notice how the key is displayed. If this box is left unchecked, the key column will be displayed in the lookup field. Because the key has no meaning other than helping you relate tables, hide it so that anyone using the lookup column sees only the values that you want them to see and not the values in the primary key field.

j. Click **Hide key column**, and then click **Next**.

k. Select **Enable Data Integrity** and **Restrict Delete**.

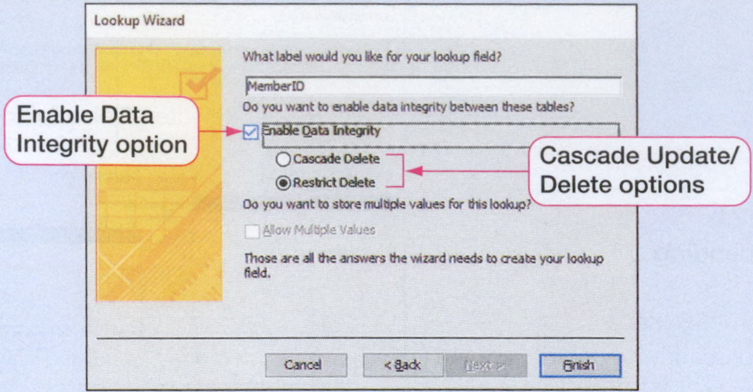

Figure 21 Finalizing the tblMember lookup field
Access 2016, Windows 10, Microsoft Corporation

l. Click **Finish**. Click **Yes** when prompted to save the table. Access will automatically create the relationship between tblMemberLessons and tblMember.

m. Click **Datasheet View** on the Status bar.

Notice how the lookup field displays the member's last name in the MemberID field. It is now much easier to determine which member has scheduled a lesson.

n. Click **Design View** on the Status bar, and then click the **MemberID** field if necessary. Under Field Properties, click the **Lookup** tab.

Notice that the Lookup Wizard configured many of the settings for you.

o. Change the Column Heads property to Yes, and then **Save** your changes.

SIDE NOTE

Double-Check Spelling

When creating a custom lookup field, always double-check your spelling before moving to the next screen in the wizard.

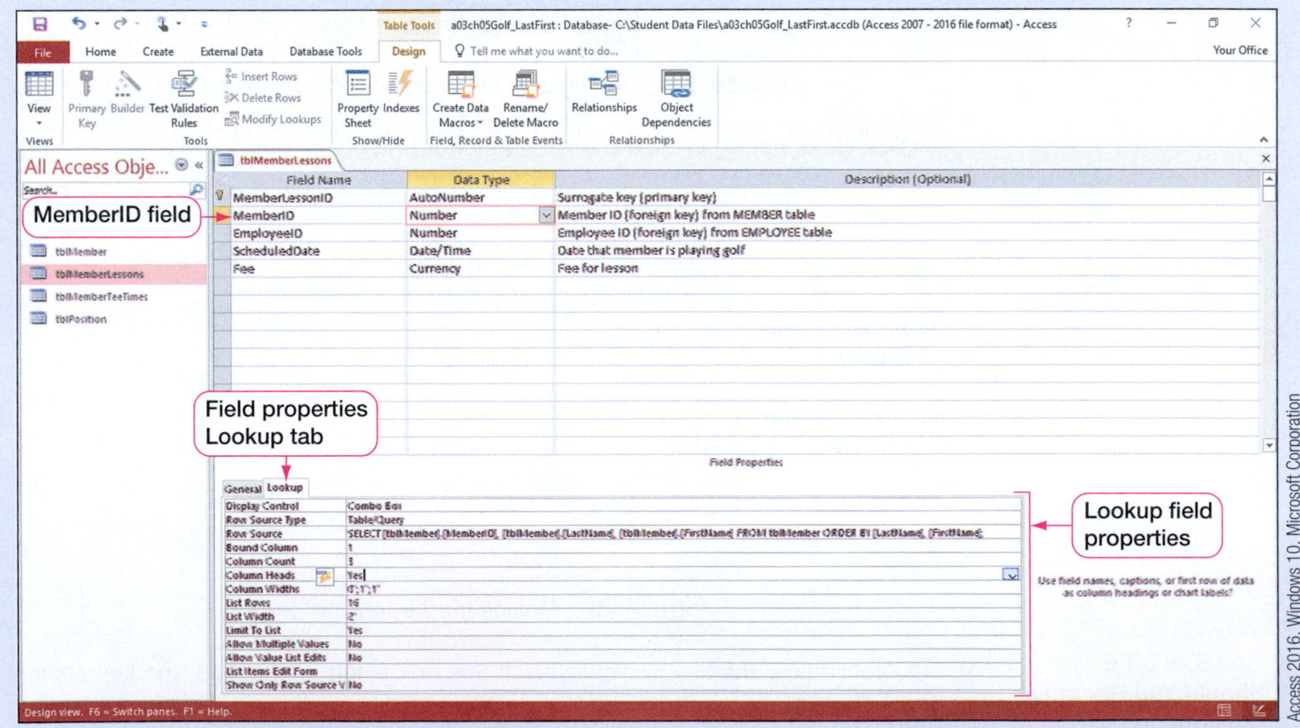

Figure 22 Column Heads field property on the Lookup tab

p. Click **Datasheet View** on the Status bar, click inside the **MemberID** field for the first record, and then click the **Selection** arrow to expand your lookup field's list.

Notice that there are headings in the columns.

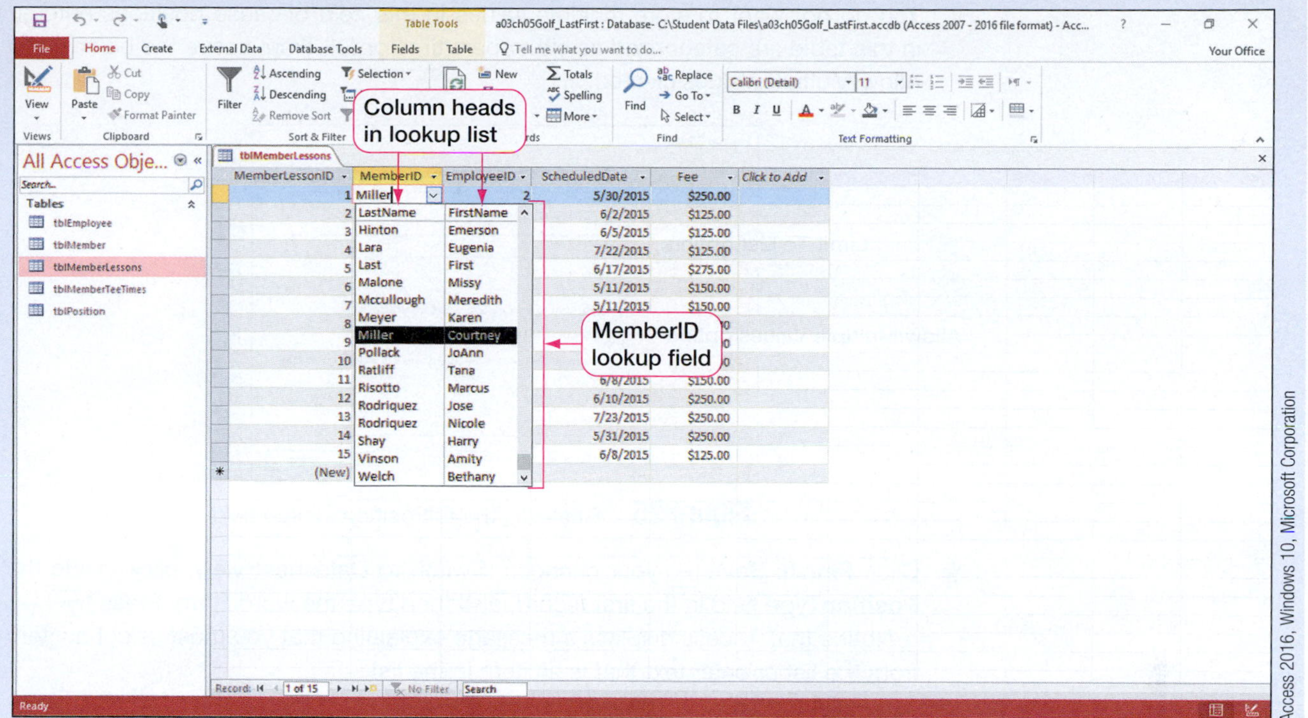

Figure 23 Lookup field with column heads

q. **Close** [X] tblMemberLessons.

r. In the Navigation Pane, right-click **tblPosition**, click **Design View**, and then click the **PositionType** field. Select **Lookup Wizard** from the Data Type list. The Lookup Wizard dialog box opens.

s. Select **I will type in the values that I want**, and then click **Next**.

t. Enter the following options:

Row 1: Full-time

Row 2: Part-time

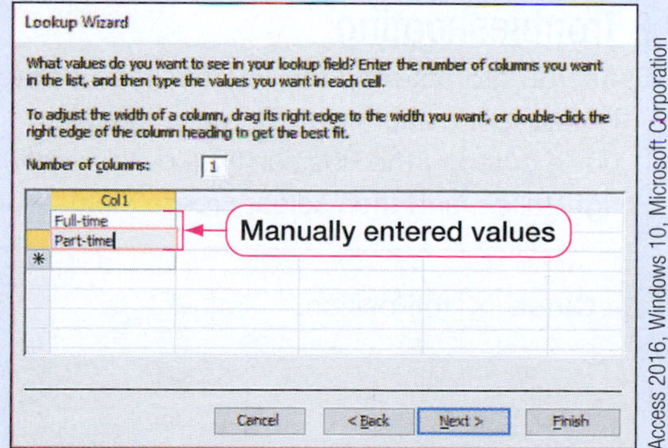

Figure 24 Values entered into the Lookup Wizard dialog box

Troubleshooting

When typing the values for a list, press [↓] or [Tab] to move down to the next row. Pressing [Enter] will cause the wizard to move to the next step.

u. Click **Next**. You want to limit the user's selection to the list because there are only part-time and full-time positions at the golf resort. Check the **Limit To List** box.

v. You do not want to store multiple values in this field because positions entered in this table are categorized as either part-time or full-time. Leave the box next to Allow Multiple Values cleared.

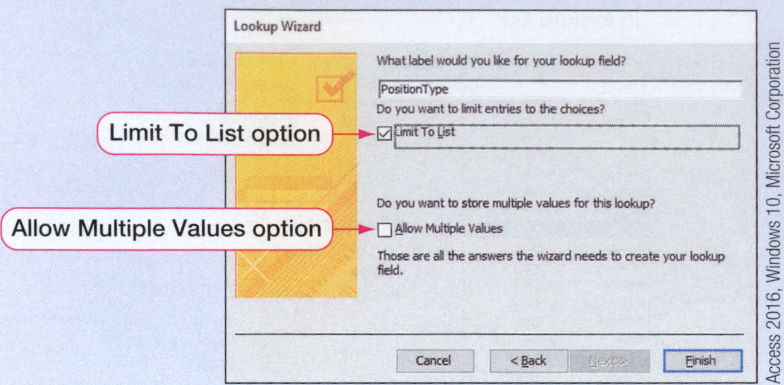

Figure 25 Finalizing the tblPosition lookup field

w. Click **Finish**. **Save** your changes. Switch to Datasheet view, click inside the **PositionType** field in the first record, and then type the word Both. Press Enter.

Notice that Access displays a message explaining that you must select an item from the list or enter text that is an item in the list.

x. Click **OK**, and then select **Full-time** from the list.

y. Enter the following from the list in the PositionType field.

Caddy Master: Full-time

Golf Caddy: Part-time

Golf Course Manager: Full-time

Golf Technician: Full-time

Head Golf Professional: Full-time

Part-time Golf Professional: Part-time

Pro Shop Attendant: Part-time

Pro Shop Manager: Full-time

Troubleshooting

As you are entering the PositionType data, you may not be able to see the EmployeePosition field. To make it easier to view the EmployeePosition field while entering the PositionType data, highlight the EmployeePosition field, right-click, and then select Freeze Fields from the menu.

z. **Close** tblPosition.

QUICK REFERENCE — **Define Custom Lookup Field Properties**

Property	Description
Display Control	You can set the control type to Text Box, List Box, or Combo Box. Combo Box is the most common choice for a lookup field.
Row Source Type	Choose whether to fill the lookup field with values from another table or query or from a list of values that you enter.
Row Source	Specify the table, query, or list of values that provides the values for the lookup field. When the Row Source Type property is set to Table/Query or Field List, this property should be set to a table or query name. When the Row Source Type property is set to Value List, this property should contain a list of values separated by semicolons.
Bound Column	Specify the column in the row source that supplies the value stored by the lookup field. This value can range from 1 to the number of columns in the row source.
Column Count	Specify the number of columns in the row source that can be displayed in the lookup field. To select which columns to display, you provide a column width in the Column Widths property.
Column Heads	Specify whether to display column headings.
Column Widths	Enter the column width for each column. If you do not want to display a column, such as an ID column, specify 0 for the width.
List Rows	Specify the number of rows that appear when you display the lookup field.
List Width	Specify the width of the control that appears when you display the lookup field.
Limit To List	Choose whether you can enter a value that is not in the list. If you have referential integrity set to Yes, this is irrelevant.
Allow Multiple Values	Indicates whether the lookup field allows multiple values to be selected. You cannot change the value of this property from Yes to No. To remove the option, delete the relationship(s) to the field, and rerun the Lookup Wizard.
Allow Value List Edits	Specify whether you can edit the items in a lookup field that is based on a value list. When this property is set to Yes and you right-click a lookup field that is based on a single-column value list, you will see the Edit List Items option. If the lookup field has more than one column, this property is ignored.
List Items Edit Form	Name an existing form to use to edit the list items in a lookup field that is based on a table or query.
Show Only Row Source Values	Show only values that match the current row source when Allow Multiple Values is set to Yes.

Configure Fields Using the Calculated, Yes/No, AutoNumber, Attachments, Hyperlinks, and OLE Objects Data Types

Another Access data type is called a **Calculated data type**. A Calculated data type allows the results of a calculation to be displayed in a read-only field. The calculation must refer to other fields in the same table and is created in the **Expression Builder**. The Expression Builder is a tool that helps you to create formulas and functions.

This feature can be useful for many reasons. For example, in an Invoice table, an ExtenededPrice field could be calculated by multiplying the Quantity and Price fields. In an Inventory table, the CurrentQuantityOnHand could be calculated by subtracting the TotalProductsSold from TotalProductsOnHand. In a Customer table, two or more fields could be joined — **concatenated** — such as with FirstName and LastName fields for address labels.

Some database designers say that adding calculated fields in a table violates normalization rules. In some situations, they are right. However, sometimes it is acceptable to break the rules. For example, if you know that you will need the calculation in every object — query, form, and report — based on the table and you know that the expression will not change over time, then use this data type. Additionally, if having the calculation in the table makes your data easier to understand, then this is an acceptable data type to use.

CONSIDER THIS | Could the Calculated Data Type Cause Challenges?

The Calculated data type in a table was introduced in Access 2010. Do you think that the use of this data type will affect the speed or size of a database at all? Give examples of when using Calculated data types in a table is and is not appropriate.

REAL WORLD ADVICE | Using the Expression Builder

The Expression Builder is a tool you can use to help write expressions, such as calculations in forms, reports, and queries, along with field properties in tables. You can easily retrieve names of fields and controls in your database as well as built-in functions that are available when you write expressions. The Expression Builder allows you to build expressions from scratch or select from many prebuilt expressions. Think of the Expression Builder as a way to retrieve and insert fields and functions you might have trouble remembering, such as identifier names for fields, tables, forms, or queries, functions, and arguments.

Configuring Fields Using the Calculated Data Type

In this exercise, you will create a new field with a calculated data type that will automatically concatenate the values from two different fields.

To Configure Fields Using the Calculated Data Type

a. In the Navigation Pane, right-click **tblEmployee**, and then click **Design View**.

b. Create a new field named NameTag, and then select the **Calculated** data type. The Expression Builder dialog box will open as soon as you change the data type to Calculated.

c. Double-click **FirstName** to add it to the Expression box.

d. Type &. This is the concatenation symbol that will allow you to combine data from different fields.

SIDE NOTE
The Table Name Is Listed
The Expression Elements box already displays the table you are using.

CHAPTER 5

SIDE NOTE

Square Brackets Around Field Names

Access adds square brackets around field names to denote that the data will come from an existing field.

e. Type " to indicate literal characters, press Spacebar, and then type " again.
   This will display a space after the name in the FirstName field.

f. Type & again, and then double-click **LastName** to add it to the Expression box.
   This will display the value in the LastName field after the space character.

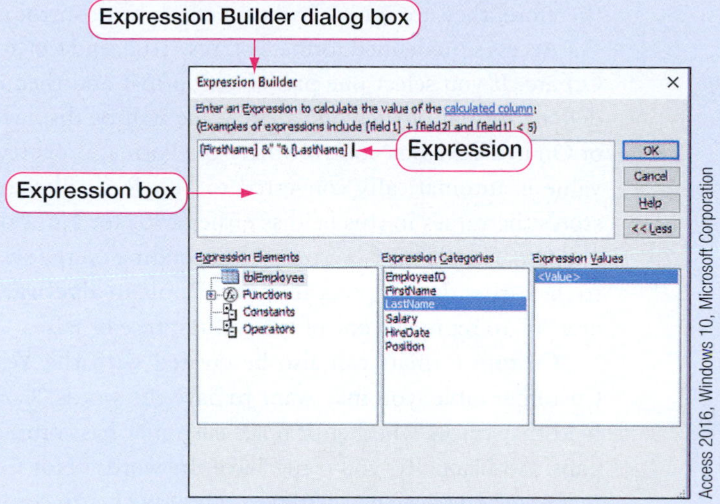

Figure 26 Expression Builder dialog box

g. Click **OK**.
   Notice that your expression is displayed in the Expression property under Field Properties.

h. Type Used for printing name tags into the Description field.

i. **Save** your changes.

j. To see how the Calculated field property works, switch to Datasheet view, resize the NameTag field to see all the data, and then enter the following record.

FirstName	LastName	Salary	HireDate	Position
Ken	Condon	67725	Today's date	Assistant Golf Professional

Notice that Access automatically adds the FirstName and LastName to the NameTag field.

Troubleshooting

A Calculated field is a read-only field and cannot be edited. If you made errors in entering the FirstName or LastName, make the changes you need to make in those fields. Access will automatically update the NameTag field.

Configuring Fields Using the Yes/No Data Type

The **Yes/No data type** allows you to set the Format property to either the Yes/No, True/False, or On/Off predefined format or to a custom format for the Yes/No data type. Access uses a check box as the default display for the Yes/No data type. A **check box** shows whether an option is selected by using a check mark to indicate that the option is selected. Predefined and custom formats apply only to data that is displayed in a box; therefore, they are ignored when a check box control is used.

Access's predefined formats of Yes, True, and On are equivalent, just as No, False, and Off are. If you select one predefined format and then enter an equivalent value, the predefined format of the equivalent value will be displayed. For example, if you enter True or On in a Text Box control where the Format property is set to the Yes/No data type, the value is automatically converted to Yes. Regardless of which format is selected, Access stores the values in this field as either a "0" for No, False, and Off or a "–1" for Yes, True, and On. The "0" and "1", or "–1" depending on the system you are using, are a throwback to the earlier days of programming. **Boolean algebra**, which is still used today, uses a "1" or a "0" to represent one of two values: true or false.

Custom formats can also be created with the Yes/No data type. For example, in a Customer table, you may want to have the words "Completed" or "Not Completed" in a field that tracks whether or not a customer has completed a survey sent out by the company. Additionally, you could have the words "Not Completed" displayed in red font so it is easier to view the customers who have yet to complete the survey.

QUICK REFERENCE | **The Three Parts of a Custom Yes/No Data Type**

The Yes/No data type can use custom formats containing up to three sections.

1. First section: This section has no effect on the Yes/No data type. However, a semicolon is required and used as a placeholder.
2. Second section: This part contains the text to display in place of Yes, True, or On values.
3. Third section: This part contains the text to display in place of No, False, or Off values.

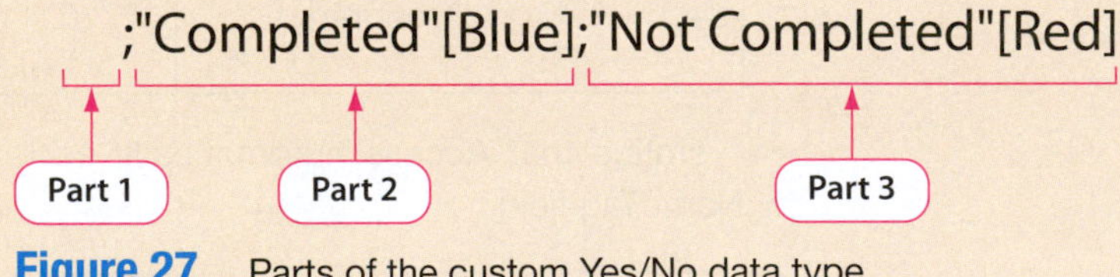

Figure 27 Parts of the custom Yes/No data type

In this exercise, you will create a new field with a Yes/No data type to easily determine which employees have competed their new hire orientation.

To Configure Fields Using the Yes/No Data Type

a. Click **Design View** on the Status bar to switch to the Design view of the tblEmployee table.

b. Create a new field called Orientation, and then select the **Yes/No** data type.

c. Type Is new hire orientation complete? into the Description field.

d. **Save** your changes.

SIDE NOTE

Check Box or Text Box

Checking a box is certainly easier than typing text. Choose a format on the basis of your customization needs and personal preferences.

e. To see how the Yes/No field property works, switch to Datasheet view, and then click the **check box** for Ken Condon's record, indicating that his orientation has been completed.

f. Switch to Design view, and then, if necessary, click the **Orientation** field.

g. Under Field Properties, click the **Lookup** tab, click the **Display Control** property, and then click the **Display Control property arrow**.

Notice the different options you have. Instead of a check box, you can format a Yes/No field as a text box or combo box.

h. Under Field Properties click the **General** tab.

i. Switch to Datasheet view, and change the following employees' orientation status to "Completed" by clicking the **check box** in the Orientation field.

John Schilling
Robert Lange
Ginger Liu
Juan Martinez
Samual Dancer
Paul Kimons
Aleeta Herriott
Lilly Baine
Dennis Matrell
Antonio Ruweeze

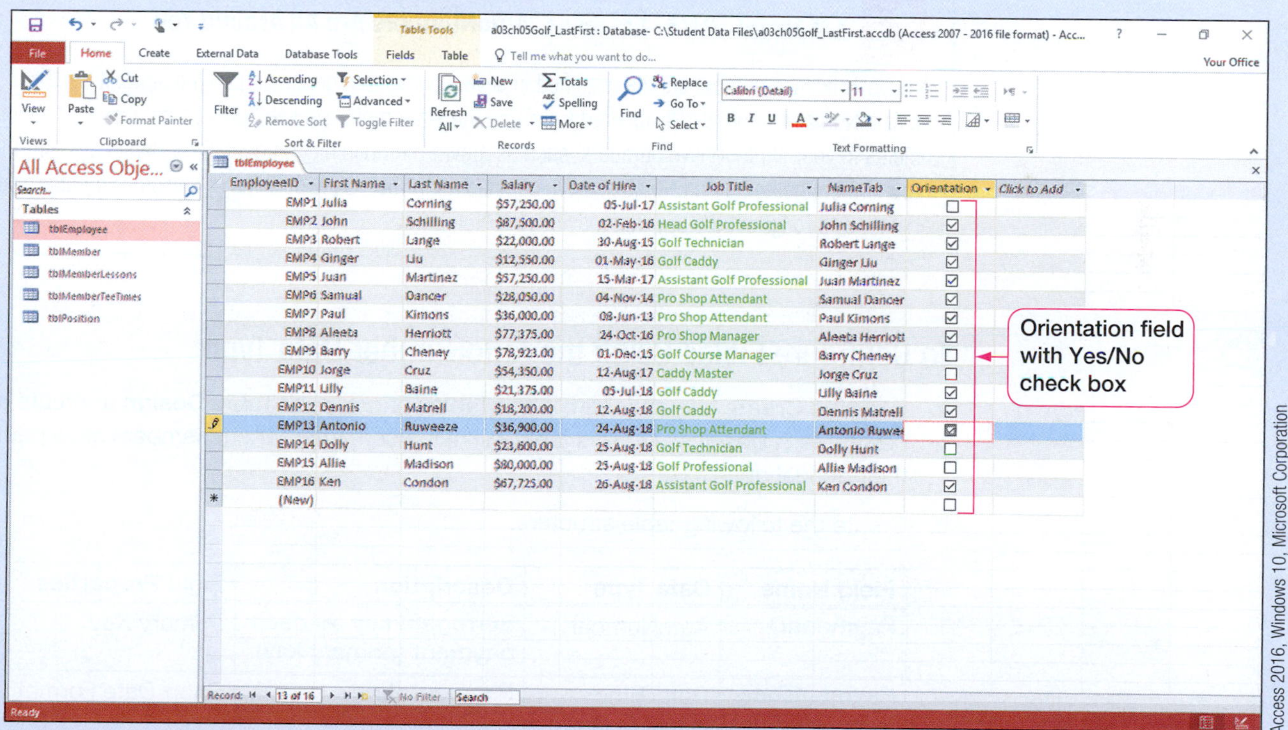

Figure 28 Yes/No field displayed as a check box

j. **Close** ☒ tblEmployee.

Configuring Fields Using the AutoNumber Data Type

A primary key uniquely identifies a record in a table. A **surrogate key** is an artificial column added to a table to serve as a primary key that is unique and sequential when records are created. However, these unique, sequential values are meaningless to users from a value standpoint; they are meaningful only in regard to creating relationships between tables.

An ideal surrogate key is short and numeric, and it never changes. In Access, a surrogate key is known as the **AutoNumber data type**. The AutoNumber data type stores an integer that Access creates automatically as you add new records. These AutoNumbers can be categorized as increment or random. An **increment AutoNumber** is the most common and is the default setting in Access in selecting the AutoNumber data type. A **random AutoNumber** will generate a random number that is unique to each record within the table. Either type of AutoNumber will serve as a good primary key. AutoNumbers are a great method for ensuring that records are uniquely identified.

Some challenges do exist in working with AutoNumbers, and one in particular causes some stress with users. An AutoNumber of a deleted record will never be used again. For example, if you have a table with ten records and the primary key is an AutoNumber — meaning that the records are numbered incrementally from 1 through 10 — and you delete record number 7, Access will never use 7 again in the AutoNumber field. If this happens to you, do not think you did something wrong. This is simply how relational databases operate. Because of the way that Access does not reuse numbers, they are not designed to count records and should never be used for that purpose.

CONSIDER THIS | AutoNumbers Are All Around You

A driver's license number can be assigned in several ways, but depending on the state, it can be an AutoNumber automatically created for you in the state motor vehicle bureau's database. Think of objects in your life that have numbers, such as a gym membership, student ID, or debit card. Are the numbers on the items AutoNumbers? Which ones might be? Can you think of any other numbers you encounter throughout the day that may be AutoNumbers?

To Configure Fields Using the AutoNumber Data Type

a. Click the **Create** tab, and then, in the Tables group, click **Table Design** to create a new table in Design view. This table will help users track when members have paid their annual dues.

b. Create the following table structure.

Field Name	Data Type	Description	Field Properties
PaymentID	AutoNumber	Surrogate key for each payment (primary key)	Primary Key
PaymentDate	Date/Time	Payment date	Short Date Format
AmountPaid	Currency	Payment amount	
MemberID	Lookup Wizard		

c. When the Lookup Wizard opens, click **I want the lookup field to get the values from another table or query**.

d. Click **Next**, and then select **tblMember**.

e. Click **Next**, and then select the following fields to be included in your lookup field: **MemberID**, **LastName**, and **FirstName**.

CHAPTER 5

f. Click **Next**, and then select the following ascending sort order for the data in your lookup field: **LastName**, **FirstName**.

g. Click **Next** two times, and then select **Enable Data Integrity** and **Restrict Delete**.

h. Click **Finish**, and then click **Yes** when Access prompts you to save the table.

i. **Save** your table as tblPayment, and then click **OK**.

j. In the Description field of the MemberID field, type This is the member who made the payment.

k. **Save** your changes.

Troubleshooting

Sometimes you may see a warning message that states, "tblPayment has been changed since the last time you opened it, either by another user or because another instance was opened on your own machine." If you know you have not made changes outside the database, click Yes.

SIDE NOTE
The Lookup Fields Do Not Display All the Data
Lookup fields that have multiple fields will display only the data that is displayed in the first column.

l. To see how the AutoNumber data type works, switch to Datasheet view, and then enter the following records. You may have to scroll down in the list to find the names.

PaymentDate	AmountPaid	MemberID
1/26/2018	1200	Duke
2/23/2018	1500	Risotto

Notice that as you enter the data, Access automatically enters the PaymentID for you.

m. Delete the **record** where the PaymentID is **1**. Click **Yes** to confirm the deletion of this record.

n. Enter the following record to see how the AutoNumber data type behaves when a record is deleted.

PaymentDate	AmountPaid	MemberID
3/5/2018	500	Pollack

Notice that as you enter the data, Access enters a PaymentID of 3.

SIDE NOTE
AutoNumbers Are Used Once
Once a number has been used in a table, Access never uses that AutoNumber again, even if a record has been deleted.

o. To see how the random AutoNumber data type works, switch to Design view.

p. Click the **PaymentID** field, and then, under Field Properties select the **New Values** property.

q. Change the New Values property from Increment to **Random**. As soon as you do, Access will warn you that once you change this property, you will not be able to change it back.

r. Click **Yes**, and then save your changes.

s. To see how the random AutoNumber data type works, switch to Datasheet view, and then enter the following records.

PaymentDate	AmountPaid	MemberID
4/8/2018	800	Allen
5/25/2018	2250	Britt

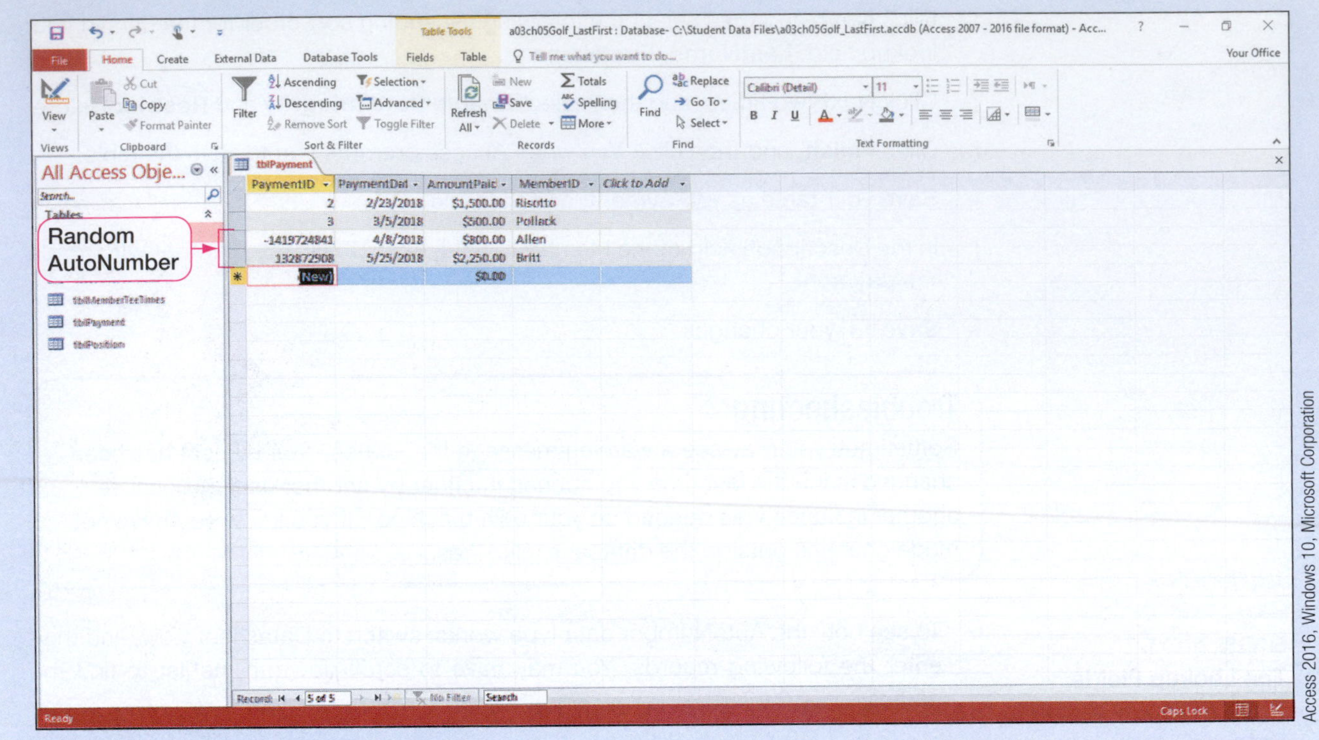

Figure 29 Random AutoNumber

> **Troubleshooting**
> Because Access creates a random AutoNumber, there is no knowing what number will appear. The number can be positive or negative. Whatever value Access enters and displays is acceptable.

t. **Close** [X] tblPayment.

Configuring Fields Using the Attachments, Hyperlinks, and OLE Objects Data Types

Images, spreadsheet files, documents, charts, and other types of supported files can be attached to the records in a database, much the way files are attached to an e-mail message. Access allows attached files to be viewed and edited, depending on how the database designer configures the **attachment** field properties. Since attachments increase the size of the database, database developers need to ensure that attachments will not use too much storage space.

In Access, fields that contain e-mail or website addresses should be defined as the Hyperlink data type. A **hyperlink** is an address that specifies a protocol — such as HTTP or FTP — and a location of an object, document, World Wide Web page, or other destination on the Internet, an intranet, or a local computer. An example is http://www.paintedparadiseresort.com. If the field is not defined as a hyperlink, Access will store it as plain text. This means that users will not be able to click it to navigate to a particular website or to launch an e-mail application and write an e-mail message.

When working with e-mail addresses, Access adds "mailto:" at the beginning of the e-mail address. The **Mailto command** is a common type of hyperlink that helps to generate a link for sending e-mail. With the Mailto command, the data is recognized as an email address and not a link to a website or document. Users will be able to click the link and compose their e-mail in their default e-mail client.

Because many companies have files that are stored on the company's server so that multiple employees have access to them, a **universal naming convention (UNC)** path can also be entered in a hyperlink field. This is a naming convention that provides a link to the machine and location where a file is stored. A UNC name uses the syntax *\\server\share\path\filename* and works the same way a Uniform Resource Locator (URL) works for a web address.

Access can also store images inside a database field by using the OLE Object data type. **OLE**, which stands for Object Linking and Embedding, is a technology developed by Microsoft that creates a **bitmap** or image of an object. The OLE Object data type can be used in much the same way as a bitmap, but it is less efficient than a bitmap because it consumes a great deal of space within the database. OLE is a legacy data type that needs to be included for existing databases, but attachments are far more functional and efficient and do not even use an OLE object. A **legacy data type** is an old or outdated data type that is still used — usually because it still works for the user — even though newer technology or more efficient methods exist. An attachment is the more efficient of the two data types because it does not consume as much space.

To Configure Fields Using the Attachments, Hyperlinks, and OLE Objects Data Types

a. In the Navigation Pane, right-click **tblEmployee**, and then click **Design View**.

b. Add the following new fields.

Field Name	Data Type	Description
EmailAddress	Hyperlink	E-mail address
Photo	OLE Object	Golf photo
OrientationSignOff	Attachment	Form verifying orientation completion

c. **Save** your changes. To see how the Hyperlink data type works, switch to Datasheet view, and then enter the following data. Resize the field so you can see what you are typing.

EmployeeID	NameTag	EmailAddress
EMP4	Ginger Liu	liug@paintedparadise.com
EMP12	Dennis Matrell	matrelld@paintedparadise.com
EMP16	Ken Condon	condonk@paintedparadise.com

Notice that a hyperlink is automatically created once you enter the e-mail addresses.

d. To insert an OLE Object into the Photo field, right-click the **Photo** field in Ginger Liu's record, and then select **Insert Object**. The Microsoft Access dialog box opens.

e. Click **Create from File**.

SIDE NOTE
Why Is the Photo Not Visible?
An OLE Object data type does not display the picture in the table. The Attachment data type for pictures allows a thumbnail to display on forms and reports.

f. Browse for the employee photos in your student data files. Insert the following employee photo in the Photo field.

EmployeeID	NameTag	Photo
EMP4	Ginger Liu	**a03ch05Liu.jpg**

g. Click the **Link** check box, and then click **OK**.
Notice that once the photo has been inserted into the Photo field, the object is displayed as a Package.

Troubleshooting

Sometimes Access can be a little tricky when you are entering objects such as photos or attachments. If you enter one and Access will not let you enter any others, click in another field and check to see whether Access will let you right-click into the OLE Object field. If that still does not work, close and then reopen the table.

SIDE NOTE
Why Check Link?
Not checking Link will cause Access to embed the image in the database, which takes up more storage space.

h. Right-click the Photo field in Dennis Matrell's record, and then select **Insert Object**.

i. In the Microsoft Access dialog box, click **Create from File**.

j. Browse for the following employee photo in your student data files, and then insert the photo in the Photo field.

EmployeeID	NameTag	Photo
EMP12	Dennis Matrell	**a03ch05Matrell.jpg**

k. Click the **Link** check box, and then click **OK**.

l. Right-click the **Photo field** in Ken Condon's record, and then select **Insert Object**.

m. In the Microsoft Access dialog box, click **Create from File**.

n. Browse for the following employee photo in your student data files. Insert the following employee photo in the Photo field.

EmployeeID	NameTag	Photo
EMP16	Ken Condon	**a03ch05Condon.jpg**

o. Click the **Link** check box, and then click **OK**.

p. To insert an attachment into the OrientationSignOff field, double-click the **Paperclip** in Ginger Liu's record. The Attachments dialog box opens.

q. Click **Add**, and then browse for and double-click **a03ch05Liu.pdf** in your student data files. The a03ch05Liu.pdf should now be displayed in your Attachments dialog box.

r. Click **OK** to close the Attachments dialog box. Then double-click the **Paperclip** in Ginger Liu's record again.

s. To view the attachment, double-click **a03ch05Liu.pdf** in the Attachments dialog box. The PDF document will open in another window.

SIDE NOTE
Numbers in Parentheses
In the Attachment field, the numbers in the parentheses indicate how many attachments exist in that field.

Troubleshooting

If the PDF document did not open, you may not have Adobe Acrobat Reader installed on your computer. You can download this free application at http://www.adobe.com.

t. **Close** [X] the PDF document, and then close the Attachments dialog box by clicking **OK**.

u. **Close** [X] tblEmployee, and then click **Yes** when prompted to save.

v. If you need to take a break before finishing this chapter, now is a good time.

Filtering Data

Filtering is very useful when only selected and required data needs to be viewed or printed in a database. Filters provide only a temporary view of the data, so filters are often saved as queries if the same criteria are to be used over and over again. In this section, you will learn how to filter data using Filter by Form, Filter by Selection, and advanced filter options.

Create Filters to View Specific Records

Three types of filtering exist. Access provides the ability to filter records containing similar values of data for a specific field. For example, records containing the value of "Santa Fe" in the City field may be of interest. The **Filter by Form** type could be used, which allows data to be filtered by using a form or datasheet. The Filter by Form method creates a blank table for the selected table. This blank table contains all the fields of the table with a list for each field. Each list contains all the unique values of records for each field. This method allows for the easy selection of the field values for which to use to filter the table records.

In some cases, the **Filter by Selection** method may not be very helpful because it may require extra steps to find the initial value to use as the filter. Filter by Selection displays only the rows in a table containing a value that matches a selected value in a row by filtering data in Datasheet view. In the above scenario, you may find that the Filter by Form method is better.

Because the Filter by Form or Filter by Selection filters may not give enough options, as they are fairly basic, an advanced filter may prove useful. An **advanced filter** is a filter for which the user defines the filter criterion. For example, an advanced filter could be used to locate products that have been sold during the past seven days. After applying an advanced filter, one can further limit the results to those that have a price over $100. However, using advanced filters requires writing expressions.

Creating Filters

In this exercise, you will explore how to create various filters on the tblMember table.

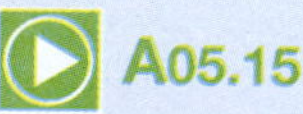

To Create Filters

a. If you took a break, open the **a03ch05Golf** database.

b. In the Navigation Pane, double-click **tblMember**.
   Notice that there are 30 records in tblMember.

c. To filter by selection, click the **City** field of Record 1.

d. On the Home tab, in the Sort & Filter group, click the **Selection** arrow.

e. Four options are displayed. Select **Equals "Santa Fe"**.
   Notice that all 13 members who live in Santa Fe are displayed. Additionally, the Filter button appears at the top of the field where the filter has been applied.

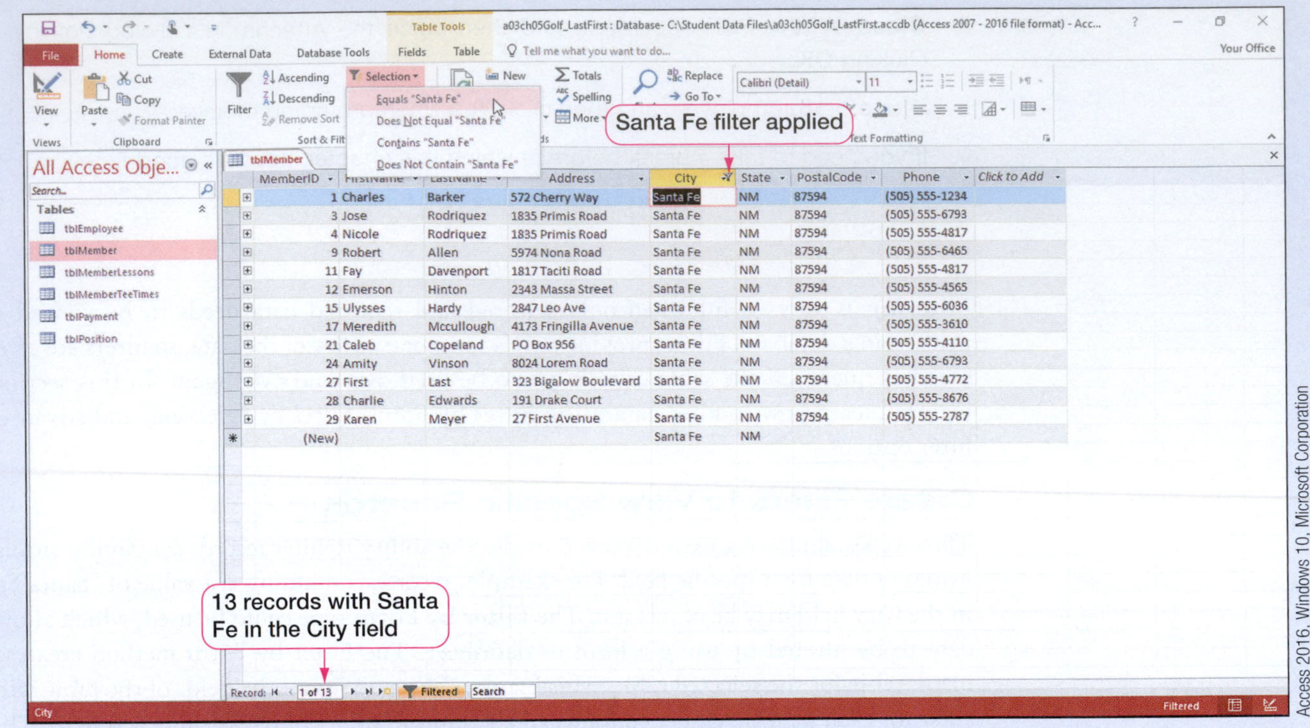

Figure 30 Filter by Selection applied

f. On the Home tab, in the Sort & Filter group, click **Toggle Filter**.
   Notice that the filter is now removed.

g. Click **Toggle Filter** again, and the filter is reapplied.

h. Click **Toggle Filter** again to remove it.

i. To filter by form, on the Home tab, in the Sort & Filter group, click **Advanced**, and then click **Filter By Form**.

j. Click in a few of the fields.
   Notice that "Santa Fe" remains in the City field and each field has a list and looks much like a form. An Or tab also appears at the bottom of the table.

k. Select **Eagle Nest** from the list in the City field.

l. On the Home tab, in the Sort & Filter group, click **Toggle Filter**. Three records meet the selected criteria.

m. On the Home tab, in the Sort & Filter group, click **Advanced**, and then click **Filter By Form**.

n. Leave **Eagle Nest** in the City field. At the bottom of the tblMember: Filter by Form pane, click the **Or** tab.
   This will allow you to search for one criterion or another. The Or operator indicates that either of the criteria can be in a record in order to display it in the filter results.

o. In the State field select **AZ**, and then click **Toggle Filter**.
   Notice that four records meet the filter criteria. The Filter is displayed at the top of the City and State fields, indicating that you have applied a filter to both fields.

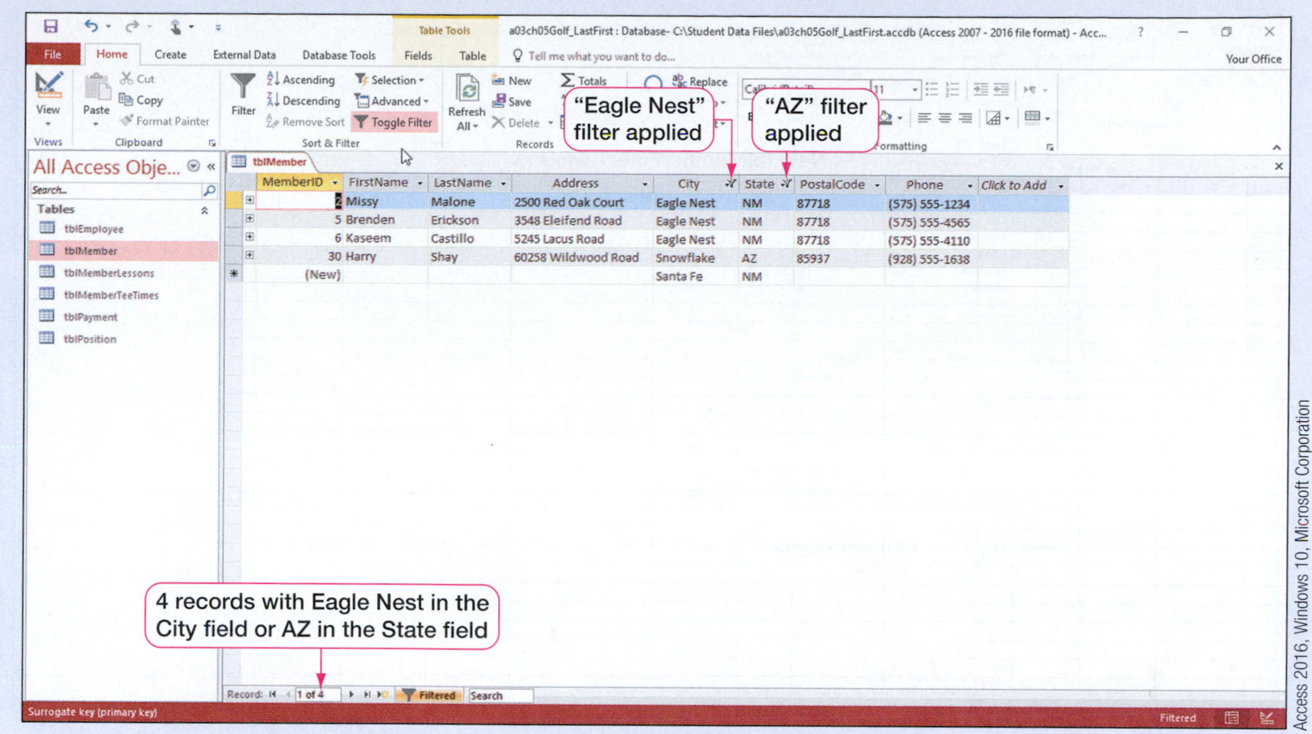

Figure 31 Filter by Form applied

p. Click **Advanced**, click **Clear All Filters**, and then click **Advanced**.

q. Select **Advanced Filter/Sort**. The tblMemberFilter1 pane opens.

r. Select the following fields, and enter the following criteria in the tblMemberFilter1 grid.

Field	Field Name	Criteria
1	City	Santa Fe
		Cowles (enter under "or" line below Criteria)

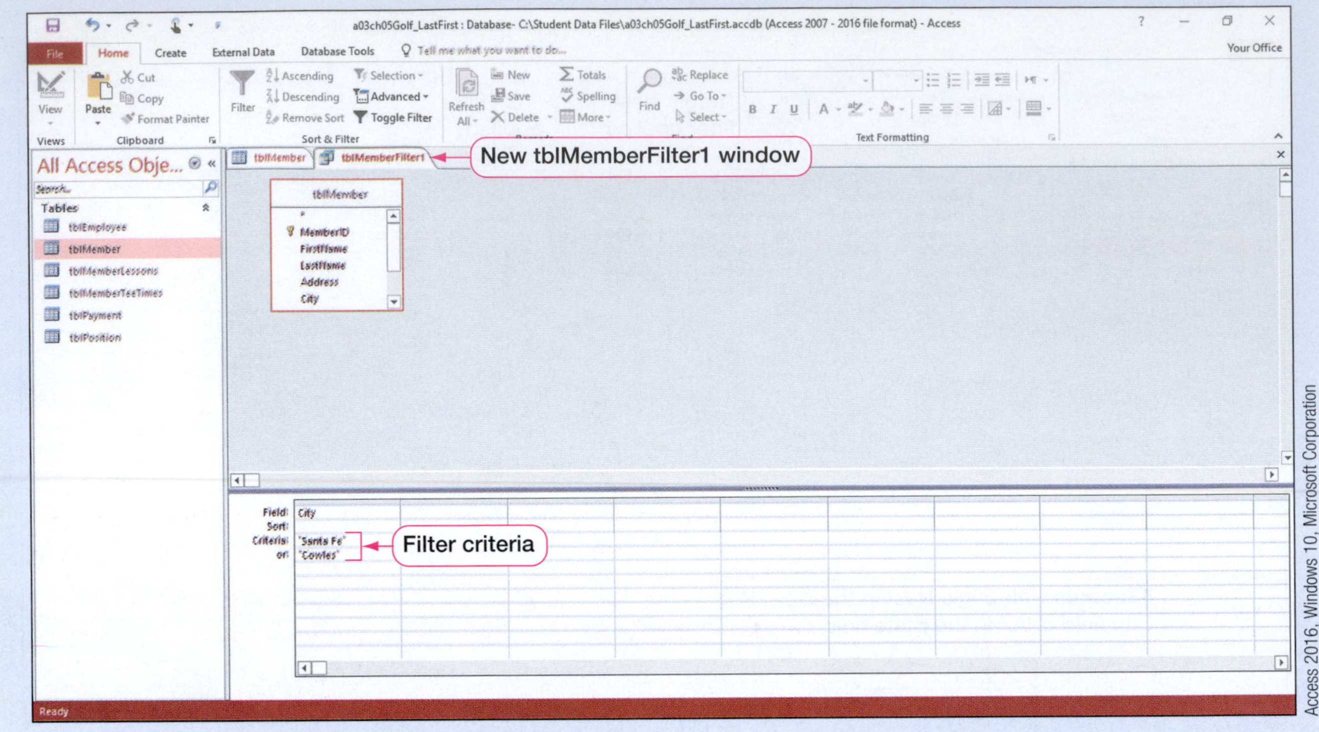

Figure 32 Advanced Filter applied

s. Click **Toggle Filter**.
   Notice that the results of the Advanced Filter are now displayed in tblMember.

t. Click the **File** tab. Click **Save As**, click **Save Object As**, and then save your filter with the name qrySantaFeMembers. Under **As**, select **Query** from the list.

u. Click **OK**.
   Notice that there is a new object named qrySantaFeMembers. This is the query you just created and saved.

v. **Close** [X] qrySantaFeMembers, **Close** [X] tblMemberFilter1, and then **Close** [X] tblMember. When Access prompts you to save the changes to tblMember, click **No**.

w. If you need to take a break before finishing this chapter, now is a good time.

Reducing Redundancy

Many times, employees will store data in an Excel spreadsheet because they know how to use Excel but not Access. Although Excel is a great tool for many tasks, it may not allow users to create the sophisticated queries that they need for decision making. Because of this, there are times that you will want to import an Excel spreadsheet into Access and work with the data. However, Excel spreadsheets often contain redundant data. **Redundancy** in data occurs when the same data is entered multiple times in multiple places. Redundant data can lead to data entry errors, inconsistent data, and other issues that can negatively affect decision making. Relational database management systems, such as Access, work most efficiently if redundant data is minimal or eliminated altogether. In this section, you will learn how to reduce redundancy by using the Table Analyzer Wizard.

Use the Table Analyzer Wizard

By using the Access **Table Analyzer Wizard**, you can divide a table created from imported data, such as an Excel spreadsheet, into several tables and can automatically create the relationships you need between them. The Table Analyzer Wizard minimizes the need for data reentry, saving you valuable time and resources. However, the Table Analyzer Wizard cannot restructure all the imported data properly.

Using the Table Analyzer Wizard

In this exercise, you will use the Table Analyzer Wizard to reduce redundancy in the tblMember table.

To Use the Table Analyzer Wizard

a. If you took a break, open the **a03ch05Golf** database.

b. In the Navigation Pane, click **tblMember** to select it. Click the **Database Tools** tab, and then, in the Analyze group, click **Analyze Table**. The Table Analyzer Wizard opens to the first introduction dialog box.

Troubleshooting

After clicking Analyze Table, you may see an error that says a potential security concern has been identified. Because there are no macros in this database, it is safe to click OK.

c. Click **Next**. The next introduction screen is displayed.

d. Click **Next** again, and then select **tblMember** if necessary.

e. Click **Next**, and then, if necessary, click **Yes, let the wizard decide**.

f. Click **Next**.

g. Access will create two new tables: Table1 and Table2. Double-click the **current table names**, and then rename them as follows.
Table1: tblMemberData
Table2: tblCityZip

h. Click **Next**.
The primary key in the new tblCityZip table will be an AutoNumber, which is an ideal primary key. Access has **Generated Unique ID** as the first field in this table, which implies AutoNumber. You may have to resize the tables to see the whole table and field names.

i. Click **Next**.

SIDE NOTE
Minimized Navigation Pane
After you finish using the Table Analyzer Wizard, the Navigation Pane may be closed. If so, click the Shutter Bar Open/Close button.

j. There are no typographical errors that need to be fixed. Click **Next**. Access will ask whether you are sure you want to move on. Click **Yes**.

k. Access asks whether you want to create a query that resembles your old table. Because your old table will be saved automatically, you will not need a query with the same data. Click **No, don't create the query**.

l. Click **Finish**. Both tables you just created — tblMemberData and tblCityZip — will open.
The tblMemberData table has a new tblCityZip_ID field with a caption of Lookup to tblCityZip that contains the city, state, and ZIP Code for each member.

Troubleshooting

Access sometimes opens the Help window to offer further assistance with analyzing the table. Just close it if it opens.

Troubleshooting

Access sometimes displays an error message that says it cannot tile the tables horizontally. Just close the message if it opens.

m. **Close** [X] tblMemberData and tblCityZip.

n. Save the database, exit Access, and then submit your file as directed by your instructor.

REAL WORLD ADVICE — **Why Worry About Analyzing Tables?**

When Access creates new tables in the Table Analyzer Wizard, it is looking for a way to minimize storage space in the analyzed table by storing data more efficiently. When a table contains redundant data in one or more fields, such as a city or state, you can use the Table Analyzer Wizard to move the data into related tables. This process is called normalization.

QUICK REFERENCE — **About the Table Analyzer Wizard**

Access takes you through a series of screens when you are working through the wizard:

- Looking at the Problem — This contains an explanation and examples of how duplicate data causes problems in a database.
- Solving the Problem — This contains an explanation and examples of how Access may split the table into multiple tables if there is redundant data in your table.
- Select Table — Select the table you want to analyze.
- What Fields Go in What Tables Decision — This is where you determine whether you want Access to decide or you want to select what fields go in what tables.
- Review Grouping — This is where you will either review or edit what Access has created or where you will create your new tables, depending on your decision in the previous step.
- Create Primary Keys — Bold fields will indicate what the new primary keys will be. You can either keep them the way they are or edit them.
- Correct Typographical Errors — The wizard gives you the opportunity to fix any errors in your data.
- Create a Query — Access can create a query that resembles your old table. This is a smart thing to have as a backup copy.

CHAPTER 5

Concept Check

1. Explain why it is important to worry about the way data is entered into a database. p. 279
2. What are the similarities and differences between an input mask and custom formatting? p. 279–292
3. Why are data validation rules helpful in business? p. 293
4. Why are captions also known as aliases? p. 296
5. What is an index? Why would you define an index in a table? p. 298
6. How can the creation of too many constraints or rules, such as requiring data, on a field or fields cause challenges for users? p. 301
7. How do default values assist in data entry? p. 302
8. How do lookup fields help to improve the efficiency of the data entry process? p. 304–305
9. What is the Calculated data type, and why do some database designers say it may be an inappropriate data type? p. 312
10. Define the three types of data filters, and give an example of when each may be used. p. 321
11. How does the Table Analyzer Wizard help to reduce redundancy? p. 324–325

Key Terms

Advanced filter 321
Attachment 318
AutoNumber data type 316
Bitmap 319
Boolean algebra 314
Bound value 304
Calculated data type 312
Caption property 296
Check box 314
Concatenate 312
Custom formatting 287
Data type 304
Data validation rule 293
Default value 302
Display Value 304
Expression Builder 312
Field format 287
Field validation rule 293
Filter by Form 321
Filter by Selection 321
Filtering 321
GIGO principle 279
Hyperlink 318
Increment AutoNumber 316
Index 298
Input mask 279
Input Mask Wizard 280
Legacy data type 319
Lookup field 304
Lookup field properties 305
Lookup Wizard 304
Mailto command 319
Multiple-field index 300
Multivalued field 304
Null 301
OLE 319
Random AutoNumber 316
Record validation rule 293
Redundancy 324
Required property 301
Single-field index 299
String 303
Surrogate key 316
Table Analyzer Wizard 325
Universal naming convention (UNC) 319
Validation text 293
Validation Text property 293
Yes/No data type 314
Zero-length string 301

Visual Summary

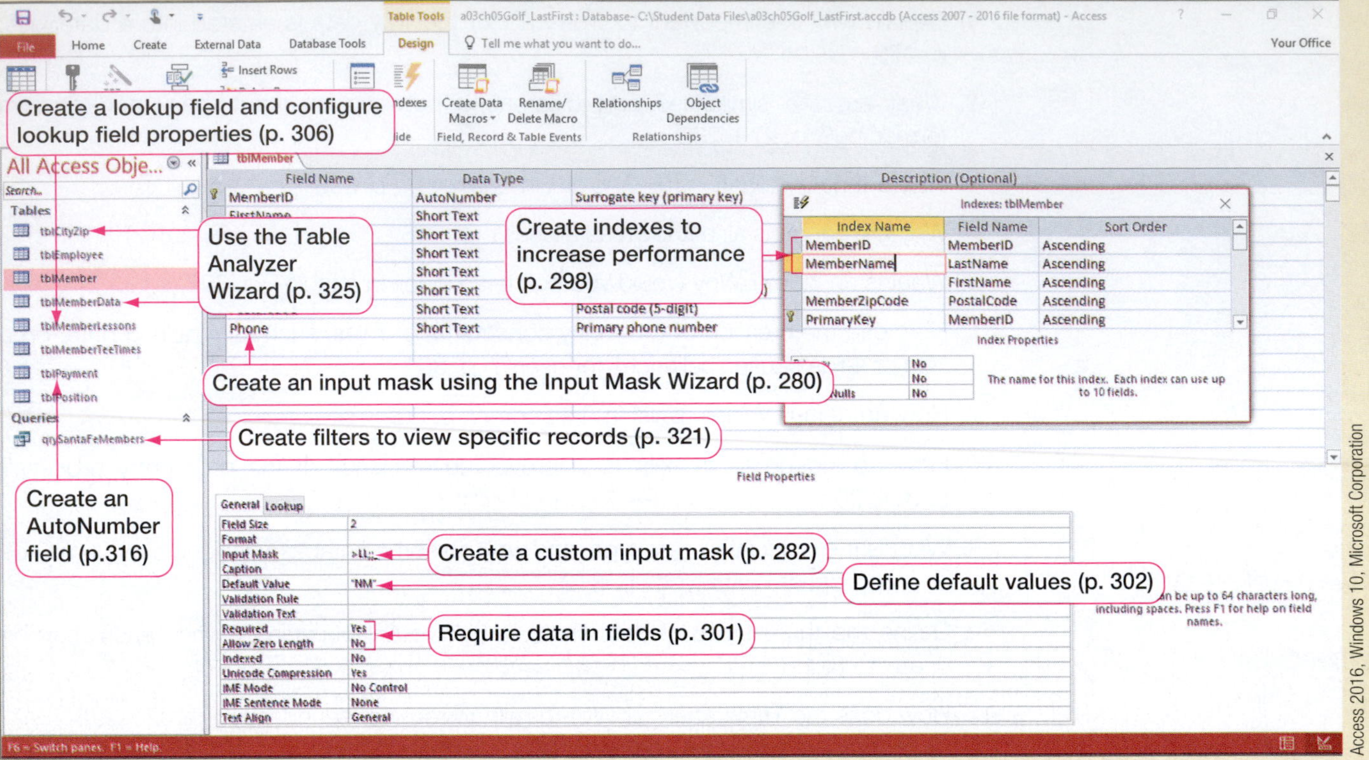

Figure 33

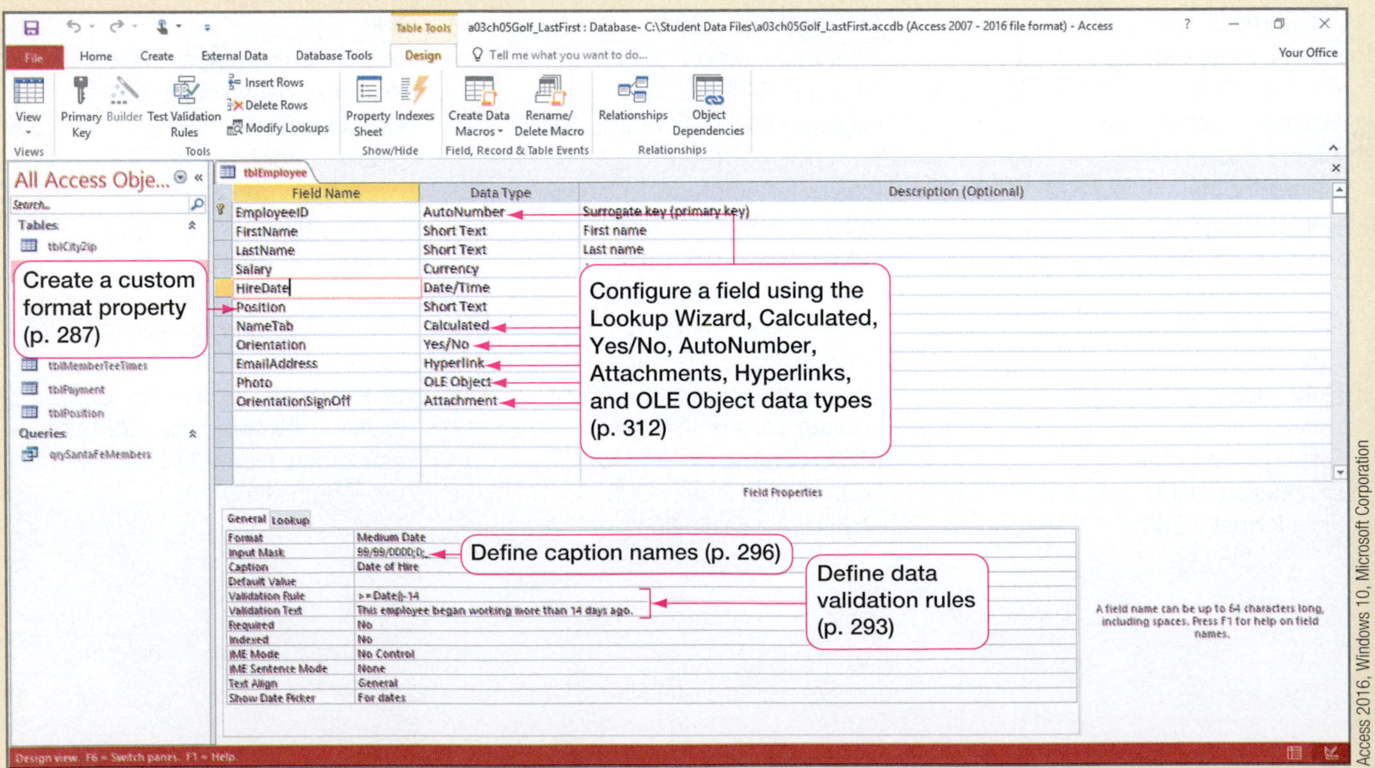

Figure 34

Practice 1

Student data file needed:

 a03ch05Scheduling.accdb

You will save your file as:

 a03ch05Scheduling_LastFirst.accdb

Scheduling Employees at the Red Bluff Golf Course & Pro Shop

Human Resources

Generally, the Red Bluff Golf Course manager schedules one caddy for every two reservations because not every golfer uses a caddy. Golfers can choose to use a caddy, carry their own bag, or rent a golf cart. You have been asked to add a table — including advanced formatting and controls — to track the golf caddies' work schedule.

a. Open the **a03ch05Scheduling** database, and then save it as a03ch05Scheduling_LastFirst using your last and first name. If necessary, enable the content.

b. Open **tblEmployee**, add your first and last name in record 1, and then close tblEmployee.

c. Click the **Create** tab, and then, in the Tables group, click **Table Design**. This new table will help to track the caddies' work schedules.

d. Add the following fields, data types, and descriptions.

Field Name	Data Type	Description
ScheduleID	AutoNumber	Surrogate key for each scheduled employee shift (primary key)
EmployeeID	Number	EmployeeID (foreign key) from tblEmployee
ScheduledDate	Date/Time	Date employee is scheduled to work
StartTime	Date/Time	Time employee's shift begins
EndTime	Date/Time	Time employee's shift ends
OnTime	Yes/No	Did employee arrive on time?

e. Save the table as tblEmployeeSchedule_iLast using your first initial and last name, and then create the following field properties.

Field Name	Field Properties
ScheduleID	• Under the Format field property, add the following custom format: "SID-0"0. • Ensure that the New Values field property is set to **Increment**.
EmployeeID	• Create a lookup field by changing the data type to **Lookup Wizard**. Select your data from the existing tblEmployee table, and then click **Next**. Select **EmployeeID**, **LastName**, and **FirstName**. Click **Next**, and then sort in **Ascending order** by **LastName** and **FirstName**. Click **Next**. Keep the Key Column hidden, click **Next**, click **Enable Data Integrity**, and then click the **Restrict Delete** option. Click **Finish**. Save the table when prompted. • Under **Field Properties**, add Employee as the caption. • Under **Field Properties**, change the Required property to **Yes**.
ScheduledDate	• Under the Format field property, apply the **Long Date** format. • Add the Short Date Input Mask. • Add Date as the caption. • Change the Required property to **Yes**.

Field Name	Field Properties
StartTime	• Under the Format field property, add the **Medium Time** format. • Add **Medium Time** as the Input Mask. • Add Shift Begins as the caption. • Add 8:00 AM as the Default Value. • Change the Required property to **Yes**.
EndTime	• Under **Field Properties**, add the **Medium Time** format. • Add **Medium Time** as the Input Mask. • Add **Shift Ends** as the caption. • Add 6:00 PM as the Default Value.
OnTime	• Under **Field Properties**, add On Time? as the caption.

f. While still in Design view, add a **Calculated field** with the following properties.

Field Name	Data Type	Description
PostedSchedule	Calculated	Calculated field of employee's ScheduledDate, StartTime, and EndTime

Field Properties
• Enter the following fields into the Expression Builder dialog box, and then separate each one with the appropriate notation as follows. • [ScheduledDate]&", "&[StartTime]&"–"&[EndTime]. Click **OK**. • Under **Field Properties**, add Posted Schedule as the caption.

g. Save your changes, and then switch to **Datasheet** view. Add the following records to test the properties in your new table, and resize your fields as needed to view the data.

Employee	Date	Shift Begins	Shift Ends	On Time
Antonio Ruweeze	7/4/2018	12:00 PM	6:00 PM	Yes
Mary Lou Lovelace	7/8/2018	8:00 AM	6:00 PM	No
Dennis Matrell	7/4/2018	8:00 AM	12:00 PM	Yes
FirstName LastName (using your first and last name)	7/15/2018	8:00 AM	6:00 PM	Yes

h. Switch to **Design** view, and then create a multiple-field index. On the Table Tools Design tab, in the Show/Hide group, click **Indexes**.

i. Enter the following index properties, starting at the first blank row in the Indexes dialog box.

Index Name	Field Name	Sort Order
ScheduleTime	StartTime	Ascending
	EndTime	Ascending

j. Index Properties

Primary	No
Unique	No
Ignore Nulls	No

k. Save your changes, and then close the Indexes dialog box.

l. Close **tblEmployeeSchedule_iLast**, and then close the database.

m. Save the database, exit Access, and then submit your file as directed by your instructor.

Problem Solve 1

Student data file needed:

 a03ch05Events.accdb

You will save your file as:

 a03ch05Events_LastFirst.accdb

Event Planning at the Red Bluff Golf Course & Pro Shop

Production & Operations

From weddings to conferences, the resort is a popular destination. The resort has several facilities that can accommodate groups from 30 to 600 people. Packages and prices vary by size of group, room, and other services, such as catering. The Event Planning & Catering team works closely with clients to ensure the clients have everything they need for their event. The resort stocks several choices of decorations, table arrangements, and centerpieces. These include professional, simple, themed, and luxurious.

a. Open the **a03ch05Events** database, and save it as a03ch05Events_LastFirst using your last and first name. If necessary, enable the content.

b. On the Create tab, in the Tables group, click **Table Design**. This table will help to track specific items requested for an event.

c. Add the following fields, data types, and descriptions.

Field Name	Data Type	Description
EventItemID	AutoNumber	Surrogate key for each selected item (primary key)
EventID	Number	This is the scheduled event.
ClientID	Number	Client ID (foreign key) from the tblClient table
DecorID	Number	What the client wants to have at the event
Theme	Short Text	Can be professional, simple, themed, or luxurious

d. **Save** the new table as tblEventItems, and then create the following field properties.

Field Name	Field Properties
EventItemID	• Under Field Properties, add the following custom format: "ITEM"0. • Ensure that the New Values field property is set to **Increment**.
EventID	• Create a lookup field by changing the data type to **Lookup Wizard**. Select your data from the existing tblEvents table, and then click **Next**.Select **EventID**, **EventName**, and **EventDate**. Click **Next**. Sort in **Descending** order by **EventDate**. Click **Next**. Hide the **Key Column**.Click **Next** two times. Click **Enable Data Integrity**, and then click Restrict Delete. • Click **Finish**. Save the table when prompted. Under Field Properties, enter Event as the caption. • Under Field Properties, change the Required property to **Yes**.
ClientID	• Create a lookup field by changing the data type to **Lookup Wizard**. Select your data from the existing tblClients table, and then click **Next**. Select **ClientID**, **LastName**, and **FirstName**. Click **Next**. Sort in **Ascending** order by **LastName** and **FirstName**. Click **Next**. Keep the Key Column hidden. Click **Next**. Click **Enable Data Integrity**, and then click **Restrict Delete**. Click **Finish**. Save the table when prompted. • Under Field Properties, enter Client as the caption. • Under Field Properties, change the Required property to **Yes**.

Field Name	Field Properties
DecorID	• Create a lookup field by changing the data type to **Lookup Wizard**. Select your data from the existing tblDecorations table, and then click **Next**. Select **DecorID**, **DecorItem**, and **Color**. Click **Next**. Sort in **Ascending** order by **DecorItem** and **Color**. Click **Next**. Keep the Key Column hidden. Click **Next**. Click **Enable Data Integrity**. Click **Finish**. Save the table when prompted. • Under Field Properties, enter Item as the caption. • Under Field Properties, change the Required property to **Yes**.
Theme	Create a lookup field by changing the data type to **Lookup Wizard**. Click **I will type in the values that I want**. Click **Next**. Enter the following options. Row 1: Professional Row 2: Simple Row 3: Themed Row 4: Luxurious Click **Next**, click **Limit to List**, and then click **Finish**. Under Field Properties, change the Field Size property to 12.

e. **Save** your changes, and then switch to **Datasheet** view. Add the following records to test the field properties in your new table.

Event	Client	Item	Theme
Wedding Reception 11/23/2018	Bennett	Tablecloth White	Luxurious
Wedding Reception 11/23/2018	Bennett	Napkins White	Luxurious
Wedding Reception 11/23/2018	Bennett	Candles with Flowers Silver	Luxurious
Wedding Reception 11/23/2018	Bennett	Fountain (large)	Luxurious

f. **Close** the tblEventItems table. **Open** the tblEvents table in **Datasheet** view to create a query from a filter.

g. Click the **Location** field, and then, on the Home tab, in the Sort & Filter group, click **Selection**.

h. Select all events being held in the Eldorado Room. **Save** this filter as a query named qryEldoradoRoom by using the **Save Object As** option.

i. **Close** qryEldoradoRoom.

j. On the Home tab, in the Sort & Filter group, click **Advanced**, click **Clear All Filters**, and then click **Advanced**.

k. Select **Advanced Filter/Sort**. The tblEventsFilter1 pane opens.

l. Select the following fields, and then enter the following criteria in the tblEventsFilter1 grid.

Field	Field Name	Criteria
1	**EventName**	
2	**EventDate**	
3	**StartTime**	
4	**EndTime**	>5pm

m. On the Home tab, in the Sort & Filter group, click **Toggle Filter**.

Notice that the results of the Advanced Filter are now displayed in the tblEvents table.

n. **Save** this filter as a query named qryEveningEvents by using the **Save Object As** option.

o. **Close** qryEveningEvents.

p. **Close** tblEvents and tblEventsFilter1. Do not save the changes when prompted.

q. On the Database Tools tab, in the Analyze group, click **Analyze Table**. The Table Analyzer Wizard opens to the first introduction screen.

r. Click **Next** two times, and then select **tblEvents** if necessary.

s. Click **Next**, and then click **Yes, let the wizard decide**.

t. Click **Next**. Access will create three new tables: **Table1**, **Table2**, and **Table3**. Double-click the current table names, and rename them as follows.

   Table1: tblEventData

   Table2: tblEventName

   Table3: tblEventLocation

u. Click **Next** two times. Access asks whether you want to create a query that resembles your old table. Because your old table will be saved automatically, you will not need a query with the same data. Click **No, don't create the query**.

v. Click **Finish**. All three tables you just created will open. Close the tblEventData, tblEventName, and tblEventLocation tables. Click **Yes** if Access prompts you to save any changes.

w. Save the database, exit Access, and then submit your file as directed by your instructor.

Critical Thinking

In this exercise, you created a new table to track specific items requested for each event and modified several field properties. How have those modifications improved the database design and ease of use?

Perform: How Others Perform

Student data files needed:

a03ch05CookingClub.accdb

a03ch05Recipe.pdf

a03ch05CrabCakes.jpg

You will save your file as:

a03ch05CookingClub_LastFirst.accdb

Modifying a Recipe Database

Production & Operations

You are the new administrative assistant of Chelsea's Cooking Club. You have been asked to keep track of recipes for the club. The database was built to easily store recipes, create shopping lists, and manage ingredients. Unfortunately, the previous administrative assistant was unsure of herself in building the database, and it appears to not be functioning as you would like. The president of the club has asked you to modify the database to ensure ease of use and functionality.

When saving any objects in this project add _iLast, using your first initial and last name, to the end of the name.

a. Open the **a03ch05CookingClub** database, and save it as a03ch05CookingClub_LastFirst using your last and first name. If necessary, enable the content.

b. Open **tblStore**, add your first and last name, address, city, state, zip code, and phone number in record 5, and then close tblStore.

c. Open **tblRecipe** in Design view, and make the following changes.

   - Add an AutoNumber for the primary key, and create a custom format.
   - Add an attachment field that will allow for a printable version of the recipe.
   - Add an OLE object field that will allow a photo of the dish to be inserted.

- Change the RecipeType field to a lookup field, and then enter the following values: Breakfast, Lunch, Dinner, Dessert, Appetizer, Other. Be sure to limit to list, and do not allow multiple values.
- Change the Servings data type to Number.
- Ensure that all captions and field sizes are appropriate, and make changes as necessary.

d. Switch to Datasheet view, and then make the following changes to record 1.
  - Change RecipeType to Appetizer.
  - Insert **a03ch05Recipe.pdf** into the PrintFriendly field.
  - Insert **a03ch05CrabCakes.jpg** into the Photo field.

e. Normalize the tblIngredient table using the Table Analyzer Wizard. Appropriately name the new tables that are created in the wizard. Do not create the query of the original table.

f. Open the newly created ingredients table from the Table Analyzer Wizard, and then make the following changes.
  - Create a custom format in the IngredientID field.
  - Change the Store field to a lookup field that looks up the store name in tblStore. Sort in Ascending order, hide the key column, enable data integrity, restrict related records from being deleted, and do not allow multiple values.
  - Ensure that all captions and field sizes are appropriate, and make changes as necessary.

g. Create a new table in Design view that will permit you to track what ingredients are used in which recipes.
  - Save the table as tblRecipeIngredient_iLast using your first initial and last name.
  - Add an AutoNumber for the primary key, and then create a custom format.
  - Add a lookup field that looks up the ingredient name in the normalized Ingredients table. Sort in ascending order, hide the key column, enable data integrity, restrict related records from being deleted, and do not allow multiple values.
  - Add a lookup field that looks up the recipe name in tblRecipe. Sort in ascending order, hide the key column, enable data integrity, restrict related records from being deleted, and do not allow multiple values.

h. Open the Relationships window, and then ensure that all tables are related and referential integrity is enforced.

i. Consider how the data will be used. Create two queries by using either Filter By Form, Filter By Selection, or Advanced Filter. Save both queries.

j. Close the database, exit Access, and then submit your file as directed by your instructor.

Additional Cases

Additional Workshop Cases are available on the companion website and in the instructor resources.

Microsoft Access 2016

Chapter 6 | PATTERN MATCHING AND FUNCTIONS IN QUERIES

OBJECTIVES

Prepare Case

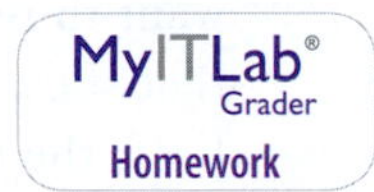

Customer Service

Human Resources

The Red Bluff Golf Club Database

The Red Bluff Golf Club needs useful information in order to run its business efficiently. Barry Cheney, the manager, has asked you to create queries to track the golfers who have scheduled tee times and private lessons. Additionally, you need to create queries for decision making, such as scheduling golf pros for private lessons or determining how many golf caddies are needed on a busy day. To keep the file small while you work with the database, Barry removed most of the data and left only some sample data for you to manipulate. Once Barry has accepted your changes, he will load all the data and implement the new database.

ARochau/Fotolia

Student data file needed for this chapter:

 a03ch06Golf1.accdb

You will save your file as:

a03ch06Golf1_LastFirst.accdb

Working with Advanced Criteria and Calculations

The most important function of a database is to create useful information for decision making. Queries enable you to retrieve data, filter data, calculate data totals, update data, append data, and delete records in bulk. Becoming proficient in building queries will improve your ability to understand and manage data. Building queries helps to turn data into useful information and is critical in creating high-quality information. Knowing the features of query design allows you to perform advanced analyses quickly.

Once you have high-quality information, you now have knowledge about your organization, which can help you make decisions about your business. This **knowledge** is defined as applied information once you have made the decision. For example, what if you want to reward your high-value customers on their birthdays? You could create a query that shows all customers who have spent more than $500 over the past six months and limit the results to those who were born in the current month. In this section, you will create advanced queries that use wildcard characters in string comparisons, find records with the "most" or "least" values, and create parameter queries. Additionally, you will create queries that use the Concatenate function as well as Not, In, and other advanced operators.

QUICK REFERENCE | **Understanding Expressions**

In Access, the term "expression" is synonymous with "formula" in Excel. An expression consists of several possible elements that you can use — alone or in combination — to yield a result. Those elements include the following.

1. Identifiers — The names of a field, a control on a form or report, or the properties of the fields or controls
2. Operators — Such as + or – signs
3. Logical operators — Includes And, Or, and Not
4. Functions — A large number of predefined functions within Access, including Sum, Count, and Avg (average), just to name a few
5. Constants — Values that do not change, such as strings of text or numbers that are not calculated by an expression.

You can use expressions in a number of ways, such as performing calculations, retrieving values of a control on a form or report, supplying criteria to a query, and more.

Use Wildcard Characters in String Comparisons

Wildcard characters, such as an asterisk (*) or a question mark (?), substitute for other symbols or characters when used in the criteria of a query. Many times, when creating a query, you will know exactly what you want to find. However, you may want to search for both the singular and plural forms of a word, words that begin with the same root, words that can be spelled in different ways, or words that you are not sure how to spell. For example, you may be searching for a customer who lives in Pittsburgh. Users may have misspelled the city's name when they entered the data. Pittsburgh — with an "h" — is in Pennsylvania. Yet, there are places named Pittsburg — without an "h" — in California, Ohio, Kansas, New Hampshire, and Texas. You could use a wildcard — Pittsburg* — and retrieve customers who live either in Pittsburgh or in Pittsburg.

Opening the Starting File

To create queries using wildcards, you first need to open a database. In this exercise, you will open the Golf database.

A06.00

To Save the Golf Database

a. Start **Access**, click **Open Other Files** in the left pane, and then double-click **This PC**. Navigate through the folder structure to the location of your student data files, and then double-click **a03ch06Golf1**. The golf database opens.

b. Click the **File** tab, save the file as an **Access Database**, and click **Save As**. Navigate to the location where you are saving your project files, and then change the filename to a03ch06Golf1_LastFirst using your last and first name. Click **Save**. If necessary, enable the content.

Working with Wildcard Characters and the Like Operator

You can use wildcard characters to find a range of values. Many times, these are combined with the Like operator. The **Like operator** finds values in a field that match a specific pattern. For example, you may want to search for all products that begin with the letters "ch"; that would return products such as cheese, chips, chocolate, and chicken. Or you may want to query a JobTitle field to search for any employees who have a manager position. By using a wildcard and the Like operator, the results of your search may include senior manager, assistant manager, manager of sales, and manager. In this exercise, you will use the Like operator and wildcard characters to query the database.

REAL WORLD ADVICE Do Not Use Like Without a Wildcard

Access will allow you to use the Like operator without a wildcard. Access then treats it just like an exact match. However, the processing time is longer when you use the Like operator without a wildcard than when you search for an exact match. Therefore, best practice dictates that you use Like only when using one of the wildcards.

A06.01

To Use Wildcard Characters in String Comparisons

a. Click the **Create** tab, and then in the Queries group, click Query Design.

b. Click **tblEmployee**, click **Add**, and then **Close** [X] the Show Table dialog box.

c. Add the **FirstName**, **LastName**, **Salary**, **HireDate**, and **Position** fields to the query design grid.

d. In the Criteria row, under **Position**, type Like "*caddy", and then click **Run**.

Notice that four records are returned in the data set that have the word "Caddy" at the end of the field. The asterisk replaced any characters that preceded the word "Caddy" in the Position field.

e. Click **Save** [Save icon] on the Quick Access Toolbar, and then save your query as qryCaddy.

SIDE NOTE
Pin the Ribbon
If your ribbon is collapsed, pin your ribbon open. Click the Home tab. In the lower right-hand corner of the ribbon, click Pin the Ribbon [Pin icon].

SIDE NOTE
What Will the Asterisk Before "Caddy" Do?
The asterisk will return all records that have the word "caddy" at the end of the field.

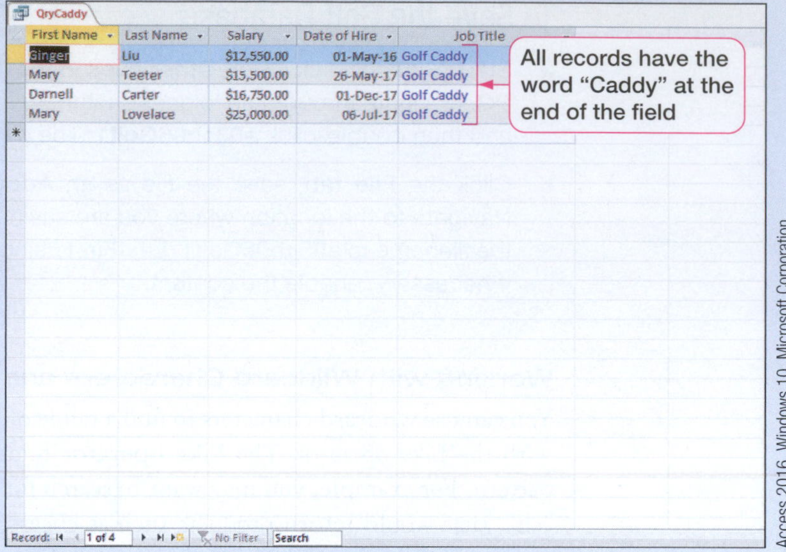

QryCaddy

First Name	Last Name	Salary	Date of Hire	Job Title
Ginger	Liu	$12,550.00	01-May-16	Golf Caddy
Mary	Teeter	$15,500.00	26-May-17	Golf Caddy
Darnell	Carter	$16,750.00	01-Dec-17	Golf Caddy
Mary	Lovelace	$25,000.00	06-Jul-17	Golf Caddy

Access 2016, Windows 10, Microsoft Corporation

Figure 1 Datasheet view of the qryCaddy query

> **SIDE NOTE**
> **What Will the Asterisk Before and After Golf Do?**
> To match specific text anywhere within a string, type an asterisk at the beginning and at the end of a string of text.

f. Switch to **Design** view, and then in the Criteria row under **Position**, delete **Like *caddy**.

g. In the **Criteria** row under Position, type Like "*golf*".

h. Click the **File** tab. Click **Save As**, click **Save Object As**, and then click **Save As**. **Save** the query as qryGolf, and then **run** the query.

Notice that all records returned in the data set have the word "Golf" somewhere within the field. The asterisk replaced any characters that were before and/or after the word "Golf" in the Position field.

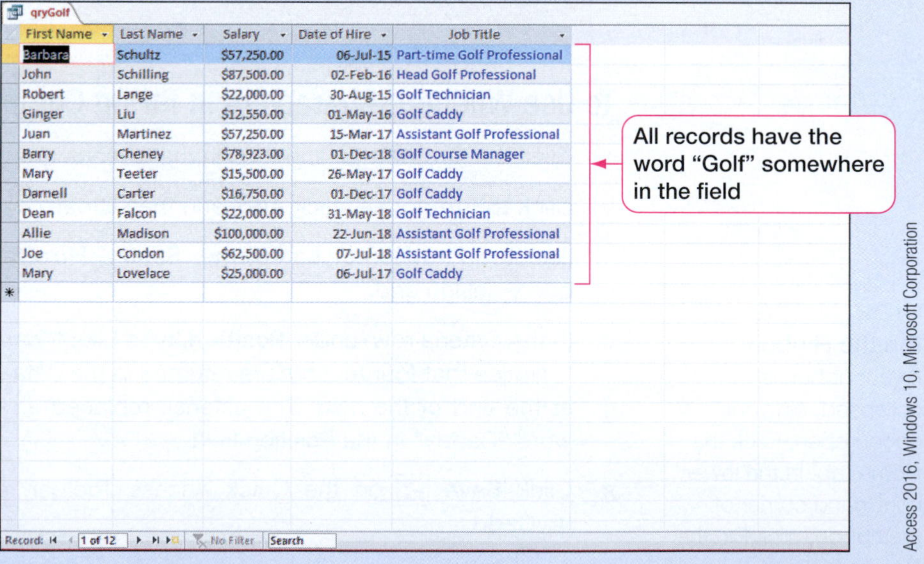

qryGolf

First Name	Last Name	Salary	Date of Hire	Job Title
Barbara	Schultz	$57,250.00	06-Jul-15	Part-time Golf Professional
John	Schilling	$87,500.00	02-Feb-16	Head Golf Professional
Robert	Lange	$22,000.00	30-Aug-15	Golf Technician
Ginger	Liu	$12,550.00	01-May-16	Golf Caddy
Juan	Martinez	$57,250.00	15-Mar-17	Assistant Golf Professional
Barry	Cheney	$78,923.00	01-Dec-18	Golf Course Manager
Mary	Teeter	$15,500.00	26-May-17	Golf Caddy
Darnell	Carter	$16,750.00	01-Dec-17	Golf Caddy
Dean	Falcon	$22,000.00	31-May-18	Golf Technician
Allie	Madison	$100,000.00	22-Jun-18	Assistant Golf Professional
Joe	Condon	$62,500.00	07-Jul-18	Assistant Golf Professional
Mary	Lovelace	$25,000.00	06-Jul-17	Golf Caddy

Access 2016, Windows 10, Microsoft Corporation

Figure 2 Datasheet view of the qryGolf query

> **SIDE NOTE**
> **Are Words in the Criteria Row Case Sensitive?**
> Access has been developed to work regardless of which case you use in the Criteria row.

i. **Close** [X] the query.

j. Click the **Create** tab, and then in the Queries group, click **Query Design**.

k. Click **tblMember**, click **Add**, and then **Close** [X] the Show Table dialog box.

l. Add the **FirstName**, **LastName**, **Address**, **City**, **State**, and **ZipCode** fields to the query design grid.

m. In the **Criteria** row under LastName, type Like "[A-E]*".

n. Sort the LastName field in **Ascending** order.

o. Save your query as qryMemberAE, click **OK**, and then click **Run**.
Notice that all members whose last names begin with "A" through "E" are displayed in ascending order.

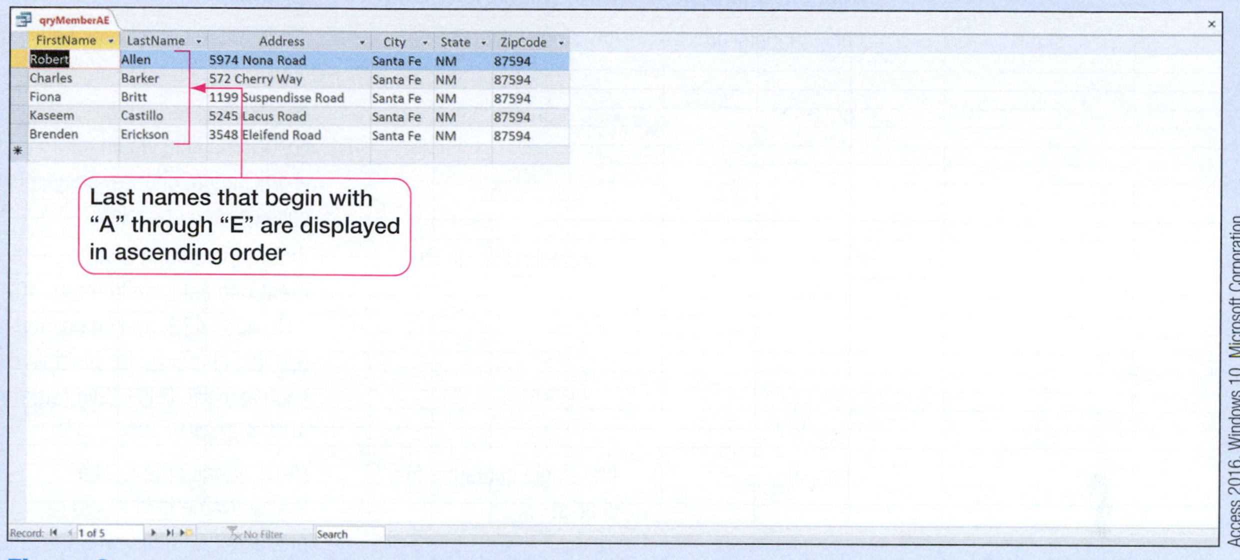

FirstName	LastName	Address	City	State	ZipCode
Robert	Allen	5974 Nona Road	Santa Fe	NM	87594
Charles	Barker	572 Cherry Way	Santa Fe	NM	87594
Fiona	Britt	1199 Suspendisse Road	Santa Fe	NM	87594
Kaseem	Castillo	5245 Lacus Road	Santa Fe	NM	87594
Brenden	Erickson	3548 Eleifend Road	Santa Fe	NM	87594

Figure 3 Datasheet view of the qryMemberAE query

p. **Close** [X] the query.

q. Click the **Create** tab, and then in the Queries group, click **Query Design**.

r. Add **tblMemberLessons** and **tblMember** to the query workspace, and then **Close** [X] the Show Table dialog box.

s. Add the **FirstName**, **LastName**, **ScheduledDate**, and **Fee** fields to the query design grid.

t. In the **Criteria** row under Fee, type Like "2#0".

u. **Save** the query as qryLessonFees, click **OK**, and then click **Run**.
Notice that all fees that begin with "2" and end with "0" are displayed.

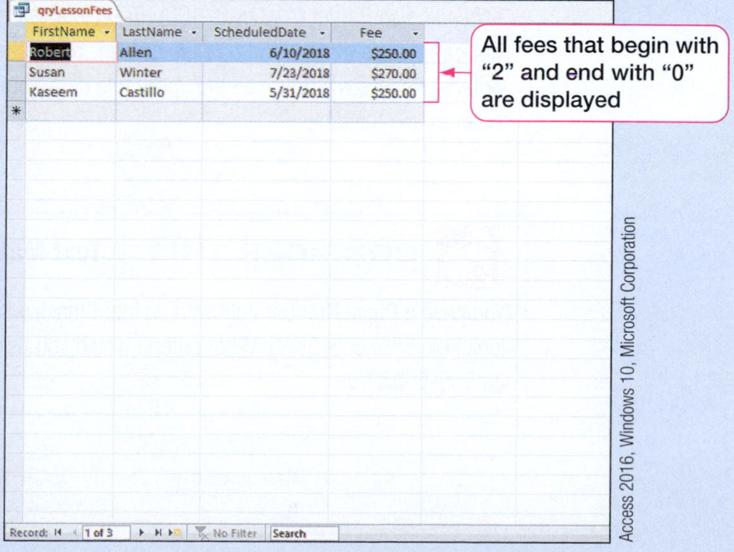

FirstName	LastName	ScheduledDate	Fee
Robert	Allen	6/10/2018	$250.00
Susan	Winter	7/23/2018	$270.00
Kaseem	Castillo	5/31/2018	$250.00

Figure 4 Datasheet view of the qryLessonFees query

v. Close [X] the query.

QUICK REFERENCE | Using Wildcard Characters in Access

Built-in pattern matching provides a handy tool for making string comparisons in queries. The chart lists the wildcard characters you can use with the Like operator and the number of characters they can match.

Wildcard Characters	What Wildcards Match	Example
? or _ (underscore)	Any single character	C?t in criteria of a Notes field would return cat, cot, and cut.
* or %	Zero or more characters	ch* in the criteria of a FoodName field would return churros, chimichanga, cheese, chips, chives, chicken, and chocolate.
#	Any single digit (0–9)	4#2 in the criteria of an AreaCode field would return 402, 412, 422, 432, and so on. You could use this character for multiple digits such as 4##. This would return 400, 401, 402, 403, 404...499.
[charlist]	Any single character in a charlist	[A-D]* in the criteria of a ProductName field would return any products that begin with the letter A, B, C, or D.
[!charlist]	Any single character not in a charlist	[!A-D]* in the criteria of a ProductName field would return any products that begin with the letters E through Z, inclusive.
- (hyphen)	Any character within a range	b[a-o]ll in the criteria of a field would return ball, bell, and bill, but not bull.

You can use a group of one or more characters — a **charlist** — enclosed in square brackets ([ ]) to match any single character in an expression. A charlist can include almost any characters and digits. Additionally, when you specify a range of characters, the characters must appear in ascending sort order (A–Z or 0–100). [A–Z] is a valid pattern, but [Z–A] is not. Finally, Access is not **case sensitive** in regard to the criteria. You can enter lowercase or uppercase letters in the criteria. Access will return all the applicable data, regardless of the case used when the data was entered into the table.

CONSIDER THIS | Text Matching and Input Masks

You have a PhoneNumber field with an input mask with symbols stored. Most numbers would look like (555) 555-5555. What criteria would you use to find seven-digit phone numbers such as 555-5555?

REAL WORLD ADVICE | **You Do Not Always Have to Type the Word "Like"**

Microsoft has made it a little easier for a novice to enter criteria in the query design grid. If you type an asterisk (*) or a question mark (?) and press Tab, Access recognizes the wildcard that you entered. Access will automatically enclose your string in quotes along with entering the word "Like". Thus, as a novice, you can write queries with relative ease.

Find Records with the "Most" or "Least" Values

An occasion may exist when you want to view only a **subset** — a portion or part of a group of records — of your query data set by selecting either a percentage or a fixed number of records. For example, you may want to view the customers who have the bottom 10% of overall customer purchases. You could then design your marketing plan to target them because they may not appear to be as loyal as other customers. Instead of viewing a percentage of your data, you may want to see the top three salespeople within the company. This would help you to determine the best salespeople who are eligible for a promotion, raise, or bonus.

Retrieving Top Values

You can use a **Top Values query** when you need to find records that contain the top values in a field. You can use a Top Values query to answer such questions as the following.

- Which is the most or least expensive product sold at our company?
- Which departments generated the greatest or least sales last year?
- What products are the top ten most popular?
- Which products are in the top or bottom 5% of sales?
- Which employees' sales are in the top or bottom 10% in the company?

A Top Values query first sorts and then filters your data to return the top values within a field. You can use a Top Values query to search for numeric, currency, and date values. In this exercise, you will create a top 25% query and bottom two or lowest values query.

A06.02

SIDE NOTE
Sorting Fields
Before running the query, you must sort data in ascending or descending order in fields containing your top or bottom values.

To Create a Top Values Query

a. Click the **Create** tab, and then in the Queries group, click **Query Design**.

b. Add **tblMemberLessons** to the query workspace, and then **Close** [X] the Show Table dialog box.

c. Add the **ScheduledDate** and **Fee** fields to the query design grid.

d. Click **Run** to view all records.
   Notice that there are nine different prices listed in the 15 records displayed.

e. Switch to **Design** view, and then sort Fee in **Descending** order.

f. Click the **Design** tab. In the Query Setup group, click the **Return (Top Values)** arrow, and then select **25%** from the Return (Top Values) list.

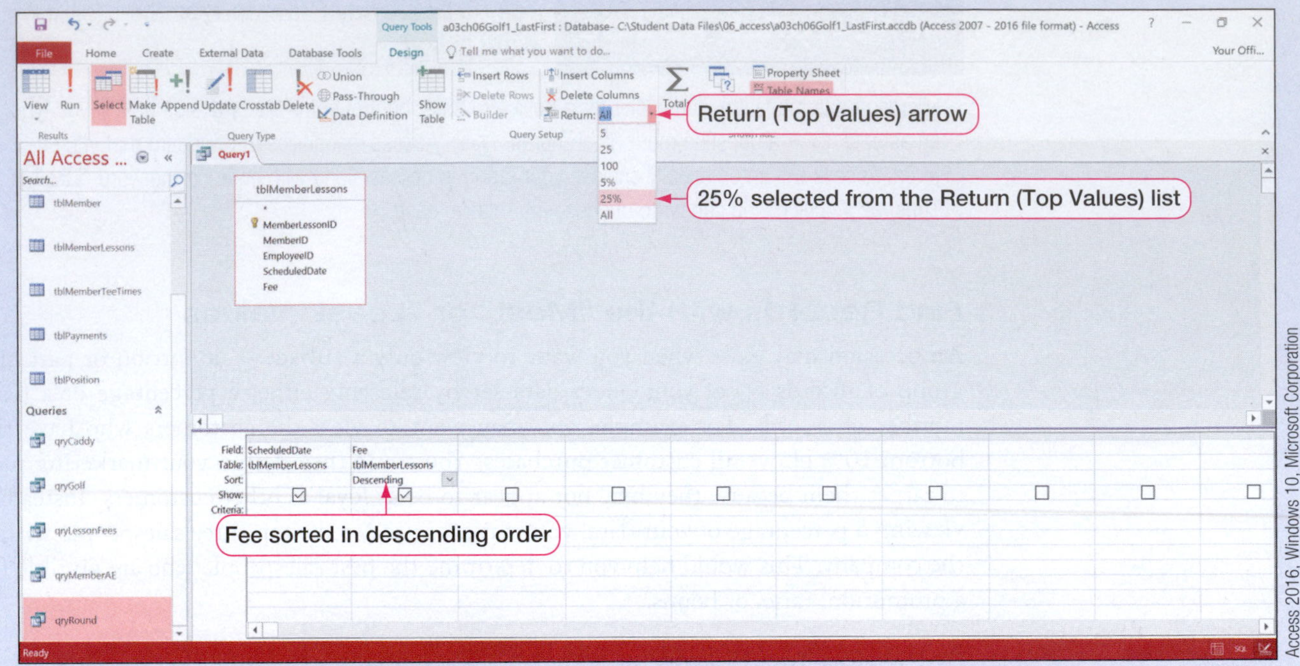

Figure 5 Design view of the Query1 query

g. **Save** the query as qryTop25, click **OK**, and then click **Run**.

Notice that four records have fees that fall within the top 25% (highest 25%) of fee values.

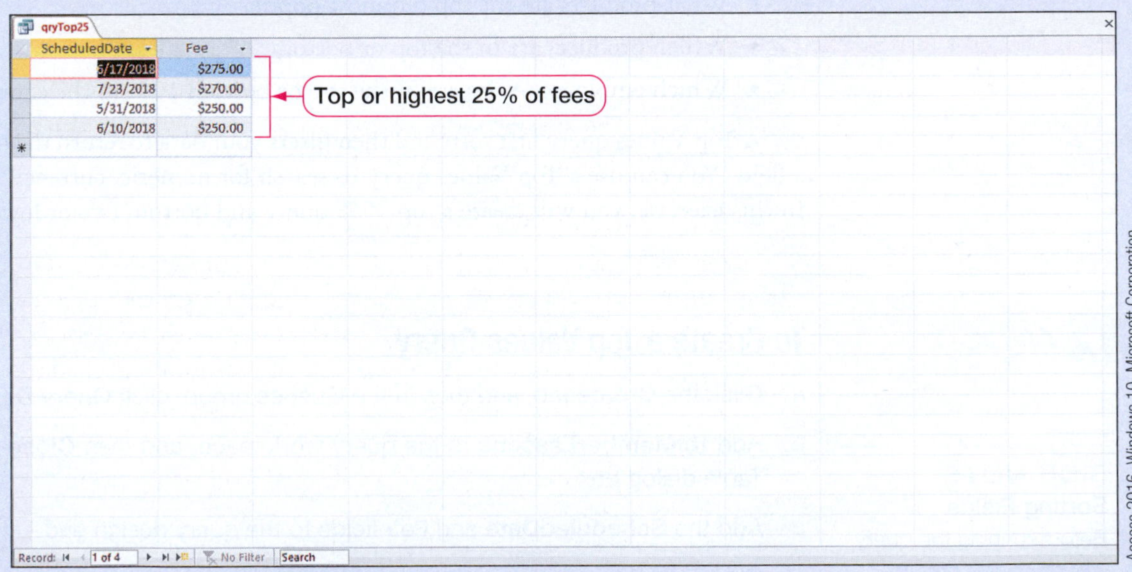

Figure 6 Datasheet view of the qryTop25 query

SIDE NOTE

Using the Return (Top Values) List

You can either enter the number or percentage of records that you want or select an option from the list.

h. Switch to **Design** view, and then change the sort order in the Fee field from Descending to **Ascending**.

i. Delete the **25%** in the Return (Top Values) box, and then type **2**.

Troubleshooting

After deleting 25% and typing 2, Access may add a "5" after the two. Because 25% is one of the list options, Access is guessing that you want that value. If this occurs, press Delete to remove the "5".

j. Click the **File** tab. Click **Save As**, click **Save Object As**, and then click **Save As**.

k. Save the query as qryBottom2, click OK, and then click **Run**.
Notice that by sorting the field in ascending order, Access now displays the two bottom — or lowest — values.

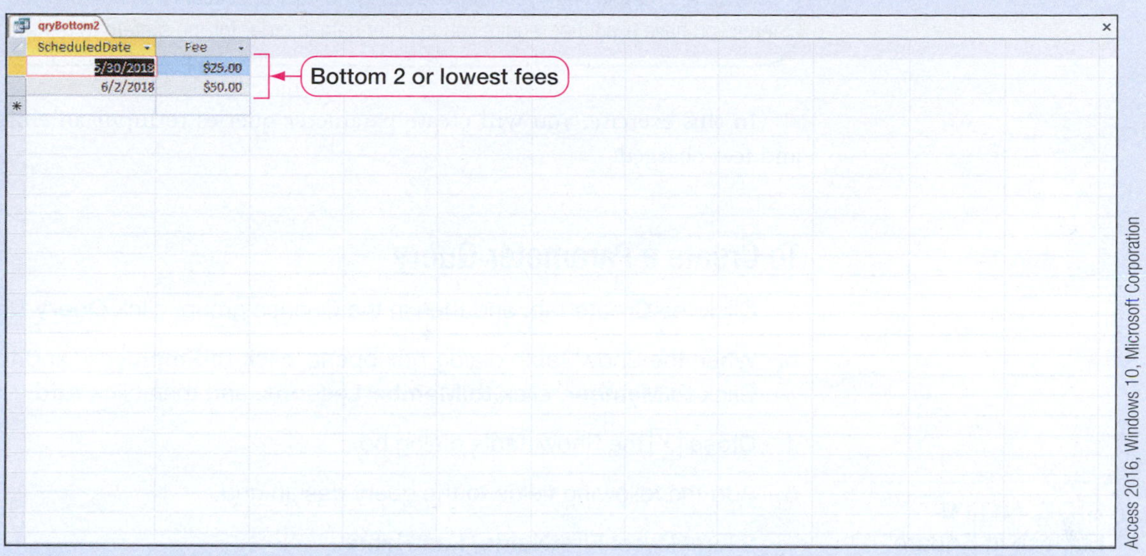

Figure 7 Datasheet view of the qryBottom2 query

l. **Close** the query.

Create Parameter Queries

Queries can be designed to prompt you for criteria without having to make changes in Design view. The criteria for selecting records are determined when the query is run rather than when the query is designed.

Using Parameters in a Query

Parameter queries can be designed when you need to change the criteria for a search each time the query is run. In this case, a variable parameter can be used. When a parameter query is run, you are prompted to enter the value for each parameter or variable. Using parameters in queries is exceptionally powerful and converts static queries, in which the criteria are already entered into the query design grid, to flexible, dynamic queries that are customized to a user's needs. The use of parameters can significantly reduce the number of queries you need to create, make queries more useful, and simplify database maintenance.

Parameters can easily be added to a query. Rather than entering the value of criteria, enter the prompt you want the user to see when the query is run, and enclose the prompt within square brackets. The value the user enters will replace the parameter and create a data set based on what the user enters. For example, the parameter [Enter ZIP Code] could be entered in the Criteria row of a ZIP Code field. When a user runs the query, the user is prompted to enter a ZIP Code, and the records matching the value entered are retrieved. This type of query can put the user in control of creating queries, even if the user has never used Access.

Parameters can be used for any data type within a table, and you can specify what type of data a parameter should accept. Specifying **parameter data types** is particularly important when you have numeric, currency, or date/time data. When you specify a data type that the parameter should accept, users see a more helpful error message if they enter the wrong type of data, such as entering text when currency should be entered.

CONSIDER THIS | Have You Used Parameter Queries?

Think about the systems you have previously used. Perhaps you have called the bank to update information — maybe a new address or phone number — and before you can speak with customer service, you have to enter your Social Security number or account number. Can you think of other systems you have used that require you to enter data in order for the system to retrieve your information?

In this exercise, you will create parameter queries to input an employee's last name and fees charged.

A06.03

To Create a Parameter Query

a. Click the **Create** tab, and then in the Queries group, click **Query Design**.

b. When the Show Table dialog box opens, click **tblEmployee**, and then press Ctrl. Click **tblMember**, click **tblMemberLessons**, and then click **Add**.

c. **Close** ☒ the Show Table dialog box.

d. Add the following fields to the query design grid.

tblEmployee: **FirstName**, **LastName**

tblMember: **FirstName**, **LastName**

tblMemberLessons: **ScheduledDate**, **Fee**

e. In the **Criteria** row of the Employee's LastName field, type [Enter the Employee's Last Name], and then save the query as qryParameter.

SIDE NOTE

Enclose in Square Brackets

Place parameter names inside of square brackets or Access adds quotation marks around text typed in the Criteria row.

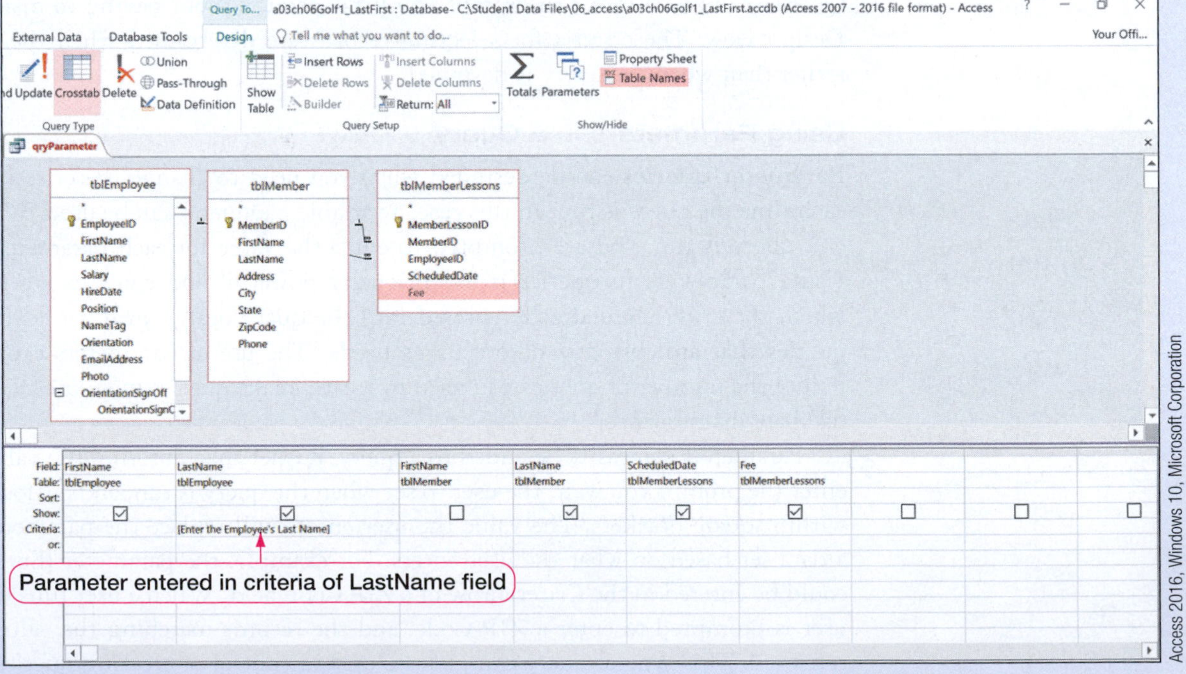

Figure 8 Design view of the qryParameter query

f. Click **Run**. When prompted to enter the employee's last name, type Schilling, and then click **OK**.

Notice that John Schilling's four scheduled private lessons are easy to retrieve with a parameter query.

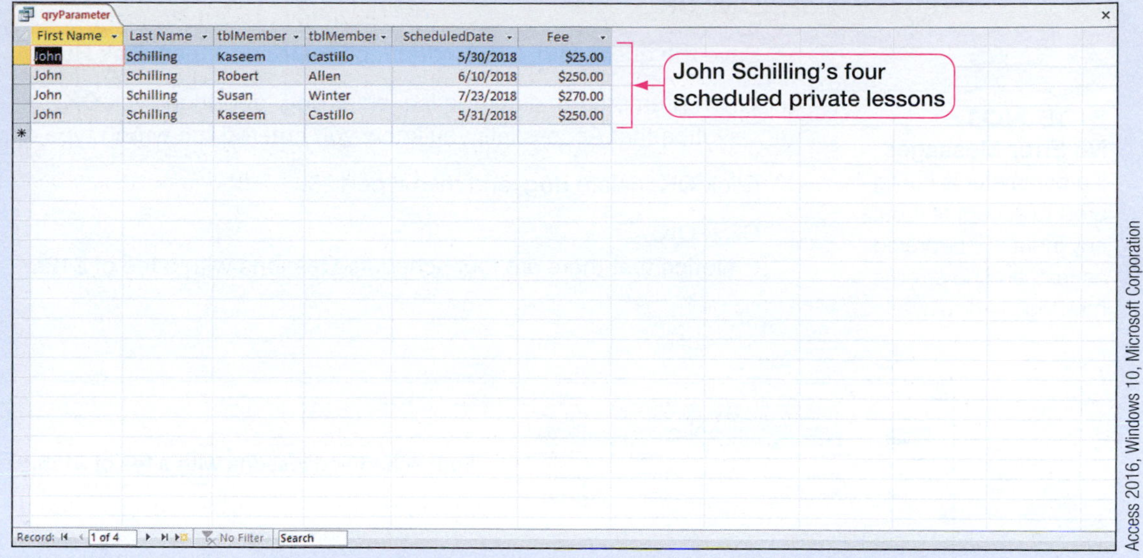

Figure 9 Datasheet view of the qryParameter query

g. **Close** [X] the query.

h. Click the **Create** tab, and then in the Queries group, click **Query Design**.

i. When the Show Table dialog box opens, click **tblMember**, and then press Ctrl. Click **tblMemberLessons**, and then click **Add**.

j. **Close** [X] the Show Table dialog box.

k. Add the following fields to the query design grid.

tblMember: **FirstName**, **LastName**

tblMemberLessons: **ScheduledDate**, **Fee**

l. In the **Criteria** row of the Fee field, type [Enter the Fee].

m. Click the **Design** tab, and then in the Show/Hide group, click **Parameters**. The Query Parameters dialog box opens.

n. Type the following into the Query Parameters dialog box.

Parameter	Data Type
[Enter the Fee]	Currency

SIDE NOTE
Parameter Prompts Must Match
Make sure that each parameter matches the prompt that you use in the Criteria row of the query design grid.

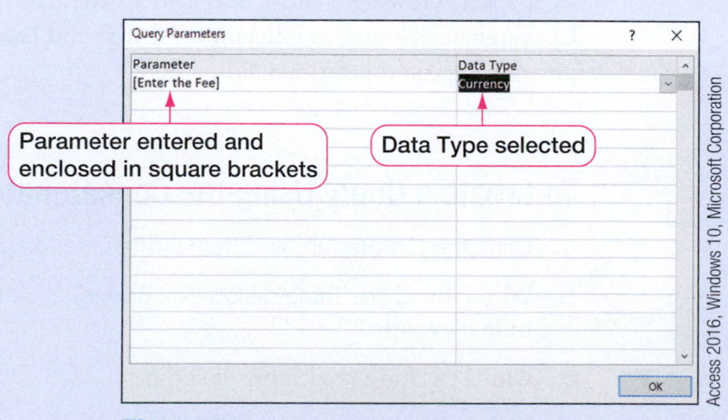

Figure 10 Query Parameters dialog box

o. Click **OK**.

p. Save the query as qryParameter2, click **OK**, and then click **Run**.

q. When prompted to enter the fee, enter dog, and then click **OK**.
Notice that Access lets you know you entered the wrong type of data.

r. Click **OK**, delete **dog**, and then type 125.

s. Click **OK**.
Notice that there are four scheduled lessons with a fee of $125.

SIDE NOTE
No Error Messages
If a parameter is configured to accept text data, any input is interpreted as text, and no error message is displayed.

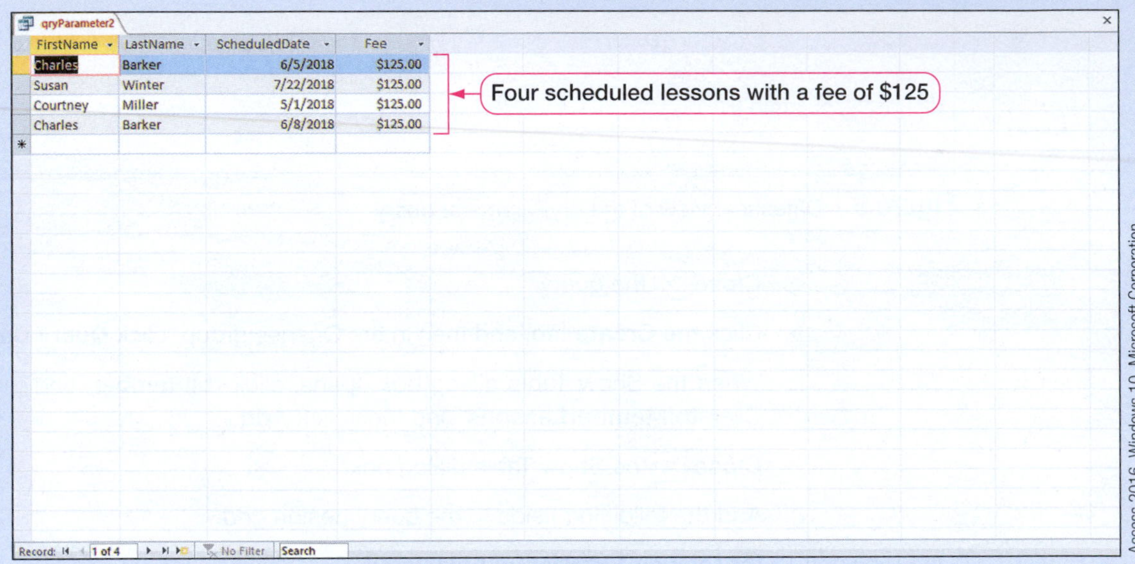

Figure 11 Datasheet view of the qryParameter2 query

t. **Close** the query.

Concatenate Strings Using the & Operator

You can use the **Concatenate operator** (&) when you want to join two strings together in an expression and create a single field. For example, if you have an Employees table that contains the fields FirstName and LastName, you can use concatenation to create a text string that displays the values of the employee's first name and last name fields separated by a space, creating a full name field in the data set. In this exercise, you will use the Concatenate operator to join employee first and last name fields and to join an employee's position type and position fields.

 A06.04

To Create a Query Using the Concatenate Operator

a. Click the **Create** tab, and then in the Queries group, click **Query Design**.

b. When the Show Table dialog box opens, click **tblEmployee** and **tblPosition**, and then click **Add**.

c. **Close** the Show Table dialog box.

d. Right-click the **first blank field** in the query design grid, and then select **Zoom**. The Zoom dialog box opens and gives you more room to work.

Troubleshooting

After selecting Zoom, you may see an error that says a potential security concern has been identified. Because there are no macros in this database, it is safe to click OK.

> **SIDE NOTE**
> **The Zoom Dialog Box**
> When entering a long expression, you can use the Zoom dialog box to see everything you are typing.

e. In the **Zoom** dialog box, type Employee:[FirstName]&" "&[LastName]. Be sure to type a space between the quotation marks.

f. Click **OK**.

g. Right-click the **next blank field** in the query design grid, and then select **Zoom**.

h. In the Zoom dialog box, type Job Title:[PositionType]&" "&[Position]. Click **OK**.

i. **Save** the query as qryConcatenate, click **OK**, and then click **Run**. If necessary, resize your fields to view all the data.

   Notice that Access joined data from multiple fields into one field — Employee and Job Title.

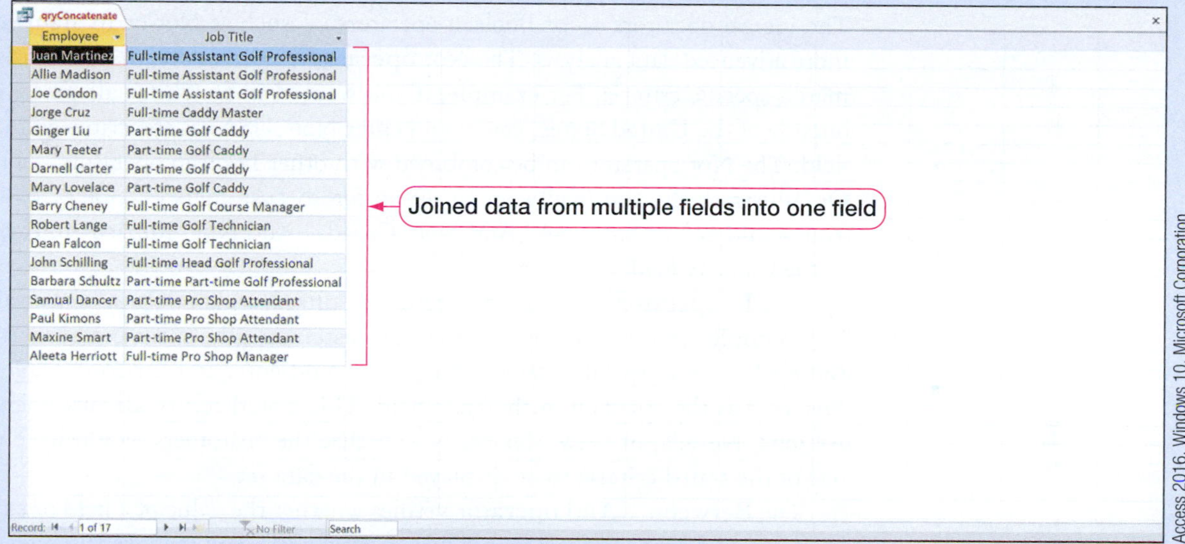

Employee	Job Title
Juan Martinez	Full-time Assistant Golf Professional
Allie Madison	Full-time Assistant Golf Professional
Joe Condon	Full-time Assistant Golf Professional
Jorge Cruz	Full-time Caddy Master
Ginger Liu	Part-time Golf Caddy
Mary Teeter	Part-time Golf Caddy
Darnell Carter	Part-time Golf Caddy
Mary Lovelace	Part-time Golf Caddy
Barry Cheney	Full-time Golf Course Manager
Robert Lange	Full-time Golf Technician
Dean Falcon	Full-time Golf Technician
John Schilling	Full-time Head Golf Professional
Barbara Schultz	Part-time Part-time Golf Professional
Samual Dancer	Part-time Pro Shop Attendant
Paul Kimons	Part-time Pro Shop Attendant
Maxine Smart	Part-time Pro Shop Attendant
Aleeta Herriott	Full-time Pro Shop Manager

Figure 12 Datasheet view of the qryConcatenate query

Troubleshooting

After clicking OK from within the Zoom dialog box, you might not see the entire expression you just entered in the query design grid. Your field just needs to be resized. It can be resized just as you would resize a column in Excel or a field in an Access table.

j. **Close** [X] the query.

REAL WORLD ADVICE **Have You Seen Concatenate in Action?**

Have you ever logged into a website and there is a welcome message at the top of the web page? For example, "Hi Joe Condon!" As you know from working in Access, storing customers' full names in one field violates the principle of normalization. Developers of the website have used concatenation in the source code of the page. In business, you can use this type of coding on reports, paychecks, and other professional documents.

QUICK REFERENCE | **Using the & Operator**

At first glance, using the ampersand to concatenate fields can appear complicated. However, if you break it into sections, it can actually be quite simple. Below are some notes to remember about the & operator.

1. You are creating a **virtual field**. This means that the concatenated field imitates its "real" equivalent or equivalents, such as combining FirstName and LastName fields. This concatenated field will not be saved in the table, only in your query. However, you can create this type of field in a table by using the Calculated data type.
2. When writing an expression, including the use of the & operator, everything to the left of the colon is the field name; everything to the right of the colon is the expression.
3. If you are using multiple tables that have the same field name in two or more tables, be sure to preface your field name with the table name, separated by an exclamation point: [tblEmployee]![FirstName].

Use Advanced Query Operators

The logical operators — or Boolean operators — such as Not or In are used to perform more advanced data analysis. The **Not operator** is used to search for records that do not match specific criteria. For example, if you wanted to search for all customers who live outside of the United States, you would enter Not "USA" as the criterion in the Country field. The Not operator can be combined with other Boolean operators, such as And and Or. Illustratively, you may want to search for all customers outside of North America. You would enter Not "USA" And Not "Canada" And Not "Mexico" in the Criteria row of the Country field.

The **In operator** can be used to return results that contain one of the values in a list. For example, you may want to search for customers who meet certain criteria, such as those who live in specific states. Thus, you would enter In ("Arizona", "Nevada", "New Mexico") as the criterion in the State field. This would return all customers who live in Arizona, Nevada, or New Mexico. Notice that the customers would have to meet only one of the stated criteria to be displayed in the data set.

The **Between…And operator** verifies whether the value of a field or expression falls within a stated range of numeric values. For example, you may want to view all products with a selling price between $1 and $10, or you may want to view all customers who live in a certain range of ZIP Codes. By using the And operator in conjunction with the Between operator, you are testing to see whether your values are greater than or equal to the lower value — such as $1 — and less than or equal to the higher value, such as $10. In the above example, the results would include $1 or $10.

You also can combine the Not and Between…And operators to return records that do not fall within a stated range of numeric values. For example, you may want to view all products with selling prices that are not between $5 and $10, or you may want to view all customers who do not live in a certain range of ZIP Codes.

Because Access treats values entered into the Between…And operator as actual characters, wildcard characters cannot be used in this operator. For example, if you want to find all clients who were born in the 1960s or 1970s, you cannot use 196* and 197* to find all years that start with 196 and 197. You could write a more advanced expression to allow for wildcard usage, but it would be easier to write your expression as Between 1960 And 1979.

A06.05

To Create a Query Using the Not, In, And, and Between...And Operators

a. Click the **Create** tab, and then in the Queries group, click **Query Design**.

b. Add **tblEmployee** to Design view, and then **Close** [X] the Show Table dialog box.

c. Add the **FirstName**, **LastName**, and **Salary** fields to the query design grid.

d. In the Criteria row of the Salary field, type Between 50000 And 75000, and then save the query as qryBetween.

e. Click **Run**.

Notice that the employees listed have salaries that are between $50,000 and $75,000.

CHAPTER 6

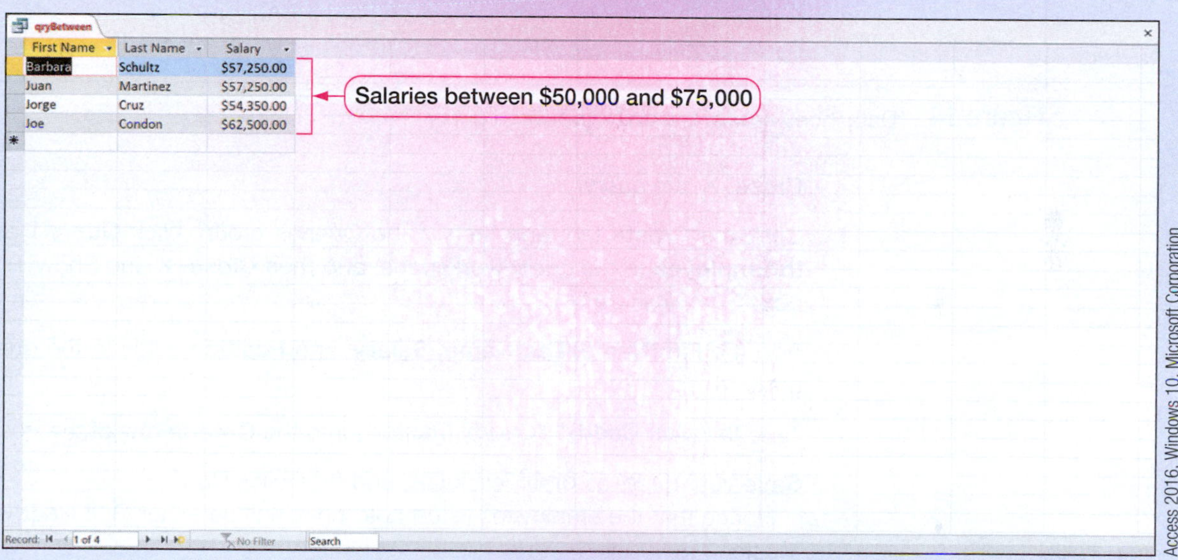

Figure 13 Datasheet view of the qryBetween query

f. Switch to **Design** view, and then modify your expression in the Criteria row of the Salary field. Type Not Between 50000 And 75000.

g. Click the **File** tab. Click **Save As**, click **Save Object As**, and then click **Save As**.

h. Save your query as qryNotBetween, click **OK**, and then click **Run**.

Notice that the employees listed have salaries that are not between $50,000 and $75,000.

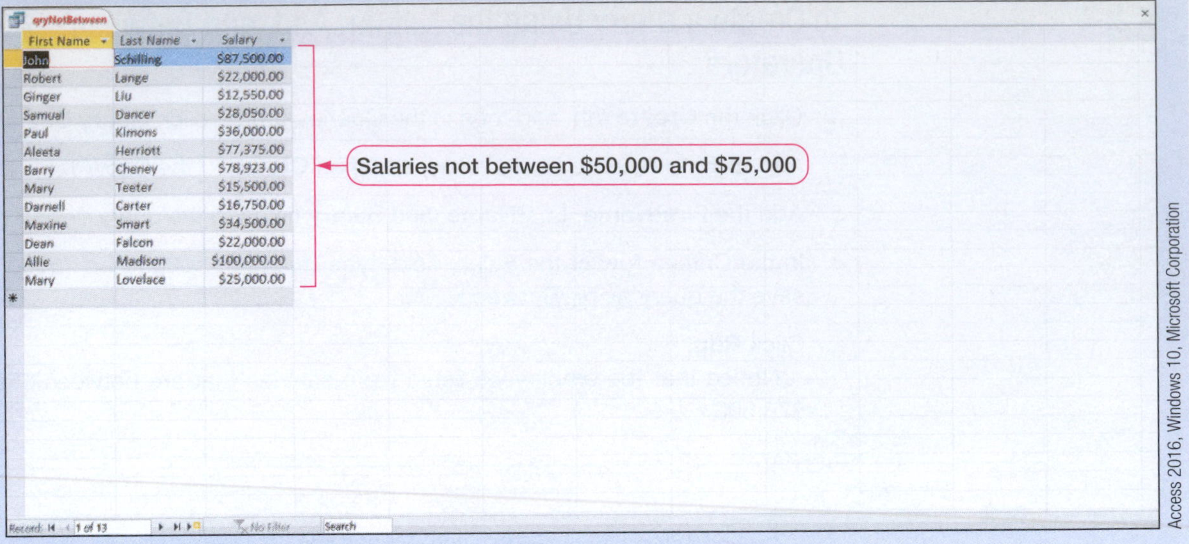

First Name	Last Name	Salary
John	Schilling	$87,500.00
Robert	Lange	$22,000.00
Ginger	Liu	$12,550.00
Samuel	Dancer	$28,050.00
Paul	Kimons	$36,000.00
Aleeta	Herriott	$77,375.00
Barry	Cheney	$78,923.00
Mary	Teeter	$15,500.00
Darnell	Carter	$16,750.00
Maxine	Smart	$34,500.00
Dean	Falcon	$22,000.00
Allie	Madison	$100,000.00
Mary	Lovelace	$25,000.00

Figure 14 Datasheet view of the qryNotBetween query

i. **Close** ☒ the query.

j. Click the **Create** tab, and then in the Queries group, click **Query Design**. Add **tblEmployee** to the query workspace, and then **Close** ☒ the Show Table dialog box.

k. Add the **FirstName**, **LastName**, **Salary**, and **Position** fields to the query design grid.

l. Type In ("Golf Caddy","Caddy Master") into the **Criteria** row of the Position field.

m. **Save** your query as qryIn, click **OK**, and then click **Run**.
Notice that the employees listed hold positions as either Golf Caddy or Caddy Master.

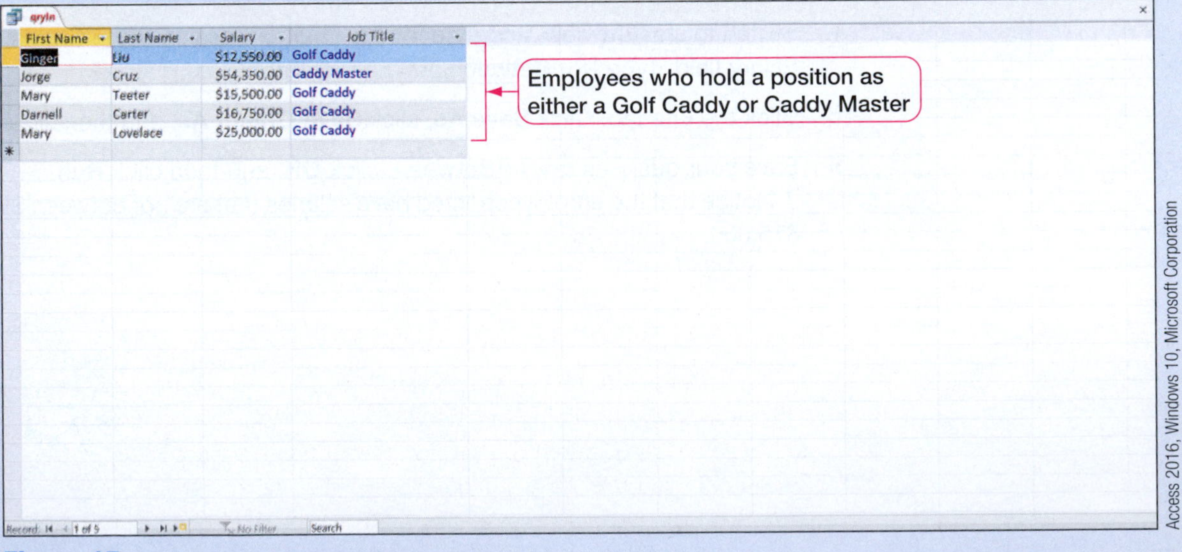

First Name	Last Name	Salary	Job Title
Ginger	Liu	$12,550.00	Golf Caddy
Jorge	Cruz	$54,350.00	Caddy Master
Mary	Teeter	$15,500.00	Golf Caddy
Darnell	Carter	$16,750.00	Golf Caddy
Mary	Lovelace	$25,000.00	Golf Caddy

Figure 15 Datasheet view of the qryIn query

n. **Close** ☒ the query.

o. If you need to take a break before finishing this chapter, now is a good time.

REAL WORLD ADVICE | **Date Fields Are a Great Place for Using Parameters**

There are many areas — accounting, marketing, sales, and so forth — within an organization that have a tremendous need for reports that fall within a specific date range. Generally, a business operating in the United States will need to file a quarterly tax return to report wages it has paid, tips its employees have reported to their employer, federal income tax withheld, Social Security and Medicare taxes withheld, and the employer's share of Social Security and Medicare taxes. This is mainly to ensure that the business is on track with tax payments and will not have a large amount due at the end of the year. Think about how the Between...And function and a parameter could be combined to print a quarterly report of all the taxes that have been paid. Typically, you could just create a query using the Between...And function and manually enter the dates you need into Design view. However, what happened when the dates change? What if the user does not know how to modify a query? In these cases, it would be best to incorporate a parameter within the Between...And function so the user can simply enter the quarter's start and end date. To do so, you would simply enter Between [Enter Start Date] And [Enter End Date] into the Criteria row in Query Design view.

CONSIDER THIS | **Using Advanced Operators Together**

For very advanced data analysis, you can combine two or more advanced operators to help sort through the data. For example, if you wanted to retrieve specific products — coats or boots — that were available in specific colors — black or brown — you could enter the criteria for both of these in one query. You would essentially be asking Access to find "coats or boots" and "black or brown". What examples could you create that would combine multiple advanced operators?

Using Advanced Functions in Queries

Knowing how to write queries in Access by using advanced functions, such as the IIf function, allows you to perform advanced analyses quickly without knowing any type of programming language. In this section, you will create queries using the IIf function, the IsNull function, date functions, and the Round function.

Create IIf Functions

The IIf function can be used to determine if a specific condition is true or false and then specify an action to be taken depending on the result. The IIf function introduces decision making into a database. Depending on whether or not specified criteria are met, the IIf function returns a different result depending on the outcome of the condition.

Creating Basic IIf Function for Individual Conditions

The **IIf function** in Access, which stands for Immediate If, is similar to the IF function in Excel. The result of this function returns one value if a specified condition is true or another value if it is false. You can use the IIf function anywhere you can use expressions. For example, you may have a database that you use to manage your store's inventory. You can use the IIf function to assist in determining what items need to be reordered. You could write an IIf function that checks to see if your current on-hand values in the Quantity field fall below a certain level. You would enter IIf([Quantity]<=3,"Reorder","OK"), which returns the string "Reorder" for any values in the Quantity field that are less than or equal to 3 and "OK" if the value is greater than 3, which means that you do not need to reorder that specific product. In this exercise, you will use the IIf function to determine which employees have earned a raise and calculate the amount of the new salary.

QUICK REFERENCE	IIf Function Syntax

The IIf function syntax, noted as IIf(expr, truepart, falsepart), has three arguments:

1. expr: Field or expression you want to evaluate. This argument is required.
2. truepart: Value or expression returned if expr is true. This argument is required.
3. falsepart: Value or expression returned if expr is false. This argument is required.

A06.06

To Create a Query Using the IIf Function

a. If you took a break, open the **a03ch06Golf1** database.

b. Click the **Create** tab, and then in the Queries group, click **Query Design**. Add **tblEmployee** to the query workspace, and then **Close** [X] the Show Table dialog box.

c. Add the **FirstName**, **LastName**, and **Salary** fields to the query design grid.

d. Right-click the **first blank field** in the query design grid, and then select **Zoom**.

e. In the Zoom dialog box, type Raise Assessment:IIf([Salary]<=30000,"Give Raise","No Raise"), and then click **OK**.

f. Right-click the **next blank field** in the query design grid, and then select **Zoom**.

g. In the Zoom dialog box, type New Salary:IIf([Salary]<=30000,[Salary]*1.03,[Salary]).

For the employees who earned a salary increase, you want to calculate what the new salary will be if the employees receive a 3% raise.

h. Click **OK**, and then click **Run**. If necessary, resize the fields to see the data.

Notice that the New Salary field is not in Currency format.

i. Switch to **Design** view, and then click the **New Salary** field.

j. Click the **Design** tab, and then in the Show/Hide group, click **Property Sheet**. Format the field as **Currency**, and then close the Property Sheet.

k. **Save** the query as qryIIf, click **OK**, and then click **Run**.

Notice that on the basis of your IIf function, Access determined which employees have earned a raise and calculated the amount of the new salary. If the employee did not earn a raise, the current salary was listed in the New Salary field.

> **SIDE NOTE**
> **Symbols Are Important**
> When writing complex expressions, include all symbols. If even one symbol is excluded or incorrect, an error will occur.

qryIIf

First Name	Last Name	Salary	Raise Assessr	New Salary
Barbara	Schultz	$57,250.00	No Raise	$57,250.00
John	Schilling	$87,500.00	No Raise	$87,500.00
Robert	Lange	$22,000.00	Give Raise	$22,660.00
Ginger	Liu	$12,550.00	Give Raise	$12,926.50
Juan	Martinez	$57,250.00	No Raise	$57,250.00
Samual	Dancer	$28,050.00	Give Raise	$28,891.50
Paul	Kimons	$36,000.00	No Raise	$36,000.00
Aleeta	Herriott	$77,375.00	No Raise	$77,375.00
Barry	Cheney	$78,923.00	No Raise	$78,923.00
Jorge	Cruz	$54,350.00	No Raise	$54,350.00
Mary	Teeter	$15,500.00	Give Raise	$15,965.00
Darnell	Carter	$16,750.00	Give Raise	$17,252.50
Maxine	Smart	$34,500.00	No Raise	$34,500.00
Dean	Falcon	$22,000.00	Give Raise	$22,660.00
Allie	Madison	$100,000.00	No Raise	$100,000.00
Joe	Condon	$62,500.00	No Raise	$62,500.00
Mary	Lovelace	$25,000.00	Give Raise	$25,750.00

Record: 1 of 17 | No Filter | Search

New salary calculation with raise included

Whether or not employee receives a raise

Access 2016, Windows 10, Microsoft Corporation

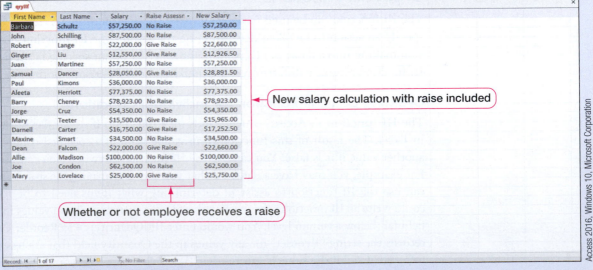

Figure 16 Datasheet view of the qryIIf query

l. **Close** [X] the query.

CHAPTER 6

Creating Nested IIf Functions for Various Conditions

There are many occasions when businesses need to test for multiple conditions. You saw in the previous section how a basic IIf function allows you to test for one of two conditions. You can also create a **nested IIf function** by placing one IIf function inside another, allowing you to evaluate a series of dependent expressions as shown in Figure 17. A **dependent expression** is an expression that relies on the outcome of another expression.

To continue with the preceding example, you might want to test for several different inventory levels and then display the appropriate status depending on which value exists. Perhaps you want to see which items will soon have to be reordered, as noted by "Reorder Soon" in the second or nested IIf function. To add this condition to the IIf function from the previous example, you would enter IIf([Quantity]<=3,"Reorder", IIf([Quantity]<=5,"Reorder Soon","OK")), which returns the string "Reorder" for any values in the Quantity field that are less than or equal to 3, "Reorder Soon" for any values that are either equal to 4 or 5, and "OK" if the value is greater than 5, which means you do not need to reorder that specific product any time soon. Notice how the second IIf function becomes the false condition of the first IIf function. In this exercise, you will use a nested IIF function to determine whether an employee will receive a raise and, if so, what the amount of the raise will be.

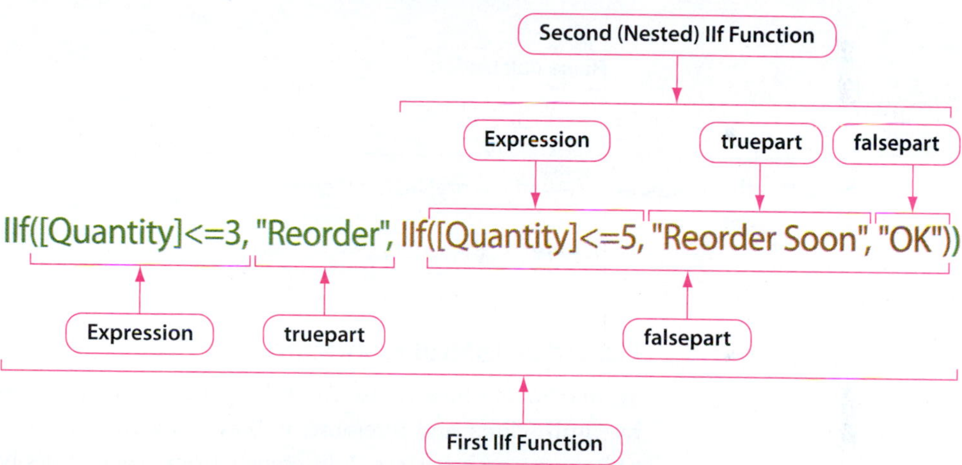

Figure 17 Nested IIf function

A06.07

To Create a Query Using Nested IIf Functions

a. Click the **Create** tab, and then in the Queries group, click **Query Design**. Add **tblEmployee** to the query workspace, and then **Close** [X] the Show Table dialog box.

b. Add the **FirstName**, **LastName**, and **Salary** fields to the query design grid.

c. Right-click the **first blank field** in the query design grid, and then select **Zoom**.

d. In the Zoom dialog box, type Raise Assessment:IIf([Salary]<=30000,"7% Raise", IIf ([Salary]<=60000,"4% Raise","No Raise")), and then click **OK**.

e. Right-click the **next blank field** in the query design grid, and then select **Zoom**.

f. In the Zoom dialog box, type Amount of Raise:IIf([Salary]<=30000,[Salary]*.07,IIf ([Salary]<=60000, [Salary]*.04,0)), and then click **OK**.

For the employees who received a salary increase, you want to calculate what the amount of the salary increase will be depending on the percentage of the increase. If the employee will not receive a raise, a zero will be displayed.

SIDE NOTE
Count Your Parentheses
The number of opening parentheses and the number of closing parentheses in your expression should always be the same.

g. Click the **Design** tab, and then in the Show/Hide group, click **Property Sheet**. Format the field as **Currency**, and then close the Property Sheet.

h. **Save** the query as qryNestedIIf, click **OK**, and then click **Run**. If necessary, resize the fields to see the data.

Notice that the Raise Assessment field has been determined and the Amount of Raise field has been calculated for you.

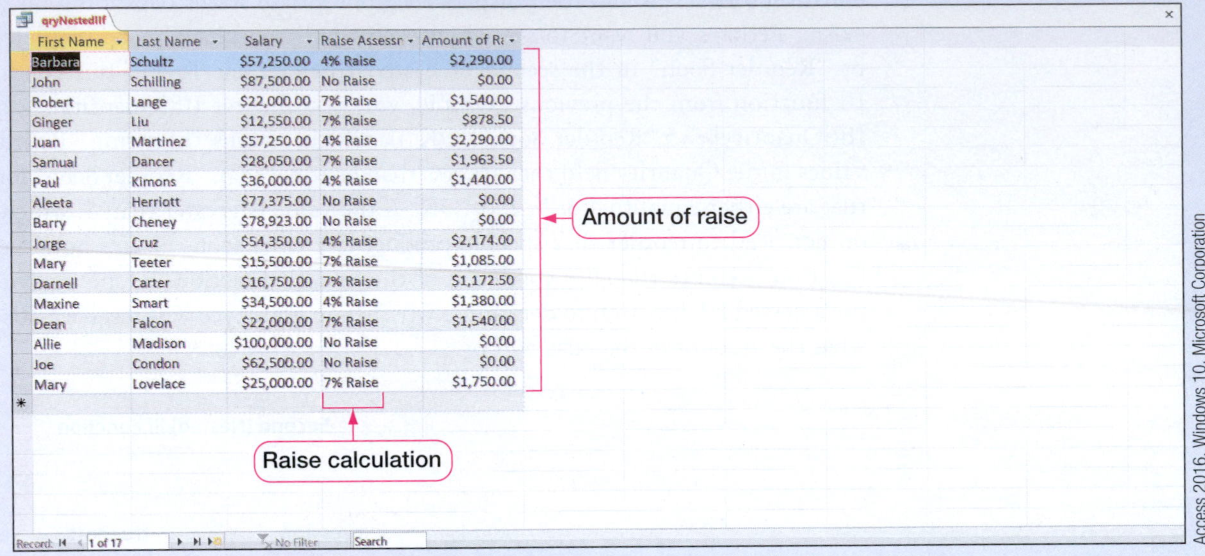

First Name	Last Name	Salary	Raise Assessr	Amount of Ra
Barbara	Schultz	$57,250.00	4% Raise	$2,290.00
John	Schilling	$87,500.00	No Raise	$0.00
Robert	Lange	$22,000.00	7% Raise	$1,540.00
Ginger	Liu	$12,550.00	7% Raise	$878.50
Juan	Martinez	$57,250.00	4% Raise	$2,290.00
Samual	Dancer	$28,050.00	7% Raise	$1,963.50
Paul	Kimons	$36,000.00	4% Raise	$1,440.00
Aleeta	Herriott	$77,375.00	No Raise	$0.00
Barry	Cheney	$78,923.00	No Raise	$0.00
Jorge	Cruz	$54,350.00	4% Raise	$2,174.00
Mary	Teeter	$15,500.00	7% Raise	$1,085.00
Darnell	Carter	$16,750.00	7% Raise	$1,172.50
Maxine	Smart	$34,500.00	4% Raise	$1,380.00
Dean	Falcon	$22,000.00	7% Raise	$1,540.00
Allie	Madison	$100,000.00	No Raise	$0.00
Joe	Condon	$62,500.00	No Raise	$0.00
Mary	Lovelace	$25,000.00	7% Raise	$1,750.00

Access 2016, Windows 10, Microsoft Corporation

Figure 18 Datasheet view of the qryNestedIIf query

i. **Close** ☒ the query.

Use the IsNull Function

To understand how to use the **IsNull function**, you need to understand what is meant by "null." First and foremost, null is not zero. Null is used to indicate that a value is unknown, and it is treated differently from other values because it has no value. Instances exist when it is necessary to search for records that contain fields with null values.

Working with Fields That Contain No Valid Data

The IsNull function returns a Boolean value — true or false — that indicates whether or not an expression contains any data. For example, consider a human resources database that you would use to manage current and past employees' data. To create a list of current employees, you could build a query that searches for missing values in the Date Terminated field, showing that the value would be null for all active employees.

Because the IsNull function, written as IsNull(expression) or IsNull([field]), returns a result of either true or false, it is commonly nested or combined with other functions, such as an IIf function. Consider the previous example of using a human resources database to manage current and past employees' data. You could nest the IsNull function inside an IIf function to return values other than true and false, such as Current Employee and Terminated Employee.

It is important to note that using the IsNull function is slightly different from using Is Null and Is Not Null in a query's criteria. When you use Is Null and Is Not Null as field criteria in the query design grid, you are checking to see whether a field contains valid data. For example, if you use **Is Null** in the criteria of a Date Terminated field, the data set would include all the employees' names and the empty Date Terminated field. Using the **Is Not Null** criteria would return each employee name and the date in which each employee was terminated.

In this exercise, you will query to find which employees need to have their photos taken.

A06.08

To Create Queries Using Null Criteria and the IsNull Function

> **SIDE NOTE**
> **Hide the Photo Field**
> It is best to uncheck the Show field box after first running the query to verify that it was written correctly.

a. Click the **Create** tab, and then in the Queries group, click **Query Design**. Add **tblEmployee** to the query workspace, and then **Close** [X] the Show Table dialog box.

b. Add the **FirstName**, **LastName**, and **Photo** fields to the query design grid.

c. To create a list of the employees who need to have their employee photos taken, type Is Null into the **Criteria** row of the Photo field.

d. **Save** the query as qryPhotoIsNull, click **OK**, and then click **Run**. Notice that there are 16 employees who need to have their photo taken.

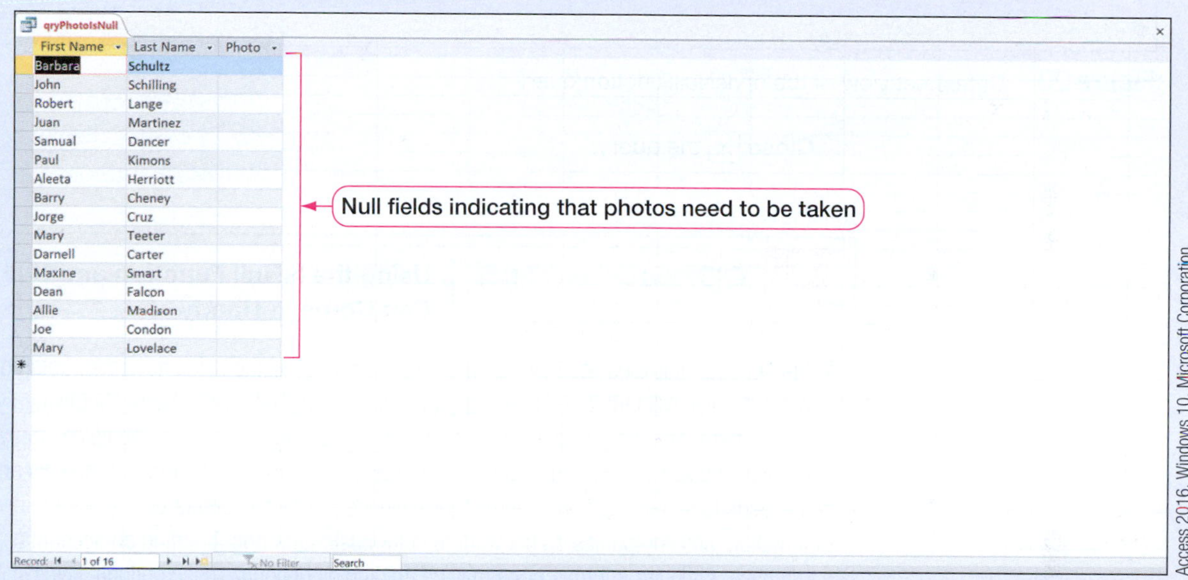

Figure 19 Datasheet view of the qryPhotoIsNull query

e. Switch to **Design** view.

f. To create a list of the employees who have an employee photo, edit the **Criteria** row of the Photo field by typing Is Not Null.

> **SIDE NOTE**
> **Editing a Query and Saving the Changes**
> Remember to use Save Object As. Otherwise, you will overwrite the previously saved query.

g. Click the **File** tab. Click **Save As**, click **Save Object As**, and then click **Save As**.

h. Save your query as qryPhotoIsNotNull, click **OK**, and then click **Run**. Notice that there is one employee who has an employee photo.

i. **Close** [X] the query.

j. Click the **Create** tab, and then in the Queries group, click **Query Design**. Add **tblEmployee** to the query workspace, and then **Close** [X] the Show Table dialog box.

k. Add the **FirstName** and **LastName** fields to the query design grid.

l. To create a list of all employees and whether or not they need to have a photo taken, type PhotoStatus:IIf(IsNull([Photo]),"Needs Photo","Has Photo") into the first blank field in the query grid.

m. **Save** the query as qryIsNullFunction, click **OK**, and then click **Run**. Notice that all employees are listed along with whether or not their photo needs to be taken.

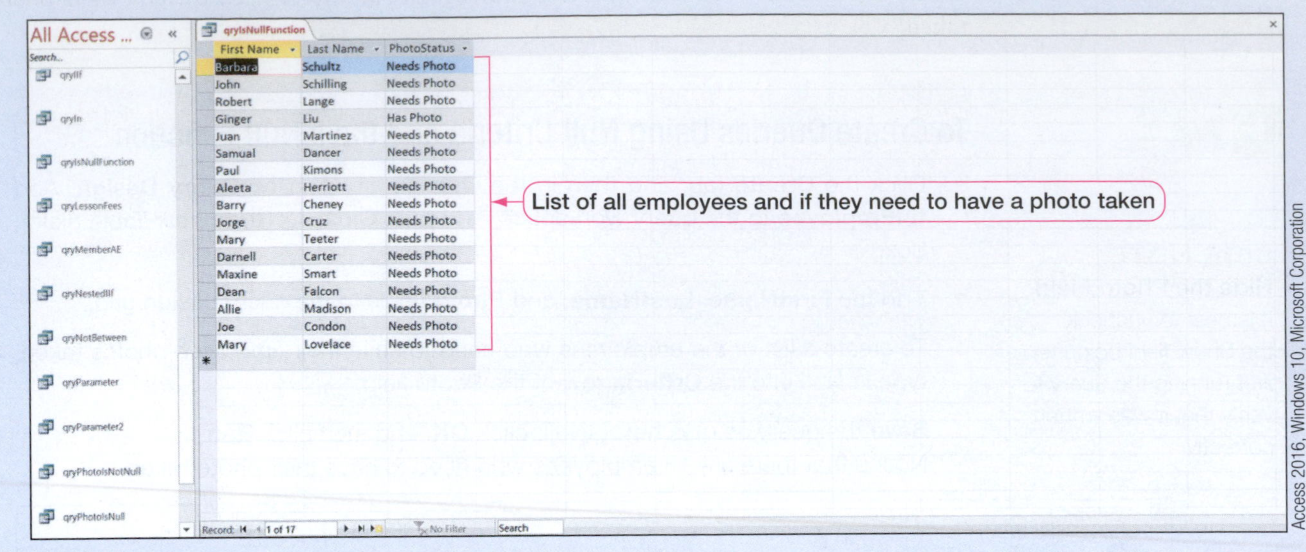

Figure 20 Datasheet view of the qryIsNullFunction query

n. **Close** [X] the query.

CONSIDER THIS | **Using the IsNull Function and Null Criteria Can Come in Handy**

In the Access databases you have been using, most if not all the fields have data entered into them. In business, you will find that databases can contain many null fields. Think about when you fill out an online form. Not every field is required, meaning that you can leave some fields empty, or null. Companies make key data required for tasks such as determining their target markets and allow some fields to remain null for customer convenience. Some customers do not want to give all of their information, and companies do not want to deter customers from creating an account or making a purchase. Although a form's fields may be marked as optional, these optional fields still have to exist in the database table to store data when a customer does give the information. Do you always complete an online form, or are there times when you leave fields empty? Are there ever times you do not complete an online form because there are too many required fields? How do you think this affects the company's database?

Use Date Functions

Access includes a variety of techniques that enable the use of dates and date ranges in the criteria of a query. Date functions are useful when working with the complex logic in a database that contains dates. Two of the more commonly used date functions are the Date and Now functions. They behave similarly, as they can be used in expressions. Additionally, both functions retrieve a date and/or time according to your computer's system date and time. The **Date function** returns the current system date. This can be very helpful if you want to track the date when a record was entered into a table and the time of day is not a concern. The **Now function** retrieves the current system date and time. For example, you may want to have a time stamp of when a document was uploaded to a system, such as a student uploading an assignment to a course management system. If an assignment is due at 1:00 PM, the Now function could log the date and time in which the upload occurred. The instructor would then know whether the student met the deadline.

The Date and Now functions are more commonly used in a table's field properties. However, if you are using a live database and are inserting records with today's date, then these two functions would work very well. In this section, you will build queries using the DateDiff, DateAdd, DateSerial, and DatePart functions.

REAL WORLD ADVICE | **Should You Use the Now Function or the Date Function?**

Avoid mixing the Now and Date functions. If you set the default value of a field to Now, Access will record the time. If you then query that field with the criteria of a date without specifying a time, you might not get the results you expect. For example, if your criteria is >12/28/2016, Access will return any records greater than >12/28/2016 at midnight. Thus, a field placed at 12/28/2016 at 8 AM would be returned in the results. The criteria of >12/28/2016 suggests that you wanted only dates starting on 12/29/2016 at midnight in the results. Generally, use the Now function only when you need time, and make sure you are familiar with the data when writing queries.

Using the DateDiff Function to Determine a Time Interval

The **DateDiff function** is used to determine the difference between two dates. Generally, one date is obtained from a field, and the second date is obtained by using the Date function. Many instances exist in which you could use the DateDiff function. For example, suppose you have a form that you use to automatically refill customer prescriptions. In the Orders table, you have a field named Refill On that contains the earliest date that the prescription can be refilled. You can use the DateDiff function with a text box on the form to display the number of days left before the prescription can be refilled and shipped. In this exercise, you will use the DateDiff function to determine how many days or months it has been since a member has paid their dues.

QUICK REFERENCE | **Five Parts of a DateDiff Function**

The DateDiff function syntax, noted as DateDiff(interval, date1, date2, [firstdayofweek], [firstweekofyear]), has five arguments:

1. The first part, interval, is the interval of time — day, month, year, and so on — used to calculate the difference between date1 and date2. This argument is required.
2. The second and third parts, date1 and date2, are the dates you want to use in the calculation. These can include a field name or expression. These arguments are required.
3. The fourth part, firstdayofweek, is a constant that indicates the first day of the week. If not specified, Access assumes that you want to begin on Sunday. This argument is optional.
4. The fifth part, firstweekofyear, is a constant that indicates the first week of the year. If not specified, Access assumes the week in which January 1 occurs. This argument is optional.

To Create a Query Using the DateDiff Function

a. Click the **Create** tab, and then in the Queries group, click **Query Design**. Add **tblPayments** to the query workspace, and then Close the Show Table dialog box.

b. Add the **MemberID** and **PaymentDate** fields to the query design grid.

c. Right-click the **first blank field** in the query design grid, and then select **Zoom**.

d. To see how many days it has been since a member paid the club's annual dues, in the Zoom dialog box type DaysSincePmt: DateDiff("d",Date(),[PaymentDate]), and then click **OK**.

SIDE NOTE

What Does a Minus Sign Mean?

Negative numbers in your field mean that the days have passed. Positive numbers mean that the date has yet to happen.

e. **Save** the query as qryDateDiffDays, click **OK**, and then click **Run**.
   Notice that you are given how many days ago or in advance a member paid his or her annual dues.

f. Switch to **Design** view.

g. Modify the **DaysSincePmt** expression to see how many months it has been since a member paid the club's annual dues by typing MonthsSincePmt: DateDiff("m", Date(),[PaymentDate]).

h. Click **OK**, and then click **Run**.
   Notice that you are given how many months ago or in advance a member paid his or her annual dues.

i. Click the **File** tab, click **Save Object As** to save the query as qryDateDiffMonths, and then close the query.

Using DateAdd Function to Subtract a Time Interval

You can use the **DateAdd function** to add or subtract a specific time interval from a date. For example, you can use DateAdd to calculate a date ten days from today or a time 30 minutes from now. Business professionals work with dates on a regular basis. A human resources manager may want to calculate when a newly hired employee is eligible for benefits. Additionally, the human resources manager may want to calculate the earliest date an employee can retire.

REAL WORLD ADVICE | **Using the 1900 Date System**

Access uses the 1900 date system to store dates: January 1, 1900, is day 1; January 2, 1900, is day 2; and so forth. When you enter a date into a Date/Time field, Access identifies it as a date and compares it to the calendar to make sure it is an actual date. If you try to enter a date that does not exist, such as September 31, an error message will appear. Access then stores the date as an integer number called the date serial. You do not need to know the date serial number to use a date field in a calculated field; however, you do need to make certain that you enter a valid date.

QUICK REFERENCE | **Three Parts of a DateAdd Function**

The DateAdd function syntax, noted as DateAdd(interval, number, date), has three arguments, all of which are required:

1. The first part, interval, contains a string expression that represents the interval of time you want to add or subtract.
2. The second part, number, refers to the numeric expression that indicates the number of intervals you want to add. It can be positive to calculate dates in the future, or it can be negative to calculate dates in the past.
3. The third part, date, is the date to which the interval is added.

CHAPTER 6

QUICK REFERENCE	Settings for the Date Interval
Setting	**Description**
yyyy	Year
q	Quarter
m	Month
y	Day of year
d	Day
w	Weekday
ww	Week
h	Hour
n	Minute
s	Second

REAL WORLD ADVICE | **Use Date Interval Settings Carefully**

Although date intervals make it easy to calculate dates in Access, it is very important to use the date intervals carefully. For example, DateDiff for the "yyyy" in Access calculates without regard to the day. If you enter the wrong interval, you can get inaccurate results in a query. Be certain you are selecting the appropriate one.

Many times, you can test your output using simple math. For example, Date()+10 would result in the same output as using the DateAdd function to add 10 to the current date: DateAdd("d", 10, Date()). Simplify your functions as much as possible. If you can calculate the same result by entering a function that is half the length, you decrease the possibility of creating errors while typing in your function.

CONSIDER THIS | **Calculating Age with Date Functions**

Many companies use an employee's date of birth to calculate such dates as retirement or benefits eligibility. Is the DateDiff function with a year interval appropriate for calculating age? Why or why not?

In this exercise, you will use the DateAdd function to determine when a member's next annual dues need to be paid.

A06.10

To Create a Query Using the DateAdd Function

a. Click the **Create** tab, and then in the Queries group, click **Query Design**. Add **tblMember** and **tblPayments** to the query workspace.

b. Add the following fields to the query design grid.

   tblMember: **FirstName**, **LastName**

   tblPayments: **Amount**, **PaymentDate**

c. Right-click the **first blank field** in the query design grid, and then select **Zoom**.

d. To see when members' next annual membership dues will need to be paid, in the Zoom dialog box, type Next Due Date: DateAdd("y",365,[PaymentDate]). Click **OK**.

SIDE NOTE
Renaming Fields in a Query
You can choose to use spaces in field names of a query because you are naming it only for display purposes.

e. **Save** the query as qryDateAdd1, click **OK**, and then click **Run**.

Notice that all due dates have been created and look the same as those of the previous year; just the year has changed. However, look at Robert Allen's record. Access does calculate correctly if someone were to pay during a leap year.

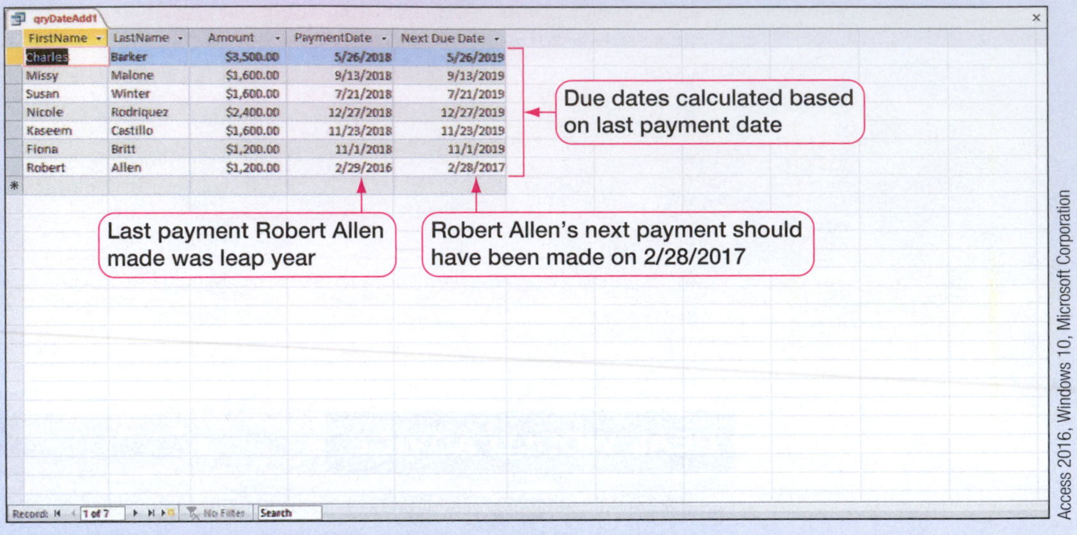

qryDateAdd1

FirstName	LastName	Amount	PaymentDate	Next Due Date
Charles	Barker	$3,500.00	5/26/2018	5/26/2019
Missy	Malone	$1,600.00	9/13/2018	9/13/2019
Susan	Winter	$1,600.00	7/21/2018	7/21/2019
Nicole	Rodriquez	$2,400.00	12/27/2018	12/27/2019
Kaseem	Castillo	$1,600.00	11/23/2018	11/23/2019
Fiona	Britt	$1,200.00	11/1/2018	11/1/2019
Robert	Allen	$1,200.00	2/29/2016	2/28/2017

Figure 21 Datasheet view of the qryDateAdd1 query

f. Switch to **Design** view.

g. Modify the **Next Due Date** field to add 52 weeks onto the date that the dues were last paid by typing Next Due Date: DateAdd("ww", 52. [PaymentDate]).

h. Click the **File** tab. Use **Save Object As** to save the query as qryDateAdd2, click **OK**, and then click **Run**.

Notice that Access now calculates 52 weeks from the last payment date. Robert Allen's last payment was on Wednesday, February 29, 2016. His next payment would be exactly 52 weeks from his last payment. Accounting for leap year, the next payment should have been paid on Wednesday, February 27, 2017.

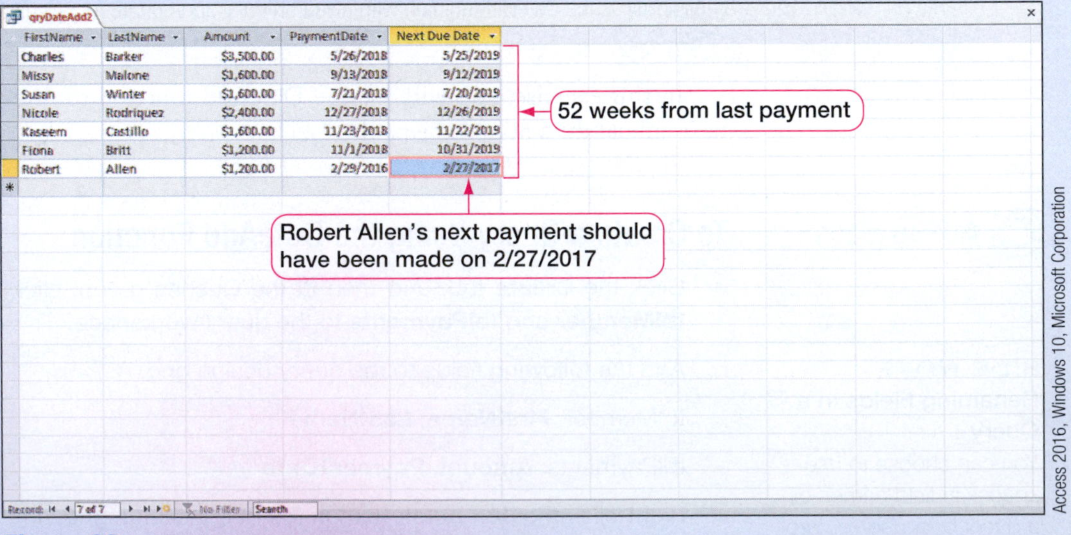

qryDateAdd2

FirstName	LastName	Amount	PaymentDate	Next Due Date
Charles	Barker	$3,500.00	5/26/2018	5/25/2019
Missy	Malone	$1,600.00	9/13/2018	9/12/2019
Susan	Winter	$1,600.00	7/21/2018	7/20/2019
Nicole	Rodriquez	$2,400.00	12/27/2018	12/26/2019
Kaseem	Castillo	$1,600.00	11/23/2018	11/22/2019
Fiona	Britt	$1,200.00	11/1/2018	10/31/2019
Robert	Allen	$1,200.00	2/29/2016	2/27/2017

Figure 22 Datasheet view of the qryDateAdd2 query

i. **Close** [X] the query.

Using the DateSerial Function to Return a Date (Year, Month, and Day)

To display specific dates, you can use the **DateSerial function**, written as DateSerial(year, month, day), to manipulate the day, month, and year of a date. DateSerial is very flexible because you can manipulate each part individually or together in any combination that meets your needs.

The best way to understand the power of this function is through an example. When the human resources manager wants to prepare paperwork for an employee's retirement, the manager can use the DateSerial function to calculate 90 days before the employee's 65th birthday. Naturally, you would take the employee's birth date and add 65 years. Then take that date and subtract three months. Using the DateSerial function, you can do this in one step. The Employee table includes a field representing Date of Birth called DOB. The function would be written as DateSerial(Year([DOB])+65, Month([DOB])–3, Day([DOB])). Thus, if an employee was born on July 5, 1967, the date returned would be April 5, 2032. In this exercise, you will use the DateSerial function to determine when an employee is eligible for benefits.

To Create a Query Using the DateSerial Function

a. Click the **Create** tab, and then in the Queries group, click **Query Design**. Add **tblEmployee and tblPosition** to the query workspace, and then **Close** [X] the Show Table dialog box.

b. Add the following fields to the query design grid.

   tblEmployee: **FirstName**, **LastName**, **HireDate**

   tblPosition: **PositionType**

c. In the **Criteria** row for the PositionType field, type "Full-time", and then clear the **Show** check box.

d. Right-click the **first blank field** in the query design grid, and then select **Zoom**.

e. Each full-time employee is eligible for health benefits after 90 days of employment, which means that the benefits begin on the 91st day of employment. To determine the date when eligibility begins, in the Zoom dialog box, type BenefitsBegin:DateSerial(Year([HireDate]),Month([HireDate]),Day([HireDate])+91). Click **OK**.

Troubleshooting

The DateSerial function returns a number that represents a date from January 1, 1900, through December 31, 9999. If the date specified by the three arguments falls outside the acceptable range of dates, an error will occur.

f. Click the **File** tab. Use **Save Object As** to save the query as qryDateSerial, click **OK**, and then click **Run**.

   Notice that Access calculated the dates on which all full-time employees became eligible for benefits.

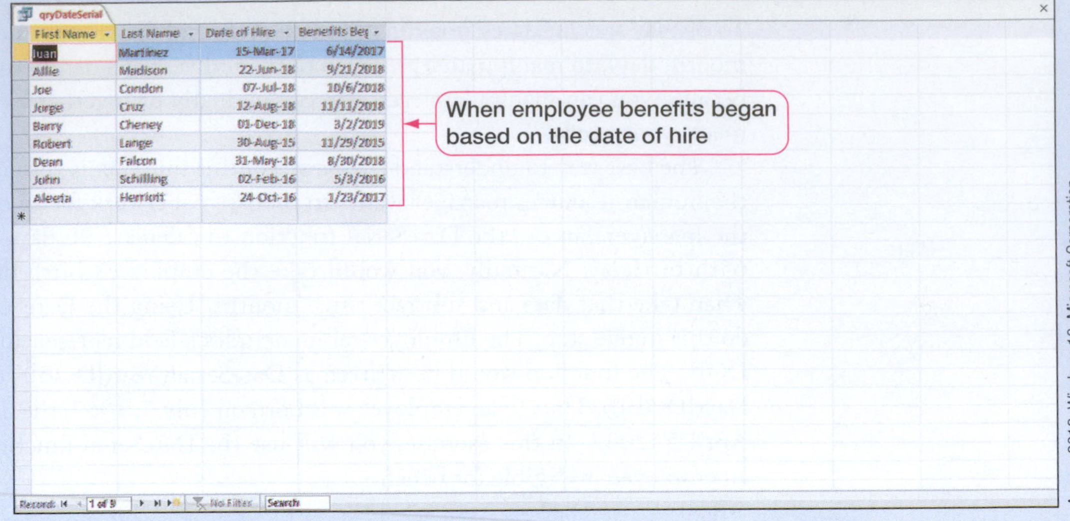

Figure 23 Datasheet view of the qryDateSerial query

Troubleshooting

Be careful where you place the numbers used to calculate. For example, in the above function, the 91 is placed after the close parenthesis — Day([HireDate])+91 — because the parentheses are enclosing the Day function argument, not the calculation.

g. **Close** [X] the query.

QUICK REFERENCE	Three Parts of a DateSerial Function

The DateSerial function syntax — noted as DateSerial(year, month, day) — has three arguments, all of which are required.

1. The first part, year, is a number between 1900 and 9999, inclusive, or a numeric expression. A numeric expression is any expression that evaluates to a number. The expression can be any combination of variables, constants, functions, and operators.
2. The second part, month, refers to either an integer or any numeric expression.
3. The third part, day, refers to either an integer or any numeric expression.

Using the DatePart Function to Evaluate a Date

You can use the **DatePart function** to examine a date and return a specific interval of time. For example, you can use DatePart to calculate the day of the week for an order's ship date. As presented in the DateAdd function, an interval is the interval of time that is returned. For example, perhaps you want to compare the number of golfers you had this summer compared to last summer. Each tee time contains a Scheduled Date. You can use the DatePart function to extract the year from the Scheduled Date in order to group your records in the query. In this exercise, you will use the DatePart function to determine when an employee has reached his or her five-year anniversary and is eligible for a bonus.

To Create a Query Using the DatePart Function

a. Click the **Create** tab, and then in the Queries group, click **Query Design**. Add **tblEmployee** to the query workspace, and then **Close** [X] the Show Table dialog box.

b. Add the **LastName**, **FirstName**, and **HireDate** fields to the query design grid.

c. Right-click the **first blank field** in the query design grid, and then select **Zoom**.

d. Each employee is eligible for a bonus after five years of service. To determine the year when eligibility begins, in the Zoom dialog box, type 5 Year Anniversary: DatePart("yyyy", ([HireDate]))+5, and then click **OK**.

e. **Save** the query as qryDatePart, click **OK**, and then click **Run**.

Notice by looking at the HireDate field that some employees have already earned the five-year anniversary bonus.

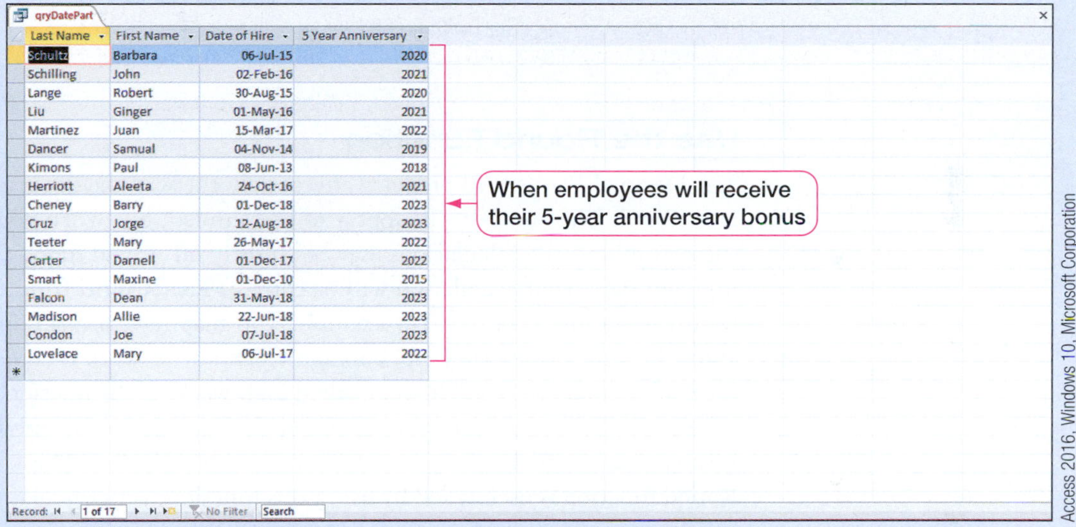

Last Name	First Name	Date of Hire	5 Year Anniversary
Schultz	Barbara	06-Jul-15	2020
Schilling	John	02-Feb-16	2021
Lange	Robert	30-Aug-15	2020
Liu	Ginger	01-May-16	2021
Martinez	Juan	15-Mar-17	2022
Dancer	Samual	04-Nov-14	2019
Kimons	Paul	08-Jun-13	2018
Herriott	Aleeta	24-Oct-16	2021
Cheney	Barry	01-Dec-18	2023
Cruz	Jorge	12-Aug-18	2023
Teeter	Mary	26-May-17	2022
Carter	Darnell	01-Dec-17	2022
Smart	Maxine	01-Dec-10	2015
Falcon	Dean	31-May-18	2023
Madison	Allie	22-Jun-18	2023
Condon	Joe	07-Jul-18	2023
Lovelace	Mary	06-Jul-17	2022

Figure 24 Datasheet view of the qryDatePart query

f. **Close** [X] the query.

QUICK REFERENCE — Four Parts of a DatePart Function

The DatePart function syntax, noted as DatePart(interval, date, [firstdayofweek], [firstweekofyear]), has four arguments.

1. The first part, interval, contains a string expression that represents the interval of time you want to return. This argument is required.
2. The second part, date, refers to the date you want to evaluate. This argument is required.
3. The third part, firstdayofweek, is a constant that indicates the first day of the week. If not specified, Access assumes that you want to begin on Sunday. This argument is optional.
4. The fourth part, firstweekofyear, is a constant that indicates the first week of the year. If not specified, Access assumes that you want to begin with the week of January 1. This argument is optional.

QUICK REFERENCE | The DatePart Function Argument Settings

Setting	Description
1	Sunday (default)
2	Monday
3	Tuesday
4	Wednesday
5	Thursday
6	Friday
7	Saturday

Setting	Description
1	Start with the week in which January 1 occurs (default).
2	Start with the first week that has at least four days into the new year.
3	Start with first full week of the year.

Use the Round Function

The Decimal Places field property affects only the way the data is displayed, not the way it is stored. The number will appear to be rounded, but when you calculate figures with these numbers, the calculations may be slightly off. If you round the field when calculating your data, your calculation will be correct. The **Round function** behaves differently from the Format property. For example, you may have a form on which employees can enter the times when they clock in and clock out of work each day, and these times are used to calculate the total hours worked each week. If the fraction portion of the number is below 0.5, then you may want to round the number down, and if the fraction portion is greater than or equal to 0.5, then the fraction should be 0.5. This is a scenario in which the Round function is useful, and by using this function, your calculations will be accurate. In this section, you will create a query using the Round function.

Rounding to a Specific Number of Decimal Places

In Access, the Round function returns a number rounded to a specific number of decimal places. This is different from formatting a field to a specific number of decimals. When you format a field property as Decimal and set the Decimal Places property to 1, the values displayed will automatically round to the nearest tenth in this case. The key to this formatting option is how the data is displayed; this format does not affect how the data is stored. For example, if you enter 2.64 into this field, it will be displayed as 2.6; however, the data is actually stored as 2.64. The number will appear to be rounded, but when you calculate these numbers, the total may not calculate correctly. In this exercise, you will use the Round function to round employees' salaries to whole numbers.

QUICK REFERENCE | The Precision Argument

When using the Round function, you can also determine the precision of the rounding. The **precision** argument allows you to determine how many decimal places you want to round your numbers to. The syntax would be Round (expression, [precision]). The precision argument is an optional argument. Access will round to two decimals — hundredths — if the precision is not entered. Because currency is rounded to two decimals, the precision is generally not entered.

REAL WORLD ADVICE

Could Omitting the Round Function Really Make a Difference?

An extra half of a penny in your employees' paychecks might not seem like a huge problem, but do the math. If your database is not calculating properly because a round function is missing, it can cost your company a lot of money. For example, if you had 100 hourly employees, and they were being paid an extra half of a penny per hour, and the average hours worked per employee was 32, it would cost your company $832 annually. However, think about the companies who have thousands or tens of thousands of employees. If you work for a company that has 10,000 employees — such as a large banking firm — this small database error would cost the company nearly $85,000 a year!

A06.13

To Create a Query Using the Round Function

SIDE NOTE
Calculated Fields in Expressions
Calculated fields can be used in expressions within your query by enclosing the field name in square brackets.

a. Open the **qryRound** query in **Design** view.

b. Right-click the **first blank field** in the query design grid, and then select **Zoom**.

c. The New Salary field has already been calculated. However, Red Bluff wants to pay salaries in whole numbers. To round the New Salary field, in the Zoom dialog box, type Final Salary: Round([New Salary]), and click **OK**.

d. Click the **Design** tab, and then in the Show/Hide group, click **Property Sheet**. Format the Final Salary field as **Currency**. Close the Property Sheet.

e. Click the **File** tab. Use **Save Object As** to save your query as qryRound2, click **OK**, and then click **Run**.

Notice by looking at the Final Salary field that the values in the New Salary field are rounded to the nearest dollar.

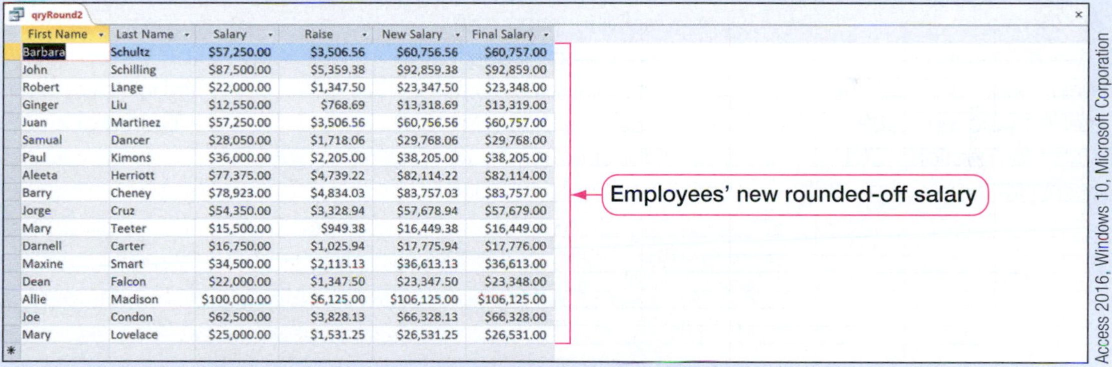
qryRound2

First Name	Last Name	Salary	Raise	New Salary	Final Salary
Barbara	Schultz	$57,250.00	$3,506.56	$60,756.56	$60,757.00
John	Schilling	$87,500.00	$5,359.38	$92,859.38	$92,859.00
Robert	Lange	$22,000.00	$1,347.50	$23,347.50	$23,348.00
Ginger	Liu	$12,550.00	$768.69	$13,318.69	$13,319.00
Juan	Martinez	$57,250.00	$3,506.56	$60,756.56	$60,757.00
Samual	Dancer	$28,050.00	$1,718.06	$29,768.06	$29,768.00
Paul	Kimons	$36,000.00	$2,205.00	$38,205.00	$38,205.00
Aleeta	Herriott	$77,375.00	$4,739.22	$82,114.22	$82,114.00
Barry	Cheney	$78,923.00	$4,834.03	$83,757.03	$83,757.00
Jorge	Cruz	$54,350.00	$3,328.94	$57,678.94	$57,679.00
Mary	Teeter	$15,500.00	$949.38	$16,449.38	$16,449.00
Darnell	Carter	$16,750.00	$1,025.94	$17,775.94	$17,776.00
Maxine	Smart	$34,500.00	$2,113.13	$36,613.13	$36,613.00
Dean	Falcon	$22,000.00	$1,347.50	$23,347.50	$23,348.00
Allie	Madison	$100,000.00	$6,125.00	$106,125.00	$106,125.00
Joe	Condon	$62,500.00	$3,828.13	$66,328.13	$66,328.00
Mary	Lovelace	$25,000.00	$1,531.25	$26,531.25	$26,531.00

Figure 25 Datasheet view of the qryRound2 query

f. **Close** [X] the query.

g. Close [X] the database, exit Access, and then submit your file as directed by your instructor.

CONSIDER THIS

Databases Can Have Thousands of Records — or More!

Remember that the database you are using was scaled down by Barry Cheney, the Red Bluffs manager, and now contains only an extremely small amount of stored data. Think about running queries using advanced criteria and calculations in a database that has hundreds or thousands of records in a table. How could these types of advanced queries save you time? Improve efficiency? Help with decision making?

Concept Check

1. What is the purpose of using wildcards in a query? p. 336
2. What is a Top Values query? Give an example of why you would want to create a subset of your data. p. 341
3. What is the purpose of a parameter query? What happens when a parameter query is executed? p. 343
4. Explain how you would use the Concatenate operator. p. 346
5. What is a logical operator? Give three examples, and state what they do. p. 346
6. Explain the difference between an IIf function and a nested IIf function. Give two examples of when you would use each one. p. 351
7. Explain the term Null. What would be the result of the IsNull function? p. 354
8. Describe the DateDiff, DateAdd, DateSerial, and DatePart functions, and give an example of each. p. 357–363
9. What is the difference between the Round function and formatting? p. 364

Key Terms

Visual Summary

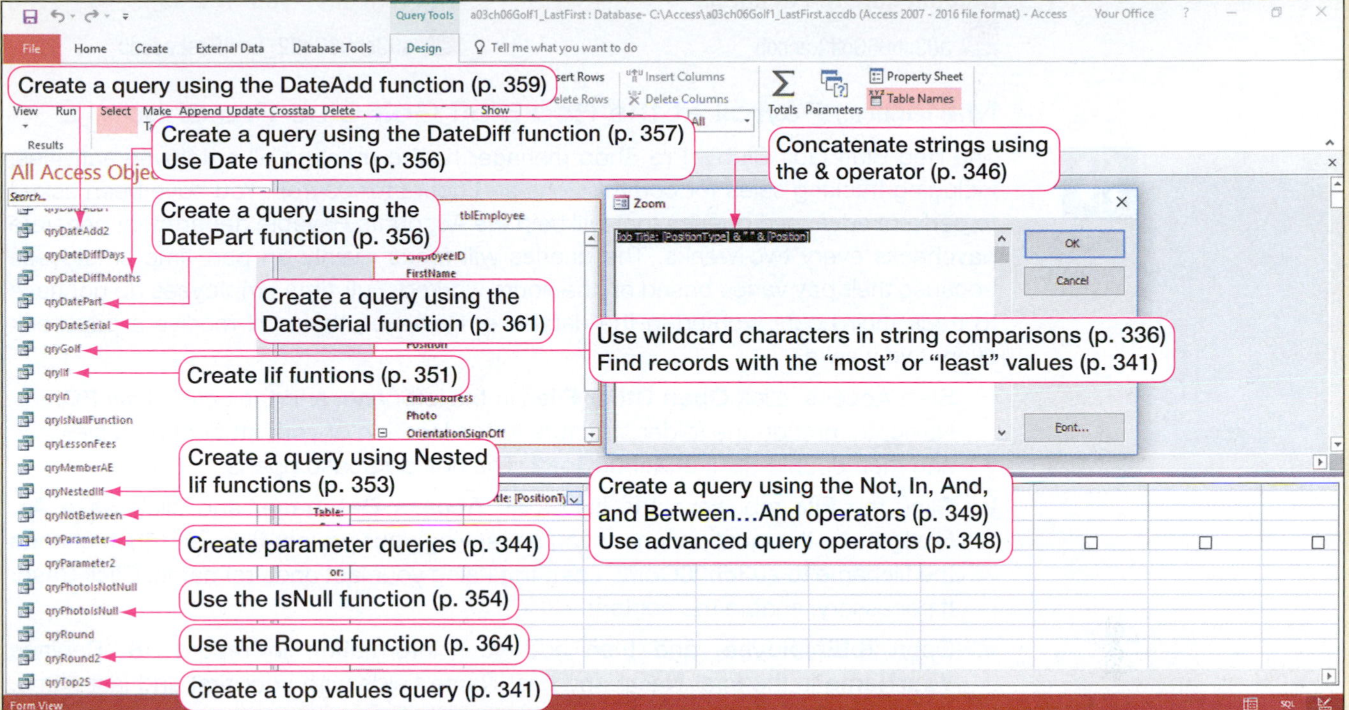

Create a query using the DateAdd function (p. 359)
Create a query using the DateDiff function (p. 357)
Use Date functions (p. 356)
Create a query using the DatePart function (p. 356)
Create a query using the DateSerial function (p. 361)
Create Iif funtions (p. 351)
Create a query using Nested Iif functions (p. 353)
Create parameter queries (p. 344)
Use the IsNull function (p. 354)
Use the Round function (p. 364)
Create a top values query (p. 341)
Concatenate strings using the & operator (p. 346)
Use wildcard characters in string comparisons (p. 336)
Find records with the "most" or "least" values (p. 341)
Create a query using the Not, In, And, and Between…And operators (p. 349)
Use advanced query operators (p. 348)

Figure 26

Access 2016, Windows 10, Microsoft Corporation

Practice 1

Student data file needed:

 a03ch06Golf2.accdb

You will save your file as:

 a03ch06Golf2_LastFirst.accdb

Managing Payroll at the Red Bluff Golf Club Pro Shop

Finance & Accounting

The Red Bluff Golf Club's Pro Shop manager has to manage all employee activities, including tracking sales for commissions and hours for payroll. You have been asked to perform advanced queries that will help the Accounts Payable department generate paychecks every two weeks. The queries will focus mainly on part-time employees because their pay varies based on the hours worked. Full-time employees do not have to track their hours worked in the database. However, they still receive a paycheck every two weeks.

a. Start **Access**, click **Open Other Files** in the left pane, and then click **This PC**. Navigate through the folder structure to the location of your student data files, and then double-click **a03ch06Golf2**. The golf database opens.

b. Click the **File** tab, save the file as an **Access Database**, and click **Save As**. Navigate to the location where you are saving your project files, and then change the filename to a03ch06Golf2_LastFirst using your last and first name. Click **Save**. If necessary, enable the content.

c. Open **tblEmployee**, and then add your information in record **18**. Replace **YourName** in the First Name and Last Name fields with your first and last name. Close tblEmployee.

d. Create a query that calculates full-time employees' payroll for the two-week period from January 2, 2018, through January 15, 2018.

- Click the **Create** tab, and then in the Queries group, click **Query Design**. Add the **tblEmployee**, **tblPayroll**, and **tblPosition** tables to the query workspace. Close the Show Table dialog box.
- Add the following fields to the query design grid.

  tblEmployee: **FullName**, **Salary**

  tblPayroll: **MaritalStatus**, **FTBenefits**, **BenefitsFee**

  tblPosition: **PositionType**
- In the **Criteria** row, under PositionType, type "Full-time".
- Calculate each full-time employee's paycheck before taxes. Because they get paid every two weeks and they are salaried employees, you can calculate the gross income by dividing the Salary field by 26, the number of pay periods in a year. Gross income is the amount an employee is paid before any deductions are taken — taxes, benefits, and so forth. Click the **first blank field** in the query design grid, and then type GrossIncome:[Salary]/26.
- To format GrossIncome as Currency, right-click the **GrossIncome** field, and then select **Properties** to open the Property Sheet. Click the **General** tab, and then under Format select **Currency**.
- Run the query, save it as qryFulltimePay_iLast, using your first initial and last name, and then switch to **Design** view.

e. Modify the qryFulltimePay_iLast query to calculate full-time employees' estimated taxes and net pay for the two-week period from January 2, 2018, through January 15, 2018.

- Nest the IIf and Round functions to estimate the taxes that will be deducted from the gross pay. You will name this new field EstTaxes. If an employee is single, 30% of his or her gross income goes to taxes. If an employee is married, 25% of his or her gross income goes to taxes. Because this is just an estimate of how much the employee will pay in taxes, you want to use the Round function to work in whole dollars. Click the **next blank field** in the query design grid, and then type EstTaxes:IIf([MaritalStatus]="Single",Round([GrossIncome]*0.3), Round([GrossIncome]*0.25)). Format this field as **Currency**.

- Create a new calculated field named NetPay (GrossIncome minus BenefitsFee and EstTaxes). Click the **next blank field** in the query design grid, and then type NetPay: [GrossIncome]-[BenefitsFee]-[EstTaxes]. Format this field as **Currency**.
- Run the query, save it as qryFullTimeNetPay_iLast, using **Save Object As**, and then close the query.

f. Create a query that will help the human resources department keep track of the days off each employee has taken throughout the year.

- Click the **Create** tab, and then in the Queries group, click **Query Design**. Add the **tblTimeCard** table to the query workspace. Close the Show Table dialog box.
- Add **EmployeeID**, **TotalHours**, **DateWorked**, and **WorkCode** to the query design grid.
- Use the Between...And function to ensure that you are displaying records only for the year 2018. In the **Criteria** row, under DateWorked, type Between 12/31/2017 And 1/1/2019.
- In the Criteria row, under **WorkCode**, type In("Vacation","Sick Day","Comp Day","Training").
- Run the query, save it as qryOtherHoursTotal_iLast, and then close the query.

g. Create a query that shows the employees who have selected benefits but for whom the human resources department has yet to enter the fee.

- Click the **Create** tab, and then in the Queries group, click **Query Design**. Add the **tblPayroll**, **tblEmployee**, and **tblPosition** tables to the query workspace. Close the Show Table dialog box.
- Add **Employee**, **MaritalStatus**, **PTBenefits**, **BenefitsFee**, and **PositionType** to the query design grid.
- In the **Criteria** row under BenefitsFee, type Is Null.
- In the **Criteria** row under PositionType, type "Part-time".
- Run the query, save it as qryFees_iLast, and then close the query.

h. Create a query that will determine how much part-time employees will pay for benefits.

- Click the **Create** tab, and then in the Queries group, click **Query Design**. Add the **tblEmployee**, **tblPayroll**, and **tblPosition** tables to the query workspace. Close the Show Table dialog box.
- Add the following fields to the query design grid.

  tblEmployee: **EmployeeID**, **FullName**

  tblPayroll: **MaritalStatus**, **PTBenefits**

  tblPosition: **PositionType**
- In the **Criteria** row under PositionType, type "Part-time".
- Because part-time employees pay different fees for their benefits, you want to nest the IIf and IsNull functions to calculate the total benefits fees for each employee. To do this, you will create a new field named BenefitsFee that determines the employees' fee. Employees can only select one option and are charged accordingly. If an employee has not selected any benefit option, he or she will not need to pay a fee—thus, the fee will be $0. If an employee has selected Dental, the fee is $5. If the employee has selected Vision, the fee is

$10. If the employee has selected Medical, the fee is $25. Right-click the **first blank field** in the query design grid, select **Zoom**, and then type BenefitsFee:IIf(IsNull([PTBenefits]),0,IIf([PTBenefits]="Dental",5,IIf([PTBenefits]="Vision",10,25))). Click **OK**. Format the field as **Currency**.

- Run the query, save it as qryPTBenefitsFee_iLast, and then close the query.

i. Close the database, exit Access, and submit your file as directed by your instructor.

Problem Solve 1

Student data file needed:

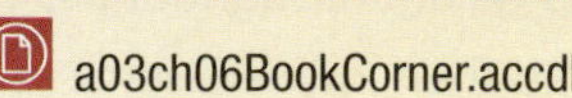

You will save your file as:

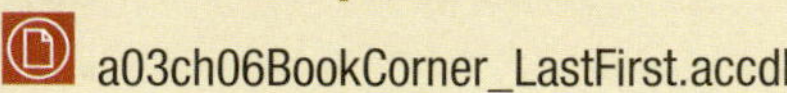

Sales & Marketing

Production & Operations

Querying the Book Corner Bookstore Database

The Book Corner is a small, local bookstore that sells to both recreational readers and the local college student population. The manager uses Access to track inventory, customers, and transactions. You have been asked to perform advanced queries that will help the management team make important business decisions. To keep the file small while you work with the database, the store manager removed most of the data and left only some sample data. Once the store manager has accepted your changes, she will load all the data and implement the new database.

a. Open the **a03ch06BookCorner** database, and then save it as a03ch06BookCorner_LastFirst using your last and first name.

b. Open **tblCustomer**, and then add your information in record **25**. Replace **YourName** in the First Name and Last Name fields with your first and last name. Close tblCustomer.

c. Create a query based on the **tblShipments** and **tblTransaction** tables that display the **TransID** and a calculated field entitled DaysToShip that calculates the number of days it took to ship the items from the date purchased, using the DateDiff function. Sort the results in **Descending** order by **DaysToShip**. Save the query as qryDaysToShip, and then close the query.

d. Create a query that is based on the **tblInventory** table. Display **InventoryID**, **Price**, and a new calculated field called NewPrice. The NewPrice should be 25% more if the book is OutofPrint and 10% more if not. Both values should be rounded to the nearest dollar. Format the NewPrice field as **Currency**. Save the query as qryNewPriceRounded, and then close the query.

e. Create a query based on the **tblAuthor** and **tblInventory** tables that contains a calculated concatenated field called Description. The Description field should display the following for all books in the database: Author: **FirstName LastName**; Title: **BookTitle**; Genre: **BookGenre**. Save the query as qryBookDescription, and then close the query.

f. Create a query based on the **tblCustomer**, **tblTransaction**, **tblTransactionDetails**, and **tblInventory** tables that will return the top 25% of customers based on a calculated field called Revenue. Display **CustomerID** and **Revenue**. Calculate Revenue by multiplying the price and quantity, format Revenue as **Currency**, and sort the results in **Descending** order. Save the query as qryTop25%Customers, and then close the query.

g. Create a query based on the **tblInventory** table to help determine when to order additional copies based on the NumberInStock. Display **InventoryID**, **BookTitle**, and a calculated field called OrderStatus. If there are seven or more copies in stock, then display None. If there are between four and six copies in stock, then display **Critical**. For those with fewer than four in stock, then display **Urgent**. Be sure to limit the results to only books that are not OutofPrint. Be sure to check to see if the the book is out of print by using Null criteria. Save the query as qryOrderStatus, and then close the query.

h. Create a query based on the **tblInventory** table to help determine which books in the fiction and literary genres were written during the 19th century (1800–1901). Display **BookTitle**, **AuthorID**, **YearPublished**, **BookGenre**, and **Condition**. Save the query as qry19thCentury, and then close the query.

i. Create a query based on the **tblInventory**, **tblTransaction**, and **tblTransactionDetails** tables to help determine which "Your Office" books have been shipped within a specific 90-day period. Display **CustomerID**, **BookTitle**, **TransactionDate**, and **Qty**. Use a parameter and the Between...And function that allows you to enter a start date and end date when you run the query. Use a wildcard and the Like operator to ensure that only books with "Your Office" in the title are included. Test your query by using 7/1/2018 as your start date and 9/30/2018 as your end date. Save the query as qry90Days, and then close the query.

j. Create a query based on the **tblTransaction** table to help determine the date when a purchase should be shipped. Display **TransID**, **CustomerID**, **TransactionDate**, **Shipped**, and a calculated field entitled ShipByDate that calculates the date by which the order should be shipped, using the DateAdd function. Orders should be shipped within seven days from the date when the order was placed. Sort the results in **Ascending** order by **ShipByDate**. Save the query as qryShipByDate, and then close the query.

k. Close the database, exit Access, and submit your file as directed by your instructor.

Perform 1: Perform in Your Life

Student data file needed:

 a03ch06BusClub.accdb

You will save your file as:

 a03ch06BusClub_LastFirst.accdb

Leading a Business Club at a Community College

Production & Operations

You have been elected president of your school's business club. Before you took over as president, the club had been keeping all membership records manually. Because you took a class that taught you how to organize and manage data in an Access database, you have decided to create a database and convert all processes that have traditionally been completed by hand. You have already created the tables and are now ready to build your queries.

a. Open the **Access** database **a03ch06BusClub**. Save your file as a03ch06BusClub_LastFirst using your last and first name. If necessary, enable the content.

b. Open tblMember, and then add your information in the first record, making up data to fill in each of the fields.

c. Create a query that concatenates the member's first and last names followed by their major and class standing. Name the concatenated field Details. Use commas to separate the full name, major, and class standing (freshman, sophomore, junior, or senior). Save your query as qryMemberDetails_iLast. Close the query.

d. Create a query that lists all members' first and last names and ZIP Codes. Display only the ZIP Codes that do not begin with either 4 or 7. Sort in Ascending order by ZIP Code, and then save your query as qryZipCodes_iLast. Close the query.

e. Create a query that lists all members whose last names begin with letters "D" through "N". Include the members' first and last names, e-mail addresses, and phone numbers. Sort in ascending order by last name, and then save your query as qryContactList1_iLast. Close the query.

f. Create a query that lists all sophomore and junior members whose last names do not begin with letters "D" through "N". Include the members' first and last names, e-mail addresses, phone numbers, and class standings. Sort in ascending order by last name, and then save your query as qryContactList2_iLast. Close the query.

g. Create a query to view all meeting details that fall within a specific 30-day period. Add a parameter that allows you to enter a start date and end date. Use 8/01/2016 as the start date and 9/01/2016 as the end date to test your query. Save your query as qry30Days_iLast. Close the query.

h. Create a query that determines the members' standing for the summer 2017 semester based on dues paid. If they have paid less than $5, they are in poor standing; if they have paid less than $15, they are in fair standing; and if they have paid $15 or more, they are in good standing. Save your query as qryStanding_iLast. Close the query.

i. Create the following queries using Date functions.
   - Using the DateDiff function, calculate how many days have passed between the most recent meeting on 06/18/2016 and the first meeting on 5/2/2016. Make certain the calculation displays only one time. Save your query as qryDays_iLast. Close the query.
   - Meetings are held every two weeks, and the most recent meeting occurred on 9/2/2018. Using the DateAdd function, calculate the date when the next meeting will be held. Save your query as qryNextMeeting_iLast. Close the query.
   - Executive board meetings are to be held every 45 days. However, no meeting has been held since 1/1/2017. Using the DateSerial function, calculate when the next meeting should have been held. Save your query as qryBoardMeeting_iLast. Close the query.

j. Close the database, exit Access, and then submit your file as directed by your instructor.

Additional Cases

Additional Workshop Cases are available on the companion website and in the instructor resources.

Access Business Unit 3 CAPSTONE

Ensuring Consistent Data and Advanced Querying

This business unit had two outcomes:

Learning Outcome 1:

Control how data is entered by using input masks, data validation rules, lookup fields, custom formatting, requiring data, and work with field captions and create indexes.

Learning Outcome 2:

Create useful information for decision making by creating queries to retrieve data, filter data, calculate data totals, update data, append data, and delete data in bulk.

In Business Unit 3 Capstone, students will demonstrate competence in these outcomes through a series of business problems at various levels from guided practice to problem solving an existing database and performing to create new databases.

More Practice 1

Student data file needed:

 a03Menu.accdb

You will save your file as:

 a03Menu_LastFirst.accdb

Building and Querying the Indigo5 Menu Items Database

Production & Operations

The Painted Paradise Golf Resort & Spa is home to a world-class restaurant with a top chef, Robin Sanchez. The cuisine is balanced and modern. From steaks to pasta to local southwestern meals, this restaurant attracts local patrons in addition to resort guests. Chef Sanchez has been using an Access database to manage menu items. She would like you to modify the tables and then query the data so she can manage her menu much easier.

a. Start **Access**, click **Open Other Files** in the pane, and then double-click **This PC**. Navigate through the folder structure to the location of your student data files, and then double-click **a03Menu**. A database opens displaying tables and queries related to the spa.

b. Click the **File** tab, save the file as an **Access Database**, and click **Save As**. Navigate to the location where you are saving your project files, and then change the filename to a03Menu_LastFirst using your last and first name. Click **Save**. If necessary, in the Security Warning, click **Enable Content**.

c. Create a new table that will help track Indigo5's menu items. Click the **Create** tab, and then in the Tables group, click **Table Design**.

d. Add the following fields, data types, and descriptions.

Field Name	Data Type	Description
MenuID	AutoNumber	The menu ID automatically assigned to each menu item (primary key)
RecipeID	Number	The recipe ID assigned to each recipe in tblRecipes (foreign key)
Season	Short Text	Season this menu item is served
Meal	Short Text	Time of day this is served
Special	Yes/No	Is this item one of the daily specials?
Price	Currency	The price that guests are charged

e. While still in Design view modify the field properties as follows.

Field Name	Field Properties
MenuID	• On the **Design** tab, in the Tools group, click **Primary Key**. • Under the **Format** field property, type "MENU0"0 for the custom format.
RecipeID	• Change the data type to a lookup field by selecting **Lookup Wizard** in the Data Type menu. Select **I want the lookup field to get values from another table or query**, and then click **Next**. Select **tblRecipes**, and then click **Next**. Select **RecipeID** and **RecipeName**, and then click **Next**. Sort in Ascending order by **RecipeName**, and then click **Next**. Keep the key column hidden, and then click **Next**. Enable **Data Integrity**, select **Restrict Delete**, and then click **Finish**. • Under Field Properties, type Recipe as the caption. • Change the Required property to **Yes**.
Season	• Change the data type to a lookup field by selecting **Lookup Wizard** in the Data Type menu. Select **I will type in the values that I want**, and then click **Next**. Type the values Fall, Winter, Spring, Summer, and then click **Next**. Limit the user's selection to what is on the list, allow multiple values, and then click **Finish**.
Meal	• Change the data type to a lookup field by selecting **Lookup Wizard** in the Data Type menu. Select **I will type in the values that I want**, and then click **Next**. Type the values Breakfast, Lunch, Dinner, Late Night, Anytime, and then click **Next**. Limit the user's selection to what is on the list, allow multiple values, and then click **Finish**.

f. Save the table as tblMenu. While still in Design view, add a Calculated field named Cost. When Calculated is selected as the Data Type, the Expression Builder will open. Cost is calculated by multiplying the Price by 40%. Type the following as the Expression: [Price]*.40. Add the description as shown in the table below.

Field Name	Data Type	Description
Cost	Calculated	The cost for the restaurant to prepare this item

g. While still in Design view modify the field properties as follows.

Cost	• Format the Result Type as **Currency**.

h. Save your changes, and then switch to **Datasheet** view. Enter the following records to test the properties in your new table. Resize the fields as needed to view the data.

Recipe	Season	Meal	Special	Price
Avocado Salad	Spring, Summer	Lunch	No	$18.95
Black Beans	Fall, Winter	Lunch	No	$12.95
YourName's Chicken Soup	Fall, Winter	Lunch	No	$6.95
Gambas al Ajillo (Shrimp with Garlic)	Fall, Spring, Summer, Winter	Dinner, Lunch	Yes	$26.95
Pasta Napolitana	Spring, Summer	Dinner	Yes	$18.95
Pueblo Green Chili Stew	Winter	Lunch	No	$14.95

Recipe	Season	Meal	Special	Price
Eggs Benedict	Fall, Spring, Summer, Winter	Breakfast	No	$11.95
Fresh Mozzarella and Basil Pizza	Fall, Spring, Summer, Winter	Dinner, Late Night, Lunch	No	$24.95
Goat Cheese Pizza	Fall, Spring, Summer, Winter	Dinner, Late Night, Lunch	No	$24.95
Reuben Panini	Fall, Spring, Summer, Winter	Dinner, Late Night, Lunch	No	$12.95
Spinach and Mushroom Frittata	Spring, Summer	Breakfast	No	$13.95

i. Close tblMenu. If you are prompted to save your changes, click **Yes**.

j. Click the **Database Tools** tab, and then in the Relationships group, click **Relationships**. If necessary, create a one-to-many relationship between **RecipeID** in tblRecipes and **RecipeID** in tblMenu. Enforce referential integrity. Do not cascade update or cascade delete. Save your changes if necessary, and then close the Relationships window.

k. Click the **Create** tab, and then in the Queries group, click **Query Design**. Use the query design grid and the data in **tblMenu** to create a query that displays the spring and summer lunch menu using the In operator. The query results should display **RecipeID**, **Season**, **Meal**, **Special**, and **Price** from tblMenu. In the Criteria row of the Season field, type In("Spring","Summer"). In the Criteria row of the Meal field, type "Lunch". Run your query, and then save it as qrySpSuLunch_iLast using your first initial and last name. Close the query.

l. Click the **Create** tab, and then in the Queries group, click **Query Design**. Use the query design grid and the data in **tblMenu** to create a Top Values query. The query results should display **RecipeID**, **Season**, **Meal**, **Special**, and **Price**. Sort in **Descending** order by Price. Enter **3** in the Return (Top Values) box to view the three highest-priced items. Run your query, and then save it as qryTopValues_iLast using your first initial and last name. Close the query.

m. Click the **Create** tab, and then in the Queries group, click **Query Design**. Use the query design grid and the data in **tblMenu** and **tblRecipes** to create a parameter query that allows you to enter two parameters. The query results should display **RecipeID**, **Season**, **Meal**, **Special**, **Price**, **Cost**, **Subcategory**, and **TimeToPrepare**. In the Criteria row of the Season field, type [Enter the season]. In the Criteria row of the Meal field, type [Enter the Meal]. Test your query using **Fall** for Season and **Lunch** for Meal. Save your query as qryParameters_iLast using your first initial and last name, and then close the query.

n. Click the **Create** tab, and then in the Queries group, click **Query Design**. Use the query design grid and the data in **tblMenu** to create a query that uses the Round function. The query results should display **RecipeID**, **Season**, **Meal**, **Special**, **Price**, **Cost**, and a new field named Rounded Cost. Use the Round function to round the data stored in the Cost field with a precision of **1**. In the first blank field on the query design grid, type Rounded Cost: Round([Cost],1). Format the field as **Currency**. Run your query, and then save it as qryRound_iLast using your first initial and last name. Close the query.

o. Click the **Create** tab, and then in the Queries group, click **Query Design**. Use the query design grid and the data in **tblMenu** and **tblRecipes** to create a query that uses the Like function and wildcards. The query results should display **RecipeID**, **Season**, **Meal**, **Special**, **Price**, **RecipeName**, and **Instructions**. Use the Like function and wildcards to view all menu items whose recipe name begins with the letters "A" through "G". In the Criteria row of the RecipeName field, type Like "[A-G]*". Sort in **Ascending** order by **RecipeName**. Run your query, and then save it as qryLike1_iLast using your first initial and last name. Close the query.

p. Click the **Create** tab, and then in the Queries group, click **Query Design**. Use the query design grid and the data in **tblIngredients** to create a query that uses the Like function and wildcards. The query results should display **Ingredient**. Use the Like function and wildcards to view all ingredients whose name begins with the letters "D" through "P". In the Criteria row of the Ingredient field, type Like "[D-P]*". Sort in **Ascending** order by **Ingredients**. Run your query, and then save it as qryLike2_iLast using your first initial and last name. Close the query.

q. Close the database, exit Access, and then submit your file as directed by your instructor.

Problem Solve 1

Student data file needed:

a03Hotel.accdb

You will save your file as:

a03Hotel_LastFirst.accdb

Using the Hotel Database for Advanced Querying

Finance & Accounting

The area of Painted Paradise Resort & Spa that generates the most revenue is the hotel. Guests can charge anything from the resort to their room. Therefore, the hotel staff must track all of these charges, such as those from the spa, golf shop, gift shop, restaurants, movies, personal trainers, and sessions with golf professionals. Hotel guests who use these services are eligible for a discount. You have been asked to create a new table that tracks guest payments and to create queries that will help management with decision making.

a. Open the Access file, **a03Hotel**. Save your file as a03Hotel_LastFirst using your last and first name. If necessary, enable the content. Open **tblGuests**, and then replace YourName in record 25 with your first and last name.

b. Create a new table named tblPayments that will track guest payments upon guest check-out. Add the following fields, data types, and descriptions.

Field Name	Data Type	Description
PmtID	AutoNumber	The payment ID automatically assigned to each transaction (primary key)
GuestID	Number	An alphanumeric code unique to every guest matching a guest in tblGuests (foreign key)
ReservationID	Number	An alphanumeric code unique to every reservation and matches a reservation in tblReservations (foreign key)
PmtAmount	Currency	The amount the guest paid
PmtDate	Date/Time	The date the guest made the payment
PmtMethod	Short Text	How the customer paid (Cash, Check, MasterCard, Visa, American Express, Discover)
AuthNumber	Short Text	The authorization number if paid by credit or debit card. Authorization numbers can begin with the number zero.

c. Create the following field properties.

Field Name	Field Properties
PmtID	• Change the format to "PMT0"0. • Make this field the primary key. • New values need to be sequential — Increment.
GuestID	• Create a Lookup field using the tblGuests table. Select **GuestID**, **GuestLastName**, and **GuestFirstName**. Sort in **Ascending** order by GuestID. Keep the key column hidden. • Type Guest as the caption. • Make data in this field required for both new and existing records.
ReservationID	• Change the format to "RBH"0. • Type RSVP ID as the caption. • Make data in this field required for both new and existing records.
PmtAmount	• Type Amount as the caption.
PmtDate	• This field should be formatted as "Medium Date" but should have an input mask of Short Date with a four-digit year. Make certain that when users enter data, an underscore is displayed in the field where users can enter digits. • Type Date as the caption.
PmtMethod	• Create a lookup field that lists the following values: Cash, Check, MasterCard, Visa, American Express, Discover. Limit the user's selection to what is on the list. Allow multiple values. • Type Method as the caption.
AuthNumber	• Set the maximum number of characters for the field to 6. • Type Auth # as the caption.

d. Enter the following data in the tblPayments table.

GuestID	ReservationID	PmtAmount	PmtDate	PmtMethod	AuthNumber
Bennett	5	$1,229.00	01-Jan-18	American Express	22597
Cote	6	$168.30	02-Jan-18	Cash	
Wong	7	$483.23	03-Jan-18	MasterCard	877456
Bridges	8	$346.50	03-Jan-18	Check	
Finch	10	$31.19	15-Feb-18	Cash	
Sharp	11	$395.80	15-Feb-18	Visa	01123
Woodward	12	$391.31	28-Feb-18	Visa	08556
Mcmahon	14	$137.62	02-Apr-18	Cash, Discover	22113
Wenner	16	$807.49	10-Apr-18	American Express	88945
YourName	17	$1,682.71	06-Jul-18	Discover	612876

e. Open the **Relationships** window and add the table tblPayments. Create a one-to-many relationship between **GuestID** in the tblGuest and **GuestID** in the tblPayments. Enforce referential integrity. Create a one-to-many relationship between **ReservationID** in the table tblReservations and the **ReservationID** in the table tblPayments. Enforce referential integrity.

f. Use the data in **tblReservations** and **tblRoomCharges** to create a query that calculates the attendant's gratuity on a room service order (18%) or spa treatment (25%). Your query results should display **ReservationID**, **CheckInDate**, **ChargeCategory**, **ChargeAmount**, and Gratuity, where Gratuity is a calculated field. If the ChargeCategory is not a spa treatment or room service, a zero should be displayed in the field. Format the Gratuity field as Currency. Sort in **Ascending** order by CheckInDate. Run the query, and then save it as qryTips. Close the query.

g. Use the data in **tblReservations** and **tblGuests** to create a query that calculates the guest's total room charges. Your query results should display **GuestFirstName**, **GuestLastName**, **ReservationID**, **CheckInDate**, **NightsStay**, **RoomRate**, **DiscountType**, and TotalRoomCharges, where TotalRoomCharges is a calculated field. Subtract any discount from the total charges. In addition to the discount data in the database, AARP and AAA members receive a 10% discount. Military personnel receive a 20% discount. Guests without a discount should still have their total room charges calculated. Sort in **Ascending** order by ReservationID. Format the calculated field as Currency. Run the query, and then save your query as qryTotalRoomCharges. Close the query.

h. Use the data in **tblGuests**, **tblChargeDetails**, and **tblRoomCharges** to create a query that enables you to enter the guest's full name — first and last name separated by a space — to find out what services the guest had while staying at the resort. Concatenate the GuestFirstName and GuestLastName fields into a new field named Guest. Be sure to leave a space between the GuestFirstName and GuestLastName fields. The Parameter should ask the user to **Enter a Guest's First and Last Name**. Your query results should also list **ChargeCategory**, **ChargeAmount**, and **Purchase**. Combine the Not and Like operators to ensure that your results do not include any Gifts/Sundries in the results. Test your query using your **first name** and **last name**. Save your query as **qryParameter**. Close the query.

i. Use the data in **tblReservations** and **tblPayments** to create a query that finds all reservations between 6/1/2017 and 6/1/2018. The query results should display **ReservationID**, **CheckInDate**, **NightsStay**, **NumberOfGuests**, **RoomType**, **RoomRate**, **PmtAmount**, **PmtDate**, and **PmtMethod**. Show only the guests who paid by credit card — MasterCard, Visa, American Express, and Discover. Sort in **Ascending** order by PmtAmount. Run the query, and then save it as qryDates. Close the query.

j. Use the data in **tblReservations**, **tblPayments**, and **qryTotalRoomCharges**, to create a query to see what the total charges will be for each guest. Your query results should display **ReservationID**, **CheckInDate**, **NightsStay**, **RoomRate**, and **TotalRoomCharges** from qryTotalRoomCharges, **PmtAmount** from tblPayments, and **DiscountType** from tblReservations. Create a new field named AmountDue that calculates whether an amount is due. (Hint: If the total room charges are more than the payment amount, then the guest owes money) Create a new field named RefundDue that calculates whether a refund is owed to a guest. Format the AmountDue and RefundDue fields as **Currency**. Run the query, and then save it as qryTotalCharges. Close the query.

k. Use the data in **tblReservations** and **tblGuests** to create a Top Values query that displays the 11 highest room rates being charged to guests who have made a reservation. The query results should display **GuestFirstName** and **GuestLastName** from tblGuests and then **CheckInDate**, **NightsStay**, and **RoomRate** from tblReservations. Enter 11 in the Return (Top Values) box. (Hint: Do not forget to sort your data.) Run the query, and then save it as qryTopValues. Close the query.

l. Close the database, exit Access, and then submit the file as directed by your instructor.

Problem Solve 2

Student data file needed:

 a03Hotel2.accdb

You will save your file as:

 a03Hotel2_LastFirst.accdb

More Advanced Querying in the Hotel Database

Finance & Accounting

Guests at the motel may charge anything from the resort to their room. The hotel staff must track all of these charges, such as those from the spa, golf, gift shop, restaurants, movies, personal trainers, and sessions with golf professionals. Hotel guests who use these services are eligible for a discount. You have been asked to create queries that will help management with decision making.

a. Open the Access file **a03Hotel2**. Save your file as a03Hotel2_LastFirst using your last and first name. If necessary, enable the content. Open **tblGuests**, replace YourName in record 25 with your first and last name, and then close tblGuests.

b. Use the data in **tblReservations** to create a parameter query that allows you to look up reservations by entering the check-in date and number of nights the guests are staying. The query results should display **ReservationID**, **GuestID**, **NumberOfGuests**, **RoomType**, **RoomRate**, and **DiscountType**. Run the query, enter 5/28/2018 as the date, and then enter 3 as the number of nights' stay to test it. Save your query as qryDateStay. Close the query.

Critical Thinking

In creating this parameter query, what other information would be helpful in this query and why? Would another type of query be more beneficial?

c. Use the data in **tblRoomCharges** to create a Top Values query that displays the five lowest charge amounts. The query results should display **RoomChargeID**, **GuestID**, **ChargeCategory**, and **ChargeAmount**. Run the query, and then save it as qryLowestCharges. Close the query.

d. Use the data in **tblRoomCharges** and **tblChargeDetails** to create a Top Values query that displays the highest charge amount when the purchase was made in either Terra Cotta Brew, Indigo5, or Silver Moon Lounge. The query results should display **RoomChargeID**, **ChargeCategory**, **ChargeAmount**, and **Purchase**. (Hint: Do not forget to sort your data.) Run the query, and then save it as qryTopCharge. Close the query.

e. Use the data in **tblReservations** to create a query that displays the guests who have reservations for all rooms except double rooms and who have an AAA, AARP, or Military discount. The query results should display **GuestID**, **CheckInDate**, **RoomType**, **RoomRate**, and **DiscountType**. Run the query, and then save it as qryNotDoubleRoom. Close the query.

f. Use the data in **tblReservations** and **tblGuests** to create a query that lists the guests who reside in any state except for AK, MT, or IA and who will be paying between $200 and $350 for their room. The query results should display **GuestFirstName**, **GuestLastName**, **Address**, **City**, **State**, **ZipCode**, **RSVPDate**, **CheckInDate**, **RoomRate**, and Months where Months is a new field that calculates how many months in advance the reservations were booked. Sort in **Ascending** order by CheckInDate. Run the query, and then save it as qryMonths. Close your query.

g. Use the data in **tblReservations** and **tblGuests** to create a query that lists the guests who reside in AK, PA, or OH. The query results should display **GuestFirstName**, **GuestLastName**, **Address**, **City**, **State**, **ZipCode**, **RSVPDate**, **CheckInDate**, **RoomRate**, and Weeks, where Weeks is a new field that calculates how many weeks in advance the reservations were booked. Sort in **Ascending** order by CheckInDate. Run the query, and then save it as qryWeeks. Close your query.

h. Use the data in **tblReservations** and **tblGuests** to create a query that calculates the guests' checkout date on the basis of when they check in and how many nights they are staying. The query results should display Guest, **ReservationID**, **CheckInDate**, **NightsStay**, **NumberOfGuests**, **RoomType**, **RoomRate, and** CheckOutDate, where Guest is a new field that combines each guest's first name and last name separated by a space and CheckOutDate is a calculated field that determines the date of checkout. Sort in **Ascending** order by GuestLastName. Run the query, and then save it as qryCheckOutDate. Close your query.

i. Use the data in **tblReservations** and **tblGuests** to create a query that determines the discount that qualifying customers will receive. The query results should display **GuestFirstName**, **GuestLastName**, **NightsStay**, **DiscountType**, and Discount %, where Discount % is a new field that displays the percentage qualifying customers will have deducted from their bill when they check out. If customers have an AAA discount, they will receive 10% off. If customers have an AARP discount, they will receive 15% off. If customers have a military discount, they will receive 20% off. Additionally, if customers are staying more than three days and do not have an AAA, AARP, or military discount, they will receive 5% off. If they do not receive a discount, then display **No Discount** in the field. Run the query, and then save it as qryDiscounts. Close your query.

j. Management wants to be able to make a follow-up call two weeks after the guest has checked out of the resort to ask about the guest's stay. Use the data in **tblReservations** and **tblGuests** to create a query that displays the date that is two weeks after the guest checked out of the resort. The query results should display **GuestFirstName**, **GuestLastName**, **Phone**, **CheckInDate**, **NightsStay**, and Follow-up Date, where Follow-up Date is a new field that displays the date that is two weeks after the check-out date. Use the DateAdd Function. Sort in **Ascending** order by Follow-up Date. Run the query, and then save it as qryFollowUp. Close the query.

k. Close the database, exit Access, and then submit the file as directed by your instructor.

Perform 1: Perform in Your Life

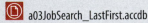

Student data file needed:	You will save your file as:
Blank Access database	a03JobSearch_LastFirst.accdb

Creating a Job Search Database

General Business

The Job Search database will help you track your internship or job search process, including contacting prospective employers and following up after interviews. Even if you are not currently looking for employment, this database will help keep track of associates you may need to contact in the future. After creating each table, you will need to enter data into each table. Ensure that at least one table has 20 records, including one with your name. If you prefer, you can make up fictitious reasonable data rather than using real data.

a. Start **Access**, and then click the **Blank desktop database**. Save the database as a03JobSearch_LastFirst using your last and first name.

b. To ensure consistency and an ease of understanding the information, create three tables named tblCall, tblCompany, and tblContact.

c. Add fields to each table. Include appropriate data types, such as Lookup, Yes/No, Attachment, Hyperlink, OLE Object, and Calculated.

d. Add appropriate field properties such as Required, Default values, Input Masks, Formats, Captions, AutoNumbers, Validation rules, and Validation text.

e. Create appropriate indexes in each table.

f. Use the data in your tables to create at least two queries about your job search efforts. Include functions, operators, and expressions.

g. Use the data in your tables to create at least one parameter query.

h. Use the data in your tables to create two queries that include a Date function.

i. Use the Table Analyzer to ensure that your tables are normalized. Modify the database as needed.

j. Close the database, exit Access, and then submit the file as directed by your instructor.

Perform 2: Perform in Your Career

Student data file needed:

 a03Inventory.accdb

You will save your file as:

 a03Inventory_LastFirst.accdb

Modifying an Inventory Database

Production & Operations

Gaby's Green Groceries, Inc., is a grocery store that specializes in organic and locally produced foods as well as some unique specialty items. As an inventory manager, you were asked to modify an existing database to make it more functional for completing tasks such as when to reorder items and to track inventory within your company. Consider the marketing and sales departments as you modify your database. The employees in these departments need to know current inventory levels and when inventory will be replenished so they can better serve the company's clients. You will deliver results of your queries to the marketing and sales departments upon completion. Enter data into each table. Ensure that at least one table has 20 records. If you prefer, you can make up reasonably fictitious data rather than using real data.

a. Start **Access**, and open the student data file **a03Inventory**. Save the database as a03Inventory_LastFirst using your last and first name. Add your first and last name to tblSuppliers.

b. To ensure consistency when entering data and ease of understanding the information, modify your tables to include appropriate data types and field properties. Include one calculated field and one Yes/No field.

c. Create appropriate indexes in each table.

d. Create a parameter query using the Between…And operator and the IIf function.

e. Create a query using the Concatenate operator.

f. Create a query using IsNull in the criteria.

g. Create a query that includes an IIf and nested IIf function.

h. Use Date functions in two of your queries.

i. Create a query that uses a wildcard character and the Like function.

j. Create a query using either the Not or In operator.

k. Create a Top Values query.

l. Close the database, exit Access, and then submit the file as directed by your instructor.

Perform 3: Perform in Your Team

Student data file needed:

a03Cupcakes.accdb

You will save your files as:

a03Cupcakes_TeamName.accdb

a03Cupcakes_TeamName.docx

Managing Employees at Jellybean's Cupcakes

Human Resources

You are the owner and manager of Jellybean's Cupcakes, a bakery franchise specializing in traditional and trendy cupcakes. The human resources (HR) manager has been having a difficult time keeping track of training efforts and tracking which training sessions employees have attended. You want to work with your HR manager to ensure that all employees are receiving adequate training. Until one month ago, all data was kept in a notebook. You have entered the paper records into a database. Your HR manager has suggested that you create a shared OneDrive folder so you can share the database with your team. After creating the database and running queries, you will distribute the information to each bakery manager via the shared OneDrive folder. This will create an environment that will help all managers, along with the human resources department, track current employees along with training efforts for all the bakeries' employees.

a. Select one team member to set up the document by completing steps b–d.

b. Open your browser, and navigate to https://www.onedrive.live.com, https://www.drive.google.com, or any other instructor-assigned location. Be sure all members of the team have an account on the chosen system, such as a Microsoft or Google account.

c. Open **a03Cupcakes**, and then save the file as **a03Cupcakes_TeamName** replacing TeamName with the name assigned to your team by your instructor.

d. Share the database with the other members of your team. Make sure that each team member has the appropriate permission to edit the database.

e. Hold a team meeting and discuss the requirements of the remaining steps. Make an action and communication plan. Consider which steps can be done independently and which steps require completion of prior steps before starting.

f. Perform the following tasks.
   - Open tblEmployee, add your team name in record 1, and then close tblEmployee.
   - Modify the tables using appropriate data types and field properties as you see fit.
   - Add the following fields to tblEmployee.

Field Name	Data Type	Description
E-mail	Hyperlink	The employee's e-mail address
Resume	Attachment	The employee's resume
Photo	OLE Object	The employee's photo

- Create appropriate indexes in each table.
- Using filter options, create two filters using Filter by Form. Save both as queries.
- Using filter options, create two filters using Filter by Selection. Save both as queries.
- Create a query that displays all employees attending any introductory training session, indicated by 101 in the session name.
- So that the HR department can e-mail a reminder to all employees registered for a training session, create a query that calculates the date two weeks before the date when the session will be held.
- So that the HR department can plan appropriately for upcoming training sessions, create a parameter query that allows users to find all training sessions that fall between two specific dates.
- To ensure that all your employees are of legal age to work, create a query that calculates each employee's current age. Sort the query in Ascending order by Current Age.
- Create a top values query that uses the query that calculates each employee's current age. Find the top 25% of employee ages.
- Analyze tblEmployee using the Table Analyzer Wizard. Make appropriate changes as you see fit.
- Close the database, and then upload the database to your shared OneDrive or other cloud account.
- Create a Word document, and then write a memo to the HR manager explaining that the database you will use to manage your employees has been uploaded. Also let the HR manager know that if she thinks of other queries that need to be created, she can feel free to add them, or she can let you know and you can help her add them. Include your instructor's name in the cc field. Additionally, each team member must list his or her first and last name as well as the specifics of his or her contributions. Save your memo as a03Cupcakes_TeamName, close the memo, and then upload it to the shared cloud folder if necessary.
- Upon request, invite your instructor to join the shared cloud folder.

g. Close the database, exit Access, and then submit the files as directed by your instructor.

Perform 4: How Others Perform

Student data file needed:

 a03RealEstate.accdb

You will save your file as:

 a03RealEstate_LastFirst.docx

Being an Entrepreneur: Rhubarb Realtors

General Business

You are the president of Rhubarb Realtors, a small real estate agency. Your intern created a database for you and your employees to use for tracking properties. At first glance, you notice that it is missing quite a few field properties within the tables that would make the database more functional and easier to use. You also noticed that there are no queries, which would help to answer many questions about the properties you have listed. You need to assess the database and apply changes to make it more useful.

a. Start **Access**, and open the student data file **a03RealEstate**. Save the database as a03RealEstate_LastFirst. Open **tblAgents**, add your first and last name in record 1, and then close tblAgents.

b. Consider each table's structure. Make any changes that you deem necessary to field properties, data types, descriptions, and indexes.

c. Add or delete fields that will enhance the database. Consider data types such as Hyperlink, Attachment, and OLE Object.

d. Consider how the data will be used. Create the following queries to assist in decision making.
   - Create a query that uses the Between…And operator.
   - Create a query of all homes built between two specified years that are either a Ranch, Split Level, or 2 story house.
   - Create a query that calculates a 7% commission if the house has been sold.
   - Create a query that uses the DateAdd function.
   - Create a query that uses the DateDiff function.
   - Create two queries that use the IIf function.
   - Create a query that uses a nested IIf function.
   - Create two parameter queries.
   - Create a query that uses the Round function.
   - Create a Top Values query.

e. Close the database, exit Access, and then submit the file as directed by your instructor.

Access Business Unit 4

Leveraging Queries for Business Information and Intelligence

Microsoft Access is a useful tool for small organizations and workgroups to easily collect and store data about their organization and to ensure that the data collected is accurate, consistent, and reliable. However, the benefits of Access do not stop there. With advanced querying techniques and SQL, it is possible not only to retrieve data from one or more tables, but also to create business intelligence with revenue calculations, determine container sizes for efficient shipping of products, and so much more. This business unit will explain ways to get more from the data stored in your databases.

Learning Outcome 1:

Use queries to calculate various values, such as sales volume for an organization, and easily view how sales volume breaks down by employee, product category, and so on. Use subqueries to calculate what percentage of total revenue came from the sales of specific services. Use SQL to query a database in a way that is easily transferrable to any other relational database management system.

Real World Success 

"Being able to include 'knowledge of SQL' on my resume was extremely helpful when I was applying for internships. Knowing how to create queries in Access, using the query design or query wizard, goes only so far at organizations that use other relational database management systems designed for large companies. Since SQL is an international standard, it is easily transferrable to many other DBMSs."

- Robert, student

Learning Outcome 2:

Use action queries to archive historical data, update many records at once, and delete records from tables and related tables. Modify the types of joins between tables to gain additional insights about the company, such as which products have never been sold.

Real World Success 

"After graduation, I obtained a job in the marketing department of a local sports team. I had never imagined that as a marketing major I would need to know Access. My manager had three different databases that she was using to manage our department. Through the use of action queries, I was able to merge all the tables into one database and cleanse the data to make the database more efficient to use."

- Beth Ann, recent graduate

Microsoft Access 2016

Chapter 7 | AGGREGATED CALCULATIONS, SUBQUERYING, AND SQL

OBJECTIVES

Prepare Case

Production & Operations

The Turquoise Oasis Spa Database: Querying with Advanced Calculations

The Turquoise Oasis Spa generates revenue through its spa services, such as facials, mud baths, and massages. Meda Rodate, the manager of the spa, needs useful information to run the business efficiently. She has hired you as an intern and has given you a copy of the database. To keep the file small while you work with the database, she removed most of the data and left only some sample data. Meda has asked you to query the data for decision making, such as scheduling employees, booking client services, and managing services. Once Meda accepts your changes, she will load all of the data and implement the new database.

Gennadiy Poznyakov/Fotolia

Student data file needed for this chapter:

 a04ch07SpaDecisions.accdb

You will save your file as:

 a04ch07SpaDecisions_LastFirst.accdb

CHAPTER 7

Understanding the GROUP BY Clause in Aggregated Calculations

Grouping data in a query can be very informative. By using the **GROUP BY clause**, you can combine records with identical values in a specified field list into a single record. Unless the field data type is Memo or OLE Object data, any field in a table can use the GROUP BY clause. When you use tables to record transactions or store regularly occurring numeric data, it is useful to be able to review that data in an aggregate, such as a sum or average. In this section, you will learn how to calculate sales volume and use the GROUP BY clause to summarize duplicate data.

An **aggregated calculation** returns a single value calculated from multiple values in a column. Common aggregate functions include Average, Count, Maximum, Median, Minimum, Mode, and Sum. You may need to create a custom field that includes an aggregate calculation.

Opening the Spa Decisions Database

To begin creating queries using the GROUP BY clause, you first need to open the database. In this exercise, you will open the Spa Decisions database.

A07.00

To Open the Spa Decisions Database

a. Start **Access**, click **Open Other Files** in the left pane, and then double-click **This PC**. Navigate through the folder structure to the location of your student data files, and then double-click **a04ch07SpaDecisions**. A database opens displaying tables related to the spa, the services it provides, and various transactions.

b. Click the **File** tab, save the file as an **Access Database**, and click **Save As**. Navigate to the location where you are saving your project files, and then change the filename to a04ch07SpaDecisions_LastFirst using your last and first name. Click **Save**. If necessary, enable the content.

Use the GROUP BY Clause in Aggregated Calculations

An aggregate function differs from a calculated field in that when you create a calculated field, you are calculating or summarizing data across a single row at a time. However, when you create an aggregated field, you are calculating or summarizing data across entire groups of rows. The word **aggregate** simply means a summative calculation, such as a total or average, or summarizing data.

Many managers need summarized data to make decisions. For example, the spa sells many different products. If a select query is created on the data, it would simply list all the products. However, the GROUP BY clause could group the data by category — such as soap, lotion, and hair care — and calculate the total sales in each category with the Sum aggregate function. By having summary data, a manager can learn which category is the best seller and see which category generates the least revenue. This information could assist in making business decisions related to marketing and inventory replenishment.

Not all data in a table can be summed or averaged, since they are not numbers; an example is employee names. Another way in which the GROUP BY clause can be used is to take a count, such as a count of orders or a count of customers. For example, Meda Rodate may want to view how many customers each employee served in a given day or week. The GROUP BY clause could group the data by employee and count the customers with the Count aggregate function. Businesses can look at this as sales volume, or the quantity of items sold, such as bottles of shampoo or massages given.

REAL WORLD ADVICE | **Making Management Decisions with Grouped Data**

In the world of business, specifically sales, summarized data can help managers make decisions. The data are current, relevant, and concise, and depending on the nature of the organization and goals set forth by the strategic sales plan, the data can help them to grow their business. Some decisions that the spa manager could make include the following.

- Reorder inventory to ensure that proper stocking levels are maintained.
- Advertise items that are not selling as well as others.
- Train employees on selling techniques.
- Place items on sale if the products are generating the lowest revenue.
- Determine whether sales figures are on target to meet sales goals.

CONSIDER THIS | **How Do You Use Grouped Data?**

Have you ever used grouped data? What about when you are calculating your grade point average (GPA) or quality point average (QPA)? Many students not only calculate their overall GPA or QPA, but also calculate what their GPA or QPA is for their major. Is this considered grouping data? Why or why not?

Calculating Revenue and Sales Volume

Two common questions that managers of retail businesses ask themselves are "How much sales revenue did we generate?" and "What was our sales volume?" **Sales volume** is the number of items sold or services rendered during the normal course of business. This figure is taken over a specific period of time — such as week, month, or year — and can be expressed in dollars or percentages. In this exercise, you will create a query using the Group By and Sum aggregate functions to determine total sales revenue and sales volume for the spa.

A07.01

SIDE NOTE

Pin the Ribbon

If your ribbon is collapsed, pin your ribbon open. Click the Home tab. In the lower right-hand corner of the ribbon, click Pin the Ribbon [pin].

To Calculate Revenue and Sales Volume

a. Click the **Create** tab, and then, in the Queries group, click **Query Design**. In the Show Table dialog box, click **tblProduct**, press Ctrl, click **tblPurchase**, and then click **Add**. **Close** [X] the Show Table dialog box.

b. On the Design tab, in the Show/Hide group, click **Totals**.

c. Add the following fields to the query design grid: **ProductDescription**, **Price**, and **Quantity**.

d. In the first blank column, create a new field by typing Revenue: [Price] * [Quantity].

e. In the Total row of the query design grid, select the following options.
ProductDescription: Leave as Group By
Price: Leave as Group By
Quantity: Select **Sum**
Revenue: Select **Sum**

Notice that you can modify how you want the data to be displayed by using the SUM aggregate function.

SIDE NOTE
Rearranged Query Design
You may notice that once a query has been saved, closed, and reopened, the aggregate function is moved into the Field row, and Expression is selected in the Total row. This occurs whenever a query has an aggregate function applied to a calculated field. It has to do with how Access converts a query design into SQL.

f. Rename the Quantity field by typing SalesVolume: in front of the field name Quantity.

Troubleshooting
When renaming a field, be sure to include the colon (:) after the new field name, and do not delete the field. Otherwise, Access will not know which field to aggregate.

g. Save the query as qryRevAndVol.

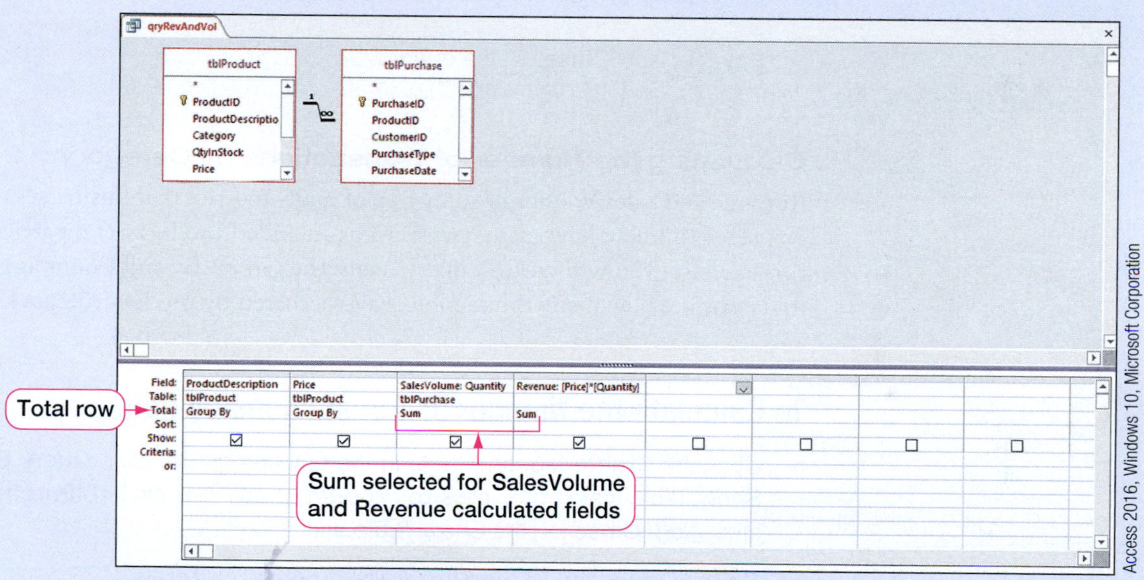

Figure 1 Design View of the qryRevAndVol query

SIDE NOTE
Resizing Fields
It is best practice to resize fields so that all data can be seen.

h. On the Design tab, in the Results group, click **Run**. Resize your fields if you cannot see all the data and column headings.

The results of the query include product descriptions along with the sales volume, and revenue. Because the query included the tblProduct table and the tblPurchase table, the results include only products whose ProductID is also in the tblPurchase table, meaning products that have been sold.

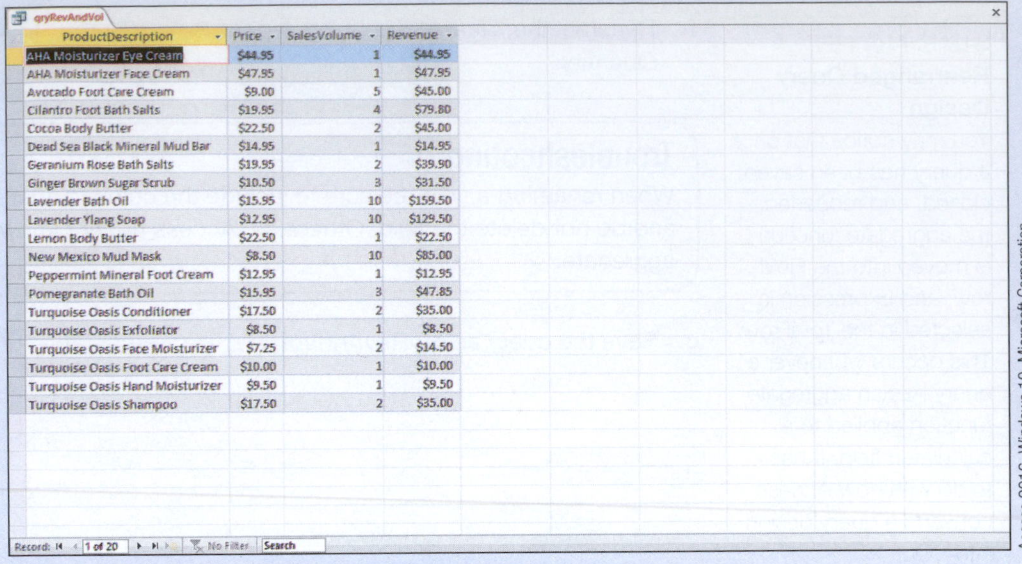

qryRevAndVol

ProductDescription	Price	SalesVolume	Revenue
AHA Moisturizer Eye Cream	$44.95	1	$44.95
AHA Moisturizer Face Cream	$47.95	1	$47.95
Avocado Foot Care Cream	$9.00	5	$45.00
Cilantro Foot Bath Salts	$19.95	4	$79.80
Cocoa Body Butter	$22.50	2	$45.00
Dead Sea Black Mineral Mud Bar	$14.95	1	$14.95
Geranium Rose Bath Salts	$19.95	2	$39.90
Ginger Brown Sugar Scrub	$10.50	3	$31.50
Lavender Bath Oil	$15.95	10	$159.50
Lavender Ylang Soap	$12.95	10	$129.50
Lemon Body Butter	$22.50	1	$22.50
New Mexico Mud Mask	$8.50	10	$85.00
Peppermint Mineral Foot Cream	$12.95	1	$12.95
Pomegranate Bath Oil	$15.95	3	$47.85
Turquoise Oasis Conditioner	$17.50	2	$35.00
Turquoise Oasis Exfoliator	$8.50	1	$8.50
Turquoise Oasis Face Moisturizer	$7.25	2	$14.50
Turquoise Oasis Foot Care Cream	$10.00	1	$10.00
Turquoise Oasis Hand Moisturizer	$9.50	1	$9.50
Turquoise Oasis Shampoo	$17.50	2	$35.00

Record: 1 of 20 No Filter Search

Figure 2 Datasheet View of the qryRevAndVol query

i. **Save** and **Close** the query.

Calculating the Number of Transactions by Category

Revenue and Sales Volume are only two of many metrics that businesses track. It may also be useful to know how many transactions included products of a particular category. In this exercise, you will create a query using the Group By and Count aggregate functions to determine how many transactions have occurred by product category.

A07.02

To Calculate the Number of Transactions by Category

a. Click the **Create** tab, and then, in the Queries group, click **Query Design**. In the Show Table dialog box, click **tblProduct**, press Ctrl, click **tblPurchase**, and then click **Add**. **Close** the Show Table dialog box.

b. On the Design tab, in the Show/Hide group, click **Totals**.

c. Add the following fields to the query design grid: **Category** and **PurchaseID**.

d. In the Total row of the query design grid select the following.
Category: Leave as Group By
PurchaseID: Select **Count**

e. Rename the PurchaseID field by typing NumOfPurchases: in front of the field name PurchaseID.

f. On the Design tab, in the Results group, click **Run**. Resize your fields if you cannot see all the data and column headings.

The results of the query show how many purchases included items from each of the product categories.

g. Save the query as qryPurchasesByCategory.

SIDE NOTE
Sum Versus Count
Sum can be performed only on number and currency fields. Count can be done on any field data type, including text.

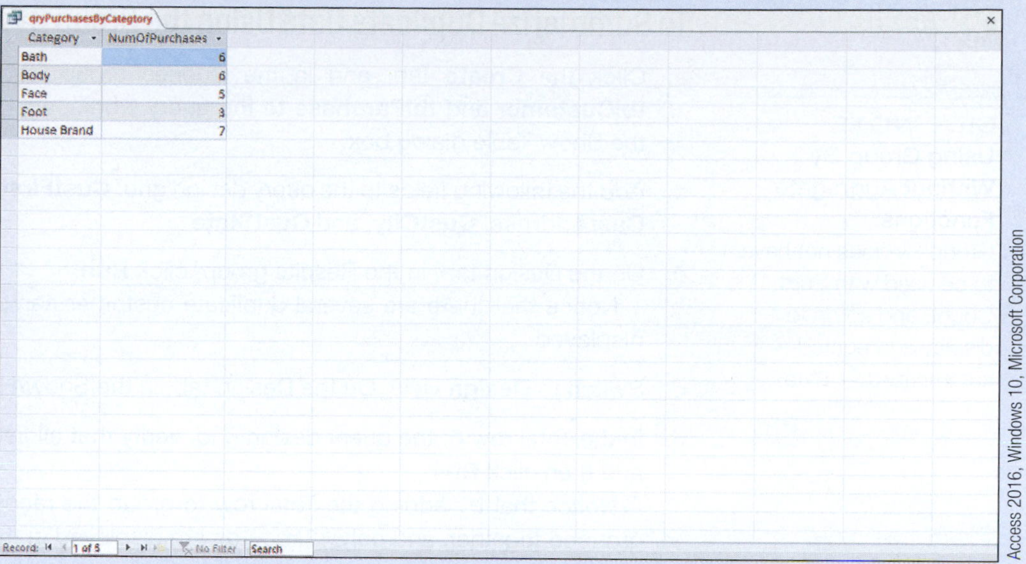

Figure 3 Datasheet View of qryPurchasesByCategory

h. **Close** [X] the query.

CONSIDER THIS | How Could You Use the Grouped Data?

Now that you can see how each product performed with regard to revenue and volume and how each product category performed with regard to number of transactions, what decisions could you make? What would you do about the low number of purchases for items in the Foot category? Do you think the spa's house brand should have higher sales and volume? What would you do to increase sales?

CONSIDER THIS | What Happens If You Forget a Step?

What would happen if you forgot to select an aggregate function in the Total row of the query design grid? What would happen if you selected the Count aggregate function instead of the Sum aggregate function? What would the data look like? How could this affect decision making?

Summarizing Duplicate Data Using the GROUP BY Clause

Another way a GROUP BY clause can be used is to summarize multiple records in a table. For example, what if you wanted a list of names of and mailing addresses of all customers who have made a purchase during a given period of time? You could simply add a transactions table to the Query Design view and include only the customers who have made a purchase. Additionally, you could exclude people who were added to the Customers table but never made a purchase; maybe they canceled their appointments, for example. Initially, those who made many purchases will be listed multiple times. However, you could add the Total row to group them and therefore remove duplicates.

The column or columns listed in the GROUP BY clause are used to group the data set. When the query is run, Access performs the grouping first, to retrieve the structure used to perform the aggregate expressions. In this exercise, you will create a query listing all customers who have made purchases at the spa. You will use the GROUP BY clause to ensure that each customer is listed only once regardless of how many purchases he or she has made.

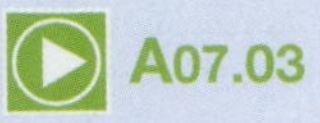

A07.03

To Summarize Duplicate Data Using the Group By Aggregate Function

SIDE NOTE

Using Group By Without Aggregate Functions

Group By does not have to be used with Sum, Count, and so on to display aggregated — summarized — data.

a. Click the **Create** tab, and in the Queries group, click **Query Design**. Add **tblCustomer** and **tblPurchase** to the query workspace, and then click **Close** in the Show Table dialog box.

b. Add the following fields to the query design grid: **CustFirstName**, **CustLastName**, **CustAddress**, **CustCity**, and **CustState**.

c. On the Design tab, in the Results group, click **Run**.

   Notice that there are several duplicate customer names within the 27 records displayed.

d. Switch to **Design** view. On the Design tab, in the Show/Hide group, click **Totals**.

e. In the Total row of the query design grid, verify that all fields are set to **Group By**, and then click **Run**.

   Notice that by adding the Total row to group the records, the duplicates were grouped together, and only 12 records are displayed in the data set.

f. **Save** the query as qryCustomersWithPurchases.

g. **Close** the query. If you need to take a break before finishing this chapter, now is a good time.

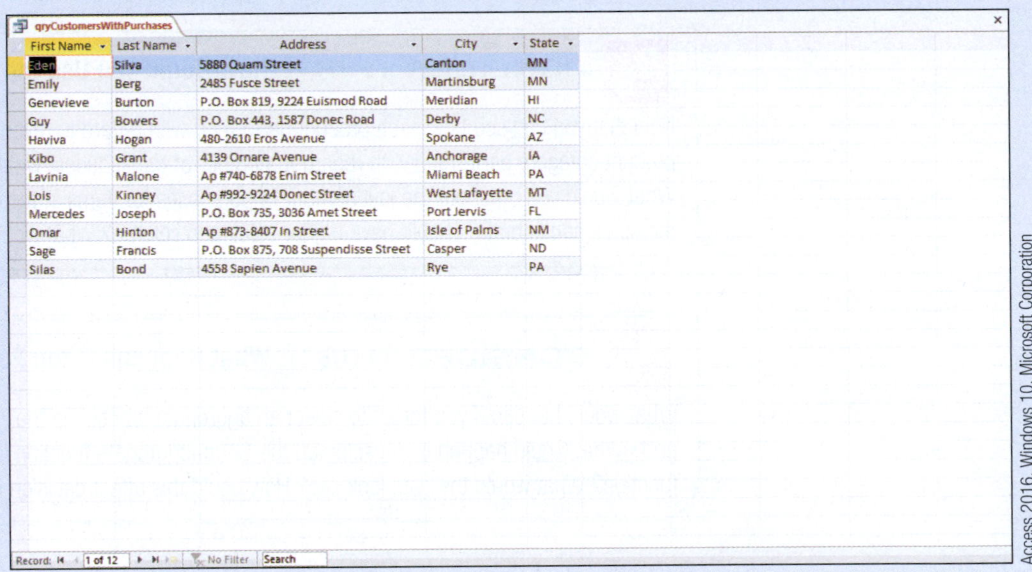

qryCustomersWithPurchases

First Name	Last Name	Address	City	State
Eden	Silva	5880 Quam Street	Canton	MN
Emily	Berg	2485 Fusce Street	Martinsburg	MN
Genevieve	Burton	P.O. Box 819, 9224 Euismod Road	Meridian	HI
Guy	Bowers	P.O. Box 443, 1587 Donec Road	Derby	NC
Haviva	Hogan	480-2610 Eros Avenue	Spokane	AZ
Kibo	Grant	4139 Ornare Avenue	Anchorage	IA
Lavinia	Malone	Ap #740-6878 Enim Street	Miami Beach	PA
Lois	Kinney	Ap #992-9224 Donec Street	West Lafayette	MT
Mercedes	Joseph	P.O. Box 735, 3036 Amet Street	Port Jervis	FL
Omar	Hinton	Ap #873-8407 In Street	Isle of Palms	NM
Sage	Francis	P.O. Box 875, 708 Suspendisse Street	Casper	ND
Silas	Bond	4558 Sapien Avenue	Rye	PA

Record: 1 of 12 No Filter Search

Figure 4 Datasheet View of qryCustomersWithPurchases

Understanding the WHERE Clause in Aggregated Calculations

The **WHERE clause** allows you to limit the results of your query by specifying criteria that field values must meet without using that field to group the data mathematically. When using the WHERE clause within your select query, you need to enter query criteria. Access selects the records that meet the condition listed in the query criteria. For example, suppose your customer service representatives need to be able to retrieve customers' e-mail addresses or phone numbers throughout the day, but the representative knows only the customer's last name. You could use the WHERE clause to limit the results of the query and make it easier for your employees to find the information they need. In this section, you will calculate sales revenue from a variety of perspectives using the WHERE clause.

REAL WORLD ADVICE | **When Do You Need to Use the WHERE Clause?**

Determining when you need the WHERE clause can be difficult at first. Generally, though not in all cases, you want to use the WHERE clause on a field that is needed to define the criteria but you do not want the field to display in the query results. If you clear the Show box, then Access will still use the field to group the records. You can also use the WHERE clause to compare values. You can use other comparison operators, such as greater than (>), less than (<), or equals (=).

Use the WHERE Clause in Aggregated Calculations

Revenue is one of the most important pieces of information that a company uses to learn more about its financial progress. **Revenue** — or gross sales — is income that a company receives from its normal business activities, that is, the sale of goods and services to customers. Using the WHERE clause can assist with this calculation. For example, you may want to calculate all sales for which the date falls in a specific range, such as a fiscal year. A **fiscal year** is a period that businesses and other organizations use for calculating annual financial statements. The fiscal year can be different from a calendar year and can vary among different businesses and organizations because they can choose whatever dates they want to use as the "year." For example, if your company uses a fiscal year, you may need to add all sales that are between July 1 of this year and June 30 of the next year. Additionally, you may want to calculate the revenue for a specific department, such as spa services, for the fiscal year.

In the business world, other criteria must be considered to accurately calculate revenue. Another valuable calculation is net revenue. **Net revenue** — or net sales — is the revenue minus sales returns, sales allowances, and sales discounts. For example, if customers return products or are given a special discount — such as 10% off — because a product they want to purchase is damaged, the returns and discounts have to be accounted for and subtracted from your gross sales. By using the WHERE clause to limit the results, you can make it easier to find the specific data you want and calculate results accurately.

REAL WORLD ADVICE | **Setting Up Queries Incorrectly Could Give Zero Results**

In these complicated queries, you can actually get zero results if the entire total row is not set correctly. Think about querying departments with revenue over $10,000. If you put the criteria of >=10000 under revenue but have not specified the sum on the revenue, then you will get zero results — unless one item purchased exceeds $10,000.

Calculating Revenue from Specific Spa Services

In this exercise, you will calculate the revenue generated from the sale of services involving waxing. To do this, you will utilize the Sum aggregate function and the GROUP BY and WHERE clauses.

To Calculate Revenue from Specific Spa Services

a. If you took a break, open the **a04ch07SpaDecisions** database.

b. Click the **Create** tab, and then, in the Queries group, click **Query Design**.

c. Add **tblSchedule** and **tblService** to the query workspace, and then **Close** [X] the Show Table dialog box.

d. Add the following fields to the query design grid: **Service**, **Fee**, and **Type**.

e. On the Design tab, in the Show/Hide group, click **Totals**. In the Total row of the query design grid, select the following.
Service: Leave as **Group By**
Fee: Select **Sum**
Type: Select **Where**

SIDE NOTE
Clear the Show Check Box
Access clears the Show check box once "Where" is selected. A data set cannot display a field that is part of an aggregated function.

f. Type the following into the Criteria row of the Type field: *Wax*. Press Enter.
Notice that Access changed the criterion you typed to Like "*Wax*". Access will add the Like operator whenever a wildcard is used in a criterion.

g. Rename the Fee field by typing Revenue: in front of the field name Fee.

h. **Save** the query as qryRevenueForWaxServices.

i. On the Design tab, in the Results group, click **Run**.
Notice that Access totaled all wax services performed on clients and grouped the results by each wax service that was given.

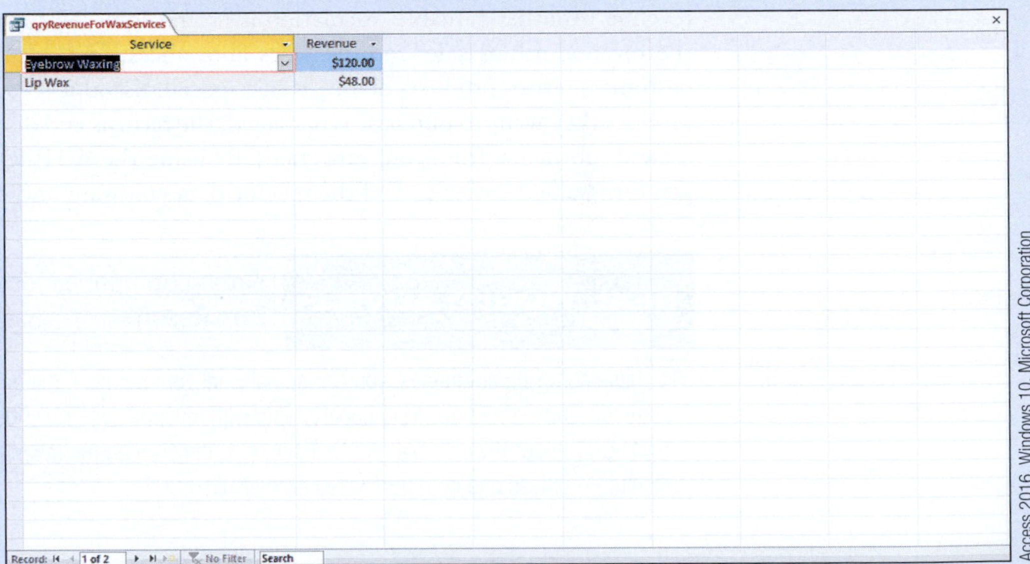

Figure 5 Datasheet View of qryRevenueForWaxServices

j. **Close** [X] the query.

Calculating Net Revenue from Specific Spa Services

In this exercise, you will calculate the net revenue from specific spa services by deducting 38% from the revenue to take into account sales returns, sales allowances, and sales discounts.

A07.05

To Calculate Net Revenue from Specific Spa Services

a. Click the **Create** tab, and then, in the Queries group, click **Query Design**. Add **tblSchedule** and **tblService** to the query design, and then **Close** [X] the Show Table dialog box.

b. On the query design grid, right-click the **Field row** in the first blank column, and then click **Zoom**.

c. In the Zoom dialog box, type Net Revenue: [Fee]*(1-0.38)
Notice that for some of the spa services given, 38% of the gross revenue needs to be deducted because of sales returns, sales allowances, and sales discounts.

d. Click **OK**. With the Net Revenue calculated field still selected, in the Show/Hide group on the Design tab, click **Property Sheet**.

e. Click the **Format** property, and then select **Currency** from the Format property dropdown box.

f. Add the following fields to the query design grid: **Fee** and **Type**.

g. Rename the Fee field by typing Gross Revenue: in front of the field name Fee.

h. On the Design tab, in the Show/Hide group, click **Totals**.
In the Total row of the query design grid, select the following.
Net Revenue: Select **Sum**
Gross Revenue: Select **Sum**
Type: Select **Where**

i. In the Criteria row of the Type field, type Body Massage, and then **Save** the query as qryNetRevForBodyMassages.

j. On the Design tab, in the Results group, click **Run**. Resize your fields if you cannot see all the data and column headings.
Notice that you now can see the Gross Revenue — the sum of the Fee field — and the Net Revenue for the Body Massage category.

SIDE NOTE
Sales Returns, Sales Allowances, and Sales Discounts
In business, sales returns, sales allowances, and sales discounts are tracked individually and totaled at the end of the year or when needed. Once totaled, they are deducted from the gross revenue.

SIDE NOTE
Subtract from 1
When you are subtracting a decimal from 1, you are really subtracting the decimal from 100%; the equivalent of 100% in decimal format is 1.00 or 1.

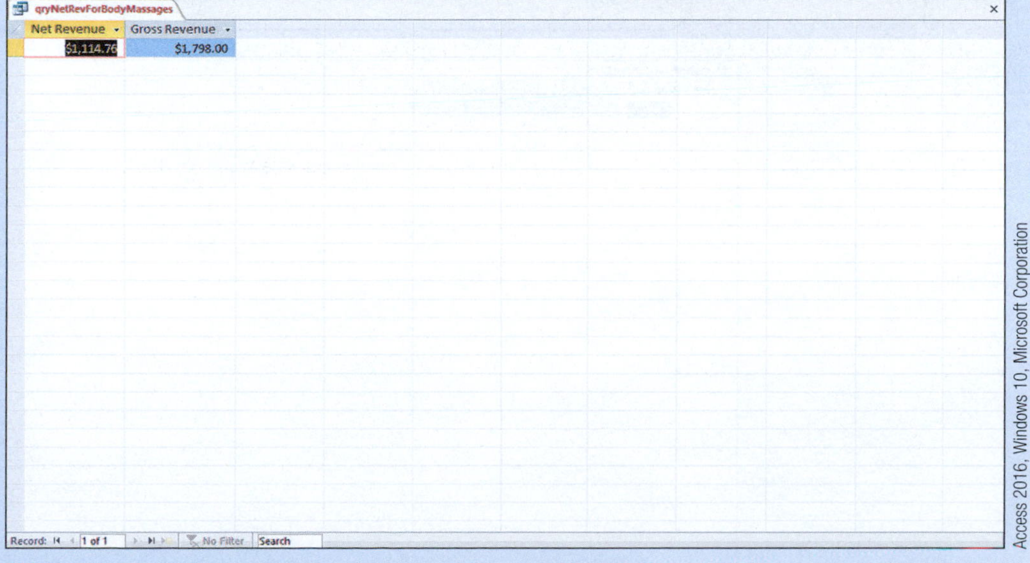

Access 2016, Windows 10, Microsoft Corporation

Figure 6 Datasheet View of qryNetRevForBodyMassages

k. **Close** [X] the query.

l. Click the **Create** tab, and then, in the Queries group, click **Query Design**. Add **tblSchedule** and **tblService** to the query workspace.

m. **Close** [X] the Show Table dialog box, right-click the **first blank field** on the query design grid, and then click **Zoom**.

SIDE NOTE
Convert Percent to Decimal
When typing a percentage in an expression, you must convert it to a decimal. If you don't, an invalid syntax error will occur.

n. In the Zoom dialog box, type Net Revenue:[Fee]*(1-0.16).
Notice that for some spa services that were given, 16% of the gross revenue needs to be deducted because of sales returns, sales allowances, and sales discounts.

o. Click **OK**. With the Net Revenue calculated field still selected, in the Show/Hide group on the Design tab, click **Property Sheet** if necessary.

p. Click the **Format** property, and then select **Currency** from the Format property dropdown box.

q. Add the following fields to the query design grid: **Fee** and **Type**.

r. Rename the Fee field by typing Gross Revenue: in front of the field name Fee.

s. On the **Design** tab, in the Show/Hide group, click **Totals**. In the Total row of the query design grid, select the following.
Net Revenue: Select **Sum**
Gross Revenue: Select **Sum**
Type: Leave as **Group By**

t. You can modify the query to view the net revenue of a specific category. In the Criteria row of the Type field, type "Hands & Feet".

u. **Save** [save] the query as qryNetRevForHands&Feet, and then click **Run**. Resize your fields if you cannot see all the data and column headings.
Notice that you now can see the Gross Revenue and the Net Revenue for the Hands & Feet category.

Troubleshooting

If the results of the query are empty, be sure you have added quotation marks around the criterion. Since this criterion includes the ampersand (&) symbol, if quotation marks are not added, Access will treat each word as a separate criterion.

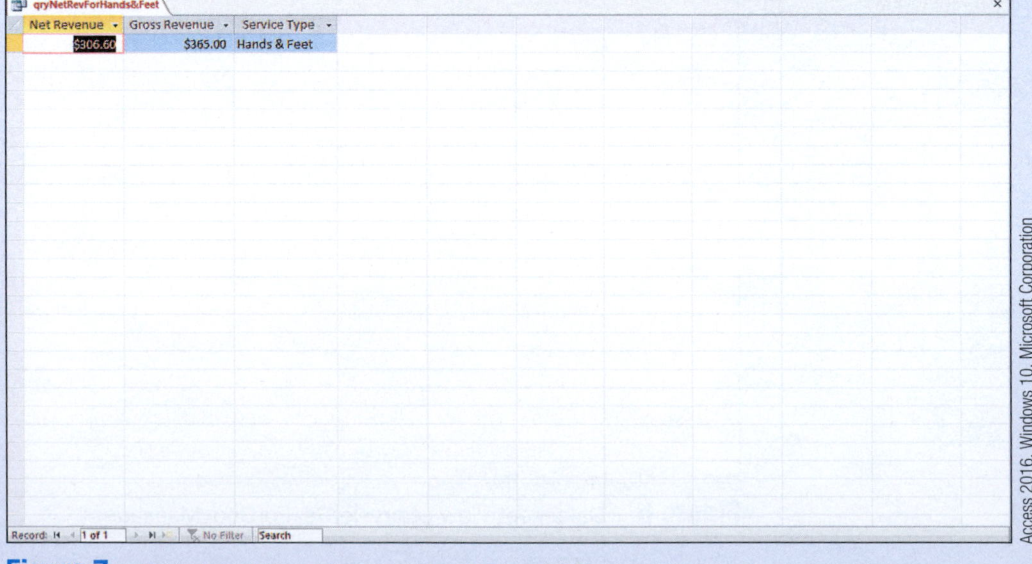

Figure 7 Datasheet View of qryNetRevForHands&Feet

v. **Save** [save] and **Close** [X] the query. If you need to take a break before finishing this chapter, now is a good time.

CHAPTER 7

QUICK REFERENCE | Standard Aggregate Functions in the Query Design Grid

Function	Use
Group By	Groups the data
Sum	Calculates the total
Avg	Calculates the average
Count	Counts the number of records
Min	Displays the minimum value
Max	Displays the maximum value
StDev	Calculates the standard deviation
First	Displays the value in the first record
Last	Displays the value in the last record
Var	Calculates the variance
Expression	Allows an expression to be entered
Where	Limits the results without grouping the data by the field

Functions and uses of aggregate functions

REAL WORLD ADVICE | Calculated Fields and Aggregate Functions

When you combine calculated fields and aggregate functions, pay careful attention to the aggregate function and what data it is aggregating. If you use an aggregate function around a calculated field, Access first calculates each record and then performs the aggregation. For example, if you have a custom field named Average Markup with the formula Average(([RetailPrice]-[WholeSaleCost])/[WholeSaleCost]), Access first calculates the markup for each product and then averages all of the markups.

Business Calculations Using Subquerying

Some managers may want to calculate the sales volume — how much has been sold of a particular item or items. Some of the salon and spa's products were sold to clients who wanted to take their favorite products home with them. A manager would want to keep track of how many items are sold per day, week, or month. Therefore, the need to first take a count of each item is critical to having an accurate calculation.

What is physical volume? **Physical volume** measures how much space is within an object. For example, clients can phone in orders or place orders online to be shipped to the client. The manager would then want to pack the products as efficiently as possible and use the smallest available shipping box to pack and ship the orders, as doing so will save on shipping costs.

Because decision making is an important part of a manager's daily routine, some managers may want to calculate the percentages of physical volume, sales volume, or sales revenue to determine how the business is performing or to monitor inventory. Once Access provides this information, they will be able to make staffing, training, marketing, and inventory decisions. In this section, you will create subqueries that calculate the percentage of sales revenue, the percentage of sales volume, physical volume, and the percentage of physical volume.

Create Subqueries Using Business Calculations

Because more sophisticated queries require more advanced manipulation of data, you may need to create a subquery. A **subquery** is simply a select query that is nested inside of another select query. This is used when you want to create a query from previously queried data. For example, when you are calculating the percentage of sales volume or the percentage of physical volume, a subquery will make the calculation easier.

Creating a Query on a Query

A subquery can easily be created by first building separate queries, using one as the source for the other, and then writing a "master" query that pulls the data from the first two queries together. The quarterly queries act like subqueries. The separate queries run first, and the master query runs last. For instance, you may want to write a report showing Turquoise Oasis Spa sales for the first quarter, the second quarter, and then both quarters. Because the date ranges are mutually exclusive, they cannot be positioned in the same query. In this exercise, you will calculate the daily gross revenue using a query and a subquery.

To Create a Query on a Query

a. If you took a break, open the **a04ch07SpaDecisions** database.

b. Click the **Create** tab, and then, in the Queries group, click **Query Design**.

c. Add **tblPurchase** and **tblProduct** to the query workspace, and then **Close** [X] the Show Table dialog box.

d. Add the following fields to the query design grid: **PurchaseType**, **PurchaseDate**, **Quantity**, **ProductDescription**, and **Price**.

e. On the Design tab, in the Show/Hide group, click **Totals**. In the Total row of the query design grid, select the following.
PurchaseType: Leave as **Group By**
PurchaseDate: Leave as **Group By**
Quantity: Select **Sum**
ProductDescription: Leave as **Group By**
Price: Leave as **Group By**

f. Rename the Quantity field by typing SalesVolume: in front of the field name Quantity.

g. **Save** the query as qrySalesVolumeByDate. On the Design tab, in the Results group, click **Run**. Resize your fields if you cannot see all the data and column headings.
Notice that you now can see the total quantity sold on a given day for each product.

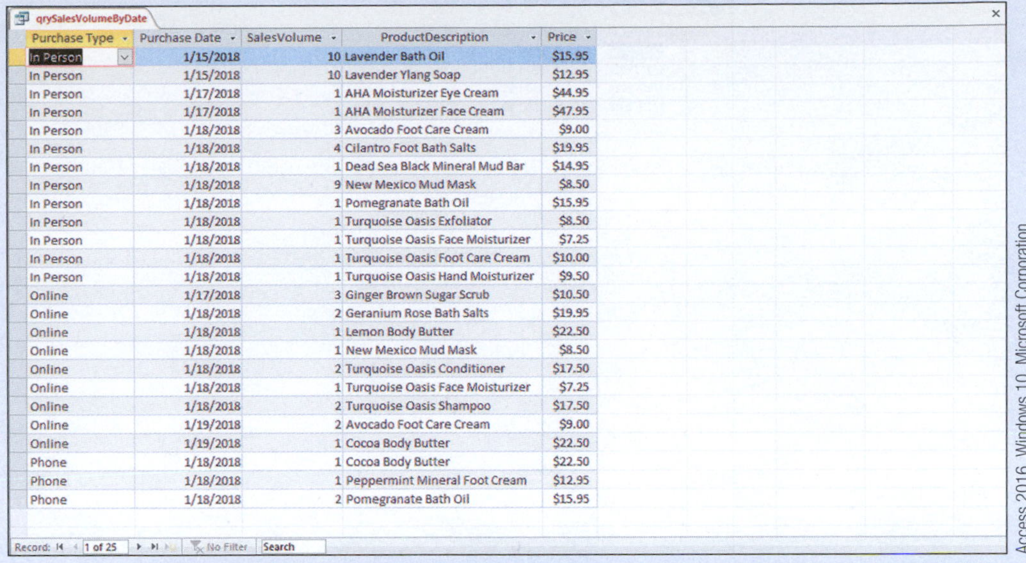

qrySalesVolumeByDate

Purchase Type	Purchase Date	SalesVolume	ProductDescription	Price
In Person	1/15/2018	10	Lavender Bath Oil	$15.95
In Person	1/15/2018	10	Lavender Ylang Soap	$12.95
In Person	1/17/2018	1	AHA Moisturizer Eye Cream	$44.95
In Person	1/17/2018	1	AHA Moisturizer Face Cream	$47.95
In Person	1/18/2018	3	Avocado Foot Care Cream	$9.00
In Person	1/18/2018	4	Cilantro Foot Bath Salts	$19.95
In Person	1/18/2018	1	Dead Sea Black Mineral Mud Bar	$14.95
In Person	1/18/2018	9	New Mexico Mud Mask	$8.50
In Person	1/18/2018	1	Pomegranate Bath Oil	$15.95
In Person	1/18/2018	1	Turquoise Oasis Exfoliator	$8.50
In Person	1/18/2018	1	Turquoise Oasis Face Moisturizer	$7.25
In Person	1/18/2018	1	Turquoise Oasis Foot Care Cream	$10.00
In Person	1/18/2018	1	Turquoise Oasis Hand Moisturizer	$9.50
Online	1/17/2018	3	Ginger Brown Sugar Scrub	$10.50
Online	1/18/2018	2	Geranium Rose Bath Salts	$19.95
Online	1/18/2018	1	Lemon Body Butter	$22.50
Online	1/18/2018	1	New Mexico Mud Mask	$8.50
Online	1/18/2018	2	Turquoise Oasis Conditioner	$17.50
Online	1/18/2018	1	Turquoise Oasis Face Moisturizer	$7.25
Online	1/18/2018	2	Turquoise Oasis Shampoo	$17.50
Online	1/19/2018	2	Avocado Foot Care Cream	$9.00
Online	1/19/2018	1	Cocoa Body Butter	$22.50
Phone	1/18/2018	1	Cocoa Body Butter	$22.50
Phone	1/18/2018	1	Peppermint Mineral Foot Cream	$12.95
Phone	1/18/2018	2	Pomegranate Bath Oil	$15.95

Record: 1 of 25 No Filter Search

Figure 8 Datasheet View of qrySalesVolumeByDate

h. **Save** and **Close** the query.

i. Click the **Create** tab, and then, in the Queries group, click **Query Design**.

j. In the Show Table dialog box, click the **Queries** tab, and then add **qrySalesVolumeByDate** to the query workspace. **Close** the Show Table dialog box.

k. Add the following field to the query design grid: **PurchaseDate**.

l. Right-click the **Field row** of the first blank column on the query design grid and then click **Zoom**.

m. In the Zoom dialog box, type GrossRevenue: [SalesVolume]*[Price]. This will calculate the gross revenue for each product. Click **OK**.

n. On the Design tab, in the Show/Hide group, click **Totals**. In the Total row of the query design grid, select the following.
PurchaseDate: Leave as **Group By**
GrossRevenue: Select **Sum**

o. Format the GrossRevenue field as **Currency**, and then **Save** the query as qryGrossRevByDate.

p. On the Design tab, in the Results group, click **Run**. Resize your fields if you cannot see all the data and column headings.
Notice that you now can see the gross revenue for each of the four days.

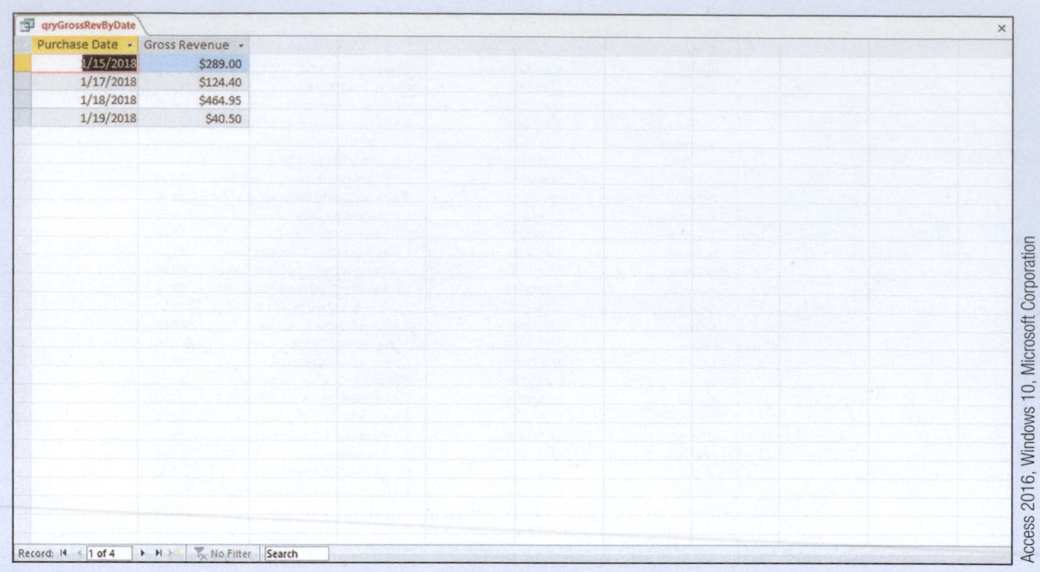

Figure 9 Datasheet View of qryGrossRevByDate

q. **Save** and **Close** the query.

Calculating the Percentage of Sales Revenue

In business, the percentage of sales revenue can be valuable information and can teach a manager a lot about the business. The **percentage of sales revenue** compares the portion of the gross revenue to the total gross revenue. As a manager, you may want to forecast or predict what next year's sales revenue will be on the basis of past sales; this is usually calculated on the basis of the past three years of data. Or you may want to see how each category is performing this year in comparison to last year's sales figures. For example, Meda Rodate may want to see how each product category's sales contributed to the overall sales of the spa. When calculating the percentage of sales revenue, you need to consider the method used to calculate percentage of sales revenue — the number of units sold — as well as the time period over which you plan on measuring the sales.

To calculate the percentage of sales revenue, you first need to calculate the total sales revenue in one query. Then you need to create a query that uses the total sales revenue calculation to calculate the percentage of sales revenue, where the percentage of a whole is the individual item divided by the grand total. For example, if the sales revenue for all spa services given last month was $27,325, the spa manager could create a query that divides the total sales revenue of each service given last month, such as Sea Salt Scrub, by the sales revenue for all spa services given last month. If the sales revenue for Sea Salt Scrubs was $1,768, the query results would illustrate that Sea Salt Scrubs contributed to 6.47% of the total sales revenue.

In this exercise, you will create two queries that, together, will calculate the percentage of gross revenue that each product category has generated for the spa.

To Calculate the Percentage of Sales Revenue

a. Click the **Create** tab, and then, in the Queries group, click **Query Design**. Add **tblPurchase** and **tblProduct** to the query design, and then **Close** the Show Table dialog box.

b. On the query design grid, right-click the **first blank field**, and then click **Zoom**.

c. In the Zoom dialog box, type TotalRevenue: [Quantity]*[Price], and then click **OK**.

d. Click the **Design** tab, and then, in the Show/Hide group, click **Totals**.

e. In the Total row of the query design grid, select the following.
TotalRevenue: Select **Sum**

f. **Save** the query as qryTotalRevenue.

g. On the Design tab, in the Results group, click **Run**. Resize your field if you cannot see all the data and column headings.

Figure 10 Datasheet View of qryTotalRevenue

Notice that you can see the spa's total revenue — the total dollars generated through the sales of its products. You need to calculate what the total revenue is before you can calculate the percentage of sales revenue.

h. **Save** and **Close** the query.

i. Click the **Create** tab, and then, in the Queries group, click **Query Design**. Add **tblPurchase** and **tblProduct** to the query design, and then **Close** the Show Table dialog box.

j. Add the following fields to the query design grid: **Category**.

k. On the query design grid, right-click the **first blank field**, and then click **Zoom**.

l. In the Zoom dialog box, type CategoryRev:[Quantity]*[Price], and then click **OK**.

m. Click the **Design** tab, and then, in the Show/Hide group, click **Totals**.

n. In the Total row of the query design grid, select the following.
Category: Leave as **Group By**
CategoryRev: Select **Sum**

o. **Save** the query as qryCategoryRev.

p. On the Design tab, in the Results group, click **Run**. Resize your fields if you cannot see all the data and column headings.

Category	CategoryRev
Bath	$327.05
Body	$243.45
Face	$177.90
Foot	$57.95
House Brand	$112.50

Access 2016, Windows 10, Microsoft Corporation

Figure 11 Datasheet View of qryCategoryRev

Notice that you can see the revenue generated for each product category. Now that you have calculated the total revenue and the revenue for each product category, you can calculate the percentage of gross revenue that each product category has generated for the spa.

q. **Save** and **Close** the query.

r. Click the **Create** tab, and then, in the Queries group, click **Query Design**.

s. In the Show Table dialog box, click the **Queries** tab, add **qryTotalRevenue** and **qryCategoryRev** to the query workspace, and then **Close** the Show Table dialog box.

t. Add the following fields to the query design grid: **Category** and **CategoryRev**.

u. In the **first blank field** of the query design grid, open the Zoom dialog box, and then type the expression PctOfGrossRev:[CategoryRev]/[TotalRevenue].

This is the equation needed to calculate what percentage of each category's sales contributed to the gross revenue. To calculate this, the category total revenue is divided by the overall gross revenue.

v. Click **OK**, and then format the PctOfGrossRev field as **Percent**.

w. **Save** the query as qryPctOfGrossRevenue, and then click **Run**. Resize your fields if you cannot see all the data and column headings.

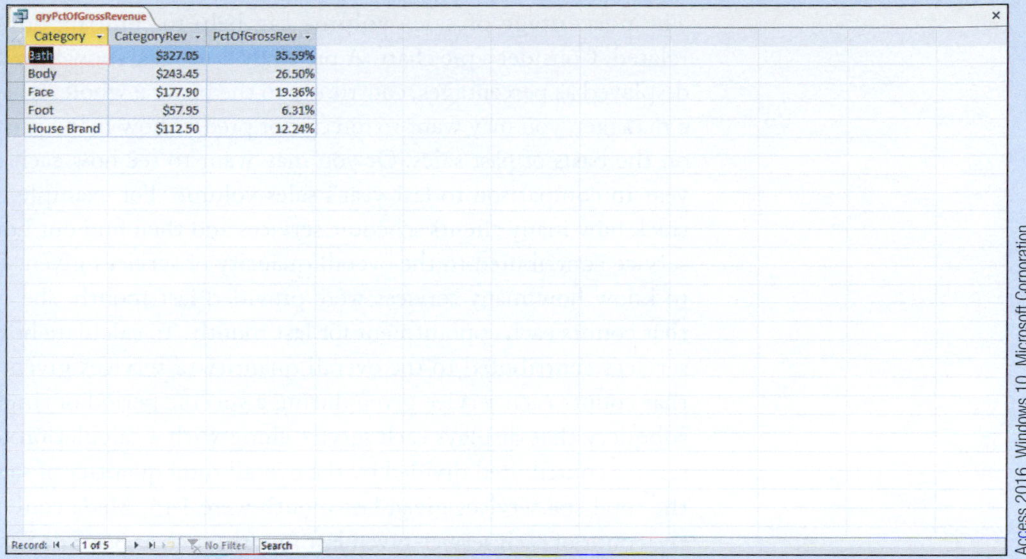

qryPctOfGrossRevenue

Category	CategoryRev	PctOfGrossRev
Bath	$327.05	35.59%
Body	$243.45	26.50%
Face	$177.90	19.36%
Foot	$57.95	6.31%
House Brand	$112.50	12.24%

Figure 12 Datasheet View of qryPctOfGrossRevenue

Notice that you can see the revenue generated for each product category as well as the percentage of revenue within each category that contributed to the overall gross revenue.

x. On the Home tab, in the Records group, click **Totals**.

Not only can you view the percentage of revenue, you can also format the query output to see the grand totals of each field. Notice that a Total row appeared at the bottom of your datasheet.

y. Click the **Total** row of the PctOfGrossRev field, and then select **Sum** from the list.

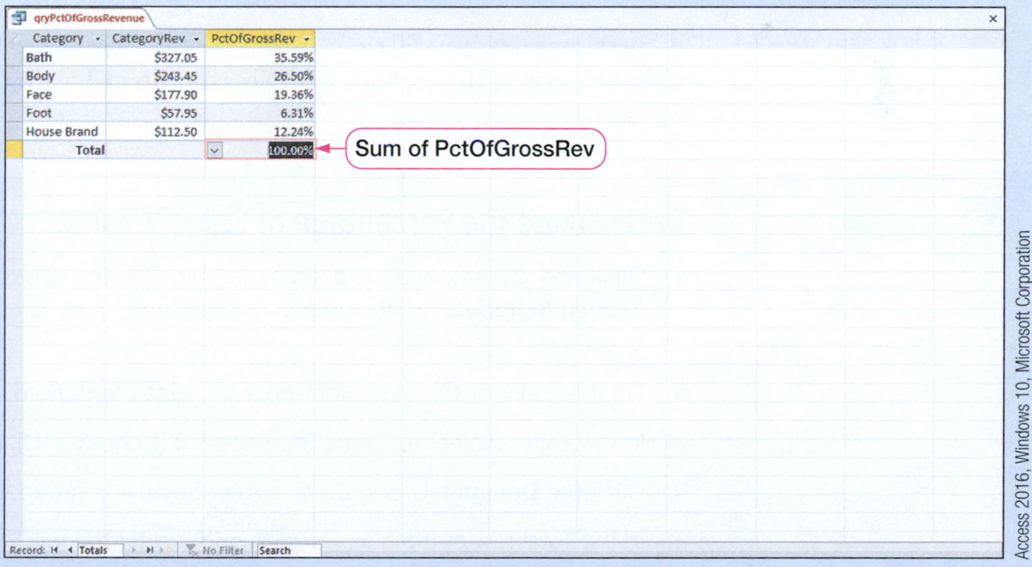

qryPctOfGrossRevenue

Category	CategoryRev	PctOfGrossRev
Bath	$327.05	35.59%
Body	$243.45	26.50%
Face	$177.90	19.36%
Foot	$57.95	6.31%
House Brand	$112.50	12.24%
Total		100.00%

Figure 13 Datasheet View of qryPctOfGrossRevenue with Total row

Notice that you can use this as a way to communicate information better, and it can also help you double-check that your percentage calculations add up to 100%.

z. **Save** and **Close** the query.

Calculating the Percentage of Sales Volume

The **percentage of sales volume** can help to compare how two or more numbers are related. Consider a pie chart. A pie chart is used to show how certain categories, generally displayed as percentages, contribute to the pie as a whole, where the total pie is 100%. As a manager, you may want to forecast or predict how many products you will sell next year on the basis of past sales. Or you may want to see how each category is performing this year in comparison to last year's sales volume. For example, Meda Rodate may want to track how many clients schedule services and then find out how the total quantity of each service contributed to the overall quantity of services given. For example, if Meda wants to know how many services were provided last month, she could simply create a query that counts each appointment for last month. To calculate how the quantities of different services contributed to the overall quantity of services given, you need to create a query that counts each service given during a specific period of time. Then you need to create a subquery that displays each service along with a calculation of the total quantity of each service contributed divided by the overall total quantity of services given. For example, if the total spa services given last month were 143, Meda could create a query that divides the count of each service given last month, such as Sea Salt Scrub, by the total spa services given last month. If 26 Sea Salt Scrubs were given last month, the query results would illustrate that 18.2% of all services given were Sea Salt Scrubs.

How Could a Manager Use the Percentage of Sales Volume Data?

Once you can see how services performed relates to the total sales volume, what decisions could you make? What if a service did not sell as well as it did last year? How would that affect marketing? Would you not offer the service anymore? What if you notice that a particular service is more popular than you initially thought? How would that affect staffing?

In this exercise, you will create two queries that, together, will calculate the percentage of scheduled services that each spa service has contributed to the overall number of scheduled services.

To Calculate the Percentage of Sales Volume

a. Click the **Create** tab, and then, in the Queries group, click **Query Design**. Add **tblSchedule** to the query design, and then **Close** the Show Table dialog box.

b. On the query design grid, right-click the **first blank field**, and then click **Zoom**.

c. In the Zoom dialog box, type ServicesVol: [ScheduleID], and then click **OK**.

d. Click the **Design** tab, and then, in the Show/Hide group, click **Totals**.

e. In the Total row of the query design grid, select the following.
ServicesVol: Select **Count**

f. **Save** the query as qryTotalServices.

g. On the Design tab, in the Results group, click **Run**. Resize your field if you cannot see all the data and column headings.

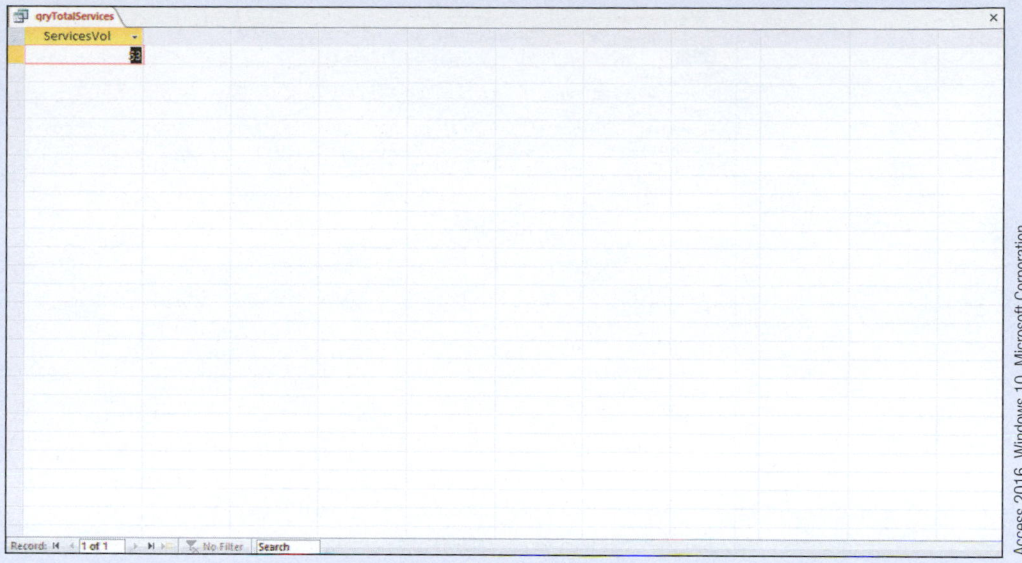

Figure 14 Datasheet View of qryTotalServices

Notice that you calculated the total number of services scheduled. This needs to be done before you can calculate the percentage of services for each service type. Notice that a total of 53 services were scheduled.

h. **Save** and **Close** the query.

i. Click the **Create** tab, and then, in the Queries group, click **Query Design**. Add **tblSchedule** and **tblService** to the query design, and then **Close** the Show Table dialog box.

j. Add the following field from tblService to the query design grid: **Type**.

k. On the query design grid, right-click the **first blank field**, and then click **Zoom**.

l. In the Zoom dialog box, type ServicesVolByType:[ScheduleID], and then click **OK**.

m. Click the **Design** tab, and then, in the Show/Hide group, click **Totals**.

n. In the Total row of the query design grid, select the following.
Type: Leave as **Group By**
ServicesVolByType: Select **Count**

o. **Save** the query as qryServicesVolumeByType.

p. On the Design tab, in the Results group, click **Run**. Resize your fields if you cannot see all the data and column headings.

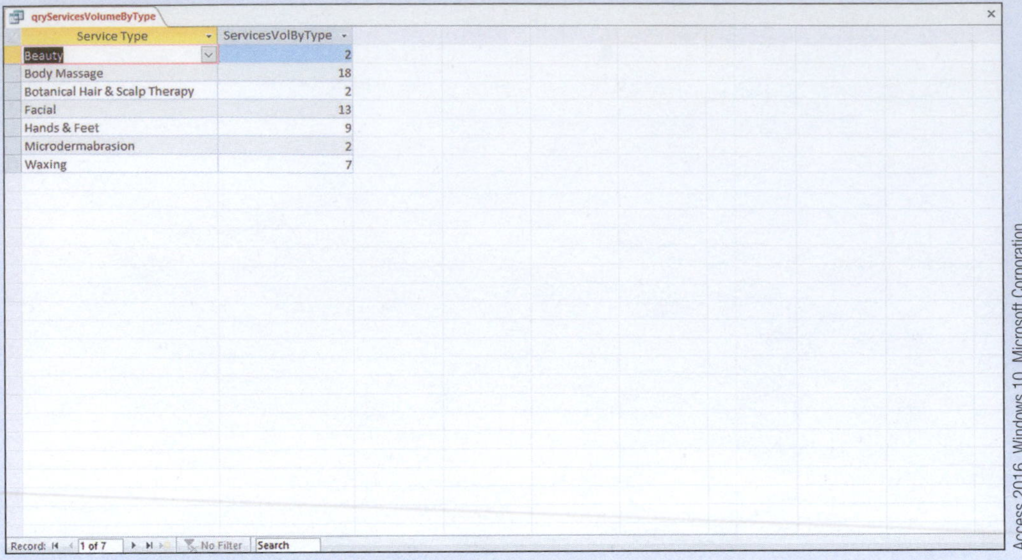

qryServicesVolumeByType

Service Type	ServicesVolByType
Beauty	2
Body Massage	18
Botanical Hair & Scalp Therapy	2
Facial	13
Hands & Feet	9
Microdermabrasion	2
Waxing	7

Record: 1 of 7 No Filter Search

Figure 15 Datasheet View of qryServicesVolumeByType

Notice that you calculated the number of services scheduled for each service type offered by the spa.

q. **Save** and **Close** the query.

r. Click the **Create** tab, and then, in the Queries group, click **Query Design**.

s. In the Show Table dialog box, click the **Queries** tab, add **qryTotalServices** and **qryServicesVolumeByType** to the query workspace, and then **Close** the Show Table dialog box.

t. Add the following field to the query design grid: **Type**.

u. In the **first blank field** of the query design grid, open the Zoom dialog box, and then type the expression PctOfServicesVol:[ServicesVolByType]/[ServicesVol].

This is the equation needed to calculate what percentage of each category's sales contributed to the gross revenue. To calculate this, the category total revenue is divided by the overall gross revenue.

v. Click **OK**, and then format the PctOfServicesVol field as **Percent**.

w. **Save** the query as qryPctOfServicesVolume, and then click **Run**. Resize your fields if you cannot see all the data and column headings.

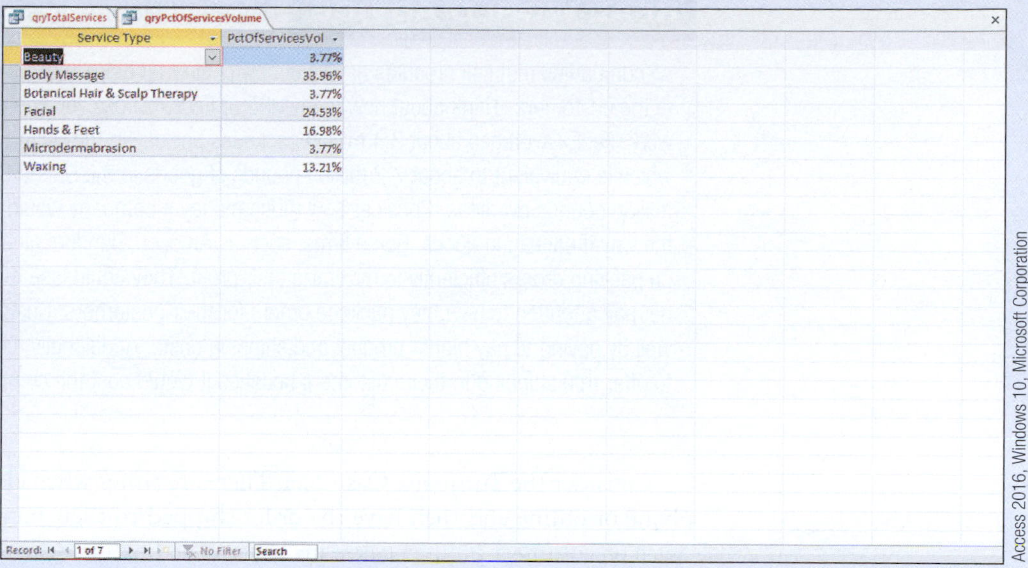

Figure 16 Datasheet View of qryPctOfServicesVolume

Notice that you can see the percentage of services scheduled for each service type offered by the spa.

x. **Save** and **Close** the query.

REAL WORLD ADVICE **Why Are You Renaming Fields?**

In the previous exercise, you used the Count aggregate function on the ScheduleID field for two queries. If you had not named each field differently, your calculation to determine the percentage of services volume would have been [CountOfScheduleID]/[CountOfScheduleID]. This would have confused Access, as you would have had two fields with the same name. In that case, you would have had to specify the table or query name before the field name like this: [qryServicesVolumeByType]![CountOfScheduleID]/[qryTotalServices]![CountOfScheduleID]. Renaming the fields is easier than having to specify the table or query from which each field came.

Calculating Physical Volume

Sometimes you might hear a question such as "How much can the box hold?" You need to calculate physical volume to determine the answer to this question. For example, many companies sell products online and have to determine the best size of box to use for packing the order. The best size box will also include space for packaging materials, such as packing peanuts or bubble wrap. This space around the object is referred to as the packaging volume. The **packaging volume** is the difference between the volume of the shipping container and the volume of the object you are shipping. Because some shipping companies apply surcharges for larger boxes, it is important to use the best size box to keep the overall shipping charge as low as possible. Imagine some of the largest online retailers you know and how much money using the correct box size can generate in terms of cost savings. If you know how to calculate packaging volume, you can calculate the remaining space in the box and then select the appropriate size box for shipping.

REAL WORLD ADVICE | **Shipping Merchandise Is Big Business**

All companies that sell products have a supply chain that helps move products from the suppliers to the customers. Think about how many UPS or FedEx trucks you see as you drive to school or work. FedEx averages about 3.4 million packages per day in the United States and internationally, which is equivalent to about 7.2 million pounds of goods in the United States a day and about 3.6 million pounds overseas. Consider how much money a company would waste if it did not optimize the way it packaged goods. Some firms, such as Amazon, conduct all their business online and rely on packing orders efficiently to maximize their profit. They could lose millions of dollars if they did not pay attention to how they package orders for their customers. Customers would feel the loss as well by having to pay higher product and shipping costs. Additionally, companies would not be able to offer free shipping to their customers because it would cost the company too much money.

Consider the Turquoise Oasis Spa. There are times when clients will place an order via phone or online and then have the order shipped to their home. If you know how much space or volume a product takes up within the box, you can determine what size box to use for the entire shipment. Calculating physical volume can help the spa's employees to manage shipping supplies.

In this exercise, you will create a query that will calculate the physical volume for shipping bars of soap using cubic inches, the standard unit for measuring volume in the United States.

To Calculate Physical Volume

a. Click the **Create** tab, and then, in the Queries group, click **Query Design**. Add **tblProduct** to the query workspace, and then **Close** [X] the Show Table dialog box.

b. Add the following fields to the query design grid: **ProductDescription** and **Size**.

c. In the Criteria row of the ProductDescription field, type "*soap*" to include any product with the word "soap" anywhere in the product description.

d. On the query design grid, right-click the **first blank field**, and then click **Zoom**.

e. In the Zoom dialog box, type PhysicalVolume: [Width]*[Length]*[Depth].
To calculate the volume of space that each bar of soap takes up, you need to multiply (length)*(width)*(depth). The result will be in cubic inches.

f. Click **OK**.

g. On the query design grid, right-click the **next blank field**, and then click **Zoom**.

h. In the Zoom dialog box, type TotalPkgVolume: Int(136/[PhysicalVolume]).
Notice that you are now calculating the total number of bars of soap that can fit into the spa's smallest carton. The result will also be in cubic inches.

i. Click **OK**.

j. **Save** the query as qryPhysicalVolumeSoaps. On the Design tab, in the Results group, click **Run**. Resize your fields if you cannot see all the data and column headings.

SIDE NOTE

What Does Int Do?

Because you cannot send a portion of a bar of soap, the Int — Integer — function truncates the decimal and returns only the integer portion of the TotalPkgVolume quotient.

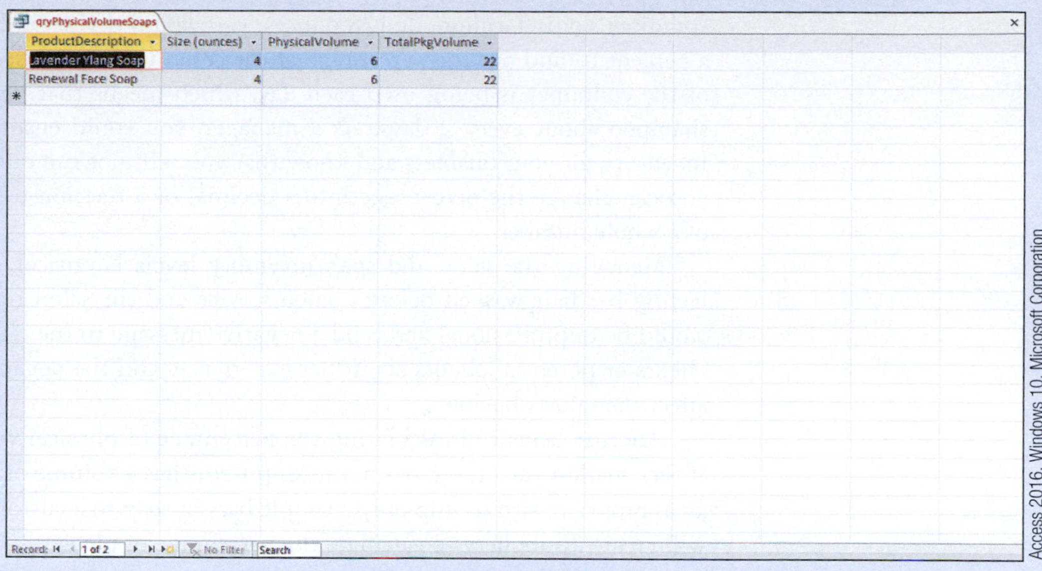

qryPhysicalVolumeSoaps

ProductDescription	Size (ounces)	PhysicalVolume	TotalPkgVolume
Lavender Ylang Soap	4	6	22
Renewal Face Soap	4	6	22

Figure 17 Datasheet View of qryPhysicalVolumeSoaps

Notice that you can ship up to 22 bars of soap in the smallest available shipping carton.

k. **Save** and **Close** the query.

REAL WORLD ADVICE **Things to Note in Calculating Physical Volume**

When you are calculating physical volume, consider the following.

- The basic formula for calculating physical volume is length × width × depth.
- If the item is not a perfect rectangle, take the average width and length. For example, if the object is 6 inches at its widest point and 2 inches at its most narrow point, use 4 inches for the width.
- If you are wrapping the item in bubble wrap, take your measurements after the item has been wrapped.
- If you take your measurements in inches, your final calculation will be in cubic inches; if you take them in centimeters, your final calculation will be in cubic centimeters; and so on.
- Finally, consider the overall dimensions of the package. A 6 × 3 × 1 bar of soap — 18 cubic inches in volume — will not fit in a 3 × 3 × 3 box even though the box, at 27 cubic inches, has 50% more volume.

Calculating the Percentage of Physical Volume

Consider a 1-gallon container of shampoo. Some of the salon and spa's supplies are purchased in pints, quarts, half gallons, or gallons. However, in shampooing customers' hair in the salon, you would not use an entire bottle of shampoo on one client. Being able to first convert these measurements is critical to having an accurate calculation. In a first query, if you use two 1-ounce pumps of shampoo on one client and you purchased a 1-gallon container of shampoo, you would have to calculate how many ounces are in the 1-gallon container of shampoo. It does not make a difference if you convert the gallons to ounces or ounces to gallons, but it tends to be easier to go from large measures to small measures. The key is to be consistent.

In a second query, you can easily find the daily **percentage of physical volume** used by dividing the amount used per day by the total amount that comes in the 1-gallon container. For example, if you use 54 one-ounce pumps of shampoo per day and the container holds 1 gallon, or 128 ounces, you would divide 54 by 128, then format it as a percent to find out the percentage of the container being used each day. Thus, 42.2% of the container is being used each day, which means that you would use 1 gallon of shampoo about every 2 days. As a manager, you could ensure that you have enough inventory for your business and know that you will not run out of product. If necessary, you can change the percentage into a decimal or a fraction to calculate the percentage of a whole number.

Managing the salon and spa's inventory levels is critical. Imagine that a client is having her hair washed before a salon service and the salon runs out of shampoo. This would be unprofessional and send a negative message to the client. She might tell other clients or potential clients about her experience, and the negative word of mouth could affect the salon's business.

Another benefit of calculating the percentage of physical volume involves shipping. If the smallest carton the spa has to ship items has a volume of 136 cubic inches, is that an appropriate size to ship only a couple bars of soap to a customer? In this exercise, you will create a subquery to calculate the percentage of physical volume a bar of soap takes up in the smallest shipping carton.

A07.10

To Calculate the Percentage of Physical Volume

a. Click the **Create** tab, and then, in the Queries group, click **Query Design**. In the Show Table dialog box, click the **Queries** tab, and then add **qryPhysicalVolumeSoaps** to the query workspace. **Close** [X] the Show Table dialog box.

b. Add the following fields to the query design grid: **ProductDescription** and **PhysicalVolume**.

c. On the query design grid, right-click the **first blank field**, and then click **Zoom**.

d. In the Zoom dialog box, type PctOfPhysicalVolume: [PhysicalVolume]/136.

   To calculate the percentage of physical volume, you need to divide the volume of the item by the total volume the package can hold. Divide the volume by 136, which is the size of the smallest carton that the spa has to ship items to customers: 136 cubic inches.

e. Click **OK**, and then format the PctOfPhysicalVolume field as **Percent**.

f. **Save** the query as qryPctOfPhysicalVolumeSoaps. On the Design tab, in the Results group, click **Run**. Resize your fields if you cannot see all the data and column headings.

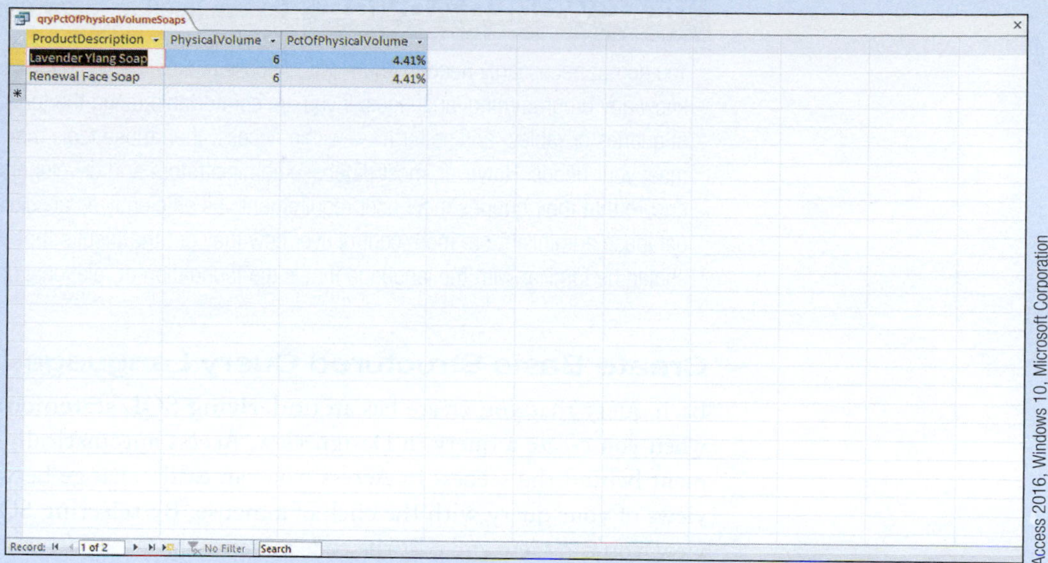

Figure 18 Datasheet View of qryPctOfPhysicalVolumeSoaps

Notice that each bar of soap consumes 4.41% of the volume in the smallest shipping carton.

g. **Save** and **Close** the query. If you need to take a break before finishing this chapter, now is a good time.

CONSIDER THIS | **Should the Spa Have Smaller Boxes?**

If a customer ordered two bars of soap and would like to have the items shipped to his home, is the spa's smallest box the best way to do so? If one bar takes up 4.41% of space in the carton, that means two bars takes up 8.82%. Some shipping companies not only charge by the weight of the package, but may also charge by the dimensions of the package. At times, companies will pack one shipment in multiple boxes because it is less expensive than packing the entire order in one large box. Do you think the spa should order and ship some products in smaller boxes? Would a padded envelope work better for some orders?

Understanding Structured Query Language

Structured Query Language (SQL) — pronounced SEE-quel — is an internationally recognized standard database language used by many relational databases, although many databases incorporate modified versions of the current standard SQL. The benefit of learning SQL is that once you know it, you can easily adapt to other relational database management systems. In this section, you will learn SELECT statement basics, how to view SQL statements, how to create a basic SQL query, how to use the WHERE and ORDER BY clauses, how to use the HAVING clause with AS and GROUP BY, how to create a union query, how to perform an INNER JOIN and OUTER JOIN, and how to create a SQL subquery.

REAL WORLD ADVICE **Do You Need to Know SQL?**

You do not necessarily need to know SQL. Access makes it easy to create objects without having to know any programming languages. If you are comfortable using the tools — wizards, Design view of queries or tables, and so forth — within Access, then those tools may be more than enough to meet your needs. However, most database administrators and developers rely on writing SQL to ensure that their queries meet user requirements as efficiently as possible. Knowing SQL also gives database administrators more control over how they get the results they want. Regardless, you should be familiar with the language that is the foundation of relational databases.

Create Basic Structured Query Language (SQL) Queries

Each query that you create has an **underlying SQL statement**, which means that even when you create a query in Design view, Access automatically generates the SQL statement behind the scenes. In Access, you can easily change between the Design and SQL views of your query with the click of a mouse. By selecting SQL view instead of Design view, you can view and edit the code as necessary.

The challenge in learning how to write SQL in this manner is that Access does add additional syntax that is not necessarily needed for a SQL query to run properly.

Viewing SQL Statements in Access

Access is a great way to begin learning SQL, and viewing SQL statements is extremely easy to do. In this exercise, you will create a simple query and then switch to SQL View to view the SQL created by Access in the background.

A07.11

To View SQL Statements in Access

a. If you took a break, open the **a04ch07SpaDecisions** database.

b. Click the **Create** tab, and then, in the Queries group, click **Query Design**. Add **tblCustomer** to the query workspace, and then **Close** the Show Table dialog box.

SIDE NOTE
Extra Words and Symbols
Remember that many programs use a modified version of SQL. If standard SQL is typed into the SQL view, the query will still run properly.

c. Add the following fields to the query design grid: **CustFirstName**, **CustLastName**, **CustEmail**, and **CustState**.

d. In the Criteria row of the CustState field, type "MN".

e. **Save** the query as qryCustomersMN. On the Design tab, in the Results group, click **Run**. Resize your fields if you cannot see all the data and column headings.
   Notice that there are three customers who live in Minnesota.

f. On the Home tab, in the Views group, click the **View** arrow, and then select **SQL View**.

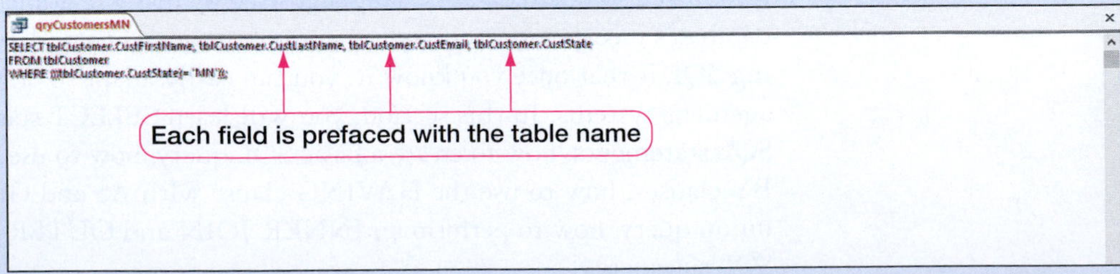

Access 2016, Windows 10, Microsoft Corporation

Figure 19 SQL View of qryCustomersMN

Notice that Access created the SQL statement in the background as you created your query in Design view. Access prefaced each field name in the SELECT statement with the table name and added parentheses in the WHERE statement.

g. **Save** and **Close** the query.

Understanding SELECT Statement Basics

In Access, SQL can be used to query data, just like when you create a select query in the query design grid. As long as you know the basic structure of a SQL SELECT statement, it is fairly easy to create a SQL query. The fundamental framework for a SQL query is the SQL **SELECT statement**. The SELECT statement contains two required clauses — SELECT and FROM — as shown in Table 1. The SELECT clause specifies the columns or fields you want to return in your data set. The FROM clause specifies the table or tables in which the columns are located. Both of these clauses are required in a SQL SELECT statement.

Clause	Required?	Include	Explanation	Example
SELECT	Yes	Field name(s)	Includes one or more columns from which data are retrieved	SELECT EmpFirstName, EmpLastName
FROM	Yes	Table name(s)	Name of the table(s) from which the columns are located	FROM tblEmployee

Table 1 Basic SELECT statement clauses

For example, the following SELECT statement would list all the employees' first and last names along with their addresses, cities, states, and ZIP Codes, which are all the fields stored in the tblEmployee table. The SELECT statement ends with a semicolon. If you forget to add it, Access will automatically add it for you.

```
SELECT EmpFirstName, EmpLastName, Address, City, State, ZipCode
FROM tblEmployee;
```

If you want to retrieve all the information about all employees in tblEmployee, you could use an asterisk (*) as a shortcut for retrieving all of the fields. The results would be the same as the previous example; however, it is much more efficient to write the SQL statement in this manner.

```
SELECT *
FROM tblEmployee;
```

Creating a Basic Query with SQL

SQL is used to interact with your data, and whenever a query is run, Access uses SQL to filter the data and perform all the data functions of its Query Design tool. If you know SQL, you can create several types of queries in Access by typing your SQL statement in SQL view. In this exercise, you will use SQL to create a basic query that will display all fields in the tblInvoice table.

A07.12

To Create a Basic Query with SQL

a. Click the **Create** tab. In the Queries group, click **Query Design**, and then **Close** [X] the Show Table dialog box.

b. On the Design tab, in the Results group, click the **View** arrow, and then select **SQL View**.

   Notice that Access has already started writing the SELECT clause.

c. Delete **SELECT;**, and then type

   SELECT *
   FROM tblInvoice;

d. **Save** the query as qryInvoicesSQL. On the Design tab, in the Results group, click **Run**.

SIDE NOTE

Using an Asterisk

The asterisk selects and returns all fields in the table when you run the query.

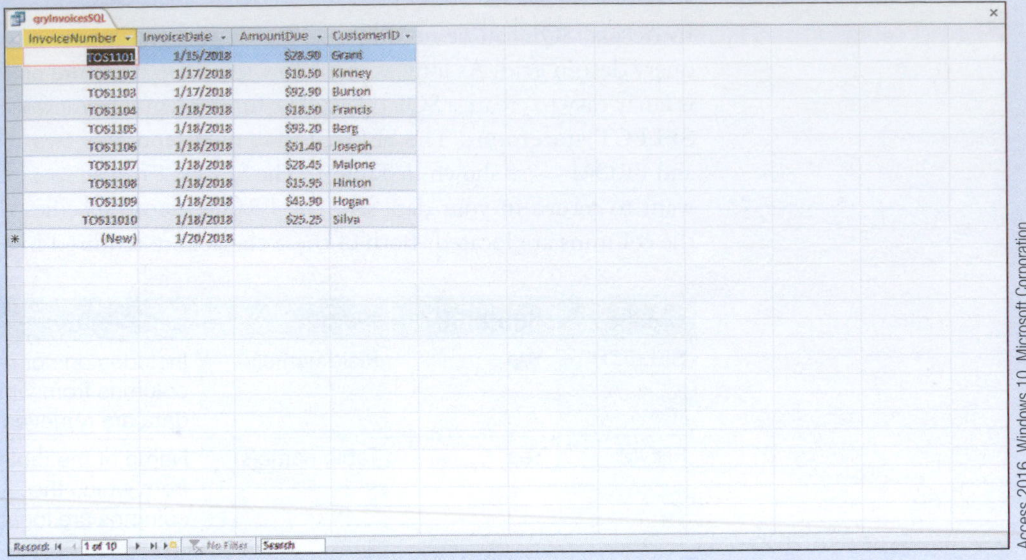

Access 2016, Windows 10, Microsoft Corporation

Figure 20 Datasheet View of qryInvoicesSQL

Notice that there are ten records in your data set.

e. **Close** ☒ the query.

Using the WHERE Clause

The WHERE clause, which is optional in a SELECT statement, narrows the query results by specifying which rows in the table will be returned in the data set. If the WHERE clause is omitted, all rows will be used. The SELECT statement

```
SELECT EmpFirstName, EmpLastName
FROM tblEmployee
WHERE EmpLastName Like "[A-M]*"
```

lists the results shown in Figure 21. Notice that the results display only the employees' whose last names begin with the letters "A" through "M".

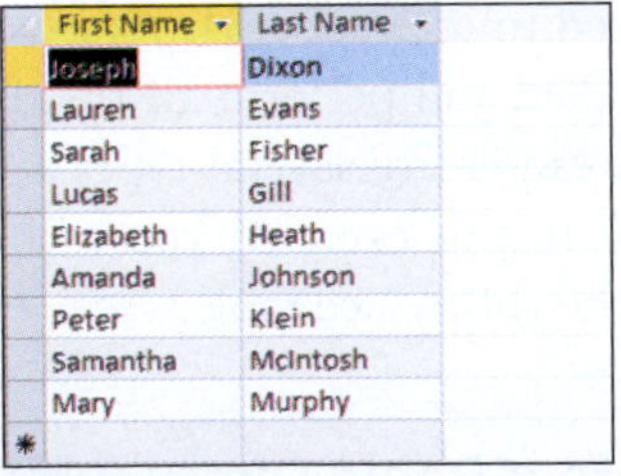

First Name	Last Name
Joseph	Dixon
Lauren	Evans
Sarah	Fisher
Lucas	Gill
Elizabeth	Heath
Amanda	Johnson
Peter	Klein
Samantha	McIntosh
Mary	Murphy

Figure 21 Datasheet view of the above SQL

Access 2016, Windows 10, Microsoft Corporation

To write effective Access queries, you need to master the WHERE clause. The WHERE clause allows you to limit the results of your query based on conditions that you specify. In this exercise, you will create three queries using SQL. One will display the data in the tblInvoice table with invoice dates between 1/15/2018 and 1/17/2018. One will display Services in the tblService table that have a fee of at least $75.00. Another will display all customer information for those living in Utah, Minnesota, Hawaii, and Pennsylvania.

To Use the WHERE Clause

a. Click the **Create** tab. In the Queries group, click **Query Design**, and then **Close** the Show Table dialog box.

b. On the Design tab, in the Results group, click the **View** arrow, and then select **SQL View**.

c. Delete **SELECT;**, and then type the following.
   SELECT *

d. Press Enter to move to the next line, and then type the following.
   FROM tblInvoice.

e. Press Enter to move to the next line, and then type the following.
   WHERE InvoiceDate BETWEEN #1/15/2018# AND #1/17/2018#;

f. **Save** the query as qrySelectInvoicesSQL. On the Design tab, in the Results group, click **Run**.

SIDE NOTE
Should You Separate Lines?
You can write a SELECT statement all on one line. It is generally written on separate lines to make it easier to read and edit.

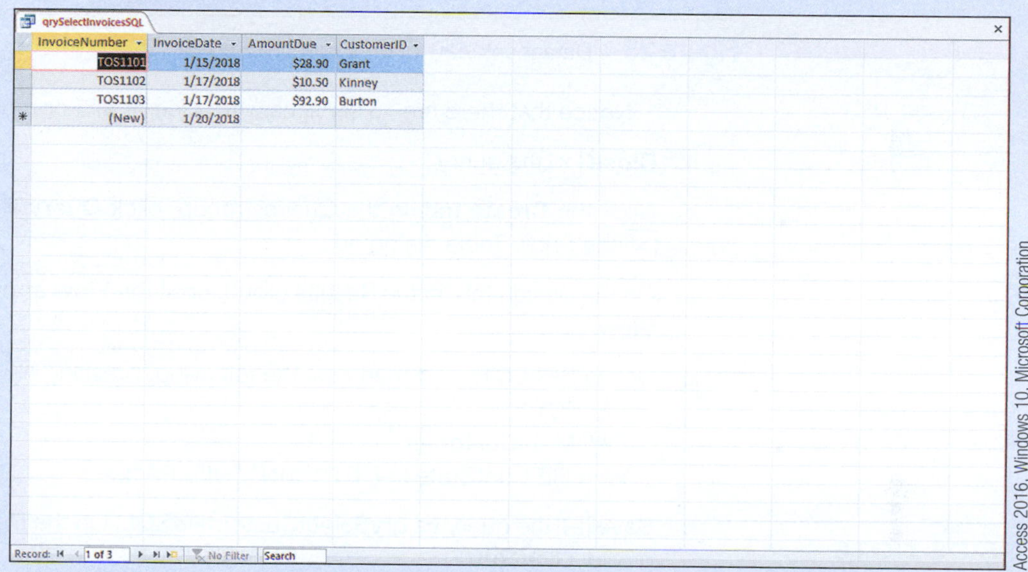

InvoiceNumber	InvoiceDate	AmountDue	CustomerID
TOS1101	1/15/2018	$28.90	Grant
TOS1102	1/17/2018	$10.50	Kinney
TOS1103	1/17/2018	$92.90	Burton
(New)	1/20/2018		

Figure 22 Datasheet View of qrySelectInvoicesSQL

Notice that there are three records in your data set.

Troubleshooting

If a syntax error dialog box appears, check your spelling, and make sure no spaces are in the field or table names.

g. **Close** the query.

h. Click the **Create** tab. In the Queries group, click **Query Design**, and then **Close** the Show Table dialog box.

i. On the Design tab, in the Results group, click the **View** arrow, and then select **SQL View**.

j. Delete **SELECT;**, and then type SELECT ServiceName, Description, Fee.

k. Press Enter to move to the next line, and then type FROM tblService.

l. Press Enter to move to the next line, and then type WHERE Fee >= 75;

m. **Save** the query as qryExpensiveServicesSQL. On the Design tab, in the Results group, click **Run**.

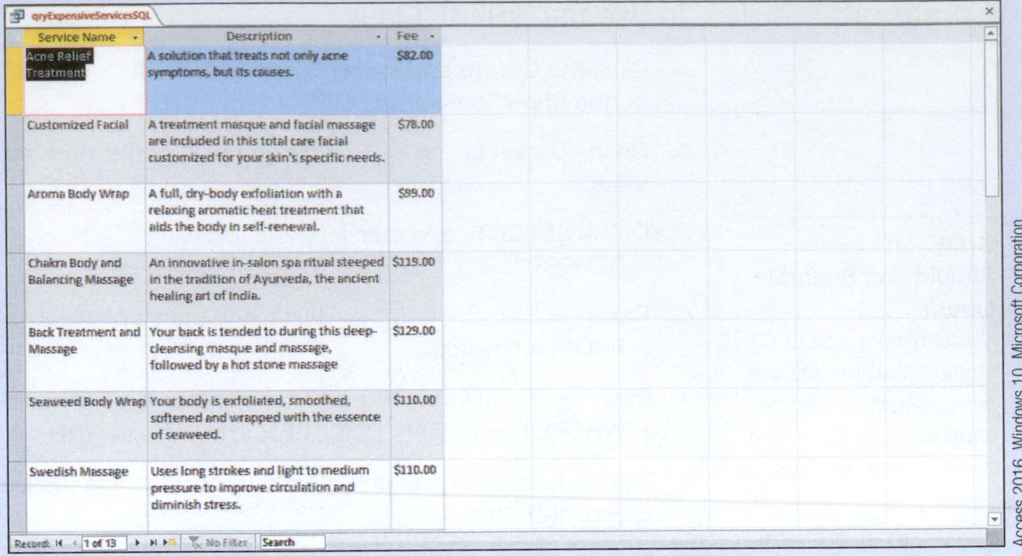

qryExpensiveServicesSQL

Service Name	Description	Fee
Acne Relief Treatment	A solution that treats not only acne symptoms, but its causes.	$82.00
Customized Facial	A treatment masque and facial massage are included in this total care facial customized for your skin's specific needs.	$78.00
Aroma Body Wrap	A full, dry-body exfoliation with a relaxing aromatic heat treatment that aids the body in self-renewal.	$89.00
Chakra Body and Balancing Massage	An innovative in-salon spa ritual steeped in the tradition of Ayurveda, the ancient healing art of India.	$119.00
Back Treatment and Massage	Your back is tended to during this deep-cleansing masque and massage, followed by a hot stone massage	$129.00
Seaweed Body Wrap	Your body is exfoliated, smoothed, softened and wrapped with the essence of seaweed.	$110.00
Swedish Massage	Uses long strokes and light to medium pressure to improve circulation and diminish stress.	$110.00

Record: 1 of 13 | No Filter | Search

Access 2016, Windows 10, Microsoft Corporation

Figure 23 Datasheet View of qryExpensiveServicesSQL

Notice that there are 13 services with a fee of $75 or more in your data set.

n. **Close** [X] the query.

o. Click the **Create** tab. In the Queries group, click **Query Design**, and then **Close** [X] the Show Table dialog box.

p. On the Design tab, in the Results group, click the **View** arrow, and then select **SQL View**.

q. Delete **SELECT;**, and then type the following, pressing Enter after each line.

```
SELECT *
FROM tblCustomer
WHERE CustState In ("UT","MN","HI","PA");
```

r. **Save** [Save] the query as qrySelectCustomersSQL. On the Design tab, in the Results group, click **Run**.

SIDE NOTE

Using Other Operators

Other operators can be used, such as AND and OR, in place of the IN operator. Thus, you could type CustState = "UT" OR CustState ="MN" and so on.

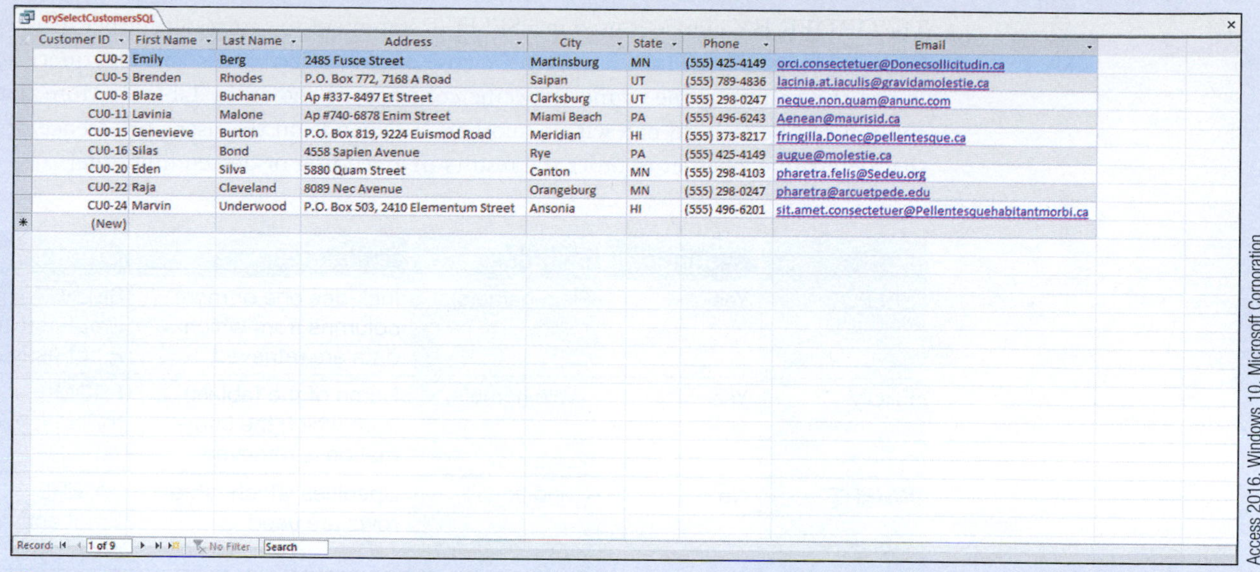

qrySelectCustomersSQL

Customer ID	First Name	Last Name	Address	City	State	Phone	Email
CU0-2	Emily	Berg	2485 Fusce Street	Martinsburg	MN	(555) 425-4149	orci.consectetuer@Donecsollicitudin.ca
CU0-5	Brenden	Rhodes	P.O. Box 772, 7168 A Road	Saipan	UT	(555) 789-4836	lacinia.at.iaculis@gravidamolestie.ca
CU0-8	Blaze	Buchanan	Ap #337-8497 Et Street	Clarksburg	UT	(555) 298-0247	neque.non.quam@anunc.com
CU0-11	Lavinia	Malone	Ap #740-6878 Enim Street	Miami Beach	PA	(555) 496-6243	Aenean@maurisid.ca
CU0-15	Genevieve	Burton	P.O. Box 819, 9224 Euismod Road	Meridian	HI	(555) 373-8217	fringilla.Donec@pellentesque.ca
CU0-16	Silas	Bond	4558 Sapien Avenue	Rye	PA	(555) 425-4149	augue@molestie.ca
CU0-20	Eden	Silva	5880 Quam Street	Canton	MN	(555) 298-4103	pharetra.felis@Sedeu.org
CU0-22	Raja	Cleveland	8089 Nec Avenue	Orangeburg	MN	(555) 298-0247	pharetra@arcuetpede.edu
CU0-24	Marvin	Underwood	P.O. Box 503, 2410 Elementum Street	Ansonia	HI	(555) 496-6201	sit.amet.consectetuer@Pellentesquehabitantmorbi.ca
(New)							

Record: 1 of 9 No Filter Search

Figure 24 Datasheet View of qrySelectCustomersSQL

Notice that there are nine customers who live in either Utah, Minnesota, Hawaii, or Pennsylvania in your data set.

s. **Close** [X] the query.

QUICK REFERENCE **Operators Allowed in the WHERE Clause**

Operator	Description
=	Equal
<>	Not equal
>	Greater than
<	Less than
>=	Greater than or equal
<=	Less than or equal
BETWEEN...AND	Between an inclusive range
LIKE	Search for a pattern
IN	The exact value you want to return for at least one column
AND	All conditions must be true to return a value
OR	At least one condition must be true to return a value

REAL WORLD ADVICE **Design View Versus SQL View**

Everything you have learned how to do in Design view can also be done in SQL view. If you are not sure how to write the SQL statement for a particular query, you can create it in Design view and then switch to SQL view to see how Access generated the code. Even though Access adds some extra words to the SQL statement, it is still correct and will return the proper data set. Additionally, when you make changes to the query in SQL view, Access modifies Design view to represent the updated SQL statement.

Using the ORDER BY Clause

The **ORDER BY clause** is used in a SELECT statement to sort results either in ascending or descending order. The ORDER BY clause orders or sorts the result of a query according to the values in one or more specific columns, as shown in Table 2. More than one column can be ordered one within another. It depends on the user's preference or needs that determine whether to order the results in ascending or descending order.

Clause	Required?	Include	Explanation	Example
SELECT	Yes	Field name(s)	Includes one or more columns from which data are retrieved	SELECT EmpFirstName, EmpLastName
FROM	Yes	Table name(s)	Name of the table(s) from which the information is retrieved	FROM tblEmployee
WHERE	No	Conditions	Specifies which table rows are used	WHERE EmpLastName Like "[A-M]*"
ORDER BY	No	Field name(s)	Allows you to sort fields in ascending or descending order. The default order is ascending.	ORDER BY EmpLastName, EmpFirstName ASC or DESC

Table 2 SELECT statement clauses with ORDER BY clause

The ORDER BY clause is optional. However, if you want your data displayed in sorted order, then you must use ORDER BY. The default sorting order in Access is ascending — A–Z — order. In this exercise, you will create two queries using SQL that will control the sort order by using the ORDER BY clause.

A07.14

To Use the ORDER BY Clause

a. Click the **Create** tab. In the Queries group, click **Query Design**, and then **Close** [X] the Show Table dialog box.

b. On the Design tab, in the Results group, click the **View** arrow, and then select **SQL View**.

c. Delete **SELECT;**, and then type the following, pressing Enter after each line.

```
SELECT Customer, Service, DateOfAppt
FROM tblSchedule
ORDER BY DateOfAppt DESC;
```

d. **Save** the query as qryScheduleSortedSQL. On the Design tab, in the Results group, click **Run**.

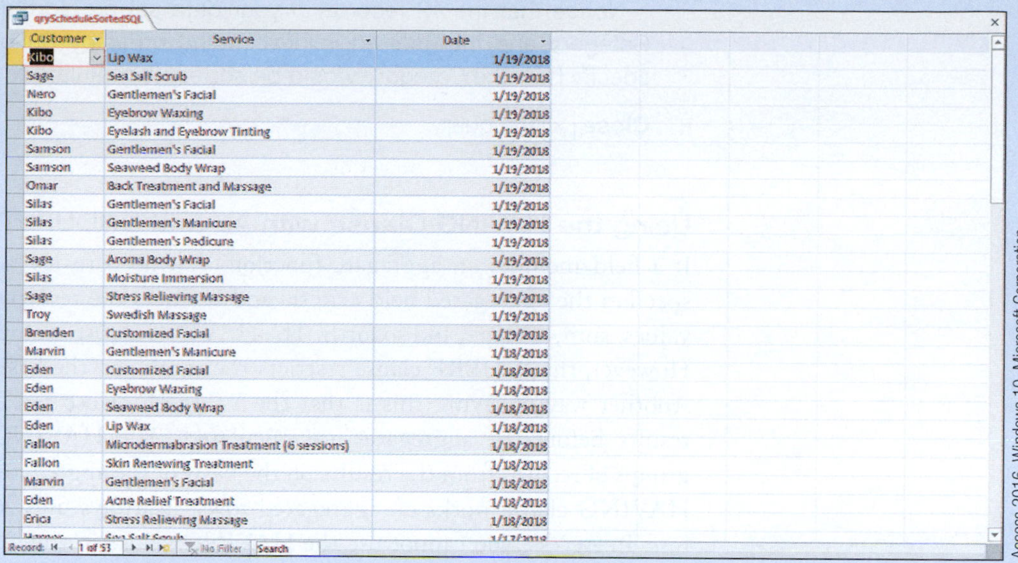

qryScheduleSortedSQL

Customer	Service	Date
Kibo	Lip Wax	1/19/2018
Sage	Sea Salt Scrub	1/19/2018
Nero	Gentlemen's Facial	1/19/2018
Kibo	Eyebrow Waxing	1/19/2018
Kibo	Eyelash and Eyebrow Tinting	1/19/2018
Samson	Gentlemen's Facial	1/19/2018
Samson	Seaweed Body Wrap	1/19/2018
Omar	Back Treatment and Massage	1/19/2018
Silas	Gentlemen's Facial	1/19/2018
Silas	Gentlemen's Manicure	1/19/2018
Silas	Gentlemen's Pedicure	1/19/2018
Sage	Aroma Body Wrap	1/19/2018
Silas	Moisture Immersion	1/19/2018
Sage	Stress Relieving Massage	1/19/2018
Troy	Swedish Massage	1/19/2018
Brenden	Customized Facial	1/19/2018
Marvin	Gentlemen's Manicure	1/18/2018
Eden	Customized Facial	1/18/2018
Eden	Eyebrow Waxing	1/18/2018
Eden	Seaweed Body Wrap	1/18/2018
Eden	Lip Wax	1/18/2018
Fallon	Microdermabrasion Treatment (6 sessions)	1/18/2018
Fallon	Skin Renewing Treatment	1/18/2018
Marvin	Gentlemen's Facial	1/18/2018
Eden	Acne Relief Treatment	1/18/2018
Erica	Stress Relieving Massage	1/18/2018

Record: 1 of 53 No Filter Search

Access 2016, Windows 10, Microsoft Corporation

Figure 25 Datasheet View of qryScheduleSortedSQL

Notice that the 53 records in your data set are sorted in descending order by DateOfAppt. You needed to specify descending in the SQL statement because ascending is the default sort order.

e. **Close** [X] the query.

f. Click the **Create** tab. In the Queries group, click **Query Design**, and then **Close** [X] the Show Table dialog box.

g. On the Design tab, in the Results group, click the **View** arrow, and then select **SQL View**.

h. Delete **SELECT;**, and then type the following, pressing Enter after each line.

```
SELECT ProductDescription, Category, QtyInStock, Price, Size
FROM tblProduct
WHERE Size > 12
ORDER BY Category, Price DESC;
```

SIDE NOTE

Sorting Both Fields

If you want both Category and Price sorted in descending order, you need to type DESC after both fields, not just Price.

i. **Save** [Save] the query as qryBulkProductsSQL. On the Design tab, in the Results group, click **Run**.

qryBulkProductsSQL

ProductDescription	Category	QtyInStock	Price	Size (ounces)
Lavender Ylang Bath Salts	Bath	30	$19.95	16
Cilantro Foot Bath Salts	Bath	30	$19.95	16
Geranium Rose Bath Salts	Bath	40	$19.95	16
Lemon Body Butter	Body	26	$22.50	16
Cocoa Body Butter	Body	29	$22.50	16
Lavender Seaweed Dead Sea Salt Body Scrub	Body	19	$19.95	16
Lavender Dead Sea Salt Body Scrub	Body	27	$19.95	16
Ginger Brown Sugar Scrub	Body	34	$10.50	16
Peppermint Mineral Foot Cream	Foot	9	$12.95	16
Turquoise Oasis Bath Salts	House Brand	27	$19.95	16
Turquoise Oasis Conditioner	House Brand	49	$17.50	23
Turquoise Oasis Shampoo	House Brand	49	$17.50	23

Record: 1 of 12 No Filter Search

Access 2016, Windows 10, Microsoft Corporation

Figure 26 Datasheet View of qryBulkProductsSQL

Notice that the 12 records in your data set are sorted in ascending order by Category and then sorted in descending order by Price. Because you did not specify how the Category would be sorted, it defaulted to ascending order.

j. **Close** [X] the query.

Using the HAVING Clause with AS and GROUP BY

If a field includes an aggregate function, you need to use a **HAVING clause**, which specifies the aggregated field criteria and restricts the results on the basis of aggregated values: sum, average, and so forth. The HAVING clause is similar to the WHERE clause. However, the WHERE clause restricts the results on the basis of individual row values. Another way of saying this is that the WHERE clause can eliminate records from the results before the aggregates are calculated. The HAVING clause eliminates entire groups of records from the results on the basis of the aggregated calculations. Because the HAVING clause works on aggregated rows, it always uses an aggregate function as its test. In Access, you cannot use the HAVING clause in the query design grid; therefore, you must switch to SQL.

When writing a SQL SELECT statement that includes a HAVING clause, you must also use a GROUP BY clause. It is also considered best practice to us an AS clause to rename any fields being aggregated. When you do not name an aggregated field in a query, regardless of whether you are working in SQL view or Design view, Access names it for you with a name such as SumOfQuantity. Thus, the **AS clause** allows you to name or rename a field, which is displayed in the data set. The GROUP BY clause is used in conjunction with the aggregate functions to group the data set by one or more columns.

In this exercise, you will create two queries using SQL. Both of these queries will use the HAVING clause as well as the AS and GROUP BY clauses. One query will return any customers who purchased more than five items on any given day. Another query will return any invoices with a total amount due of $25.00 or less.

To Use the HAVING Clause with the AS and GROUP BY Clauses

a. Click the **Create** tab. In the Queries group, click **Query Design**, and then **Close** [X] the Show Table dialog box.

b. On the Design tab, in the Results group, click the **View** arrow, and then select **SQL View**.

c. Delete **SELECT;**, and then type the following, pressing Enter after each line.

```
SELECT CustomerID, PurchaseDate, ProductID, Sum(Quantity) AS Total
FROM tblPurchase
GROUP BY CustomerID, PurchaseDate, ProductID
HAVING (Sum([Quantity]))>5;
```

d. **Save** the query as qryLargePurchaseCustomersSQL. On the Design tab, in the Results group, click **Run**.

SIDE NOTE

Field Names Using the AS Clause

In SQL view, the renamed field in the AS clause is not recognized as a field and cannot be used in a HAVING clause.

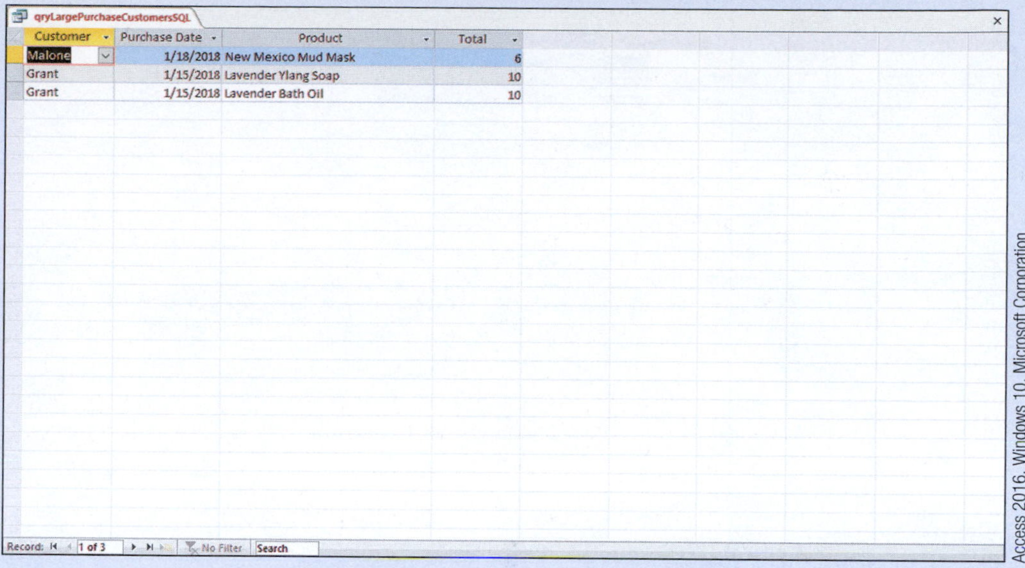

Figure 27 Datasheet View of qryLargePurchaseCustomersSQL

Notice that there are three clients who have purchased a total of five or more products from the spa. If you had typed a criterion of >5 under the Sum([Quantity]) field in the query design grid, Access would have summed any quantity that is individually greater than 5. The HAVING clause displays records in which the sum of the Quantity field is greater than 5.

e. **Close** ☒ the query.

f. Click the **Create** tab. In the Queries group, click **Query Design**, and then **Close** ☒ the Show Table dialog box.

> **SIDE NOTE**
> **Using the Asterisk**
> Even though you are selecting all the tblInvoice table fields, you cannot use an asterisk in a query that has the GROUP BY clause.

g. On the Design tab, in the Results group, click the **View** arrow, and then select **SQL View**.

h. Delete **SELECT;**, and then type the following, pressing Enter after each line.

```
SELECT InvoiceNumber, InvoiceDate, Sum([AmountDue]) AS Total, CustomerID
FROM tblInvoice
GROUP BY InvoiceNumber, InvoiceDate, CustomerID
HAVING Sum([AmountDue])<=25;
```

i. **Save** the query as qrySmallInvoicesSQL. On the Design tab, in the Results group, click **Run**.

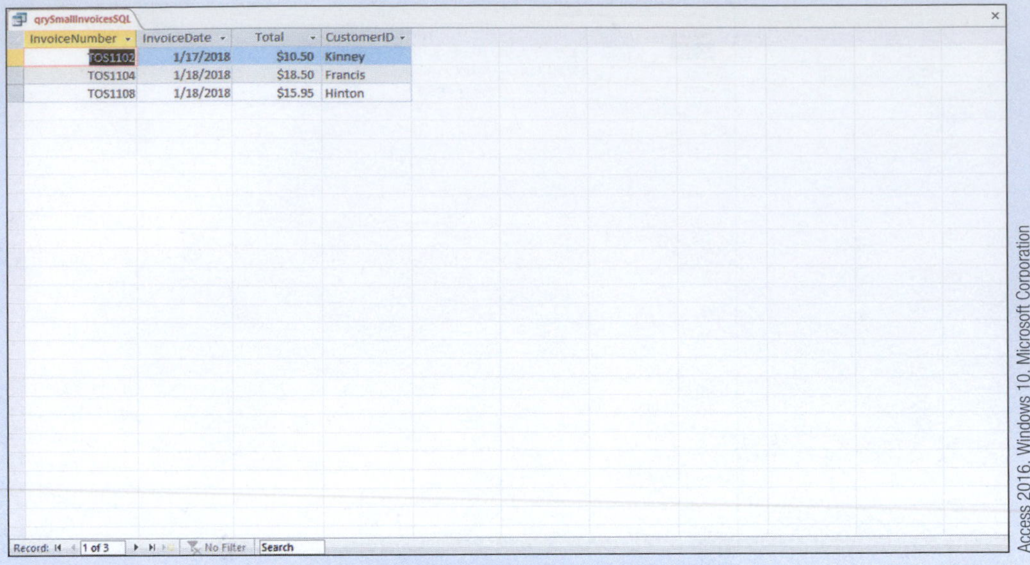

Access 2016, Windows 10, Microsoft Corporation

Figure 28 Datasheet View of qrySmallInvoicesSQL

Notice that there are three clients who have invoices totaling $25 or less.

j. **Close** [X] the query.

Incorporate Joins into Structured Query Language (SQL) Queries

A **join** is used to combine the data from two or more tables. The data set is created on the basis of a field or fields that two tables share: primary and foreign keys. The goal is to extract meaningful data from the data set. Joins are performed on the basis of a **predicate**, which specifies the condition to use to perform a join. A join can be either an inner join or an outer join, depending on how you want the data set to perform. In this section, you will write inner, outer, right, and full join queries along with union queries in SQL.

Creating Queries Using the INNER JOIN Clause

The **INNER JOIN clause** is used to return only the rows that actually match on the basis of the join predicate. An inner join is a join in which the values in the columns being joined are equal, that is, contain a relationship based on a common field. Additionally, compared to using a comparison operator, such as the FROM or WHERE clause, the output of an inner join will include where the two tables intersect or overlap, as shown in Figure 29.

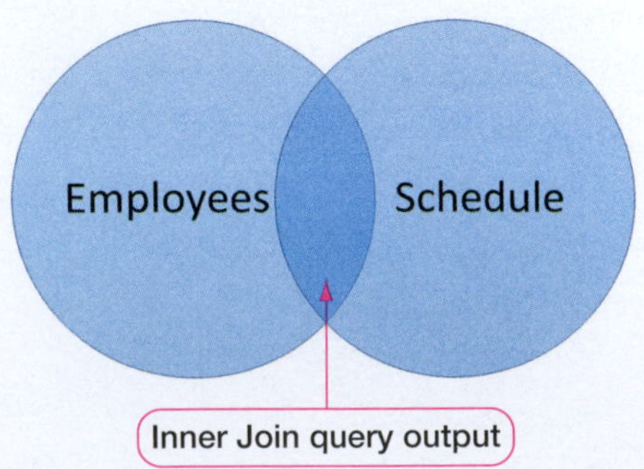

Figure 29 Output of Inner Join lies in the intersection of both circles

The following SELECT statement

```
SELECT EmpFirstName, EmpLastName, Customer, Service, DateOfAppt
FROM tblEmployee
INNER JOIN tblSchedule ON tblEmployee.EmployeeID = tblSchedule.Employee;
```

lists the results shown in Figure 30. Notice that the results display all employees who have an appointment scheduled. Additionally, the DateOfAppt field belongs in tblSchedule, which is why the INNER JOIN clause needed to be used. The INNER JOIN is letting Access know that the EmployeeID within tblEmployee — the primary key — is the same data as what is stored in the Employee field within tblSchedule, the foreign key.

In this exercise, you will create several queries using SQL and the INNER JOIN clause to retrieve data from multiple tables.

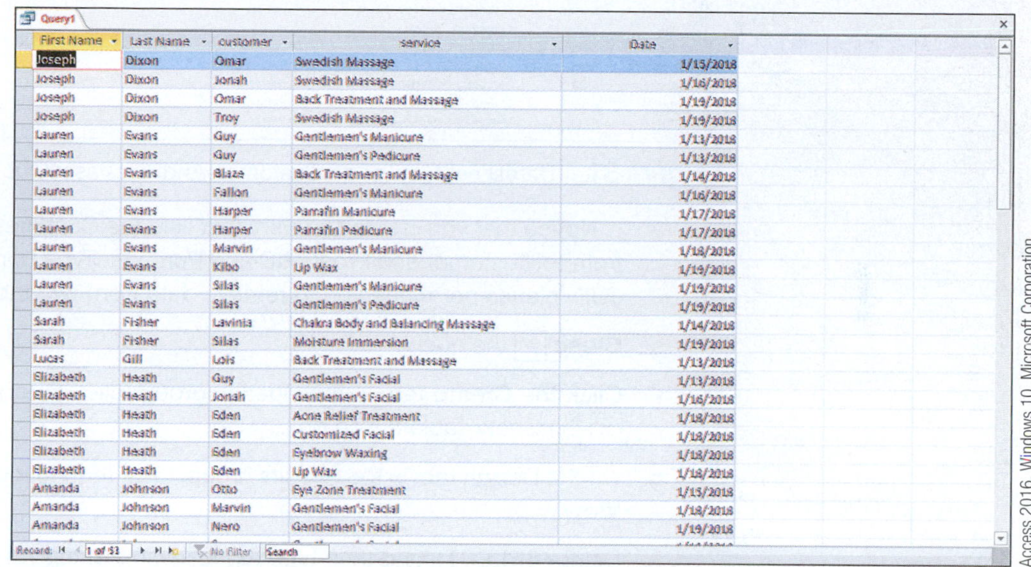

Query1

First Name	Last Name	customer	service	Date
Joseph	Dixon	Omar	Swedish Massage	1/15/2018
Joseph	Dixon	Jonah	Swedish Massage	1/16/2018
Joseph	Dixon	Omar	Back Treatment and Massage	1/19/2018
Joseph	Dixon	Troy	Swedish Massage	1/19/2018
Lauren	Evans	Guy	Gentlemen's Manicure	1/13/2018
Lauren	Evans	Guy	Gentlemen's Pedicure	1/13/2018
Lauren	Evans	Blaze	Back Treatment and Massage	1/14/2018
Lauren	Evans	Fallon	Gentlemen's Manicure	1/16/2018
Lauren	Evans	Harper	Parrafin Manicure	1/17/2018
Lauren	Evans	Harper	Parrafin Pedicure	1/17/2018
Lauren	Evans	Marvin	Gentlemen's Manicure	1/18/2018
Lauren	Evans	Kibo	Lip Wax	1/19/2018
Lauren	Evans	Silas	Gentlemen's Manicure	1/19/2018
Lauren	Evans	Silas	Gentlemen's Pedicure	1/19/2018
Sarah	Fisher	Lavinia	Chakra Body and Balancing Massage	1/14/2018
Sarah	Fisher	Silas	Moisture Immersion	1/19/2018
Lucas	Gill	Lois	Back Treatment and Massage	1/13/2018
Elizabeth	Heath	Guy	Gentlemen's Facial	1/13/2018
Elizabeth	Heath	Jonah	Gentlemen's Facial	1/16/2018
Elizabeth	Heath	Eden	Acne Relief Treatment	1/18/2018
Elizabeth	Heath	Eden	Customized Facial	1/18/2018
Elizabeth	Heath	Eden	Eyebrow Waxing	1/18/2018
Elizabeth	Heath	Eden	Lip Wax	1/18/2018
Amanda	Johnson	Otto	Eye Zone Treatment	1/15/2018
Amanda	Johnson	Marvin	Gentlemen's Facial	1/18/2018
Amanda	Johnson	Nero	Gentlemen's Facial	1/19/2018

Record: 1 of 53 No Filter Search

Figure 30 Datasheet View of Inner Join query

Access 2016, Windows 10, Microsoft Corporation

A07.16

To Create Queries Using the INNER JOIN Clause

a. Click the **Create** tab. In the Queries group, click **Query Design**, and then **Close** [X] the Show Table dialog box.

b. On the Design tab, in the Results group, click the **View** arrow, and then select **SQL View**.

c. Delete **SELECT;**, and then type the following, pressing Enter after each line.

   SELECT CustFirstName, CustLastName, ProductID, PurchaseType
   FROM tblCustomer INNER JOIN tblPurchase ON tblCustomer.CustomerID = tblPurchase.CustomerID;

d. **Save** the query as qryCustomersAndPurchasesSQL. On the Design tab, in the Results group, click **Run**.

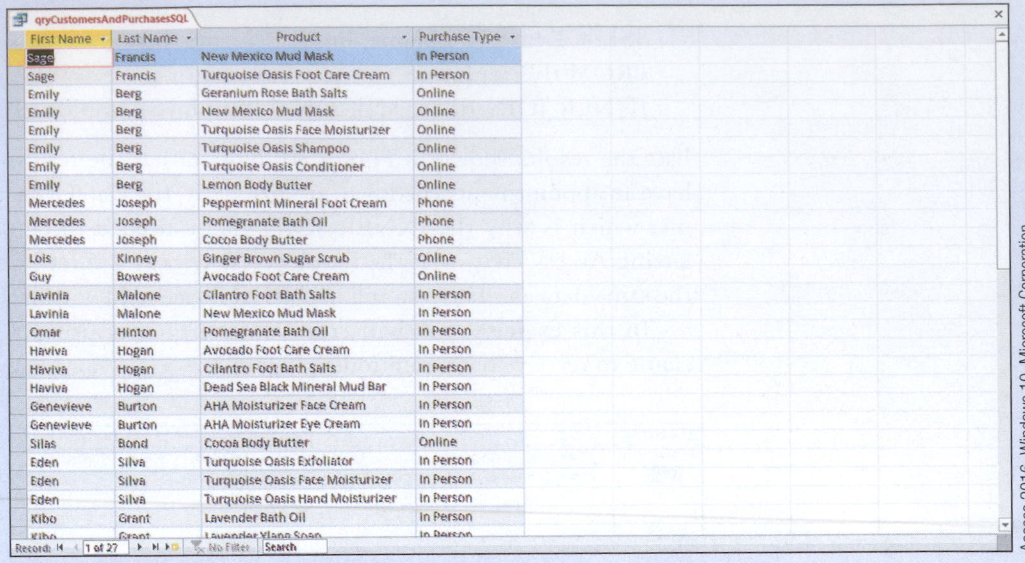

Figure 31 Datasheet View of qryCustomersAndPurchasesSQL

Notice that you created a query that lists the CustFirstName and CustLastName from tblCustomer and ProductID and PurchaseType from tblPurchase. The INNER JOIN clause permitted you to retrieve data from two tables.

e. **Close** [X] the query.

f. Click the **Create** tab. In the Queries group, click **Query Design**, and then **Close** [X] the Show Table dialog box.

g. On the Design tab, in the Results group, click the **View** arrow, and then select **SQL View**.

h. Delete **SELECT;**, and then type the following, pressing Enter after each line.

   SELECT ServiceName, Customer, Employee, Description, Fee
   FROM tblService INNER JOIN tblSchedule ON tblService.ServiceID =
   tblSchedule.Service;

i. **Save** the query as qryCustomersAndServicesSQL. On the Design tab, in the Results group, click **Run**.

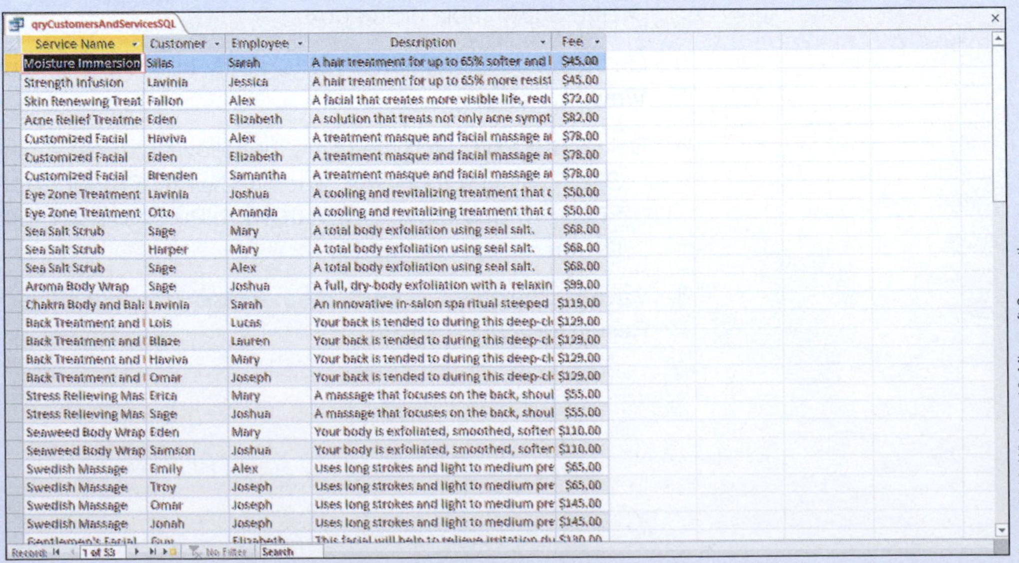

Figure 32 Datasheet View of qryCustomersAndServicesSQL

Notice that even though your query lists the ServiceName, Description, and Fee from tblService and Customer and Employee from tblSchedule, you were able to reorder the fields on the basis of how you typed the fields into SQL view.

j. **Close** [X] the query.

k. Click the **Create** tab. In the Queries group, click **Query Design**, and then **Close** [X] the Show Table dialog box.

l. On the Design tab, in the Results group, click the **View** arrow, and then select **SQL View**.

m. Delete **SELECT;**, and then type the following, pressing Enter after each line.

```
SELECT Employee, DateOfAppt, Count(ServiceName) AS TotalServices
FROM tblService
INNER JOIN tblSchedule ON tblService.ServiceID = tblSchedule.Service
GROUP BY Employee, DateOfAppt
ORDER BY DateOfAppt, Count(ServiceName) DESC;
```

n. **Save** the query as qryTotalServicesByEmployeeByDateSQL. On the Design tab, in the Results group, click **Run**.

Notice that you can see how many appointments each employee has on a given day.

SIDE NOTE

Different SQL Clauses

You can combine different SQL clauses to create a more focused query.

SIDE NOTE

Changes to the SQL

If the SQL is viewed after it has been saved and closed, you will notice that Access adds the table name before each field name. It is necessary to type the table name only if the field to which you are referring exists in multiple tables.

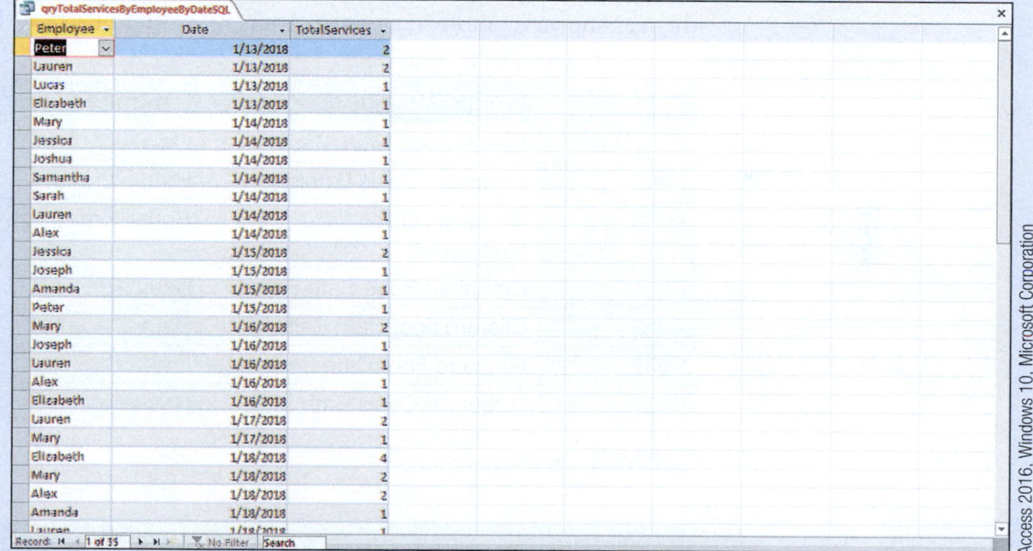

qryTotalServicesByEmployeeByDateSQL

Employee	Date	TotalServices
Peter	1/13/2018	2
Lauren	1/13/2018	2
Lucas	1/13/2018	1
Elizabeth	1/13/2018	1
Mary	1/14/2018	1
Jessica	1/14/2018	1
Joshua	1/14/2018	1
Samantha	1/14/2018	1
Sarah	1/14/2018	1
Lauren	1/14/2018	1
Alex	1/14/2018	1
Jessica	1/15/2018	2
Joseph	1/15/2018	1
Amanda	1/15/2018	1
Peter	1/15/2018	1
Mary	1/16/2018	2
Joseph	1/16/2018	1
Lauren	1/16/2018	1
Alex	1/16/2018	1
Elizabeth	1/16/2018	1
Lauren	1/17/2018	2
Mary	1/17/2018	1
Elizabeth	1/18/2018	4
Mary	1/18/2018	2
Alex	1/18/2018	2
Amanda	1/18/2018	1
Lauren	1/18/2018	1

Record: 1 of 35 No Filter Search

Access 2016, Windows 10, Microsoft Corporation

Figure 33 Datasheet View of qryTotalServicesByEmployeeByDateSQL

o. **Close** [X] the query.

Creating Queries Using OUTER JOINS

The **OUTER JOIN clause** returns all rows from at least one of the tables within the FROM clause as long as those rows meet any WHERE or HAVING search conditions. The OUTER JOIN clause is used whenever multiple tables are accessed through a SQL SELECT statement that returns all of the records from one table and only those records from the other table in which the joined fields match.

Outer joins are subdivided into left outer joins, right outer joins, and full outer joins, depending on which table's rows are shown in the data set: left, right, or both. The **LEFT**

JOIN clause is used when you want to return all rows in the left table even if no matching rows exist in the right table. For example, you can create a query that includes all the records from the Product table and related transactions in the Purchase table as shown in Figure 34.

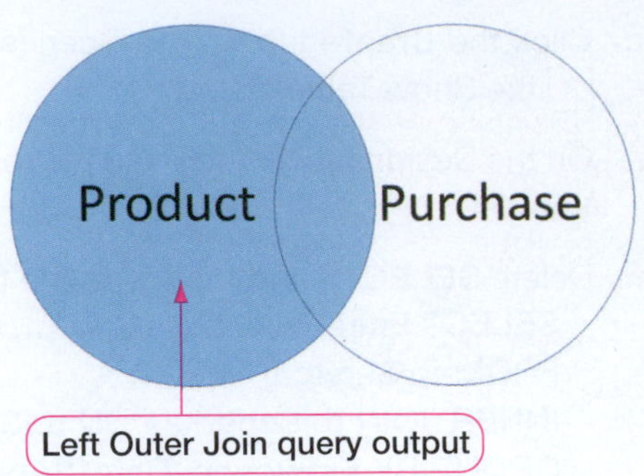

Figure 34 Output of left join lies in the intersection of both circles and all the data in the Product (left) table

The data set of the following SQL query

```
SELECT ProductDescription, CustomerID, Quantity, Price, PurchaseDate
FROM Product
LEFT JOIN Purchase ON Product.ProductID = Purchase.ProductID;
```

would include all products as shown in Table 3, whether or not a customer purchased them as shown in Table 4, along with the matching purchase data as shown in Table 5.

ProductID	ProductDescription	Category	QtyInStock	Price
P001	New Mexico Mud Mask	Face	100	$ 8.50
P002	Turquoise Oasis Exfoliator	House Brand	94	$ 8.50
P003	Turquoise Oasis Face Moisturizer	House Brand	80	$ 7.25
P004	Geranium Rose Bath Salts	Bath	40	$19.95
P005	Cilantro Foot Bath Salts	Bath	30	$19.95
P006	Avocado Foot Care Cream	Foot	104	$ 9.00
P007	Turquoise Oasis Bath Salts	House Brand	27	$19.95

Table 3 tblProduct table

PurchaseID	Product	CustomerID	Qty	PurchaseDate
PUR1	Cilantro Foot Bath Salts	Grant	2	5/24/2018
PUR2	Turquoise Oasis Exfoliator	Grant	1	5/24/2018
PUR3	Geranium Rose Bath Salts	Jones	1	5/24/2018
PUR4	Geranium Rose Bath Salts	Burton	1	5/25/2018
PUR5	Cilantro Foot Bath Salts	Jones	2	5/26/2018
PUR6	Avocado Foot Care Cream	Berg	1	5/26/2018
PUR7	Turquoise Oasis Bath Salts	Berg	3	5/26/2018

Table 4 tblPurchase table

ProductDescription	CustomerID	Qty	Price	PurchaseDate
New Mexico Mud Mask			$ 8.50	
Turquoise Oasis Exfoliator	Grant	1	$ 8.50	5/24/2018
Turquoise Oasis Face Moisturizer			$ 7.25	
Geranium Rose Bath Salts	Jones	1	$19.95	5/24/2018
Geranium Rose Bath Salts	Burton	1	$19.95	5/25/2018
Cilantro Foot Bath Salts	Grant	2	$19.95	5/24/2018
Cilantro Foot Bath Salts	Jones	2	$19.95	5/26/2018
Avocado Foot Care Cream	Berg	1	$ 9.00	5/26/2018
Turquoise Oasis Bath Salts	Berg	3	$19.95	5/26/2018

Table 5 Data set of left join query

The **RIGHT JOIN clause** is used when you want to return only rows that have matching data in the right table even if no matching rows exist in the left table. For example, you can create a query that includes all the records from the Purchase table and related transactions in the Product table as shown in Figure 35. In this case, you may have a record of purchases for products that you no longer sell and that have been deleted from the Product table.

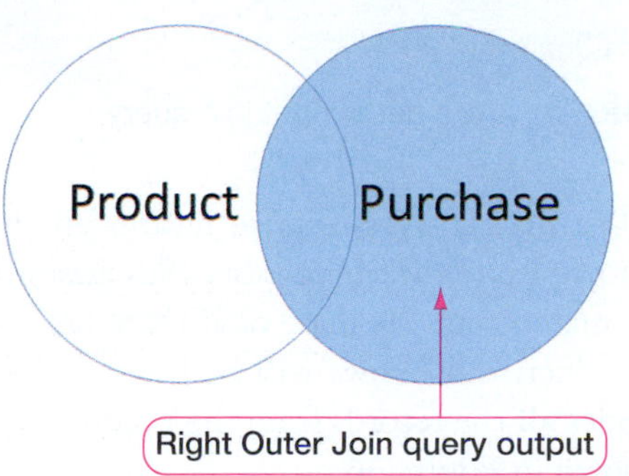

Figure 35 The output of the right join lies in the intersection of both circles and all the data in the Purchase (right) table

The data set of the SQL query
SELECT ProductDescription, Category, CustomerID, Quantity, Price, PurchaseDate FROM Product RIGHT JOIN Purchase ON Product.ProductID = Purchase.ProductID;

would include all purchases, whether or not the product still exists in the Product table as shown in Tables 6, 7, and 8.

ProductID	ProductDescription	Category	QtyInStock	Price
P001	New Mexico Mud Mask	Face	100	$ 8.50
P002	Turquoise Oasis Exfoliator	House Brand	94	$ 8.50
P003	Turquoise Oasis Face Moisturizer	House Brand	80	$ 7.25
P006	Avocado Foot Care Cream	Foot	104	$ 9.00
P007	Turquoise Oasis Bath Salts	House Brand	27	$19.95

Table 6 Product table

PurchaseID	Product	CustomerID	Qty	PurchaseDate
PUR1	Cilantro Foot Bath Salts	Grant	2	5/24/2018
PUR2	Turquoise Oasis Exfoliator	Grant	1	5/24/2018
PUR3	Geranium Rose Bath Salts	Jones	1	5/24/2018
PUR4	Geranium Rose Bath Salts	Burton	1	5/25/2018
PUR5	Cilantro Foot Bath Salts	Jones	2	5/26/2018
PUR6	Avocado Foot Care Cream	Berg	1	5/26/2018
PUR7	Turquoise Oasis Bath Salts	Berg	3	5/26/2018

Table 7 Purchase table

ProductDescription	Category	CustomerID	Qty	Price	PurchaseDate
Cilantro Foot Bath Salts		Grant	2		5/24/2018
Turquoise Oasis Exfoliator	House Brand	Grant	1	$ 8.50	5/24/2018
Geranium Rose Bath Salts		Jones	1		5/24/2018
Geranium Rose Bath Salts		Burton	1		5/25/2018
Cilantro Foot Bath Salts		Jones	2		5/26/2018
Avocado Foot Care Cream	Foot	Berg	1	$19.95	5/26/2018
Turquoise Oasis Bath Salts	House Brand	Berg	3	$19.95	5/26/2018

Table 8 Data set of right join query

The **FULL JOIN clause** returns all the rows from the left table (Product) and all the rows from the right table (Purchase). If there are records in Product that do not have matches in Purchase or if there are records in Purchase that do not have matches in Product, those rows will be listed as well. For example, you can create a query that includes all the records from the Product table and all transactions in the Purchase table, as shown in Figure 36.

Figure 36 Output of full join includes all the data from both circles

Unfortunately, the FULL OUTER JOIN clause is not supported in Microsoft Access. However, you could create a full outer join query by creating a query from two other queries because the rows in a full outer join contain all the rows from a left outer join and a right outer join, with the duplicate rows from both included just once instead of being included twice. This process, however, can be more easily completed with a union query.

In this exercise, you will create several SQL queries using the LEFT and RIGHT OUTER JOINS.

A07.17

To Create Queries Using OUTER JOINS

a. Click the **Create** tab. In the Queries group, click **Query Design**, and then **Close** the Show Table dialog box.

b. On the Design tab, in the Results group, click the **View** arrow, and then select **SQL View**.

c. Delete **SELECT;**, and then type the following, pressing Enter after each line.

```
SELECT CustFirstName, CustLastName, Service, DateOfAppt
FROM tblCustomer
LEFT JOIN tblSchedule ON tblCustomer.CustomerID = tblSchedule.Customer;
```

d. **Save** the query as qryCustomersScheduledLeftJoinSQL. On the Design tab, in the Results group, click **Run**.

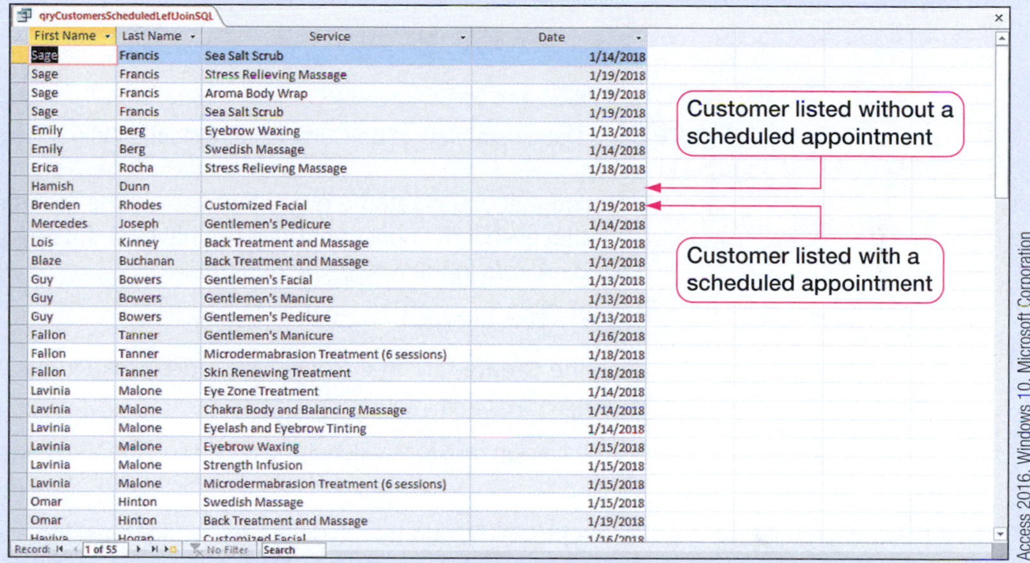

First Name	Last Name	Service	Date
Sage	Francis	Sea Salt Scrub	1/14/2018
Sage	Francis	Stress Relieving Massage	1/19/2018
Sage	Francis	Aroma Body Wrap	1/19/2018
Sage	Francis	Sea Salt Scrub	1/19/2018
Emily	Berg	Eyebrow Waxing	1/13/2018
Emily	Berg	Swedish Massage	1/14/2018
Erica	Rocha	Stress Relieving Massage	1/18/2018
Hamish	Dunn		
Brenden	Rhodes	Customized Facial	1/19/2018
Mercedes	Joseph	Gentlemen's Pedicure	1/14/2018
Lois	Kinney	Back Treatment and Massage	1/13/2018
Blaze	Buchanan	Back Treatment and Massage	1/14/2018
Guy	Bowers	Gentlemen's Facial	1/13/2018
Guy	Bowers	Gentlemen's Manicure	1/13/2018
Guy	Bowers	Gentlemen's Pedicure	1/13/2018
Fallon	Tanner	Gentlemen's Manicure	1/16/2018
Fallon	Tanner	Microdermabrasion Treatment (6 sessions)	1/18/2018
Fallon	Tanner	Skin Renewing Treatment	1/18/2018
Lavinia	Malone	Eye Zone Treatment	1/14/2018
Lavinia	Malone	Chakra Body and Balancing Massage	1/14/2018
Lavinia	Malone	Eyelash and Eyebrow Tinting	1/14/2018
Lavinia	Malone	Eyebrow Waxing	1/15/2018
Lavinia	Malone	Strength Infusion	1/15/2018
Lavinia	Malone	Microdermabrasion Treatment (6 sessions)	1/15/2018
Omar	Hinton	Swedish Massage	1/15/2018
Omar	Hinton	Back Treatment and Massage	1/19/2018

Figure 37 Datasheet View of qryCustomersScheduledLeftJoinSQL

Notice that you created a query that lists all the records from tblCustomer (the left table) even if the customer has not yet scheduled an appointment for a service and lists the related records in tblSchedule (the right table). This query makes it easy to see which customers have yet to schedule a spa service.

e. **Close** the query.

f. Click the **Create** tab. In the Queries group, click **Query Design**, and then **Close** the Show Table dialog box.

g. On the Design tab, in the Results group, click the **View** arrow, and then select **SQL View**.

h. Delete **SELECT;**, and then type the following, pressing Enter after each line.

```
SELECT InvoiceNumber, InvoiceDate, CustFirstName, CustLastName
FROM tblCustomer
LEFT JOIN tblInvoice ON tblCustomer.CustomerID = tblInvoice.CustomerID
ORDER BY CustLastName, CustFirstName;
```

i. **Save** the query as qryCustomersInvoiceLeftJoinSQL. On the Design tab, in the Results group, click **Run**.

CHAPTER 7

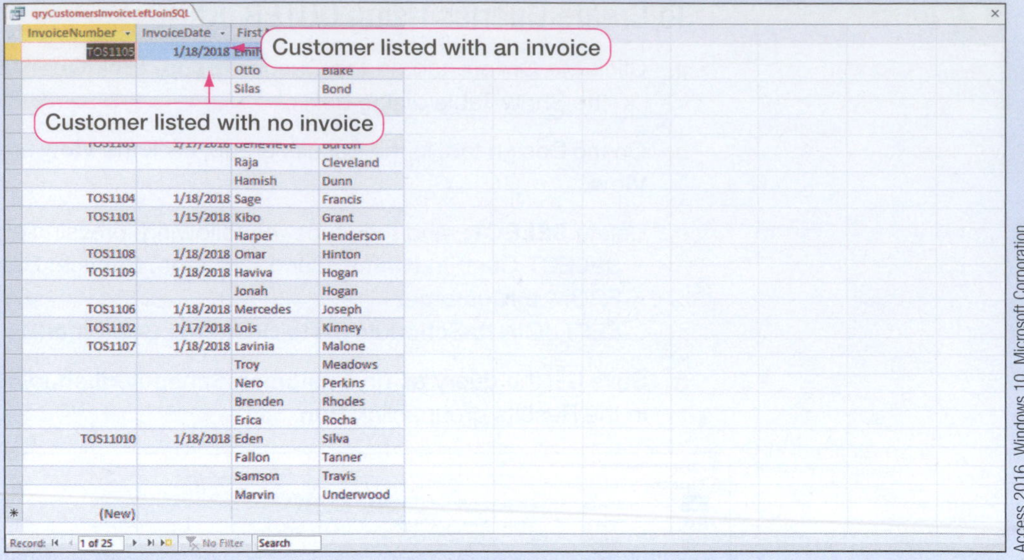

Figure 38 Datasheet View of qryCustomersInvoiceLeftJoinSQL

Notice that you created a query that lists all the records from tblCustomer (the left table) even if the customer does not have an outstanding invoice and lists the related records in tblInvoice (the right table).

j. **Close** ☒ the query.

k. Click the **Create** tab. In the Queries group, click **Query Design**, and then **Close** ☒ the Show Table dialog box.

l. On the Design tab, in the Results group, click the **View** arrow, and then select **SQL View**.

m. Delete **SELECT;**, and then type the following, pressing Enter after each line.

```
SELECT ServiceName, DateOfAppt, Customer, Fee, LengthOfService
FROM tblSchedule
RIGHT JOIN tblService ON tblSchedule.Service= tblService.ServiceID;
```

n. **Save** the query as qryScheduledServicesRightJoinSQL. On the Design tab, in the Results group, click **Run**.

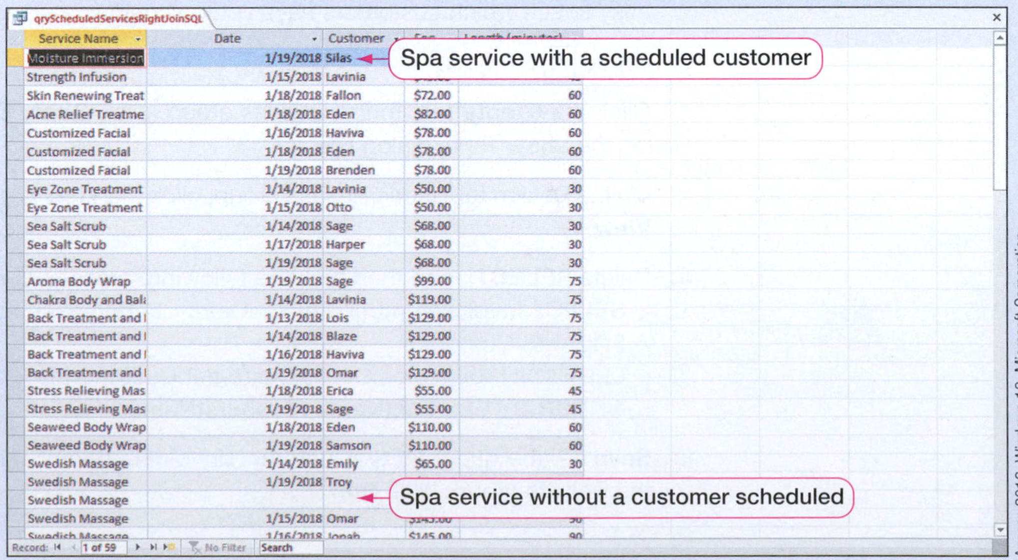

Figure 39 Datasheet View of qryScheduledServicesRightJoinSQL

Notice that you created a query that lists all the records from tblService (the right table) and the related records in tblSchedule (the left table). This query makes it easy to see which spa services have yet to be scheduled. Your query should include 59 records.

o. **Close** [X] the query.

p. Click the **Create** tab. In the Queries group, click **Query Design**, and then **Close** [X] the Show Table dialog box.

q. On the Design tab, in the Results group, click the **View** arrow, and then select **SQL View**.

r. Delete **SELECT;**, and then type the following, pressing Enter after each line.

```
SELECT EmpFirstName, EmpLastName, Service, DateOfAppt
FROM tblSchedule RIGHT JOIN tblEmployee ON tblSchedule.Employee =
tblEmployee.EmployeeID
ORDER BY EmpLastName DESC, EmpFirstName DESC;
```

s. **Save** [Save] the query as qryEmployeesScheduledRightJoinSQL. On the Design tab, in the Results group, click **Run**.

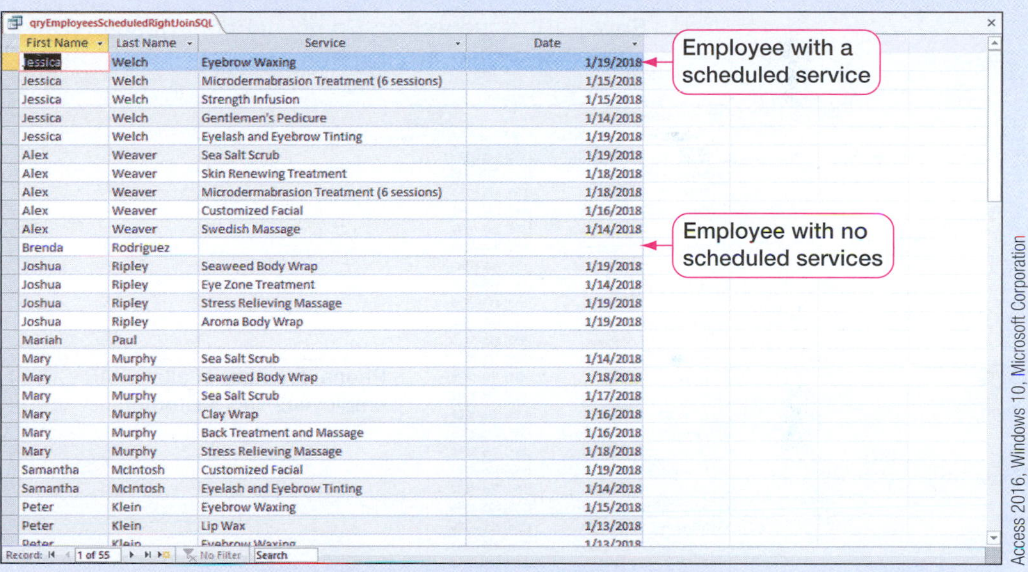

qryEmployeesScheduledRightJoinSQL

First Name	Last Name	Service	Date
Jessica	Welch	Eyebrow Waxing	1/19/2018
Jessica	Welch	Microdermabrasion Treatment (6 sessions)	1/15/2018
Jessica	Welch	Strength Infusion	1/15/2018
Jessica	Welch	Gentlemen's Pedicure	1/14/2018
Jessica	Welch	Eyelash and Eyebrow Tinting	1/19/2018
Alex	Weaver	Sea Salt Scrub	1/19/2018
Alex	Weaver	Skin Renewing Treatment	1/18/2018
Alex	Weaver	Microdermabrasion Treatment (6 sessions)	1/18/2018
Alex	Weaver	Customized Facial	1/16/2018
Alex	Weaver	Swedish Massage	1/14/2018
Brenda	Rodriguez		
Joshua	Ripley	Seaweed Body Wrap	1/19/2018
Joshua	Ripley	Eye Zone Treatment	1/14/2018
Joshua	Ripley	Stress Relieving Massage	1/19/2018
Joshua	Ripley	Aroma Body Wrap	1/19/2018
Mariah	Paul		
Mary	Murphy	Sea Salt Scrub	1/14/2018
Mary	Murphy	Seaweed Body Wrap	1/18/2018
Mary	Murphy	Sea Salt Scrub	1/17/2018
Mary	Murphy	Clay Wrap	1/16/2018
Mary	Murphy	Back Treatment and Massage	1/16/2018
Mary	Murphy	Stress Relieving Massage	1/18/2018
Samantha	McIntosh	Customized Facial	1/19/2018
Samantha	McIntosh	Eyelash and Eyebrow Tinting	1/14/2018
Peter	Klein	Eyebrow Waxing	1/15/2018
Peter	Klein	Lip Wax	1/13/2018

Figure 40 Datasheet View of qryEmployeesScheduledRightJoinSQL

Notice that you created a query that lists all the records from tblEmployee (the right table) and the related records in tblSchedule (the left table). This query makes it easy to see which employees have yet to be scheduled for a spa service.

t. **Close** [X] the query.

Creating a Union Query

A **union query**, like a query that uses the FULL JOIN clause, is used to query unrelated tables or queries and combine the results into a single data set. This type of query is different from querying related tables, as it combines two SQL SELECT statements. The data sets must have similar structures: The data types must match, though field names do not need to be the same, and the columns in each SELECT statement must be in the same order.

The salon and spa's management team wants to create a phone directory from both the Client table and the Employee table of data. If you were restricted to using the query design grid, you would have to create two queries — one for each table — and then combine the results. A union query can examine both tables at the same time and then present the results as a single data set. In this exercise, you will create a union query to display a comprehensive phone directory of customers and employees.

To Create a Union Query

a. Click the **Create** tab. In the Queries group, click **Query Design**, and then **Close** [X] the Show Table dialog box.

b. On the Design tab, in the Query Type group, click **Union**. Access will automatically switch to SQL view.

c. Type the following, pressing Enter after each line.

```
SELECT CustFirstName AS FirstName, CustLastName AS LastName,
CustPhone AS Phone
FROM tblCustomer
UNION SELECT EmpFirstName, EmpLastName, EmpPhone
FROM tblEmployee
ORDER BY LastName, FirstName;
```

d. **Save** the query as qryCompletePhoneDirectoryUnionSQL. On the Design tab, in the Results group, click **Run**.

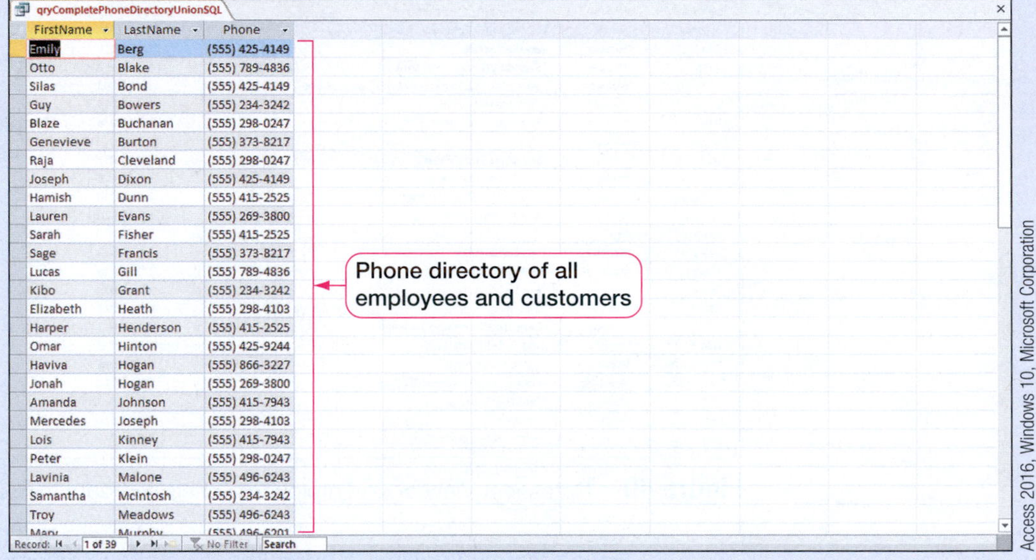

FirstName	LastName	Phone
Emily	Berg	(555) 425-4149
Otto	Blake	(555) 789-4836
Silas	Bond	(555) 425-4149
Guy	Bowers	(555) 234-3242
Blaze	Buchanan	(555) 298-0247
Genevieve	Burton	(555) 373-8217
Raja	Cleveland	(555) 298-0247
Joseph	Dixon	(555) 425-4149
Hamish	Dunn	(555) 415-2525
Lauren	Evans	(555) 269-3800
Sarah	Fisher	(555) 415-2525
Sage	Francis	(555) 373-8217
Lucas	Gill	(555) 789-4836
Kibo	Grant	(555) 234-3242
Elizabeth	Heath	(555) 298-4103
Harper	Henderson	(555) 415-2525
Omar	Hinton	(555) 425-9244
Haviva	Hogan	(555) 866-3227
Jonah	Hogan	(555) 269-3800
Amanda	Johnson	(555) 415-7943
Mercedes	Joseph	(555) 298-4103
Lois	Kinney	(555) 415-7943
Peter	Klein	(555) 298-0247
Lavinia	Malone	(555) 496-6243
Samantha	McIntosh	(555) 234-3242
Troy	Meadows	(555) 496-6243
Mary	Murphy	(555) 496-6201

Figure 41 Datasheet View of qryCompletePhoneDirectoryUnionSQL

Notice that you created a phone directory of all employees and customers, which includes a total of 39 records in the data set.

e. **Close** [X] the query.

CONSIDER THIS | **How Can You Tell an Employee from a Customer?**

Having a comprehensive phone directory can be useful but not if you can't tell which are the customers and which are the employees. Can you think of a way to modify the SQL to make this happen? Perhaps adding a new field?

Creating a SQL Subquery

A SQL **subquery** is a separate SELECT statement that is nested inside the main SELECT statement. This type of query is an alternative way of returning data from multiple tables and will be performed once for each row of the resulting data set. A subquery is usually added in the WHERE clause of the SQL SELECT statement. Most of the time, a subquery is used when you know how to search for a value using a SELECT statement but do not know the exact value.

For example, you may want to query your StoreSalesData table to find sales data for a specific district or region. However, if you do not know all the store numbers but know the district or region where the stores are located, you can write a subquery that will retrieve the information you desire, as shown in Figure 42.

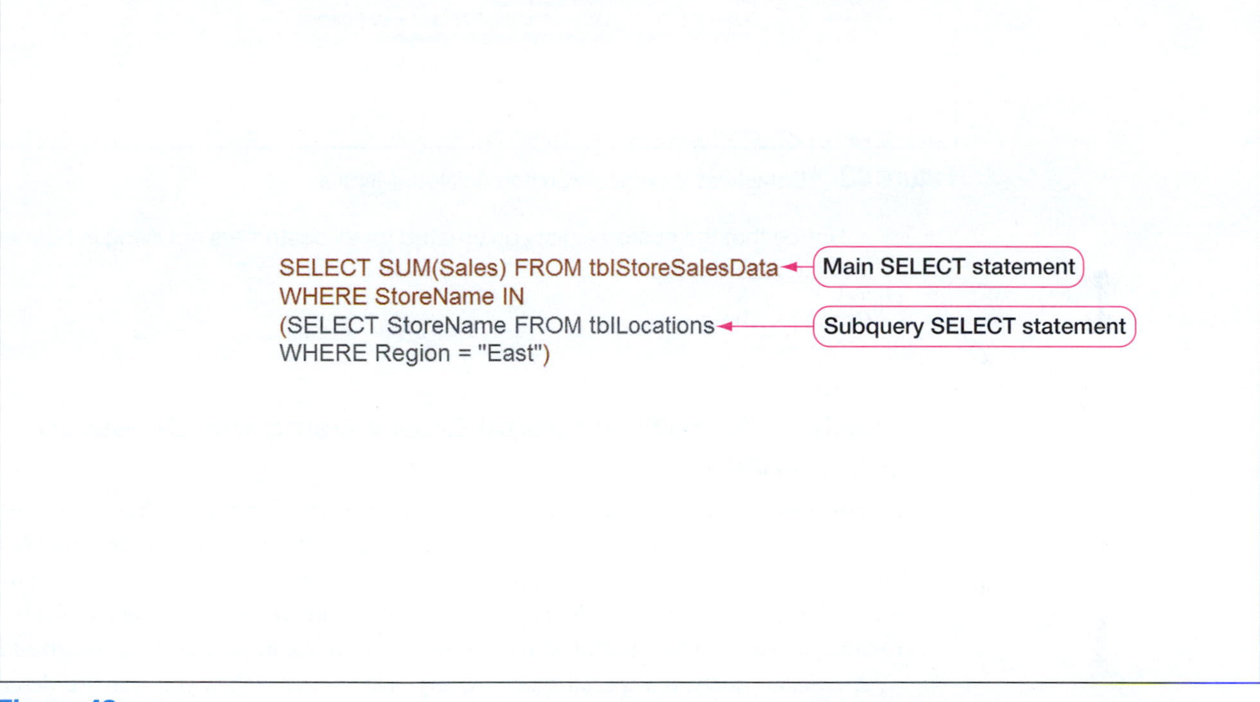

Figure 42 Structure of a SQL subquery

In this exercise, you will create a query using SQL that will display all customers who do not live in Minnesota.

To Create a SQL Subquery

a. Click the **Create** tab. In the Queries group, click **Query Design**, and then **Close** the Show Table dialog box.

b. On the Design tab, in the Results group, click the **View** arrow, and then select **SQL View**.

c. Delete **SELECT;**, and then type the following, pressing Enter after each line.

```
SELECT CustomerID, CustFirstName, CustLastName, CustState, CustEmail
FROM tblCustomer
WHERE CustomerID NOT IN (SELECT CustomerID
FROM tblCustomer
WHERE CustState = 'MN');
```

d. **Save** the query as qryCustomersNotInMNSQL. On the Design tab, in the Results group, click **Run**.

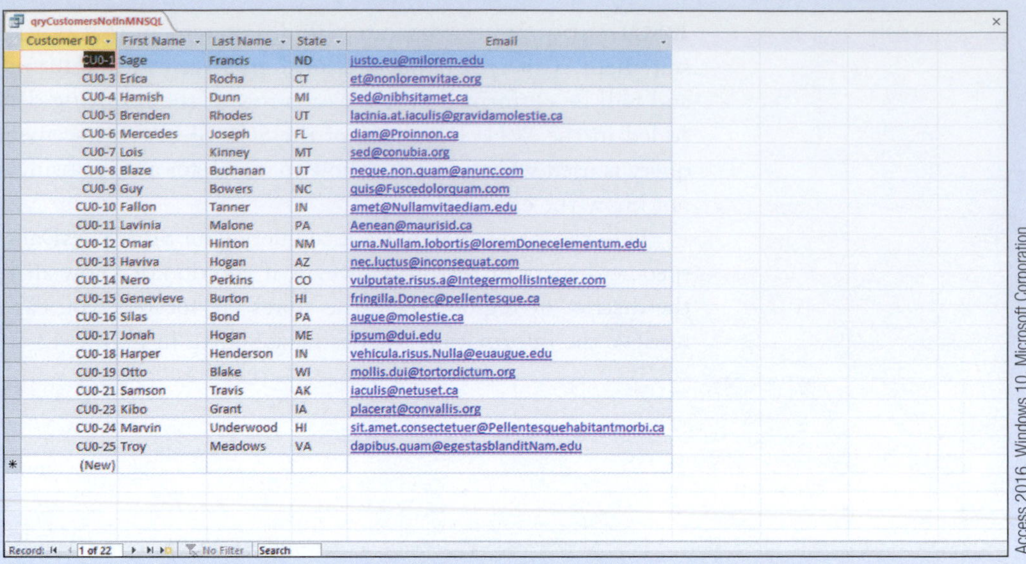

qryCustomersNotInMNSQL

Customer ID	First Name	Last Name	State	Email
CU0-1	Sage	Francis	ND	justo.eu@milorem.edu
CU0-3	Erica	Rocha	CT	et@nonloremvitae.org
CU0-4	Hamish	Dunn	MI	Sed@nibhsitamet.ca
CU0-5	Brenden	Rhodes	UT	lacinia.at.iaculis@gravidamolestie.ca
CU0-6	Mercedes	Joseph	FL	diam@Proinnon.ca
CU0-7	Lois	Kinney	MT	sed@conubia.org
CU0-8	Blaze	Buchanan	UT	neque.non.quam@anunc.com
CU0-9	Guy	Bowers	NC	quis@Fuscedolorquam.com
CU0-10	Fallon	Tanner	IN	amet@Nullamvitaediam.edu
CU0-11	Lavinia	Malone	PA	Aenean@maurisid.ca
CU0-12	Omar	Hinton	NM	urna.Nullam.lobortis@loremDonecelementum.edu
CU0-13	Haviva	Hogan	AZ	nec.luctus@inconsequat.com
CU0-14	Nero	Perkins	CO	vulputate.risus.a@Integermollisinteger.com
CU0-15	Genevieve	Burton	HI	fringilla.Donec@pellentesque.ca
CU0-16	Silas	Bond	PA	augue@molestie.ca
CU0-17	Jonah	Hogan	ME	ipsum@dui.edu
CU0-18	Harper	Henderson	IN	vehicula.risus.Nulla@euaugue.edu
CU0-19	Otto	Blake	WI	mollis.dui@tortordictum.org
CU0-21	Samson	Travis	AK	iaculis@netuset.ca
CU0-23	Kibo	Grant	IA	placerat@convallis.org
CU0-24	Marvin	Underwood	HI	sit.amet.consectetuer@Pellentesquehabitantmorbi.ca
CU0-25	Troy	Meadows	VA	dapibus.quam@egestasblanditNam.edu
*	(New)			

Record: 1 of 22 No Filter Search

Figure 43 Datasheet View of qryCustomersNotInMNSQL

Notice that the customer list you created for all customers not living in Minnesota includes 22 records.

e. **Close** [X] the query.

Create a Two-Dimensional Query Using the Crosstab Query Wizard

A **crosstab query** is different from the aggregate functions that you have been completing thus far because it groups the aggregates by the column and row headings. The added value in decision making is that crosstab queries are useful for summarizing data, calculating statistics, identifying bad data, and looking for trends. Additionally, crosstab queries can be a useful way to present data in a compact and summarized format.

A crosstab query is a special type of query that you use when you want to describe one number in terms of two other numbers. For example, suppose you wanted to know how much money was made from each service at the spa each month. This would require the construction of a crosstab query to display the information. A crosstab query uses aggregate functions and then groups the results by two sets of values — one down the side of the datasheet as rows and the other across the top as columns — and transforms rows of data to columns.

When you create a crosstab query, you specify which fields will be used as the row headings, which field's values will be used as the column headings, and which fields contain values to summarize. Only one field can be used when you specify the column heading and value to summarize. However, up to three fields can be used as row headings. Furthermore, expressions can be used to create row headings, column headings, or values to summarize. In this section, you will create and edit a crosstab query.

Using the Crosstab Query Wizard

As with other wizards in Access, the **Crosstab Query Wizard** is the easiest way to create a crosstab query. While the wizard does help automate the creation process, there are some things that the wizard cannot do for you. Even though the wizard may not be able to create the perfect crosstab query, you can use it to create a basic crosstab query and then modify the query's design within Design view.

In this exercise, you will use the Crosstab Query Wizard to create a crosstab query that will display each employee along with the total customers and a count of how many appointments each employee has per day.

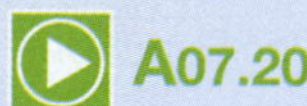
A07.20

To Use the Crosstab Query Wizard

a. Click the **Create** tab, and then, in the Queries group, click **Query Wizard**.

b. In the New Query dialog box, click **Crosstab Query Wizard**, and then click **OK**.

c. Click **Table: tblSchedule**, and then click **Next**.

d. Double-click the **Employee** field. The Employee field will be used as the row heading in the crosstab query.

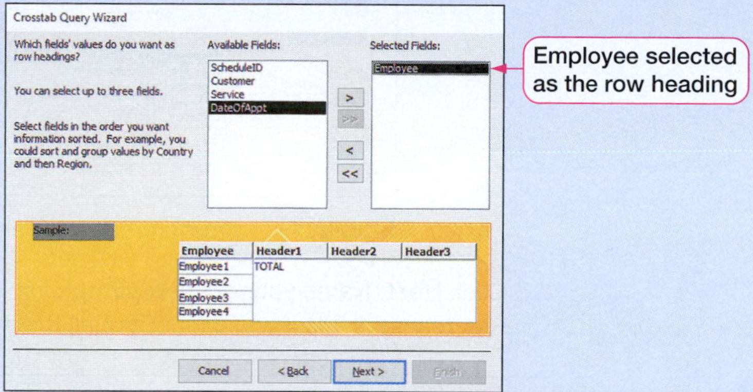

Figure 44 Crosstab Query Wizard with row heading selected
Access 2016, Windows 10, Microsoft Corporation

e. Click **Next**. Click the **DateOfAppt** field. The DateOfAppt field will be used as the column headings in the crosstab query.

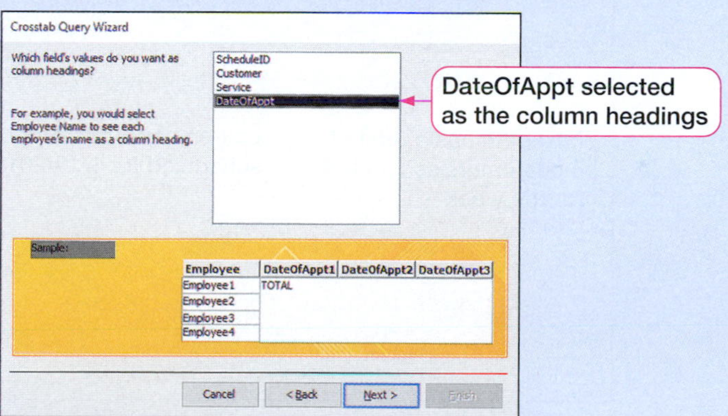

Figure 45 Crosstab Query Wizard with column heading selected
Access 2016, Windows 10, Microsoft Corporation

f. Click **Next**. Click **Date** as the interval.

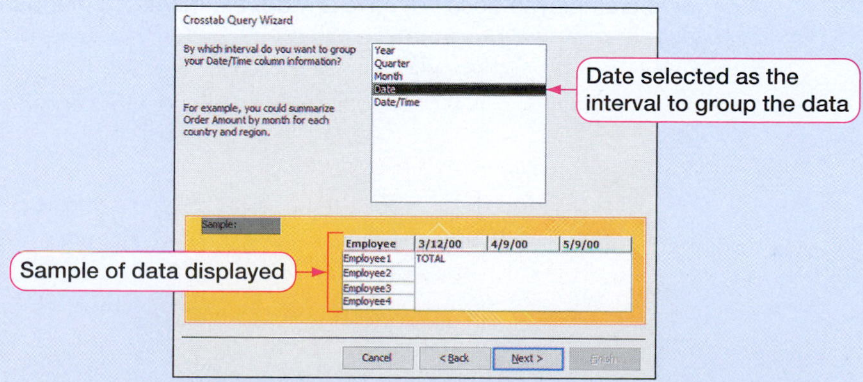

Figure 46 Crosstab Query Wizard with interval selected
Access 2016, Windows 10, Microsoft Corporation

CHAPTER 7

g. Click **Next**. Click **Customer** under Fields, and then click **Count** under Functions to view how many customers each employee has on a given day.

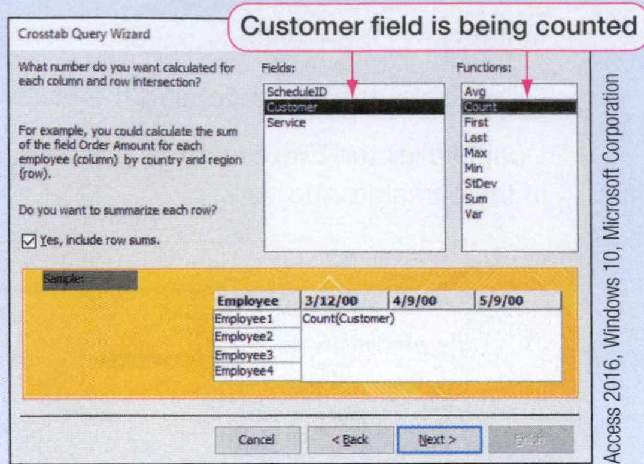

Figure 47 Crosstab Query Wizard with calculation type selected

h. Click **Next**. Name your query qryEmployeeDailySummary, and then click **Finish**. Resize your fields if you cannot see all the data and column headings.

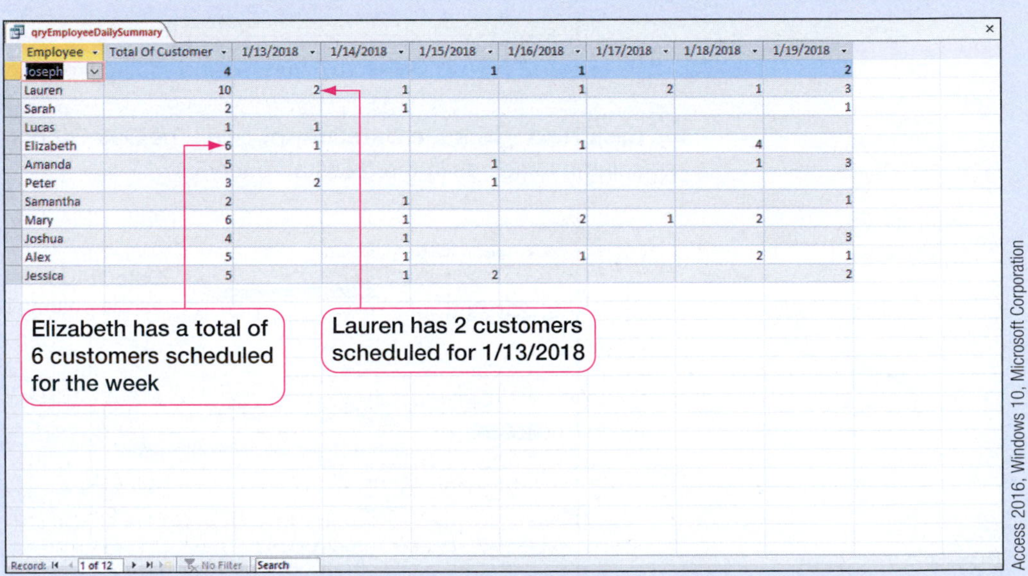

qryEmployeeDailySummary

Employee	Total Of Customer	1/13/2018	1/14/2018	1/15/2018	1/16/2018	1/17/2018	1/18/2018	1/19/2018
Joseph	4			1	1			2
Lauren	10	2	1		1	2	1	3
Sarah	2		1					1
Lucas	1	1						
Elizabeth	6	1			1		4	
Amanda	5			1			1	3
Peter	3	2		1				
Samantha	2		1					1
Mary	6		1		2	1	2	
Joshua	4		1					3
Alex	5		1		1		2	1
Jessica	5		1	2				2

Record: 1 of 12 No Filter Search

Figure 48 Datasheet View of qryEmployeeDailySummary

Notice that each employee is listed along with the total customers and a count of how many appointments each employee has per day. Empty fields indicate that the employee does not have any appointments on that particular day.

REAL WORLD ADVICE | **What the Crosstab Query Wizard Cannot Do**

Although the Crosstab Query Wizard can be very helpful in creating crosstab queries, there are a few things that cannot be done in progressing through the wizard.

1. The wizard will let you select fields from only one table. If you want to use fields from multiple tables, you need to add the tables in Design view.
2. You cannot create expressions in the wizard.
3. You cannot add a parameter prompt.
4. You cannot specify a list of fixed values to be used as column headings.

Although these tasks cannot be done within the wizard, any of them can be added to the query design grid by simply going into Design view.

Editing a Crosstab Query

When you work in Design view, you have more control over your query design, which enables features to be added that are not available in the wizard. When you edit a crosstab query in Design view, you use the Total and Crosstab rows in the design grid to specify three criteria.

- Which field value becomes the column heading
- Which field values become row headings
- Which field values are to be calculated

In this exercise, you will edit the qryEmployeeDailySummary crosstab query so that, when run, it prompts the user for an employee ID or an appointment date to view the number of appointments scheduled.

To Edit a Crosstab Query

a. Click the **File** tab, click **Save As**, use the Save Object As option, and then save your query as qryEmployeeDailySummaryEdit.

b. Switch to **Design** view, and then resize your fields in the query design grid if you cannot see all the text.

c. In the Criteria row of the Employee field, type [Enter Employee ID]. This edits the query so the manager can enter a specific employee ID and view how many appointments that employee has scheduled that week.

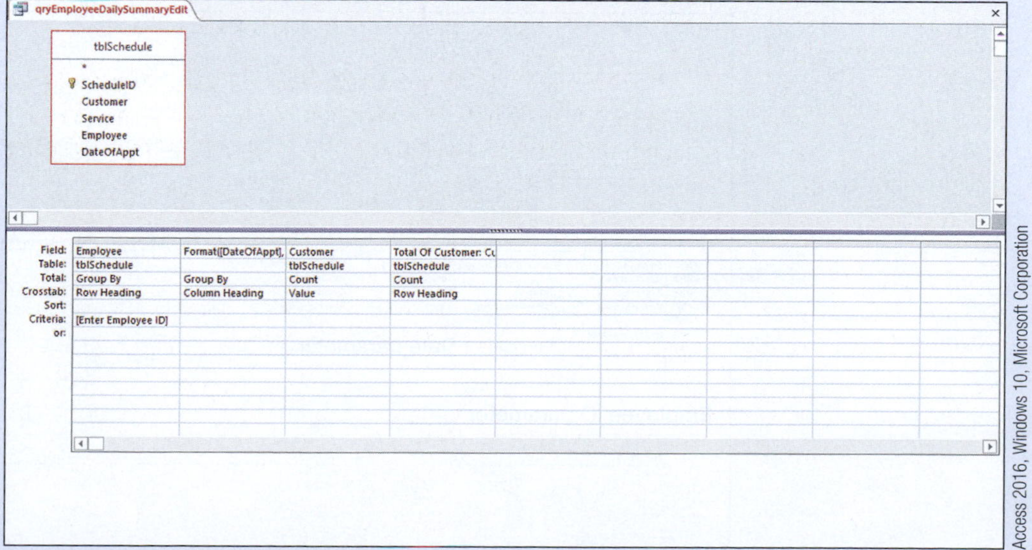

Figure 49 Design View with parameter criteria for Employee

d. On the Design tab, in the Show/Hide group, click **Parameters**.

e. In the Query Parameters dialog box, in the Parameter column, type the same parameter that you used in the Criteria row: [Enter Employee ID].

f. Press Tab. Click the **Data Type** arrow, select **Integer**, and then click **OK**.

g. On the Design tab, in the Results group, click **Run**. In the Enter Parameter Value dialog box, type **2**, and then click **OK**.

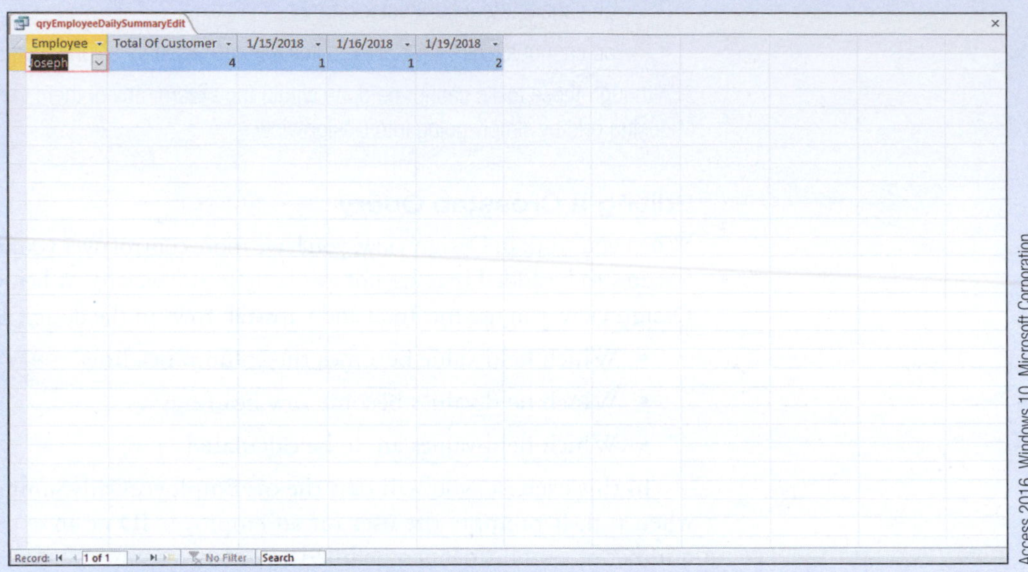

Figure 50 Datasheet View displaying summary for Employee ID 2

> **SIDE NOTE**
> **Only a Week of Data Appears**
> Remember that the spa manager gave you a portion of the data. If you had the full database, you would see every date, which could extend over months or years.

Notice how you can see only Joseph's four appointments for the week.

h. Switch to **Design** view. In the Or row, under the Format([DateOfAppt],"Short Date") field, type [Enter Date]. This will allow the manager to enter a specific employee number or a specific date.

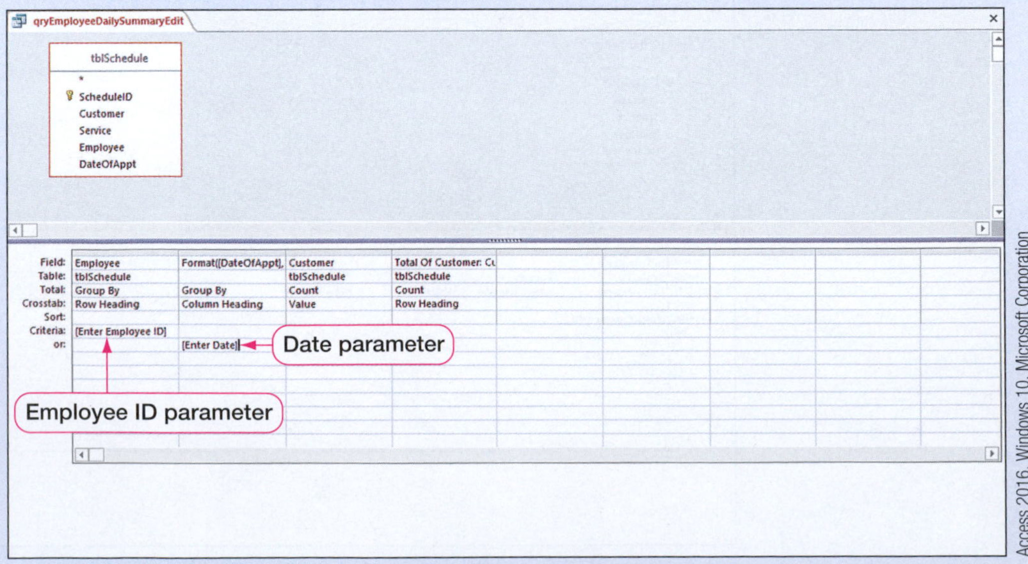

Figure 51 Design View with parameter criteria for DateOfAppt

i. On the Design tab, in the Show/Hide group, click **Parameters**.

j. In the Query Parameters dialog box, in the second row of the Parameter column, type the same parameter that you used in the Criteria row: [Enter Date].

k. Press Tab. Select **Date with Time** in the Data Type column, and then click **OK**.

l. On the Design tab, in the Results group, click **Run**. When the Enter Employee Number Parameter prompt appears, do not enter anything. Click **OK**.

m. When the Enter Date Parameter prompt appears, type 1/18/2018, and then click **OK**.

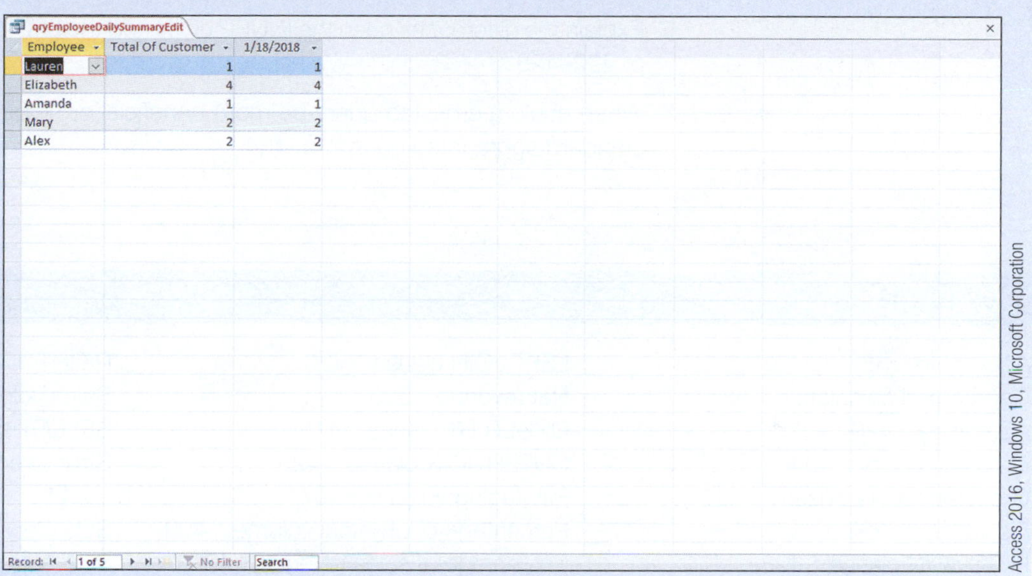

Figure 52 Datasheet View of qryEmployeeDailySummaryEdit

Notice how you can see all employees who have appointments on 1/18/2018. This happened because you did not enter a specific employee number. Therefore, Access displayed every employee number.

n. **Save** and **Close** the query. If Access prompts you to enter parameters as you are saving your changes, click **OK** twice. Exit Access, and then submit your file as directed by your instructor.

Concept Check

1. Give two more business examples of when you could use the sales revenue calculation. p. 388
2. Explain how an aggregate function differs from a calculated field. p. 392
3. Give two more business examples of when you could use the volume — either physical or sales — calculation. p. 397
4. What is the difference between using the WHERE clause and using the HAVING clause? p. 414, 420
5. Explain the differences been the INNER JOIN and the LEFT and RIGHT OUTER JOINS. p. 422–428
6. When could a crosstab query be more beneficial or helpful to use than a SELECT or standard aggregated query? p. 434

Key Terms

Aggregate 387
Aggregated calculation 387
AS clause 420
Crosstab query 434
Crosstab Query Wizard 434
Fiscal year 393
FULL JOIN clause 428
GROUP BY clause 387
HAVING clause 420
INNER JOIN clause 422
Join 422
LEFT JOIN clause 426
Net revenue 393
ORDER BY clause 418
OUTER JOIN clause 425
Packaging volume 407
Percentage of physical volume 409
Percentage of sales revenue 400
Percentage of sales volume 404
Physical volume 397
Predicate 422
Revenue 393
RIGHT JOIN clause 427
Sales volume 388
SELECT statement 413
Structured Query Language (SQL) 411
Subquery 398
SQL subquery 433
Underlying SQL statement 412
Union query 431
WHERE clause 392

Visual Summary

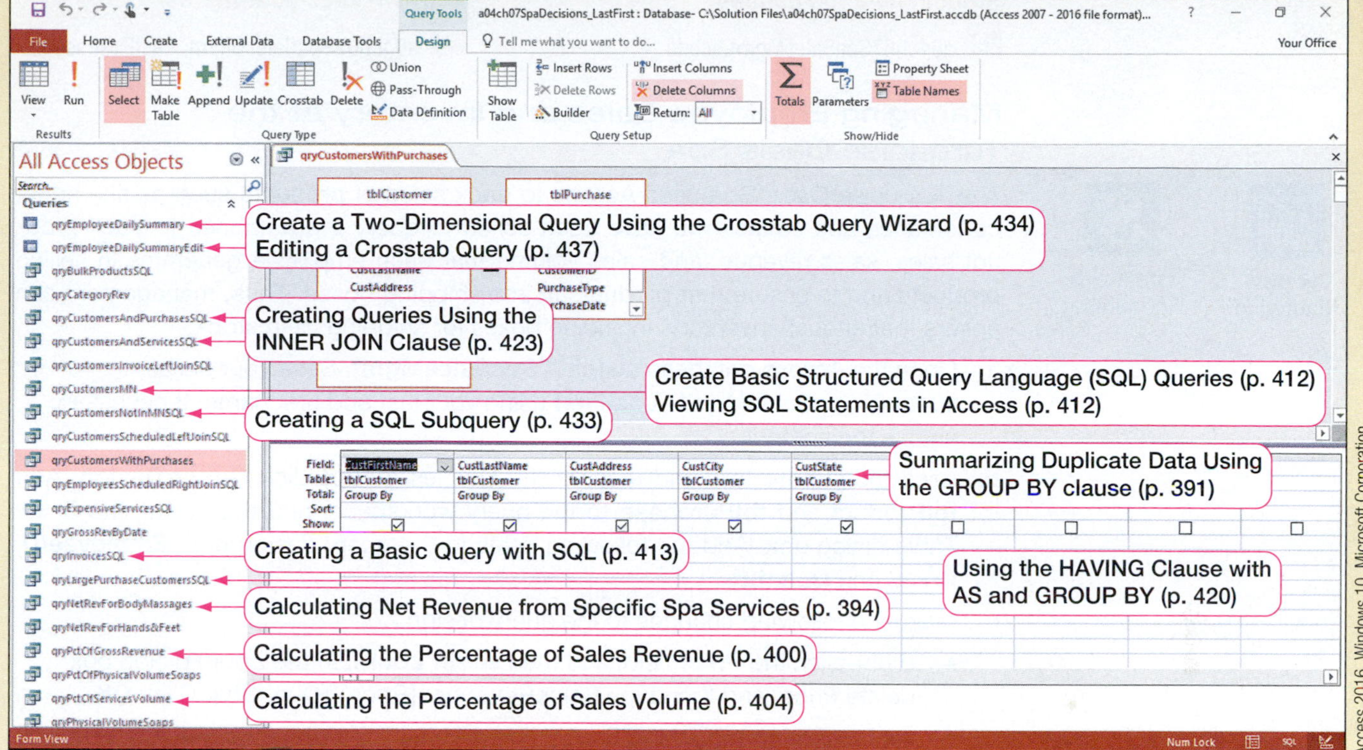

Figure 53

Access 2016, Windows 10, Microsoft Corporation

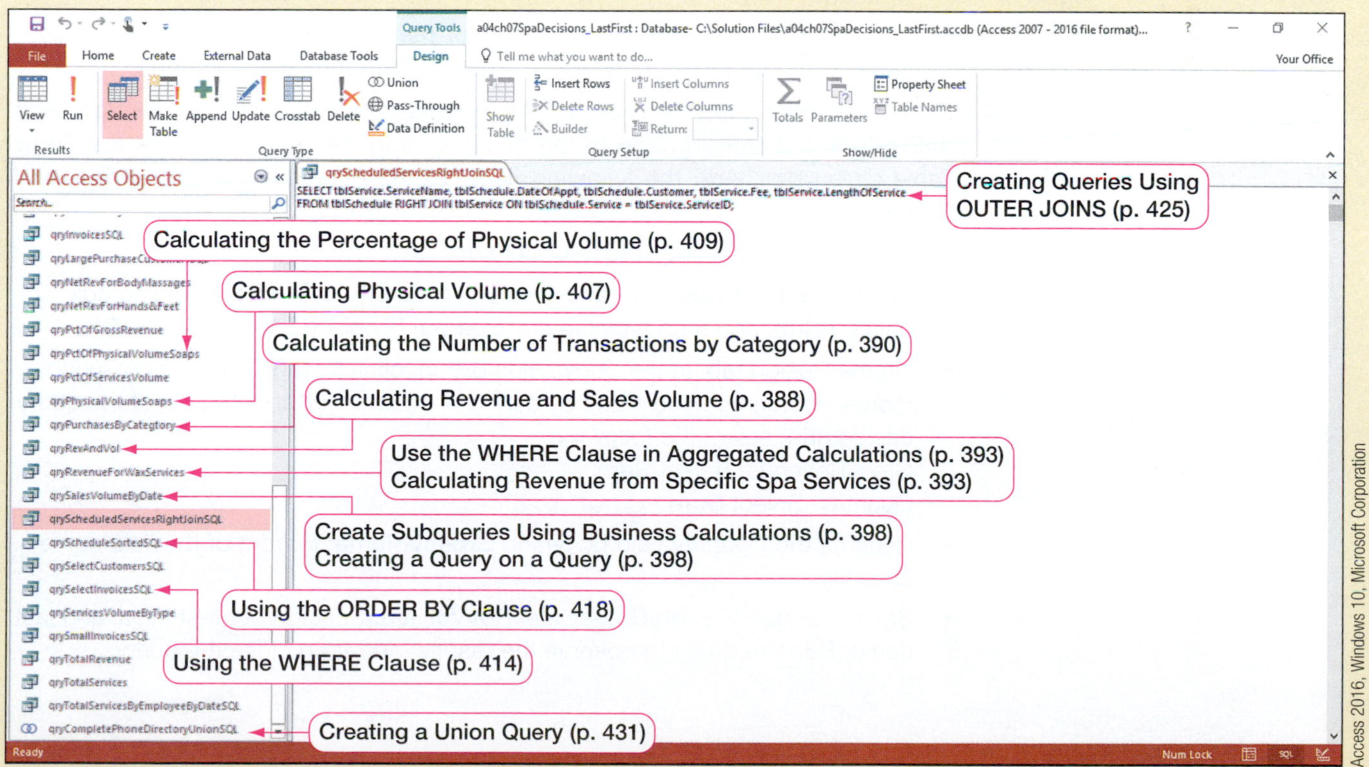

Figure 54

Access 2016, Windows 10, Microsoft Corporation

Practice 1

Student data file needed:

 a04ch07SpaSalesMgmt.accdb

You will save your file as:

 a04ch07SpaSalesMgmt_LastFirst.accdb

Managing Employee Sales and Inventory at the Turquoise Oasis Spa

The Turquoise Oasis Spa uses Access to track sales of products such as shampoo, conditioner, and soaps. You have been asked to query the database to track product sales, sales revenue, and sales volume that each employee generates in selling products and to ensure that products fit into shipping boxes. Thus, management can ensure that enough inventory, including boxes for shipping, is in stock.

a. Open the Access database **a04ch07SpaSalesMgmt**. Save your file as a04ch07SpaSalesMgmt _LastFirst using your last and first name. If necessary, enable the content.

b. Click the **Create** tab, and then, in the Queries group, click **Query Design**. Add **tblProduct** and **tblPurchase** to the query workspace, and then close the Show Table dialog box. Add the following fields to the query design grid: **EmployeeID**, **Price**, and **Quantity**.

c. Make the following changes to the query design.
   - Right-click the **Price** field, and then select **Zoom**. In the Zoom dialog box, delete Price, and then type SalesRevenue: [Price]*[Quantity]. Click **OK**.
   - On the Design tab, in the Show/Hide group, click **Totals**. To see how much money each employee made by selling products, in the Total row of the query design grid, select the following.
     SalesRevenue: Select **Sum**
     Quantity: Select **Sum**
   - Rename the Quantity field by typing SalesVolume: in front of the field name Quantity.
   - Save your query as qryEmpSalesRevVol_iLast using your first initial and last name. Run the query to observe the results, and then close the query.

d. Click the **Create** tab, and then, in the Queries group, click **Query Design**. Add **tblProduct** and **tblPurchase** to the query workspace, and then close the Show Table dialog box. Add the following fields to the query design grid: **Price**, and **Quantity**.

e. Make the following changes to the query design.
   - Right-click the **Price** field, and then select **Zoom**. In the Zoom dialog box, delete **Price**, and then type GrossRevenue: [Price]*[Quantity]. Click **OK**.
   - On the Design tab, in the Show/Hide group, click **Totals**. To see how much money each employee made by selling products, in the Total row of the query design grid, select the following.
     GrossRevenue: Select **Sum**
     Quantity: Select **Sum**
   - Rename the Quantity field by typing GrossVolume: in front of the field name Quantity.
   - Save your query as qryGrossSalesRevVol_iLast using your first initial and last name. Run the query to observe the results, and then close the query.

f. Click the **Create** tab, and then, in the Queries group, click **Query Design**. Add **qryEmpSalesRevVol_iLast** and **qryGrossRevVol_ilast** to the query workspace, and then close the Show Table dialog box. Add the following fields to the query design grid: **EmployeeID**, **SalesRevenue**, and **SalesVolume**.

g. Make the following changes to the query design.

- In the **next blank field** in the query design grid, in the Zoom dialog box, type PercentOfGrossRevenue:[SalesRevenue]/[GrossRevenue]. Format the PercentOfGrossRevenue field as **Percent**. This expression calculates how each employee's sales revenue contributed to the total gross sales revenue.
- In the **next blank field** in the query design grid, in the Zoom dialog box, type PercentOfGrossVolume:[SalesVolume]/[GrossVolume]. Format the PercentOfGrossVolume field as **Percent**. This expression calculates how each employee's sales volume contributed to the total gross sales volume.
- Sort in Descending by PercentOfGrossRevenue.
- Save your query as qryRevenueAnalysis_iLast using your first initial and last name. On the Design tab, in the Results group, click **Run**. Resize your fields if you cannot see all the data and column headings.
- On the Home tab, in the Records group, click **Totals**. Average your SalesRevenue and SalesVolume fields. This will determine whether employees are selling at, above, or below average. Sum your PercentOfGrossRevenue and PercentOfGrossVolume fields to ensure that they equal 100%.
- Save and close the query.

h. Click the **Create** tab, and then, in the Queries group, click **Query Design**. Add **tblProduct** to the query workspace, and then close the Show Table dialog box. Add the following field to the query design grid: **ProductDescription**.

i. Make the following changes to the query design.

- Determine the physical volume by calculating width × length × depth. In the **first blank field** in the query design grid, in the Zoom dialog box, type PhysicalVolume:[Width]*[Length]*[Depth].
- For each product, calculate the total number of units that can fit inside a medium sized carton. A medium sized carton is 526 cubic inches. In the **next blank field** in the query design grid, in the Zoom dialog box, type MaxUnitsInCarton:Int(526/[PhysicalVolume]).
- To calculate the percentage of physical volume, use the size of a medium-sized carton that the spa has to ship items to customers: 526 cubic inches. In the **next blank field** in the query design grid, in the Zoom dialog box, type PercentOfPhysicalVolume: [PhysicalVolume]/526, and then format the PercentOfPhysicalVolume field as **Percent**.
- On the Design tab, in the Results group, click **Run**. Resize your fields if you cannot see all the data and column headings.
- Save your query as qryVolumePercent_iLast using your first initial and last name, and then close the query.

j. Click the **Create** tab, and then, in the Queries group, click **Query Wizard** to create a crosstab query.

- Select **tblPurchase**, and then click **Next**.
- Double-click the **ProductID** field as the row heading, and then click **Next**.
- Click the **EmployeeID** field as the column heading, and then click **Next**.
- Click **Quantity** under Fields, and then click **Sum** under Functions to view the products each employee has sold. Click **Next**.
- Save your query as qryEmployeeProductSalesVolume_iLast using your first initial and last name, and then click **Finish**.

- Switch to **Design** view, add the **tblEmployee** table to the query workspace, and then make the following changes to the EmployeeID field.
  Table: Select **tblEmployee**
  Field: Select **EmpFirstName**
- On the Design tab, in the Results group, click **Run**. Resize your fields if you cannot see all the data and column headings.

k. Save and close the query. Exit Access, and then submit your file as directed by your instructor.

Problem Solve 1

Student data file needed:

 a04ch07ProShopSalesAnalysis.accdb

You will save your file as:

 a04ch07ProShopSalesAnalysis_LastFirst.accdb

Advanced Queries with the Red Bluff Golf Course & Pro Shop Database

The managers at the Red Bluff Golf Course & Pro Shop have been collecting and storing their sales data in an Access database and need you to create some queries to help them to make sound business decisions based on data.

a. Open the Access database **a04ch07ProShopSalesAnalysis**. Save your file as a04ch07ProShopSalesAnalysis _LastFirst using your last and first name. If necessary, enable the content.

b. Create a query based on tblTransactions and tblProducts that will calculate the total revenue earned for each ProductType. Add **ProductType** and a calculated field called Revenue to the Query design grid. The Revenue field should multiply Quantity and UnitPrice. Group the results by **ProductType**, sum the Revenue calculation, format the Revenue field as **Currency**, and then sort the results in **Descending** order by Revenue. Name the query qryRevenueByProductType.

c. Create a query based on tblCustomers and tblTransactions that will display the **FirstName**, **LastName**, **StreetAddress**, **City**, **State**, **Zip**, and **Phone** for any resort member who has made a purchase at the Pro Shop during the fourth quarter of 2018. Be sure that each customer is listed only once. Sort in **Ascending** order by LastName. Save the query as qry4thQuarterCustomers.

d. Create a query based on tblTransactions and tblProducts that calculates total sales volume for each ProductType during the first quarter of 2018. The query should calculate the total quantity of items sold by applying the Sum aggregate function to the **Quantity** field. Rename this field Q1SalesVolumeByType. Group the results by **ProductType**. Save the query as qryQ1SalesVolumeByType.

e. Create a query based on tblTransactions that calculates gross sales volume during the first quarter of 2018. The query should calculate the total quantity of items sold by applying the Sum aggregate function to the **Quantity** field. Rename this field TotalQ1SalesVolume. Save the query as qryTotalQ1SalesVolume.

f. Create a subquery based on **qryQ1SalesVolumeByType** and **qryTotalQ1SalesVolume** that calculates the percentage of quarter 1 sales volume for each ProductType. Your subquery should include the **ProductType** field and a calculated field named %OfQ1SalesVolumeByType that divides Q1SalesVolumeByType by TotalQ1SalesVolume. Format the calculated field as **Percent** with **2** decimal places. Sort the results in **Descending** order by %OfQ1SalesVolumeByType. Save the query as qryQ1PercentByTypeSalesVolume.

g. Create a query using SQL based on tblTransactions and tblProducts that calculates total sales volume for each ProductType. Use the INNER JOIN clause to connect the two tables. Use the AS clause to rename the calculated field that totals the Quantity field as HighSalesVolume. Group the results by **ProductType**. Use the HAVING clause to ensure that only products with a total quarter 1 sales volume of at least 200 are returned. Use the ORDER BY clause to sort the results in descending order by the calculated field. Save the query as qryHighSalesVolumeByType.

h. Close the query, exit Access, and then submit your file as directed by your instructor.

Perform 1: Perform in Your Life

Student data file needed:

 a04ch07BigEsElectric.accdb

You will save your file as:

 a04ch07BigEsElectric_LastFirst.accdb

Using SQL to Query the Big E's Electric Database

Your computer internship at a local electronics store, Big E's Electric, is coming to an end, and management is considering offering you a full-time position with the company. For this position, management is looking for someone who is not only familiar with Access but who also is able to write SQL. You have been asked to create some queries in their sales database using only SQL. Additionally, you will create a crosstab query that will help view quarterly data by employee.

a. Open the Access database **a04ch07BigEsElectric**. Save your file as a04ch07BigEsElectric_LastFirst using your last and first name. If necessary, enable the content.

b. Open tblCustomers, and then add your information in record 1. Replace YourName in the FirstName and LastName fields with your first and last name. Close tblCustomers.

c. Create a SQL query based on tblProducts that will display all the fields of those products in the Computers & Tablets category. Save your query as qryCategory_iLast using your first initial and last name.

d. Create a SQL query based on tblTransaction that will display EmployeeID, TransactionDate, and MethodOfPayment of the transactions in which the transaction is between the dates 1/1/2018 and 2/15/2018. Sort in descending order by TransactionDate. Save your query as qryTransDates_iLast using your first initial and last name.

e. Create a SQL query based on tblCustomers that will display all the fields of the customers who live in either Pennsylvania or Indiana. Sort in ascending order by LastName. Save your query as qryPAorIN_iLast using your first initial and last name.

f. Create a SQL query based on tblTransactionDetails that will display the ProductID and a calculated field named TotalSalesVolume. The calculated field should be the total of the Quantity field. Use the HAVING clause so that only products whose total sales volume has exceeded 140 are displayed. Group by ProductID and sort in descending order by TotalSalesVolume. Save your query as qryHighVolumeProducts_iLast using your first initial and last name.

g. Create a SQL union query that will display FirstName, LastName, and Phone for both customers and full-time employees. Name the query qryPhoneListAll_iLast using your first initial and last name. Sort in ascending order by LastName and then by FirstName.

h. Create a crosstab query using the Crosstab Query Wizard. Use the tblTransaction table, select EmployeeID as the row heading, select TransactionDate as the column heading, and group the TransactionDate by Quarter. Calculate the total number of transactions for each employee. Save the crosstab query as qryQtrTransactions_iLast using your first initial and last name. Modify the crosstab query by adding tblEmployees and replacing EmployeeID with LastName. Rename the LastName field to Employee, and then rename the Total of TransactionID field to TotalTransactions. Save the crosstab query as qryQtrTransactions_iLast using your first initial and last name.

i. Create a SQL query based on tblProducts and tblTransactionDetails that will display all the fields from tblProducts and the TransactionID and Quantity fields from tblTransactionDetails. Use a join to include all products, whether or not they have been purchased. Sort in ascending order by TransactionID. Save your query as qryTransactionDetails_iLast using your first initial and last name.

j. Create a SQL query based on tblTransaction and tblEmployees that will display all the fields from tblTransaction and the FirstName and LastName fields from tblEmployees. Use a join to include all employees, whether or not they have sold any products. Sort in ascending order by the employee's last name and then by first name. Save your query as qryEmpTransaction_iLast using your first initial and last name, and then close the query.

k. Close the database, exit Access, and then submit your file as directed by your instructor.

Additional Cases

Additional Workshop Cases are available on the companion website and in the instructor resources.

Microsoft Access 2016

Chapter 8 | ACTION QUERIES AND ADVANCED RELATIONSHIPS

OBJECTIVES

1. Create a new table using a make table query p. 448
2. Append data to a table p. 452
3. Edit and delete data p. 454
4. Work with update queries p. 455
5. Create, test, and run delete queries p. 460
6. Create inner joins p. 465
7. Create outer joins p. 466
8. Use the Find Unmatched Query Wizard p. 469

Prepare Case

Sales & Marketing

The Turquoise Oasis Spa: Understanding Action Queries

The Turquoise Oasis Spa generates revenue through its spa services and product sales. The spa needs updated information to run its business efficiently and to make decisions about the business. The spa manager, Meda Rodate, and the salon manager, Irene Kai, have asked you to automate the creation of tables and data updates through the use of action queries. This will make data management easier and more efficient for the managers and spa employees. Additionally, the managers will be able to track marketing campaigns by viewing the customers who have redeemed coupons and discounts.

Michaeljung/Shutterstock

Student data files needed for this chapter:

 a04ch08Marketing1
 a04ch08Marketing2
 a04ch08Spa2.accdb
 a04ch08Spa3.accdb

You will save your files as:

 a04ch08Spa2_LastFirst.accdb
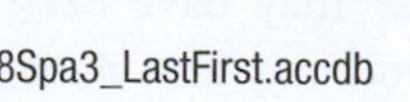 a04ch08Spa3_LastFirst.accdb
 a04ch08Marketing1_LastFirst.accdb
a04ch08Marketing2_LastFirst.accdb

Understanding Action Queries

Thus far, you have been creating select queries. Select queries are used to display and manipulate data but not to change the data. An **action query** is a query that makes changes to records or moves many records from one table to another. Action queries are used to change data in existing tables or make new tables based on a query's dataset. Access offers four different types of action queries:

- A make table query creates a new table based on a query dataset.
- An append query is similar to a make table query, except that a query dataset is appended — added — to an existing table.
- An update query allows the values of one or more fields in a query dataset to be modified.
- A delete query deletes all the records in the underlying table of a query dataset that meet specific criteria.

One important note is that action queries permanently modify the data in tables. Because there is no undo feature for action queries, it is important to be cautious in running any action query. It is a good idea to create a backup of the database in case you need to restore any of the changed data. In this section, you will create and make new table queries, delete queries, update queries, and append queries.

REAL WORLD ADVICE | **Turning Off the Action Query Warning**

When you run an action query, Access will always warn you that you are about to make a change to your data and ask you to confirm the change. You can turn the Access warnings off. However, there are dangers to doing so because you will not know for sure whether the action query executed. For example, if you are running an update query to update employee salaries by $500, you will add $500 on to each employee's salary every time you run the query. If you turn off the warning, you could accidentally increase each employee's salary by $2,500 or more. Of course, employees would not complain, but this would cause tremendous problems for the payroll department and the company's budget. If you do want to avoid being prompted when you run action queries, do the following.

1. Click the File tab.
2. Click Options.
3. In the Access Options dialog box, click Client Settings.
4. Under Editing, under Confirm, clear the Action queries check box.

Create a New Table Using a Make Table Query

When you create a database, you store your data in tables — objects that contain records and fields. For example, you can create a customer table to store a list of customers' first and last names, addresses, and telephone numbers, or an inventory table to store information about the products your company sells. Because other database objects — queries, forms, and reports — depend on tables, you should design your database by creating all of its tables first. You have learned that the manual process of creating tables can take some time if you want to create a database that is constructed properly and functions well.

There are times, however, when you will decide to store and track data that is different from what the database was initially designed for. Thus, you can use existing data to add a new table that will allow you to make better decisions about your business. The process of creating a new table can be automated through a make table query. For example, your database may have been initially built to track customers and the orders they placed. Now you may also want to track marketing efforts and the number of customers who use coupons that were mailed or e-mailed to them. You would need to create a new table to track which customers redeemed coupons and when the coupons were redeemed.

Opening the Starting Files

To create action queries, you first need to open the Spa and Marketing databases.

A08.00

To Open the Spa and Marketing Database

a. Start **Access**, click **Open Other Files** in the left pane, and then click **This PC**. Navigate through the folder structure to the location of your student data files, and then double-click **a04ch08Spa2**.

b. Click the **File** tab, save the file as an **Access Database**, and click **Save As**. Navigate to the location where you are saving your project files, and then change the filename to a04ch08Spa2_LastFirst using your last and first name. Click **Save**. If necessary, enable the content.

c. Open the **a04ch08Spa3** database. Save your file as a04ch08Spa3_LastFirst using your last and first name.

d. Open the **a04ch08Marketing1** database. Save your file as a04ch08Marketing1_LastFirst using your last and first name.

e. Open the **a04ch08Marketing2** database. Save your file as a04ch08Marketing2_LastFirst using your last and first name.

Creating a Make Table Query

A **make table query** acquires data from one or more tables and then creates a new table from the resulting dataset when you run the query. The new table can be added to the current database that you have open to build the new table. You can create a make table query by first creating a select query and then changing it to a make table query. Your initial select query can include calculated fields and expressions to return the desired data along with allowing you to verify your results before running the query.

You can also create the make table query in one database and then have Access build the table in another database. This allows you to use data in one database — the one in which the make table query resides — and copy that data into a new table within another database. For example, you may decide at some point, perhaps once you have a few years' worth of data, that you want to archive some of the older data into another database.

Archiving data is an important task in business. Managers do not want to delete historical data because it might be useful to help manage and develop their businesses. A major use of historical data is for **forecasting** — to predict or estimate future sales trends, budgets, and so forth. Archiving data from the company's **operational database** — the database used to carry out regular operations, such as payroll and inventory management, of an organization — or **transactional database** — the database used to record daily transactions — into another database, one that is used for storing older data, is a concept known as **data warehousing**. A **data warehouse** contains a large amount of different types of data that present a clear picture of the business environment at a specific point in time.

Data warehousing is a technology used to establish business intelligence. **Business intelligence (BI)** helps an organization to attain its goals and objectives by giving management a better understanding of past performance as well as information on how the organization is progressing toward its goals. **Business intelligence tools** are a classification of software applications that aid in collecting, storing, analyzing, and providing access to data that helps managers make improved business decisions.

One use of BI tools is for **data mining**, which helps to expose trends, patterns, and relationships within the data that might otherwise have remained undetected. For example, the queries that you have been creating in Access are searching for data that you know exists. You have created queries to find customers who live in specific cities and states as well as queries that help to calculate employee raises, just to name a few. With data mining, you are searching, or mining, the data within the data warehouse for unknown trends. The salon manager could mine archived data in the data warehouse to see what two products are most likely to sell together or what two services are most likely to be given to the same customer.

Think about how this can help a manager make decisions. What about forecasting? The salon manager could learn a lot about the business and use this information to help increase sales. If the manager knows that two items are most likely to sell together in one transaction, she could ensure that she has equal amounts of inventory in stock. She can also train employees to use a **suggestive sell** — a sales technique used to add more revenue to a sale by suggesting and selling another product to the customer.

Running a Make Table Query

Once your make table query is ready, the table is created when you click the Run button on the Query Tools Design tab as shown in Figure 1. The challenge with clicking Run is that you cannot see what Access is going to do, nor can you verify that the data will be displayed how you want it to look. For example, you may be creating a make table query that includes calculated fields and expressions. You probably would want to view the query dataset before actually creating a table. The way around this is to switch from Design view to Datasheet view. This enables you to preview the data that will be added to the new table before actually creating it.

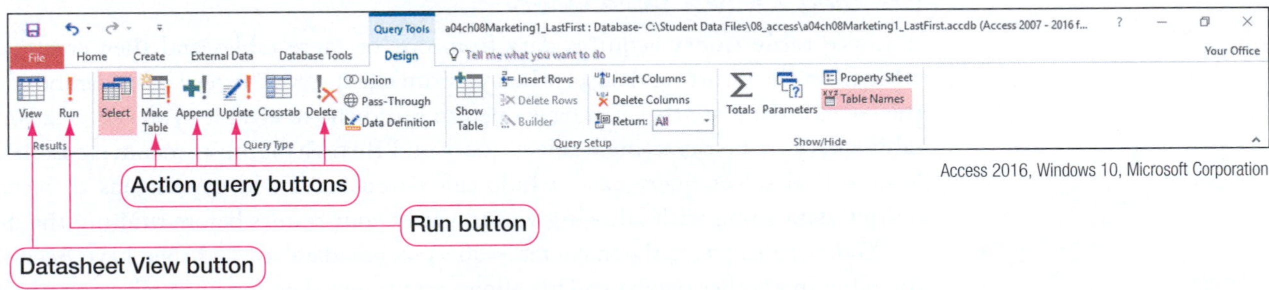

Access 2016, Windows 10, Microsoft Corporation

Figure 1 Action query buttons

> **REAL WORLD ADVICE** Archiving Data
>
> There are times when you need to copy or archive data, and you will want to make a table from data within your database. For example, you may have a table of past sales data that is used in reports. The sales figures will not change because the transactions have occurred in the past. Continually running a query to retrieve the data can take time, especially if you run a complex query against a large amount of data. Loading the historical data into a separate table and using that table as a data source can reduce time and provide a convenient data archive. Remember, however, that the data in your new table is just a snapshot — an image — of the data at a specific time. It has no relationship or link to other tables in the database.

In this exercise, you will create a make table query in the Marketing1 database to add a table to the Spa2 database.

To Create and Run a Make Table Query

a. Switch to the **a04ch08Marketing1_LastFirst** database if necessary. Click the **Create** tab, and then in the Queries group, click **Query Design**.

b. Add **tblCampaign** and **tblMailing** to the query workspace, and then **Close** [X] the Show Table dialog box.

c. Add the following fields to the query design grid: **MailingID**, **CustomerID**, and **Redeemed** from the tblMailing table and **CampaignName**, **CampaignType**, **StartDate**, **EndDate**, **DiscountCode**, **Department**, and **Details** from the tblCampaign table.

d. In the Criteria row of the Department field, type "Turquoise Oasis Spa". Clear the **Show** check box.

e. On the **Design** tab, in the Results group, click the **View** arrow, and then click **Datasheet View**.

Notice that you can see the 9 fields and 52 records that will be added to your new table.

f. Switch to **Design** view. On the Design tab, in the Query Type group, click **Make Table** to change the query type to a make table query.

g. In the Make Table dialog box, type tblCampaign in the Table Name box to name your new table.

h. Click **Another Database**, click **Browse**, navigate to the location where you are saving your files, and then select the **a04ch08Spa2_LastFirst** database. In the Make Table dialog box, click **OK** two times.

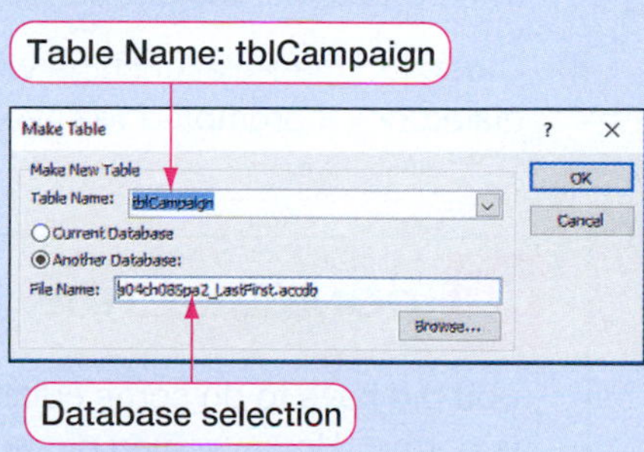

Figure 2 Make Table dialog box

Access 2016, Windows 10, Microsoft Corporation

i. On the **Design** tab, in the Results group, click **Run**. Click **Yes** in the Microsoft Access dialog box to confirm that you want to paste 52 rows into a new table. **Save** [💾] the query as qryMakeTable. **Close** [X] the query, and then **Close** [X] the a04ch08Marketing1_LastFirst database.

j. Switch to the **a04ch08Spa2_LastFirst** database, and then open the **tblCampaign** table.

Notice that all 52 records were exported from the a04ch08Marketing1_LastFirst database but that all the formatting, such as a check box for the Redeemed field, was not copied.

SIDE NOTE
Pin the Ribbon
If your ribbon is collapsed, pin your ribbon open. Click the Home tab. In the lower right-hand corner of the ribbon, click Pin the Ribbon [📌].

SIDE NOTE
Verify the Action
The only way to verify that an action query worked correctly is to look in the table to see whether the proper action occurred.

Troubleshooting

If you do not see the tblCampaign table in the a04ch08Spa2_LastFirst database, close the database and then reopen it.

k. Switch to **Design** view, and then make the following changes to the field properties and descriptions.

Field	Field Properties	Description
MailingID	Change this field to the **primary key** Change the format to **"MID"0**	**The Mailing ID (primary key)**
CustomerID	Change the caption to **Customer**	**The Customer ID (foreign key)**
Redeemed	Change the lookup control to a check box	**Was the coupon re-deemed?**
CampaignName	Change the caption to **Campaign Name**	**The campaign name**
CampaignType	Change the caption to **Campaign Type**	**The campaign type**
StartDate	Change the caption to **Start Date**	**The campaign start date**
EndDate	Change the caption to **End Date**	**The campaign end date**
DiscountCode	Change the caption to **Discount Code**	**The POS discount code**
Details		**The details of the campaign**

SIDE NOTE
Saving Relationships
If you move or resize tables, you will be prompted to save your changes. If you create only the relationship, Access will automatically save that change for you.

l. **Save** the changes, and then **Close** tblCampaign.

m. Click the **Database Tools** tab, and then in the Relationships group, click **Relationships**. Find **tblCampaign** in the Relationships window, and then create a relationship between **CustomerID** in the tblCampaign table and **CustomerID** in the tblCustomer table. Enforce referential integrity.

n. **Close** the Relationships window, and then click **Yes** in the Microsoft Access dialog box if prompted to save your changes.

CONSIDER THIS | **Why Not Just Create the New Table from Scratch?**

You did have to do some editing after running your make table query, and this is normal. However, you did not have to create the fields, select the field types, and enter the data. Some minor editing took a few minutes. Additionally, you still would have had to create the relationship, whether you built the table from scratch or created it from a make table query. How long would it have taken you if you created it from scratch? What if the table had two or three times as many fields? Could you have created it faster from scratch?

Append Data to a Table

You can use an append query when you need to add new records to an existing table by using data from other sources such as an Excel workbook, a Word document, a text file, or another database. An **append query** selects records from one or more data sources and copies the selected records to an existing table.

Creating an Append Query

Suppose that you have access to another database that contains a table of potential customers. However, you already have a table in your existing database that stores this type of data. Therefore, you decide to import the list of potential customers from the other database. To avoid having to import it into a new table and then manually enter the data into your existing table, you can use an append query to copy the records into your existing table. For example, the Painted Paradise Resort & Spa's marketing department regularly updates its database with new marketing campaigns, customers, and redemption status of discounts. If the spa manager wants to ensure that she has current data for decision making, she needs to regularly add new records to the table that is storing the marketing data in the spa database. An append query could help the spa's manager easily and regularly add new records to the existing table.

REAL WORLD ADVICE | **Benefits of Using an Append Query**

- You can append — add — multiple records to a table at one time. If you copy data manually, you usually have to do it multiple times. By using an append query, you eliminate the copy-and-paste process, which can ensure that no mistakes are made and all records are appended.
- You can review the data that will be appended before you run the query. You can view your selection in Datasheet view and modify the data as needed before you append any data. This can be helpful if your query includes criteria or expressions.
- You can use criteria to refine your selection. For example, you might want to append only customers who live within a certain state.
- You can append records when some of the data source fields do not exist in the destination table. For example, suppose that your existing customer table has 11 fields and the external prospective customers table only has 10 of the 11 fields. You can still use an append query to copy and add the data from the 10 fields that match — and the fields MUST match to be able to do this.

Running an Append Query

The data is not appended to your table until you click the Run button on the Design tab. Before you append the records, you can switch to Datasheet view for a preview of the records that will be affected by the action query. If you need to modify your dataset, you can switch back to Design view and make the needed changes. This can be done as many times as necessary before actually running the query. It is important to emphasize that you cannot undo an append query. If you make a mistake, you must either restore your database from a backup or correct your error, either manually or by using a delete query. Therefore, you should back up your database or the destination table before running an append query.

In this exercise, you will use an append query to add new records to the tblCampaign in the Spa2 database.

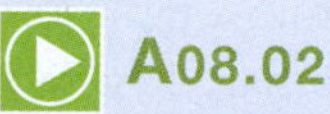

To Create and Run an Append Query

a. Switch to the **a04ch08Marketing2_LastFirst** database if necessary. Click the **Create** tab, and then in the Queries group, click **Query Design**.
   The marketing department has added the spring promotions for the Turquoise Oasis Spa, and you need to append the new promotional data to the tblCampaign table in the a04ch08Spa2_LastFirst database.

b. Add **tblCampaign** and **tblMailing** to the query workspace, and then **Close** [X] the Show Table dialog box.

c. Add the following fields to the query design grid: **MailingID**, **CustomerID**, and **Redeemed** from the tblMailing table, and then add **CampaignName**,

CampaignType, **StartDate**, **EndDate**, **DiscountCode**, **Department**, and **Details** from the tblCampaign table.

d. In the Criteria row of the Department field, type "Turquoise Oasis Spa". Clear the **Show** check box of the Department column.

e. In the Criteria row of the StartDate field type #4/1/2018#.

f. On the Design tab, in the Query Type group, click **Append** to change the query type to an append query.

g. When the Append dialog box opens, click the **table name** arrow, select append the data to the **tblCampaign** table, and then click **Another Database**. Click **Browse**, navigate to the location where you are saving your files, and then select the **a04ch08Spa2_LastFirst** database. Click **OK** two times.

SIDE NOTE
Previewing Data
Switching to Datasheet view allows you to preview the records that will be added to the other table before you actually run the query.

h. On the **Design** tab, in the Results group, click the **View** arrow, and then click **Datasheet View** to preview the data that will be included in your table. You should have 78 records that will be appended automatically to the tblCampaign table in the a04ch08Spa2_LastFirst database.

i. Switch to **Design** view, and then in the Results group, click **Run**. In the Microsoft Access dialog box, click **Yes** to confirm that you want to append 78 rows.

j. Save the query as qryAppendData and then **Close** the query.

k. Switch to the **a04ch08Spa2_LastFirst** database, and then open the **tblCampaign** table.

Notice how all 78 records were exported from the a04ch08Marketing2_LastFirst database along with the formatting, and you now have 130 records in your tblCampaign table.

l. **Close** the tblCampaign table, switch to the **a04ch08Marketing2_LastFirst** database, and then **Close** the a04ch08Marketing2_LastFirst database.

Edit and Delete Data

Because many databases contain a tremendous amount of data, it would be extremely time consuming to manually update data record by record. For example, many new area codes have been created in the United States over the past several years. It would take too much time to have an employee look through each customer's record and modify the area code as needed. This is when an update query can be helpful. An **update query** can be used to add, change, or delete data in one or more existing records. Update queries are similar to the Find and Replace dialog box but are much more powerful.

You also have the option of using a delete query depending on the type of deletion you need to perform. A **delete query** is used to remove entire records from a table at one time. Delete queries remove all the data in each field, including the primary key. When you need to delete old records from your database, you could search through the table and delete each individual record, which could take some time, or you could use a delete query to delete them all at once. A delete query cannot be used to delete an actual table from the database, but it can be used to delete all of the data from within a table.

Running update and delete queries are different than using the Cascade Update Related Fields and Cascade Delete Related Records properties in the Relationships window. When you set the Cascade Update Related Fields property, Access updates the primary key in all related tables if it changes on the one side of the relationship. When you set the Cascade Delete Related Records property, Access deletes the related records in all related tables if the key field is deleted on the one side of the relationship. If you want to delete data from several related tables, you must enable the Enforce Referential

Integrity and Cascade Delete Related Records properties for each relationship. This allows your query to delete data from the tables on the one and many sides of the relationship.

Be careful that you fully understand what Cascade Update and Cascade Delete do before using them. A vast amount of data can be updated or deleted at once and unintentionally if you are not careful. For example, if you delete an employee by accident — you should never do so on purpose, even if the person is no longer employed by your company — then it would wipe out every transaction the employee was associated with. This is why best practice is to create a backup of your database before making any major changes in the data.

Work with Update Queries

You can use an update query when you have to update or change existing data in multiple records. As a best practice, there are two steps that you must follow to create and run an update query. First, create a select query that identifies the records to update, and then change the query to an update query that, upon running, will update the records.

A **simple update query** involves updating data in one table, allowing you to specify two values: the value you want to replace and the value to be used as a replacement. To create and run an update query, first begin with a select query that identifies the records to be updated. Then change the query to an update query and click Run. The important thing to remember is that although the data types for each table field do not have to match, they must be compatible.

A simple update query can be an easy way to update large amounts of data. For example, perhaps an employee no longer works at the salon, and there are dozens of future appointments that need to be changed to a different employee's name. If this employee — perhaps the person you hired to fill the former employee's position — is now going to handle these appointments, you could create an update query that changes the name of the employee for all future appointments from the former employee to the new employee. In this exercise, you will create two update queries to extend the end date of an in-house promotion and to change the details of the promotion.

To Create and Run a Simple Update Query

a. Switch to the **a04ch08Spa2_LastFirst** database, if necessary. Click the **Create** tab, and then in the Queries group, click **Query Design**.

   The marketing department has extended the date for all in-house promotions that currently expire on 3/31/2018, and you need to update the data in the tblCampaign table in the a04ch08Spa2_LastFirst database.

b. Add **tblCampaign** to the query workspace, and then **Close** the Show Table dialog box.

c. Add the following fields to the query design grid: **MailingID**, **CampaignType**, and **EndDate**.

d. In the Criteria row of the CampaignType field, type "In-house Promotion".

e. In the Criteria row of the EndDate field, type #3/31/2018#.

f. On the **Design** tab, in the Query Type group, click **Update** to change the query type to an update query. In the Update To property row of the EndDate field, type #6/30/2018#, and then **Save** the query as qryUpdateData.

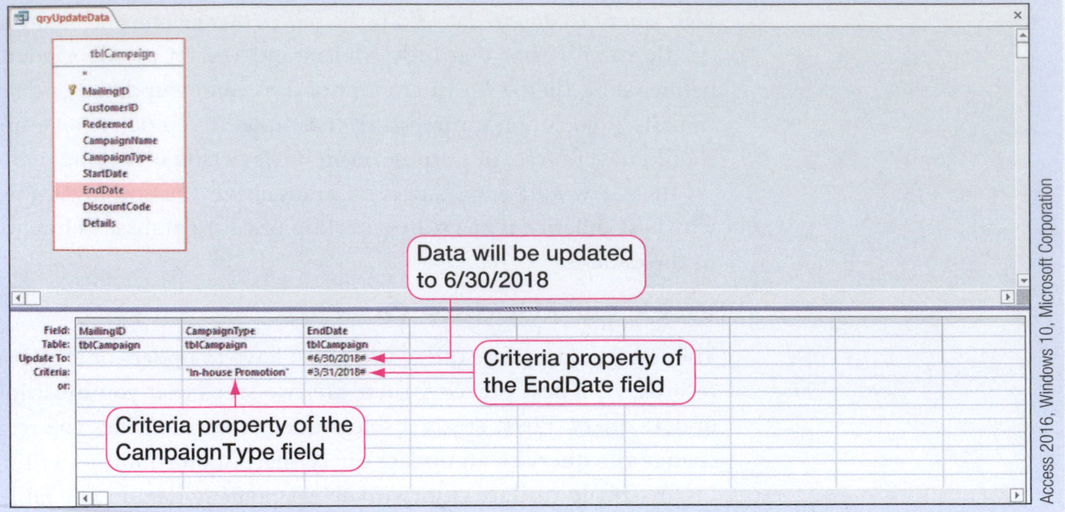

Figure 3 Design view of the qryUpdateData query

> **SIDE NOTE**
> **What Is Access Showing?**
> When you preview the data, notice that Access does not show you how the data will look after the update but shows you which records will be updated.

g. Switch to **Datasheet** view to preview the data that will be included in your update. You should have 52 records that will be updated automatically in your table.

h. Switch to **Design** view, and then in the Results group, click **Run**. Click **Yes** in the Microsoft Access dialog box when Access asks you to confirm that you want to update 52 rows.

i. **Close** [X] the query.

j. Open the **tblCampaign** table.
   Notice that all In-house Promotions now have an EndDate of 6/30/2018. **Close** [X] tblCampaign.

k. Click the **Create** tab, and then in the Queries group, click **Query Design**. The marketing department has changed the details for all in-house promotions, and you need to update the data in the tblCampaign table. Add **tblCampaign** to the query workspace. **Close** [X] the Show Table dialog box.

l. Add the following fields to the design grid: **CampaignType** and **Details**.

m. In the Criteria property row of the CampaignType field, type "In-house Promotion".

n. On the **Design** tab, in the Query Type group, click **Update** to change the query type to an update query.

o. In the **Update To** property row of the Details field, type [Details] & " " & "Minimum purchase of $50 is required.". **Save** the query as qryUpdateDetails.
   You are doing this to modify the specifics of the promotion. The marketing department has informed you that to receive this promotion, a client has to spend a minimum of $50. To keep the text that is already in the Details field and add the additional information, you can concatenate the existing data with the marketing department's update.

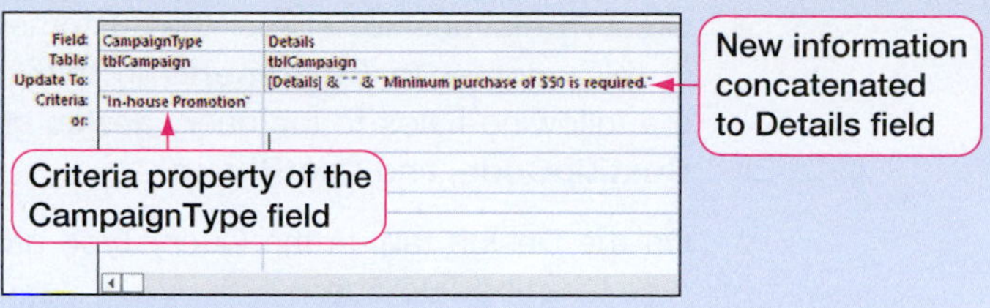

Figure 4 Design view of the qryUpdateDetails query

Access 2016, Windows 10, Microsoft Corporation

> **SIDE NOTE**
> **Concatenating Data Saves Time**
> Access did not delete what was in the field before the update; it simply concatenated what was already in the field with the new data.

p. Switch to **Datasheet** view to preview the data that will be included in your table.
   You should have 52 records that will be updated automatically in your table. Notice that Access does not show you how the records will be updated but rather just that 52 records will change.

q. Switch to **Design** view, and then in the Results group, click **Run**. Click **Yes** in the Microsoft Access dialog box when Access asks you to confirm that you want to update 52 rows. **Close** [X] the query.

r. Open the **tblCampaign** table.
   Notice that all In-house Promotions have been adjusted in the Details. For example, some entries are listed as **Receive 10% off any service. Minimum purchase of $50 is required.**

s. **Close** [X] the tblCampaign table.

Creating Complex Update Queries

There are times when you need to update data from one table to another through the use of a **complex update query**. When you do this, the data types for both the source and destination fields must either match or be compatible. Additionally, when you update data from one table to another and use compatible data types instead of matching data types, Access converts the data types of the fields in the destination table. As a result, some of the data in the destination fields may be **truncated**, that is, it may be shortened or trimmed.

In this exercise, you will create an update query to add the ZIP Codes and update the area codes in the tblCustomer table from the tblMktglImport table.

A08.04

To Create and Run a Complex Update Query

a. In the **a04ch08Spa2_LastFirst** database, open **tblMktgImport** and **tblCustomer**.
   The marketing department has updated some of their customer data, and you need to update the tblCustomer table with the new data from the marketing department's database. The table from the marketing department's database has already been imported into your database. Changes in data between the two tables are the addition of data in the Zip Code field and the update of area codes and exchanges. Close [X] tblMktgImport and tblCustomer.

b. Click the **Create** tab, and then in the Queries group, click **Query Design**.

c. Add **tblCustomer** and **tblMktgImport** to the query workspace, and then **Close** [X] the Show Table dialog box.

d. Create a relationship between the CustomerID fields in each table. Drag **CustomerID** in tblCustomer to **CustomerID** in tblMktgImport. From the **tblCustomer**, add the following fields to the query design grid: **CustomerID**, **CustCity**, **CustState**, **CustZipCode**, and **CustPhone**.

e. On the Design tab, in the Query Type group, click **Update** to change the query type to an update query.

f. To update data from one table to another and match the fields between the two tables, type the following into the Update To row.

Field	Update To
CustCity	[tblMktgImport]![CustCity]
CustState	[tblMktgImport]![CustState]
CustZipCode	[tblMktgImport]![CustZipCode]
CustPhone	[tblMktgImport]![CustPhone]

Resize the columns in the design grid to see what you have entered.

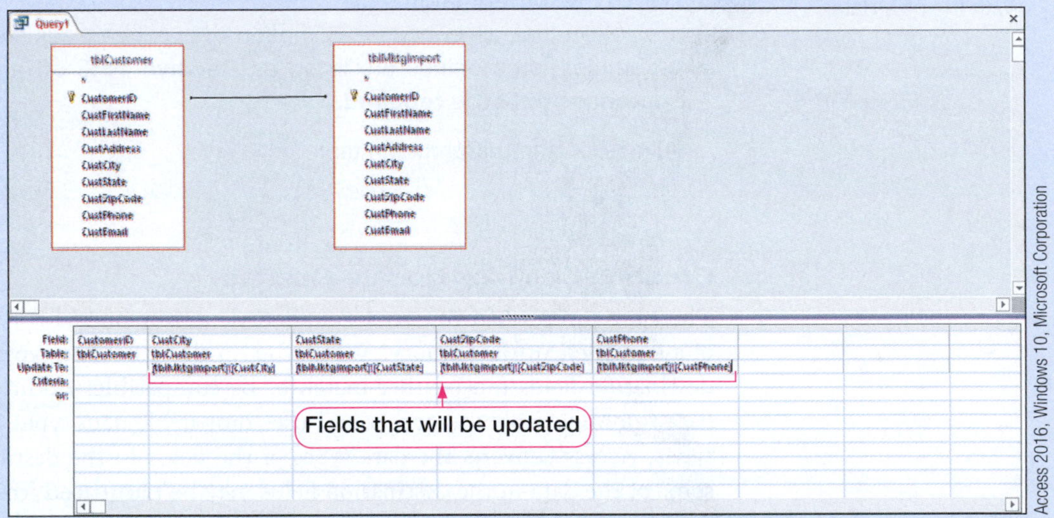

Figure 5 Design view of a complex update query

g. Switch to **Datasheet** view to preview the data that will be included in your update. You should have 25 records that will be updated automatically in your table.

h. Switch to **Design** view, and then in the Results group, click **Run**. Click **Yes** in the Microsoft Access dialog box when Access asks you to confirm that you want to update 25 rows.

i. **Save** the query as qryComplexUpdate, and then **Close** the query.

j. Open the **tblCustomer** table.
Notice that all applicable data — area code and ZIP Code — have been updated.

k. **Close** tblCustomer.

QUICK REFERENCE | **Restrictions on Data Type Conversions**

The following table outlines the restrictions on how to convert data types and briefly describes any data loss that might occur during conversion.

Table 1 Restrictions on data type conversions

Convert to	Convert from	Changes or Restrictions
Text	Memo	Deletes all except the first 255 characters.
	Yes/No	The value –1 converts to Yes. The value 0 converts to No.
	Hyperlink	Truncates links longer than 255 characters.
Memo	Yes/No	The value –1 converts to Yes. The value 0 converts to No.
Number	Text	Must consist of numbers, valid currency, and decimal separators. The number of characters in the Text field must fall within the size set for the Number field.
	Memo	Must contain only text and valid currency and decimal separators. The number of characters in the Memo field must fall within the size set for the Number field.
	Number with a different field size or precision	Must not be larger or smaller than what the new field size can store. Changing precision might cause Access to round some values.
	Date/Time	Dates depend on the size of the Number field. To accommodate all possible dates, set the Field Size property of your Number field to Long Integer or greater.
	Currency	Values must not exceed or fall below the size limit set for the field.
	AutoNumber	Values must fall within the size limit set for the field.
	Yes/No	Yes values convert to –1. No values convert to 0.
Date/Time	Text	Must be a recognizable date or date/time combination.
	Memo	Must be a recognizable date or date/time combination.
	Number	Value must fall between –657,434 and 2,958,465.99998843.
	Currency	Value must fall between –$657,434 and $2,958,465.9999.
	AutoNumber	Value must exceed –657,434 and be less than 2,958,466.
	Yes/No	The value –1 (Yes) converts to December 29, 1899. The value 0 (No) converts to midnight (12:00 AM).
Currency	Text	Must consist of numbers and valid separators.
	Memo	Must consist of numbers and valid separators.
	Yes/No	The value –1 (Yes) converts to $1. The value 0 (No) converts to $0.
AutoNumber	Text	Not allowed if AutoNumber field serves as primary key.
	Memo	Not allowed if AutoNumber field serves as primary key.
	Number	Not allowed if AutoNumber field serves as primary key.
	Date/Time	Not allowed if AutoNumber field serves as primary key.
	Currency	
	Yes/No	
Yes/No	Text	Must consist only of Yes, No, True, False, On, or Off.
	Memo	Must consist only of Yes, No, True, False, On, or Off.
	Number	Zero or Null converts to No. All other values convert to Yes.
	Date/Time	Null, or 12:00:00 AM, converts to No. All other values convert to Yes.
	Currency	Zero or Null converts to No. All other values convert to Yes.

(continued)

Convert to	Convert from	Changes or Restrictions
	AutoNumber	All values convert to Yes.
Hyperlink	Text	Converts a valid hyperlink in text format to a hyperlink.
	Memo	Converts a valid hyperlink in text format to a hyperlink.
	Number	Not allowed when a Number field is part of a relationship. If the original value is in the form of a valid Internet Protocol (IP) address (four number triplets separated by a period: nnn.nnn.nnn.nnn) and the numbers happen to coincide with a Web address, the conversion results in a valid link. Otherwise, Access appends "http://" to the beginning of each value, and the resulting links are not valid.
	Date/Time	Access appends "http://" to the beginning of each address, but the resulting links will almost never work.
	Currency	Access appends "http://" to the beginning of each value, but as with dates, the resulting links will almost never work.
	AutoNumber	Not allowed when the AutoNumber field is part of a relationship. Access appends "http://" to the beginning of each value, but the resulting links will almost never work.
	Yes/No	Access converts all Yes values to –1 and all No values to 0, and appends "http://" to the beginning of each value. The resulting links do not work.

Create, Test, and Run Delete Queries

You can use an update query to delete data in one or more fields in a database. However, to delete entire records, including the primary key value that makes the record unique, you can use a delete query.

Creating Simple Delete Queries

A **simple delete query** is used to remove one or more records from a table. The number of rows deleted depends upon the criteria within the Where clause of the delete query. Typically, you use delete queries when you need to remove large amounts of data quickly. If you want to remove a very small number of records, you may want to simply delete them by hand. Undoubtedly, by running a delete query, you reduce and/or eliminate the chance of not deleting — missing — a record if the process is done manually. In this exercise, you will create a delete query to remove the two soap products from the tblProduct table in the Spa2 database.

To Create and Run a Simple Delete Query

a. In the **a04ch08Spa2_LastFirst** database, click the **Create** tab, and then in the Queries group, click **Query Design** to begin creating a query that will help the spa manager. She has decided to discontinue selling soaps because they are not generating enough revenue for the spa.

b. Add **tblProduct** to the query workspace, and then **Close** [X] the Show Table dialog box.

c. Add the **ProductDescription** field to the query design grid.

d. In the Criteria property of the ProductDescription field, type Like"*soap*".

e. Click the **Design** tab, and then in the Query Type group, click **Delete** to change the query type to a delete query.

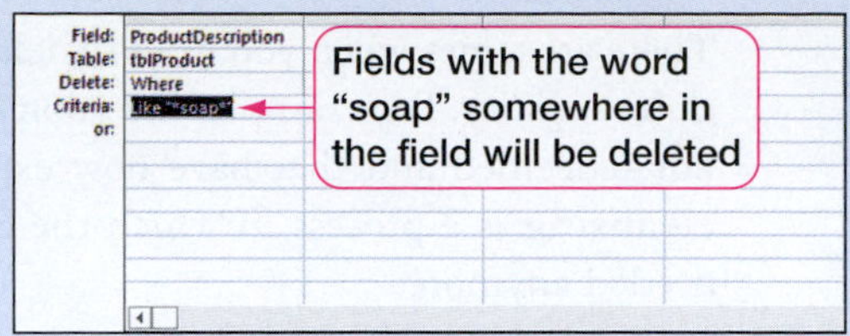

Figure 6 Design view of a delete query
Access 2016, Windows 10, Microsoft Corporation

f. Switch to **Datasheet** view to preview the data that will be deleted. You should have two records that will be deleted when you run the delete query.

g. Switch to **Design** view, and then in the Results group, click **Run**. Click **Yes** in the Microsoft Access dialog box when Access asks you to confirm that you want to delete two rows.

Troubleshooting

If you had your table open when you ran your delete query, #Deleted is displayed in the fields or records that were affected by the delete query. The message is displayed until you close and then reopen the table.

h. **Save** the query as qrySimpleDelete, and then **Close** the query.

i. Open the **tblProduct** table.
   Notice that all applicable records — Lavender Ylang Soap and Renewal Face Soap — have been deleted.

j. **Close** tblProduct.

CONSIDER THIS | What If You Try to Delete Records That Have Related Records?

What do you think would happen if you tried to run a delete query and the records had related records in another table? Would you still be able to delete the records? Would it change anything if you set your Relationships property to Cascade Delete Related Records?

REAL WORLD ADVICE | Why Use a Delete Query?

It is important to ensure that the data in your database is current. Removing unneeded data is a good organizational strategy that all database users should practice. Cleansing outdated or incorrect data creates a database that is easy to use and maintain. Of course, before performing a delete query, you should always back up your database just in case you either make a mistake or think you might want to use the data to be deleted at a later point in time. Data can become unneeded for a few reasons.

- Real-world changes — You may need to delete discontinued products or employees who no longer work at your company.
- Human error — Human error happens. Users could accidently enter duplicate data for a customer or an order. A delete query can make it easier to fix errors.
- Time — At times, you may need to archive older data, such as past employees or last year's sales data, and move it to an archive database or data warehouse.

Building Complex Delete Queries

There are times when you need to delete data in multiple tables. This is a more **complex delete query**. For example, the salon manager may want to remove all coupons that were not redeemed and that have now expired. This will keep the database cleansed. **Data cleansing** is a process in which the delete query will remove data that is not useful or needed anymore.

REAL WORLD ADVICE | **Cleansing Data**

Using incorrect data in business operations can be expensive. Many companies use customer information databases that record data such as contact information, addresses, and preferences. For instance, if customer addresses are inconsistent or incorrect, the company will endure the cost of resending mail or even losing customers. Although cleansing data is critical to maintain accurate records, some things need to be considered, including the following.

- Loss of information — Data can be overcleansed to the point at which important information is removed from the database. This loss can be particularly pricey if there is a large amount of deleted data.
- Time consumption — Cleansing data is not an easy or quick process. Once data has been cleansed, you would want to avoid recleansing the data in its entirety after some values in the data collection change. Therefore, the process should be repeated only on values that have changed.

In this exercise, you will create two delete queries to remove customers who are moving away and want to be removed from the mailing list and to remove appointments scheduled for a time when the spa will be closed for construction.

A08.06

To Create and Run a Complex Delete Query

a. In the **a04ch08Spa2_LastFirst** database, click the **Database Tools** tab, and then in the Relationships group, click **Relationships**.

The marketing department has been notified that two customers want to be removed from the Painted Paradise Resort & Spa's mailing list, as they are moving out of the country and will not be customers anymore. You need to delete the records from your database to ensure that the data you have is current and cleansed.

b. Right-click the **relationship line** between the tblCampaign and tblCustomer tables, and then click **Edit Relationship** to modify the relationship between tblCustomer and tblCampaign. In the Edit Relationships dialog box, click the **Cascade Delete Related Records** check box, and then click **OK**.

c. On the Design tab, in the Relationships group, click **Close**.

d. Click the **Create** tab, in the Queries group, click **Query Design**.

e. Add **tblCustomer** to the query workspace, and then **Close** [X] the Show Table dialog box.

f. Add the following fields to the query design grid: **CustomerID**, **CustFirstName**, and **CustLastName**.

g. On the **Design** tab, in the Query Type group, click **Delete** to change the query type to a delete query.

SIDE NOTE
The Relationship Line
You can also double-click the relationship line to open the Edit Relationships dialog box.

SIDE NOTE
Deleting Records on the One Side of a Relationship
To delete records on the one side of the relationship and related records on the many side, enable Referential Integrity and Cascade Delete Related Records.

h. To delete the two customers, in the Criteria property row of the CustLastName field, type "Dunn", and then in the Or property row of the CustLastName field, type "Cleveland". **Save** the query as qryComplexDelete1.

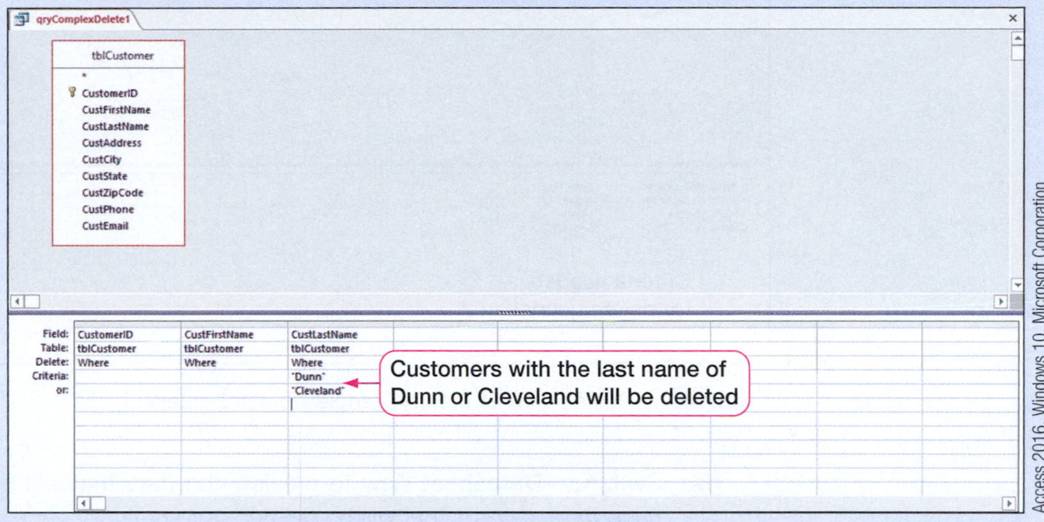

Figure 7 Design view of the qryComplexDelete1 query

i. Switch to **Datasheet** view to preview the data that will be deleted. You should have two records that will be deleted automatically once you run the query.

j. Switch to **Design** view, and then in the Results group, click **Run**. Click **Yes** in the Microsoft Access dialog box when Access asks you to confirm that you want to delete two rows.

k. **Close** the query.

l. Open the **tblCustomer** table. On the Design tab, in the Query Type group, click Make Table to change the query type to make table query.

Notice that all applicable data — customers with the last name of Dunn and Cleveland — have been deleted.

SIDE NOTE
Deleting Records on the Many Side
If you need to remove data only on the many side of the relationship, you can create and run your delete query without having to change the relationship.

m. Open the **tblCampaign** table. Notice that all applicable data — customers with the CustomerID of 4 and 22 — have been deleted. **Close** tblCampaign and tblCustomer.

n. Click the **Create** tab, and then in the Queries group, click **Query Design**.

Management has notified the spa employees and clients that the spa will be closing at 11:00 AM on January 15, 2018, to have some construction work done. You need to delete the appointments that are currently entered for that time.

o. Add **tblSchedule** to the query workspace, and then **Close** the Show Table dialog box.

SIDE NOTE
Entering Times
You can also type just >#11 AM# and press Enter. Access will automatically enter the zeros for you.

p. Add the following fields to the query design grid: **DateOfAppt** and **TimeOfAppt**.

q. Click the **Design** tab, and then in the Queries group, click **Delete** to change the query type to a delete query.

r. To delete the appointments scheduled for three clients, in the Criteria property row of the DateOfAppt field, type #1/15/2018#, and then type >#11:00:00 AM# into the Criteria property row of the TimeOfAppt field. **Save** the query as qryComplexDelete2.

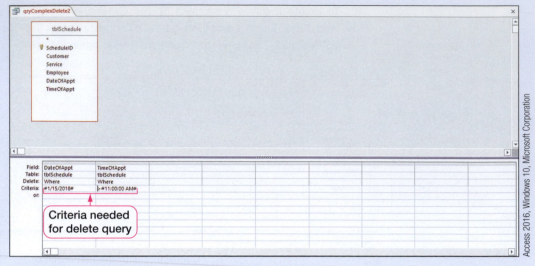

Figure 8 Design view of the qryCompleteDelete2 query

s. Switch to **Datasheet** view to preview the data that will be deleted. You should have three records that will be deleted automatically once you run the query.

t. Switch to **Design** view, and then in the Results group, click **Run**. Click **Yes** in the Microsoft Access dialog box when Access asks you to confirm that you want to delete three rows.

u. **Close** [X] the query, and then **Close** [X] the a04ch08Spa2_LastFirst database. If you need to take a break before finishing this chapter, now is a good time.

QUICK REFERENCE | **Tips for Using a Delete Query**

The reason you deleted records from the tblCustomer table and not the tblCampaign table is because tblCustomer resides on the one side of the relationship. Additionally, you did not have to change any of the other relationships because there were not any related records. In the future, you may need to edit all relationships and ensure that the Cascade Delete Related Records property is selected. You first need to decide which records exist on the one side of the relationship and which exist on the many side.

- To delete records on the one side of the relationship and the related records on the many side, enable the Referential Integrity and Cascade Delete Related Records properties.
- To delete records only on the one side of the relationship, first delete the relationship, and then delete the data.
- To remove data only on the many side of the relationship, create and run the delete query without changing the relationship.

Advanced Relationships Using Multiple Tables

When you run a database query to find data in related tables, Access automatically looks for records that have matching values on both sides of the relationship. This is what you will probably do the majority of the time. However, you can control which records will be displayed in the query dataset by using query joins. This enables you to enhance your dataset even further to find the data that you want.

A **query join** is a temporary or virtual relationship between two tables in a query that do not have an established relationship or common field with the same field name and data type. Tables that are joined in a query are related only in that query and nowhere else. The type of join used will indicate which records the query will select or perform an action on. Creating a query join will not establish a permanent relationship between the tables. Permanent relationships can be created only in the Relationships window. In this section, you will create queries that include inner and outer joins, and you will create and edit unmatched data queries.

Create Inner Joins

An **inner join**, the default join type in Access, is a join that selects only those records from both database tables that have matching values. One or more fields can serve as the join fields. Records with values in the joined field that do not appear in both of the database tables will be excluded from the query dataset. For example, consider the spa and how the managers track sales of products to customers. By creating an inner join — a union or marriage of the data — the resulting dataset could include a customer and the products that customer has purchased. However, not all products or all customers may be included in the dataset because some products may not be included on an invoice. Maybe the spa just started selling a new product and no one has purchased it yet. Some customers may not have purchased any products because they visit the spa or salon to receive services but not to purchase products.

Creating an Inner Join Query

You can use an inner join in a query to retrieve only the rows that satisfy the join conditions on the tables in the query workspace. In the simplest type of inner join, the join condition is field1 = field2. In this exercise, you will create two inner join queries.

To Create and Run Inner Join Queries

a. If you took a break, open the **a04ch08Spa3_LastFirst** database.

b. Click the **Create** tab, and then in the Queries group, click **Query Design**.

c. Add **tblPurchase** and **tblCustomer** to the query workspace, and then **Close** the Show Table dialog box.

d. Double-click the **relationship line** between tblPurchase and tblCustomer to open the Join Properties dialog box. Notice that the default selection — the CustomerID field — is set to only include rows in which the joined fields from both tables are equal. This is an inner join. Click **OK** to close the Join Properties dialog box.

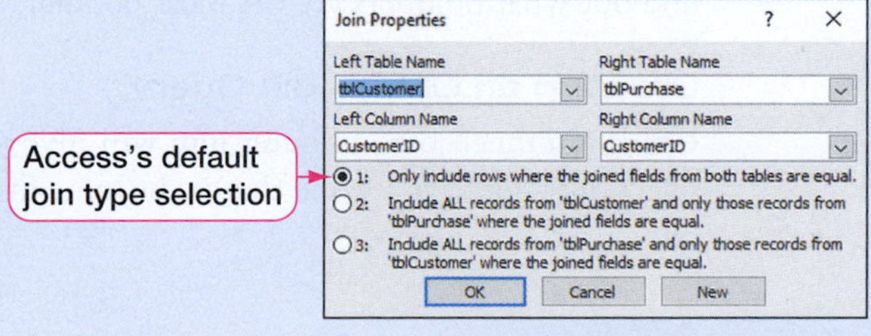

Figure 9 Join Properties dialog box

Access 2016, Windows 10, Microsoft Corporation

e. Add the following fields to the query design grid: **CustomerID**, **CustFirstName**, and **CustLastName** from tblCustomer and **ProductID**, **PurchaseDate**, and **Quantity** from tblPurchase.

f. Click the **Design** tab, and then in the Results group, click **Run**.
   Notice that there are 23 customers who have purchased products from the spa. However, if you open tblCustomer, there are 46 records. Thus, the query included only the records from both tables that matched on the CustomerID field.

g. **Save** the query as qryInnerJoin1, and then **Close** the query.

h. Click the **Create** tab, and then in the Queries group, click **Query Design**.

i. Add **tblCampaign** to the query workspace. Click the **Queries** tab, and then add **qryInnerJoin1** to the query workspace. **Close** the Show Table dialog box.

j. Create a relationship between the query and the table. Drag **CustomerID** in the qryInnerJoin query to **CustomerID** in the tblCampaign table, and then double-click the **relationship line** to open the Join Properties dialog box. Notice that the default selection is set to include only rows in which the joined fields from both tables are equal.

k. Click **OK** to close the Join Properties dialog box.

l. Add the following fields to the query design grid: **CustomerID**, **CustFirstName**, **CustLastName**, **ProductID**, **PurchaseDate**, and **Quantity** from qryInnerJoin1, and **CampaignName** and **Redeemed** from the tblCampaign.

m. On the Design tab, in the Results group, click **Run**.
   Notice that there are 143 records in the dataset and that some rows appear to be duplicated. Because the join property is set to inner join, Access is listing each purchase multiple times to coincide with each coupon the customers received. Thus, an inner join may not always be the best option for you to view data.

n. **Save** the query as qryInnerJoin2, and then **Close** the query.

Create Outer Joins

An **outer join** selects all of the records from one database table and only those records in the second table that have matching values in the joined field. One or more fields can serve as the join field. For example, consider again the spa and how the managers track sales of products to customers. An outer join query that includes these two tables could include all customers and only the products that have been purchased. Thus, you could find out what products are the most popular.

Creating an Outer Join Query

Unlike an inner join, an outer join will give you data even if the common field that you select does not have a value that is the same in both tables. In this exercise, you will create two outer join queries.

To Create and Run Outer Join Queries

a. In the **a04ch08Spa3_LastFirst** database, click the **Create** tab, and then in the Queries group, click **Query Design**.

b. Add **tblProduct** and **tblPurchase** to the query workspace, and then **Close** [X] the Show Table dialog box.

c. Double-click the **relationship line** between tblProduct and tblPurchase to open the Join Properties dialog box.

   The join is based on the relationship on the ProductID field. Notice that the default selection is set to include only rows in which the joined fields from both tables are equal — an inner join.

d. To change this to an outer join, select **Include ALL records from 'tblProduct' and only those records from 'tblPurchase' where the joined fields are equal**, and then click **OK**.

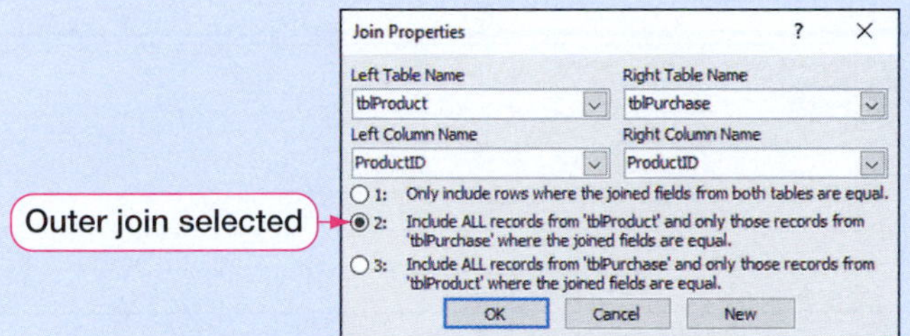

Figure 10 Join Properties dialog box with outer join

Access 2016, Windows 10, Microsoft Corporation

Troubleshooting

Be sure to read the options before automatically selecting option 2. Access randomizes how the relationships are listed in the Join Properties dialog box. On your computer, option 3 may have the join property that you want.

e. Add the following fields to the query design grid: **ProductDescription** from tblProduct and **CustomerID** from tblPurchase.

f. On the **Design** tab, in the Results group, click **Run**.

   Notice that all records from tblProduct appear, including products that no customers have purchased. However, the customers who have not purchased any products, such as Buchanan, do not appear. Additionally, products purchased by more than one customer appear multiple times.

g. **Save** the query as qryOuterJoin1, and then **Close** [X] the query.

h. Click the **Create** tab, and then in the Queries group, click **Query Design**.

i. Add **tblProduct** and **tblPurchase** to the query workspace, and then **Close** [X] the Show Table dialog box.

j. Double-click the **relationship line** between tblProduct and tblPurchase to open the Join Properties dialog box. Select **Include ALL records from 'tblProduct' and only those records from 'tblPurchase' where the joined fields are equal**, and then click **OK**.

k. Add the following fields to the query design grid: **ProductDescription** from tblProduct and **CustomerID** from tblPurchase.

l. On the **Design** tab, in the Show/Hide group, click **Totals**. In the Total row of the CustomerID field, click the **Total row** arrow, and then select **Count**.

m. In the design grid, in the field row of the CustomerID column, click to the left of the **CustomerID** field, type TotalSold: to rename the CustomerID field. **Save** the query as qryOuterJoin2.

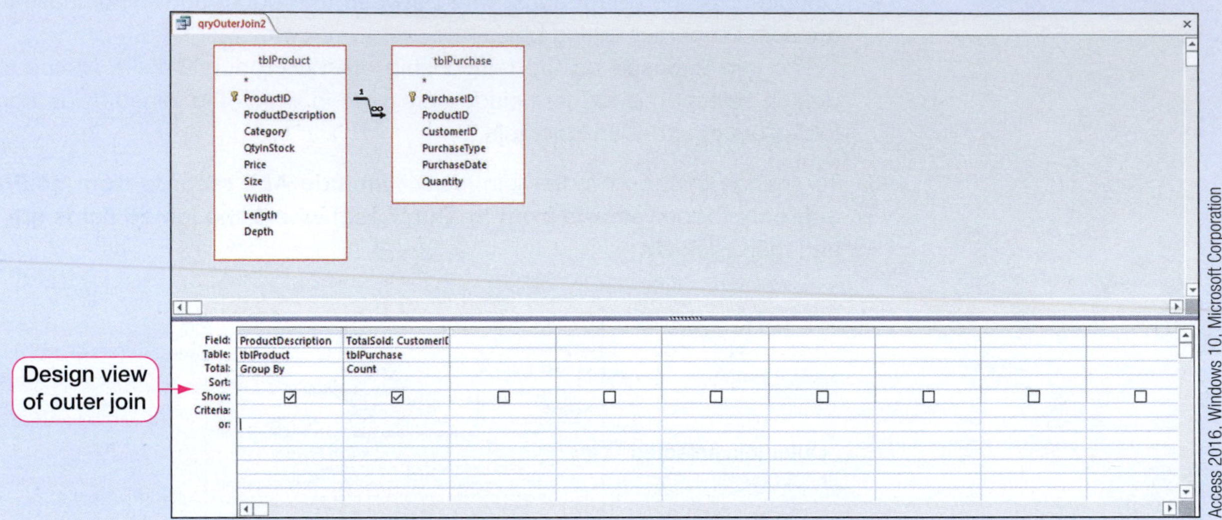

Figure 11 Design view of the qryOuterJoin2 query

n. On the Design tab, in the Results group, click **Run**.

Notice that 33 products are returned by the query. This is the same as the number of the products in tblProduct. The TotalSold field reflects the number of purchase transactions for the product. Access automatically places a zero in the fields in which there is no record of a customer purchasing this item.

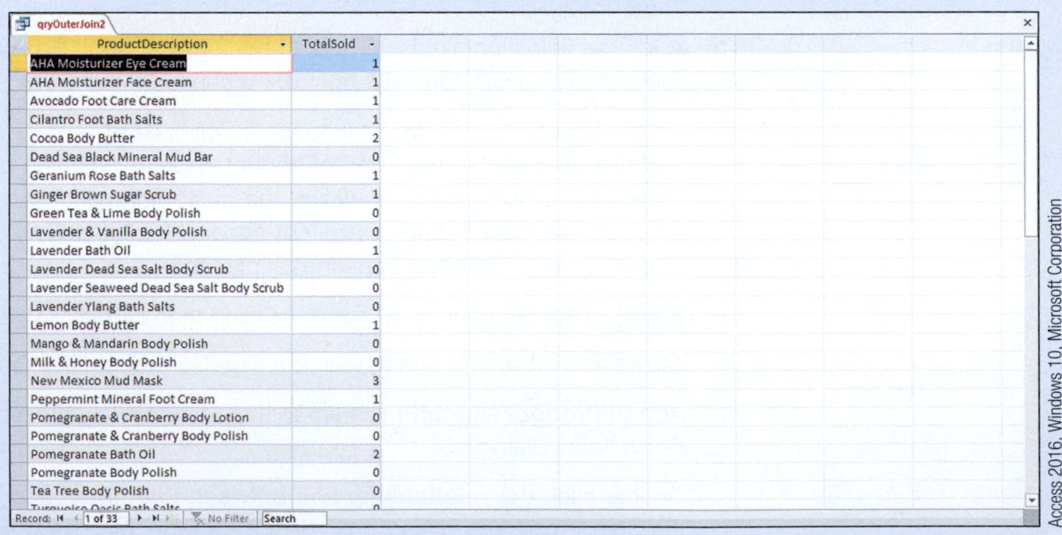

ProductDescription	TotalSold
AHA Moisturizer Eye Cream	1
AHA Moisturizer Face Cream	1
Avocado Foot Care Cream	1
Cilantro Foot Bath Salts	1
Cocoa Body Butter	2
Dead Sea Black Mineral Mud Bar	0
Geranium Rose Bath Salts	1
Ginger Brown Sugar Scrub	1
Green Tea & Lime Body Polish	0
Lavender & Vanilla Body Polish	0
Lavender Bath Oil	1
Lavender Dead Sea Salt Body Scrub	0
Lavender Seaweed Dead Sea Salt Body Scrub	0
Lavender Ylang Bath Salts	0
Lemon Body Butter	1
Mango & Mandarin Body Polish	0
Milk & Honey Body Polish	0
New Mexico Mud Mask	3
Peppermint Mineral Foot Cream	1
Pomegranate & Cranberry Body Lotion	0
Pomegranate & Cranberry Body Polish	0
Pomegranate Bath Oil	2
Pomegranate Body Polish	0
Tea Tree Body Polish	0

Figure 12 Datasheet view of the qryOuterJoin2 query

o. **Close** the query.

CHAPTER 8

SS **CONSIDER THIS** | **Outer Joins Can Be Extremely Helpful in Managing Your Business**

What would you do if you created an outer join query on your Product and Invoice tables and discovered that you stock products that have never been purchased by a customer? Should you place the products on sale? Develop a better advertising or marketing plan? Discontinue the products?

Use the Find Unmatched Query Wizard

By creating a query using the Find Unmatched Query Wizard, you will be able to edit, analyze, and cleanse data. The **Find Unmatched Query Wizard** finds records in one table that do not have related records in another table. After the wizard constructs your query, you can modify the query's design to add or remove fields or to add a join between the two tables. You can also create your own query to find unmatched records without using the wizard, but at times, it is easier to at least begin building such a query by using the wizard.

This type of query can be very helpful in business. What if the spa or salon had a walk-in client — a client who wants to have a service but did not schedule an appointment. The receptionist could find all employees who do not have an appointment scheduled for a specific time to determine who would be able to assist the walk-in client.

Additionally, you can use the Find Unmatched Query Wizard to cleanse data in a table. For example, perhaps the spa manager decided to discontinue a product or stop offering a specific service and probably will not need to use any of the transactional data in the future. The manager could find unmatched records between the Products and Purchases tables to ultimately delete the transactions in which the discontinued items reside. Thus, finding unmatched records may be the first of several steps that you will want to take — you may then want to create a delete query to help you delete records that are no longer needed.

Creating a Find Unmatched Data Query

The easiest way to determine the records that are unmatched is by using the Find Unmatched Query Wizard. After the wizard builds your query, you can modify the query's design. In this exercise, you will create unmatched queries to find employees who do not have appointments with clients and services that have not been given to clients.

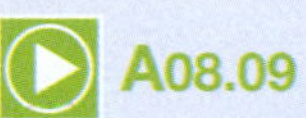

To Create Queries Using the Find Unmatched Query Wizard

a. Click the **Create** tab, and then in the Queries group, click **Query Wizard** to create a new query that will find which employees do not have any scheduled appointments with clients.

b. In the New Query Wizard dialog box, click **Find Unmatched Query Wizard**, and then click **OK**.

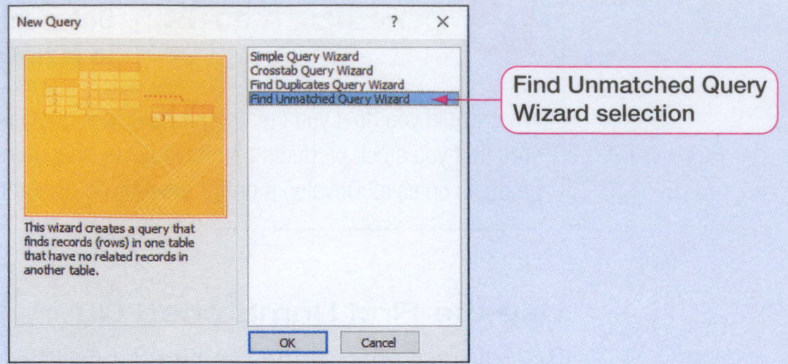

Figure 13 New Query Wizard dialog box

Access 2016, Windows 10, Microsoft Corporation

Troubleshooting

Access may display a Microsoft Access Security Notice dialog box, warning you that a potential security concern has been identified. The database you are using does not contain unsafe content. Therefore, it is safe to click Open.

c. Select **Table: tblEmployee** to select the table that contains the records you want in your query results, and then click **Next**.

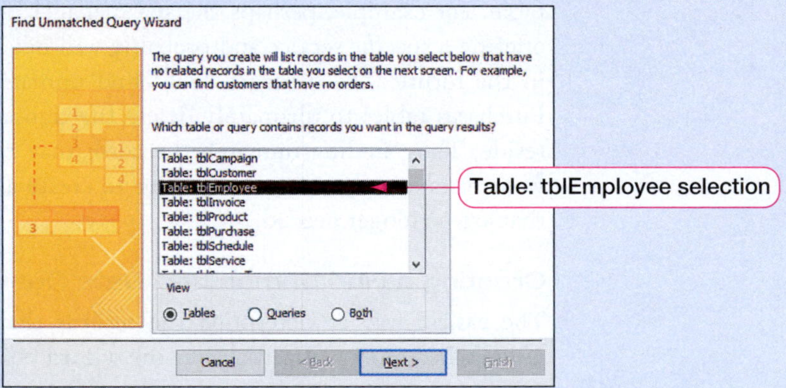

Figure 14 Select tables and/or queries to display in the query

Access 2016, Windows 10, Microsoft Corporation

d. Select **Table: tblSchedule** to select the table that contains the related records, and then click **Next**.

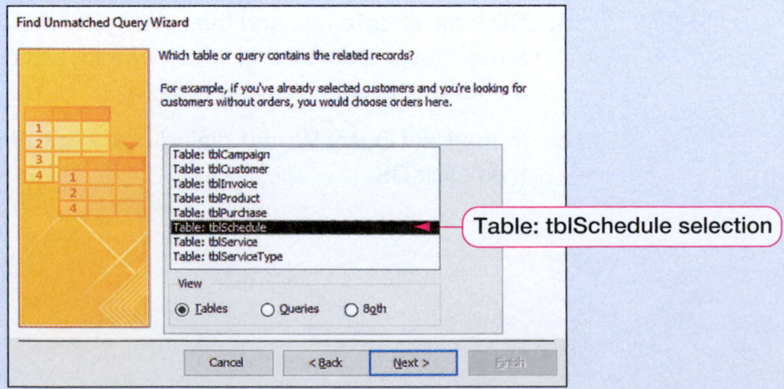

Figure 15 Select tables and/or queries that contain the related records

Access 2016, Windows 10, Microsoft Corporation

e. Under tblEmployee, select **EmployeeID** if necessary. Under tblSchedule, select **Employee** if necessary. Access prompts you to select the common field that is in both tables, and it should have already selected EmployeeID from tblEmployee and Employee from tblSchedule. Click **Next**.

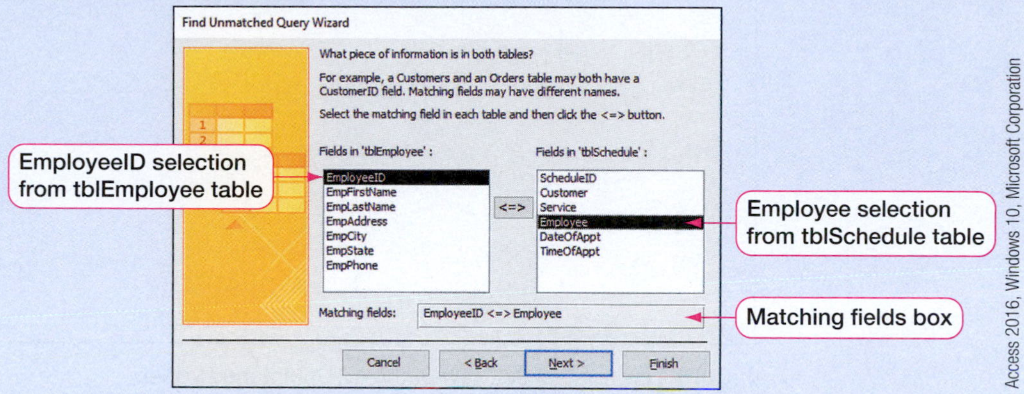

Figure 16 Determine the related field between the selected tab

Access 2016, Windows 10, Microsoft Corporation

Troubleshooting

If Access did not automatically select the related fields, click EmployeeID under Fields in 'tblEmployee', click Employee under Fields in 'tblSchedule', and then click the <=> button.

f. In the Find Unmatched Query Wizard under available fields, click **EmpFirstName**, and then click the **One Field** button [>]. Under available fields, select **EmpLastName**, and then click the **One Field** button [>]. Click **Next**.

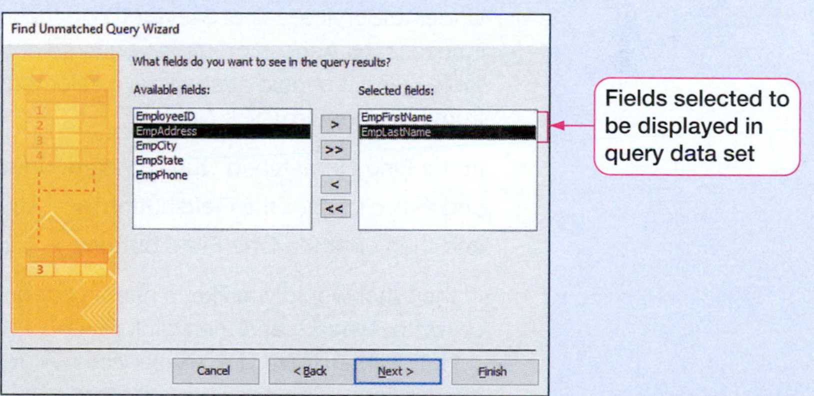

Figure 17 Unmatched fields field selection

Access 2016, Windows 10, Microsoft Corporation

g. In the What would you like to name your query? box, replace the existing text with qryUnmatched1, and then click **Finish**. Notice that there are two employees who do not have any appointments scheduled at this time.

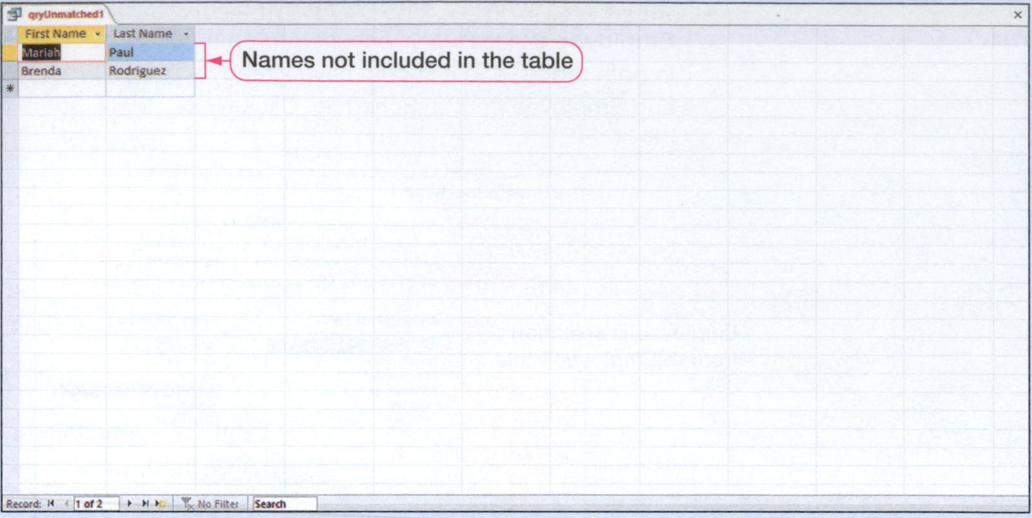

Figure 18 Datasheet view of the qryUnMatched1 query

Access 2016, Windows 10, Microsoft Corporation

h. **Close** [X] the query.

i. Click the **Create** tab, and then in the Queries group, click **Query Wizard** to create a new query that will find which services have not been given to any clients.

j. In the New Query dialog box, click **Find Unmatched Query Wizard**, and then click **OK**.

k. Select **Table: tblService** to select the table that contains the records you want in your query results, and then click **Next**.

l. Select **Table: tblSchedule** to select the table that contains the related records, and then click **Next**.

m. Under tblService, select **ServiceID** if necessary. Under tblSchedule, select **Service** if necessary. Access prompts you to select the piece of information that is in both tables, and it should already have selected ServiceID from tblService and Service from tblSchedule. Click **Next**.

n. In the Find Unmatched Query Wizard, under available fields, click **ServiceName**, and then click the **One Field** button [>]. Under available fields, select **Description**, and then click the **One Field** button [>]. Click **Next**.

o. In the What would you like to name your query? box, replace the existing text with qryUnmatched2, and then click **Finish**.

   Notice that there are six services — four with descriptions and two without descriptions — listed in your dataset.

p. Switch to **Design** view. By looking at the relationship line, you can see that Access created an outer join to allow you to view the results you were interested in seeing, that is, what you defined while progressing through the wizard.

q. In the Criteria row of the Service field, click after **Is**, press Spacebar, and then type Not. In tblService, double-click the **Fee** field to add it to the query design grid.

r. On the Design tab, in the Show/Hide group, click **Totals**. In the Total row of the Fee field, select **Sum**. In the design grid, in the field row in the Fee column, click to the left of the **Fee** field, and then type GrossRevenue: to rename the Fee field.

s. On the Design tab, in the Results group, click **Run**. Resize the fields to see all the data if necessary.

t. On the **Home** tab, in the Records group, click **Totals**. In the Total row, click the **arrow** for the GrossRevenue field, and then select **Sum**.
Notice that the spa would generate additional gross revenue of $5,339 if the spa scheduled these services once in a given day, week, or month.

u. **Save** the changes, and then **Close** the query.

v. **Close** the a04ch08Spa3_LastFirst database.

Unmatched Records Can Help You Manage Your Business

Now that you know there are 24 services that clients have never requested, should you offer some sort of discount or promotion for these services? Develop a better advertising or marketing plan? Discontinue some or all of the services?

Concept Check

1. Compare and contrast the four types of action queries. p. 448
2. Give a business example of how you could use each of the four action queries. p. 448
3. What is the difference between a simple action query and a complex action query? p. 457
4. Explain the difference between an inner join and an outer join. Why is it important to understand joins in trying to retrieve data for decision making? p. 465–466
5. How can using the Find Unmatched Query Wizard help you manage your data? p. 469

Key Terms

Action query 448
Append query 452
Business intelligence (BI) 449
Business intelligence tools 449
Complex delete query 462
Complex update query 457
Data cleansing 462
Data mining 450
Data warehouse 449
Data warehousing 449
Delete query 454
Find Unmatched Query Wizard 469
Forecasting 449
Inner join 465
Make table query 449
Operational database 449
Outer join 466
Query join 465
Simple delete query 460
Simple update query 455
Suggestive sell 450
Transactional database 449
Truncated 457
Update query 454

Visual Summary

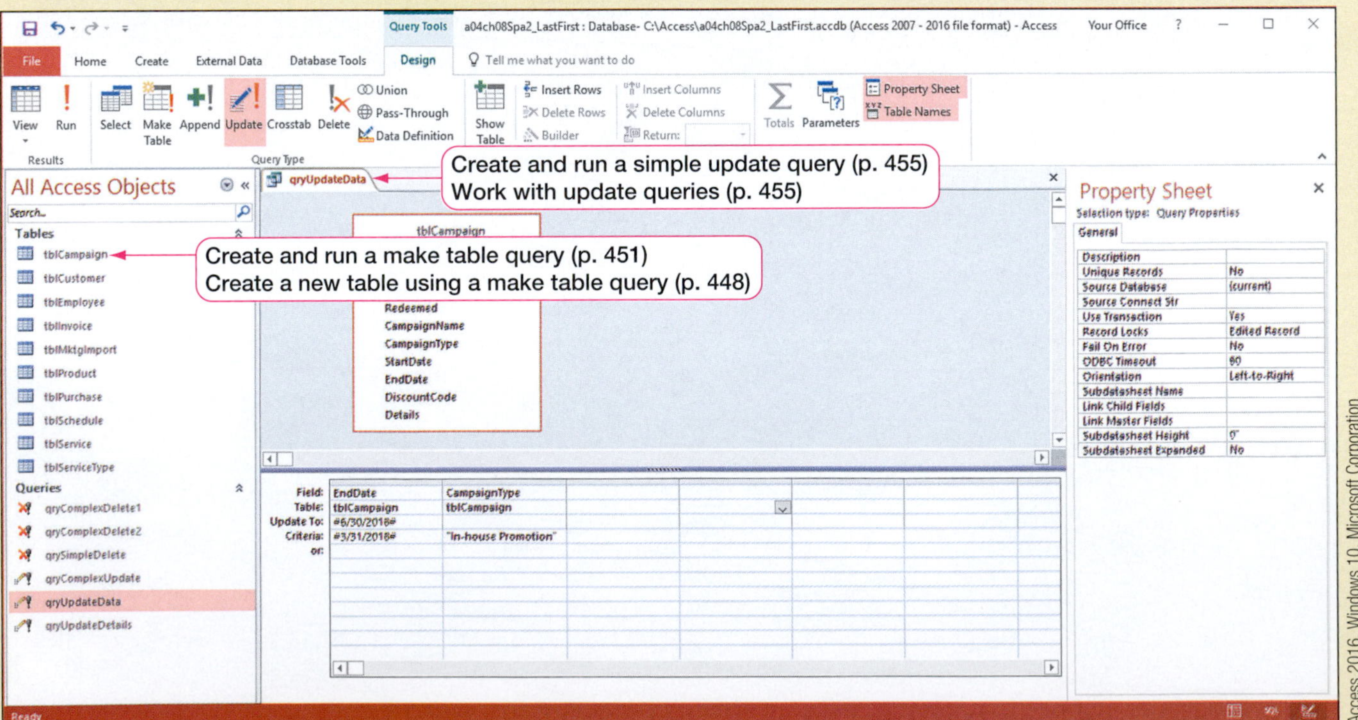

Figure 19

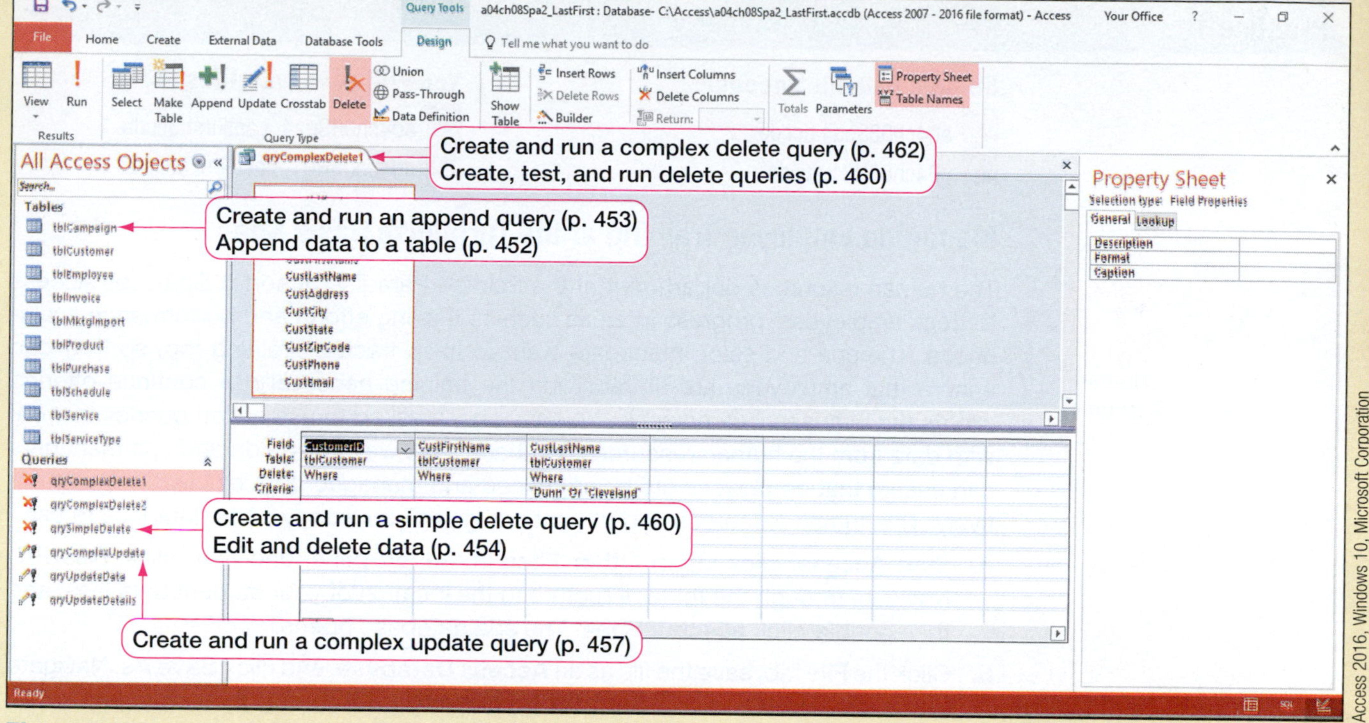

Access 2016, Windows 10, Microsoft Corporation

Figure 20

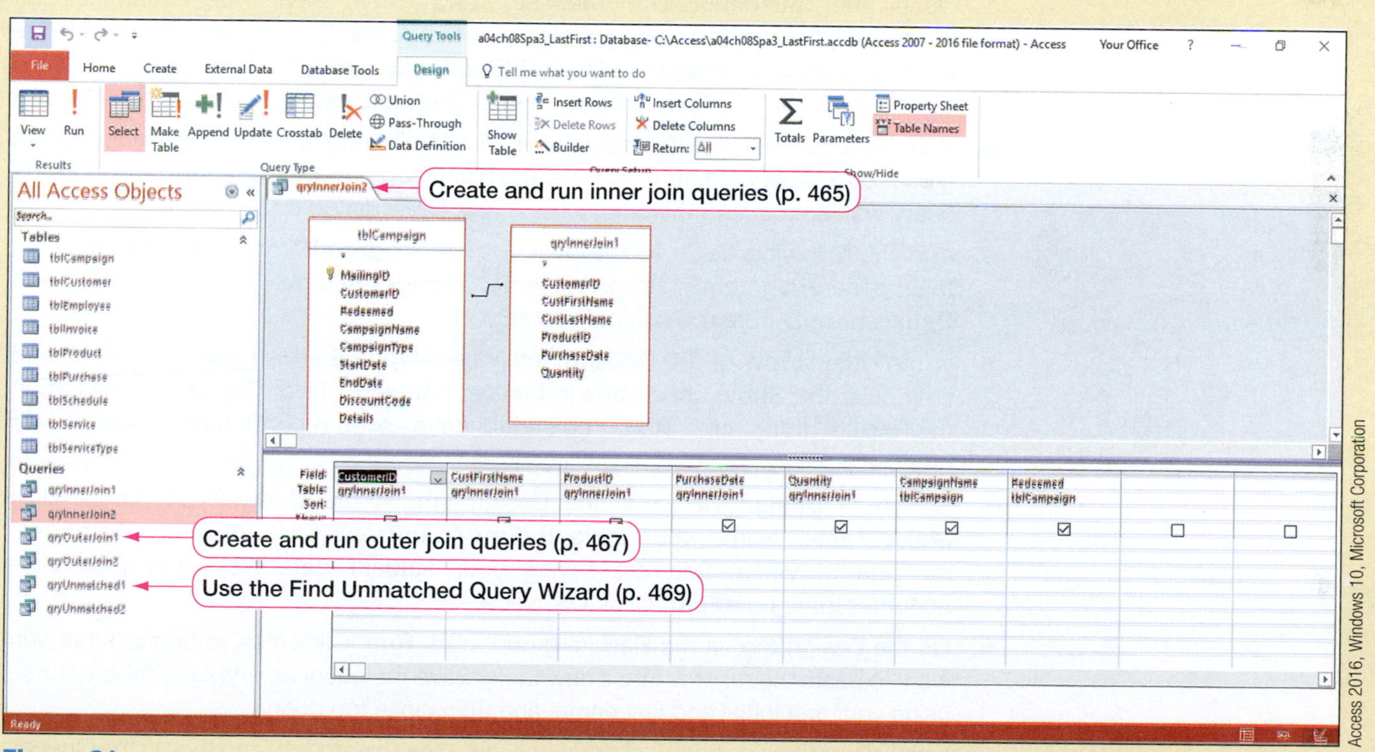

Access 2016, Windows 10, Microsoft Corporation

Figure 21

Practice 1

Student data files needed:

 a04ch08Spa4.accdb

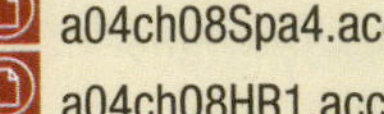 a04ch08HR1.accdb

You will save your files as:

 a04ch08Spa4_LastFirst.accdb

a04ch08HR1_LastFirst.accdb

Managing Employee Training at the Turquoise Oasis Spa

Human Resources

The human resources department at the Painted Paradise Resort & Spa uses Access to track employees' progress in areas such as training efforts and performance evaluations. The spa and salon managers want to keep track of training too, so they can ensure that employees are all receiving the training necessary to continue offering clients the best services possible. You have been asked to use action queries to work with data from the human resources database. This way, the salon and spa managers can ensure that employees are being trained and managed both efficiently and effectively. The human resources department has given you a copy of its database to use.

a. Start **Access**, click **Open Other Files** in the left pane, and then click **This PC**. Navigate through the folder structure to the location of your student data files, and then double-click **a04ch08Spa4**. The spa database opens.

b. Click the **File** tab, save the file as an **Access Database**, and click **Save As**. Navigate to the location where you are saving your project files, and then change the filename to a04ch08Spa4_LastFirst, using your last and first name. Click **Save**. If necessary, enable the content. Open tblEmployee, add your information in record **1** using your first and last name, and then close tblEmployee.

c. Open the **a04ch08HR1** database, and then save the database as a04ch08HR1_LastFirst using your last and first name. Click **Enable Content** in the security warning if necessary. Open **tblEmployee**, add your information in record **1** using your first and last name and e-mail address, and then close tblEmployee.

d. In the **a04ch08HR1_LastFirst** database, click the **Create** tab, and then, in the Queries group, click **Query Design**. Add **tblEmpTrainProg** and **tblTrainingProgram** to the query workspace, and then close the Show Table dialog box.

e. Add the following fields to the design grid: **ProgramID** and **EmployeeID** from tblEmpTrainProg and **ProgramName**, **ProgramDate**, **ProgramTime**, and **DepartmentID** from tblTrainingProgram.

f. In the Criteria row of the DepartmentID field, type Like "Turquoise Oasis*", and then clear the **Show** check box in the DepartmentID field. On the Design tab, in the Results group, click **Run**. You should have seven records that display in your data set.

g. Switch to **Design** view. On the Design tab, in the Query Type group, click **Make Table**. Name your table **tblEmpTrainProg**. Click **Another Database**, navigate to where you are saving your student data files, and then click **a04ch08Spa4_LastFirst**. Click **OK** twice.

h. On the Design tab, in the Results group, click **Run**. Click **Yes** to confirm that you want to paste the records into a new table. Save the query as qryMakeTable1_iLast, using your first initial and last name, and then close the query.

i. In the a04ch08HR1_LastFirst database, click the **Create** tab, and then in the Queries group, click **Query Design** to create a table. Add **tblEmployee** and **tblEmpDept** to the query workspace, and then close the Show Table dialog box.

j. Add the following fields to the query design: **all fields** from tblEmployee and **Department** from tblEmpDept.

k. In the Criteria row of the Department field, type Like "Turquoise Oasis*", and then clear the **Show** check box in the Department field. On the Design tab, in the Query

Type group, click **Make Table**. Name your table **tblEmployee**, click **Another Database**, and then navigate to where you are saving your student data files. Click **a04ch08Spa4_LastFirst**, and then click **OK** twice.

Because the structure of tblEmployee has changed — the addition of an e-mail address field — since it was last created in the a04ch08HR1_LastName database, you need to recreate the tblEmployee table.

l. Switch to **Datasheet** view. You should have 22 records displayed in your dataset. Switch to **Design** view. On the **Design** tab, in the Results group, click **Run**. Access will display a warning that the existing table 'tblEmployee' will be deleted before you run the query. Click **Yes** to confirm. Click **Yes** to confirm that you want to paste 22 records into a new table. Save the query as qryMakeTable2_iLast, and then close the query.

m. Close the a04ch08HR1_LastFirst database, and then switch to the **a04c08hSpa4_LastFirst** database if necessary.

n. When Access creates a table using an action query, only the basic structure is established. You need to modify the table. Open **tblEmployee** in **Design** view, and then make the following changes to the field properties and descriptions.

Field	Field Properties	Description
EmployeeID	Change this field to the primary key Change the format to "EMP"0	The Employee ID (primary key)
FirstName	Change the caption to First Name	The employee first name
LastName	Change the caption to Last Name	The employee last name
Address		The employee address
City	Change the default value to Santa Fe	The employee city
State	Format as all uppercase letters Change the default value to NM	The employee state
Phone	Change the input mask to the Phone Number format	The employee phone number
EmailAddy	Format as all lowercase letters Change the caption to E-mail Address	The employee e-mail address
JobTitle	Change the caption to Job Title	The employee job title

o. Save your changes, and then close tblEmployee.

p. You need to modify the basic table structure that Access created when you ran the make table query. Open **tblEmpTrainProg** in **Design** view, and then make the following changes to the field properties and descriptions.

Field	Field Properties	Description
Create a new AutoNumber field named EmpTrainProgID	Change this field to the primary key Change the format to "ETP"0	The Employee Training Program ID (primary key)
ProgramID	Change the caption to Program ID	The program ID (foreign key)
EmployeeID	Change the caption to Employee Change the data type to look up the employee ID in tblEmployee. Be sure to enforce referential integrity and restrict delete	The employee ID (foreign key)
ProgramName	Change the caption to Program Name	The program name
ProgramDate	Change the caption to Date	The program date
ProgramTime	Change the caption to Time	The program time

q. Save your changes, and then close tblEmpTrainProg.

r. Click the **Database Tools** tab, and then in the Relationships group, click **Relationships**. Create a relationship between **EmployeeID** in tblEmployee and **Employee** in tblSchedule. Click **Enforce Referential Integrity**, and then click Create.

s. Click the **Create** tab, and then in the Queries group, click **Query Design**. Add **tblEmployee** to the query workspace, close the **Show Table** dialog box, and then add the **EmailAddy** field to the query design grid.

t. On the **Design** tab, in the Query Type group, click **Update**. Because EmailAddy is a new field, you need to update the table to enter all employee e-mail addresses to the EmailAddy field. The format of employee e-mail addresses is initialLastname@paintedparadise.com. In the Update To row in the EmailAddy field, type **Left([First Name],1)&[LastName]&"@paintedparadise.com"**.

u. On the Design tab, in the Results group, click **Run**. Click **Yes** to update 22 rows. Save your query as qryUpdateEmail_iLast, and then close the query.

v. Open **tblEmployee**. Notice that all e-mail addresses have been added to the EmailAddy field and that the e-mail address you entered has been replaced. Close tblEmployee.

w. Click the **Create** tab, and then in the Queries group, click **Query Design**. Add **tblEmployee** and **tblEmpTrainProg** to the query workspace, close the Show Table dialog box, and then add the following fields to the query design grid: **FirstName** and **LastName** from tblEmployee and **ProgramName**, **ProgramDate**, and **ProgramTime** from tblEmpTrainProg.

x. To change the relationship to an outer join, double-click the join line to edit the Join Properties. Select **Include ALL records from 'tblEmployee' and only those records from 'tblEmpTrainProg' where the joined fields are equal**, and then click **OK**. On the Design tab, in the Results group, click **Run**. Save the query as **qryOuterJoin_iLast**, and then close the query.

y. Close the database, exit Access, and submit your files as directed by your instructor.

Problem Solve 1

Student data file needed:

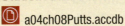

 a04ch08Putts.accdb

You will save your file as:

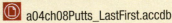

 a04ch08Putts_LastFirst.accdb

Managing Data in the Putts for Paws Database

Putts for Paws is a charity event that raises money for a local animal shelter and is hosted by the Red Bluff Golf Course. The details of the event, such as corporate sponsors, participants, and orders, are tracked by using an Access database. You have been asked to update the database so the Putts for Paws director will have an easier time managing the data from year to year. You have been given a sample database to assist the organization by creating action queries that will allow the director to maintain accurate data.

a. Open the **a04ch08Putts** database, and then save it as a04ch08Putts _LastFirst using your last and first name.

b. Open **tblParticipant**, and then add your information in record **1** using your first and last name. Close tblParticipant.

c. Create a Make Table query based on tblParticipant and tblOrder of all participants who have placed an order with the Putts for Paws Charity. Include **ParticipantID**,

FirstName, **LastName**, **ContactPhoneNumber**, **AmountPaid**, and **OrderDate**. Name the table the query will create tblParticipantOrders. Run the query, and then save your query as qryParticipantOrderTable.

d. Open tblParticipantOrders in **Design** view, and then make the following changes to the field properties and descriptions.

Field	Field Properties	Description
PartOrderID	Change the data type to **AutoNumber** Under the Format field property, add the following custom format: "PO0"0	Participant Order ID (primary key)
FirstName	Change the Field Size to 20 if necessary Add First Name as the caption	Participant first name
LastName	Change the Field Size to 25 if necessary Add Last Name as the caption	Participant last name
ContactPhoneNumber	Change the Field Size to 14 if necessary. Under Input Mask, add the **Phone Number** format Add Phone as the caption	Contact phone number
AmountPaid	Add Amount Paid as the caption	Amount paid
OrderDate	Under Input Mask, add the **Short Date** format Add Order Date as the caption	Order date
ParticipantID		Participant ID (foreign key)

e. Create a relationship between **ParticipantID** in tblParticipantOrders and **ParticipantID** in tblParticipant. Enforce referential integrity.

f. Create an Append query that will append the participants in the tblNewParticipants table to the tblParticipant table. Run the query, and then save your query as qryAppendNewParticipants.

g. Create an Update query that will update the address information and phone number for the participants in the tblParticipant table from the data that is in the tblUpdatedParticipantInfo table where the **ParticipantID** fields match. Run the query, and then save your query as qryUpdateParticipantInfo.

h. Participant Ian McShane, ParticipantID number 3, had notified Putts for Paws that he has to withdraw himself from the event. You have been asked to remove him from any and all tables in the database. Create a Delete query that will remove ParticipantID 3 from tblParticipant, tblOrder, tblOrderLine, tblParticipantOrders, and tblParticipantRole. Edit the appropriate table relationships necessary to accomplish this task. Run the query, and then save your query as qryDeleteParticipant.

i. Create an outer join query that lists all participants and participant orders, even if a participant does not have an order. Include **ParticipantID**, **FirstName**, and **LastName** from tblParticipant and then include **AmountPaid** and **OrderDate** from tblParticipantOrders. Run the query, and then save your query as qryParticipantOrders.

j. Create an outer join query that lists all participants and participant roles, even if a participant does not have a role. Include **ParticipantID**, **FirstName**, and **LastName** from tblParticipant, and then include **CorporateID** and **Role** from tblParticipantRole. Run the query, and then save your query as qryParticipantRoles.

k. Create a Find Unmatched query that displays all the participants who do not have an order. Use tblParticipant as the table you want to see in your results, and tblParticipantOrders as the table that contains the related records. Include

ParticipantID, **FirstName**, and **LastName**. Run the query, and then save your query as qryUnmatchedPartOrders.

l. Create an inner join query that includes **CompanyName** from tblCorporate and **Role** from tblParticipantRole. Run the query, and then save your query as qryCompanyRoles.

m. Close the database, exit Access, and submit your file as directed by your instructor.

Perform1: Perform in Your Life

Student data files needed:

 a04ch08Vehicle.accdb

a04ch08CarUpdate.accdb

You will save your file as:

a04ch08Vehicle_LastFirst.accdb

Managing the Vehicle Fleet at Pippy's Pizza

Finance & Accounting

Living the entrepreneurial dream of owning your own business, you open a pizza shop close to local colleges, businesses, and residential areas. Delivery business accounts for nearly 80 percent of your revenue. Most of your employees are college students and do not have cars on campus, so you decided to lease vehicles that can be used for your deliveries. You have created a database to help you manage the fleet. You want to create some queries that will help you maintain the data within the database. For example, when you purchase a vehicle, the dealership gives the new vehicle's information in a database. You want to be able to append that data to your vehicle database. Additionally, once a lease has ended and you turn the car back into the dealership, you will need to delete the vehicle and that vehicle's maintenance records.

a. Open the **Access** database **a04ch08Vehicle**. Save your file as a04ch08Vehicle_LastFirst using your last and first name. If necessary, enable the content. Open tblDealer, and then add your information in record 3.

b. Create and run the following append queries.
   - Append the data from the tblVehicle table in the a04ch08CarUpdate database to the tblVehicle table in the a04ch08Vehicle_LastFirst database. Close the query without saving it.
   - Append the data from the tblFeatures table in the a04ch08CarUpdate database to the tblFeatures table in the a04ch08Vehicle_LastFirst database. Close the query without saving it.

c. Create, run, and save two update queries.

d. Create, run, and save two delete queries.

e. Create, run, and save two outer join queries.

f. Create, run, and save two inner join queries.

g. Using the Find Unmatched Query wizard, create an unmatched data query. Run and save the query.

h. Submit the file as directed by your instructor.

Additional Cases

Additional Workshop Cases are available on the companion website and in the instructor resources.

Access Business Unit 4 CAPSTONE

Leveraging Queries for Business Information and Intelligence

This business unit had two outcomes:

Learning Outcome 1:

Use queries to calculate various values, such as sales volume for an organization, and easily view how sales volume breaks down by employee, product category, and so on. Use subqueries to calculate what percentage of total revenue came from the sales of specific services. Use SQL to query a database in a way that is easily transferrable to any other relational database management system.

Learning Outcome 2:

Use action queries to archive historical data, update many records at once, and delete records from tables and related tables. Modify the types of joins between tables to gain additional insights about the company, such as which products have never been sold.

In Business Unit 4 Capstone, students will demonstrate competence in these outcomes through a series of business problems at various levels from guided practice to problem solving an existing spreadsheet and performing to create a new database.

More Practice 1

Student data files needed:

 a04Menu.accdb

 a04ArchiveMenu.accdb

You will save your files as:

 a04Menu_LastFirst.accdb

 a04ArchiveMenu_LastFirst.accdb

Updating the Indigo5 Menu Items Database

Production & Operations

The Painted Paradise Golf Resort and Spa is home to a world-class restaurant with a top chef, Robin Sanchez. Robin regularly updates the data in her database to make certain she has all the ingredients and recipes needed to offer the high-quality food for which the restaurant is known. You have been asked to manage and cleanse the data in the Indigo5 menu items databases.

a. Start **Access**, click **Open Other Files** in the left pane, and then double-click **This PC**. Navigate through the folder structure to the location of your student data files, and then double-click **a04Menu**. A database opens displaying tables related to the restaurant's menu items and recipes.

b. Click the **File** tab, save the file as an **Access Database**, and click **Save As**. Navigate to the location where you are saving your project files, and then change the filename to a04Menu_LastFirst using your last and first name. Click **Save**. If necessary, enable the content.

c. Follow the instructions to create an outer join query that will allow Robin to see all food categories and whether or not there is a recipe associated with a category.
   - Click the **Create** tab, and then, in the Queries group, click **Query Design**.
   - Add **tblFoodCategories** and **tblRecipes** to the query workspace, and then close the Show Table dialog box.
   - Add the **FoodCategory** and **RecipeName** fields to the design grid.
   - To change the relationship to an outer join, double-click the join line to edit the Join Properties. Select **Include ALL records from 'tblFoodCategories' and only those records from 'tblRecipes' where the joined fields are equal**, and then click **OK**.

- On the Design tab, in the Results group, click **Run**.
- AutoFit the columns so that all data are visible.
- Save the query as qryRecipeCats_iLast using your first initial and last name.
- **Close** the query.

d. Follow the instructions to create a query that lists each recipe and its ingredients.
   - Click the **Create** tab, and then, in the Queries group, click **Query Design**.
   - Add **tblIngredients**, **tblRecipeIngredients**, and **tblRecipes** to the query workspace, and then close the Show Table dialog box.
   - Add the following fields to the design grid: **RecipeName** from tblRecipes and **Ingredient** from tblIngredients.
   - On the Design tab, in the Results group, click **Run**.
   - AutoFit the columns so that all data are visible.
   - Save the query as qryRecipeIngredients_iLast, and then close the query.

e. Follow the instructions to create a Find Unmatched query that will retrieve all ingredients in the tblIngredients table that are not listed in the tblRecipeIngredients table.
   - Click the **Create** tab, and then, in the Queries group, click **Query Wizard**
   - In the New Query dialog box, click **Find Unmatched Query Wizard**, and then click **OK**.
   - Under Which table or query contains records you want in the query results?, select **tblIngredients**, and then click **Next**.
   - Under Which table or query contains the related records?, select **Table: tblRecipeIngredients**, and then click **Next**.
   - Verify that **IngredientID** is selected as the matching field, and then click **Next**.
   - Under What fields do you want to see in the query results?, double-click **IngredientID** and then double-click **Ingredient** to each field to the Selected fields area. Click **Next**.
   - Under What would you like to name your query?, replace the existing text with qryUnusedIngredients_iLast. Click **Finish**.
   - AutoFit the columns so that all data are visible.
   - **Save** and **close** the query.

f. Follow the instructions to create a query that will update the price of each menu item.
   - Click the **Create** tab, and then, in the Queries group, click **Query Design**.
   - Add **tblMenu** to the query workspace, and then close the Show Table dialog box.
   - Add the **Price** field to the design grid.
   - On the Design tab, in the Query Type group, click **Update**. Because the restaurant has been awarded a Michelin star — a hallmark of fine dining quality — the chef can justify charging more money for her dishes.
   - In the Update To row of the Price field, type [Price]+5.
   - On the Design tab, in the Results group, click **Run**. In the Microsoft Access dialog box, click **Yes**.
   - Save the query as qryPriceUpdate_iLast, close the query, and then close the database.

g. Follow the instructions to open the a04ArchiveMenu database.
   - Click the **File** tab, click **Open** in the left pane, and then double-click **This PC**.
   - Navigate through the folder structure to the location of your student data files, and then double-click **a04ArchiveMenu**.
   - Click the **File** tab, save the file as an **Access Database**, and click **Save As**. Navigate to the location where you are saving your project files, and then change the filename to a04ArchiveMenu_LastFirst using your last and first name. Click **Save**. If necessary, enable the content.

h. Follow the instructions to create a query that will append the old recipes in the tblRecipesOld table to the tblRecipes table in the a04Menu_LastFirst database.

- Click the **Create** tab, and then, in the Queries group, click **Query Design**.
- Add **tblRecipesOld** to the query workspace, and then close the Show Table dialog box.
- Add the following fields to the design grid: **RecipeName**, **FoodCategoryID**, **TimeToPrepare**, **Servings**, and **Instructions**.
- On the Design tab, in the Query Type group, click **Append**. The Append dialog box opens.
- Click **Browse**, navigate to the location where you are saving your project files, and double-click **a04Menu_LastFirst**.
- Click the Table Name arrow, select **tblRecipes**, and then click **OK**.
- On the Design tab, in the Results group, click **Run**. In the Microsoft Access dialog box, click **Yes**.
- Save the query as qryRecipes_iLast and then close the query.

i. Follow the instructions to create a query that will make a table of all the records from tblReviews in the a04ArchiveMenu_LastFirst database and save it to the a04Menu_LastFirst database.

- Click the **Create** tab, and then, in the Queries group, click **Query Design**.
- Add **tblReviews** to the query workspace, and then close the Show Table dialog box.
- Add the following fields to the design grid: **ReviewID**, **Reviewer**, **ReviewDate**, **Stars**, and **RecipeID**.
- On the Design tab, in the Query Type group, click **Make Table**. The Make Table dialog box opens.
- In the Table Name box, type tblReviews, select **Another Database**, and then click **Browse**.
- Navigate to the location where you are saving your project files, double-click **a04Menu_LastFirst**, and then click **OK**.
- On the Design tab, in the Results group, click **Run**. In the Microsoft Access dialog box, click **Yes**.
- Save the query as qryReviewsTable_iLast and then close the query.

j. Follow the instructions to reopen the a04Menu_LastFirst database.

- Click the **File** tab, click **Open** in the left pane, and then double-click **This PC**.
- Navigate through the folder structure to the location where you are saving your project files, and then double-click **a04Menu_LastFirst**.

k. Right-click **tblReviews**, and then select **Design View**. Make the following changes to the structure of the table.

Field Name	Field Properties
ReviewID	In Format, type "R0"0.
Reviewer	Change the field size to 35.
ReviewDate	In Caption, type Date.
Stars	In Decimal Places, select **2**.
RecipeID	In Caption, type Recipe.

l. Save the changes, in the Microsoft Access dialog box, click **Yes**, and then close the tblReviews table.

m. Follow the instructions to create a relationship between tblRecipes and tblReviews and modify existing relationships.
   - Click the **Database Tools** tab.
   - In the Relationships group, click **Relationships**, and then click **Show Table**.
   - Select **tblReviews**, click **Add**, and then click **Close**.
   - Drag **RecipeID** in tblRecipes to **RecipeID** in tblReviews.
   - Click to select **Enforce Referential Integrity**.
   - Click to select **Cascade Delete Related Records**, and then click **Create**.
   - Double-click the **relationship line** between tblRecipes and tblRecipeIngredients.
   - Click to select **Cascade Delete Related Records**, and then click **OK**.
   - Double-click the **relationship line** between tblRecipes and tblMenu.
   - Select **Cascade Delete Related Records**, and then click **OK**.
   - Double-click the **relationship line** between tblRecipes and tblFoodCategories.
   - Select **Cascade Delete Related Records**, and then click **OK**.
   - Click **Save**, and then, in the Relationships group, click **Close**.

n. Follow the instructions to create a query that will delete all pizza recipes from the tblRecipes table and all items from any related tables.
   - Click the **Create** tab, and then, in the Queries group, click **Query Design**.
   - Add **tblRecipes** to the query workspace, and then close the Show Table dialog box.
   - Add the **RecipeName** field to the design grid.
   - In the Criteria row of the RecipeName field, type *pizza*, and then press **Enter**.
   - On the Design tab, in the Query Type group, click **Delete**.
   - On the Design tab, in the Results group, click **Run**. In the Microsoft Access dialog box, click **Yes**.
   - Save the query as qryPizza_iLast and then close the query.

o. Close the database, exit Access, and then submit your files as directed by your instructor.

Problem Solve 1

Student data file needed:

 a04HotelRevenue.accdb

You will save your file as:

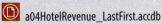

 a04HotelRevenue_LastFirst.accdb

Calculating Revenue and Maintaining the Hotel Database

Finance & Accounting

The area of Painted Paradise Golf Resort & Spa that generates the most revenue is the hotel. Guests may charge anything from the resort to their room. Therefore, the hotel area must track all of the guests' charges, such as those from the spa, golf shop, gift shop, restaurants, movies, personal trainers, and sessions with golf professionals. Hotel guests who use these services are eligible for a discount. You have been asked to create useful information through the use of queries and have been given a scaled-down version of the hotel's database to use.

a. Open the Access database **a04HotelRevenue**. Save your file as a04HotelRevenue_LastFirst using your last and first name. If necessary, enable the content.

b. Create a query, using the **tblReservations** table that calculates the total revenue from all room reservations along with the total number of reservations grouped by room type.
   - Add the **RoomType** field to the design grid.
   - Create a calculated field named RoomRevenue that multiples the **RoomRate** and the **NightsStay** fields.

- Use the Total row to sum the RoomRevenue calculated field for each room type.
- Add the **ReservationID** field to the design grid and use the Total row to count the total number of reservations for each room type.
- Rename this field NumOfReservations.
- The query should include the following fields in the order listed: **RoomType**, **RoomRevenue**, and **NumOfReservations**.
- Run the query, adjust the column widths so that all data are visible, and then save the query as qryRoomRev.
- Close the query.

Critical Thinking Which room type had the highest revenue and most reservations? What assumptions can you make about the guests of the hotel on the basis of this room type? Which room type has the biggest impact on revenue with the smallest change in reservations?

c. Create a query that calculates gross sales revenue and total reservations, using the **tblReservations** table.
   - Create a calculated field named GrossRoomRev that multiplies the **RoomRate** and **NightsStay** fields.
   - Use the Total row to sum the **GrossRoomRev** calculated field.
   - Include a new field named TotalReservations that counts the **ReservationID** field.
   - If necessary, rearrange the order of the fields to be **GrossRoomRev** and then **TotalReservations**.
   - Run the query, adjust the column widths so that all data are visible, and then save the query as qryGrossRoomRev.
   - Close the query.

d. Create a query that will use the fields in the **qryRoomRev** and **qryGrossRoomRev** queries to display the room revenue and number of reservations along with the percentage of sales revenue and percentage of reservations for each room type.
   - Organize and name the fields so they appear as **RoomType**, **RoomRevenue**, %OfRoomRev, **NumOfReservations**, and %OfReservations.
   - Format the percent fields as **Percent** with **2** decimal places.
   - Run the query, and adjust the column widths so that all data are visible.
   - Add totals to sum the **RoomRevenue**, **%OfRevenue**, **NumOfReservations**, and **%OfReservations**.
   - Save the query as qryRoomRevAnalysis, and then close the query.

e. Create an Append query that appends updated data from the accounting department, which has been imported into the database and stored in **tblNewRoomCharges**.
   - The query should append all records from the **tblNewRoomCharges** table to the **tblRoomCharges** table.
   - Run the query, save it as qryAppendRoomCharges, and then close the query.

f. Create a Delete query that deletes all the records in the **tblNewRoomCharges** table.
   - Run the query, save it as qryDeleteRecords, and then close the query.

g. Create a Make Table query to store data about older reservations, which will eventually be exported to a data warehouse.
   - The new table should include the **ReservationID**, **GuestID**, **CheckInDate**, **NightsStay**, **NumberOfGuests**, **RoomRate**, **DiscountType**, and **EmployeeID** fields from the **tblReservations** table with check-in dates on or before 12/31/2017.
   - Name the new table tblArchivedReservations.
   - Run the query, save it as qryArchivedReservations, and then close the query.

h. Create an Update query that adds a $5 delivery charge to all **room service** orders in the tblRoomCharges table.
   - Run the query, and then save the query as qryUpdateRecords.
   - Close the query.

i. Create an Update query that subtracts $25 from the room rate for VIP guest **Paula Cote** in the **tblReservations** table.
   - Run the query, save it as qryUpdateVIPRecord, and then close the query.

j. Create an outer join query that displays **all fields** from **tblRoomCharges** and the **Purchase** field from **tblChargeDetails** to include all records from tblRoomCharges and only the records from tblChargeDetails in which the joined fields are equal.
   - Run the query, and adjust the column widths so that all data are visible.
   - In Datasheet view, add a total row at the bottom of the data set that totals the **Amount** field.
   - Save the query as qryRoomCharges, and then close the query.

k. Create a query using SQL that will display the **GuestID** from **tblCharges** and a new field named TotalCharges that calculates the total room charges for each guest.
   - Group by GuestID.
   - Use the HAVING Clause to display only records in which the TotalCharges are greater than $300.00.
   - Sort the results in Descending order by TotalCharges.
   - Run the query, and adjust the column widths so that all data are visible.
   - Save the query as qrySQLHighCharges, and then close the query.

l. Close the database, exit Access, and then submit your file as directed by your instructor.

Problem Solve 2

Student data files needed:

 a04HotelReservations.accdb

a04Employees.accdb

You will save your files as:

 a04HotelReservations_LastFirst.accdb

 a04Employees_LastFirst.accdb

Managing Employees with Advanced Querying

Finance & Accounting

Management at the resorts' hotel is responsible for tracking employees' hours worked, training sessions attended, and annual evaluations. Additionally, management wants to track the guests whom the employees assist and the sales revenue that each employee generates. You have been asked to create queries that will help management manage the hotel employees.

a. Open the Access database **a04Employees**. Save your file as a04Employees_LastFirst using your last and first name. If necessary, enable the content.

b. Create a Make Table query to create a table of all employee training records.
   - The new table should include the **TrainingID** and **EmpID** fields from the **tblEmpTraining** table.
   - Name your new table tblEmpTraining, and save it in the a04HotelReservations database, located with your student data files.
   - Run the query, save the query as qryEmpTraining, and then close the query.
   - Close the **a04Employees_LastFirst** database.

c. Open the Access database **a04HotelReservations**. Save your file as a04HotelReservations_LastFirst using your last and first name.

d. Create a relationship between **tblEmployees** and **tblEmpTraining**, and then enforce referential integrity.

e. Create a relationship between **tblEmpTraining** and **tblTraining**, and then enforce referential integrity.

f. Create a relationship between **tblEmployees** and **tblEvaluations**, and then enforce referential integrity.

g. Use the data in tblReservations to create a query that lists the employees and counts the total guests that each employee has checked in to the hotel.
- The query results should list **EmployeeID** and **GuestID**.
- Group the query by **EmployeeID**, and then count the number of guests.
- Rename the **GuestID** field to NumOfGuests.
- Run your query, adjust the column widths so that all data are visible, and then save it as qryEmpTotalGuests.
- In Datasheet view, add a total row at the bottom of the data set that sums the **NumOfGuests** field.
- Save and close the query.

h. Use the data in **tblReservations** to create a query that lists the employees and calculates the total revenue that each employee has generated.
- The query results should list **EmployeeID**, and there should be a new field named GrossRevenue that multiplies the **RoomRate** and **NightsStay** fields.
- Group the query by **EmployeeID**, and then sum the **GrossRevenue** field.
- Sort in Descending order by **GrossRevenue**.
- Run your query, adjust the column widths so that all data are visible, and then save it as qryEmpGrossRevenue.
- In Datasheet view, add a total row at the bottom of the data set that sums the GrossRevenue field.
- Save and close the query.

i. Use the data in **tblReservations** to create a query that calculates total revenue.
- Create a new field named TotalRevenue that multiplies the room rates by the number of nights and then sum the calculated field.
- Run the query, adjust the column widths so that all data are visible, and then save it as qryTotalRevenue.
- Close the query.

j. Use the data in **qryEmpGrossRevenue** and **qryTotalRevenue** to calculate each employee's percentage of gross revenue.
- The query should include **EmployeeID**, **GrossRevenue**, and a calculated field named PercentOfGrossRevenue, where PercentOfGrossRevenue equals GrossRevenue divided by TotalRevenue.
- Format PercentOfGrossRevenue as **Percent** with **2** decimal places.
- Run the query, adjust the column widths so that all data are visible, and then save it as qryPercentOfGrossRevenue.
- In Datasheet view, add a total row at the bottom of the data set that sums the **PercentOfGrossRevenue** field.
- Save and close the query.

k. Use the data in qryTrainingInfo to create a **Crosstab query** that displays the number of employees who attended each training session.
- Use **EmployeeName** as the Row Heading and **TrainingSession** as the Column Heading, and then count the **SessionDate** field.
- Save the query as qryEmpTraining.

- In Design view, change the field heading of the **Total Of SessionDate** field to Total.
- In Datasheet view, add a total row at the bottom of the data set that averages the **Total** field, and then sums the remaining fields.
- Adjust the column widths so that all data are visible.
- Save and close the query.

l. Create an Update query that adds 60 minutes to all Customer Service training sessions in the tblTraining table.
   - Run the query, save it as qryUpdateTimes, and then close the query.

m. Create a Delete query that deletes **Halla Reid** from the **tblEmployees** table and all related data. You will need to edit the appropriate relationships to **Cascade Delete Related Records** in order to do this.
   - Run the query, save it as qryDeleteEmp, and then close the query.

n. Create an outer join query that displays all fields from **tblTraining** and the **EmpID** field from **tblEmpTraining** that includes all records from tblTraining and only those records from tblEmpTraining in which the joined fields are equal.
   - Run the query, save it as qryEmpSessions, and then close the query.

o. Close the database, exit Access, and then submit your files as directed by your instructor.

Perform 1: Perform in Your Life

Student data file needed:

a04KBDOrg.accdb

You will save your file as:

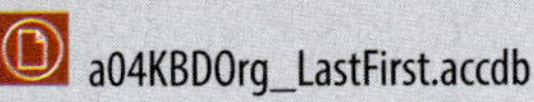

a04KBDOrg_LastFirst.accdb

Kappa Beta Delta Database

General Business

Kappa Beta Delta (KBD), a business school student organization, uses a database to keep track of membership data as well as company data for those who attend events. You need to manage the data, as it has not been used in the most efficient way possible. You also need to calculate the revenue generated through membership dues. When saving queries in this project, add _iLast, using your first initial and last name, to the end of the name.

a. Open the Access database **a04KBDOrg**. Save your file as a04KBDOrg_LastFirst using your last and first name. If necessary, enable the content.

b. Open tblMembers, and then add your information in the last record in the table.

c. Create a query that calculates the gross revenue from member dues.

d. Create at least one delete query that will help you to delete members after they have graduated.

e. Create a subquery that calculates the percentage of revenue for each semester. Add totals to your data set in Datasheet view.

f. Create a query with an outer join that lists all members and the total amount of dues they have paid since they joined the organization. Add data aggregates to the data set in Datasheet view.

g. Create two queries that use the Where function.

h. Create a Group By query that performs an aggregated calculation.

i. Create two queries that use an inner join.

j. Create two queries that perform aggregated calculations.

k. Create a crosstab query that counts the number of students who attended each meeting.

l. Close the database, exit Access, and then submit your file as directed by your instructor.

Perform 2: Perform in Your Career

Student data file needed:

 a04Resale.accdb

You will save your file as:

 a04Resale_LastFirst.accdb

Resale Shop Database

Production & Operations

As a manager of a local resale shop that helps to raise money for worthy causes, you were asked to query an existing database to track such things as gross revenue for each campaign. Additionally, you will need to manage the data through the use of action queries. This will ensure that your data is current and cleansed. When saving queries in this project, add _iLast, using your first initial and last name, to the end of the name.

a. Open the Access database **a04Resale**. Save your file as a04Resale_LastFirst using your last and first name. If necessary, enable the content.

b. Open tblContributors, and then add your information in record 1.

c. Create a query that calculates gross revenue and percent of gross revenue for all donations on the basis of the campaign. Add data aggregates to the data set when in Datasheet view.

d. Create a query that calculates the volume and percent of volume for all donations on the basis of the campaign. Add data aggregates to the data set when in Datasheet view.

e. Create a crosstab query that uses the ContributorID and CampaignID fields from tblEvents as the row headings and the EventID field as the column heading. Use Sum as the interval, and then total the Amount field. Modify the column heading to display the event name as the heading. Change the field name of the TotalOfAmount field to Total. Add totals to sum all fields in Datasheet view.

f. Create an outer join query that lists all campaigns and the contributors and donation amount where the joined fields are equal.

g. Create a Find Unmatched query that lists all non-contributors — those who did not donate to any campaign.

h. Use an action query to change the MailingList field value to No for the non-contributors.

i. Use an action query to delete the Red Cross campaign from tblCampaigns. Delete all related records.

j. Close the database, exit Access, and then submit your file as directed by your instructor.

Perform 3: Perform in Your Team

Student data files needed:

 a04Beverages.accdb

 Blank Word document

You will save your files as:

 a04BeveragesFolder_TeamName

 a04Beverages_TeamName.accdb

 a04BeveragesPlan_TeamName.docx

Querying the Beverage Database

You are the bar manager at a local restaurant that specializes in home-cooked meals for breakfast, lunch, and dinner. The general manager has given you a scaled-down version of the database with one day's worth of beverage transactions. You need to manage the inventory of beverage items to ensure that you have enough beverages for each day you are open for business. You and your team will collaborate to create several useful queries in the database. You may choose to use Microsoft's OneDrive, Google Drive, or any other cloud service to collaborate with your team on this database.

Because databases can be opened and edited by only one person at a time, it is a good idea to plan ahead by assigning tasks to each team member and setting times when the tasks are to be completed. You will create a Word document to develop the plan before beginning work on the database.

a. Select one team member to set up the Word document and Access database by completing steps b-e.

b. Open your browser, and navigate to https://www.onedrive.live.com, https://www.drive.google.com, or any other instructor-assigned location. Create a new folder, and then name it a04BeveragesFolder_TeamName using the name assigned to your team by your instructor. Be sure all members of the team have an account on the chosen system, such as a Microsoft or Google account.

c. Open the Access database **a04Beverages**. Save your file as a04Beverages_TeamName. If necessary, enable the content. Open **tblSuppliers**, and then add your team information in record **1**.

d. Upload the **a04Beverages_TeamName** database to the **a04BeveragesFolder_TeamName** folder, and then share the folder with the other members of your team. Make sure that the other team members have permission to edit the contents of the shared folder and that they are required to log in to access it.

e. Create a new Word document in the team folder, and then name it a04BeveragesPlan_TeamName.

f. In the Word document, each team member must list his or her first and last name as well as a summary of his or her planned contributions. As work is completed on the database, this document should be updated with the specifics of each team member's contributions.

g. In Access, you and your team members will need to create the following queries. When saving queries in this project, add _iLast, using your first initial and last name, to the end of the name.
   - Create a query that calculates the percentage of physical volume that a serving size of milk and orange juice take up in their respective containers.
   - Create a query that calculates the number of servings per container. Format the physical volume calculation as Standard with 2 decimal places.
   - Create an inner join query that lists all suppliers and the beverages they supply.
   - Create a query that calculates the sales volume of the amount of inventory that is used in a typical day. Group your data by the sales date and beverage name. Add data aggregates to sum the sales volume calculation in Datasheet view.
   - Create a query that calculates gross revenue by sales date.
   - Create a subquery that determines how much inventory you would need to order each week. Format the containers needed calculation as an integer.
   - Create a simple query that calculates the net revenue for each beverage. The restaurant makes 66% on each beverage sold. Display beverages that have net revenue of at least $1.25.
   - Using the query from the previous step, create a query that calculates the revenue for each beverage sold.
   - Create a union query that lists all suppliers and beverage names. Rename your displaying field as Name.
   - Create a query that lists the beverage name and total beverages sold, where the totals are between 10 and 20. Rename your total beverages sold field as TotalSold.

h. Close the database, exit Access, and then submit your files as directed by your instructor.

Perform 4: How Others Perform

Student data files needed:

 a04CarRental.accdb

 Blank Word document

You will save your files as:

 a04CarRental_LastFirst.accdb

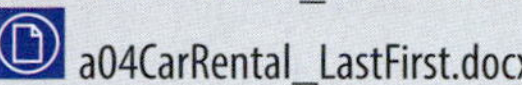 a04CarRental_LastFirst.docx

Cappy's Car Rental

Production & Operations

You are the owner of Cappy's Car Rental, a small rental car company. Your intern created a database for you and your employees to use for tracking rentals and assessing monthly performance. At first glance, you notice that it has very few queries. You believe that queries would help to answer many questions about the cars you have rented. You need to evaluate the database, create useful queries, evaluate the existing queries, and cleanse the data, as the intern left a fair amount of older data in the tables. When saving queries in this project, add _iLast, using your first initial and last name, to the end of the name.

a. Open the Access database **a04CarRental**. Save your file as a04CarRental_LastFirst using your last and first name.

b. Open **tblCustomers**, and then add your information in record 1.

c. Open **Word**, create a new blank document, and then save it as a04CarRental_LastFirst using your last and first name. This will be used to answer the questions below.

d. Consider how the data will be used. Create five queries that can be used to assist you and your employees with decision making. In your Word document, explain what question each query would answer, such as calculating sales revenue within a specific date range.

e. Create three action queries. In your Word document, explain what each query would do if you clicked Run, such as updating prices or deleting older data. If you would need to make changes to relationships for the query to run properly, note that as well.

f. Evaluate and modify the two existing queries to make them easier to read and use. In your Word document, explain what changes you made and why.

g. Save and submit your files as directed by your instructor.

Access Business Unit 5

Producing Professional Forms and Reports

Forms provide Access users a quick and simple interface for entering and navigating data. However, Access forms can be constructed to show data in much more detail by using subforms, multi-item forms, and tab controls. Forms can be enhanced by altering the properties of fields on the forms. Specifying default field values or changing the tab order on a form will make it easier to use. Like forms, reports can greatly enhance the value of a database. Reports can be customized with summary fields, calculated fields, and conditional formatting to create professional and easy-to-print documents. Reports can also be used in tandem with parameter queries and forms to provide more specific data in the report.

Learning Outcome 1:

Define bound and unbound forms, modify a variety of form properties, and create specialized and multipage forms using tab controls.

Real World Success 

"My boss was trying to organize a huge reception for out-of-town customers and guests. He had all the data he needed in various tables, but he was trying to manage all the data lookup and data entry from just the tables. I showed him how to create forms, especially forms with tabs, and he was thrilled. It not only reduced the amount of time he had to spend on managing the data, but it also turned me into his Access go-to person."

- Rebecca, MBA student and intern

Learning Outcome 2:

Create, modify, group, and sort reports that summarize data; create calculated fields for reports; utilize parameters and conditional formatting for reports; and create mailing labels with reports.

Real World Success 

"I never understood why Access was so popular. I could enter data in a table in Excel so much faster and could sort and filter the data to see what I needed. When my first boss asked me for a report based on the data I had in my Excel table, he was not too impressed with what I had printed. After all, it was just rows and columns from Excel. He had someone show me how to import the data into Access and then create a report, and then I understood why Access was so popular! The data was the same, but the report looked so much more professional and was much easier to read. Now I use Access all the time to create reports from my data."

- Lindsay, 2014 graduate

Microsoft Access 2016

Chapter 9 | ADVANCED FORM SETTINGS AND FORM TYPES

OBJECTIVES

1. Define bound and unbound forms p. 495
2. Modify the form property sheet p. 497
3. Modify the form header p. 504
4. Modify the form in Design view p. 506
5. Create specialized forms p. 521
6. Create a multipage form using tab controls p. 522

Prepare Case

Customer Service

Enhancing Data Entry at the Red Bluff Golf Course & Pro Shop

The Red Bluff Golf Course & Pro Shop generates revenues through golfers signing up for tee times and taking golf lessons. You have provided a database to Barry Cheney, the golf club manager, in which he can track employees and members. He and his staff have been experimenting with forms but have had little luck. He would like to have an interface to the database by which any of the golf club workers can easily sign members up for lessons and tee times. You will assist Barry and his staff by setting up forms that they can use as the interface.

Will Hughes/Shutterstock

Student data files needed for this chapter:

 a05ch09Golf.accdb

 a05ch09RedBluff.jpg

You will save your file as:

 a05ch09Golf_LastFirst.accdb

Working with Form Properties

A **form** is an object used to enter new records into a table, edit or delete existing records in a table, or display existing records in a table. A form can present a single record at a time rather than displaying all records the way that a table does. This presentation makes it easier for a person using the database to focus on a single record and thus helps to prevent data entry errors.

Forms have three views.

- **Form view** shows the data in the form. This is the view you use to enter or change data. You cannot change the form design in this view. This is the view that the golf course employees will use when they are performing their jobs.
- **Layout view** shows a modified form design and the data. Some of the form design, such as field lengths and fonts, can be changed in this view. The data cannot be changed. This view gives you an easy way to resize fields and check form appearance while you are creating the form.
- **Design view** shows the form design but not the data. Any aspect of the report design can be changed; however, the data cannot be changed. This view is used for creation of the form.

In this section, you will explore the different properties that are available for form fields and controls.

Define Bound and Unbound Forms

A **bound form** is a form that is directly connected to a data source such as a table or query and that can be used to enter, edit, or display data from that data source. When you create a form from a table using a wizard, the form is bound to the table you choose in the wizard setup. The field labels are the captions defined for the fields in the table design. The formatting for the fields and the field lengths are also based on the field definitions in the table design. All of these can be changed after the form has been created. An **unbound form** is not linked directly to a data source. Unbound forms can be used to specify parameters, create buttons to print reports, provide navigation menus, and other similar operations.

Opening the Starting File

In this exercise, you will start working with the golf database that has already been created. There are multiple tables that list employees, members, and other data relevant to running the golf course. There are three queries that you will use for calculated controls when creating your forms. There is also a form created with a subform that you will help to enhance later in the chapter.

A09.00

To Open the Golf Database

a. Start **Access**, click Open Other Files in the left pane, and then double-click **This PC**. Navigate through the folder structure to the location of your student data files, and then double-click **a05ch09Golf**. The golf database opens.

b. Click the **File** tab, click **Save As**, and save the file as an **Access Database**, and click **Save As**. Navigate to the location where you are saving your project files, and then change the file name to a05ch09Golf_LastFirst using your last and first name. Click **Save**. If necessary, enable the content.

Creating a Bound Form

The database used by the golf club contains tables, queries, and forms, but the forms are not fully functional yet. The first form Mr. Cheney would like is a form that can be used to add members one at a time. In this exercise, you will use the Form Wizard to create this form and then make some changes in Layout view.

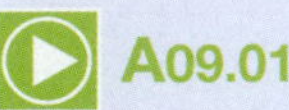

SIDE NOTE

Pin the Ribbon

If your ribbon is collapsed, pin your ribbon open. Click the Home tab. In the lower right-hand corner of the ribbon, click Pin the Ribbon [pin icon].

To Create a Bound Form

a. Click the **Create** tab, and then, in the Forms group, click **Form Wizard**.

b. Click the **Tables/Queries** arrow, select **tblMember**, and then click **Select all fields** [>>] to select all the fields in the table.

c. Click **Next**, make sure that Columnar is selected, and then click **Next**.

d. In the form title, type frmAddMember, verify that **Open the form to view or enter information** is selected, and then click **Finish**.

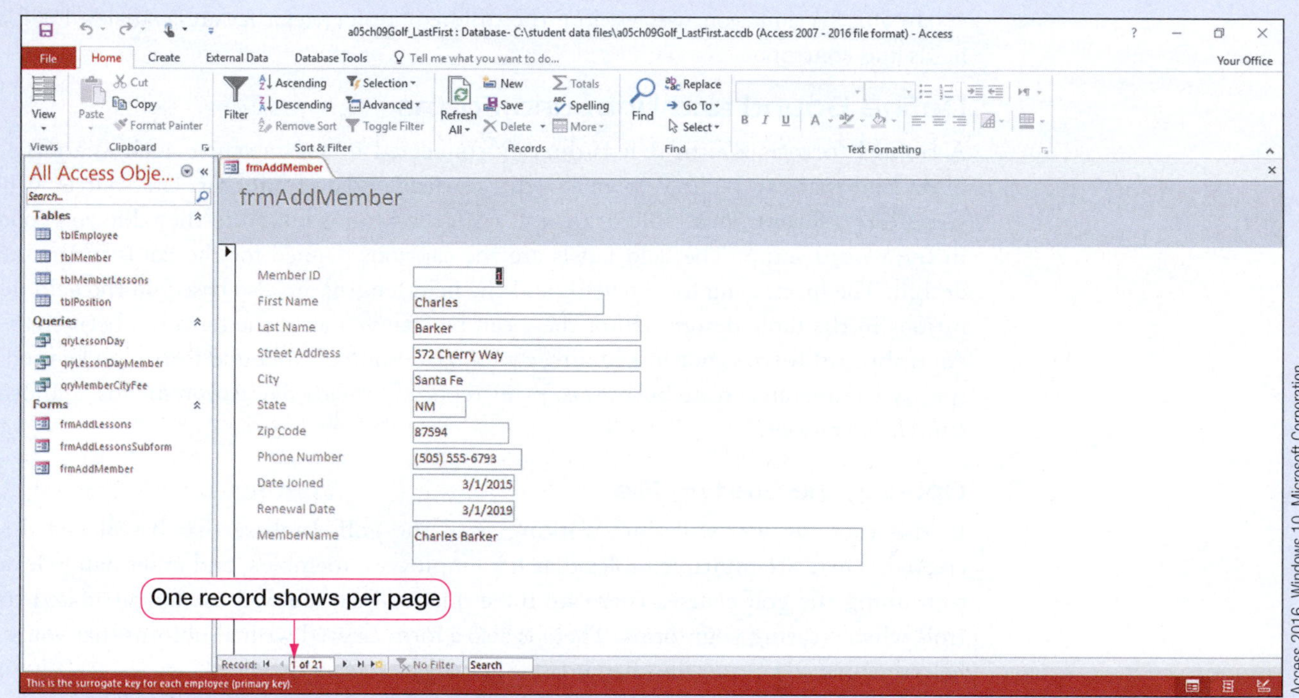

Access 2016, Windows 10, Microsoft Corporation

Figure 1 Form named frmAddMember

Making Changes in Layout View

Recall that Layout view allows a database developer to see a form with data in the fields and make changes to the form layout. Layout view is an ideal view for resizing fields in a form, since you can see the data as you are making changes. In frmAddMember, the MemberName field is a calculated field composed of FirstName and LastName, so Access set its length longer than needed. In this exercise, you will change the length of this field in Layout view.

QUICK REFERENCE	Switch to Layout View

To switch to Layout view for a form, you can use the Ribbon or the status bar, or you can right-click in the Navigation Pane.

- To use the Ribbon: On the Home tab, in the Views group, click the View arrow, and then select Layout View.
- To right-click: In the Navigation Pane, right-click the form you want to open, and select Layout View.
- To use the status bar: On the status bar, click Layout View.

A09.02

To Change the Size of a Field

a. Switch to **Layout** view.

b. Click the **MemberName field value** in the form detail.

c. Move the pointer to the **right border** of the field until it becomes a double-headed arrow ↔. Move the **border** to the left until it lines up with the address and city fields above.

d. Move the pointer to the **lower border** of the field until it becomes a double-headed arrow ↔. Move the **border** up until the field is a single line.

e. **Save** the form.

Modify the Form Property Sheet

Every field on a form has certain characteristics or properties stored in the **property sheet**. There are also characteristics of the form and sections within the forms stored in their respective property sheets. Making changes to these properties will change the formatting determined by the table design.

The property sheet has five tabs: Format, Data, Event, Other, and All. The Format tab is where properties that change the display of a field or form part are listed. The Data tab shows the field source property — where the value comes from — and other properties that affect the values that can be entered into a field. On the Event tab, you can set procedures to determine what happens when a user performs an action, such as clicking on a field. The Other tab contains all other properties that are not on one of the other tabs, such as name or data sheet caption. Finally, the All tab repeats all the properties.

QUICK REFERENCE	Property Sheet Tab options	
Property Sheet Tab	**Properties Included**	**Examples**
Format tab	Properties related to the formatting and design of a field or form	For a field • Decimal places • Width • Font For a form or form part • Background color • Special effects
Data tab	Properties related to the source of a field and how the field data is entered	For a field • Source for the field • Input masks • Validation rules
Event tab	Macro procedures that should be used when a user performs an action	Actions to be taken upon • A click • An update • On double-click
Other tab	Any properties not included elsewhere	For a field • Field name • Caption for a form • Printing information
All tab	All properties	Repeats all properties from the other tabs

The property sheet is opened by selecting the Design tab and, in the Tools group, clicking Property Sheet. The Data tab shows properties including the field source and the properties that affect the values that can be entered into the selected field, or control. A **control** is an object on a form or report that displays data, performs actions, and lets you view and work with information. A **bound control** is a field that retrieves its data from an underlying table. The properties on the Data tab are similar to the properties you use when defining a field in a table.

QUICK REFERENCE	Property Sheet Data Tab Options for Bound Controls
Property	**Options**
Control Source	The source for the data in a bound control. This may also be a calculated field.
Text Format	The format applied to the entered text.
Input Mask	Defines input rules for a field.
Default Value	Allows you to define a value that will automatically appear in a blank record.
Validation Rule	Defines the range of data that will be accepted in a field.
Validation Text	The error message that will appear if entered data violates the validation rule.
Filter Lookup	Specifies whether values will appear in a bound text box control when using the Filter By Form option.
Enabled	Stronger than the Lock property, this determines whether data can be entered or copied using the form.
Locked	Determines whether data can be entered into the field using the form.

For an **unbound control**, such as a field label, the Data tab has only a Smart Tags property. An unbound control does not have a data source and is often used for labels, display controls, and calculated controls, as there are few properties related to how the control is stored in the database. The properties shown on a tab are context sensitive and show only properties that apply to the selected control.

Changing Default Values for a Field

The **Default Value**, an option on the Data tab in the Property Sheet pane, allows you to define a value that will automatically appear in a new blank record. If a field has a typical value, you can define it here and speed up data entry.

Most members of the golf club are from Santa Fe, New Mexico. In this exercise, you will enter those values as default values for the city and state. The user will be able to change these values but will not need to enter them for members who live in Santa Fe.

SIDE NOTE
Select the Control First
To see the properties of a control, the control on the form must be selected first.

To Change Default Values

a. In the form detail, click the **City field value**.

b. Click the **Design** tab. If necessary, in the Tools group, click **Property Sheet**. The Property Sheet pane will open and show the properties for the City text box.

c. In the Property Sheet pane, click the **Data** tab. Click **Default Value**, type Santa Fe, and then press Tab.

d. Access places quotation marks around the value because it is a text value. Adding a default value does change the City field value of existing records to Santa Fe. The default is used only when adding a new blank record.

e. In the form detail, click the **State field value**. In the Property Sheet pane, click **Default Value**, type NM, and then press Tab.

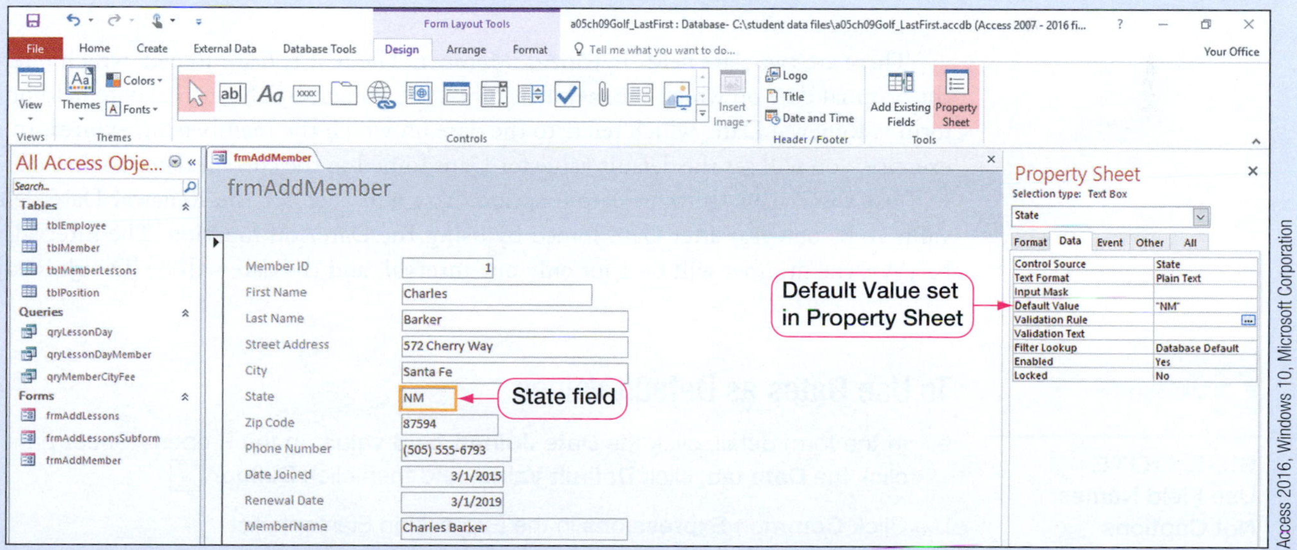

Figure 2 Default Value for State field changed to NM

f. **Save** the form.

Some table properties, such as the default value of a field, will transfer to a form. For example, if the default value in the City field of the tblMember table had been set to Santa Fe, the same field on the form would have reflected this. While these settings can be set in either the form or the table, it is best practice to set them in the table.

Using Dates and Calculations as the Default Value

You can also use Date functions and calculations as the default value. The Access function **Current Date** automatically puts the current date — based on your computer's system date — in the field. The **DateAdd function** allows you to add an interval to a date. The advantage of using this function is that it always returns a valid date. The DateAdd function has the following format: DateAdd(interval,number,date). Interval can be a day, month, year, or more, as shown in Table 1. Number is how many of the intervals you want to add to the date shown. You use year rather than 365 days so that Access will automatically take into account the possibility of a leap year.

Argument	Function Wanted	How Indicated
Interval		
	Year	yyyy
	Quarter	q
	Month	m
	Day	d
	Weekday	w
	Day of year	y
	Week	ww
	Hour	h
	Minute	n
	Second	s
Number		
	Add	Positive value
	Subtract	Negative value

Table 1 DateAdd function formatting

There are two date fields in frmAddMember. The first is Date Joined, which refers to the original date on which the member joined the golf club. The second date field on the form is Renewal Date, which refers to the date on which the membership expires. In this exercise, you will set the default value for Date Joined to the current date. To do that, you will use the Access Current Date function. You will then set the Renewal Date default value to be one year after Date Joined by using the DateAdd function. The interval will be yyyy, the number will be 1 for only one interval, and the date will be [DateJoined].

A09.04

SIDE NOTE

Use Field Names, Not Captions

When creating calculations, you must use the field name and not the field caption so Access knows which field to include in the calculation.

To Use Dates as Default Values

a. In the form detail, click the **Date Joined field value**. In the Property Sheet pane, click the **Data** tab, click **Default Value**, and then click **Builder** [...].

b. Click **Common Expressions** in the Expression Elements list.

c. Double-click **Current Date** in the Expression Categories list, and then click **OK**.

d. In the form detail, click the **Renewal Date field value**. Click **Default Value**, and then click **Builder** [...]. In the Expression Builder dialog box, under **Enter an Expression to define the control property value**, type =DateAdd("yyyy",1,[Date Joined]). Click **OK**.

This will create a default value of one year from the date joined that was entered earlier.

e. Switch to **Form** view. On the Navigation bar, click **New (blank) record**.
Notice that the new blank record has default values of Santa Fe, NM; the current date; and a renewal date one year from the current date entered in the Date Joined field.

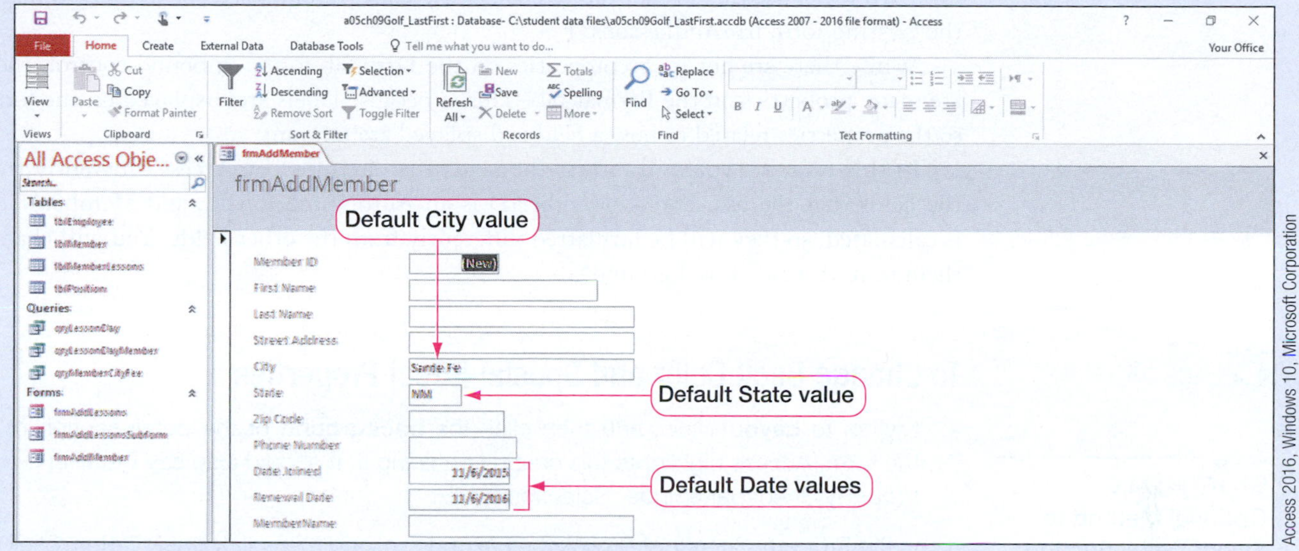

Figure 3 New Record with default City, State, and Date values

f. On the Navigation bar, click **First record** to return to the first record for Charles Barker.

g. **Save** the form.

REAL WORLD ADVICE Default Date Versus Calculated Date

Both date fields that were just set to default dates with functions may seem like calculated fields, but they are not. It is important to understand the difference because a calculated date will change, and a default date will not. What this means is that the Date Joined will always be the current day by default, and the Renewal Date will always be one year later for all new records added in the form.

However, if you change the Date Joined after it has been entered, the Renewal Date will not change — or recalculate — as you might expect. For the Renewal Date to change when the Date Joined is changed, the Source Control, not the Default Value, of the bound field would have to be changed to a calculated field.

CONSIDER THIS Allowing the Default Date to Be Changed

You set the default date to today's date but allowed the date to be changed. You could also not have allowed changes. When would you want to use a default that can be changed, and when would you want to force the value to be a default that cannot be changed? Would it depend on the data being entered, the person doing the data entry, both, or some other variable?

Changing the Background Color of the Form and Properties for Unbound Controls

The properties on the Format tab determine how the control is displayed on a form. The box for each value can be resized or moved — Width, Height, Top, Left. The border can be changed, the font can be changed, and a scroll bar can be added. None of these properties change how the field is stored in the database, but they do make it easier to use the form. You will use the Format tab to change the background color of the form to match the existing form frmAddLessons.

While there are not many properties on the Data tab for an unbound control, there are many properties on the Format tab. This is because labels are displayed on the form, so the properties related to how a field is displayed are relevant.

In this exercise, you will format the fields that are filled by Access differently than the fields that the user enters. MemberID is an AutoNumber field, and MemberName is calculated, so they will be formatted differently from the other fields. You will change them to have a faded background.

A09.05

To Change Back Color and Special Effect Properties

SIDE NOTE

Optional Method to Select Detail Section

You can also select the detail section by clicking the Selection type arrow at the top of the Property Sheet pane and then selecting Detail.

a. Switch to **Layout** view, and then click the **background** of the detail section of the form. Access highlights this area by outlining it. It should also say Detail in the Property Sheet pane under Selection type.

b. In the Property Sheet pane, click the **Format** tab, and then click **Back Color**. Click **Builder** [...], and then select **White, Background 1, Darker 15%**.

c. In the form detail, click the **MemberID field value**. In the Property Sheet pane, on the Format tab, click the **Special Effect** arrow [▾], and then select **Sunken**.

d. Click **Back Color**, click **Builder** [...], and then select **White, Background 1, Darker 15%**.

e. In the form detail, click the **MemberName field value**, click the **Special Effect** arrow [▾], and then select **Sunken**.

f. Click **Back Color**, click **Builder** [...], and select **White, Background 1, Darker 15%**.

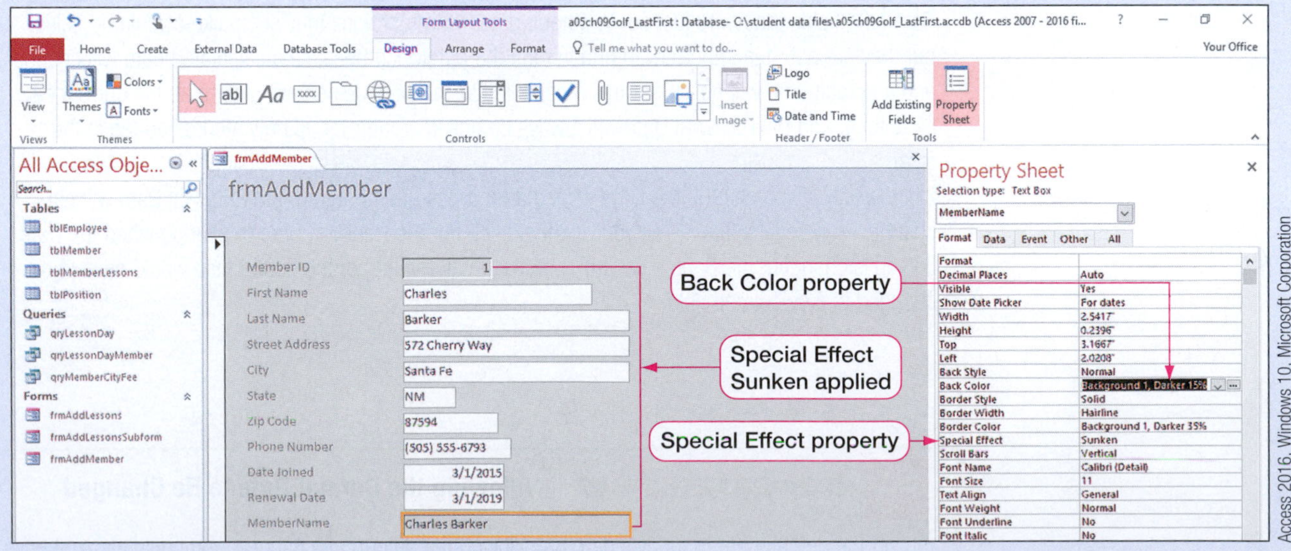

Figure 4 Member ID and MemberName sunken and filled with back color

g. **Save** [💾] the form.

REAL WORLD ADVICE	Use Formatting Sparingly

While it is possible to change the formatting for each label and field control, too much formatting can be distracting and make a form harder to use. Instead, use varied formatting only if you have a reason for that variation. Two examples of when you might make this choice: (1) Use a bright color to highlight a single important control, and (2) use one color for protected fields and another color for unprotected fields.

Displaying the Date Picker

The **Date Picker** is a popup calendar that allows a user to enter a date by clicking a date in the calendar. By default, the Date Picker will appear next to any date field unless the date field has an input mask. On frmAddMember, the Date Joined field has an input mask that was set in the table properties of tblMember. In this exercise, you will have to remove the input mask for the date picker to be displayed.

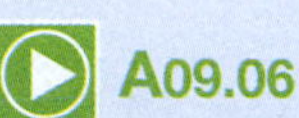

To Change the Date Format

a. In the form detail, click the **Date Joined field value**. In the Property Sheet pane, click the **Data** tab, select the **Input Mask** value, and then press Delete to delete the value.

The input mask requires the date to be typed in a particular way. The Date Picker requires the data to be selected. The data cannot be entered in both ways. Thus, the input mask will take precedence over the data picker.

b. Switch to **Form** view, and click the Date Joined text box.

Notice the Date Picker that appears next to the Date Joined field. This indicates that the date picker is available to use for this field.

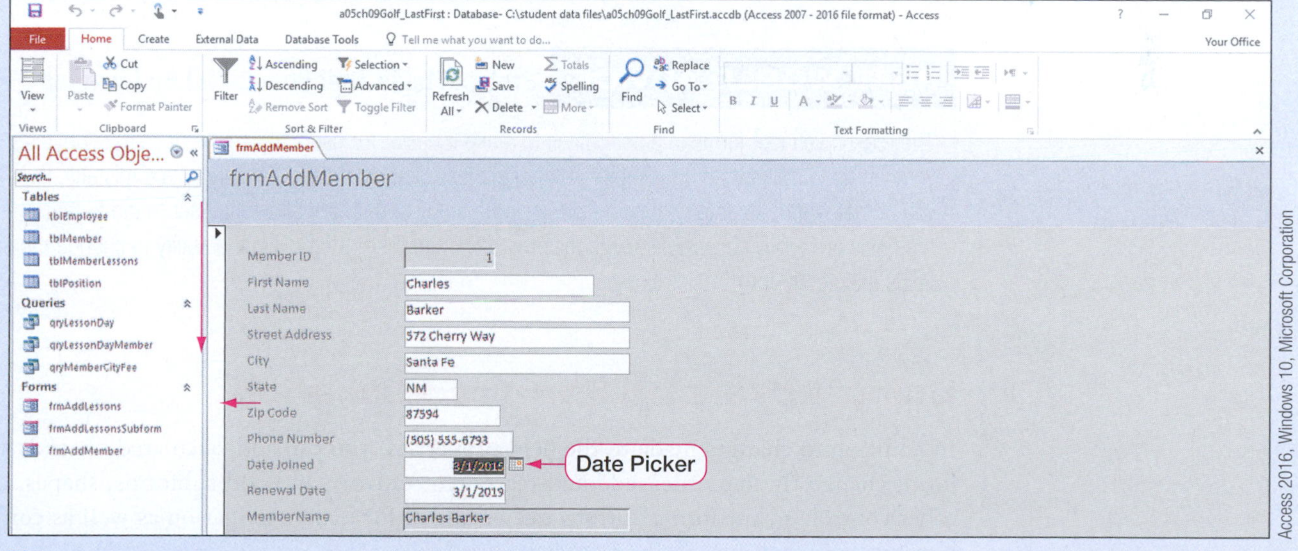

Figure 5 Date Picker activated for Date Joined field

c. **Save** the form.

Preventing Fields from Being Updated

The **Locked property** of a form determines whether data can be entered into the field by using the form. A value of No means that data can be entered; a value of Yes means that the field is locked and data cannot be entered. The **Enabled property** is stronger than a lock. If the enabled property is No, the data cannot be entered or copied. The default is that bound controls are unlocked and enabled.

When a field is locked, it may confuse the user if Tab stops at that field for data entry. The **Tab Stop property** determines whether the field can be selected in using Tab to navigate through the fields on a form. To avoid any confusion, locked fields can be skipped in using Tab.

The frmAddMember form currently allows a user to edit all fields. While MemberID and MemberName are deemphasized, a user could still try to change them. In this exercise, you will lock the fields and also change the form so the fields are skipped when a user tabs from field to field.

A09.07

To Prevent Fields from Being Updated

a. Switch to **Layout** view, and then, in the form detail, click the **Member ID field value**. In the Property Sheet pane, click the **Data** tab, click the **Locked** arrow, and then select **Yes**.

b. Click the **Other** tab, click the **Tab Stop** arrow, and then select **No**.

c. In the form detail, click the **MemberName field value**. In the Property Sheet pane, click the **Data** tab, click the **Locked** arrow, and then select **Yes**.

d. Click the **Other** tab, click the **Tab Stop** arrow, and then select **No**.

e. **Close** the Property Sheet pane, and then **Save** the form. If you need to take a break before finishing this chapter, now is a good time.

REAL WORLD ADVICE | **Protect Fields That Should Not Be Changed**

The reason you use forms to enter data is to make it easier for users to use the database. Anything you can do to make the form simpler will make it less likely that the user will make a mistake. If you do not want a user to change a field, lock the fields and do not allow the user to tab to it. If the fields are easily accessible, users may try to change them. Removing the ability to change the fields makes the form easier to use.

Using Advanced Form Modification

In addition to changes made to the field properties, you can add calculated controls to a form; change the tab order; add and rearrange controls; and add subforms, shapes, and other controls to the form. Buttons can be added for easier navigation as well as combo boxes to help look up specific records.

In addition to the detail section of the form, the form also has a header section and footer section. Titles, logos, dates, times, and other controls, both bound and unbound, can be added to the header and footer to further enhance a form. In this section, you will modify an existing form using more advanced form modification techniques.

Modify the Form Header

Every form has a header section. The header section can be used to add a form title, logo, date, or time as well as other unbound controls. The color of the header can also be changed. On frmAddMember, you will make changes to the header, including changing the color and title. You also will add a logo, the date, and the time to the form.

Editing the Form Header

A **logo** is an unbound control that can be added to the header of a form. It is an embedded picture that includes a blank header box, generally to the right of the picture. The logo can be placed only in the header and will not change as you view different records using the form.

In this exercise, you will add the golf logo to the form header, delete the blank header box, and then change the title of the form to be more meaningful to the form users.

CHAPTER 9

A09.08

To Edit the Title and Add a Logo

a. If you took a break, open the **a05ch09Golf_LastFirst** database and, if needed, navigate to the **frmAddMember** form in **Layout** view.

b. In the form header, double-click the title **frmAddMember**. Select the **current text**, and then replace the text with Add a New Member. If necessary, click outside of the text box to deselect it, then resize the title so that it fits on one line.

c. Click the **Design** tab, and then, in the Header/Footer group, click **Logo**. Navigate to your student data files, click **a05ch09RedBluff**, and then click **OK** to insert the logo.

d. Click the **blank header** box to the right of the logo you just added, and then press Delete to remove that control from the form.

Troubleshooting

If you delete the title by mistake, click Undo on the Quick Access Toolbar, reselect the blank header box to the right of the logo, and press Delete again. The blank header box will be longer than the title when you select it.

e. Click the **logo** to select it, and then point to the bottom right corner of the logo until your pointer becomes a diagonal arrow. Resize the logo so that the height is the same as the height of the header area and the width is about the same width as the title. Move the **logo** to the right of the title.

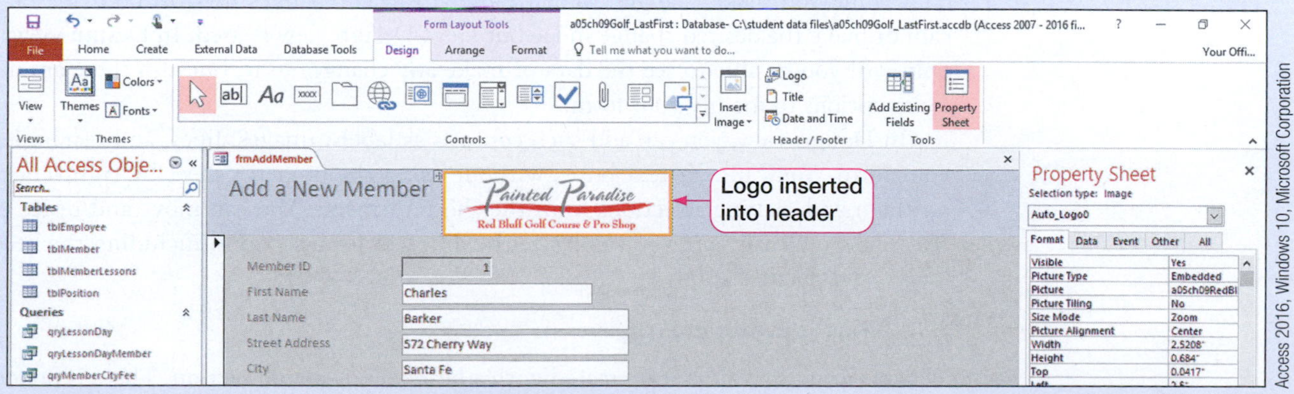

Figure 6 Logo added in form header

f. **Save** the form.

Adding the Date and Time and Changing the Background Color

The date and time can also be added to the header so every time the form is opened, the current date and time will appear. This will also be helpful if the form or record is printed because it will have the current date. You can add the date, the time, or both. Both the date and the time have three formatting options to choose from.

The background color of the header can be changed to match other forms and reports or to make the form unique.

In this exercise, you will add the date and time and use the default formatting options. You will also change the background color of the form header to white to match the existing form frmAddLessons.

A09.09

To Add the Date and Time and Background Color

a. Click the **Design** tab, and then, in the Header/Footer group, click **Date and Time**.

b. In the Date and Time dialog box, accept the defaults **Include Date** and **Include Time**, and then click **OK**.

   The current date and time have been added to the top right corner of the form.

c. Click the **form header** to select it. If necessary, on the Design tab, in the Tools group, click **Property Sheet**. In the Property Sheet pane, click the **Format** tab, and click **Back Color**. Click **Builder** [...], and then select **White, Background 1**.

d. **Save** [save icon] the form.

REAL WORLD ADVICE | **Using Date and Time as a Record Keeper**

Forms are useful to print out one record at a time. In business, it is helpful to document information, especially when you are giving it to someone else in the organization. If you print a database record using a form, by including the current date and time you will have printed documentation about that record, not only when it was printed, but also when it was current.

Modify the Form in Design View

So far, all the modifications to the form have been in Layout view, where you can see the data while you make changes. When more advanced changes need to be made or you cannot make the desired change in Layout view, Design view is used. In Design view, not only will you be able to see the data or make any changes to it, but also there are many more options to modify your form.

In Design view, you can add such controls as labels, images, lines, and rectangles to your form. You can edit text boxes without using the property sheet by right-clicking on them and making selections from the shortcut menu. You can move and resize controls independently, and you can resize the different form sections, including the header, footer, and detail sections.

Inserting a Form Footer

When a form is created, it is created with a header and a detail section. There is no footer when the form is first created, but footers are useful to add labels and other identifying information about the form.

A footer must be created in Design view, but it can later be modified in Layout view. In this exercise, you will insert a footer and format it to match the rest of the form.

A09.10 To Add a Form Footer

a. Switch to **Design** view. Since a footer has not been inserted yet, you will not see anything below the bottom bar that says Form Footer.

b. Point to the **bottom edge** of the bar that says Form Footer until you see the **pointer** [+], and then pull the **edge** down to the **1"** mark on the vertical ruler. The footer will be Background 1, so you will change it to match the form detail. Click anywhere in the **form footer**.

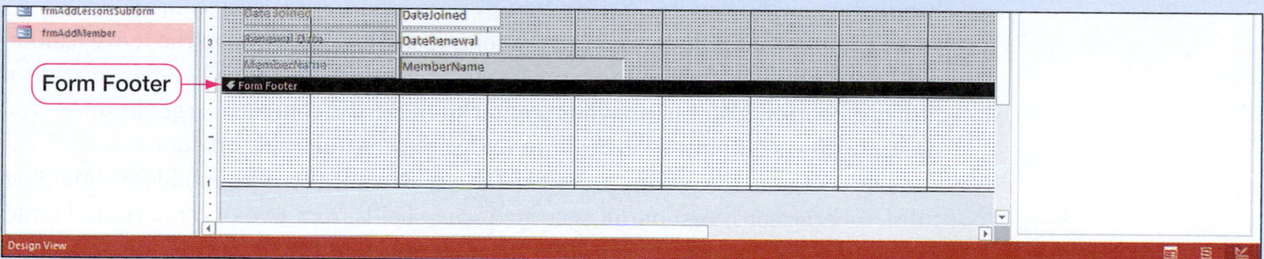

Figure 7 Form Footer on frmAddMember

Access 2016, Windows 10, Microsoft Corporation

c. In the Property Sheet pane, on the Format tab, click **Back Color**. Click **Builder** [...], and then select **White, Background 1, Darker 15%**. **Close** [X] the Property Sheet pane.

d. Test the form by entering a new record. Switch to **Form** view. On the Navigation bar, click **New (blank) record** [▶*]. In the First Name field, type your first name, and then, in the Last Name field, type your last name. In the Street Address field, type 1200 Reservoir Street, and then accept the default city and state values. In the Zip Code field, type 87593, press Tab, and in the Phone Number field, type 5055554882. Accept the **default** for the Date Joined, and accept the default for the Renewal Date.

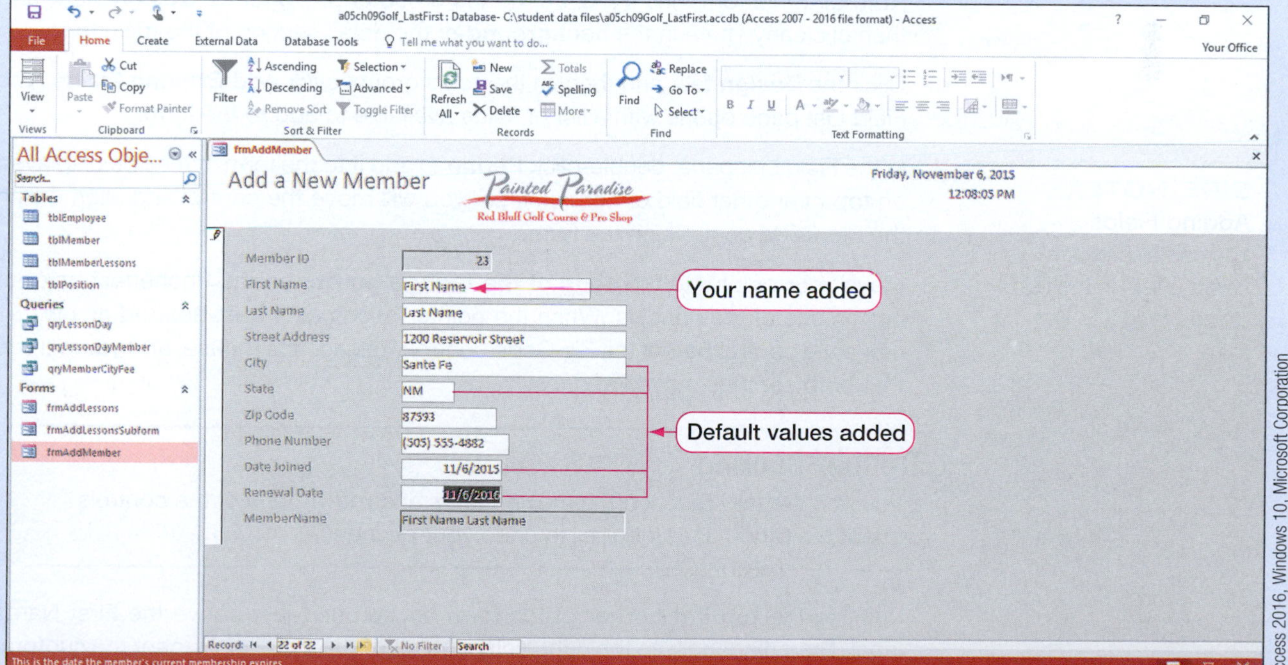

Access 2016, Windows 10, Microsoft Corporation

Figure 8 New record added to frmAddMember

e. **Save** [💾], and then **Close** [X] the form.

Adding and Stacking Fields

Any form can be modified, whether it is created from one table or multiple tables. Often, you will decide to add or delete a field after the form has been created.

When you add an existing field, Access adds two controls. One is the bound control — a text box — tied to a table field. The second is an unbound control that labels the text box. The two controls are attached to each other. They can be moved as a pair or separately. When a control is selected, Access outlines the control in orange. There are eight boxes or handles on the orange outline. The large gray handle in the top left corner is called the **move handle**. It is used to move the controls in the form. The smaller orange handles are sizing handles. **Sizing handles** are used to resize the control.

If you use your pointer to move the control without clicking on the move handle, you will move both controls at the same time. If you click the move handle, you will move just one control. You can use your pointer to move the control a large distance. You can use the arrow keys on the keyboard to nudge the control a short distance.

The staff used the wizard to create a form with a **subform** from tables tblMember and tblMemberLessons. A subform is created when fields from two or more related tables are used to create a form. The fields from the first table selected become the main form fields, and the fields from the second and subsequent tables become the subform fields. In this exercise, you will add the Phone field to the main form as it was omitted when the form was originally created. You will also align the fields by stacking them so they are lined up neatly on the form.

To Add a New Field and Align It with an Existing Field

a. In the Navigation Pane, right-click **frmAddLessons**, select **Copy**, and then right-click a blank area of the Navigation Pane. Select Paste, name the new form frmAddLessonsFixed, and then click **OK**.

b. In the Navigation Pane, double-click **frmAddLessonsFixed** to open the form. Note that this form has a main form and a subform. Switch to **Design** view, and then click anywhere in the **background** of the detail section of the main form.

c. Click the **Design** tab, and then, in the Tools group, click **Add Existing Fields**. The Field List pane opens with a list of fields available to add to the form.

d. In the Field List pane, double-click **Phone** to add it to the form. It may be displayed on top of another field or control; if so, you will move the control and align it with the Zip Code controls on the form.

e. Move your pointer to the **edge of the orange border** on the Phone text box but not on one of the handles. When the pointer becomes a **four-headed arrow**, move the control **below** the Zip Code control. Release the mouse, and you will see that both controls moved at once.

SIDE NOTE
Adding Fields
You can also click to select a field in the field list and drag it to the form.

Troubleshooting

If you accidentally touched the move handle and moved one of the controls without the other, use Undo to undo your change.

f. Point to the **top left corner** of the form background just above the First Name label. Drag diagonally to the right, selecting **all of the controls** except the subform and the subform label. Access indicates that all the controls are selected by outlining them in orange.

> **SIDE NOTE**
> **Arranging Controls**
> You can also use the Arrange tab to arrange a group of controls automatically on a form.

g. Click the **Arrange** tab, and then, in the Table group, click **Stacked**.
   Access arranges all the member controls in a stacked layout. The stacked layout can be thought of as an invisible table with matching bound and unbound controls for each field in a row. All the unbound controls are in one column; all the bound controls are in the second column.

h. With the controls still selected, on the Arrange tab, in the Position group, click **Control Padding**, and then select **Narrow**. This will reduce the amount of vertical space between each control.

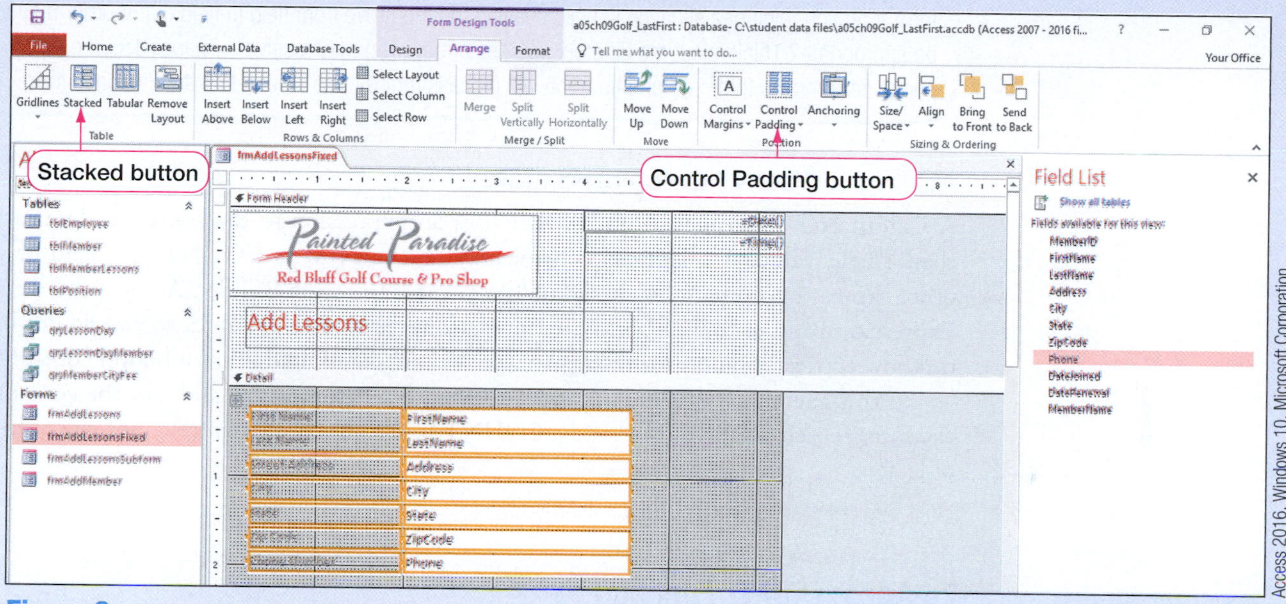

Figure 9 Stacked fields with padding adjusted

i. **Close** the Field List pane, and **save** the form.

Changing Tab Order

Fields and other controls are placed on a form either in the order in which they are added in the Form Wizard or in the order in which they appear in the source table. The **tab order**, or the order in which you move from one control to another when you press Tab, is based on the initial location of the control on the form. Moving a control to a new spot on the form does not change the tab order of the control. When you add a new field to the form, unless it is placed after all the other controls, you will have to adjust the tab order. The tab order is changed in the Tab Order dialog box, which is accessed from Design view.

In this exercise, you will change the tab order so Phone Number comes after Zip Code when you press Tab.

A09.12

To Change Tab Order

a. Click the **Design** tab, and then, in the Tools group, click **Tab Order**.

b. In the Section pane of the Tab Order dialog box, verify that **Detail** is selected. In the Custom Order list, click the **selection** box to the left of the Phone field to select the row.

c. Point to the **selection** box to the left of **Phone**, and then drag the row up to just below **ZipCode**. You will see a thick black line to show where the row will be moved. Click **OK**.

d. Switch to **Form** view, and then test the tab order by tabbing through the fields. When you press Tab, the fields should be selected in order from top to bottom.

e. **Save** the form.

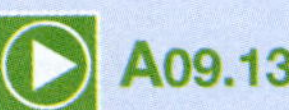

CONSIDER THIS | Out-of-Order Fields

Forms can be created to match field order in a table, but there are other considerations in planning a form. Can you think of a situation in which having the tab move from field to field out of order might be appropriate? Think about the different sources of data you may receive — paper documents, phone calls, online forms — and how you will process that data to input it into the database form.

Adding a COUNT Calculated Field

A **Calculated control** is a control that uses an expression as the source of data rather than a field value. A calculated control may be the SUM or COUNT of a field or any other expression value Access has available in the Expression Builder. Access provides the Expression Builder to help build the calculations, similar to a wizard, so you do not have to know the exact syntax for the expression. A calculated field is an unbound control.

In this exercise, you will open the subform in a new window and add the control to the form footer. Then you will add a COUNT function to the form to count the number of lessons.

A09.13

To Add a COUNT Function

a. Switch to **Design** view, and then click the **subform** so it is outlined in orange. With your pointer **on the border**, right-click, and then select **Subform in New Window**.

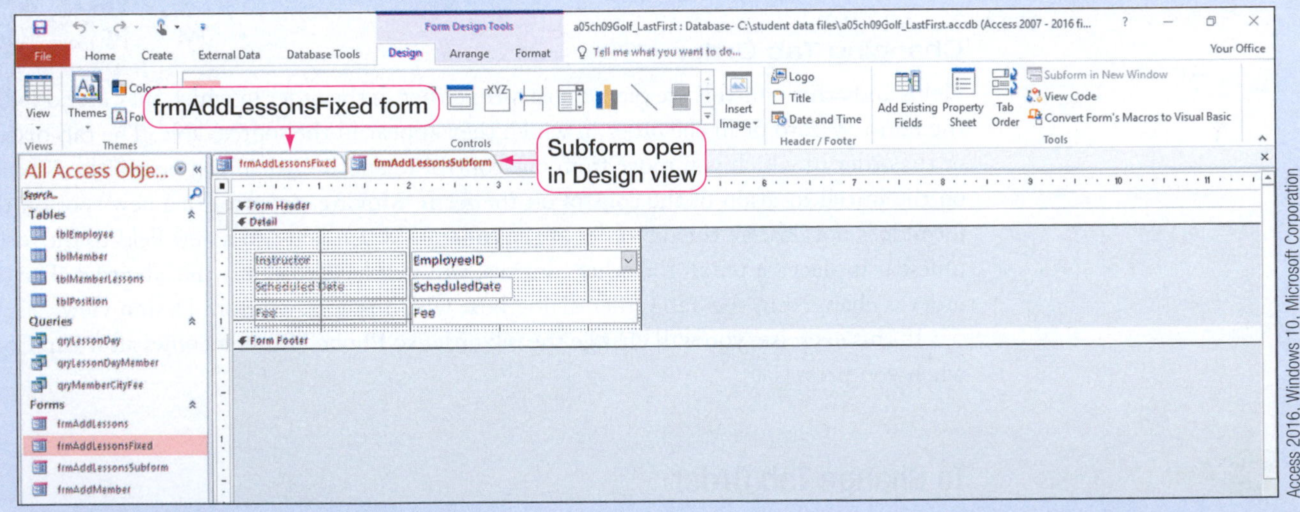

Figure 10 Subform open in new window

b. Point to the Form Footer bar, and then, when the **pointer** changes to ✛, pull down the **bottom edge** of the Form Footer bar to the **1"** mark on the vertical ruler.

c. Click the **Design** tab, and then, in the Controls group, click **Text Box** ab|. Move your pointer to the **footer**, and then click the **1"** vertical grid line in the middle of the footer.

> **Troubleshooting**
>
> If you put your controls too close to the left edge of the footer, the controls will overlap. You can use Undo and try again, or you can use the two move handles to move each field separately.

d. On the Design tab, in the Tools group, click **Property Sheet** to open the property sheet for the new control.

> **SIDE NOTE**
>
> **Entering Functions**
>
> You can type a function directly in the control rather than using the Expression Builder, or you can type it into the Expression Builder.

e. In the Property Sheet pane, click the **Data** tab, and then click **Control Source Builder** . In the Expression Builder, type =COUNT(, and in the Expression Categories pane, double-click **ScheduledDate**, and then type). The expression should look like this: =COUNT([ScheduledDate]). Any extra spaces will be removed once you save the expression. Click **OK**.

f. In the Property Sheet pane, click the **Other** tab, click **Name**, and then replace the text with LessonCount.

g. Select the new **label** on the form, and then replace the text with Lesson Count.

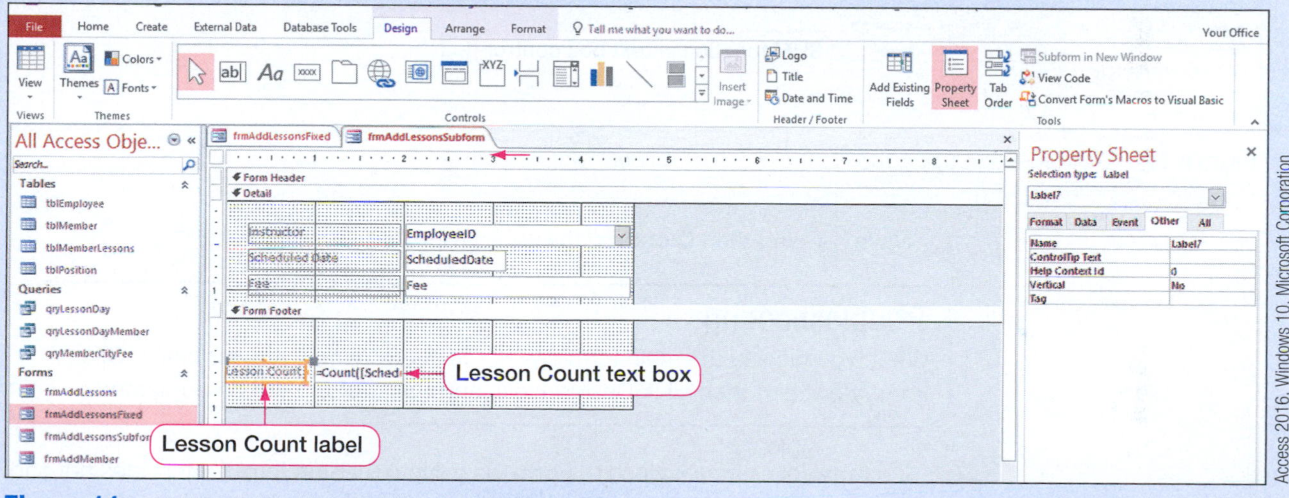

Figure 11 COUNT function added to subform footer

h. **Save** the subform.

Adding a SUM Calculated Field

The SUM function can also be added to the subform. In this exercise, you will add a calculated control to calculate the total lesson fees in the subform footer.

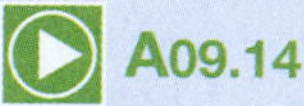

A09.14

To Add a SUM Function

a. On the **Design** tab, in the Controls group, click **Text Box** . Move the pointer to the footer below the Lesson count controls, and then click the **1"** vertical grid line. If necessary, move the Lesson Count control up to make room.

b. With the new text box selected, in the Property Sheet pane, click the **Data** tab, and then click **Control Source Builder** .

c. In the Expression Builder box, type =SUM(, and in the Expression Categories pane, double-click **Fee**, and then type). The expression should look like this: =SUM([Fee]). Any extra spaces will be removed once you save the expression. Click **OK**.

d. In the Property Sheet pane, click the **Other** tab, click **Name**, and then replace the text with FeeTotal. **Close** the Property Sheet pane.

e. Select the new label in the form footer, and then replace the text with Fee Total.

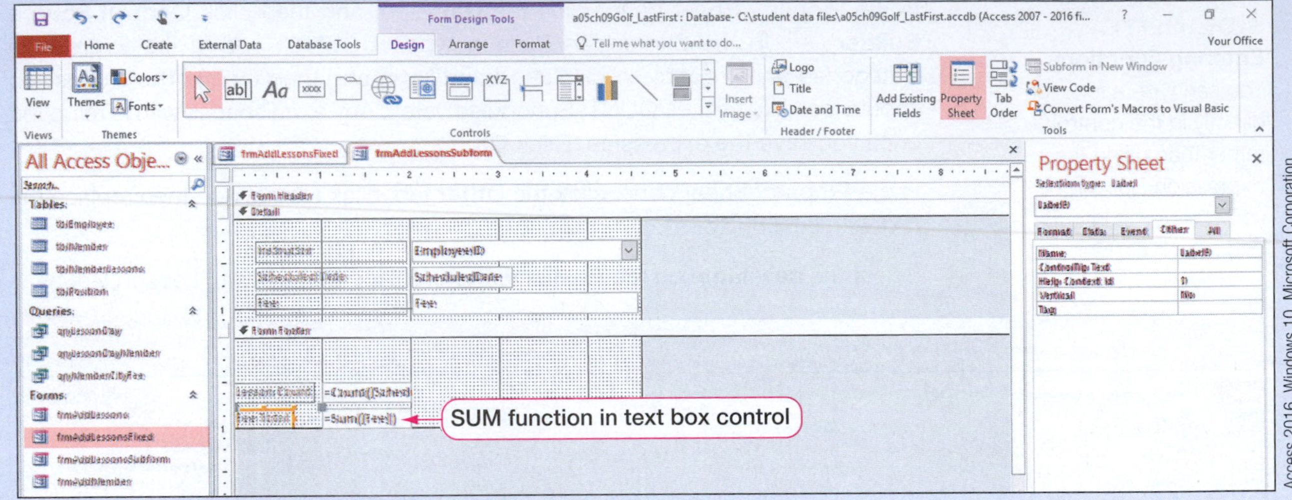

Figure 12 SUM function using the Control Source Builder

f. **Save**, and then **Close** the subform.

> **Troubleshooting**
>
> When you display the main form again, the subform may appear blank. Click Form View, and then click Design View, and the subform will be populated.

g. On frmAddLessons, switch to **Form** view. Note that the form footer does not show in the subform when the subform is viewed as part of the main form.

h. **Save** the form.

Adding Fields from a Subform to the Main Form

On a form with a subform, the footer of the subform is not visible, so any controls that were added to the subform will not be seen in Form view, even though you can see them in Design view. You have calculated the count and sum fields, but you need to show them on the main form. In this exercise, you will create new controls on the main form and use the fields from the subform as their control source.

To Add Fields from the Subform to the Main Form

a. Switch to **Design** view, and on the **Design** tab, in the Controls group, click **Text Box**. Place your pointer in the **detail section** of the form, and then click the **1"** vertical grid line just below Phone Number to place the text box.

b. Open the Property Sheet pane, click the **Data** tab, and then click **Control Source Builder**.

c. In the Expression Elements pane, double-click **frmAddLessonsFixed**, and then click **frmAddLessonsSubform**. This changes the fields in the Expression Categories pane to the fields from the subform.

Troubleshooting

If the fields do not show in the Expression Categories pane, click Cancel, then switch to Form view and then back to Design view. Click Control Source Builder again, and continue with step c above.

d. In the Expression Categories pane, double-click **LessonCount**. This will build the expression [frmAddLessonsSubform].Form![LessonCount]. This creates a reference to the LessonCount calculated field on frmAddLessonsSubform. Click **OK**.

e. In the Property Sheet pane, click the **Other** tab, click **Name**, and then replace the text with LessonCount.

f. Select the new **label** in the form detail, and then replace the text with Lesson Count. Resize the label control if necessary.

g. On the Design tab, in the Controls group, click **Text Box** [ab|]. Place the pointer in the detail section of the form, and then click the **4"** vertical grid line to the right of **Lesson Count** to place the text box.

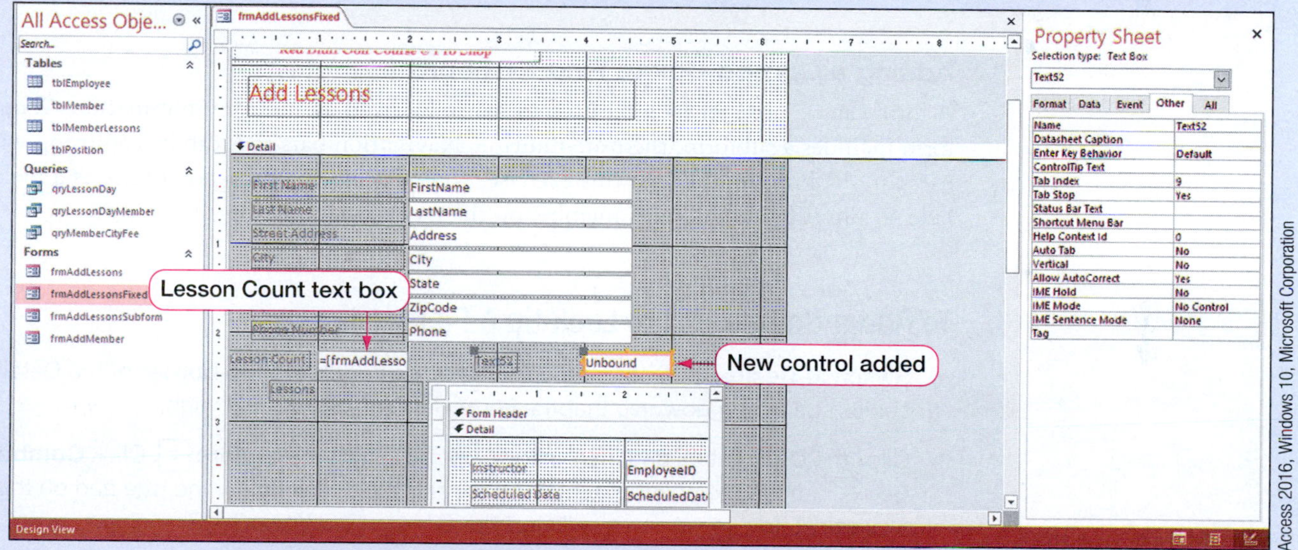

Figure 13 New text box added in Design view

h. In the Property Sheet pane, click the **Data** tab, and then click **Control Source Builder** [...].

i. In the Expression Elements pane, double-click **frmAddLessonsFixed**, and then click **frmAddLessonsSubform**.

j. In the Expression Categories pane, double-click **FeeTotal**. This will build the expression [frmAddLessonsSubform].Form![FeeTotal]. This creates a reference to the FeeTotal calculated field on frmAddLessonsSubform. Click **OK**.

k. In the Property Sheet pane, click the **Other** tab, click **Name**, and then replace the text with TotalFees.

l. Click the **Format** tab, click the **Format** arrow, and then select **Currency**.

SIDE NOTE
Moving Controls
If you need to adjust a control's placement, remember that the move handle moves each control individually.

m. Double-click the new **label** on the form, and replace the text with Total Fees. **Close** the Property Sheet pane, and switch to **Form** view to see the new controls.

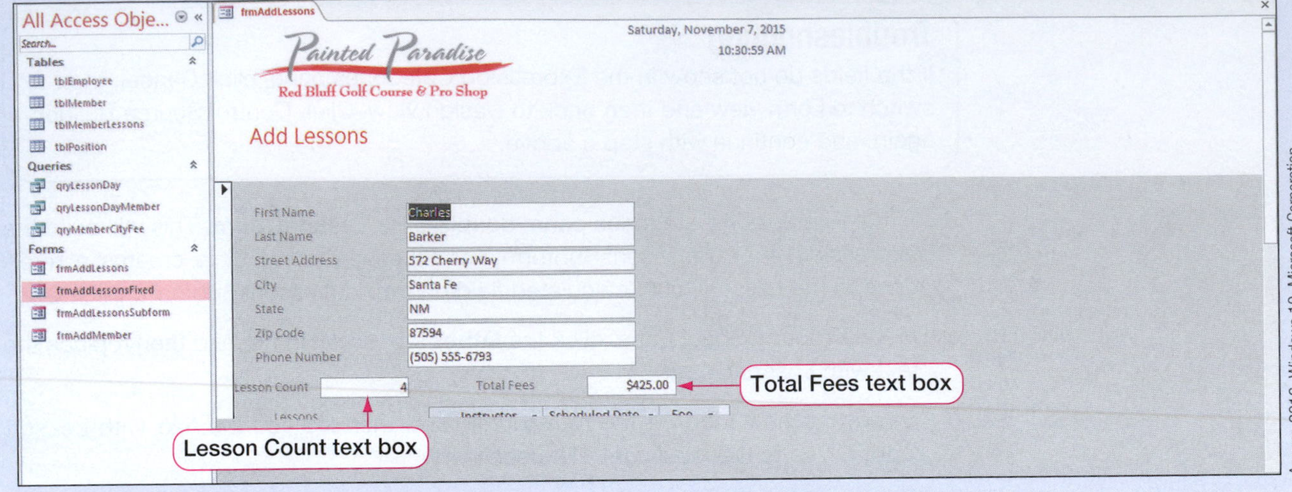

Figure 14 New text boxes in Forms view

n. **Save** the form.

Adding a Combo Box to Find a Record

A form can be used for looking up information as well as entering information. When a form includes a subform, there are multiple Navigation bars that can be confusing when users are looking for data. In this exercise, you will add a combo box to use as a lookup field to simplify looking up a member on the form.

To Add a Combo Box to Look Up a Field Value

a. Switch to **Design** view, and then place the pointer on the **top border** of the Detail section bar. Drag down so that the Form Header section is **2"** high.

b. Click the **Design** tab, and then, in the Controls group, click **More**. Click **Combo Box**, move the pointer to the **header**, and then click below the **title** and on the **1"** vertical grid line. Access will start the Combo Box Wizard.

> **Troubleshooting**
>
> If the Combo Box Wizard does not open, click More in the Controls group, and then click Use Control Wizards to turn that feature on.

c. Click **Find a record on my form based on the value I selected in my combo box**, and then click **Next**.

d. Double-click **LastName** and **FirstName**, in that order, to add them to the Selected Fields pane, and then click **Next**.

e. Accept the default to **Hide key column**, and then click **Next**.

f. Type Member Name as your label, and then click **Finish**.

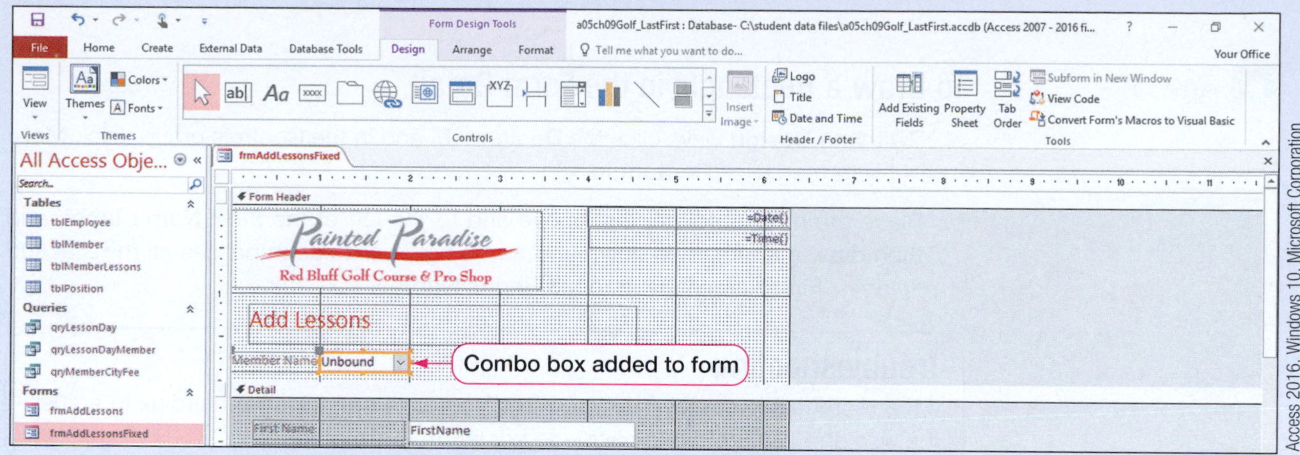

Access 2016, Windows 10, Microsoft Corporation

Figure 15 Combo box added to form header

g. If necessary, drag the new **combo** box so all the text in the label is visible, and then switch to **Form** view to test the lookup box.

h. **Save** the form.

CHAPTER 9

CONSIDER THIS | **Lookup Options**

Adding a combo box to look up a field value can be extremely helpful. Can you think of any times when a lookup field may not be appropriate on a form? Think about all the privacy laws that businesses of all types have to follow. How would those privacy laws affect how or whether you use lookup options?

Anchoring Controls

Different sized windows may show more or less of your form, just as different sized monitors or monitors with different resolutions may show the form a little differently. To preserve the relative position of your controls on a form regardless of the window size, monitor size, or monitor resolution, you can anchor the controls so they are always in the same relative position on the form. In this exercise, you will anchor the date and time controls so they always appear in the top right corner of the form.

To Anchor Controls

a. Switch to **Layout** view, click the **Date** field, and while holding Shift, click the **Time** field to select both fields.

b. Click the **Arrange** tab, and then, in the Position group, click **Anchoring**, and then select **Top Right**. If these fields already appear in the top right corner of the form, try changing the window size. The fields should always be in the top right corner, no matter the size of the window in which the form is open.

c. **Save** the form.

Adding Shapes to a Form

Not only can you add text controls and calculated controls to the form, but you can also add shapes and lines to the form. In this exercise, you will use the Rectangle tool in Design view to add a rectangle to this form so the Lesson Count and Total Fees fields stand out from the rest of the fields.

To Draw a Rectangle in the Form Detail

a. Switch to **Design** view, click the **Design** tab, and in the Controls group, click **More** [▾], and then click **Rectangle** [▭].

b. Place the mouse pointer just above and to the left of the **First Name label**, and then draw the rectangle down and to the right so it encompasses all the stacked fields — First Name label through Phone Number text box.

> **Troubleshooting**
>
> If the rectangle is not the size you want, you can use the sizing handles to adjust the size and use the move handle to adjust the position.

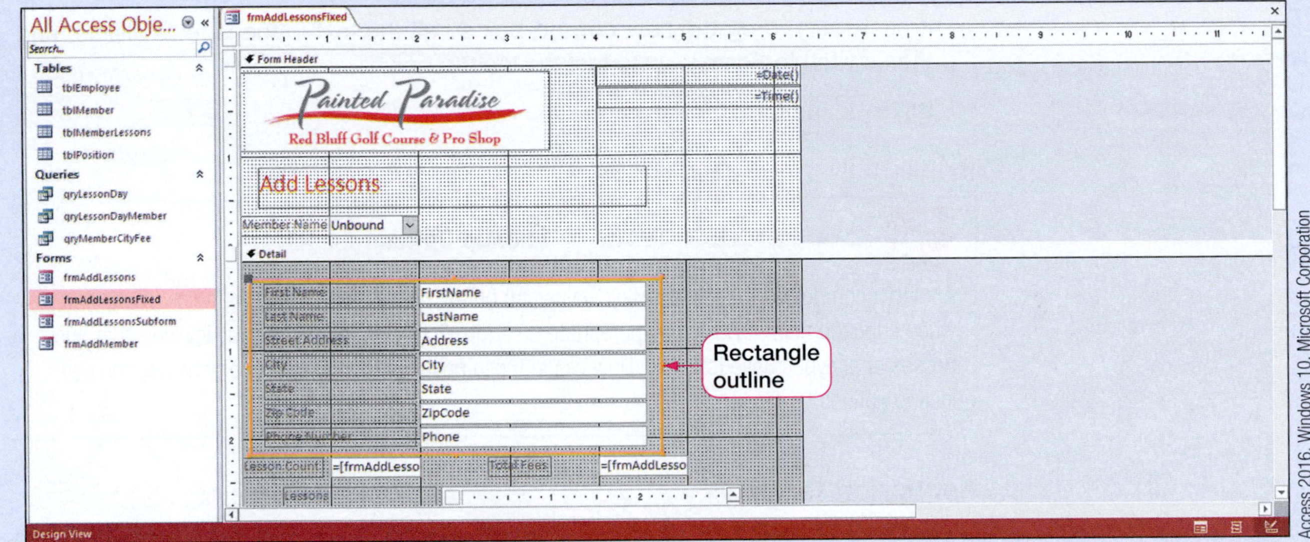

Figure 16 Rectangle shape added to the form

c. Switch to **Form** view to see the rectangle.

d. **Save** [💾] the form.

Adding Navigation Buttons

To make navigating your forms easier, you can add buttons to the form. Buttons are available in several categories and are listed in Table 2. Record Navigation buttons replicate most of the navigation tools available on the Navigation bar. You can create buttons to go to the first, next, last, and previous records. Record Operations buttons allow the user to add, delete, and undo a record. Form Operations buttons open, close, and print forms.

Category	Actions
Record Navigation	Find Next
	Find Record
	Go To First Record
	Go To Last Record
	Go To Next Record
	Go To Previous Record
Record Operations	Add New Record
	Delete Record
	Duplicate Record
	Print Record
	Save Record
	Undo Record
Form Operations	Apply Form Filter
	Close Form
	Open Form
	Print a Form
	Print Current Form
	Refresh Form Data

Table 2 Form Button categories and actions

The Add Lessons form is very easy to use, but it is still navigated by using the Navigation bars. In this exercise, you will add buttons to use for navigation.

A09.19

To Add Record Navigation Buttons

a. Switch to **Design** view, click the **Design** tab, and then, in the Controls group, click **Button** [xxxx].

b. Click the form detail at the **5"** horizontal grid line at the **.5"** mark on the vertical ruler — next to the LastName text box. If not enough of the form is showing, Access will expand the section to fit the button. Access will start the Command Button Wizard.

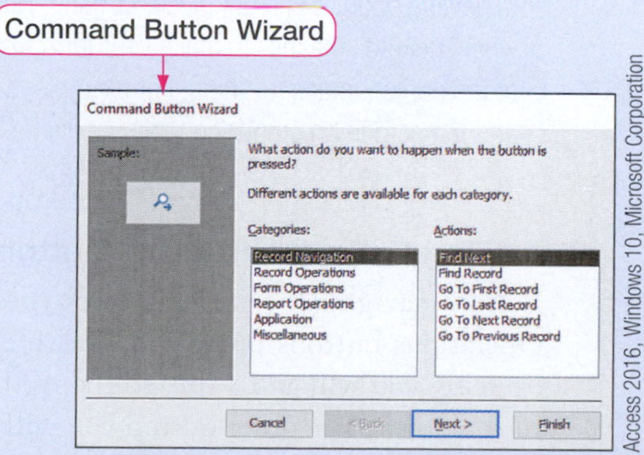

Figure 17 Command Button Wizard

c. In the Categories pane, ensure that **Record Navigation** is selected. In the Actions pane, click **Go To Next Record**, and then click **Next**.

d. Click the option button for **Text**, replace the text with Next Member, and then click **Next**.

e. Replace the **text** with cmdNextMember, and then click **Finish**.

f. On the Design tab, in the Controls group, click **Button** [xxxx]. Place your pointer below the **Next Member** button, and then click the form.

g. In the Categories pane, click **Record Navigation**. In the Actions pane, click **Go To Previous Record**, and then click **Next**.

h. Click the option button for **Text**, replace the text with Previous Member, and then click **Next**.

i. Replace the text with cmdPreviousMember, and then click **Finish**.

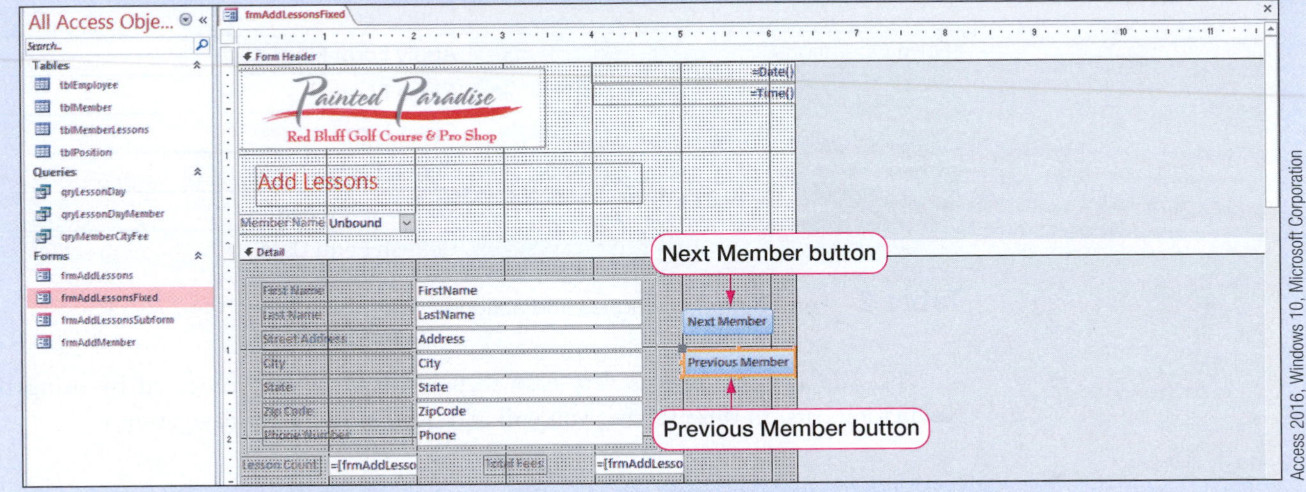

Figure 18 Two new buttons added to the form

j. **Save** the form.

REAL WORLD ADVICE Record Versus Member

Access suggests text for command buttons that includes the word "Record." In this case, the word "Record" is a technical database term. You know that a record is a row in a table and that it contains data about a person, place, or thing. However, a user without database training will not know what "Record" means. To make your form user friendly, replace the word "Record" with the name of the person, place, or thing. For example, a record in a member table should be called "Member," and a record in an employee table should be called "Employee."

Adding Form Operations Buttons

Besides navigation buttons, other types of buttons can also be added to a form. Form Operations buttons provide you with easier ways to work with the form itself. In this exercise, you will add a link to the Add Member form that will allow the user to switch to that form. The other button you will add will close the form.

To Add Record Operations Buttons

a. Click the **Design** tab, and then, in the Controls group, click **Button**. Place your pointer below the **Previous Member** button, and then click the form.

b. In the Categories pane, click **Form Operations**. In the Actions pane, click **Open Form**, and then click **Next**.

c. Click **frmAddMember**, and then click **Next**. Click **Open the form and show all the records**, and then click **Next**.

d. Click **Text**, replace the text with Add a New Member, and then click **Next**.

e. Name the button cmdAddMember, and then click **Finish**.

f. In the Controls group, click **Button**. Place the pointer below the **Add a New Member** button, and then click the form.

g. In the Categories pane, click **Form Operations**. In the Actions pane, click **Close Form**, and then click **Next**.

h. Click **Text**, accept **Close Form**, and then click **Next**.

i. Select the **button name**, replace the text with cmdCloseForm, and then click **Finish**.

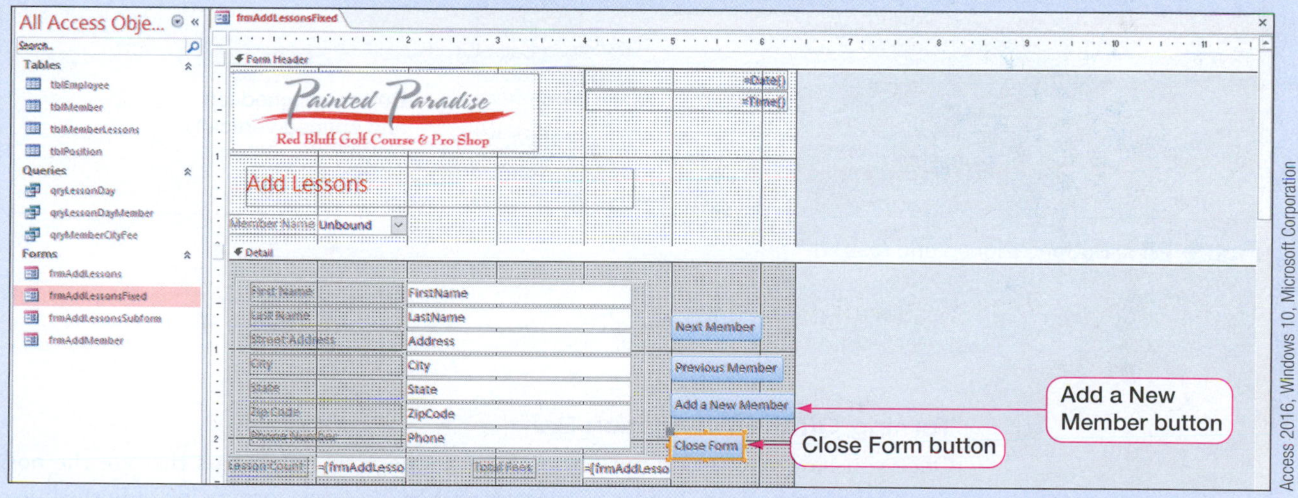

Figure 19 Form with four buttons added

j. **Save** the form.

Aligning Controls

You can use the grid to line up controls on a form manually, or you can use the many align tools available. Using the align tools will give your form a finished and polished look. In this exercise, you will line up all four buttons with one another, make them the same size, and make sure they are spaced evenly on the form.

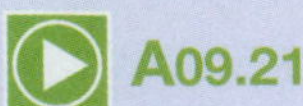

To Align Buttons

a. Click the **Next Member** button to select it. Then, while holding Shift, click the **Previous Member** button, the **Add a New Member** button, and the **Close Form** button to select all four buttons. Click the **Arrange** tab, and in the Sizing & Ordering group, click **Align**, and then select **Left**. This will align the buttons on their left edges.

b. In the Sizing & Ordering group, click **Size/Space**, and then select **Equal Vertical**. This will evenly space the buttons vertically so there is the same amount of space between each pair of buttons.

c. Click **Size/Space**, and then select **To Widest**. This will make all buttons the same width on the basis of the widest button selected.

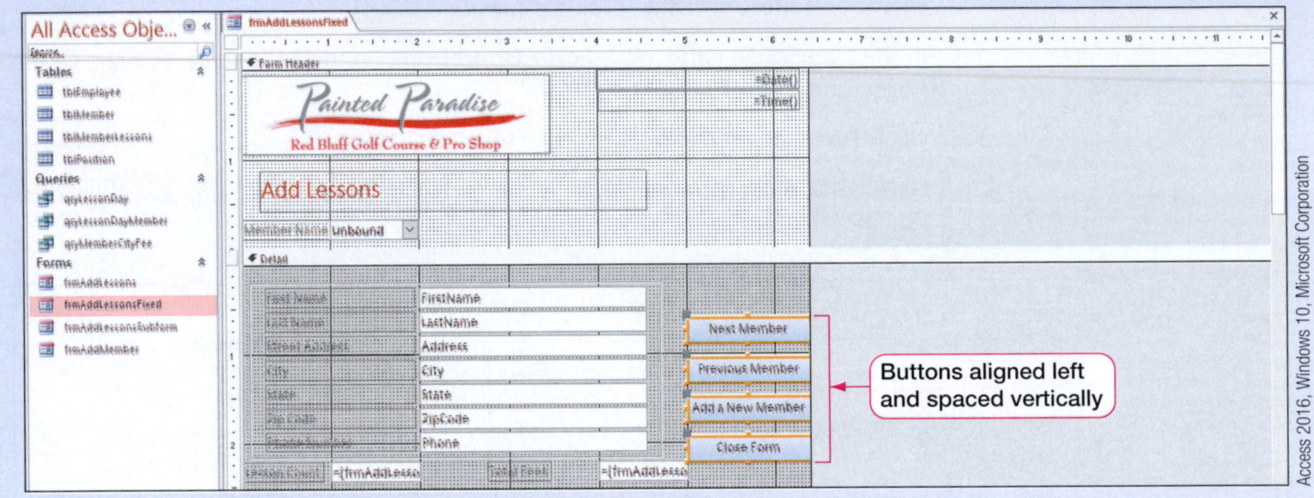

Figure 20 Buttons aligned and resized

d. **Save** the form.

Turning Off the Navigation Bar

Once you have navigation buttons on a form, the Navigation bars that are the normal part of the forms can be hidden so the user will navigate the form using only the buttons. In this exercise, you will turn off the Navigation bars for both the main form and the subform. You will also turn off the Record Selector on the far left side of the form.

To Turn Off the Navigation Bar

a. Click the **Design** tab, and then, in the Tools group, click **Property Sheet** to open the form's property sheet.

b. In the Property Sheet pane, click the **Selection type** arrow at the top of the pane, and then select **Form**. This changes the property sheet to show the properties of the entire form.

c. Click the **Format** tab, click **Navigation Buttons**, click the Navigation Buttons **arrow**, and then select **No**. This removes the navigation buttons from the form.

d. Click **Record Selectors**, click the **Records Selectors** arrow, and then select **No**. This removes the record selectors from the form.

e. In the detail section of the form, click the **Form selector** on the subform. This changes the property sheet to show the properties of the subform.

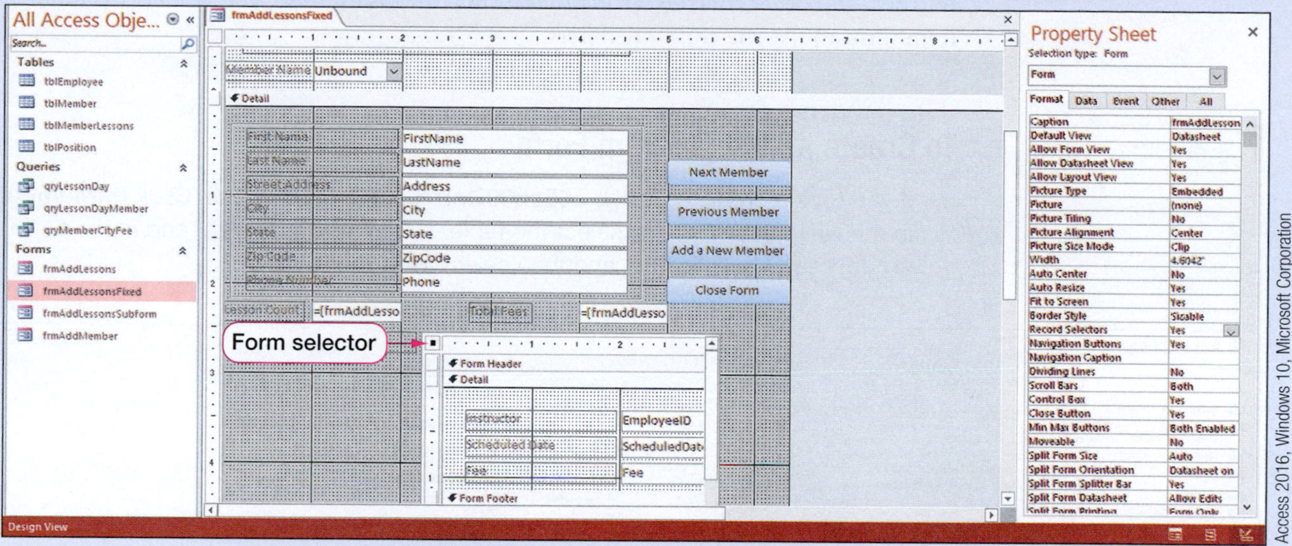

Figure 21 Subform selected in Property Sheet pane

f. In the Property Sheet pane, on the Format tab, click **Navigation Buttons**, click the Navigation Buttons **arrow**, and then select **No**.

g. **Close** the Property Sheet pane, and then **Save** the form. Switch to Form view, and then test your buttons. Note that if you click **Add New Member**, you will open frmAddMember. **Close** frmAddMember. On **frmAddLessons**, click **Close Form** to close the form. If necessary, click **Yes** to save the objects.

h. If you need to take a break before finishing this chapter, now is a good time.

REAL WORLD ADVICE **Picture Versus Text**

Access allows you to use pictures or text for buttons. Use text unless the meaning of the picture is absolutely obvious. For example, does an image of a door mean close or open? "Exit" is not the obvious interpretation. If the meaning is not obvious, use words to label the button. The picture of a printer is universal, and the undo button is well known. The others may need explanation and are better left as text.

Creating Advanced Forms

Forms do not have to show only one record at a time. Forms can show multiple records at a time in a **multiple-item form**, or continuous form.

Forms can also be multiple pages, each of which is controlled by a tab. This way, you can view multiple forms in one window by clicking on different tabs.

In this section, you will create different types of advanced forms to illustrate the different uses for forms in Access.

Create Specialized Forms

On the Create tab, there is a More Forms button that lists different types of forms available to create. Before you choose a form, you should have an object in the Navigation Pane selected. Whatever is selected in the Navigation Pane, whether it is a table or a query, will become the source for the form you choose to create.

Creating a Multiple-Item Form

While the multiple-item form looks very similar to a data sheet, it can be customized as a form. The data is arranged in rows and columns, but you can add graphical elements, buttons, and other controls, as in other forms. In this exercise, you will create a multiple-item form to list the club's members.

A09.23

To Create a Multiple-Item Form

a. If you took a break, open the **a05ch09Golf_LastFirst** database. Click **tblMember** in the Navigation Pane to select the table. Click the **Create** tab, and in the Forms group, click **More Forms**, and then select **Multiple Items**.

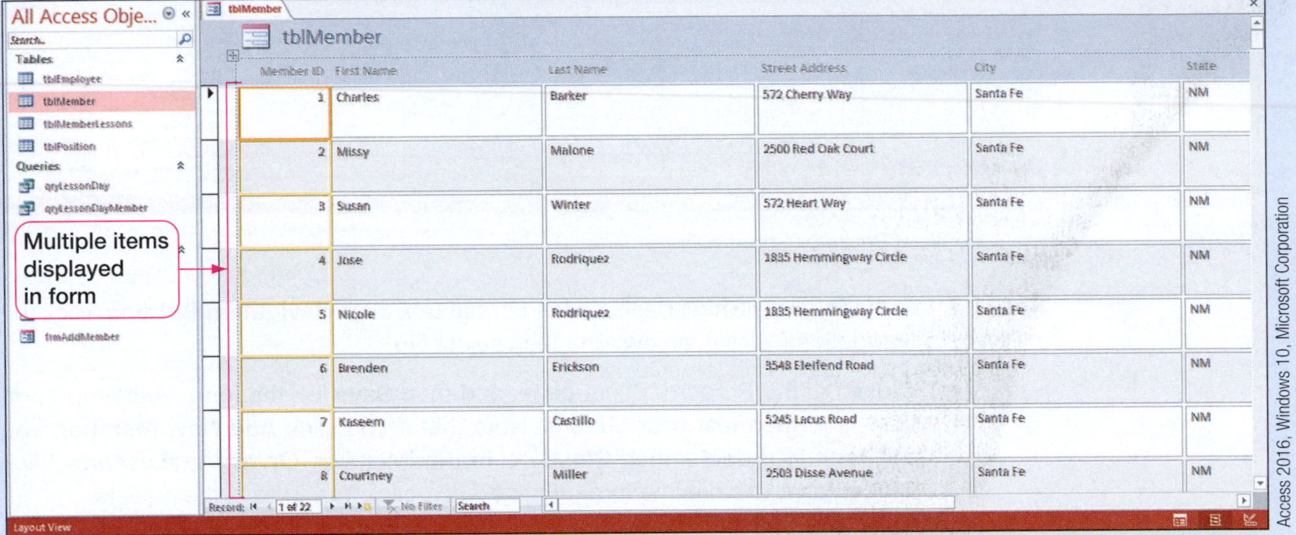

Access 2016, Windows 10, Microsoft Corporation

Figure 22 Multiple-Items Form Created

b. Scroll right to find **Date Joined**, and then click the first **Date Joined field value**. Click the **Design** tab, and in the Tools group, click **Property Sheet**. In the Property Sheet pane, click the **Data** tab, click **Input Mask**, and then select the text. Press Delete to remove the input mask.

c. On the form detail, click the **Renewal Date field value**, and then, in the Property Sheet pane, on the Data tab, click **Input Mask**. Select the text, and then press Delete to remove the input mask. The Date Picker will now be displayed.

d. At the top of the Property Sheet pane, click the **Selection type** arrow, and then select **Form Header**. Click the **Format** tab, and then click **Back Color**. Click **Builder** [...], and then select **White, Background 1, Darker 15%**. **Close** [X] the Property Sheet pane.

e. Click the form **title**, and then change it to Multiple Members Form. Click the form **icon** to the left of the title, and then press Delete.

f. **Save** [save icon] the form, and type frmMultipleMembers. Click **OK**, and then **Close** [X] the form.

Create a Multipage Form Using Tab Controls

A multipage form can be used to show two different forms on one page or to show groups of fields from multiple tables, and it allows you to switch between them, using tabs you create on the form. Multipage forms can be created by using either the Page Break tool or the Tab Control tool. The Page Break tool creates a continuous flow between forms so you can use the Page Up and Page Down keys to move between forms. The **Tab Control** tool creates tabs, with one tab per page, so you switch between pages using the tabs.

Modifying an Existing Form to Add a Tab Control

You will create a modified version of frmAddLessons that has three tabs with all the member information. In this exercise, you will start by creating a copy of frmAddLessons and then modifying that form.

A09.24

To Copy an Existing Form and Add a Tab Control

a. Right-click **frmAddLessonsFixed** in the Navigation Pane, and then select **Copy**. Point to a **blank area** in the Navigation Pane, **right-click**, and then select **Paste**. Type frmMemberPortal, and then click **OK**. Double-click **frmMemberPortal** on the Navigation Pane to open the form.

> **Troubleshooting**
>
> The tab on the open form may still show "frmAddLessons" — in Form and Layout view — even though you changed the object name when you copied and pasted. You can leave it that way, or you can change the tab name in the Property Sheet pane by selecting the form, clicking the Format tab, selecting Caption, and then changing it to frmMemberPortal.

b. Switch to **Design** view, right-click the **subform**, and then select **Cut**.

c. Click the **Design** tab, and in the Controls group, click **Tab Control** , and then click the **1"** vertical grid line in the **detail area** below Lesson Count to insert the tab control. The page numbers on the tabs that appear on the Tab Control in Figure 23 may be different from the page numbers that appear in the tabs in your file.

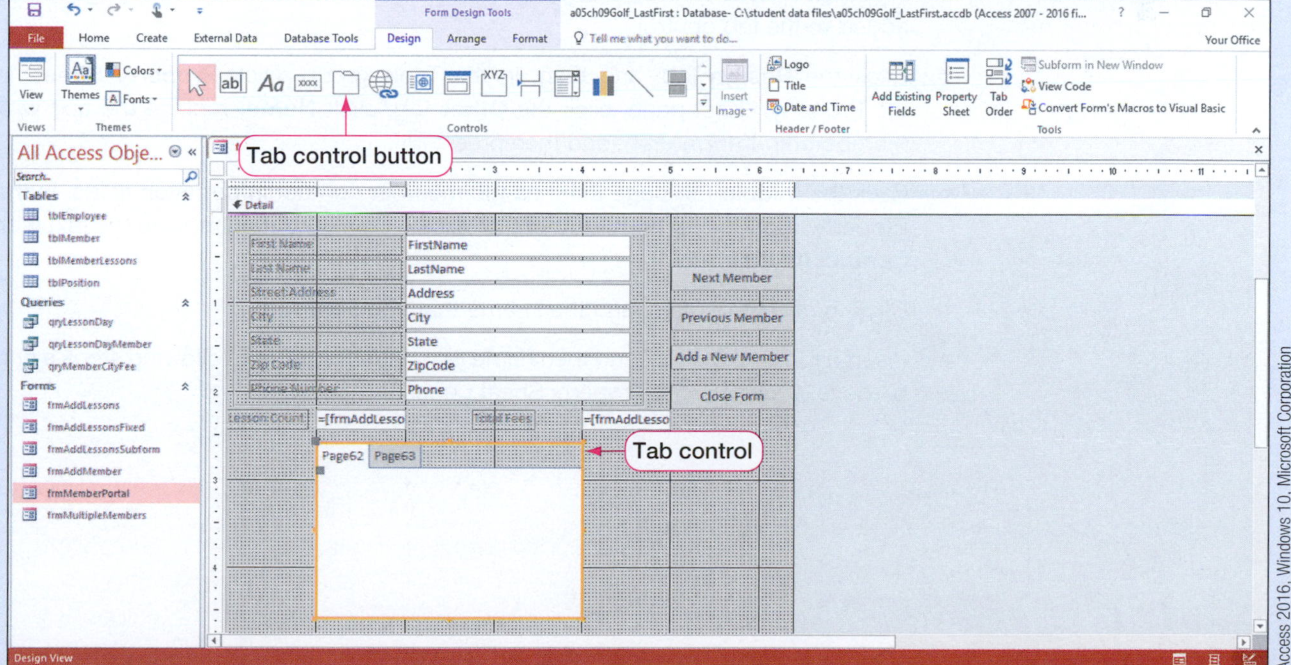

Figure 23 Tab control added to form with two tabs

d. Right-click the **blank** area of the tab control, and then select **Paste**. This will paste the subform on the first tab page. Select the **Lessons** label control, and then press Delete.

e. Click the **First Name** label, click the **selection** box at the top left corner of the stacked controls, and then right-click the **First Name** label. Select **Cut**.

f. Click the **second** tab of the tab control twice to select it, right-click the **blank** area, and then select **Paste**. This will paste all the stacked controls on the second tab page.

g. Select the rectangle shape in the form detail that was around the stacked controls, and press Delete. Move the **Next Member** button so that the top left corner is on the **.5"** mark on the horizontal ruler and the **.5"** mark on the vertical ruler. Move the **Previous Member**, **Add New Member**, and **Close Form** buttons next to the **Add Member** button so they are in a horizontal line.

h. Press and hold Shift, and then select all four buttons. Click the **Arrange** tab, and in the Sizing & Ordering group, click **Align**, and then select **Top**.

i. In the Sizing & Ordering group, click **Size/Space**, and then select **Equal Horizontal**.

j. **Save** the form.

Inserting a Tab Page and Changing Tab Captions

By default, the tab control will be inserted with two tabbed pages. You can add more pages as necessary. In this exercise, you will add two more pages to include additional member information and summary details. Every tab is named "Page" with a number. In this exercise, you will change tab names to something more meaningful.

To Insert New Tab Pages and Change the Tab Names

a. Right-click the **tab control**, and then select **Insert Page**. A new blank page will be added to the tab control.

b. Click the **Design** tab, and then, in the Tools group, click **Property Sheet**. In the Property Sheet pane, click the **Other** tab, click **Name**, replace the text with Membership Information, and then press Tab.

c. Click the **middle** tab page that has the member contact information fields. In the Property Sheet pane, on the Other tab, click **Name**, and then replace the text with Contact Information.

d. Click the **first** tab page, and then name that page Lessons.

e. Insert a fourth tab page, and then name that page Summary, following steps a and b above. **Close** the Property Sheet pane.

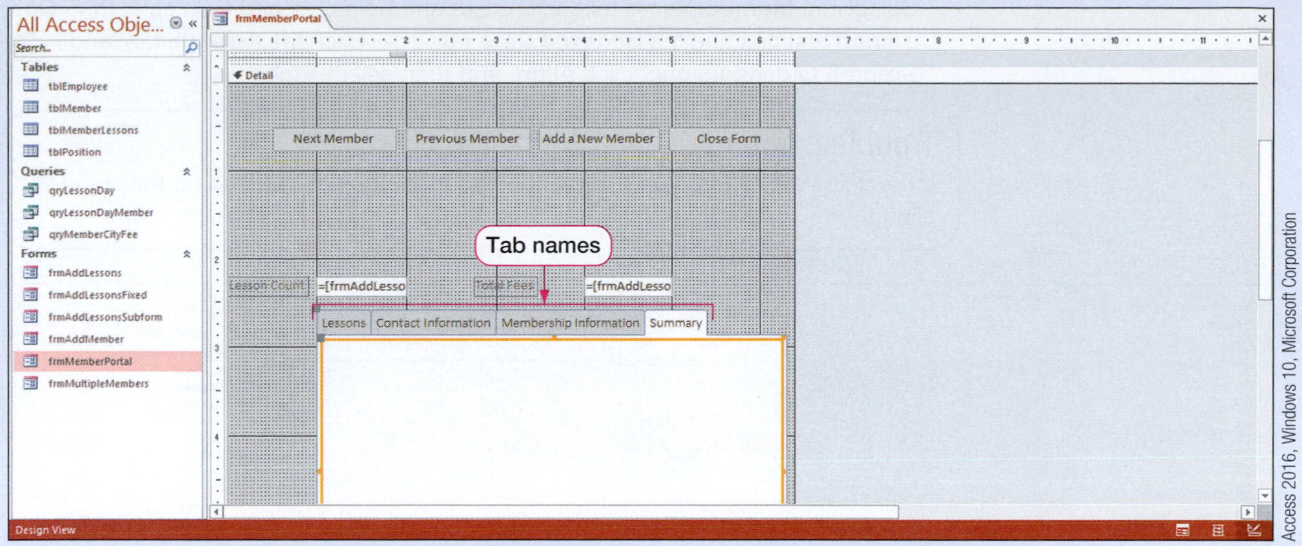

Figure 24 Tabs added to Tab Control and renamed

f. **Save** the form.

Inserting Existing Fields in a Tab Page

You can add existing fields and other controls to the tabbed pages. As long as the tables in the database are related in a one-to-many relationship, you can add fields from other tables in the tab control. In this exercise, you will add fields from tblMember that are not already on the form. You will also move the summary controls — Lesson Count and Total Fees — to the Summary tab page.

A09.26

To Insert Existing Fields in a Tab Page

a. On the tab control, click the **Membership Information** tab. Click the **Design** tab, and in the Tools group, click **Add Existing Fields**.

b. Click **MemberName**, and then drag it to the top left corner of the **Membership Information** page.

Troubleshooting

If you cannot see the list of fields from tblMember, click Show all tables at the top of the Field List, and then double-click tblMember to expand the table and see the fields available.

Troubleshooting

If you double-click the MemberName field, it will be added to the main form. If this happens, click Undo or delete the control and repeat step b.

c. Click **DateJoined**, and then drag it to the **Membership Information** tab below MemberName. Click **DateRenewal**, and then drag it to the **Membership Information** tab below DateJoined. **Close** the Field List pane.

d. Select the **MemberName label**, press and hold Shift, and then select the **Date Joined** label and the **Renewal Date** label. Click the **Arrange** tab, and in the Sizing & Ordering group, click **Align**, and then select **Left**.

e. Select the **MemberName** text box, press and hold Shift, and then select the **Date Joined** text box and the **Renewal Date** text box. Click the **Arrange** tab, and in the Sizing & Ordering group, click **Align**, and then select **Right**.

Troubleshooting

If the fields are too far apart, move them closer together, and repeat the steps to align them.

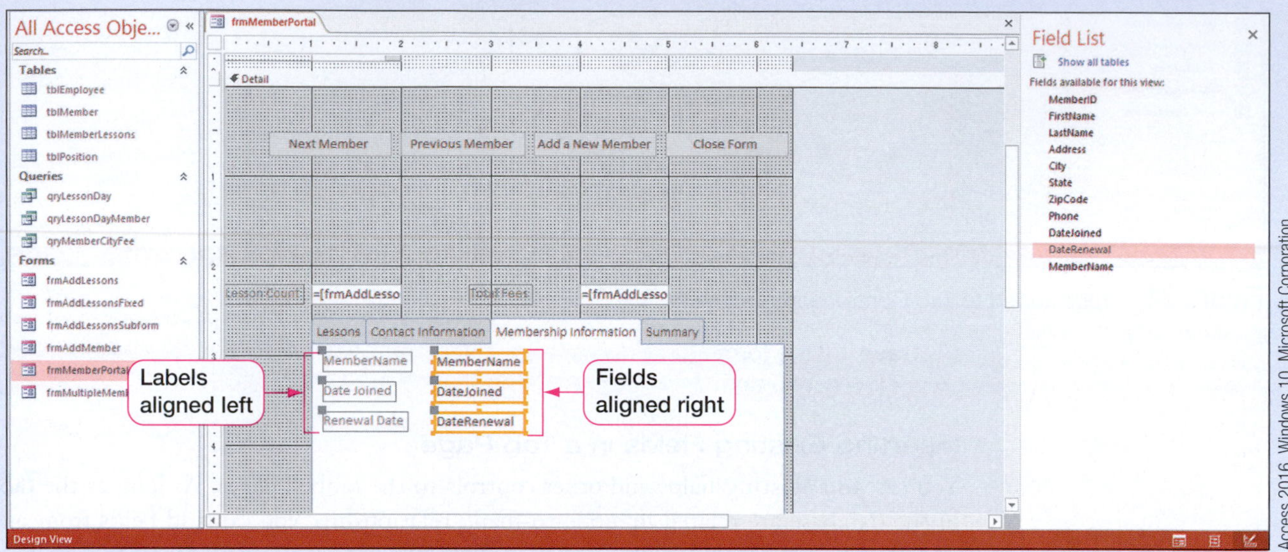

Figure 25 Fields added and aligned on Membership Information tab

f. With the MemberName, DateJoined, and DateRenewal fields selected click the right border of the MemberName field and drag it to the 3.5" horizontal ruler mark.

g. In the form detail, select the **Lesson Count** label, press and hold V, CTRL and then select the **Lesson Count** text box, the **Total Fees** label, and the **Total Fees** text box. Right-click the **selected controls**, and then select **Cut**.

h. Click the **tab control**, and then click the **Summary** tab. Right-click a **blank area** of the page, and then select **Paste**.

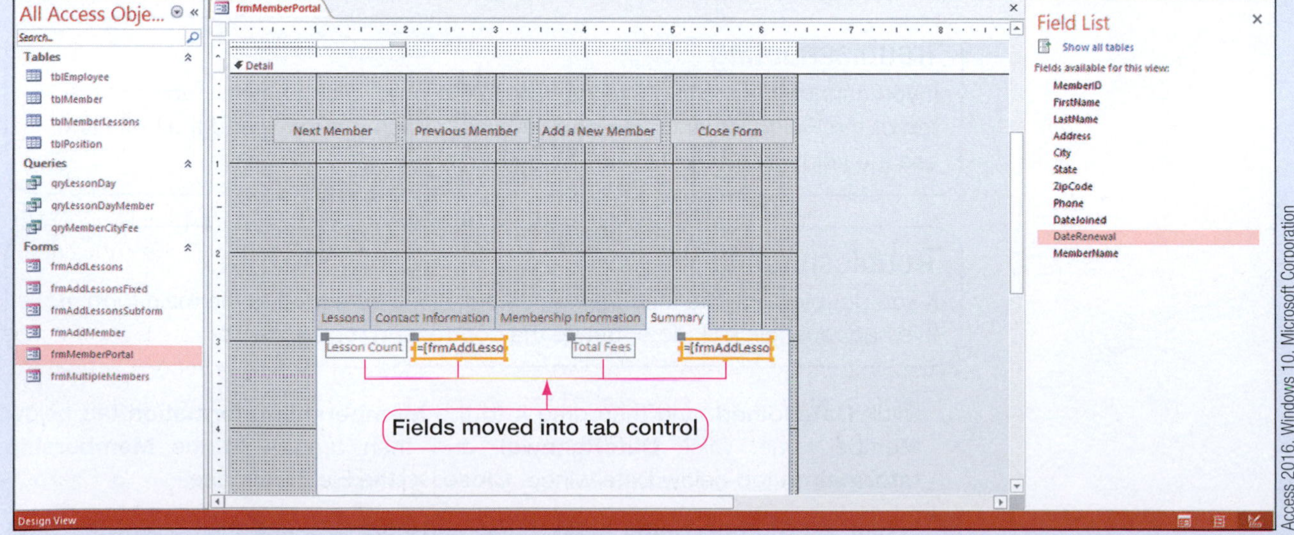

Figure 26 All fields moved from form to tab control pages

i. **Save** the form.

Rearranging, Moving, and Resizing the Tab Control

When you have all your pages added to the tab control and all the controls added to the tabbed pages, you can move the tab control, if necessary, and resize it so all the controls fit well on each page. In this exercise, you will move the tab control to fit just under the navigation buttons on the form, and you will resize the tab control to reduce the amount of blank space on each page. You will also rearrange the pages in the tab control so they are in a different order.

A09.27

SIDE NOTE

Size of the Tab Control

The tab control is as wide as the widest control. So if Access prevents you from making a page narrower, it is because another page needs that amount of space.

To Rearrange, Move, and Resize the Tab Control

a. Click the **tab control** to select it, point to the **orange border**, and then move the tab control to just below the navigation buttons on the **1"** horizontal grid line and **1"** vertical grid line.

b. Right-click the **tab control**, select **Page Order**, and then click **Summary**. Click **Move Up** three times to move Summary to the top of the list, and then click **OK**.

c. Click the **Summary** tab. Select the **Lesson Count** label, press and hold Shift, select the **Lesson Count** text box, and then move them so the Lesson Count label is in the top left corner of the page. Select the **Total Fees** label and text box, and move them below the Lesson Count controls. Use the **Align** options to left-align the labels and right-align the text boxes.

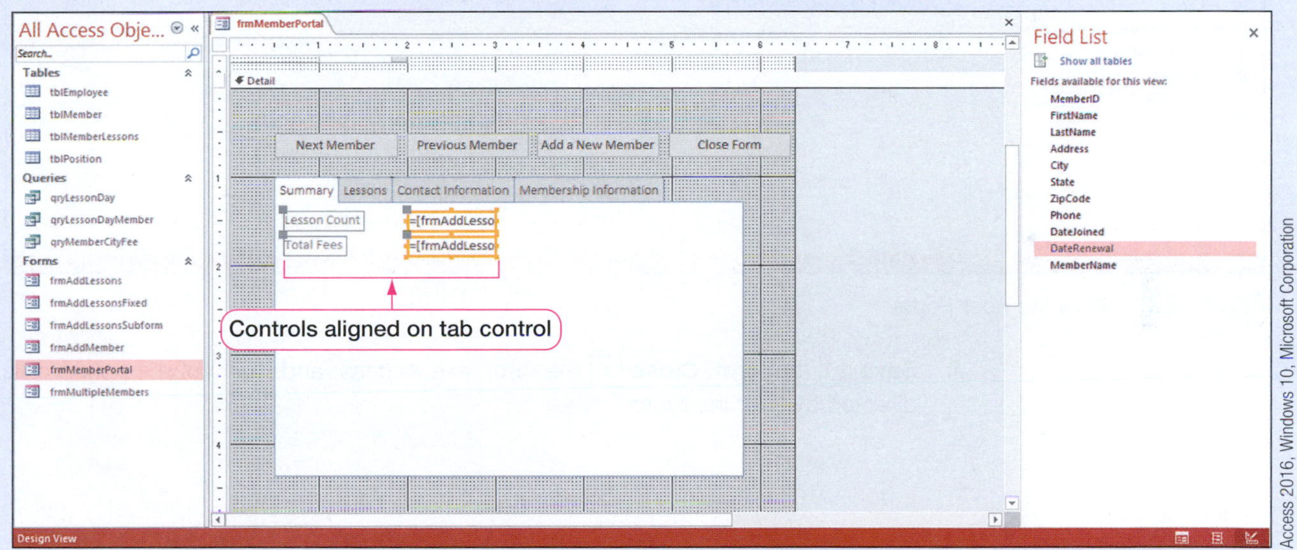

Figure 27 Summary page controls rearranged and aligned

d. Click the **Lessons** tab, click the **subform** to select it, and then, if necessary, move it to the top left corner of the page. Point to the **bottom edge** of the subform, and then drag it up so the footer is hidden.

e. Click the **Contact Information** tab. Click to select the **First Name** label. Because these controls were stacked earlier, you can click the **Select** button ⊞ at the top left of the controls to select all the controls at once. Drag the controls so the First Name label is in the top left corner of the page.

f. Click the **Membership Information** tab, select all **six controls**, and then, if necessary, move them so the MemberName is in the top left corner of the page.

g. Click the **tab control** to select it. The orange box should include the pages and the tabs. Point to the **right sizing handle** on the right side of the selection, and then drag to the left until the right side of the control is inside of the Membership Information tab. This will resize the tab control to the widest control on any of the pages.

h. Double-click the **title** in the header, and then change it to Member Portal.

Troubleshooting

If you cannot click the title because the blank header box from the logo is in the way, click the blank header box, press Delete to delete it, and then select the title.

i. Switch to **Form** view to see your form and test your tabs. Select a name from the Member Name box in the header of the form to see the detail about that member.

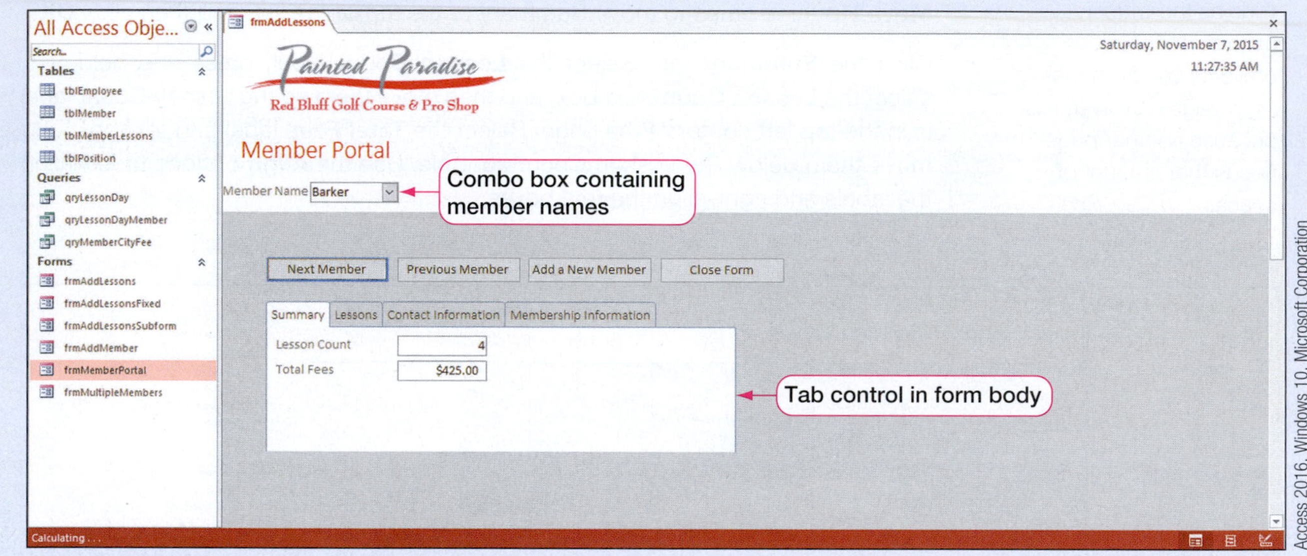

Figure 28 Final Member Portal

j. **Save** the form. **Close** the form, exit Access, and then submit your file as directed by your instructor.

Concept Check

1. What is the difference between a bound control and an unbound control? Suppose you have a form for entering customers into the table. What would be an example of a bound control on this form? An unbound control? p. 498–499
2. What does the tab order do, and why would you ever change it? p. 509
3. What types of controls would you include in a form header? How do you get the form header to show? p. 514
4. What types of controls would you include in a form footer? How do you get the form footer to show? p. 510
5. Forms provide an easy-to-use interface for nontechnical users. What are some features of forms that you can use to make forms easier to use? p. 516
6. What is the advantage to using a multiple-item form even though it looks very similar to a data sheet? p. 522

Key Terms

Bound control 498
Bound form 495
Calculated control 510
Control 498
Current Date 500
Date Picker 503
DateAdd function 500
Default Value 499
Design view 495
Enabled property 504
Form 495
Form view 495
Locked property 504
Logo 505
Move handle 508
Multiple-item form 521
Property sheet 497
Sizing handles 508
Subform 508
Tab Control 523
Tab order 509
Tab Stop property 504
Unbound control 499
Unbound form 495

Visual Summary

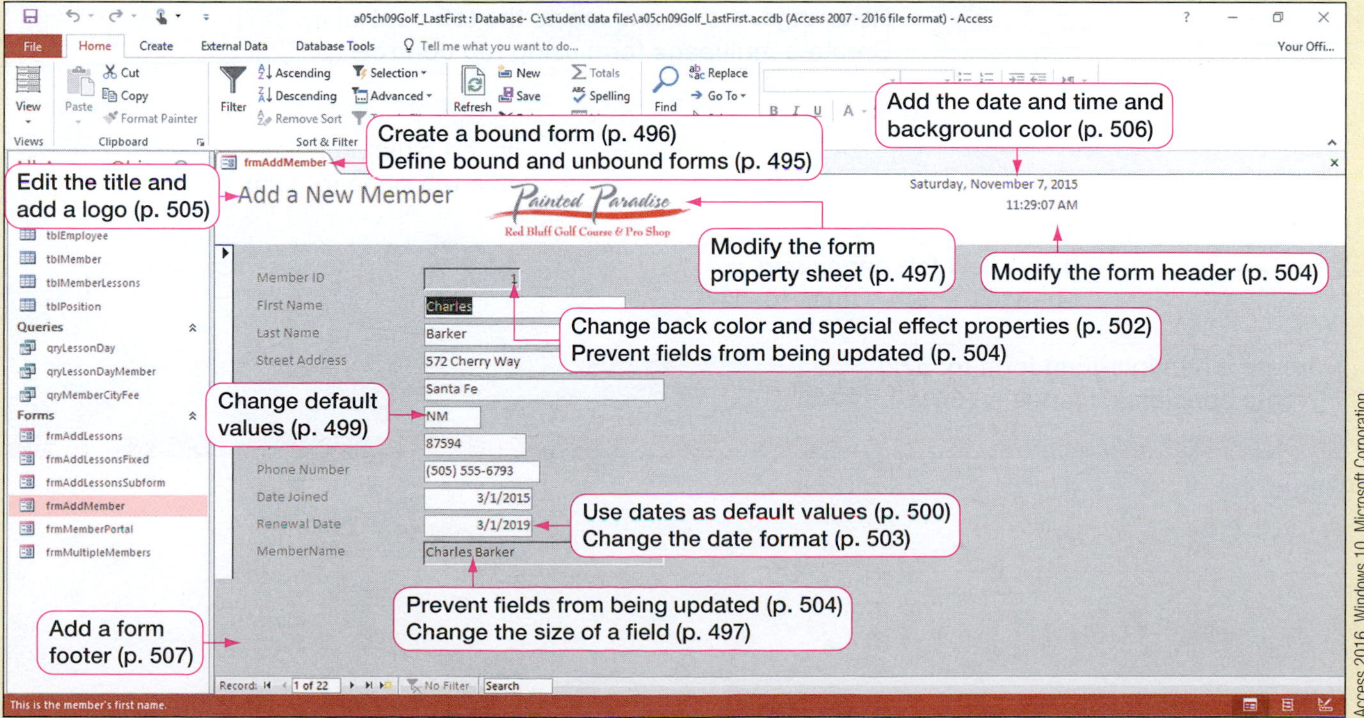

Figure 29

Access 2016, Windows 10, Microsoft Corporation

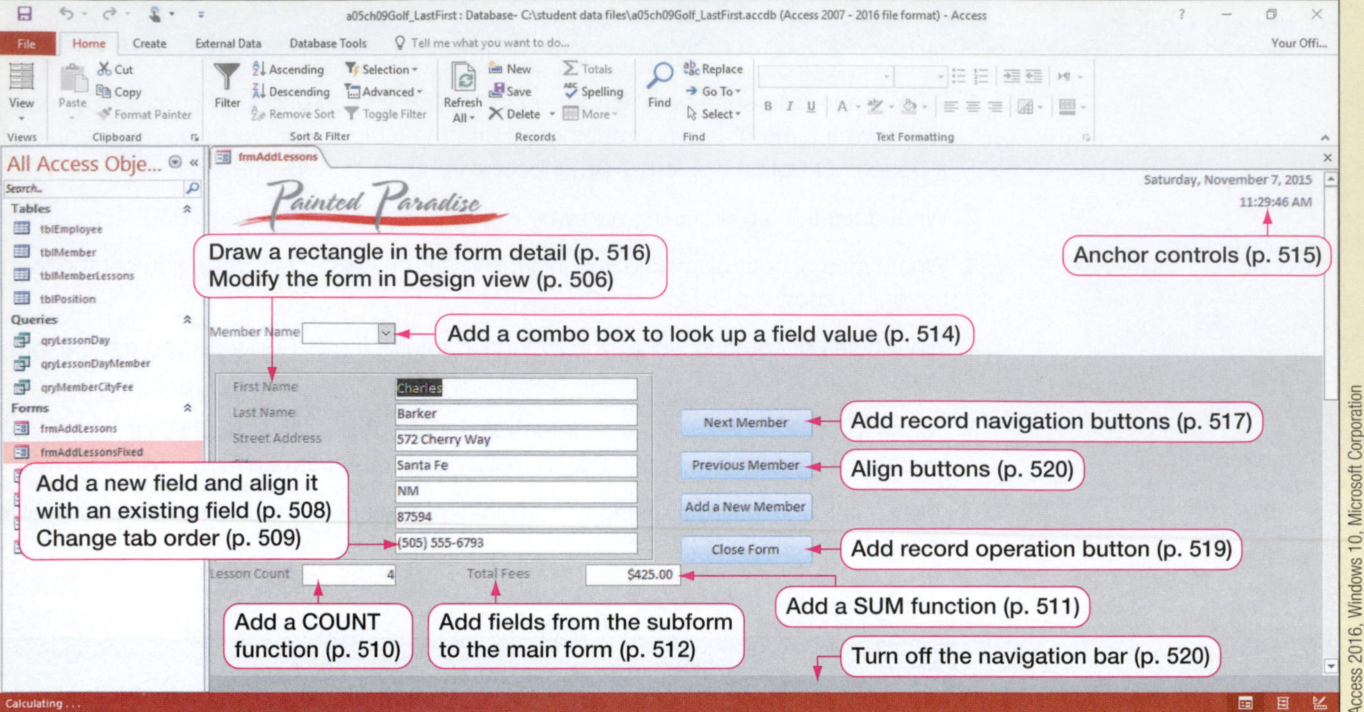

Figure 30

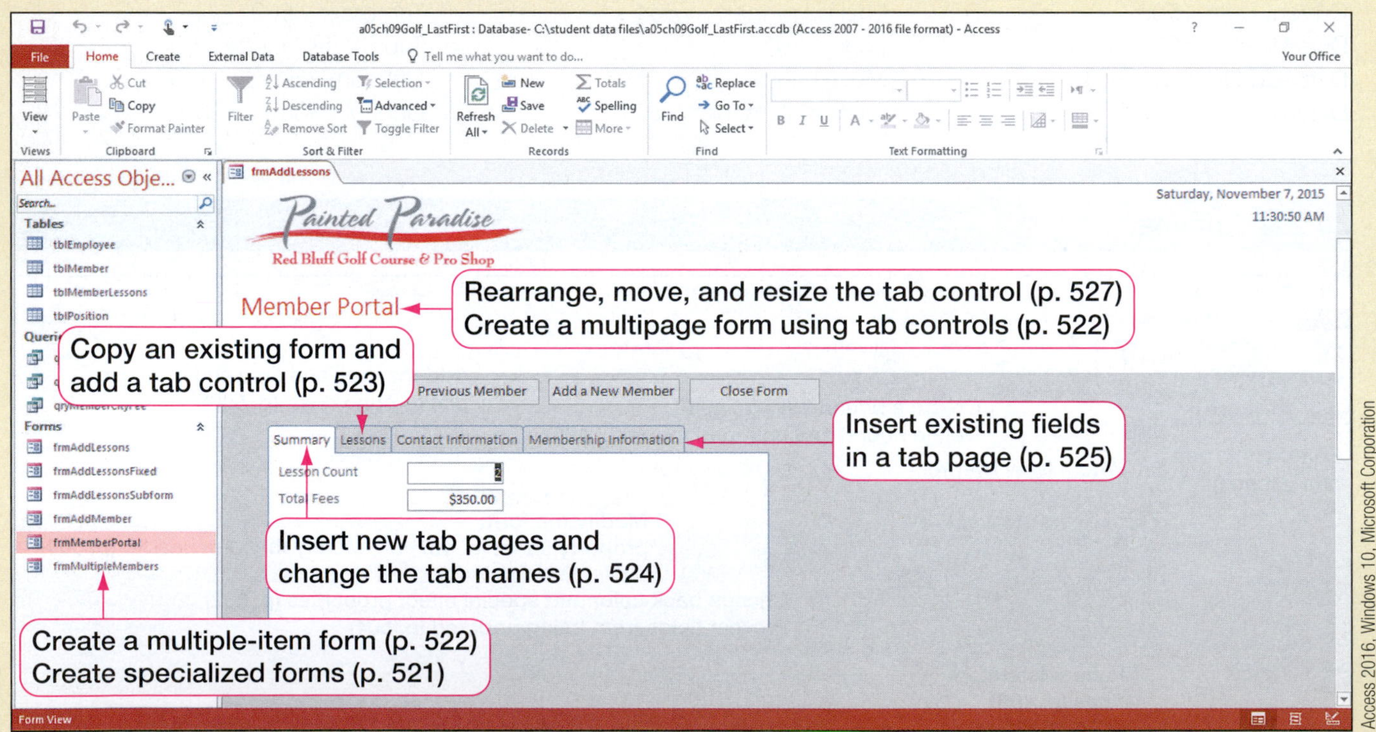

Figure 31

Practice 1

Student data file needed:

 a05ch09Putts.accdb

You will save your file as:

 a05ch09Putts_LastFirst.accdb

Enhancing the Putts for Paws Database with Forms

Customer Service

Red Bluff Golf Course & Pro Shop runs a charity golf event that raises money for a local animal shelter. You have been asked to improve the usability of the database by providing a form interface.

a. Start **Access**, click **Open Other** Files in the left pane, and then double-click **This PC**. Navigate through the folder structure to the location of your student data files, and then double-click **a05ch09Putts**. The golf database opens.

b. Click the **File** tab, click **Save As**, and save the file as an **Access Database**, and click **Save As**. Navigate to the location where you are saving your project files, and then change the file name to a05ch09Putts_LastFirst using your last and first name. Click **Save**. If necessary, enable the content.

c. Create a form to add a participant to the tournament.
   - Click the **Create** tab, and then, in the Forms group, click **Form Wizard**.
   - Click the **Tables/Queries** arrow, select **tblParticipant**, and then select all fields from **tblParticipant**. Click **Next**, accept **Columnar**, and then click **Next**.
   - Name the form frmParticipant_iLast using your first initial and last name, and then click **Finish**.
   - Switch to **Layout** view.
   - Click the **header**, select the title **frmParticipant_iLast**, and then replace the text with Add Participant by iLast using your first initial and last name. If necessary, resize the title to fit it on one line.
   - Switch to Design view, select the title, and then resize it so the right edge lines up with the 4" mark on the horizontal ruler.
   - Switch to Layout view, and then, on the Design tab, in the Header/Footer group, click **Logo**. Navigate to your student data files, and then select **a05ch09RedBluff**. Delete the blank header box to the right of the logo. Move the logo below the title, and then resize it to fit between the title and the bottom of the header.
   - On the **Design** tab, in the Header/Footer group, click **Date and Time**, accept the defaults, and then click **OK**.
   - Select the **Date** and **Time** fields, click the **Arrange** tab, and in the Position group, click **Anchoring**, and then select **Top Right**.
   - Click the **Design** tab, and in the Tools group, click **Property Sheet**, and then select **FormHeader** from the Selection type list. Click the **Format** tab, click **Back Color Builder**, and select **White, Background 1**.
   - In the Property Sheet pane, select **Detail** from the Selection type list. Click the **Format** tab, click **Back Color Builder**, and then select **White, Background 1, Darker 15%**.
   - In the form detail, click the **State field value**, click the **Data** tab, click **Default Value**, and then type NM.
   - Click the **ParticipantName field value**. Move the pointer to the **right border** of the field until it becomes a double-sided arrow. Move the border to the left until it lines up with the right border of the StreetAddress field. Move your pointer to the **lower border** of the field until it becomes a double-headed arrow. Move the border up until the field is a single line.

- With ParticipantName still selected, in the Property Sheet pane, on the Data tab, click the **Locked** property, and then select **Yes**. Click the **Other** tab, click **Tab Stop**, and then select **No**.
- With ParticipantName still selected, click the **Format** tab, click **Special Effect**, and then select **Sunken**. Click **Back Color Builder**, and then select **White, Background 1, Darker 15%**.
- Switch to **Form** view, and then change the **name** of the first participant to your name.
- Save and close the form.

d. Modify an existing form to see participant's orders.

- Right-click **frmParticipantOrders** in the Navigation Pane, and select **Copy**. Right-click a blank area in the Navigation Pane, and then select **Paste**. Type frmParticipantOrders_iLast using your first initial and last name.
- Switch to **Design view**, and change the title to Participant Orders by iLast using your first initial and last name.
- On the Design tab, in the Controls group, click **Combo Box**. Move your pointer to the **header**, and then click in the header to place the **combo box** to the right of the title.
- In the Combo Box Wizard, click **Find a record on my form based on the value I selected in my combo box**, and then click **Next**.
- Double-click **LastName** and **FirstName** in that order, and then click **Next**.
- Accept **Hide key column**, and then click **Next**.
- Type Participant Name, and then click **Finish**.
- If necessary, drag the new **combo box** so the **left edge** of the label lines up with the **3"** mark on the horizontal ruler.
- Save the form.

e. Add a tab control to a form.

- On **frmParticipantOrders_iLast**, in **Design** view, delete the **Orders** label and the **Order Details** label.
- Right-click the **Orders** subform, and then select **Cut**.
- On the Design tab, in the Controls group, click **Tab Control**, and then click to add the control to just below the **FirstName** label. Right-click the **first** tab page, and then select **Paste**.
- Right-click the **Order Details** subform, and then select **Cut**. Click the **second** tab page, right-click, and then select **Paste**.
- Right-click the **tab control**, and select **Insert Page**. Select all the **LastName** and **FirstName** controls, right-click, and then select **Cut**. Right-click the **new** tab page, and then select **Paste**.
- On the Design tab, in the Tools group, click **Add Existing Fields**, and then drag **StreetAddress**, **City**, **State**, **ZipCode**, and **ContactPhoneNumber** to add them to the third page of the tab control just below **FirstName**.
- Select all the **controls** on the page. Click the **Arrange** tab, and then, in the Table group, click **Stacked**; in the Position group, click **Control Padding**, and then select **Narrow**.
- Click the **first** tab. Click the **Design** tab, and then, in the Tools group, click **Property Sheet**. Click the **Other** tab, click **Name**, and then replace the text with Orders. Repeat these steps to name the second tab Order Details and the third tab Participant Information.

- Right-click the **tab** control, click **Page Order**, and then move up **Participant Information** so it is before the **Orders** page.
- Save the form.

f. Add buttons to a form and remove navigation buttons.

- With **frmParticipantOrders_iLast** open and in Design view, click the **Design** tab, and then, in the Controls group, click **Button**. Move your pointer to the top left corner of the **Detail** section of the form, and then click to add the button.
- In the Command Button Wizard, click **Record Navigation**, click **Go To Next Record**, and then click **Next**. Click **Text**, replace the text with Next Participant, and then click **Next**. Name the button cmdNextParticipant, and then click **Finish**.
- In the Controls group, click **Button**. Place your pointer to the right of the Next Participant button, and then click the **form**. Click **Record Navigation**, click **Go To Previous Record**, and then click **Next**. Click **Text**, type Previous Participant, and then click **Next**. Name the button cmdPreviousParticipant, and then click **Finish**.
- In the Controls group, click **Button**. Place your pointer to the right of the Previous Participant button, and then click the **form**. Click **Form Operations**, click **Open Form**, and then click **Next**. Click **frmParticipant_iLast**, and then click **Next**. Click **Open the form and show all the records**, and then click **Next**. Click **Text**, replace the text with Add a New Participant, and then click **Next**. Name the button cmdAddParticipant, and then click **Finish**.
- In the Controls group, click **Button**. Place your pointer to the right of the **Add a New Participant** button, and then click the **form**. Click **Form Operations**, click **Close Form**, and then click **Next**. Click **Text**, and then click **Next**. Name the button cmdCloseForm, and then click **Finish**.
- Select all **four buttons**. Click the **Arrange** tab. In the Sizing & Ordering group, click **Align**, and then select **Top**.
- In the Sizing & Ordering group, click **Size/Space**, and then select **To Widest**. Click **Size/Space**, and then select **Equal Horizontal**.
- In the Property Sheet pane, select **Form** for Selection type, click the **Format** tab, click **Navigation Buttons**, and then select **No**.
- Save the form.

g. Use subform calculations in a form.

- On **frmParticipantOrders_iLast**, click the **Orders** tab on the tab control, right-click the **Order** subform, and then select **Subform in New Window**.
- Drag the footer down **1"**. Click the **Design** tab, and in the Controls group, click **Text Box**, and then click the **1"** vertical grid line in the footer.
- In the Property Sheet pane, click the **Data** tab, and then click **Control Source Builder**.
- In the Expression Builder, type =SUM([AmountPaid]), and then click **OK**.
- In the Property Sheet pane, click the **Other** tab, click **Name**, and then replace the text with TotalPaid. Double-click the **label** in the footer, and then type Total Paid.
- Save and close the subform window.
- Click the **Order Details** tab on the tab control. Open the subform in a new window, drag the **footer** down **1"**, and add a **text box** in the footer with the Control Source =COUNT([Quantity]), the name TotalQuantity, and the label Total Quantity. Save and close the subform, and then save the form.

- Right-click the **tab control**, and then select **Insert Page**. In the Property Sheet pane, click the **Other** tab, click **Name**, and then replace the text with Order Summary.
- On the Design tab, in the Controls group, click **Text Box**, and then click the **Order Summary** page to add the text box.
- In the Property Sheet pane, click the **Data** tab, and then click **Control Source Builder**. In the Expression Builder, in the Expression Elements pane, double-click **frmParticipantOrders_iLast**. Click **frmOrderSubform**. In the Expression Categories pane, double-click **TotalPaid**, and then click **OK**. (Hint: If fields are not visible for frmOrderSubform, switch to Form view and then back to Design view.)
- In the Property Sheet pane, click the **Other** tab, click **Name**, and then replace the text with TotalPaid. Click the **Format** tab, click **Format**, and then select **Currency**. Click the **label** on the Order Summary page, and then replace the text with Total Paid.
- Repeat the steps above to add the **Total Quantity** field from frmOrderLineSubform to the Order Summary page, but do not change the format to Currency. Name the field TotalQuantity, and give it the label Total Quantity.
- Select the **Total Paid** label and the **Total Quantity** label. Click the **Arrange** tab, and in the Sizing & Ordering group, click **Align**, and then select **Left**. Select the **Total Paid** text box and the **Total Quantity** text box, click **Align**, and then select **Right**. Select all four controls, and then move them to the top left corner of the page.
- Switch to **Form** view to make sure your fields are all visible on all the tabs.
- Save and close the form.

h. Close the database, exit Access, and submit your file as directed by your instructor.

Problem Solve 1

Student data file needed:

 a05ch09UHS.accdb

You will save your file as:

 a05ch09UHS_LastFirst.accdb

University High School Database

Customer Service

University High School has transitioned to a new system in which one counselor is assigned to a team of students every year. To manage this process, a database has been created with which to keep track of students and counselors. Each counselor is assigned to a team that consists of many students. Only a sample of records have been added, and now they need forms to be able to view and enter data. You will create forms to help make viewing and entering data easier for the staff.

a. Open the Access file **a05ch09UHS**. Save your file as a05ch09UHS_LastFirst using your last and first name.

b. Using the Form Wizard, create a form that will show for each staff member the students they have assigned to them. From tblStaff, select **StaffName**, and from tblStudents, select **all fields** except ID, TeamID, and StudentName. View the form by **tblStaff**, select **Datasheet** layout, and name the form frmStaffMember and the subform frmStaffMemberSubform.

c. Resize the Staff Name field so it appears on one line and the right edge lines up with the **4" vertical grid line**. Change the title to Staff Member Assignments by iLast using your first initial and last name. Fit the title on one line.

d. Insert the default value of the date and time in the header, and anchor the controls to the **Top Right**. Change the back color of the form header to **Green, Accent 6, Lighter 60%**.

e. Insert a combo box in the header to **Find a record on my form based on the value I selected in my combo box**, select **StaffLastName** and **StaffFirstName**, hide the key column, and change the label to Counselor Name. Move the combo box below the title, and resize the text box so the right edge lines up with the **3.5" mark** on the horizontal ruler.

f. Resize the subform so all fields are showing. Move the subform to align with the Staff Name label. Save and close the form.

g. Create a form that will serve as a portal for the school counselors. Copy **frmStaffMember**, and paste it in the Navigation Pane as a new form named frmCounselorCorner. Open **frmCounselorCorner**.

h. Change the title of the form to Counselor Corner by iLast using your first initial and last name. Insert a **Tab Control** on the form so the top left corner is at the **.5"** vertical grid line and the **1"** horizontal grid line. Cut and paste the subform to the first page of the Tab Control.

i. Delete the **frmStaffMember** label, and move the subform to the top left corner of the tab control page. Open the subform in a new window. Drag the Form Footer down to the **1"** mark on the vertical ruler.

j. In the Form Footer, add a **text box**. Create a function to count the number of students based on the StudentFirstName field. Name the field StudentCount. Change the label on the subform to Student Count. Save and close the subform.

k. Rename the first page of the tab control Student List. Rename the second page Counselor Information. Insert a new page, and name it Student Summary. Move the **Student Summary** page between the Student List and Counselor Information pages.

l. On the Student Summary page, add a text field that will show the new calculated field. Name the field StudentCount, and change the label to Student Count. On the Counselor Information page, add the existing fields **StaffName**, **Address**, **City**, **State**, **Zip** from tblStaff. Stack the fields on the page, and move the stack to the top left corner.

m. In the frmCounselorCorner form details, add the **TeamID** field under the Staff Name. Align the Staff Name and TeamID labels to the left. Align the StaffName and TeamID text boxes to the left.

n. Change the **Back Color** of the form detail section to **Green, Accent 6, Lighter 80%**. Change the Staff Name field and the TeamID field to **Locked**, Sunken and **Green, Accent 6, Lighter 80%**, and change the **tab stop** to **No** for both fields. Save and close the form.

o. Create a multiple-item form from **tblStudents** that will show a listing of all students at the school. Change the header Back Color to **Green, Accent 6, Lighter 60%**. Delete the form icon in the header, and change the title to Student List by iLast using your first initial and last name. Delete the **Student Name** field. Name the form frmStudentList.

p. Using the Form Wizard, create a form from **tblStudents**, and include all fields. Name the form frmAddStudent. Change the title to Add a Student by iLast using your first initial and last name. Set the default value of the **City** field to Brownsburg, set the default value of the **State** field to IN (enter using quotation marks — "IN" — or Access thinks you are entering an incomplete formula), and set the default value of the **Zip** field to 46112. Resize the **Student Name** field so it is as wide as the Address field and on only one line. Save and close the form.

q. Close your database, exit Access, and submit your file as directed by your instructor.

Perform 1: Perform in Your Career

Student data file needed:

 a05ch09PetStore.accdb

You will save your file as:

 a05ch09PetStore_LastFirst.accdb

Make a Pet Store Database Friendly

Production & Operations

A pet store owner started creating a database to keep records of animals, breeds, purchases, and customers. Data has been added to the tables, but there are no forms or reports for entering data or looking up data. You have been asked to help create forms to add data to the tables and to look up data that is already in the tables. You will use different kinds of forms for this task.

a. Open the **Access** database **a05ch09PetStore**. Save your file as a05ch09PetStore_LastFirst using your last and first name. If necessary, enable the content.

b. Open **tblCustomer**, change the **FirstName** and **LastName** in the first record to your actual name, and then close the table.

c. Create a form to add data to tblAnimal. Include all the fields from the table. Change the title to Add Animals by iLast, using your first initial and last name, and then save the form as frmAddAnimals_iLast using your first initial and last name.

d. Use the form wizard to create a form with a subform, that is a form using two tables, to show all the animal information and all animal purchase information:
   - Save the form as frmPurchases_iLast using your first initial and last name, and save the subform as frmPurchasesSubform_iLast using your first initial and last name.
   - Change the title to Animal Information by iLast using your first initial and last name.
   - Include the date and time in the header, anchored to the top right.
   - Lock all the animal information fields in the main form, and then turn off the tab stops.

e. Add four buttons: Next Animal, Previous Animal, Add Animal, and Close Form. The Add Animal button should open frmAddAnimals_iLast.
   - Turn off the Navigation bars for both the form and the subform.
   - Resize any fields as necessary, and make sure all fields are visible on the form and the subform. Make the form look professional.

f. Create a form with a tab control that will look up the customer name and show three tabs: Customer, Purchases, and Summary.
   - Save the form as frmCustomer_iLast using your first initial and last name, and save the subform as frmCustomerSubform_iLast using your first initial and last name.
   - The title of the form should be Customer Lookup by iLast using your first initial and last name.
   - Add a combo box in the header to look up the customer name.
   - Change the header to a different color.
   - Add three buttons: Next Customer, Previous Customer, and Close Form.

- Remove the Record Selectors and Navigation Buttons from the frmCustomer_iLast form.
- The first tab of the tab control should show the customer contact information.
- The second tab of the tab control should show the customer's purchases.
- The third tab of the tab control should show the total number of purchases a customer has made and the total amount the customer has spent.
- Resize any fields as necessary, and make sure all fields are visible on the form and the subform. Make the form look professional.

g. Create a multiple-item form to display all customers in tblCustomer. Change the title to Customer List by iLast using your first initial and last name, and then delete the form icon from the header. Save the form as frmCustomerList_iLast using your first initial and last name.

h. Close your database, exit Access, and then submit your file as directed by your instructor.

Additional Cases

Additional Workshop Cases are available on the companion website and in the instructor resources.

Microsoft Access 2016

Chapter 10 | ADVANCED REPORTS AND MAILING LABELS

OBJECTIVES

Prepare Case

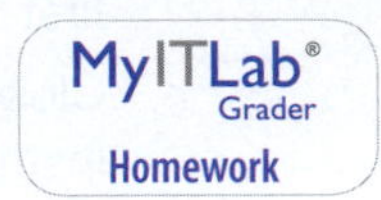

Customer Service

Enhancing Database Reports at the Red Bluff Golf Club

The Red Bluff Golf Club generates revenues through golfers signing up for tee times and taking golf lessons. You have provided a database to Barry Cheney, the golf club manager, that he can use to track employees and members. Some forms and reports have already been created, but Barry would like to see more to help him manage memberships and lessons. You will assist Barry and his staff by setting up reports that they can use on a regular basis.

Lichtmeister/Shutterstock

Student data file needed for this chapter:

 a05ch10Golf.accdb

You will save your file as:

 a05ch10Golf_LastFirst.accdb

Creating Customized Reports

An Access **report** provides data in an easy-to-read and professional-looking format suitable for printing. A report is designed to fit well on the printed page, with breaks built in for each page. Column headers automatically repeat on each page, and the pages are automatically numbered. Reports provide ways to report on data by groups, such as by each customer or by product. Totals can be calculated for each group, and grand totals can be shown. The source of data for a report can be a table or a query.

QUICK REFERENCE	Query, Form, or Report?

There are three ways to display data from a database: a query, a form, and a report. When would you use each?

- Queries are the most versatile of the three for finding data in your database. They allow complex data selection and data calculation. But the output from a query is tabular and not always suitable for presentation to a client or manager. If you want to share the results of a query in printed form, you will often create a report from the query.
- Forms are usually used for data input, and they are best suited for output on the screen. In fact, many types of forms are very difficult to print, as they can run for many pages with formatting that is unsuitable for the printed page, such as a lack of page breaks and page numbers.
- Reports are designed for printing. You can use them to provide an easy-to-understand output for a client or manager. You can also create mailing labels and other specialized printable formats.

Reports can be created with the same controls that are available in forms. You can also create mailing label reports or other types of labels.

Reports can be created in four different ways: with the Report tool, with the Report Design tool, with the Blank Report tool, and with the Report Wizard. The **Report tool** creates a report with one mouse click. The report displays all of the fields from the table or query that you select. The **Report Design tool** creates a blank report in Design view to which you can manually add fields or other controls. The **Blank Report tool** creates a blank report in Layout view. You can insert fields or other controls while you see the data. Finally, the **Report Wizard** guides you through creating a report by asking you questions. The report is then created on the basis of your answers to the questions.

QUICK REFERENCE	Report Views Available

Reports have four views.

- Report view shows how the report will look in a continuous page layout. If a report has multiple pages, this view shows the report as one continuous layout without individual page headers or footers. Reports cannot be changed in this view.
- Print Preview shows how the report will look on the printed page. In this view, you can see the page breaks and how they will appear on paper. This view allows you to change the page layout from landscape to portrait view and to change margins.
- Layout view shows the report and the data. Some of the report design properties, such as column widths and fonts, can be changed in this view. You can add controls in this view. Layout view is ideal for making changes when seeing the data as you make the change would be useful.
- Design view shows the report design but not the data. Any aspect of the report design can be changed in this view.

In this section, you will create a report using the Report Wizard that includes summary fields for subtotals and grand totals. Then you will work with already created reports to modify the existing fields, controls, groups, and totals.

Use the Summary Options in Report Wizard

One of the features of Access reports is the ability to summarize your data. For example, if you have numeric data such as sales quantity, you might want to calculate a grand total of that quantity. When you are creating a report with a wizard, calculations such as sums, averages, minimums, and maximums are available as standard summation. In Design view, you can build even more complex formulas and edit existing ones.

Opening the Starting File

The Red Bluff Golf Club needs a report showing the members to whom the golf course employees have given lessons. The report needs to be grouped by the employee who gives the lessons. In this exercise, you will open the database and create this report.

A10.00

To Open the Golf Database

a. Start **Access**, click **Open Other Files** in the left pane, and then click **This PC**. Navigate through the folder structure to the location of your student data files, and then double-click **a05ch10Golf**. A database opens displaying tables and queries related to the spa.

b. Click the **File** tab, save the file as an **Access Database**, and click **Save As**. Navigate to the location where you are saving your project files, and then change the filename to a05ch10Golf_LastFirst using your last and first name. Click **Save**. If necessary, enable the content.

Adding Subtotals and Totals

Reports have a grouping feature that allows for records to be presented in sets. One common way to utilize grouping is to use one-to-many relationships in your database and use a record from the one side to group records from the many side. For example, suppose your database has a one-to-many relationship between customers and orders; that is, a customer can place many orders, and an order is placed by one customer. You might report on orders by first showing the customer and then grouping all of the customer's orders together. In the Report Wizard, the one-to-many grouping is the first grouping suggested to you. You can also group other fields together. You could choose to group orders by date placed or by state of shipment. Once you create report groups, you can add summary calculations for each group.

In this exercise, you will create a report for the golf course that groups the member lessons by employee so that when you look up an employee, you will see all the lessons that employee has scheduled. The report will also add a subtotal of the fees to be paid to each employee and a grand total of the fees paid to all the employees.

A10.01

To Create a Report with Subtotals and Totals Using the Summary Wizard

SIDE NOTE
Pin the Ribbon
If your ribbon is collapsed, pin your ribbon open. Click the Home tab. In the lower right-hand corner of the ribbon, click Pin the Ribbon.

SIDE NOTE
Order Makes a Difference
The order in which you select the fields in the Report Wizard will determine how the fields are laid out on the report.

a. Double-click **tblMember** to open it, navigate to **record 21**, the last record, and then change the **First Name** and **Last Name** to your first name and last name. **Close** tblMember.

b. Click the **Create** tab, and then, in the Reports group, click **Report Wizard.** Select the fields for your report in this order: From **tblEmployee**, select **EmployeeLastName** and **EmployeeFirstName**; from **tblMemberLessons**, select **ScheduledDate**; from **tblMember**, select **LastName** and **FirstName**; from **tblMemberLessons**, select **Fee**.

Troubleshooting

If you make a mistake in selecting the fields in the order above, move them all back to Available Fields and start over. For the report to work correctly, the fields need to be added in the exact order listed above.

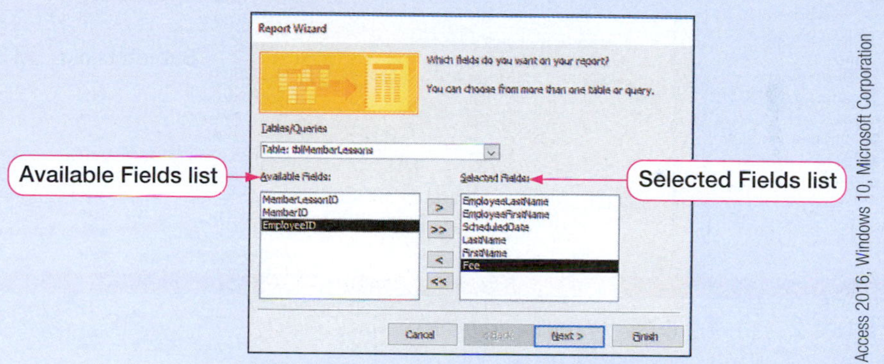

Figure 1 Fields selected in the Report Wizard

c. Click **Next**. Accept the grouping by **tblEmployee**, and then click **Next**. Click **Next** again — you will not select any other grouping — and click the first sort box arrow, and then select **ScheduledDate**. Click the next **sort box** arrow, select **LastName**, click the third **sort box** arrow, and then select **FirstName**. Make sure all are in **Ascending** order.

d. Click **Summary Options**. Because Fee is the only field with numeric data that you selected, Access gives you only the option to calculate summary values for Fee. Click the **Sum** check box, and then click **OK**.

e. Click **Next**, accept the **Stepped** layout, accept **Portrait** orientation, and then click **Next**.

f. In the title box, type rptEmployeeLessons, and then click **Finish**.

SIDE NOTE
Fields Too Narrow
If a field shows ### instead of values, it means that the field is not wide enough to display the values. This is corrected by resizing the field.

g. On the **Print Preview** tab, in the Close Preview group, click **Close Print Preview**. On the Design tab, in the Views group, click the **View** arrow, and then click **Layout View**. Click the first **Fee** field, point to the **left edge** of the field, and then, when the pointer changes to the **horizontal resize pointer**, drag to the left to widen the field.

h. Click the first **Subtotal** field, point to the **left edge** of the field, and then, when the pointer changes to the **horizontal resize pointer**, drag to the left to widen the field.

i. Scroll down to the end of the report, select the **Grand Total** field, point to the **left edge** of the field, and then, when the pointer changes to the **horizontal resize pointer** ↔, drag to the left to widen the field.

j. Click **Print Preview** on the status bar to see how the report will print, and then **Save** the report.

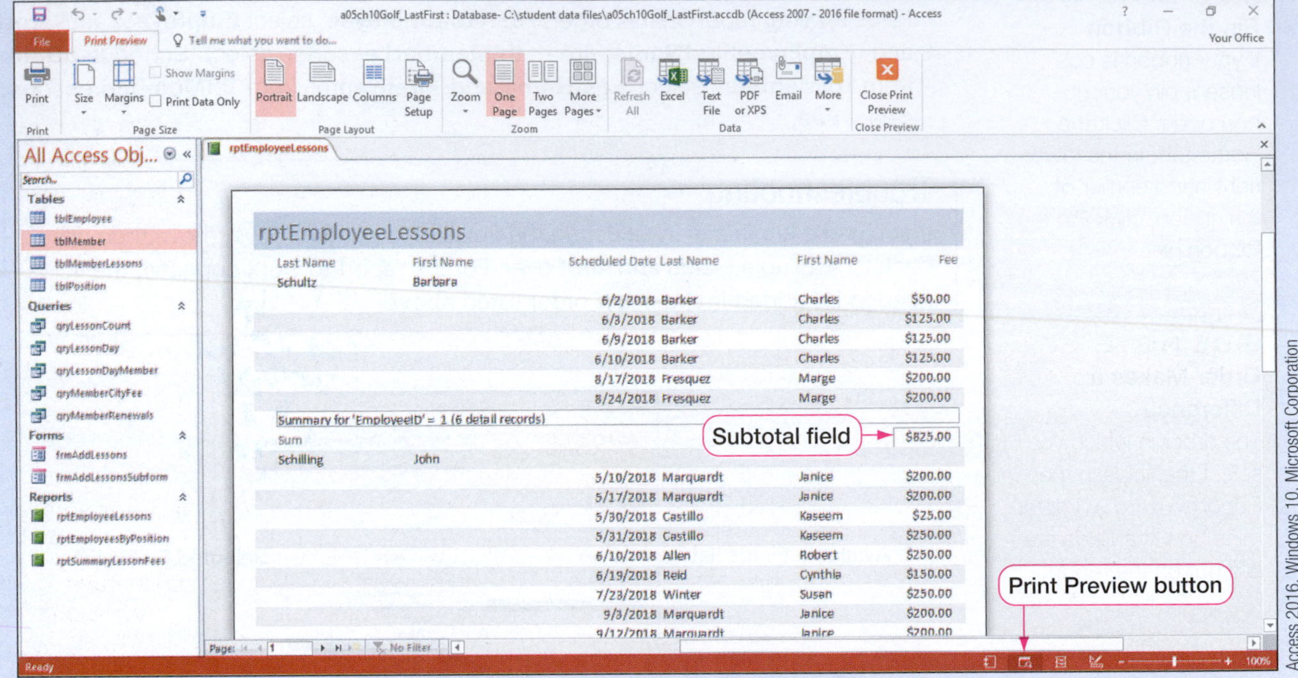

Access 2016, Windows 10, Microsoft Corporation

Figure 2 Print Preview of rptEmployeeLessons

Modify the Report in Design View

A report with subtotals and totals has seven areas in Design view, as shown in Figure 3.

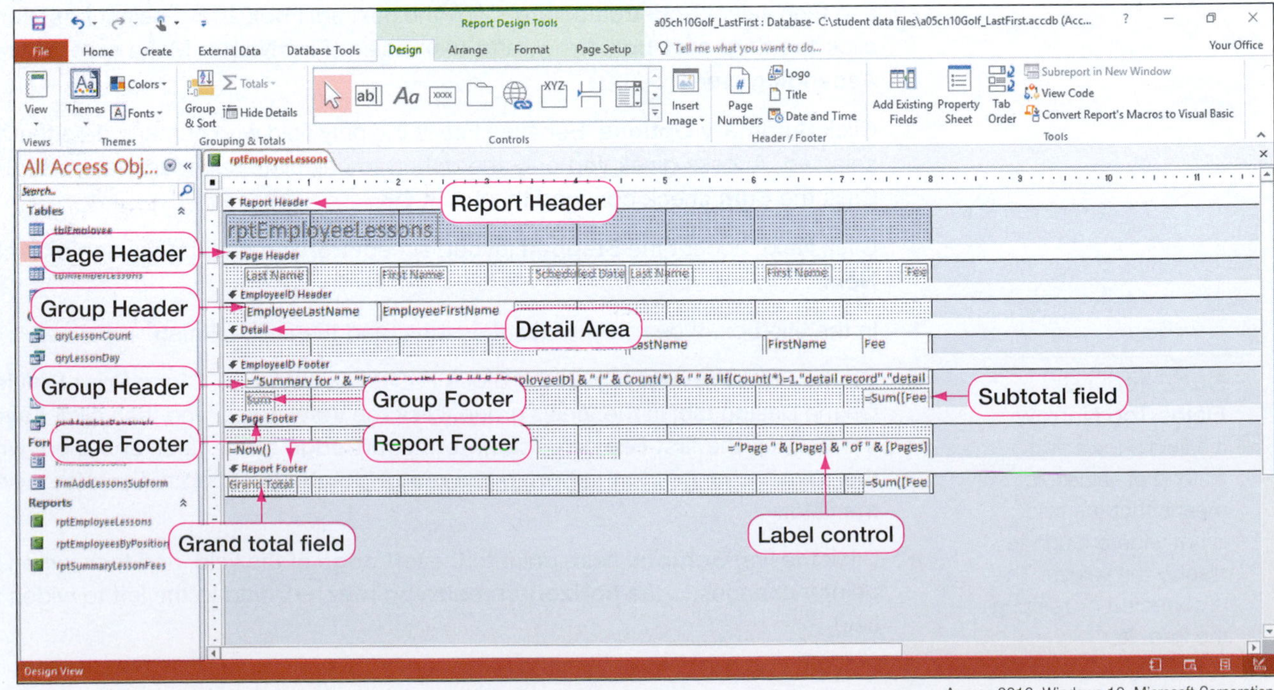

Access 2016, Windows 10, Microsoft Corporation

Figure 3 Design view of report with totals and subtotals

The **Report Header** contains the information printed once at the beginning of a report. The default title is the name of the report. If you add a logo or date and time, they also appear in the Report Header.

The **Page Header** contains the information printed at the top of every page of a report. The default information contained here is the column headers, which are taken from the captions from the table design. If no captions were defined, the values are field names. These are label controls. A **label control** is a control that contains descriptive information, typically a field name. The Employee Lessons report has the column headers for both the grouping fields and the detail fields.

The **Group Header** contains the information printed at the beginning of every group of records. In Design view, the Group Header bar is labeled with the primary key of the record by which the report was grouped, in this case the EmployeeID from tblEmployee. Recall that when the wizard grouped by tblEmployee, the EmployeeLastName and EmployeeFirstName were the two fields in the grouping header. You see the bound controls for these two fields in the Group Header. The field labels are shown in the Page Header.

The **Detail area** shows the fields from the underlying record source. These are the bound controls showing values. The field labels are shown in the Page Header.

The **Group Footer** contains the information printed at the end of every group of records on a report. It is shown if you chose summary options in the Report Wizard. The Group Footer is labeled with the primary key of the record by which the report was grouped, in this case the EmployeeID from tblEmployee. The fields shown include a calculated control that shows a count of detailed records and a calculated control that represents the summary field(s) you chose. The label showing which summary option you picked is on the left side of the footer. The calculated summary field is on the right.

The **Page Footer** shows the information printed at the end of every page of a report. By default, two controls are shown: the current date using the Now function and a calculated control representing the page number for this page.

The **Report Footer** shows the information printed once at the end of a report. It is shown if you chose summary options in the Report Wizard. The fields shown are the calculated control(s) that represents the summary field(s) you chose. The Label control showing that it is the grand total is on the left side of the footer. The calculated summary field is on the right.

CONSIDER THIS | End of Page or End of Report

The page footer show the same information at the bottom of every page, whereas the report footer shows information only once at the end of the report. What types of information would be helpful at the end of every page, other than page numbers? What type of information would be better placed at the end of the report? Is there any information you might want in both places?

Selecting and Modifying Controls in Design View

In this exercise, you will change the title of the report in the page header, and then you will delete the Summary field that appears after each group of members.

QUICK REFERENCE	Design View Areas		
Area	**Purpose**	**Where Displayed**	**When the Report Wizard Shows It**
Report Header	To introduce the report; includes the title and often a logo	At the beginning of the report	By default
Page Header	Includes column headings	At the top of each page	By default
Group Header	To introduce the group; shows the values of the grouping variables	At the beginning of each grouping	When your report has grouping
Detail Area	Shows the detailed fields	Within groups	By default
Group Footer	To end the group; used to contain subtotals for the group	At the end of each grouping	When your report has grouping and you chose summary options
Page Footer	To end a page; defaults to showing the date and the page number	At the end of each page	By default
Report Footer	To end the report; can contain grand totals	At the end of the report	When you chose summary options

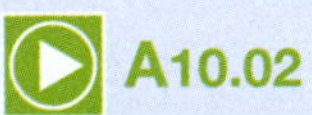

To Modify the Headers and Footers in Design View

a. Switch to **Design** view, double-click the title **rptEmployeeLessons**, select the **text**, and then type Employee Lessons by iLast using your first initial and last name.

b. Click the **control** in the EmployeeID footer that begins **="Summary for**, and then press Delete to delete the control.

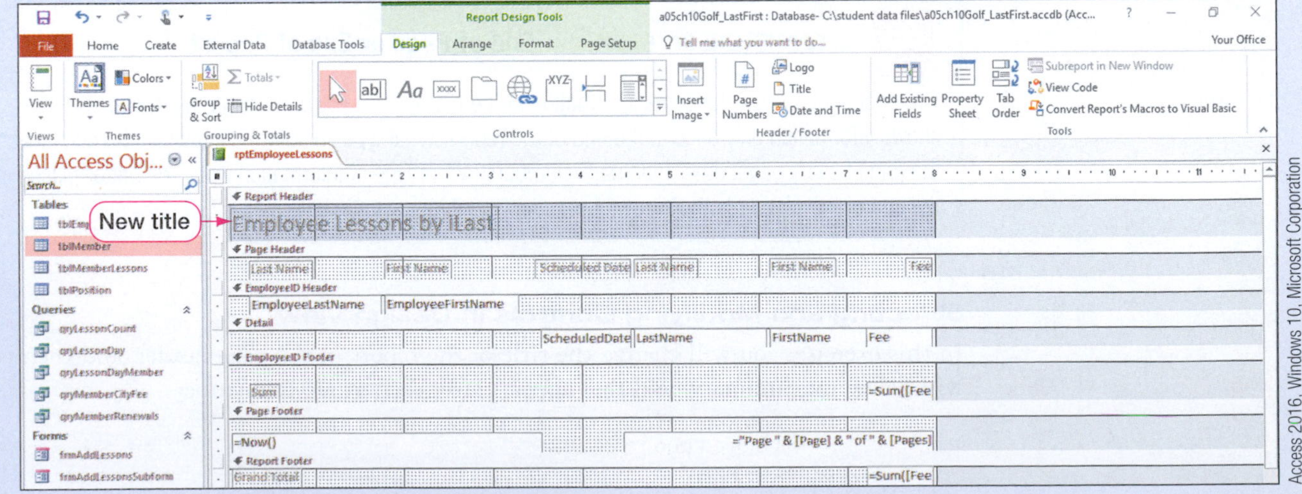

Figure 4 Title changed and Summary control deleted

c. Click **Print Preview** to see how the report will look when printed, and then **Save** the report.

Moving, Resizing, and Aligning Fields in Design View

When a control is selected, in either Layout view or Design view, the control is outlined in orange. There are eight boxes called handles on the outline. The large gray handle in the top left corner is called the move handle. The **move handle** is used to move the control. The smaller orange handles are sizing handles. **Sizing handles** are used to resize the control.

When fields are added or moved, you can align them with other fields so the alignment is correct. Controls may be aligned by their top, left, right, or bottom borders, or they may be aligned to the grid.

In Design view, the report grid is made up of vertical lines as well as rows and columns of dots. By default, the **snap to grid** option for reports is turned on, which means that when you add or move a control in a report, it will automatically align to a point on the grid. If that option is not turned on, then you can manually align a control to the grid so it is lined up exactly with one of the points — dots — on the grid.

In this exercise, you will resize and align the Subtotal Fees and the Total Fees controls in the EmployeeID footer and in the report footer, and you will rename the labels. You will also align the Subtotal and Grand Total labels with their corresponding text boxes after you move them. You will also resize a field in the page footer.

To Move, Modify, and Align Labels in a Footer

a. Switch to **Design** view, and then click the **Sum label**. Point to the label, and then, when the pointer changes to a **four-headed** arrow, move the label to the right so that the **left edge** lines up with the **5"** mark on the horizontal ruler.

b. Double-click the **Sum label**, and then type Subtotal Fees. Click the **Subtotal Fees** label, press and hold Shift, and then select the **=Sum([Fee])** text box. Click the **Arrange** tab, and in the Sizing & Ordering group, click **Align**, and then select **Top**. This will align the label and text box by their top borders.

c. Click the **Grand Total** label in the Report Footer. Point to the **label**, and when the pointer changes to a **four-headed** arrow, move the label to the right so that the **left edge** lines up with the **5"** mark on the horizontal ruler.

d. Double-click the **Grand Total** label, and then type Total Fees.

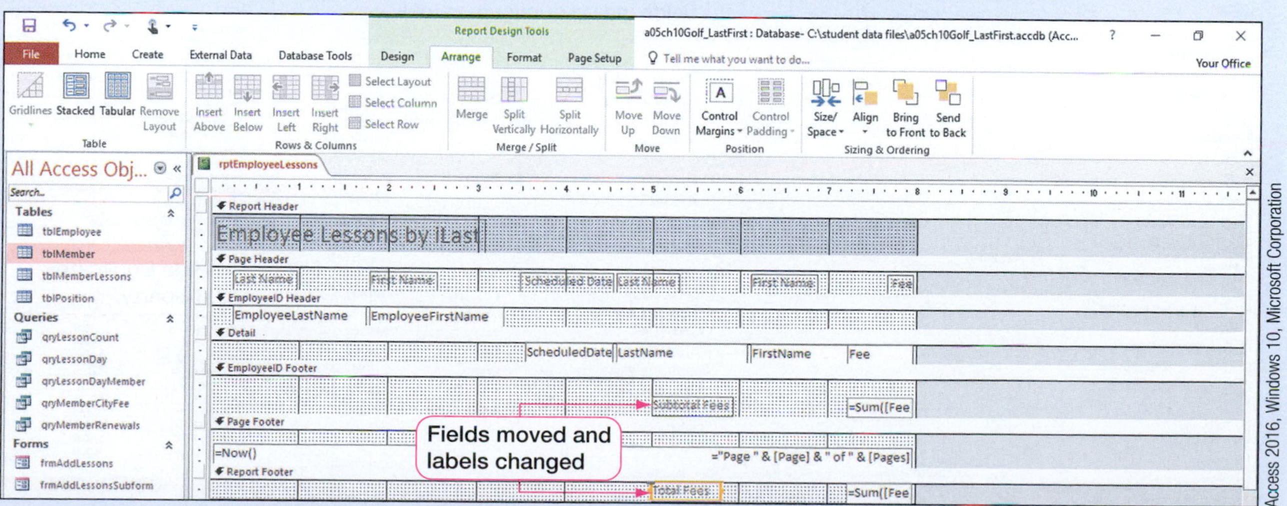

Figure 5 Subtotal and Total fields moved and edited

e. Click **Print Preview** to see how the report will look when printed, and then **Save** the report.

Change Report Properties

Like fields on a form, every field on a report has certain characteristics or properties about the field stored in a property sheet. The **property sheet** is a multitabbed pane that opens and shows all the characteristics that can be changed for whichever part of the form is selected. Different parts of the report will have different properties. For example, the background of the form will have a Back Color property but not a decimal places property as a number field does.

You will change the properties of the report so the duplicate member names — for members with multiple lessons — will be hidden. Since the report is sorted by member last name, all the records for one member will be consecutive, and hiding the duplicates will not hinder reading the report correctly.

Modifying the Hide Duplicates Property

On the Employee Lessons report, lessons are sorted by date and then by the member's name. This means that if an employee gives multiple lessons to a member, the member's name is repeated for each lesson. In this exercise, you will hide these duplicate values for Last Name and First Name.

To Hide Duplicate Values

SIDE NOTE

To See Grouping and Sorting

Click Group & Sort on the Design tab to open the Group, Sort, & Total pane. This will show how the report is grouped and sorted.

a. Switch to **Layout** view, and then click **Barker** in the first row of the second Last Name column.

b. If necessary click the **Design** tab, and then, in the Tools group, click **Property Sheet**. In the Property Sheet pane, click the **Format** tab, click the **Hide Duplicates** arrow, and then select **Yes**.

c. In the form detail, click **Charles** in the first row of the second First Name column. On the Format tab, click the **Hide Duplicates** arrow, and then select **Yes**.

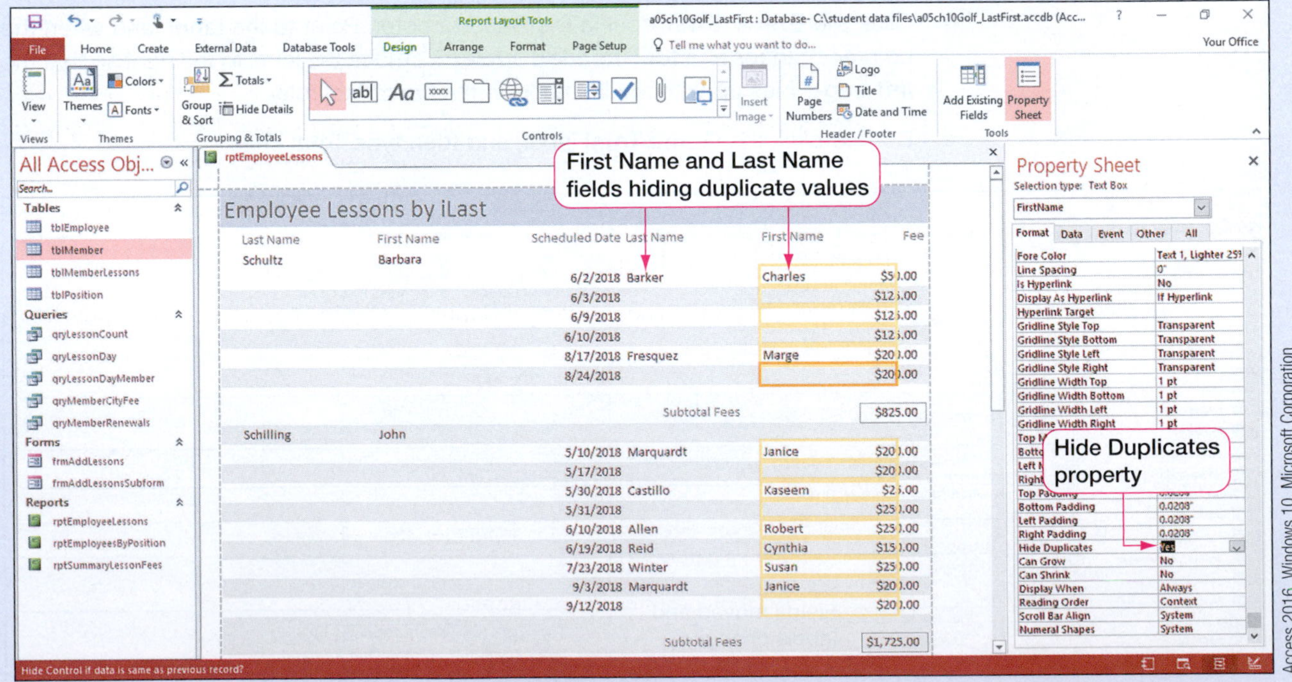

Figure 6 Duplicate field values hidden on report

d. **Close** the Property Sheet pane, and then click **Report View** to preview the report. **Save** and then **Close** the report.

Add and Remove Fields from a Report

When you create a report using the Report Wizard, you tell the wizard which fields you want, and the wizard formats the report with headers and footers for any grouping you choose. However, you may want to change the fields on existing reports or add or change the grouping. You can add and delete fields in either Layout view or Design view. In the next exercise, you will make these changes in Layout view, where you can see how the report will look with the changes.

Removing Fields from a Report

To remove a field from a report, you must remove both the bound control and the label control, or you will end up with data that is not labeled or a label without data. The golf course managers use a report named rptEmployeesByPosition, but it pops up a dialog box every time they open it. You determine that the dialog box is opening because Access is looking for a field on the report that does not exist in any of the database tables. In this exercise, you will remove that field, since it is not being used.

To Remove a Field from a Report

a. Open **rptEmployeesByPosition**, and click **OK** at the Enter Parameter Value prompt. Switch to **Layout** view, click the first **Orientation** check box, and then press Delete to delete the bound control.

b. Right-click the **Orientation** label in the header, and then select **Delete**. This will delete the label control.

c. **Save** the report.

Adding Fields to a Report

To add a field to a report, you will use the Field List, which will automatically add both the bound control and the label control for the field you choose to add. When you add fields to a report, you may have to change the tab order so that when you press Tab to move from field to field, the fields are selected in a logical order.

In this exercise, you will add a Salary field to the rptEmployeesByPosition report. The report is grouped by position and shows each employee by their hire date. You will also change the tab order so the fields are selected in the correct order.

To Add a Field to a Report

a. If necessary click the **Design** tab, and then, in the Tools group, click **Add Existing Fields**. This will open the Field List pane.

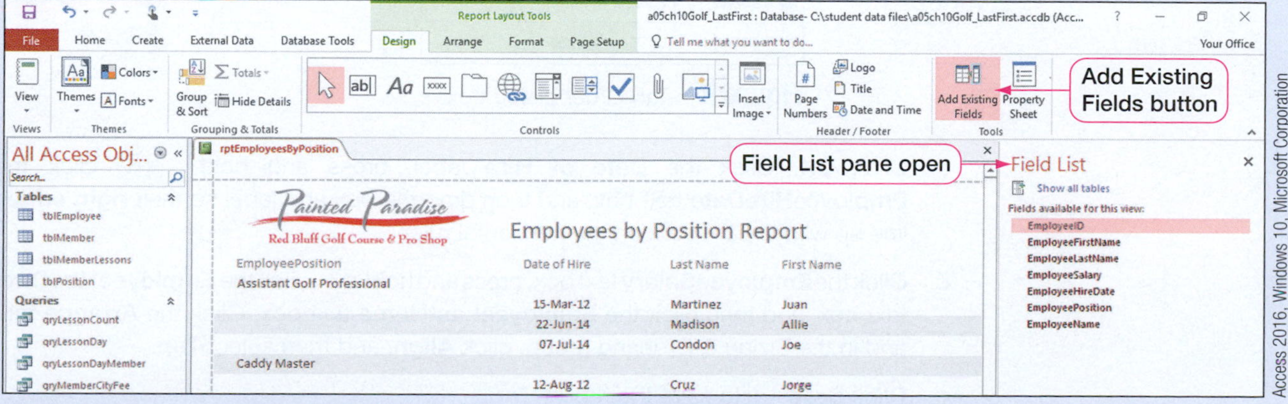

Figure 7 Field List pane open

b. Double-click **EmployeeSalary** in the Field List pane, and the field will be added to the left side of the report, overlapping Employee Position. **Close** [X] the Field List pane.

> ### Troubleshooting
> If the EmployeeSalary field is not listed, click **Show all tables** at the top of the Field List pane. This will list additional fields available to use on the report.

c. Click the **layout selector** [⊞] in the top left corner of the highlighted controls. When the pointer becomes a **four-headed** arrow [✥], drag the controls to the right of **EmployeePosition**, and release the mouse button.

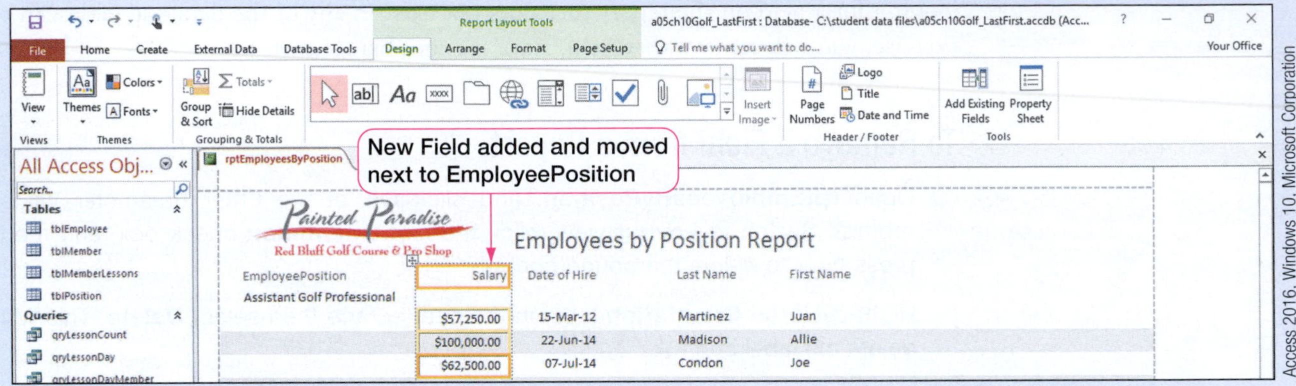

Figure 8 Salary field added and moved

d. Switch to **Design** view. On the Design tab, in the Tools group, click **Tab Order**. Click the **EmployeeSalary** field to select it, and then, using the **selection** box [ ] to the left of the field name, drag the field to the top of the **Custom Order** list.

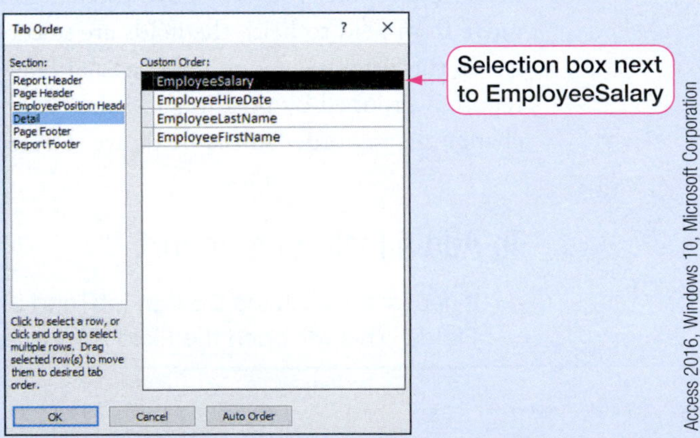

Figure 9 Tab Order dialog box

e. Click **OK**. Click the **Date of Hire** label, press and hold Shift, click the **EmployeeHireDate** text box, and then drag the box and label so their **right edges** line up with the **5"** mark on the horizontal ruler.

f. Click the **EmployeeSalary** text box, press and hold Shift, click the **EmployeeHireDate** text box, and then click the **EmployeeLastName** text box. Click the **Arrange** tab, and in the Sizing & Ordering group, click **Align**, and then select **Top**.

g. Click **Save** [💾] to save the report.

> **CONSIDER THIS** | **Field Without a Label?**
>
> Even though you can add and delete the bound control and the label separately, most of the time you will add or delete them together. Can you think of any time when you would want to show the bound control without the label?

Use the Group, Sort, and Total Pane

Grouping and sorting allow you to organize your report and to add totals and subtotals. When you create a report using the Report Wizard, one of the steps asks you how you want to group the report, and another asks how you want to sort the report. You can add, delete, or change the grouping and sort options manually on an existing report without having to use the Report Wizard. Grouping and sorting options can be changed in either Layout view or Design view.

Earlier, you created a report using the wizard to add grouping, sorting, and subtotals. Now you will change those options on rptEmployeesByPosition, which is an existing report that is grouped on EmployeePosition and sorted by EmployeeHireDate.

Opening the Group, Sort, and Total Pane

When you add a group or sort to a report, you have to open the Group, Sort, and Total pane. This opens at the bottom of your report window and allows you to add, delete, and change all the group, sort, and total options.

In this exercise, you will change rptEmployeesByPosition so it shows Employee Salary subtotals for each Employee Position and a grand total for all Employee Salaries.

A10.07

To Change Group, Sort, and Total Options on a Report

a. Click the **Design** tab, and in the Grouping & Totals group, click **Group & Sort**.

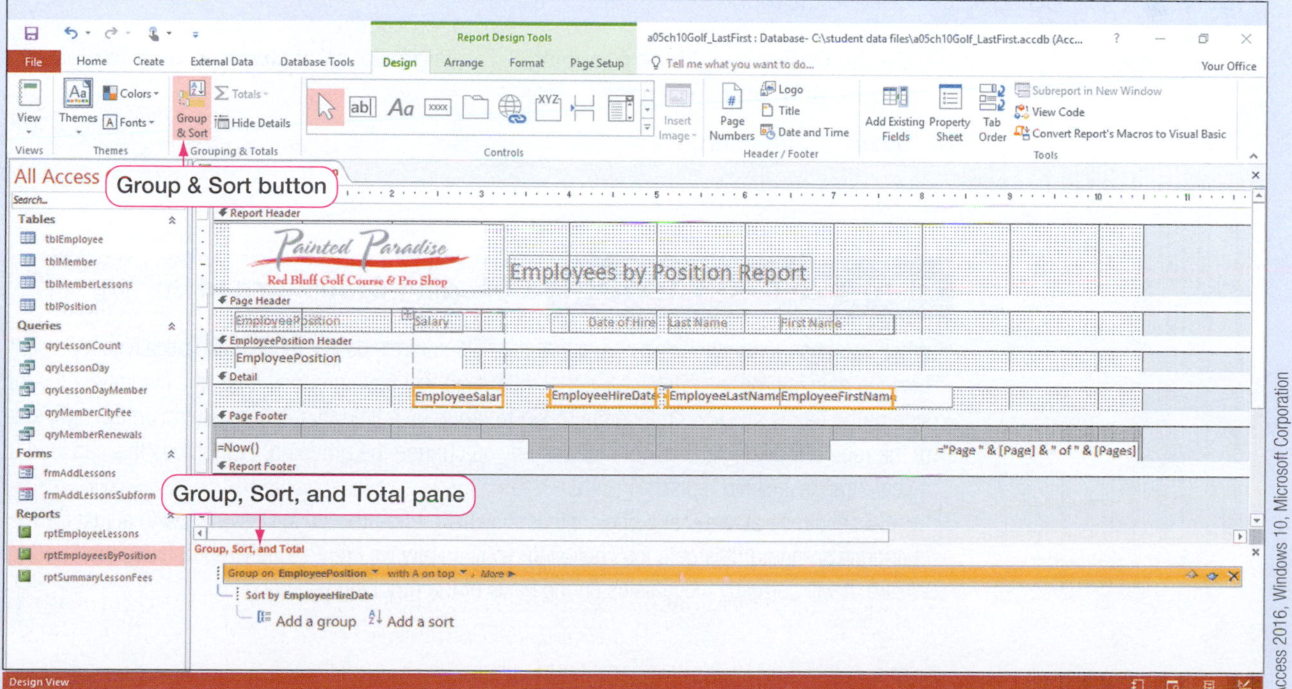

Figure 10 Group, Sort, and Total pane open in Design view

b. On the first row that says Group on EmployeePosition, click **More**. This opens the options for the group of records. Click the arrow next to **with no totals**, click the **Total On** arrow, and then select **EmployeeSalary**. Verify that **Sum** is selected in the Type box, and then click both the **Show Grand Total** check box and the **Show subtotal in group footer** check box.

c. Click outside the **Totals** box to close it, and then click **Less** on the Group on EmployeePosition row.

   You should see a new field called =Sum([EmployeeSalary]) in the EmployeePosition Footer and in the Report Footer. The first calculated field in the EmployeePosition Footer is the subtotal field, and the second calculated field in the Report Footer is the grand total field.

Troubleshooting

If you do not see the new fields, scroll to the bottom of the report.

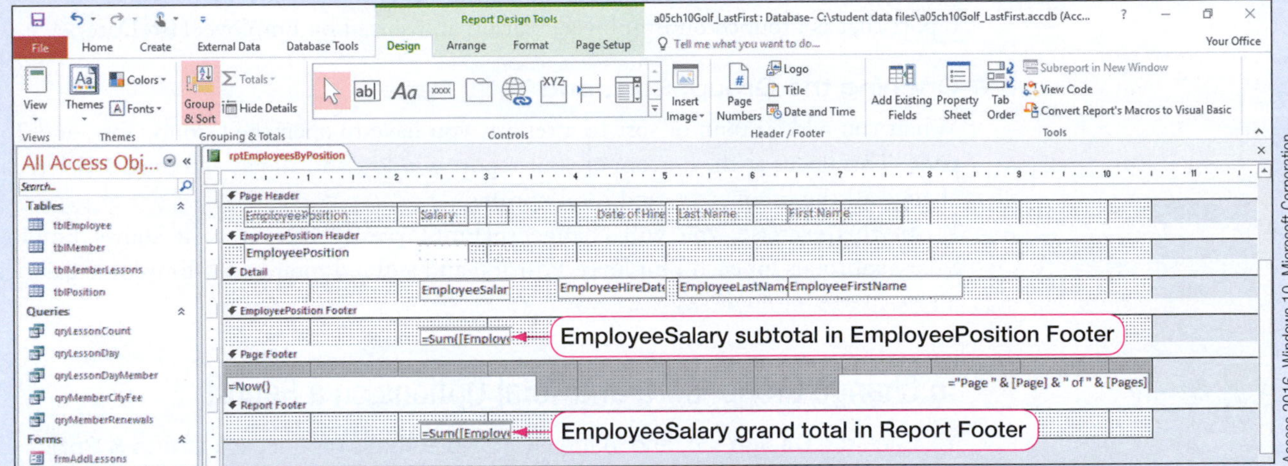

Figure 11 Calculated fields added to the report

d. On the Design tab, in the Grouping & Totals group, click **Group & Sort** to close the Group, Sort, and Total pane.

e. **Save** the report.

REAL WORLD ADVICE Changing Grouping and Sorting

When you change the grouping of a report, the field controls do not move automatically to represent how the data is grouped. This means that if the field you have grouped on is in a column on the left side of the report and you change the report to group by a field that is in a column on the right side of the report, those fields will not move when you change the grouping. Sometimes this can lead to a very strange-looking report.

You should be aware that some controls may have to be moved in Design view to adjust for the change in sorting. If this gets too confusing, you can always create a new report using the Report Wizard. It will correctly move fields on the basis of the grouping you choose.

Hiding Details on a Summary Report

The rptEmployeesByPosition report shows the Employee Position and each employee who holds that position along with the employees' individual salaries and total salaries. There are times when showing summary detail is either unnecessary or not appropriate. The details can be easily hidden on a report by using the Hide Details option. This option may be applied in either Layout view or Design view.

CONSIDER THIS | To Hide or Not to Hide

You have the option in a report to hide detail. When might this option be helpful? What type of data can you envision having to summarize? Under what circumstances might you hide the detail?

In this case, Barry Cheney, the golf course manager, would like a report that shows just the total amount of salaries for each position, without the detail for each employee because the employee information is confidential. In this exercise, you will hide the salary details of the employees so that the report shows only total salaries by position.

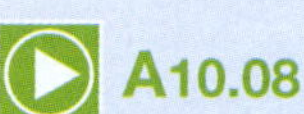

To Hide Detail Lines on a Report

a. Switch to **Layout** view, click the **Design** tab, and then, in the Grouping & Totals group, click **Hide Details**.

   The only rows on the report should now be the Employee Position and the total salaries for each position.

Troubleshooting

If your report does not look like the report in Figure 12, switch to Design view, open the Group, Sort, and Total pane and double-check that the EmployeeSalary subtotal is showing in the group footer and not the group header. If Show subtotal in group header is checked, uncheck it, and then click Show subtotal in group footer.

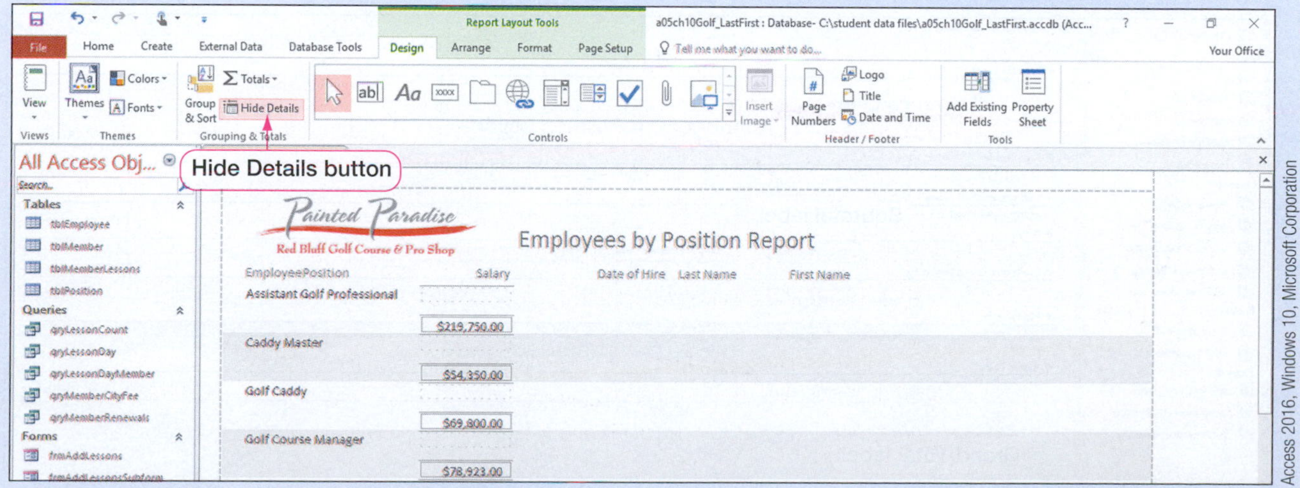

Figure 12 Report with details hidden

b. On the Design tab, in the Grouping & Totals group, click **Hide Details** again to unhide the details. Now you should see all the employees and their individual salaries, as well as the subtotals of the salaries.

c. Click **Hide Details** again to hide the details, and then **Save** the report.

Add Labels and Shapes to a Report

When you create groups and totals, calculated fields are often added to the report without a label. An example of this is the grand total and subtotals of the Employee Salary field that you added in the previous section. You can add labels to go with a calculated field, and then you can add lines and shapes to help bring attention to different parts of a report, such as the totals.

Adding Labels to a Report

When Access adds a field to a report without a label, it is good practice to add a label manually so the user of the report knows what he or she is looking at. In this exercise, you will add a label for the subtotal in the EmployeePosition Footer and for the grand total of Employee Salary in the report footer. Because the labels are not actually related to the calculated field, they will be unbound controls.

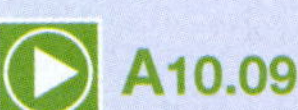

A10.09

To Add a New Label to a Report

a. Switch to **Design** view, click the **Design** tab, and in the Controls group, click **Label** Aa. Click the **1"** mark on the horizontal ruler in the Report Footer, and then type Grand Total.

b. Click the **Grand Total** label, press and hold Shift, and then click the **calculated** field. Click the **Arrange** tab, in the Sizing & Ordering group, click **Align**, and then select **Top**.

c. Click the **Design** tab, and in the Controls group, click **Label** Aa, click the **1"** mark on the horizontal ruler in the EmployeePosition Footer, and then type Position Subtotal.

d. Click the **Position Subtotal** label, press and hold Shift, and then click the **calculated** field. Click the **Arrange** tab, and in the Sizing & Ordering group, click **Align**, and then select **Top**.

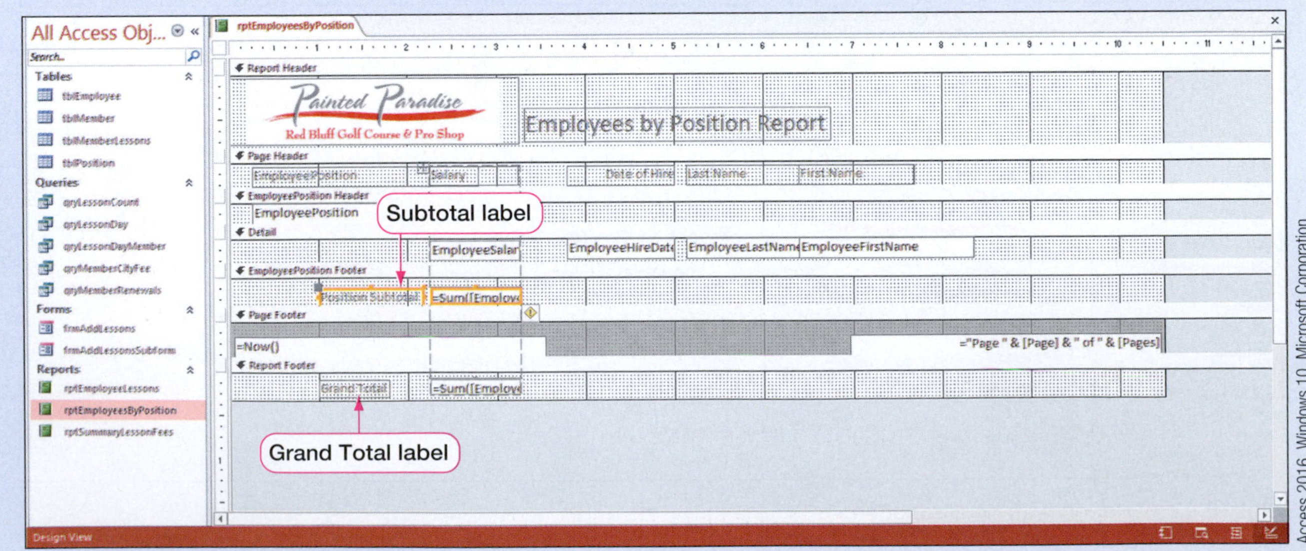

Figure 13 Labels added to report

Adding a Horizontal Line to a Report

You can add a line or other shape to a report to highlight different controls. A line is an unbound control that can be moved and resized like any other control on the report. A line also has properties like other controls, although they all have to do with formatting, since there is no data connected to the line.

In this exercise, you will draw a line just above the grand total in the Report Footer so this number stands out as a calculated total on the report. You will then change the line properties so the line has a different color, a different width, and a different border style.

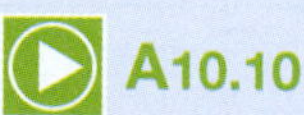

A10.10

To Add a Horizontal Line to a Report

a. Click the **Design** tab, and in the Controls group, click **Line**, press and hold Shift, and click the **1"** mark on the horizontal ruler in the Report Footer at the top of the Grand Total label. Drag the line to the right until you stop at the **4"** mark on the horizontal ruler.

Troubleshooting

If you have trouble keeping the Line control horizontal, you may be trying to drag it before placing the line. First, click to place the Line control in the footer. Once the line appears, you can easily drag it horizontally by holding down Shift.

b. On the Design tab, in the Tools group, click **Property Sheet**. In the Property Sheet pane, click the **Format** tab, click the **Border Style** arrow, and then select **Dash Dot Dot**.

c. Click the **Border Width** arrow, and then select **1pt**.

d. Click **Border Color**, click **Builder**, and then select **Dark Red**, the first color in the bottom row. **Close** the Property Sheet pane, and then click **Report View** to see your changes.

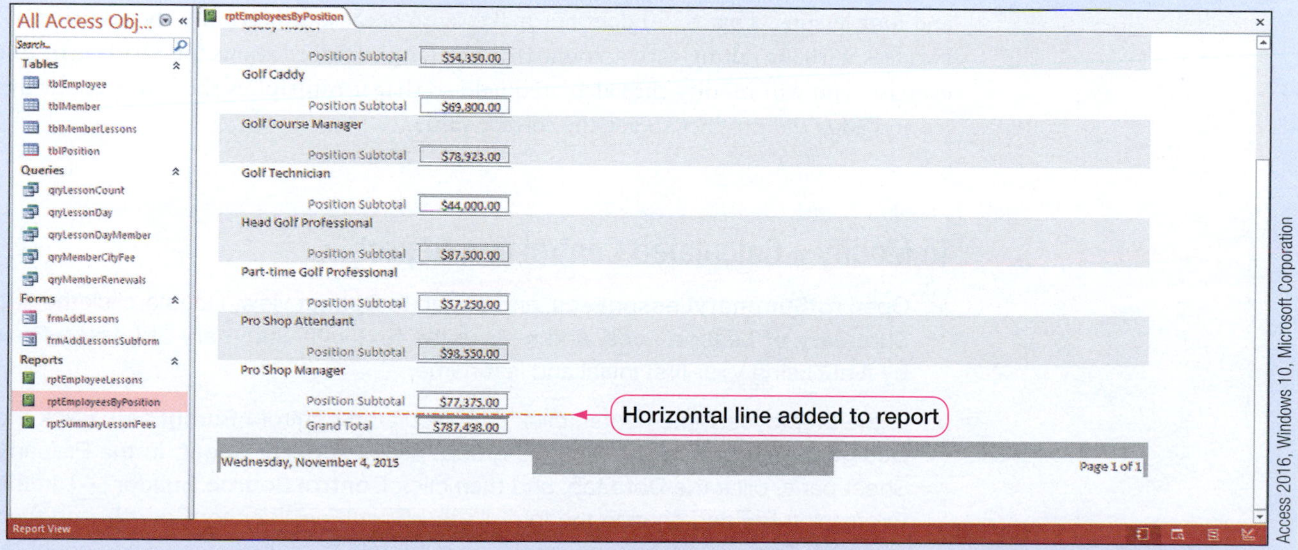

Figure 14 Horizontal line formatted and shown in Report view

e. Click **Save**, and then **Close** the report.

Modify Calculated Fields in a Report

The Report Wizard summary functions can be helpful to create simple calculations on a report, but sometimes they do not or cannot complete the calculations the way you want. For example, the rptSummaryLessonFees report shown in Figure 15 was created from a query to show each employee, the employees' fees, and the number of lessons for each fee. When the summary functions of SUM were chosen in the Report Wizard for Fee and LessonCount, they added the totals but did not take into account the number of lessons at each different fee amount.

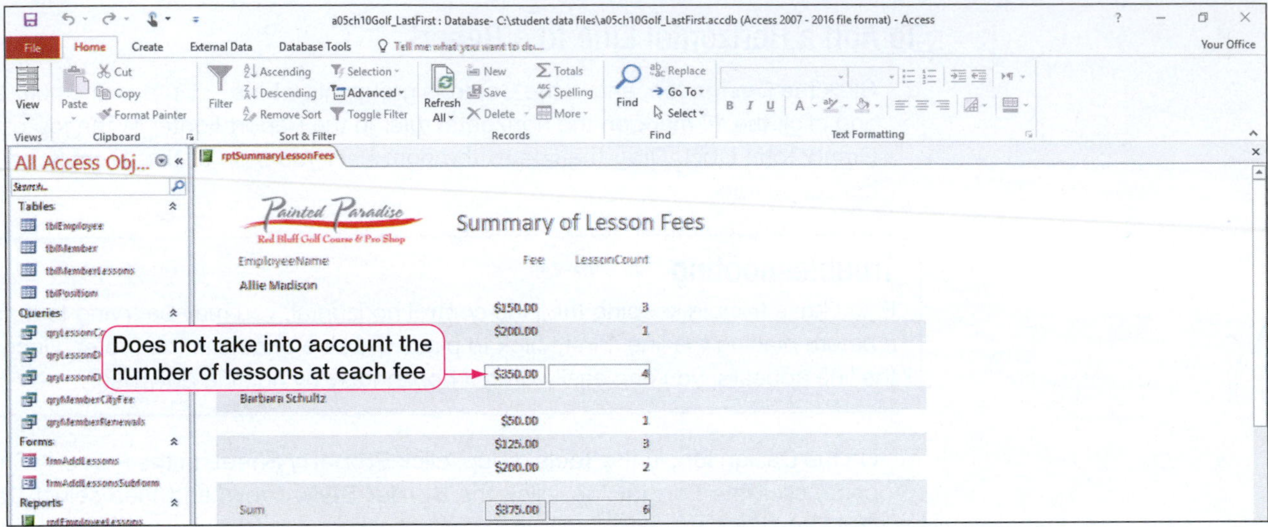

Figure 15 rptSummaryLessonFees

Access 2016, Windows 10, Microsoft Corporation

Modifying Existing Calculated Fields

In Figure 15, you can see why the summary fields did not give the intended results. Look at the data for Allie Madison. She taught three lessons for a fee of $150.00 each. She taught one lesson with a fee of $200. The group summary shows a total of $350 in fees and four lessons. That $350 does not make sense because it is simply the addition of the two fees without taking into account that she taught three lessons for $150 each. In this exercise, you will modify the calculated field so that it multiplies the lesson count by the fee and adds the product to get the correct value.

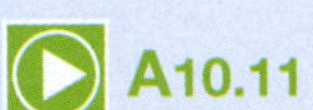 A10.11

To Modify a Calculated Control in a Report

a. Open **rptSummaryLessonFees**, and switch to **Design** view. Double-click the title **Summary of Lesson Fees**, and replace the **text** with Summary of Lesson Fees by iLast using your first initial and last name.

b. In the EmployeeName Footer, click the calculated control **=Sum([Fee])**. Click the **Design** tab, and then, in the Tools group, click **Property Sheet**. In the Property Sheet pane, click the **Data** tab, and then click **Control Source Builder** [...]. In the Expression Builder, change the formula to =Sum([Fee]*[LessonCount]), and then click **OK**. This will change the employee subtotals to multiply the lesson count by the related fee and then add the total fees.

c. In the **Report Footer**, click the calculated control **=Sum([Fee])**. In the Property Sheet pane, on the Data tab, click **Control Source Builder** [...], and then, in the Expression Builder, change the formula to =Sum([Fee]*[LessonCount]). Click **OK**.

This will change the grand total. **Close** [X] the Property Sheet pane. Switch to **Layout** view, and then verify that **Allie Madison** has a subtotal Fee of $650.

Troubleshooting

If you see a prompt that asks you to enter a parameter value, you mistyped the expression for the calculation. Click Cancel, and correct the expression.

d. Switch to **Design** view, click the **Sum** label in the EmployeeName Footer, and replace the text with Employee Summary.

e. Switch to **Layout** view. Scroll down, click **John Schilling's Employee summary**, and then drag the **left edge** of the box to the left so the dollar sign is shown fully. Click the **Grand Total** fees box, and then repeat resizing of the field. **Save** and then **Close** [X] the report. If you need to take a break before finishing this chapter, now is a good time.

Creating Parameter Reports

Recall that parameter queries are queries in which the user enters the criteria, or parameters, when the query is run, and the results are based on the parameters entered. A **parameter** is a value that can be changed each time you run the query. These flexible queries can be customized to a user's needs. Reports can then be created from parameter queries to have that same flexibility. In this section, you only create not only a parameter report, but also a form for entering the parameters. This will require some modification of the original query, which you will also do.

Create a Parameter Report

A report created from a **parameter query** (a query that uses prompts for criteria) will work just like a parameter query: When you open the report, you will be prompted for values to search for, and only those values will appear on the report. In this section, you will create a report from an existing parameter query. You will create a form for entering the parameters in order to more easily run the report. You will also add conditional formatting to the report to highlight values that meet certain criteria.

Creating a Report from a Parameter Query

Barry Cheney would like a report that shows membership renewals between a specific start and end date. In this exercise, you will make a copy of qryMemberRenewals and create the report from that new query. The query is a parameter query that finds all records with a renewal date between a start date entered and an end date entered.

To Create a Report from a Parameter Query

a. If you took a break, open the **a05ch10Golf_LastFirst** database.

b. Click the **Create** tab, and then, in the Reports group, click **Report Wizard**. Click the **Tables/Queries arrow**, select **qryMemberRenewals**, and then click **add all fields** [>>]. Click **Next**. Do not add any grouping levels. Click **Next**, click the first **sort** box arrow, select **DateRenewal**, and then click **Next**. Accept the **Tabular** layout, select **Landscape** orientation, and then click **Next**. Name your report rptMemberRenewals, and then click **Finish**.

c. The first parameter box will open prompting you for a Start Date value. Type 5/1/2019, and then click **OK**.

d. The second parameter box will open prompting you for an End Date value. Type 7/1/2019, and then click **OK**. Your report will open with two records that have a renewal date between the start date you entered and the end date you entered.

e. Click the **Print Preview** tab and then, in the Close Preview group, click **Close Print Preview**. Select the report title **rptMembershipRenewals**, and then replace the text with Membership Renewals by iLast using your first initial and last name.

f. **Save** and then **Close** the report.

Creating a Form for Entering Parameters

An unbound form can be helpful as an input tool for parameter reports. Rather than opening the report and having parameter windows open one by one, a form can have controls for entering each of the parameters. In this exercise, you will create an unbound form with two controls: one for the start date and one for the end date. These dates will be unbound and will stay active only while the form is open. You will format these controls to be date fields. Because it is a good idea to use a default value, you will use the current date for the default in both the start date and end date text boxes.

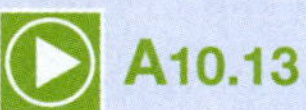
A10.13

To Create a Form for Entering Parameters

a. Click the **Create** tab, and then, in the Forms group, click **Blank Form**.

b. Switch to **Layout** view, and then click the **Design** tab, and then, in the Header/Footer group, click **Title** to add a title to the form. Replace the text with Renewal Date Form by iLast using your first initial and last name.

c. **Close** the Field List pane. On the Design tab, in the Controls group, click **Label** *Aa*. Move your pointer to the top left corner of the form details area, and then click the **form**. Type Enter Dates for Renewal Queries and Reports.

d. Select the label, click the **Format** tab, and in the Font group, click the **Font Color**, and then select **Red**. Click the **Font Size** arrow, and then select **14**.

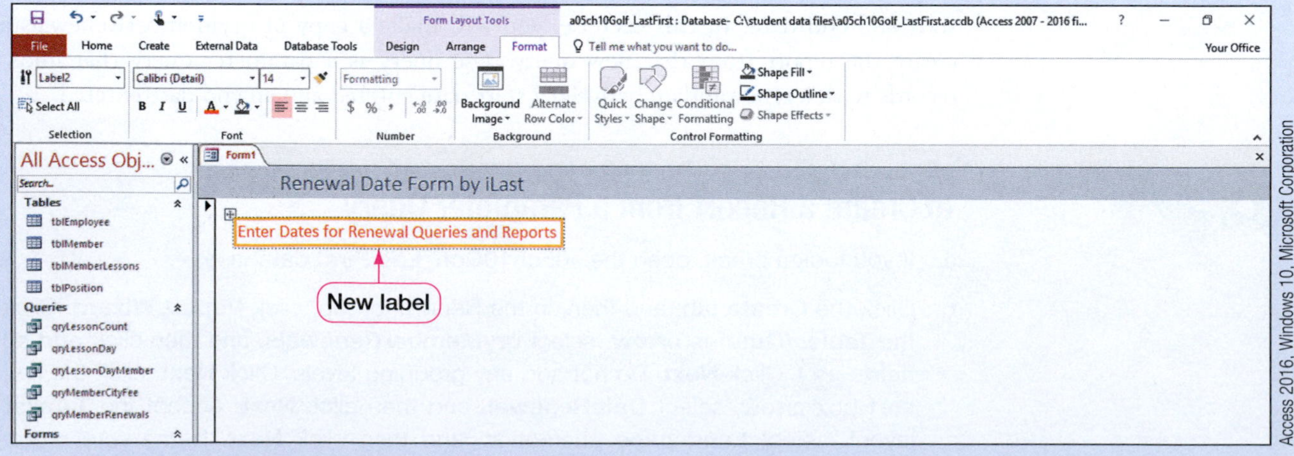

Figure 16 Label added to form

e. Click the **Design** tab, and then, in the Controls group, click **Text Box** [ab|]. Click the form to insert the text box below the **Enter Dates for Renewal Queries and Reports** label. The field will automatically be stacked below the label.

f. Click the new **label**, and then replace the text with Start Date.

g. Click the **text** box, and then, on the Design tab, in the Tools group, click **Property Sheet**. In the Property Sheet pane, click the **Format** tab, click the **Format** arrow, and then select **Short Date**.

h. In the Property Sheet pane, click the **Data** tab, click **Default Value**, and then type =Date(). This will make the default value the current date. Click the **Other** tab, click **Name**, and then replace the text with StartDate.

> **SIDE NOTE**
> **Other Field Properties**
> Additional properties such as validation rules, validation text, and input masks can be added to form fields through the Properties Sheet.

i. On the Design tab, in the Controls group, click **Text Box** [ab|]. Click the **form** to insert a text box immediately below **Start Date**. Click the **label**, and then replace the text with End Date.

j. Click the new **text** box, and in the Property Sheet pane, click the **Format** tab, click the **Format** arrow, and then select **Short Date**. Click the **Data** tab, click **Default Value**, and then type =Date(). Click the **Other** tab, click **Name**, and then replace the text with EndDate. **Close** [X] the Property Sheet pane.

k. Click the **blank space** above **Start Date**. Click the **Arrange** tab, and then, in the Rows & Columns group, click **Select Row**. This will select the blank placeholder and the label you entered. In the Merge/Split group, click **Merge**. This merges the two controls in the first row so they line up better with the start date and end date labels.

l. Click the **first date** text box, and then, on the Arrange tab, in the Merge/Split group, click **Split Horizontally**. Repeat for the **second date** text box. This splits the one long control into two smaller controls to make the data entry field smaller.

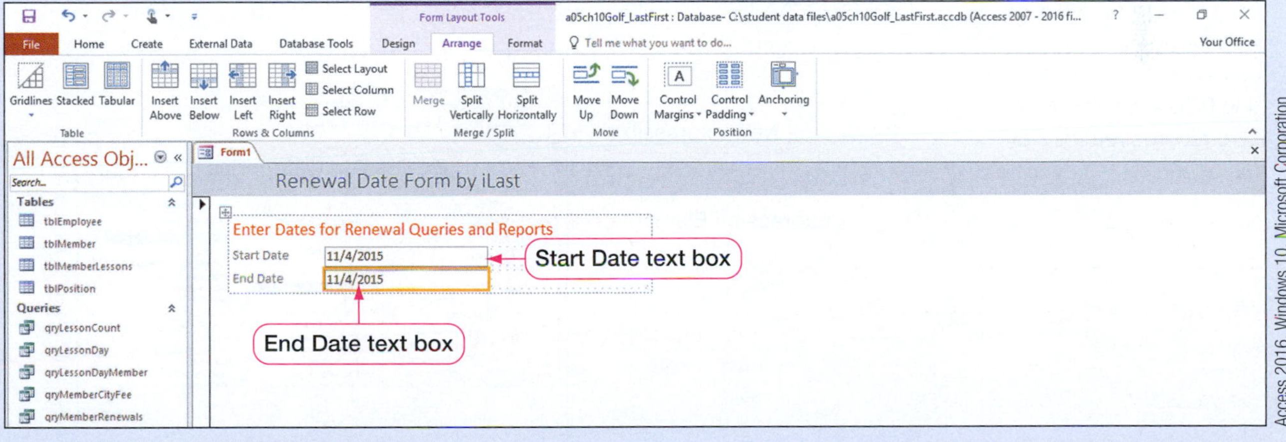

Figure 17 Renewal Date Form

m. Switch to Form view. Type 5/1/2019 for the Start Date and 7/1/2019 for the End Date.

n. **Save** [save icon] the form, type frmMemberRenewals.

Modifying a Query to Use New Form Fields

The form you just created will provide controls to enter the parameter values for the parameter query qryMemberRenewals, on which the report rptMemberRenewals is based. The query was created to accept values from the parameter windows, but since the values will now be entered into a form, the query needs to be updated to get the values from the form. In this exercise, you will change the query so the parameter values point to the values entered in the form and not in the parameter windows as in a normal parameter query.

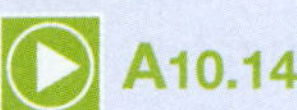

To Change Query Criteria to Use Fields from a Form

a. In the Navigation Pane, right-click **qryMemberRenewals**, and then select **Design View**.

> **Troubleshooting**
>
> If you double-click the query to open it instead of using the right-click, you will be prompted to enter two parameter values. Click OK through each of the prompts to open the query, and then switch to Design view.

b. Scroll to the right, delete the criteria under **DateRenewal**, and then leave the insertion point in the **Criteria row**. Click the **Design** tab, and then, in the Query Setup group, click **Builder**. Type Between in the Expression pane.

c. In the Expression Elements pane, click **a05ch10Golf_LastFirst** to expand it. Double-click **Forms**, double-click **All Forms**, and then click **frmMemberRenewals**.

d. In the Expression Categories pane, double-click **StartDate**, type and in the Expression pane above, and then, in the Expression Categories pane, double-click **EndDate**. Your expression should read Between Forms![frmMemberRenewa ls]![StartDate] and Forms![frmMemberRenewals]![EndDate].

SIDE NOTE

Omitting a Date

If one date is omitted from the criteria, Access will interpret the criteria as between one date and 0. The result will be zero records returned by the query.

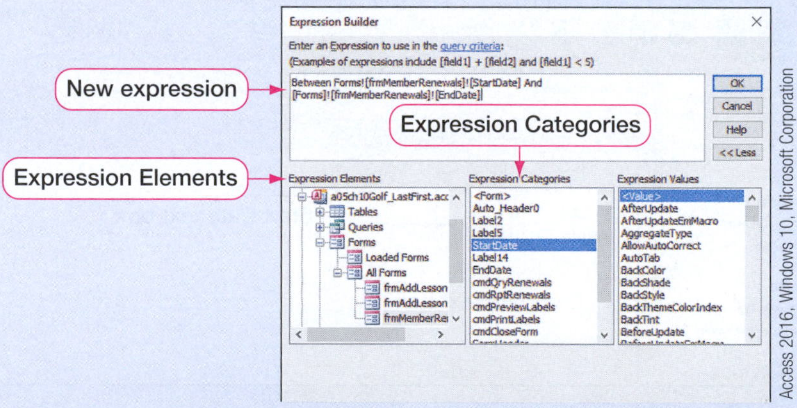

Figure 18 New expression in Expression Builder

e. Click **OK**. Click the **Design** tab, and then, in the Results group, click **Run** to run the query. You should see the same two records as the last time you ran the query with the earlier parameters. The difference is that the query is now using the dates from the frmMemberRenewals forms for the parameters.

f. **Save** and then **Close** the query.

REAL WORLD ADVICE **Running the Parameter Report**

Once you change the query to accept the parameters from the form rather than the prompts when you open the report, you will want to use only the form to run the report and the query.

When the query was first created, the prompt was entered as Between [Start Date] and [End Date], so the prompt windows showed the text "Start Date" and "End Date". Now that you are using the form parameters, the prompts will show the name of the form and the name of the field and will look something like this: "Forms![frmMemberRenewals_initialLastname]![StartDate]".

If a prompt were to open with this text, the user might not know what to do with it. Therefore, once a form has been created and the query points to the form, the report and query should be run only from the form.

Modifying a Report to Use New Form Fields

When reports are built from parameter queries, running the report yields different results depending on the parameter values entered. Because reports are designed to be printed, that means that after some time has passed, it might not be easy to recall what parameter value was used to run that particular report. In this exercise, you will add the parameter values to the report header so that they can be easily identified.

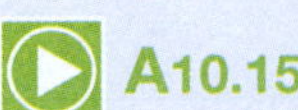
A10.15

To Add Form Fields to the Parameter Report

a. In the Navigation Pane, right-click **rptMemberRenewals**, and then select **Design View**. Use your pointer to drag the **bottom edge** of the **Report Header** to the **1 inch** mark on the vertical ruler.

Troubleshooting

If you double-click the report to open it instead of using the right-click, you will be prompted to enter two parameter values. Click OK through each of the prompts to open the report, and then switch to Design view.

b. Click the **Design** tab, and in the Controls group, click **Text Box** [ab|]. Click the **Report Header** below the title to insert a text box. If necessary, drag the **control** with the move handle so that the **left edge** of the Label control lines up with the **.5 inch** mark on the horizontal ruler. Click the label, and then replace the text with Start Date.

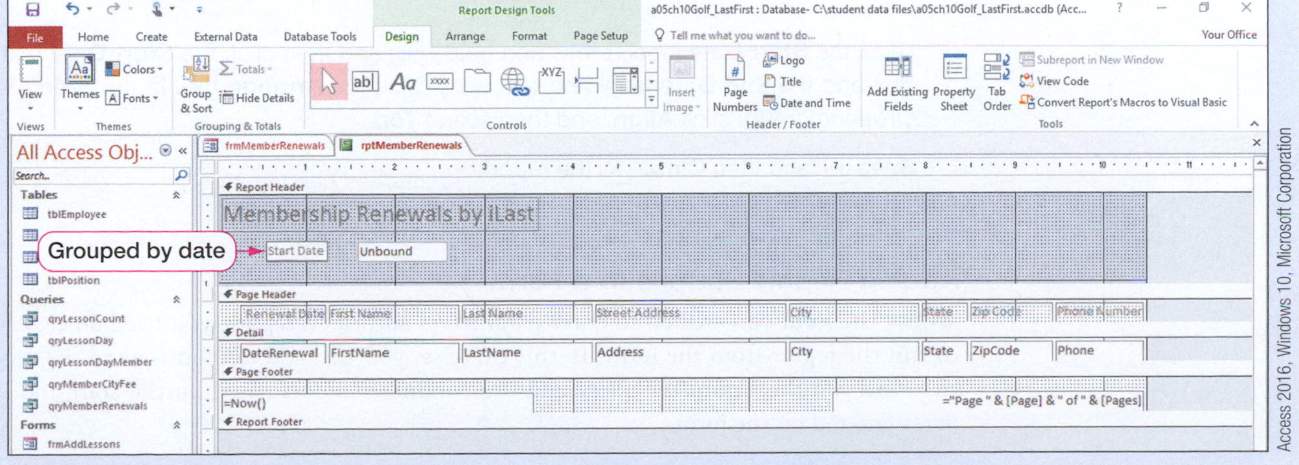

Figure 19 Text box added to report header

c. Click the **text** box, and then, on the Design tab, in the Tools group, click **Property Sheet**. In the Property Sheet pane, click the **Format** tab, click the **Format** arrow, and then select **Short Date**.

d. In the Property Sheet pane, click the **Data** tab, and then click **Control Source Builder** [ab|]. In the Expression Elements pane, double-click **a05ch10Golf_LastFirst**, double-click **Forms**, double-click **All Forms**, and then click **frmMemberRenewals**. In the Expression Categories pane, double-click **StartDate**, and then click **OK**.

e. On the Design tab, in the Controls group, click **Text Box** [ab|]. Click the **Report Header** to the right of the **Start Date** text box. If necessary, drag the control with the move handle so that the **left edge** of the label control lines up with the **3 inch** vertical grid line. Click the **label**, and then replace the text with End Date.

f. Click the **text box**, and in the Property Sheet pane, on the **Format** tab, click the **Format** arrow, and then select **Short Date**.

g. Click the **Data** tab, and then click **Control Source Builder** [ab|]. In the Expression Elements pane, double-click **a05ch10Golf_LastFirst**, double-click **Forms**, then double-click **All Forms**, and then click **frmMemberRenewals**. In the Expression Categories pane, double-click **EndDate**, and then click **OK**. **Close** [X] the Property Sheet pane.

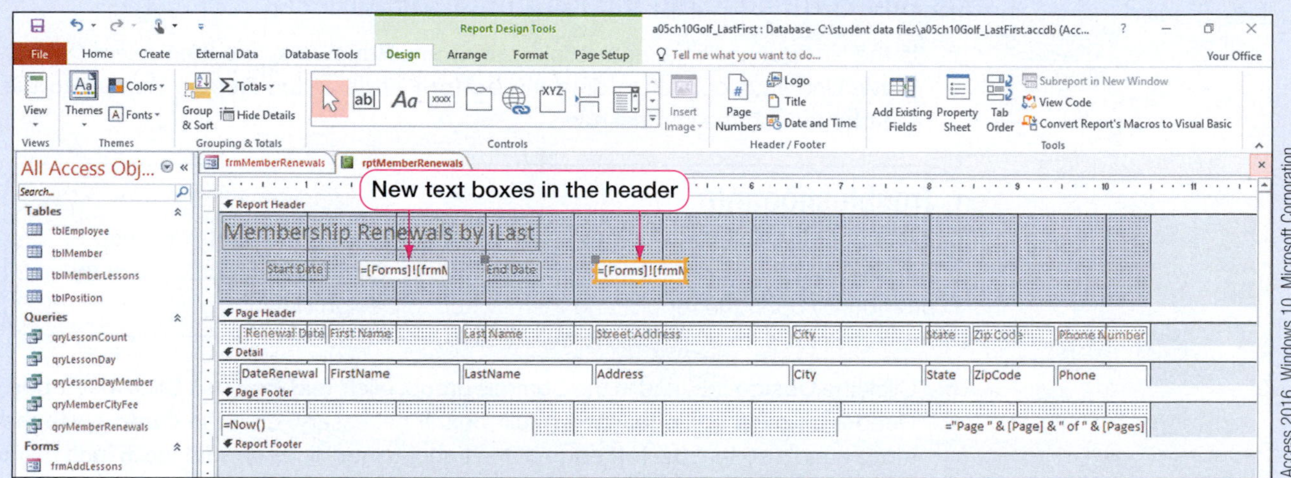

Figure 20 Text boxes added and formatted in report header

h. Click the **Start Date** label, press and hold Shift, and then click the **Start Date** text box and the **End Date** label and text box. Click the **Arrange** tab. In the Sizing & Ordering group, click **Align**, and then select **Top**.

i. **Save** [save icon] and then **Close** [X] the report.

Adding Report Buttons to a Form

To use the form you created to enter parameters and run a report, you need an easy way to run the report from the form. In this exercise, you will add two buttons to the report that will run the parameter query and the parameter report based on the start and end dates entered on the form.

A10.16

To Add Report Buttons to a Form

a. With the **frmMemberRenewals** form open, switch to **Design** view. Drag to reduce the **Detail section** of the form to the **2 inch** mark on the vertical ruler.

b. Click the **Design** tab, and then, in the Controls group, click **Button** [xxxx]. Move your pointer below the **End Date** label, and then click the **form**. The Command Button Wizard opens.

c. In the Categories pane, click **Miscellaneous**. In the Actions pane, click **Run Query**, and then click **Next**.

d. Click **qryMemberRenewals**, and then click **Next**. Click **Text**, replace the text with Run Renewals Query, and then click **Next**. Name the button cmdQryRenewals, and then click **Finish**.

e. On the Design tab, in the Controls group, click **Button** [xxxx]. Move your pointer to the right of the existing button, and then click the **form**. The Command Button Wizard opens.

f. In the Categories pane, click **Report Operations**. In the Actions pane, click **Open Report**, and then click **Next**.

g. Click **rptMemberRenewals**, and then click **Next**. Click **Text**, replace the text with Run Renewals Report, and then click **Next**. Name the button cmdRptRenewals, and then click **Finish**. Align the buttons by their top edge.

h. **Save** the form, and then switch to **Form** view. In **Start Date**, type 5/1/2019. In End Date, type 7/1/2019. Alternatively, you can use the date picker for each field to pick the dates.

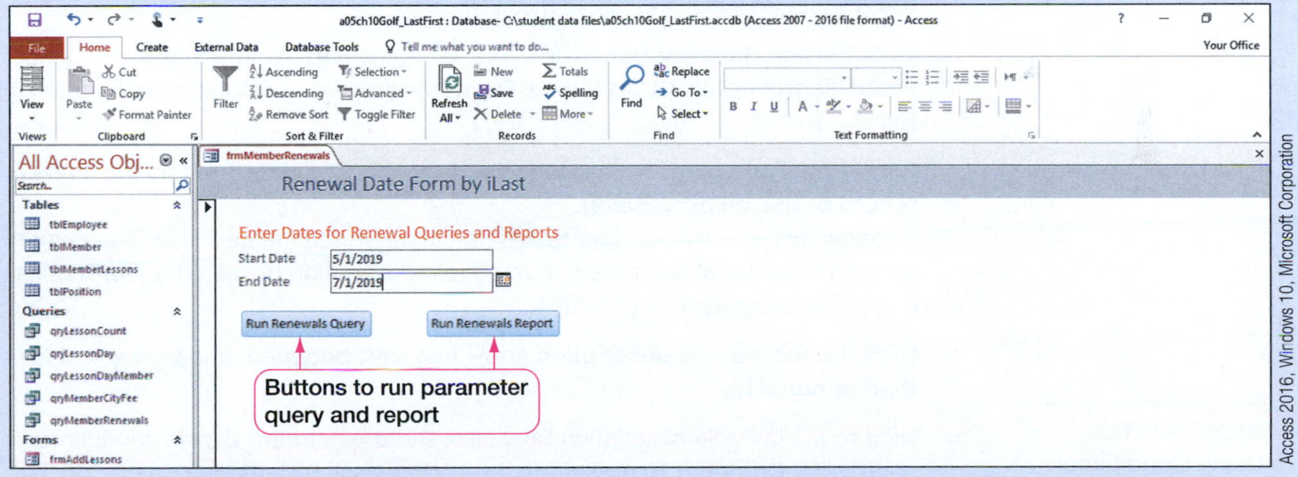

Figure 21 New buttons added to form

i. Click **Run Renewals Query**. The query opens, showing the two members who have renewals between the two dates you entered. **Close** [X] the query, but leave the form open.

j. Click **Run Renewals Report** using the same two dates entered above. The report opens, showing the two members who have renewals between the two dates you entered. The dates are also filled in in the header. **Close** [X] the report. Click **Save** if you are prompted to save changes.

Use Conditional Formatting in a Report

Conditional formatting formats a control on the basis of one or more comparisons to a set rule. These comparisons can be based on the value of the control or on a calculation that includes other values; for example, you could highlight values that are zero or negative. You can also compare the value to the value in other records; for example, you could highlight the value that is highest or lowest.

The Conditional Formatting Rules Manager dialog box is used to set the conditions. You can access the dialog box in Layout or Design view.

Adding Conditional Formatting to a Report

Barry wants a report that will show at a glance which memberships have already expired. In this exercise, you will create a simple report with member names and renewal dates and use conditional formatting to highlight the expired memberships with red text.

A10.17

To Add Conditional Formatting to a Report

a. Click the **Create** tab, and then click **Report Wizard**. Click the **Tables/Queries** arrow, select **tblMember**, and then add **DateRenewal**, **DateJoined**, and **MemberName** to the **Selected Fields**. Click **Next**.

b. Do not add any additional grouping, and then click **Next**. Sort in ascending order by **DateRenewal**, and then click **Next**. Accept the **Tabular** layout and **Portrait** orientation, and then click **Next**. Change the title of the report to rptExpiredMemberships, and then click **Finish**.

c. On the Print Preview tab, in the Close Preview group, click **Close Print Preview**, switch to **Layout** view, and then change the title to Expired Memberships by iLast using your first initial and last name.

d. Click the first **Renewal Date** field value. Click the **Format** tab, and in the Control Formatting group, click **Conditional Formatting** to start the Conditional Formatting Rules Manager.

e. Click **New Rule**, and then accept the selection **Check values in the current record or use an expression**.

   Below this, you will see four boxes that allow you to create a rule. You need to select a value for at least the first three rule description boxes. The fourth box is only for entering a range of values.

f. Click the second **rule description** arrow that says **between**, and then select **less than or equal to**.

g. Next to the last rule description box, click **Build** [...]. In the Expression Elements pane, click **Common Expressions**. In the Expression Categories pane, double-click **Current Date**, and then click **OK**.

   This tells Access to compare the value in the field with the current date. If the field value is less than or equal to the current date, then the font color — which will be chosen next — will be changed to red.

h. Click **Font color** [A], select **Red**, and then click **OK**. Verify that the rule says **Value <= Date()**.

SIDE NOTE
Using Conditional Formatting Conservatively
Using too many colors or an overly complicated color pattern in conditional formatting rules can be distracting. Be concise and clear in using conditional formatting.

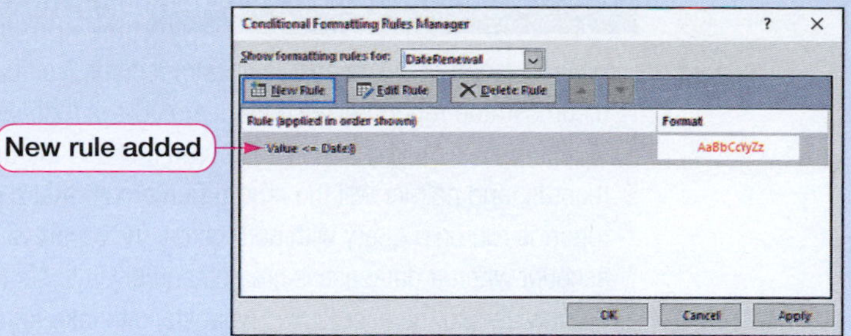

Figure 22 Conditional Formatting Rules Manager

Access 2016, Windows 10, Microsoft Corporation

Troubleshooting

If the rule is not correct, click Edit Rule, and change the options. You can also delete the rule and start again by clicking Delete Rule.

i. Click **OK** again. The report should have anywhere from three to six dates highlighted, depending on the current date.

j. **Save** and **Close** the report. If you need to take a break before finishing this chapter, now is a good time.

Creating Mailing Labels

Access has a specialized report that can be used for mailing labels, name tags, or other types of labels. Because Access is often used to keep track of customers, employees, or other types of people, this is a common use of Access. You could also export the names and addresses to Word and then create the mailing labels in Word, but doing it directly in Access saves a step.

Because mailing labels are actually reports, they have the four views that all reports have: Print Preview, Report view, Layout view, and Design view. Because of the mailing label format, the views look different from those you have seen before. In Print Preview, the labels look the way they will look when you print them. In this section, you will create mailing labels from a query. You will also add buttons to an existing form to request a Print Preview of the labels and to print the labels.

Create Mailing Labels

Access has built-in label formats for many of the leading label makers. The wizard allows you to pick the correct format. You can create labels based on data in tables or queries.

Creating Address Mailing Labels

The golf club needs mailing labels for members whose memberships are expiring soon so the golf club can mail a renewal letter. In this exercise, you will use qryMemberRenewals as the source to create these labels. Because the query will show results only when date parameters have been entered, you will need to enter parameters for the report. If no parameters have been entered and the query is not open when you first create the report, you will get error messages instead of results. To prevent this from happening, you will run the query first. Because the query is based on parameters entered in a form, you will open the form first, enter parameters, run the query, and then create the report.

REAL WORLD ADVICE | **Reports Based on Queries**

When a report is based on a table with records, you can run the report, and there will always be records in the report because there are always records in the table. When you run a report from a query, unless the query has been run first and the query is open, the query will not have any records, and neither will the report! Remember that a query does not store any records, so if a report is run on a query with no records, the report will have no records. This should be taken into account when a database is created and given to someone else to use. Instructions should always be provided so the user knows what steps to take to run a query or report successfully. While not discussed in this chapter, a macro can be created to run a query and then a report if necessary.

To Create Mailing Labels

a. If you took a break, open the **a05ch10Golf_LastFirst** database.

b. Open **frmMemberRenewals**, and type 1/1/2019 for the start date and 3/1/2019 for the end date. Click **Run Renewals Query**.

c. With both the form and query still open, click the **Create** tab, and in the Reports group, click **Labels**. The Label Wizard starts.

   The first task is to match your labels with the standard labels that are part of the wizard. The easiest way to do that is to look at the box or sheet of labels. If you do not have a standard label, you can specify a customized size. The golf club uses Avery C2160 labels, so you will select that type of label.

d. If necessary, click the **Filter by manufacturer** arrow, select **Avery**, select Product number **C2160**, and then click **Next**.

e. Click the **Font name** arrow, select **Times New Roman**, click the **Font size** arrow, and then select **11**. Click the **Font weight** arrow, select **Normal**, and then click **Next**.

f. Double-click **FirstName** to move it to the prototype label. Press Spacebar, double-click **LastName**, and then press Enter.

Troubleshooting

The field selection looks like the field selection in other wizard dialog boxes, but there are important differences. First, you must format your labels yourself. You will need to type spaces, commas, and line breaks. Second, there is no field back button. If you put the fields in the wrong order, it is sometimes easiest to go back a step in the wizard dialog box and try again.

If you omitted the space, click between the two fields, and press Spacebar.

g. Double-click **Address**, press Enter, double-click **City**, and then type , — a comma. Press Spacebar, double-click **State**, press Spacebar, and then double-click **ZipCode**.

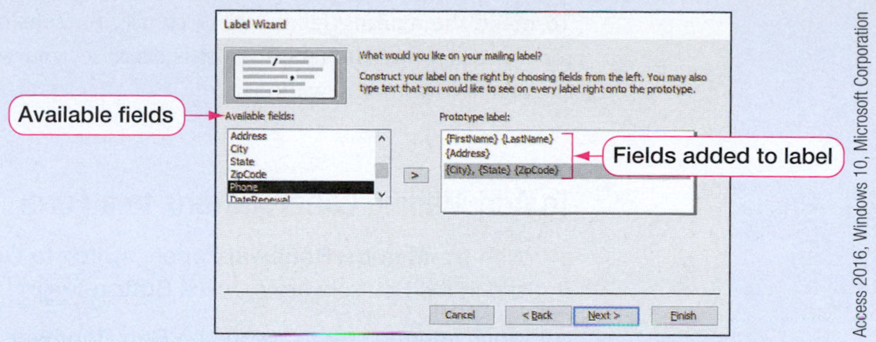

Access 2016, Windows 10, Microsoft Corporation

Figure 23 Complete address added in Label Wizard

h. Click **Next**. In the Available fields list, double-click **ZipCode** to add it to **Sort by**, and then click **Next**.

i. Name the report rptLabels and then click **Finish**.

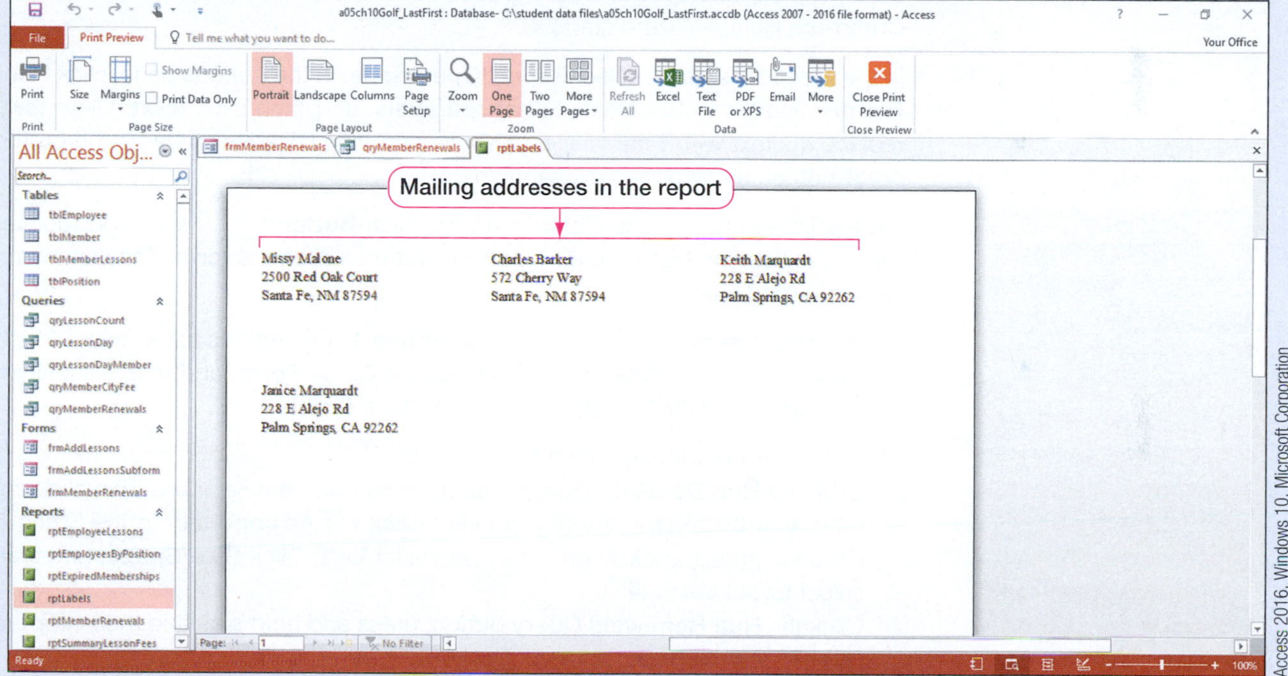

Access 2016, Windows 10, Microsoft Corporation

Figure 24 Finished Labels

j. **Save** and **Close** the label report. **Close** qryMemberRenewals, and leave frmMemberRenewals open.

Troubleshooting

When you clicked Finish, did the mailing labels report ask you for parameters? Make sure that frmMemberRenewals is open with parameters entered. If you close the form, Access will not know what dates you want.

Adding Mailing Label Buttons to a Form

To make the mailing labels easier to use, buttons can be added to a form to launch the report containing the labels. In this exercise, you will add buttons to preview and print the labels to your renewal form.

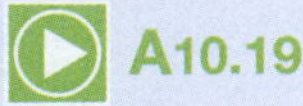

To Add Mailing Label Buttons to a Form

a. With **frmMemberRenewals** open, switch to **Design** view. Click the **Design** tab, and in the Controls group, click **Button** [xxxx].

b. Move your pointer to below the **Run Renewals Query** button, and then click the form. The Command Button Wizard starts.

c. In the Categories pane, select **Report Operations**. In the Actions pane, select **Preview Report**, and then click **Next**. Select **rptLabels**, and then click **Next**. Click **Text**, replace the text with Preview Mailing Labels, and then click **Next**. Name the button cmdPreviewLabels and then click **Finish**.

d. On the Design tab, in the Controls group, click **Button** [xxxx]. Move your pointer to the **right** of the Preview Mailing Labels button, and then click the **form**. The Command Button Wizard starts.

e. In the Categories pane, select **Report Operations**. In the Actions pane, click **Print Report**, and then click **Next**. Select **rptLabels**, and then click **Next**. Click **Text**, replace the text with Print Mailing Labels, and then click **Next**. Name the button cmdPrintLabels, and then click **Finish**.

f. On the Design tab, in the Controls group, click **Button** [xxxx]. Move your pointer below the Preview Mailing Labels button, and then click the **form**. The Command Button Wizard starts.

g. In the Categories pane, select **Form Operations**. In the Actions pane, select **Close Form**, and then click **Next**. Click **Text**, accept **Close Form**, and then click **Next**. Name the button cmdCloseForm, and then click **Finish**.

h. Align the buttons with one another.
   - Click the **Run Renewal Query** button, press and hold Shift, and then click the other **two buttons** in the first column. Click the **Arrange** tab. In the Sizing & Ordering group, click **Align**, and then select **Left**. Click **Size/Space**, and then select **Equal Vertical**.
   - Click the **Run Renewals Query** button, press and hold Shift, and then click the **Run Renewals Report** button. Click **Align**, and then select **Top**.
   - Using Shift, select the **Preview Mailing Labels** and **Print Mailing Labels** buttons. Click **Align**, and then select **Top**.
   - Using Shift, select **Run Renewals Report**, **Print Mailing Labels**, and **Close Form** buttons. Click **Align**, and then select **Left**.
   - Using Shift, select **all five buttons**. Click **Size/Space**, and then select **To Widest**.

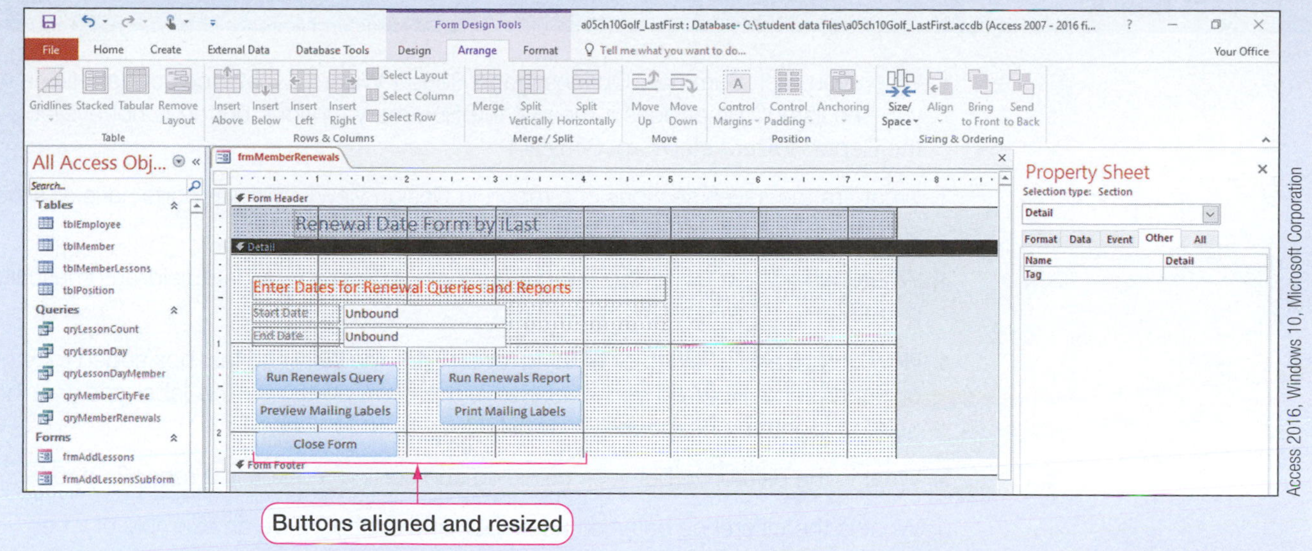

Figure 25 Buttons resized and aligned

i. **Save** the form, and then switch to **Form** view. In **Start Date**, type 1/1/2019. In **End Date**, type 3/1/2019. Click the **Preview Mailing Labels** button. The labels report opens, showing the members who have renewals between the two dates. **Close** the report.

j. Click the **Close Form** button, and then exit Access.

REAL WORLD ADVICE — Preview Before You Print

When you create a report, it is a good idea to preview it before you print it or send it in PDF form to someone else. Sometimes formatting changes make the report go to two pages when you did not intend that. On mailing labels, it is common for the address to not quite fit into the label or for you to have omitted a space between fields.

Concept Check

1. When you click Summary Options in the Report Wizard, what types of data fields will you see listed? What does it mean if the Summary Options button is not available in the Report Wizard step? p. 543-544
2. What are the seven sections of a report in Design view? Will all reports have all seven sections all the time? Why or why not? p. 543
3. Where would you go to set the current date to show in a date field automatically? p. 543
4. How do you add a field to an existing report? Are the label and text box added together or separately? How do you delete a field on a report? Are the label and text box deleted together or separately? p. 547
5. What is the difference between grouping and sorting records in a report? p. 549
6. What is the difference between a text box and a label? Give an example of when you would use each. p. 552
7. What does the Builder button in the Control Source property box allow you to do? p. 554
8. What is a parameter report? When would a parameter report be more useful than a regular report? p. 555
9. What is conditional formatting, and when would you use it? p. 562
10. What can you use for sources of data for mailing labels? Is there anything special you would do for mailing labels based on parameter queries? p. 539

Key Terms

Blank Report tool 539
Conditional formatting 562
Detail area 543
Group Footer 543
Group Header 543
Label control 543
Move handle 545
Page Footer 543
Page Header 543
Parameter 555
Parameter query 555
Property sheet 546
Report 539
Report Design tool 539
Report Footer 543
Report Header 543
Report tool 539
Report Wizard 539
Sizing handle 545
Snap to grid 545

Visual Summary

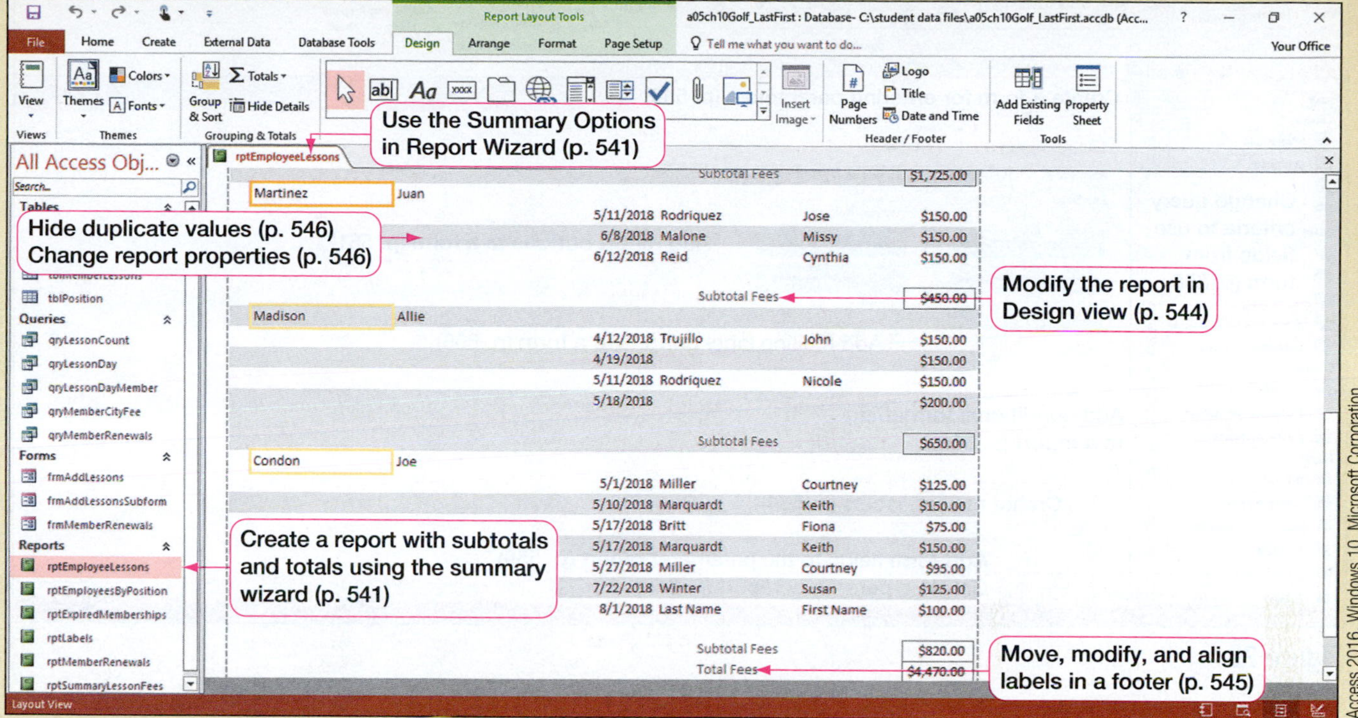

Figure 26

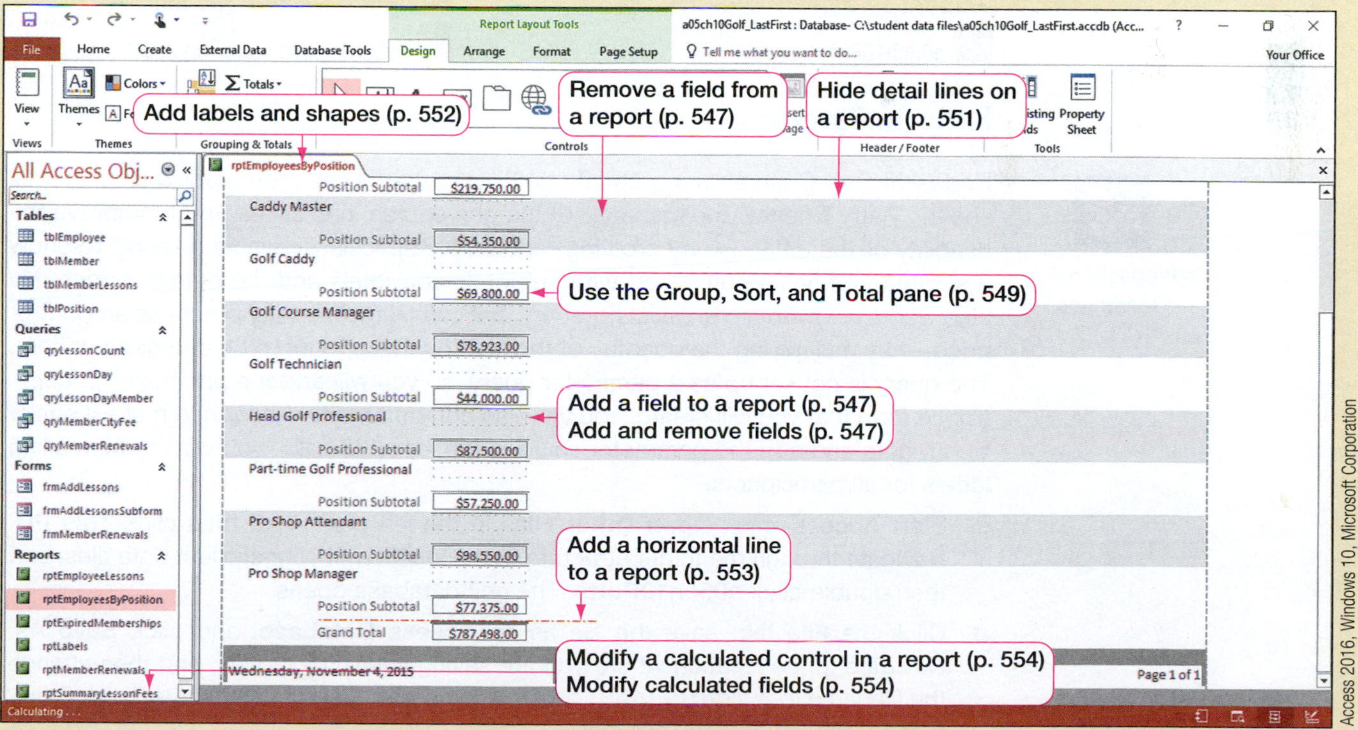

Figure 27

Access 2016, Windows 10, Microsoft Corporation

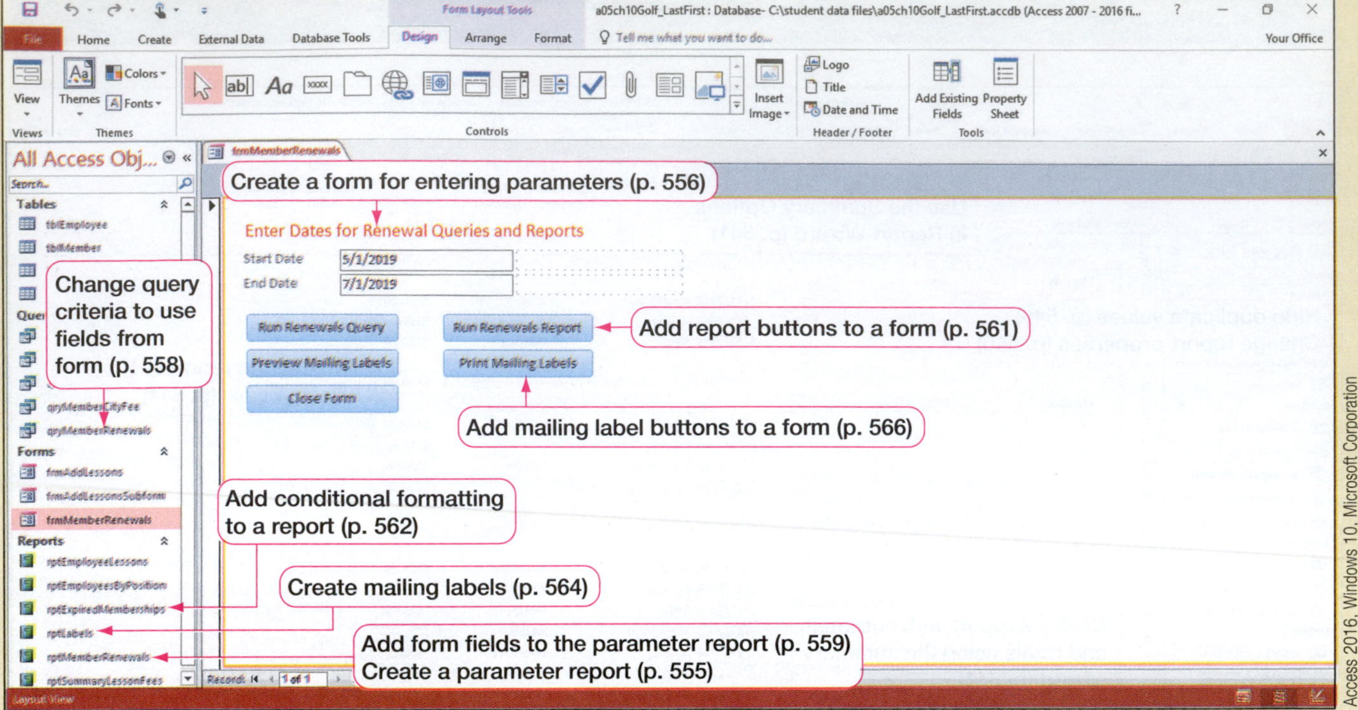

Figure 28

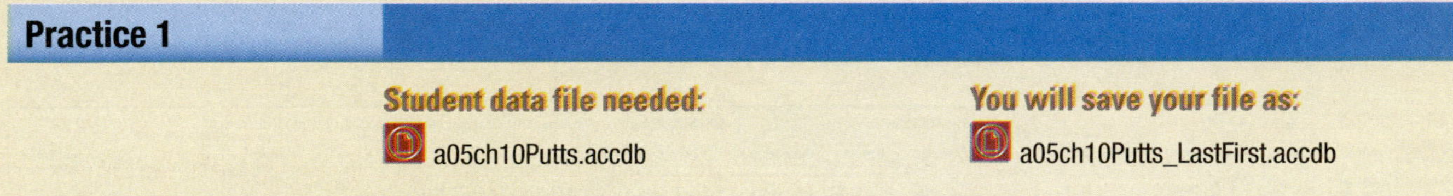

Practice 1

Student data file needed:

a05ch10Putts.accdb

You will save your file as:

a05ch10Putts_LastFirst.accdb

Putts for Paws

Production & Operations

Red Bluff Golf Course runs a charity golf event that raises money for a local animal shelter. Barry Cheney, the manager of the golf course, has asked you to improve the usability of the database by creating reports. He specifically wants a report to show a summary of items purchased with subtotals and totals and the details hidden. He also wants a way to run an existing query that calculates the total purchase amount — price — by multiplying the quantity of the item by the amount to be charged per item. The query is not set up as a parameter query, so you will add the parameter to come from a form that you will create. You will also add buttons to the form to make it easier to navigate and add the parameter value to the report. Finally, you will create mailing labels for all participants.

a. Start **Access**, click **Open Other** Files in the left pane, and then click **This PC**. Navigate through the folder structure to the location of your student data files, and then double-click **a05ch10Putts**. The golf database opens.

b. Click the **File** tab, save the file as an **Access Database**, and click **Save As**. Navigate to the location where you are saving your project files, and then change the filename to a05ch10Putts_LastFirst using your last and first name. Click **Save**. If necessary, enable the content.

c. Open **tblParticipant**, change the **FirstName** and **LastName** in the first record to your actual name, and then close the table.

d. The first report you will create will show each item's description, the quantity purchased, and then a subtotal and a grand total for each item.

- Click the **Create** tab, and then, in the Reports group, click **Report Wizard**.

- From tblItem, select **ItemDescription**. From tblOrderLine, select **Quantity**, and then click **Next**.
- Group by **tblItem**, and then click **Next**. Sort by **Quantity** in ascending order, and then click **Summary Options**. Click the **Sum** check box, and then click **OK**. Click **Next**. Accept the **Stepped layout** and **Portrait** orientation, and then click **Next**.
- Change the title of your report to rptItemsPurchased_iLast using your first initial and last name, and then click **Finish**.
- Switch to **Layout** view, and then change the title to Items Purchased by iLast using your first initial and last name.
- Click the line that begins **"Summary for 'ItemID'"**, and then press Delete.
- Click the **Design** tab, and then, in the Grouping & Totals group, click **Hide Details**.
- Switch to **Design** view. In the Page Footer, click the calculated Date control, **=Now()**. Use your pointer to drag the **right edge** left to the **2 inch** mark on the horizontal ruler.
- In the ItemID Footer, move the **Sum** label so the **left edge** lines up with the **3 inch** vertical grid line. Change the label to Total Items.
- In the Report Footer, move the **Grand Total** label so the **left edge** lines up with the **3 inch** vertical grid line.
- Switch to **Report** view to check your report formatting. Save and close the report.

e. You will create a report to show by participant the order date, item description, quantity, and the price of each item they purchased. Then you will subtotal the purchases by participant and have a grand total for all purchases.

- Open **qryOrdersCalcPrice**, click the **File** tab, click **Save As**, select **Save Object As**, and then click **Save As**. In the Save As dialog box, type qryOrdersCalcPrice_iLast using your first initial and last name, and then click **OK**. Close the query.
- Click the **Create** tab, and then click **Report Wizard**. From qryOrdersCalcPrice_iLast, select **all fields** except ItemID. Click **Next**.
- Group by **ParticipantName**, click **Next**, and then sort in ascending order by **OrderDate** and **ItemDescription**.
- Click **Summary Options**, and select **Sum** for **Quantity**, **Price**, and **TotalCost**. Click **OK**.
- Click **Next**, select the **Outline** layout, change to **Landscape** orientation, and then click **Next**.
- Change the title of your report to rptParticipantPurchases_iLast using your first initial and last name, and then click **Finish**.
- Switch to **Layout** view, and change the title to Participant Purchases by iLast using your first initial and last name.
- Click the line that begins **Summary for 'ParticipantName'**, and then press Delete.
- Switch to **Design** view. Select the **Total Cost** label, **Total Cost** text box, **Total Cost summary** in the ParticipantName Footer, and the **Total Cost summary** in the Report Footer. Move them all so their left edges lines up with the **7.5 inch** mark on the horizontal ruler. Then drag the right edges to line up with the **8.5 inch** mark on the horizontal ruler.
- Select the **Price** label, **Price** text box, **Price summary** in the ParticipantName footer, and **Price summary** in the Report Footer. Drag the right edges to line up with the left edge of the Total Cost boxes.

- In the ParticipantName footer, change the label from **Sum** to Participant Total.
- Select the **TotalCost subtotal** text box and the **TotalCost grand total** text box. Click the **Design** tab. In the Tools group, click **Property Sheet**, and then change the Format of both fields to **Currency**.
- Select the **page number** footer control in the Page Footer. Drag the **control** to the left so the **right edge** lines up with the right edge of the **TotalCost subtotal** text box. Drag the **right edge** of the report body to the **8.5 inch** horizontal line.
- Switch to **Report** view to check your report formatting. Save and close your report.

f. Now you will create a form to enter the item requested. This value will then be applied to the qryOrdersCalcPrice_iLast as a parameter value. Once the data has been found in the query, rptParticipantPurchases_iLast can be run with the specific value entered in the form. This will allow the golf course employees to search for purchase information on a particular item.
   - Click the **Create** tab, and then, in the Forms group, click **Blank Form**.
   - In the Header/Footer group, click **Title**, and then replace the title with Item Report by iLast using your first initial and last name.
   - Close the Field List pane. Click the **Label** control, move your pointer to the **top left corner** of the form detail, and then click to place the label. Type Enter Item for Queries and Reports.
   - Click the **Combo Box** control, and then click the **form** below the label. Select **I want the combo box to get the values from another table or query**, and then click **Next**. Select **Table: tblItem**, and then click **Next**. Double-click **ItemDescription**, and then click **Next**. Sort by **ItemDescription**, and then click **Next**. Adjust the width of the column to fit, and then click **Next**. Accept the name **ItemDescription**, and then click **Finish**.
   - Click the **ItemDescription** combo box, and then click **Property Sheet** in the Tools group. In the Property Sheet pane, click the **Other** tab, and click **Name**, and then type ItemDescription.
   - Select the **ItemDescription** label, and then double-click the **right edge** to adjust the width.
   - Click in the **first row** in the layout, click the **Arrange** tab, and then, in the Rows & Columns group, click **Select Row**. In the Merge/Split group, click **Merge**.
   - Save your form as frmRequestItems_iLast using your first initial and last name. Close the property sheet pane, and close the form.

g. Now you will modify qryOrdersCalcPrice_initialLastname to use the item description from the form you just created. This will make the query a parameter query.
   - Open **qryOrdersCalcPrice_iLast**, switch to **Design** view, and then click the **Criteria** row under ItemID. Click the **Design** tab, and then, in the Query Setup group, click **Builder**. In the Expression Elements pane, double-click **a05ch10Putts_LastFirst**, double-click **Forms**, double-click **All Forms**, and then click **frmRequestItems_iLast**.
   - In the Expression Categories pane, double-click **ItemDescription**, and then click **OK**.
   - Save and close your query.

h. Next you will modify the report rptParticipantPurchases_iLast to put the item description selected in the form in the report header:
   - In the Navigation Pane, right-click **rptParticipantPurchases_iLast**, and then select **Design View**.
   - Click the **Design** tab, and then, in the Controls group, click **Text Box**. Click to the right of the **report title** in the report header to insert a text box.

- Select the **label**, and then change the text to Item Selected.
- Move and resize the label so the **left edge** lines up with the **5 inch** vertical grid line and the **right edge** lines up with the **6 inch** vertical grid line.
- Select the **text** box, and then, in the Property Sheet pane, on the Data tab, click **Control Source Builder**. In the Expression Elements pane, double-click **a05ch10Putts_LastFirst**, double-click **Forms**, double-click **All Forms**, and then click **frmRequestItems_iLast**.
- In the Expression Categories pane, double-click **ItemDescription**, and then click **OK**. In the Property Sheet pane, click the **Other** tab, click **Name**, and then type Description.
- Close the Property Sheet pane. Save and close your report.

i. You will add buttons to frmRequestItems_iLast to run the query and report.

- Open **frmRequestItems_iLast**, and switch to **Design** view. Drag the bottom edge of the Detail area to the **2.5 inch** mark on the vertical ruler.
- Click the **Design** tab, and then, in the Controls group, click **Button**. Click below the combo box label to start the Command Button Wizard.
- Select **Miscellaneous**, select **Run Query**, and then click **Next**. Select qryOrdersCalcPrice_iLast using your first initial and last name, and then click **Next**. Select **Text**, and then type Run Calculate Price Query. Click Next. Name the button cmdQryCalcPrice, and then click **Finish**.
- In the Controls group, click **Button**, and then click below the first button. Select **Report Operations** and **Open Report**, and then click **Next**. Select **rptParticipantPurchases_iLast**, and then click **Next**. Select **Text**, type Run Participants Purchases Report, and then click **Next**. Name the button cmdRptRun, and then click **Finish**.
- Select both buttons, and then click the **Arrange** tab. In the Sizing & Ordering group, click **Align**, and then select **Left**. In the Sizing & Ordering group, click Size/Space, and then select **To Widest**.
- Drag the **form footer** down until it is on the **.5 inch** mark on the vertical ruler.
- Switch to **Form** view. Test your form by selecting **Cart sponsor** in the combo box. Click **Run Calculate Price Query**, and you should get four records. Close the query, and then click **Run Participants Purchases Report**. You should see the same four records. Close the report.
- Save and close your form.

j. Create mailing labels for all participants.

- In the Navigation Pane, click **tblParticipant**, click the **Create** tab, and then, in the Reports group, click **Labels**.
- If necessary, filter by manufacturer **Avery**, select Product Number **C2160**, and then click **Next**.
- Change the font to **Times New Roman**, and then change the font size to **11**. Click **Next**.
- Add **First Name**, press Spacebar, add **Last Name**, and then press Enter.
- Add **StreetAddress**, and then press Enter.
- Add **City**, type , — a comma — and then press Spacebar, add **State**, press Spacebar, and then add **ZipCode**. Click **Next**.
- Sort by **LastName**, and then **FirstName**. Click **Next**.
- Name your report rptLabels_iLast using your first initial and last name, and then click Finish.
- Save and close your report.

k. Close your database, exit Access, and submit your file as directed by your instructor.

Problem Solve 1

Student data file needed:

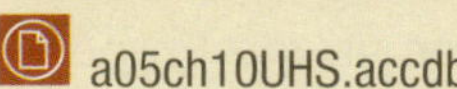

a05ch10UHS.accdb

You will save your file as:

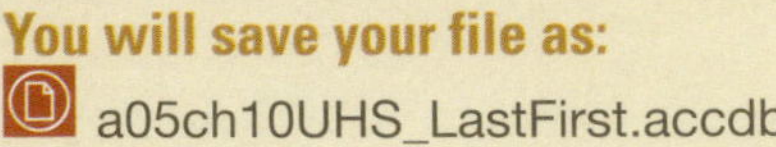

a05ch10UHS_LastFirst.accdb

University High School Database

Customer Service

University High School has transitioned to a new system in which one counselor is assigned a group of students every year. To manage this process, a database has been created with two tables, one for students and one for the counselors. Each counselor is assigned to a team with many students on each team. There are currently no reports for this database, and the school administrators would like to be able to look up a grade or range of grades and to see counselors and students assigned to that grade. There is a query that will look this information up, but they would like a report and a form to enter the parameters in. Then they would like mailing labels for all students so that the administrators can send out letters to parents.

a. Open the Access file **a05ch10UHS**. Save your file as a05ch10UHS_LastFirst using your last and first name.

b. Open **tblStudents**, change the **FirstName** and **LastName** in the first record to be your actual name, and then close the table.

c. Create a report from qryByGrade that displays all students grouped by grades. Include all the fields and group by **Grade**. Sort the report by **Team** and then by **StudentLastName**, and include a Summary option to **Average** the **Age** field. Choose **Landscape** orientation and **Outline** layout, and then name the report rptStudentsByGrade.

d. Enter 9 for the first parameter date and 12 for the next parameter date. Modify the report by deleting the **Summary for Grade** text box. Resize the **Page number** text box so the **right edge** lines up with the **10 inch mark** on the horizontal ruler. If necessary, resize the **form body** to the **10 inch mark**.

e. Hide the duplicate values for **Counselor First Name** and **Counselor Last Name**. Change the report title to Students By Grade by iLast using your first initial and last name. Save and close the report.

f. Create a form for entering grade parameters. Name the form frmStudentsByGrade, and add the title Students By Grade by iLast using your first initial and last name. Add a label that says Enter the grade range to run student query and student report.

g. Add a **text box** for the starting grade. Change the label to Starting Grade, and name the text box StartingGrade in the property sheet. Add another **text box** for the ending grade. Change the label to Ending Grade, and name the text box EndingGrade in the property sheet. Merge the first row so the text box is lined up with the left side of the stacked controls.

h. Add a **button** to the form below the Ending Grade label to run **qryByGrade**, show the text Run Student Grade Query, and name the button cmdQryGrade. Add a second **button** to the right of the first button to open rptStudentsByGrade, show the text Run Student Grade Report, and name the button cmdRptGrade. Add a third **button** to the right of the second button to close the form, show the text Close Form, and name the button cmdCloseForm. Align the buttons by their **top edges**, size them to the **widest**, and space them **equal horizontally**. Save the form.

i. Modify **qryByGrade** so the query uses the parameters from the form. Save and close the query.

j. Modify **rptStudentsByGrade** so the grade parameters entered in the form are shown in the header. (Hint: Change the source control.) Change the label of the

StartingGrade field to Starting Grade, and line up the **left edge** with the **4.5 inch** mark on the horizontal ruler, and then name it StartingGrade. Add a second **text box** for the EndingGrade, change the label to Ending Grade, and line up the **left edge** with the **7 inch** vertical grid line, and name it EndingGrade.

k. Select the **title**, the **starting date** label and **text box**, and the **ending date** label, and align all the controls to their **bottom edges**. Save and close the report. Test the form by entering a range of grades, then run the query and run the report. Close the query, the report, and the form.

l. Create mailing labels for all students. Select **Avery** for the manufacturer and **C2160** for the product number. Select **Times New Roman**, font size **11**, **normal** font weight. Add the **StudentFirstName**, **StudentLastName**, and **Team**, separated by spaces, to the first line. Add **Address** to the second line. Add **City**, **State**, and **Zip** to the last line, with a comma and space between city and state. Sort by **student last name**, and name the report rptLabels.

m. Close your database, exit Access, and submit your file as directed by your instructor.

CHAPTER 10

Critical Thinking

The students in this database are grouped into teams. Assume that the counselors or other school faculty members need a report of all students on a single team. Considering the steps above, how could you create a report that would selectively show students on the basis of the Team selected by the faculty? What objects would you need to create in the database to make this possible?

Perform 1: Perform in Your Career

Student data file needed:

 a05ch10PetStore.accdb

You will save your file as:

a05ch10PetStore_LastFirst.accdb

Pet Store Reporting

Production & Operations

A pet store owner started creating a database to keep records of animals, breeds, purchases, and customers. Data has been added to the tables, but there are no forms or reports for entering data or looking up data. There is currently a parameter query that prompts for a range of dates to look up the date of birth for the animals, but there is no report associated with the query. You have been asked to create a parameter report from the parameter query as well as a form for entering beginning and ending dates for the purchase query. The form will include buttons to run the query and report. The report will need to include the date parameters in the header.

a. Open the **Access** database **a05ch10PetStore**. Save your file as a05ch10PetStore_LastFirst using your last and first name. If necessary, enable the content.

b. Create a report from qryAnimalDOB, and name it rptAnimalsByDOB_iLast using your first initial and last name. The report will count the number of animals born each month. You also need to do the following.

- Show all the fields grouped by date of birth by month.
- Sort by date of birth.
- Change the title to Animals by Month of Birth by iLast using your first initial and last name.
- Move or resize the fields as necessary so all the fields and data are visible.
- Hide duplicate values for the Animal type field.

c. Create a form called frmAnimalsDOB_iLast using your first initial and last name. To enter the beginning and ending parameter dates, do the following.
   - Add a title to the form and a label so the user knows what the form is for.
   - Add three buttons to the form: one to open qryAnimalDOB, one to open rptAnimalsByDOB_iLast, and one to close the form. Format the buttons to be professional in appearance. Arrange the buttons and provide text to display on the buttons.

d. Modify qryAnimalDOB to use the parameters entered in the form.

e. Modify rptAnimalsByDOB_iLast so the date parameters are shown in the header of the report.

f. Create mailing labels for all the customers, and then name the report rptCustomerLabels_iLast using your first initial and last name.

g. Close your database, exit Access, and then submit your file as directed by your instructor.

Additional Cases

Additional Workshop Cases are available on the companion website and in the instructor resources.

Producing Professional Forms and Reports

This business unit had two outcomes:

Learning Outcome 1:

Define bound and unbound forms, modify a variety of form properties, and create specialized and multi-page forms using tab controls.

Learning Outcome 2:

Create, modify, group, and sort reports that summarize data; create calculated fields for reports; utilize parameters and conditional formatting for reports; and create mailing labels with reports.

In Business Unit 5 Capstone, students will demonstrate competence in these outcomes through a series of business problems at various levels from guided practice to problem solving an existing database and performing to create new databases.

More Practice 1

Student data files needed:

 a05Menu.accdb

 a05MenuLogo.jpg

You will save your file as:

 a05Menu_LastFirst.accdb

Indigo5 Restaurant

Production & Operations

Robin Sanchez, the chef of the resort's restaurant, Indigo5, has a database of recipes and ingredients. She uses this database to plan menus and create shopping lists. She has asked you to provide forms and reports to make the database easier to use. First, you will create a form listing recipes by food category. Next, you will help her find all recipes that include an ingredient that she has in stock. You will create a query to find those recipes and a report from the query that lists the recipes. You know you want a form to do the lookup for these recipes, so you will start with the form. Robin would also like a report on recipes by category that shows the minimum and maximum preparation times for each category.

a. Start **Access**, click **Open Other Files** in the left pane, and then double-click **This PC**. Navigate through the folder structure to the location of your student data files, and then double-click **a05Menu**. A database opens displaying tables and queries related to the spa.

b. Click the **File** tab, save the file as an **Access Database**, and click **Save As**. Navigate to the location where you are saving your project files, and then change the filename to a05Menu_LastFirst using your last and first name. Click **Save**. If necessary, in the Security Warning, click **Enable Content**.

c. Create a form for finding details about a specific recipe. You will start by creating a form with a subform. You will add a combo box to find a specific recipe and then add a tab control to organize the recipe details. You will also remove the navigation bars and replace them with buttons.

- Click the **Create** tab, and then, in the Forms group, click **Form Wizard**. Add the following fields: From tblRecipes, select **RecipeName**; from tblIngredients, select **Ingredient**; from tblRecipeIngredients, select **Quantity**; and from tblRecipes, select **TimeToPrepare** and **Servings**. Accept the default view and default layout. Name the form frmRecipes_iLast, and name the subform frmRecipesSubform_iLast using your first initial and last name.
- Switch to **Design** view, and then change the title of the form to Find Recipes by iLast using your first initial and last name. Drag the header down to the **1.5 inch** mark on

the vertical ruler. Resize so the title appears on one line, and move the title so the **top edge** lines up with the **1 inch** mark on the vertical ruler. Insert the logo **a05MenuLogo** in the header. Resize the logo so the **bottom edge** is at the **1 inch** mark on the vertical ruler and the **right edge** is at the **3.5 inch** mark on the horizontal ruler.

- On the Design tab, click **Date and Time** to add the current date and time to the header, accepting the default formats. Click the **Arrange** tab, and then click **Anchoring** to anchor both fields to the top right of the form.
- Click the **Design** tab, and then click **Combo Box** to add a combo box in the form header to the right of the title. In the Combo Box Wizard dialog box, click **Find a record on my form based on the value I selected in my combo box**, and then click **Next.** Double-click **RecipeName**, accept the default to **Hide key column**, and then change the label of the combo box to Recipe Name. Align the combo box and label with the bottom of the title. Resize the combo box text box to fit between the **5 inch** and **7 inch** marks on the horizontal ruler.
- Right-click the **frmRecipes subform**, and then select **Cut**. Click the **Design** tab, click **Tab Control**, and then add a tab control to the form just below the **Servings** label. Right-click the **first page** of the tab control, and then select **Paste** to paste the subform.
- Delete the subform label, and then move the subform to the top left corner of the tab control. In the **Property Sheet** pane, change the name of the page to Ingredients.
- Select and cut the **Prep Time** label, the **TimeToPrepare** text box, the **Servings** label, and the **Servings** text box. Paste these **fields** in the top left corner of the second tab page, and then change the name of the tab page to Details.
- Right-click the **tab control**, and then select **Insert Page**. Name the new page Directions. On the Design tab, click **Add Existing Fields**, and then drag the field **Instructions** to the third tab page. Delete the **Instructions** label, and then move the text box to the top left corner of the tab page. Adjust the height of the field to approximately **1.5 inches**.
- Move and resize the **tab control** so the top left corner is at the **1 inch** mark on the vertical ruler and at the **.5 inch** mark on the horizontal ruler and the bottom right corner is at the **4.5 inch** mark on the vertical ruler and at the **6.5 inch** mark on the horizontal ruler. Right-click the **tab control**, and then select **Page Order**. Change the order of the tab pages to **Details**, **Ingredients**, and **Directions**.
- In the Property Sheet pane, select **Detail**, click the **Format** tab, and then using the **Build** button, change the back color to **White, Background 1, Darker 15%**. Select the **form header**, and then change the back color to **White, Background 1**.
- Click the value for **RecipeName** in the form Detail. In the Property Sheet, click the **Data** tab, change **Locked** to **Yes**. Click the **Other** tab, change **Tab Stop** to **No**.
- On the Design tab, click **Button** to add a button to the form detail to the right of the tab control. Select **Record Navigation**, and select **Go To Next Record**. Select **Text**, type Next Recipe, and then name the button cmdNextRecipe. Place a second button on the form below the first. Select **Record Navigation**, and select **Go To Previous Record**. Select **Text**, type Previous Recipe, and then name the button cmdPreviousRecipe.
- Place a third button below the second button. Select **Form Operations**, and select **Close Form**. Select **Text**, and then accept **Close Form**. Name the button cmdCloseForm.
- Select all three buttons. Click the **Arrange** tab, and then click **Align** to align the buttons **Left**. Click **Size/Space**, and select **To Widest**, and then click **Size/Space**, and select **Equal Vertical**.

- In the Property Sheet pane, click **Selection type**, select **Form**, click the **Format** tab, and then change the **Navigation Buttons** to **No**. Change **Record Selectors** to **No**.
- View, save, and close the form.

d. Create a form to request recipes by ingredient.

- Click the **Create** tab, and then click **Blank Form**. Click the **Design** tab, click **Title**, and then name the report Request Ingredient by iLast using your first initial and last name.
- On the Design tab, in the Controls group, click **Combo Box**, and then insert the combo box in the detail area of the form. Click **I want the combo box to get the values from another table or query**. Click **Table: tblIngredients**, double-click **Ingredient**, and then sort by **Ingredient** in ascending order. Adjust the width of the column to fit, and then name your combo box Ingredient.
- Open the **Property Sheet** pane, and then change the name of the text box to Ingredient.
- Click save, and then name your form frmRequestIngredient_iLast using your first initial and last name.
- Switch to **Form** view, and then request **Garlic**.
- Leave the form open.

e. Copy and update **qryRecipeIngredient** to find the recipes that include the ingredient picked on the new form.

- Right-click **qryRecipeIngredient** in the Navigation pane, and then select **Copy**. Right-click the Navigation pane, and then select **Paste**. Name the new query qryRecipeIngredient_iLast using your first initial and last name.
- Open **qryRecipeIngredient_iLast** in **Design** view. Click **Builder** to add criteria to **IngredientID** that selects **Ingredient** from **frmRequestIngredient_iLast**.
- Run your query to test it, and then save and close the query.

f. Create a recipe report from **qryRecipeIngredient_iLast**.

- Click the **Create** tab, click **Report Wizard**, and select the following fields: From qryRecipeIngredient_iLast, select **RecipeName**, **TimeToPrepare**, **Servings**, and **Instructions**. Group by **TimeToPrepare**, and then sort in ascending order by **RecipeName**. Accept the **Stepped** layout, and then change the orientation to **Landscape**. Name your report rptRecipeReport_iLast using your first initial and last name.
- Switch to **Layout** view, and change the title of your report to Recipe Prep Time by iLast using your first initial and last name.
- Switch to **Design** view. On the Design tab, click **Text Box**, and then add a text box to the report header to the right of the title. Change the label to Ingredient Selected, and then move the **left edge** of the label so it lines up with the **4 inch** vertical grid line. Select the **text** box, and then open the Property Sheet pane. On the Data tab, click **Control Source Builder** to point the control source to the **Ingredient** field on **frmRequestIngredient_iLast**. Click the **Other** tab, and then name the text box Ingredient.
- Open the report in **Print Preview** to test it, and then save and close the report and form.

g. Add buttons to frmRequestIngredients_iLast to open the recipe report and query and to close the form.

- The first button you create should show the text Recipe Report, open **rptRecipeReport_iLast**, and be named cmdOpenReport.
- The second button you create should show the text Recipe Ingredient Query, open **qryRecipeIngredient_iLast**, and be named cmdIngredientQuery.

- The last button you create should close the form, show the text Close Form, and be named cmdCloseForm.
- All buttons should line up under the **Ingredient** label and display all text.
- Save and close the form.

h. Create a report of recipes by category with minimum and maximum preparation times.
   - Click the **Create** tab, and then click **Report Wizard**. Select the following fields: From tblFoodCategories, select **FoodCategory**; from tblRecipes, select **RecipeName**, **TimeToPrepare**, and **Servings**.
   - Group by **FoodCategory**, sort by **RecipeName**, and in Summary Options, select **Min** and **Max** for **TimeToPrepare**. Accept the default layout, and then change the title of your report to rptTimesToPrepare_iLast using your first initial and last name.
   - Change the title of your report to Recipe Times to Prepare by iLast using your first initial and last name. Delete the line that starts **Summary for 'Food**.
   - Move the Min label and the Max label so their **left edges** are on the **4 inch** vertical grid line. Change them to read Minimum Prep Time and Maximum Prep Time, respectively.
   - Switch to **Print Preview** to check your report, and then save and close the report.

i. Close the database, exit Access, and then submit your file as directed by your instructor.

Problem Solve 1

Student data files needed:

 a05Events.accdb

 a05Logo.jpg

You will save your file as:

 a05Events_LastFirst.accdb

Creating Forms for Event Reservations

Production & Operations

Patti Rochelle, corporate event planner, has a database that she uses to track group reservations with the conference rooms that are booked for the event. You will create forms to help her manage events. You will create a form showing each event planned with group, event, and reservation details.

a. Open the Access file **a05Events**. Save your file as a05Events_LastFirst using your last and first name. If necessary, enable the content.

b. Create a new form with fields from tblEvent that displays information about the events in the database. Select **EventName**, **EventStart**, and **EventLength**. From tblGroup, select **GroupName**, **ContactFirstName**, **ContactLastName**, and **ContactPhone**. Name the form frmEvents.

c. Change the title to Events by iLast using your first initial and last name. Add the Date and Time with the default settings, and anchor the fields to the top right corner of the form. Change the heading Back Color to **White, Background 1**. Change the form detail Back Color to **White, Background 1, Darker 15%**.

d. Expand the header to the **1.5 inch** mark on the vertical ruler. Move the title so its top edge is lined up with the **1 inch** mark on the vertical ruler. Insert the logo **a05Logo.jpg**. Resize the logo so the right edge is lined up with the **4 inch** mark on the horizontal ruler and the bottom edge is lined up with the **1 inch** mark on the vertical ruler.

e. Drag the bottom of the form detail to the **3 inch** mark on the vertical ruler. Insert a tab control. Select both the labels and the text fields for **GroupName**, **ContactFirstName**, **ContactLastName**, and **ContactPhone**; then cut them from the main form and paste them on the first page of the tab control. Cut and paste the **EventStartDate** and **EventLengths** controls on the second tab page.

f. Name the first tab page Group Details, and move the controls so the **Group Name** label is in the top left corner of the page.

g. Name the second tab page Event Details, and move the controls so the **Event Start Date** label is in the top left corner of the page.

h. Insert a new page to the tab control, and name it Reservation Details. Add the following fields to the page: From tblConfRes, add **ReservationDate**, **DaysReserved**, and **RoomCharge**; from tblConfRooms, add **RoomName** and **Capacity**. Arrange the fields in a stacked table, and move them to the top left corner of the page.

i. Move the tab control so the top edge lines up with the **1 inch** mark on the vertical ruler and the left edge lines up with the **1 inch** mark on the horizontal ruler. Change the order of the tabs so the Event Details come before the Group Details.

j. Create a calculated field to multiply the **DaysReserved** by the **RoomCharge** fields. Insert the calculated field on the Reservation Details page to the right of the Room Charge controls. Name the field TotalCharge, and change the label to Total Charge. Format the field as **Currency**. Align the Total Charge controls with the Room Charge Controls by Top.

k. Add buttons to the form between the Event Name controls and the tab control: Go to next record with the text label Next Event and the button name cmdNextEvent; go to previous record with the text label Previous Event and the button name cmdPreviousEvent; close the form with the text label Close Form and the button name cmdCloseForm.

l. Align the buttons so the left edge of the first button is lined up with the **1 inch** mark on the horizontal ruler and the right edge of the last button is lined up with the **5 inch** mark on the horizontal ruler. Size the buttons **To Widest**, and space them **Equal Horizontal**. Save and close the form.

m. Use the Form Wizard to create a new form from qryReservedRooms that displays which rooms have been reserved. Include all the fields, and name the form frmReservedRooms.

n. Change the title to Reserved Rooms by iLast using your first initial and last name. Add the Date and Time using the default settings to the header, and anchor both controls to Top Right. Change the header Back Color to **White, Background 1**. Change the form detail Back Color to **White, Background 1, Darker 15%**.

o. In the form detail, delete the **Group Name** controls. Add a combo box to the header just below the title that will find a record on your form on the basis of the value you select in your combo box, using the **GroupName** field from qryReservedRooms. Name the combo box GroupName, and change the label to Group Name. Line up the top of the controls to the **.5 inch** mark on the vertical ruler. Resize the text box so the right edge is lined up with the **4 inch** mark on the horizontal ruler.

p. Select the **Total Charge** controls, and move them so the top edges are lined up with the **3.5 inch** mark on the vertical ruler. Draw a rectangle around the Total Charge label and text box. The top left corner of the rectangle should be at the **.2 inch** mark on the horizontal ruler and at the **3 inch** mark on the vertical ruler. The bottom right corner should be at the **5 inch** mark on the horizontal ruler and at the **4 inch** mark on the vertical ruler. Change the rectangle Special Effect to **Sunken**. Save and close the form.

q. Create a multiple items form from tblGroup that shows details on each group in the database. Change the title to Groups by iLast using your first initial and last name. Delete the form icon from the header. Save the form as frmGroups. Close the form.

r. Close the database, exit Access, and then submit the file as directed by your instructor.

Problem Solve 2

Student data file needed:

 a05Events2.accdb

You will save your file as:

 a05Events2_LastFirst.accdb

Creating Reports for Event Reservations

Production & Operations

Patti Rochelle, corporate event planner, has a database that she uses to track group reservations with the conference rooms that are booked for the event. You will create reports to help her manage events and provide her staff with more detailed information.

First, you will create a report that shows room charges expected for reservations in different rooms. This will show the staff how each room is being used and how much revenue is being generated.

a. Open the Access file **a05Events2**. Save your file as a05Events2_LastFirst using your last and first name. If necessary, enable the content.

b. Use the Report Wizard to create a report that displays each room with the number of days reserved and the total room charges. Select **RoomName**, **ReservationDate**, **DaysReserved**, **RoomCharge**, and **TotalCharge** from qryReservedRooms. Group by **RoomName**, and then sort by **ReservationDate**. Sum **DaysReserved** and **TotalCharge**. Change to **Landscape** orientation, and then name your report rptRoomCharges.

c. Change the title of the report to Room Charges. Remove the Summary for **'RoomName'** line.

d. Move the **Sum** label in the RoomName footer so its left edge is at the **3.5 inch** mark on the horizontal ruler. Change the label to Totals. Format the **TotalCharge** subtotal and grand total text fields to currency.

e. Select one of the **Grand Total** labels, and delete it. (Hint: The two labels are on top of each other, so move one first and then delete one.) Move the remaining **Grand Total** label so the left edge lines up with the **3.5 inch** mark on the horizontal ruler.

f. Select the remaining three **Grand Total** controls in the Report Footer, and drag them down so their top edges line up with the **.5 inch** mark on the vertical ruler. Add a horizontal line above the controls, starting at the **3 inch** mark on the horizontal ruler and ending at the **10 inch** mark on the horizontal ruler.

g. Move the page number label to fit on the page. Save and close the report.

h. Use the Report Wizard to create a report that shows the events and charges by Group. Select **GroupName**, **EventName**, **EventStart**, and **TotalCharge** from qryReservedRooms. Accept the grouping by **GroupName** and then **EventName**. Use the **Stepped** layout and **Landscape** orientation. Name your report rptGroupEventCharges. Change the title of your report to Group Event Charges.

i. Open the Group, Sort, and Total pane, and show the sum of **Total Charge** for each group as a grand total and in the group footer. Format the subtotal and grand total text boxes as **Currency**. Add a label in the GroupName Footer with the text Group Charges. Line up the left edge with the **7 inch** mark on the horizontal ruler. Add a label to the Report Footer with the text Total Event Charges. Align it **Right** with the Group Charges text box.

j. Add conditional formatting to the **Group Charges** subtotal so the values will appear red and bold if the amount is greater than $10,000. Resize the **Total Charges** label and text boxes so they all fit on one page. Resize the page number label to fit on the page. Save and close the report.

k. Use the Report Wizard to create a report from the parameter query called qryRoomName. This report will show the event details for a specific room. Include the following fields in this order: **EventStart**, **EventName**, **RoomName**, **DaysReserved**, and **TotalCharge**.

View the data by **tlbEvent**, group by **EventStart** by month, do not add any sorting, and choose **Landscape** orientation. Name the report rptRoomDates.

l. Delete the **EventStartbyMonth** label, and extend the left edge of the EventStartDate label to the **2 inch** mark on the horizontal ruler. Resize the **Total Charge** label and text box to fit on one page. Move the page number control to fit on the page. Resize the **Days Reserved** label to see all the text. Change the title to Room Date Report. Save and close the report.

m. Create a blank form to enter the room name parameter. Add a label that says Enter a room name to see reservations for. Select the first row, and merge the fields. Change the font color to **Red**, and change the font size to **14**.

n. Add a combo field below the label to find values from **tblConfRooms**. Select **RoomName**, sort in **RoomName** order, and change the label to Room Name. Name the combo box RoomName. Save the form as frmRoomReport.

o. Add a button to the form below the Room Name label to run **qryRoomName**. Show the text Run Room Query on the button, and name the button cmdRoomQuery. Add a button below the Run Room Query button to open **rptRoomDates**. Show the text Open Room Report, and name the button cmdRoomReport. Add a third button below the second one to close the form. Accept the default text, and name the button cmdCloseForm. Make all the buttons big enough to see all the text.

p. Modify **qryRoomName** so the **ConfRoomID** criterion uses the **RoomList** combo box value.

q. Modify **rptRoomDates** so the room ID is entered in a field in the header of the report. Name the field Room, change the label text to Room, and change the source to be **RoomName** from frmRoomReport. Test the buttons, save, and close the form.

r. Close the database, exit Access, and then submit the file as directed by your instructor.

Critical Thinking

Given the reports and forms created in the prior exercise, what improvements could be made to the database? What changes would add value to Painted Paradise Resort & Spa's event planning?

Perform 1: Perform in Your Life

Student data file needed:

 a05Club.accdb

You will save your file as:

 a05Club_LastFirst.accdb

Make Your Club's Database User Friendly

Customer Service

You have developed a database for a club that you belong to. You use the database to track the names of the club members, events, and member attendance at the events. Make the database user friendly by providing forms and reports.

a. Start **Access**, and then open the **a05Club** database. Save the database as a05Club_LastFirst using your last and first name.

b. Open **tblMember**, and change the Last Name and First Name of the first record to your actual first and last name. Close the table tblMember.

c. Create a form to add records to the tblMember table. Name the form. frmAddMembers_iLast using your first initial and last name, change the title to Add a Member by iLast using your first initial and last name, and add the date and time so it always appears in the top right corner.

d. Create a new form with a tab control, then name the form frmMemberEvents_iLast, and name the subform frmMemberEventsSubform_iLast using your first initial and last name.

- The first tab should have the contact information of the member.
- The second tab should have the related event information, including the name of the event, date of the event, name of the place, event charge, whether the member paid, and the amount paid.
- The third tab should have summary information showing the total amount the member has paid for events and the number of events he or she is signed up for.
- Rename each tab with an appropriate name, rename the title, and format and resize fields as necessary.
- Add four buttons to frmMemberEvents_iLast: Next Member, Previous Member, Add a Member, and Close Form. The Add a Member button should open the form to add a new member. The buttons should be the only form of navigation on the form and subform.
- Add a combo box to the header to look up a member's first and last name and show all records related to that member.
- Change the title of the form, and then add the date and time anchored to the top right corner of the form.

e. Create a parameter report from qryEventDates using starting and ending date parameters for events. Name the report rptEventAttendance_iLast using your first initial and last name.

- View the report by **tblEvent**, and then group it by the event date. Sort appropriately. (Hint: For best results, use the Outline layout and Landscape orientation.)
- Include a count of the number of members per event on the report.
- Create a blank form to make the date selections. Include buttons to run the query and the report. Name the form frmEventReporting_iLast using your first initial and last name.
- Modify the query so it uses the dates from the form.
- Modify the report so the dates entered on the form are also in the report header.
- Add a button to the form to run **qryEventDates**. Add a button to open **rptEventAttendance_iLast**.

f. Create a report that shows the member name and the events each member is signed up for. Sort by the event date, and then sum the event charges for each member. Name the report rptMemberEvents_iLast using your first initial and last name. Change the title and labels to something more descriptive. Make sure all the fields are visible.

g. Close the database, exit Access, and then submit the file as directed by your instructor.

Perform 2: Perform in Your Career

Student data file needed:

a05Inventory.accdb

You will save your file as:

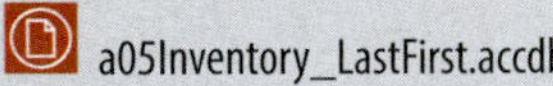

Creating Reports and Forms for Gibby's Great Groceries

Production & Operations

As an inventory manager for Gibby's Great Groceries, Inc., you were asked to modify an existing database to make it more functional for completing tasks such as reordering items and tracking inventory within your company.

a. Start **Access**, and then open **a05Inventory** database. Save the database as a05Inventory_LastFirst using your last and first name.

b. Create a form with a subform for viewing inventory and transaction data. Add a combo box to the form to find an inventory item within the form. Add buttons to navigate and close the form. Align all controls and buttons to make the form look professional. Name the form frmInventory_iLast, and name the subform frmInventorySubform_iLast using your first initial and last name.

c. Create a report to show all the transactions. Show the details by transaction type and item name. Add subtotals to show how many of each item has been sold for each type of transaction. Hide duplicate values where appropriate. Name the report rptTransactionSummary_iLast using your first initial and last name.

d. Create a blank form with a combo box to look up the name of an item. Name the form frmItemLookup_iLast using your first initial and last name.

e. Create a report from qryItem to show the transactions for that item, and then name the report rptItemTransactions_iLast using your first initial and last name.
   - Add a subtotal for item quantity and a label to identify the total. Insert a line between the last line item and the subtotal.
   - Modify the query so the data comes from the form.

f. Add buttons to the **frmItemLookup_iLast** form to preview the report, print the report, run the query, and close the form. Arrange the buttons on the form to look professional.

g. Create a form with a tab control that has three tabs. Show all item details on the first, transaction details as a datasheet form on the second, and supplier details on the third.
   - Add three buttons to the form: two to navigate to the next and previous records and one to close the form. Arrange the buttons on the form to look professional.
   - Name the form frmItemSummary_iLast using your first initial and last name. Name the transaction details datasheet form frmItemSubtotal_iLast using your first initial and last name.

h. Close the database, exit Access, and then submit the file as directed by your instructor.

Perform 3: Perform in Your Team

Student data file needed:

 a05ProShop.accdb

 Blank Word document

You will save your files as:

 a05ProShop_TeamName.accdb

 a05ProShop_TeamName.docx

Creating Forms and Reports for the Pro Shop

Production & Operations

You and your teammates have just taken over management of a pro shop at the local country club. One of the first things you want to do is analyze the data the shop has been collecting in an Access database. The database consists of four tables and one query: tblCustomers, tblProducts, tblSalesReps, tblTransactions, and qryCustomerTransactions. Unfortunately, that is all the database consists of. You and your teammates need to create forms for looking up data and reports to use to manage the shop. You may choose to use Microsoft's OneDrive or Google's Google Docs to collaborate on this database. Split your team up as directed by your instructor. Your team will divide up the steps as directed by your instructor. The first person will retrieve the database from the cloud, make his or her changes to it, and then upload the file for the next person to download until all team members have made their changes and the database is complete.

a. Select one team member to set up the database by completing steps b–d.

b. Open your browser and navigate to https://www.onedrive.live.com, https://www.drive.google.com, or any other instructor-assigned location. Be sure all members of the team have an account on the chosen system, such as a Microsoft or Google account.

c. Open **a05ProShop**, and then save the file as a05ProShop_TeamName using the name assigned to your team by your instructor.

d. Share the database with the other members of your team. Make sure that each team member has the appropriate permission to edit the database.

e. Hold a team meeting, and discuss the requirements of the remaining steps. Make an action and communication plan. Consider which steps can be done independently and which steps require completion of prior steps before being started.

f. Create a form that will allow you to enter customer information. Include all the fields. Change the title. Change the default value of Status to Member. Name the form frmAddCustomer.

g. Create a form that will show, by Customer name, all customer transactions. Include date, product, price, and quantity. Name the form frmCustomerTransactions, and name the subform frmCustomerTransactionsSubform. Change the title, change the date and time in the header, and then anchor the header to the top right. Delete unnecessary labels, and align all objects to create a professional-looking form.

h. Copy **frmCustomerTransactions**, and then paste it as frmCustomerPortal.

- Modify the form to have a combo box in the header to look up the customer name.
- Include a tab control in which one tab shows customer transactions and another tab shows two calculated fields. The first tab control determines the total cost of the customer transactions, the second tab control determines the number of transactions, and the third tab control has all the customer details. Name the tabs appropriately.
- Add buttons to frmCustomerTransactions that will allow the user to navigate to the next customer or the previous customer, add a button that will add a customer, and add a button that will close the form.

i. Create a report to show the transactions by month with the transaction date, product type, and quantity sold. Change the title to something more meaningful.

- Include a subtotal of each month's quantities and a grand total.
- Add conditional formatting to show all quantities of five or more in bold and red font.
- Save the report as rptTransactionsByMonth.

j. Copy **rptTransactionsByMonth**, and then save it as rptTransactionSummary.

- Hide the details in rptTransactionSummary so all that the report shows is the month and the total number of items sold each month, with a grand total.
- Delete any unnecessary labels, and then change the title to something meaningful.
- Add a horizontal line between the last subtotal and grand total amount.

k. Create a blank form to enter a start date and end date to look up a range of transactions. Name the form frmTransactionDates.

- Create a report from qryCustomerTransactions to show all transactions by ProductType, including the Transaction Date, Quantity, UnitPrice, and TotalTransaction fields. Name the report rptProductTransactions.
- Format, move, and resize any fields as required.
- Add subtotals for Quantity and TotalTransaction.
- Modify the query so the data comes from the form.
- Add buttons to the form to preview the report, print the report, run the query, and close the form.
- Add the parameter dates to the report header.

l. Upload the final version to the cloud tool you are using, and then direct your instructor to the account. Make sure that your instructor has permission to edit the contents of the shared folder.

m. Create a new Word document in the assignment folder in OneDrive, and then name it a05ProShop_TeamName using the name assigned to your team by your instructor.

n. In the Word document, each team member must list his or her first and last name as well as a summary of his or her contributions. As work is completed in the database, the document should be updated with the specifics of each team member's contributions.

o. Close the database, exit Access, and then submit the files as directed by your instructor.

Perform 4: How Others Perform

Student data file needed:	You will save your files as:
 a05AppStore.accdb	 a05AppStore_LastFirst.accdb
 Blank Word document	 a05Answers_LastFirst.docx

Phil's Phone App Store Database

An intern has created a database that Phil's Phone App Store can use to sell apps for smartphones. The database is not working well, and Phil has asked you for help.

Authors can write many apps. Each app is sold to many customers. Customers can buy many apps.

a. Start **Access**, and then open **a05AppStore**. Save the database as a05AppStore_LastFirst using your last and first name.

b. Create a Word document a05Answers_LastFirst, using your last and first name, in which you will answer the questions.

c. The form frmAuthorSalesApp is used to show the names of authors and the apps each author has written along with the charges and royalties. The form is cluttered and not as useful as it could be. What changes would you recommend? You do not have to fix it; just describe the problems and what you would do to fix them.

d. The rptSalesByAuthor shows sales by author. It is based on qryFindApps. Fix it for Phil.
   - Fix the report to have subtotals and grand totals.
   - Fix the report to be more attractive and easier to read.

e. Phil wants to be able to select sales by app. The intern created frmFindAppSales to enter the app name and then run qryFindApps. It is not working well.
   - Fix either the form or the query or both to make it work.
   - Fix the form to make it attractive.

f. The report showing royalties on app sales, rptAppRoyaltiesByAuthor, looks odd to Phil. What is the matter with it? You do not need to fix it; just describe the problems and what could be done to fix them.

g. Close the database, exit Access, and then submit the files as directed by your instructor.

Access Business Unit 6

Developing a Polished User Interface and Experience

Having easy access to an organization's data can benefit people at all levels, from the data entry crew members who enter new records into the database to the managers who rely on up-to-date reports to make decisions. Microsoft Access can provide all users, regardless of their knowledge of Access, the forms, reports, and other objects they need for their job. Because not everyone knows how to use Access, developing user interfaces to assist the users in navigating the database is an essential skill to develop. This business unit will explain ways to enhance an Access database with new functionality using macros and how to create a user-friendly interface that will provide users with easy access to all the forms and reports they need.

Learning Outcome 1:

Use navigation forms to provide users with access to all the forms and reports they need via a well-organized, user-friendly interface. Also learn how to enhance the user experience by utilizing command buttons to increase the usability of forms and modify the start-up options to automatically display the interface when the database is opened.

Real World Success 

"The database our company uses was developed without any navigational system. Since then, it has grown to include dozens of forms and reports. Finding the right form to enter data into or find information on had become a very time-consuming task. By utilizing navigation forms, we were able to create a single location within the database that organized our forms and reports in a logical, easy-to-use fashion. The navigation form also allows our employees to decrease the time needed to complete tasks in the database."

\- James, alumnus

Learning Outcome 2:

Use various types of macros to enhance the functionality of a database, automate routine tasks, and enhance the overall user experience.

Real World Success 

"In my first position after graduation, I was asked to work on a database that was used to create 15 different reports. Each week, I had to run dozens of queries, print some reports, and export other reports as PDF files. Then I would have to attach the PDF files to e-mails to be sent out. By creating macros, I was able to automate all of these processes, including automatically attaching PDF versions of reports to e-mails. As a result, I was able to turn the time spent previously with the database into more productive ventures."

\- Thomas, alumnus

Microsoft Access 2016

Chapter 11 | DEVELOP NAVIGATION FORMS AND THE USER INTERFACE

OBJECTIVES

Prepare Case

Production & Operations

General Business

The Turquoise Oasis Spa Database: Creating a User Interface

The Turquoise Oasis Spa has a well-built database with queries, forms, and reports. However, there are a lot of objects, and navigating them with the Navigation Pane has become tedious and sometimes confusing. Meda Rodate, the spa manager, has asked you to develop a navigational system and user interface to make the whole database more user-friendly and easier to navigate, especially for someone who is new to Access. Three navigation forms have already been created, but they must be accessed from the Navigation Pane. You will create a new navigation form for the customer forms and reports, create a navigation form that accesses all the navigation forms already created, and develop an application from the database.

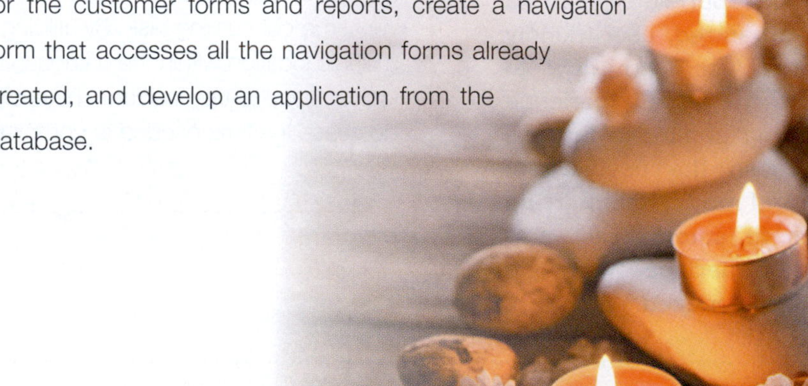

Africa Studio/Shutterstock

Student data files needed for this chapter:

 a06ch11SpaApplication.accdb

 a06ch11TurquoiseOasisLogo.jpg

You will save your file as:

 a06ch11SpaApplication_LastFirst.accdb

Creating Navigation Forms

A well-designed database includes properly thought-out tables, forms, and reports. An equally important aspect of a well-designed database is how the user will navigate and access objects within the database. Whether the user is a novice or experienced with Access, a well-planned navigation system and **user interface** provides a more streamlined experience. A user interface is part of the computer application or operating system through which the user interacts with a computer or software. A well-designed user interface acts like a menu system — or home page — for users so they do not have to search for objects in the Navigation Pane.

Ideally, a database user should have access to the data through forms and reports. By restricting access to the tables in Datasheet view, the integrity of the data and structure of the data are not at risk. Users should be allowed to enter, edit, and delete data but not to modify the structure or design of the database. In this section, you will create a navigation system built into a well-designed user interface to allow the user to move seamlessly from object to object to complete the task at hand.

REAL WORLD ADVICE | **Where Did the Switchboard Go?**

Many Access users are familiar with the Switchboard, a form used for database navigation. In Access 2010, the Switchboard was replaced by a new, up-to-date, Internet-style navigation form that can be built directly from the ribbon.

For those who still want to use the Switchboard, it is available in Access 2016; however, it is not built into the ribbon as it was in past versions. The Switchboard Manager can be launched by adding a command to the Quick Access Toolbar, by adding a command to the ribbon, or by running it automatically in the Immediate window using a VBA command. If your database contains a Switchboard, consider the benefits of building a navigation form in its place.

View a Navigation Form

The **navigation form** provides a familiar Internet-style interface that allows you to access multiple objects in the database from one central location. Similar to websites, the navigation form allows for top-level navigation commands across the top of the page or vertical navigation along the side of the page as well as second-level navigation buttons directly below the top or along the side of the page. Commands are highlighted when selected, providing visual cues as you navigate the form.

REAL WORLD ADVICE | **Custom Web Apps**

If you want your application to not only look like a website but also exist on a website, Access can help. A feature introduced in Access 2013 is the ability to create customized web apps. A customized web app is a web-based application that can be created by using templates. A template for custom web apps can be found in the Access Welcome screen. A SharePoint site is required to create a custom web app.

Opening the Starting File

In this exercise, you will open the Spa Application database to view examples of navigation forms. You will then build additional navigation forms and create a main menu that will, along with the use of command buttons, make a refined user interface.

A11.00

To Open the Starting File

a. Start **Access**, click **Open Other Files** in the left pane, and then double-click **This PC**. Navigate through the folder structure to the location of your student data files, and then double-click **a06ch11SpaApplication**. A database opens displaying tables, forms, and reports related to the spa, the services it provides, and various transactions.

b. Click the **File** tab, save the file as an **Access Database**, and click **Save As**. Navigate to the location where you are saving your project files and then change the filename to a06ch11SpaApplication_LastFirst using your last and first name. Click **Save**. If necessary, enable the content.

Opening and Using Navigation Forms

In this exercise, you will look at three different navigation forms that have already been developed in the database. Each navigation form represents a different area of the spa: employees, products, and services. By viewing each navigation form, you will get an idea of what the format should be for the remaining navigation forms that you will create.

A11.01

To Open and Use Navigation Forms

SIDE NOTE

Pin the Ribbon

If your ribbon is collapsed, pin your ribbon open. Click the Home tab. In the lower right-hand corner of the ribbon, click Pin the Ribbon [icon].

a. Notice the long list of objects in the Navigation Pane. Double-click **frmEmployeeNavigation** to open the form.

This navigation form provides access to all the forms and reports related to the employees listed in the database. The blue navigation buttons on the left side represent forms, and the green navigation buttons represent reports.

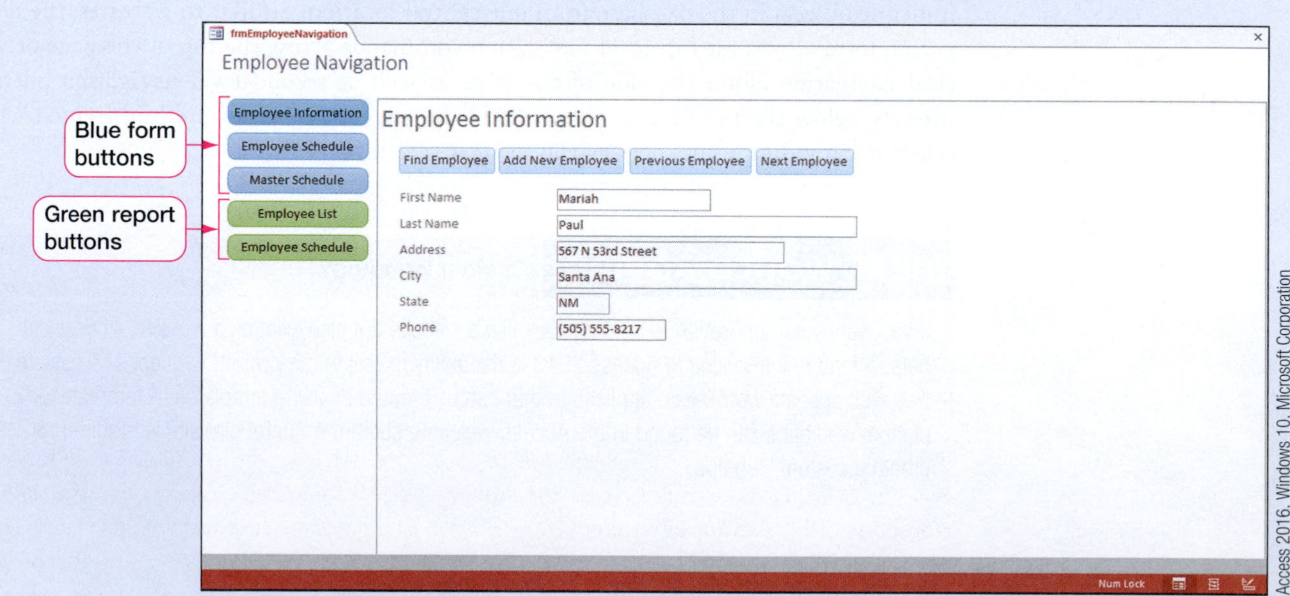

Figure 1 Employee navigation form

b. Click the blue **Master Schedule** button on the left side of the navigation form to open the Master Schedule form. Click the green **Employee Schedule** button on the left side to open the Employee Schedule report.

   Notice how the color and outline change slightly when a button is selected.

c. **Close** ☒ frmEmployeeNavigation.

> **SIDE NOTE**
> **Scroll Bars**
> Scroll bars may or may not appear on your screen depending on the screen resolution and size.

d. Double-click **frmProductNavigation** in the Navigation Pane to open the Product Navigation form. Notice that the form and reports on the left side are related to the products offered by the spa. Click each one to see the related form or report.

e. Double-click **frmServicesNavigation** in the Navigation Pane to open the Services Navigation form. Notice that the forms and report on the left side are related to the services offered by the spa. Click each one to see the related form or report.

f. **Close** ☒ frmServicesNavigation and frmProductNavigation.

REAL WORLD ADVICE | **Color-Coding**

Color-coding can be used effectively to distinguish between different tasks or objects on a navigation form. In the previous example, different colors were used to distinguish reports from forms. Colors can also be used to group related tasks or groups of tasks. For example, all tasks related to customers, regardless of which navigation form they are found on, could be one color, while all tasks related to employees could be a different color. This gives you an option to group tasks on one navigation form or on many and still have them be easy to find.

QUICK REFERENCE | **Edit the Navigation Form**

As you are developing your navigation form, if there are modifications you need to make in the form or report within the navigation form, you can make those modifications right in the navigation form.

1. Click the button with the form or report that needs to be modified.
2. On the Home tab, in the Views group, click the View arrow, and then select Layout View.
3. Make the modifications to the form or report, and then click Save to save the changes. If you forget to save the changes right away, Access will prompt you to save them when you close the navigation form.

Create a Navigation Form

Access provides six different predefined layouts for navigation forms that are customizable, and they can be redesigned even after they have been created. The predefined layouts use a drag-and-drop method to add new objects to the navigation form. The **navigation control bar** is an area of a navigation form that allows for the addition of new forms, reports, or other database objects. All you do is drag a database object onto the navigation control bar, and a new navigation button is added to the form. When the button is clicked, the corresponding form or report will be displayed in the **subform control**. A subform control embeds one form into another form. If you drop the form or report anywhere on the form other than the navigation control bar, the form or report will be added to the form itself rather than as a navigation button.

Using a Predefined Layout to Create a Navigation Form

Of the six predefined layouts to choose from, three provide one level of navigation, either horizontal or vertical, and three provide two levels of navigation, either horizontal or a combination of horizontal and vertical. In this exercise, you will develop a navigation form for customer navigation that uses a vertical navigation form similar to those you viewed in the previous exercise.

To Use a Predefined Layout to Create a Navigation Form

a. Click the **Create** tab, and in the Forms group, click **Navigation**, and then click **Vertical Tabs, Left**. A new navigation form will open in Layout view.

> **Troubleshooting**
>
> You may see the Field List open on the right side of your window. You can close this by clicking the Design tab and then clicking Add Existing Fields in the Tools group or by clicking the Close button on the Field List.

b. Drag **frmCustomer** from the Navigation Pane to the **[Add New]** button on the navigation form.

c. Drag **frmCustomerInvoices** from the Navigation Pane to the **[Add New]** button on the navigation form.

d. Continue adding **frmCustomerSchedule**, **frmCustomerPurchases**, **rptCustomerList**, and **rptScheduleByCustomer** to the **[Add New]** button on the navigation form.

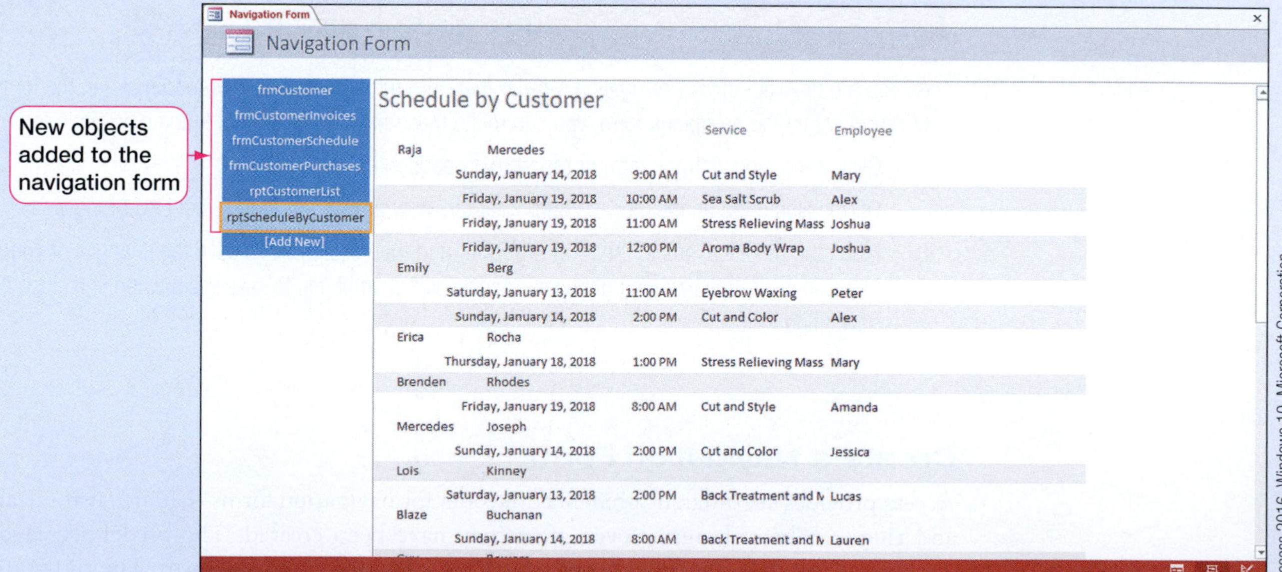

Figure 2 Customer navigation form with six navigation buttons on the left side

e. Save the form as frmCustomerNavigation.

Modify a Navigation Form

Once a navigation form has been created, additional forms and reports can be added to the form, deleted from the form, or rearranged on the form.

Once buttons have been added to the navigation form, the captions — or text — can be changed or replaced with icons instead of the button caption to further customize the form. Many of the shapes available in Access 2016 were specifically designed to use with navigation controls such as Next, Previous, and Exit.

Adding Objects to a Navigation Form

Forms and reports can be easily added to the form by dragging the object from the Navigation Pane to the [Add New] button; therefore, it is important to be able to see your Navigation Pane as you work on the navigation form. In this exercise, you will add additional forms and reports to the navigation form.

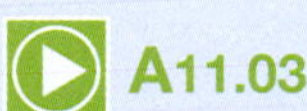

To Add Objects to a Navigation Form

a. Drag **rptPurchaseByCustomer** from the Navigation Pane to the **[Add New]** button to add the report to the navigation form.

b. Drag **frmMasterSchedule** from the Navigation Pane to the **[Add New]** button to add the form to the navigation form.

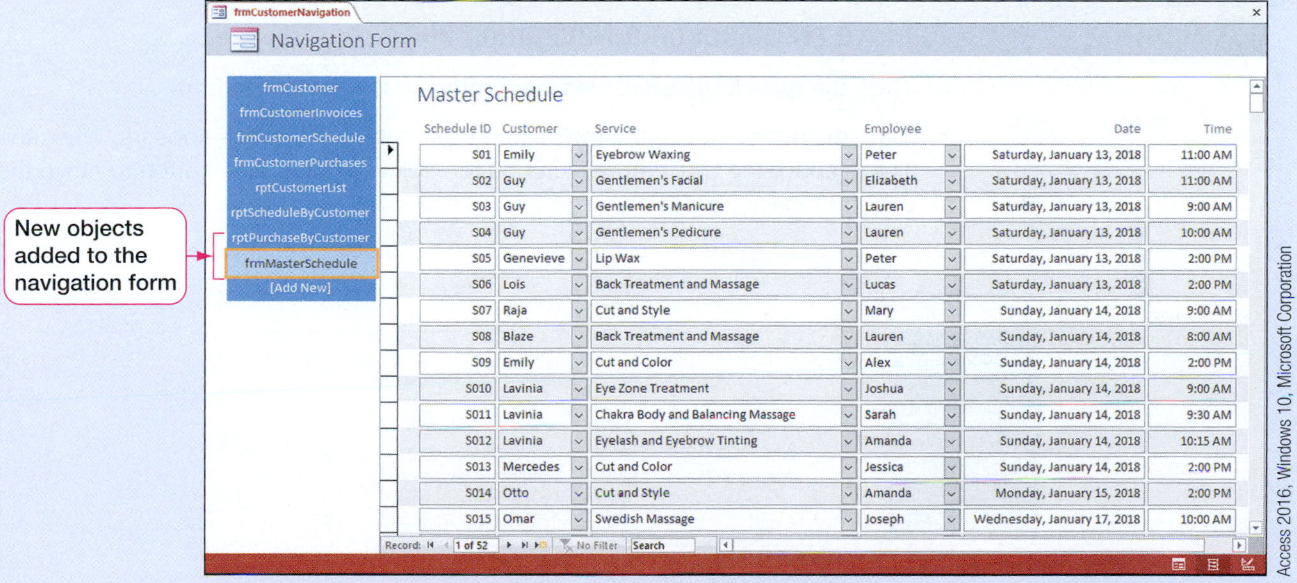

Figure 3 New objects added to the navigation form

c. **Save** the navigation form.

Deleting an Object from a Navigation Form

If necessary, objects may be deleted from a navigation form. When an object is deleted from the navigation form, only the button is deleted, the actual object is still available in the navigation pane of the database. In this exercise, you will delete a form object from the navigation form.

A11.04

To Delete an Object from a Navigation Form

a. Ensure that the frmMasterSchedule button on the navigation form is selected.

b. Press Delete to delete the object from the navigation form.

SIDE NOTE

Alternate Method

An alternate method of deleting the button is to select the button, right-click, and then select Delete from the menu.

Troubleshooting

When you delete an object from a navigation form, make sure the button is selected with an orange border around it. If you are in edit mode with the insertion point blinking in the text instead of the button selected with the orange border, you will delete the text rather than the button.

c. **Save** the navigation form.

Moving an Object on a Navigation Form

Existing objects on a navigation form can easily be rearranged. In this exercise, you will rearrange the order of the objects on the navigation form.

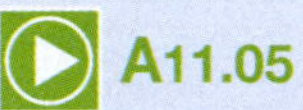

A11.05

To Move an Object on a Navigation Form

a. Click the **rptScheduleByCustomer** button on the navigation form.

b. Drag the **button** above the rptCustomerList button until a line appears. When the line is above the **rptCustomerList** button, release the mouse button to move the report to the new position.

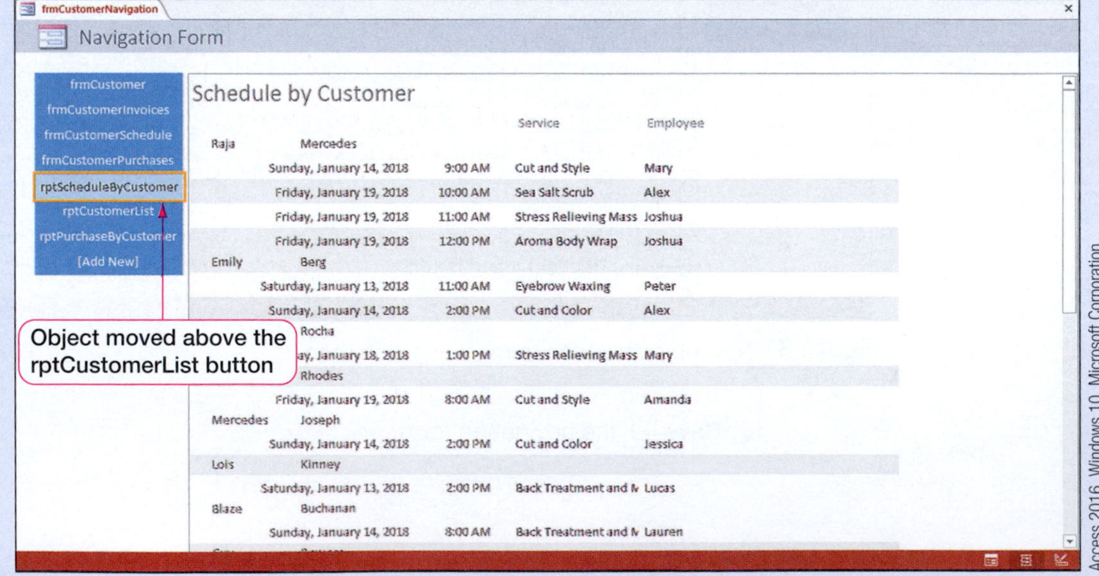

Figure 4 rptScheduleByCustomer object moved to new position

c. **Save** the navigation form.

Modifying the Appearance of Buttons on a Navigation Form

Navigation buttons can be modified to customize the form. The button shape and color can be changed. A theme can be added either to the navigation form or to the whole database, including the navigation form. In this exercise, you will add a theme to the database and change the shape and color of the buttons.

CHAPTER 11

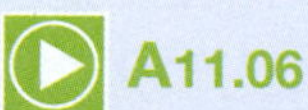

To Modify the Appearance of Buttons on a Navigation Form

a. Double-click the navigation form **title text**, select the text, type Customer Navigation, and then press Enter. Select the icon to the left of the title, and then press Delete.

b. On the Design tab, in the Tools group, click **Property Sheet**. Under Selection type, click the **selection** arrow, and then select **FormHeader**. On the Format tab, locate and click inside the **Back Color** property. Click the **Build button** [...], and then select **White, Background 1**, the first row in the first column under Theme Colors. **Close** [X] the Property Sheet pane.

c. Click the **frmCustomer** button. Click the **Format** tab, and in the Control Formatting group, click **Change Shape**, and then click **Rounded Rectangle**.

d. Double-click the **frmCustomer** button to edit the button text. Type Customer to replace the existing text, and then press Enter.

e. On the Format tab, in the Font group, click **Format Painter**. Click the **frmCustomerInvoices** button to change the button shape to match the Customers button, and then change the button text to Invoices.

f. Using the **Format Painter**, change the shape of the **frmCustomerSchedule** and **frmCustomerPurchases** buttons to match the Customers button. Change the button names to Appointments and Purchases.

g. Click the button **rptScheduleByCustomer**. Click the **Format** tab, and in the Control Formatting group, click **Change Shape**, and then click **Rounded Rectangle**.

h. Change the rptScheduleByCustomer button name to Appointment Report.

i. Using the **Format Painter**, change the shape of the **rptCustomerList** and **rptPurchaseByCustomer** buttons to match the Appointment Report button. Change the button names to Customer List and Purchase Report.

j. Click the **Design** tab, and in the Themes group, click **Themes**, and then click **Integral**. This changes the theme for all the objects in the database, including the navigation form.

SIDE NOTE
Alternate Method
An alternate method of renaming the buttons on a navigation form is to use the Caption property, located on the Format tab of the Property Sheet.

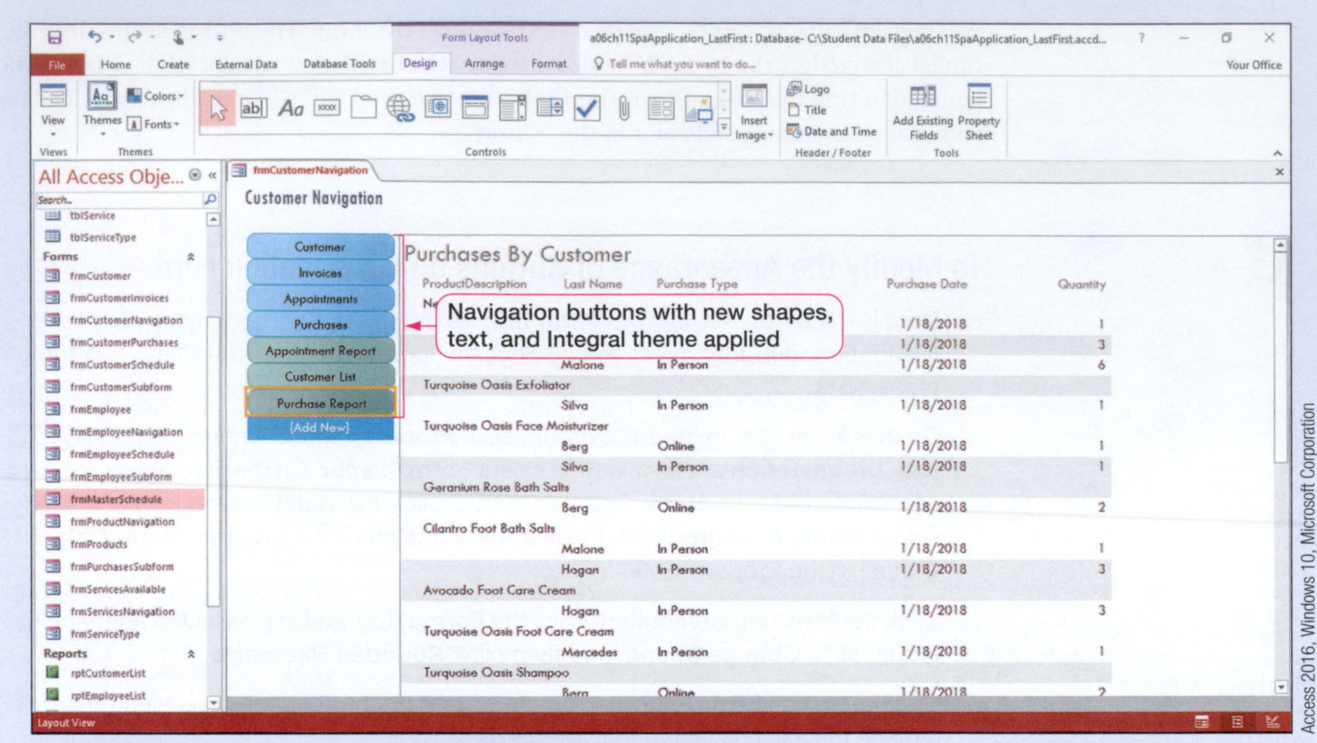

Access 2016, Windows 10, Microsoft Corporation

Figure 5 Customer navigation form with modified appearance

k. **Save** and **close** the navigation form. If you need to take a break before finishing this chapter, now is a good time.

> **REAL WORLD ADVICE** — **Navigation Forms and Tab Controls: When to Use Each?**
>
> Although tab controls and navigation forms look similar, the two objects function very differently. In a tab control, the tabbed windows are hidden behind each other and are all open at the same time. You can picture the layout as pieces of paper laid on top of each other with a tab at the top of each page. As you click a tab, the piece of paper with the selected tab is moved to the top of the pile. In a navigation form, the tabs open a new form or report in the same subform control each time, so only one object is open at a time. This is useful when you want to provide a hierarchy of options — navigation tabs and second-level navigation options. Navigation forms provide for better database performance, since only one object at a time is open. They also trigger updates and requery the object's data source.

Refining the User Interface

Navigation forms do not display data from a table; therefore, a navigation form is an unbound object. Because the user does not have to move from record to record or from page to page, some of the form navigation properties can be removed. The navigation buttons and record selectors can be removed because they are not needed. The ability to access a shortcut menu can be disabled, as can the option to copy data and close the object. Any operations that would distract the user from the purpose of the navigation form should be disabled or removed.

If you find your navigation form cluttered with too many objects, you can create multiple navigation forms and have one form open another. The key to making multiple navigation forms is to have them arranged in a way that makes intuitive sense. A navigation form with only reports and another with only forms may not simplify the process of navigating through your database. It is, in effect, replicating the Navigation Pane. Instead, you should consider grouping forms and reports by task or by function, as seen in Figure 6.

By grouping the different business functions, you create an intuitive and well-defined user interface. A user should be able to complete all related tasks under a single navigation form rather than having to move from form to form to find different tasks. Think of how a good website works: On the Home page, there are links to go to other pages. On each page of the website, you are then able to view related information about one topic. To go to a new topic, you go to a new page. You can create a similar experience using multiple navigation forms that are all linked together. In the Spa example, you might want to have different pages to navigate service, product, employee, and customer tasks as shown in Figure 6.

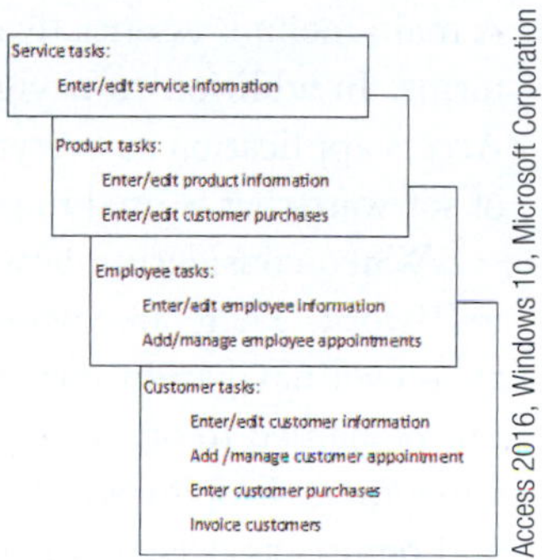

Figure 6 Different task lists

To accomplish this, you can create a main navigation form that has four navigation buttons: Services, Products, Employees, and Customers. Clicking one of the buttons opens another navigation form with additional objects related to the area you clicked.

A well-refined user interface will make sense to any user, even one with no Access experience. The user should be able to look at the navigation form and locate the form or report that he or she needs. In this section, you will create a user interface that includes a navigation form, custom form buttons, and modified start-up options for the database.

CONSIDER THIS | Websites Compared to Access

An Access user interface can be set up to look and work just like a web page. Think about websites you enjoy visiting. Other than the content, what makes a web page attractive? Is it how easy things are to find? Is it the consistent color theme? When designing a user interface, think about what makes an interface interesting and easy to use, and look for ways to implement these aspects in your user interface.

REAL WORLD ADVICE **Planning Is Everything**

How do you decide, as the designer, what a good user interface will look like? What makes sense to you may not make sense to the final user, so to make the best decisions for the application, it is important to understand your end user and the job he or she has to do. The more information you get directly from the user, the better your application will be.

Consider spending time with users, doing the following.

- Interviewing the users about the tasks they complete with the application
- Asking what changes the users would make to improve the application
- Asking what the users do not like about the application
- Observing what the users do and taking notes to refer to when you are designing the application

Create a Main Menu

A main menu is essentially a navigation form that provides access to additional navigation forms. In addition to navigation forms, a main menu can have a command to close the Access application so everything the user needs is in one place. An **application** is a piece of software that is used to perform one task or multiple tasks.

When considering how the main menu will work, you have to look at how the tabs will work. There are two different ways to create a main menu form. You can create a two-level navigation form with top-level tabs and second-level tabs. The top-level tabs can be named to organize groups of tasks. For example, the top-level tabs may be called Customers, Employees, Products, and Services. The second-level tabs could be the forms and reports associated with each task group. For example, the second-level tabs could be forms for customer data entry and reports for customer lists. An example can be seen in Figure 7.

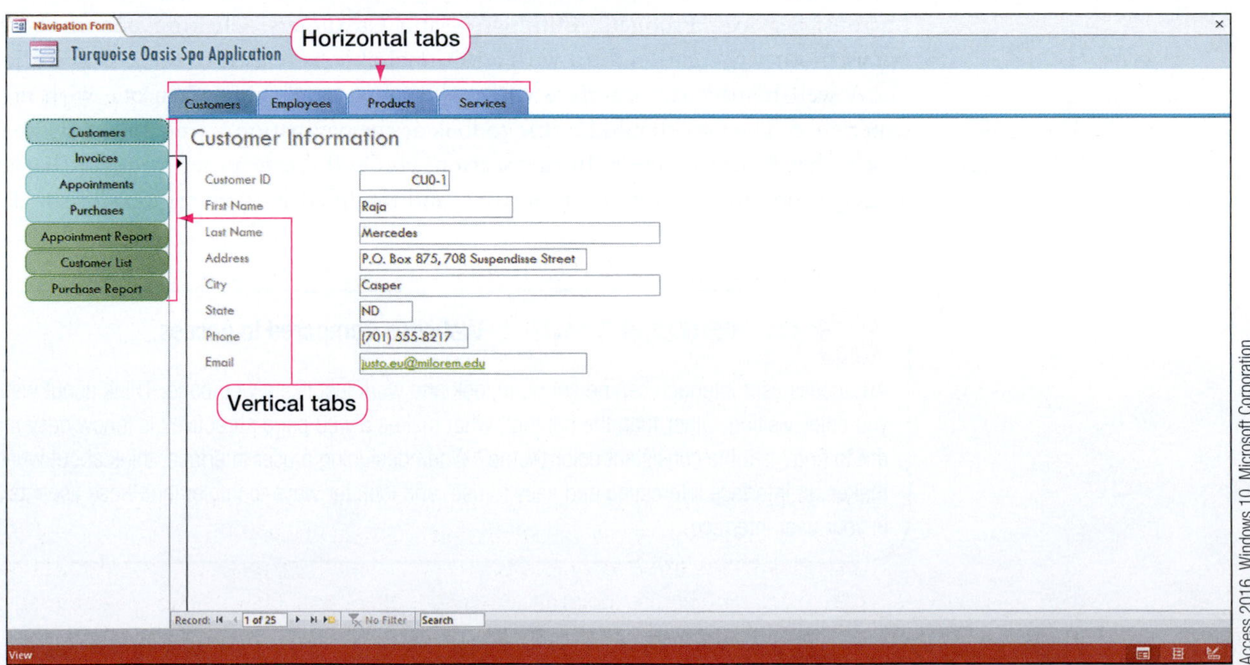

Figure 7 Navigation form with horizontal and vertical tabs

Another option is to create a navigation form for each group of tasks with only top-level tabs. Each top level points to the related forms and reports. Thus, the main menu navigation form has only top-level tabs that open the individual navigation forms for each task group. For example, you can create a customer navigation form, an employee navigation form, and so on. Each top-level tab in the main menu navigation form can open one of the individual navigation forms. As seen in Figure 8, the effect is the same as the method described above, but the look is different.

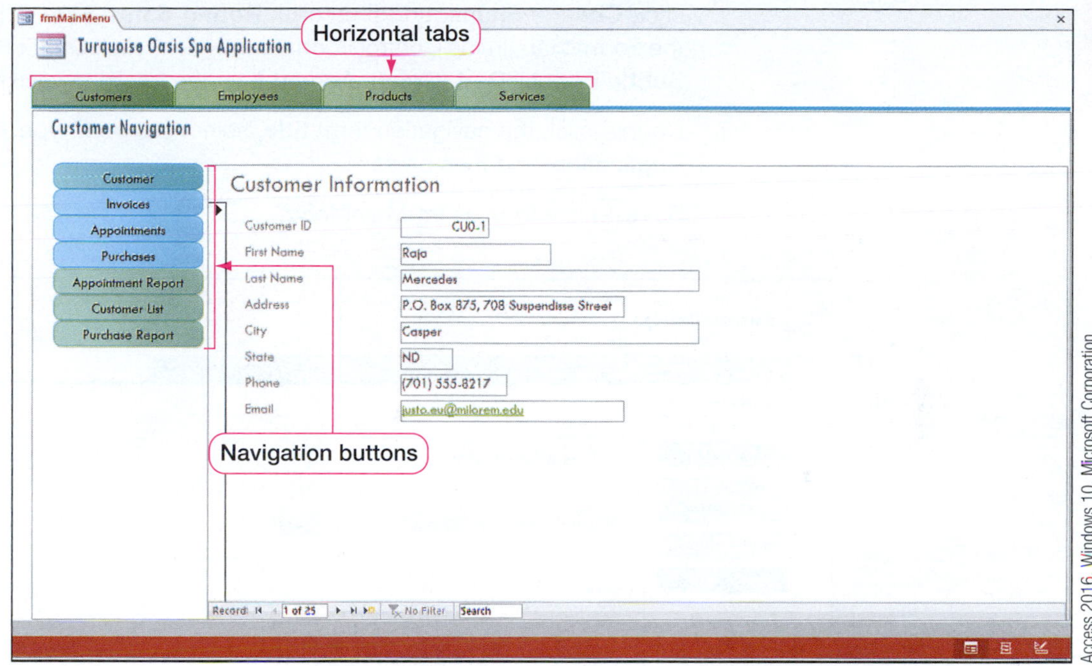

Access 2016, Windows 10, Microsoft Corporation

Figure 8 Navigation form using other navigation forms with only top-level tabs

Creating a Main Menu Navigation Form

The spa database you are working with has four different navigation forms. In this exercise, you will create a new navigation form to access each of those navigation forms. You will then add command buttons to navigate records and close the database.

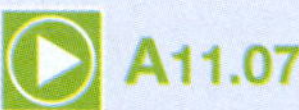 A11.07

To Create a Main Menu Navigation Form

a. If you took a break, open the **a06ch11SpaApplication** database.

b. Click the **Create** tab, and in the Forms group, click **Navigation**, and then click **Horizontal Tabs**.

c. **Close** [X] the Field List pane if necessary.

d. On the Design tab, in the Tools group, click **Property Sheet**. Under Selection type, click the **selection** arrow, and then select **FormHeader**. On the Format tab, locate and click inside the **Back Color** property. Click the **Build button** [...], and then, in the first row in the first column under Theme Colors, select **White, Background 1**.

e. **Close** [X] the Property Sheet pane.

f. Drag **frmCustomerNavigation** from the Navigation Pane to the **[Add New]** button.

g. One at a time, drag **frmEmployeeNavigation**, **frmProductNavigation**, and **frmServicesNavigation** to the **[Add New]** button.

h. Double-click the **frmCustomerNavigation** tab, select the **text**, type Customers, and then press Enter. Repeat for the remaining tabs, and name them Employees, Products, and Services.

i. Click the **Customers** tab on the navigation form. Press and hold Shift, and then click the **Services** tab. Click the **Format** tab, and in the Control Formatting group, click **Change Shape**, and then click **Round Same Side Corner Rectangle**. On the Format tab, in the Control Formatting group, click **Quick Styles**, and then click **Subtle Effect - Dark Green, Accent 5**, in the fourth row, sixth column.

j. Double-click the navigation form **title**, select the **text**, type Turquoise Oasis Spa Application, and then press Enter.

k. **Save** the form as frmMainMenu.

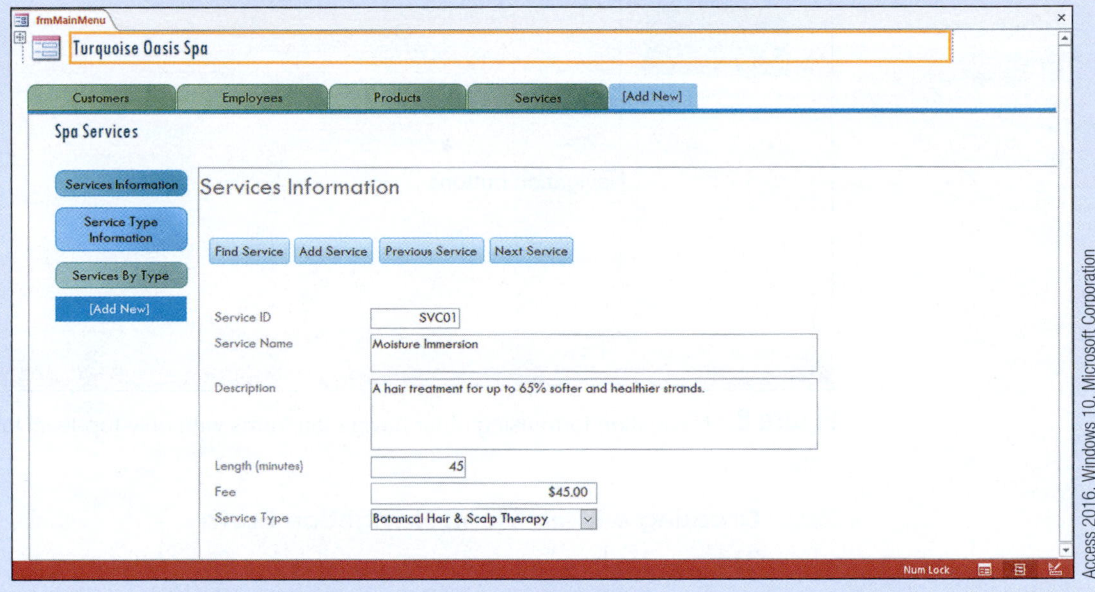

Figure 9 Main menu navigation form with horizontal tabs

Adding an Image to the Main Menu

Meda Rodate would like you to add the Turquoise Oasis Spa logo to the new main menu. By default, Access adds a form icon to new navigation forms. This icon can be deleted or replaced with a custom image. In this exercise, you will replace the default image with the Turquoise Oasis Spa logo.

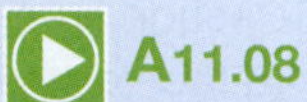

To Add an Image to the Main Menu

a. On frmMainMenu, click the **icon** to the left of the title, and then click the **Design** tab.

b. In the Controls group, click **Insert Image**. Click **Browse**, navigate through the folder structure to the location of your student data files, and then double-click **a06ch11TurquoiseOasisLogo**.

c. On the Design tab, click **Property Sheet**. In the Property Sheet pane, on the Format tab, click inside the **Size Mode** property, click the arrow, and then click **Zoom**.

d. Type 3 for the **Width**, and then type 0.8 for the **Height** of the image.

e. **Close** [X] the Property Sheet pane.

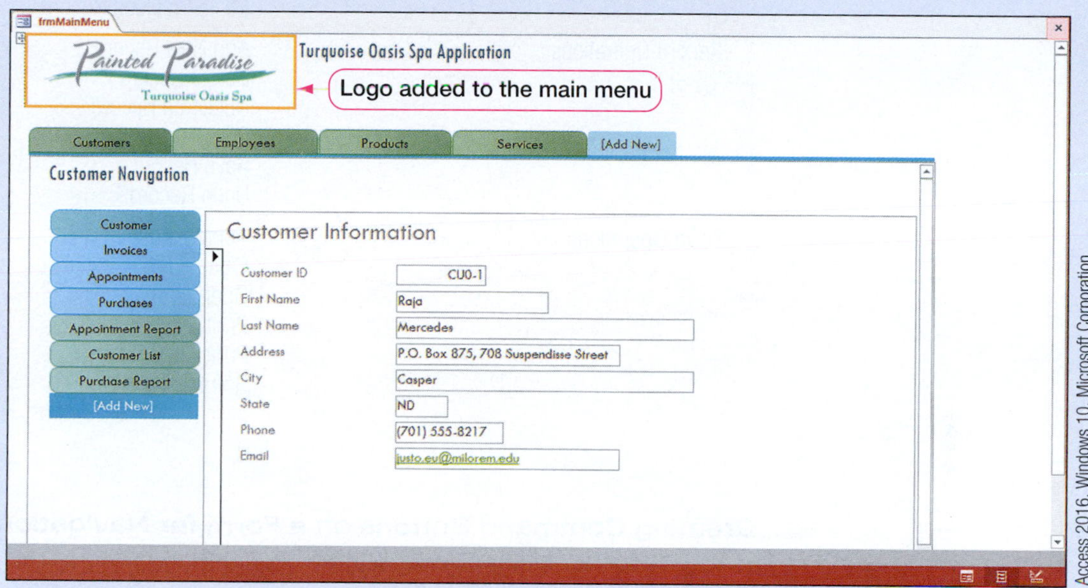

Figure 10 Logo added to main menu navigation

f. **Save** [Save] and **Close** [X] the form.

Add Command Buttons to the Navigation Form

The navigation forms help to organize the user interface to the database. But individual records are still navigated with the navigation bars. For users who are unfamiliar with Access, buttons near the top of forms are more intuitive than the navigational arrows at the bottom of a form. In this section, you will add some buttons for navigation and turn off the navigation bar.

Command buttons are available in several categories. Record navigation buttons replicate most of the navigation tools available on the Navigation bar. You can create buttons to go to the first, next, last, and previous records. Record operations buttons allow the user to add, delete, and undo a record. Form operations buttons open, close, and print forms. Command buttons can be added to the navigation form, but they can also be added to forms and reports that are accessed through the navigation form.

QUICK REFERENCE	Form Command Buttons Available
Category	**Actions**
Record Navigation	Find Next Find Record Go To First Record Go To Last Record Go To Next Record Go To Previous Record
Record Operations	Add New Record Delete Record Duplicate Record Print Record Save Record Undo Record
Form Operations	Apply Form Filter Close Form Open Form Print a Form Print Current Form Refresh Form Data

Creating Command Buttons on a Form for Navigation

If you open the Employee Navigation form, Product Navigation form, or Service Navigation form, you will notice that there are buttons on the navigation forms for the user to click to find a record, add a record, or go to the previous and next records. In this exercise, you will add similar buttons to the Customer form as well as an Exit Database button on the main menu navigation form.

To Create Command Buttons on a Form for Navigation

a. Double-click **frmCustomer** in the Navigation Pane to open the form.

b. On the Home tab, in the Views group, click the **View** arrow, and then select **Design View**.

c. Press Ctrl + A to select all objects on the form. Press and hold Shift and then click the form title to deselect it. Drag all of the **controls** in the form detail section down so that the top textbox is on the **.5"** mark on the vertical ruler.

d. On the Design tab, in the Controls group, click the **Button** [xxxx] form control, and then click in the **top left corner** of the form detail section to add the button. The Command Button Wizard opens automatically.

e. In the Command Button Wizard, under the Categories list, verify that **Record Navigation** is selected. On the Actions list, click **Find Record**, and then click **Next**.

f. Click **Text**, in the text box, select the **text**, and then type Find Customer.

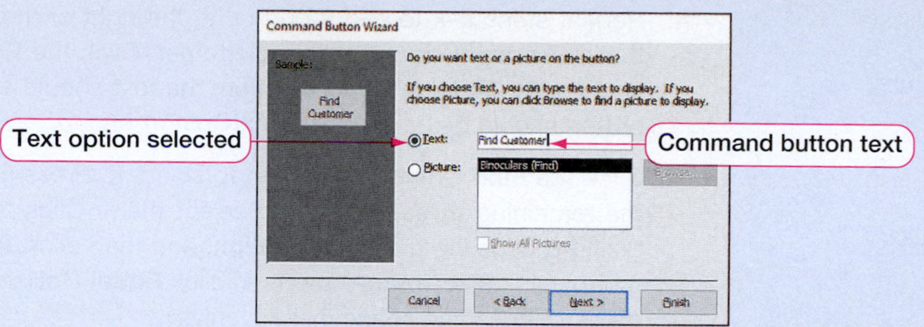

Figure 11 Customized command button text

Access 2016, Windows 10, Microsoft Corporation

g. Click **Next**.

h. Name the button cmdFindCustomer, and then click **Finish**.

i. On the Design tab, in the Controls group, click the **Button** [XXXX] form control, and then click to the **right** of the first button.

j. On the Categories list, click to select **Record Operations**, and then, on the Actions list, verify that **Add New Record** is selected. Click **Next**.

k. Click **Text**, select the **text**, type Add New Customer, and then click **Next**. Name the button cmdAddNewCustomer, and then click **Finish**.

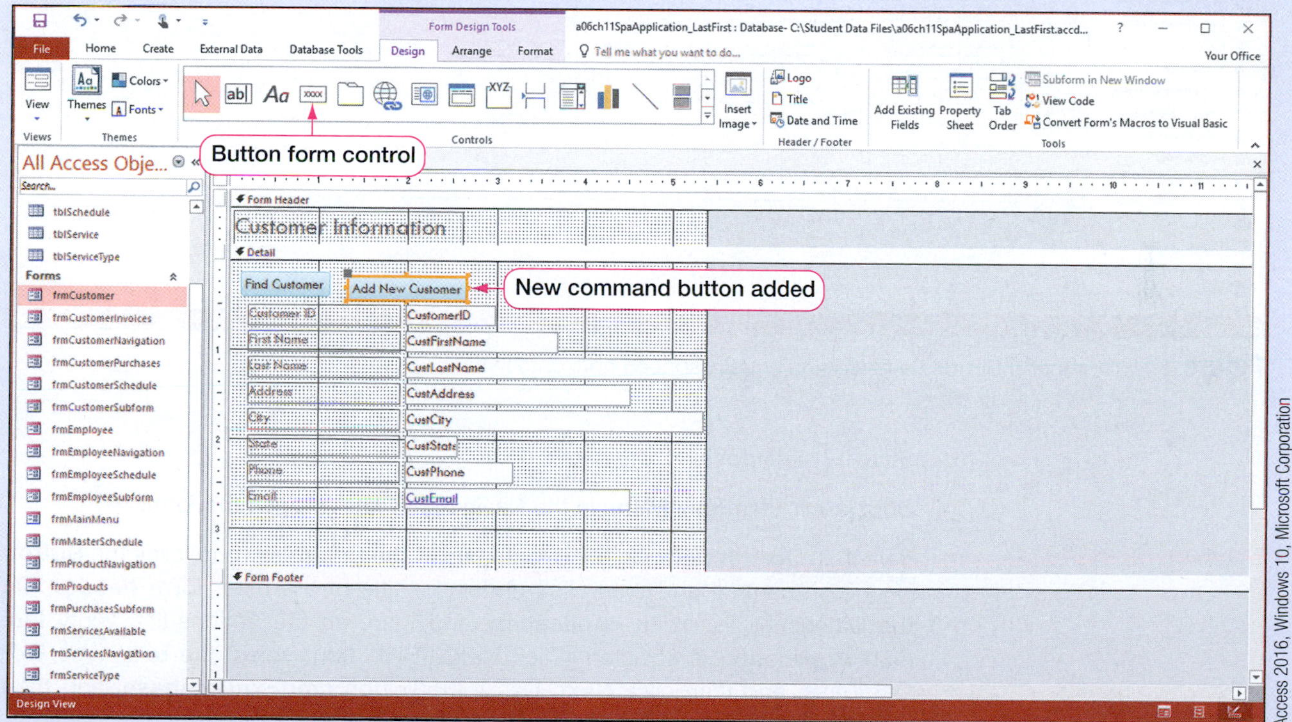

Access 2016, Windows 10, Microsoft Corporation

Figure 12 Two command buttons added to the form

l. Repeat steps d–k to add a button, to the right of the Add New Customer button, that takes the user to the previous customer. Click the **Record Navigation** category and the **Go To Previous Record** action; the text should say Previous Customer, and the button should be named cmdPreviousCustomer.

m. Repeat steps d–k to add a button, to the right of the Previous Customer button, that takes the user to the next customer. Click the **Record Navigation** category and the **Go To Next Record** action; the text should say Next Customer, and the button should be named cmdNextCustomer.

n. Click the **Find Customer button** to select it. Press and hold Shift, and then click the remaining **three buttons** to select them. Click the **Arrange** tab, and in the Sizing & Ordering group, click **Align**, and then click **Top**. In the Sizing & Ordering group, click **Size/Space**, and then click **Equal Horizontal**. This will align the tops of the buttons and space them evenly.

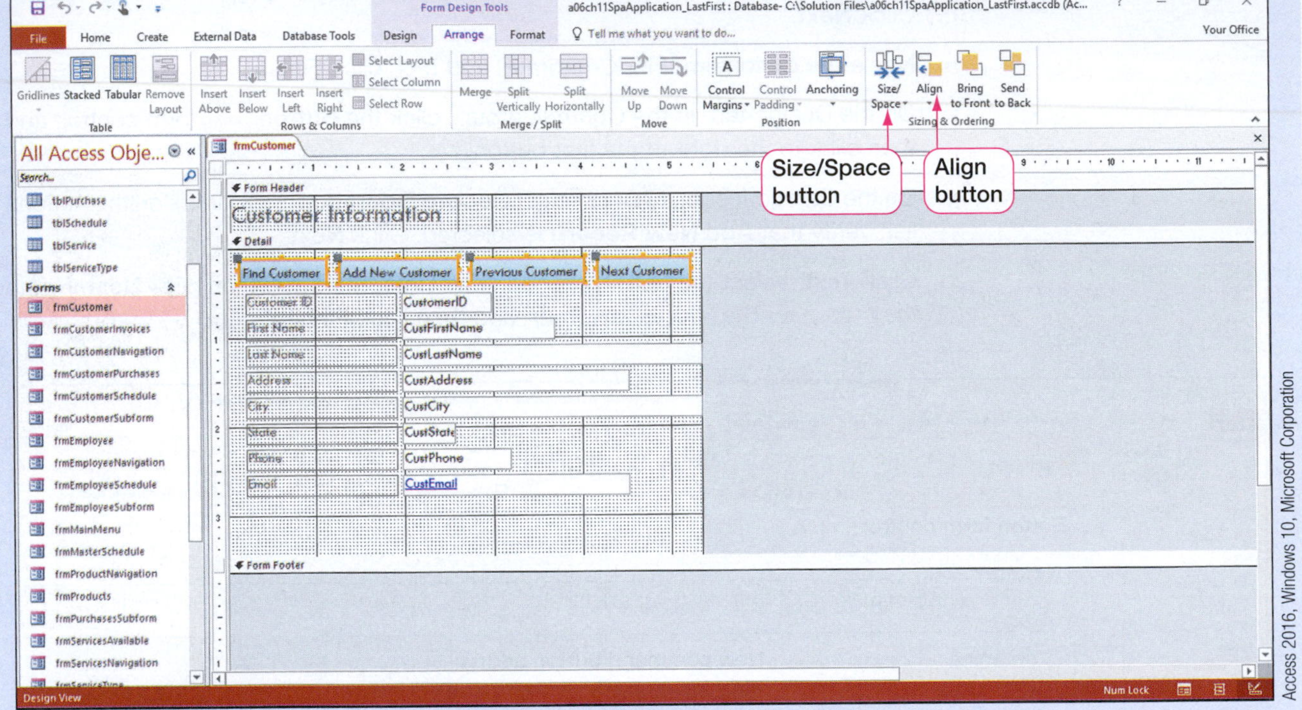

Figure 13 Command Buttons aligned and equally spaced horizontally

o. **Save** and **close** the form.

p. Double-click **frmMainMenu** in the Navigation Pane to open the form.

q. Switch to **Design** view. On the Design tab, in the Controls group, click the **Button** form control, and then click under the title of the main **form header**. On the Categories list, click **Application**, and then, on the Actions list, verify that **Quit Application** is selected. Click **Next**. Click **Text**, select the **text**, type Exit Database, and then click **Next**. Name the button **cmdExitDatabase**, and then click **Finish**. Switch to **Form** view.

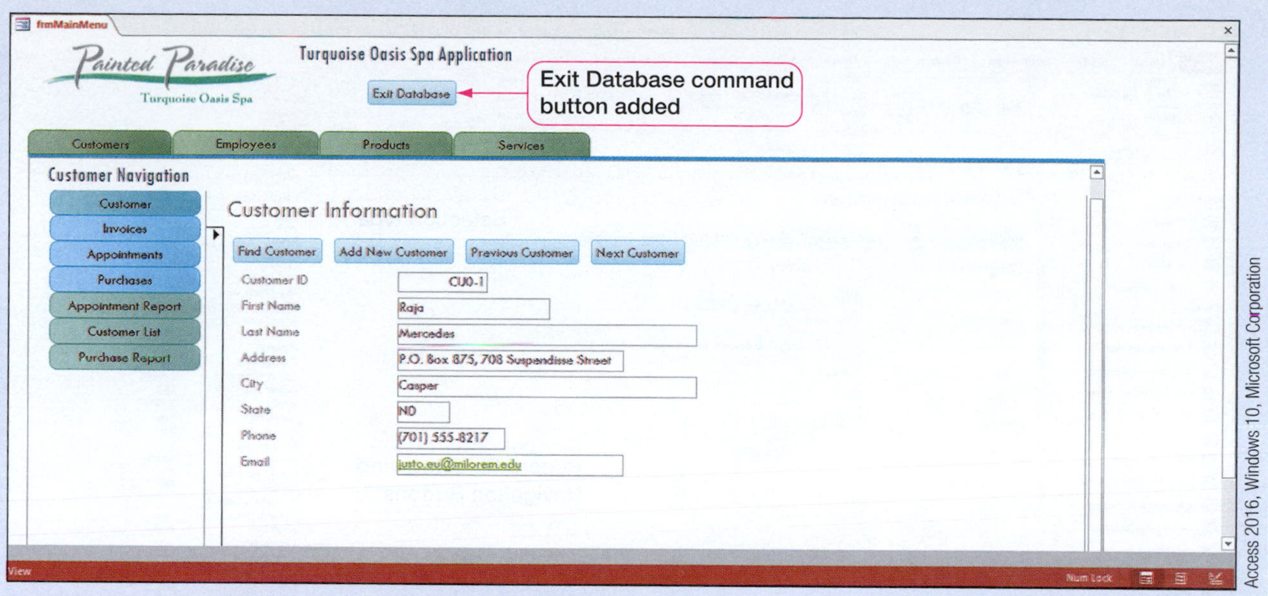

Access 2016, Windows 10, Microsoft Corporation

Figure 14 Exit database command button added to the form

r. **Save** the form. Click the **Exit Database** button to check that your button is working properly. Access should close.

Removing Navigation Arrows and Record Selectors on a Form

If you look at any of the forms with command buttons added, the navigation arrows and record selectors have all been removed, which forces the user to use the buttons to manage the records. With the addition of the command buttons, the navigation arrows and record selectors create duplicate functionality. In this exercise, you will remove the record selectors and navigation arrows from the Customer form.

A11.10

To Remove Navigation Arrows and Record Selectors on a Form

a. Open the Access database **a06ch11SpaApplication**. In the Navigation Pane, double-click **frmCustomer** to open the form.

b. Switch to **Layout** view. On the Design tab, in the Tools group, click **Property Sheet**.

c. Under Selection type, click the **selection** arrow, and then click **Form**.

d. On the Format tab in the Property Sheet pane, click the **Record Selectors** arrow, and then click **No**.

e. Click the **Navigation Buttons** arrow, and then click **No**.

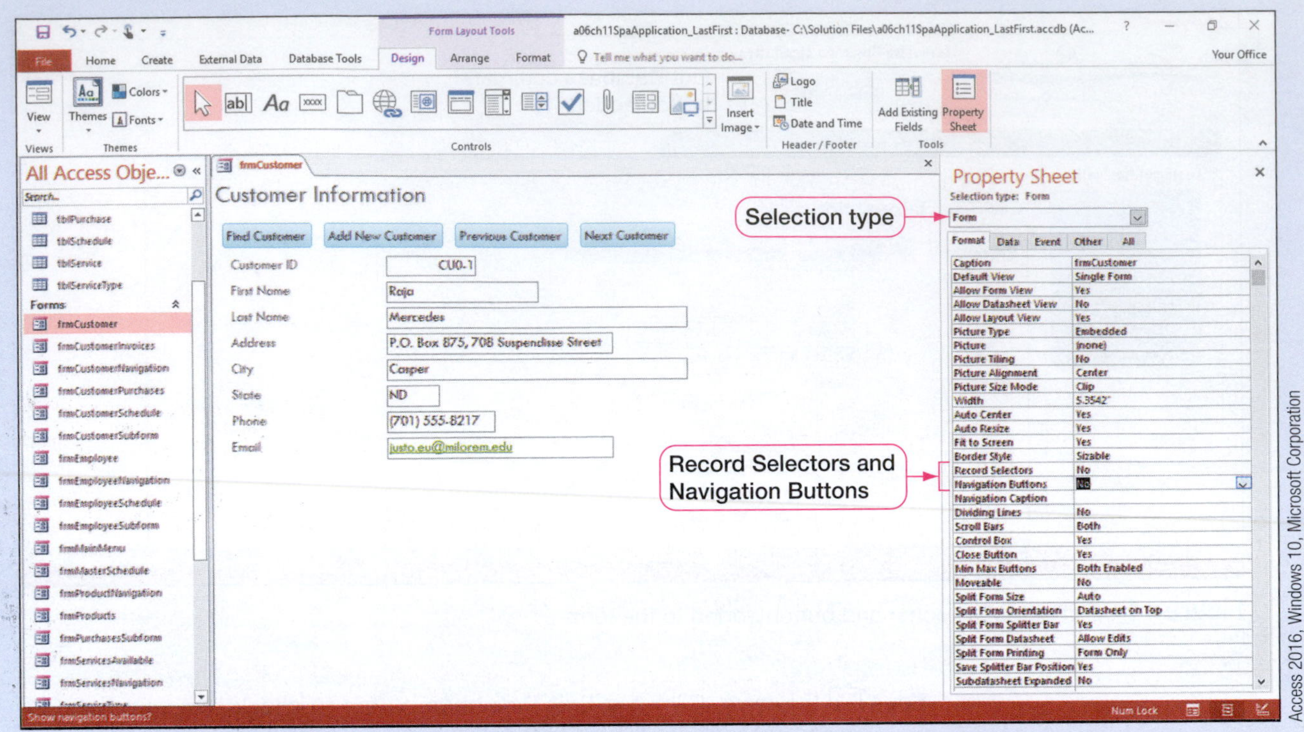

Figure 15 Record selectors and navigation buttons properties set to no

f. **Close** ☒ the Property Sheet pane.
   Notice that the record selectors and navigation arrows are hidden.

g. **Save** and **Close** ☒ the form.

Set Start-Up Display Options and Test the Application

Once your database has been designed, the forms and reports have been created, and a navigation system and user interface is in place, you will have an application for others to use. To make the application as user-friendly as possible, you can name the application and then remove options available to database designers. By doing this, you reduce the chance of changes being made to the data or the database structure, either intentionally or accidentally, by an end user. These options may include removing access to certain application options, such as the Navigation Pane, the ribbon, and various toolbar options.

You also will want to show a start-up form when your database opens. The **start-up form** is the form that opens automatically when you open the database. This is generally the navigation form that will act as your main menu.

Optional commands, such as the command to compact and repair the database when it is closed, may also be set to run automatically so the user does not have to worry about maintenance tasks.

Making Changes to the Start-Up Options

Changing the application title helps to better identify the application and give it an identity separate from the actual database. Selecting a start-up form will determine which form opens when the application is started. Restricting access to the Navigation Pane requires the user to use the user interface you have developed. In this exercise, you will change the application title to "Turquoise Oasis Spa" and designate your main menu navigation form as the start-up form.

CONSIDER THIS | **Creating a Pleasant Experience**

In the interest of protecting the data in your database or creating a more efficient application, what options could you think of limiting? Should you password protect your application? How would this be more or less confusing? Should you allow only certain changes to be made to the data, such as allowing editing but not deleting? How would these options affect the usability of your application?

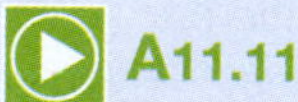

To Make Changes to the Start-Up Options

a. Click the **File** tab, click **Options**, and then click **Current Database**. Under the Application Options section, click the **Application Title**, and then type Turquoise Oasis Spa.

b. Click the **Display Form** arrow, and then click **frmMainMenu**. This will be the form that opens when the application is opened.

c. Click the **Compact on Close** check box. This automatically compacts and repairs the database every time it is closed.

   A database grows dynamically as data is added or manipulated. However, the database does not shrink automatically when data is deleted or the manipulation is complete; this means that the size of the database may be unnecessarily large. Databases may also become fragmented as data is added and deleted. To maintain optimal performance of the database, you should compact and repair the database each time it is closed.

SIDE NOTE
Show Navigation Pane
If the Navigation Pane is hidden, press F11 to unhide it as long as the option to disable special keys is not selected in the database options.

d. Under the Navigation section, clear the **Display Navigation Pane** check box. This hides the Navigation Pane.

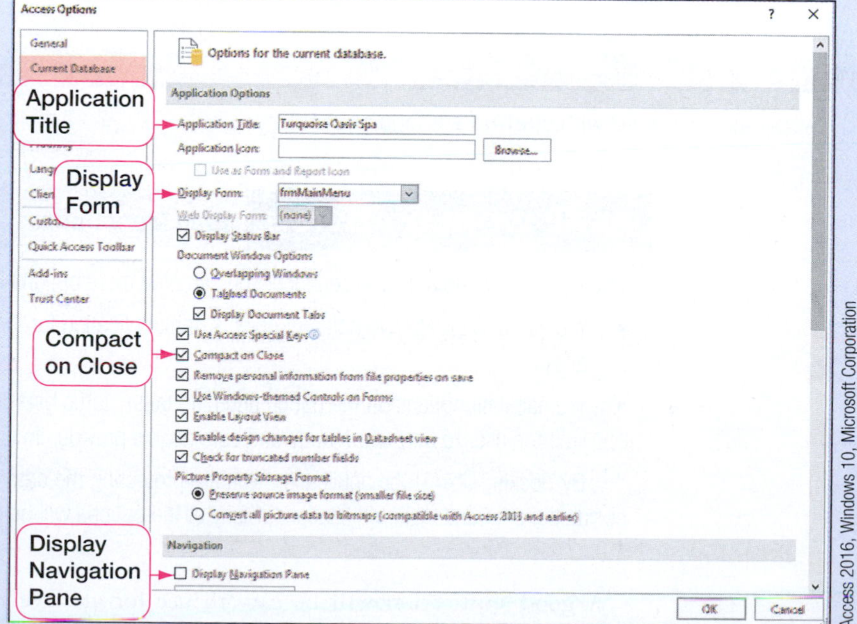

Figure 16 Access Options window

e. Click **OK** to close the Access Options window.

f. Click **OK** when the message **You must close and reopen the current database for the specified option to take effect** is displayed.

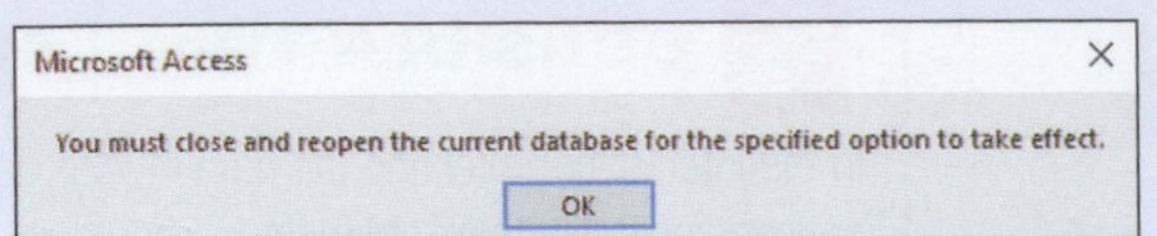

Figure 17 Message displayed after start-up changes have been made

Access 2016, Windows 10, Microsoft Corporation

g. **Close** [X] the database, and reopen the **a06ch11SpaApplication** database.
When the database reopens, frmMainMenu should open automatically. Also notice that the name of the application, not the database, is on the title bar.

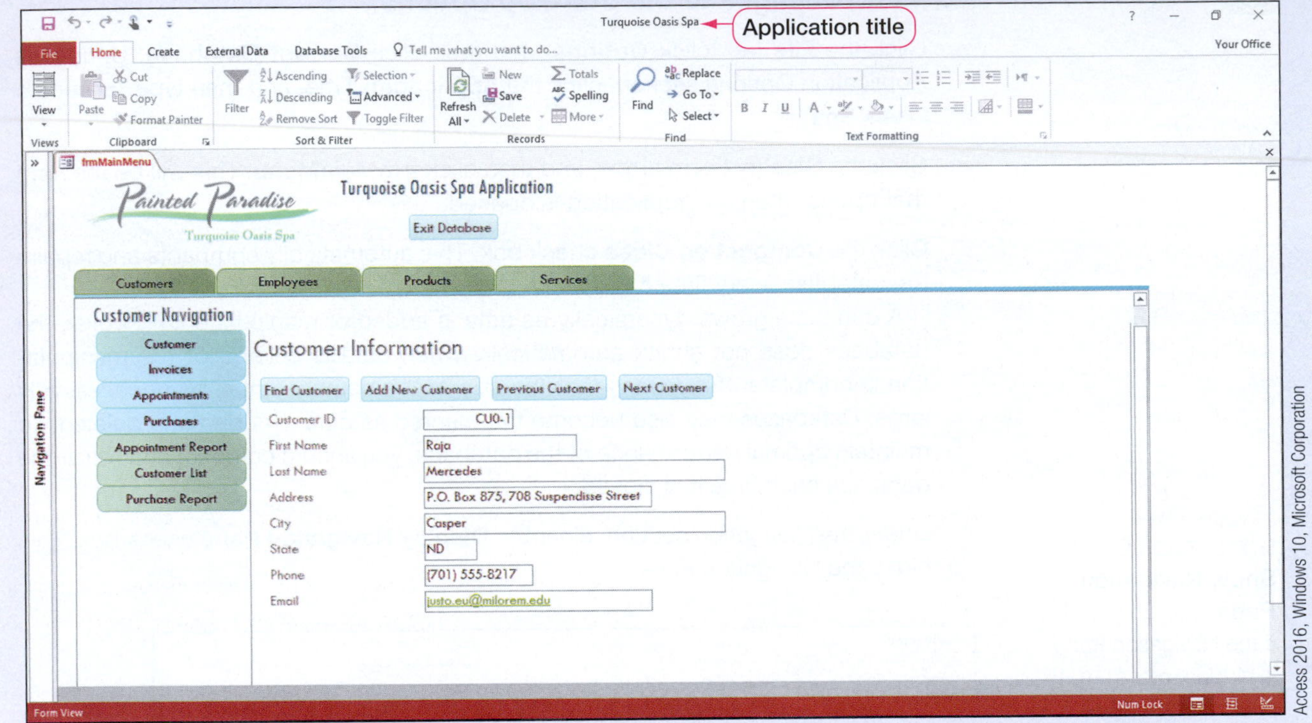

Access 2016, Windows 10, Microsoft Corporation

Figure 18 Application opened with start-up settings applied

REAL WORLD ADVICE Even More Options

To create a more fluid user experience, you can hide more options in the start-up form.

- You can also create two different objects: the application for the user and the database for the designer.
- You can limit options on the ribbon and hide tabs, status bars, and shortcut menus. This would limit the user to only commands and buttons you provide, limiting the accessibility of the data.

By "locking down" the application, you are protecting the data and database structure from accidental or intentional modifications. Many of the options will be presented in Chapter 14.

A good application will be easy to use for all levels of Access users, not just the designer. Before your application is released to all users, the best practice is for it to undergo usability testing. **Usability testing** consists of testing an application with a user before releasing an application for wider use.

The goal of usability testing is to observe people using the application to discover what errors they may make with it and to identify areas that require modification. The four areas of usability testing are as follows.

- **Performance** — How much time and how many steps are required to complete a task?

- **Accuracy** — How many mistakes did the user make?
- **Recall** — How much did the user remember after a period of nonuse?
- **Emotional response** — How did the user feel about the tasks completed?

Usability testing requires observing a user under controlled circumstances to determine how he or she will use the application for its intended purpose. It has nothing to do with the user's opinion of the application, only how he or she interacts with it.

For successful usability testing, a realistic scenario should be set up in which the user is given a list of tasks to perform in the application. In the spa example, this could include entering a new customer, changing an existing appointment, and printing a report. While the user is performing these tasks, an observer is watching and taking notes but not interacting with the user. The user should be allowed to make mistakes, which are noted by the observer. These mistakes will allow the designer to see what modifications may need to be made to the application.

CHAPTER 11

CONSIDER THIS | **Finding a Tester**

All applications should be tested before they are given to the final user. If you are the only person available, you should at least run through the application as if you were a user. Unfortunately, you understand how the application should work and might not be able to be objective. What are some options for you to find a tester of your application? Could you ask a coworker, family member, or roommate?

Viewing the User Interface as a User

If you cannot test the user interface with an actual person, then you can at least view the user interface as a user rather than the developer. This will give you a better idea of what the user will see and whether modifications are required. In this exercise, you will follow a portion of a previously developed plan to test the user interface as a user rather than the developer.

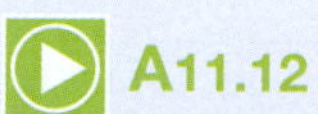

To View the User Interface as a User

a. Make sure that frmMainMenu is opened in Form view.

b. Using Table 1, begin to test the application as a user. As you complete a task, fill in the Action Taken section and the Comments section of the table. This is what the developer will use to make any modifications to the application if necessary.

Task	Action Taken	Comments
Enter a new customer		
Enter a new customer invoice		
Enter a new product		
Print the product list report		
Exit the database		

Table 1 Task list

c. In addition to the above steps, click each **tab** to launch the form or report. Only one form or report should open at a time, and it should be the one labeled on the tab.

d. **Close** ☒ the database, exit Access, and then submit your file as directed by your instructor.

Concept Check

1. To what elements should a database user have access? Why should a database user not have access to the entire database? p. 591
2. What is a navigation form? How is it different from the Navigation Pane? p. 593
3. What is the difference between navigation forms and tab controls? When would you use each? p. 598
4. What are some important considerations in constructing a user interface for your database? p. 598
5. What are some benefits of using command buttons on a form? p. 603
6. What is the difference between an Access application and a database? What is usability testing, and why is it important? p. 608

Key Terms

Application 600
Navigation control bar 593
Navigation form 591
Start-up form 608
Subform control 593
Usability testing 610
User interface 591

Visual Summary

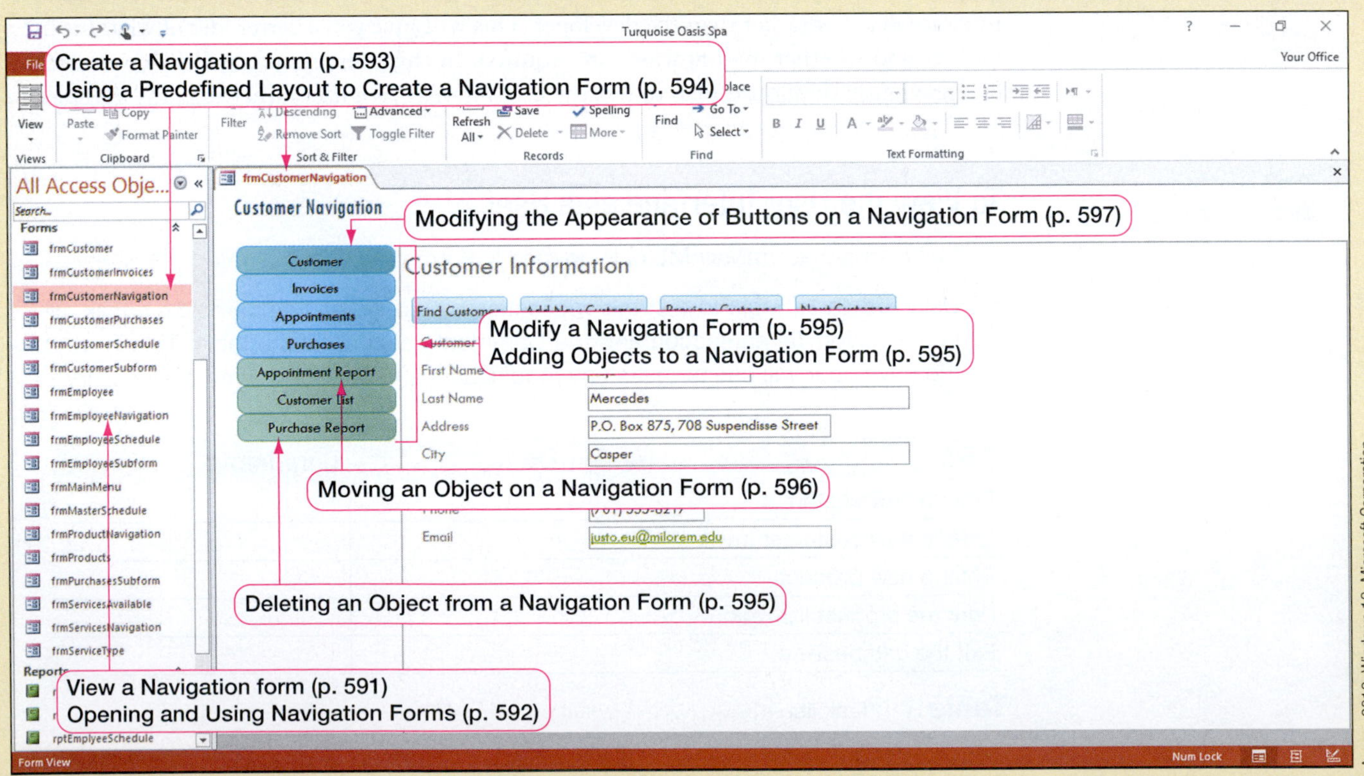

Figure 19

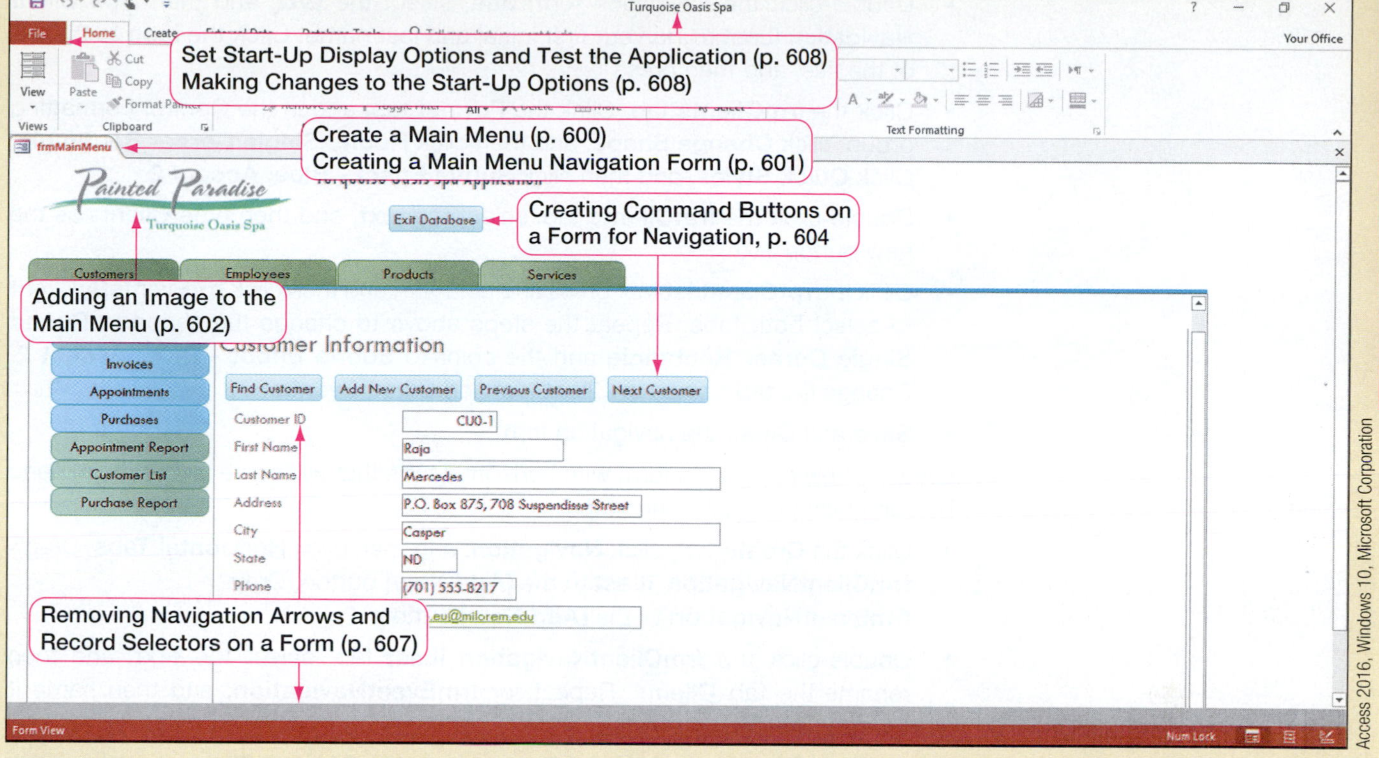

Figure 20

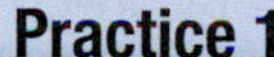

Practice 1

Student data files needed:

a06ch11Events.accdb

a06ch11EventPlanningLogo.jpg

You will save your file as:

a06ch11Events_LastFirst.accdb

Event Planning

Production & Operations

You have been asked to create an application for the Event Planning database. The application needs to include a main navigation form built from individual navigation forms. It will also need command buttons on various forms to increase the ease of use of the database. Finally, the start-up options need to be configured to open the application and the new navigation form.

a. Open the Access database **a06ch11Events**. Save your file as a06ch11Events_LastFirst using your last and first name. If necessary, enable the content.

b. Create a navigation form with horizontal tabs to provide easy access to all the client forms and reports by completing the following steps.

- Click the **Create** tab, and in the Forms group, click **Navigation**, and then click **Horizontal Tabs**. Drag **frmClients** from the Navigation Pane to the **[Add New]** button on the navigation form. Continue by adding **rptEventsByClient** and **rptClientList** to the **[Add New]** button on the navigation form.
- On the Design tab, click the **View** arrow, and then click **Layout View**. Save the form as frmClientNavigation_iLast using your first initial and last name.
- On the Design tab, click **Themes**, and then click **Integral**.
- Click the **rptClientList** tab, and then drag the tab to the left of the **rptEventsByClient** tab.

- Double-click the navigation form **title**, select the **text**, and then type Client Navigation iLast using your first initial and last name. Click the **icon** to the left of the title, and then press Delete.
- Click the **frmClients** tab. Click the **Format** tab, and in the Control Formatting group, click **Change Shape**, and then click **Round Single Corner Rectangle**. Click **Quick Styles**, and then click **Subtle Effect - Blue, Accent 2**.
- Double-click the **frmClients** tab, select the **text**, and then type Clients as the new button text.
- Click the **rptClientList** tab, press and hold Shift, and then click **rptEventsByClient** to select both tabs. Repeat the steps above to change the shape to **Round Single Corner Rectangle** and the color to **Subtle Effect - Blue, Accent 2**. Change the tab names to Client List and Client Events.
- **Save** and **Close** the navigation form.

c. Create a new navigation form with horizontal tabs that will serve as the main menu by completing the following steps.
  - Click the **Create** tab, click **Navigation**, and then click **Horizontal Tabs**. Drag **frmClientNavigation_iLast** to the **[Add New]** button. Drag **frmEventNavigation** to the **[Add New]** button.
  - Double-click the **frmClientNavigation_iLast** tab, select the **text**, and then rename the tab Clients. Repeat for **frmEventNavigation**, and then name it Events.
  - Click the **Clients** tab. Click the **Format** tab, click **Change Shape**, and then click **Snip Single Corner Rectangle**. Click **Quick Styles**, and then click **Intense Effect - Turquoise, Accent 1**. Repeat for the Events tab.
  - Double-click the **navigation form** title, select the **text**, and then type Event Planning Application.

d. Click the **icon** to the left of the title, and then click the **Form Layout Tools Design** tab, click **Insert Image**. Click **Browse**, navigate through the folder structure to the location of your student data files, and then double-click **a06ch11EventPlanningLogo**.

e. On the Design tab, click **Property Sheet**. In the Property Sheet pane, click the **Format** tab. Click the **Size Mode** arrow, and then click **Zoom**. Type 3 for the **Width**, and then type 0.8 for the **Height** of the image.

f. Click the **Selection type** arrow, and then click **FormHeader**. On the Format tab, click the **Back Color** box. Click the **Build button**, and then select **White, Background 1**, the first row in the first column under Theme Colors.

g. **Save** the form as frmEventsMainMenu_iLast using your first initial and last name, and then **Close** the form.

h. In the Navigation Pane, double-click **frmClients** to open the form. On the Home tab, in the Views group, click the **View** arrow, and then click **Design View**. Press Ctrl + A to select all form controls. Press and hold Shift and then click the form title to deselect it. Drag all **controls** in the form detail section down to the **.5"** mark on the vertical ruler.

i. On the Design tab, in the Controls group, click the **Button** form control, and then click in the **top left corner** of the form detail section to add the button.

j. On the Categories list, verify that **Record Navigation** is selected. On the Actions list, click **Find Record**, and then click **Next**. Click **Text**, select the text, type Find Client, and then click **Next**. Name the button cmdFindClient, and then click **Finish**.

k. In the Controls group, click the **Button** form control, and then click next to the first button. On the Categories list, click **Record Operations**. On the Actions list, click

Add New Record, and then click Next. Click Text, select the text, type Add New Client, and then click Next. Name the button cmdAddNewClient, and then click Finish.

l. Repeat to add two more buttons: Next Client and Previous Client. Click the **Record Navigation** category and **Go To Next Record** action; the text should say Next Client, and the button should be named cmdNextClient. Click the **Record Navigation** category and **Go To Previous Record** action; the text should say Previous Client, and the button should be named cmdPreviousClient.

m. Click the **first button** to select it. Press and hold Shift, and then click to select the remaining **three buttons**. Click the **Arrange** tab, click **Align**, and then click **Top**. Click **Size/Space**, and then click **Equal Horizontal**.

n. **Save** and **Close** the form.

o. Complete the following steps to add a command button to frmEventsMainMenu_iLast that will exit Access when clicked.
   - Double-click **frmEventsMainMenu_iLast** in the Navigation Pane.
   - Switch to **Design** view. On the Design tab, in the Controls group, click the **Button** form control, and then click under the text **Event Planning Application** in the **form header**.
   - On the Categories list, click **Application**. On the Actions list, click **Quit Application**.
   - Click **Next**, click **Text**, select the **text**, and then type Exit Database. Click **Next**. Name the button cmdExitDatabase, and then click **Finish**. Switch to **Form** view.
   - **Save** the navigation form.
   - Click **Exit Database** to check that the button does exit Access.

p. Open **a06ch11Events_LastFirst**. In the Navigation Pane, double-click **frmClients** to open the form. Switch to **Layout** view, and then click **Property Sheet**. Under Selection type, click the **selection** arrow, and then click **Form**.

q. Click the **Format** tab in the Property Sheet pane. Click the **Record Selectors** arrow, and then select **No**. Click the **Navigation Buttons** arrow, and then select **No**.

r. **Close** the Property Sheet pane, **Save** and **Close** the form.

s. Complete the following steps to modify the start-up options for the database.
   - Click the **File** tab, click **Options**, and then click **Current Database**.
   - Under the Application Options section, click the **Application Title** text box, and then type Events Database.
   - Click the **Display Form** arrow, and then select **frmEventsMainMenu_iLast**.
   - Click the **Compact on Close** check box.
   - In the Navigation section, click **Display Navigation Pane** to deselect the option.
   - Click **OK** to close the Access Options window, click **OK** again.

t. **Close** the database, exit Access, and then submit your file as directed by your instructor.

Problem Solve 1

Student data files needed:

 a06ch11ProShop.accdb

a06ch11ProShopLogo.jpg

You will save your file as:

 a06ch11ProShop_LastFirst.accdb

Navigation Forms in the Red Bluff Golf Course & Pro Shop Database

Production & Operations

The Red Bluff Golf Course & Pro Shop database is in need of some usability enhancements. You have been asked to create some navigation forms that will improve the usability of the database and make it easier for all sales to be recorded accurately and efficiently.

a. Open Access database **a06ch11ProShop**. Save your file as a06ch11ProShop_LastFirst using your last and first name. If necessary, enable the content.

b. Remove the navigation buttons and record selectors from **frmCustomers**, **frmProducts**, **frmSalesReps**, and **frmTransactions**.

c. Create a command button on each of the forms that will add a new record from Record Operations. Place the button just below the Previous Record and Next Record buttons and centered with the Find button. Reference the following table for naming purposes.

Form Name	Text Label	Button Name
frmCustomers	Add New Customer	cmdAddNewCustomer
frmProducts	Add New Product	cmdAddNewProduct
frmSalesRep	Add New Rep	cmdAddNewRep
frmTransactions	Add New Transaction	cmdAddNewTransaction

d. Save the changes, and close the forms. Create a navigation form with Vertical Tabs, Left and make the following changes.
   - Add **frmSalesReps**, **frmProducts**, **frmCustomers**, and **frmTransactions** to the navigation control bar.
   - Rename the tabs to be Sales Reps, Products, Customers, and Transactions.
   - Change the shape of the tabs to **Round Single Corner Rectangle**, and apply the **Colored Outline – Gray-50%, Accent 1** Quick Style to the navigation buttons.
   - Replace the icon from the form header with the a06ch11ProShopLogo image. Change the Size Mode property to **Zoom**, modify the Width property to 3, and modify the Height property to 0.8. Change the Back Color of the form header to **White, Background 1**.
   - Change the title to Red Bluff Golf Course & Pro Shop.
   - Add a command button under the form title in the form header that, when clicked, closes the database. The text label should be Exit Database, and the button name should be cmdExitDatabase.

e. Save the navigation form as frmRedBluffMainMenu.

f. Make the following modification to the Current Database settings.
   - Change the Application Title to Red Bluff Golf Course & Pro Shop Database.
   - Make the database display the **frmRedBluffMainMenu** when opened.
   - Hide the Navigation Pane.

g. Save the database, exit Access, and then submit your file as directed by your instructor.

Perform 1: Perform in Your Life

Student data file needed:

 a06ch11TabletRentals.accdb

You will save your file as:

 a06ch11TabletRentals_LastFirst.accdb

Tablet Rental Database Application

Your college business club has received a grant to test a new version of electronic textbooks. As part of the grant, several tablet computers have been purchased that come preloaded with the new electronic textbooks. These tablets are to be loaned to business students to allow them to test the devices and the use of the electronic textbooks. As part of the grant, you have been asked to enhance the database that tracks each device, the textbooks loaded onto the devices, and who has been given a device on loan. You will enhance the database by adding navigation forms, using command buttons for easier record navigation, and performing a usability test.

a. Open the Access database **a06ch11TabletRentals**. Save your file as a06ch11TabletRentals_LastFirst using your last and first name. If necessary, enable the content.

b. Create a navigation form to increase the usability of the database.
   - Add tabs for the frmEText, frmStudents, and frmTablet forms. Select a shape and a style for these tabs. Change the names of the tabs to ETexts, Students, and Tablets.
   - Add tabs for the rptBookPairings and rptTabletAssignments reports. Select a shape and a style for the tab that differentiate these two tabs from the ones you used for the forms. Change the name of the tabs to Book Pairings and Tablet Assignments.
   - Add an image to the navigation form in place of the default image inserted by Access. This could be your school's official logo or an image of your choosing. Change the title of the navigation form to Tablet Assignment Database. Save the form as frmTabletNavigation_iLast using your first initial and last name.
   - Add a command button to the navigation form that exits the database.

c. Change the appropriate setting such that the new navigation form is shown by default and the Navigation Pane is hidden.

d. Modify the frmEText, frmStudents, and frmTablet forms to make common tasks for the users more intuitive.
   - On the frmEText form, add four buttons: one to move to the next EText, one to move to the previous EText, one to find an EText, and one to add an EText.
   - On the frmStudents form, add four buttons: one to move to the next student, one to move to the previous student, one to find a student, and one to add a student.
   - On the frmTablet form, add four buttons: one to move to the next Tablet, one to move to the previous Tablet, one to find a Tablet, and one to add a Tablet.
   - Remove the record selectors and navigation buttons from the frmEText, frmStudents, and frmTablet forms.
   - Use Tablet Assignments as the title for the database, and then change the appropriate setting such that the database compacts and repairs on close.

e. Perform usability testing on each of the forms individually and on the navigation form. Use the following table to track your comments.

Task	Action(s) Taken	Comments
Enter a new tablet computer		
Navigate through the tablet computer records		
Enter new student information		
Navigate through the student computer records		
Enter new EText information		
Navigate through the EText computer records		
Pair an EText with a tablet		
Assign a tablet to a new student		
Print the Book Pairings report		
Print the Tablet Assignments report		
Exit the database		

f. Close the database, exit Access, and then submit your file as directed by your instructor.

Additional Cases

Additional Workshop Cases are available on the companion website and in the instructor resources.

Microsoft Access 2016

Chapter 12 | CREATE A REFINED USER EXPERIENCE WITH MACROS

OBJECTIVES

1. Modify database settings for protection from macro viruses p. 620
2. Understand the Macro Designer p. 623
3. Understand how to test and troubleshoot macros p. 627
4. Improve database design and function by automating manual processes p. 630
5. Reduce processing time by combining routine tasks p. 633
6. Create macro groups p. 637
7. Create macros that run when the database opens p. 640
8. Improve the functionality of forms and reports p. 644
9. Implement complex business rules with data macros p. 649

Prepare Case

Sales & Marketing

Production & Operations

The Turquoise Oasis Spa Database: Automating Tasks and Increasing Functionality

Employees of the Turquoise Oasis Spa use the company database to store employee and customer information, record transactions, track inventory, schedule spa services, produce reports, and so on. The spa is continuing to experience growth as it offers new products and services, catering to more and more clients. Meda Rodate, the spa manager, has realized that the current database no longer meets the needs of the business. She has asked you to automate some routine tasks to increase the efficiency of the database and create additional functionality to improve the overall usability of the database.

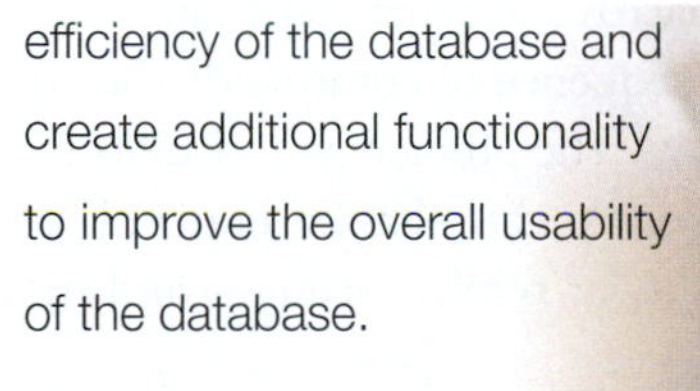

Anna Omelchenko/Shutterstock

Student data files needed for this chapter:

 a06ch12SpaApplication.accdb

 a06ch12SpaProducts.xlsx

You will save your files as:

 a06ch12SpaApplication_LastFirst.accdb

 a06ch12rptScheduleByCustomer_LastFirst.pdf

 a06ch12rptLowInventory_LastFirst.xlsx

Understanding the Purpose of Macros

A well-designed database application takes into consideration efficiency and usability, among other things. Macros can help to improve both the efficiency and the usability of a database. **Macros** are database objects that provide a method of automating routine database tasks. They can add functionality to reports and form, as well as the controls that forms and reports contain. **Arguments** are values that provide information about the action being carried out by the macro.

There are three different kinds of macros in Microsoft Access: stand-alone, embedded, and data macros. **Stand-alone macros** are separate database objects that are displayed in the Navigation Pane. Stand-alone macros can be executed directly in the Navigation Pane by double-clicking the macro object, by clicking Run in Design view, or by attaching the macro to a database object, like a button or text field. **Embedded macros** are stored as part of a database object such as a form or report or any control such as a button. Embedded macros are not displayed in the Navigation Pane and are executed only when the objects in which they are embedded trigger events. **Data macros** are stored in Access tables and are triggered by table events. Data macros are typically used to implement business logic in tables and to automatically set values in fields. In this section, you will learn the purpose of macros as well as how to build, edit, and troubleshoot them.

Modify Database Settings for Protection from Macro Viruses

Turquoise Oasis Spa collects and stores personal information about its clients in the database, such as addresses, phone numbers, and credit card information. Ensuring that this personal information is kept safe and secure is very important to the company. Before the explanation of how to create macros in the database, it is important to discuss some of the security risks associated with macros and what steps can be taken to mitigate those risks.

A macro is a sequence of commands that run automatically, and as mentioned above, macros can improve the efficiency and usability of a database. However, the sequence of commands in a macro can also be harmful when executed. Harmful macros have been known to add, edit, or remove data — and may spread to other databases or even to the user's computer.

Open the Starting File

The Turquoise Oasis Spa database already contains two stand-alone macros. In this exercise, you will open the Spa database and review the security warnings provided by Access.

A12.00

To Open the Starting File

a. Start **Access**, click **Open Other Files** in the left pane, and then double-click **This PC**. Navigate through the folder structure to the location of your student data files, and then double-click **a06ch12SpaApplication**. A database opens displaying tables, forms, and reports related to the spa, the services it provides, and various transactions.

b. Click the **File** tab, save the file as an **Access Database**, and click **Save As**. Navigate to the location where you are saving your project files, and then change the filename to a06ch12SpaApplication_LastFirst using your last and first name. Click **Save**. If necessary, enable the content.

Creating a Trusted Location

When it comes to macros in Microsoft Office documents, there are four security options from which to choose: disable all macros without notification, disable all macros with notification, disable all macros except digitally signed macros, and enable all macros. Enabling all macros is not recommended because macros may contain potentially dangerous code.

To ensure the security of the computers and data collected at Painted Paradise, all macros have been disabled with notification by default. This means that any macro that exists in a Microsoft Office document cannot be run unless the user explicitly enables that content. The Turquoise Oasis Spa database is located in a specific location on the Painted Paradise network. This location can be designated as a trusted location. A **trusted location** is typically a folder on your hard drive or a network share where trusted files are located. External documents that could potentially contain harmful macros should not be put into a trusted location. Such files should be placed in another location until they can be scanned or otherwise verified to be safe. Any file that you put in a trusted location can be opened without being checked by the Trust Center security feature, making it easier for the end user to reap the benefits of macros. An alternative option to creating a trusted location is to modify the macro settings to enable all macros. However, for a variety of security reasons, this is not recommended in most situations.

In this exercise, you will designate a folder and its subfolders on your computer as a trusted location.

A12.01

SIDE NOTE
Pin the Ribbon
If your ribbon is collapsed, pin your ribbon open. Click the Home tab. In the lower right-hand corner of the ribbon, click Pin the Ribbon [pin icon].

To Create a Trusted Location

a. Click the **File** tab, and then click **Options**.

b. Click **Trust Center** on the left, and then click **Trust Center Settings**.

c. Click **Trusted Locations** on the left side of the Trust Center dialog box, and then, in the bottom-right corner, click **Add new location**.

d. Click **Browse**, navigate through the folder structure to the location where you are saving your files, and then click **OK**.

e. Click the **Subfolders of this location are also trusted** check box to ensure that all databases in the directory are trusted.

f. Click **OK** to close the Trusted Location dialog box, click **OK**, and then click **OK** to close the Access Options dialog box.

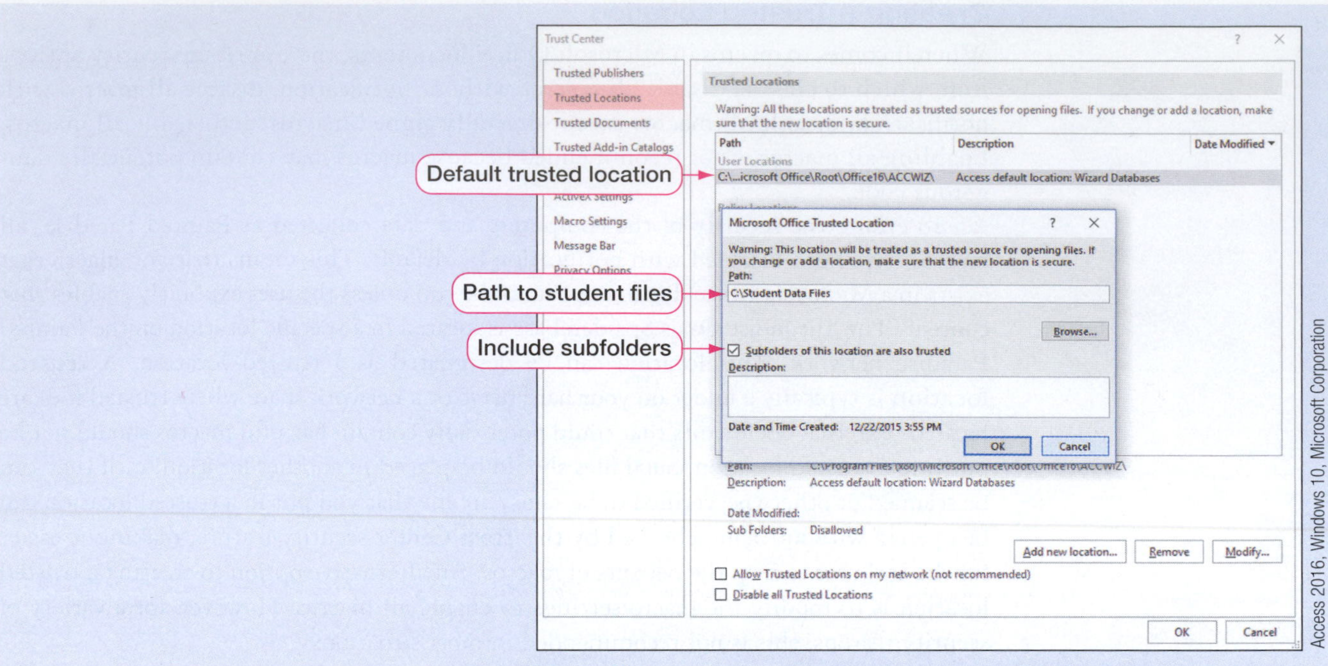

Figure 1 Trusted Locations dialog box

QUICK REFERENCE — Macro Settings

Macro settings are part of the Trust Center settings and can be modified on the basis of the needs of the organization. Below are the setting options and their descriptions.

Setting	Description
Disable all macros without notification	All macros and security alerts about macros are disabled.
Disable all macros with notification	This is the default setting. It disables all macros and provides security alerts if there are macros present.
Disable all macros except digitally signed macros	This setting is the same as the Disable all macros with notification option except that digitally signed macros will be enabled by default.
Enable all macros	Allows all macros to run. This setting makes your computer vulnerable to potentially malicious code and is not recommended.

REAL WORLD ADVICE — Selecting the Appropriate Macro Setting

If the database is in a location defined as a trusted location, the macros in the database will be ignored by the Trust Center security system. Depending on the nature of the organization, the policy may be to disable all macros. However, the most common settings are Disable all macros with notification and Disable all macros except digitally signed macros. Both of these settings help to mitigate the risk of a macro virus and still allow useful macros to run without establishing a trusted location.

Understand the Macro Designer

The **Macro Designer** is an interface for building and editing macros. This interface makes it easy to build robust database applications, increase the productivity of business users, and reduce code errors. It also has the ability to troubleshoot and run macros directly from the interface.

Open and View the Macro Designer

The management of Turquoise Oasis Spa has asked you to improve the usability and efficiency of the database by creating macros. To create macros, you must use the Macro Designer. In this exercise, you will familiarize yourself with the Macro Designer and all of its components.

A12.02

To Open and View the Macro Designer

a. Scroll down to the bottom of the Navigation Pane.

b. Right-click **mcrSampleMacro**, and then click **Design View**.

This mcrSampleMacro is a simple macro consisting of two actions. When executed, the macro will perform the OpenReport action, opening the rptEmployeeList report, and then it will send the report to the printer using the RunMenuCommand action.

> **Troubleshooting**
>
> Double-clicking an object in the Navigation Pane normally opens that object. Macros are different, however. Double-clicking a macro in the Navigation Pane will run the macro instead of opening it.

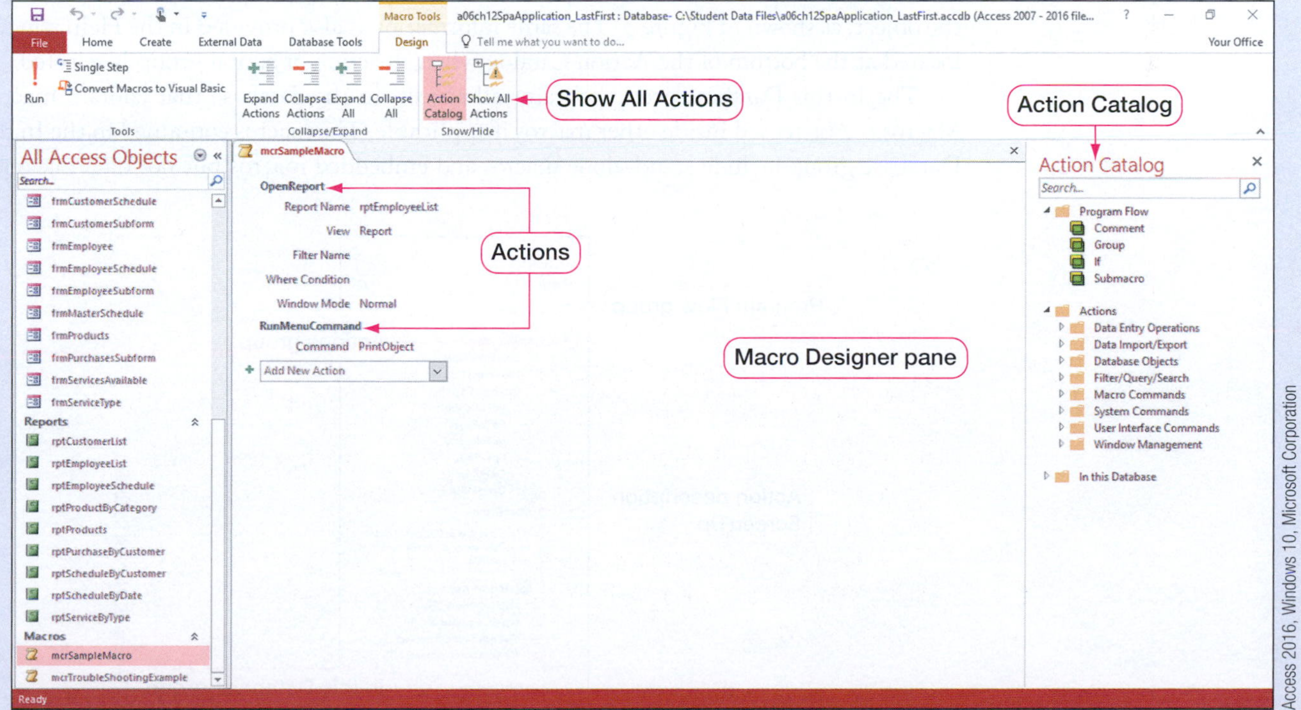

Figure 2 Macro Designer

As shown in Figure 2, the Macro Designer pane consists of all the actions and logic that make up the macro. An **action** is a self-contained instruction that can be combined with other instructions to automate tasks and is considered to be the basic building block of a macro. Actions can be added to the macro by simply selecting one from the Add New Action list or by searching the Action Catalog to the right of the Macro Designer pane. The **Action Catalog** is a searchable set of macro actions that can retrieve actions on the basis of keywords. The Action Catalog consists of three different groups: Program Flow, Actions, and In this Database.

The Program Flow group contains a list of blocks that can control the order in which actions are executed or help to structure the macro, as shown in Table 1.

Block Name	Purpose
Comment	A form of internal documentation that can help explain the purpose of the macro
Group	Allows for actions and program flow to be part of a named group to better organize the view of the macro in the Macro Designer. The group can be collapsed, expanded, and moved together.
If	Implements logic into a macro that will execute actions based on whether or not a condition is true. Program flow can be used to incorporate complex business rules into the database.
Submacro	Allows for a named collection of actions to be grouped together. Submacros can be incorporated into other macros by using the RunMacro or OnError actions, but they cannot be executed directly from the Navigation Pane.

Table 1 List of Program Flow Blocks

The Actions group contains several different categories of actions grouped together according to purpose and function that can be used to build a macro. As you point to each action group and action, Access displays a ScreenTip that explains the general purpose of the object, as shown in Figure 3. The same information is also provided in the Help window located at the bottom of the Action Catalog when an action or action group is selected.

The In this Database group contains all objects in the database that contain macros. Macros can be reused inside other macros if applicable. The macros contained in the In this Database group include stand-alone macros and embedded macros but not data macros.

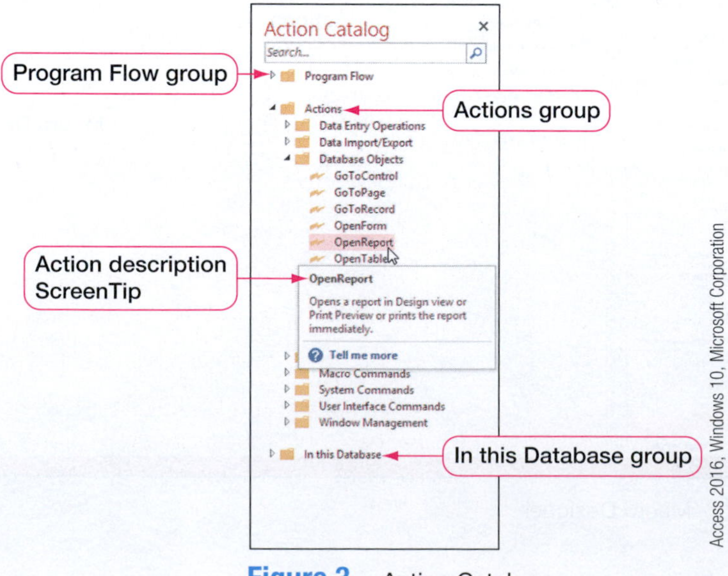

Figure 3 Action Catalog

Editing a Macro

Even a simple macro such as mcrSampleMacro can be improved to create a better user experience. In this exercise, you will improve the macro by adding a comment that explains the purpose of the macro and an additional action that displays a message box informing the user that the report is being sent to the printer.

A12.03

To Edit a Macro

SIDE NOTE

Alternate Method

Alternatively, you could search for the MessageBox macro in the Action Catalog and either double-click the action or drag it to the macro.

a. In the Action Catalog, in the Program Flow group, drag **Comment** to the top of the Macro Designer pane, above the OpenReport macro action.

Troubleshooting

If the Action Catalog is not visible on the right, you can toggle between showing and hiding it by clicking the Action Catalog button in the Show/Hide group located on the right of the Design tab.

b. In the comment field, type This macro opens the Employee List Report and sends it to the printer.

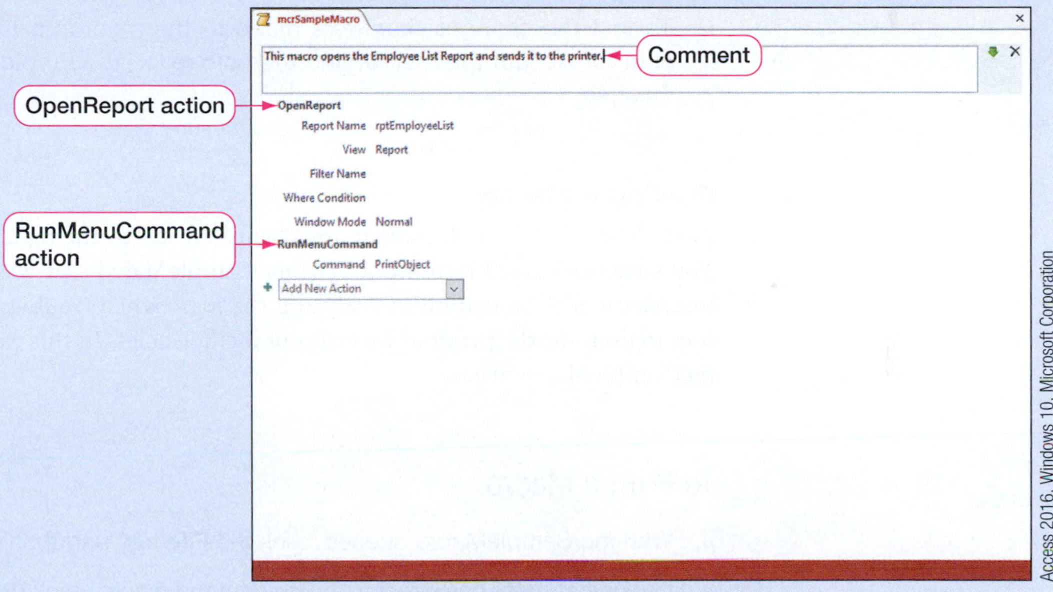

Figure 4 Comment added to mcrSampleMacro

c. On the Add New Action box, click the **arrow**, and then select **MessageBox** from the list of actions.

SIDE NOTE

Moving Actions in a Macro

Actions can also be moved around by dragging them to the desired location.

d. In the Message argument, type The report is now being sent to the printer.

e. Verify that **Yes** is selected as the value for the Beep argument. Click the **Type** arrow, and then select **Information**.

f. In the Title of the message argument, type Printing Report.

g. At the far right of the MessageBox, click the **Move up** arrow to move the action above the RunMenuCommand action. This will cause the message box to be displayed before the report is sent to the printer.

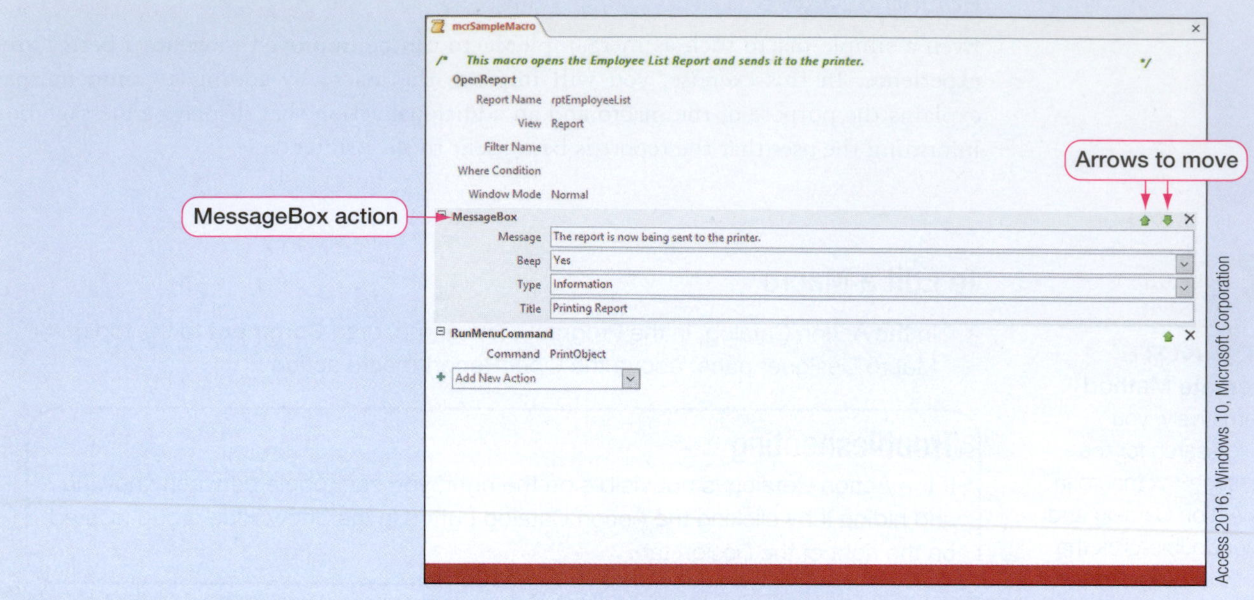

Figure 5 mcrSampleMacro edited

h. **Save** [Save icon] the macro.

i. To test the changes that were made to the macro, in the Tools group, click **Run** to execute the macro, and then **close** [X] the Employee List report when finished.

Printing a Macro

Meda Rodate likes to document any changes made to the databases in case of an audit. You have been asked to print out the mcrSampleMacro that was just modified. Printing macros can also be helpful in analyzing the logic when troubleshooting by allowing the user to examine the printout for errors or inefficiencies. In this exercise, you will print the mcrSampleMacro macro.

A12.04

To Print a Macro

a. With mcrSampleMacro opened, click the **File** tab, and then click **Print**.

b. If your instructor has directed you to print the macro, click **Print**. In the Print Macro Definition dialog box, select the options to print the **Properties**, **Actions and Arguments**, and **Permissions by User and Group** if necessary, and then click **OK**. If you are not printing the macro, click **Cancel**.

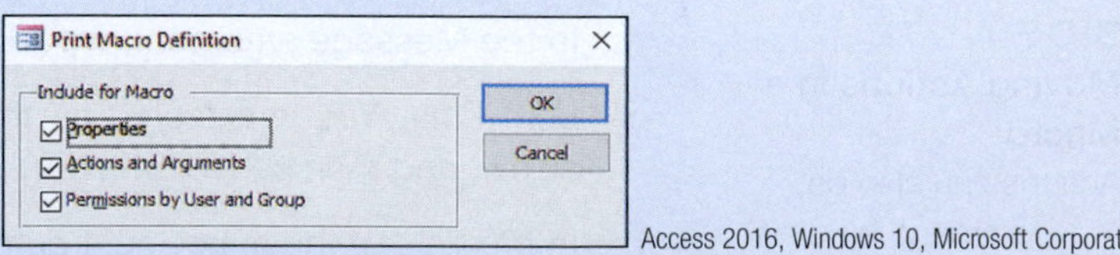

Figure 6 Print Macro Definition dialog box

c. **Close** [X] the macro.

In addition to the actions and arguments that make up mcrSampleMacro, the printout includes the database name, directory path, date, and additional information about the properties of the macro.

REAL WORLD ADVICE | **Sharing and Backing Up Macros**

Both the number and complexity of macros can grow over time as the business grows and its needs change. Access allows macros to be copied from the Macro Designer and pasted into a text editor as XML. The XML then can be copied easily from the text editor and pasted directly into the Macro Designer. To copy the macro quickly, with the macro opened in Design view, press Ctrl and type A to select all of the macro actions, and then press Ctrl and type C to copy the action. Pasting the macro into a text editor allows for easy sharing of the macro. It is also a quick method of creating backups.

Understand How to Test and Troubleshoot Macros

Macros can become very complex with multiple steps and logic built in. It is very important to test macros thoroughly to ensure that they function as intended. It is also important to test macros to ensure that they do not result in errors. These errors can create problems within your database and cause users to have concerns about seeing an unexpected error message.

Figuring out which actions are causing the macro to result in an error can be a tedious task. The **Single Step** feature is located next to the Run button on the Design tab in the Tools group; it allows you to observe the flow of a macro and the results of each action, isolating any action that causes an error or produces unwanted results.

When the Single Step feature is turned on, the macro executes one action at a time and pauses between actions. After each action, the Macro Single Step dialog box appears, showing the name of the macro, the value of any conditions, the name of the action about to be executed, and the arguments for the action. In addition to this information, the dialog box provides three choices on what to do next.

- Step executes the action shown in the dialog box.
- Stop All Macros stops all actions in the macro and closes the dialog box.
- Continue resumes normal operation of the macro and exits the single step process.

Single Stepping Through a Macro

An employee of Turquoise Oasis Spa had attempted to create a macro that would open the frmCustomer form, create a new record, and place the pointer in the first name field. However, the macro is not working properly, and you have been asked to troubleshoot and fix the macro. In this exercise, you will be using the Single Step feature to assist you in the process.

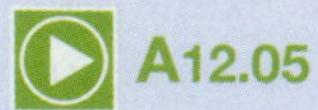

A12.05

To Single Step Through a Macro

SIDE NOTE

Macro Paused with MessageBox Action

The MessageBox action pauses a macro so the message can be displayed. You need to click OK for the macro to continue.

a. In the Navigation Pane, right-click the **mcrTroubleShootingExample** macro, and then click **Design View**.

b. On the Design tab, in the Tools group, click **Single Step**, and then click **Run**.

Notice the Macro Single Step dialog box and all of the information displayed. The macro name is at the top, along with the action name toward the bottom. Just below the action name are the arguments for the action. This is a MessageBox action that displays a message to the user. To the right is an Error Number of 0. This means that no error has been detected with this action.

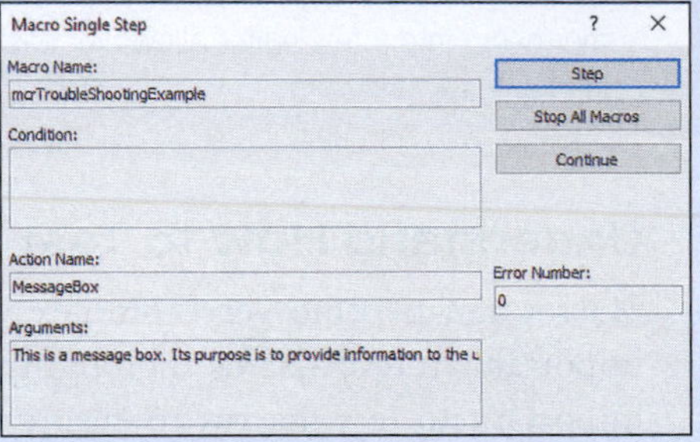

Figure 7 Macro Single Step MessageBox action

Access 2016, Windows 10, Microsoft Corporation

c. Click **Step** to execute the MessageBox action, and then click **OK** to close the message box.

d. The next action is the GoToRecord action with an Error Number: 1, which indicates that there is an error. Click **Step** to execute this action to get additional information.

An information box is displayed with information about the GoToRecord action. The second statement provides some useful information: "The type of object the action applies to isn't currently selected or isn't in the active view."

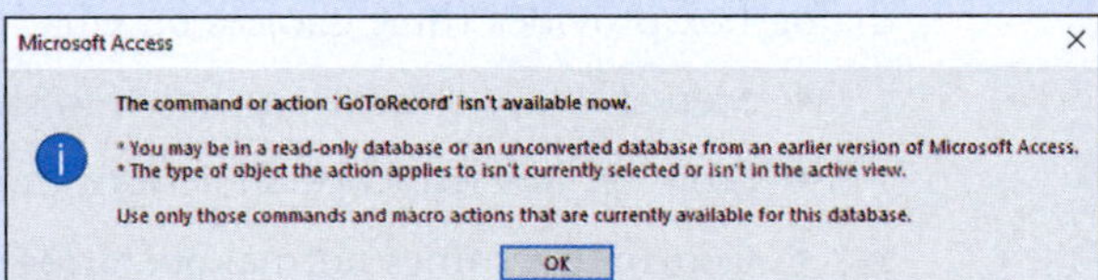

Figure 8 Error message for GoToControl action

Access 2016, Windows 10, Microsoft Corporation

e. Click **OK**. The Macro Single Step dialog box now provides only the option to Stop All Macros so that the GoToRecord action error can be addressed. Click **Stop All Macros**.

Notice the order of the actions in the macro. This macro has been designed to go to a specific record and then to a specific field in that record before the form is even opened. The error message that was displayed indicates that this is the root cause of the macro failure.

CHAPTER 12

f. Place the pointer over the **OpenForm** action, and then click the **Move up** arrow twice in the OpenForm action to move it so it is above the GoToRecord action and below the MessageBox action.

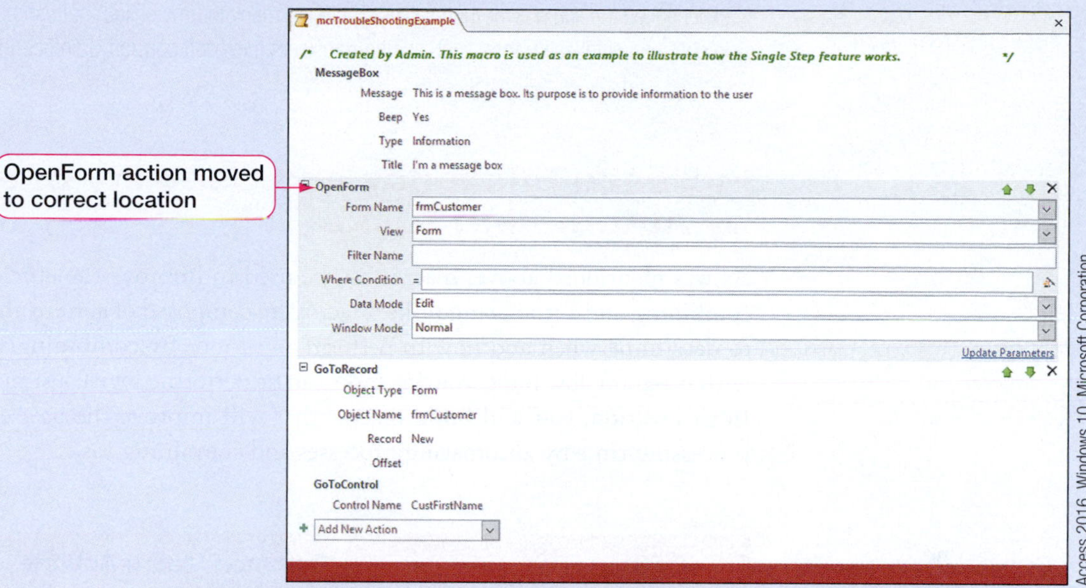

Figure 9 mcrTroubleShootingExample macro corrected

g. **Save** the change, and then go through the single step process again to ensure that there are no additional errors with the macro.

h. Click the **Single Step** button to turn off the Single Step feature. **Close** the frmCustomer form, and then **close** the macro.

i. Double-click the **mcrTroubleShootingExample** macro in the Navigation Pane to run it and ensure that the macro runs as expected.

j. **Close** the frmCustomer form. If you need to take a break before finishing this chapter, now is a good time.

Troubleshooting

If the Single Step feature is on when the macro ends, then it remains on. If you run another macro, it will automatically display the Macro Single Step dialog box again. To turn single stepping off, either click Continue in the dialog box or, on the Design tab in the Tools group, click the Single Step button so it is not highlighted.

REAL WORLD ADVICE Single Stepping Macros

If part of your macro is functioning correctly, then you can begin single stepping at a specific point in the macro. Simply add the Single Step macro action at the point where you wish to begin.

REAL WORLD ADVICE | **Error Codes in Macros**

Error codes provided in the Single Step feature and informational dialog boxes do not always provide enough information to resolve the error. If you receive an error, rest assured that many other people have experienced the same error themselves. There are many forums online that can be used to find solutions to common database errors, such as http://answers.microsoft.com/en-us/office/forum/access.

Increase Efficiency and Usability of a Database by Automating Tasks

As was mentioned above, macros can be used to improve the efficiency of a database by combining and automating tasks. Macros are composed of actions that often contain logic to determine when and how to perform an action. By combining various macro actions with program flow logic, routine tasks can be performed with a simple click of the mouse. In this section, you will build macros that will improve the user experience and reduce processing time by automating processes and combining tasks.

QUICK REFERENCE | **Common Macro Actions**

Action Name	Description
ApplyFilter	Applies a filter to a table, form, or report to restrict or sort the records in the object
AutoExec	An AutoExec macro is a macro that is named AutoExec. It is executed automatically when the database is opened.
Beep	Produces a beep tone through the computer's speakers
CloseWindow	Closes the specified window, or the active window if none is specified
DisplayHour-glassPointer	Provides a visual indication that the macro is running
ExportWithFor-matting	Outputs the data in the specified database object to one of several possible output formats
FindRecord	Finds the first record, or the next record if the action is used again, that meets a speci-fied criteria
GoToControl	Moves the focus to a specified field or control on the active datasheet or form
MessageBox	Displays a message box containing a warning or informational message
OpenForm	Opens a form in a specified view: Design, Form, or Layout
OpenReport	Opens a report in a specified view: Design, Print Preview, or Report
QuitAccess	Exits Microsoft Access
RunMacro	Runs a macro
SelectObject	Selects a specified object so you can run an action that applies to the object

Improve Database Design and Function by Automating Manual Processes

Meda Rodate, the manager of the Turquoise Oasis Spa, frequently requests copies of a report that lists the customers who have scheduled services for a particular date. The current process consists of looking through the report and copying the information for the date requested into a word-processing program before sending it to management.

This process takes too much time and is prone to errors because the information is being copied manually from one location to another. A macro can automate the process and reduce the risk of errors.

Exporting Database Objects Using Macros

In this exercise, you will create a macro that opens the desired report, applies a filter to show only the information for services on a particular date, and exports the report as a PDF-formatted file.

A12.06

To Export Database Objects Using Macros

a. If you took a break, open the **a06ch12SpaApplication** database.

b. Click the **Create** tab, and then, in the Macros & Code group, click **Macro**.

c. In the Action Catalog, under the Program Flow group, double-click **Comment** to add a comment to the macro.

d. In the Comment box, type This macro applies a filter to the customer schedule report and exports the report as a PDF.

SIDE NOTE

Where Conditions and Filters

A parameter query could be created to prompt the user for a service date. The query name could then be entered into the Filter Name field.

Troubleshooting

By default, the Action Catalog and Add New Action combo box show only actions that will execute in nontrusted databases. To see all actions, click Show All Actions in the Show/Hide group on the Design tab.

e. Click the **Add New Action** arrow, and then select **OpenReport** from the list of actions to add the action to the macro.

f. Click the Report Name **arrow**, and select **rptScheduleByCustomer**, and then verify that **Report** is selected as the value for the View argument.

g. In the Where Condition argument, type [DateOfAppt]=[Enter a date of service, Example (5/2/2018)].

This expression uses the field that stores the appointment date and prompts the user for a date to use as a criterion for the filter. The message "Enter a date of service, Example (5/2/2018)" will be displayed in a parameter box when the macro is executed.

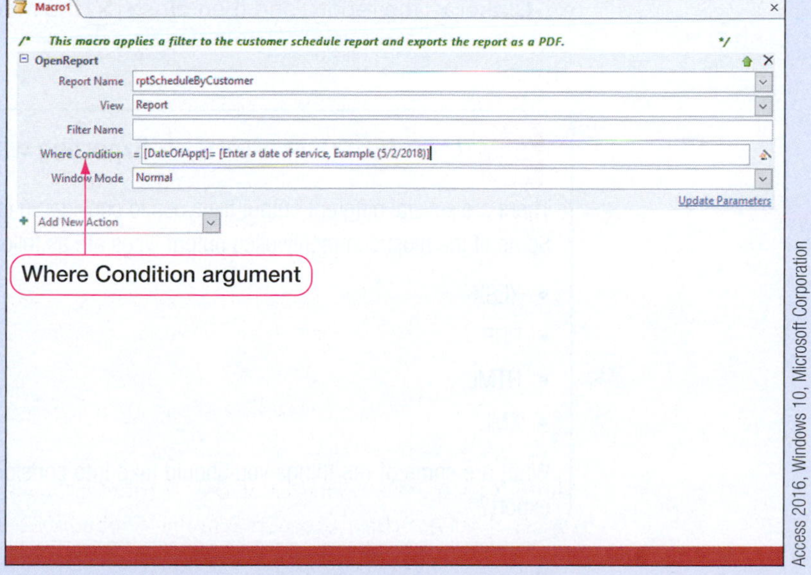

Figure 10 Design view of the macro in progress

> **SIDE NOTE**
> **Output File**
> A specific file name and location can be entered in the Output File box, such as C:\Reports\CustomerSchedule.pdf.

h. Click the **Add New Action** arrow, and then select **ExportWithFormatting** from the list of actions to add the action to the macro.

i. Select **Report** for the Object Type, and then select **rptScheduleByCustomer** for the Object Name.

j. Select **PDF Format (*.pdf)** as the Output Format. Leave the Output File argument blank, and keep all other settings the same.

k. **Save** the macro as mcrCustomerServicesList.

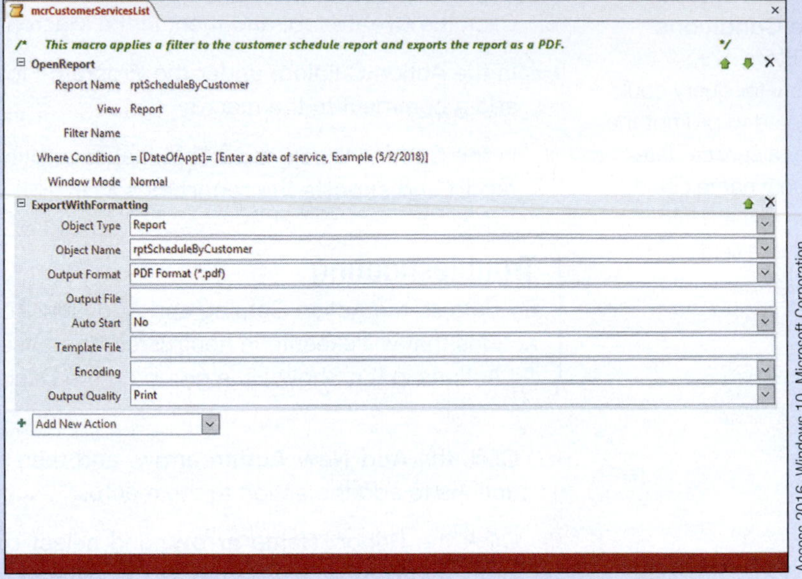

Access 2016, Windows 10, Microsoft Corporation

Figure 11 mcrCustomerServicesList macro completed

l. To test the macro, on the Design tab, in the Tools group, click **Run**. In the Enter Parameter Value dialog box, type 1/19/2018, and then click **OK**.

m. **Save** the report to your student files as a06ch12rptScheduleByCustomer_LastFirst using your last and first name.

n. **Close** the report, and then **close** the macro.

CONSIDER THIS | **Exporting with an Appropriate File Type**

There are several different output file types to consider in exporting database objects using macros. Some of the most commonly used output types are as follows.

- XLSX
- PDF
- HTML
- XML

What are some of the things you should take into consideration when deciding which file type to export?

REAL WORLD ADVICE **Comments Make Macros Easier to Understand and Maintain**

Comments that describe the purpose of a macro or complex program flows are considered best practice but are often neglected by database programmers. Appropriate comments that provide useful information about the macro and its purpose can be extremely valuable to the organization. They also can save time if a new employee is required to take over the database design and programming.

Reduce Processing Time by Combining Routine Tasks

Turquoise Oasis Spa routinely adds new products to meet the demands of their clients. When new products are acquired, the information is sent in a spreadsheet with the product name and other information. This data needs to be entered into the database, a task that is currently done manually by copying and pasting.

Automating an Import and Update Process

In this exercise, you will develop a macro that will automate the process of importing new products into the database by executing a query that will convert the product name to proper case and then will append the modified records to the products table.

You will be adding several actions to this macro that will import the data from a spreadsheet into a temporary table, and then the data will need to be cleaned by executing an update query. The cleaned data then will be added to the products table by executing an append query. Finally, the data will be removed from the temporary table by executing a delete query.

Macros can be used to automate complex sets of actions. It is important to carefully think through all the actions that a macro will be executing to complete the tasks before beginning work on creating the macro. Taking the time to create a process flow that describes the actions and reasons for those actions can save time and reduce the chance of errors.

Step	Purpose	Specifics
Import new records to a temporary table	To update the list of products	The new product list needs to be modified before importing it into the tblProduct table.
Set warning messages off	To suppress common database warnings	Before action queries are executed, Access issues warnings and prompts that require a user response.
Run the qryUPDATE_ProductDescription query	To clean the data imported	Converts all product names to proper case.
Run qryAPPEND_NewProducts	To append new products to the tblProduct table	Appends newly modified data into the tblProduct table.
Run qryDELETE_TempNewProducts	To delete the contents of the temporary table	Prevents excess data from being stored in a temporary table.

Table 2 Process flow table example

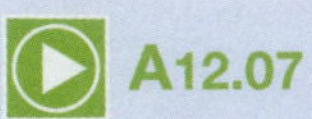

SIDE NOTE

Bypass Warnings

The SetWarnings action allows the user to bypass all prompts that accompany various actions in a database, such as running an update query.

To Automate an Import and Update Process

a. Click the **Create** tab, and then, in the Macros & Code group, click **Macro**.

b. In the Action Catalog, double-click **Comment** to add a comment to the macro. In the comment field, type This macro automates the process of importing new products into the products table.

c. If necessary, on the Design tab, in the Show/Hide group, click **Show All Actions**.
   By default, Access shows only a subset of possible actions in Add New Action box. If you select Show All Actions, Access will display all possible actions in the Add New Action list.

d. Click the **Add New Action** arrow, and then select **ImportExportSpreadsheet** from the list of actions to add the action to the macro. If necessary, select **Import** as the Transfer Type and **Excel Workbook** as the Spreadsheet Type.

Troubleshooting

If an action is not available in the Add New Action box, be sure to click Show All Actions. Each time Access is closed, the action list is restored to showing only macros that are allowed in databases that have not been trusted regardless of changes made to the Trust Center settings.

e. For the Table Name argument, type tblTempNewProducts.

f. The File Name field must include the complete path to the file being imported. Navigate to the student files using Windows Explorer, click in the **address bar** of Windows Explorer, and then, with the path selected, press Ctrl + C to copy the path. Press Ctrl + V to paste the path in the File Name field, click at the end of the path, and then type \a06ch12SpaProducts.xlsx into the File Name argument.

g. In the Has Field Names argument, select **Yes**.

h. Click the **Add New Action** arrow, select **SetWarnings** from the list of actions to add it to the macro, click the **Warnings On** argument, and if necessary, select **No**.
   It is important to note that when you turn off warnings using the Macro Designer, warnings will automatically be turned back on when the macro is finished. However, if the macro is converted to VBA, the warnings will remain off permanently. Therefore, it is good practice to turn the warnings back on before ending the macro.

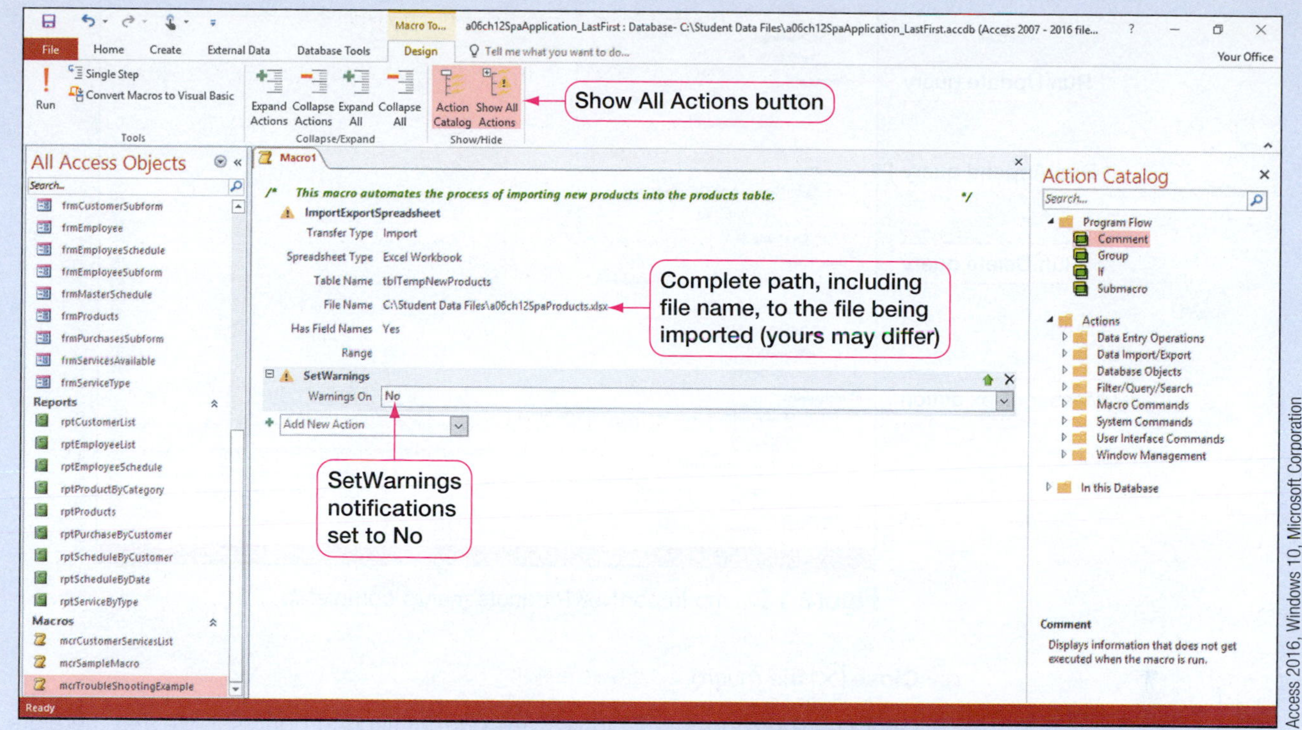

Access 2016, Windows 10, Microsoft Corporation

Figure 12 Design view of the macro in progress

> **SIDE NOTE**
> **Message Box**
> Message boxes are useful to alert the user that an action has been completed, but message boxes can also be used for custom error messages.

> **SIDE NOTE**
> **Beep**
> The frequency and duration of the beep depend on the hardware, which varies between computers.

i. Select **OpenQuery** from the Add New Action list. You will be selecting an action query that will update the new product's names from all capital letters to all proper case so the product names are formatted consistently throughout the table.

j. Select **qryUPDATE_ProductDescription** for the Query Name argument. If necessary, select **Datasheet** for View, and then, if necessary, select **Edit** for Data Mode.

k. Add another **OpenQuery** action to this macro. Select **qryAPPEND_NewProducts** for the Query Name. If necessary, select **Datasheet** for View, and then, if necessary, select **Edit** for Data Mode. This action will execute the append query that will add the modified products to the product table.

l. Add another **OpenQuery** action to this macro. Select **qryDELETE_TempNewProducts** for the Query Name. If necessary, select **Datasheet** for View, and then, if necessary, select **Edit** for Data Mode. This action will execute the delete query that will remove the products from the temporary table.

m. Click the **Add New Action** arrow, select **SetWarnings** from the list of actions to the macro, click the **Warnings On** argument, and if necessary, select **Yes**.

n. Add the **MessageBox** action to this macro. Type New products have been added to the database. as the Message, and then, if necessary, select **Yes** for Beep. This will produce a sound from the computer speakers when the message box appears.

o. Select **Information** for the Message Box Type, and then type New Products Added as the Title.

p. **Save** the macro as mcrImportNewProducts.

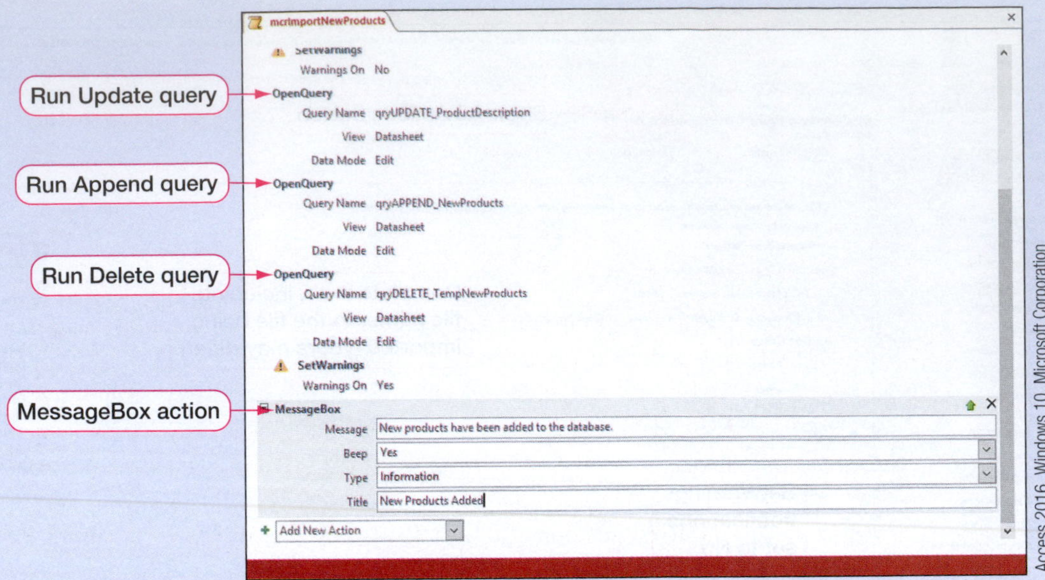

Figure 13 mcrImportNewProducts macro completed

q. **Close** [X] the macro.

r. Open the **tblProduct** table to view the current list of products. Note that there are 25 records. **Close** [X] the tblProduct table.

s. To test the macro, double-click **mcrImportNewProducts** in the Navigation Pane.

t. Click **OK** when prompted by the message box, open the **tblProduct** table, and then view the added records. Note that there are now 30 records. **Close** [X] the tblProduct table.

Troubleshooting

Upon running this macro, if you get an error message stating, "The Microsoft Access database engine could not find the object," then you most likely entered the file path incorrectly in the File Name field in the first action. Verify that the path and file name are correct.

REAL WORLD ADVICE — Set Warnings Action

The SetWarnings action is often used to suppress warning messages when you are performing various tasks such as running update queries and delete queries. This action must be used with caution, as some warnings do provide helpful information, and the option to not perform a particular action could cause irreversible damage to the data.

The SetWarnings action does not prevent an error message from being displayed if the error forces the macro to stop running. For example, if the file with new products was incorrectly named and placed in the same directory, the macro would fail with the first action.

CONSIDER THIS | **Preventing Errors**

A properly designed process will prevent users from making errors. What would happen if you tried to import the same file more than once? What role would the primary or composite key play in that process? What if warnings were turned off?

Create Macro Groups

Creating macro groups can make a large number of macros in a database easier to manage and maintain. A **macro group** is two or more macros that are similar in function that are stored under the same macro name. When a macro group is created, only the name appears in the Navigation Pane, regardless of how many submacros the macro group contains. For example, a macro group could contain a submacro for every report in a database that exports and or prints each report and appear only once in the Navigation Pane. Although Access does not require the submacros in a macro group to be similar, it is best practice to create logical groups based on function and purpose.

When a macro group is executed directly in the Navigation Pane or by clicking Run in Design view, only the first submacro is executed. The most common way to run a submacro is to assign it to an event on a form or report. You can also run submacros by creating an AutoKeys macro. An **AutoKeys macro** is a macro group that assigns keys on the keyboard to execute each submacro. The macro must be named AutoKeys, and each submacro must be named with the key or key combinations on the keyboard that will be used to execute the macros. To name a key assignment macro, use ^ to indicate Ctrl, + for Shift, and { } around key names that are more than one letter long. You are restricted to numbers, letters, Insert, Delete, and the function keys in conjunction with Shift and Ctrl. If the key assignment is a combination that normally does something else, then the submacro key assignment will override the normal function. For example, pressing Ctrl + F, which normally opens the Find and Replace dialog box, would no longer work if you created a new macro with the same key combination.

QUICK REFERENCE | **Key Assignments**

Key	Macro Syntax
Press F5	{F5}
Press Ctrl and type r	^r
Press Shift+F3	+{F3}
Press Insert	{INS}
Press Ctrl+F2	^{F2}
Press Delete	{DEL}

Creating a Macro Group

The Turquoise Oasis Spa database contains several reports that provide information related to employee schedules, inventory, and client services. These reports are often printed and shared with members of management. In this exercise, you will create a macro group that will automate the steps of opening each report, sending it to the printer, and then closing the report.

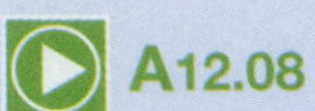

To Create a Macro Group

a. Click the **Create** tab, and in the Macros & Code group, click **Macro**.

b. In the Action Catalog, double-click **Comment** to add a comment to the macro. In the Comment field, type **The following macro group will open specific reports, send them to printer, and then close the reports.**

c. In the Program Flow group, under the Action Catalog, double-click **Submacro** to add it to the macro, and then, in the Submacro name box, type **PrintEmployeeSchedule** to give it a name.

d. In the submacro block, click the **Add New Action** arrow, and then select **OpenReport**. Select **rptEmployeeSchedule** for the Report Name. If necessary, select **Report** for the View argument, and then, if necessary, select **Normal** for Window Mode.

e. In the submacro block, click the **Add New Action** arrow, and then select **RunMenuCommand**. Click the **Command** arrow, and then select **PrintObject** for the Command argument.

f. In the submacro block, click the **Add New Action** arrow, and then select **CloseWindow**. Click the **Object Type** arrow, select **Report**, click the **Object Name** arrow, select **rptEmployeeSchedule**, and then click the **Save** arrow and select **No**. Because you are not editing the report, there are no changes that need to be saved.

SIDE NOTE
Submacro Names
Each submacro in a macro group must have a unique name.

SIDE NOTE
PrintObject Action
If you add the PrintObject action to the macro, it will automatically insert the RunMenuCommand action and select PrintObject as the Command.

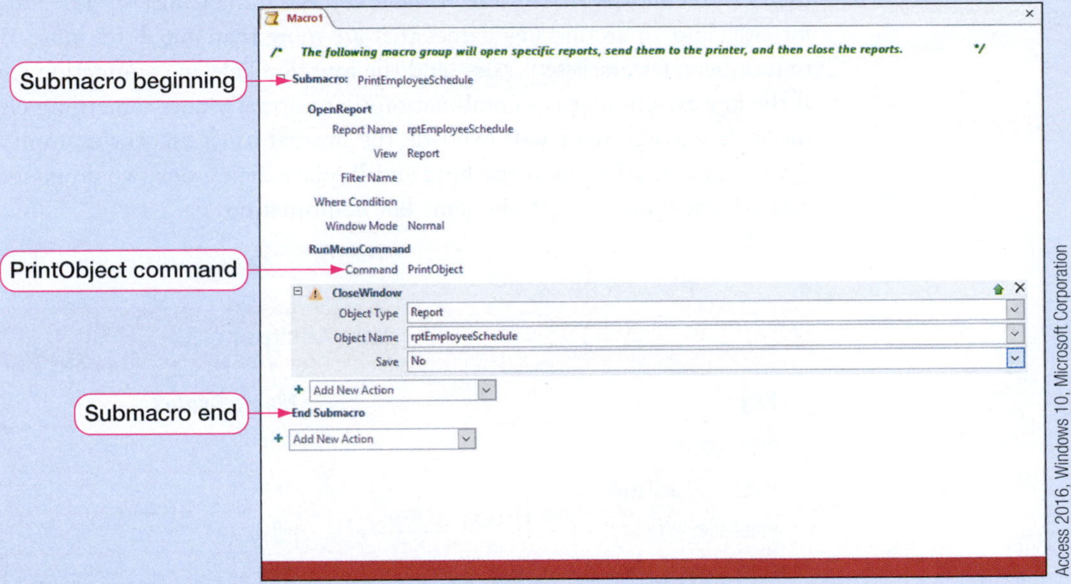

Figure 14 Design view of the macro in progress

g. Repeat steps e–g to create two more submacros for two additional reports.

- Create one submacro named **PrintProductInventory** that opens, prints, and closes the rptProducts report. Do not save the report.
- Create another submacro named **PrintCustomerSchedule** that opens, prints, and closes the rptScheduleByCustomer report. Do not save the report.

h. **Save** the macro as **mcrPrintReports**, and then **close** the macro.

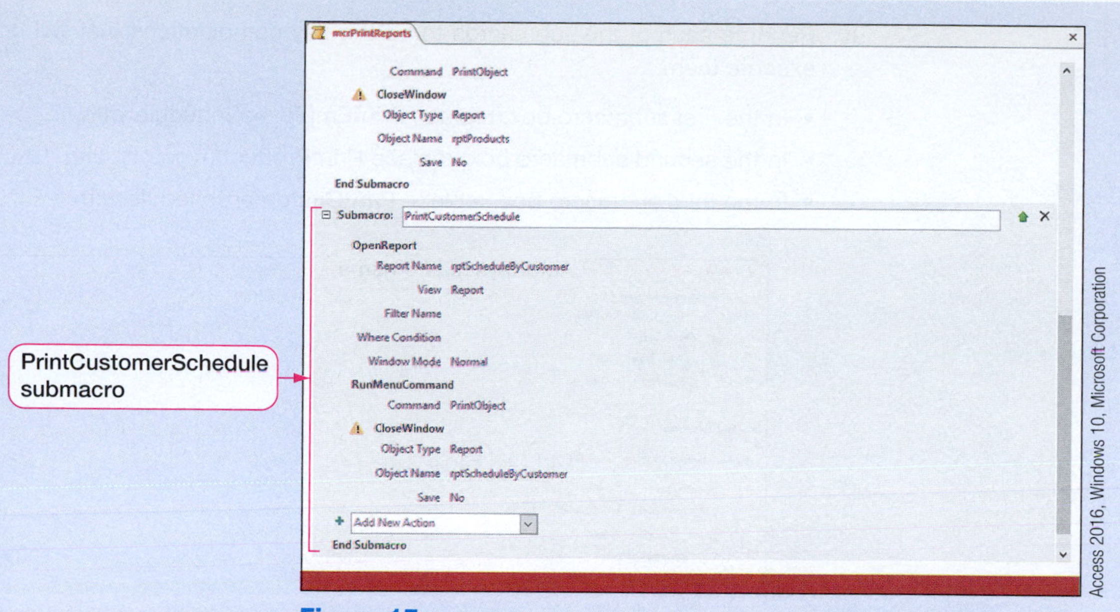

Figure 15 mcrPrintReports macro completed

REAL WORLD ADVICE **Cutting Paper Waste**

Today's businesses rely more and more on information contained in reports to make decisions. However, many businesses are cutting waste by exporting reports and having them sent in an e-mail instead of having them printed directly from a database. You can take advantage of macros in Access for exporting or e-mailing documents to cut back on paper waste.

Creating a Key-Assignment Macro

In this exercise, because submacros cannot be executed in the Navigation Pane, you will make the process easier by assigning keys to each submacro so that the reports can be printed simply by pressing keys on the keyboard.

To Create a Key Assignment Macro

a. Right-click the **mcrPrintReports** macro group in the Navigation Pane, select **Copy**, right-click anywhere in the Navigation Pane, and then select **Paste** to create a copy of the macro group.

b. In the Paste As dialog box, type AutoKeys, and then click **OK**. Now that the macro group has been saved as AutoKeys, key combinations can be assigned to each submacro so that they can be executed from the keyboard.

c. In the Navigation Pane, right-click the **AutoKeys** macro, and then select **Design View**. In the comment at the top of the macro, click at the end of the text, and then type Each submacro has an assigned set of keys used to execute.

d. Rename each of the submacros to be the key combinations that will be used to execute them.

- In the first submacro box, replace PrintEmployeeSchedule with ^i.
- In the second submacro box, replace PrintProductInventory with ^e.
- In the third submacro box, replace PrintCustomerSchedule with ^{F1}.

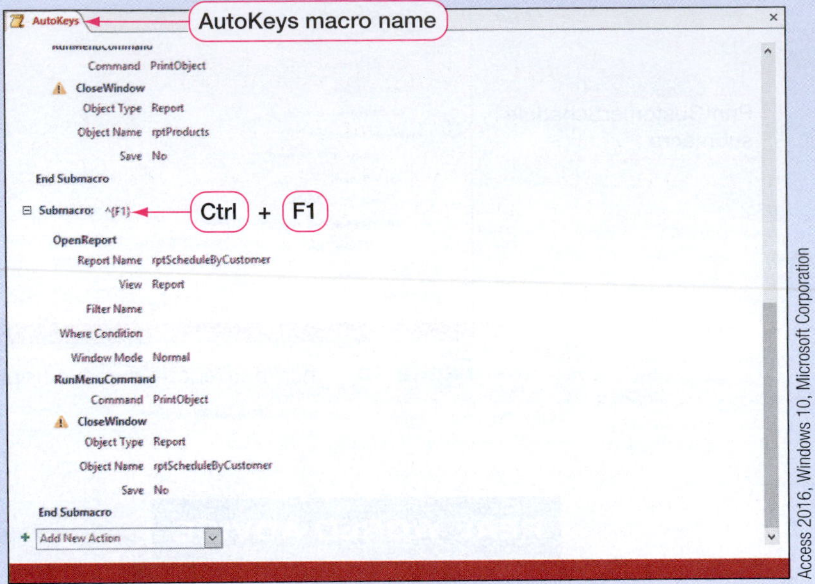

Figure 16 Completed AutoKeys macro

e. **Save** the changes to the macro group, and then **close** the macro.

f. Test out the new key-assigned macro group. Press and hold Ctrl and then press E, I, or F1 to print the employee schedule, inventory, or the customer schedule report.

Troubleshooting

For the AutoKeys macro to run the database, the database may have to be closed and reopened.

REAL WORLD ADVICE Maintaining Descriptive Submacro Names

Submacros can easily be added to other macros by using the RunMacro or OnError actions, or they can be easily assigned to events. For this reason, it is important to maintain a copy of the original macro group with descriptive submacro names before renaming them in an AutoKeys macro.

Create Macros That Run When the Database Opens

If you want a set of actions to run every time a database is opened, then you can create an **AutoExec macro**. The name "AutoExec" is reserved for use by a macro that will run automatically before any other macros when a database is opened.

Creating an AutoExec Macro

Every morning, invoice information is entered into the database for any spa service with a remaining balance that has been charged to the customer's hotel room. In this exercise, you will create an AutoExec macro that will automatically minimize the Navigation Pane for optimal viewing, open the invoice form, go to a new record, and insert the pointer in the InvoiceDate field.

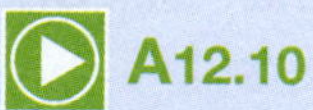
A12.10

To Create an AutoExec Macro

a. Click the **Create** tab, and then, in the Macros & Code group, click **Macro**.

b. In the Action Catalog, double-click **Comment** to add a comment to the macro. In the Comment field, type This macro will run each time the database is opened. It minimizes the Navigation Pane, opens the Invoice form in a new record, and sets the focus on the Invoice Date field.

c. Click the **Add New Action** arrow, and then select the **SelectObject** action. Click the **Object Type** arrow, select **Form**, click the **Object Name** arrow, and then select **frmCustomerInvoices**.

d. Click the **In Database Window** arrow, and then select **Yes**.
By selecting Yes for the In Database Window argument of the SelectObject action, you are selecting the object in the Navigation Pane and making the Navigation Pane the active window.

e. Click the **Add New Action** arrow, and then select the **MinimizeWindow** action.
The MinimizeWindow action minimizes the active window, which in this case is now the Navigation Pane.

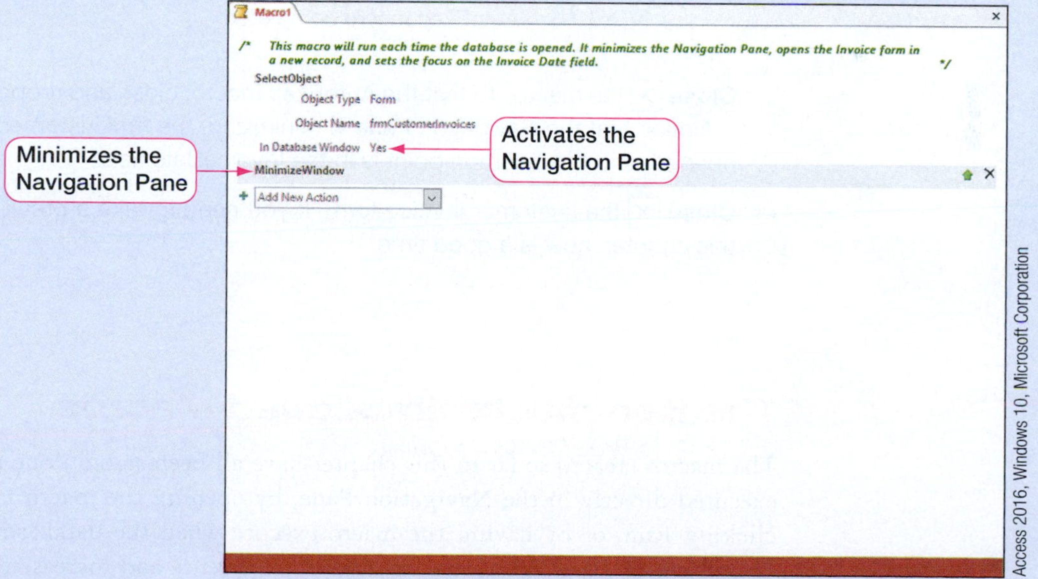

Figure 17 Design view of the macro in progress

f. Click the **Add New Action** arrow, select the **OpenForm** action, click the **Form Name** arrow, and then select **frmCustomerInvoices**.

g. Verify that **Form** is selected as the value for the View argument. Click the **Data Mode** arrow, and then select **Edit**.
Selecting Edit for the Data Mode allows data to be entered and/or modified in the form.

h. Verify that **Normal** is selected as the value for the Windows Mode argument.

i. Add the **GoToRecord** action to the macro. Select **Form** as Object Type, select **frmCustomerInvoices** as Object Name, and select **New** for the Record argument in order to go to a new record in the form.

j. Click the **Add New Action** arrow, and then select the **GoToControl** action to the macro. Type InvoiceDate as the Control Name.

SIDE NOTE

Bypassing the AutoExec Macro

An AutoExec macro can be bypassed by holding down Shift when you open the database.

k. **Save** the macro, in the Save As dialog box type AutoExec, and then click **OK**.

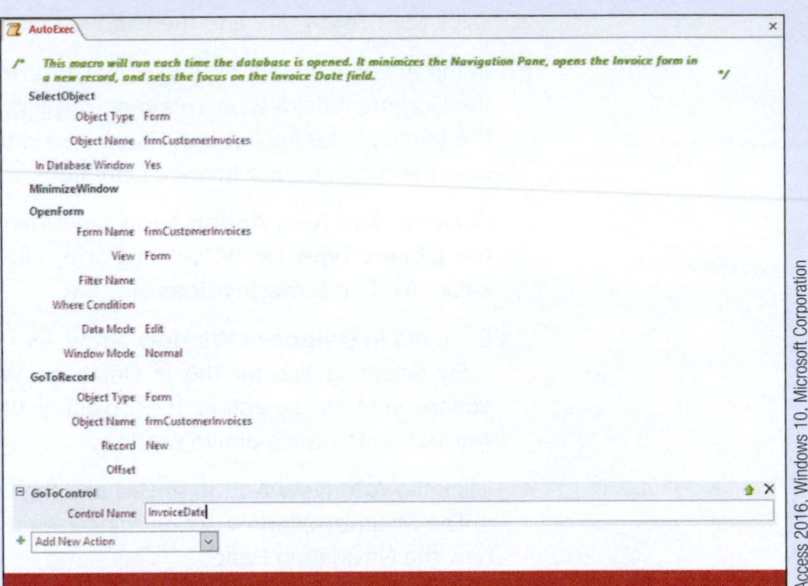

Figure 18 AutoExec macro completed

l. **Close** the macro. To test the AutoExec macro, close and reopen the database. Notice that the Navigation Pane is minimized, the frmCustomerInvoices form is opened, and the insertion point is in the InvoiceDate field.

m. **Close** the customer invoice form. If you need to take a break before finishing this chapter, now is a good time.

The Benefits of Embedded Macros

The macros created so far in this chapter have all been stand-alone macros that can be executed directly in the Navigation Pane, by opening the macro in Design view and clicking Run, or by having the macro execute when the database opens. Embedded macros can be used to create a better user experience and increase the functionality of a database.

Embedded macros are triggered by database events. A **database event** occurs when an action is completed on any given object. The action could be, for example, a simple click of the mouse or entering information into a specific field. When the specific event occurs the macro executes the actions.

QUICK REFERENCE | **Common Events and Descriptions**

Many different events occur in a database. Below is a table of the common events used to increase the effectiveness of macros and their descriptions.

Event Name	Description
On Click	Event occurs when a user presses and releases the left mouse button over an object
On Open	Event occurs when a form or report is opened
Before Update	Event occurs before an existing record is modified
After Update	Event occurs after an existing record has been modified
On Got Focus	Event occurs when the user presses Tab to focus on an object
On Lost Focus	Event occurs when the user presses Tab to move the focus from one object to another
On Dbl Click	Event occurs when a user presses and releases the left mouse button twice over an object
On Enter	Event occurs when a text-based control is clicked, whether it contains text or not
On Exit	Event occurs after a text-based control is used and the user presses Tab to move to the next control

It is important to note that the simple act of moving from one field in a form to another field triggers several different database events. Knowing the order in which the events take place is critical in determining which event to associate a macro with. For example, if you have two macros that are to be run in a certain order, you want to make sure that the events they are associated with occur in that order.

QUICK REFERENCE | **Order of Common Events for Controls**

Events occur in form controls when you move the focus to another control or update and change data in a control.

A control is selected.

1. Enter
2. Got focus

A control is exited.

1. Exit
2. Lost focus

Data in a text box control is changed.

1. Key down
2. Key press
3. Dirty
4. Change
5. Key up

Data in a control is updated and exited.

1. Before update
2. After update
3. Exit
4. Lost focus

In addition to events associated with controls, such as text boxes and command buttons, there are many events associated with mouse activity. In this section, you will build macros that are event driven to create a more interactive user experience with a database.

QUICK REFERENCE	Order of Common Mouse Events

Events occur when a mouse button is pressed while the mouse pointer is on a control on a form.

Click a control.

1. Mouse down
2. Mouse up
3. Click

A control has focus, and the mouse selects another control.

1. Exit
2. Lost focus
3. Enter
4. Got focus
5. Mouse down
6. Mouse up
7. Click

Double-click a control.

1. Mouse down
2. Mouse up
3. Click
4. Double-click
5. Mouse up

Move the mouse pointer over a control.

1. Mouse move (This event is separate from other mouse events.)

Improve the Functionality of Forms and Reports

Forms can also be enhanced by embedding macros into the form or form controls to increase the functionality and improve the user experience. By being embedded, the macro becomes portable, and if you export the form into another database, any macros that are embedded will remain with the form object.

Embedding a Macro to Improve User Experience

Users of the Turquoise Oasis Spa database currently enter sales information in the frmCustomerPurchases form. If the patron is a returning customer, there is no easy way to locate the customer's record before adding the transaction information. In this exercise, you will first create a Datasheet form from the tblCustomer table, which is ideal for searching. You will then embed a macro into the Datasheet form that will open the frmCustomerPurchases form for the record selected.

To Embed a Macro to Improve User Experience

a. If you took a break, open the **a06ch12SpaApplication** database, and if necessary, **close** [X] the customer invoice form.

b. Press F11 to open the Navigation Pane. Select the **tblCustomer** table in the Navigation Pane.

c. Click the **Create** tab, and in the Forms group, click **More Forms**, and then select **Datasheet** in the list.

Notice that the Datasheet form is arranged just like a table.

d. **Save** the datasheet form as frmCustomerList.

e. Click the column heading **Customer ID** to select the Customer ID column.

f. If necessary, on the Form Tools Datasheet tab, in the Tools group, click **Property Sheet** to display the Property Sheet pane.

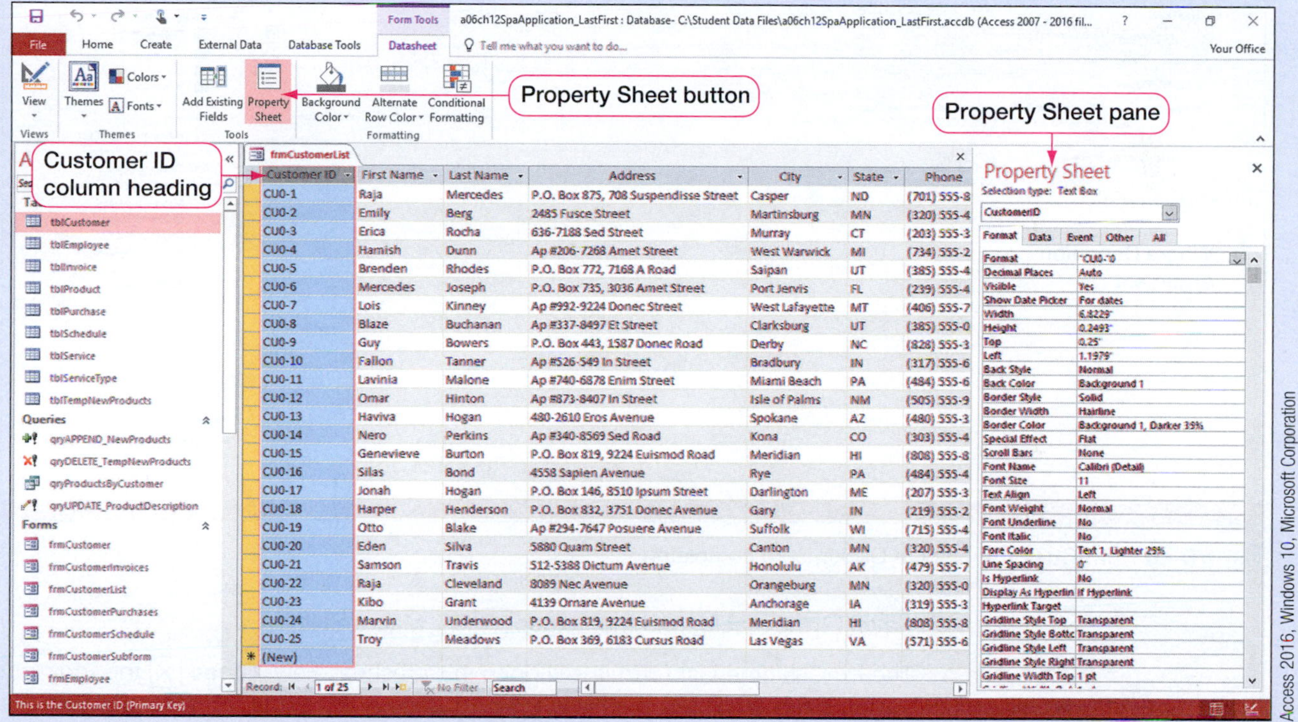

Access 2016, Windows 10, Microsoft Corporation

Figure 19 frmCustomerList property sheet

g. Click the **Event** tab in the property sheet, locate the On Click event, and then click the **Expression Builder** [...].

h. In the Choose Builder dialog box, verify that **Macro Builder** is selected, and then click **OK**.

i. In the Action Catalog, double-click **Comment** to add a comment to the macro. In the Comment field, type This embedded macro will open the frmCustomerPurchases form for the Customer ID selected in frmCustomerList.

j. Click the **Add New Action** arrow, select the **OpenForm** action, click the **Form Name** arrow, and select **frmCustomerPurchases**.

k. Verify that **Form** is selected as the value for the View argument.

l. In the **Where Condition** argument type [CustomerID]=[Forms]![frmCustomerList]![CustomerID].

This expression ensures that the record displayed in frmCustomerPurchases has the same CustomerID as the one clicked in frmCustomerList.

m. Click the **Data Mode** arrow, select **Edit**, click the **Window Mode** arrow, and then select **Dialog**.

The dialog windows mode allows the form to display as a pop-up window on top of the already opened form. This creates a more fluid user experience and allows the user to quickly see the invoice information.

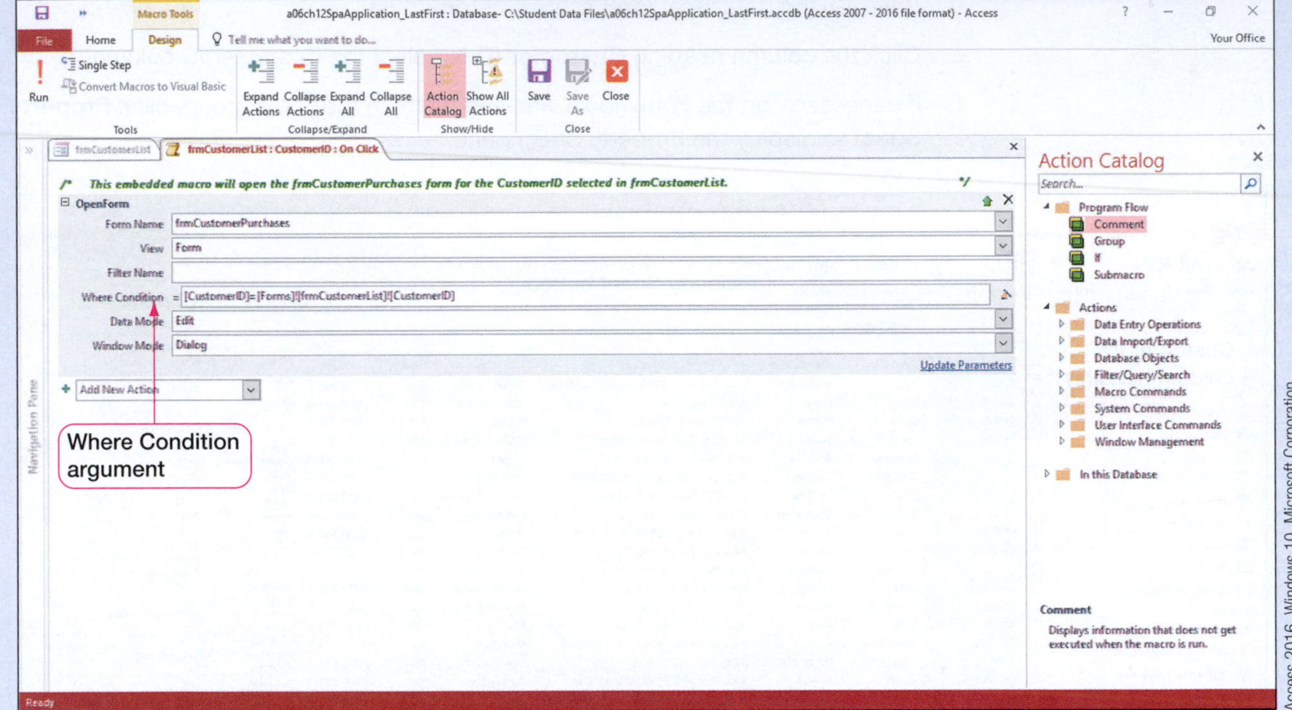

Figure 20 frmCustomerList On Click macro completed

n. **Save** the macro, and then **close** the Macro Builder.

o. The frmCustomerList form is still open in Datasheet view. **Close** the Property Sheet pane. To test this macro, click Customer ID **CU0-5** in the Customer ID field, and then observe that the frmCustomerPurchases form open to the same customer record.

p. **Close** the frmCustomerPurchases form, and then **close** the frmCustomerList form. Click **Yes** if you are prompted to save changes.

Embedding a Macro to Increase Functionality

The rptProducts report contains a list of all the product details, including the quantity in stock. Management is often asking for the products that are running low so that more can be ordered. Although reports can be filtered by using the Filter feature on the Home tab, it is not a simple process. In this exercise, you will embed a macro that will apply a filter to the rptProducts report that will prompt the user for a number. The report will then show only the products that have fewer than that number in stock. The report will then be attached to an e-mail that can be sent to the appropriate person(s).

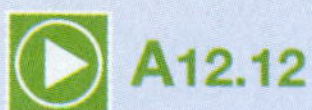

To Embed a Macro to Increase Functionality

a. Right-click the **rptProducts** report in the Navigation Pane, and then select **Design View**.

b. On the Design tab, in the Controls group, click the **Button** [xxxx] form control.

c. Click to create a button to the right of the Product List report title in the **Report Header**. Position the button in between the **4"** and **5"** markings on the horizontal ruler at the top.

d. On the Design tab, **Property Sheet**. In the Property Sheet pane click the **Format** tab, and then change the Caption property to Low Inventory.

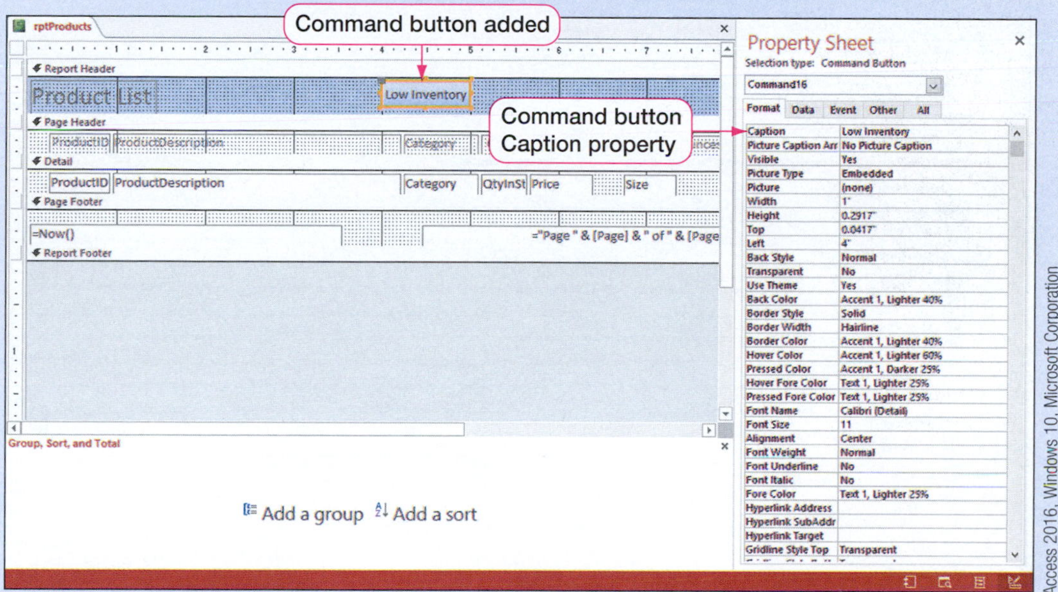

Figure 21 Design view of report with Low Inventory command button

e. Click the **Event** tab on the Property Sheet, click in the **On Click** event, and then click the **Expression Builder** [...].

f. In the Choose Builder, verify that **Macro Builder** is selected, and then click **OK**.

g. In the Action Catalog, double-click **Comment** to add a comment to the macro. In the Comment field, type This macro will apply a filter to the report, prompting the user for a number. The report will display products with fewer items in stock than the number provided and attach the filtered report to an e-mail.

h. Click the **Add New Action** arrow, and then select **SetFilter**. In the **Where Condition** argument, type [QtyInStock]<[Enter a quantity for which to return all products with fewer in stock].

This expression will prompt the user for a quantity and will then filter the report to show only records in which the QtyInStock value is less than the quantity provided.

i. Click the **Add New Action** arrow, select the **EMailDatabaseObject** action, click the **Object Type** arrow, select **Report**, click the **Object Name** arrow, and then select **rptProducts**.

j. Click the **Output Format** arrow, and then select **Excel 97 - Excel 2003 Workbook (*.xls)**.

> **SIDE NOTE**
> **Message Text Character Limit**
> The Message Text argument has a 255 character limit, just as a Text data type in tables does.

k. Leave the To, Cc, and Bcc arguments blank. You may want to enter your own e-mail address in the To argument for testing purposes.

l. In the **Subject** argument, type Low Inventory Report.

m. Leave the Message Text argument blank.

n. In the **Edit Message** argument, verify that **Yes** is selected. This allows the user to review and/or edit the e-mail before sending.

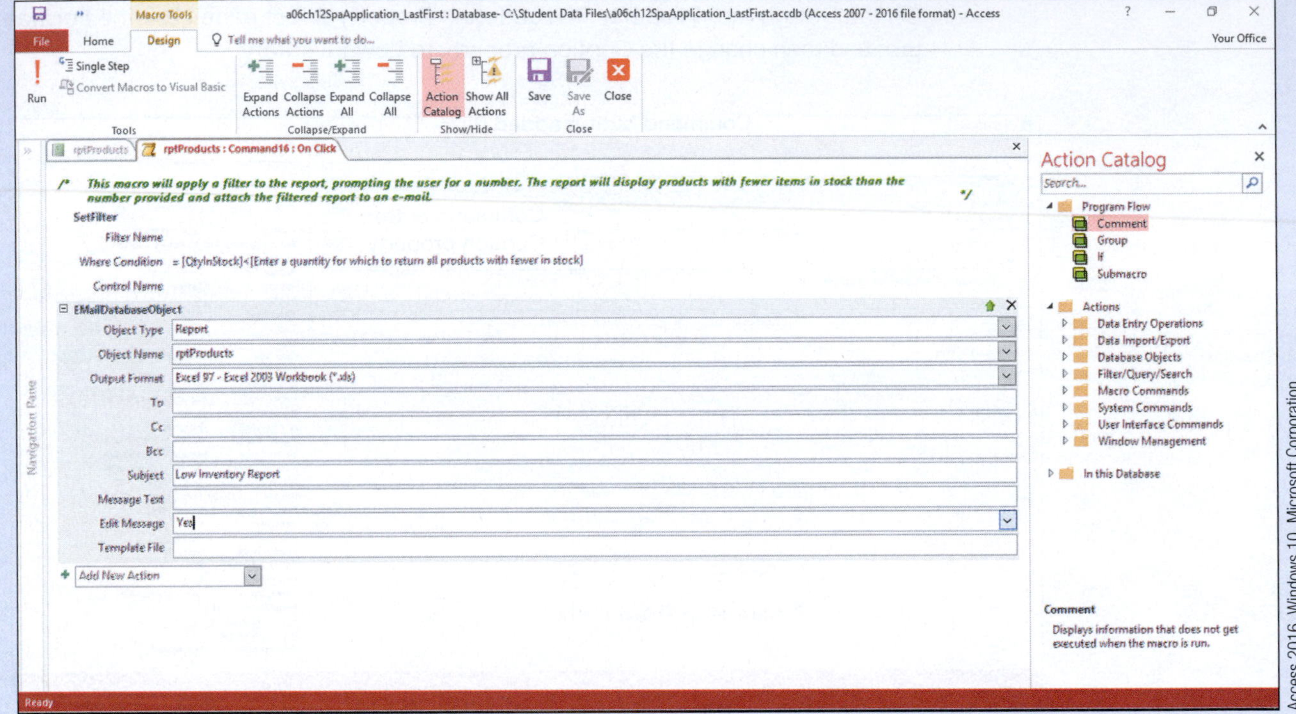

Access 2016, Windows 10, Microsoft Corporation

Figure 22 rptProducts command button macro completed

o. **Save** the macro, and then **close** the Macro Builder.

p. To test the macro, on the Home tab, in the Views group, click the **View** arrow, and then select **Report View**. Click the **Low Inventory** button. In the **Enter Parameter Value** dialog box, type 25, and then click **OK**.

q. Once your e-mail client is opened, right-click the **attached report**, and then click **Save As**. Navigate to the location where you are saving your project files, and then change the filename to a06ch12rptLowInventory_LastFirst using your last and first name.

r. **Close** your e-mail window, **close** the report, and then click **Yes** to save changes.

> **Troubleshooting**
> The EMailDatabaseObject action uses the default e-mail client on the user's computer. This is typically Outlook, Outlook Express, or Thunderbird. The database object being attached to the e-mail is stored in a temporary table that the user must have permissions to access or the object will fail to attach to the e-mail.

Implement Complex Business Rules with Data Macros

Access databases can be enhanced to enforce complex business rules with the use of macros. For example, when a shipment of new products arrives at a warehouse, the items in the shipment must be entered into inventory. A data macro could be constructed that, when a shipment is entered into a database as received, automatically updates the inventory amounts for the products in another table. Remember that data macros are database objects stored in Access tables and are triggered by table events. Data macros are typically used to implement business logic into tables and automatically set values in fields. Since these macros are stored in tables, the logic associated with the macros is automatically applied to any forms or queries that use the tables. This functionality allows for much more complex data validation.

Macros can be associated with five table events: Before Change, Before Delete, After Insert, After Update, and After Delete. These table events can be divided into two categories: Before events and After events. **Before events** occur before any changes are made to the table data, and **After events** occur after the changes have been successfully made. Before events are very simple and support only a few of the data macro actions, whereas After events are more robust and support the full range of data macro actions.

Data macros are limited in what they can do, as they have only a limited number of data actions available for use. **Data actions** are a specific, limited set of macro actions that can be used in a data macro. Certain data actions are available for certain table events. For example, data macros associated with Before events cannot prevent a record from being updated or deleted. They can only set a local variable or raise an error if conditions warrant.

QUICK REFERENCE — **Table-Level Events**

Event	Description
After Insert	After a new record has been added to this table
After Update	After any field in a record in this table has been updated
After Delete	After a record in this table has been deleted
Before Delete	When a record in this table is about to be deleted
Before Change	When a record in this table is about to be updated

QUICK REFERENCE — **Common Data Actions Enter Intro Text**

Action	Description
CancelRecordChange	Cancels the changes made to a record before the changes are committed
DeleteRecord	Deletes a record
ExitForEachRecord	Immediately exits a ForEachRecord data block
OnError	Can specify what should happen if an error occurs in a macro
RunDataMacro	Runs a named data macro
SendEmail	Sends an e-mail message from a default e-mail client
SetField	Assigns a value to a field; has to be used inside a CreateRecord or EditRecord data block
StopMacro	Stops the currently running macro; typically used when a condition makes it necessary to stop the macro

Data macros can incorporate the use of data blocks. A **data block** contains an area to add one or more data actions, and it executes all the actions contained as part of its operation. Data blocks can be used only with After events, with the exception of the LookupRecord data block, which can also be used with Before events.

QUICK REFERENCE | **Data Blocks**

Data Block	Description
CreateRecord	Actions within this block are used to create a record.
EditRecord	Actions within this block are used to edit a record.
ForEachRecord	Actions within this block will run on each record returned by the query argument.
LookupRecord	Actions within this block will run with the record selected by the query argument.

Creating a Data Macro

Currently, when a customer makes a purchase at the spa, the employee must manually adjust the inventory levels to indicate the change in the quantity in stock. You have been asked to automate this process to eliminate errors and increase the accuracy of the product inventory. In this exercise, you will create a data macro that will be triggered after a record has been created in the tblPurchase table and that will deduct the Quantity ordered from the QtyInStock field in the tblProduct table.

A12.13

To Create a Data Macro

a. Double-click the **tblPurchase** table in the Navigation Pane to open it in Datasheet view.

b. Click the **Table** tab, and then, in the **After Events** group, click **After Insert**.

c. In the Action Catalog, double-click **Comment** to add a comment to the macro. In the Comment field, type This macro will update the product inventory when a new record is created in the Purchase table.

d. In the Action Catalog, under the Data Blocks group, double-click the **LookupRecord** to add the data block to the macro.

e. In the Look Up A Record In argument, select the **tblProduct** table.

f. In the **Where Condition** argument, type [tblProduct].[ProductID]=[tblPurchase].[ProductID].
This expression ensures that the record that will be edited is the record that has the same ProductID as the record being created in the tblPurchase table.

g. In the LookupRecord data block, click the **Add New Action** arrow, and then select **EditRecord**.

h. In the EditRecord data block, click the **Add New Action** arrow, and then select **SetField**.

i. In the **Name** argument, type tblProduct.QtyInStock for the field you want to edit.

j. In the **Value** argument, type [tblProduct].[QtyInStock]-[tblPurchase].[Quantity].
This expression will subtract the number of items being purchased from that item's inventory.

SIDE NOTE
SQL in the Where Condition Argument
SQL SELECT statements such as SELECT tblProduct. [ProductID], tblProduct. [QtyInStock]FROM tblProduct; can also be used in the Where Condition argument.

SIDE NOTE
The SetField Action
The SetField action can be used only inside of an EditRecord or CreateRecord data block.

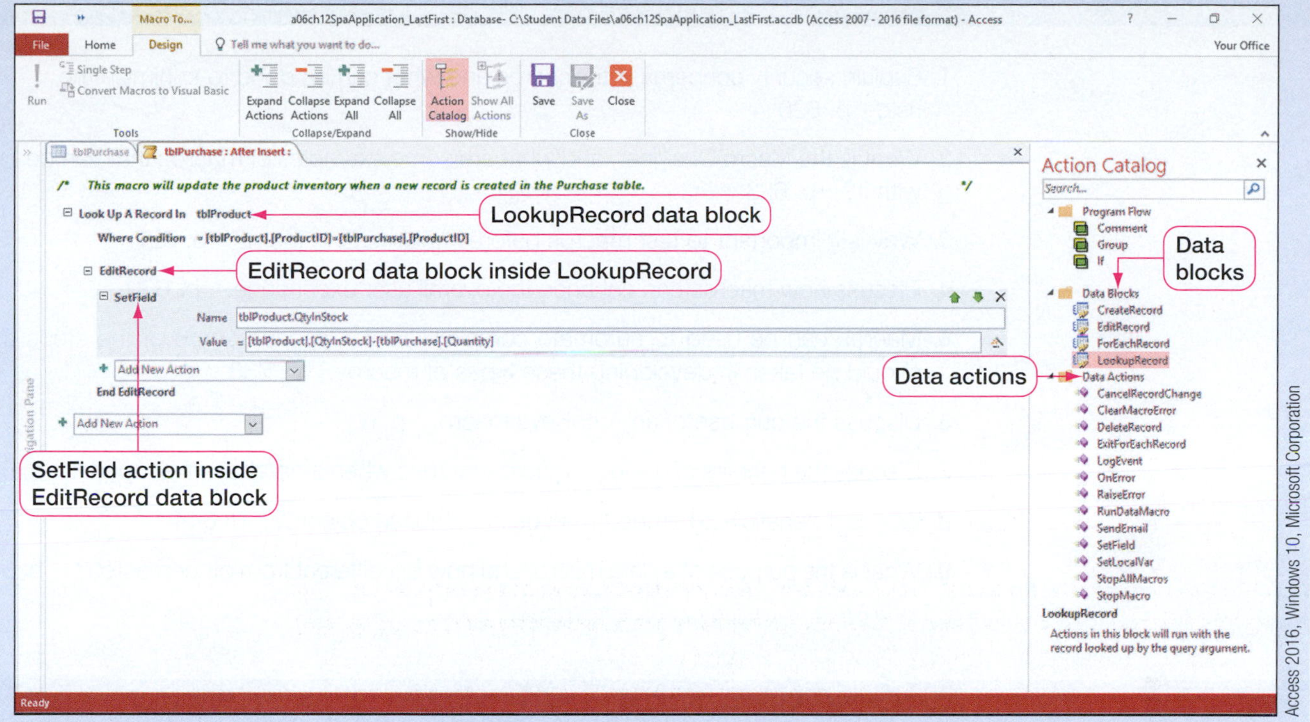

Access 2016, Windows 10, Microsoft Corporation

Figure 23 tblPurchase after insert data macro completed

k. **Save** the macro, **close** the Macro Builder, and then **close** the tblPurchase table.

l. Open the **tblProduct** table, take note of the quantity in stock for the New Mexico Mud Mask item, and then **close** the tblProduct table.

m. Open the **tblPurchase** table, and on the Navigation bar, click **New Record**. Click the **Product** arrow, select **New Mexico Mud Mask**, click the **Customer** arrow, select **Blake Otto**, click the **Purchase Type** arrow, and then select **Online**.

m. In the **Purchase Date** field, type 01/16/2018, and in the **Quantity** field, type 5.

o. **Close** the tblPurchase table, and then open the **tblProduct** table to verify that there are now five fewer New Mexico Mud Mask items in stock. **Close** the tblProduct table.

p. **Close** the database, exit Access, and then submit your files as directed by your instructor.

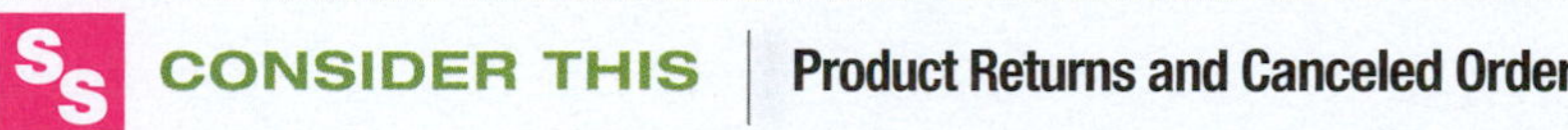

CONSIDER THIS | **Product Returns and Canceled Orders**

Products are often returned and online orders canceled for various reasons. How could data macros be modified to automate the process of updating the inventory amount if a product is returned?

Concept Check

1. Explain security concerns with macros and what can be done to minimize the risk. p. 620
2. What is the Macro Designer, and what are some examples of macros that can be built with it? p. 623
3. Why is it important to test macros before implementing them? p. 627
4. Discuss how macros can enhance the overall user experience. p. 630
5. Macros can be used to automate complex tasks. Describe some of the steps that should be taken in developing these types of macros. p. 633
6. Discuss the purpose of an AutoKeys macro. p. 637
7. Discuss the benefits of having a macro that runs when a database first opens. p. 640
8. Why is it beneficial to embed macros in database objects? p. 644
9. What is the purpose of a data macro, and how is it different from other macros?. p. 649

Key Terms

Action 624
Action Catalog 624
After event 649
Argument 620
AutoExec macro 640
AutoKeys macro 637
Before event 649
Data action 649
Data block 650
Data macro 620
Database event 642
Embedded macro 620
Macro 620
Macro Designer 623
Macro group 637
Single Step 627
Stand-alone macro 620
Trusted location 621

Visual Summary

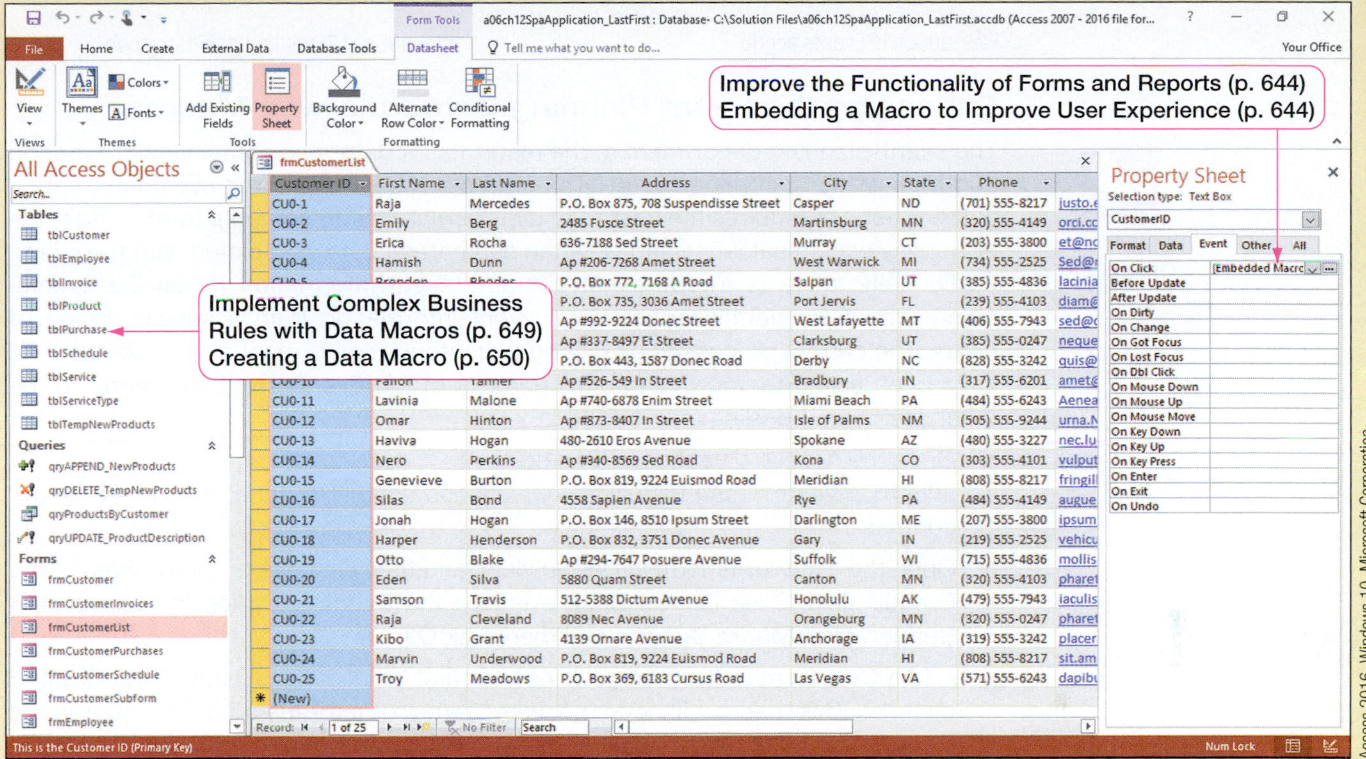

Improve the Functionality of Forms and Reports (p. 644)
Embedding a Macro to Improve User Experience (p. 644)
Implement Complex Business Rules with Data Macros (p. 649)
Creating a Data Macro (p. 650)

Figure 24

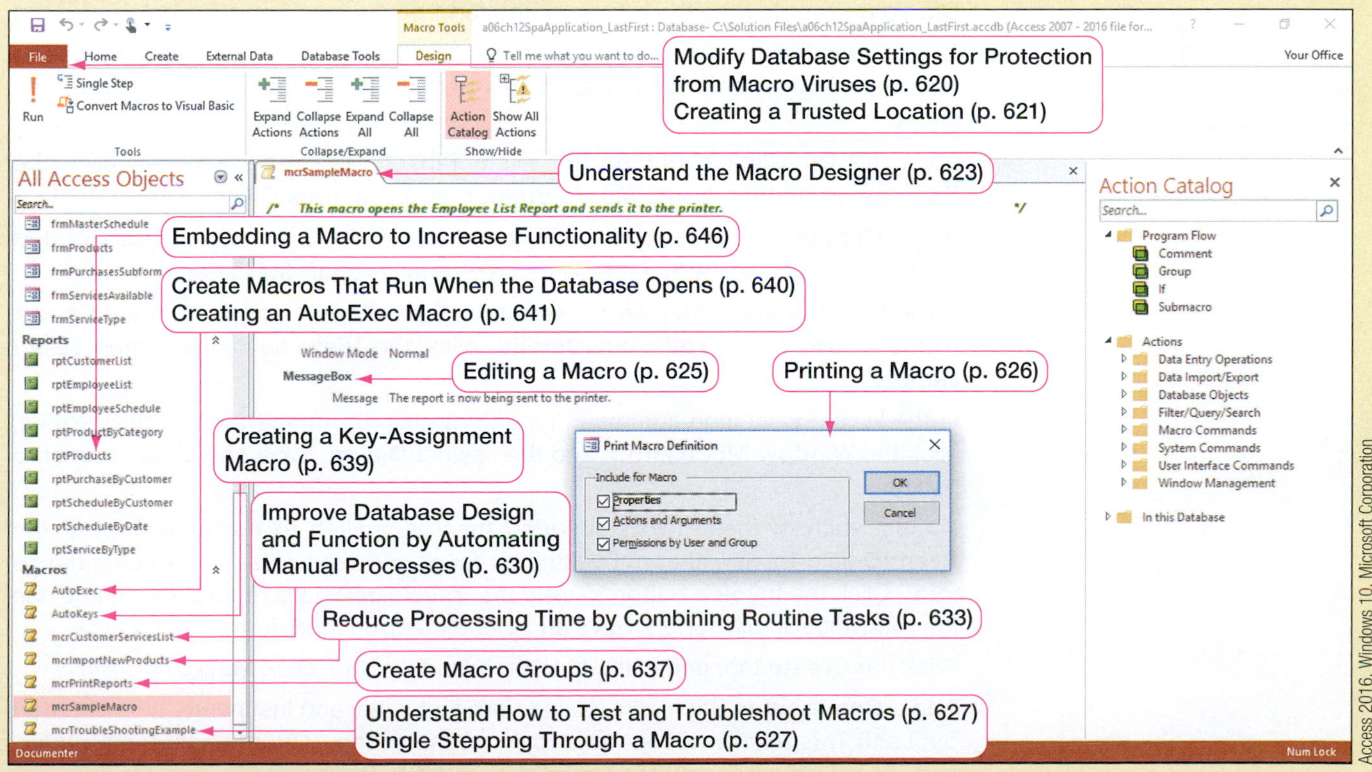

Modify Database Settings for Protection from Macro Viruses (p. 620)
Creating a Trusted Location (p. 621)
Understand the Macro Designer (p. 623)
Embedding a Macro to Increase Functionality (p. 646)
Create Macros That Run When the Database Opens (p. 640)
Creating an AutoExec Macro (p. 641)
Editing a Macro (p. 625)
Printing a Macro (p. 626)
Creating a Key-Assignment Macro (p. 639)
Improve Database Design and Function by Automating Manual Processes (p. 630)
Reduce Processing Time by Combining Routine Tasks (p. 633)
Create Macro Groups (p. 637)
Understand How to Test and Troubleshoot Macros (p. 627)
Single Stepping Through a Macro (p. 627)

Figure 25

Practice 1

Student data file needed:

 a06ch12Events.accdb

You will save your file as:

 a06ch12Events_LastFirst.accdb

Enhancing the Event Planning Database with Macros

Production & Operations

The event-planning department at the resort has a database containing information about past and upcoming events. The current process of adding event information to the database requires the user to enter information into separate forms, and there is no easy way to calculate and view the estimated costs associated with the event. Additionally, there is a report that contains event information for all the events. Management frequently requests the event information from a specific range of dates. The current process of extracting that information is manual and tedious. You have been asked to improve the functionality of the Events form and report in the database by embedding macros.

a. Open the Access database, **a06ch12Events**. Save your file as a06ch12Events _LastFirst using your last and first name. If necessary, enable the content.

b. Open the **frmEvents** form in Design view, and then view the property sheet of the EventID field. Click the **On Click** event on the **Event** tab, click the **Expression Builder**, click **Macro Builder**, and then click **OK**.

c. Add a **Comment** to the macro. Using your first initial and last name, type Created by iLast. This macro will open the event items form for the active event. Add the **OpenForm** action to the macro, select **frmEventItems** for the Form Name, and then, for the View argument, select **Form**.

d. Type the following expression in the Where Condition argument: [EventID]=[Forms]![frmEvents]![EventID], select **Edit** for Data Mode, select **Dialog** for the Window Mode argument, and then save and close the Macro Builder.

e. Click the **Design** tab, and in the Controls group, select the **Button** form control. Drag a **rectangle** near the bottom of the form below the Client ID label.

f. Click **Cancel** in the Command Button Wizard dialog box, and then rename the button Invoice by editing the Caption property on the Format tab in the property sheet.

g. Click the **On Click event** on the Event tab of the Property Sheet, click the **Expression Builder**, select **Macro Builder**, and then click **OK**.

h. Add a **Comment** to the macro. Using your first initial and last name, type Created by iLast. This macro will open the invoice details report for the active event.

i. Click the **Add New Action** arrow, select the **OpenReport** action, click the **Report Name** arrow, select **rptInvoiceDetails**, click the **View** arrow, and then select **Report**.

j. In the Where Condition argument, type [EventID]=[Forms]![frmEvents]![EventID], click the **Window Mode** arrow, and then select **Dialog**. Save and close the macro builder.

k. To test each of these two embedded macros, switch to **Form** view, click the **EventID** field to view the frmEventItems form, and then close the frmEventItems form. Click the **Invoice** button to view the rptInvoiceDetails report, and then close the rptInvoiceDetails report. Save and close the frmEvents form.

l. Click the **Create** tab, and in the Macros & Code group, click **Macro**.

m. Add a **Comment** to the macro. Using your first initial and last name, type Created by iLast. This macro will open a report and filter the contents based on a user-provided date range and then send the report to the printer.

n. Click the **Add New Action** arrow, select the **OpenReport** action, click the **Report Name** arrow, select **rptEventsByDate**, click the **View** arrow, and then select **Report**.

o. In the **Where Condition** argument, type [EventDate] Between [Enter first date (mm/dd/yy)] And [Enter second date (mm/dd/yy)]. Click the **Window Mode** arrow, and then select **Normal**.

p. Click the **Add New Action** arrow, and select the **PrintObject** action.

q. Click the **Add New Action** arrow, and select the **CloseWindow** action, click the **Object Type** arrow and select **Report**, click the **Object Name** arrow, and select **rptEventsByDate**, and then click the **Save** arrow and select **No**.

r. Save the macro as mcrPrintEventsByDateRange, and then close the macro.

s. Open **rptEventsByDate** in Design view, and then, in the Controls group, select the **Button** control. Create a **button** to the right of the Report title in the **Report Header**. Place the **left edge** of the button on the **3"** mark on the horizontal ruler at the top.

t. If necessary, click **Property Sheet**, and then, in the Format tab of the Property Sheet pane, replace the text in the Caption box with Events by Date Range. Resize the button so that all text is visible.

u. Click the **Event** tab, and then click the **On Click** event arrow. Select **mcrPrintEventsByDateRange** from the list.

v. Save the changes to the report. Switch to **Report** view, click the **Events by Date Range** button, and then type **01/01/18** for the first date and **03/31/18** for the second date.

w. Cancel or print as directed by your instructor.

x. Save the database, exit Access, and then submit your file as directed by your instructor.

Problem Solve 1

Student data files needed:

a06ch12PuttsForPaws.accdb

a06ch12NewParticipants.xlsx

You will save your file as:

a06ch12PuttsForPaws_LastFirst.accdb

Automating Tasks in the Putts for Paws Database

Putts for Paws is an annual charity event that takes place at the Painted Paradise Golf Resort & Spa and raises money for a local animal shelter. You have been asked to enhance the event's current database by creating macros that will improve the database's efficiency and functionality.

a. Open the Access database **a06ch12PuttsForPaws**. Save your file as a06ch12PuttsForPaws_LastFirst using your last and first name. If necessary, enable the content.

b. Create a macro that will import the data contained in the **a06ch12NewParticipants** spreadsheet into the **tblParticipant** table.

- Add a comment to the macro, and type This macro imports the list of new participants into the tblParticipant table.
- Add a MessageBox to the macro. Type the message as You are about to import new participants into the participants table.
- Select **Yes** for the Beep argument and **Information** for the Type argument.
- Type Importing Participants for the Title.

- If necessary, Show All Actions. Add **SetWarnings** to the macro, and select **No** for Warnings On.
- Add the **ImportExportSpreadsheet** action to the macro, and complete the necessary arguments to Import the spreadsheet.
    - Select **Import** for the Transfer Type.
    - Select **Excel Workbook** for the Spreadsheet Type.
    - Type tblParticipant for the Table Name.
    - In the File Name argument, type the path to the Excel spreadsheet to be imported, and at the end of the file path, type \a06ch12NewParticipants.xlsx, and then select **Yes** for Has Field Names argument.

c. Save the macro as mcrImportNewParticipants.

d. Run the macro, verify that the new participants have been added to the **tblParticipant** table, and save all changes.

e. Create an After Insert Data Macro in the **tblOrderLine** table so that when a new record is recorded, the quantity ordered is automatically deducted from the quantity available in the tblItem table.

- Insert a comment at the top of the macro, and type This macro automatically deducts the quantity ordered from the quantity available in the tblItems table.
- Add the necessary Data Blocks and Data Actions to complete the task.
- Save and close the macro.

f. Test the macro by entering the following record into the tblOrderLine table and confirming that the quantity available in the tblItem table for CART Item ID changes from 40 to 37.

OrderID	LineNum	ItemID	Quantity
11	2	CART	3

g. Create a command button on the frmParticipant form that, when clicked, will open the frmOrder form to the participant's order form if an order had been previously placed or a new record if an order has not been placed.

- Type Place Order for the button's name, and place it in between the Add Record and Find Record buttons.
- Add a comment to the top of the macro, and type: This macro will open the frmOrder form to the participant's record if applicable and a new record if not.
- Add the OpenForm action, and fill in the necessary arguments to complete the task. Have the form open in Form View, select Edit for Data Mode, and select-Normal for Window Mode. Type [ParticipantID]=[Forms]![frmParticipant]![ParticipantID] in the Where Condition argument.
- Apply an Intense Effect – Red, Accent 2 Quick Styles to the button.
- Change the shape of the button to a **Rounded Rectangle**. Test the macro.
- Save and close the macro.

h. Close the database, exit Access, and then submit your file as directed by your instructor.

Critical Thinking

In this project, you created several macros to enhance the functionality of the database. Describe how one of the macros that you created could be modified to improve its functionality and/or the user experience.

Perform 1: Perform in Your Career

Student data file needed:

 a06ch12TicketSales.accdb

You will save your file as:

 a06ch12TicketSales_LastFirst.accdb

Campus Event Tickets

You have recently started working for a business on your campus that sells a variety of tickets. For any given event on campus, your business gets a specific number of tickets to sell. Currently, the business is using a database to track this data. You have been asked to enhance the functionality of the database. Specifically, your supervisor would like the database to open with the Navigation pane hidden and the Transactions form displaying a new record. On the Transactions form, she would like a button that would allow employees to create new customer records. Once new transactions are entered, the number of tickets available in the Events table will need to be updated. Last, your supervisor would like to be able to print reports by using keyboard shortcuts.

a. Open the Access database **a06ch12TicketSales**. Save your file as a06ch12TicketSales_LastFirst using your last and first name. If necessary, enable the content. For each macro created, in a comment along with a brief description of the macro's function, include Created by iLast., using your first initial and last name.

b. Create an After Insert macro on the tblTransactions table that will update the number of tickets available in the tblEvents table when a new transaction is recorded.

c. Add a command button to the frmTransactions form that will open the frmCustomers form to a new record. The frmCustomers form should open in Dialog mode. This will allow employees to add a new customer before a transaction is completed.

d. Create an AutoKeys macro that prints the rptEventRoster and rptTicketsAvailable reports. Assign a key combination to each of the macro groups.

e. Create an AutoExec macro that, on start-up, will minimize the Navigation Pane and open the frmTransactions form to a new record.

f. Close the database, exit Access, and then submit your file as directed by your instructor.

Additional Cases

Additional Workshop Cases are available on the companion website and in the instructor resources.

Access Business Unit 6 CAPSTONE

Developing a Polished User Interface and Experience

This business unit had two outcomes:

Learning Outcome 1:

Use navigation forms to provide users with access to all the forms and reports they need via a well-organized, user-friendly interface. Also learn how to enhance the user experience by utilizing command buttons to increase the usability of forms and modify the start-up options to automatically display the interface when the database is opened.

Learning Outcome 2:

Use various types of macros to enhance the functionality of a database, automate routine tasks, and enhance the overall user experience.

In Business Unit 6 Capstone, students will demonstrate competence in these outcomes through a series of business problems at various levels from guided practice to problem solving an existing database and performing to create new databases.

More Practice 1

Student data files needed:

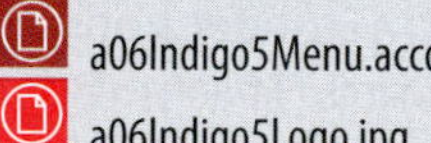

a06Indigo5Menu.accdb

a06Indigo5Logo.jpg

You will save your file as:

a06Indigo5Menu_LastFirst.accdb

Improving Navigation of the Indigo5 Restaurant Database

Production & Operations

Indigo5 is a five-star restaurant that caters to local patrons as well as clients of the resort and spa. The Menu database is used to store information about ingredients, recipes, and specials. The database consists of several forms used for entering new information as well as a few reports. You will create a navigation system that will give the employees access to the essential forms and reports. You will also implement business logic, using a data macro to automatically set the cost of each menu item.

a. Start **Access**, click **Open Other Files** in the left pane, and then double-click **This PC**. Navigate through the folder structure to the location of your student data files, and then double-click **a06Indigo5Menu**. A database opens displaying tables related to the restaurant's menu items and recipes.

b. Click the **File** tab, save the file as an **Access Database**, and click **Save As**. Navigate to the location where you are saving your project files, and then change the filename to a06Indigo5Menu_LastFirst using your last and first name. Click **Save**. If necessary, enable the content.

c. Follow these steps to create command buttons at the top of the Food Categories form that will allow the user to easily navigate the categories and add new ones.

- Right-click the frmFoodCategories form, and then click **Design View**. Click the **Food Category ID text box**, press and hold Shift, and then click all the text boxes and labels in the form detail. Move them all down about **1"**.
- Add a **Button** form control in the **top left corner** of the detail section. In the Command Button Wizard, verify that **Record Navigation** is selected in the Categories list, click **Go To Previous Record** in the Actions list, and then click **Next**. Click **Text**, and then type Previous Category as the button text. Click **Next**, type cmdPreviousCategory as the button name, and then click **Finish**.

- Add two additional command buttons each to the right of the previous. Refer to the table below for the specific values for the Command Button Wizard.

Category	Action	Button Text	Button Name
Record Navigation	Go To Next Record	Next Category	cmdNextCategory
Record Operations	Add New Record	Add Category	cmdAddCategory

- Select all three buttons, click the **Arrange** tab, and in the Sizing & Ordering group, click **Align**, and then click **Top** from the list of options. Click **Space/Size**, and then click **Equal Horizontal** to make all the buttons equally spaced apart.
- With the buttons still selected, click the **Format** tab, and in the Control Formatting group, click **Quick Styles**, and then click **Moderate Effect - Blue, Accent 1** — the fifth row of the second column.

d. Follow these steps to hide the navigation buttons and record selectors on the form.
- Click the **Design** tab, and in the Views group, switch to **Layout** view.
- Click the **Design** tab, and in the Tools group, click **Property Sheet**. Under Selection type in the Property Sheet pane, click the **selection** arrow, and then select **Form**.
- On the Format tab in the property sheet, locate the **Record Selectors** property, and set the value to **No**.
- Locate the **Navigation Buttons** property, and set the value to **No**.

e. Referencing the table below, make similar modifications to the **frmIngredients**, **frmRecipes**, and **frmMenu** forms. Place the buttons in a similar position as described above, apply the same Quick Styles format to the navigation buttons, and then set the Record Selectors and Navigation Buttons properties to **No**.

Form Name	Button Text	Button Name
frmIngredients	Previous Ingredient	cmdPrevIngredient
	Next Ingredient	cmdNextIngredient
	Add Ingredient	cmdAddIngredient
frmRecipes	Previous Recipe	cmdPrevRecipe
	Next Recipe	cmdNextRecipe
	Add Recipe	cmdAddRecipe
frmMenu	Previous Item	cmdPrevItem
	Next Item	cmdNextItem
	Add Item	cmdAddItem

f. Save and close all opened forms.

g. Click the **Create** tab, and in the Forms group, click **Navigation**, and then click **Vertical Tabs, Left**. Save the navigation form as frmMenuNavigation_iLast using your first initial and last name.

h. Follow the steps to create a main menu navigation form for the database.
- If necessary, close the Field List pane. On the Design tab, in the Tools group, click **Property Sheet**. Under Selection type, click the **selection** arrow, and then click **FormHeader**. On the Format tab, locate **Back Color**. Click the **Builder button**, and then select **White, Background 1**, the first row in the first column under Theme colors.
- Drag the **frmMenu** form from the Navigation Pane to the **[Add New]** vertical tab.

- Drag the **frmRecipes** form from the Navigation Pane to the **[Add New]** vertical tab.
- Continue adding the **frmFoodCategories** and **frmIngredients** forms and the **rptMenuItems** and **rptRecipeDetails** reports to the **[Add New]** vertical tabs in the navigation form.
- Double-click the **frmMenu** tab, select the **text**, and then rename the tab Menu. Double-click the **frmRecipes** tab, select the **text**, and then rename the tab Recipes. Double-click each of the remaining tabs, select the **text**, and then rename the tabs Food Categories, Ingredients, Menu Items, and Recipe Details.
- Click the **Menu** tab, press and hold Shift, and then click the **Ingredients** tab. Click the **Format** tab, and in the Control Formatting group, click **Change Shape**, and then click **Rounded Rectangle**. Click **Quick Styles**, and then click **Subtle Effect - Blue, Accent 1** — the fourth row in the second column.
- Click the **Menu Items** tab, press and hold Shift, and then click the **Recipe Details** tab. On the Format tab, in the Control Formatting group, click **Change Shape**, and then click **Round Single Corner Rectangle**. Click **Quick Styles**, and then click **Light 1 Outline, Colored Fill - Blue, Accent 1** — the third row in the second column.
- Click the **icon** to the left of the title. Click the **Design** tab, and in the Controls group, click **Insert Image**. Click **Browse**, navigate through the folder structure to the location of your student data files, and then double-click **a06Indigo5Logo** to insert the new image.
- Click **Property Sheet**, and then, if necessary, in the Property Sheet pane, click the **Format** tab. Click the **Size Mode** box, click the **Size Mode** arrow, and then click **Zoom**. Type 3 for the **Width**, and then type 0.8 for the **Height** of the image.
- Double-click the **Navigation form** title, select the **text**, and then type Menu Navigation.
- Save and close the form.

i. Follow the steps to create a data macro that will automatically set the price of a menu item to be 160% of its cost.
   - In the Navigation Pane, double-click the **tblMenu** table to open it. Click the **Table Tools Table** tab, and in the Before Events group, click **Before Change**.
   - Add a **comment** to the data macro, using your first initial and last name, that reads Created by iLast. This data macro will automatically set the Price field to be 160% of the amount in the Cost field.
   - Add the **SetField** action to the macro. Type **Price** in the Name argument, and then type [Cost]*1.6 for the Value argument. This will automatically set the price of the menu item to be 160% of whatever cost is entered.
   - Save and close the data macro.

j. Test the data macro by creating a new record in the tblMenu table using the information below.

MenuID	Recipe ID	Season	Meal	Special	Price	Cost
	Spinach and Mushroom Frittata	Spring, Summer	Breakfast			3.54

Notice that once you save the form or change records, the Price field is automatically set to $5.66. Changing an existing cost will also cause the data macro to update the price value. Close the table.

k. Follow the steps to modify the start-up options of the database.

- Click the **File** tab, click **Options**, and then click **Current Database**. Under the Application Options section, click the **Application Title** text box, and then type Indigo5 Database.
- Click the **Display Form** arrow, and then select **frmMenuNavigation_iLast**.
- Click the **Compact on Close** check box. In the Navigation section, click **Display Navigation Pane** to deselect the check box.
- Click **OK** to close the Access Options dialog box, and then click **OK** again.

l. Close the database. Start **Access**, and then open **a06Indigo5Menu_LastFirst**. When the database reopens, the only form to open should be frmMenuNavigation_iLast. Also notice that the name of the application is on the title bar.

m. Close the database, exit Access, and then submit your file as directed by your instructor.

Problem Solve 1

Student data file needed:

a06HotelManagement.accdb

You will save your file as:

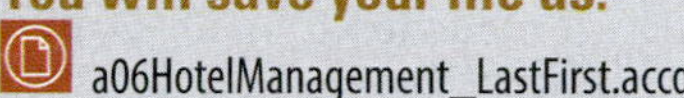

Combining a User Interface with an AutoKeys Macro

Production & Operations

The hotel database consists of several forms and reports that employees and managers use on a daily basis to enter information in and retrieve information from. You have been asked to create a user-friendly navigation system to access all the forms required to enter a reservation. You will also create macros that will print and e-mail reports using key combinations on the keyboard.

a. Open the Access database, **a06HotelManagement**. Save your file as a06HotelManagement_LastFirst using your last and first name. If necessary, enable the content.

b. Remove navigation buttons and record selectors from the frmEmployees, frmGuests, frmReservations, and frmRoomCharges forms.

c. Create a horizontal navigation form, and then add frmReservations, frmRoomCharges, frmGuests, and frmEmployees in that order.

- Rename the tabs to be Reservations, Room Charges, Guests, and Employees.
- Remove the icon in the form header, and then edit the text to be Hotel Navigation.
- Apply the Organic theme to the navigation form.
- Save the form as frmHotelNavigation.

d. Create an AutoKeys macro that consists of several submacro groups. Each group will open a specific report, queue the report to the printer, and close the report without prompting to save.

- Add a Comment to the macro describing the purpose of the macro.
- See the table below for specifics.

Report Name	Key Combination
rptTotalRoomChargesByCategory	Ctrl + F2
rptTotalRoomCountByType	Ctrl + F3
rptRoomChargesByReservation	Ctrl + F4

- Create an expression in the Where Condition argument for rptRoomChargesByReservation that will prompt the user to enter a reservation number and will show results only for that reservation number in the report.
- Type Enter a Reservation number for a list of room charges as the message prompt.

e. Modify the appropriate database settings to hide the Navigation Pane, and then have the navigation form be displayed when the database is opened.

f. Test all macros. When testing the macro that prompts you for a reservation ID type 7 to view a report of room charges.

g. Close the database, exit Access, and then submit your file as directed by your instructor.

Problem Solve 2

Student data file needed:
a06Inventory.accdb

You will save your file as:
a06Inventory_LastFirst.accdb

Managing Inventory

Production & Operations

You have been managing inventory for an accounting office using an Access database. Your supervisor has asked you to enhance the database to make it more user friendly.

a. Open the Access database **a06Inventory**. Save your file as a06Inventory_LastFirst using your last and first name. If necessary, enable the content.

b. Create an After Insert macro on the tblTransactionDetails table that will add the Quantity field from the tblTransactionDetails table to the QuantityInStock field in the tblProducts table when a new record is entered.

c. Add a comment at the beginning of the After Insert macro describing the purpose of the macro.

d. Make the following changes to the frmProducts and frmPurchases forms.
   - Remove navigation buttons and record selectors.
   - Apply the **Slice** theme to the database.
   - Add buttons to the frmProducts and frmPurchases forms that can be used to find a particular record in the form. Place the buttons at the top of the detail section of the form. Refer to the table below for labels and names.

Form Name	Text Label	Button Name
frmProduct	Add Product	cmdAddProduct
frmProduct	Previous Product	cmdPreviousProduct
frmProduct	Next Product	cmdNextProduct
frmPurchases	Add Purchase	cmdAddPurchase
frmPurchases	Previous Purchase	cmdPreviousPurchase
frmPurchases	Next Purchase	cmdNextPurchase

e. Be sure all buttons are aligned, that they are spaced equally, and that all label text is visible.

f. Save changes, and close the forms.

g. Create a navigation form with vertical tabs on the left, and then make the following changes.
   - Add frmProducts, frmPurchases, rptCurrentInventory, and rptTransactionsByDate in that order.
   - Change the shapes of the vertical tabs containing the forms to Round Same Side Corner Rectangle, and apply **Subtle Effect, Dark Blue, Accent 1** — the second column in the fourth row.
   - Change the shapes of the vertical tabs containing the reports to Snip Single Corner Rectangle, and apply **Subtle Effect, Dark Green, Accent 3** — the fourth column in the fourth row.

- Rename the tabs to be Products, Purchases, Current Inventory, and Transactions by Date.
- Remove the icon in the form header, and then edit the text to be Inventory Navigation.
- Save the form as frmInventoryNavigation.

h. Make the following changes to the database settings.
- Change the Application title to Inventory Database.
- Make the database compact on close.
- Hide the Navigation Pane when the database opens.

i. Close the database, exit Access, and then submit your file as directed by your instructor.

Critical Thinking

Conduct a usability test on the solution file. In what ways has the user experience been improved? Are there areas in which usability could be improved upon?

Perform 1: Perform in Your Life

Student data file needed:

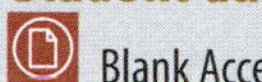

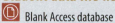

Blank Access database

You will save your file as:

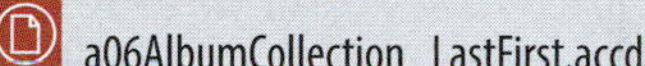

a06AlbumCollection_LastFirst.accdb

Vinyl Album Database

You have a growing collection of vinyl albums and have decided that, because the popularity of vinyl records is on the rise, you want to try to catalog them. Create a database that will keep track of artists, albums, and where and when the records were purchased or acquired. Once the tables are created, you will create some forms to make data entry easier and create various reports. You will then create a navigation form to provide easy access to these forms and reports. When saving any objects in this project, add _iLast, using your first initial and last name, to the end of the name.

a. Start **Access**, and then create a new blank database. Save the database as a06AlbumCollection_LastFirst using your last and first name.

b. The tables you create should allow you to track the following at a minimum.
- The names of the musicians/artists
- The album name, artist, and genre and the location and date purchased
- The location name and contact information: e-mail address, website, address, and phone number

c. Create any necessary queries to create two reports for this database.
- Create one report that lists the albums purchased from each location. Save the report as rptAlbumsByLocation_iLast.
- Create one report that lists the albums purchased each month. Save the report as rptAlbumsByMonth_iLast.

d. Create forms for the tables so that information can be entered easily into the tables. You may want to use subforms to combine data entry into multiple tables.
- Add navigation buttons to each form that will allow users to Find, Go To Previous Record, Go To Next Record, and Add New Record.
- Apply a style and shape of your choosing to the navigation buttons.
- Be sure to remove any unnecessary record selectors and navigation buttons from any of the forms.

e. Create a navigation form with vertical tabs on the left, and then add the forms and reports.
   - Rename the tabs appropriately.
   - Apply a style and shape of your choosing to the tabs.
   - Using your first initial and last name, change the title of the navigation form header to **iLast's Music Collection**.
   - Save the navigation form as **frmAlbumNavigation_iLast**.

f. Create an AutoKeys macro that will export each of the reports created as a PDF file to your student files folder.
   - Assign the rptAlbumsByLocation_iLast report a key combination by pressing Ctrl + A.
   - Assign the rptAlbumsByMonth_iLast report a key combination by pressing Ctrl + B.
   - Add a comment to the macro that contains your first initial and last name and a brief description of the purpose of the macro.

g. Test your AutoKeys macros.

h. Have frmAlbumNavigation_iLast be displayed when the database opens, hide the Navigation Pane, and give the application a title of **Music Collection**.

i. Close the database, exit Access, and then submit your file as directed by your instructor.

Perform 2: Perform in Your Career

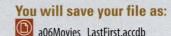

Student data file needed:
Blank Access database

You will save your file as:
a06Movies_LastFirst.accdb

Manny's Movies Database

Production & Operations

Manny's Movies is a company that arranges screenings of independent movies created by local filmmakers. Manny's Movies needs a database that can keep track of employees, local filmmakers, venues, scheduled screenings, available films, and a contact list of fans who want to receive e-mail updates on upcoming events. You will create a database with the tables and forms required to track the appropriate information. You will then create several macros to increase the functionality of the database and enhance the user's experience. When saving any objects in this project, add _iLast, using your first initial and last name, to the end of the name.

a. Start **Access**, and then create a new blank database. Save the database as **a06Movies_LastFirst** using your last and first name.

b. The tables you create should allow you to track the following at a minimum.
   - Name, address, phone number, and e-mail address of employees, local filmmakers, fans, and venues that host screenings
   - Title, filmmaker, and genre of the available films
   - Each screening should include the date, time, venue, film title, and cost of admission.

c. Create two reports for this database.
   - One report should list the film titles available for each filmmaker. Save this report as rptFilmsByFilmmakers_iLast.
   - One report should list the screenings occurring each month. Save this report as rptScreeningsByMonth_iLast.

d. Create forms for the tables so that information can be entered easily into the tables.

- Add navigation buttons to each form that will allow users to Find Record, Go To Previous Record, Go To Next Record, and Add New Record.
- Apply a style and shape of your choosing to the navigation buttons.

e. Create an AutoExec macro that will minimize the Navigation Pane and display the Screenings form when the database opens and have the insertion point placed in the venue field of a new record. Include a comment in the macro that contains your first initial and last name and a brief description of the purpose of the macro.

f. Embed a macro into the On Load event of the rptFilmsByFilmmakers_iLast report that will prompt the user for a filmmaker's last name and then display the films for that filmmaker. Include a comment in the macro that contains your initial and last name and a brief description of the purpose of the macro.

g. Embed a macro into the On Click event of a command button on the rptScreeningsByMonth_iLast report that will export the report as a PDF to your student file folder. Include a comment in the macro that contains your initial and last name and a brief description of the purpose of the macro.

h. Test your macros.

i. Close the database, exit Access, and then submit your file as directed by your instructor.

Perform 3: Perform in Your Team

Student data files needed:

 a06Wellness.accdb

Blank Word document

You will save your files as:

 a06Wellness_TeamName.accdb

 a06WellnessPlan_TeamName.docx

Employee Wellness Program

Human Resources

Your employer has begun an employee wellness program. To lower health care costs at the company, the human resources department is encouraging all employees to eat healthy foods and exercise more. As part of this initiative, your team has been asked to develop a database that will allow company employees to log basic calories and food intake. The database will also allow for tracking the type and minutes of exercise by each employee. A basic database has been created for your team. You will need to make the following changes to the database.

a. Select one team member to set up the database by completing steps b–e.

b. Open your browser, and navigate to either **https://www.onedrive.live.com**, **https://www.drive.google.com**, or any other instructor-assigned location. Create a new folder, and then name it a06WellnessFolder_TeamName using the name assigned to your team by your instructor.

c. Open the Access database **a06Wellness**. Save your file as a06Wellness_TeamName using the name assigned to your team by your instructor. If necessary, enable the content.

d. Upload the **a06Wellness_TeamName** database to the a06WellnessFolder_TeamName folder, and then share the folder with the other members of your team. Make sure that the other team members have permission to edit the contents of the shared folder and that they are required to log in to access the folder.

e. Because databases can be opened and edited by only one person at a time, it is a good idea to plan ahead by determining what each team member will be responsible for contributing. Create a new Word document in the assignment folder, and then name it a06WellnessPlan_TeamName using the name assigned to your team by your instructor.

f. In the Word document, each team member must list his or her first and last name as well as a summary of planned contributions. As work is completed on the database, this document should be updated with the specifics of each team member's contributions.

g. You will need to complete the following actions in the database.
   - Create forms for entering new foods, consumed foods, and exercises into the database.
   - Create a navigation form that organizes the three forms created in the prior action. Change the default title on the navigation form to your team name. Choose an appropriate picture to replace the default picture on the navigation form.
   - Choose a theme for the database.

h. You will need to complete the following actions with the navigation form.
   - Add the **rptCalories** and **rptExercise** reports to the navigation form.
   - Choose a shape and style combination for the buttons representing forms on the navigation form.
   - Choose a different shape and style combination for the buttons representing the reports on the navigation form.

i. Add navigation buttons to each form that will allow users to Find, Go To Previous Records, Go To Next Record, and Add New Record. Remove any record selectors and navigation buttons from the forms.

j. Create an AutoExec macro that, when the database is opened, will hide the Navigation Pane and open the navigation form. Add a comment to the macro that contains your team name and a brief description of the purpose of the macro.

k. Create an AutoKeys macro. Choose a key combination that prints the rptExercise report. Choose a second key combination that prints the rptCalories report. Add a comment to the macro that contains your team name and a brief description of the purpose of the macro.

l. Close the database, exit Access, and then submit your files as directed by your instructor.

Perform 4: How Others Perform

Student data files needed:

a06HipHopFundRaising.accdb

 Blank Word document

You will save your files as:

 a06HipHopFundRaising_LastFirst.accdb

 a06HipHopFundRaising_LastFirst.docx

Hip-Hop Fund-Raising Database

Production & Operations

You have just taken a new job at a local fundraising organization called Hip-Hop Fund-Raising. Hip-Hop Fund-Raising seeks out local hip-hop talent to perform concerts that are held to raise funds for various charities. A database has been created to track the various aspects of the organization. As you navigate through the database, you will notice some design flaws in the navigation forms as well as error messages when you attempt to run some of the macros. You will need to make some changes to this database to increase its usability, and you will explain the problems and how to solve them.

a. Open the Access database, **a06HipHopFundRaising**. Save your file as a06HipHopFundRaising_LastFirst using your last and first name.

b. Open **Word**, create a new blank document, and then save it as a06HipHopFundRaising_LastFirst using your last and first name. This will be used to explain your changes and list improvements.

c. When the database is opened, an error message is displayed. Explain what is causing the error and what can be done to correct it, and then make the appropriate change.

d. There is a data macro associated with the tblDonations table After Insert event that is not working. Explain why it is not working properly, and then make the appropriate changes so that it does.

e. The mcrOpenContributors macro is causing error messages to be displayed when executed. Use the single step process to determine where the macro is failing, and then make appropriate corrections. Explain why the macro was failing and what you did to correct it.

f. The frmHipHopNavigation form needs some work to make it user friendly. List the things you think are missing from the navigation form in terms of both content and design. Once you have made your list, implement those changes to improve the design and function of the frmHipHopNavigation navigation form.

g. Save and close the Word document.

h. Close the database, exit Access, and then submit your files as directed by your instructor.

Access Business Unit 7

Implementing and Automating a Database with VBA

Developing VBA procedures can really enhance the functionality and usability of a database. Understanding how to structure the code when writing procedures can also make it much easier to maintain and update the procedures as needs evolve. Allowing multiple users to access the database is also essential for many organizations. This business unit will explain how to write, test, and edit VBA procedures; prepare a database for multiple users; encrypt a database; modify the startup options to prevent unauthorized changes; and more.

Learning Outcome 1:

Develop VBA procedures to enhance the functionality and usability of a database. Learn how to structure VBA procedures to improve readability and utilize comments to document the procedures.

Real World Success 

"During an internship at a public accounting firm, I used VBA to enhance the functionality of one of their databases. For example, each day several Excel files with the contact information of prospective clients were imported into a table. I was able to improve the process, allowing for multiple Excel files to be imported simultaneously using VBA."

- Lauren, recent alumnus

Learning Outcome 2:

Learn how to implement a database for multiple users, how to make a database compatible with earlier versions of Access, and how to prevent unauthorized changes to the database with encryption and by modifying the startup options.

Real World Success 

"I created a database for a colleague that she implemented in her business. Later she mentioned that errors had begun to appear when the database was in use. Upon inspection, I learned that some of her employees had modified the database incorrectly, resulting in errors. Once the database was fixed, I created a front-end database for my colleague's employees and showed her how to modify the start-up options to help prevent similar errors in the future."

- Chloe, alumnus

Microsoft Access 2016

Chapter 13 | USE VBA IN ACCESS

OBJECTIVES

1. Understand the functionality of VBA p. 671
2. Convert existing macros to VBA p. 671
3. Edit and structure VBA procedures p. 675
4. Create and use loops in VBA p. 684
5. Create VBA procedures p. 689
6. Use comments to document VBA procedures p. 692
7. Debug and add error handling to a procedure p. 694
8. Compile a database p. 697
9. Secure VBA in a database p. 699

Prepare Case

Finance & Accounting

The Red Bluff Golf Course & Pro Shop Putts for Paws Charity Database

The Red Bluff Golf Course & Pro Shop sponsors the charity tournament Putts for Paws to raise money for the local pet shelter. The scope of the database is limited to tracking the monies being raised for the Putts for Paws event. Participants in the tournament are assigned roles, and any role may donate money to the event. You have been asked to add increased functionality to the database. Some of the functionality that must be added cannot be accomplished with macros but must be accomplished by using VBA. This will make tasks such as importing data and data entry more efficient.

Linn Currie/Shutterstock

Student data files needed for this chapter:

 a07ch13Putts.accdb

 a07ch13List.xlsx

You will save your files as:

 a07ch13Putts_LastFirst.accdb

 a07ch13Putts_LastFirst.accde

Introducing VBA Basics

Microsoft Office contains a powerful programming language called **Visual Basic for Applications**, more commonly known as VBA. The tools for using this language are installed by default in most instances. Many people incorrectly think that you need to be a programmer to use any of it. However, VBA allows anyone to make a wide variety of enhancements to any Microsoft Office application. In this section, you will use VBA to enhance the functionality of databases.

Understand the Functionality of VBA in Access

VBA is particularly valuable in automating repetitive tasks. In this way, using VBA is similar to using macros, but VBA provides additional tools. These tools allow you to create more robust and dynamic tasks such as automatically populating a form field or prompting a user to select a file for importing. The code that you will write in this chapter is called a procedure in VBA. Each **procedure** contains a series of statements or instructions that are executed as a unit.

To better understand VBA, it is helpful to consider two common approaches to programming. **Object-oriented programming** uses objects — such as a form in Access — to design applications. **Objects** are combinations of data and code that are treated as a single unit. The application can respond to events that occur in relation to the object. **Event-driven programming** uses an event — such as moving to the next record of a form — to trigger the execution of code. VBA is triggered by events within a database. The code can then invoke other events or make changes to objects within the application.

In Microsoft Access, this object hierarchy has been replicated in the structure of the application. Access contains a top-level Application object that then contains other objects such as forms or buttons. These objects have changeable properties such as background colors or the value of a text box. Objects also have **methods**, which are actions — such as SaveAs — that control the object's behavior.

VBA in one Microsoft Office application can also be used to interact with other Office applications. For example, VBA can be used to export tables from Access to an Excel spreadsheet or to populate an e-mail message in Outlook with data from an Access form.

Convert an Existing Macro to VBA

Sometimes the best way to learn what VBA can do is to see how Office itself uses VBA. Consider the Putts for Paws charitable event. The event organizers must track participants and the donations made by these participants. The golf course has recently added a web service that allows participants to register for the event online. This system produces an Excel file on a daily basis that lists any new participants who have registered for the event. Because the event has become so successful, the number of participants has increased dramatically, and many new participants are signing up. Barry Cheney, manager of the Red Bluff Golf Course & Pro Shop, has asked you to modify the Putts for Paws database such that it can easily import these new Excel lists.

REAL WORLD ADVICE | **Why Not Use a Saved Import?**

Saved Imports in Access are extremely useful for automating the repetitive task of importing a file into Access. However, this process works only when the file name and location are always the same. Mobile users or users working with file names that change frequently can become frustrated with Saved Imports. Any change in the file structure renders the Saved Import useless. VBA can accommodate for changes.

Opening the Starting File

A macro already exists in the Putts for Paws database that would import a spreadsheet from the correct folder on the user's computer. The mcrImportParticipants macro imports a list of participants from the file a07ch13List.xlsx into the table tblParticipant. This macro will result in an error if the file is not named exactly as listed previously or if it is in a different location. Currently, the macro is set up to import the a07ch13List.xlsx file from the C:\Temp folder of the user's computer. The macro is embedded in a button on the Imports tab of the frmPuttsMenu navigational form in the Putts database. In this exercise, you will open the Putts database.

A13.00

To Open the Starting File

a. Start **Access**, click **Open Other Files** in the left pane, and then double-click **This PC**. Navigate through the folder structure to the location of your student data files, and then double-click **a07ch13Putts**. A database opens displaying tables, forms, reports, and other objects related to the Putts for Paws charity tournament.

b. Click the **File** tab, save the file as an **Access Database**, and click **Save As**. Navigate to the location where you are saving your project files, and then change the file name to a07ch13Putts_LastFirst using your last and first name. Click **Save**. If necessary, enable the content.

Troubleshooting

Depending on the configuration of your computer, you may not always be prompted to enable content when you first open a database in Access. Entering the Trust Center and setting the Macro Settings to Disable all macros with notification will display the Security Warning any time you open a database that contains macros or Visual Basic. Conversely, by establishing a Trusted Location, you have the option of enabling all content in databases that are stored in the specified location.

Converting an Existing Macro to VBA

Because the Macro Builder in Access does not allow for file selection to occur in importing files with the ImportExportSpreadsheet macro action, this process is limited in its functionality. In this exercise, you will convert this macro into VBA in order to edit the macro to allow the user to select the file to import. Additionally, Barry Cheney wants users to be able to select multiple files for import. He has mentioned that some participants are still being tracked manually in a different Excel spreadsheet.

 A13.01

SIDE NOTE

Pin the Ribbon

If your ribbon is collapsed, pin your ribbon open. Click the Home tab. In the lower right-hand corner of the ribbon, click Pin the Ribbon.

To Convert an Existing Macro to VBA

a. Right-click the **mcrImportParticipants** macro in the Navigation Pane, and then click **Design View**.

b. On the Design tab, in the Tools group, click **Convert Macros to Visual Basic**.

c. Clear the check box to **Add error handling to generated functions**, and leave the check box for **Include macro comments** selected. Error handling and commenting will be discussed later in this chapter, but the conversion process will give a demonstration of this process.

SIDE NOTE

Opening the Visual Basic Editor

Converting a macro will open the Visual Basic Editor. You can also access the Visual Basic Editor on the Database Tools tab in the Macro group or with the keyboard shortcut Alt + F11.

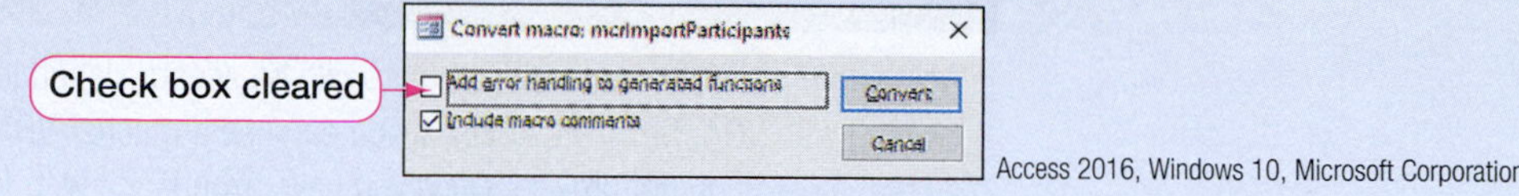

Figure 1 Convert macro dialog box

d. Click **Convert**, and then click **OK** in the Convert macros to Visual Basic message box that appears.

The Visual Basic Editor window will now open.

e. If necessary, Maximize the Visual Basic Editor.

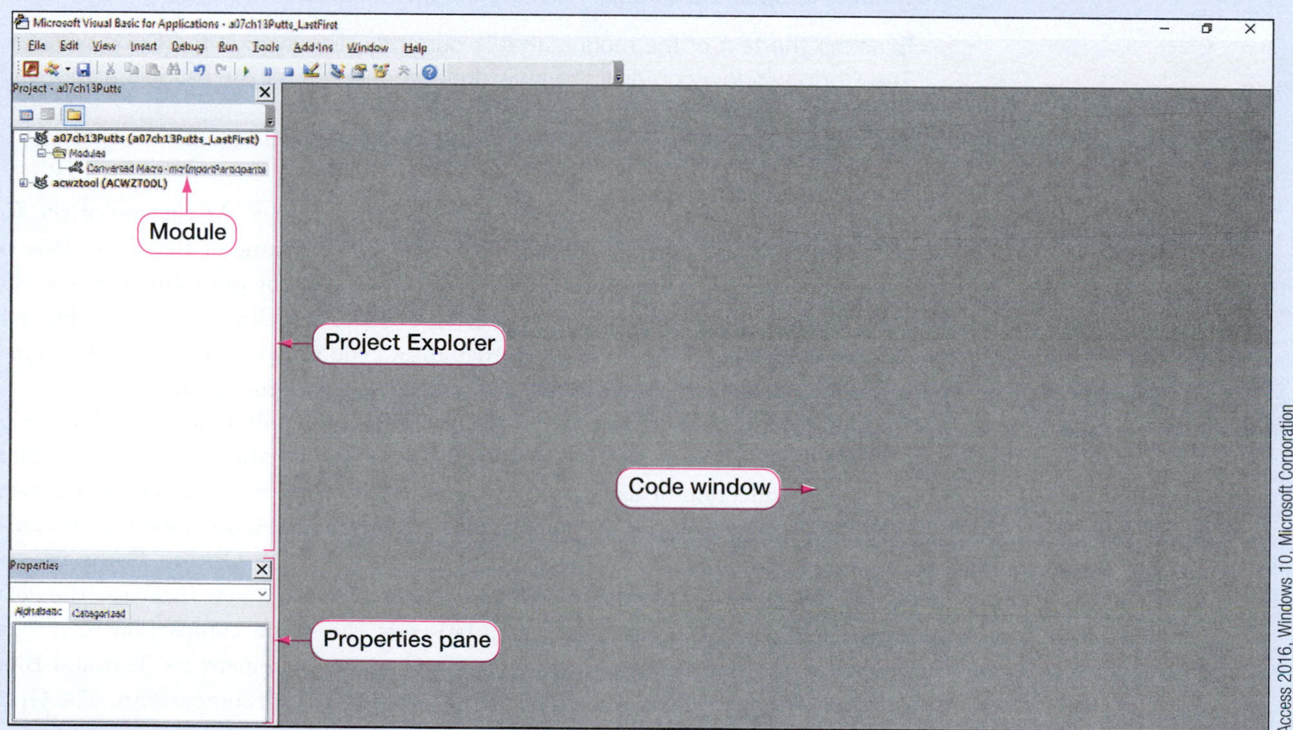

Figure 2 The Visual Basic Editor

Opening the Converted Macro in the Visual Basic Editor

The **Visual Basic Editor** is the tool built into Microsoft Office that is used for creating and editing VBA. At the top of the screen is the title bar with the name of the database that is currently open and being edited. Directly under the application title are the Menu bar and Standard toolbar that are visible by default. On the left side of the Visual Basic Editor is the Project Explorer. The **Project Explorer** contains a list of the currently open Access Database objects that contain VBA procedures and a list of modules within the current database. VBA in an Access database can be embedded either in a specific Access object — such as a form or a button — or within a module. A **module** is used to store a VBA procedure that can be referenced or called by other procedures or events in the database. This is helpful, especially when a single procedure might be used in several different instances in a database. For example, a message box with a common statement could be created as a procedure and then used in other procedures throughout the database.

The larger window on the right of the Visual Basic Editor is the **Code window**. This is where you can edit the text of any procedure.

REAL WORLD ADVICE | **Macros Versus VBA**

Anything that can be done with a macro can be accomplished in VBA. In fact, most macros are created with VBA. So why use VBA if you can use a macro? VBA provides additional functionality that macros do not provide. Once you have experience with VBA, it is often faster and more efficient to create a few lines of code than to create macros. In fact, best practice is to try not to switch back and forth between VBA and macros.

A13.02

To Open the Converted Macro in the Visual Basic Editor

a. Double-click **Converted Macro - mcrImportParticipants** in the Project Explorer window to open the module. If necessary, Maximize ☐ the Code window.

b. Examine the text of the module that is currently displayed in the Code window. The Code window contains the individual procedures for the module along with other items discussed later in the workshop.

The contents of the Code window are shown in Figure 3. At the top of the Code window is the Object box. The **Object box** displays the name of the object that contains the procedure, such as a form or command button. If the procedure exists within a module, the Object box will display (General). Next to the Object box is the Procedure box. The **Procedure box** provides a list that allows you to navigate quickly between the Declarations section and the individual procedures in the open module.

The **Declarations section** contains declarations that apply to all procedures within the module. **Declarations** define user-defined data types, variables, arrays, and constants. An **array** is a collection of data of the same type. For example, an array can be used to store all the different job titles in a company. By default, all Access modules contain the Option Compare statement in the Declarations section. The **Option Compare** statement sets the string comparison method for the module. In a new database, the default statement is Option Compare Database. This sets the string comparison to the database default. The two settings for the Option Compare statement are Text and Binary. The **Option Compare Text** setting results in case-insensitive comparisons. The **Option Compare Binary** setting examines the ASCII values for the characters contained in a string and is therefore case sensitive.

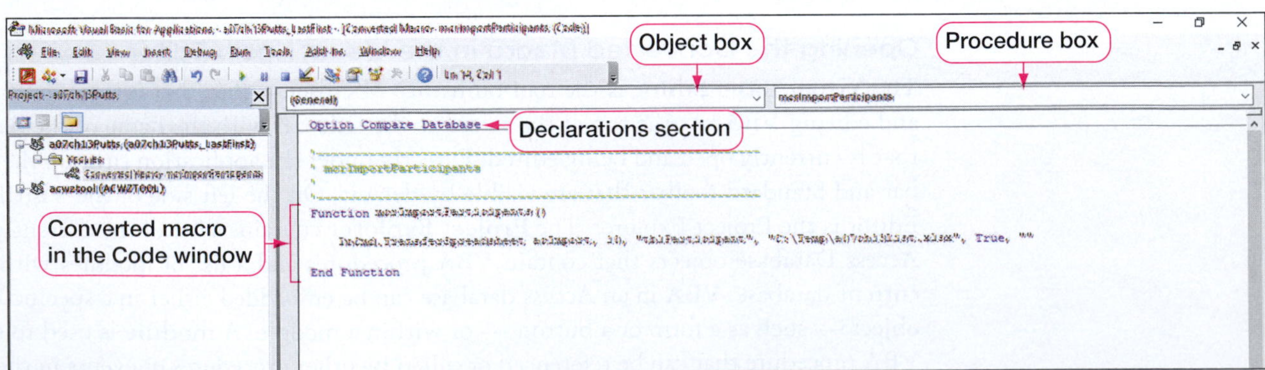

Access 2016, Windows 10, Microsoft Corporation

Figure 3 Converted macro in the Visual Basic Editor

CONSIDER THIS | **Text Versus Binary**

Using the Option Compare Text statement causes Access to evaluate the strings "text" and "Text" as equal in a VBA procedure. Using Option Compare Binary would result in the same two strings being evaluated as not equal in a VBA procedure. The database default is binary. Are there benefits to changing the default setting?

After the Declarations section is the first procedure of the module. Modules can contain multiple procedures. The procedure in this module is the macro that was converted to VBA. In this instance, the procedure is a function. A **function** executes instructions and returns a value to another procedure. Functions are called by other procedures, whereas a **Sub procedure** runs on its own or can be called by another procedure. A Sub procedure performs a set of instructions and can pass multiple values to other procedures. Each function you create starts with the statement "Function" followed by the name you give the function. In this case, the name is mcrImportParticipants. The function can contain multiple tasks and must end with the statement "End Function".

Edit and Structure VBA Procedures

In the conversion process, a comment was placed above the function in the newly created module. Comments are strings of text that will not be processed as part of the procedure and appear as green text. Comments will be discussed later in this chapter. Before examining the individual lines of the procedure, look over the format of the text in the Code window. An important aspect of writing VBA is to keep the code legible so that you and others can interpret what is happening. This means using indentation, comments, and line breaks liberally.

You need to take extra steps to keep the code legible and to document what steps you are taking and why. This makes it easier for you and others who work within the database to understand what the procedure is doing while you or they are editing it. One of these steps will be using Tab to create indentations in the code.

Be aware that VBA procedures lack word wrapping in the Code window. Because the Code window does not word wrap like Microsoft Word or other word-processing programs, lengthy strings of code will extend continuously to the right. This creates code that is extremely difficult to read. To break a line of code across two lines, a line continuation character can be used. A **line continuation character** consists of a single space followed by a single underscore character as the last character in a line of code. This tells the Visual Basic Editor that the two lines of code should be treated as one.

REAL WORLD ADVICE | **Lines of Code in VBA**

The Visual Basic Editor interprets statements of code on a line-by-line basis. In other words, typing part of a statement on a line of the Visual Basic Editor and pressing Enter before the end of the statement will invoke an error. If you need to break a lengthy line of text across two lines of the Code window, type a line continuation character at the end of a line, and continue your statements on the next line of the Code window.

Examining the DoCmd Object and Breaking a Statement

The **DoCmd object** allows Access actions to be performed from within VBA. This can include opening a report, telling Access not to show warning messages, or closing an object. Typing DoCmd into the Code window or using the Object Browser will show a list of all methods associated with the DoCmd object. The Object Browser can be opened by clicking [icon] on the Standard toolbar in the Visual Basic Editor. The **Object Browser** lists all VBA objects along with the associated methods and properties for each object. In this exercise, you will examine the DoCmd object in more detail.

A13.03

To Examine the DoCmd Object and Break a Statement

a. Examine the line of code that begins with the DoCmd object.

   Notice that this line of code is indented. Indentations indicate that you are taking action within the procedure. Liberal use of white space combined with line indentation creates a more legible procedure.

b. Examine the statement that follows DoCmd.

   The TransferSpreadsheet method is used to import an Excel spreadsheet into the database. The properties associated with a method will allow for further control of how the method behaves. In this example, the TransferSpreadsheet method uses several properties to control actions, such as which folder to open by default and whether to import, export, or link to the spreadsheet file.

c. On the line of the Code window that begins with DoCmd, click after the **comma** that follows the number 10. Press Spacebar, type _ and then press Enter.

   Using a line continuation character will allow you to break a single statement across two lines of code without creating errors in the code.

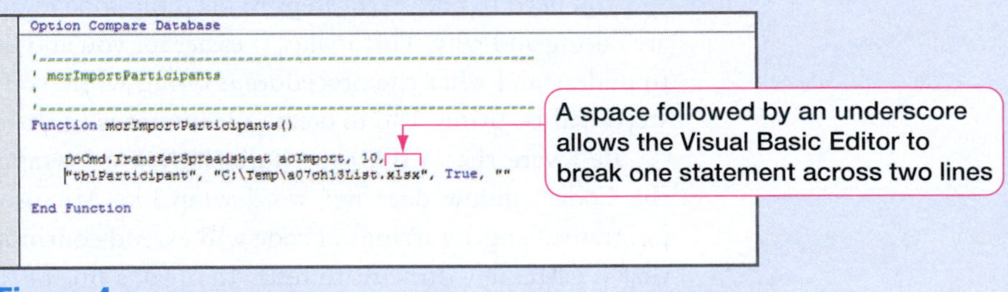
Option Compare Database
'---
' mcrImportParticipants
'
'---
Function mcrImportParticipants()
DoCmd.TransferSpreadsheet acImport, 10, _
"tblParticipant", "C:\Temp\a07ch13List.xlsx", True, ""
End Function
A space followed by an underscore allows the Visual Basic Editor to break one statement across two lines

Figure 4 DoCmd object Access 2016, Windows 10, Microsoft Corporation

Examine the TransferSpreadsheet Method

For importing, exporting, and linking tasks, VBA uses the Transfer methods. The particular method used is specific to the object that is the focus of the task. The **TransferSpreadsheet method** allows Access to import, export, or link to spreadsheet files specifically. This object has six arguments. An **argument** is a constant, variable, or expression that is passed to a procedure.

Table 1 lists the arguments for the TransferSpreadsheet method.

Argument Name	Description	Example
TransferType	This argument refers to the type of action that is to take place with the object.	acImport, acExport, acLink
SpreadsheetType	This argument refers to the type of spreadsheet that will be imported by the database.	acSpreadsheetTypeExcel12 or the number 10
TableName	This is the name of the Access table that will be used during the process in the Transfer Type argument. This can also be a select query in which the data from the query can be exported. When importing, Access will append records to an existing table. If no table exists, Access will import the records into a new table.	"tblName"
FileName	This is the name of the spreadsheet file to be used during the process selected in the TransferType argument.	"C:\Temp\FileName.xlsx" When a specific file is used, the path and file name must be given in quotation marks.
HasFieldNames	This argument specifies whether the spreadsheet contains field names in the first row of the spreadsheet. If the spreadsheet does contain field names, this argument should be set to Yes. If the spreadsheet does not contain field names, this argument should be set to No. The default is No.	Yes/No and True/False can be used interchangeably here.
Range	This optional argument can be used to define a specific range of cells from the spreadsheet to import. If this argument is left blank, Access will import or link the entire worksheet.	"Data" or "" for blank

Table 1 TransferSpreadsheet method arguments

To Examine the TransferSpreadsheet Method

a. Notice that in this TransferSpreadsheet method, after the text DoCmd, the Transfer Type is set to acImport. This tells Access to import the file.

b. Notice that the Spreadsheet type is set to 10. This is the numeric equivalent of the default for this argument, Excel Spreadsheet.

c. Notice that the TableName argument is the tblParticipant table and the table name is in quotation marks. This argument requires the name of the table to be a text string.

d. Notice that the FileName argument contains "C:\Temp\a07ch13List.xlsx". This is the path and name of the spreadsheet that will be imported. Here, this value is a fixed path and file name, just as it was in the original macro. Using VBA, you will need to change it to make this procedure more flexible.

SIDE NOTE

Property Names

In typing an argument, there are often numeric equivalents for the property names. Right-click and select Quick Info after typing an argument to view the numeric equivalent.

e. Notice that the HasFieldNames argument is set to True. This tells Access the spreadsheet does have the appropriate column headers.

Troubleshooting

A HasFieldNames argument set to True requires an exact match. If the column headings in the target Excel spreadsheet do not match the Access field names, an error message will be displayed, and the data will not be imported.

f. Notice that the Range argument displays "", the equivalent of a blank to indicate the default value. This directs Access to import the entire worksheet.

g. Notice that the End Function statement ends the function. When the procedure comes to this statement, it will not process any remaining code.

For this macro to work as required by Barry Cheney, it must allow the user to select the correct file or files from a dynamic location on the user's computer. VBA can be used to add this functionality and control how the user interacts with the resulting processes.

Understanding the FileDialog Object

To allow users to select one or more files for importing, some new code must be inserted prior to the DoCmd object. The **FileDialog object** can be used to allow the user to select the file or files needed for the import process. The FileDialog object has the following four properties, which control how the object is executed in the procedure.

QUICK REFERENCE | **FileDialog Object Properties**

Property	Description	Property Name in VBA
Open	This option allows the user to select one or more files that can be opened in the host application.	msoFileDialogOpen
SaveAs	This option allows the user to select a single file that can then be used to save the current file.	msoFileDialogSaveAs
FilePicker	This option allows the user to select one or more files. The file paths are stored in the Select-edItems method of the FileDialog object.	msoFileDialogFilePicker
FolderPicker	This option allows the user to select a path (folder). The file path text is stored in the Select-edItems method of the FileDialog object.	msoFileDialogFolderPicker

The FileDialog object also has several methods that can be used to customize the behavior of the File Dialog window. In this example, the methods AllowMultiSelect, Title, and SelectedItems will be used. The AllowMultiSelect method lets users select multiple files for import. The Title method allows you to set a customized title for the File Dialog window. The SelectedItems method stores the names of the files that are selected for import.

REAL WORLD ADVICE **The AutoComplete Feature**

VBA uses an AutoComplete feature similar to that found in other Microsoft Office applications, such as writing field names in query criteria. For example, typing "FileDialog." in the Visual Basic Editor, as seen in Figure 5, will open a list of objects and methods that are found within the FileDialog object. These can be selected with the pointer or by typing enough of the desired item to prompt Access to highlight the item, which you then can complete by pressing Tab.

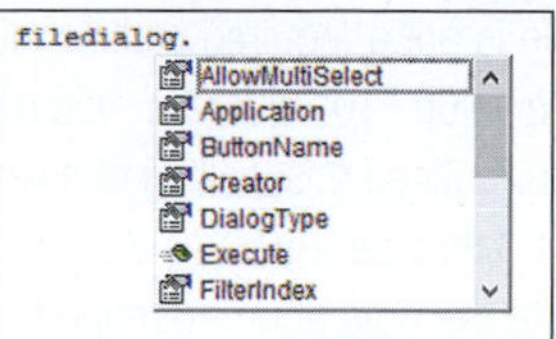

Access 2016, Windows 10, Microsoft Corporation

Figure 5 FileDialog object showing the AutoComplete feature

The first step in creating the File Dialog process is to declare a variable as a FileDialog object. Creating and declaring variables will make the procedure more efficient and easier to follow as more statements are added. **Variables** are placeholders that can be set to a hard-coded value or to an object within VBA and then later modified during the execution of the procedure. The different variable data types are listed in Table 2. Because you can customize the names of variables in VBA, you can create variables that are easy to remember and identify. The **Dim statement** begins the process of declaring a variable. This is followed by the name the user wants to define as a variable. This can be any string that does not begin with a number and is not a reserved word in VBA. Following the name of the variable is the As Type portion of the statement.

Name	Description	Example
Byte	An integer from 0 to 255	125
Boolean	Used in true or false variables	True or False
Integer	Numeric data type for whole numbers	125
Long	Numeric data type for large integer numbers	9,000,000,000
Currency	Numeric data type that allows for 4 digits to the right of the decimal and 15 to the left	1234.67
Single	Numeric data type used for numbers that can contain fractions	125.25
Double	Numeric data type used for large numbers that can contain fractions	9,000,000,000.25
Date	Stores date and time data	7/1/2013 8:35:56 AM
String	A variable length of text characters	"Your import is complete"
Object	Used to create a variable that stores a VBA object	FileDialog
Variant	The default data type if none is specified; can store numeric, string, date/time, empty, or null data	125 or "One hundred and twenty-five"

Table 2 Variable types

User-defined types can also be created in VBA modules and assigned to a variable with the Dim statement. In this instance, a variable will be created and set to be equal to the FileDialog object. This allows for easy use of the FileDialog object later in the procedure.

Variables do not have to be defined by using the Dim statement. Not formally defining variables often leads to errors in your VBA as the result of misspellings of variable names. This is required only if the Option Explicit statement is used in the Declarations section of the module. The **Option Explicit statement** will force any variables in a procedure to be defined by using the Dim statement.

CONSIDER THIS | Using Option Explicit

VBA can interpret variable names without the use of the Dim statement. By default, defining a variable is not a required action. You could simply type MyVariable = 10, and the procedure would use the value "10" wherever you used the variable "MyVariable". This can lead to problems such as an unnoticed misspelling of a variable name. Additionally, any undefined variables will be of the Variant data type. Because Variant covers such a wide variety of data types, the application must evaluate the data and determine the appropriate data type. This increases the processing time. Using the Option Explicit statement in the Declarations section — the first line of the Code window — forces the definition of any variable names, preventing this type of situation from occurring. What are the advantages of using Option Explicit?

REAL WORLD ADVICE | What Is the Best Way to Identify the Properties of an Object?

The properties associated with an object can be referred to by name but also can sometimes be referred to by a defined constant. For example, with the FileDialog object, you can choose to use the File Open dialog box by typing msoFileDialogOpen or, more simply, by typing the number 1. Using the defined constant will accomplish the same desired outcome as typing msoFileDialogOpen. The difference is that using the defined constant may be faster to type, but it may not be as intuitive to decipher in reviewing the procedure later on.

Adding the FileDialog Object to the Procedure

In this exercise, you will incorporate the FileDialog object into the VBA procedure that will begin the process of allowing the user to select multiple spreadsheets to import into the participant table.

To Add the FileDialog Object to the Procedure

a. Place the insertion point on the blank line above the **DoCmd.TransferSpreadsheet** action in the Code window.

b. Press Enter, and then press Tab to indent the code.

c. Type Dim ParticipantDialog as Object, and then press Enter.
   This creates a variable called ParticipantDialog. This variable can be reused throughout the procedure and will be more efficient when you set the object properties later on.

d. Type Set ParticipantDialog = Application.FileDialog(msoFileDialogOpen), and then press Enter twice. A Microsoft Visual Basic for Applications message box may appear before you have completed this line of code. If so, click **Yes**, and then see the Troubleshooting tip for further explanation of this message box.

SIDE NOTE

Manually Adding Object Libraries

Plug-in applications and legacy object libraries may need to be added manually. This can be accomplished by clicking the Tools menu and selecting References.

Troubleshooting

Objects in VBA exist in library files. Objects become available in the Code window when these library files are referenced in the Visual Basic Editor. The FileDialog object is not included in the default libraries that are referenced in Access 2016. Access will automatically install a reference for the correct object library when you enter the FileDialog object into the Code window. The message box in Figure 6 is displayed when Access adds the appropriate library for the FileDialog object. If the proper library file did not load, add the Microsoft Office 16.0 Object Library to the list of references.

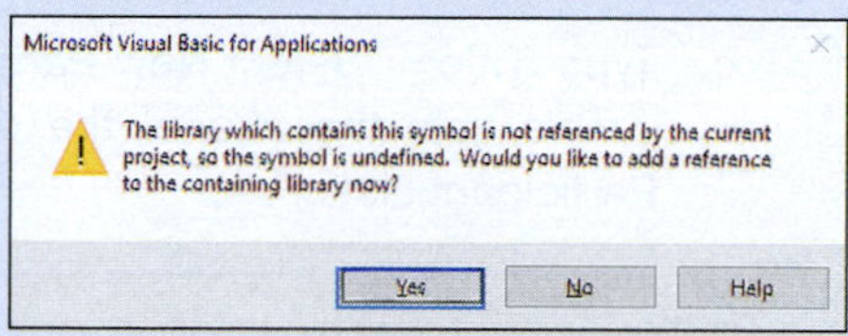

Figure 6 Add a library reference
Access 2016, Windows 10, Microsoft Corporation

e. Examine the Set statement. The Set statement tells the application that the variable ParticipantDialog will be used as a FileDialog object.

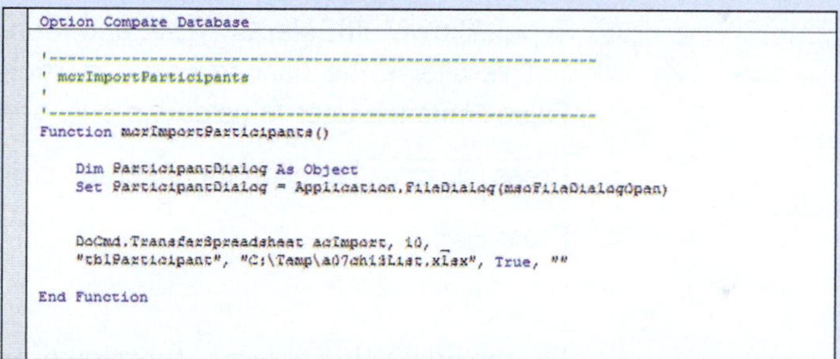

Figure 7 FileDialog object added to the procedure
Access 2016, Windows 10, Microsoft Corporation

CONSIDER THIS | Using the Filters Method

The Filters property of the FileDialog object can be useful for customizing the File Open dialog box. By using this method, the VBA procedure can reset the filter on the dialog box so that only spreadsheet files are initially viewed. This prevents a user from accidentally selecting the incorrect file type. To accomplish this, use the .Filters method. To be safe, start by clearing out any existing filters (.Filters.Clear). Then add the filters you want the user to see. For example, .Filters.Add "Excel Spreadsheet", "*.xlsx" will allow users to select any .xlsx files. Filters.Add "All Files", "*.*" adds an all files option that displays any file in the current folder. Why might it be useful to restrict which files a user can select in a dialog box?

Using the With Statement

Once a variable has been assigned to serve as a placeholder for the FileDialog object, there are several properties that can be set. The **With statement** allows for an efficient way of using several methods or setting multiple properties on a single object. Without it, the developer would be required to type the object's full name for each method used or property set. With statements are simple to use and provide for enormous time savings in coding. To use a With statement type "With ObjectName", where "ObjectName" is the object you want to modify. Inside of a With statement, each method used or property to edit is preceded only by a single period. Each With statement must be accompanied by an "End With" statement. While With statements can be nested to apply settings to multiple properties within an object, they can act on only one object at a time. In this exercise, you will incorporate the With statement into the VBA procedure to set multiple properties of the FileDialog object.

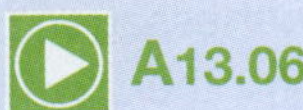

To Use the With Statement

a. Ensure that the insertion point is on the line above the **DoCmd** object. Type With ParticipantDialog, press Enter, and then press Tab.
   This inserts an indentation to create a more legible code structure.

b. Type .Title = "Select New Participant List(s)", and then press Enter.
   This sets the title of the dialog box that appears to display "Select New Participant List(s)".

Troubleshooting

Inside the With statement, be sure to type a period character before the method or property you are working with. In the prior step, typing "Title" without the period character will result in an error.

c. Type .AllowMultiSelect = True, and then press Enter.
   This allows the user to select multiple files to import. Setting this method to False limits the user to selecting only one file at a time.

d. Press Backspace to align the insertion point with the With statement.

e. Press Enter.

For the FileDialog object to function properly, the procedure must determine whether the user selected any files. Alternatively, the user could end the operation by clicking the Cancel button in the File Dialog window. If this happens, the procedure should end after the Cancel button is clicked. An If statement can be implemented within the With statement to determine the outcome of the user's actions.

REAL WORLD ADVICE Capitalization

While VBA is by default case sensitive, when you type the name of a variable, method, or property, the Visual Basic Editor will automatically capitalize the text for you. For example, if you want the FileDialog property .AllowMultiSelect, typing .allowmultiselect will be automatically corrected to the appropriate case.

Using If Statements in VBA

If statements in VBA work similarly to those found in Access and Excel, though the syntax is slightly different. Each If statement must follow the basic syntax.

```
If [Condition] Then
[Statement]
Else
[Statement]
End If
```

REAL WORLD ADVICE **When to Nest If Statements in VBA**

You can nest If statements to take into account multiple logical tests. In VBA, there is an alternative to nesting If statements. If statements in VBA can use ElseIf before the Else statement in order to continue to consider additional conditions being met. The use of the ElseIf statement would look like this.

```
IF [Condition1] Then
[Statement]
ElseIf [Condition2] Then
[Statement]
Else
[Statement]
End If
```

The .Show method of the FileDialog object displays the selected type of dialog box to the user and returns to the procedure a True value if one or more files were selected. If no files were selected, .Show returns a False value.

In this exercise, you will incorporate an If statement into the VBA procedure so that if .Show returns a value of True, the procedure will import the files to the appropriate table. If .Show returns a value of False, a message will be displayed stating that the operation was canceled and the procedure should be exited.

To Use If Statements in VBA

a. Ensure that the insertion point is on the line above the **DoCmd** object, and then press Tab to indent the current line.

b. Type If .Show = True then, and then press Enter.

c. Press Tab to create an indentation.

d. Type Dim ImportFileName as Variant to define a variable that will hold the names of the files selected by the user. Using the Variant type is required here and will be discussed later.

e. Click before the **DoCmd** statement, and highlight the two lines of this code. Press Tab twice to align this statement with the prior Dim statement.
This allows the import to run if the .Show property is true. Because the procedure will need to account for multiple files, additional code will be required. This will be revisited in the next step.

f. Click after the last argument of the DoCmd statement, press Enter, and then press Backspace. This aligns the pointer with the same column as the If portion of the statement.

g. Type Else, and then press Enter. This begins the False portion of the If statement.

h. Press Tab, and then type Msgbox "You canceled the import" to create a new message box.
This message box will tell the user that the import process has been stopped by clicking Cancel in the File Dialog box.

i. Press Enter, and then press Backspace.

j. Type End If, and then press Enter.

k. Press [Backspace]. This aligns the pointer with the same column as the With Statement.

l. Type **End With**, and then press [Enter].

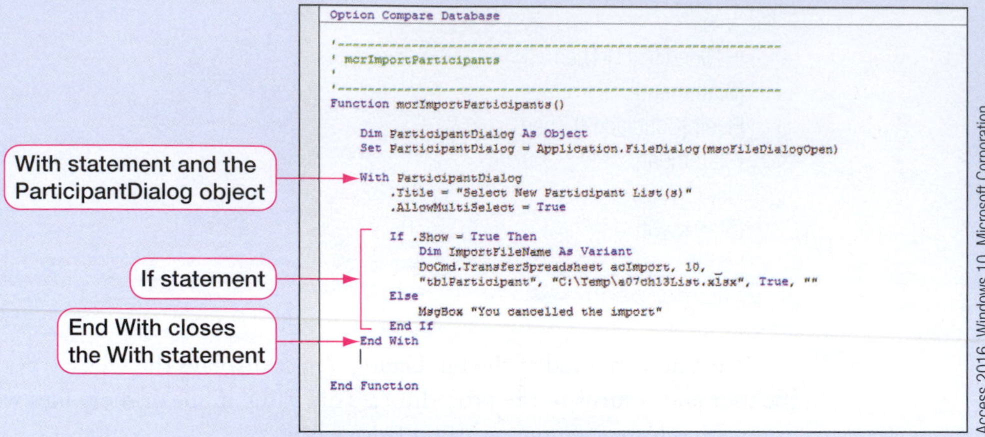
With statement and the ParticipantDialog object
If statement
End With closes the With statement
Option Compare Database
'--
' mcrImportParticipants
'
'--
Function mcrImportParticipants()
Dim ParticipantDialog As Object
Set ParticipantDialog = Application.FileDialog(msoFileDialogOpen)
With ParticipantDialog
.Title = "Select New Participant List(s)"
.AllowMultiSelect = True
If .Show = True Then
Dim ImportFileName As Variant
DoCmd.TransferSpreadsheet acImport, 10, _
"tblParticipant", "C:\Temp\a07ch13List.xlsx", True, ""
Else
MsgBox "You cancelled the import"
End If
End With
End Function
Access 2016, Windows 10, Microsoft Corporation

Figure 8 Import procedure

REAL WORLD ADVICE	Message Boxes in VBA

The Msgbox function is an extremely useful function. In VBA, a message box can display customized text and buttons in addition to the standard OK, Cancel, and Yes/No buttons that are familiar in Microsoft applications. Similar to the process of commenting code, message boxes provide a convenient method of keeping your users informed about the status of the application that they are using.

The procedure that has been created and edited to this point will function as follows: When the procedure is executed, first it declares the variable ParticipantDialog as an Access object. The procedure then defines the variable as a FileDialog object with a File Open parameter. Next, by using a With statement, the title of the File Open dialog box is set, and the object is enabled to accept multiple file selections from the user. Alternatively, Access will display a message box stating that the user canceled the import if the Cancel button in the dialog box is clicked. To complete the procedure, a loop will be added to the True portion of the If statement to account for situations in which the user selects multiple files for importing.

Create and Use Loops in VBA

When the user selects a file to import, the procedure stores the name of the file in the SelectedItems property of the FileDialog object. It then imports that file into the appropriate table. If the user were to select multiple files, each file name would be stored in the same property and imported. The process for importing the appropriate files listed in the .SelectedItems FileDialog property happens on a file-by-file basis. In other words, each file that is selected will force the procedure to access a new file name and import the file as an individualized action.

This type of repetitive action is often one of the main reasons macros or VBA are used to automate a process in Access. **Loops** are used to execute a series of statements multiple times. Loops are similar to If statements in that they evaluate a condition and act depending on the status of the condition. Loops offer a distinct difference in that they allow the statements contained within the loop to be executed multiple times depending on the constraints of the loop. Figure 9 demonstrates a programmatic loop. The number of times the loop runs can be determined in two ways: Loops can run until a condition is determined to be true or false. Loops can also be set to run until they have executed a specific number of times. This can be determined by counting the number of repetitions that have run or by counting the number of items on which the loop should act.

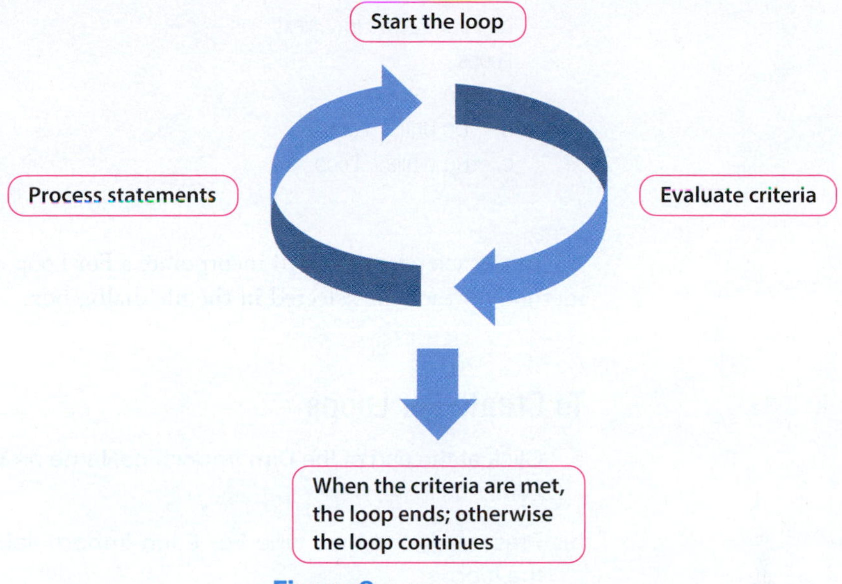

Figure 9 A loop

Loops can be conceptually difficult to understand, but they have a simple structure in the actual procedure. In the example of the FileDialog object, the procedure should store a file name for each file selected by the user. The problem with this specific situation is that the number of files may differ from day to day. On Monday, there might be three files to import, while on Tuesday, there might only be one. Fortunately, VBA has a statement that handles this very situation.

Creating For Loops

The For Each...In...Next statement executes the nested statements for each item in a defined set of objects. In this example, the For Each...In...Next statement selects the name of each file selected by the user. When there are no more file names to record, the loop exits. The syntax for a For Each...In...Next statement contains three parts and looks like the following.

```
For Each [element as data type] In [group]
[Statements]
Next
```

The element is a variable that refers to the item that requires an action, such as a file name. The group is the object that contains the collection of items over which the statements will be repeated. The statements section contains any actions to be carried out. Once the For Each...In...Next statement has carried out the required actions on all of the available items, the procedure continues with the statement in the procedure after the Next statement.

QUICK REFERENCE | **Types of Loops in VBA**

1. For Loops
   a. For...Next
   b. For Each...In...Next
2. Loops
   a. Do Loop
   b. Do Until...Loop
   c. Do While...Loop

In this exercise, you will incorporate a For Loop that will use the TransferSpreadsheet method for each file selected in the file dialog box.

To Create For Loops

a. Click at the end of the **Dim ImportFileName as Variant** statement, and then press Enter.

b. Press Tab, and then type For Each ImportFileName In .SelectedItems to begin the loop.
   The loop will continue until there are no additional file names in the .SelectedItems method.

c. Click before the **DoCmd** statement, and then highlight the two lines of the DoCmd. Press Tab twice to indent the DoCmd statement within the For Each statement.

d. Select the text **"C:\Temp\a07ch13List.xlsx"**, and then press Delete to remove it.

e. Type ImportFileName with no quotation marks.
   This replaces the text in the FileName property of the TransferSpreadsheet statement with the variable you created to hold a file name selected by the user. Because a variable name is used in place of a text string, no quotation marks are needed.

f. Press End, and then press Enter.
   Remember that the TransferSpreadsheet method imports the file to the appropriate Access table. In the loop, each time a file is imported, the loop starts over again with the next file name that was stored in the .SelectedItems property.

g. Press Backspace, and then type Next to complete the loop.
   This aligns the insertion point with the same column as the For Each statement. The Next portion of the statement exits the loop once all files have been imported.

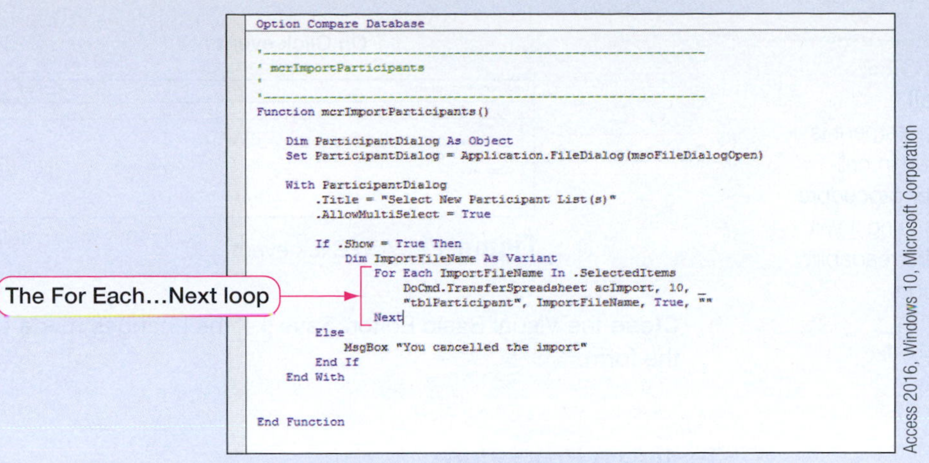

Option Compare Database
'--
' mcrImportParticipants
'
'--
Function mcrImportParticipants()
Dim ParticipantDialog As Object
Set ParticipantDialog = Application.FileDialog(msoFileDialogOpen)
With ParticipantDialog
.Title = "Select New Participant List(s)"
.AllowMultiSelect = True
If .Show = True Then
Dim ImportFileName As Variant
For Each ImportFileName In .SelectedItems
DoCmd.TransferSpreadsheet acImport, 10, _
"tblParticipant", ImportFileName, True, ""
Next
Else
MsgBox "You cancelled the import"
End If
End With
End Function
The For Each...Next loop
Access 2016, Windows 10, Microsoft Corporation

Figure 10 Finished procedure

h. **Close** the Visual Basic Editor. Close ☒ the mcrImportParticipants macro.

This completes the For Each...In...Next statement and the procedure as a whole. Now, regardless of how many files the user selects the user for import, Access will process each file separately.

Using a Call Statement to Run a Procedure

The last step before testing the procedure is to change the assignment of the button on the frmImports form. Because the button was originally set up to run a macro when clicked, you need to change this setting to run the new procedure. To accomplish this, you need to call the function that was created by converting the import macro. The **Call statement** will run another Sub procedure or function from within a procedure by transferring to the called routine. In this exercise, you will edit the Import New Participants button on the frmImports form to call the mcrImportParticipants procedure when clicked.

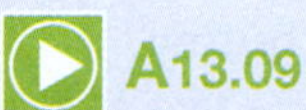
A13.09

To Use a Call Statement to Run a Procedure

a. In the Navigation Pane, right-click **frmImports**, and then click **Design View**.

b. On the Design tab, in the Tools group, click **Property Sheet** to open the Property Sheet pane if necessary.

c. In the Design window, click the **Import New Participants** button.

d. If necessary, in the Property Sheet pane, click the **Event** tab. The On Click event lists the macro mcrImportParticipants as the action to take when the button is clicked.

e. Click the **On Click arrow**, and then select **[Event Procedure]**.

f. Click the Build button [...].

This will open the Visual Basic Editor. The Code window will display a new Private Sub statement. This Sub will be run when the command button is clicked.

g. On the blank line of the Sub, press Tab. Type Call mcrImportParticipants to call the newly created VBA procedure.

SIDE NOTE
Using Call
The Call statement is not required in calling another procedure. However, using it will improve the readability of your code.

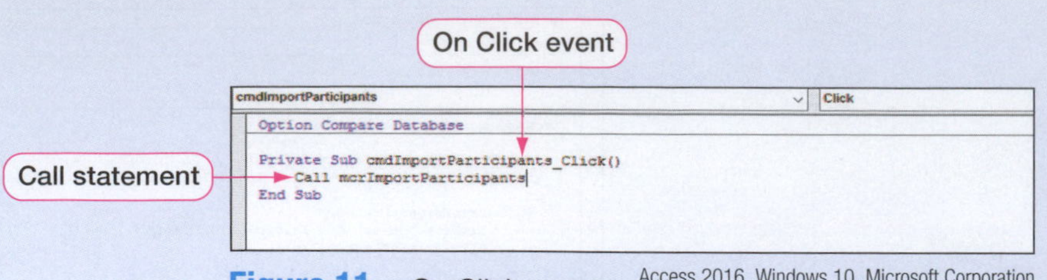

Figure 11 On Click event

Access 2016, Windows 10, Microsoft Corporation

h. **Close** the Visual Basic Editor. **Save** the changes made to the form. **Close** the form.

Testing a Procedure

Once code has been completed, it is important to test the process. You have been provided with a file of new participants for the Putts for Paws events. These participants need to be imported into the database. In this exercise, you will use your newly created procedure to import these new participants.

CONSIDER THIS | **What Can Happen with an Untested Procedure?**

What type of consequences might occur if an untested procedure runs and contains errors? What about a procedure that imports data into a database? What could happen to the list of Red Bluff's participants?

A13.10

To Test a Procedure

a. In the Navigation Pane, double-click **frmPuttsMenu** to open the Putts for Paws Database navigation form.

b. Click the **Imports** tab, and then click the **Import New Participants button.**
   You will be presented with a File Open dialog box. Notice that the title of the dialog box is the same as you specified in your procedure.

c. Navigate through the folder structure to the location of your student data files, and then double-click **a07ch13List.xlsx**.

d. To verify that the import was successful, click the Participants tab, and then click **Last Record** to view the last record in the tblParticipant table. The last record should now be ParticipantID number 1009.

e. In the frmPuttsMenu form, click the **Imports** tab, and then click the **Import New Participants** button again.

f. Click **Cancel** to stop the import process. You will be presented with a message box stating that you canceled the import.

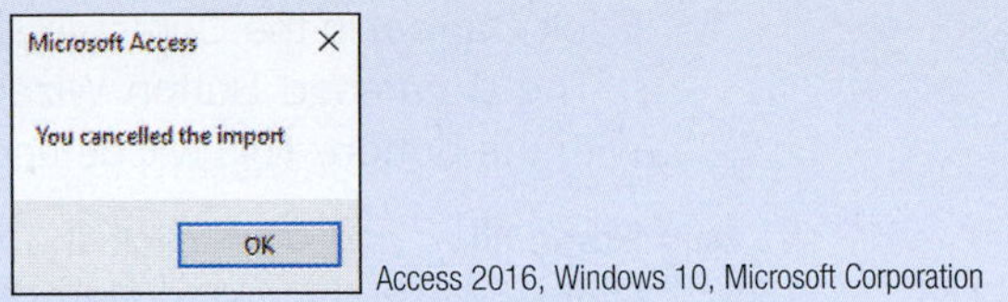

Access 2016, Windows 10, Microsoft Corporation

Figure 12 Cancellation message box

g. Click **OK**. In developing VBA, it is important to test every action a user might take.

h. If you need to take a break before finishing this chapter, now is a good time.

CHAPTER 13

Adding VBA to an Access Database

VBA can be added to Access databases in a variety of ways. As was previously demonstrated, VBA can be added to modules and called from other objects in the database, such as buttons. This is a robust option, as the same procedure can be called from multiple objects in the database. Like macros, VBA can also be embedded into an object, such as a form. If the object is then copied to another database, the VBA procedure is copied with the object. In this section, you will add VBA procedures to a form within the Putts for Paws Database.

REAL WORLD ADVICE | **Creating VBA Procedures from Scratch**

There will not always be a macro to begin with, and often what you will be trying to accomplish with VBA will be more involved than what a macro can be set up to do in Access. Unlike other Microsoft applications, in Access, it is not always the best practice to begin with a recorded macro.

Create VBA Procedures

Barry Cheney has asked you to modify the frmParticipant form of the Putts for Paws database. The database has been set up such that each entity that donates can specify a billing address that is separate from the entity's designated mailing address. This works well when the two addresses are different, but when the addresses are the same, the result is a duplicate data entry. To increase the efficiency of the data entry process, you have been asked to provide a method of automation to the form. Barry has requested a button that will copy the billing address fields into the mailing address fields.

Adding a Command Button to a Form

In this exercise, you will add a button to the form that will allow a user to copy the billing address data into the mailing address data with a simple button click.

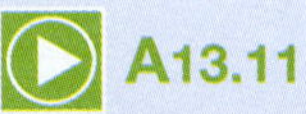
A13.11

To Add a Command Button to a Form

a. If you took a break, open the **a07ch13Putts** database, and then open the **frmPuttsMenu** form.

b. On the Home tab, in the Views group, click the **View** arrow, and then select **Layout View**.

c. Click the **Participants** tab.

d. On the Design tab, in the Controls group, click the **Button** form control.

e. Move the pointer between the **BillingZipCode label** and the **MailingStreetAddress label**, and then click to place the Button form control.

f. Click **Cancel** in the Command Button Wizard.

The Command Button Wizard cannot be used to associate a VBA procedure with the button. This will be accomplished in the Property Sheet pane.

g. Press Ctrl, and then click the **empty cell** in the table to the right of the button. Right-click in the cell, point to **Merge/Split** on the shortcut menu, and then select **Merge**.

The button should act as a separator between the mailing and billing addresses. Merging the button across the table will create a clear break between the two addresses and allow enough room for the button to have a descriptive caption.

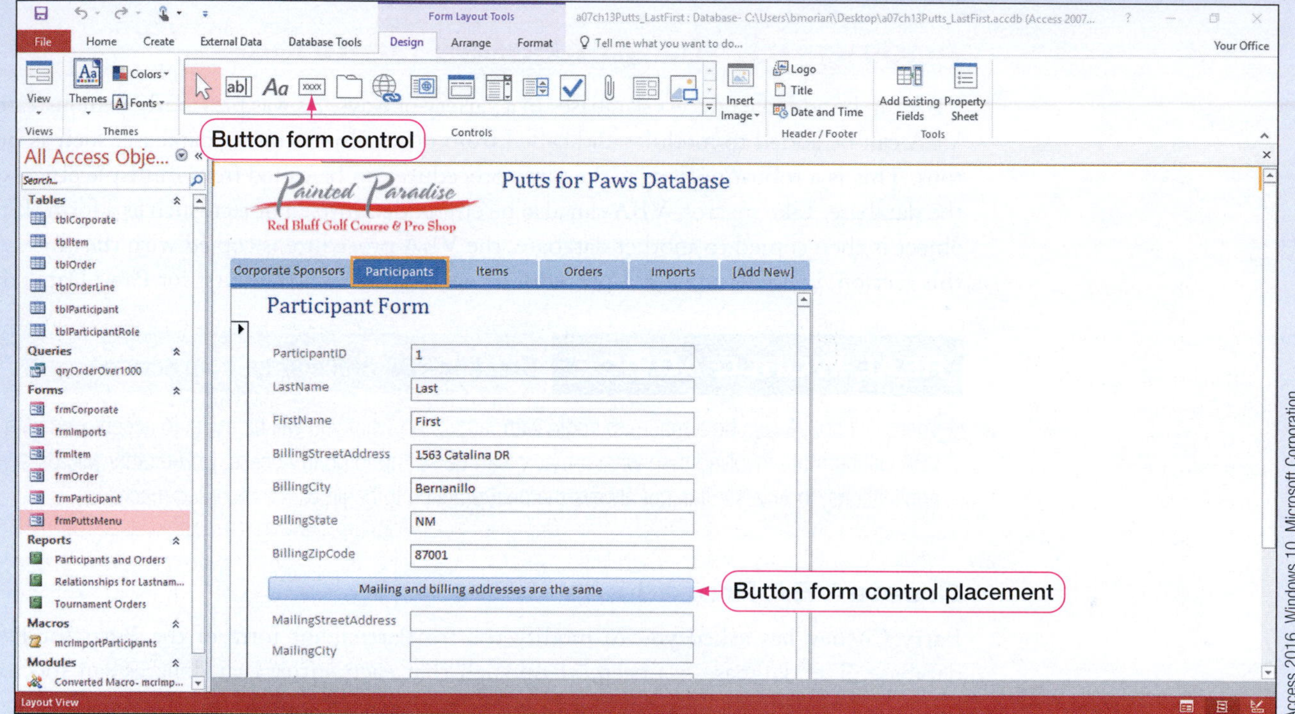

Figure 13 Button form control positioned on the Participants form

h. If necessary, click **Property Sheet** to make the Property Sheet pane visible.

i. In the Property Sheet pane, click the **All** tab. In the **Name** field of the property sheet, replace the existing text with cmdCopyBillingAddress.

j. In the Caption field, replace the existing text with Mailing and billing addresses are the same.

k. **Save** the changes to the form.

REAL WORLD ADVICE Renaming Command Buttons

When a new button is created on a form, Access assigns the button a name, such as Command65. When you are using the wizard to assign functions to a button, this naming convention may not be an obstacle because you will be able to change the caption on the button as part of the wizard. However, when you are creating a button to assign Visual Basic code, this can present problems because the name of the button is too vague. Instead, it is helpful to rename the button to describe the event that will take place. Thus, when you search through your code later, you can quickly find and identify an event button that needs to be modified.

Using the Me Keyword in a Procedure

The process needed in this example is to copy the data from the billing address fields to the mailing address fields when the button cmdCopyBillingAddress is clicked. Access provides some useful shortcuts to assign VBA procedures to controls on objects such as forms. To quickly copy values from one form object to another, you can take advantage of the Me keyword. The **Me keyword** functions like a declared variable that refers to the current object.

To Use the Me Keyword in a Procedure

a. Click the **Home** tab, in the Views group, click the **View** arrow, and then select **Design View**.

> **Troubleshooting**
> To edit the VBA code of an Access object, the object — such as a form — must be opened in Design view. Opening the object in Layout view, which is often used to create and edit forms, will result in a Microsoft Access error.

SIDE NOTE
Accessing the VBA Code for an Object
Often, the most efficient way to access the VBA code related to an event or object is through its property sheet in Design view.

b. If necessary, click the **Participants** tab, and then click the **Mailing and billing addresses are the same** button.

c. In the Property sheet, click the **Event** tab, and then, in the field for **On Click**, click the **Build** button [...].

d. In the Choose Builder dialog box, select **Code Builder**, and then click **OK**.
This opens the Visual Basic Editor. The basic syntax of the procedure in the Code window has been automatically completed. The Option Compare Database statement is in the Declaration section of the Code window. In the Project Explorer, a new Microsoft Access Class object has been created for the form that is being edited. The object Form_frmParticipant will contain any VBA procedures created to run in response to events occurring on this form.

e. Examine the first line of the procedure.
A Sub statement was automatically created when you chose the Code Builder option. The name of the Sub procedure, cmdCopyBillingAddress_Click(), indicates that the procedure will be run when a user clicks the cmdCopyBillingAddress button. In this procedure, the value property of the individual fields can be used to set one field value equal to that of another field value. In this example, you will use the Me keyword to identify the fields to copy.

SIDE NOTE
Private Sub
A Private Sub is a procedure that is accessible only by other procedures in the module in which it is located. In this exercise, for example, the cmdCopyBillingAddress_Click() procedure cannot be used on another form.

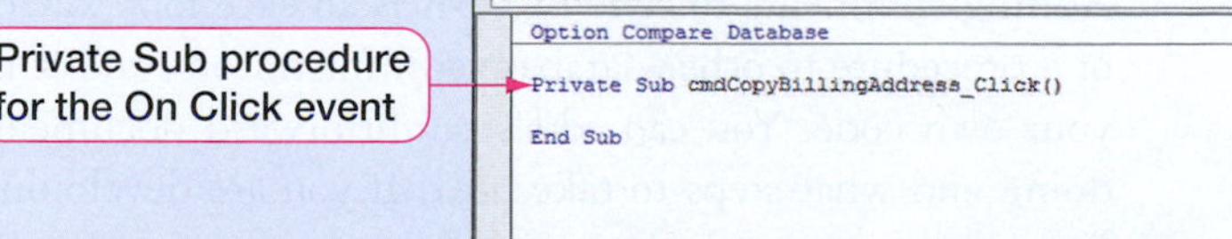

Figure 14 cmdCopyBillingAddress On Click event

f. Click the **blank line** in the Code window under the Private Sub statement, and then press Enter.

g. Press Tab.
This will create an indentation for your next statement. The Visual Basic Editor will use this indentation point as a reference for subsequent statements. Pressing Enter after typing a statement will align the pointer with the column in which the previous statement begins.

h. Type Me.MailingStreetAddress.Value = Me.BillingStreetAddress.Value, and then press Enter.

   This uses the Me keyword as the Form object in place of typing Form![frmParticipant] to access the Form objects. The statement in its entirety sets the field value of MailingStreetAddress to that of the BillingStreetAddress value.

i. Type Me.MailingCity.Value = Me.BillingCity.Value, and then press Enter.

j. Type Me.MailingState.Value = Me.BillingState.Value, and then press Enter.

k. Type Me.MailingZipCode.Value = Me.BillingZipCode.Value, and then press Enter.

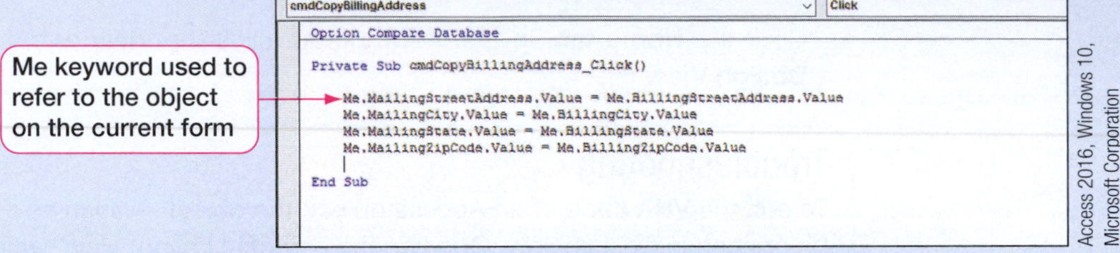

Figure 15 On Click event procedure

l. **Close** the Visual Basic Editor, and then **Save** the changes to the form.

m. Click the **Home** tab, and then, in the Views group, click **View** to return to Form view.

n. To test the new procedure on ParticipantID number 1, click the **Participants** tab, and then click the **Mailing and billing addresses are the same** button. Verify that the information in the Billing Address fields was copied to the Mailing Address fields.

REAL WORLD ADVICE | **The Procedure Box and Object Box Shortcuts**

Both the Procedure box and the Object box can be used to create event procedures from within the Visual Basic Editor. With the Object box, you can select the desired object to which the event should be attached, and the corresponding Private Sub structure will appear in the Code window. Once you are editing a specific object, you can use the Procedure box to select the action that you want a procedure to run in response to an event.

Use Comments to Document VBA Procedures

Adding comments to code in VBA is an excellent way of communicating the intentions of a procedure to other database administrators, and it is a good way of keeping track of your own code. You can add straightforward documentation on what the procedure is doing and what steps to take next. If you are developing more complicated procedures, you might want to leave yourself notes about what still needs to be completed or what statements are not working as expected.

Using the Edit Toolbar

Adding comments in the Code window begins with typing an apostrophe. The apostrophe character tells the Visual Basic Editor to ignore any text following the apostrophe on a line of the Code window. Comments can take an entire line of the Code window or begin after another statement in the Code window. By default, the Visual Basic Editor also changes the font color of any commented text to green. Commenting works only on a line-by-line basis, though. In this exercise, you will explore the commenting functionality on the Edit tool bar in the Visual Basic Editor.

To Use the Edit Toolbar

a. If necessary, press Alt + F11 to open the Visual Basic Editor.

b. On the Menu bar, click **View**, point to Toolbars, and then click **Edit**.
   The Edit toolbar will appear as a floating toolbar. It can be docked by clicking the title bar and dragging it to the top of the Visual Basic Editor window. If no modules are currently open, the buttons on the Edit toolbar will be grayed out.

c. Click the **title bar** of the Edit toolbar, and then drag it to the right of the Standard toolbar to dock it at the top of the Visual Basic Editor.

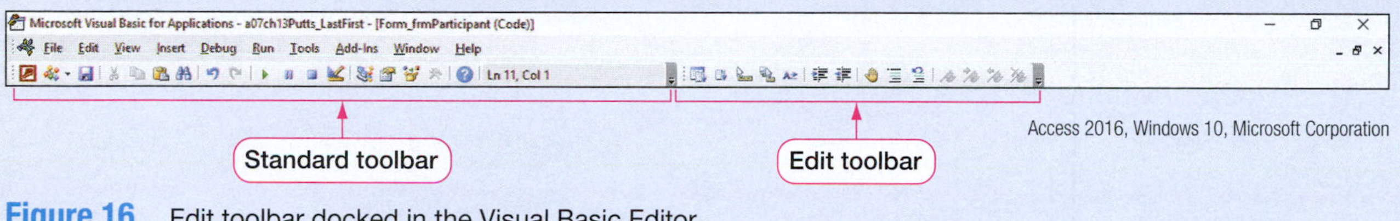

Access 2016, Windows 10, Microsoft Corporation

Figure 16 Edit toolbar docked in the Visual Basic Editor

The Edit toolbar has many useful features built into it. The comment block feature can be used to identify large or small strings of text in a procedure as a comment. It also includes buttons for increasing and decreasing indentations and listing the properties and methods of a statement in the Code window. Figure 16 shows the Edit toolbar as it appears in the Visual Basic Editor.

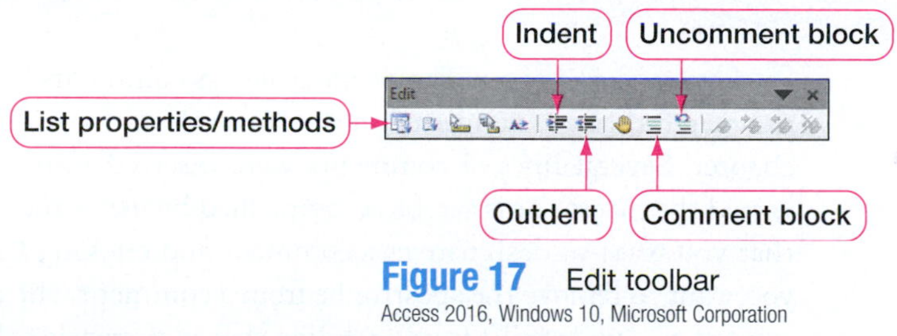

Figure 17 Edit toolbar

Access 2016, Windows 10, Microsoft Corporation

Adding Comments to a Procedure

The procedure that was created to copy the mailing address of the charity participants has no documentation associated with it. In this exercise, you will add an appropriate comment to the procedure that will inform future database administrators of who wrote the procedure and its purpose.

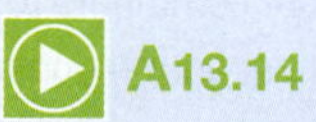

To Add a Comment to a Procedure

a. If necessary, in the Project Explorer window, double-click the **Form_frmParticipant** object to open it.

b. Click the **line** under Private Sub in the Code window to place the insertion point.

c. Type Created by iLast using your first initial and last name. Pressing Enter at this point would result in a Visual Basic Compile error because the text above does not contain any VBA statements.

d. On the Edit toolbar, click **Comment Block**.
   Notice that an apostrophe now appears in the first character space of the line and the color of the text is now green. The Visual Basic Editor will now ignore this entire line of text when the procedure is executed.

e. Press Enter, and then type **This procedure will copy the Billing Address information to the Mailing Address fields**. On the Edit toolbar, click **Comment Block**.

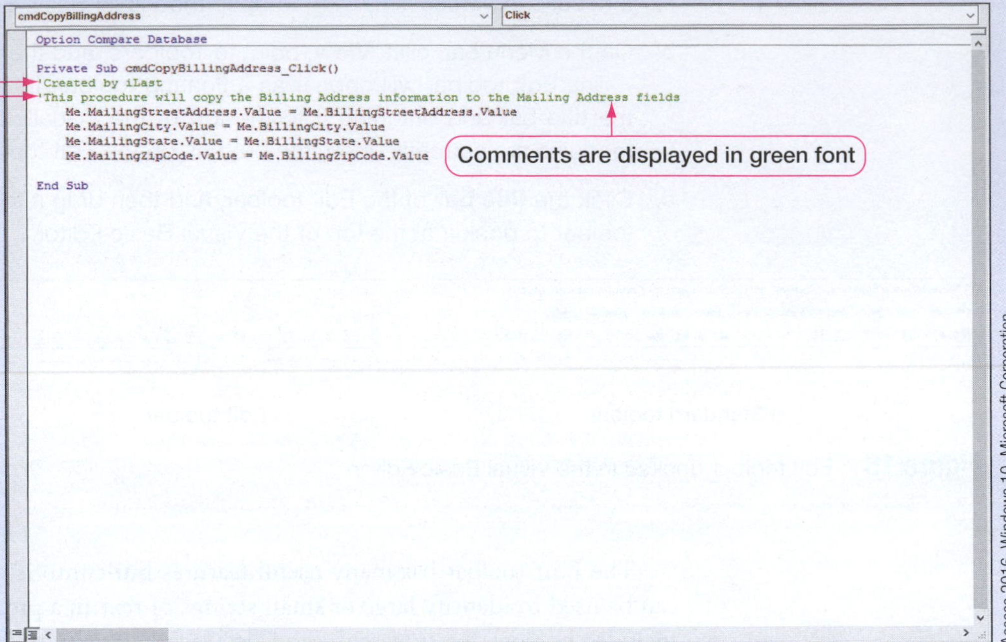

Figure 18 Comments in a procedure

f. **Close** the Form_frmParticipant object.

Larger blocks of text can be identified as comments by using this technique. Consider the macro that was converted in the "Convert an Existing Macro to VBA" section of this chapter. Several lines of comments were inserted into the procedure when Access converted the macro. This can be accomplished by using the pointer to select each line of text that you want to designate as a comment and clicking Comment Block. Likewise, if you want to remove the apostrophe from a comment, clicking Uncomment Block will remove the apostrophe from each line that is currently selected.

CONSIDER THIS | **Commenting in VBA Code**

Comments are often overlooked, but they are an important aspect of coding. If you have ever examined a database someone else has created, it can be very difficult to discern a complex series of queries or decipher the relationships between poorly named objects in a database. Likewise, attempting to understand the rationale for an action in a database might be nearly impossible without comments to explain the original developer's intent. Sometimes, later on, even you may not remember your rationale for the action in a database you created. Much of the same is true with VBA. What benefits are there to commenting your code? Can you imagine a situation in which commenting is unnecessary?

Debug the VBA in a Database and Add Error Handling

Creating a procedure that runs perfectly on the first run or in all situations is virtually impossible. No matter how experienced you might be at writing VBA, a simple typo or misplaced statement can invoke a Visual Basic error. If they are not handled correctly, these errors generally open the Visual Basic Editor in Debugging mode. While this might be acceptable to a developer, the standard user will be confused by the event and should not be given access to the raw VBA code.

Debugging is the process of identifying and reducing the number of errors that can occur within your code. **Error handling** is the process of anticipating and controlling errors. You want your application to inform the user of a problem, and your application or procedure should exit cleanly. VBA has some error-handling features installed such that when an error is encountered, the procedure will be halted, and you will receive an error message. You can also add customized error handling to a VBA procedure using a few key statements.

Adding Error Handling to a Procedure

The On Error statement provides a wide array of ways to handle errors that might arise throughout the course of a procedure. The **On Error statement** can enable or disable an error-handling routine and specify the location of the routine within the procedure. Using the GoTo statement can redirect the procedure to a line label or a specific line number. **Line labels** can be used like bookmarks in a procedure. The combination of On Error statements and line labels allows basic error handling to be built into any VBA procedure. It is important to note that not all errors that occur are negative. For example, when you are searching for the name of a person in a table, the message you receive that the name cannot be found is the result of an error. The message is simply a controlled response to the error.

Consider the VBA procedure created to import additional participants into the Putts database. If the Excel file being imported does not contain the appropriate column headings, Access will encounter an error and stop the import process. Because the process originates in a VBA procedure, the error will result in the termination of the process, and by default, it will open the Visual Basic Editor in Debug mode. To prevent this from occurring, some simple error handling can be added to the procedure to control the outcome of any errors.

After an error occurs, an **Exit statement** can be used to terminate the procedure. The Exit statement works similarly to the End Function statement in that both terminate the function. Using Exit Function is different, as additional code can be added after this function is used, whereas using End Function will not allow additional code to be added to the procedure.

In this exercise, you will incorporate error handling into the procedure that imports new participants.

CONSIDER THIS | Referring to Specific Lines of Code

The Visual Basic Editor allows for two ways of referring to a line of code. Line labels are one method. On the Standard toolbar, the Code window tracks the line number and column number of the placement of your pointer. You can use a line number in much the same way you can use a line label to reference a specific place in a procedure. Would there be any differences in referencing with line labels versus line numbers?

A13.15

To Add Error Handing to a Procedure

a. If necessary, in the Project Explorer, double-click the **Converted Macro - mcrImportParticipants** module to view it in the Code window. You do not need to close other modules if they are open.

b. Click to place the insertion point on the line below the **Function** statement, type 'Created by iLast, and then press Enter.

Troubleshooting

Not typing the apostrophe character before the comment will result in an error in the Visual Basic Editor.

c. Type **'This procedure imports new participants into the Putts database**, and then press Enter.

d. Type **On Error GoTo ImportParticipants_Err**, and press Enter.

Later in this exercise, you will create a line label named ImportParticipants_Err. If an error occurs during the execution of this procedure, Access will immediately move to the portion of the code that starts on the line that contains the identified line label.

e. Click to place the insertion point above the **End Function** statement. Type **ImportParticipants_Exit:**, and then press Enter.

This line label will serve as a bookmark. If no errors occur, the procedure will end on the next line. Be sure to include the colon after the line label.

f. Press Tab, type **Exit Function**, and then press Enter.

The Exit Function statement here serves as a stopping point for the procedure. If no error has occurred, the procedure will not execute any statements after the Exit Function statement.

g. Press Enter, and then press Backspace. Next you will insert a bookmark that will be used in the event that an error does occur in the code.

h. Type **ImportParticipants_Err:**, and then press Enter.

This is a line label and will serve as a bookmark. If an error occurs, the code will move to this line and continue running the procedure.

i. Press Tab to indent the line, type **Msgbox Error$**, and then press Enter.

The Msgbox object will display a message box to the user. The contents of the message box can be a fixed text string or a variable that can be defined elsewhere in the procedure. Here, "Error$" will display the error that Access encountered during the import process in the message box.

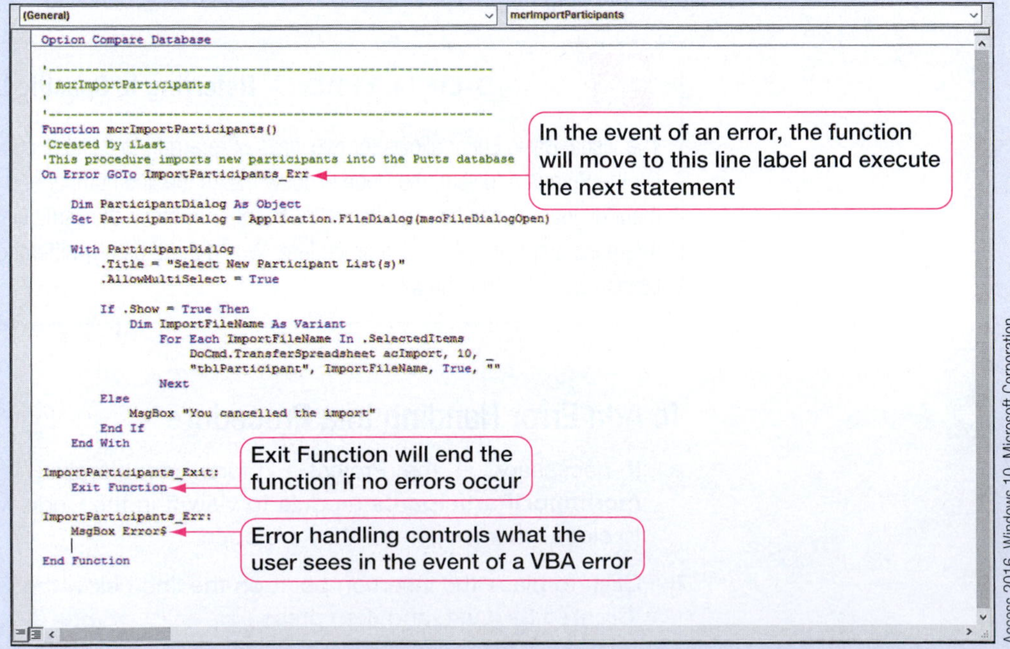

(General)
mcrImportParticipants
Option Compare Database
'--
' mcrImportParticipants
'
'--
Function mcrImportParticipants()
'Created by iLast
'This procedure imports new participants into the Putts database
On Error GoTo ImportParticipants_Err
Dim ParticipantDialog As Object
Set ParticipantDialog = Application.FileDialog(msoFileDialogOpen)
With ParticipantDialog
.Title = "Select New Participant List(s)"
.AllowMultiSelect = True
If .Show = True Then
Dim ImportFileName As Variant
For Each ImportFileName In .SelectedItems
DoCmd.TransferSpreadsheet acImport, 10, _
"tblParticipant", ImportFileName, True, ""
Next
Else
MsgBox "You cancelled the import"
End If
End With
ImportParticipants_Exit:
Exit Function
ImportParticipants_Err:
MsgBox Error$
End Function
In the event of an error, the function will move to this line label and execute the next statement
Exit Function will end the function if no errors occur
Error handling controls what the user sees in the event of a VBA error

Access 2016, Windows 10, Microsoft Corporation

Figure 19 Error handling and comments added to the mcrImportParticipants procedure

j. **Save** the procedure. If you need to take a break before finishing this chapter, now is a good time.

CONSIDER THIS | **On Error Resume Next**

The On Error statements can be constructed to respond in a variety of ways when an error occurs in a procedure. The On Error Resume Next statement is used to skip the statement immediately after it in the event of an error. No error message will be displayed when this statement is used, as it turns off VBA's usual error-handling procedures. In what types of situations might this statement be useful?

QUICK REFERENCE | **Printing VBA Code**

1. Open the module you want to print.
2. On the File menu, click Print.
3. To select a printer, click Setup.
4. Click OK to print to the selected printer.

Compiling and Securing Your VBA

Before you implement a database that contains VBA, you should check all modules for potential errors. This will prevent users from encountering unnecessary and confusing errors while using the database. You should consider securing your VBA so that it is not altered. Unsecured VBA can be altered either intentionally or unintentionally, but it can be easily secured to prevent this. In this section, you will compile the database to check for errors in the code and then secure the database so that the VBA code cannot be edited.

Compile VBA Modules

Errors in VBA procedures can occur while the code is being written or when the code is executed. A **syntax error** occurs when a completed line of code is entered that the Visual Basic Editor does not recognize. Syntax errors occur within the Visual Basic Editor once the pointer leaves a line of code that the Code window cannot interpret. This type of error is identified immediately and can then be corrected. How can you detect errors that are not caught until the execution of a procedure? Compiling your code before running it is one way of finding errors before the execution of a VBA procedure. When you compile the VBA in your database, Access examines all of the VBA contained in modules or objects for errors. Thus, you can find the errors in a procedure before users stumble across them.

Compiling VBA Modules to Identify VBA Errors

Access compiles an individual procedure before the procedure is executed. Using the Visual Basic Editor to compile your database forces Access to compile all existing modules, not just the one being executed. This catches any errors in procedures within those modules. For example, declaring a variable more than once in a procedure will result in an error when the procedure is executed. This error will not be identified when the code is being written; rather, it will be identified when the module is compiled. Compiling code before the first execution of a procedure is a simple yet important process. In this exercise, you will use the Visual Basic Editor to compile the database and identify any VBA errors.

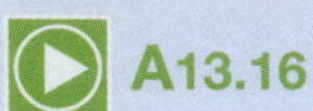

To Compile VBA Procedures to Identify VBA Errors

a. If you took a break, open the **a07ch13Putts** database, open the Visual Basic Editor, and then open the **Converted Macro - mcrImportParticipants** module.

b. On the Menu bar, click **Debug**, and then click **Compile a07ch13Putts**.
   If there are no syntax errors with your VBA procedures, Access returns you to the Visual Basic Editor. If an error exists, a compile error occurs, and Access indicates what the error is and opens the relevant module to the incorrect line of code. To demonstrate this, you will first create a typical syntax error that the Visual Basic Editor will immediately identify. Then you will create an error that will not be identified until the code is compiled.

c. Click **Insert Module** to create a new module.
   This will create a new module entitled Module1. Notice that the Option Compare Database statement is in the Declarations section by default.

d. Type Sub TestCompile, and then press Enter twice.
   When you press Enter, the parentheses are added after the name of the Sub, and the End Sub statement is inserted by default by the Visual Basic Editor on the last line of the procedure.

e. Type dim, and then press Enter.
   This will invoke a Visual Basic compile error. This happens because the Dim statement cannot exist without a variable name.

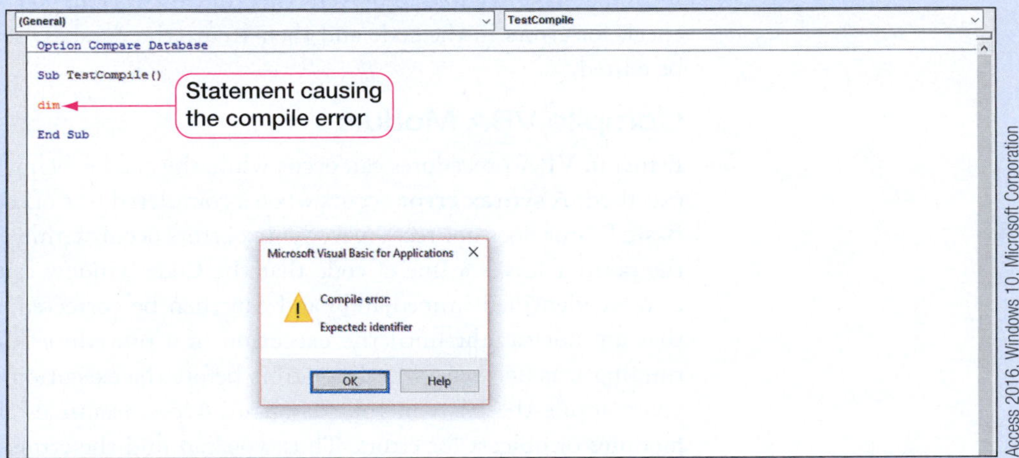

Figure 20 Compile error

Troubleshooting

If a VBA error occurs while Access is running a procedure, you are offered the choice of ending the procedure or entering debugging mode. Choosing to end the procedure halts the execution of any code and returns you to the database. Choosing to enter debugging mode opens the Visual Basic Editor with the incorrect line of code highlighted in yellow. Once you fix the code as needed, click Reset in the Standard toolbar to return the application to a state in which it can again run procedures.

SIDE NOTE
Variant Data Types
Typing Dim Test and pressing Enter will not invoke a compile error because if no data type is specified in the procedure, the Variant data type is used by default.

f. Click **OK** in the Compile error message box.
   Notice that the Visual Basic Editor has changed the font color of the incorrect line of code to red to indicate the location of the error. Additionally, your pointer is now located in the place where the error was detected.

g. Your insertion point should be located after the dim keyword. Press Spacebar, type test as string, and then press Enter.

h. Type Dim test as String once more, and then press Enter.
This time, no syntax error occurs. The error here — duplicated variable names — will not be detected until the procedure is compiled.

i. On the Menu bar, click **Debug**, and then click **Compile a07ch13Putts**. The duplicate variable names invoke a compile error.

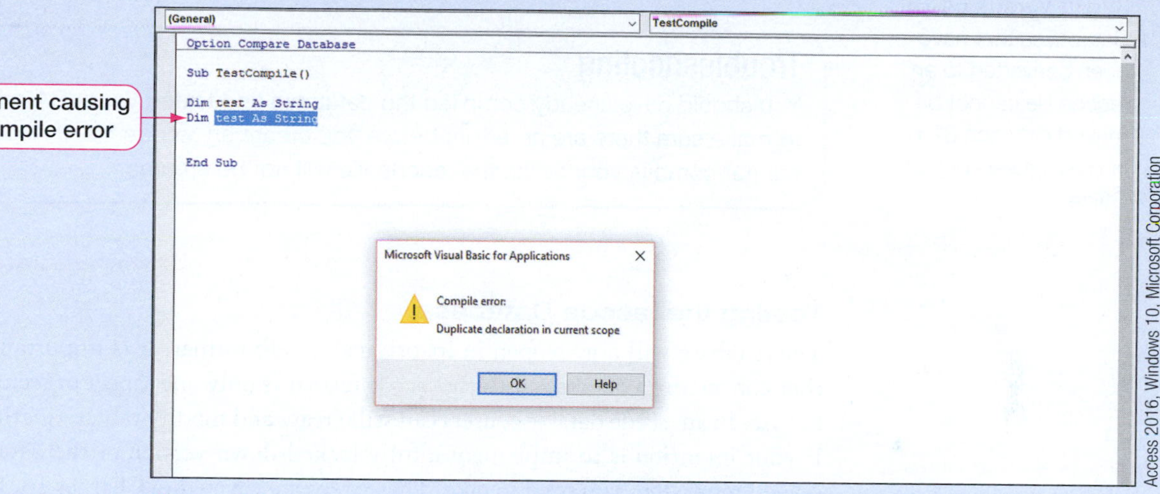

Figure 21 Compile error

j. Click **OK** in the Compile error message box. In this instance, the Visual Basic Editor highlights the incorrect line of code but does not change the font color.

k. Select the second instance of the **Dim test As String** line of code, and then press Backspace. This deletes the duplicated instance of the Test variable declaration.

l. On the Menu bar, click **Debug**, and then click **Compile a07ch13Putts**.
This time, when the database is compiled, no errors occur, and you are returned to the Visual Basic Editor without further messages. Your code has successfully compiled!

m. Save the procedure, accepting the name **Module1**. **Close** the Visual Basic Editor. If necessary, close any open objects in the database, saving any changes.

Secure VBA in a Database

Once the VBA in an Access database has been compiled, it is ready to be used within the database environment. Before deploying the database you may want to consider securing the macros and Visual Basic procedures in a database. This is important so that the VBA in a database is not edited by accident, resulting in errors or incorrect execution of VBA procedures.

Creating a .accde File

The default file format in Access 2016 is the .accdb extension. This format, without additional security measures, allows for full editing of the database by the user. Access provides the .accde format as a method of securing some aspects of the database. In an .accde file, VBA procedures will not be viewable to the user, and any errors that might occur during the execution of a VBA procedure will not result in the Visual Basic Editor being displayed. Additionally, forms and reports can be opened but not edited in .accde versions of a database. In this exercise, you will save the Putts database in .accde format, which will create a new copy of the database that can then be given to the user.

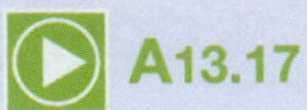 A13.17

To Create a .accde File

a. Click the **File** tab, and then click **Save As**.

b. Under Save Database As, and then under Advanced, click **Make ACCDE**.

c. Click **Save As**.

d. Navigate to the location where you are saving your project files, and then click **Save**.

SIDE NOTE
32-Bit Versus 64-Bit
Databases that have been converted to an .accde file cannot be moved between 32-bit and 64-bit versions of Office.

Troubleshooting
You should have already compiled the database and tested your VBA procedures to make sure there are no errors before you create an .accde file. If Access cannot compile your code, the .accde file will not be created.

Testing the .accde Database

The database will now reopen in its original .accdb format. It is important to remember that converting a database into the .accde format is only one aspect of securing a database for use. In an .accde database, users can still create and modify tables, queries, and macros. If your intention is to implement a fully locked-down version of the database, there are several more steps you need to take. These steps are covered in Chapter 14. In this exercise, you will test that the .accde database works as expected.

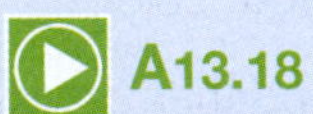 A13.18

To Test the .accde Database

a. Click the **File** tab, and then click Close to close the a07ch13Putts_LastFirst database.

b. Click the **File** tab, and then click **Open**.

c. Navigate to the location where you are saving your project files, and then double-click **a07ch13Putts_LastFirst.accde**.

Troubleshooting
When .accde databases are created, the only difference in the file name may be the last letter of the file extension. Depending on your system settings, you may or may not be able to see the extensions of files on your computer. An alternative way to identify .accde files is to look at the icon for the file. Access databases with the .accdb extension have the icon, while .accde databases have a padlock visible on the icon.

If the file is not in a trusted location, you will see a warning message. This message is to alert the user that there are macros and/or VBA code present within the database that could potentially be malicious.

d. If you encounter this message, click **Open**.

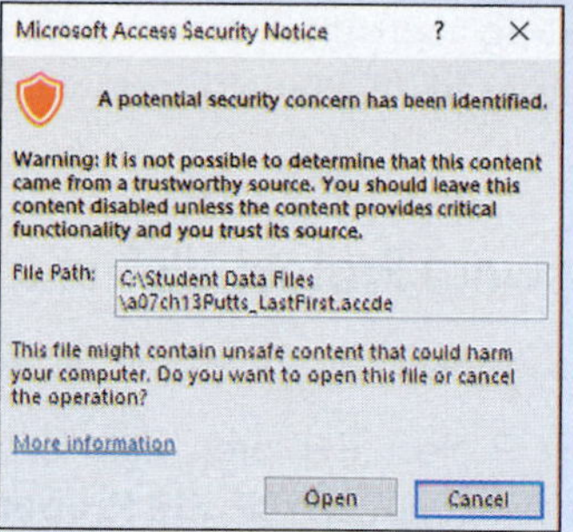

Access 2016, Windows 10, Microsoft Corporation

Figure 22 Microsoft Access Security Notice

e. In the Navigation Pane, right-click the module **Converted Macro - mcrImportParticipants**. Notice that Design view is grayed out and cannot be selected.

f. Press Alt + F11 to open the Visual Basic Editor, and then click ⊞ next to the **a07ch13Putts_LastFirst** object to expand the view.

g. Click ⊞ next to the Modules objects to expand the view.

h. Double-click the **Converted Macro - mcrImportParticipants** module. You will receive a message stating that the project is not viewable.

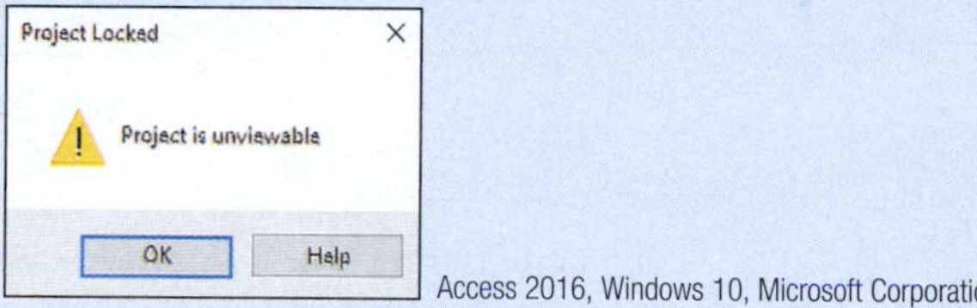

Access 2016, Windows 10, Microsoft Corporation

Figure 23 Project Locked dialog box

i. Click **OK**, and then **close** the Visual Basic Editor.

j. Click the **File** tab, and then click **Close** to close the a07ch13Putts_LastFirst.accde database.

k. Click the **File** tab, and then click **Open**.

l. Navigate to the location where you are saving your project files, and then double-click **a07ch13Putts_LastFirst.accdb**.

REAL WORLD ADVICE **.accdb and .accde Files**

Once a database has been saved as an .accde file, it cannot be converted back to the .accdb file format. Therefore, no changes can be made to macros or VBA modules within the database. Instead, any changes would have to be made in the original .accdb file that would then need to be converted. This is critical because any changes that have been made to the database would be lost — or must be made again in the original file. This includes data entered into tables or new Access objects such as tables or queries that have been added to the database.

Protecting VBA in a Database with a Password

Access provides several methods of securing a database. These security measures can affect many aspects of the database and are extremely useful tools for deploying databases to users. These security features are explored in Chapter 14. The Visual Basic Editor provides a method of securing the VBA in a database without implementing more general security measures. This can allow for full editing of the database by the user without compromising the integrity of the VBA code. Any VBA code in a database can be secured by providing a separate password via the Visual Basic Editor.

In this exercise, you will password protect the VBA in the Putts database.

To Password Protect VBA in a Database

a. Press Alt + F11 to open the Visual Basic Editor.

b. In the Project Explorer, right-click the **a07ch13Putts_LastFirst** database, and then select **a07ch13Putts Properties**.

c. In the a07ch13Putts - Project Properties dialog box, click the **Protection** tab.

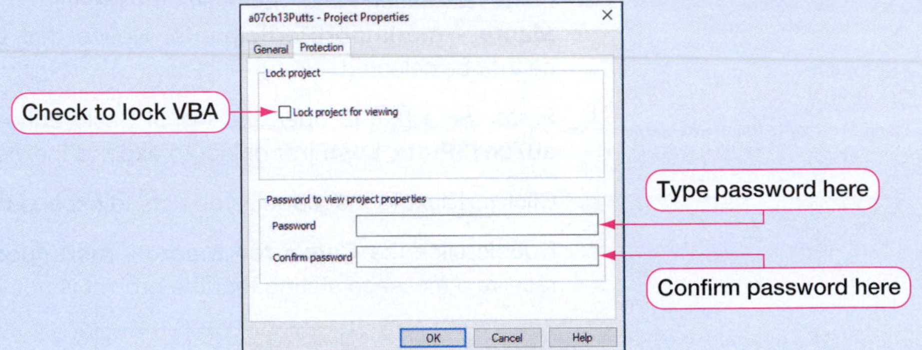

Figure 24 Password protecting your VBA

Access 2016, Windows 10, Microsoft Corporation

d. Check the **Lock project for viewing** check box.

e. In the Password to view project properties area, click in the **Password** box, and then type Zpe!82bv, which is the password supplied by Barry Cheney.

f. Click in the **Confirm password** box, type Zpe!82bv, and then click **OK**.

g. **Close** the Visual Basic Editor.

h. **Close** the database, **exit** Access, and then submit your files as directed by your instructor.

The a07ch13Putts - Project Properties dialog box will return you to the Visual Basic Editor without a confirmation message that the password was set. The Visual Basic Editor can still be opened by any database user. When a module or object is opened, before any code is displayed, the Visual Basic Editor will prompt you for the VBA password.

Concept Check

1. Discuss the difference between object-oriented programming and event-driven programming. p. 671
2. Macros and VBA can accomplish many of the same goals. When is it advantageous to use VBA? When would it be advantageous to use macros? p. 671
3. What is the benefit of using indentations and line continuation characters in building a procedure? p. 675
4. What benefit does looping offer in VBA? p. 684
5. What are two locations in Access where VBA procedures can be stored? Provide an example of each. p. 689
6. Discuss two purposes of adding comments to VBA procedures. p. 692
7. What are the benefits of debugging and error handling? p. 694
8. Why is it important to compile the VBA in a database before putting it into use? p. 697
9. What are the differences between .accdb and .accde files? p. 699

Key Terms

Argument 676
Array 674
Call statement 687
Code window 673
Debugging 694
Declaration 674
Declarations section 674
Dim statement 679
DoCmd object 676
Error handling 694
Event-driven programming 671
Exit statement 695
FileDialog object 678
Function 675
Line continuation character 675
Line label 695
Loop 684
Me keyword 691
Method 671
Module 673
Object 671
Object box 674
Object Browser 676
Object-oriented programming 671
On Error statement 695
Option Compare 674
Option Compare Binary 674
Option Compare Text 674
Option Explicit Statement 680
Procedure 671
Procedure box 674
Project Explorer 673
Sub procedure 675
Syntax error 697
TransferSpreadsheet method 676
Variable 679
Visual Basic Editor 673
Visual Basic for Applications 671
With statement 681

Visual Summary

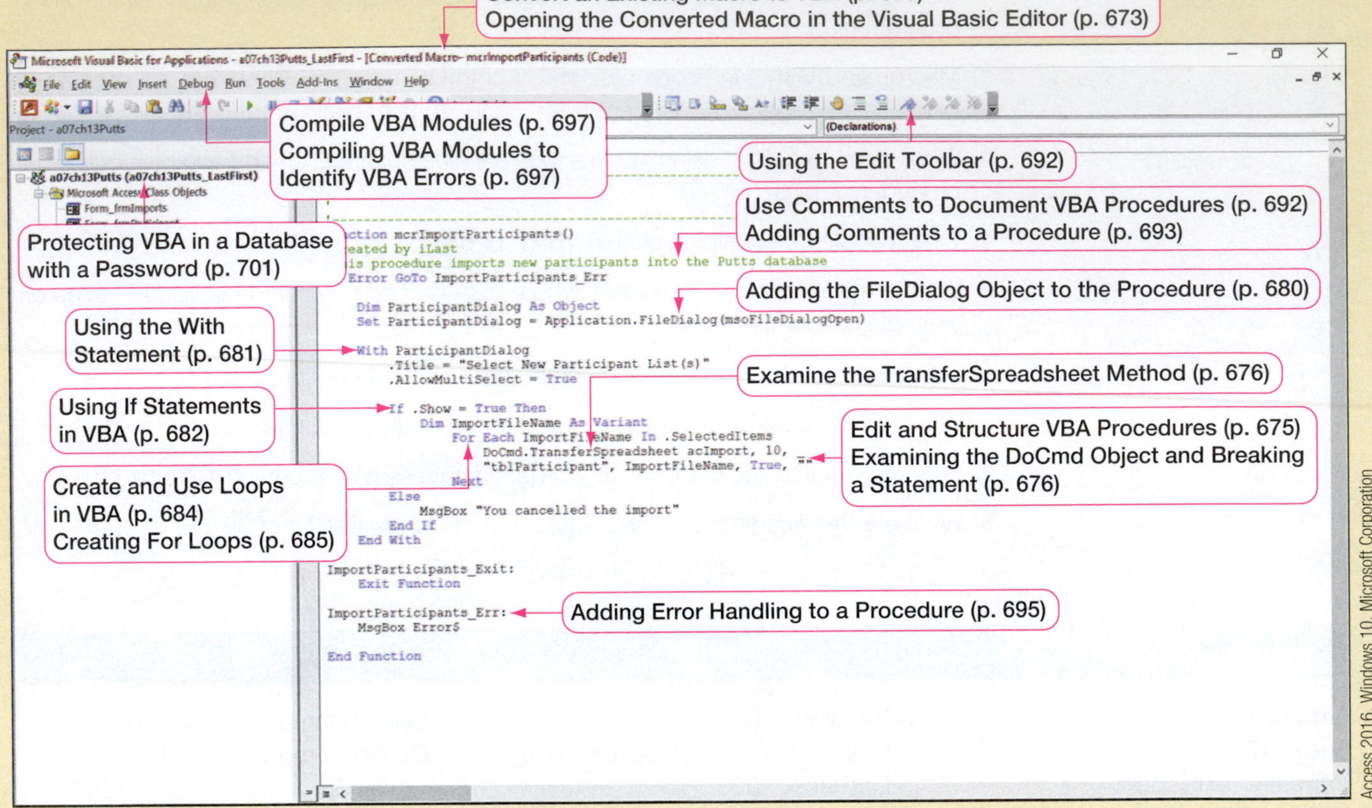

Access 2016, Windows 10, Microsoft Corporation

Figure 25

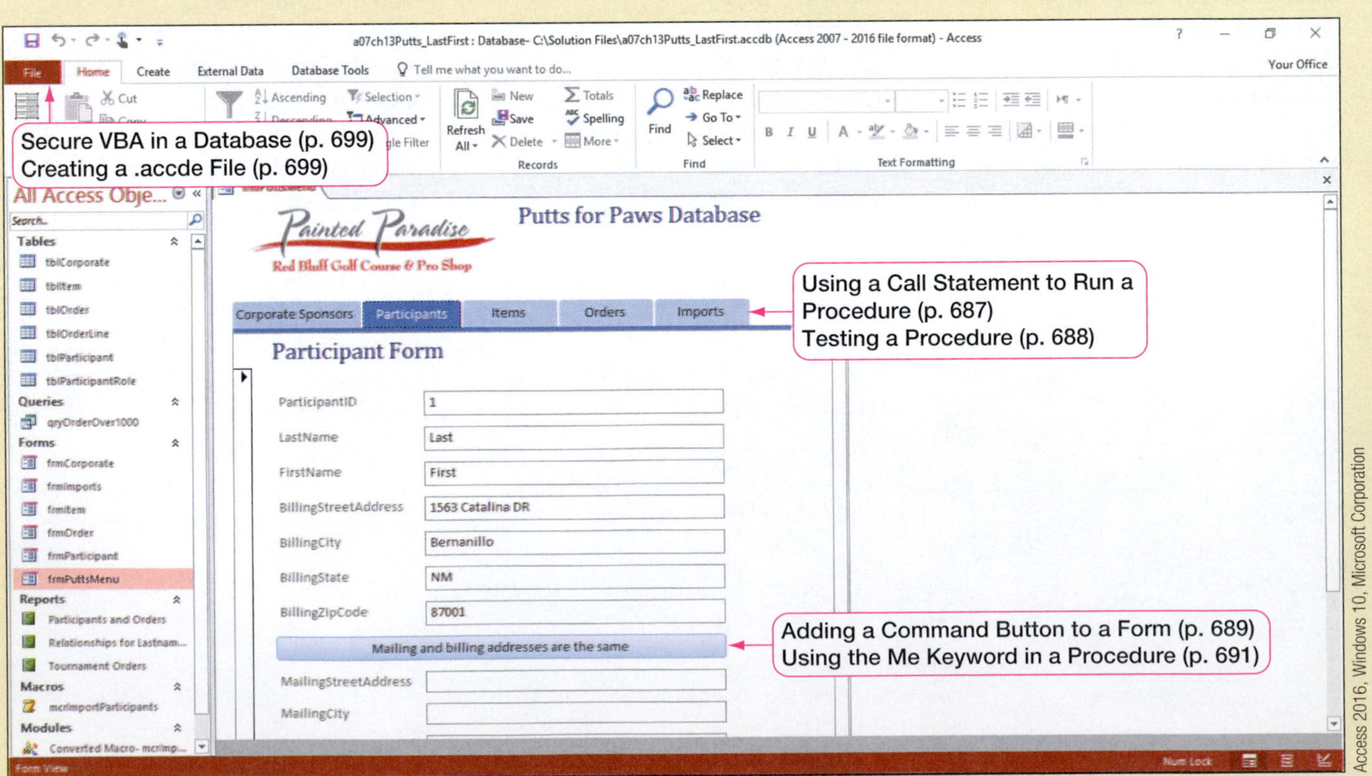

Access 2016, Windows 10, Microsoft Corporation

Figure 26

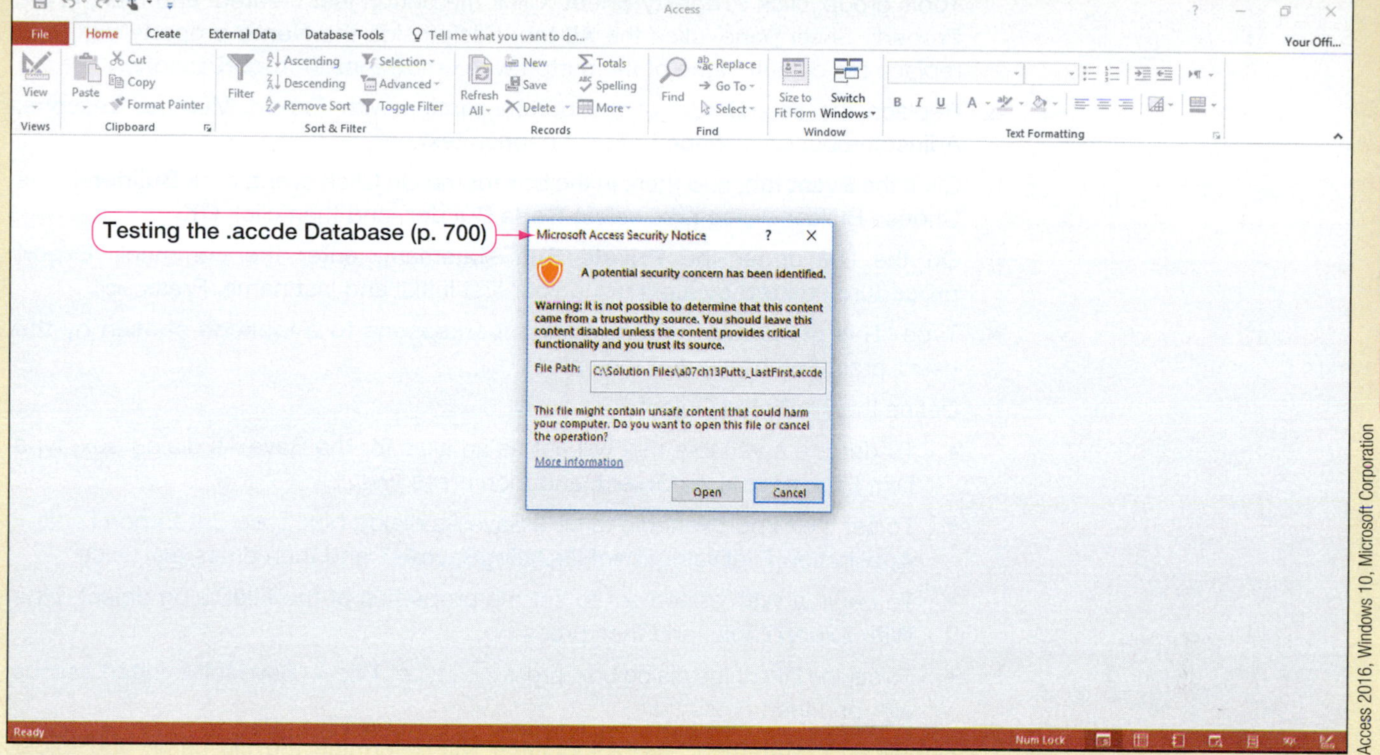

Figure 27

Practice 1

Student data file needed:

a07ch13Golf.accdb

You will save your files as:

a07ch13Golf_LastFirst.accdb

 a07ch13tblMemberLessons_LastFirst.xlsx

Red Bluff Golf Course & Pro Shop

Production & Operations

Having been impressed by your work on databases in the past, Barry Cheney has asked you to build some enhancements into the database that is used to track golf lessons and tee times. The data kept in the tblMemberLessons table will need to be analyzed regularly. Barry would like this data to be in a Microsoft Excel spreadsheet to facilitate this analysis. He has asked that you create a button on the Members tab of the frmGolfMenu navigational form that will export this file. He would also like you to protect the VBA with a password.

a. Start **Access**, and then open the student data file **a07ch13Golf**. Click the **File** tab, and save the file as an **Access Database** in the folder or location designated by your instructor with the name a07ch13Golf_LastFirst using your last and first name. If necessary, enable the content.

b. In the Navigation Pane, right-click the **frmGolfMenu** form, and then click **Layout View**.

c. On the Form Layout Tools Design, in the Controls group, click the **Button** form control. Place the button in the Members tab form header to the right of the name of the form. If necessary, click **Cancel** on the Command Button Wizard dialog box.

d. On the Design tab, click the **View** arrow, click **Design View**, and then click **Yes** to save changes. If the property sheet is not visible, click the **Design** tab, and in the

Tools group, click **Property Sheet**. Click the button just created, and then, in the Property Sheet pane, click the **All** tab. Click inside the **Name** property box, and replace the default name of the button with cmdExportMemberLessons.

e. Replace the default text of the button caption with Export Member Lessons. Adjust the button's shape to fit the caption text.

f. Click the **Event** tab, and then, in the box for the On Click event, click **Builder**. In the Choose Builder dialog box, select **Code Builder**, and then click **OK**.

g. On the line under the **Private Sub** statement, enter the comment 'Export procedure created by iLast using your first initial and last name. Press Enter.

h. Type 'This procedure exports tblMemberLessons to a location chosen by the user., press Enter twice, and then press Tab.

i. Define the FileDialog Object.
   - To declare a variable that will act as an alias for the Save As dialog box, type Dim ExportTable as Object, and then press Enter.
   - To set the Export variable to be a Save As dialog box, type Set ExportTable = Application.FileDialog(msoFileDialogSaveAs), and then press Enter twice.
   - To begin a With statement to set the properties of the FileDialog object, type With ExportTable, and then press Enter.
   - To set the title of the dialog box, press Tab, type .Title = "Save tblMemberLessons as", and then press Enter.

j. Create an If statement and a loop that will determine the file name and folder selected by the user or exit the procedure if no items are selected.
   - Type If .Show = True Then, and then press Enter.
   - Press Tab, and then type Dim Filename As Variant to declare a variable to store the file name selected by the user. Press Enter.
   - Type For Each Filename in .SelectedItems to begin the loop, press Enter, and then press Tab.
   - Type DoCmd.TransferSpreadsheet acExport, acSpreadsheetTypeExcel12xml, "tblMember", Filename, True, "", and then press Enter.
   - Press Backspace to align the insertion point with the **For Each** statement, type Next to complete the loop, and then press Enter. Press Backspace to align the insertion point with the If statement.
   - Type Else, press Enter, and then press Tab.
   - Type Msgbox "You canceled the export." to create a message box telling the user that the export was canceled. Press Enter, and then press Backspace.
   - Type End If to end the If statement, press Enter, and then press Backspace.
   - Type End With, and then press Enter.

k. Add comments and error handling to the export procedure.
   - Place the insertion point in the **blank line** under the two comment lines. Type On Error GoTo ExportMemberLessons_Err to begin the error-handling process, and then press Enter.
   - Place the insertion point above the **End Sub** statement. Type Exit Sub to create an exit point for situations in which the procedure executes as expected, and then press Enter twice.
   - Type ExportMemberLessons_Err: to add a line label that corresponds with the On Error statement added previously. Press Enter, and then press Tab.
   - Type Msgbox Error$ to return any error message received to a message box.

l. On the Menu bar, click **Debug**, and then click **Compile a07ch13Golf**. If there are no errors in the procedure you created, you will be returned to the Visual Basic Editor. If there are errors, resolve them, and compile the database again to confirm that all errors were corrected.

m. Save the VBA.

n. Password protect the VBA in the database, and then test the new export.

- In the Project Explorer, right-click the **a07ch13Golf** database, click **a07ch13Golf Properties** from the shortcut menu that appears, and then click the **Protection** tab.
- Click the **Lock project for viewing** check box.
- In the Password to view project properties area, click the **Password** box, and then type 423abg70, which is the password supplied by Barry Cheney.
- Click the **Confirm password** box, retype your password, and then click **OK**.
- Close the Visual Basic Editor.
- On the Home tab, in the Views group, click the **View** arrow, and then click **Form View**.
- Click **Export Member Lessons** to test the export. In the Save As dialog box, browse to where you are saving your files, and then type a07ch13tblMemberLessons_LastFirst to save the exported table.
- Click **Export Member Lessons** again to test the result of canceling the export. In the Save As dialog box, click **Cancel**, and then click **OK** on the message box that appears.

o. Close the database, exit Access, and then submit your files as directed by your instructor.

CHAPTER 13

Problem Solve 1

Student data file needed:

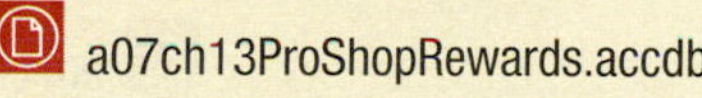

a07ch13ProShopRewards.accdb

You will save your file as:

a07ch13ProShopRewards_LastFirst.accdb

Sales Rep Performance at the Pro Shop

Sales & Marketing

Management

The Red Bluff Pro Shop is piloting a rewards program for its top sales representatives. Management would like the rep's ID on the rep summary form to change its format if the sales rep meets specific criteria. Once this functionality has been added, management would like the code to be password protected and the database settings modified to prevent employees from accidently modifying any of the tables or forms.

a. Open the Access database **a07ch13ProShopRewards**. Save your file as a07ch13ProShopRewards_LastFirst using your last and first name. If necessary, enable the content.

b. Open the **frmSalesRepSummary** form, and use the Code Builder to create a VBA procedure for the On Current event.

- Below the End Sub line for the Form_Current event that was created, create a VBA procedure named RepPerformance.
- Type the following comment: 'Created by iLast, using your first initial and last name, on the first line of the function.
- Type 'This procedure will change the format of the ID field based on specific conditions. on the next line.

c. The procedure should change the format of the ID field based on the following criteria: Revenue is greater than $2,500 or sales volume is greater than 15.
   - Incorporate an If statement into the procedure to check for either criterion.
   - Use the Me keyword to refer to the objects and properties needed.
d. Indent the next lines of code to make the procedure easier to read. If either criterion is met, the following properties should be changed.
   - The BackThemeColorIndex property of the ID field should be Accent 4 a value of 7 in VBA.
   - The BackTint property should be lighter by 50%, a value of 50 in VBA.
   - The ForeTint property should be Background 1, a value of 1 in VBA.
e. Use the backspace to align the Else statement to the If statement.
f. Indent the next lines of code to make the procedure easier to read. If neither criterion is met, the following properties should be changed.
   - The BackThemePropertyColorIndex property should be Background 1, a value of 1 in VBA.
   - The BackTint property should be 0, a value of 100 in VBA.
   - The ForeTint property should be Text Dark, a value of 100 in VBA.
g. Call the RepPerformance procedure in the Form_Current procedure of the frmSalesRepSummary form.
h. Use the Code Builder to create an event procedure for the On Load event. Call the RepPerformance procedure in the Form_Load procedure.
i. Test the new procedure by viewing Sales Reps 3 and 4.
j. Lock the VBA project for viewing, and password protect it with the following password: Cb32!d.
k. Close the database, exit Access, and then submit your file as directed by your instructor.

Perform 1: Perform in Your Career

Student data file needed:

 a07ch13Outfitters.accdb

You will save your file as:

 a07ch13Outfitters_LastFirst.accdb

Campus Outfitters

Production & Operations

You have recently begun working for a business near your campus that specializes in selling camping and adventure products to students. The business is still relatively new and is growing rapidly. You have been asked to help enhance the company's inventory database. The company manager would like the form that displays products to visually indicate products whose inventory has fallen below specified levels. The manager would also like the process of importing new inventory into the database to be automated. Currently, when new inventory is received, the store is e-mailed a spreadsheet from the vendor containing the shipment details.

a. Open the Access database **a07ch13Outfitters**. Save your file as a07ch13Outfitters_LastFirst using your last and first name. If necessary, enable the content.
b. Create a new procedure for the On Load event for the frmProduct form. Create a new procedure as a Private Sub, and name it LowInventory. This routine should evaluate the inventory of the database on the following criteria.
   - If the category is 1 (Water Sports) or 3 (Footwear) and the inventory level is below 5, the ProductName field should appear with set BackThemeColorIndex property set to Accent 1, a value of 4 in VBA. The ForeThemeColorIndex property should be set to Background 1, Lighter 25%, a value of 1 in VBA.

- For all other categories, if the inventory level is below 20, the ProductName field should appear with set BackThemeColorIndex property set to Accent 1, a value of 4 in VBA. The ForeThemeColorIndex property should be set to Background 1, Lighter 25%, a value of 1 in VBA.
- If the above conditions are not met, the ProductName field should appear with set BackThemeColorIndex property set to Background 1, a value of 1 in VBA. The ForeThemeColorIndex property should be set to Text 1, Lighter 25%, a value of 0 in VBA.
- Call this event from the frmProducts **On Load**, **After Update**, and **On Current** events.
- Insert a comment in the LowInventory procedure that contains your first initial and last name as well as the purpose of the procedure.

c. Insert a command button at the top of the frmProducts form. Use the code builder to create an **On Click** event for the button. In the Visual Basic Editor, create code that will prompt the user of the database to import new inventory that has arrived. The procedure should allow multiple files to be selected.

d. Include error handling in the procedure that, in the event of an error, will show the error to the user.

e. Compile the VBA to check for possible errors. If there are errors, resolve them, and compile the database again to confirm that all errors were corrected.

f. Protect the VBA in the database by locking the project for viewing and assigning the password CSd13Pn# as the password.

g. Close the database, exit Access, and then submit your file as directed by your instructor.

Additional Cases

Additional Workshop Cases are available on the companion website and in the instructor resources.

Microsoft Access 2016

Chapter 14 | IMPLEMENT YOUR DATABASE

OBJECTIVES

Prepare Case

Production & Operations

The Red Bluff Golf Course & Pro Shop Putts for Paws Charity Database

The Red Bluff Golf Course & Pro Shop sponsors a charity tournament, Putts for Paws, to raise money for the local pet shelter. The scope of the database is limited to tracking the monies being raised for the Putts for Paws event. Participants in the tournament are assigned roles, and any role may donate money to the event.

Now that a fully functioning database has been constructed, you have been asked to implement the database.

Blueorange Studio/Shutterstock

Student data files needed for this chapter:

a07ch14Putts.accdb

a07ch14Corporate.xlsx

a07ch14Icon.ico

You will save your files as:

a07ch14Putts_LastFirst.accdb

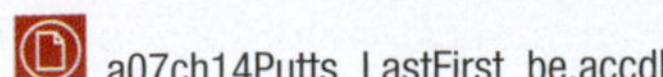

a07ch14Putts_LastFirst_be.accdb

a07ch14Putts_LastFirst2003.mdb

Implementing a Database

How do you prepare your database for multiple users? What are the best practices for implementing a database? These are very broad questions with many important ideas to consider. For this workshop, the design of the database has been completed, and how data is entered into the database has been determined. Now you will consider how the database itself is accessed. Before this can happen, a few questions must be answered: How many people will be using the database? Should the tables for the database be stored in a centralized location? If so, how will the users access those tables? Are there macros or VBA that need to be locked? This workshop will address these concerns and more about the implementation of databases.

When securing a database, the developer must be careful to ensure that the database is protected adequately. Any database objects to which the user will not need access should be hidden from view or otherwise protected so that they cannot be deleted or modified — either by accident or maliciously. Often, these objects include tables, macros, and Visual Basic code within the database. Securing a database is a detailed process and must be completed carefully. There might be several ways of opening or editing an object in Access; all of these methods must be accounted for in securing a database.

Once the database is secure, it can be implemented or distributed to users. Several implementation methods exist. The appropriate method can vary depending on the number of users and how data is accessed by the database. Some users may have older versions of Access. These users require a copy of the database that is compatible with these previous versions. If a large number of users will be accessing the database, Access provides a helpful utility called the Database Splitter to provide greater access to the database. In this section, you will prepare a database for implementation.

Understand Shared and Exclusive Modes to Access a Database

When a database is opened in Access, it is opened in Shared Mode by default. A database is opened in **Shared Mode** when multiple users are allowed access to the database at the same time. A database opened in **Exclusive Mode** allows only one user at a time the ability to open and edit the database. When security is being established in a database for implementation, Access routinely requires opening the file with Exclusive Access. Exclusive Access also ensures that no other users will be able to open the database while changes are being made. It is important to note that some of the changes in this workshop will take effect only after the database or database object has been closed and reopened.

REAL WORLD ADVICE | **Setting the Default Open Mode**

You can set the default open mode to either Shared or Exclusive. This setting is located in the Access Options under Client Settings, Advanced, and Default open mode. However, Access allows for this option as a setting only on individual computers. It cannot be set for individual databases. If the default open mode is set to Exclusive, all databases will be opened exclusively. If the open mode is set to Exclusive, no other users will be able to use the database.

Opening the Starting File

You have been asked by Barry Cheney, manager of the Red Bluff Golf Course & Pro Shop, to make modifications to the Putts for Paws database, as it will be used by numerous employees in several locations. The file will need to be secured to prevent any of the users from inadvertently modifying the database. The database will also need to be used by multiple users efficiently. In this exercise, you will open the Putts for Paws database.

A14.00

To Open the Starting File

a. Start **Access**, click **Open Other Files** in the left pane, and then double-click **This PC**. Navigate through the folder structure to the location of your student data files, and then double-click **a07ch14Putts**. A database opens displaying tables, forms, reports, and other objects related to the Putts for Paws charity tournament.

b. Click the **File** tab, save the file as an **Access Database**, and click **Save As**. Navigate to the location where you are saving your project files and then change the filename to a07ch14Putts_LastFirst using your last and first name. Click **Save**. If necessary, enable the content.

Opening a Database with Exclusive Access

If you are making changes to a database that is available to multiple users, you may want to ensure that only you have the database open. By opening a database with Exclusive Access, you will ensure that no other users can open the database and thus prevent you from being able to make changes. In this exercise, you will open the Putts for Paws database with exclusive access.

 A14.01

To Open a Database with Exclusive Access

SIDE NOTE

Shared and Exclusive Access

Saving a database with a different file name leaves the file in Shared Access mode.

a. Click the **File** tab, and then click **Close**.

b. Click the **File** tab, click **Open** in the left pane, and then double-click **This PC**. Navigate to the location where you are saving your project files, and then click to select **a07ch14Putts_LastFirst**.

c. Click the **Open arrow**, and then select **Open Excusive**. If necessary, enable the content.

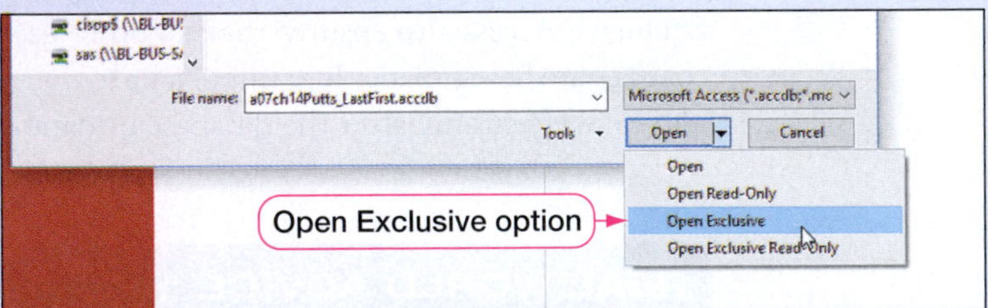

Figure 1 Open Exclusive to provide greater access to the database

Access 2016, Windows 10, Microsoft Corporation

Prepare a Database for a Single User

Other chapters in this text have discussed the importance of carefully choosing the data type for a field in a table, establishing table relationships, and best practices for building queries. These practices are important in database design in part because they can improve database performance. In this section, you will prepare a database for a single user.

Using the Performance Analyzer

The **Performance Analyzer** is a tool in Access that analyzes and suggests ways to optimize the performance of a database. The Performance Analyzer can review individual Access objects or the entire database at one time.

After you run the Performance Analyzer, it provides three types of analysis results. Access can perform suggestions and recommendations for you. **Recommendations** are actions that Access believes will improve the performance of your database. **Suggestions** are actions that Access believes will improve your database performance but may have consequences that should be considered first. The Performance Analyzer provides a description of these consequences when you select a specific suggestion. **Ideas** are similar to suggestions, but the user must perform these actions. If you decide to pursue an idea from the Performance Analyzer, Access will provide instructions to complete the task. In this exercise, you will run the Performance Analyzer tool on the Putts for Paws database.

A14.02

To Use the Performance Analyzer

a. Click the **Database Tools** tab, and then, in the Analyze Group, click **Analyze Performance**.

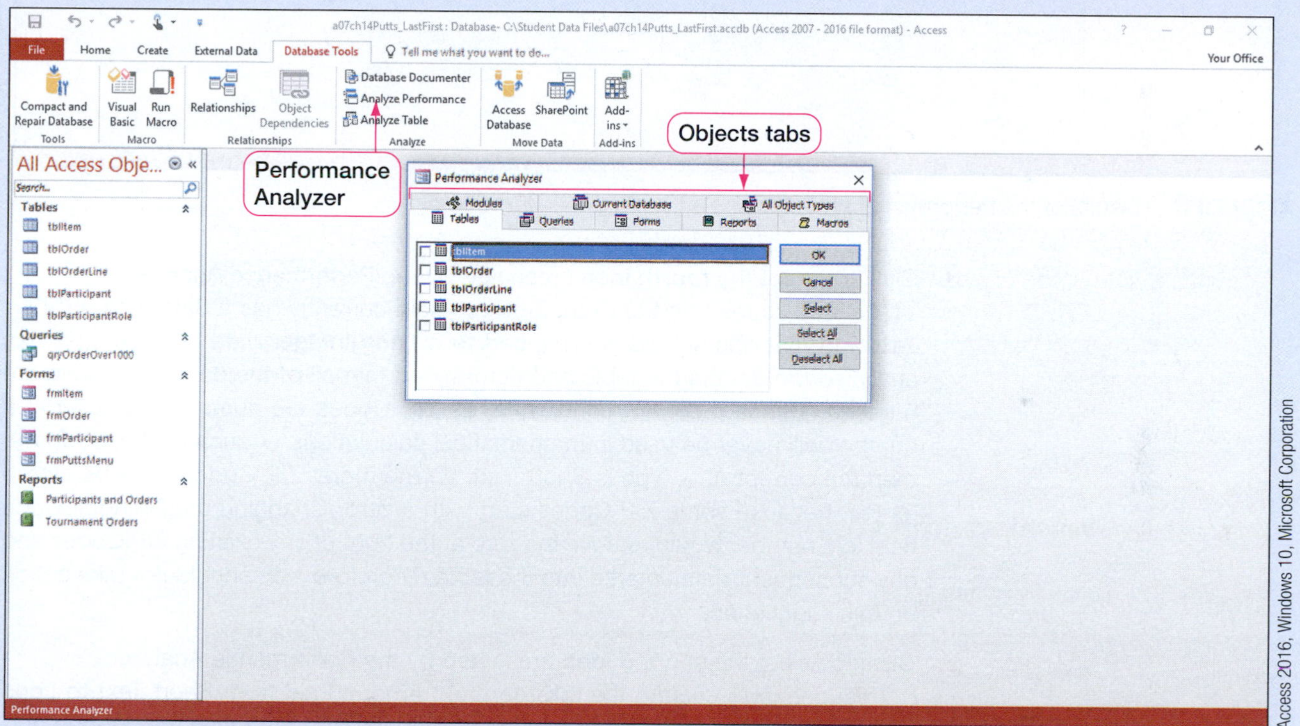

Figure 2 Performance Analyzer

SIDE NOTE

Pin the Ribbon

If your ribbon is collapsed, pin your ribbon open. Click the Home tab. In the lower right-hand corner of the ribbon, click Pin the Ribbon [icon].

b. In the Performance Analyzer dialog box, click the **All Object Types** tab, and then click the **Select All** button. This will check all items, including macros and VBA modules, within the database to be analyzed.

c. Click **OK**.

Any recommendations, suggestions, or ideas will be displayed in the Analysis Results section of the dialog box. A description of the results is provided in the Analysis Notes section of the window. As was mentioned previously, some of the optimizations that the Performance Analyzer will make may have consequences that should be carefully considered. For example, consider the first idea presented by the Performance Analyzer. The idea is to save your database in MDE format. This concept will be revisited later in this chapter.

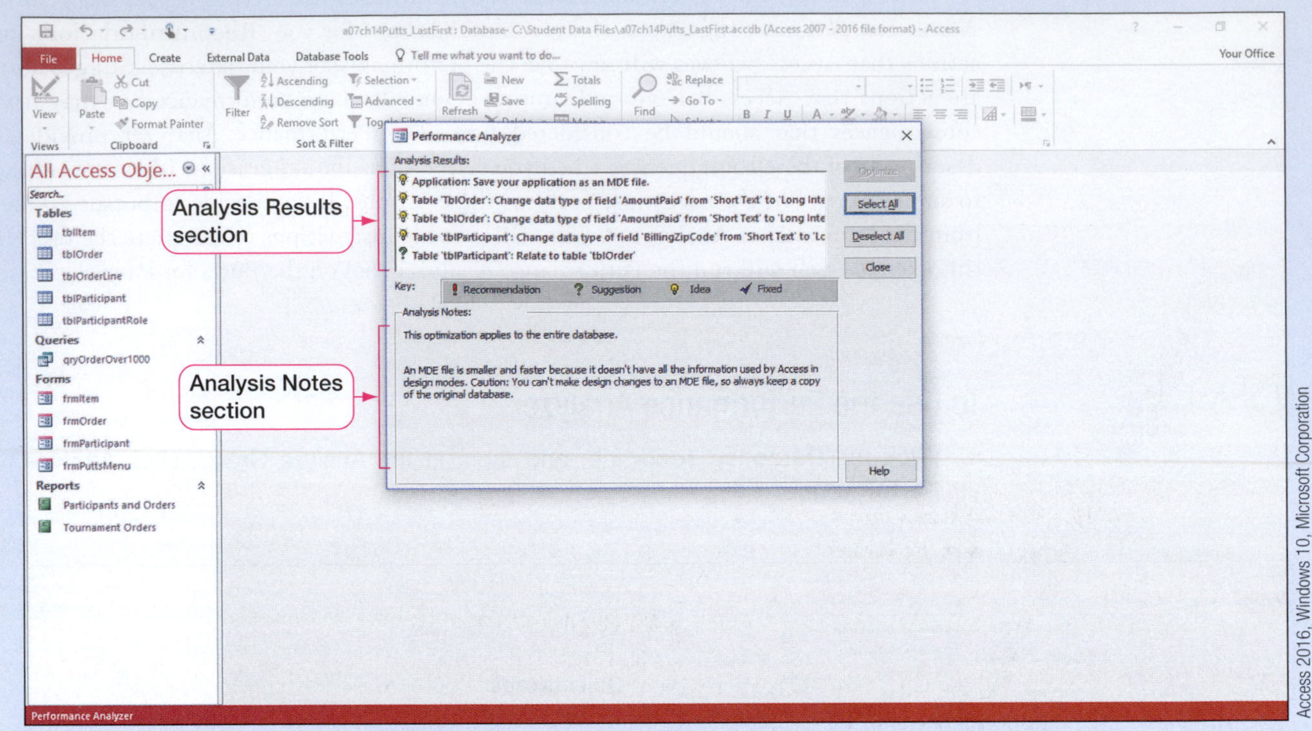

Figure 3 Results of the Performance Analyzer

d. Click to select the **fourth idea** presented by the Performance Analyzer.

The idea states that the BillingZipCode field currently has a data type of Short Text and that this should be changed to a Long Integer data type. Access has analyzed the data in the table and determined that all of the data in this field are numeric. This is a correct conclusion, as ZIP Codes are numeric. However, if a number will never be used in mathematical calculations — such as ZIP Codes — then the correct data type is Short Text. Furthermore, ZIP Codes must be stored as text because some ZIP Codes start with a zero. Changing the BillingZipCode field to a number would remove the zero at the front of any existing ZIP Codes and any subsequent data entered into the table. Therefore, you should not take action on this suggestion.

e. Click to select the **second idea** presented by the Performance Analyzer.

This idea is to change the tblOrder field AmountPaid from Short Text to Long Integer. This idea complies with the best practice of a database that storing currency data in a text field can lead to problems with data management. Because this is an idea, you will need to make this change manually.

f. Click **Close** to exit the Performance Analyzer.

Making Changes to a Database to Improve Performance

Data in a database that will be used in mathematical calculations should be stored as an appropriate number field, such as Currency or Number. Since the tblOrder table field AmountPaid is stored as Short Text, only a count of text records can be performed on the field. The AmountPaid field cannot be used to provide a sum or average. If you attempt to run the qryOrderOver1000 query, you will receive a Microsoft Access error stating that there is a data type mismatch in the criteria of the query. This error results because the criteria of the query looks for values greater than 1000 in the AmountPaid field. Since the field is short text, this criterion results in an error.

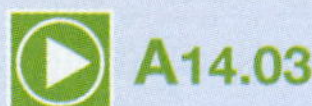

To Make Changes to a Database to Improve Performance

a. In the Navigation Pane, double-click the **tblOrder** table to open it in Datasheet view.

b. Select the **AmountPaid** field. Click the **Fields** tab, and in the Formatting group, click the **Data Type** arrow, and then click **Currency**.

c. Click **Yes** in the warning Message box that appears. Notice that the data in the AmountPaid field is now displayed as currency.

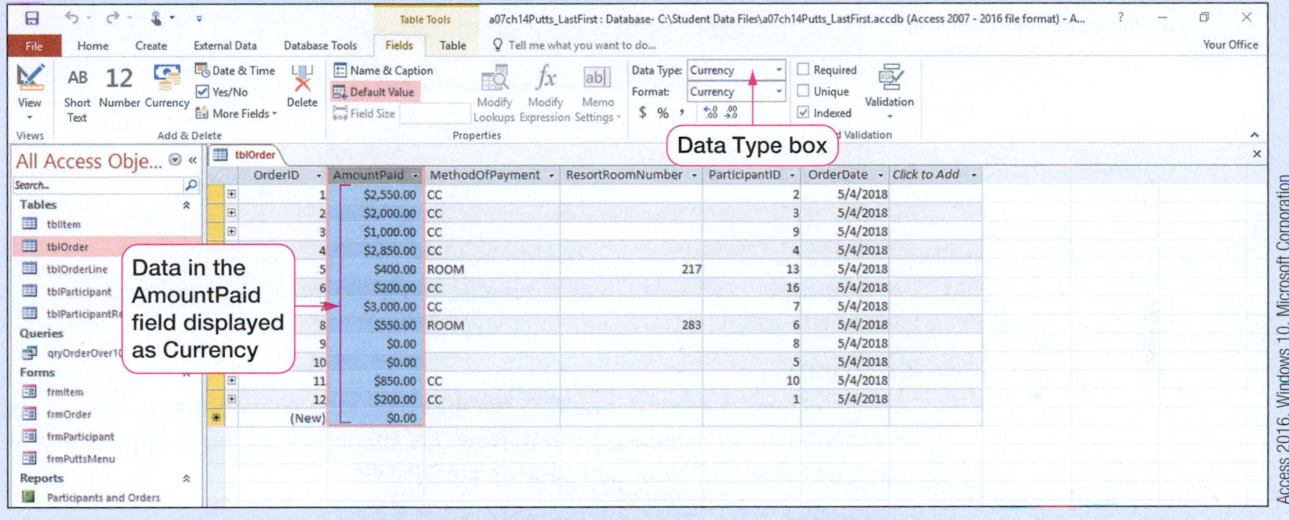

Figure 4 AmountPaid field changed to Currency data type

d. **Save** your changes, and then **close** the tblOrder table.

Making Changes to a Database with the Performance Analyzer

The Performance Analyzer listed several possible optimizations that could improve database performance. These should be reviewed to determine whether additional enhancements could be made. In this exercise, you will run the Performance Analyzer tool again and allow the tool to optimize the database further.

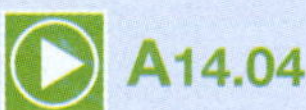

To Make Changes to a Database with the Performance Analyzer

a. Click the **Database Tools** tab, and then, in the Analyze group, click **Analyze Performance**.

b. In the Performance Analyzer dialog box, click the **All Object Types** tab, click **Select All**, and then click **OK**.
Examine the options presented by the Performance Analyzer. Some of the same ideas and suggestions appear, though now the idea to change the AmountPaid data type is no longer present.

c. In the Analysis Results box, click the suggestion that reads **Table 'tblParticipant': Relate to table 'tblOrder'**.
This is a suggestion by the Performance Analyzer to create a relationship between the tblParticipant table and the tblOrder table. This suggestion complies

with the best practices of database design, as the tblOrder table contains listings of orders participants have made. Because this is a suggestion, the Performance Analyzer can begin this process for you.

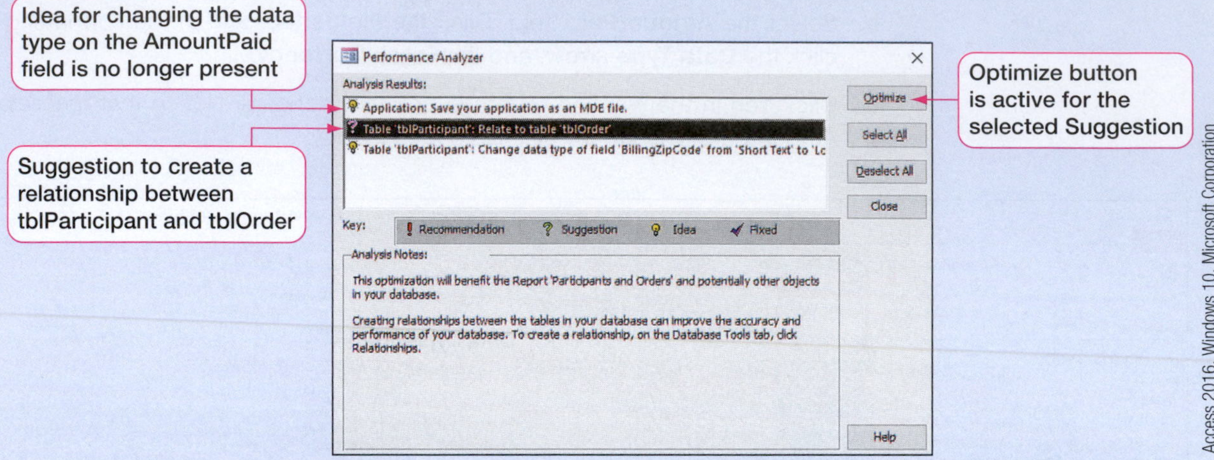

Figure 5 Performance Analyzer after correcting the AmountPaid field

d. Click **Optimize**.

A checkmark will appear next to the suggestion, indicating that Access made the change to the database for you. Now you should review the change to ensure that it complies with your database design.

e. Click **Close**. Click the **Database Tools** tab, and then, in the Relationships group, click **Relationships**.

Examine the relationship created by the Performance Analyzer. Notice that the relationship does not enforce referential integrity.

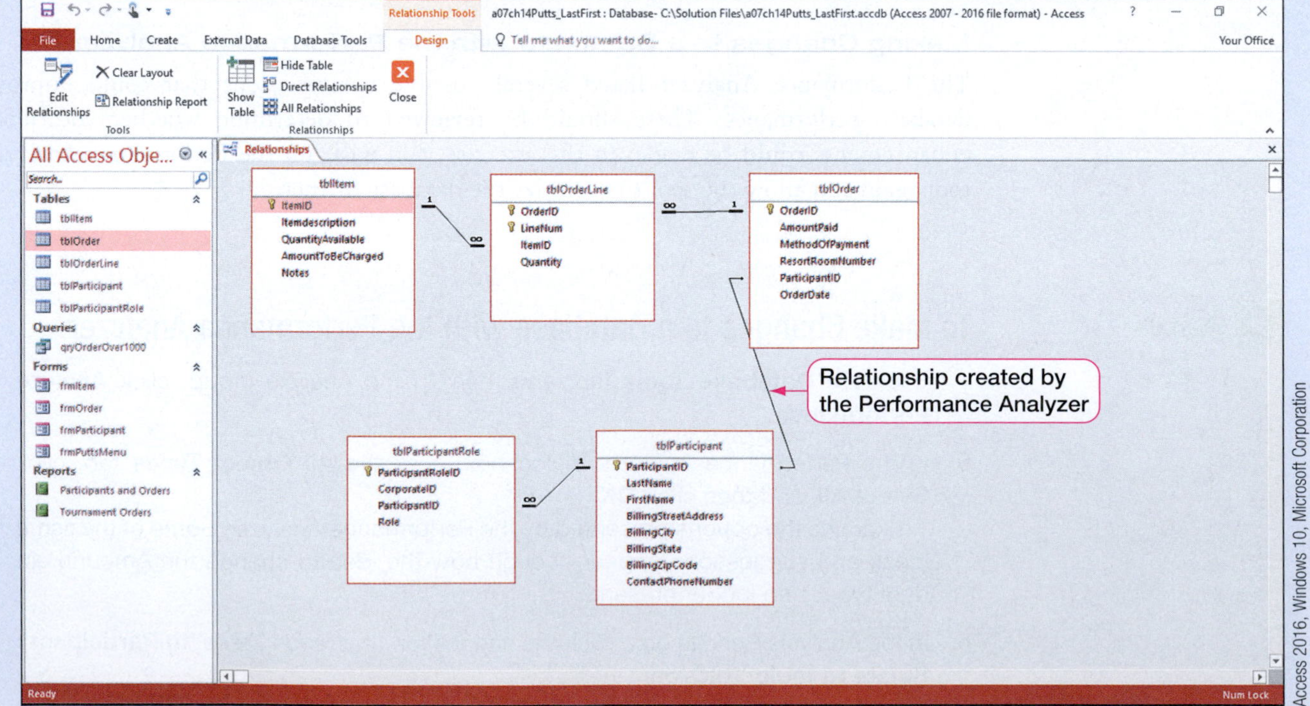

Figure 6 Relationships in the Putts for Paws database

f. Right-click the **relationship line** between tblParticipant and tblOrder, and then select **Edit Relationship**.

g. Click the **Enforce Referential Integrity** check box, and then click **OK**. This will create a one-to-many relationship between the tblParticipant table and the tblOrder table.

h. On the Design tab, in the Relationships group, click **Close**.

Understand Compatibility Between Different Versions of Access

As with most types of software, each new version of Access has features that previous versions did not. Common features of Access 2016 that are not compatible with Access 2003 are as follows.

- Calculated fields in tables
- Data macros
- Multivalued lookup fields
- Fields with the Attachment data type
- Long Text fields that have the append only property set to Yes
- Navigation controls
- Links to unsupported external files

To convert an .accdb file to the Access 2003 format, these features must first be removed. This includes navigation forms and any links to .xlsx files. The .accdb file type was first implemented in Access 2007, but there are features new to Access 2013 that will not open or are limited in Access 2007. Some of these features include data macros and calculated fields in tables.

Access 2003 and prior versions use the file type .mdb. While Access 2016 can convert directly to Access versions 2002-2003 or 2000, it cannot directly convert to Access 97 or prior versions. To accomplish this, a database would first need to be converted into a 2002-2003 or 2000 version. The database would then be opened in an earlier version of Access and, from there, be converted to an Access 97 database.

Saving an Access Database as a Previous Version

Barry Cheney has stated that while all new computers in the office are using Access 2013, there are several computers in the Red Bluff Golf Course & Pro Shop still using Access 2003. In this exercise, you will create a copy of the database in Access 2003 format.

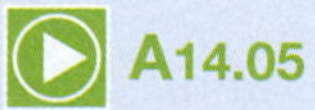
A14.05

To Save an Access Database as a Previous Version

a. Click the **File** tab, and then click **Save As**.

b. Under Save Database As, and under Database Files Types, click **Access 2002-2003 Database (*.mdb)**.

c. Click **Save As**.

You will receive a message box stating that you cannot save the current database in an earlier version because a feature is not backward-compatible. The message box lists possible features that could be causing the problem but does not identify the issue with this specific conversion.

SIDE NOTE

Rich Text Long Text Fields

Versions of Access before 2007 will not recognize Long Text fields formatted as Rich Text. Instead, the text will be displayed with corresponding HTML tags.

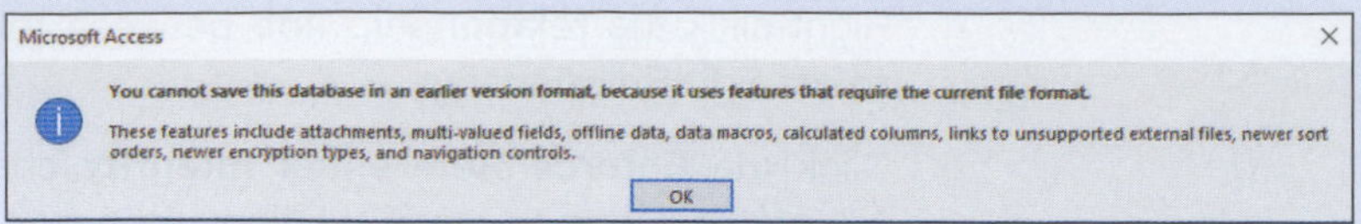

Figure 7 Access conversion error message

Access 2016, Windows 10, Microsoft Corporation

d. Click **OK**.

   The incompatible feature in this database is a Long Text field in the tblItem table. The Append Only property of this Long Text field is set to Yes.

e. In the Navigation Pane, right-click the table **tblItem**, and then select **Design View**.

f. Click the **Notes** field. In the Field Properties pane, click inside the **Append Only** property, click the **arrow**, and then select **No**.

g. Save the table. Click **Yes** in the warning message stating that all history in the Notes column will be lost, and then **Close** the table.

h. Click the **File** tab, and then click **Save As**.

i. Under Save Database As, under Database Files Types, click **Access 2002-2003 Database (*.mdb)**, and then click **Save As**. Navigate to the location where you are saving your files, name the file a07ch14Putts_LastFirst2003, using your last and first name, and then click **Save**.

j. If necessary, click **Enable Content**. The database will be converted to an Access 2003 .mdb file type and will remain open. Notice that the Navigation Pane view has changed. It now displays only the tables. Click the **Navigation Pane arrow**, and then click **All Access Objects**. All database objects are now visible.

k. Click the **File** tab, and then click **Close**.

REAL WORLD ADVICE | **Multiple Versions of Access**

It is not uncommon in large corporations or in companies that are composed of several smaller units for there to be multiple IT systems in place. In some cases, you might find multiple versions of Microsoft Office running in a company. In situations like this, backward compatibility is always a concern. When designing databases, carefully consider which versions of Access are in use and which features are not backward compatible.

Prepare a Database for Multiple Users

There are times when you will need to access data that is not contained in the database currently open in Access. Importing can bring this data into the local table structure, but this is not always the best option. When data is shared among many databases and is stored in a central location on a computer network, Access provides the ability to link to the data. In this section, you will prepare a database for multiple users.

Linking Tables

A **linked table** provides a link to data stored in another database or application. The data contained in the application becomes available to Access as a table.

Access can link to a table in another Access database, to an Excel spreadsheet, or to tables in SQL and Oracle databases. Linking to data is a best practice when the core data is shared among other users or applications or when Access is used as a means of viewing and querying SQL and Oracle database systems. This can reduce data redundancy and provide an efficient way of interacting with the data.

Data for the Putts for Paws corporate partners is currently being stored in the Excel spreadsheet a07ch14Corporate. In this exercise, you will link this data to the Putts for Paws database so it can be used later in the planning of the event.

CHAPTER 14

To Link Tables

a. Click the **File** tab, click **Open** in the left pane, and then double-click **This PC**. Navigate to the location where you are saving your project files, and then double-click **a07ch14Putts_LastFirst**.

b. Click the **External Data** tab, and then, in the Import & Link group, click **Excel**.

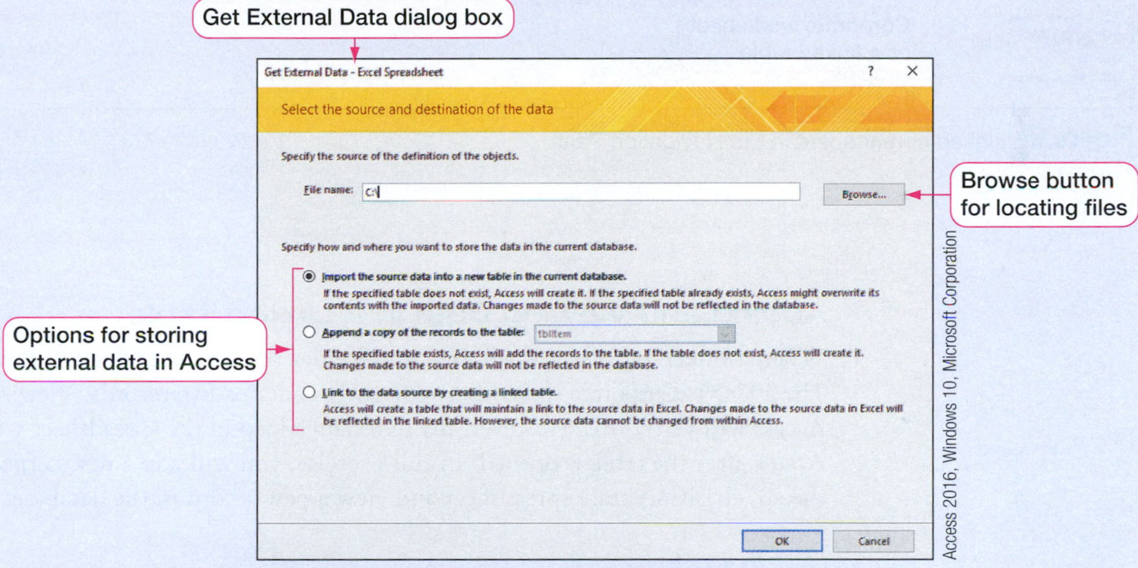

Figure 8 Get External Data dialog box

c. In the Get External Data dialog box, click the **Browse** button, navigate through the folder structure to the location of your student data files, and then double-click **a07ch14Corporate**.

d. Click **Link to the data source by creating a linked table**, and then click **OK**.
The Link Spreadsheet Wizard dialog box is now visible. The wizard will display a list of worksheets and named ranges present in the file you selected.

e. Click **Next**.
The wizard will now ask whether you want to use the spreadsheet column headings as field names in your table. The column headings in the spreadsheet are appropriate field names in Access.

f. Click the **First Row Contains Column Headings** check box, and then click **Next**.
The wizard has now finished linking the spreadsheet and needs a name for the new table. Access will suggest "Corporate" as the table name.

g. Type tblCorporate to replace the existing text in the Linked Table Name box, and then click **Finish**.

h. Click **OK** in the message box that appears telling you that the spreadsheet is now linked.

The tblCorporate table now appears in the Navigation Pane. Notice the blue arrow to the left of the Microsoft Excel symbol. This indicates that the table is linked. Data can be added, changed, or deleted from a linked table; however, the structure of the table cannot be changed.

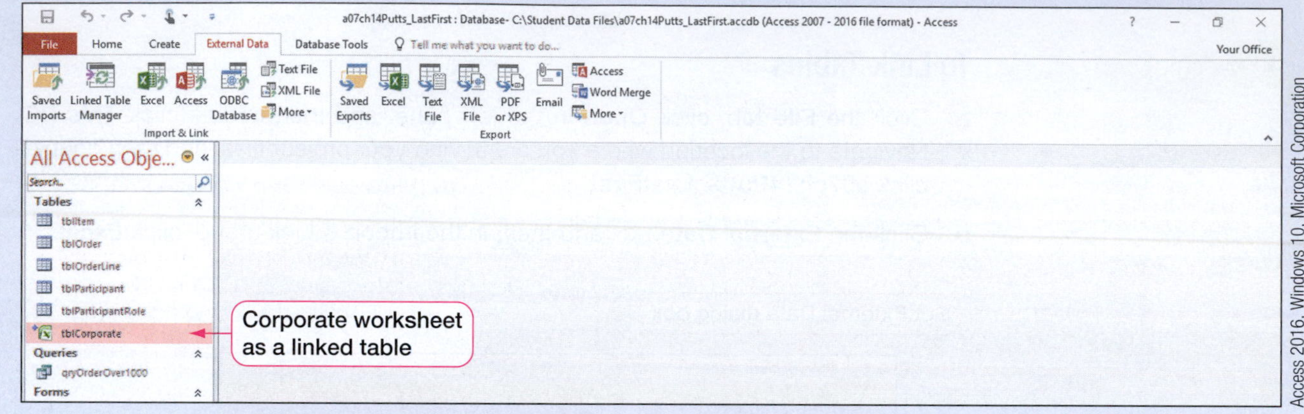

Figure 9 Linked spreadsheet in the Navigation Pane

Adding and Viewing Data in a Linked Table

When a linked table is opened, Access refreshes the data contained in the linked object. The a07ch14Corporate spreadsheet currently contains five records. Viewing this table in Access will verify this. However, any new data added to the spreadsheet will be visible in Access after the table is opened. In this exercise, you will add a new corporate partner to the a07ch14Corporate spreadsheet and view a new record in the database.

To Add and View Data in a Linked Table

a. Start **Excel**, click **Open Other Workbooks** in the left pane, and then double-click **This PC.** Navigate through the folder structure to the location of your student data files, and then double-click **a07ch14Corporate**.

> **Troubleshooting**
>
> If the a07ch14Corporate spreadsheet is opened while the tblCorporate table is open in Access, Excel will notify you that the file is locked for editing. You will have the options to open a read-only copy of the file, to be notified when the file is available for full use, or to cancel.

b. Click cell **A7** of the Corporate worksheet, type 6, and the press Tab. In cell B7, type your first and last name, and press Enter.

c. **Save** the workbook, and then **Close** Excel.

d. In the a07ch14Putts_LastFirst database, in the Navigation Pane, double-click **tblCorporate**. If necessary, adjust the **width** of the Company Name column to view the data. Your name should be displayed as the sixth record in the table.

e. **Close** [X] the table, and if necessary, click **Yes** to accept changes to the layout of the table.

REAL WORLD ADVICE **Linking Access to SharePoint**

Access data can be published outside of the database in many ways. Data can be exported in formats such as PDF and Microsoft Excel spreadsheets. Access objects can also be published to Microsoft SharePoint sites. SharePoint is an online collaboration tool that allows teams to organize and update information online. Access can synchronize forms and reports between the online client and the offline database. You can also make changes to your Access database and update the data online.

Using the Database Splitter

In implementing a database system for multiple users, it can be helpful to divide the database objects into two separate database files. This splitting of the database creates a front-end system and a back-end system. The **front-end database** is deployed directly to users and contains non-data objects such as queries, reports, forms, macros, and VBA modules. Front-end databases can be deployed locally to users' computers. This allows users, if given proper permissions, to modify the file to include objects for their individualized use. Front-end databases allow for the creation of temporary objects, such as temporary tables.

Back-end databases contain the tables from the original database. The front-end database accesses these tables by linking to them. This is beneficial, as the back-end database can be stored in a central location where a company's technical support can ensure that the data is protected and backed up regularly. It is important to remember that the back-end database cannot be on a shared drive with limited file permissions. In other words, the back-end database must allow the front-end database the ability to add and delete data to its tables.

For database developers, splitting databases is beneficial, as changes can be made to the front-end database without having to take the entire database offline. A new form or query can be developed and moved into the front-end system without having to shut down the back-end system. In this exercise, you will split the Putts for Paws database into a front-end database and a back-end database.

A14.08

To Use the Database Splitter

a. Click the **Database Tools** tab, and then, in the Move Data group, click **Access Database**. This launches the Database Splitter wizard.

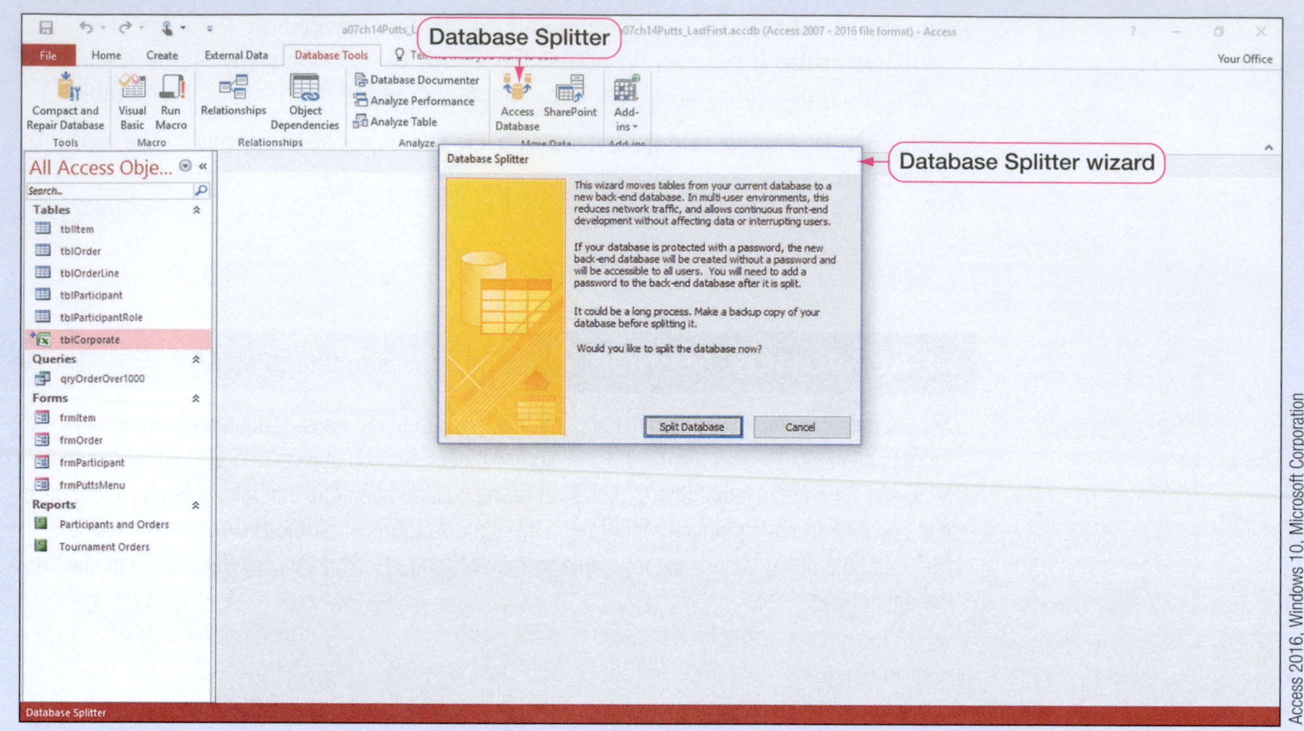

Figure 10 Splitting an Access database

b. Click **Split Database**.

This will open the Create Back-end Database dialog box. The Database Splitter wizard will first create the back-end database.

c. Navigate to the location where you are saving your project files. Notice that the name of the file being created is a07ch14Putts_LastFirst_be. The "be" appended to the end of the file name stands for "back-end". Click **Split**.

d. Click **OK** in the Database Splitter message box stating that the database has been successfully split. The database that is currently open is now the front-end database.

e. Examine the Navigation Pane. Notice that all of the tables are now linked. This is indicated with the blue arrow next to the table icon. This front-end database can now be deployed to multiple users.

SIDE NOTE

Linked Tables in Split Databases

If the back-end database is moved, the links in the front-end database must be updated.

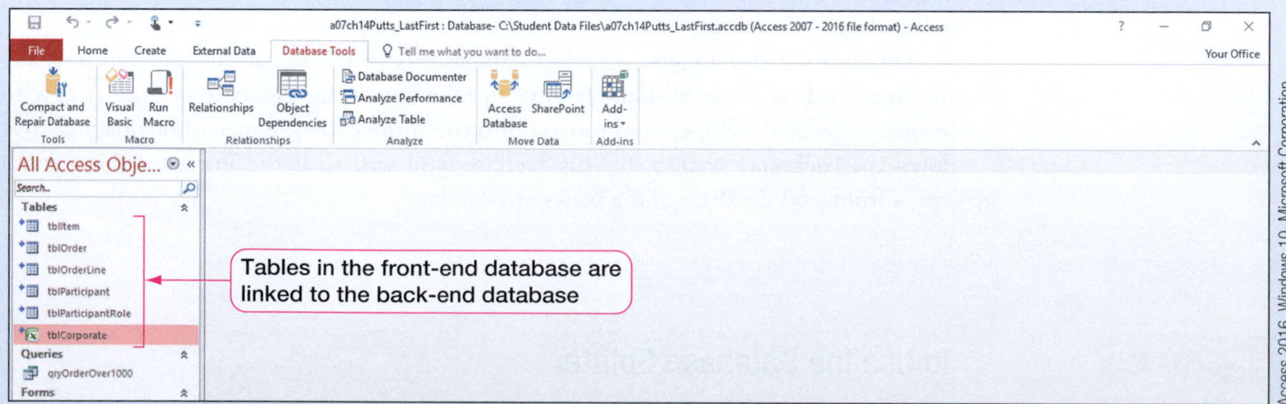

Figure 11 Linked tables in the front-end database

f. In the folder containing the a07ch14Putts_LastFirst database, create a folder called Putts_be. Move the **a07ch14Putts_LastFirst_be** database into the Putts_be subfolder.

Using the Linked Table Manager

Access cannot update the data in the database from a linked object if the object has been moved from its original location. Linked tables are dependent on the location of the object, not the database that contains the link. This means that databases containing a linked table can be moved at will with no ill effects. However, the file containing the linked object must remain in the same location in order for the link to function properly.

If a linked object is moved, the Linked Table Manager can be used to refresh the link. The **Linked Table Manager** lists the file location of all linked tables in a database. If the location of a linked object changes, the Linked Table Manager can be used to refresh those links. Attempting to access a linked object that has been moved from its original location will result in an error similar to the one displayed in Figure 12.

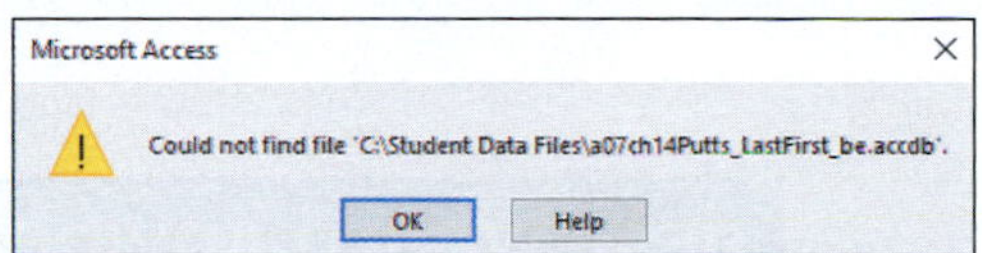

Figure 12 Error message stating that a linked object could not be found

Access 2016, Windows 10, Microsoft Corporation

Because the back-end database was moved to a different location, the links to the objects contained within it will need to be refreshed.

A14.09

To Use the Linked Table Manager

a. Click the **External Data** tab, and then, in the Import & Link group, click **Linked Table Manager**.

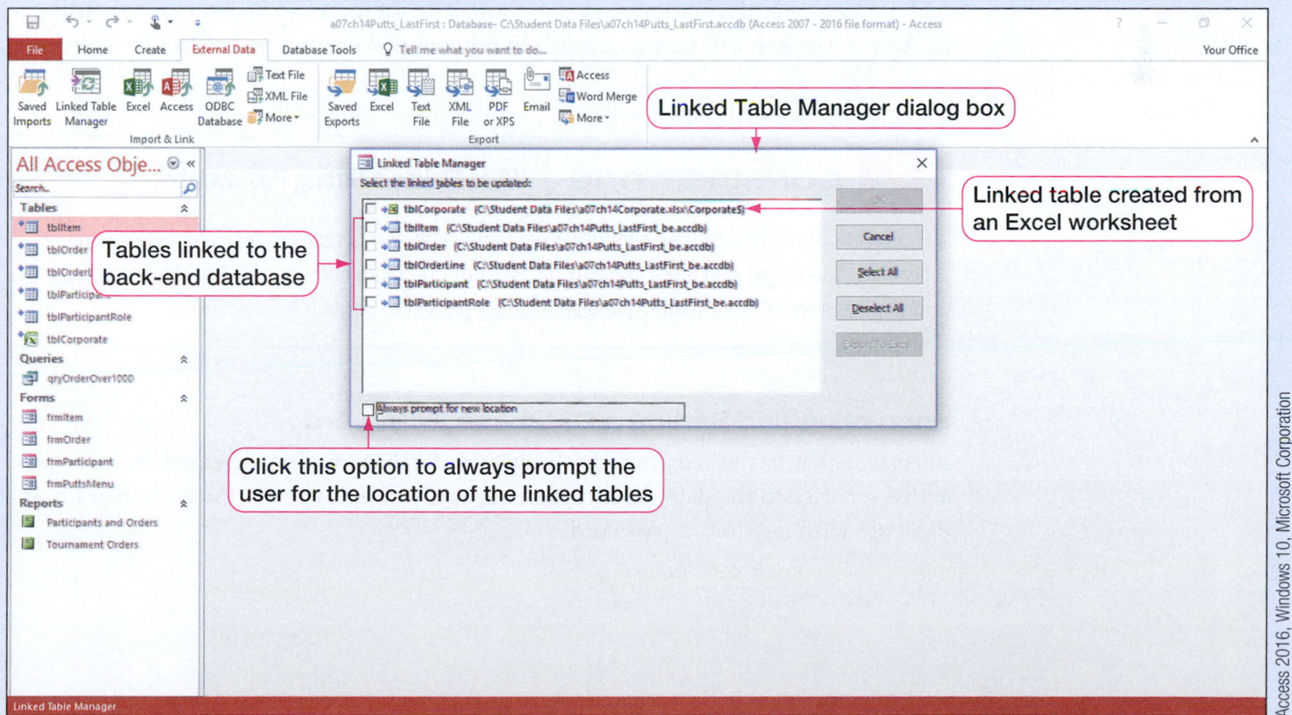

Figure 13 Linked Table Manager

b. Click the **tblItem**, **tblOrder**, **tblOrderLine**, **tblParticipant**, and **tblParticipantRole** check boxes, and then click **OK**.

SIDE NOTE

The File Path of the Linked Tables

The file paths in Figure 13 might be different in your database. This depends upon the configuration of your computer.

c. In the Select New Location dialog box, navigate to the **Putts_be** folder, and then double-click to open it. Select the **a07ch14Putts_LastFirst_be** database, and then click **Open**.

d. Click **OK** in the Linked Table Manager message box stating that all selected linked tables have been successfully refreshed.

e. Click **Close** to close the Linked Table Manager.

f. Double-click one of the tables in the Navigation Pane to ensure that its contents can be viewed. **Close**  the table.

g. Click the **File** tab, and then click **Close**.

REAL WORLD ADVICE | **Linked Data in Earlier Versions of Access**

If you have an Access 2016 database with links to external data that is not compatible with prior versions of Access, there is a solution. Try importing the data and then deleting the external links. This will provide the database with the ability to convert to a previous version of Access.

Encrypt a Database with Passwords

Ultimately, to protect a database and its information, passwords and encryption can be implemented. **Encryption** is the process of changing text-based information into a state in which a key is required in order to read the information. An algorithm or cipher is used to process the data from text into an unreadable state. The process of **decryption** will make encrypted information readable again. The information is decrypted by using a key. In Access, the key will be a password. In other applications, the key can be a separate file.

CONSIDER THIS | **What Makes a Strong Password?**

Passwords should be created carefully. Common words and phrases in any language should be avoided. The longer and more complex a password, the more secure it will be. How do you build a strong password? What features should a strong password contain?

Encrypting and Setting a Database Password

Barry Cheney has asked that the front-end database file you created be encrypted for added security to the data. In this exercise, you will encrypt the Putts for Paws front-end database with a required password.

To Encrypt and Set a Database Password

a. Click the **File** tab, click **Open** in the left pane, and then double-click **This PC**. Navigate to the location where you are saving your project files, select the **a07ch14Putts_LastFirst** database, click the **Open** arrow, and then click **Open Exclusive**.

> **Troubleshooting**
> To encrypt the database, it must be opened with Exclusive Access. When Access closes and reopens a database, as it does during the split database operation, the front-end database will be opened with Shared Access.

b. Click the **File** tab.

c. Click **Encrypt with Password**. In the Set Database Password dialog box, type 917abf70, retype your password in the Verify box, and then click **OK**.

You will receive a Microsoft Access warning stating that row-level locking will be ignored.

> **Troubleshooting**
> Row-level locking is used to ensure that when two users are editing a table, they cannot edit the same row — record — of data. This is not compatible in an encrypted database. Access will disable this feature and provide the warning message shown in Figure 14.

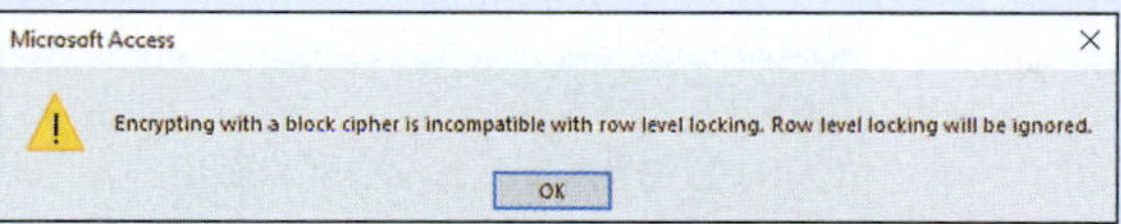

Figure 14 Row-level locking warning message

d. Click **OK**. The database will now prompt the user for a password when the database is opened. It is best practice to test opening the database to ensure that it prompts the user for a password. Click the **File** tab, and then click **Close**.

e. Click the **File** tab, then click **Open** in the left pane, and then double-click **This PC**. Navigate to the location where you are saving your project files, and double-click **a07ch14Putts_LastFirst**. In the Password Required dialog box, type 917abf70, and then click **OK**.

f. If you need to take a break before finishing the chapter, now is a good time.

Setting the User's Experience

Access features several options to assist a database developer in controlling the user's experience in a database. To begin securing a database, there are several key features in Access that should be disabled or modified. This includes controlling the way users navigate in the database, preventing users from editing certain Access objects, controlling what tabs the user will see on the ribbon, adding a customized icon for the database, and setting a password on the database. To set a password, the database must first be opened with Exclusive Access. In this section, you will control the user interface of an Access database.

Modify the Start-up Options in a Database

To ensure the integrity of the database, access to several features must be eliminated. Barry Cheney has asked that users not be able to create new objects in the database or be able to import or export data using the ribbon. When any of these functions are required, they will be built into the database forms as buttons or other controls. Likewise, any information stored in the database that users will need to access will be included on the navigation form that is displayed when the database is opened.

Preventing a table from being opened directly requires hiding the Navigation Pane. To prevent the creation of new database objects, the Create tab on the ribbon must be hidden. Importing and exporting data can be prevented by hiding the External Data and Database Tools tabs. Hiding the Database Tools tab will also take one step toward securing any VBA or macros in the database.

Often, in Access, there are several ways of accomplishing any single task. For example, the Visual Basic Editor can be opened by using a button on the ribbon or by pressing the keyboard shortcut Alt+F11. To properly secure a database, each of these options must be considered in order to adequately prevent an object from being accessed. Ultimately, any direct access to the VBA code must be locked down. The Alt+F11 keyboard shortcut is one of the special keys in Access.

Using Special Keys

Special keys are a set of four keyboard shortcuts that can be disabled in securing a database. A list of special keys is provided in Table 1. To properly secure a database, special keys should be disabled, because they allow users access to the Navigation Pane and the Visual Basic Editor even if these items are initially hidden from view in the database. To begin securing the Putts for Paws database, you will hide tabs on the ribbon, hide the Navigation Pane, and disable special keys.

Key or Key Combination	Description	Why Should This Be Disabled?
F11	Shows or hides the Navigation Pane	Prevents users from accessing tables or other objects to protect the integrity of the database
Ctrl + G	Shows the Immediate Window in the Visual Basic Editor; launches the Visual Basic Editor if it is not already open	Prevents users from accessing or creating Visual Basic code in the database
Ctrl + Break	Stops Access from retrieving records from a server	Applies when Access is designed to work as the front-end application to a SQL server
Alt + F11	Opens the Visual Basic Editor	Prevents users from accessing or creating Visual Basic code in the database

Table 1 Table of special keys

Setting Start-up Preferences

The first step in securing the database as requested by Barry Cheney is to examine the current database options. In this exercise, you will modify the start-up preferences in the Putts for Paws database. These options will affect only the database that is currently open.

A14.11

To Set Start-up Preferences

a. If you took a break, open the **a07ch14Putts** database.

b. Click the **File** tab, and then click **Options**. In the navigation options on the left side of the Access Options dialog box, click **Current Database**.

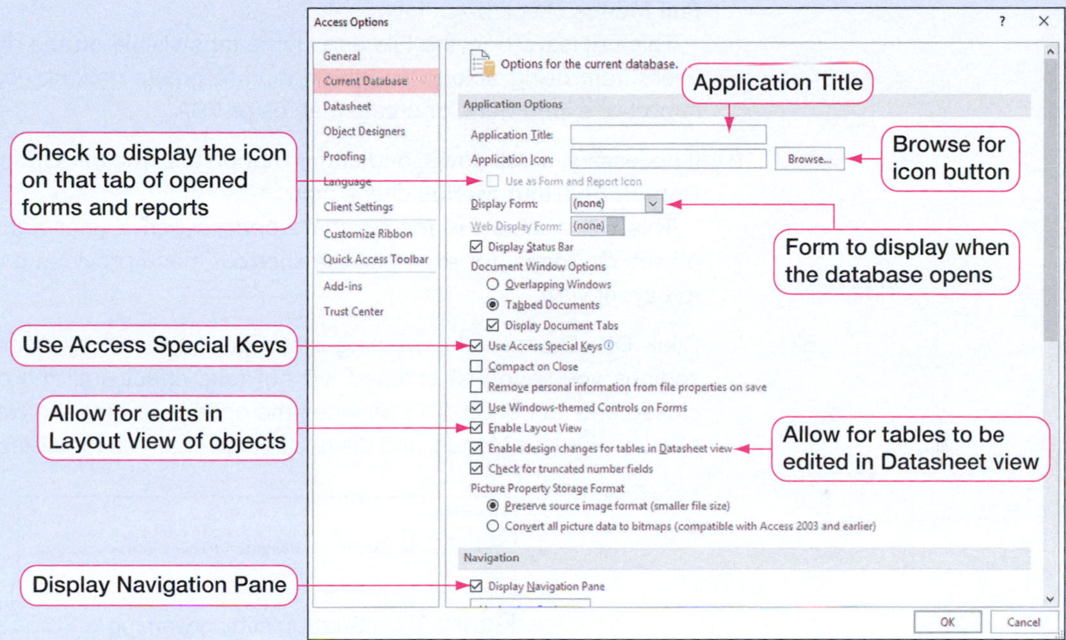

Figure 15 Access Options for the Putts for Paws database

c. In the **Application Title** box, type Putts for Paws Database. This will replace the file name on the title bar in the Access window.

d. To the right of the Application Icon box, click **Browse**. Navigate to the location of your student data files, and double-click **a07ch14Icon**.

e. Click the **Use as Form and Report Icon** check box. The icon selected in the previous step will now replace the default Access icon that normally appears on the left side of the tab when forms or reports are opened.

f. Click the **Display Form** arrow, and then select **frmPuttsMenu**. This will automatically open the frmPuttsMenu form when the database is opened.

g. Clear the **Use Access Special Keys** check box. This step disables the four special keys described previously.

h. Clear the **Enable Layout View** check box. By removing the Layout view option from the Views group on the ribbon, you will prevent users from being able to edit forms and other Access objects.

Troubleshooting

Changes to the options in an Access database might require that a specific Access object that is open when the changes are made be closed and reopened. For example, disabling the Layout view feature will not take effect on an open form. Before the changes take effect, the form must be closed and reopened.

i. Clear the **Display Navigation Pane** check box.

This will hide the Navigation Pane, preventing users from opening any of the objects found there. Combined with disabling special keys, this will lock users out of accessing any objects in the Navigation Pane. Users could still access the Navigation Pane if the Use Access Special Keys option were checked.

j. If necessary, scroll down, and under Ribbon and Toolbar Options, clear the **Allow Full Menus** check box.

This will leave only the File and Home tabs visible on the ribbon. This restricts users from being able to use the ribbon to create new objects in the database, import or export data, or create macros or VBA.

k. If necessary, scroll down, and under Ribbon and Toolbar Options, clear the **Allow Default Shortcut Menus** check box.

This will disable the menus that appear when a user right-clicks an Access object. On forms, for example, the shortcut menu provides a means of changing to Layout view.

l. Click **OK**. Examine the warning message displayed by Access. Several of the settings you have just enacted will not take effect until the database has been closed and reopened. This includes the options to hide the Navigation Pane, Full Menus, Shortcut Menus, and disable design changes for tables in Datasheet view.

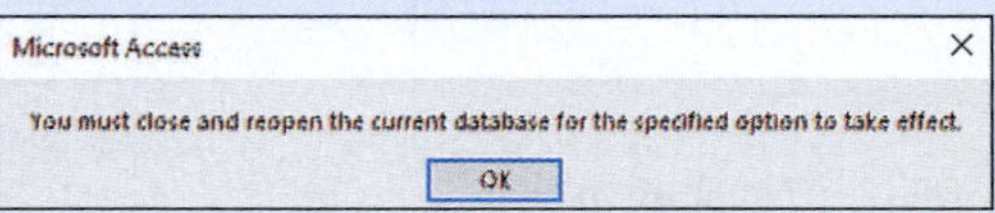

Figure 16 Start-up setting warning

Access 2016, Windows 10, Microsoft Corporation

m. Click **OK**.

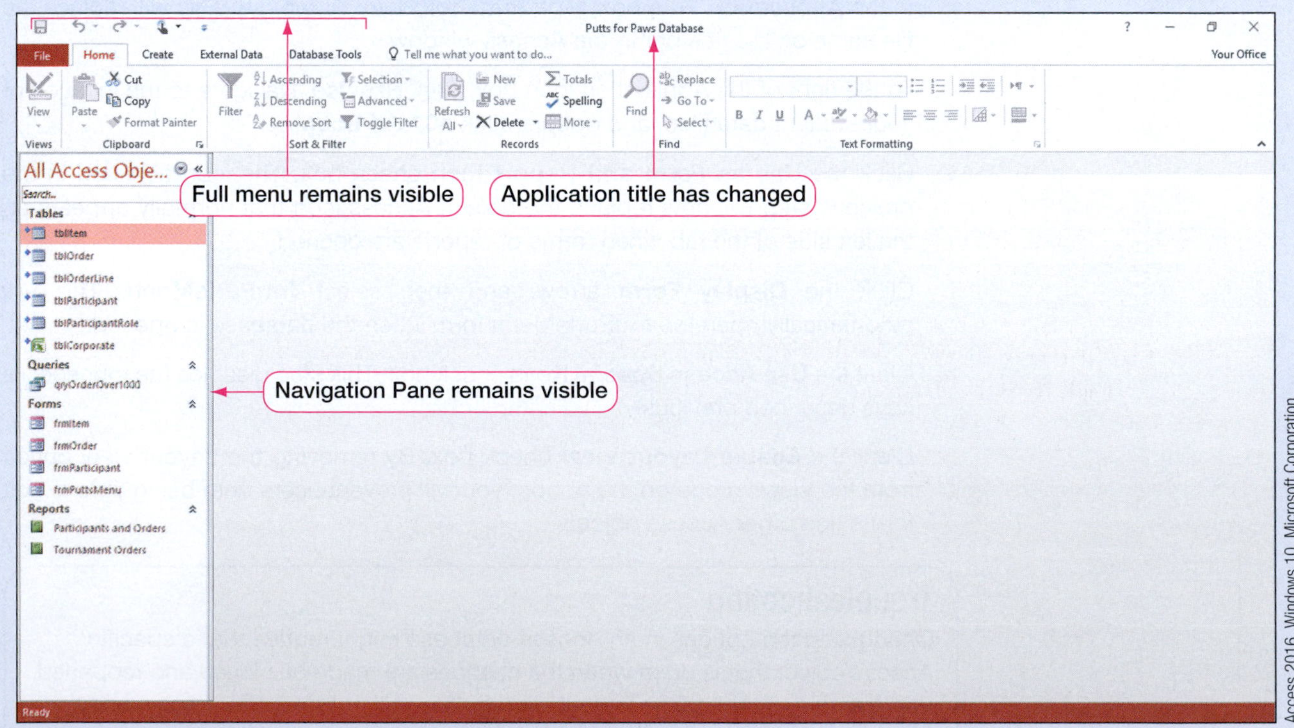

Access 2016, Windows 10, Microsoft Corporation

Figure 17 Access options before closing the database

n. Click the **File** tab, and then click **Close**.

Testing the Start-up Settings

You should always test any changes you make to the user interface of a database. This gives you a chance to verify that all options are correctly set. It also allows you to experience the database as other users will.

To Test the Start-up Settings

A14.12

a. To test the changes that have been made to the database, click the **File** tab, click **Open** in the left pane, and then double-click **This PC**.

b. Navigate to the location where you are saving your project files, and then double-click **a07ch14Putts_LastFirst**.

c. Type 917abf70 for the password to open the file when prompted.
   Notice that only the File and Home tabs on the ribbon are available. Likewise, the frmPuttsMenu navigation form opened with the database, but the Navigation Pane is not visible.

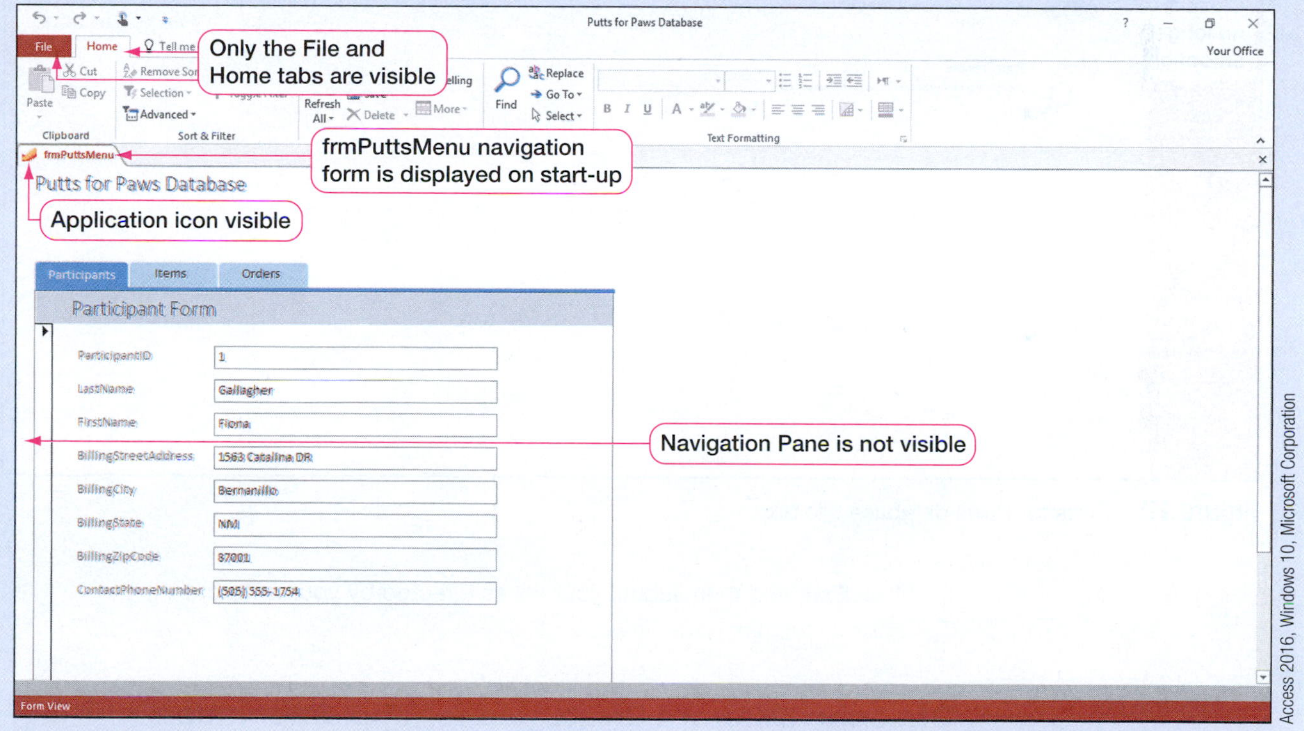

Figure 18 Putts for Paws database

SIDE NOTE

Bypass Startup Options

To bypass any startup options, an AutoExec macro, or an Open event procedure, hold down Shift while opening the database.

d. Press Alt + F11. Normally, this will open the Visual Basic Editor. However, because special keys have been disabled, nothing will happen as a result of this key combination.

e. Click the **File** tab to examine the changes to this view.

The available options are now limited. Users are allowed to print objects and exit the database. The Privacy Options button will open the Access Options dialog box. Users can also reset the Current Database options from this menu.

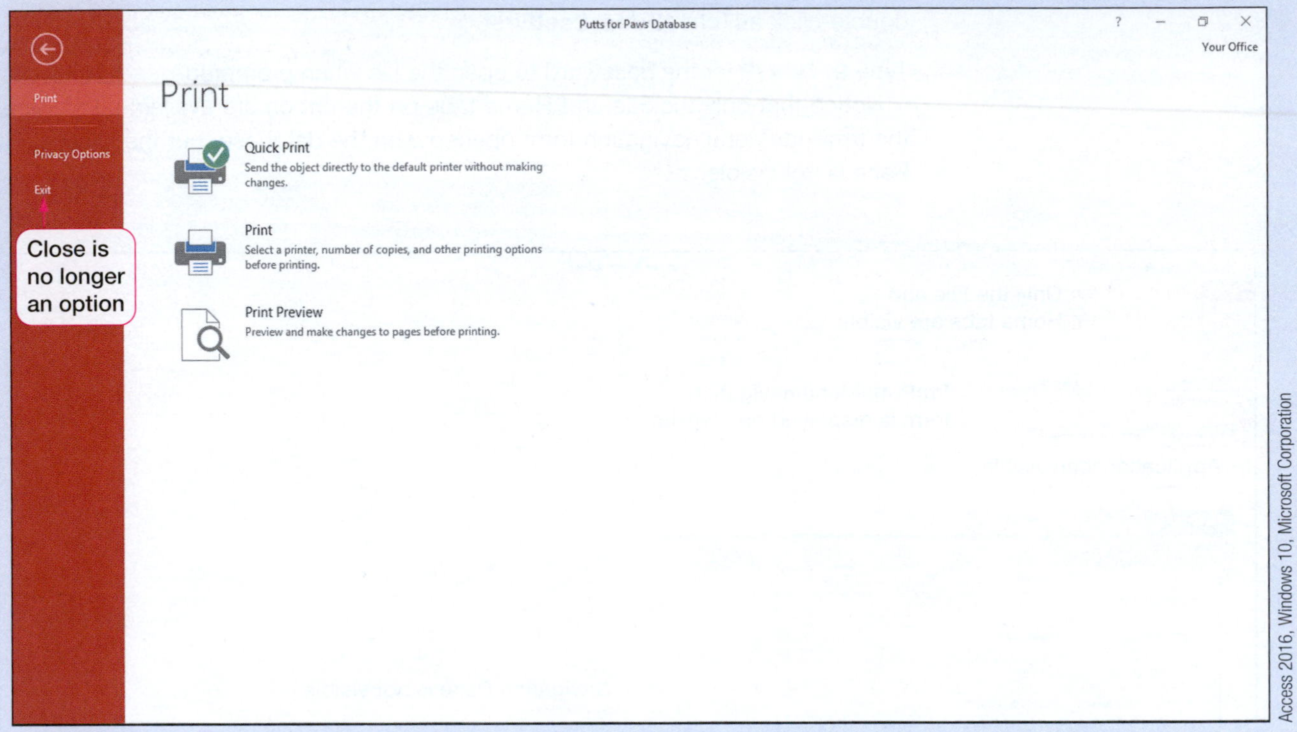

Figure 19 Putts for Paws database File tab

f. Click **Exit**, and then submit your file as directed by your instructor.

Describe Different Strategies for Implementation

Selecting a method of implementing your database — or any information technology solution — is a critical decision. There are several approaches to choose from and many important factors to consider. Cost, time, and the functionality of the new system are three of the most important factors to consider. It is important that you choose an approach that fits your business, employees, and technical environment. Your new database will most likely be replacing a legacy system. This might be a paper-based system or a software-based system. **Legacy software** is technology that is out of date but still in use. Legacy software exists because the software still meets the basic needs of the business. Often, users prefer a legacy system. They are familiar with the system, and any flaws in the system have usually been eliminated. It can be intimidating to learn a new system or business process, so implementations can be fraught with anxiety about the unknown.

You might choose to implement your database all at once. This **cold turkey implementation** approach involves implementing your database in its entirety and replacing the legacy system all at once. This method leaves little room for error. Once the new system is in place, the legacy system is no longer in use. If errors are found in the new system, they must be corrected in the absence of an alternative process. On the other hand, this approach gets users into the new system quickly and limits the need for maintaining more than one active solution.

Other methods involve a more gradual approach. In **piloted implementations**, small groups of a company's employees start using the new database. Gradually, more groups come on board as the system is perfected until the entire organization is using the new system. In **parallel implementations**, the legacy system and new system are used concurrently. In **phased implementations**, a portion of the new system is put into place and perfected before additional pieces of the system are moved into use. These three strategies offer robust ways to test a system and correct errors before a new system is put into full use. This provides a backup if the new system needs to be taken out of use, and it limits the loss of productivity if such an event happens. Conversely, these implementation approaches can take more time to complete and lead to increased costs, as two systems must be maintained until the new system completely replaces the legacy system.

Concept Check

1. For what reasons would you want to open an Access database in Exclusive mode? p. 711
2. Once the Performance Analyzer has run, what are the differences in the three types of results that it will present? Should these results always be acted upon? Why or why not? p. 712
3. What compatibility issues exist between Access 2003 and Access 2016? p. 717
4. What types of objects can be used to create linked tables in Access? What are the consequences of poor file management in regard to linked tables? p. 718
5. Define encryption. Describe situations in which encrypting a database would be beneficial. p. 724
6. What are the advantages of customizing the start-up options of a database? p. 726
7. Discuss the different methods of implementing a new database in an organization. What are the benefits and drawbacks of each method? p. 730

Key Terms

Back-end database 721
Cold turkey implementation 730
Decryption 724
Encryption 724
Exclusive Mode 711
Front-end database 721
Ideas 713
Legacy software 730
Linked table 718
Linked Table Manager 723
Parallel implementation 731
Performance Analyzer 712
Phased implementation 731
Piloted implementation 731
Recommendations 713
Shared Mode 711
Special keys 726
Suggestions 713

Visual Summary

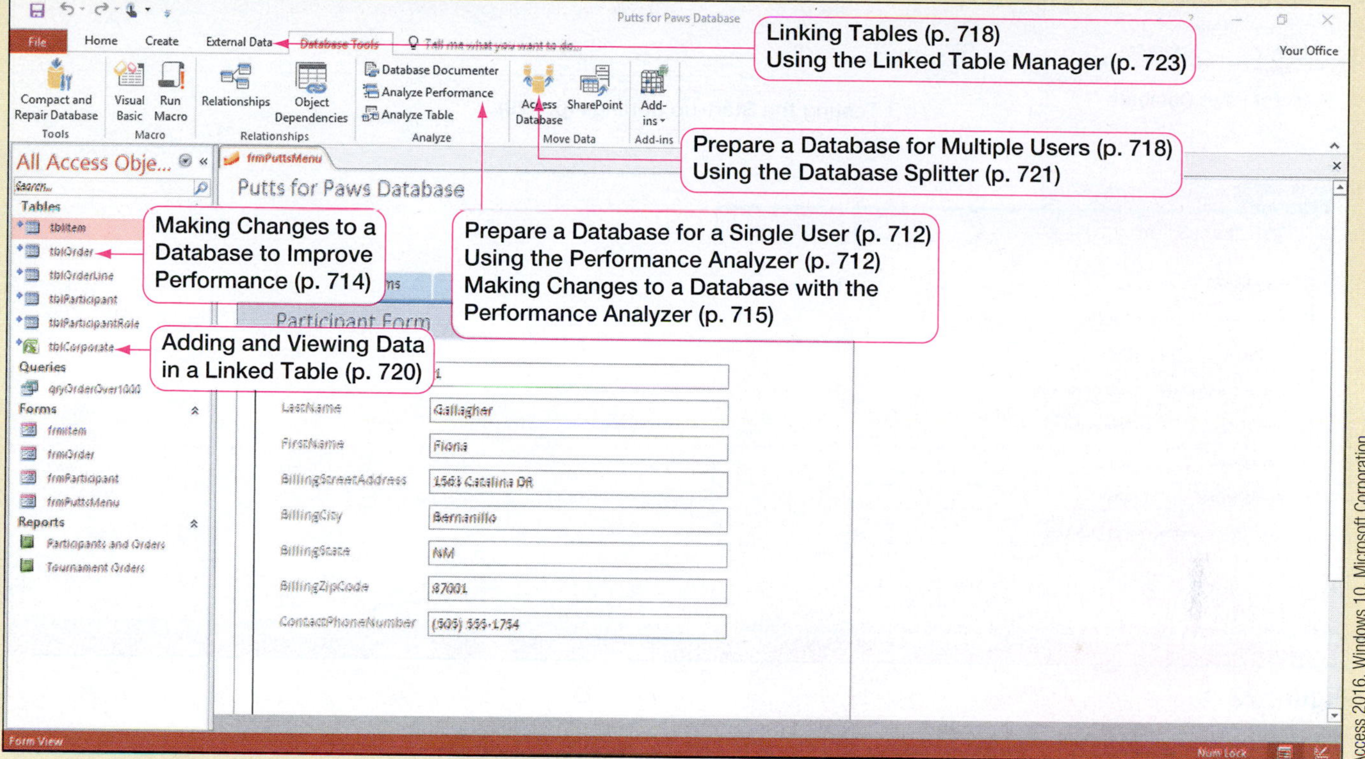
Linking Tables (p. 718)
Using the Linked Table Manager (p. 723)
Prepare a Database for Multiple Users (p. 718)
Using the Database Splitter (p. 721)
Making Changes to a Database to Improve Performance (p. 714)
Prepare a Database for a Single User (p. 712)
Using the Performance Analyzer (p. 712)
Making Changes to a Database with the Performance Analyzer (p. 715)
Adding and Viewing Data in a Linked Table (p. 720)
Putts for Paws Database
Access 2016, Windows 10, Microsoft Corporation

Figure 20

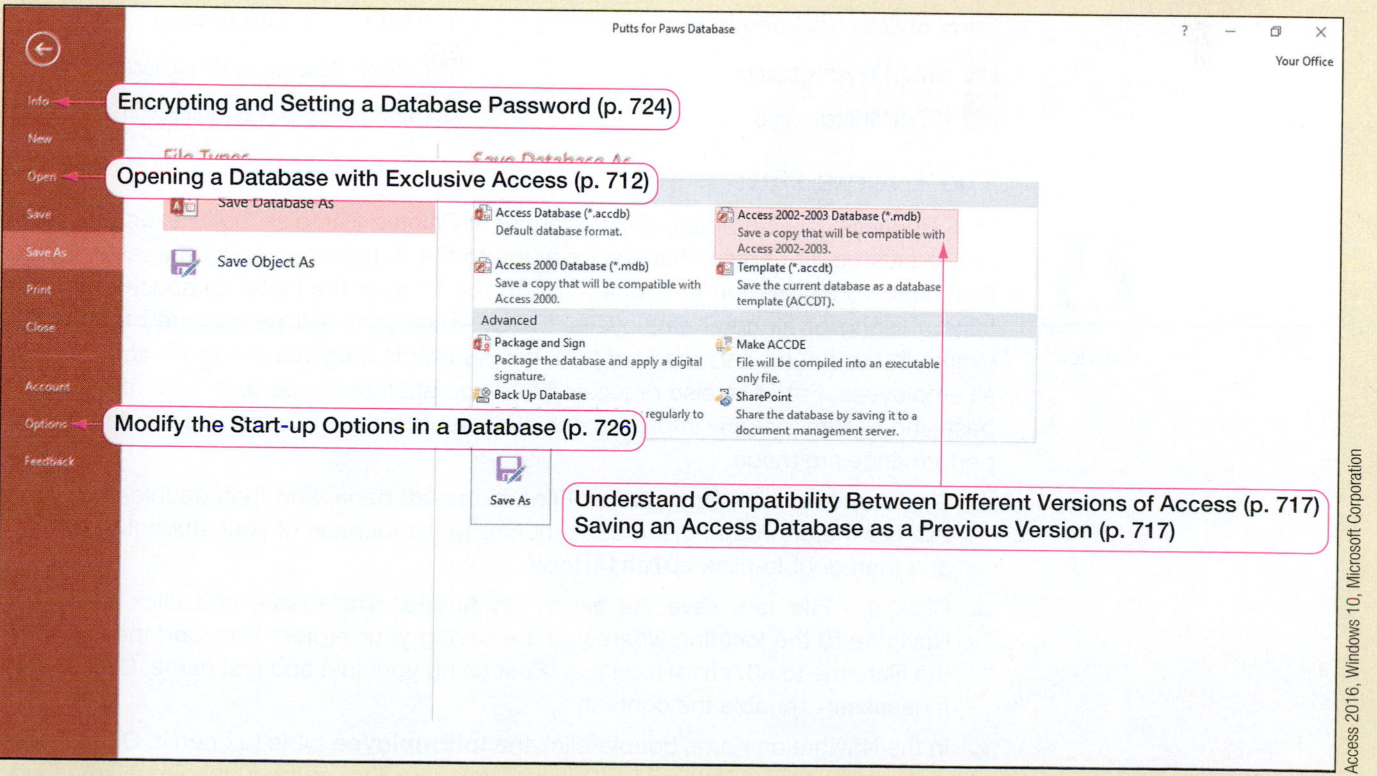
Putts for Paws Database
Encrypting and Setting a Database Password (p. 724)
Opening a Database with Exclusive Access (p. 712)
Modify the Start-up Options in a Database (p. 726)
Understand Compatibility Between Different Versions of Access (p. 717)
Saving an Access Database as a Previous Version (p. 717)
Access 2016, Windows 10, Microsoft Corporation

Figure 21

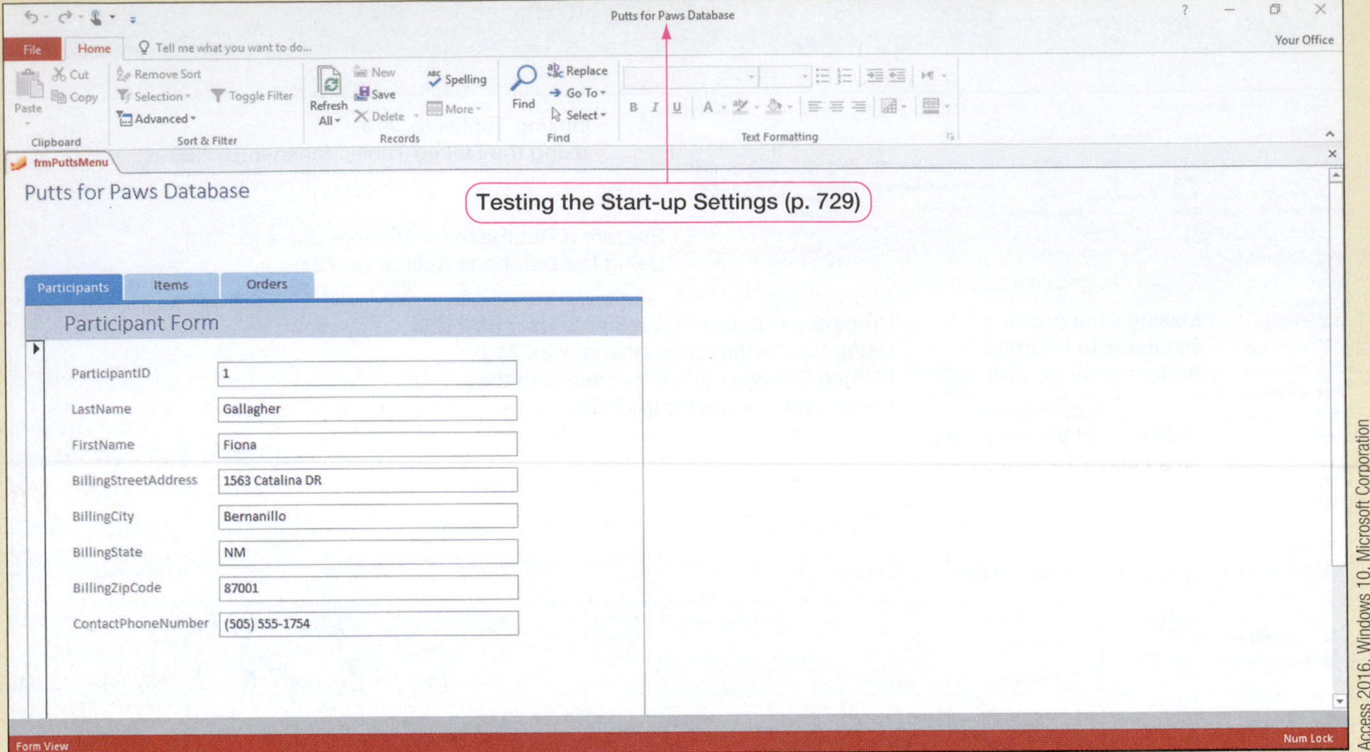

Access 2016, Windows 10, Microsoft Corporation

Figure 22

Practice 1

Student data files needed:

a07ch14Events.accdb

a07ch14Hotel.accdb

You will save your files as:

a07ch14Events_LastFirst.accdb

a07ch14Hotel_LastFirst.accdb

The Events Database

Customer Service

Patti Rochelle, the Corporate Event Planner at Painted Paradise Golf Resort and Spa, has requested that some changes be made to the database used by the resort hotel. First, she would like you to create a link to the table in the Hotel database that contains a listing of all hotel employees. These employees will be assigned to specific events in the future, and the Events database needs easy access to an active list of all employees. Patti has also requested that you analyze the performance of the database and ensure that any improvements that can be made to speed up the database's performance are made.

a. Start **Access**, click **Open Other Files** in the left pane, and then double-click **This PC**. Navigate through the folder structure to the location of your student data files, and then double-click **a07ch14Hotel**.

b. Click the **File** tab, save the file as an **Access Database**, and click **Save As**. Navigate to the location where you are saving your project files, and then change the filename to a07ch14Hotel_LastFirst using your last and first name. Click **Save**. If necessary, enable the content.

c. In the Navigation Pane, double-click the **tblEmployee** table to open it. On the New record line, type 6 in the AreaID field. Type your first name in the FirstName field, and then type your last name in the LastName field.

d. **Close** the table, click the **File** tab, and then click **Close**.

e. Click the **File** tab, click **Open** in the left pane, and then double-click **This PC**. Navigate through the folder structure to the location of your student data files, and then double-click **a07ch14Events**.

f. Click the **File** tab, save the file as an **Access Database**, and click **Save As**. Navigate to the location where you are saving your project files, and then change the filename to a07ch14Events_LastFirst using your last and first name. Click **Save**. If necessary, enable the content.

g. Create a link to the tblEmployee table in the Hotel database by completing the following steps.
   - Click the **External Data** tab, and then, in the Import & Link group, click **Access**.
   - In the Get External Data dialog box, click **Browse**. Navigate to the location where you are saving your project files, and double-click **a07ch14Hotel_LastFirst**.
   - In the Get External Data - Access Database dialog box, click **Link to the data source by creating a linked table**, and then click **OK**.
   - In the Link Tables dialog box, select **tblEmployee**, and then click **OK**.

h. Analyze and improve the performance of the database by completing the following steps.
   - Click the **Database Tools** tab, and then, in the Analyze group, click **Analyze Performance**.
   - In the Performance Analyzer dialog box, click the **All Object Types** tab.
   - Click **Select All**, and then click **OK** to run the Performance Analyzer.
   - Select the suggestion **Table 'tblEvents': Relate to table tblEventItems'**, and then click **Optimize**. This will improve the performance of the qryEventList query.
   - Click the idea **Table 'tblMenuChoice': Change data type of field 'CostPerPerson' from Short 'Text' to 'Double'** to examine it. The CostPerPerson field is the price each person would be charged for a meal and should be converted to Currency. Click **Close**.
   - In the Navigation Pane, double-click the **tblMenuChoice** table to open it.
   - Select the **CostPerPerson** field, and then click the **Fields** tab.
   - In the Formatting group, click the **Data Type** arrow, and then select **Currency**. Because currency fields are smaller than text fields, Access will warn you that the potential exists for losing data. This will not be an issue in this table. Click **Yes**.
   - **Save** your changes, and **Close** the table.

i. To encrypt the database with a password, it will need to be opened with Exclusive Access. Click the **File** tab, and then click **Close**.

j. Click the **File** tab, click **Open** in the left pane, and then double-click **This PC**. Navigate to the location where you are saving your project files, and then click to select **a07ch14Events_LastFirst**. Click the **Open** arrow, and then select **Open Exclusive**. If necessary, enable the content.

k. Encrypt the database with a password, and modify the start-up options by completing the following steps.
   - Click the **File** tab, and then click **Encrypt with Password**.
   - In the Password field, type 321efd68, and then, in the Verify field, type 321efd68. Click **OK**.
   - Click **OK** in the message that Access will ignore row-level locking.

- Click the **File** tab, and click **Options**. From the navigation options on the left side of the Access Options dialog box, click **Current Database**.
- In the Application Title box, type Painted Paradise Resort & Spa.
- Click **OK** to close the Access Options dialog box.

l. Close the database, exit Access, and then submit your files as directed by your instructor.

Problem Solve 1

Student data files needed:

 a07ch14Spa.accdb

 a07ch14Schedule.xlsx

You will save your files as:

 a07ch14Spa_LastFirst.accdb

 a07ch14Spa_LastFirst_be.accdb

Turquoise Oasis Spa Database

Production & Operations

Business is going well at the Turquoise Oasis Spa, and management is expanding its service and product offerings. This also means that additional staff will be hired to manage all the transactions. You have been asked to make changes to their existing database to make it easier and more secure to share with multiple employees. The spa managers have also begun outsourcing their scheduling and would like to create a linked table in the database to the spreadsheet where the scheduling information is being stored.

a. Open the Access database **a07ch14Spa**. Save your file as a07ch14Spa_LastFirst using your last and first name. If necessary, enable the content.

b. Split the database into front-end and back-end systems to better accommodate multiple users. Name the back-end database a07ch14Spa_LastFirst_be.

c. Create a linked table to the **a07ch14Schedule** Excel spreadsheet. Ensure that the column headings are used as the field names of the table, and keep the default name of tblSchedule.

d. Run the Performance Analyzer on All Object Types in the database. Examine the second and third ideas presented, and make the appropriate changes to the database to optimize performance. (Hint: For the idea of relating the tblEmployee table to the other tables in the database, examine the tables, and look for a table where EmployeeID is used as a foreign key. Since the tables are in the back-end database, you will need to create the relationships there.)

e. Change the navigational options for the front-end database.
   - The Application Title should display Turquoise Oasis Spa.
   - The **frmTurquoiseNavigation** form should open when the database starts, and the Navigation pane should be hidden.
   - Special Keys, Layout View, and design changes to tables in Datasheet view should be disabled in the database.
   - Full Menus and Default Shortcut Menus should be disabled in the database.
   - Close the database, exit Access, and then submit your files as directed by your instructor.

Critical Thinking

When it comes to modifying the start-up options of a database, it is not a one-size-fits-all approach. What are some things you should consider about the end users before deciding how to modify the navigational options?

Perform 1: Perform in Your Life

CHAPTER 14

Student data files needed:

 a07ch14Pet.accdb

 a07ch14Donations.xlsx

You will save your files as:

 a07ch14Pet_LastFirst.accdb

 a07ch14Pet_LastFirst2003.mdb

 a07ch14Pet_LastFirst_be.accdb

Allan's Adopt-A-Pet Database

You have been hired as a database administrator for Allan's Adopt-A-Pet, a pet adoption service, to enhance a database that helps to keep track of the service's animals, customers, and adoptions. Your supervisor has requested that you make the appropriate changes to the database so that it can easily be used by multiple people and to implement appropriate security measures to prevent unintentional or malicious modifications to the database.

a. Open the Access database **a07ch14Pet**. Name your file a07ch14Pet_LastFirst using your last and first name. If necessary, enable the content.

b. Add your first and last name to the tblCustomer table, and then close the table.

c. Save a copy of the database in Access 2002-2003 database (*.mdb) format. Save the file as a07ch14Pet_LastFirst2003. Close the database, and then open the **a07ch14Pet_LastFirst** database.

d. Split the database into front-end and back-end systems to make it easier for multiple users to use the database. Name the back-end database a07ch14Pet_LastFirst_be.

e. Create a linked table using the a07ch14Donations Excel spreadsheet. Name the table tblDonations.

f. Encrypt the a07ch14Pet_LastFirst database, and protect it from unauthorized access. You will need to close the database and open it with Exclusive Access first. Use td74#nhy as the password for the database.

g. Change navigational options for the front-end database to match the following criteria.

   - Add an appropriate application title.
   - The **frmPetNavigation** form should open when the database starts, and the Navigation Pane should be hidden.
   - Modify other settings so that the users are limited in what they can access in the database, in order to protect it.

h. Close the database, exit Access, and then submit your files as directed by your instructor.

Additional Cases

Additional Workshop Cases are available on the companion website and in the instructor resources.

Access Business Unit 7 CAPSTONE

Implementing and Automating a Database with VBA

This business unit had two outcomes:

Learning Outcome 1:

Develop VBA procedures to enhance the functionality and usability of a database. Learn how to structure VBA procedures to improve readability and utilize comments to document the procedures.

Learning Outcome 2:

Learn how to implement a database for multiple users, how to make a database compatible with earlier versions of Access, and how to prevent unauthorized changes to the database with encryption and by modifying the startup options.

In Business Unit 7 Capstone, students will demonstrate competence in these outcomes through a series of business problems at various levels from guided practice to problem solving an existing database and performing to create new databases.

More Practice 1

Student data files needed:

 a07Indigo5Menu.accdb

 a07Ingredients1.xlsx

 a07Ingredients2.xlsx

You will save your files as:

 a07Indigo5Menu_LastFirst.accdb

 a07Indigo5Menu_LastFirst_be.accdb

 a07Indgo5Menu_LastFirst.accde

Indigo5 Menu Database

Production & Operations

Painted Paradise is home to the world-class restaurant Indigo5. The manager of Indigo5, Alberto Dimas, is looking for ways to use technology to make the restaurant more efficient. His discussions with Chef Robin Sanchez have led to the further development of the database that is utilized to maintain the menus and ingredients used at Indigo5.

Currently, the database includes a list of all menus in use and the ingredients used in each recipe. Functionality was recently added to assist Indigo5 in maintaining an inventory of ingredients as well. A macro was added that will update the inventory of ingredients on the basis of the data in a temporary table; after the inventory is updated, the temporary table is deleted. You will convert the macro to VBA and create an import procedure that will allow Robin Sanchez to select multiple files from local food distributors to import into the database. After the import takes place, the original macro should then run. After the entire process is finished, a message box should alert the database user that the process has been completed. When this process is complete, Alberto has requested that the database be modified to allow multiple users and prevent the creation of new database objects.

a. Start **Access**, click **Open Other Files** in the left pane, and then double-click **This PC**. Navigate through the folder structure to the location of your student data files, and then double-click **a07Indigo5Menu**. A database opens displaying tables related to the restaurant's menu items and recipes.

b. Click the **File** tab, save the file as an **Access Database**, and click **Save As**. Navigate to the location where you are saving your project files, and then change the filename to a07Indigo5Menu_LastFirst using your last and first name. Click **Save**. If necessary, enable the content.

c. Convert the **mcrUpdateIngredients** macro to VBA, including error handling and comments when converting the macro, by completing the following steps.

   - In the Navigation Pane, right-click the **mcrUpdateIngredients** macro, and then click **Design View**.

- On the Design tab, in the Tools group, click **Convert Macros to Visual Basic**. In the Convert macro: mcrUpdateIngredients dialog box, click **Convert**, and then click **OK**.
- In Project Explorer, double-click **Converted Macro- mcrUpdateIngredients** to open the Code window.
- Insert a comment between the Function statement and the On Error statement. Type 'This procedure updates the ingredients in the database., and then press Enter.
- Insert another comment under the first one. Type 'This procedure was created by iLast using your first initial and last name.

d. Add an import process to the procedure. The process should allow for multiple Excel spreadsheets to be imported into the tblTempIngredients table.

- To begin a new line of code, click **under** the On Error statement, press Enter, and then press Tab.
- Type Dim IngredientDialog As Object, and then press Enter. This declares a variable that will serve as the FileDialog object.
- Type Set IngredientDialog = Application.FileDialog(msoFileDialogOpen) to set the variable as the FileDialog object, and then press Enter.
- To use a With statement to handle the IngredientDialog object more efficiently, press Enter, type With IngredientDialog, and then press Enter.
- Press Tab to indent the next line of code. For the title of the file dialog window, type .Title = "Import ingredients into the database", and then press Enter.
- To allow multiple spreadsheets to be imported at the same time, type .AllowMultiSelect = True, and then press Enter.

e. Use an If statement to determine whether any files were selected for import. Use a For Each Next statement to loop through the process of importing each spreadsheet selected by the user. The user should be notified with a message box if no spreadsheets were selected.

- Press Enter, and then type If .Show = True Then.
- Press Enter, and then press Tab.
- To declare a variable that will hold the names of the files to be imported, type Dim ImportFile As Variant, and then press Enter.
- Press Tab, type For Each ImportFile In .SelectedItems, press Enter, and then press Tab.
- Type DoCmd.TransferSpreadsheet acImport, acSpreadsheetTypeExcel12, _ to begin the DoCmd, and then press Enter. The line continuation character will allow the Visual Basic Editor to break the statement across two lines of the code window.
- Type "tblTempIngredients", ImportFile, True, "", press Enter, and then press Backspace.
- Type Next to end the For Each Next statement after it has looped through all of the selected files. Press Enter.

f. Create a message box that alerts users that the process is complete and then a message that displays if the user cancels the import process.

- Press Backspace, and then type MsgBox "Finished importing new ingredients." Press Enter, and then press Backspace.
- Type Else, and then press Enter.
- Press Tab. To create a message box that will inform users that they have canceled the import procedure, type MsgBox "You have canceled the import process.", and then press Enter.
- Press Backspace, type End If, and then press Enter.
- Press Backspace, type End With, and then press Enter.

g. Compile the code to check for any possible errors in the procedure.
   - Click **Debug** on the menu bar, and then click **Compile a07Indigo5Menu**.
   - If no message appears, your code compiled successfully. If a message appears indicating a problem with your code, fix the problem, and then compile the VBA again.
   - Close the Visual Basic Editor, and then close the mcrUpdateIngredients macro.

h. Assign the new procedure to a button on the frmIngredients form.
   - In the Navigation Pane, right-click the **frmIngredients** form, and then click **Design View**.
   - Select all of the form **labels** and **fields** and the **subform** in the Detail portion of the form, and then move them down to the .5" marker.
   - Click the **Design** tab, and then, in the Controls group, click the **Button** form control.
   - Insert the new command button **above** the IngredientID label and text box. In the Command Button Wizard, click **Cancel**.
   - If necessary, click the **Design** tab, and then, in the Tools group, click **Property Sheet**.
   - In the Property Sheet pane, click the **All** tab, click in the **Name** field, highlight the default name of the command button, and then type **cmdImportNewIngredients**.
   - Click in the **Caption** field, highlight the default caption text, and then type **Import New Ingredients**.
   - Click the **Event** tab, and in the On Click field, click **Build**. In the Choose Builder dialog box, click **Code Builder**, and then click **OK**.
   - The Visual Basic Editor will open to a new Private Sub procedure in the Form_frmIngredients object. Click the **blank line** of code after the Private Sub statement.
   - Type **Call mcrUpdateIngredients**, and then close the Visual Basic Editor.
   - Adjust the width of the new command button to include the full caption text.
   - Save the **frmIngredients** form, and then close it.

i. Split the database to accommodate more users.
   - Click the **Database Tools** tab, and then, in the Move Data group, click **Access Database**.
   - Click **Split Database**, navigate to where you are saving your files, and then save the back-end file as **a07Indigo5Menu_LastFirst_be**. Click **Split**, and then click **OK** in the confirmation message that Access split the database.

j. Alberto has requested that the front-end database display only the File and Home tabs on the ribbon. The database should have a title, and Alberto would like to prevent users from editing forms by right-clicking them.
   - Click the **File** tab, click **Options**, and then click **Current Database** in the Navigation Pane.
   - In the Application Title box, type **Indigo5 Menu Database**.
   - Under Ribbon and Toolbar Options, clear the **Allow Full Menus** check box so that only the Home and File tabs are displayed. If any Add-in applications are installed for Access, the Add-ins tab will appear.
   - Under Ribbon and Toolbar Options, clear the **Allow Default Shortcut Menus** check box. This prevents the shortcut menus from appearing when a user right-clicks a form or report.
   - Click **OK**, and then click **OK** in the message box informing you that the changes you have made will not be enabled until the database has been closed and reopened.

k. To further secure the database, save a copy of the front-end file as an ACCDE file. This will prevent users from being able to access any VBA or macros in the database.
   - Click the **File** tab, and then click **Save As**.
   - In the Advanced list, click **Make ACCDE**, and then click **Save As**. Navigate to where you are saving your files, and then save the ACCDE file as **a07Indigo5Menu_LastFirst**.

l. Test the finished ACCDE file by importing two files of ingredients into the database.
- Click the **File** tab, and then click **Exit**.
- Start **Access**, open the **a07Indigo5Menu_LastFirst.accde** database, and then, in the Microsoft Access Security Notice dialog box, click **Open**.
- In the Navigation Pane, double-click the **frmIngredients** form to open it.
- Click **Import New Ingredients** to begin the import process. Navigate through the folder structure to the location of your student data files, press and hold Ctrl, and then click **a07Ingredients1** and **a07Ingredients2**. Click **Open**.
- Click **OK** in the message box stating that your import has finished.
- Close the **frmIngredients** form, and in the Navigation Pane, double-click the **tblIngredients** table to open it. Examine the ingredient Rice. The value in the InStock field is now 13. Close the tblIngredient table.

m. Close the database, exit Access, and then submit your files as directed by your instructor.

Problem Solve 1

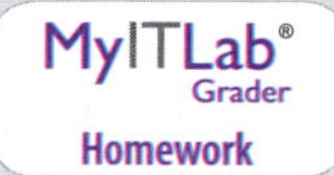

Student data files needed:

 a07HotelAdsAnalysis.accdb
 a07SpaAds.xlsx
 a07GolfAds.xlsx
 a07Icon.ico

You will save your file as:

a07HotelAdsAnalysis_LastFirst.accdb

Advertisements in the Hotel

Customer Service

The hotel at the Painted Paradise Golf Resort & Spa has several large-screen televisions that run promotional slide shows from other units of the resort, such as the Indigo5 restaurant and the Terra Cotta Brew coffee shop. Along the bottom of each display is a ticker line. The ticker line displays advertisements and announcements from the different areas of Painted Paradise. Each area will send its information to the hotel in an Excel spreadsheet with fixed column headings. Several files might be received in any given time period. Create a flexible import system in the database that will allow multiple Microsoft Excel spreadsheets to be imported at one time. Analyze the performance of the database, and optimize any reasonable suggestions.

a. Open the Access database **a07HotelAdsAnalysis**. Save your file as a07HotelAdsAnalysis_LastFirst using your last and first name. If necessary, enable the content.

b. Create a button on the frmImports form that will initiate the import process by completing the following steps.
- Place a **button** at the top of the Detail portion of the frmImports form. Name the button cmdImportNewAds. The caption of the button must read Import New Advertisements.
- Assign an event procedure to the **On Click** event of the button.

c. The import procedure must allow for multiple Excel spreadsheets to be imported into the tblAdvertisements table.
- Insert a comment that states This procedure imports new advertisements into the Hotel database. Press Enter.
- Add another comment that states This procedure was created by iLast using your first initial and last name. Press Enter twice.

d. As part of the procedure, include error trapping.
- Include an On Error statement after the comments.
- Use a GoTo statement to redirect the procedure to an ImportAds_Err line label.

e. In the procedure, construct a process in which a user can import multiple Excel spreadsheets into the tblAdvertisements table. A template of the Excel files that the other resort areas are using has been provided for you. The files include column headings that match the Advertisements table in the a07ps3Hotel database.
   - Use AdsDialog as the object name.
   - The file dialog box must have the title Import Advertisement List(s).
   - If the import is canceled, a message should be displayed. The message must display the text You canceled the import.

f. Complete the error trapping in the procedure.
   - If an error occurs, use the line label ImportAds_Exit line label to exit the procedure.
   - Include the line label ImportAds_Err to display the error message to the user.

g. Compile the database before exiting the Visual Basic Editor. If an error occurs during the compile process, fix the error and compile that database again.

h. Test the import process by importing the **a07GolfAds** and **a07SpaAds** Excel files.

i. Run the Performance Analyzer on the database.
   - The Performance Analyzer will recommend using the Option Explicit statement in your VBA procedure. Complete this process.

j. Secure the user interface of the database by completing the following steps.
   - The Application Title should be Advertising Database. Use **a07Icon** as the Application Icon for forms and reports.
   - Only the File and Home tabs on the Ribbon should be visible.
   - Users should not be able to edit forms or reports in Layout view or by right-clicking a database object.
   - Users should not be able to edit tables in Datasheet view.
   - Users should not be able to use special keys in the database.

k. Encrypt the database to protect it from unauthorized access.
   - Use 824zpq91 as the password.

l. Close the database, exit Access, and then submit your file as directed by your instructor.

Critical Thinking

Currently, this database tracks only the message, start and end dates, and areas of the advertisements displayed on the large screens throughout the hotel. What else could be tracked to gauge the effectiveness of these advertisements?

Problem Solve 2

Student data files needed:

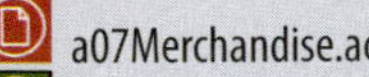

a07Merchandise.accdb

a07NewItems1.xlsx

a07NewItems2.xlsx

You will save your files as:

a07Merchandise_LastFirst.accdb

a07Merchandise_LastFirst_be.accdb

Merchandise Sales

Sales & Marketing

You have decided to take the summer and tour with one of your favorite bands. To earn money for the summer, you have arranged to sell merchandise for the band before and after concerts. You have been given a database that the band uses to manage the inventory at their merchandise tent. You have been asked to make enhancements to the database to allow for multiple users. You have also been asked to convert a macro in the database into VBA to make the import of new merchandise into the database easier.

a. Open the Access database **a07Merchandise**. Save your file as a07Merchandise_LastFirst using your last and first name. If necessary, enable the content.

b. The mcrImportItems macro imports a single Excel spreadsheet from a fixed location into the tblTransactions table. Convert the mcrImportItems macro to a VBA function, and modify it to prompt the user for multiple files to import.
   - Open the **mcrImportItems** macro in Design View.
   - Convert the macro to Visual Basic. Convert the macro with error handling but not with comments.
   - Insert a new line under the name of the function, and insert a comment that includes your first initial and last name as the author of the procedure. Insert another comment that describes what the function will do.
   - Add code to the converted macro that will prompt the user to locate the files to be imported. Use InventoryDialog as the name of the object variable. The function must allow for multiple files to be imported, and the title of the dialog box should read **Select File(s) to Import**.
   - Add line continuation characters to your code as needed. If the user cancels the import, a message box that reads You canceled the import should appear.

c. Open the rptInventoryReport report in Design View. Add a command button to the form to the right of the title of the report. Change the caption of the button to read Import New Inventory.

d. Add an On Click event using the code builder. In the newly created On Click event, call the mcrImportItems function. Save changes to the form, and switch to Report View.

e. Test the import function by importing the **a07NewItems1** and **a07NewItems2** Excel workbooks. Refresh the report to see the changes to the inventory in the database.

f. Split the database into front-end and back-end components. Save the back-end file as a07Merchandise_LastFirst_be.

g. Secure the front-end component of the database by completing the following steps.
   - The Application Title should be Merchandise Database.
   - Only the File and Home tabs on the Ribbon should be visible.
   - Users should not be able to edit forms or reports in Layout view or by right-clicking a database object.
   - Users should not be able to edit tables in Datasheet view.
   - Users should not be able to use special keys in the database.

h. Encrypt the database to protect it from unauthorized access. Use 74!tr364 as the password.

i. Close the database, exit Access, and then submit your files as directed by your instructor.

Perform 1: Perform in Your Career

Student data file needed:

 a07Repair.accdb

You will save your files as:

 a07Repair_LastFirst.accdb

 a07Repair_LastFirst_be.accdb

Home Repair with a Heart

Production & Operations

A small home repair business that employs several contractors and specializes in home improvement projects needs help with its database. You were recently hired to increase the functionality of the database by analyzing its performance. You also need to make appropriate changes to the database so it can easily be used by multiple people and that the appropriate security measures can be taken to prevent unintentional or malicious modifications to the database.

a. Open the Access database **a07Repair**. Save your file as a07Repair_LastFirst using your last and first name. If necessary, enable the content.

b. Add your first name and last name, address, and phone to the tblCustomers table.

c. Run the Performance Analyzer on all database objects. Create any relationships between tables suggested by the Performance Analyzer.

d. Split the database to better accommodate multiple users. Name the back-end database a07Repair_LastFirst_be.

e. Modify the appropriate settings for the front-end database to make it more secure.
   - Type an appropriate Application Title.
   - The navigation form should be the form displayed when the database opens.
   - Special keys should be disabled.
   - Users should not be able to edit tables in Datasheet view.
   - Users should not be able to edit forms or reports in Layout view.
   - Do not display the Navigation pane when the database is opened.
   - Only the File and Home tabs on the Ribbon should be visible.

f. Encrypt the database using the password er7jhMk!

g. Close the database, exit Access, and then submit your files as directed by your instructor.

Perform 2: Perform in Your Life

Student data file needed:

 Blank Access database

You will save your file as:

 a07FamilyTree_LastFirst.accdb

My Family Tree

In this project, you will create a family tree in an Access database. The database should be constructed with you as the central focus of the project. In other words, when you enter a family member into the database, that person's relationship status will be relative to you. A database of this nature will include intensive data entry, so build the database with this in mind. Organize the forms in a logical and efficient fashion. You will use VBA to assist you in automating tasks when possible. Family tree information may be private information. You will take steps to secure your database not only to prevent unintentional editing of database objects but to protect any sensitive information in the database.

a. Start **Access**, and then create a new blank database. Save the database as a07FamilyTree_LastFirst using your last and first name.

b. Create a table that will list the different relationship possibilities. At a minimum, this should include items such as mother, father, brother, sister, and the like.

c. Create a table that will hold the personal information for your family members. Create an attachment field that can contain a picture.

d. Create a navigational form that contains two tabbed forms. The first should be a form to enter data into the personal information table. The second should be a form that is not based on a table that can hold command buttons.

e. On the blank form, create a command button. This command button will have an import script that will run on the On Click event. Name the command button **cmdImportFamilyData**.

f. As part of this project, you could export the personal information table as an Excel spreadsheet. This spreadsheet can serve as a data entry template that you can e-mail to family members. They could complete the form and send it back to you.

- Create an import process that would allow you to select these files and import them into the personal information table. Assume that you may be selecting more than one file at a time. Add appropriate comments to describe the purpose of the procedure and to indicate who the author of the procedure is, using your first initial and last name.
- Compile the code in the database before exiting the Visual Basic Editor.
- In the Visual Basic Editor, lock the project for viewing, and provide a password to the VBA properties. Use 853ahe90 for the password.

g. Analyze the performance of your database, and then optimize your database where appropriate.

h. This database will contain private information. Full names and dates of birth are common aspects of a family tree. Encrypt the database with a password, using 284enu49 for the password.

i. Close the database, exit Access, and then submit your file as directed by your instructor.

Perform 3: Perform in Your Team

Student data files needed:

 a07Scheduling.accdb

 a07Scheduling.xlsx

You will save your files as:

 a07Scheduling_TeamName.accdb

 a07Scheduling_TeamName_be.accdb

Scheduling at a Medical Facility

Production & Operations

You have been hired as the manager of a call center at a regional medical facility. The facility houses a wide range of medical services, including general physicians, x-ray services, and a lab service. You have been asked to deploy a database to a small portion of the facility before the database is expanded to additional units.

There are several requirements for the database. Its performance must be improved. It must be prepared for multiple users. All computers running the database will be using Access 2016. However, users should not be able to create new objects in the database or modify existing objects in the database. The information in the database will be private data and must be protected with a password.

a. Select one team member to set up the document by completing steps b–e.

b. Open your browser, and navigate to https://www.onedrive.live.com, https://www.drive.google.com, or any other instructor-assigned location. Create a new folder, and then name it a07SchedulingFolder_TeamName, using the name assigned to your team by your instructor.

c. Open the Access database, **a07Scheduling**. Save your file as a07Scheduling_TeamName. If necessary, enable the content.

d. Upload the **a07Scheduling_TeamName** database to the a07SchedulingFolder_TeamName folder, and then share the folder with the other members of your team. Make sure that the other team members have permission to edit the contents of the shared folder and that they are required to log in to access it.

e. Create an import process that will allow a user to import a clinician's availability from a Microsoft Excel spreadsheet.
   - The command button cmdImportAppointments has been created on the frmSchedulingMenu form. Assign a function to this button that will run in response to the On Click event.
   - For the import process, assume that multiple spreadsheets can be imported at the same time.

- The procedure should import Excel spreadsheets to the tblAppointments table. The clinic physicians will have an Excel template to fill out so that the fields in the spreadsheet match that of the database.
- Add comments to the procedure to explain what the procedure is doing.
- Add a comment to the procedure listing your team name as the author of the procedure.
- Add error handling to the procedure. The error handling should show the user the error encountered and then exit the function.
- Provide a title to the dialog box that will be presented to the user.
- If the import is canceled, a message box should alert the user that he or she has canceled the import.
- Compile the database before closing the Visual Basic Editor.

f. Split the database into a front-end system and a back-end system. Name the back-end database **a07Scheduling_TeamName_be**.

g. Secure the front-end database by encrypting it with a password.
   - Close the database, and open it with Exclusive Access. Use the password **727ebc67**.

h. Secure the user interface of the front-end system.
   - The application title should be **Scheduling Database**.
   - The **frmSchedulingMenu** form menu should be displayed when the database is opened.
   - Prevent users from using special keys.
   - Only the File and Home tabs should be visible on the Ribbon.
   - Prevent users from editing tables in Datasheet view.
   - Prevent users from editing forms and reports in Layout view or by right-clicking a database object.
   - The Navigation Pane should not be visible when the database is opened.

i. Test the import process. Click the **Import Clinician Appointments** button to import the **a07Scheduling** Excel file.

j. Close the database, exit Access, and then submit your files as directed by your instructor.

Perform 4: How Others Perform

Student data file needed:

 a07Projects.accdb

You will save your files as:

 a07Projects_LastFirst.accdb

 a07Projects_LastFirst2003.mdb

Project Management Database

Production & Operations

You are the project manager at a midsize technology company. As your company has grown, the task of tracking projects with the current paper-based process has become overwhelming. The company has decided to build an Access database that will better track projects. You have been asked to review the database and fix any errors or improve any inefficiencies that can be found. Additionally, some users will be using Access 2003 to view the database. Create a copy of the database in 2003 format.

a. Open the Access database **a07Projects**. Save your file as **a07Projects_LastFirst** using your last and first name. If necessary, enable the content.

b. Open the **frmProjectSummary** form. Examine the Project Start Date field.

c. The BackThemeColorIndex property of this field is supposed to change under two conditions: (1) when the number of days from the project start date to the date last updated is greater than 30 and the project status is "development" and (2) when the number of days from the project start date to the date last updated is greater than 60 days and the project status is "implementation." If neither of these conditions is met or if the project status is completed, the BackThemeColorIndex property of the Project Start date field should be **Background 1** — a value of 1 in VBA.

d. Examine Project ID number 1.
   - The correct format is presented when the form is first opened. Change from Project ID 1 to 2, then back to 1. Why does the format stay the same when records are changed? There are two reasons why this problem is occurring. You will need to correct both before proceeding.
   - Update the status of Project ID 3 to "Complete" by clicking **Completed** from the Project Status list. Save the form. This should remove the formatting from the Project Start Date field. Why did the format remain?
   - Examine Project ID 1. Could a better choice of background and font colors be used to highlight the data? Change the colors used to provide a more legible result.
   - Add comments to the procedure that explain the process.

e. Analyze the performance of the database. Make any changes categorized as suggestions or ideas.

f. Save the database in **Access 2003** format. This will fail initially. Examine the tables, and resolve any issues that might prevent this from happening. Save the database in Access 2003 format as **a07Projects_LastFirst2003**.

g. Close the database, exit Access, and then submit your files as directed by your instructor.

Microsoft Access 2016

Appendix A | NORMALIZE A DATABASE FOR EFFECTIVE DESIGN

OBJECTIVES

1. Identify insertion, deletion, and update anomalies in data p. 749
2. Modify a table to satisfy the first normal form p. 752
3. Modify a table to satisfy the second normal form p. 756
4. Modify a table to satisfy the third normal form p. 760
5. Join tables together in relationships with referential integrity enforced p. 763
6. Understand entity relationship diagrams p. 765

Prepare Case

Production & Operations

Painted Paradise Resort & Spa Employee Training Preparation

Aidan Matthews, the chief technology officer at Painted Paradise Resort & Spa, wants all of the resort to be electronic. The Terra Cotta Brew coffee shop was one of the last areas of the resort still not tracking data electronically. The prior intern for the resort started an Excel spreadsheet to track the sales. When the employees started to use it, they found it to be cumbersome. Furthermore, it requires too much time to enter data. Aidan has given you a copy of the Excel spreadsheet with four transactions in it. He wants you to analyze the data, import it into a database, remove duplications, and normalize the database.

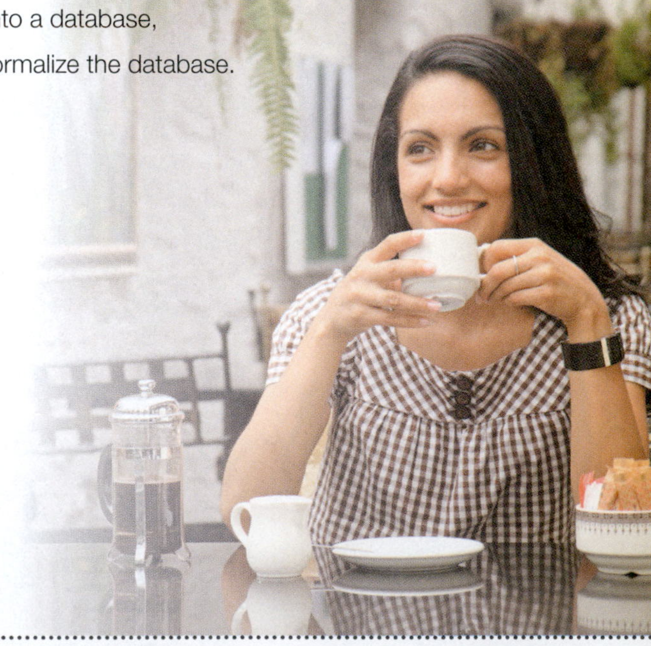

Konradbak/Fotolia

Student data files needed for this appendix:

 a00AppendixTerraCotta.accdb

 a00AppendixTerraCotta.xlsx

 a00AppendixImport.xlsx

You will save your files as:

 a00AppendixTerraCotta_LastFirst.accdb

 a00AppendixTerraCotta_LastFirst.xlsx

Normalizing a Database

Designing the table structure for a database is not an easy task. Some of the best relational database designers start a design and then, after working with it for a while, throw it in the trash and start over. A poor relational database designer tends to structure a database like an Excel spreadsheet, which results in redundancy, inefficiencies, and anomalies. As in a well-written paper, one set of business requirements can lead to several different yet equally good database designs. **Normalization** is the process of minimizing the duplication of information in a relational database through effective database design. In addition to minimizing duplication, normalization prevents anomalies, avoids the need for redesigning as the database is expanded, and provides a better structure for querying. The goal of normalization is that every field in a relation — a table — is directly dependent on every part of the key for the relation. While normalization is not the only component to a well-designed database, it is an important start.

In this appendix, you will learn how to implement the normalization process. Before starting, you should understand the basics of a database, including the following terms: attribute, cardinality, composite key, entity, foreign key, join, junction table, many-to-many relationship, natural primary key, numeric key, one-to-many relationship, one-to-one relationship, primary key, record, and table. These concepts can be found in earlier chapters and the glossary.

The process of normalization holds each table to a progressive series of criteria known as **normal forms (NF)**. There are several levels of normal forms. Each level represents the table's vulnerability to redundancy, anomalies, and inaccuracies. The **highest normal form (HNF)** is the level that a table satisfies along with all levels below. Thus, if a table has an HNF of 2NF, then the table complies with the first and second normal forms. If a table reaches the 3NF level, then the table is considered normalized. If a database is stated to be 3NF, this means that all tables in the database meet the criteria for the first three normal forms. Higher levels than 3NF do exist; however, discussion of the higher levels is beyond the scope of this appendix.

Types of Anomalies

One goal of normalization is to minimize anomalies. **Anomalies** are unmatched or missing data that are caused by limitations in database design. Anomalies can be categorized into three types: insert, delete, and update. An **insertion anomaly** forces you to enter data about two different entities when you have data on only one entity. For example, suppose the database has a table with the following fields: TransactionDate, CustomerFirstName, CustomerLastName, ProductName, ProductPrice, and Quantity. This table requires data about the customer, the product, and the transaction. If a customer wants to be anonymous in his or her purchase, the employee filling out this table will have only the TransactionDate, ProductName, ProductPrice, and Quantity. Therefore, this table requires the user to enter data about the customer when the user knows only the data about the product and transaction. This is an insertion anomaly.

A **deletion anomaly** forces you to delete two different pieces of data when you wanted to delete only one piece of data, resulting in information loss. As in the prior example, suppose the database has a table with the following fields: TransactionDate, CustomerFirstName, CustomerLastName, ProductName, ProductPrice, and Quantity. If a user wishes to cancel an order, then deleting the record will delete the customer, product, and transaction data. This is a deletion anomaly.

An **update anomaly** forces you to change data in multiple records, such as when you need to change the name of a product and you must change multiple rows to make the update. Update anomalies can be difficult to detect. Again, suppose the database has a table with the following fields: TransactionDate, CustomerFirstName, CustomerLastName, ProductName, ProductPrice, and Quantity. Suppose a customer made several different purchases and then changed her name. The user of the database would have to change the last name for every time the customer had made a purchase in the past. This is an update anomaly.

Opening a Nonnormalized Dataset in Excel

Identifying the anomalies in the spreadsheet will better prepare you for converting the data into Access tables. In this exercise, you will open an Excel file containing a dataset that is not normalized.

A00.00

To Open a Nonnormalized Dataset in Excel

a. Start **Excel**, click **Open Other Workbooks** in the left pane, and then click **This PC**. Navigate through the folder structure to the location of your student data files, and then double-click the **a00AppendixTerraCotta** workbook. If necessary, enable editing.

b. Click the **File** tab, click **Save As**, and then double-click **This PC**. In the **Save As** dialog box, navigate to the location where you are saving your project files, and then change the file name to a00AppendixTerraCotta_LastFirst using your last and first name. Click **Save**.

Identifying Anomalies

Examples of each type of anomaly exist in the Excel spreadsheet containing transactions for the coffee shop. In this exercise, you will identify anomalies.

To Identify Anomalies

SIDE NOTE
Pin the Ribbon
If your ribbon is collapsed, pin your ribbon open. Click the Home tab. In the lower right-hand corner of the ribbon, click Pin the Ribbon [pin icon].

SIDE NOTE
Preventing Update Anomalies
You may think a field is highly unlikely to change. However, if it is even remotely possible that the field will change, you must account for that in the database design to avoid an update anomaly.

a. On the ItemsOrdered worksheet, examine the data in cells A2:N9, representing four different items purchased by customers.

Field Name	Description
ID	An automatically generated number to represent each order
Date	Date the order was placed
EmployID	ID of employee who took the order
EmpFirst	First name of employee who took the order
EmpLast	Last name of employee who took the order
Address	Address of employee who took the order
City	City of employee who took the order
State	State of employee who took the order
Zip	ZIP Code of employee who took the order
ProductName	Name of the product the customer ordered. Notice that additional products are dropped down to the next row in Excel.
RetailPrice	The price the business normally charges a customer for the product before any applicable discounts. Importantly, this is not the wholesale cost — the price the business pays for the product.
PricePaid	Price the customer paid for the product. This may be different from the retail price if the customer received a discount.
Qty	Quantity the customer ordered
Subtotal	RetailPrice multiplied by Qty

Table 1 Data in the spreadsheet tracking orders

b. Examine the ProductName data in cells **J2:J9**.

Terra Cotta brew just added a new product, a breakfast soufflé. This new product cannot be added until it has been sold for the first time. This is an insertion anomaly.

c. Click the empty cell **J10**. On the **Home** tab, in the Font group, click the **Fill Color arrow**, and then click **Orange, Accent 2, Lighter 60%** to identify this as an insertion anomaly.

d. Examine the data in cells **J7:L7**.

This order of orange juice sold by Suzanne Kay was erroneous and needs to be deleted. Notice that this is the only entry for orange juice. Therefore, if this order is deleted, the information that orange juice costs $2.00 will be lost. This is a deletion anomaly.

e. Select cells **J7:L7**. On the **Home** tab, in the Font group, click the **Fill Color arrow**, and then click **Green, Accent 6, Lighter 60%** to identify this as a deletion anomaly.

f. Examine the data in cells **E2:E9**.

James Kilroy just got married to Jessica McAfee. He decided to change his last name to McAfee-Kilroy. Because James has sold more than one order, his information would need to be updated in multiple places — once for every order he took. This is an update anomaly.

g. Select cells **E2:E4**. On the **Home** tab, in the Font group, click the **Fill Color arrow**, and then click **Blue, Accent 1, Lighter 80%** to identify this as an update anomaly.

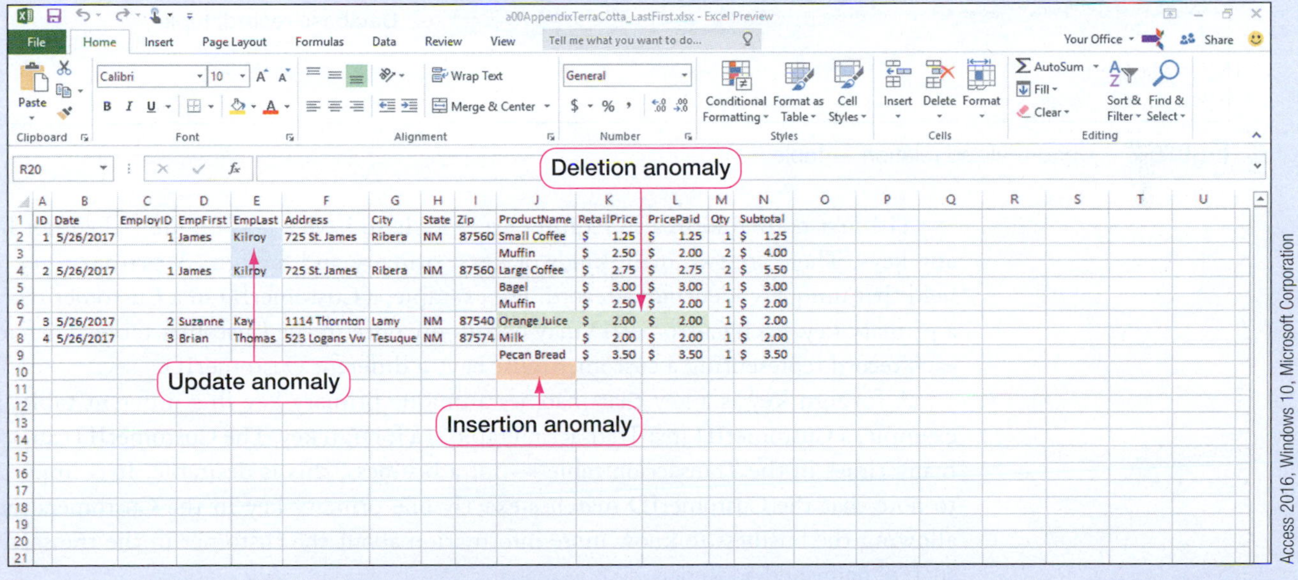

	A	B	C	D	E	F	G	H	I	J	K	L	M	N
1	ID	Date	EmployID	EmpFirst	EmpLast	Address	City	State	Zip	ProductName	RetailPrice	PricePaid	Qty	Subtotal
2	1	5/26/2017	1	James	Kilroy	725 St. James	Ribera	NM	87560	Small Coffee	$ 1.25	$ 1.25	1	$ 1.25
3										Muffin	$ 2.50	$ 2.00	2	$ 4.00
4	2	5/26/2017	1	James	Kilroy	725 St. James	Ribera	NM	87560	Large Coffee	$ 2.75	$ 2.75	2	$ 5.50
5										Bagel	$ 3.00	$ 3.00	1	$ 3.00
6										Muffin	$ 2.50	$ 2.00	1	$ 2.00
7	3	5/26/2017	2	Suzanne	Kay	1114 Thornton	Lamy	NM	87540	Orange Juice	$ 2.00	$ 2.00	1	$ 2.00
8	4	5/26/2017	3	Brian	Thomas	523 Logans Vw	Tesuque	NM	87574	Milk	$ 2.00	$ 2.00	1	$ 2.00
9										Pecan Bread	$ 3.50	$ 3.50	1	$ 3.50

Figure 1 Insertion, deletion, and update anomalies

h. Examine the data, and identify other insertion, deletion, and update anomalies.

What if this data set had 2,000 orders? It would be difficult to query, prone to typos causing inconsistent data, and inefficient at storing data.

i. Notice that many of the Excel rows are blank and that each order could span several rows.

This format is not conducive to being converted into Access tables and breaks the first normal form. Aidan Matthews, the chief technology officer, knows this and has already converted the data into a better starting point in another file.

j. **Save** the spreadsheet, exit Excel, and then submit your file as directed by your instructor.

The First Normal Form

The **first normal form (1NF)** dictates that the table must not have repeating groups of values in a single column — atomicity — and that it must have a key. Also, in 1NF, each non-key field needs some sort of dependency on the key. A record is considered **atomic** when none of the values are repeating or concatenated for a single column. In Figure 2, each order has a repeating group for ProductName, PricePaid, Qty, and SubTotal. In other words, each order may have several different products that were purchased. Therefore, each row in the spreadsheet is not atomic. Rather, each database record equivalent — also known as a **tuple** — may be in more than one row because of this repeating group. Thus, the field of ProductName — also known as an attribute — can have multiple values. If the values are repeated in the rows that are currently blank, each row will become atomic, and each row will represent one database record or tuple. In doing this, it may seem that you are adding in redundancy rather than decreasing it. However, the redundancy will be taken care of as you progress through the normal forms.

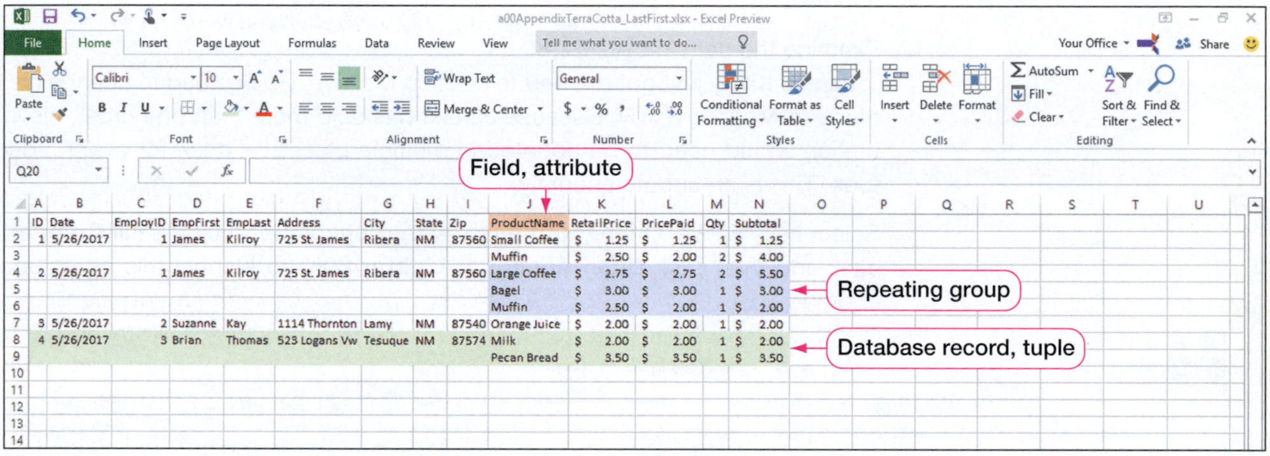

ID	Date	EmployID	EmpFirst	EmpLast	Address	City	State	Zip	ProductName	RetailPrice	PricePaid	Qty	Subtotal
1	5/26/2017	1	James	Kilroy	725 St. James	Ribera	NM	87560	Small Coffee	$ 1.25	$ 1.25	1	$ 1.25
									Muffin	$ 2.50	$ 2.00	2	$ 4.00
2	5/26/2017	1	James	Kilroy	725 St. James	Ribera	NM	87560	Large Coffee	$ 2.75	$ 2.75	2	$ 5.50
									Bagel	$ 3.00	$ 3.00	1	$ 3.00
									Muffin	$ 2.50	$ 2.00	1	$ 2.00
3	5/26/2017	2	Suzanne	Kay	1114 Thornton	Lamy	NM	87540	Orange Juice	$ 2.00	$ 2.00	1	$ 2.00
4	5/26/2017	3	Brian	Thomas	523 Logans Vw	Tesuque	NM	87574	Milk	$ 2.00	$ 2.00	1	$ 2.00
									Pecan Bread	$ 3.50	$ 3.50	1	$ 3.50

Figure 2 Unnormalized relation — table

The first normal form also requires every table to have a key. Figure 2 does not have any keys. There are two main kinds of keys: primary and foreign. A **primary key** is a field that uniquely identifies a record. For example, a CustomerID in a Customer table is a primary key. Each CustomerID may occur only once in the Customer table. Therefore, each record representing a customer must have a different CustomerID.

A **foreign key** is a key that matches a unique primary key in a different table. For example, a CustomerID in a Transaction table is a foreign key. The CustomerID can occur many times in the Transaction table — for a business, this is desirable. It is important to note that the CustomerID matches exactly one primary key in the Customers table, allowing the business to know more information about the customer in the transaction, such as name and address.

Each primary key and each foreign key can also be described as one of three subtypes: natural, artificial, or surrogate. A **natural key** is created from naturally occurring data generated outside of this database, such as driver's license number or e-mail address. An **artificial key** is created from non-naturally occurring data that is visible to the user, such as sequential numbering from the AutoNumber data type. Finally, a **surrogate key** is created from non-naturally occurring data that is *not* visible to the user. In Access, an ID field created with an AutoNumber data type could be used as a surrogate key if the user never sees the AutoNumber. Whenever possible for best practice, a natural key is preferred over an artificial or surrogate key.

A database designer can also use more than one field to identify a primary or foreign key. When multiple fields are used, it is referred to as a **composite key** or **concatenated key**. For example, suppose a table called Reviews has the following fields: CustomerID, ProductID, and Review. The table should allow each customer to review each product once. What should the primary key of the table be? Consider the following options.

1. CustomerID is the primary key. Then the CustomerID can appear only once in the table. Thus, each customer could review only exactly one product — which is not desirable.
2. ProductID is the primary key. Then the ProductID can appear only once in the table. Thus, each product could be reviewed only by exactly one customer — which is also not desirable.
3. AutoNumber is used to make an artificial or surrogate primary key. Then one customer could review the *same* product many times — which is also not desirable. Imagine an angry customer who really wants to make a product look poor providing multiple bad reviews.
4. CustomerID and ProductID are a composite/concatenated primary key. Then the combination of a customer and a product can occur only once in the table. In other words, each customer can review each product exactly once — which is exactly what is desired and is best practice for this example.

Thus, in this example and using the best practice of option 4, the Review table should have three different keys.

1. CustomerID, by itself, is a foreign key to a Customer table. Assuming that CustomerID is non-naturally occurring and is not hidden from the user, CustomerID is an artificial foreign key.
2. ProductID, by itself, is a foreign key to a Products table. Assuming that ProductID is non-naturally occurring and is not hidden from the user, ProductID is an artificial foreign key.
3. The unique combination of CustomerID and ProductID is the primary, composite key. Assuming that the foreign keys are artificial, this key could also be referred to as an artificial, composite, primary key.

During the process of designing a database, a table may have candidate keys. **Candidate keys** are fields in the table that could be used as the primary key if desired. For example, a Customer table could have a Candidate key of user name and e-mail address. Candidate keys can be multiple fields — composite — as well. If no candidate keys exist, typically an artificial or surrogate key is created, using something like an AutoNumber field. Once the database has been finalized, any unused candidate keys are known as **alternate keys**.

REAL WORLD ADVICE | **Why Would You Use a Surrogate Key?**

Using a surrogate key has its pros and cons. If the key never has a foreign key, you do not need a surrogate key. The advantage with a surrogate key is that it can help to prevent some cascading changes from primary to foreign key errors. However, a surrogate key can increase the file size and can require more joins. Many database designers debate the need for surrogate keys. However, if you have a primary key with a foreign key that may need to be changed frequently or more than normal, you should consider using a surrogate key.

CONSIDER THIS | Appropriate Keys

In this example, product name is unique to each product. However, is it the best key to use? Could two products ever have the same product name? What if you separated the size from the product name, with "small" and "coffee" in different fields? Would a surrogate key be better?

QUICK REFERENCE | Types of Keys

The two main types of keys are primary and foreign.

Name	Definition	Example
Primary key	Uniquely identifies a record in that table	CustomerID in the customer table
Foreign key	Matches a unique primary key in a different table	CustomerID in the transactions table

Each primary key and each foreign key is also one of the following three subtypes.

Name	Definition	Example
Natural key	Created from naturally occurring data generated outside of this database	EmailAddress in the customer table
Artificial	Created from non-naturally occurring data that is visible to the user	CustomerID created from an Access AutoNumber and visible to the user
Surrogate	Created from non-naturally occurring data that is not visible to the user	CustomerID created from an Access AutoNumber and not visible to the user

Other keys:

Name	Definition	Example
Composite key or concatenated key	A key that uses multiple keys	CustomerID and ProductID in a Review table that allows each customer to review each product once
Candidate key	In designing a database, fields in the table that could be used as the primary key if desired	EmailAddress in a customer table before any keys have been designated
Alternate key	A candidate key that is not used in the final table	EmailAddress in a customer table where CustomerID is an artificial primary key

Determining Keys and Satisfying Atomicity

Figure 3 shows the Terra Cotta Brew spreadsheet that contains the data the database needs to track. Each row had the values copied down to create an atomic table. However, it still does not have a key specified. What are the potential candidate keys? Each row represents a product purchased in an order. The ID field represents a single order. Since one order may span several rows, ID by itself cannot be a key. There is also a ProductName field. Each product name is unique, but it may be purchased on multiple occasions. However, when considered together, the product name and order ID fields in combination are unique. Thus, in this example, the key is a composite key with ID — representing the order — and ProductName — representing the product ordered.

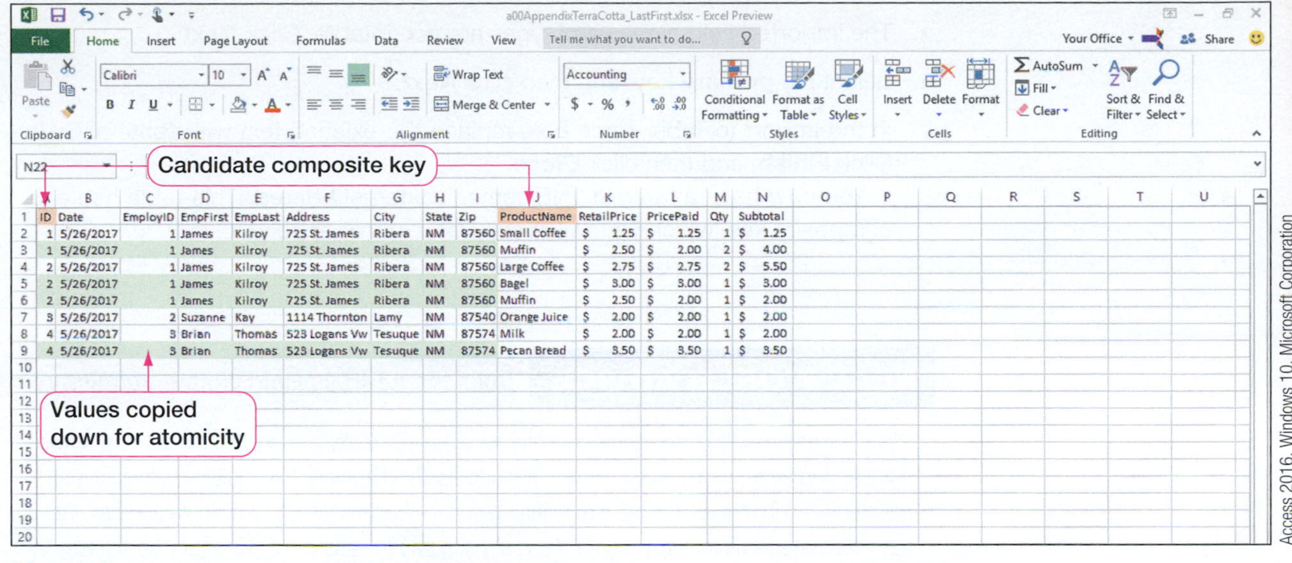

ID	Date	EmployID	EmpFirst	EmpLast	Address	City	State	Zip	ProductName	RetailPrice	PricePaid	Qty	Subtotal
1	5/26/2017	1	James	Kilroy	725 St. James	Ribera	NM	87560	Small Coffee	$ 1.25	$ 1.25	1	$ 1.25
1	5/26/2017	1	James	Kilroy	725 St. James	Ribera	NM	87560	Muffin	$ 2.50	$ 2.00	2	$ 4.00
2	5/26/2017	1	James	Kilroy	725 St. James	Ribera	NM	87560	Large Coffee	$ 2.75	$ 2.75	2	$ 5.50
2	5/26/2017	1	James	Kilroy	725 St. James	Ribera	NM	87560	Bagel	$ 3.00	$ 3.00	1	$ 3.00
2	5/26/2017	1	James	Kilroy	725 St. James	Ribera	NM	87560	Muffin	$ 2.50	$ 2.00	1	$ 2.00
3	5/26/2017	2	Suzanne	Kay	1114 Thornton	Lamy	NM	87540	Orange Juice	$ 2.00	$ 2.00	1	$ 2.00
4	5/26/2017	3	Brian	Thomas	523 Logans Vw	Tesuque	NM	87574	Milk	$ 2.00	$ 2.00	1	$ 2.00
4	5/26/2017	3	Brian	Thomas	523 Logans Vw	Tesuque	NM	87574	Pecan Bread	$ 3.50	$ 3.50	1	$ 3.50

Figure 3 1NF relation — table — with a composite key

The additional forms of normalization will require this data to be broken up into multiple tables. The composite key is only a candidate composite key at this point. The fields identified as potential keys may end up in separate tables.

Once this data has been imported into Access and the composite primary key of ID and ProductName has been designated, it will satisfy 1NF. However, it would still be subject to the insertion, deletion, and update anomalies. Later in this appendix, you will further modify the database as you progress through the normal forms, creating several — not just one — table. In this exercise, you will import the data into an Access table, but you will not actually designate the key yet.

 A00.02

To Satisfy Atomicity for the First Normal Form

SIDE NOTE

Field Size

While field size is not the focus of this appendix, new fields are created at maximum field size upon import. Best practice dictates changing field sizes appropriately.

a. Open the Excel file **a00AppendixImport**.

Notice the changes to this file compared to the spreadsheet prepared by the intern. As can be seen in Figure 3, Aidan Matthews copied down the Date, EmpFirst, EmpLast, Address, City, State, and Zip fields, temporarily creating more redundancy. Each customer order is represented by several rows — for example, the first customer order is in rows 2 and 3. Even though this is two rows in the spreadsheet, after further modification, each customer order will ultimately be represented by one database record. Further, each column represents a database field. By copying each row so the data is repeating, you make each row atomic and a separate database record.

b. Click **Close** ☒.

c. Open the blank Access file **a00AppendixTerraCotta**. Note that the database is empty. Save your file as **a00AppendixTerraCotta_LastFirst** using your last and first name. If necessary, enable the content.

d. Click the **External Data** tab, and then, in the Import & Link group, click **Excel**.

e. Click **Browse**, locate and select **a00AppendixImport**, and then click **Open**. Ensure that **Import the source data into a new table in the current database** is selected, and then click **OK**.

f. Ensure that **First Row Contains Column Headings** is selected, and then click **Next**.

g. The imported field names and types are acceptable. Click **Next**.

h. Select **No primary key**, and then click **Next**.

i. In the Import to Table name box, replace the existing text with tblItemsOrdered. Click **Finish**, and then click **Close**.

You now have a table in 1NF named tblItemsOrdered. This table has a composite key, which you will specify later in this appendix.

REAL WORLD ADVICE | **Does the Address Field Violate Atomicity?**

While the address field represents only one address, it is really a concatenated value of street number and street name. In that sense, the address field actually has multiple values in it and is not atomic even though it is not a repeating group — because it is just a single address. You could have separate fields for street number and street name to satisfy 1NF. For many businesses, a single field for address is sufficient. You will want to look at the business requirements when creating your tables and keep the future in mind. If you would never want to query how many employees live on the same street, separating the values is not necessary. However, if you were building a database for a delivery service, you would want to separate the values for street number and street name into two fields.

The Second Normal Form

The **second normal form (2NF)** requires that the table has no fields with partial dependencies on a composite or concatenated key and satisfies 1NF. A **dependency** exists when a field relates to a key. For example, the order date is dependent on the order ID. Although several orders can be placed on the same day, one order cannot be placed on more than one date. Thus, order date is dependent on the key of order ID.

A **determinant** is a field that determines the value of another field. For example, the orderID determines the order date. An order can be placed on one specific date. Thus, if you know the key orderID, you should be able to determine the order date.

A **partial dependency** exists when the field depends on one part of a composite or concatenated key. In other words, the field is determined by only one piece of a multi-field key. A **transitive dependency** exists when a field depends on another field in the table, which then depends on a candidate key. A depends on B and B depends on C; thus, A implies C. If C is a candidate key and B is not a candidate key, this is a transitive dependency. For 2NF, transitive dependency is acceptable, but partial dependency is not.

Ask yourself whether each field could still be there if one part of the key were removed. For example, can employee first name remain if the product name is not part of the composite key? The answer is yes. If you answer yes for even one field, the table is not in 2NF. Thus, employee first name is not dependent on the product that was purchased — ProductName — and so this is a partial dependency. To get a table to satisfy 2NF, you break the table up into several tables. Dependencies are frequently shown in a **functional dependency diagram** as shown in Figure 4.

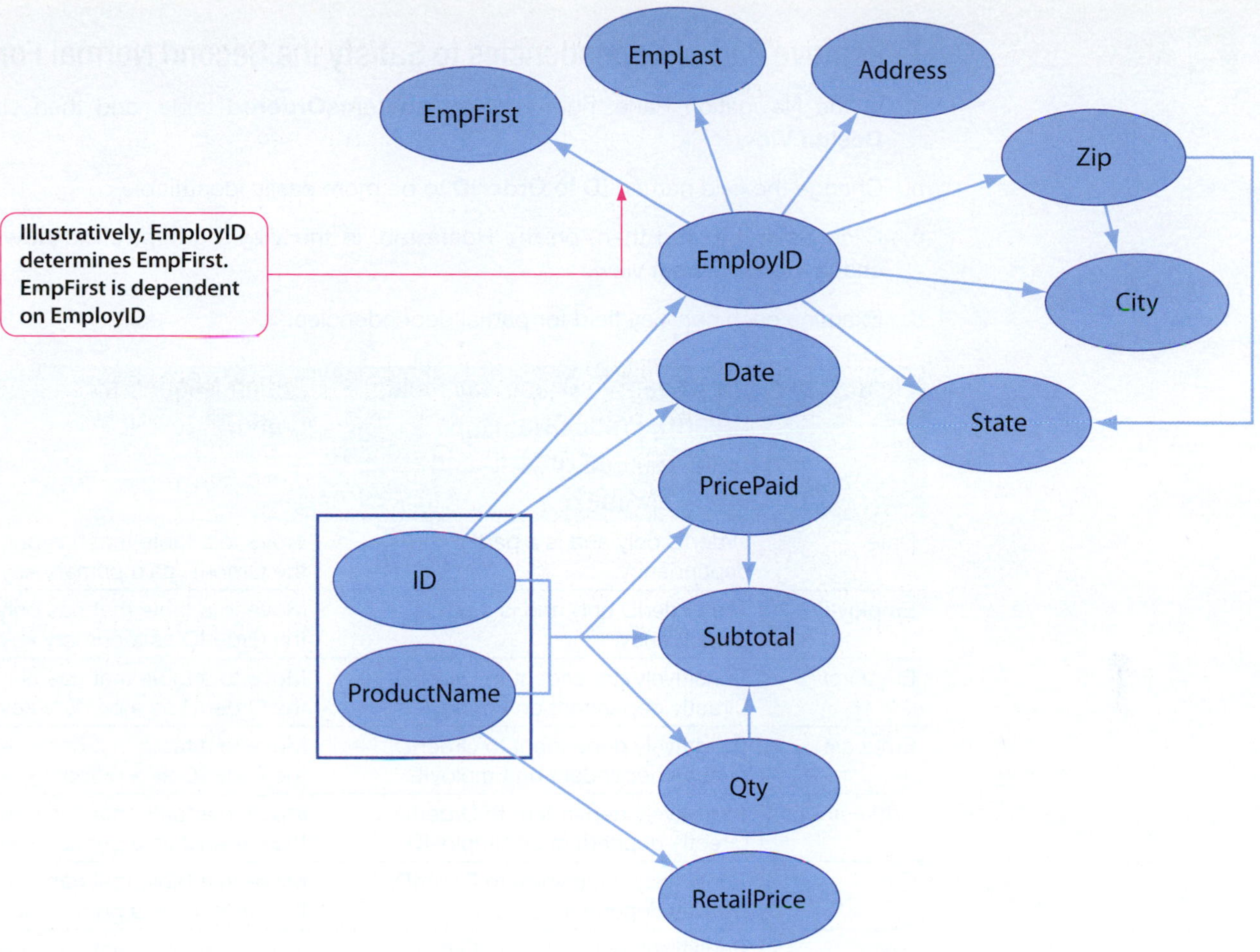

Figure 4 Functional dependency diagram of tblItemsOrdered

To better understand Figure 4, notice the following.

- The box around ID and Product Name indicates that ID and Product Name are currently the composite primary key if all fields stay in one table.
- The arrows leading to Price Paid, Subtotal, and Quantity show that those fields are dependent on both ID and Product Name.
- The arrows leading from just ID to Employ ID and Order Date show that those two fields are dependent on only ID.
- The arrows leading from Employ ID to EmpFirst, EmpLast, Address, Zip, City, and State show that those fields are dependent on Employ ID.
- The arrows that point from Zip to City and to State show that City and State are dependent on Zip. In other words, if you know the ZIP Code, you can determine the city and state.
- The arrows pointing from Product Name to Retail Price show that Retail Price is dependent on Product Name.

In looking at Figure 4, it starts to become clearer that the data needs to be separated out into multiple tables to satisfy 2NF. Only three fields — Price Paid, Subtotal, and Qty — are dependent on *both* ID and Product Name.

Removing Dependencies

To construct a database based on the provided data that satisfies 2NF, the tblItemsOrdered table will need to be split into multiple tables. In this exercise, you will make duplicate copies of the original table and remove dependent data from them.

To Remove Partial Dependencies to Satisfy the Second Normal Form

a. In the Navigation Pane, right-click the **tblItemsOrdered** table, and then click **Design View**.

b. Change the field named **ID** to **OrderID** to be more easily identifiable.

c. Click **Save** , and then, on the Home tab, in the Views group, click **View** to change to Datasheet view.

d. Examine each non-key field for partial dependencies.

Field Name	Dependent to Which Key Field: OrderID, ProductName, or Concatenated OrderID and ProductName?	Action Needed to Conform to 2NL
Date	OrderID only and is a partial dependency.	Move to a table that has only the OrderID as a primary key.
EmployID	The OrderID only and is a partial dependency.	Move to a table that has only the OrderID as a primary key.
EmpFirst	Transitively dependent to OrderID. Directly dependent on EmployID.	Move to a table that has only the OrderID as a primary key.
EmpLast	Transitively dependent to OrderID. Directly dependent on EmployID.	Move to a table that has only the OrderID as a primary key.
Address	Transitively dependent to OrderID. Directly dependent on EmployID.	Move to a table that has only the OrderID as a primary key.
City	Transitively dependent to OrderID. Directly dependent on Zip.	Move to a table that has only the OrderID as a primary key.
State	Transitively dependent to OrderID. Directly dependent on Zip.	Move to a table that has only the OrderID as a primary key.
Zip	Transitively dependent to OrderID. Directly dependent on EmployID.	Move to a table that has only the OrderID as a primary key.
RetailPrice	The ProductName only and is a partial dependency.	Move to a table that has only the ProductName as a primary key.
PricePaid	Because this price is specific to this order — may be a discounted amount — and this particular product, it is dependent on both OrderID and ProductName.	Remain in this table.
Qty	Because this quantity is specific to this order and this particular product, it is dependent on both OrderID and ProductName.	Remain in this table.
Subtotal	Transitively dependent on the composite key OrderID and ProductName. Directly dependent on PricePaid and Qty.	Remain in this table for now.

Table 2 Table evaluating partial dependency

e. Click the **File** tab, click **Save As**, and then click **Save Object As**. Under Database File Types, verify that Save Object As is selected. Click **Save As**.

f. In the Save As dialog box, in the Save 'tblItemOrdered' to box, type tblInventory. Click **OK**.

> **Troubleshooting**
>
> If Access responds with an error message stating that there is no primary key defined, click No. You will add a key later.

g. On the **Home** tab, in the Views group, click **View**.

h. Delete **all fields except ProductName and RetailPrice**. For each field that you need to delete, right-click the **field's name**, and then select **Delete Rows**. When prompted, click **Yes** to confirm that you want to delete the field. Access responds with an error message when you delete some of the fields. The error message states that deleting a field requires Microsoft Access to delete one or more indexes. This deletion is acceptable. Click **Yes** when prompted with this error.

h. Delete **all fields except ProductName and RetailPrice**. For each field that you need to delete, right-click the **field's name**, and then select **Delete Rows**. When prompted, click **Yes** to confirm that you want to delete the field. Access responds with an error message when you delete some of the fields. The error message states that deleting a field requires Microsoft Access to delete one or more indexes. This deletion is acceptable. Click **Yes** when prompted with this error.

Now, the tblInventory contains two fields, ProductName and RetailPrice — the amount a customer pays for the product when no discounts exist. While the data only has these two fields, later the business could add more fields about the product. For example, where is the product purchased by the business? What is the amount the business pays for the item — the wholesale cost?

j. On the Home tab, in the Views group, click **View**. In the Field Name column, click the **ProductName** field. On the **Design** tab, in the Tools group, click **Primary Key** to designate ProductName as a natural primary key.

You have separated the ProductName portion of the original concatenated or composite key into its own table.

> **Troubleshooting**
>
> If you get an error that prevents you from adding the primary key, check carefully that you deleted the second occurrence of the product named "Muffin".

k. **Save** and **Close** the tblInventory table.

l. In the Navigation Pane, double-click **tblItemsOrdered** to open it in Datasheet view. Click the **File** tab, click **Save As**, and then click **Save Object As**. Click **Save As**.

m. In the Save As dialog box, in the Save 'tblItemsOrdered' to box, type **tblOrders**, and then click **OK**.

> **Troubleshooting**
>
> If Access responds with an error message stating that there is no primary key defined, click No. You will add a key later.

n. Make sure tblOrders is open in Datasheet view. On the Home tab, in the Views group, click **View**.

o. Delete **RetailPrice** because that field is now in the tblInventory table. If prompted, click **Yes** to confirm the deletion.

p. Delete **ProductName**, **PricePaid**, **Qty**, and **Subtotal.** These fields will remain in the original tblItemsOrdered table. If prompted, click **Yes** to confirm deletion, and then click **Yes** again for the index message.

Access responds with an error message. This says that deleting a field requires Microsoft Access to delete one or more indexes. This deletion is acceptable.

q. Click **Save**. On the Design tab, in the Views group, click **View**.

r. Delete the record for the second occurrences of the **OrderIDs 1** and **4**. Delete the record for the second and third occurrences of the **OrderID 2**. Click **Yes** to confirm deletion.

s. On the Home tab, in the Views group, click **View**. Click the **OrderID** field. On the Design tab, in the Tools group, click **Primary Key** to designate OrderID as an artificial primary key.

t. **Save** and **Close** tblOrders.

u. In the Navigation Pane, right-click **tblItemsOrdered**, and then click **Design View**.

v. Delete **all fields except OrderID**, **ProductName**, **PricePaid**, **Qty**, **and Subtotal**. If prompted, click **Yes** to confirm deletion, and then click **Yes** again if necessary for index error messages.

w. Select both **OrderID** and **ProductName**. On the Design tab, in the Tools group, click **Primary Key** to designate OrderID and ProductName as the concatenated or composite key.

You have separated the ProductName portion of the original concatenated or composite key into its own table named tblInventory. You also have moved the field — RetailPrice — that was dependent on only that portion of the ProductName into the new table tblInventory.

The tblItemsOrdered and tblInventory tables now satisfy at least 2NF in a practical sense. In the strictest sense, tblOrders is not even 1NL, as Address is a multivalued field: street number and street name. Also, tblOrders and tblItemsOrdered still suffer from insertion, deletion, and update anomalies.

x. **Save** and **Close** tblItemsOrdered.

The Third Normal Form

The **third normal form (3NF)** requires that the table has to be free of transitive dependencies and that the table satisfies both 1NF and 2NF. Remember that a transitive dependency exists when a field depends on another field in the table and that field depends on a candidate key. A depends on B and B depends on C; thus, A implies C. If C is a candidate key and B is not a candidate key, this is a transitive dependency. When multiple overlapping candidate keys exist, you also should satisfy an additional criterion. Known as the **Boyce–Codd normal form (BCNF, 3.5NF)**, this additional criterion requires that all determinants are candidate keys and that the table satisfies 1NF, 2NF, and 3NF. By normalizing to BCNF, you are eliminating all functional dependencies.

Ask yourself, "If I update this field, does another field in the table also need to be updated?" If the answer is yes, then you have a transitive dependency. For example, think about a ZIP Code. If you need to change the ZIP Code, then you may also have to change the city and state. In its strictest sense, 3NF would have a table of cities and ZIP Codes and a table of cities and states, and the original table would require you to enter only the ZIP Code. However, this level of normalization would create more joins, increase complexity, and potentially decrease the speed of the database system. Therefore, the business requirements must be taken into consideration.

Other times, you clearly want to normalize to 3NF. Think about the employee last name in the orders table. The employee's last name is a non-key field. Is the OrderID a determinant for the employee's last name? No. Instead, EmployID determines the employee's last name. Therefore, employee's last name is dependent on something other than the OrderID and needs to be moved into its own table.

Satisfying the Third Normal Form

In this exercise, you will move fields, such as the employee's last name, to proper tables to satisfy 3NF.

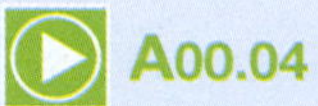

To Satisfy the Third Normal Form

a. In the Navigation Pane, double-click the table **tblOrders** to open it in Datasheet view.

b. Examine each non-key field for transitive dependencies.

Non-key Field Name	On What Field Is This Field Dependent and Is It a Candidate Key?	Action Needed to Conform to 3NL
Date	OrderID — a candidate key	Remain in this table.
EmployID	OrderID — a candidate key	Remain in this table.
EmpFirst	EmployID — a non-candidate key	Move to a table with EmployID as the primary key.
EmpLast	EmployID — a non-candidate key	Move to a table with EmployID as the primary key.
Address	EmployID — a non-candidate key	Move to a table with EmployID as the primary key.
City	State — a non-candidate key	Move to a table with EmployID as the primary key.
State	City — a non-candidate key	Move to a table with EmployID as the primary key.
Zip	EmployID — a non-candidate key	Move to a table with EmployID as the primary key.

Table 3 Table evaluating 3NL for tblOrders

c. Click the **File** tab, click **Save As**, and then click **Save Object As**. Click **Save As**. In the Save As dialog box, in the Save 'tblOrders' to box, type tblEmployees, and then click **OK**.

d. On the Home tab, in the Views group, click **View**.

e. Delete the **OrderID** and **Date** fields. If prompted, click **Yes** to confirm deletion. Click **Yes** again as needed. Access responds with an error message. This says that deleting the field requires Access to delete the primary key. If needed, click **Yes** to confirm. You will reset the primary key later.

f. Click **Save** . On the Home tab, in the Views group, click **View**.

g. Delete the record for the second occurrence of the **EmployID 1**, and then click **Yes** to confirm deletion.

h. Add a record to the tblEmployees with the following values.

- EmployID — 4
- EmpFirst — Your First Name
- EmpLast — Your Last Name
- Address — 123 Elm Street
- City — Lamy
- State — NM
- Zip — 87540

i. On the Home tab, in the Views group, click **View**. Click the **EmployID** field, and then, in the Design tab, in the Tools group, click **Primary Key** to designate EmployID as an artificial primary key.

j. **Save** and **Close** the tblEmployees table.

k. In the Navigation Pane, right-click the **tblOrders** table, and then click **Design View**.

l. Delete **all the fields except OrderID**, **Date**, **and EmployID**. If prompted, click **Yes** to confirm deletion.

m. **Save** and **Close** the tblOrders table.

n. In the Navigation Pane, double-click the **tblItemsOrdered** table to open it in Datasheet view.

o. Examine each non-key field for transitive dependencies.

Non-key Field Name	On What Field Is This Field Dependent and Is It a Candidate Key?	Action Needed to Conform to 3NL
PricePaid	The Order ID and ProductName, a candidate key	Remain in this table.
Qty	The Order ID and ProductName, a candidate key	Remain in this table.
Subtotal	PricePaid and Qty, both non-candidate keys. Further, subtotal is a value that can easily be calculated in queries.	Delete this field.

Table 4 Table evaluating 3NL for non-key fields in tblItemsOrdered

p. On the Home tab, in the Views group, click **View**. Delete the **Subtotal** field. If prompted, click **Yes** to confirm deletion. Subtotal is a calculation that should be done in a query, not in the table.

q. **Save** and **Close** the tblItemsOrdered table.

The tblItemsOrdered, tblInventory, and tblOrders tables are all in 3NF. The table tblEmployee is not even in 1NF because of the transitive dependencies of State and City and the multivalued column of Address. For a database to be considered normalized, all tables need to be in 3NF. However, most expert database designers consider leaving the state and city in the Employees table and placing the Street Number and Name in the same column as an acceptable variation from normalization.

QUICK REFERENCE | **Normal Forms**

Normal Form Level	Description
First normal form (1NF)	The table must not have repeating groups of values in a single column — atomicity — and it must have a key.
Second normal form (2NF)	The table has no fields with partial dependencies on a composite or concatenated key and satisfies 1NF.
Third normal form (3NF)	The table has to be free of transitive dependencies and has to satisfy all lower levels of NF.
Boyce–Codd normal form (BCNF, 3.5NF)	All determinants are candidate keys and satisfy all lower levels of NF.

Table 5 Table of normal forms

Join Tables Together in Relationships with Referential Integrity

Once the tables are set, the database needs relationships to join the data from various tables. A **one-to-many relationship (1:M or 1:N)** is a relationship between two tables in which one record in the first table corresponds to many records in the second table. One-to-many is called the cardinality of the relationship. **Cardinality** indicates the number of instances of one entity that relates to one instance of another entity. For example, each employee can be in the employees table only exactly one time. However, an employee can be in the orders table many times — once for each sale. These two tables are related by a one-to-many relationship using the EmployID key.

A **many-to-many relationship (M:N)** is a relationship between tables in which one record in one table has many matching records in a second table and one record in the related table has many matching records in the first table. For example, a product can be in many different orders. Also, each order can have many products in inventory. Because these two tables do not have a common field, in Access this kind of many-to-many relationship must have an additional table in between these two. This intermediate table is referred to by several synonymous terms: "intersection," "junction," or "link table."

A **one-to-one relationship (1:1)** is a relationship between tables in which a record in one table has only one matching record in the second table. In a small business, a department might be managed by no more than one manager, and each manager might manage no more than one department. That relationship in the business is a one-to-one relationship.

Access allows you to add some **integrity constraints** — or rules — to your database to help ensure the data's validity. The entity integrity constraint requires that all primary keys have a value — that is, that they not be null. **Referential integrity** in relationships requires that only values that have a corresponding value in the primary table can be entered for a foreign key. **Cascade update** will update a foreign key automatically when the primary key changes. For example, if you change an employee's ID, cascade update will change every instance in the orders table. **Cascade delete** will delete every record with the foreign key if the record with the value is deleted from the primary table. For example, if you deleted an employee — which is not good practice — it would delete every order that the employee processed. Finally, **domain integrity constraints** are rules that are specific for each field. For example, setting the data type of currency for price will require that the data entered is numeric.

Joining Tables with Relationships

Setting all the constraints for this database is beyond the scope of this appendix, but doing so is an important next step in database creation. Relationships should be created to ensure that the database operates efficiently. In this exercise, you will add three relationships between the tables.

 A00.05

SIDE NOTE

Adding Tables

You can also use the Ctrl key to select multiple tables at once (that are not in contiguous order) to add to the relationships window.

To Join Tables with Relationships

a. Click the **Database Tools** tab in the Relationships group, and then click **Relationships**.

b. In the Show Table dialog box, tblEmployees should already be selected. Press and hold Shift, click **tblOrders** to select all four tables in the list, and then click **Add**.

c. Click **Close** to close the Show Table dialog box. Drag the tables in the Relationships window so you have enough space between the tables to form the relationships. Move the tblEmployees table to the right of the other tables, after tblOrders.

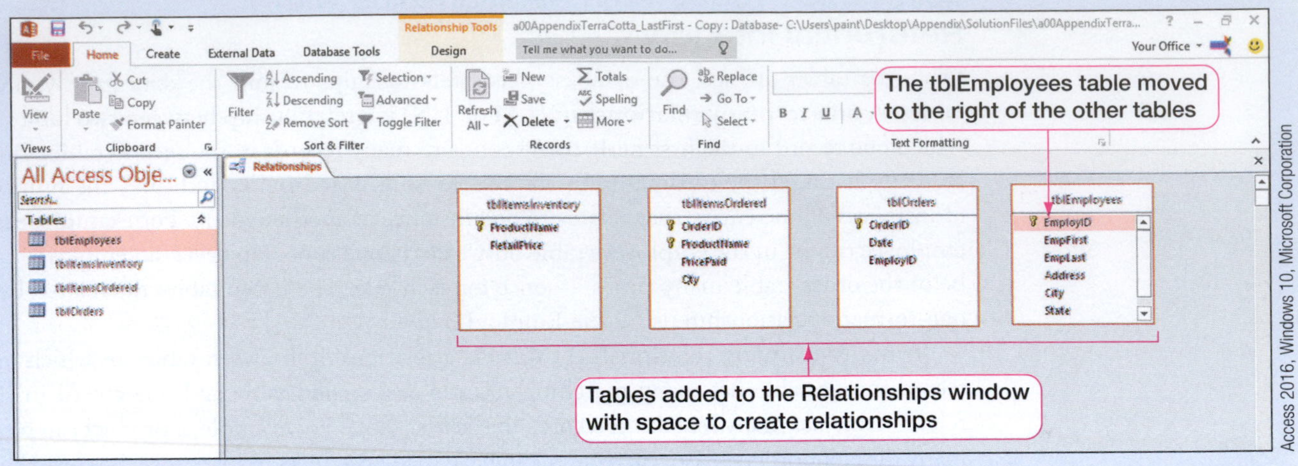

Figure 5 Tables added to the Relationships window

> **SIDE NOTE**
> **Order of Tables**
> The order or arrangement of the tables in the relationship view does not matter. The relationships between fields are the important part.

d. Point your mouse pointer to the **EmployID** field from tblEmployees. Drag the primary key field **EmployID** from tblEmployees if your mouse pointer is over **EmployID** in tblOrders. Let go of the left mouse button. This does not move the field but instructs Access to create a relationship between the two tables using those two fields.

e. Access displays the Edit Relationships dialog box. Click **Enforce Referential Integrity** to select it, and then click **Create**.

> **Troubleshooting**
> If you get the error message "Microsoft Access cannot create this relationship and enforce referential integrity," double-check that your data is all correct and that you did not delete a record by accident.

> **SIDE NOTE**
> **Creating Relationships**
> Alternatively, you could drag from EmployID in tblOrders to EmployID in tblEmployees.

f. Drag the primary key **OrderID** from tblOrders to **OrderID** in tblItemsOrdered.

g. Access displays the Edit Relationships dialog box. Click **Enforce Referential Integrity** to select it, and then click **Create**.

h. Drag the primary key **ProductName** from tblItemsOrdered to **ProductName** in tblInventory.

i. Access displays the Edit Relationships dialog box. Click **Enforce Referential Integrity** to select it, and then click **Create**.

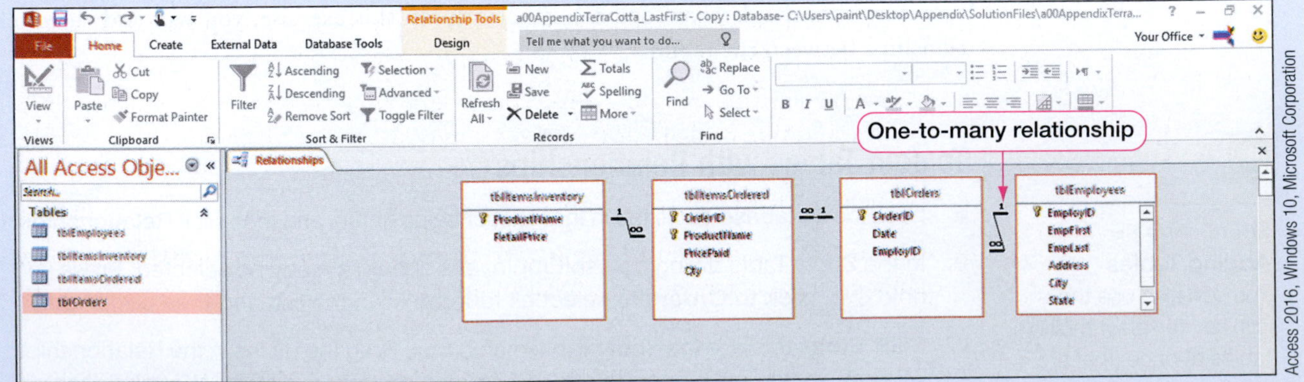

Figure 6 Final Relationships window

j. **Save** and **Close** the Relationships window. Exit Access, and then submit your files as directed by your instructor.

Understanding an Entity Relationship Diagram

Many ways of visually expressing the database structure exist. Best practice is to use one of these methods both in designing the database and in documenting the database. An **entity relationship diagram (ERD)** is a common way to visually express the tables and relationships in your database. An ERD does not tell you anything about data flow; it is a fixed view of the database structure.

There are variations in how designers represent ERDs. For example, some designers may prefer the crow's feet approach. The crow's feet approach will list the tables in a database as rectangles with lines and symbols representing the types of relationships between them. An example of a crow's feet diagram displaying a one-to-many relationship is shown in Figure 7.

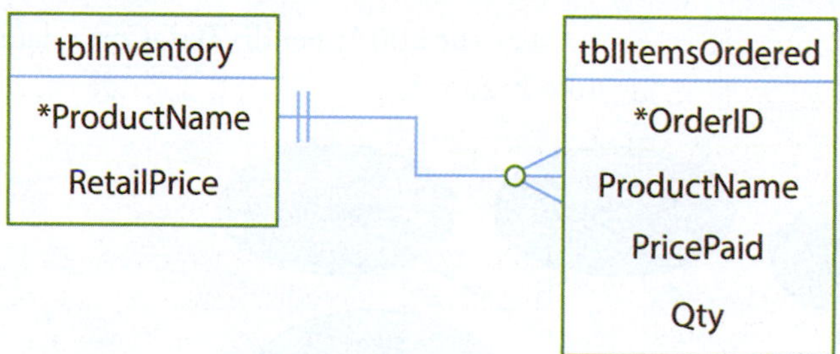

Figure 7 Crow's feet diagram

Here, the tblInventory table is related to the tblItemsOrdered table by the ProductName field. The asterisk next to the field name designates the primary key field in each table. The line between the tables represents the relationship between the two ProductName fields. The lines intersecting the relationship next to the tblInventory table symbolizes that exactly one record will exist for each product in the table. The circle and lines next to the tblItemsOrdered table symbolize that for a product in the tblInventory table, zero or many records may exist in the tblItemsOrdered table.

Alternatively, under the entity relationship model, the following basic shapes are used to create an ERD: rectangle, diamond, and oval. Some common variations in the shapes are included in Figure 8. However, discussing all the variations is beyond the scope of this appendix.

1. Identify your entities. Remember that entities are people, places, or items that you want to keep data about. Entities in ERDs are usually nouns and are drawn in rectangles. Depending on the type of entity, several variations exist.
   a. Strong entities have a primary key. These are drawn in a normal rectangle.
   b. Weak entities do not have a primary key. Rather, they have a primary key from another table — a foreign key — and a discriminator value in the table that forms the key. These are drawn in a double rectangle.
   c. Bridge entities are tables that form a join or linking table for a many-to-many relationship. Bridge entities use a composite key. A composite key consists of two foreign keys that together combine for a unique value. These are drawn in a diamond with a rectangle around it.
2. Identify the relationships. Remember that relationships are associations between tables based on common fields. Relationships in ERDs are usually verbs and are drawn in diamonds.
3. Identify the attributes. Remember that attributes are information about the entity, or the data. Consider the business requirements of the system. Ask yourself, "What fields are needed in queries? What common fields and keys are needed for the relationships?" You may find a new entity and need to revise your ERD in this step. Attributes in ERDs are generally drawn inside an oval. Depending on the type of attribute, several variations exist.

a. Key attributes are underlined.

b. A second inside circle is used for multivalued attributes, such as an address that contains both street number and street name.

c. Derived values are represented with a dashed oval line. For example, the value of City is derived from the value of Zip, which is not a candidate key.

4. Determine the cardinality of the relationships. This may require you to add a join or linking table. Cardinality in ERDs is listed depending on the type of relationship.

   a. 1:N or 1:M for one-to-many relationships

   b. N:M for many-to-many relationships

   c. 1:1 for one-to-one relationships

For the a00AppendixTerraCotta database, an entity relationship diagram would look like Figure 8.

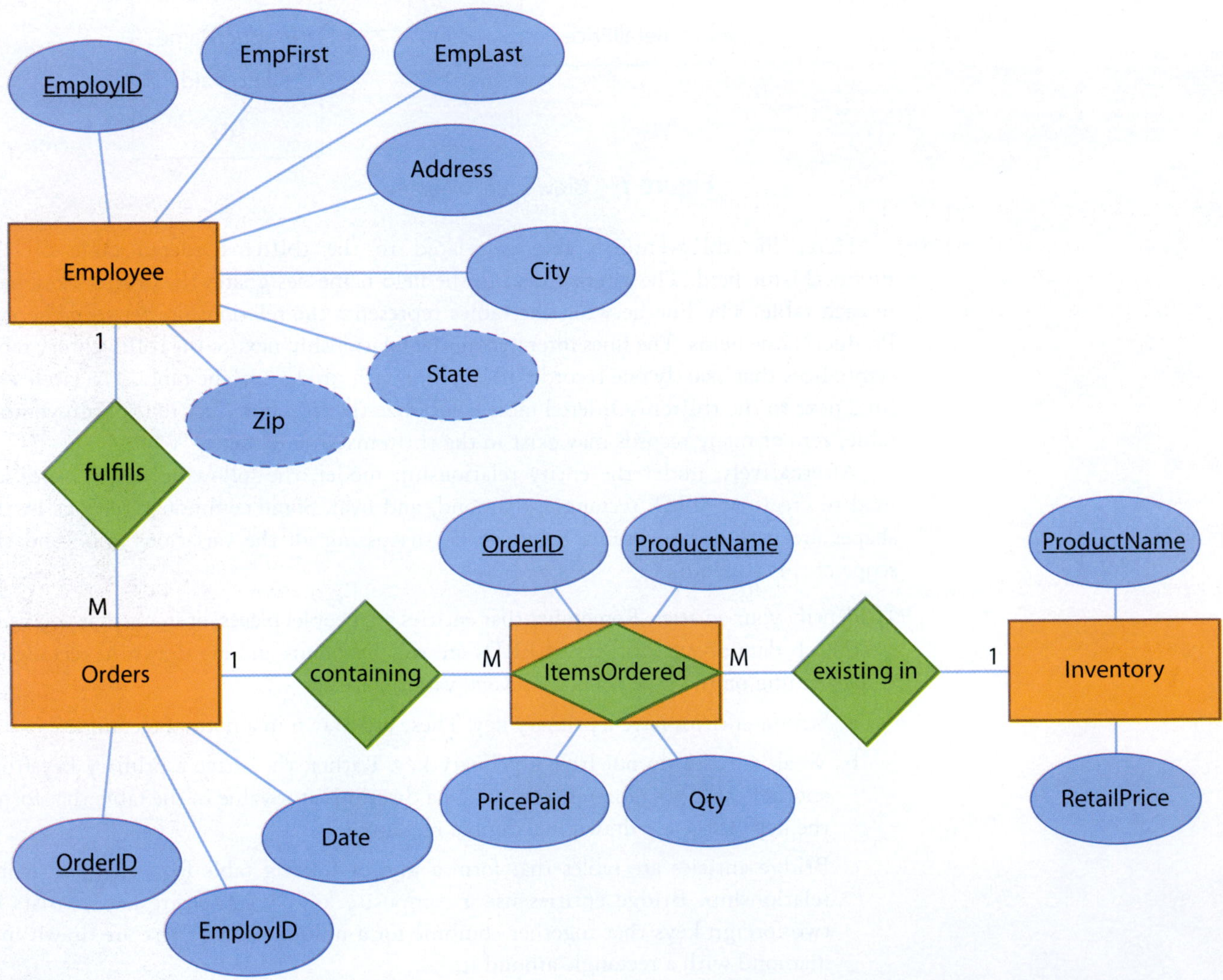

Figure 8 Entity Relationship diagram

Concept Check

1. Describe examples of insertion, update, and delete anomalies. p. 749
2. What is a repeating group? p. 752
3. Describe what partial and transitive dependencies are. p. 756
4. You are analyzing a table within a database that manages inventories of office supplies. The table you are analyzing, tblReceivedSupplies, is used to track the arrival of new supplies. You notice that the fields SupplyID, SupplyName, Date, and Quantity all exist within the table. To meet the criteria for 3NF, which of these non-key fields would need to be deleted and why? What other table should exist to meet the criteria for normalization? p. 760
5. Describe three types of relationships that can exist between tables in a database. p. 763
6. Explain the purpose of an entity relationship diagram. p. 765

Key Terms

Alternate key 753
Anomaly 749
Artificial key 752
Atomic 752
Boyce–Codd normal form (BCNF, 3.5NF) 760
Candidate key 753
Cardinality 763
Cascade delete 763
Cascade update 763
Composite or concatenated key 752
Deletion anomaly 749
Dependency 756
Determinant 756
Domain integrity constraint 763
Entity relationship diagram (ERD) 765
First normal form (1NF) 752
Foreign Key 752
Functional dependency diagram 756
Highest normal form (HNF) 749
Insertion anomaly 749
Integrity constraint 763
Many-to-many relationship (M:N) 763
Natural key 752
Normal form (NF) 749
Normalization 749
One-to-many relationship (1:M or 1:N) 763
One-to-one relationship (1:1) 763
Partial dependency 756
Primary key 752
Referential integrity 763
Second normal form (2NF) 756
Surrogate key 752
Third normal form (3NF) 760
Transitive dependency 756
Tuple 752
Update anomaly 749

Visual Summary

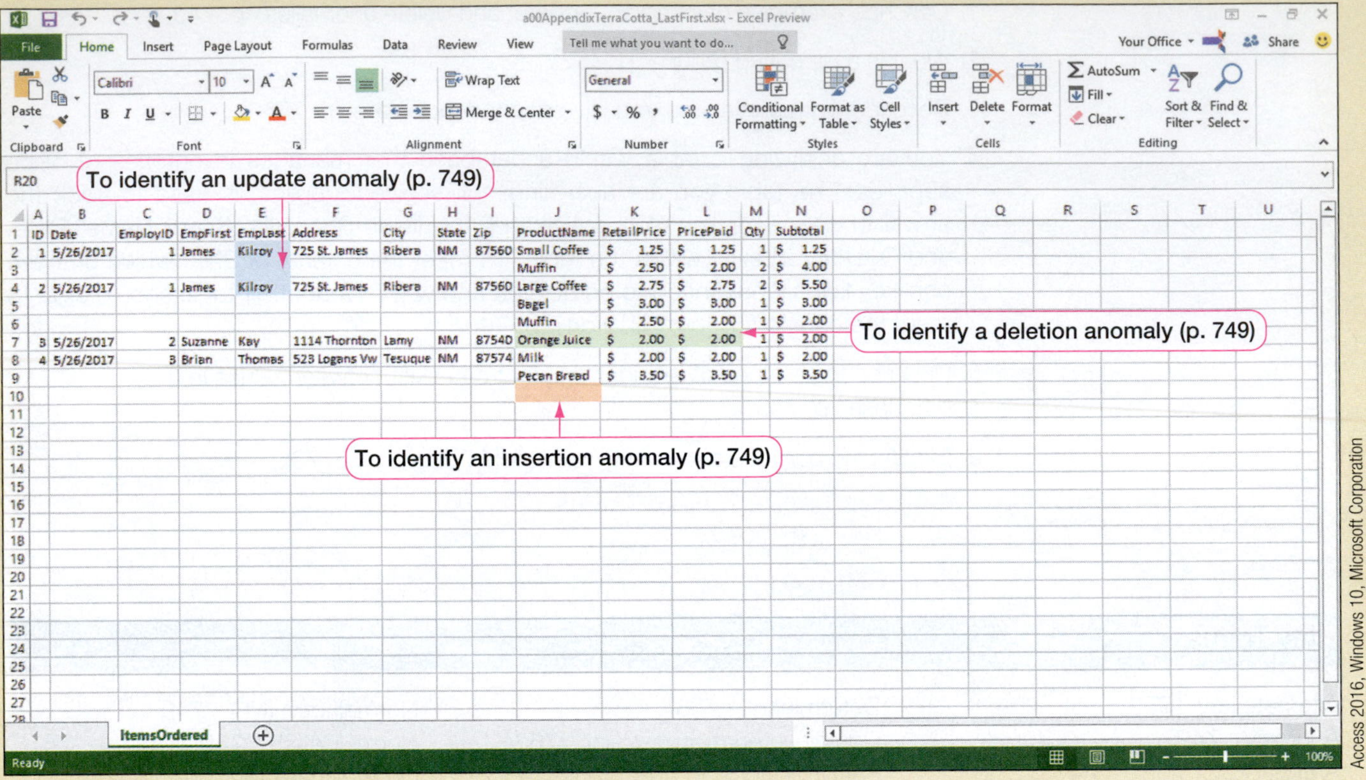

Figure 9

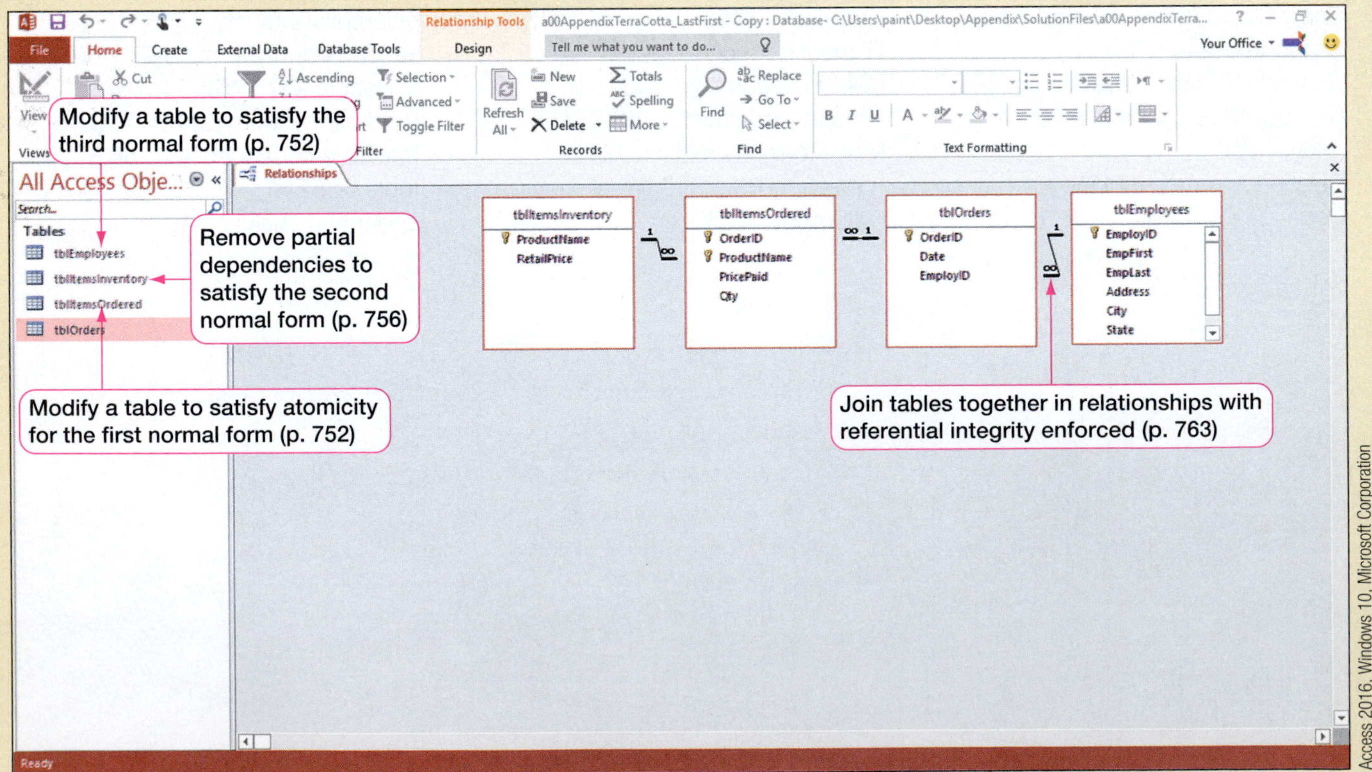

Figure 10

Problem Solve 1

Student data files needed:

 Blank Access database

 a00ps1AppendixRentals.xlsx

You will save your file as:

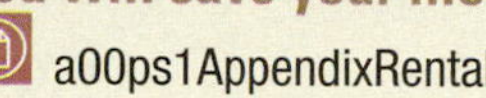 a00ps1AppendixRentals_LastFirst.accdb

Normalizing Data for Karl's Car Rentals

Finance & Accounting

Karl runs a car rental business and has hired you to help take his business paperless. As part of the process, he would like to create an Access database to manage the business customers, inventory of cars, and rental transactions. Each customer should be stored in the database only one time. Each customer can have multiple rentals. Each rental should include only one vehicle.

a. Start **Access**, and then create a new blank database. Save the database as a00ps1AppendixRentals_LastFirst using your last and first name.

b. Import the **a00ps1AppendixRentals** spreadsheet into the a00ps1AppendixRentals database as a new table. Do not identify a primary key. Name the table tblTransactions using your first initial and last name.

c. Open the **tblTransactions** table, and save it as a new table named tblVehicles. Complete the table design by completing the following steps.
   - In Design view, delete the fields **CustomerID**, **First Name**, **Last Name**, **Phone**, **Rental Date**, and **DueDate**.
   - In Datasheet view, delete the **second entry** in the table for the Chevrolet, Sedan, Gray, 2 door.
   - Add a new field named VehicleID with the **Number** data type. Enter values for each vehicle, starting with **1** and ending with **9**. Make this field the **primary key** on the table.
   - Save changes, and close the tblVehicles table.

d. Open the **tblTransactions** table, and save it as a new table named tblCustomers. Complete the table design by completing the following steps.
   - In Design view, delete the fields **Make**, **Model**, **Color**, **Doors**, **Rental Date**, and **DueDate**.
   - Make the CustomerID field the primary key on the table.
   - Save changes, and close the tblVehicles table.

e. Open **tblTransactions**. Complete the table design by completing the following steps.
   - In Design view, delete the fields **First Name**, **Last Name**, **Phone**, **Make**, **Model**, **Color**, and **Doors**.
   - Add a new field named **TransactionID** with the data type **Number**.
   - Add TransactionID number for all rows in the table, starting with **1** and ending with **10**.
   - Make the TransactionID the **primary key** on the table.
   - Add a new field named **VehicleID** with the data type **Number**.
   - Enter the following values for the VehicleID numbers according to the TransactionIDs.

     1. 1
     2. 6
     3. 8
     4. 4
     5. 7
     6. 3
     7. 9

8. 2
9. 5
10. 8

• Close the table.

f. If necessary, delete Table1.

g. In the Relationships window, show all three tables. Create **relationships** between the tables based on the appropriate fields, and enforce **referential integrity**. Save changes, and close the relationships window.

h. **Close** the database, exit Access, and then submit your file as directed by your instructor.

Critical Thinking

This database ended up with only three tables — in reality, it would need many more to be a functional database. If you wanted to track all credit cards used by a customer — it's possible for repeat customers to use a different card each time — how would you do that? Assume that all transactions are credit, never cash.

Perform 1: Perform in Your Career

Student data files needed:

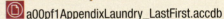

 Blank Access database

 a00pf1AppendixLaundry.xlsx

You will save your file as:

a00pf1AppendixLaundry_LastFirst.accdb

Louis' Laundry

Production & Operations

You have a part-time job at Louis' Laundry, a local laundry service. In addition to dry cleaning, Louis' Laundry does alterations. At present, all transactions get entered into an Excel spreadsheet. When a customer drops off an order, he or she is given a ticket with a number. A separate ticket is given for alterations and laundry. You have finally convinced Louis that a database would be a better solution, and Louis has agreed to pay you to create one. You will start with the spreadsheet and then normalize the tables.

a. Start **Access**, and then create a new blank database. Save the database as a00pf1AppendixLaundry_LastFirst using your last and first name.

b. Populate the database with the data from **a00pf1AppendixLaundry.xlsx**. When saving any tables in this project, add _iLast, using your first initial and last name, to the end of the name.

c. Normalize the database. Note in the field descriptions in Design view whether each field is a candidate key — and if so, what kind — or non-key. If a candidate key is not the determinant of a non-key field, place a short explanation why in the description. For each key or candidate key, note whether it is artificial or natural. Also, note any other derivations from HNF of BCNF.

d. Add your name as one of the employees.

e. Add appropriate keys and relationships.

f. If your instructor requests, create an entity relationship diagram for your database. Ask your instructor whether to use Word, PowerPoint, paper, or some other program to create the diagram.

g. **Close** the database, exit Access, and submit your file as directed by your instructor.

Perform 2: How Others Perform

Student data file needed:

 a00pf2AppendixSashas.accdb

You will save your file as:

 a00pf2AppendixSashas_LastFirst.accdb

Sasha's Laugh House

Production & Operations

An intern has created a database that Sasha's Laugh House, a local comedy club, uses to schedule acts. The database is not normalized. Each act can perform many shows. Each show has several acts. Each act charges a single act fee, and all tickets to a single show are the same price. Each show has only one employee responsible for booking the acts. Sasha has noticed that data errors have started to occur and has asked you to evaluate and fix the database.

a. Open the Access database **a00pf2AppendixSashas**, and review the database. Save your file as a00pf2AppendixSashas_LastFirst using your last and first name. When saving any tables in this project, add _iLast, using your first initial and last name, to the end of the name.

b. Normalize the database. Note in the field descriptions in Design view whether each field is a candidate key — and if so, what kind — or non-key. If a candidate key is not the determinant of a non-key field, place a short explanation why in the description. Also, note any other derivations from HNF of BCNF.

c. Change the second employee — EmployID 2 — to be your name in the tblEmployee table.

d. Add at least two additional fields you think Sasha might find helpful. Add a description in Design view explaining the purpose of each field. Leave the data for these fields blank.

e. Ensure that you have specified all keys and added relationships.

f. In the Navigation Pane, right-click each table, and then select Table Properties. In the Description for each table, specify the HNF for the table before changes and after your changes.

g. Close the database, exit Access, and then submit your file as directed by your instructor.

Appendix B

Microsoft Office Specialist Access 2016			
Chapter	MOS Obj #	Objective	Your Office Heading
1.	Create and Manage a Database		
	1.1	Create and Modify Databases	
Ch1	1.1.1	Create a Blank Desktop Database	Creating a New Database and Templates
Ch1	1.1.2	Create a Database from a Template	Creating a New Database and Templates
Ch1 Ch2	1.1.3	Create a Database by Using Import Objects or Data from Other Sources	Importing a Table (Ch1) Importing from a Named Range (Ch2) Importing from a Text File (Ch2) Importing a Worksheet (Ch2)
Online	1.1.4	Delete Database Objects	Delete Tables, Queries, Forms, and Reports
	1.2	Manage Relationships and Keys	
Ch2	1.2.1	Create and Modify Relationships	Create a One-to-Many Relationship Create a Many-to-Many Relationship
Ch2	1.2.2	Set the Primary Key	Understand and Designate Keys
Ch2	1.2.3	Enforce Referential Integrity	Understand Referential Integrity
Ch2	1.2.4	Set Foreign Keys	Understand and Designate Keys
Ch2	1.2.5	View Relationships	Understand Relationships between Tables
	1.3	Navigate Through a Database	
Ch1	1.3.1	Navigate Specific Records	Understand the Purpose of Tables
Ch11	1.3.2	Create and Modify a Navigation Form	Create a Navigation Form
Ch11 Ch14	1.3.3	Set a Form as the Startup Option	Set Start-Up Display Options and Test the Application (Ch11) Setting Startup Preferences (Ch14)
Ch1	1.3.4	Display Objects in the Navigation Pane	Customize the Navigation Pane
Ch1	1.3.5	Change Views of Objects	Understanding Queries, Forms, and Reports
	1.4	Protect and Maintain Databases	
Ch1	1.4.1	Compact a Database	Compact and Repair a Database
Ch1	1.4.2	Repair a Database	Compact and Repair a Database
Ch1	1.4.3	Back Up a Database	Backing Up a Database
Ch14	1.4.4	Split a Database	Using the Database Splitter
Ch14	1.4.5	Encrypt a Database with a Password	Encrypting and Setting a Database Password
Online	1.4.6	Recover Data from Backup	Recovering Data from a Backup
	1.5	Print and Export Data	
Ch4	1.5.1	Print Reports	Create a Report Using the Report Wizard
Ch1	1.5.2	Print Records	Printing Query Results
Online	1.5.3	Save a Databases as a Template	Saving Databases as Templates
Ch4 Online	1.5.4	Export Objects to Alternative Formats	Save a Report to a PDF (Ch4) Exporting to Excel, Text Files, and XML (Online)

Microsoft Office Specialist Access 2016			
Chapter	MOS Obj #	Objective	Your Office Heading
2.	**Build Tables**		
	2.1	**Create Tables**	
Ch2 Ch8	2.1.1	Create a Table	Create a Table in Design View Create a New Table Using a Make Table Query
Ch2	2.1.2	Import Data into Tables	Import Data from Other Sources
Ch14	2.1.3	Create Linked Tables from External Sources	Linking Tables
Ch1	2.1.4	Import Tables from other Databases	Understand the Purpose of Tables
Online	2.1.5	Create a Table from a Template with Application Parts	Creating a Table from a Template with Application Parts
	2.2	**Manage Tables**	
Online	2.2.1	Hide Fields in Tables	Hiding Fields in Tables
Online	2.2.2	Add Total Rows	Adding Total Rows in Tables
Ch2	2.2.3	Add Table Descriptions	Create a Table in Design View
Online	2.2.4	Rename Tables	Renaming Tables
	2.3	**Manage Records in Tables**	
Ch4	2.3.1	Update Records	Navigate and Edit Records in Datasheets
Ch2	2.3.2	Add Records	Enter Data Manually
Ch2 Ch8	2.3.3	Delete Records	Enter Data Manually (Ch2) Create, Test, and Run Delete Queries (Ch8)
Ch2 Ch8	2.3.4	Append Records from External Data	Import Data from Other Sources (Ch2) Append Data to a Table (Ch8)
Ch3	2.3.5	Find and Replace Data	Find and Replace Records in the Datasheet
Ch3	2.3.6	Sort Records	Sort Table and Query Results
Ch3 Ch5	2.3.7	Filter Records	Applying a Filter to a Dataset (Ch3) Create Filters to View Specific Records (Ch5)
	2.4	**Create and Modify Fields**	
Ch2	2.4.1	Add Fields to Tables	Creating a Table in Design View
Ch5	2.4.2	Add Validation Rules to Fields	Define Data Validation Rules
Ch5	2.4.3	Change Field Captions	Define Caption Names Using the Caption Property
Ch2	2.4.4	Change Field Sizes	Create a Table in Design View
Ch2	2.4.5	Change Field Data Types	Create a Table in Design View
Ch5	2.4.6	Configure Fields to Auto-Increment	Configuring Fields Using the AutoNumber Data Type
Ch5	2.4.7	Set Default Values	Define Default Values
Ch2 Ch5	2.4.8	Using Input Masks	Understand Masks and Formatting (Ch2) Understand the Purpose and Benefits of Input Masks (Ch5)
Ch2	2.4.9	Delete Fields	Deleting a Field from a Table

Microsoft Office Specialist Access 2016			
Chapter	**MOS Obj #**	**Objective**	**Your Office Heading**
3.	**Create Queries**		
	3.1	**Create a Query**	
Ch1	3.1.1	Run a Query	Understand the Purpose of Queries
Ch7	3.1.2	Create a Crosstab Query	Create a Two-Dimensional Query Using the Crosstab Query Wizard
Ch6	3.1.3	Create a Parameter Query	Using Parameters in a Query
Ch8	3.1.4	Create an Action Query	Understand Action Queries
Ch3	3.1.5	Create a Multi-Table Query	Creating a Query from Multiple Tables
Ch3	3.1.6	Save a Query	Create Queries in Design View
	3.2	**Modify a Query**	
Online	3.2.1	Rename a Query	Renaming a Query
Ch3	3.2.2	Add Fields	Create Queries in Design View
Online	3.2.3	Remove Fields	Removing Fields from a Query
Ch3	3.2.4	Hide Fields	Define Selection Criteria for Queries
Ch1	3.2.5	Sort Data Within Queries	Understand the Purpose of Queries
Ch3	3.2.6	Format Fields Within Queries	Create Aggregate Functions
	3.3	**Create Calculated Fields and Grouping within Queries**	
Ch3	3.3.1	Add Calculated Fields	Create Calculated Fields
Ch3	3.3.2	Set Filtering Criteria	Define Selection Criteria for Queries
Ch3	3.3.3	Group and Summarize Data	Create Aggregate Functions
Ch3	3.3.4	Group Data by Using Comparison Operators	Define Selection Criteria for Queries
Ch3 Ch6	3.3.5	Group Data by Using Arithmetic and Logical Operators	Define Selection Criteria for Queries (Ch3) Use the GROUP BY Clause in Aggregated Calculations (Ch6)
4.	**Create Forms**		
	4.1	**Create a Form**	
Ch1 Ch9	4.1.1	Create a Form	Understand the Purpose of Forms (Ch1) Creating Advanced Forms (Ch9)
Online	4.1.2	Create a Form from a Template with Application Parts	Understanding Application Parts
Ch1	4.1.3	Save a Form	Understand the Purpose of Forms
	4.2	**Configure Form Controls**	
Ch4	4.2.1	Move Form Controls	Resizing and Changing Controls
h4 9	4.2.2	Add Form Controls	Creating a Form (Ch4) Adding a Picture to a Form (Ch4) Modify the Form in Design View (Ch9)
e	4.2.3	Modify Data Sources	Modifying Data Sources for a Form
	4.2.4	Remove Form Controls	Resizing and Changing Controls
	4.2.5	Set Form Control Properties	Modify the Form Property Sheet
	4.2.6	Manage Labels	Resizing and Changing Controls
	4.2.7	Add Sub-Forms	Creating Subforms (Multi-table Forms)

Microsoft Office Specialist Access 2016			
Chapter	**MOS Obj #**	**Objective**	**Your Office Heading**
	4.3	**Format a Form**	
Ch9	4.3.1	Modify Tab Order	Changing Tab Order
Ch4	4.3.2	Configure Print Settings	Printing a Record from a Form
Online	4.3.3	Sort Records By Form Field	Sorting Records in a Form
Ch4	4.3.4	Apply a Theme	Change the Form Theme
Online	4.3.5	Control Form Positioning	Controlling Form Positioning with Margins, Padding, and Anchoring
Ch9	4.3.6	Insert Backgrounds	Adding the Date and Time and Changing the Background Color
Ch4 Ch9	4.3.7	Insert Headers and Footers	Creating a Form (Ch4) Inserting a Form Footer (Ch9)
Ch4	4.3.8	Insert Images	Adding a Picture to the Form
5.	**Create Reports**		
	5.1	**Create a Report**	
Ch4 Ch10	5.1.1	Create a Report Based on The Query or Table	Creating Customized Reports (Ch4) Creating Parameter Reports (Ch10)
Online	5.1.2	Create a Report in Design View	Creating a Report from Design View
Ch4	5.1.3	Create a Report by Using a Wizard	Understand the Purpose of Reports
	5.2	**Configure Report Controls**	
Ch4 Ch10	5.2.1	Group and Sort Fields	Customize a Report (Ch4) Use the Group, Sort, and Total Pane (Ch10)
Online	5.2.2	Modify Data Sources	Modifying Data Sources for Reports
Ch4 Ch10	5.2.3	Add Report Controls	Creating a Single-Table Report (Ch4) Add and Remove Fields from a Report (Ch10)
Ch4 Ch10	5.2.4	Add and Modify Labels	Create a Report Using the Report Wizard (Ch4) Add Labels and Shapes to a Report (Ch10)
	5.3	**Format a Report**	
Online	5.3.1	Format a Report into Multiple Columns	Formatting Reports into Multiple Columns
Ch4 Ch10	5.3.2	Add Calculated Fields	Creating Totals Using the Report Wizard (Ch4) Adding Subtotals (Ch4) Modify Calculated Fields in a Report (Ch10)
Online	5.3.3	Control Report Positioning	Controlling Report Positioning with Margins and Padding
Ch4	5.3.4	Format Report Elements	Creating a Multiple-Table Report
Ch4	5.3.5	Change Report Orientation	Create a Report Using the Report Wizard
Ch4	5.3.6	Insert Header and Footer Information	Create a Report Using the Report Wizard
Online	5.3.7	Insert Images	Inserting an Image to a Report
Online	5.3.8	Apply a Theme	Applying a Theme to a Report

Glossary

A

Action A self-contained instruction that can be combined with other instructions to automate tasks and is considered to be the basic building block of a macro.

Action Catalog A searchable set of macro actions that can retrieve actions based on keywords. The Action Catalog consists of three different groups: Program Flow, Actions, and In this Database.

Action query A query that makes changes to records or moves many records from one table to another. Action queries are used to change the data in existing tables or make new tables based on a query's data set.

Active cell The cell that is the recipient of an action, such as a click, calculation, typing, or paste; identified by the thick green border. Only the active cell can have data entered into it.

Add-ins for Office Enhancements for the features in Office that can be installed from the Microsoft Store.

Adobe PDF file A file format that is easy to send through e-mail and preserves the original document look and feel so it opens the same way every time for the recipient.

Advanced filter A filter that hides records that do not match the criteria that you chose; it can have several criteria in multiple fields, combined with sorting.

After event A type of data macro that occurs after a change has been successfully made to the table data.

Aggregate A summative calculation, such as a total or average.

Aggregate function Perform arithmetic operations, such as averages and totals, on records displayed in a table or query.

Aggregated calculation A calculation that returns a single value, calculated from multiple values in a column. Common aggregate functions include Average, Count, Maximum, Median, Minimum, Mode, and Sum.

Append query A query that selects records from one or more data sources and copies the selected records to an existing table.

Append row The first blank row at the end of the table in Access.

Application A piece of software designed to perform one task or multiple tasks.

Application Start screen The first screen that is seen when a program is opened but an existing program file is not open. In this screen, you can select a blank document, workbook, presentation, database, or one of many application-specific templates.

Argument A constant, variable, or expression that is passed to a procedure.

Array A collection of data of the same type.

AS clause When used in a SQL SELECT statement, the AS clause allows you to name or rename a field, which will be displayed in the data set.

Attachment A data type that stores images, spreadsheet files, documents, charts, and other types of supported files to the records in your database, much the way you attach files to an e-mail message.

Attribute Information about an entity.

AutoExec macro A macro that will run automatically before any other macros when a database is opened.

AutoFit A method to change the column width of the data to match the widest data entered in that field.

AutoKeys macro A macro group that assigns keys on the keyboard to execute each submacro. The macro must be named AutoKeys, and each submacro must be named with the key or key combinations on the keyboard that will be used to execute the macros.

AutoNumber data type A data type that stores an integer that is generated automatically for each new record.

AutoRecovery A feature that will attempt to recover any changes made to a document since your last save if something goes wrong.

B

Back-end database Contains the tables from the original database.

Backstage view Provides access to the file-level features, such as saving a file, creating a new file, opening an existing file, printing a file, and closing a file, as well as program options.

Backup database An extra copy of a database created in case the database is lost. Access appends the current date to the file name.

Before event A type of data macro that occurs before any changes are made to the table data.

Between…And operator An operator that verifies whether the value of a field or expression falls within a stated range of numeric values and is combined with the And or Or operator. For example, to find data that falls between two dates, you would type Between 2/3/2016 And 8/6/2016.

Bitmap An image of an object

Blank Report tool An Access tool with which you can create a blank report in Layout view.

Boolean algebra 0 and 1 are used to represent one of two values: true or false. The 0 and 1 — or –1 depending on the system you are using — are a throwback to the earlier days of programming but are still used today.

Bootcamp Mac software that allows the user to decide which operating system, Mac operating system or Windows, to run.

Bound control A control on a report or form whose data source is a field in the table.

Bound form A form that is directly connected to a data source, such as a table or query, and that can be used to enter, edit, or display data from that data source.

Bound value A control on a report or form whose data source is a field in the table.

Bullet A symbol that appears before each item to create a list of items, or identifies a summary point.

Business intelligence Helps an organization to attain its goals and objectives by giving it a better understanding of past performance as well as information on how the organization is progressing toward its goals.

Business intelligence tools (BI) A classification of software applications that aid in collecting, storing, analyzing, and providing access to data that helps managers make improved business decisions.

C

Calculated control A control whose source of data is an expression rather than a field.

Calculated data type A data type that allows you to display the results of a calculation in a read-only field.

Call statement A statement that runs another Sub procedure or function from within a procedure by transferring to the called routine.

Caption property The text that is displayed for the field name when the field name appears in queries, forms, or reports.

Cardinality The number of instances of one entity that relate to one instance of another entity. Cardinality is expressed as one-to-many, many-to-many, or one-to-one.

Case sensitive Query results will return all matching data when a user enters lowercase or uppercase letters in the criteria property, regardless of the case that was used when the data was entered.

Cell The intersection of a row and a column in a table or worksheet.

Charlist A group of one or more characters.

Check box A control in which a check mark is used to indicate when the option is selected.

Close The command to close an Office file without exiting the associated program.

Cloud computing Computing resources, either hardware or software, being used by another computer over a network. Files that are stored in a remote location can be stored, accessed, and edited.

Code window The larger window on the right of the Visual Basic Editor where you can edit the text of any procedure.

Cold turkey implementation Involves implementing your database in its entirety and replacing the legacy system all at once.

Compacting An Access feature that rearranges objects in your database to use disk space more efficiently.

Comparison operator An operator used in a query to compare the value in a database to the criteria value entered in the query.

Complex delete query A query used to delete data between multiple tables.

Complex update query A query used to update data between multiple tables.

Composite key A primary key composed of two fields.

Concatenate To join two or more fields.

Concatenate operator A function that helps to join data from multiple fields to create a single text string of data. This is done by using an ampersand (&) to create a single field by combining data in multiple fields. For example, to concatenate first and last name fields, you would type FullName:[FirstName]& " " &[LastName], where FullName would become the name of the concatenated field.

Conditional formatting A method of formatting a control on the basis of one or more comparisons to a set of rules. These comparisons can be based on the value of the control or on a calculation that includes other values.

Contextual tabs A ribbon tab that contains commands related to selected objects so you can manipulate, edit, and format the objects. This ribbon tab does not appear unless the object is selected.

Control An object on a form or report that displays data, performs actions, and lets you view and work with information.

Crosstab query A special type of query used when you want to describe one field in terms of two or more other fields in the table.

Crosstab Query Wizard A wizard that helps to create a basic crosstab query. For a more advanced query, changes would need to be made in the query's Design view after finishing the wizard.

Current Date A function that automatically puts the current date in a field based on your computer's system date.

Custom formatting Formatting that is used to customize the way numbers, dates, times, and text are displayed and printed.

D

Data Facts about people, events, things, or ideas.

Data action A specific, limited set of macro actions that can be used in a data macro.

Data block Contains an area to add one or more data actions and executes all the actions contained as part of its operation. Data blocks can be used only with After events, with the exception of the LookupRecord data block, which can also be used with Before events.

Data cleansing A process of removing data that is not useful or needed anymore.

Data macro Stored in Access tables and triggered by table events. Data macros are typically used to implement business logic in tables and to automatically set values in fields.

Data mining The act of using business intelligence tools is called data mining, which helps to expose trends, patterns, and relationships within the data that might otherwise have remained undetected.

Data type The characteristic that defines the kind of data that can be entered into a field, such as numbers, text, or dates. The data type tells Access how to store and display the field.

Data validation rule A rule that prevents inaccurate data from being entered and consequently stored in a database. Validation rules can be set for a specific field or an entire table.

Data warehouse Data warehouses contain large amounts and different types of data that present a clear picture of business environments at specific points in time.

Data warehousing The exporting of older data from transactional and operational databases into a storage database, called a data warehouse.

Database A collection of data.

Database event Occurs when an action is completed on any given object. The action could be, for example, a simple click of the mouse or entering information into a specific field.

Database management system (DBMS) Database management software that can be used to organize, store, manipulate, and report on your data.

Datasheet view A view of an Access object that shows the data.

Date Function A function that returns the current system date.

Date Picker A pop-up calendar that allows a user to enter a date by clicking the date in the calendar.

DateAdd function This function can be used to add or subtract a specific time interval from a date. For example, Date()+10 would result in the same output as using the DateAdd function to add 10 to the current date — DateAdd("d", 10, Date()).

DateDiff function A function that can be used to add or subtract a specific time interval from a date. For example, Date()+10 would result in the same output as using the DateAdd function to add 10 to the current date: DateAdd("d", 10, Date()).

DatePart function A function that can be used to examine a date and return a specific interval of time. For example, if each employee is eligible for a bonus after five years of service, you can determine the year when eligibility begins by typing 5 Year Anniversary:DatePart("yyyy", ([HireDate]))+5.

DateSerial function A function, written as DateSerial(year, month, day), that can be used to manipulate the day, month, and year of a date. For example, if each full-time employee is eligible for health benefits after 90 days of employment, which means that the benefits begin on the 91st day of employment, you could determine the date when eligibility begins by typing Benefits Begin:DateSerial(Year([HireDate]),Month([HireDate]), Day([HireDate])+91).

Debugging The process of identifying and reducing the number of errors that can occur within your code.

Declaration Defines user-defined data types, variables, arrays, and constants.

Declarations section Contains declarations that apply to all procedures within the module.

Decryption The process of making encrypted information readable again by using a key (password).

Default value A value that is automatically entered into a field when a new record is created.

Delete query A query that is used to remove entire records from a table at one time. Delete queries remove all the data in each field, including the primary key.

Delimiter A character used in a text file to separate the fields; it can be a paragraph mark, a tab, a comma, or another character.

Dependent expression An expression that relies on the outcome of another expression.

Design view A view of an Access object that shows the detailed structure of a table, query, form, or report.

Detail area The section of a report that displays the records from the underlying table or query.

Dialog box A user window that provides more options or settings beyond those provided on the ribbon.

Dialog Box Launcher An icon in a group that opens a corresponding dialog box or task pane.

Dim statement The statement that begins the process of declaring a variable.

DoCmd object An object that allows Access actions to be performed from within VBA. This can include opening a report, telling Access not to show warning messages, or closing an object.

Document A letter, memo, report, brochure, resume, or flyer.

E

Edit mode A mode that allows you to edit or change the contents of a field or change the name of a file or folder.

Embedded macro A macro that is stored as part of a database object such as a form or report or any control such as a button. Embedded macros are not displayed in the Navigation Pane and are executed only when the objects in which they are embedded trigger events.

Enabled A property option that allows a field to have the value changed or copied. By default, all fields are enabled.

Encryption The process of changing text-based information into a state in which a key is required in order to read the information.

Entity Person, place, item, or event about which you want to keep data.

Error handling The process of anticipating and controlling errors.

Event-driven programming Programming that uses an event — such as moving to the next record of a form — to trigger the execution of code.

Exclusive Mode Allows only one user at a time the ability to open and edit the database.

Exit statement A statement that can be used to terminate the procedure.

Expression Builder A tool that helps you build calculated fields correctly by providing a list of expressive elements, operators, and built-in functions.

F

Field A specific piece of information that is stored in every record and, when formatted, appears as a column in a database table. An item of information in a worksheet column that is associated with something of interest.

Field format A method of customizing the way numbers, dates, times, and text are displayed and printed by using predefined formats or custom formats.

Field size The maximum length of a data field or a range of values.

Field validation rule A rule that verifies the value entered in a field. If the validation rule is violated, Access prevents the user from leaving the current field until the problem has been fixed.

File extension Three or four characters after the file name that is preceded by a period and that is used by the Windows operating system to determine which programs should be used to open a file.

File path The physical location of the file starting with a letter that represents the drive and separating folders with a "\".

FileDialog object An object that can be used to allow the user to select the file or files needed for the import process.

Filter A condition applied temporarily to a table or query to show a subset of the records.

Filter by Form A method of filtering data in a form or spreadsheet by creating a blank table for the selected table.

Filter by Selection Selecting a value in a record and filtering the records that contain only the values that match what has been selected.

Filtering A function that allows you to view and print only the desired and required information from a database.

Find command A command used to find records in a database with a specific value.

Find Duplicates Query Wizard Finds duplicate records in a table or a query.

Find Unmatched Query Wizard Finds records in one table that do not have related records in another table.

Fiscal year A period businesses and other organizations use for calculating annual financial statements. This can be different from a calendar year and can vary among different businesses and organizations because they can choose whatever dates they want to use as the "year."

Font A style of displaying characters, numbers, punctuation, and special characters. Also the way letters in words look, including the size, weight, and style.

Forecasting Using historical data to predict or estimate future sales trends, to develop budgets, and so forth.

Foreign key A field in a table that stores the value of the primary key of a related table for the purpose of creating a relationship.

Form An object that allows you to enter or view your table data.

Form view Data view of a form.

Format Specifies how data is displayed.

Format Painter A tool that allows you to copy a format and apply it to other selections.

Front-end database Deployed directly to users and contains non-data objects such as queries, reports, forms, macros, and VBA modules.

FULL JOIN clause Used when you want to return all the rows from the left table and all the rows from the right table in a SQL query.

Function Executes instructions and returns a value to another procedure.

G

Gallery A set of menu options that appear when you click the arrow next to a button.

GIGO principle Stands for Garbage In, Garbage Out, meaning that inputting inconsistent or inaccurate data leads to inconsistent or inaccurate output.

Grand total Controls added to a report to perform calculations on all records.

Group A collection of records along with some introductory and summary information about the records. A logical grouping of commands on the ribbon.

GROUP BY clause A function that can help to combine records with identical values in a specified field list into a single record.

Group Footer A footer that contains the information printed at the end of every group of records; used to display summary information for the group.

Group Header A header that contains the information printed at the beginning of every new group of records, for example, the group name.

H

HAVING clause If a field includes an aggregate function, a HAVING clause specifies the aggregated field criteria and restricts the results based on aggregated values.

Help A window opened via the Help button or the F1 key.

Hyperlink An address that specifies a protocol (such as HTTP or FTP) and a location of an object, document, World Wide Web page, or other destination on the Internet, an intranet, or local computer, for example,http://www.paintedparadiseresort.com.

I

Ideas Similar to suggestions, but the user must perform these actions.

IIF function A function, whose name stands for Immediate If, that is similar to the IF function in Excel. This function returns one value if a specified condition is true or another value if it is false. For example, for employees who received a salary increase, you can calculate what the new salary will be if employees receive a 3% raise by typing New Salary:IIf([Salary]<=30000,[Salary]*1.03, [Salary]).

Importing The process of copying data from another file, such as a Word file or Excel workbook, into a separate file, such as an Access database.

In operator An operator that can be used to return results that contain one of the values in a list of values. For example, if you want to search for customers who meet certain criteria, such as those who live in specific states, you would type In("Arizona", "Nevada", "New Mexico") as the criterion in the State field.

Increment AutoNumber The most common and the default setting in Access when selecting the AutoNumber data type.

Index This stores the location of records based on the field that you choose.

Information Data that has been manipulated and processed to make it meaningful.

Inner join The default join type in Access, an inner join selects only those records from both database tables that have matching values.

INNER JOIN clause Used to return only the rows that actually match based on the join predicate.

Input mask A way to control how data is entered by creating a typing guide. In most cases, an input mask controls the way that data is stored.

Input Mask Wizard A tool that provides input masks for most common formatting needs and helps to automate the process of establishing an input mask.

Is Not Null By entering this into a field's criteria in the Design view of a query, the results will include records that contain valid data. For example, to create a list of the employees who have not had an employee photo taken, you could type Is Not Null in the Criteria property of the Photo field.

Is Null By entering this into a field's criteria in the Design view of a query, the results will include records that do not contain valid data.

IsNull function A function that is used to indicate that a value is unknown and is treated differently than other values because it has no value. For example, to create a list of the employees who have had an employee photo taken, you could type Is Null in the Criteria property of the Photo field.

J

Join lines The lines connecting tables in the Relationship tab.

Join A connection between two tables based on a common field, used to create a relationship.

Junction table A table that breaks down a many-to-many relationship into two one-to-many relationships.

K

Keyboard shortcut Keyboard equivalents for software commands that allow you to keep your hands on the keyboard instead of reaching for the mouse to perform actions.

KeyTips A form of keyboard shortcut. Pressing the Alt button will display KeyTips (or keyboard shortcuts) for items on the Ribbon and the Quick Access Toolbar.

Knowledge Applied information once you make the decision.

L

Label control A control on a form or report that contains descriptive information, typically a field name.

Layout Selector A tool that allows you to move a whole table at one time.

Layout view Shows data and allows limited changes to a form or report design.

LEFT JOIN clause Used when you want to return all rows in the left table even if no matching rows exist in the right table.

Legacy data type An old or outdated data type that is still used — usually because it still works for the user — even though newer technology or more efficient methods exist.

Legacy software Technology that is out of date but still in use.

Like operator An operator that helps to find values in a field that match a specified pattern. For example, you could find all employees who have the job title with the word caddy by typing Like "*caddy*" in the Criteria property under Position.

Line continuation character Consists of a single space followed by a single underscore character as the last character in a line of code.

Line label Can be used like a bookmark in a procedure.

Linked table A table that provides a link to data stored in another database or application.

Linked Table Manager Lists the file location of all linked tables in a database. If the location of a linked object changes, the Linked Table Manager can be used to refresh those links.

Live Preview A feature that shows the results that would occur in your file if you were to click that particular option.

Locked A property option that determines whether the value in a field can be entered using a form.

Logical operator An operator used in a query used to combine two or more criteria.

Logo An unbound control that can be added to the header of a form.

Lookup field A table field that has values that come either from a table, a query, or a value list.

Lookup field properties Can be set to change the behavior of a lookup column.

Lookup Wizard This automatically populates the appropriate field properties and creates the appropriate table relationships.

Loop Used to execute a series of statements multiple times.

M

Macro A database object that provides a method of automating routine database tasks. Macros can add functionality to reports and forms as well as the controls that forms and reports contain.

Macro Designer An interface for building and editing macros.

Macro group Two or more macros that are similar in function that are stored under the same macro name.

Mailto command A common type of hyperlink that helps to generate a link for sending e-mail.

Main form The primary or first table selected in creating a form.

Make table query A query that acquires data from one or more tables and then automatically loads the resulting data set into a new table once you run the query.

Many-to-many relationship A relationship between tables in which one record in one table has many matching records in a second table and one record in the second table has many matching records in the first table.

Maximize The button located in the top right corner of the title bar that enlarges a window to its maximum size, which offers the largest workspace.

Me keyword Functions such as a declared variable that refers to the current object.

Method An action — such as SaveAs — that controls the object's behavior.

Mini toolbar A toolbar that appears after text has been selected and that contains buttons for the most commonly used formatting commands, such as font, font size, font color, center alignment, indents, bold, italic, and underline.

Minimize The button that reduces a window to a taskbar button.

Module Used to store VBA procedures that can be referenced or called by other procedures or events in the database.

Most Recently Used list A list maintained by Office of your most recently modified files: documents, spreadsheets, databases, and presentations.

Move handle The spot in the top left corner of an object that, when selected, allows the object to be moved.

Multiple-field index An index that stores the location of records on the basis of the fields that you choose.

Multiple-item form A form that looks similar to a datasheet but that can be customized as a form.

Multiplier effect When Access joins two tables without a common field, each record in the first table is matched with each record in the second table.

Multivalued field A field that helps to keep track of multiple related facts about a subject.

N

Named range A cell or group of cells that have been given a name, other than the default column and row cell address reference, that can then be used within a formula or function.

Natural primary key A primary key that has a logical relationship or meaning in the data.

Navigation bar Provides a way to move through records in table, query, report, and form objects.

Navigation control bar An area of a navigation form that allows for the addition of new forms, reports, or other database objects.

Navigation form A form that provides a familiar Internet-style interface that allows you to access multiple objects in the database from one central location.

Navigation mode A mode that allows you to move from record to record or from field to field using keystrokes and the Navigation bar.

Navigation Pane The pane that in File Explorer displays locations where users can find files, such as Quick Access, OneDrive, This PC, Network, and possibly more, depending on the computer. Also a pane that enables you to move around within your document, search for content, and manipulate the organization of headings; provides a set of related features for navigating and searching for content.

Nested IIF function A function that nests IIf functions, or places one inside another, allowing a series of dependent expressions to be evaluated. For example, if you wanted to determine how much of a raise each employee received, you can type Raise Assessment:IIf([Salary]<=30000,"7% Raise",IIf([Salary]<=60000,"4% Raise","No Raise")).

Net revenue The revenue minus sales returns, sales allowances, and sales discounts. Also known as net sales.

Normalization The process of minimizing the duplication of information in a relational database through effective table design.

Not operator An operator that is used to search for records that do not match specific criteria and can be combined with other operators. For example, you may want to search for all customers outside of North America. You would enter Not "USA" And Not "Canada" And Not "Mexico" in the Criteria property of the Country field.

Now function A function that retrieves the current system date and time.

Null A term used to indicate that a field is blank.

Number data type A data type that can store only numeric data. The data field will be used in calculations.

Numeric key A primary key with a number data type. AutoNumber is often used for numeric keys.

O

Object box Displays the name of the object that contains the procedure such as a form or command button.

Object Browser Lists all VBA objects along with the associated methods and properties for each object.

Object A table, form, query, or report. An item that can be selected and manipulated independently of surrounding text.

Object-oriented programming Programming that uses objects — such as a form in Access — to design applications.

Office Background An artistic design displayed in the upper right in the title bar of Office.

Office Backstage A feature that provides access to the file-level commands, such as saving a file, creating a new file, opening an existing file, printing a file, and closing a file, as well as program options and account settings.

Office Theme A color scheme used by Office.

OLE Stands for Object Linking and Embedding, a technology developed by Microsoft that creates a bitmap or image of an object. OLE objects allow you to store images inside a database field.

On Error statement A statement that can enable or disable an error-handling routine and specify the location of the routine within the procedure.

OneDrive An online cloud computing technology provided by Microsoft and integrated with Office 2016 that offers a certain amount of free collaborative storage space.

One-to-many relationship A relationship between two tables in which one record in the first table corresponds to many records in the second table; the most common type of relationship in Access.

One-to-one relationship A relationship between tables in which a record in one table has only one matching record in the second table.

Operational database The database that is used to carry out an organization's regular operations, such as payroll and inventory management.

Option Compare A statement that sets the string comparison method for the module.

Option Compare Binary A setting that examines the ASCII values for the characters contained in a string and is therefore case sensitive.

Option Compare Text A setting that results in case-insensitive comparisons.

Option Explicit Statement A statement that forces any variables in a procedure to be defined by using the Dim statement.

ORDER BY clause Used in a SELECT statement to sort results in either ascending or descending order.

Orphan The first line of a paragraph when the line is alone at the bottom of a page.

Outer join A join that selects all of the records from one database table and only those records in the second table that have matching values in the joined field. One or more fields can serve as a join field.

OUTER JOIN clause Used when you want to return all rows from at least one of the tables within the FROM clause as long as those rows meet any WHERE or HAVING search conditions in a SQL query.

P

Packaging volume The difference between the volume of the shipping container and the volume of the object you are shipping.

Page Footer A footer that contains the information printed at the end of every page in a report; often used to display page numbers.

Page Header A header that contains the information printed at the top of every page of a report.

Pane A smaller window that often appears to the side of the program window and offers options or helps you to navigate through completing a task or feature.

Parallel implementation The legacy system and new system are used concurrently.

Parameter A value that can be changed each time you run the query.

Parameter data type When this is defined, users see a more helpful error message if they enter the wrong type of data, such as entering text when currency should be entered.

Parameter query A type of query that can be designed when search criteria is unknown. When a parameter query is run, the user is prompted to enter the value for each parameter.

Percentage of physical volume This calculation can compare how much an object holds in comparison to how much space is being used.

Percentage of sales revenue This calculation can compare a portion of the gross revenue to the total gross revenue.

Percentage of sales volume This calculation compares how two numbers are related, such as this year's sales and last year's sales. Consider the method used to calculate sales volume as well as the time period over which you plan to measure the sales volume.

Performance Analyzer A tool in Access that analyzes and suggests ways to optimize the performance of a database.

Phased implementation A portion of the new system is put into place and perfected before additional pieces of the system are moved into use.

Physical volume How much space an object can hold.

Piloted implementation Small groups of a company's employees start using the new database. Gradually, more groups come on board as the system is perfected until the entire organization is using the new system.

Portable document format (PDF) A file type that preserves most formatting attributes of a source document regardless of the software in which the document was created.

Precision This allows you to determine how many decimal places you want to round your numbers to when using the Round function.

Predicate Specifies the condition to use to perform an inner or outer join.

Presentation An oral performance aid that uses slides or stand-alone silent presentation, such as that at a kiosk.

Primary key The field that uniquely identifies a record in a table.

Primary sort field The first field chosen in a multiple field sort.

Print Preview Backstage view of how a document, workbook, presentation, table, or other object will appear when printed.

Procedure Contains a series of statements or instructions that are executed as a unit.

Procedure box A list that allows you to navigate quickly between the Declarations section and the individual procedures in the open module.

Project Explorer Contains a list of the currently open Access Database objects that contain VBA procedures and a list of modules within the current database.

Property sheet A list of properties for fields in which you can make precise changes to each property associated with the field.

Protected View A view of the file in which the contents can be seen and read but cannot be edited, saved, or printed until editing is enabled. By default, Office will open files from e-mail or a web browser in this view.

Q

Query An object that retrieves specific data from one or more database objects either tables or other queries and then, in a single datasheet, displays only the data you specify.

Query by example A type of query in which a sample of the data is set up as criteria.

Query design grid Selected fields in a query. Shown at the bottom of a query's Design view.

Query join A temporary or virtual relationship between two tables in a query that do not have an established relationship or common field with the same field name and data type.

Query workspace Displays the source for data in the query. Shown at the top of a query's Design view.

Quick Access Toolbar Located at the top left of the Office window, it can be customized to display commonly used buttons.

R

Random AutoNumber This will generate a random number that is unique to each record within the table.

Recommendations Actions that Access believes will improve the performance of a database.

Record All of the categories of data that pertain to one person, place, thing, event, or idea and that are formatted as a row in a worksheet or database table.

Record selector The small box at the left of a record in Datasheet view and Form view that is used to select an entire record.

Record validation rule A rule that determines whether a record is valid, or meets all criteria, when a record is saved. In other words, you need to compare and validate the values in one field against the values in another field in the same record.

Redundancy Data that is repeated in more than one place in the database, an indicator of poor design.

Relational database Three-dimensional database software that can connect data in separate tables to form a relationship when common fields exist and can offer reassembled information from multiple tables.

Relationship An association between two tables based on a common field.

Replace command A command used to automatically replace values in a table or query.

Report An object that summarizes the fields and records from a table or query in an easy-to-read format suitable for printing.

Report Design tool An Access tool with which you can create a blank report in Design view.

Report Footer A footer that contains the information printed once at the end of a report; used to print report totals or other summary information for the entire report.

Report Header A header that contains the information printed once at the beginning of a report; used for logos, titles, and dates.

Report tool The Access tool that creates a report with one mouse click, which displays all of the fields from the record source that you select.

Report view A view that allows you to see what the printed report will look like in a continuous page layout.

Report Wizard An Access feature that guides you through creating a report by asking you questions.

Required property A property that can be used to specify whether a value is required in a field, ensuring that the field is not left blank.

Restore Down A button that, when a window is at its maximum size, will restore the window to a previous, smaller size. When a window is in the Restore Down mode, this button expands the window to its full size.

Revenue Income that a company receives from its normal business activities, that is, from the sale of goods and services to customers. Also known as gross sales.

Ribbon The row of tabs with buttons across the top of the application where you will find most of the commands for the application. The ribbon differs from program to program, but each program has two tabs in common: the File tab and the Home tab.

Ribbon Display Options Three options for ribbon display: Auto-Hide Ribbon, Display Tabs, and Display Tabs and Command.

RIGHT JOIN clause Used when you want to return only rows that have matching data in the right table even if no matching rows exist in the left table in an SQL query.

Roaming settings A group of settings that offer synced user-specific data that affects the Office experience.

Round function A function that returns a number rounded to a specific number of decimal places.

S

Sales volume The number of items sold or services rendered during the normal course of business. These figures would be taken over a specific period of time and can be expressed in either dollars or percentages.

ScreenTip A small box that provides a name or other information about the object to which you are pointing.

Secondary sort field The second and subsequent fields chosen in a multiple field sort.

SELECT statement The fundamental framework for a SQL query is the SQL SELECT statement.

Shared Mode When multiple users are allowed access to the database at the same time.

Short Text data type A data type that can store either text or numeric characters.

Shortcut menu A list of context-sensitive commands related to a selection that appears when you right-click.

Simple delete query A query that is used to remove one or more records from a table or another query. The number of rows deleted depends upon the criteria within the Where clause of the delete query.

Simple update query A query that involves updating data in one table, allowing you to specify two values: the value you want to replace and the value to be used as a replacement.

Single Step A feature of Access that allows you to observe the flow of a macro and the results of each action, isolating any action that causes an error or produces unwanted results.

Single-field index An index set on an individual field, such as a primary key.

Sizing handle The small boxes around a selected control that allow you to resize the control.

Sizing handles The small boxes around a selected control that allow you to resize the control.

Snap to grid An option for reports that automatically aligns new controls to a point on the grid in Design view.

Sort field A field used to determine the order of the records in a table.

Sorting The process of rearranging records into a specific order.

Special keys A set of four keyboard shortcuts that can be disabled in securing a database.

Special operator An operator used to compare text values in a query.

Split form A form created from one table with a Form view and a Datasheet view in the same window.

Spreadsheet A two-dimensional grid that can be used to model quantitative data and perform accurate and rapid calculations with results ranging from simple budgets to financial and statistical analyses.

SQL subquery A separate SELECT statement that is nested inside the main SELECT statement.

Stand-alone macro A separate database object that is displayed in the Navigation Pane. Stand-alone macros can be executed directly in the Navigation Pane by double-clicking the macro object, by clicking Run in Design view, or by attaching the macro to a database object, such as a button or text field.

Start-up form The form that opens automatically when you open the database.

String A set of characters that can include spaces, symbols, and numbers.

Structured Query Language (SQL) An internationally recognized standard database language that is used by every relational database, although many databases incorporate modified versions of the current standard SQL.

Sub procedure A procedure that runs on its own or can be called by another procedure. Sub procedures perform a set of instructions and can pass multiple values to other procedures.

Subform A subform is created when fields from two or more related tables are used to create a form. The fields from the first table become the main form fields, and the fields from the second and subsequent tables become the subform fields.

Subform control A control that embeds one form into another form.

Subquery A select query that is nested inside another select query.

Subreport The report section created for the secondary table records in creating a report from two or more tables.

Subset A portion or part of a query data set.

Subtotals Controls added to a report to perform calculations on a group of records.

Suggestions Actions that Access believes will improve a database's performance but that may have consequences that should be considered first.

Suggestive sell A sales technique that is used to add more revenue to a sale by suggesting to the customer that he or she purchase another product.

Surrogate key An artificial column added to a table to serve as a primary key that is unique and sequential when records are created. In Access, the AutoNumber data type is used as a surrogate key.

Syntax error An error that occurs when a completed line of code is entered that the Visual Basic Editor does not recognize.

T

Tab Control A control that creates tabs, with one tab per page in a form.

Tab order The order in which fields on a tab are accessed by using the Tab key.

Tab Stop A property that determines whether the field can be selected when using the Tab key to navigate through the fields on a form.

Table An organized grid of information, arranged in rows and columns.

Table Analyzer Wizard A tool that is designed to read a large table of data and convert it into an efficient database by looking for repetitive information in the table and determining which information might be better served by the use of a lookup field.

Tell me what you want to do A help tool in the title bar of Office applications that can launch commands in addition to accessing traditional help.

Template A file with predefined layouts, theme colors and fonts, and sample content that enables you to quickly produce a professional, consistent slide show.

Text box control A bound control. Represents the actual value of a field.

Text filter Filters that allow you to create a custom filter to match all or part of the text in a field that you specify.

Theme A set of design elements such as fonts, styles, colors, and effects associated with a theme name that enables you to create professional, color-coordinated documents quickly.

Toggle button A type of button that turns the feature on with one click and turns the feature off with a second click.

Top Values query A query that is used to find records that contain the top or bottom values in a field.

Total row A temporary row that can be added to the end of a datasheet that allows for statistical calculations of field values.

Transactional database The database that is used to record daily transactions.

TransferSpreadsheet method A way to allow Access to import, export, or link to spreadsheet files specifically.

Truncated Data that is shortened or trimmed because of a change in the database, such as reducing the Field Size property.

Trusted location A folder on your hard drive or a network share where trusted files are located.

U

Unbound control A control that does not have a data source and is often used for labels and other display controls.

Unbound form A form that is not linked directly to a data source and is used to specify parameters, create buttons to print reports, provide navigation menus, and similar operations.

Underlying SQL statement Even when you create a query in the QBE grid, Access automatically generates the SQL statement in the background.

Union query Used to query unrelated tables or queries and combine the results into a single dataset.

Universal naming convention (UNC) A naming convention for files that provides a link to the machine and location where the file is stored. A UNC name uses the syntax \\server\share\path\filename and works the same way in which a Uniform Resource Locator (URL) works.

Update query A query that can be used to add, change, or delete data in one or more existing records. Update queries are similar to the Find and Replace dialog box but are much more powerful.

Usability testing Testing an application with a user before releasing an application for wider use.

USB drive A small and portable storage device, popular for moving files back and forth between a lab, office, and/or home computer.

User interface Part of the computer application or operating system through which the user interacts with the computer or software.

V

Validation text A message designed to helps users understand why there is a problem.

Validation Text property A property that allows you to specify the error message that helps users understand why there is a problem.

Variable A placeholder that can be set to a hard-coded value or to an object within VBA and then later modified during the execution of the procedure.

View One of several perspectives of an object.

Virtual field This means that the concatenated field initiates its "real" equivalent or equivalents, such as combining FirstName and LastName fields.

Virtualization Software that mimics Windows in order to run Office on a Mac.

Visual Basic Editor The tool built into Microsoft Office that is used for creating and editing VBA.

Visual Basic for Applications A powerful programming language contained in Microsoft Office that allows for a variety of enhancements to any Microsoft Office application.

W

WHERE clause Allows you to limit the results of your query by specifying criteria that field values must meet without using that field to group the data.

Wildcard characters Characters, such as an asterisk (*) or question mark (?), that substitute for other characters when used in a selection.

With statement A statement that allows for an efficient way of using several methods or setting multiple properties on a single object.

Wizard A step-by-step guide for performing complex tasks.

Workbook An Excel file that contains one or more worksheets.

Y

Yes/No data type A data type that allows you to set the Format property to either Yes/No, True/False, or On/Off predefined formats or to a custom format for the Yes/No data type.

Z

Zero-length string Text that contains no characters and is created by typing two sets of double quotes without a space in between them ("").

Index

C

E

F

G

S

T